MEE Essay Analyses

Released Multistate Essay Examination Analyses

AmeriBar
Phone (800) 529-2651 • Fax (800) 529-2652

MEE Essay Analyses

Copyright 2014

All rights reserved. No part of this book may be reproduced in any form or by any means without express consent of AmeriBar and the National Conference of Bar Examiners.

ISBN 1-44049-238-7

TABLE OF CONTENTS

Agency & Partnership

(February 2000)

Legal Problems:

1. Does a general partner of a limited partnership have an obligation to inform the limited partners of an offer to purchase the limited partnership's sole asset?

2. Can a general partner of a limited partnership dissolve the limited partnership without obtaining the approval of the limited partners? If so, what are the limited partners' rights?

3. Can the limited partners take each of the desired actions without losing their status as limited partners and subjecting themselves to unlimited liability?

DISCUSSION

Point One: (33%)

As general partner, Able had an obligation to inform the limited partners of the offer from Historical Society.

A general partner of a limited partnership has fiduciary duties to the limited partners of the partnership similar to that which a partner of a general partnership has to the other general partners. Revised Uniform Limited Partnership Act (RULPA) § 403(b). These duties are the duty of care and the duty of loyalty. See Revised Uniform Partnership Act (RUPA) § 404(a). Able's failure to inform the limited partners of the offer from Historical Society was a violation of its fiduciary obligations as general partner. First, if the limited partners had a right under the partnership agreement to approve or disapprove the sale, the failure violated the implied right to information under the Uniform Partnership Act. (UPA § 18; RUPA § 403). Second, to the extent the offer was partnership property and Able would benefit from thwarting the sale, the withholding of information by Able violated its fiduciary duties under *UPA* § 21 (1). In addition, Able's failure to inform the limited partners of the offer to purchase the partnership's major asset was a violation of Able's general common-law fiduciary duty. *See, e.g., Meinhard v. Salmon,* 249 N.Y. 458, 463-464, 164 N.E. 545, 546 (1928). (Partners owe one another the "duty of the finest loyalty.")

Point Two: (33%)

Able can dissolve the limited partnership, but such a dissolution would be wrongful. In a wrongful dissolution, the limited partners would wind up Dwight LLP, and could sell the Dwight Building to Historical Society.

A nonjudicial dissolution of a limited partnership can occur at a time specified in the limited partnership agreement, upon the happening of an event specified in the limited partnership agreement, or upon the written consent of all partners. RULPA § 801(1), (2), (3). In this case, the facts do not specify that the Dwight LLP partnership agreement provides for a time for dissolution. It does provide that on the sale of the Dwight Building, the partnership would terminate; however, this event has not occurred nor has the unanimous consent of the limited partners to the dissolution of the Dwight LLP been obtained. Therefore, Able cannot properly dissolve the limited partnership. The general partner can withdraw, but the limited partners have 90 days in which to decide to continue the partnership. RULPA § 801(4). Those are the only means under the statute by which a limited partnership can be dissolved as a matter of right.

In a general partnership, each partner has the ability to dissolve the partnership even if the dissolution is not as a matter of right. UPA § 31 (2). Although there is no parallel provision under RULPA, that act does contemplate an effective but wrongful dissolution by a general partner. RULPA § 803 (" . . . the general partners who have not wrongfully dissolved. . ."). Thus it appears that Able could dissolve the limited partnership but that such a dissolution would be wrongful.

If Able wrongfully dissolves the limited partnership, the limited partners would have the right to wind up the limited partnership's affairs. "[T]he general partners who have not wrongfully dissolved a limited partnership or, if none, the limited partners, may wind up the limited partnership's affairs. . . ." RULPA § 803. The winding up of a limited partnership is no different than the process of winding up a general partnership. Winding up is generally the process of completing old business of the partnership and distributing the partnership's assets to the partners. *Ellebracht v. Siebring,* 525 F. Supp. 113,116 (W.D. Mo. 1981), *aff'd,* 676 F.2d 706 (8th Cir. 1982). Part of the winding up process is the conversion of the partnership's assets into cash for distribution to the partners. Reuschlein & Gregory, *The Law of Agency and Partnership* 344 (2d ed. 1990). As part of the winding up of the partnership, the limited partners would have the right to sell the Dwight Building to Historical Society.

Point Three: (33%)

The limited partners may dissolve the limited partnership, push for a sale to Historical Society, and remove Able as general partner without the possibility of unlimited liability. The limited partners may require their approval for all actions taken by the general partner, but, in doing so, they increase their exposure to the possibility for unlimited liability.

A limited partner who is not also a general partner can be held liable for the obligations of a limited partnership if the limited partner "participates in the control of the business." RULPA § 303(a). However, the Act provides a safe harbor for certain types of activities that are deemed not to constitute participation in the control of the business. RULPA § 303(b). Action by the limited partners to dissolve the limited partnership (RULPA § 303(b)(6)(i)), to sell all or substantially all of the limited partnership's assets (RULPA § 303(b)(6)(ii)), or to remove the general partner (RULPA § 3 03(b)(6)(v)) are all within the safe harbor and therefore those actions by themselves will not expose the limited partners to any unlimited general partner-type liability.

A decision by the limited partners to keep Able as general partner but to require their approval for every action Able takes is not within the safe harbor provisions of the statute. RULPA § 303(b). It is likely that such oversight of all of the day-to-day decision-making of a general partner in its operation of the limited partnership would constitute participation in the control of the business. RULPA § 303(a).

However, even if such oversight was deemed to constitute participation in control of the partnership, the limited partners would not be automatically liable as general partners. Reliance by a third party is required in order to impose greater liability upon a limited partner. "[I]f the limited partner participates in the control of the business, he is liable only to persons who transact business with the limited partnership reasonably believing, based upon the limited partner's conduct, that the limited partner is a general partner." RULPA § 303(a). Here, Bank knew of the limited partners' status; thus, there was no reliance by Bank. If the limited partnership were to continue its operations, it would be necessary to contract with various third parties to complete the restoration work. It would be likely that if Able was required, in each instance, to defer to the approval of the limited partners in the partnership's dealings with such third parties, they could have a reasonable belief that the limited partners were controlling the business and acting as a general partner.

Agency & Partnership

(February 2001)

Legal Problems:

1. Is a general partner responsible for the debts of a general partnership if the partnership has insufficient funds to meet the debt, when the partners did not expressly authorize the debt?

2. Is a general partner who advances his own funds to purchase goods for the partnership entitled to reimbursement from the partnership?

3. Is a general partner who contributes more services to the general partnership than the other partners entitled to remuneration from the partnership?

4. May a majority, but less than all, of the partners bind the general partnership to a transaction outside the ordinary course of business without approval of all of the partners?

DISCUSSION

Point One: (20-30%)

Partners are agents of a general partnership for the purpose of binding the partnership and are responsible for the obligations of the partnership.

Andrew purchased the special hybrid seed without obtaining the consent of the other partners. As a general rule, partners are agents of the partnership, and, as such, their acts (including entering into contracts) bind the partnership. Uniform Partnership Act (1969) (UPA) § 9(1). "An act of a partner, including the execution of an instrument in the partnership name, for apparently carrying on in the ordinary course the partnership business or business of the kind carried on by the partnership, binds the partnership, unless the partner had no authority to act for the partnership in the particular matter and the person with whom the partner was dealing knew or had received a notification that the partner lacked authority." *Id. See also* Revised Uniform Partnership Act (1994)(RUPA) § 301(1).

In this case, the special hybrid seed was purchased in the name of ABC Partnership. Purchasing seed for a farm, including expensive disease-resistant seed, constitutes carrying on in the ordinary course of ABC's partnership business. Because Andrew has operated the farm on a day-to-day basis, the seed vendor could properly assume that the purchase of the seed was for carrying on the ordinary business of the partnership and that Andrew had authority to make the purchase. As a result, ABC is liable for payment of the seed.

Partners are jointly responsible for the debts of a general partnership. UPA § 15(b). Under

RUPA, partners are jointly and severally liable for general partnership obligations. RUPA § 306(a).

Because the contract to purchase seed is an enforceable obligation of ABC, Charles is jointly (and, under RUPA, severally) liable with Andrew and Brenda for the obligation.

Point Two: (20-30%)

A partner who uses his own funds to purchase goods for the partnership is entitled to reimbursement.

A partner is entitled to be repaid by the partnership for contributions to partnership property made by the partner individually. UPA § 18(a). Since Andrew made the $7,000 down payment from his own funds as an advance to the partnership, ABC is obligated to repay him that amount. *See also* RUPA § 401(d) ("A partnership shall reimburse a partner for an advance to the partnership beyond the amount of capital the partner agreed to contribute."). Although the facts imply that ABC does not have sufficient funds, Andrew still has the *right* to be reimbursed by the partnership. Since, as previously stated, each partner is liable for the debts of the partnership, Charles and Brenda will also be personally liable for a portion of the down payment if the partnership is unable to reimburse Andrew.

Point Three: (15-25%)

Partners are not entitled to be paid for their services to a general partnership, unless the partners have an express agreement to provide such payments, but some courts will allow remuneration based on an implied agreement.

Andrew claims that he is entitled to be paid by ABC for his services to the partnership because he contributed many more services than Brenda and Charles. As a general rule, a partner is not entitled to separate remuneration for services on the theory that a partner's compensation for his or her services is his or her share of profits. UPA § 18(f), RUPA § 401(h).

There are two exceptions to this rule. First, in the case of a winding up of the partnership, a surviving partner is entitled to reasonable compensation for services rendered in connection with winding up the business of the partnership. Since ABC is not winding up operations, this would not apply to Andrew's request.

The second exception is where the partners expressly agree to pay a partner for his or her efforts. The UPA is explicit that the rights of a partner as stated in the Act, including the right to receive remuneration, may be changed by an agreement among the partners. UPA § 18. If partners want to pay salaries, they must agree to do so. Harold Gill Reushlein & William A. Gregory, THE LAW OF AGENCY AND PARTNERSHIP § 186, at 275-76 (1990). Here the partners had no express agreement to pay any remuneration to Andrew. On that basis many courts would find that Andrew is not entitled to any compensation for his services to ABC. *Yoder v. Hooper*, 695 P.2d 1182 (Colo. Ct. App. 1984). However, other courts have permitted remuneration based on an implied agreement to compensate a partner but there are no facts here to suggest an implied agreement. *Knutson v. Laner,* 627 P.2d 66 (Utah 1981).

Point Four: (25-35%)

All partners must consent to the land swap by ABC Partnership in order for it to be binding on ABC since the action is outside the ordinary course of ABC's business.

As a general rule, matters outside the ordinary course of a partnership's business must be unanimously approved by the partners. UPA § 18(h); RUPA § 401(j). Although the UPA and the RUPA do not define the types of acts that are sufficiently outside the ordinary course of business to require the consent of all partners, the facts make clear that ABC's sale of 500 acres of farmland and purchase of land to be developed for a subdivision are not within the scope of the ordinary course of business of its farm operations. While a conveyance of land might be in the ordinary course of business when one partner had been given authority in the past to convey pieces of land, this was not the case here. *See Smith* v. *Dixon,* 238 Ark. 1018, 386 S.W.2d 244 (1965).

Because the transaction was not in the ordinary course of ABC's business and because it was not unanimously approved by the partners, Andrew's actions did not bind ABC. UPA § 9(2); RUPA § 301(2). Should XYZ claim Andrew had apparent authority to sell the land, that claim would fail because the transaction was not in the ordinary course of ABC's business. The nature of the transaction (i.e., not in the ordinary course of the partnership's business) put XYZ constructively on notice that Andrew alone might not have the authority to engage in the transaction.

Agency & Partnership

(July 2001)

Legal Problems:

1. Is a principal bound when an agent who has actual authority enters into an obligation apparently for the benefit of the principal but in fact for the benefit of a third party?

2. Is a principal bound when an agent who has actual authority enters into an obligation in violation of an undisclosed limitation placed on the agent's authority by the principal?

3. Is a principal bound when an agent whose actual authority has been terminated but who continues to have apparent authority enters into an obligation on behalf of the principal?

DISCUSSION

Point One: (25-35%)

Principal is liable to Bellseller for the church bell. Principal is bound by Agent's purchase of the church bell apparently on Principal's behalf, even though Agent was in fact operating on Greta's behalf, since Bellseller was unaware of that fact.

There is no doubt that Principal is liable. However, different jurisdictions are likely to reach this result based on different theories.

First, some jurisdictions would conclude that Agent had actual authority to bind Principal to the contract with Bellseller because Agent was expressly authorized by Principal to purchase the bell and the price that Agent agreed to pay was within the range authorized by Principal. Moreover, because the contract entered into by Agent disclosed that Principal was Agent's principal, Bellseller knew that Agent was acting as agent for a third party. This makes Principal a disclosed principal who is "subject to liability upon a contract purported to be made on his account by an agent authorized to make it for the principal's benefit, *although the agent acts for his own or another s improper purposes,* unless the [third] party has notice that the agent is not acting for the principal's benefit." RESTATEMENT (SECOND) OF AGENCY § 165. *See also U.S. Fidelity & Guaranty Co. v. Anderson Constr. Co.,* 260 F.2d 172 (9th Cir. 1958). Here, Bellseller had no knowledge that Agent was not acting for Principal's benefit, and as a result, Principal is liable to Bellseller for the price of the church bell. (In some jurisdictions, this same reasoning would be used to hold Principal liable on an "inherent authority" rationale. *See* Comment a to RESTATEMENT (SECOND) OF AGENCY § 165.) Agent, on the other hand, could be liable to Principal for breach of fiduciary duty.

Other jurisdictions would conclude that Agent did not have actual authority. Agent did not make the purchase for Principal, he made the purchase for Greta and his act of *purchasing the bell for Greta* was NOT within the actual authority given by Principal: Principal only authorized agent to make the purchase *for the benefit of Principal. See* Draft, RESTATEMENT (THIRD) OF

AGENCY § 2.01, comment e (an "act that would be within the agent's actual authority had the agent acted to serve the interests of the principal. . . falls outside actual authority [if] the agent acted to serve the agent's own purposes or other improper purposes.") Thus, although he purported to be acting for Principal, Agent probably lacked actual authority *to make this purchase for Greta,* though he would have had authority to purchase for Principal. Consequently, Principal would probably not be bound simply on the basis of actual authority.

Nevertheless, jurisdictions that conclude that Agent lacked actual authority would probably also conclude that Agent had *apparent* authority to make this purchase. Apparent authority is created "by written or spoken words or any other conduct of the principal which, reasonably interpreted, causes the third person to believe that the principal consents to have the act done on his behalf by the person purporting to act for him." *See* RESTATEMENT (SECOND) OF AGENCY § 27. *See also Mohr v. State Bank of Stanley,* 241 Kan. 42, 734 P.2d 1071, 1076 (1987); *Lewis v. Washington Metro. Area Transit Auth.,* 463 A.2d 666 (D.C. 1983). The principal must "be responsible for the information which comes to the mind of the third person," but this can occur if the principal provides "documents or other indicia of authority" to the agent that are subsequently shown to the third party. RESTATEMENT (SECOND) OF AGENCY § 27, comment a.

In this case, Principal provided Agent with written credentials which, when they were shown to Bellseller, caused Bellseller to believe that Agent was authorized to purchase the bell on behalf of Principal. Agent then purported to act within the scope of this apparent authority, and Bellseller believed him to be so acting. Consequently, Principal is liable for the contract made by Agent within the scope of his apparent authority. *See* RESTATEMENT (SECOND) OF AGENCY § 159.

In any event, the basic justification for imposing liability on Principal is simply that Principal created a situation where Bellseller reasonably relied on Agent's claims to be acting for Principal. Agency law typically protects third parties who act in reliance on appearances created by a purported principal, and a court is likely to protect Bellseller for this reason, whether the result is explained on grounds of apparent authority, inherent authority, or estoppel. *See* RESTATEMENT (SECOND) OF AGENCY § 8, comments d, e & f; § 8A.

Point Two: (25-35%)

Agent acted with actual authority to purchase the book, and with apparent authority because Tomeseller was unaware of Principal's price limitation. Therefore, Principal is liable even though Agent exceeded the terms of his authorization.

Principal specifically authorized Agent to buy the book, so Agent had actual authority to purchase the book on Principal's behalf. RESTATEMENT (SECOND) OF AGENCY § 26. However, Agent exceeded the limitation on price imposed by Principal, and therefore exceeded the scope of his actual authority. Although Agent is liable to Principal for breach of duty to obey instructions, Principal will nevertheless be liable to Tomeseller.

Agent showed the written authorization to Tomeseller, and the purchase contract identified

Principal as the principal, so Principal was a disclosed principal, and Agent had apparent authority. Apparent authority is created "by written or spoken words or any other conduct of the principal which, reasonably interpreted, causes the third person to believe that the principal consents to have the act done on his behalf by the person purporting to act for him." RESTATEMENT (SECOND) OF AGENCY § 27. *See also Mohr v. State Bank of Stanley,* 241 Kan. 42, 734 P.2d 1071, 1076 (1987); *Lewis v. Washington Metro. Area Transit Auth.,* 463 A.2d 666 (D.C. 1983). When Agent presented Tomeseller with the written authorization, which did not include the limitation, Tomeseller reasonably understood that Agent was authorized to purchase the book on Principal's behalf, creating apparent authority on behalf of Agent.

Because the price limitation was not included on the written authorization shown to Tomeseller, she was unaware of the limitation. "A disclosed or partially disclosed principal authorizing an agent to make a contract, but imposing upon him limitations as to incidental terms intended not to be revealed is subject to liability upon a contract made in violation of such limitations with a third person who has no notice of them." RESTATEMENT (SECOND) OF AGENCY § 160. *See also Hunt v. Davis,* 387 So. 2d 209 (Ala. Civ. App. 1980) (holding that secret limitations on an agent's authority do not bind third parties); *Wittlin v. Giacalone,* 171 F.2d 147 (D.C. Cir. 1948). Therefore, Principal remains liable to Tomeseller for payment of the book.

Point Three: (25-30%)

<u>Because Agent was acting with apparent authority, even though Principal had terminated all actual authority, Principal is liable to Lampseller for the purchase of the lamp.</u>

Principal had terminated the agency relationship by delivery of the letter to Agent, so Agent did not have actual authority to buy the lamp. RESTATEMENT (SECOND) OF AGENCY § 119. Agent did, however, continue to have apparent authority. Once apparent authority is created, it can be terminated only when the third party has notice of termination or when the authority is terminated due to impossibility or lack of capacity. Reuschlein & Gregory, THE LAW OF AGENCY AND PARTNERSHIP § 46 at 95, (2d ed. 1990); RESTATEMENT (SECOND) OF AGENCY § 125.

When Principal engaged Agent, Principal gave Agent credentials and form contracts used to buy antiques on Principal's behalf. Agent showed Lampseller the credentials and used Principal's form to purchase the lamp, so Lampseller could reasonably have understood that Agent had authority from Principal to buy antiques, including the lamp. When Principal entrusted Agent with "indicia of authority," Principal became obliged to give notice of any termination of that authority to third persons who relied upon Agent's possession of the credentials. Since Lampseller had no notice that Agent's credentials were no longer valid, the apparent authority continued as to Lampseller and, as a result, Principal is liable for payment to Lampseller for the $5,000 purchase price.

Agency & Partnership

(February 2002)

Legal Problems:

1. Can the limited partners decide how the day-to-day business of a limited partnership is to be conducted?

2. What rights does a limited partner have to obtain information from the general partner about the limited partnership's affairs?

3. What rights does a purchaser of a limited partnership interest have in the limited partnership if such purchase is not approved by the partnership?

DISCUSSION

Point One: (35-45%)

Carl and the other limited partners have no right to determine how the day-to-day business of Transitions is to be conducted. Management of the business is vested exclusively in Bill, the general partner.

A limited partnership is a partnership which has one or more general partners and one or more limited partners. Revised Unif. Ltd. Partnership Act (RULPA) § 101(7). A general partner of a limited partnership generally has the powers and the liabilities of a partner in a general partnership. RULPA § 403. Management of a limited partnership is entrusted to the general partners, who are personally liable for the obligations of the business. *Life Care Centers of America, Inc. v. Charles Town Assoc. Ltd. Partnership*, 79 F.3d 496, 503 (6th Cir. 1996) (dictum); *United States v. Heffner*, 916 F. Supp. 1010, 1012 n.2 (S.D. Cal. 1996) ("general partner controls the business of the limited partnership to the exclusion of the limited partners"); *Duke & Benedict, Inc. v. Wolstein*, 826 F. Supp. 1413, 1415 (M.D. Fla. 1993) ("The defendant is the general partner of this partnership and has complete control over the management and affairs of this business.").

By comparison, limited partners generally have no control over how the day-to-day business of the limited partnership is conducted. *Duke & Benedict, Inc.*, 826 F. Supp. at 1415 ("The plaintiff is the limited partner, who has no say or control as to how the partnership is run."); *In re the Cincinnatian, Ltd.*, 143 B.R. 108, 110 (S.D. Ohio 1992) (holding that limited partner was not entitled to have provision included in limited partnership agreement giving it voice in selection of manager; limited partners "do not have statutory right to exercise control of the partnership's decisions"). The role of limited partners in a limited partnership is generally passive, with only limited rights to vote on extraordinary events of the partnership, such as dissolution or sale of substantially all of the partnership's assets.

Therefore, Bill, as the sole general partner, has exclusive control over the daily management of

Transitions, and Carl and the other limited partners cannot decide how the day-to-day business of Transitions is to be conducted.

Point Two: (10-20%)

Carl, as a limited partner, has the right to inspect various records of Transitions and to obtain information about the affairs of Transitions from Bill, the general partner.

A limited partnership is required to keep specified records at its office, including the names and addresses of each partner, any income tax returns or reports for the three most recent years, and any financial statements for the three most recent years. RULPA § 105. Upon reasonable request, any limited partner may inspect and copy during ordinary business hours any of the records required to be kept by the limited partnership. RULPA §§ 105(b), 305. In addition, any limited partner has the right to obtain from the general partners upon reasonable demand "true and full information regarding the state of the business and financial condition of the limited partnership" and "other information regarding the affairs of the limited partnership as is just and reasonable." RULPA § 305.

Therefore, Carl has the right to inspect the records that Transitions is required to keep and the right to obtain from Bill, the general partner, true and full information regarding the business and financial condition of Transitions.

Point Three: (30-40%)

Edward's purchase of Donna's limited partnership interest in Transitions did not result in Edward's becoming a limited partner, although Edward did obtain Donna's financial rights in Transitions.

A limited partnership interest is personal property and, except as provided in the partnership agreement, is freely assignable in whole or in part. RULPA §§ 701, 702. However, assignment of a limited partnership interest does not entitle the assignee to become a limited partner or to exercise any of the rights of a limited partner. RULPA §§ 301, 702. Instead, assignment only entitles the assignee to receive (to the extent assigned) any distributions to which the assignor would be entitled. *Id.* In other words, a limited partner may only assign his or her economic rights in the limited partnership. *See generally* Alan R. Bromberg & Larry E. Ribstein, BROMBERG AND RIBSTEIN ON PARTNERSHIP §§ 13.04(e), 13.06(e)(2)-(f) (1988).

An assignee of a limited partnership interest may be admitted as a limited partner to the partnership only if all partners have consented to such admission, unless the partnership agreement expressly gives the transferring partner the right to admit a new partner without approval of the other partners. RULPA § 704. The facts indicate that Bill disapproves of the sale and there is no indication that the other partners approved the admission of Edward as a limited partner. Edward therefore did not become a limited partner in Transitions upon Donna's sale of her limited partnership interest to Edward. As a result, Edward cannot exercise any of the rights of a limited partner, such as the right to inspect records (RULPA §§ 105, 305), the right to obtain information regarding the limited partnership (RULPA § 305), the right to seek a judicial dissolution (RULPA § 802), or the right to bring a derivative action (RULPA § 1001).

On the other hand, the assignment of Donna's limited partnership interest to Edward did transfer Donna's economic rights in Transitions to Edward. Consequently, Edward is entitled to any distributions from Transitions to which Donna would have been entitled.

Agency & Partnership

(July 2002)

Legal Problems:

(1)(a) Did Adam act with either actual or apparent authority in contracting for the Tahitian lobby decorations?

(1)(b) Did Adam act with either actual or apparent authority in contracting with Moby for the guest room furnishings?

(2) Does Sunrise have a claim for indemnification from Adam for either of the contracts for which Sunrise is liable?

(3) Can Sunrise terminate Adam's agency prior to the expiration of the one-year term, and if so, is Sunrise liable to Adam for damages based on the early termination?

DISCUSSION

Summary: Adam acted with apparent but not actual authority with respect to the contract with Tahini. Adam acted with apparent authority because Sunrise advised Tahini of the agency agreement but not of the limitations on Adam's authority. On the other hand, Adam acted with actual authority with respect to the Moby contract which was consistent with all of the terms of the agency contract between Sunrise and Adam. Thus, Sunrise is liable to both Tahini and Moby, albeit on different theories. Sunrise can seek indemnification from Adam for its liability under the Tahini contract but not under the Moby contract. Because Adam materially breached the agency contract, Sunrise can terminate that contract prior to the end of the fixed term in the contract without any liability to Adam.

Point One(a): (20-30%)

Sunrise is liable on the contract for the purchase of the Tahitian decorations because Adam acted with apparent authority.

Adam had no actual authority to purchase the Tahitian lobby items on Sunrise's behalf. Under the Restatement (Second) of Agency, actual "authority to do an act can be created by written or spoken words or other conduct of the principal which, reasonably interpreted, causes the agent to believe that the principal desires him so to act on the principal's account." Restatement (Second) of Agency § 26. Sunrise made it clear to Adam that the items had to be within the style guidelines described in Exhibit B. The Tahitian items were inconsistent with the guidelines, and thus Adam had no actual authority to purchase them.

On the other hand, Adam did have apparent authority to purchase the Tahitian lobby items on

Sunrise's behalf. Under the Restatement, "apparent authority to do an act is created as to a third person by written or spoken words or any other conduct of the principal which, reasonably interpreted, causes the third person to believe that the principal consents to have the act done on his behalf by the person purporting to act for him." Restatement (Second) of Agency § 27. Sunrise had sent a letter to Tahini appointing Adam "to act on its behalf in the selection of interior floor and wall coverings, works of art, furniture, and plumbing and lighting fixtures for the Sunrise East Beach hotel." The Sunrise letter emphasized Adam's authority by stating: "Know that you deal with Sunrise when you deal with Adam on this project." Sunrise did not indicate to Tahini that there were any restrictions on Adam's scope of discretion or authority, and the facts do not suggest that Tahini had knowledge of any limitations through other means. As a result, it was reasonable for Tahini to conclude that Adam acted with authority when he ordered the decorations. Since Adam acted with apparent authority, Sunrise is liable to Tahini. Restatement (Second) of Agency § 140(b).

Point One(b): (10-20%)

Adam acted with actual authority in contracting with Moby for the guest room furnishings and therefore Sunrise is liable on the contract.

When Adam contracted with Moby for the guest room furnishings, he was within the budget and style limitations required by Sunrise and Moby was a local supplier. Therefore, he acted within the scope of the actual authority granted by Sunrise. Restatement (Second) of Agency § 26. Because Adam acted within the scope of the grant of actual authority, Sunrise is liable on the contract to Moby for the guest room furnishings. In addition, Adam also acted with apparent authority because Moby received the letter from Sunrise. See Point One (a) above.

Point Two: (10-20%)

Sunrise has a claim against Adam for the amount of Sunrise's liability to Tahini but does not have a claim against Adam for its liability to Moby for the guest room furnishings.

Sunrise has a claim against Adam for the amount of its liability to Tahini because Adam did not act within the scope of his actual authority and, therefore, breached his duty to follow directions. Restatement (Second) of Agency §§ 399,401.

Sunrise has no claim against Adam for reimbursement of its liability to Moby for guest room furnishings because Adam acted within the scope of his grant of authority. Restatement (Second) of Agency § 399. He followed directions and fulfilled his fiduciary obligations.

Point Three: (20-30%)

Sunrise can terminate Adam's agency at any time and end Adam's authority to bind Sunrise. Early termination of Adam's agency may expose Sunrise to liability for damages to Adam, but in this case Sunrise has a defense to such a claim.

Although the general rule is that authority conferred for a specific time terminates at the expiration of the period, Restatement (Second) of Agency §§ 105 and 118 provide that: "[a]uthority terminates if the principal. . . manifests to the [agent] dissent to its continuance." Therefore, Sunrise may terminate Adam as its agent at any time, including before the end of the one-year term. The principal has the power to terminate the agency even in violation of the agency contract: "The principal has power to revoke. . . although doing so is in violation of a contract between the parties. . ." Restatement (Second) of Agency § 118 cmt. b. However, the principal "has a duty not to repudiate or terminate the employment in violation of the contract of employment." Restatement (Second) of Agency § 450. In such a situation, the principal may be liable to the agent for damages. Restatement (Second) of Agency § 455.

Given Adam's deviation from the terms of his contract with Sunrise, Adam is not likely to recover from Sunrise for early termination. First, if a termination is based upon the agent's breach of contract, then the principal has an offset against the agent's damages. Restatement (Second) of Agency § 456. Second, "[a] principal is privileged to discharge before the time fixed by the contract of employment an agent who has committed such a violation of duty that his conduct constitutes a material breach of contract." Restatement (Second) of Agency § 409(1). That appears to be the case in this situation.

Agency & Partnership

(February 2003)

Legal Problems: (1)(a)   Does Lessor exercise sufficient control over Handy to establish Handy as Lessor's "servant" so that Lessor is liable for Handy's torts?

           (1)(b)   If Handy is Lessor's servant, is Handy's conduct within the scope of employment?

           (2)   If Handy is not a servant, did Tenant reasonably rely upon Handy's apparent authority to install an electrical outlet so that Lessor is nonetheless liable for Handy's tort?

DISCUSSION

Summary: Lessor may be held liable for Handy's tortious conduct under either of two theories. First, if the Lessor-Handy relationship is one of master and servant, Lessor is liable for Handy's torts if Handy was acting within the scope of his employment when he committed them. *See* Restatement (Second) of Agency § 219. Second, even if the relationship between Lessor and Handy does not rise to the level of a master-servant relationship, Lessor will be liable for Handy's tort if Tenant relied on statements or conduct by Handy that were within Handy's apparent authority. Restatement (Second) of Agency § 265.

Point One (a): The relationship between Handy and Lessor may be a master-servant
(30-40%)   relationship such that Lessor is liable for torts committed by Handy while acting within the scope of his employment.

A master is liable for the torts of the master's servants committed while acting in the scope of their employment. Restatement (Second) of Agency § 219(1). Handy is clearly an agent as he agreed to work for, and subject to the control of, Lessor. The more difficult question is whether Handy would be considered to be Lessor's servant.

Note: The Restatement (Third) of Agency has adopted "Employer-Employee" language in place of the traditional "Master-Servant" terminology and applicants may of course use this newer terminology.

Whether Handy performed the work for Tenant as Lessor's "servant" or as an independent contractor agent depends on the degree of control exercised by Lessor over Handy's activities. The Restatement (Second) of Agency § 2(2) provides that a "servant is an agent employed by a master to perform service in his affairs whose physical conduct in the performance of the service is controlled or is subject to the right to control by the master." Conversely, the Restatement (Second) of Agency § 2(3) provides that "an independent contractor is a person who contracts with another to do something for him but who is not controlled by the other nor subject to the other's right to control with respect to his physical conduct in the performance of the undertaking." The Restatement (Second) of Agency § 220(2) lists factors used to determine whether an agent is a servant. These factors are:

(a) the extent of control which, by the agreement, the master may exercise over the details of the work;

(b) whether or not the one employed is engaged in a distinct occupation or business;

(c) the kind of occupation, with reference to whether, in the locality, the work is usually done under the direction of the employer or by a specialist without supervision;

(d) the skill required in the particular occupation;

(e) whether the employer or the workman supplies the instrumentalities, tools, and the place of work for the person doing the work;

(f) the length of time for which the person is employed;

(g) the method of payment, whether by the time or by the job;

(h) whether or not the work is a part of the regular business of the employer;

(i) whether or not the parties believe they are creating the relation of master and servant; and

(j) whether the principal is or is not in business.

In Handy's case, the facts permit a persuasive argument on either side. Several factors suggest that Handy should be considered a servant of Lessor. First, Lessor exercises significant control over Handy, in insisting that any repair be approved by Lessor. Second, the relationship appears to be long term, not a temporary arrangement for a small number of repair jobs; it has already lasted for a year. Third, payment is by time worked, not by the particular job. Finally, the work performed is a necessary part of Lessor's business of owning and operating apartment buildings.

On the other hand, several factors support an argument for classifying Handy as an independent contractor. First, Handy, as a repairman, is engaged in a distinct occupation and business that requires some degree of special skill. Second, Handy provides his own tools. Third, Handy has his own separate repair business and appears to have taken on Lessor's work in the course of operating that separate business. Fourth, Lessor approves repairs to his properties but does not specify the methods that Handy must use.

Note: Either analysis of the servant issue is plausible. The point is that Lessor is only liable under the theory of *respondeat superior* if Handy is a servant.

Point One (b): If Handy is a servant, his actions were within the scope of employment

(15-25%)   because, although not authorized, adding an electrical outlet was incidental to authorized conduct.

Conduct is within the scope of employment if the conduct is of the "same general nature authorized or incidental to the conduct authorized." Restatement (Second) of Agency § 229(1). Factors examined in determining whether conduct is within the scope of employment include whether the conduct is the kind the servant is employed to perform; whether it occurs substantially within the authorized time and space; and whether it was performed, at least in part, to serve the master. *See* Restatement (Second) of Agency § 228.

In this case, Handy was not authorized to add the electrical outlet as Handy's contract with Lessor expressly prohibited him from doing electrical work. It also prohibited him from doing work "on the side" for a tenant. However, even forbidden activity can be within the scope of employment. Restatement (Second) of Agency § 230.

The Restatement (Second) of Agency § 229(2) sets forth factors to consider in determining whether an action is incidental to the authorized conduct so that it comes within the scope of employment. These factors include:

(a) whether or not the act is one commonly done by such servants;
(b) the time, place and purpose of the act;
(c) the previous relations between the master and the servant;
(d) the extent to which the business of the master is apportioned between different servants;
(e) whether or not the act is outside the enterprise of the master or, if within the enterprise, has not been entrusted to any servant;
(f) whether or not the master has reason to expect that such an act will be done;
(g) the similarity in quality of the act done to the act authorized;
(h) whether or not the instrumentality by which the harm is done has been furnished by the master to the servant;
(i) the extent of departure from the normal method of accomplishing an authorized result; and
(j) whether or not the act is seriously criminal.

A key fact that points to the conclusion that adding the electrical outlet was incidental to the scope of employment is the fact that Handy did the electrical work while providing Tenant with authorized services.

Point Two: Even if Handy is not a servant, or is a servant not acting within the
(50-60%)   scope of employment, Lessor is liable if Tenant reasonably believes Handy was Lessor's agent and relied on what appeared to be authority for Handy to perform the work.

Restatement (Second) of Agency § 265 sets out the general rule: "(1) A master or other principal is subject to liability for torts which result from reliance upon, or belief in, statements or other conduct within an agent's apparent authority." Section 265(2) conditions this liability upon reliance.

An agent is clothed with apparent authority when a principal "by written or spoken words or any other conduct of the principal which, reasonably interpreted, causes the third party to believe that the principal consents to have the act done on his behalf by the person purporting to act for him." Restatement (Second) of Agency § 27. The facts indicate that Lessor clothed Handy with apparent authority by advising tenants to call the "Lessor's Repair Line" when they needed repairs, and then using Handy's business phone number as the "Lessor's Repair Line." The act of using Handy's number reasonably caused Tenant to believe that Handy was authorized by Lessor to act on Lessor's behalf. There are no facts to suggest that Tenant knew or could expect to know that a person authorized to make general repairs was prohibited by contract from adding an electrical outlet.

With respect to reliance, the facts permit a persuasive argument on either side. Arguably, Tenant did not reasonably rely on Handy's apparent authority because Tenant was told that adding an electrical outlet was an improvement, not a repair, and Handy made repairs. Further, Handy indicated that there was a charge for the electrical work.

However, the alternative argument could also be made. Lessor arranged to have "Lessor's Repair Line" ring directly to Handy's office. Tenant knew that Handy was working for Lessor; in fact Handy was present doing work on behalf of Lessor. It is not unreasonable to believe that the same person designated to make repairs would also make improvements. Further, the facts indicate that Tenant believed the payment for the work ($200) was to go to Lessor.

Agency & Partnership

(July 2003)

Legal Problems: (1)   Under the theory of apparent authority, is a partnership bound by a contract entered into by a partner when that partner lacked actual authority?

(2)   Is a partner liable to the partnership for breach of fiduciary duties when the partner enters into a contract against the other partners' instructions and without providing complete information to his partners?

DISCUSSION

Summary: Carl lacked actual authority to bind the partnership by signing the contract. In this three-person partnership, Adam and Barbara had expressly limited his authority when they told him "not to finalize a deal with Jane without first discussing the terms with them." The partnership, however, may be bound by the contract if Carl had apparent authority. Whether Carl had apparent authority depends on (a) whether expanding into the pinball and video game machine business could be considered "carrying on in the ordinary course" of this partnership's business, and (b) whether Jane viewed Carl as authorized to negotiate and sign the contract on behalf of the partnership. These issues can be resolved by a fact-based analysis.

Carl is liable to the partnership for any loss arising from the contract because he is an agent of the partnership and violated his fiduciary duties to the partnership: Carl violated express instructions when he entered into the contract without first consulting with Adam and Barbara; he also failed to make adequate disclosure to Adam and Barbara.

Point One: Although Carl lacked actual authority to enter into the contract, the partnership is bound by the contract if Carl had apparent authority to act on the partnership's behalf on this matter.

Carl's Actual Authority (10-20%): Each partner is entitled to participate equally "in the management and conduct of the partnership business." Uniform Partnership Act (UPA) § 18(e), Revised Uniform Partnership Act (RUPA) § 401(f). The rules of partnership management provide for majority rule on matters arising in the ordinary course and unanimous rule on matters arising out of the ordinary course of business. UPA §18(h), RUPA § 401(j).

Carl lacked actual authority to sign the contract binding the partnership because Adam and Barbara expressly instructed Carl "not to finalize a deal with Jane without first discussing the terms with them." The express instruction from Adam and Barbara "not to finalize" restricted Carl's actual authority. In this three-partner partnership, Carl lacked unanimous or majority approval to proceed beyond investigating the opportunity. Therefore, Carl lacked actual authority and the partnership is not bound on an actual authority basis.

Carl's Apparent Authority (40-50%): As a partner, Carl is an agent of the partnership. "An act of a partner . . . for apparently carrying on in the ordinary course the partnership business or business of the kind carried on by the partnership binds the partnership, unless the partner had no authority to act for the partnership in the particular matter and the person with whom the partner is dealing knew . . . the partner lacked authority." RUPA § 301 (1997). *See also* UPA § 9(1) (1914). There is no suggestion that Jane was aware of any limitation on Carl's authority. Thus, two questions arise: (a) whether Carl had apparent authority to enter into purchase agreements on behalf of the partnership, and (b) whether the purchase of pinball and video machines was within the ordinary course of the partnership's business. These questions are appropriately viewed from Jane's perspective. *See Luddington v. Bodenvest, Ltd.,* 855 P.2d 204, 209 (Utah 1993). *See also Smith v. Dixon,* 386 S.W.2d 244 (Ark. 1965) (look to custom and past dealings between the parties or with the particular partnership).

With respect to the first question, it would be perfectly reasonable for Jane to believe that Carl had the authority to enter into a purchase agreement without consulting his partners and there is no evidence that she knew that he lacked authority in this instance. The facts state that Carl represented the partnership in past dealings with Jane, negotiating and signing contracts without input from Adam or Barbara. Thus, from Jane's perspective, when Carl signed the contract with Jane, he was carrying on business "in the usual way" in which it was always carried on for the partnership. *See RNR Investments Limited Partnership v. Peoples First Community Bank,* 812 So. 2d 561 (Fla. Ct. App. 2002) ("apparently carrying on in the ordinary course" means that partnership business must have been carried on "in the usual way").

With respect to the second question, the issue is whether the purchase of *pinball and video game machines* would appear to be a carrying on of "the *partnership* business or business of the kind carried on by the partnership." RUPA § 301 (emphasis added). The partner's act must not only be an act carrying out business "in the usual way," but it must also be an act the public would "reasonably conclude is directly and necessarily embraced within the partnership business as being incident or appropriate to such business according to the course and usage of conducting it." *Merrill v. O'Bryan,* 93 P. 917 (Wash. 1908). The act must be "apparently within the nature of the business" of the partnership. *Cummings v. Nordmark,* 438 P.2d 605, 606 (Wash. 1968). *See also Luddington v. Bodenvest Ltd.,* 855 P.2d at 210 (act must be "within the ordinary and apparent scope of the partnership business").

In this case, the partnership was engaged in the beverage distribution business. An argument could be made that Carl's purchase of pinball and video game machines was neither "partnership business" nor "business of the kind carried on by the partnership." RUPA § 301. Ownership of pinball and video games is not "directly and necessarily embraced" within the scope of a beverage business, nor is it obviously "incident or appropriate to such business." *Merrill v. O'Bryan,* 93 P. 917.

On the other hand, other beverage distribution businesses in the same geographic area as this partnership have been expanding into the pinball and video game machine business. Thus, even if the business of this partnership had been limited to beverage distribution, it is arguable that the supply of other goods and services to bars and restaurants, including game machines, is a "business of the kind carried on by the partnership" and is therefore within the "nature of the business" of this partnership. *See Cummings v. Nordmark,* 438 P.2d 605. Moreover, Jane, who was aware of the trend of beverage distributors expanding into the pinball and video game business could view this partnership's expansion as being "incident or appropriate to [its] business according to the course and usage of conducting it [in her area]." *Merrill v. O'Bryan,* 93 P. 917. *Cf.* Florida Revised Uniform Partnership Act § 301(1) (scope of partnership business is determined with reference to acts of such businesses "in the geographic area in which the partnership operates.").

The apparent authority arguments could go either way. The important task for applicants is to recognize the issue and apply the test appropriately. There is also an argument that even if Carl lacked authority to enter the contract, the partnership ratified the partnership contract when it presumably accepted the machines and began operating them.

Point Two: (40-50%)	Carl is liable to the partnership for any loss arising from the contract with Jane because Carl breached his fiduciary duty to the partnership by signing this contract in violation of the instructions from Adam and Barbara, and without providing full disclosure to Adam and Barbara.

A partner is an agent of the partnership and owes duties to the partnership and the other partners. When a partner violates a duty, the partner is liable to the partnership and other partners for the resulting loss. Carl violated his duties to the partnership and the other partners when he entered into the contract in violation of his instructions and without discussing the terms with Adam and Barbara. Although the rationale differs under the UPA and the RUPA, under either statute, Carl is liable to the partnership for the loss resulting from his breach of duty.

Carl breached several duties to the partnership. First, under the common law and the UPA, Carl is an agent of the partnership and owes a duty of obedience to his other partners, including a duty to follow reasonable instructions. *See* Restatement (Second) of Agency § 385 (1958); UPA § 4(3). Carl breached this duty by failing to follow Adam and Barbara's instruction that he not enter into any contract with Jane unless he first discussed the terms with them. (In a jurisdiction where the RUPA is applicable, one could also argue that this failure to follow instructions was "intentional misconduct" and a breach of Carl's duty of care. *See* RUPA § 404(c).)

Second, Carl had an obligation to provide full information to Adam and Barbara. That obligation was imposed by their express instruction to him "not to finalize a deal with Jane without first discussing the terms" with them. *See* UPA § 20 ("[p]artners shall render on demand true and full information of all things affecting the partnership to any partner"). In addition, courts have interpreted the UPA to require full disclosure of information material to partnership affairs even in the absence of an explicit demand, and the RUPA specifically imposes such an obligation. *See Griva v. Davison,* 637 A.2d 830 (D.C. 1994); *Silverberg v. Colantuno,* 991 P.2d 280 (Colo. App. 1998); RUPA § 403(c).

Finally, it is arguable that Carl breached his duty of care by failing to thoroughly investigate the facts before entering into the contract with Jane. The amount of money involved was substantial, and Carl arguably should have visited all 72 bars and checked all 127 machines, not just 50 bars and 98 machines, before entering the contract. The common law, the UPA, and the RUPA all impose on partners a general duty of care, including a duty to act in good faith when carrying out partnership business. *See generally* RUPA § 404.

However, the duty of care is generally violated only by "grossly negligent or reckless conduct, intentional misconduct, or a knowing violation of the law." *See* RUPA § 404(c). Although Carl may have been negligent in failing to inspect all machines and was clearly wrong in failing to consult with Barbara and Adam before finalizing the deal, these omissions may not rise to the level of gross neglect (or worse) necessary to violate the duty of care. *See Duffy v. Piazza Construction, Inc.,* 815 P.2d 267 (Wash. Ct. App. 1991). From all that appears, Carl acted in the good faith belief that he was making a good deal for the partnership, he undertook an extensive (if incomplete) examination of the relevant information before agreeing to purchase the pinball machines, and his failure to consult with Adam and Barbara, while a violation of instructions, was consistent with the way the partnership had done business in the past. Under the circumstances, a breach of the duty of care may be difficult to establish.

There is no evidence of any self-interest in the transaction, and thus there is no duty of loyalty problem.

In summary, Carl likely did not breach his duty of care. He did, however, breach his duty of obedience and his duty to provide full information. He is therefore liable to the partnership for the losses resulting from either breach.

Agency & Partnership

(February 2004)

ANALYSIS

Legal Problems: (1) Does the statement "I don't want to do this anymore. I am quitting this partnership," made by one partner, dissolve an "at will" partnership?

(2) May a partner bind a partnership to a contract made after dissolution?

(3) What is a partner's liability for partnership obligations?

DISCUSSION

Summary: The effect of Randy's "quitting" is to dissolve the partnership and to put it in a "winding up" period, at the conclusion of which it terminates. As the partnership had already dissolved, Sandy lacked actual authority to enter into the contract with Barney on behalf of the partnership. All the same, the partnership is bound by the contract with Barney because Sandy still had apparent authority to bind the partnership. Because they did not agree otherwise, Randy and Sandy share losses equally. Because Sandy paid the trade creditors, she is entitled to a $15,000 contribution from Randy.

Point One: Randy's statement "I don't want to do this anymore. I am quitting this partnership," (35-40%) dissolves the "at will" partnership. This begins a period of winding up (liquidation) during which time the partnership affairs are settled. Once winding up is complete, the partnership terminates.

The facts do not indicate that the partnership had a definite term or limited undertaking. Therefore, this was an "at will" partnership. Any partner may dissolve an "at will" partnership by his or her express will.

Under the Uniform Partnership Act (UPA), dissolution occurs when the parties cease to associate in carrying on the business together. *See* UPA § 29 ("The dissolution of a partnership is the change in the relation of the partners caused by any partner ceasing to be associated in the carrying on as distinguished from the winding up of the business."). "On dissolution the partnership is not terminated but continues until the winding up of partnership affairs is completed." UPA § 30. Winding up is "the process of settling partnership affairs after dissolution." Official Comment to § 29. Once all partnership affairs have been settled, the partnership terminates.

When Randy told Sandy "I don't want to do this anymore. I am quitting this partnership," Randy dissolved the partnership. The partnership must now undergo a period of winding up (i.e., completing the remaining business and settling debts). Once this is done, the partnership is terminated.

Under the Revised Uniform Partnership Act (RUPA), Randy's statement is an event of dissociation. Sandy has "notice of the partner's express will to withdraw as a partner." RUPA § 601(1). Therefore, under RUPA § 801(1) Randy's statement dissolves the partnership and the business must be wound up. Pursuant to RUPA § 802, "a partnership continues after dissolution only for the purpose of winding up its business. The partnership is terminated when the winding up of its business is completed."

Point Two: The partnership is probably bound by Sandy's contract with Barney, even though it

(35-40%)   occurred after dissolution, because Sandy had apparent authority to enter into the contract.

Under the UPA, upon dissolution, a partner's actual authority to bind the partnership terminates except as is necessary to wind up the business. *See* UPA § 33. The contract with Barney was for new business. When Randy dissolved the partnership (*see* Point One, above), Sandy's actual authority to enter into a contract for new business ended.

Under the RUPA, upon dissolution, a "partnership is bound by a partner's act after dissolution that . . . is appropriate for winding up the partnership business." RUPA § 804. As indicated above, the contract with Barney was for new business. There is an exception under RUPA § 803(c) that permits a partner who has not wrongfully dissociated to preserve the partnership business as a going concern for a reasonable period of time. These facts do not come within this exception. To date, the business has existed for only a year and it only had short-term contracts remaining. The contract with Barney was a long-term contract (three years).

While Sandy lacked actual authority to contract with Barney, under both the UPA and the RUPA, Sandy likely had apparent authority to bind the partnership after dissolution, so long as Barney was not aware of the dissolution and reasonably believed that Sandy was authorized to act. *See* UPA § 35(1) ("After dissolution a partner can bind the partnership . . . by any transaction which would bind the partnership if dissolution had not taken place, provided the other party to the transaction . . . though he had not so extended credit, had nevertheless known of the partnership prior to dissolution, and had no knowledge or notice of dissolution . . ."); RUPA § 804(2) ("a partnership is bound by a partner's act after dissolution that . . . (2) would have bound the partnership under § 301 before dissolution, if the other party to the transaction did not have notice of the dissolution"). RUPA § 301(1) provides a partner with apparent authority to carry on in the ordinary course the partnership's business unless the other party to the transaction knows that there is no authority.

The facts support the conclusion that Sandy had apparent authority to enter into the contract. Even though Barney had not previously done business with the partnership, the facts state that he was familiar with the partnership. Sandy, on behalf of the partnership, had been soliciting a long-term contract from him for over a month. Sandy was acting in the ordinary course of the partnership's business when soliciting a contract for widgets. Further, Barney was not aware of the dissolution. Therefore, the partnership is probably bound by Sandy's contract with Barney.

Point Three: (15-25%)	Because there is no agreement to the contrary, when Sandy paid $30,000 to the trade creditors, Sandy became entitled to a contribution of $15,000 from Randy.

When Sandy paid the entire $30,000 debt to the trade creditors, she became entitled to contribution of $15,000 from Randy. Among partners, unless the parties agree otherwise, profits are shared equally and losses are shared in the same ratio as profits. *See* UPA § 18(a) ("Each partner shall . . . share equally in the profits . . . and must contribute towards the losses . . . according to his share in the profits."); RUPA § 401(b) ("Each partner is entitled to an equal share of the partnership profits and is chargeable with a share of the partnership losses in proportion to the partner's share of the profits."). Regardless of the fact that Randy contributed twice as much capital ($10,000) as Sandy ($5,000) to the partnership, the facts indicate that they shared profits equally. Because they did not agree otherwise, Randy and Sandy would share losses in the same ratio as they shared profits.

Agency & Partnership

(July 2004)

ANALYSIS

Legal Problems: (1)   Is Owen an independent contractor or a servant (employee) of Best Care?

(2)   Did Owen have actual or apparent authority to bind Best Care to the contract to purchase the X-ray machine?

(3)   Is Best Care liable to Anita's estate for Owen's negligence on an apparent (ostensible) agency theory?

DISCUSSION

Summary: Whether Owen is an independent contractor or a servant (employee) is a question of fact. The degree of control is generally the distinguishing factor between an independent contractor and a servant (employee). Traditionally, Owen would have been an independent contractor because Best Care did not retain substantial control over how Owen was to practice medicine; however, recent opinions have moderated this position and look to the right to control rather than actual exercise of control.

Best Care is not liable on the Vision-Owen contract. Owen lacked actual authority to enter into the contract with Vision on behalf of Best Care because Vision was not a vendor in City. Further, Best Care had made no manifestations to provide Vision with a reasonable basis to believe that Owen was acting as an agent of Best Care.

Even if Owen is an independent contractor, he appears to the outside world—and to Anita in particular—to be an employee of Best Care as a result of Best Care's representations made on the billboards. Because of this apparent (ostensible) agency, Best Care would be estopped from denying liability for Owen's negligence and Anita's resulting death.

(35-45%)

Point One: Owen was probably an independent contractor and not an employee of Best Care, but the facts could be argued differently.

Owen is either an independent contractor or a servant (employee). "An independent contractor is a person who contracts with another to do something for him but who is not controlled by the other nor subject to the other's right to control with respect to his physical conduct in the performance of the undertaking. He may or may not be an agent." RESTATEMENT (SECOND) OF AGENCY § 2(3). "A servant [employee] is an agent employed by a master [employer] to perform service in his affairs whose physical conduct in the performance of the service is controlled or is subject to the right to control by the master." *Id*. at § 2(2). A number of factors are relevant in distinguishing an independent contractor from a servant. The crucial factor is the extent of control that the employer may exercise over the details of the work. *See* RESTATEMENT (SECOND) OF AGENCY § 220. Traditionally, doctors were considered independent contractors because of their high level of skill and the use of their independent judgment. *See McMurdo v. Getter*, 10 N.E.2d 139 (Mass. 1937). However, in recent years, courts have placed greater emphasis on the employer's "right to interfere or control rather than [the employer's] actual interference or exercise of control." *See Knorp v. Albert*, 28 P.3d 1024 (Kan. Ct. App. 2001); *Kelly v. Rossi*, 481 N.E.2d 1340 (Mass. 1985). Other factors used to distinguish between a servant and an independent contractor are: (1) whether the one employed is engaged in a distinct occupation or business, (2) the skill required in the particular occupation, (3) who supplies the materials to perform and the place to perform the service, (4) method of payment, and (5) how the parties characterize the transaction. RESTATEMENT (SECOND) OF AGENCY § 220 (2); *Chapman v. Black*, 741 P.2d 998 (Wash. App. 1987).

These facts could be argued either way. Here, most of the factors suggest that Owen is an independent contractor and not an employee or servant of Best Care. In particular items 1, 2, and 5 of the contract favor characterizing Owen as an independent contractor, while items 4 and 6 of the contract indicate some level of oversight and control on the part of Best Care. The self-labeling in item 1 is evidence, but is not decisive.

Point Two:	Owen had neither actual nor apparent authority to bind Best Care to the contract to purchase the X-ray machine. Thus, Best Care is not liable to
(30-40%)	Vision for breach of contract.

Agency arises where one person consents that another shall act on his behalf and, at least as respects matters within the agency, subject to his control. *See generally* RESTATEMENT (SECOND) OF AGENCY § 1(1).

Actual authority arises where the principal communicates the authority to act to the agent. *See generally* RESTATEMENT (SECOND) OF AGENCY § 7; William A. Gregory, THE LAW OF AGENCY AND PARTNERSHIP, 3d ed. § 14. A principal is bound by contracts entered into between an agent with actual authority and a third party. *See generally* RESTATEMENT (SECOND) OF AGENCY § 144.

Item 3 of the contract provides that "[e]ach doctor is authorized to purchase supplies and equipment for Best Care's emergency room from a list of approved vendors located in City and within Best Care's price guidelines." This contract provision gave Owen actual authority to buy equipment for Best Care so long as it was within specified price guidelines from suppliers located in City for Best Care's account. If Owen had acted within this authority, Best Care would be bound even if Vision was unaware of the authorization. However, Owen exceeded his authority by purchasing equipment from Vision, which was not an approved vendor and was located 450 miles away from City. Therefore, Best Care is not liable under the contract because

Owen did not have actual authority.

Further, Best Care is not liable under the theory of apparent authority. Apparent authority is created as to a "third person by written or spoken words or any other conduct of the principal which, reasonably interpreted, causes the third person to believe that the principal consents to have the act done on his behalf by the person purporting to act for him." RESTATEMENT (SECOND) OF AGENCY § 27. There are no facts to suggest that Best Care made any representations that would create a reasonable basis for Vision to believe that Owen was authorized to purchase the X-ray machine.

Point Three:	Even if Owen is an independent contractor, Best Care is liable for Owen's negligence if Anita reasonably believed that Owen was acting
(25-35%)	as an agent of Best Care.

While a master is liable for the torts of its servant (employee) conducted within the scope of employment, a principal is not necessarily liable for the torts of its independent contractor agent. *See* RESTATEMENT (SECOND) OF AGENCY §§ 219, 250. A principal, however, may be estopped from denying liability for the torts of its independent contractor if the principal has created indicia of apparent authority. *See* RESTATEMENT (SECOND) OF AGENCY § 8B. This is sometimes referred to as the "holding out" theory or ostensible agency. *See Adamski v. Tacoma General Hospital*, 579 P.2d 970 (Wash. Ct. App. 1978) (The hospital may be liable under the "holding out" theory so long as the hospital acted in some way that leads the patient to a reasonable belief that he is being treated by a hospital employee).

RESTATEMENT (SECOND) OF AGENCY § 267 provides that "one who represents that another is his servant or other agent and thereby causes a third person justifiably to rely upon the care or skill of such apparent agent is subject to liability to the third person for harm caused by the lack of care or skill of the one appearing to be a servant or other agent as if he were such." Here, Best Care publicly advertised, on billboards strategically placed throughout City, that people should come to its emergency room because "Best Care's emergency room doctors are the absolute *best* and will really *care* for you." Anita apparently saw and believed the slogan on the billboards because she expressly requested the ambulance driver to take her to Best Care because "Best Care's emergency room doctors are the absolute best." It would be reasonable for a prospective patient to conclude, based on the billboards, that all doctors in Best Care's emergency room are employees of Best Care. As it was reasonable for Anita to believe that Owen was an agent of Best Care, under the general principle that a principal is liable for the torts committed by its agents Best Care would be liable to Anita's estate for Owen's actions (negligently severing an artery so that she bled to death).

NOTE: Most jurisdictions provide that a principal who hires an independent contractor to perform an "ultrahazardous" or "inherently dangerous" activity has a nondelegable duty to exercise due care to provide for the safety of persons who may be harmed by that activity. However, the usual tort and agency law definitions of ultrahazardous activity would not cover surgery, and there is no line of authority holding that a doctor's performance of surgery falls within this rule.

Agency & Partnership

(February 2005)

ANALYSIS

Legal Problems: (1) What is the nature of the legal relationship between Scott and Ruth?

(2) Does an agent have actual authority to bind an undisclosed principal to contracts that are made in violation of the principal's instructions to the agent?

(3) Does an agent have apparent authority to bind an undisclosed principal to contracts that are made in violation of the principal's instructions to the agent?

(4) Does an agent have inherent agency power to bind an undisclosed principal to contracts that are made in violation of the principal's instructions to the agent?

DISCUSSION

Summary

Ruth was Scott's agent for purposes of operating the restaurant. However, Ruth did not have actual authority to purchase supplies from Wholesale or to employ Nora for a 20-year term because these actions violated Scott's express instructions to Ruth. Ruth also lacked apparent authority to bind Scott because Scott was an undisclosed principal, and neither Wholesale nor Nora was aware that Ruth was acting in an agency capacity. Scott did nothing to manifest to Wholesale or Nora that Ruth had authority to act on his behalf.

Nevertheless, Ruth probably had inherent agency power to bind Scott to pay for the supplies purchased from Wholesale. The purchase of restaurant supplies is the kind of transaction usually performed by a restaurant manager, and the principal is appropriately held responsible for that transaction, even if Ruth violated Scott's orders in the way in which she carried it out. By contrast, hiring an assistant manager for a 20-year term is not the type of transaction one would ordinarily expect to be performed by a restaurant manager, and Ruth's inherent agency power probably did not extend to binding Scott to such a contract.

Point One: Ruth was Scott's general agent for the operation of the restaurant. Because the agency
(10-20%) was not disclosed to persons dealing with Ruth's Family Restaurant, Scott was an "undisclosed principal."

Ruth and Scott agreed that Ruth would act as Scott's agent. Moreover, Ruth was a "general agent" for Scott, having been authorized, as manager of the restaurant, to conduct a series of transactions to ensure continuity of service for Scott, as owner of Ruth's Family Restaurant. *See* RESTATEMENT (SECOND) OF AGENCY § 3(1) (1958). However, neither party disclosed the agency relationship to outsiders. As a result, Scott was Ruth's "undisclosed principal." *See* RESTATEMENT (SECOND) OF AGENCY § 4(3) (1958) (defining undisclosed principal).

As Scott's agent, Ruth could bind Scott to contracts with Wholesale or Nora if Ruth had actual authority, apparent authority, or inherent agency power to enter such contracts. The issue in this problem is whether an agent has the power to bind an undisclosed principal to contracts that the agent enters in violation of instructions from the principal.

Point Two: Because her actions violated Scott's express instructions, Ruth had no actual authority
(20-30%)   to purchase restaurant supplies from Wholesale or to hire Nora for a 20-year term.

Actual authority "to affect the legal relations of the principal" exists only if the agent's acts are "done in accordance with the principal's manifestations of consent." RESTATEMENT (SECOND) OF AGENCY § 7 (1958). Thus, Ruth had actual authority to bind Scott only insofar as Ruth acted consistently with Scott's "manifestations of consent" to her.

Here, Ruth's acts were completely contrary to Scott's instructions. Ruth was told not to contract with Wholesale, yet she did so. Ruth was instructed to hire employees only on an at-will basis, yet she hired Nora for a 20-year term. Because these acts were done contrary to Scott's "manifestations of consent" to Ruth, they were not done with actual authority.

Point Three: Ruth had no apparent authority to bind Scott because Scott was an undisclosed
(20-30%)   principal, and neither Nora nor Wholesale was aware that Ruth was Scott's agent.

Apparent authority is created when a purported principal causes third persons to believe that the purported agent has the power to act on behalf of the principal. In other words, apparent authority depends on a person's manifestations to a third person "that another is his agent." *See* RESTATEMENT (SECOND) OF AGENCY § 8 & comment a (1958).

Ruth could not have apparent authority to bind Scott because Scott made no manifestations to anyone that Ruth was his agent. In fact, no one other than Ruth or Scott was aware of their agency relationship. Furthermore, Scott and Ruth took pains to avoid disclosing the agency, even to the extent of Ruth's signing all contracts as "Ruth, d/b/a Ruth's Family Restaurant." "Apparent authority exists only with regard to those who believe and have reason to believe that there is authority; there can be no apparent authority created by an undisclosed principal." *Id.* Neither Nora nor Wholesale was aware that Scott was Ruth's principal.

Point Four: Scott might be liable to Wholesale on the theory that Ruth had inherent agency power

(25-35%) to bind Scott to contracts for the purchase of restaurant supplies, but a court is unlikely to conclude that Ruth had inherent agency power to bind Scott to an extraordinary employment contract.

Even if Ruth lacked actual or apparent authority to bind Scott, as Scott's agent, Ruth might have had "inherent agency power" to bind Scott to transactions undertaken to benefit Scott that were similar to the types of activities authorized, even if those transactions were in violation of orders. *See* RESTATEMENT (SECOND) OF AGENCY § 8A and comment a (1958). The concept of "inherent agency power" provides a means for courts to protect persons dealing with agents even when the agent violates orders. The theory is that an agent is generally acting "in the principal's interests" and is "trusted and controlled" by the principal. When such an agent's disobedience causes a loss, it is "fairer" that the loss fall upon the principal than on a third party, at least if the agent is engaged in acts generally of a kind that would fall within his or her actual authority, but for the violation of instructions.

Inherent agency power has generally been found in precisely the kind of situation presented on these facts—an agent has been given general power to manage a business and has done acts for the principal's account, albeit in violation of instructions. *See* RESTATEMENT (SECOND) OF AGENCY §§ 161, 194-195 (1958).

Under the facts of this problem, Ruth probably did have inherent agency power to contract with Wholesale for the delivery of restaurant supplies. Ruth was a general agent and was authorized to purchase restaurant supplies. Purchasing restaurant supplies from the local supply company that offered the best prices would be a "usual" or ordinary transaction for an agent managing a restaurant. If Ruth somehow violated Scott's special instructions, Scott should nonetheless be liable to Wholesale, especially since Scott's business certainly benefited by purchasing cheaper supplies from Wholesale. *See* RESTATEMENT (SECOND) OF AGENCY § 194 (1958).

On the other hand, Scott is not likely to be held liable to Nora. Ruth's entry into a contract to employ Nora as an assistant manager for a 20-year term was not a transaction that would be "usual" in the restaurant business. Although restaurant managers regularly hire and fire employees, at-will employment contracts are the norm. An employment contract specifying a 20-year term would be extraordinary and unusual in any business; certainly a 20-year term of employment is neither usual nor necessary in employing an assistant restaurant manager. A restaurant's business manager would not ordinarily have the power to enter such a contract. Therefore, Ruth had no inherent agency power to bind Scott to a 20-year employment contract with Nora.

Another fact to consider is that Nora was Ruth's niece, which suggests that the fairness concern that undergirds inherent agency analysis may, in fact, cut in Scott's favor here. It would seem unfair to hold Scott responsible for Ruth's violation of instructions when the violation was done to benefit a member of Ruth's family.

NOTE: The draft Third Restatement of Agency eliminates the concept of inherent agency power, but would reach the same results in the case of an undisclosed agency relationship under a theory that it calls "estoppel of undisclosed principal." *See* RESTATEMENT (THIRD) OF AGENCY, TENTATIVE DRAFT NO. 2, § 2.06.

Agency & Partnership

(February 2006)

ANALYSIS

Legal Problems: (1)   Is Dealer vicariously liable for Sales's negligence?

           (a)   Do Dealer and Sales have a master-servant relationship?

           (b)   Was Sales acting within the scope of his employment?

           (2)   Has Sales violated his fiduciary duty to Dealer such that he must give Dealer the $200 that Friend paid him?

DISCUSSION

Summary

Dealer is vicariously liable for Sales's negligence. Dealer and Sales have a master-servant relationship because Dealer employed Sales to perform services on behalf of Dealer, and Dealer had the right to control the physical conduct of Sales's performance. When Sales negligently injured Ped, Sales was acting within the scope of his employment as he had been assigned the task of delivering the SUV to Rich in Smalltown.

Sales, as an agent, is a fiduciary. Sales violated his fiduciary duty to Dealer by failing to obey instructions and failing to act solely for the benefit of Dealer. Sales must give all profits arising from the agency relationship to the principal. Therefore, Sales must give the $200 to Dealer.

Point One: (5-15%)
Dealer is vicariously liable for Sales's negligence if there is a relationship between Dealer and Sales that qualifies as master and servant (*see* Point One(a)), and Sales was acting within the scope of his employment when he negligently injured Ped (*see* Point One(b)).

Masters are liable for the torts of their servants committed while acting in the scope of their employment. RESTATEMENT (SECOND) OF AGENCY § 219(1). Therefore, Dealer is vicariously liable for Sales's negligence if (a) Dealer and Sales created an agency relationship that rises to the level of master-servant, and (b) Sales was acting within the scope of his employment when he negligently injured Ped.

Point One(a): (25-35%)
Dealer and Sales created a master-servant relationship.

Agency is a fiduciary relationship "which results from the manifestation of consent by one person to another that the other shall act on his behalf and subject to his control, and the consent by the other so to act." RESTATEMENT (SECOND) OF AGENCY § 1(1).

Sales is a full-time employee of Dealer. Although (1) Dealer did not generally deliver SUVs, (2) Sales was employed as a salesperson, not a driver, (3) delivery was made after the normal workday, and (4) Rich agreed to pay Sales $75 for delivery, Sales was still an agent, acting on behalf of Dealer and subject to Dealer's control, when he delivered the SUV to Rich. Sales delivered the SUV at the request of Dealer. The delivery was for the benefit of Dealer. Dealer agreed to make the delivery because Dealer "was eager to please Rich." Sales made the delivery subject to Dealer's control. Dealer provided directions to Rich's house and instructions regarding the drive ("Drive straight to his house, no detours. Drive carefully and no speeding. I don't want any dents in that SUV."). Overall, the facts support a conclusion that an agency relationship existed between Dealer and Sales.

This agency relationship between Dealer and Sales rises to the level of master-servant. "A master is a principal who employs an agent to perform services and who controls or has a right to control the physical conduct of the [agent's] performance." Restatement (Second) of Agency § 2(1). This is a fact-based analysis. RESTATEMENT (SECOND) OF AGENCY § 220 specifies factors to be considered in determining whether an agent is a servant or, instead, an independent contractor. The most important factor is the extent of control that Dealer may exercise over the details of the work. *See Binsau v. Garstin*, 177 A.2d 639, 641 (Del. 1962); *Miller v. Component Homes, Inc.*, 356 N.W.2d 213, 217 (Iowa 1984). Dealer provided Sales with instructions regarding speed and route, which indicates the power to control the manner in which Sales performed the work in question.

Other factors that support a master-servant relationship include the following: Delivering SUVs is not a distinct occupation for Sales. Delivering SUVs is not work done by a specialist without supervision. Delivering SUVs does not require special skills or equipment. Further, Sales is a full-time employee of Dealer, and Dealer did not pay Sales any extra money for this work.

[NOTE: There are some factors that support an argument that Sales was acting as an independent contractor rather than servant. Delivering SUVs was not a regular part of Dealer's business. This was an *ad hoc* assignment, not a regular part of Sales's duties. Sales was paid separately for this work ($75 by Rich). Further, Sales delivered the SUV after his regular hours of employment. While overall, it is likely that a court would conclude that the agency relationship between Dealer and Sales rises to the level of a master-servant relationship, an applicant should receive credit for a cogent argument either way.]

Point One(b): (25-35%)
Sales was acting in the scope of his employment when he negligently injured Ped.

For Dealer to be held vicariously liable for Sales's negligence, the tort must have been committed within the scope of Sales's employment. Conduct is "within the scope of employment if, but only if" it is conduct that the person was employed to perform, it occurs substantially within the authorized time and space limits, and it is done to serve the master. RESTATEMENT (SECOND) OF AGENCY § 228. Additionally, conduct is "within the scope of employment" if it is "of the same general nature as that authorized, or incidental to the conduct authorized." RESTATEMENT (SECOND) OF AGENCY § 229(1).

An applicant might argue that delivering the SUV was not "within the scope of employment." Although Sales delivered the SUV to serve Dealer, Sales was employed as a salesperson. Additionally, the delivery was performed after the normal workday and in Smalltown, not Capital City, where the dealership was located.

However, scope of employment is determined by the manifestations of the master. It "includes only acts of the kind authorized, done within limits of time and space which approximate those created by the authorization." RESTATEMENT (SECOND) OF AGENCY § 228 cmt. a. Dealer specifically authorized Sales to deliver the SUV to Smalltown after work. Therefore, this act was authorized and within the scope of employment.

While the escapade with Friend might be a "frolic" that exceeded the scope of Sales's employment, the accident occurred after any "frolic" had ended and while Sales was completing the delivery of the SUV pursuant to Dealer's instructions.

Point Two: (20-30%)
Sales violated his fiduciary duty to Dealer and therefore must give the $200 to Dealer.

As an agent (*see* Point One(a) above), Sales owes a fiduciary duty to Dealer, his principal, with respect to matters within the scope of the agency. RESTATEMENT (SECOND) OF AGENCY § 13. This includes the duty to obey reasonable instructions and the duty to act solely for the benefit of the principal with respect to matters within the scope of his agency. *See* RESTATEMENT (SECOND) OF AGENCY §§ 385, 387. When Sales made a detour to help Friend move, Sales violated his duty to obey the reasonable instruction "Drive straight to his house, no detours. Drive carefully and no speeding." By using the SUV for his own benefit, Sales also violated his duty to act solely for the benefit of Dealer as he used the SUV to make a personal profit. As a result, Sales is liable to Dealer for the $200. *See* RESTATEMENT (SECOND) OF AGENCY §§ 403 (agent who makes a profit in violation of his duty of loyalty is liable to principal for that profit), 404 (agent who, in violation of his duty, uses principal's assets for his own gain is subject to liability for that profit).

Further, even if an applicant were to argue that Sales had not violated his duty to Dealer, Sales would still be obligated to give Dealer the $200. An "agent's primary function is to make profits for the principal, and his duty to account includes accounting for any unexpected and incidental accretions whether or not received in violation of duty." RESTATEMENT (SECOND) OF AGENCY § 388 cmt. a.

Agency & Partnership

(July 2006)

ANALYSIS

Legal Problems: (1)   (a)   Is Uncle a co-owner of a business for profit and therefore a partner of Monster Tires?

                   (b)   Did Uncle have authority to bind Monster Tires when he ordered tires from TireCo?

   (2)   Did Friend have authority to bind Monster Tires when he purchased the yacht?

   (3)   Are the partners personally liable for the obligations of the partnership?

DISCUSSION
Summary

Monster Tires is liable to TireCo for the tires Uncle ordered. Uncle is a partner of Monster Tires because he is a co-owner of a business for profit. As a partner, Uncle had at least apparent authority to bind the partnership to transactions in the ordinary course of business. Monster Tires is not liable to Custom Yachts for the yacht Friend ordered. Because the purchase of the yacht was not in the ordinary course of business of the partnership, *all* partners must authorize the purchase for it to become an obligation of the partnership. The partners are personally liable on the TireCo contract because partners in a general partnership are jointly and severally liable for all partnership obligations. Only Friend is personally liable on the Custom Yachts contract.

Point One(a) (20-30%)
Uncle did not become a partner at the time he originally lent Nephew money, but he later became a partner when he agreed to accept a one-third share of all the profits.

A partnership is defined as an association of two or more persons to carry on as co-owners of a business for profit whether or not the persons intend to form a partnership. REVISED UNIF. PARTNERSHIP ACT (RUPA) § 202(a). Uncle originally loaned money to Nephew so Nephew could buy the tire dealership. Loaning money to Nephew does not make Uncle a partner, nor does the fact that Nephew repaid the loan on the basis of 50% of the profits of the business. RUPA § 202(c)(3) (a person who shares profits is presumed to be a partner "unless the profits were received in payment . . . of a debt . . . or of interest or other charge on a loan").

Uncle's status changed, however, when Uncle agreed to forgive the loan in return for a one-third share of the profits. Now Uncle falls under the partnership presumption and Uncle is a partner. This conclusion is strengthened by the fact that Uncle at the same time also agreed to provide rent-free space to the business, something a co-owner might do for a business.

[NOTE: Better applicants should recognize that Uncle and Nephew did not initially create a partnership because Uncle did not agree to participate in a business for profit.]

Point One(b) (20-30%)
As a partner, Uncle is an agent of the partnership. He can bind the partnership to the contract to buy tires from TireCo because this is the kind of business carried on by the partnership.

Every partner is an agent of the partnership for the purposes of its business. RUPA § 301(1). If Uncle was a partner at the time of the second store opening, his act of ordering the tires bound the partnership because it was an act apparently for carrying on the ordinary course of partnership business. As a partner, Uncle had at least apparent authority to place orders with Big Rubber, Inc., TireCo, or another manufacturer. *See id.* This would be so even if Uncle did not usually order tires and, indeed, even if he was not ever involved in the day-to-day operations of the business. While it does not appear that Uncle had actual authority from his other two partners to order the tires, he could still bind the partnership unless the TireCo representative knew or had received notification prior to the time Uncle placed the order that Uncle lacked authority to do so. *Id.* Therefore, Monster Tires is liable to TireCo.

Point Two (20-30%)
Monster Tires is not liable to Custom Yachts because Friend had no authority to purchase the yacht.

Although Friend was a partner at the time he ordered the yacht, this purchase is not apparently for carrying on the ordinary course of the tire dealership business. This is so, even though Friend regularly entertains in the course of business, because the purchase of a yacht is an extraordinary transaction. Friend therefore binds the partnership only if his act was authorized by all the other partners. RUPA § 301(2). The facts indicate that Nephew and Friend agreed that Friend should purchase the yacht, but that Uncle was opposed to buying it. Because an act outside the ordinary course of business of a partnership may be undertaken only with the consent of all of the partners, RUPA § 401(j), Friend had no actual authority to buy the yacht.

Friend also did not have apparent authority to buy the yacht because Custom Yachts could not reasonably believe that buying a yacht was in the ordinary course of business of a tire dealership. Therefore, Monster Tires does not have to pay Custom Yachts.

[NOTE: Applicants who fail to see that the purpose of a yacht is not in the ordinary course of the partnership's business could conclude that Friend had actual, or apparent, authority to purchase the yacht and bind the partnership.]

Point Three (10-15%)
Uncle, Nephew, and Friend are jointly and severally liable on the contract with TireCo because that contract is an obligation of the partnership, but only Friend is liable on the Custom Yachts contract.

All partners are jointly and severally liable for all obligations of the partnership. RUPA § 306(a). The association of Uncle, Nephew, and Friend is a general partnership because the partners took no steps to create a limited partnership. The obligation to TireCo is one that occurred in the ordinary course of business. Therefore, Uncle, Nephew, and Friend are each personally liable to TireCo. However, in order to recover from them individually, TireCo must secure a judgment against both the partnership and the named partners. Furthermore, TireCo must first seek recovery from the assets of the partnership before it can attempt to levy execution against individual partners. RUPA § 307.

Only Friend is liable on the Custom Yachts contract because Friend had no authority to purchase the yacht for the partnership (*See* Point Two). Under agency law, when an agent acts without authority, a third party (here, Custom Yachts) can recover from the agent. *See* RESTATEMENT (SECOND) OF AGENCY §§ 329-30.

Agency & Partnership

(February 2007)

ANALYSIS

Legal Problems: (1) Is a limited partner entitled to (a) copies of contracts between the limited partnership and entities related to or controlled by the general partner, (b) copies of contracts generally between the limited partnership and other entities, (c) copies of the limited partnership's federal and state tax returns, and (d) copies of all correspondence between the limited partnership and all other parties for a five-year period?

(2) If the limited partners remove the general partner, are they by that act alone liable to persons who transact business with the partnership?

(3) If the limited partners, after removing the general partner, run the limited partnership until a replacement general partner can be found, are they liable to persons who transact business with the partnership?

DISCUSSION

Summary

Limited partners have a right to obtain from the general partner "upon reasonable demand" information regarding the state of the business and financial condition of the limited partnership, copies of tax returns, and such other information regarding the partnership's affairs as is just and reasonable. In this case, the tax returns are clearly required to be disclosed, the contracts are required to be disclosed under both the financial condition requirement and the other information requirement, and the correspondence is probably required to be disclosed under the other information requirement (although a court could conclude that the request is unreasonably broad).

Limited partners have the right to remove a general partner without that act being treated as an exercise of "control" of the limited partnership and without becoming liable for the limited partnership's obligations.

If, following removal of the general partner, the limited partners choose to run the partnership's business, then they will be exercising control over the limited partnership and each limited partner will be liable to persons who reasonably believe, based upon the limited partner's conduct, that the limited partner is acting as a general partner. Aggressive disclosure of the limited partners' status as limited, but not general partners, could limit such liability.

Point One (40-50%)

<u>A limited partner is absolutely entitled to copies of tax returns and is entitled to such copies of contracts and correspondence as is just and reasonable.</u>

Under the Revised Uniform Limited Partnership Act (RULPA), a limited partner has a right to "inspect and copy" partnership records that are required to be kept pursuant to § 105 of the Act, and, in addition, to obtain from the general partner "upon reasonable demand":

> "true and full information regarding the state of the business and financial condition of the limited partnership," RULPA § 305(2)(i);

> "promptly after becoming available, a copy of the limited partnership's federal, state, and local income tax returns for each year," RULPA § 305(2)(ii); and

> "other information regarding the affairs of the limited partnership as is just and reasonable." RULPA § 305 (2)(iii).

In some jurisdictions, the reasonableness of a demand will depend, in part, on the purpose for which the limited partner is seeking disclosure. *See, e.g., Madison Ave. Inv. Partners, LLC v. America First Real Estate Inv. Partners, LP*, 806 A.2d 165 (Del. Ch. 2002). Where, as here, the limited partner has substantial reason to suspect mismanagement of the limited partnership and wishes to obtain partnership documents to investigate the matter, the limited partner has a right to access those documents. *Id.*; *Somerville S Trust v. USV Partners, LLC,* 2002 WL 1832830 (Del. Ch. 2002).

Baker probably acted improperly in refusing to provide information in response to Tim's request for "copies of contracts between the limited partnership and entities related to or controlled by the general partner." This request should be covered under the first subsection of the Act because such information relates to the "business and financial condition of the limited partnership." In addition, where there is a suggestion that a general partner is engaged in self-dealing, a limited partner's request for specific information that would confirm or disprove that suggestion is surely "just and reasonable."

Tim's demands for "copies of contracts generally between the limited partnership and other entities" are also probably covered under the first and third subsections for the same reasons. Such information is potentially relevant both to the general "business and financial condition" of the partnership and to the possibility that Baker has been self-dealing.

The request for copies of the limited partnership's federal and state tax returns is specifically covered under the second subsection of the statute. In addition, tax returns are documents that the limited partnership is required to keep and that a limited partner may inspect and copy at any time. RULPA § 305(2)(ii).

Tim's request for "copies of all correspondence between [the limited partnership] and any other parties for the past five years" may go too far. This request must be honored, if at all, only if the request is "just and reasonable" under the third subsection of the statute. Whether a demand for copies of all correspondence is "just and reasonable" is certainly debatable. Under the circumstances, Tim would claim that it is a reasonable demand that would provide information useful in determining whether Baker was properly managing the business. Baker would claim that the request goes far beyond what is reasonable, and is essentially an effort to delve into all the files of the business on a fishing expedition for evidence of wrongdoing.

Point Two (20-30%)

Limited partners are not liable as general partners simply for removing a general partner.

A limited partner is generally not liable for the obligations of a limited partnership. RULPA § 303(a). *See, e.g., Zeiger v. Wilf*, 755 A.2d 608 (N.J. Super. App. Div. 2000). However, a limited partner can become so liable if "in addition to the exercise of his [or her] rights and powers as a limited partner, he [or she] participates in the control of the business." RULPA § 303(a). Thus, the question whether the limited partners would be liable for partnership obligations were they to remove Baker as general partner would be resolved by determining whether the act of removing the general partner would be "participat[ion] in the control of the business." *Id.*

Because of the inherent "difficulty of determining when the 'control' line has been overstepped," RULPA (and the parallel laws of most states) specifically enumerates certain activities in which a limited partner may engage "without being deemed to have taken part in control of the business." § 303(b), official cmt. This so-called "safe harbor" list of activities that do not constitute the exercise of control provides specifically that a "limited partner does not participate in the control of the business" for purposes of incurring liability under § 303(a) "solely by . . . proposing [or] voting . . . [on the] removal of a general partner." § 303(b)(6)(v). Thus, the limited partners in Astoria may remove Baker as general partner without gaining liability for the limited partnership's obligations.

In states that have adopted the 2001 Uniform Limited Partnership Act, the situation is even clearer. Limited partners are "not personally liable, directly or indirectly, by way of contribution or otherwise, for an obligation of the limited partnership solely by reason of being a limited partner, even if the limited partner participates in the management and control of the limited partnership." 2001 UNIFORM LTD. P'SHIP ACT § 303. The new Act provides the limited partners a "full, status-based liability shield" akin to the protection given corporate shareholders. *Id.*, official cmt.

Point Three (20-30%)

Limited partners who participate in the control of the business can be held liable for the obligations owed by the limited partnership, but only to those persons who transact business with the limited partnership in the reasonable belief that the limited partner is a general partner.

Limited partners can become liable for the obligations of the limited partnership if they participate in the control of the business in ways not within the safe harbor exceptions in RULPA § 303(b). In particular, Tim's suggestion that Tim, Uma, and Vivian jointly "run the limited partnership" after removing Baker from the role of general partner appears to contemplate a degree of involvement in the business of the partnership that exceeds what is permitted by any of the safe harbor exceptions. Moreover, the facts suggest that this management and control of the business would necessarily constitute "participat[ion] in the control of the business," as the removal of Baker would leave no one but the limited partners in control.

Participation in the control of the business can make a limited partner liable for the obligations of the limited partnership, but that liability extends only to "persons who transact business with the limited partnership reasonably believing, based upon the limited partner's conduct, that the limited partner is a general partner." RULPA § 303(a). Thus the limited partners could attempt to limit their liability when running the business by giving all the parties with which the limited partnership does business notice that they are limited, not general, partners. *See, e.g., Folgers Architects, Ltd. v. Kerns*, 612 N.W.2d 539, 550-51 (Neb. Ct. App. 2000), *rev'd in part and aff'd in part on other grounds*, 633 N.W.2d 114 (Neb. 2001).

In some jurisdictions, however, liability could be imposed, even without third-party reliance, if "a limited partner's control activities are so extensive as to be 'substantially the same as' those of a general partner." *Zeiger v. Wilf*, 755 A.2d 608, 618 (N.J. Super. App. Div. 2000). In these jurisdictions, Tim, Uma, and Vivian would be well-advised to make their limited role clear and to search diligently for a replacement general partner to make clear that their temporary control did not amount to taking on a role "substantially the same" as that of a general partner.

As noted earlier, the 2001 Uniform Limited Partnership Act "renders the control rule extinct." 2001 UNIFORM LTD. P'SHIP ACT § 303, official cmt. Under this Act, Tim, Uma, and Vivian would have no liability for partnership obligations even if they participated directly in the management and control of the limited partnership.

Agency & Partnership

(July 2007)

ANALYSIS

Legal Problems: (1)   What is the legal relationship of Talker, Fixer, and Manager?

(2)(a) Did Fixer have actual authority to hire Crafty on behalf of TFM?

(2)(b) Did Fixer have apparent authority to hire Crafty on behalf of TFM?

(3)   Can Crafty hold Talker personally liable for unpaid wages?

DISCUSSION

Summary

Talker, Fixer, and Manager are doing business as a general partnership. As partners in a general partnership, they must ordinarily act by majority rule; thus Fixer had no actual authority to hire Crafty. However, Fixer had apparent authority to hire Crafty on behalf of the partnership. Therefore, TFM is liable for Crafty's unpaid wages. As a general partner, Talker is personally liable for the partnership's debts. However, Crafty can collect those wages from Talker only if Crafty obtains a judgment against Talker and first exhausts the partnership's assets.

Point One (20-30%)

Talker, Fixer, and Manager are general partners in TFM.

A partnership is the association of two or more persons to carry on as co-owners a business for profit whether or not the persons intend to form a partnership. *See* UNIF. PARTNERSHIP ACT (UPA) §§ 101(6) & 202(a) (1997); *cf. also* UPA § 6(1) (1914) (defining partnership in same manner as UPA (1997)). "A business is a series of acts directed toward an end." UPA § 202 cmt. 1 (1997). As co-owners of a business, each partner "has the power of ultimate control." *Id.*

In order to create a partnership, the parties must intend to take actions that create a partnership, but it is not necessary that they realize they are forming a partnership or describe their business as a partnership. "[W]here intent cannot be directly ascertained, it must be established from all of the facts, circumstances, actions, and conduct of the parties." *MacArthur Co. v. Stein*, 934 P.2d 214, 217-18 (Mont. 1997). A written agreement is generally not required.

A person who receives a share of the profits of the business is presumed to be a partner in the business. UPA § 202(c)(3) (1997); *cf.* UPA § 7(4) (1914) (receipt of a share of profits of a business is prima facie evidence that one is a partner in the business). The presumption does not apply in specified situations, such as where the profits are received in payment of a debt, as interest on a loan, as wages, as rent, or for the sale of the goodwill of a business. *See* UPA § 202(c)(3)(i)-(vi) (1997); *cf.* UPA § 7(4)(a)-(e) (1914) (providing similar exceptions).

Here, there is a for-profit business and the three friends share equally in the profits of the business. There are no facts suggesting that the profits are received in payment of a debt, as interest on a loan, as wages, as rent, or for the sale of the goodwill of a business. Furthermore, the conduct of Talker, Fixer, and Manager supports the partnership presumption: each of them participates in the business on a regular basis; they meet regularly to discuss the business; and the name of the business includes initials from each of their names.

In sum, although there is no written partnership agreement, the conduct of Talker, Fixer, and Manager establishes that they have associated as co-owners of a business for profit. This association constitutes a partnership relationship. Because they have no agreement to the contrary, they have created a general partnership.

Point Two(a) (5-15%)

Fixer had no actual authority to bind the partnership to a contract of employment with Crafty.

Absent an agreement to the contrary, "[a] difference arising as to a matter in the ordinary course of business of a partnership may be decided by a majority of the partners." UPA § 401(a)(j) (1997); *see also* UPA § 18(h) (1914) (providing same rule as UPA (1997)). An act outside of the ordinary course of business requires the consent of all partners. UPA § 401(a)(j) (1997).

Hiring an employee to perform services in the partnership business is clearly a matter within the ordinary course of the business of the TFM partnership. No major change in or deviation from the cabinet restoration business is involved. Fixer was merely hiring additional help to deal with an overflow of business. *See State Comp. Ins. Fund v. Indus. Acc. Comm'n*, 82 P.2d 732, 734 (Cal. Ct. App. 1938) (general rule is that each partner has authority to bind the firm by employment of persons whose services are reasonably necessary for carrying on business); *Felice v. Felice*, 112 A.2d 581, 583 (N.J. Super. A.D. 1955) (partner can bind firm by engaging employees in ordinary course of business).

The facts of this problem make clear that a majority of the partners (two of the three) opposed the hiring of Crafty. Consequently, Fixer did not have actual authority to hire Crafty.

Point Two(b) (20-30%)

Fixer had apparent authority as a partner to bind the partnership when he hired Crafty.

Each partner has authority to bind the partnership by any act "for apparently carrying on in the ordinary course the partnership business or business of the kind carried on by the partnership . . . unless the partner had no authority to act for the partnership in the particular matter and the person with whom the partner was dealing knew or had received a notification that the partner lacked authority." UPA § 301(1) (1997); *see also* UPA § 9(1) (1914) (very similar to UPA

(1997)). The effect of UPA § 301(1) (1997) is to "characterize a partner as a general managerial agent having both actual and apparent authority co-extensive with the firm's ordinary business, at least in the absence of a contrary partnership agreement." UPA § 301 cmt. 2 (1997).

Under UPA (1997), a two-part analysis is required. First, it must be determined whether the particular act was "for apparently carrying on in the ordinary course the partnership business or business of the kind carried on by the partnership." *Id*. If it was, then the partnership is liable unless it is proven that the person dealing with the partner had actual knowledge or notification of the partner's lack of authority. *See RNR Inv. Ltd. P'ship v. Peoples First Cmty. Bank*, 812 So. 2d 561, 565-66 (Fla. Ct. App. 2002).

Here, hiring Crafty to help in cabinet restoration was in the ordinary course of a cabinet restoration business. *See* Point Two(a).

Therefore, the partnership will be bound unless it is proved that Crafty had known that Fixer lacked authority to hire Crafty, in which case Crafty would have no claim. The facts of the problem do not suggest that Crafty had knowledge of Fixer's lack of authority; therefore, Fixer had apparent authority as a partner to bind the partnership by hiring Crafty because the act appeared to be in the ordinary course of the partnership business.

[NOTE: The result under the 1914 version of UPA would be the same. *See* UPA § 9(1) (1914).]

Point Three (15-25%)

Talker is personally liable for Crafty's unpaid wages. However, to collect against Talker, Crafty must first obtain judgments against Talker and the partnership and exhaust the assets of the partnership.

A partner is jointly and severally liable for all obligations of the partnership. *See* UPA § 306(a) (1997). As discussed above, Fixer had apparent authority as a partner to bind the partnership to an employment contract with Crafty. Therefore, the unpaid wages are a partnership obligation for which Talker is jointly and severally liable.

However, to collect from Talker personally, Crafty must first obtain a judgment against Talker and against the partnership and levy execution against the partnership's assets. Ordinarily, a claimant may not take action against a partner's personal assets unless the partnership assets fail to satisfy the claimant's judgment. *See* UPA § 307(d) (1997). Moreover, under the UPA (1997), a judgment against a partnership is not, by itself, a judgment against a partner. Consequently, a judgment against a partnership may not be satisfied out of the partner's separate assets unless there is also a separate judgment against the partner. *See id.* § 307(c). However, a judgment against a partner personally may be sought in the same action as a judgment against the partnership.

In sum, the unpaid wages are a partnership obligation. Therefore, Crafty can execute against the separate assets of Talker to satisfy the claim for unpaid wages only if Crafty obtains a judgment against Talker as well as obtaining a judgment against the partnership and exhausting its assets.

[NOTE: Under the UPA (1914), a partner is jointly, as opposed to jointly and severally, liable for obligations of the partnership. *See* UPA § 15(b) (1914). Consequently, all partners must be joined as defendants in an action based upon a partnership contract unless a statute permits otherwise. *See generally* WILLIAM GREGORY, THE LAW OF AGENCY AND PARTNERSHIP § 207(A)-(C) (West 3d ed. 2001). Moreover, a partnership is not a legal entity under the UPA (1914). Therefore, a third party cannot sue the partnership and is required to sue all the individual partners unless a statute permits a suit against the partnership as an entity. *See id.* While the UPA (1914) does not require exhaustion of partnership assets prior to execution upon the separate assets of a partner, case law in a number of UPA jurisdictions imposes such a requirement. *See id.* § 207(E).]

Agency & Partnership

(July 2008)

ANALYSIS

Legal Problems: (1)   Can Green, as a judgment creditor of Amy, attach and execute upon the partnership real estate?

        (2)   What steps should Red take to collect the amount of his loan to Beck from Beck's interest in the partnership?

        (3)   Does White have a right to inspect partnership books and records and to participate in the management of the partnership?

        (4)   Can White force a dissolution and winding up of the partnership?

DISCUSSION

Summary

Green cannot attach and execute upon the partnership property because that property is owned by the partnership and is not subject to attachment and execution by a creditor of an individual partner. To collect the amount of his loan to Beck, Red must first reduce his claim to a judgment and seek a charging order against the partner's financial interest in the partnership. White does not have a right to inspect partnership books and records because non-financial partnership rights, such as the right to inspect partnership books and records, to demand information from other partners, or to participate in the management or affairs of the partnership, cannot be exercised by a creditor of an individual partner, nor can they be assigned by a partner.

White cannot force a dissolution and winding up of the partnership. A transferee of a partner's financial interest in the partnership may only seek dissolution and winding up of the partnership if the partnership is at will or, if the partnership is for a term or a particular undertaking, after the term or undertaking has been completed. Here, the partnership is for a specific term, and that term has not expired.

Point One (20–30%)
Green, a judgment creditor of Amy, an individual partner, cannot attach and execute upon the partnership real estate.

A judgment creditor of an individual partner may not attach and execute upon partnership real estate to satisfy his claim against that partner.

Under the Uniform Partnership Act (UPA) (1914), partners are tenants in partnership in specific items of partnership property. UPA § 25 (1914). The incidents of this tenancy include an equal right to use the partnership property for partnership purposes. *Id.* § 25(2)(a). However, a partner's interest in specific items of partnership property is not subject to attachment or execution except upon a claim against the partnership. *Id.* § 25(2)(c).

Under the Uniform Partnership Act (1997), the partnership is a legal entity distinct from its partners. UPA § 201(a) (1997). Partnership property is owned by the partnership and a partner is not a co-owner of such property. *Id.* § 501. Therefore, partnership property is not subject to execution by an individual partner's creditors. *Id.* § 501 cmt.

Thus, Amy has no interest in partnership real estate that could be subject to attachment and execution by a judgment creditor such as Green.

[NOTE TO GRADERS: The 1914 UPA and the 1997 UPA reach the same result through slightly different reasoning. The key point under both acts is that partnership property is not the individual property of the partners and can't be attached or executed upon by judgment creditors of an individual partner. While Amy's personal creditor cannot reach partnership property as discussed in Point Two, the creditor could reach Amy's interest in the partnership.]

Point Two (20–30%)
Red should reduce his claim against Beck to a judgment and should then seek a charging order against Beck's financial interest in the partnership.

A creditor of an individual partner who wants to pursue a partner's financial interest in the partnership must first reduce his claim to a judgment. A creditor of an individual partner who has reduced his claim to a judgment may seek a charging order against that partner's financial interest in the partnership. UPA § 28 (1914); UPA § 504 (1997). The partner's financial interest (called the "transferable interest in the partnership" under the 1997 Act) is the partner's share of profits and losses and the right to receive distributions. *See* UPA § 26 (1914); UPA § 502 (1997). This financial interest is the only interest of a partner in the partnership that can be pursued by a creditor of an individual partner.

Thus, Red should reduce his claim against Beck to a judgment and should then seek a charging order against Beck's financial interest in the partnership.

[NOTE TO GRADERS: A court may also appoint a receiver of the share of distributions due or to become due to the partner and may make such other orders as are required in the circumstances of the case. UPA § 28(1) (1914); UPA § 504(a) (1997). The court may also, at any time prior to redemption of the interest, order a foreclosure of the interest subject to the charging order. UPA § 504(b) & cmt. 2 (1997) (noting that the 1997 Act codifies the case law under the 1914 Act).]

Another way Red might collect from Beck's interest in the partnership is to convince Beck to assign him Beck's interest in the partnership in which case Red would succeed to Beck's financial interest in the partnership. *See* Points Three and Four.

Point Three (20–30%)

White, an assignee of Curt's partnership interest, has received only Curt's financial interest in the partnership; White has no right to inspect partnership books and records or to participate in the management of the partnership.

Generally a person may become a partner only with the consent of all the partners. UPA § 18(g) (1914); UPA § 401(i) (1997). Thus, a partner does not have the unilateral power to make someone a partner by transferring his or her partnership interest to them.

The assignee of a partnership interest receives only the financial interest of the partner. *See* UPA § 27(1) (1914); UPA § 503(b)(1)–(2) (1997). The 1997 Act refers to this financial interest as the partner's transferable interest in the partnership. UPA § 502 (1997). "Section 502 continues the UPA Section 26 concept that a partner's only transferable interest in the partnership is the partner's share of profits and losses and right to receive distributions, that is, the partner's financial rights." *See id.* cmt. An assignee does not acquire the right to inspect partnership books and records, or to participate (or interfere) in the management or conduct of the business. UPA § 27(1) (1914); UPA § 503(a)(3) (1997).

In sum, because White is a mere assignee of Curt's partnership interest, White has received only Curt's financial interest in the partnership; White is not a partner and has no right to inspect partnership books and records or to participate in the management of the partnership.

Point Four (20–30%)
White may not force a dissolution and winding up of the partnership because it is a partnership for a term and the term has not yet been completed.

White is a transferee of Curt's financial interest in the partnership. (*See* Point Three.) A transferee of a partner's financial interest in a partnership may seek dissolution of the partnership if the partnership is a partnership at will or, if a partnership is for a term or a particular undertaking, the term or the undertaking has been completed. UPA § 32(2) (1914); UPA § 503(b)(3) (1997). Under the 1997 Act, the court will dissolve a partnership for a term and order a winding up at the request of a transferee of a partner's financial interest after the expiration of the term and only if it is equitable to do so. *See* UPA § 801(6)(i) & cmt. 9 (1997).

In this case the partnership is a partnership for a term of 25 years, not a partnership at will, and the term has not yet expired. Therefore, a transferee of a partner's financial interest may not seek dissolution and winding up of the partnership. Consequently, White cannot force a dissolution and winding up of the partnership.

Agency & Partnership

(February 2009)

ANALYSIS

(Agency and Partnership I.A.; II.A., B.)

Legal Problems: (1) Did Taster have actual authority to buy Monumental Muffins' muffin recipe for $4,000?

     (2) Did Taster have apparent authority to buy Bakers Bonanza's tart recipe for $6,000?

     (3) Did Taster have any authority to buy Parisian Delights' cake recipe in exchange for a copy of Hanson's fruitcake recipe?

     (4) Did Taster have any authority to buy the baking oven from Ironcast Enterprises for $5,000?

DISCUSSION

Summary

Taster purported to act as Hanson's agent. An agent acts with actual or apparent authority. Taster had actual authority to buy recipes for $5,000 cash or less. Hanson's is clearly bound to the contract with Monumental Muffins because Taster had actual authority to enter into that contract. Taster had apparent authority to enter into the contract with Bakers Bonanza and Hanson's is legally bound to that contract. Taster had no authority to reveal Hanson's secret recipe, and it was unreasonable for Parisian Delights to believe that Taster had such authority, so Hanson's is not bound to that contract. Taster also had no authority to enter into the contract with Ironcast, and Hanson's is not legally bound to that contract.

Point One (10–20%)
Taster had actual authority to enter into the Monumental Muffins muffin recipe contract for $4,000 on Hanson's behalf. Therefore, Hanson's is legally bound to that contract.

When Hanson's hired Taster to act on Hanson's behalf, an agency relationship was created. *See* RESTATEMENT (THIRD) OF AGENCY § 1.01 ("Agency is the fiduciary relationship that arises when one person (a "principal") manifests assent to another person (an "agent") that the agent shall act on the principal's behalf. . . ."). As Hanson's agent, Taster had actual authority to "take action designated or implied in [Hanson's] manifestations to [Taster] and acts necessary or incidental to achieving [Hanson's] objectives. . . ." *Id*. at § 2.02(1).

The contract between Hanson's and Taster empowered Taster to enter into contracts on Hanson's behalf to buy baked-goods recipes for a price not to exceed $5,000. Thus, Taster had actual authority to enter into the contract to buy Monumental Muffins' muffin recipe for $4,000, and Hanson's is legally bound to that contract.

Point Two (30–40%)
Taster had apparent authority to enter into the contract with Bakers Bonanza to buy the almond-pecan tart recipe for $6,000 on Hanson's behalf. Therefore, Hanson's is legally bound to that contract.

An agent has apparent authority to act on behalf of a principal when "a third party reasonably believes the actor has authority to act on behalf of the principal and that belief is traceable to the principal's manifestations." RESTATEMENT (THIRD) OF AGENCY § 2.03. Apparent authority can co-exist with actual authority; it can also exist in the absence of any actual authority. *See In re Victory Corrugated Container Corp.*, 183 B.R. 373, 376–77 (Bankr. D.N.J. 1995).

Here, Taster did not have actual authority to enter into contracts exceeding $5,000. Thus, Taster did not have actual authority to contract with Bakers Bonanza for $6,000. However, Hanson's president stated at the annual baking industry trade show that Taster would be buying recipes on Hanson's behalf. These manifestations by Hanson's would reasonably cause Bakers Bonanza to believe that Taster was acting with authority when contracting to buy recipes. The manifestations were made by Hanson's president, a person entitled to speak on behalf of Hanson's. The amount involved ($6,000) was within the price range typically paid for baked-goods recipes. Therefore, Taster had apparent authority to enter into the contract to buy Bakers Bonanza's tart recipe and Hanson's is legally bound to that contract.

Point Three (20–30%)
Taster did not have authority to buy Parisian Delights' chocolate truffle cake recipe in exchange for Hanson's fruitcake recipe. Therefore, Hanson's is not legally bound to that contract.

Taster did not have actual authority to buy Parisian Delights' cake recipe in exchange for Hanson's fruitcake recipe—in fact, Taster's contract expressly forbids such an action. Nor did Taster have apparent authority to enter into the contract with Parisian Delights. Here, the facts state that baked-goods recipes typically sold for $3,000 to $6,000. There is no suggestion that the use of non-cash consideration is typical. Further, given Hanson's long history in the baking industry and its close guarding of the fruitcake recipe, Parisian Delights may well have known that Hanson's fruitcake recipe was secret and that its disclosure was not authorized. When facts suggest it may be unreasonable for a third party to believe that a purported agent has authority, the third party has the duty to make further inquiry. *See* RESTATEMENT (THIRD) OF AGENCY § 2.03. Had Parisian Delights asked Hanson's if Taster had authority to obtain recipes for non-cash consideration, Taster's lack of any authority would have been readily determinable.

[NOTE: Applicants should not receive any credit for discussing inherent authority as that doctrine is not applicable generally nor on the facts.]

Point Four (10–20%)
Hanson's is not liable to Ironcast Enterprises on the contract for the oven as Taster had no authority to enter into that contract on Hanson's behalf.

Taster had no actual or apparent authority to enter into the contract with Ironcast Enterprises to buy the baking oven on Hanson's behalf. Actual authority does not exist because the contract limited Taster's authority to acquiring recipes—contracting to buy an oven was not within the express grant of authority nor was it an act "necessary or incidental to achieving the principal's objectives." RESTATEMENT (THIRD) OF AGENCY § 2.02. Apparent authority does not exist because no acts of Hanson's reasonably interpreted could have caused Ironcast to believe that Taster had authority to buy baking equipment. Therefore, Hanson's is not legally bound on the contract to buy the oven from Ironcast for $5,000.

Agency & Partnership
(July 2009)

Legal Problems: (1)   What type of entity is the "Metropolitan Limited Partnership"?

                        (2)   Can Marketing recover from Andy, Ben, and Carol in their individual capacities for the amounts it is owed by MLP and what steps must it follow if it tries to do so?

                        (3)   Can Zack's estate recover from Andy, Ben, and Carol in their individual capacities for the wrongful death claim?

DISCUSSION

Summary

Despite being labeled a limited partnership, the Metropolitan Limited Partnership (MLP) is not a limited partnership because it lacks a general partner. Even though a Certificate of Limited Partnership was ultimately filed, that filing does not create a limited partnership when no general partner has signed the partnership agreement. By their actions in buying the land and arranging for the marketing of the venture's property, Andy, Ben, and Carol acted as co-owners of a business for profit and thereby formed a general partnership.

As partners in a general partnership, Andy, Ben, and Carol are each personally liable for partnership debts. Marketing can recover from Andy, Ben, and Carol in their individual capacities for the amounts it is owed by MLP if Marketing first obtains a judgment against each of Andy, Ben, and Carol and against MLP and levies execution on MLP's assets.

Zack's estate can recover for the wrongful death claim from Andy, Ben, and Carol in their individual capacities if it follows the same procedures. The fact that the Certificate of Limited Partnership was filed before Zack's claim arose does not change this result because that filing did not create a limited partnership.

Point One (35–45%)
Metropolitan Limited Partnership is not a limited partnership, but is a general partnership.

Despite being labeled a limited partnership, MLP is not a limited partnership. Although Andy, Ben, and Carol may have intended to form a limited partnership, they did not succeed in doing so. To create a valid limited partnership, statutory requirements must be met. A limited partnership must include a general partner who has signed the initial Certificate of Limited Partnership filed with the Secretary of State. UNIF. LTD. P'SHIP ACT §§ 201(a)(3), 204, 801(4) (1976 with 1985 amendments). Here, Warren was designated as the general partner, but never signed the agreement. Thus, MLP never had a general partner and cannot qualify as a limited partnership.

Further, to create a limited partnership, a certificate of limited partnership must be filed with the state. *Id.* § 201. Here, such a certificate was not initially filed. Even though Andy, Ben, and Carol did ultimately file the Certificate of Limited Partnership, their failure to obtain the signature of a general partner prevents the formation of a limited partnership.

Instead, the venture is a general partnership. Andy, Ben, and Carol were acting as co-owners of a business for profit. As such, they formed a partnership whether or not they subjectively intended to. *See* UNIF. P'SHIP ACT (1997) § 202(a) (". . . the association of two or more persons to carry on as co-owners a business for profit forms a partnership, whether or not the persons intend to form a partnership."). As is the case here, individuals can inadvertently form a general partnership notwithstanding their expressed intention to do something else, in this case to form a limited partnership. *See id.* § 202 cmt. 1 ("Indeed, they may inadvertently create a partnership despite their expressed subjective intention not to do so.").

Had Andy, Ben, and Carol done nothing more than purchase property, they might have avoided a partnership designation under the Uniform Partnership Act which states that neither "common property" nor "part ownership" alone is enough to establish a partnership. *See id.*   § 202(c). However, in addition to owning the property, Andy, Ben, and Carol hired a marketing company to develop a campaign to resell the land as "Metropolitan Estates." This exceeds co-ownership and thus Andy, Ben, and Carol are general partners and MLP is a general partnership.

Point Two (35–45%)
Because MLP is a general partnership and Andy, Ben, and Carol are general partners in that partnership, as such, each is personally liable for partnership debts, including the amounts owed to Marketing. However, to collect from Andy, Ben, and Carol personally, Marketing must first obtain a judgment against Andy, Ben, and Carol individually and against MLP and levy execution against MLP's assets.

As partners in the general partnership that owns the property, Andy, Ben, and Carol "are liable jointly and severally for all obligations of the partnership unless otherwise agreed by the claimant or provided by law." *See* UNIF. P'SHIP ACT (1997) § 306(a). There being no agreement or statutory provision to the contrary, Andy, Ben, and Carol are jointly and severally liable for Marketing's claim.

However, to collect from Andy, Ben, and Carol personally, Marketing must first obtain a judgment against Andy, Ben, and Carol individually and against MLP and levy execution against MLP's assets. Ordinarily, a claimant may not take action against a partner's separate assets unless the partnership assets fail to satisfy the claimant's judgment. *See id.* § 307(d). Moreover, under the Uniform Partnership Act, a judgment against a partnership is not, by itself, a judgment against a partner. Consequently, a judgment against a partnership may not be satisfied out of the partner's separate assets unless there is also a judgment against the partner. *See id.* § 307(c). A judgment against a partner personally may be sought in the same action as a judgment against the partnership.

Here, if these procedures are followed and MLP's assets fail to satisfy Marketing's claim, Marketing may recover from Andy, Ben, and Carol personally.

Point Three (10–20%)
Andy, Ben, and Carol are each personally liable for the wrongful death claim even though that claim arose after they filed the Certificate of Limited Partnership, because the limited partnership did not have a general partner.

As general partners, Andy, Ben, and Carol are jointly and severally liable for the wrongful death claim. (*See* Point Two.) Although the wrongful death claim arose after the Certificate of Limited Partnership was filed in the name of Metropolitan, that filing does not protect Andy, Ben, and Carol because it failed to create a limited partnership due to the lack of a general partner. (*See* Point One.) Therefore, the act of filing is irrelevant, and Andy, Ben, and Carol are jointly and severally liable for the wrongful death claim. To recover from them, Zack's estate must follow appropriate procedures. (*See* Point Two.)

Agency & Partnership

(July 2010)

Legal Problems: (1)   What is the legal relationship among Fran, Gina, and Hank?

                            (2)   Is Ivan entitled to Gina's share of the monthly net profits of Petals?

                            (3)   Is Ivan entitled to inspect the books and records of Petals?

                            (4)   Is Fran entitled to use the delivery truck on Sundays to take her children to their soccer games?

DISCUSSION

Summary

Fran and Gina are general partners in the Petals partnership, but Hank is only a creditor of Petals. As a transferee of Gina's right to receive net profits in Petals, Ivan is legally entitled to Gina's share of those profits. However, that assignment does not make Ivan a partner. Therefore, Ivan does not have a right to inspect the books and records of Petals. Fran is not entitled to use the delivery truck on Sundays to take her children to their soccer games.

Point One (35%)
Fran and Gina are partners in Petals. Hank is a creditor of Petals.

A partnership is defined as "the association of two or more persons to carry on as co-owners a business for profit . . . whether or not the persons intend to form a partnership." UNIFORM PARTNERSHIP ACT (UPA) (1997) § 202(a); *see also* UPA (1914) § 6(1). Here, a partnership was formed when Gina joined Fran in running Petals. Because the partnership was formed *without* the formalities required of other types of partnerships, it is a general partnership.

Fran and Gina each receive a share of the net profits of Petals, and each is therefore presumed to be a partner in the business. UPA (1997) § 202(c)(3); UPA (1914) § 7(4). This presumption is supported by the fact that Gina is to receive her share of the net profits "for as long as Petals remains in business," and that Fran and Gina each work in the business and participate in the business planning for Petals. Further, Gina agreed to share in any losses that Petals might suffer. Therefore, Fran and Gina are partners in the Petals partnership.

Hank also receives a share of the net profits of Petals and, therefore, also might be presumed to be a partner in the partnership. However, this presumption does not apply where those profits are "received in payment of a debt by installment or otherwise." UPA (1997)   § 202(c)(3)(i); UPA (1914) § 7(4)(a). The statement on the memo line of Hank's check is evidence that Hank loaned money to the partnership. Hank is entitled to receive a share of the net profits of Petals only until his loan (plus interest) to Petals is paid in full, and therefore he is not presumed to be a partner in the business. In addition, Hank did not agree to share in any losses that Petals might suffer. Further, Hank does not play any role in the day-to-day operations of Petals. Hank is a creditor of Petals, but is not a partner in the partnership.

Point Two (25%)
As the transferee of a legally transferable interest in the partnership, Ivan is legally entitled to receive distributions that Gina would otherwise have received.

As a partner in the Petals partnership (*see* Point One), Gina has a transferable interest in the profits and losses of the partnership and in her right to receive distributions. UPA (1997)   § 502; UPA (1914) § 26. The transfer of that interest is permissible and creates in the transferee a right to receive distributions to which the transferor would otherwise be entitled. UPA (1997) § 503(b)(1); UPA (1914) § 27(1). Here, Gina transferred her right to receive a share of the net profits of Petals to Ivan when she assigned all of her interest in Petals to him. Therefore, Ivan is legally entitled to receive Gina's share of the net profits of Petals.

[NOTE: An applicant might add that a partnership need not give effect to a transferee's rights until it has notice of the transfer. UPA (1997) § 503(e). Here, the partnership had such notice because Gina gave Fran a copy of the letter effecting the transfer. An applicant might also note that the transfer of a partner's right to profits and losses and the right to receive distributions does not effect a termination or dissolution of the partnership.]

Point Three (25%)
Ivan is not entitled to inspect the books and records of Petals because he is not a partner in Petals.

As a partner in the Petals partnership, Gina has a transferable interest in the partnership (*see* Point Two). That interest, however, is limited. For example, a transfer of the partnership interest does not make the transferee a partner unless the other partner or partners consent to making the transferee a partner. On our facts, such consent was not given because Fran said, "I don't want anything to do with Ivan." Therefore, Ivan did not become a partner and is not entitled to access information concerning partnership transactions nor to inspect or copy the partnership books or records. UPA § 503(a)(3); UPA (1914) § 27(1).

Point Four (15%)
The delivery truck is partnership property, and Fran is not entitled to use it on Sundays to take her children to their soccer games.

Property is partnership property if it is acquired in the name of the partnership. UPA (1997) § 204(a)(1); UPA (1914) § 8(1). Partnership property is property of the partnership and not of the partners individually. UPA (1997) § 203; UPA (1914) § 25(1). Here, the delivery truck was purchased in the partnership's name and, therefore, is partnership property and not Fran's individual property. The facts do not suggest that the partners agreed that Fran could use the delivery truck for her own purposes on Sundays, and, absent such an agreement, Fran is not entitled to use the truck to take her children to their soccer games even if the partnership is not using the truck on that day.

[NOTE: Under § 27 of the UPA (1914) and § 503 of the UPA (1997), the transfer of all or any part of a partner's interest is not a dissolution of the partnership. Thus, Gina's gift to her son Ivan of her interest in the partnership does not dissolve the partnership.]

Agency & Partnership

(July 2011)

ANALYSIS

Legal Problems

(1)(a) If Adam immediately withdraws from the partnership, what are the consequences to him?

(1)(b) If Adam immediately withdraws from the partnership, what are the consequences to the partnership?

(2)(a) If Adam gives six months' written notice and then withdraws from the partnership, what are the consequences to him?

(2)(b) If Adam gives six months' written notice and then withdraws from the partnership, what are the consequences to the partnership?

(3) If the partnership's business is wound up after Adam's withdrawal, will he be personally liable for any partnership debts incurred during the winding-up process after his withdrawal?

DISCUSSION

Summary

Adam can withdraw from PSS, without complying with the six months' written notice requirement in PSS's partnership agreement, by giving notice of dissociation. But such a notice, although effective, would be wrongful because it would violate the notice requirement set forth in the partnership agreement. Thus, Adam would be liable to the partnership and to Beth and Chris for damages caused by Adam's wrongful dissociation. Further, Adam would not be able to force the cessation of the operations of PSS and a sale of partnership assets. Beth and Chris may vote to buy out Adam's interest and continue operations instead. Even if Adam's dissociation did lead to a sale of partnership assets, Adam would not be able to participate in the winding-up process.

On the other hand, if Adam gives the six months' notice required under PSS's partnership agreement, Adam's withdrawal would dissolve the partnership and force the winding up of PSS and the sale of the partnership assets. Adam could participate in that process but could not dictate the terms of the sale.

If the partnership business is wound up, Adam would be liable as a partner for liabilities appropriately incurred during the winding-up period whether or not he gives notice properly.

[NOTE: The following jurisdictions have enacted the Uniform Partnership Act (1997): Alabama, Alaska, Arizona, Arkansas, California, Colorado, Delaware, DC, Florida, Hawaii, Idaho, Illinois, Iowa, Kansas, Kentucky, Maine, Maryland, Minnesota, Mississippi, Montana, Nebraska, Nevada, New Jersey, New Mexico, North Dakota, Ohio, Oklahoma, Oregon, South Dakota, Tennessee, Texas, Vermont, Virginia, and Washington. The remaining states have the UPA (1914).]

Point One(a) (25%)

Under the Uniform Partnership Act (1997), Adam can dissociate from PSS without complying with the six months' written notice requirement under PSS's partnership agreement. However, dissociation from the partnership without giving the required six months' notice, although effective, would be wrongful and would make Adam liable for damages. A similar result would follow under the Uniform Partnership Act (1914).

Under the Uniform Partnership Act (UPA) § 601(1) (1997), a partner can dissociate from the partnership at any time by giving notice to the partnership. Thus, Adam can dissociate from the partnership by giving the partnership a notice of dissociation. Furthermore, the right to dissociate can be exercised by the dissociating partner at any time even if the exercise of the power to dissociate was wrongful. Dissociation is wrongful if it is done in contravention of the terms of the partnership agreement. *Id.* § 602(a), cmt. 1, § 602(b)(1).

Here, Adam's dissociation would be wrongful because the partnership agreement requires the giving of six months' written notice. Because Adam's dissociation would be wrongful, Adam would be liable to the partnership and to Beth and Chris for any damages caused by his dissociation. UPA § 602(c) (1997). Furthermore, as a wrongfully dissociating partner, Adam could not participate in the winding up of the business. *Id.* § 803(a)

Generally, the provisions of the UPA (1997) are default law that can be modified by the terms of a partnership agreement. However, certain rules cannot be modified. For example, a partnership agreement cannot modify the right to dissociate except to require that a dissociation notice be in writing. *Id.* § 103(b)(6). Therefore, even though the PSS partnership agreement requires that a partner give six months' written notice before the partnership can be dissolved, Adam can effectively dissociate from PSS. And, because Adam's dissociation would be wrongful, Adam would be liable to the partnership and to Beth and Chris for any damages caused by his dissociation. *Id.* § 602(c).

The result is similar under the Uniform Partnership Act of 1914. While that act does not recognize a concept of dissociation as that term is used in UPA (1997), it does recognize the right of a partner to dissolve a partnership. A dissolution is the "change in the relation of the partners caused by any partner ceasing to be associated in the carrying on as distinguished from the winding up of the business." Uniform Partnership Act (UPA) § 29 (1914). Dissolution of a partnership is caused by "the express will of any partner when" as here, there is "no definite term or particular undertaking," specified in the partnership agreement. *Id.* § 31(b).

Under the UPA (1914), if Adam notifies the partners that he no longer wishes to be associated with the partnership, the partnership will be dissolved. As under the UPA (1997), it is irrelevant that Adam's notice is in contravention of the terms in the partnership agreement, such as a requirement, as here, that he gives six months' notice. *Id.* § 31(2). Regardless of whether he complies with the partnership agreement, Adam's notice would result in the partnership's dissolution. But, as under the UPA (1997), if Adam wrongfully caused the partnership to be dissolved in contravention of the terms of the partnership agreement, the other partners have a right to damages for the breach of the partnership agreement. *Id.* § 38(2)(a)(II).

Point One(b) (20%)
Under the Uniform Partnership Act (1997), while Adam may immediately dissociate from the partnership, his wrongful dissociation will not necessarily lead to a dissolution and winding up of PSS. Beth and Chris may elect not to wind up the business but instead to purchase Adam's interest in PSS and continue its operations. A similar result follows under the Uniform Partnership Act (1914).

Under the UPA (1997), which recognizes the partnership as a separate legal entity from its partners, a partner's wrongful dissociation from the partnership does not cause the partnership to be dissolved if the remaining partners waive the right to have the partnership terminated and its business wound up. UPA § 802(b)(1) (1997). Here, because Adam's dissociation would be wrongful (*see* Point One (a)), under Section 802(b), the partnership would be terminated and its business would up unless the remaining partners, Beth and Chris, waived those rights. If they did, the partnership would have to purchase Adam's interest, *see id.* § 701(a), for a buyout price determined in accordance with § 701(b).

If Beth and Chris did not waive the right to wind up the business and terminate the partnership but decided to wind up the business and terminate the partnership, Adam could not participate in that winding-up process. *See* Point One(a). The persons winding up the business, here Beth and Chris, could choose to continue PSS's business for a "reasonable time." *Id.* § 803(c).

Under the UPA (1914), a rightful or wrongful withdrawal results in the dissolution of the partnership. UPA § 31(1) (1914). However, under § 38(2)(b) "[t]he partners who have not caused the dissolution wrongfully, if they all desire to continue the business in the same name, ... may do so . . . ." A partner who has caused the dissolution wrongfully is not granted the same right. *Id.* § 38(2)(c). Thus, Beth and Chris could choose to continue the business. If they did choose to continue the business, Adam would be entitled to receive the value of his interest less the damages he caused by wrongfully causing the partnership's dissolution. *Id.* § 38(2)(c)(II). If Beth and Chris chose not to continue the business, Adam would have the same rights to the partnership property as Beth and Chris would have subject to any damages he would owe them. *Id.* § 38(2)(c)(I).]

Point Two(a) (20%)
Under the Uniform Partnership Act (1997), if Adam gives the required six months' notice, his dissociation would not be wrongful; Adam would be entitled to participate in the dissolution and winding up of PSS (*see* Point Two (b)).

If Adam gives the six months' notice required under PSS's partnership agreement, his dissociation would not be wrongful. *See* UPA § 602(b) (1997). Thus, he would not be liable for damages to either the partnership or Beth or Chris. *See id.* § 602(c). His dissociation would result in dissolution of the partnership with the requirement that the partnership's business be "wound up." *Id.* § 801(1); *see also* § 802(a). Because Adam's dissociation would not be wrongful, he is entitled to participate in the winding up of the partnership. *Id.* § 803(a). Thus, by giving notice as required by the partnership agreement, Adam can force the cessation of operations of PSS and the sale of its assets. Lastly, because his dissociation would not be wrongful, Beth and Chris could not cause a buyout of his interest, nor would he be liable to them for damages. *See id.* § 701(a).

A similar result follows under the Uniform Partnership Act (1914). *See* UPA §§ 37, 38(1) (1914).

Point Two(b)(20%)
If Adam gives the required six months' notice, the partnership will be dissolved and wound up. Although Adam could participate in the winding-up process, Beth and Chris would control that process.

If Adam gives the required six months' notice, PSS will be dissolved and wound up. UPA § 801(1) (1997). Furthermore, Adam can participate in the winding-up process (*see* Point Two (a)). However, Adam is still only one of three partners, all of whom may participate in the winding up. Because no facts suggest that Adam has controlling management authority, Adam may vote to conduct an immediate winding up and sale of assets, but could be consistently outvoted by Beth and Chris should they decide to continue the partnership for a reasonable time after its dissolution. *See generally id.* § 803(c). Thus, Adam cannot force an immediate cessation of operations and sale of partnership assets even if he properly gives notice under the PSS partnership agreement. A similar result should follow under the Uniform Partnership Act (1914). *See* UPA §§ 37, 38(1) (1914).

Point Three (15%)
Partnership obligations appropriately incurred during the winding up process are obligations of all partners including a dissociating partner.

Under Section 804 of the Uniform Partnership Act (1997), the partnership is bound by a partner's act after dissolution if the act was appropriate to the winding up of the partnership. If the partnership is bound, then each partner is liable for his proportionate share of the liability. *See* UPA § 806 (1997); *see also* UPA § 306 (1997) ("all partners are liable jointly and severally for all obligations of the partnership"). Thus, a dissociating partner, whether the dissociation was rightful or wrongful, cannot avoid liability for partnership debts incurred during the winding up process.

A similar result follows under the UPA § 35(1) (1914). As to contractual debts, however, the partners' liability is only joint, not joint and severable. UPA § 15(b) (1914).

Agency & Partnership

(February 2012)

ANALYSIS

Legal Problems

(1) Is Garden LLP liable for the $500,000 judgment owed to the customer when the injury that led to the judgment occurred prior to the partnership's qualification as an LLP?

(2) Are the man and woman personally liable for the $500,000 judgment owed to the customer?

(3) Is the investor personally liable for the $500,000 judgment owed to the customer?

DISCUSSION

Summary

Garden LLP is the same entity as Garden Partnership and is liable for the $500,000 judgment owed to the customer even though the injury that led to that judgment occurred prior to the partnership's qualification as an LLP.

LLP status does not relieve partners of pre-existing liability for partnership obligations incurred prior to qualification as an LLP, although it does limit their liability for obligations incurred after such qualification. Therefore, the man and woman are jointly and severally liable for the $500,000 owed to the customer because the injury that led to the judgment occurred before Garden Partnership, then a general partnership in which the man and woman were the general partners, became Garden LLP.

A new partner is not personally liable for LLP obligations incurred before the person's admission as a partner. Therefore, the investor is not personally liable for the customer's injury because the investor was not a partner in Garden LLP (or Garden Partnership) when that injury occurred.

Point One (45%)
Garden LLP is liable to the customer for the judgment because the limited liability partnership is the same entity that existed prior to its qualification as an LLP and assumes all outstanding liabilities of the prior entity.

The Uniform Partnership Act (UPA 1997) adopts an entity theory of partnership. In other words, the partnership itself is a legal entity and not a mere aggregate of individual partners. *See* UPA § 201(a) (1997) ("A partnership is an entity distinct from its partners.").

An LLP continues to be the same entity that existed prior to the filing of a statement of qualification as an LLP. *Id.* § 201(b). "[T]he filing of a statement of qualification does not create a 'new' partnership. The filing partnership continues to be the same partnership entity that existed before the filing." *Id.* § 201 cmt.

Here, since Garden LLP is the same entity as Garden Partnership, it has all of Garden Partnership's outstanding obligations, and Garden LLP is liable to the customer for the judgment.

[NOTE: In states that have not adopted the UPA 1997, the same result follows if they have both the UPA 1914 and a separate statute providing for LLPs.]

Point Two (35%)
The man and woman are jointly and severally liable to the customer because the obligation to the customer was incurred prior to Garden Partnership's qualification as an LLP.

Under the UPA (1997), the partners in a partnership are jointly and severally liable for all obligations of the partnership "unless otherwise agreed by the claimant or provided by law." UPA § 306(a) (1997). [A similar result follows from § 15 of the UPA 1914.] Because the customer has not otherwise agreed, the man and woman are jointly and severally liable for the judgment obtained against Garden Partnership unless otherwise provided by law.

Here, the UPA does not protect the man and woman. The UPA provides that when a partnership has qualified as an LLP, any obligation "incurred while the partnership is a limited liability partnership, whether arising in contract, tort, or otherwise, is solely the obligation of the partnership." *Id.* § 306(c). Here, however, the obligation to the customer arose *before* the partnership qualified as an LLP, and the limited liability protection does not apply. Garden Partnership became a limited liability partnership only upon the filing of the statement of qualification with the secretary of state. UPA § 1001. "The connection between partner status and personal liability for partnership obligations is severed only with respect to obligations incurred while the partnership is a limited liability partnership. Partnership obligations incurred before a partnership becomes a limited liability partnership . . . are treated as obligations of an ordinary partnership." *Id.* § 306 cmt. 3. Consequently, the man and woman are jointly and severally liable for the judgment owed to the customer that arose prior to Garden Partnership qualifying as an LLP.

Point Three (20%)
The investor is not personally liable to the customer because the customer's injury occurred before the investor became a partner.

A person who is admitted as a partner is not personally liable for any partnership obligation incurred prior to the admission of the person to the partnership. UPA § 306(b) (1997). In this case, the injury to the customer and, consequently, the partnership obligation arose before the investor was admitted as a partner. Therefore, the investor has no personal liability to the customer.

[NOTE: While not asked to do so by the question, an examinee may correctly point out that while the investor has no personal liability to the customer, the $50,000 that the investor contributed to the partnership is "at risk for the satisfaction of existing partnership debts." UPA § 306 cmt. 2 (1997).]

Agency & Partnership

(February 2013)

ANALYSIS

Legal Problems

(1) Is the principal or the agent, or both, liable on contracts with a third party when the principal is an "undisclosed principal"?

(2) Is the principal or the agent, or both, liable on contracts with a third party when the principal is "partially disclosed" or an "unidentified principal"?

(3) Is the principal or the agent, or both, liable on contracts with a third party for the purchase of goods when the agent exceeded his authority but the principal nonetheless accepts the goods?

DISCUSSION

Summary

The agent, but not the owner, is liable to the basket manufacturer because the owner is an undisclosed principal and the agent acted without actual or apparent authority. Both the agent and the owner, however, are liable on the burner contract because the owner is an unidentified principal and the agent had apparent authority to enter into that contract. With respect to the solar cells contract, whether the owner is liable depends upon whether a court would follow the Second or Third Restatement of Agency, which take different positions on the effect of the ratification of a contract by an undisclosed principal. Under either, the agent would also be liable on the contract, as he was a party to the contract.

[NOTE: The contracts that are the subject of this question are contracts for the sale of goods and, therefore, are governed by Article 2 of the Uniform Commercial Code. Article 2, however, does not contain agency rules. Accordingly, common law concepts of agency are applicable. UCC § 1-103(b).]

Point One (35%)
The agent, but not the owner, is liable to the basket manufacturer. The agent had no actual authority to enter into the contract to buy aluminum baskets, and because the owner was an undisclosed principal, the manufacturer had no reason to believe that the agent had apparent authority. Furthermore, the manufacturer had no reason to believe that the agent was not contracting for his own benefit.

An agent acting on behalf of a principal can bind the principal to contracts if the agent has either actual or apparent authority. An agent has actual authority when contracting on behalf of his principal if he "reasonably believes, in accordance with the principal's manifestations to the agent, that the principal wishes the agent so to act." RESTATEMENT (THIRD) OF AGENCY § 2.01 (2006). Here, the agent was told to buy only wicker baskets, not aluminum baskets. Thus, when he contracted with the basket manufacturer to buy aluminum baskets, he had no actual authority to do so.

An agent acts with apparent authority "when a third party [with whom the agent acts] reasonably believes the actor has authority to act on behalf of the principal and that belief is traceable to the principal's manifestations." Id. § 2.03. Here the owner notified basket manufacturers that she or her agent might contact them to purchase baskets, but that notification did not specifically name the agent or any other person as the owner's agent. Furthermore, the basket manufacturer had no prior dealings with the agent or the owner or any reason to think that the agent was acting for the benefit of anyone but himself. Thus, there is no basis to conclude that the basket manufacturer thought that the agent had apparent authority to act for the owner.

Generally, when an agent acts on behalf of an undisclosed principal and the agent lacks authority to enter into the contract, the agent is liable on the contract as a party to the contract, but the principal is not liable. This rule is consistent with the third party's expectations. "The third party expected the agent to be a party to the contract because the agent presented the deal as if he were acting for himself. Moreover, if the third party is unaware of the principal's existence, the third party must be relying on the agent's solvency and reliability when entering into the contract." See ROBERT W. HAMILTON, JONATHAN R. MACEY & DOUGLAS K. MOLL, CORPORATIONS, INCLUDING PARTNERSHIPS AND LIMITED LIABILITY COMPANIES 34 (11th ed. 2010). See also RESTATEMENT (THIRD) OF AGENCY § 6.03, cmt. c. Furthermore, because the third party has no idea that the agent is acting or is seemingly acting on behalf of another, there is no reason to believe that the third party would be expecting an undisclosed principal to be liable on the contract. Id.

Point Two (35%)
Because the owner is an unidentified (as opposed to undisclosed) principal, both she and the agent (as a party to the contract) probably are liable on the contract with the burner manufacturer.

When the agent contracted with the burner manufacturer, he did not have actual authority to do so, as the owner had expressly restricted the agent's authority to purchase only burners with "whisper technology." See Point One. However, the agent may have had apparent authority to buy burners without whisper technology.

An agent acts with apparent authority "when a third party [with whom the agent acts] reasonably believes the actor has authority to act on behalf of the principal and that belief is traceable to the principal's manifestations." RESTATEMENT (THIRD) OF AGENCY § 2.03 (2006). The owner indicated that an agent might contact the burner manufacturer. The notice contained no restriction regarding the type of burners that the agent was authorized to purchase. The facts indicate that burner manufacturers regularly receive such notices.

Although the agent told the burner manufacturer that he represented a well-known hot-air balloon operator, he did not disclose the owner's name. Thus, the owner was a partially disclosed or unidentified principal. *See* RESTATEMENT (SECOND) OF AGENCY § 4(2) (1958) (using term "partially disclosed principal"); RESTATEMENT (THIRD) OF AGENCY § 1.04(2)(c) (2006) (using term "unidentified principal"). An agent for a partially disclosed principal may have apparent authority. RESTATEMENT (SECOND) OF AGENCY § 159 cmt. e (1958). Based upon (1) the notice sent by the owner, (2) the agent's revelation that he was acting as an agent, and (3) the fact that burner manufacturers regularly receive such notices and sell to agents, the manufacturer may argue that it reasonably and actually believed that the agent was authorized to purchase burners without whisper technology. The manufacturer may also argue that because the agent revealed that he was an agent, his listing of the owner's address as the delivery address connects the agent to the notice given by the owner. Arguably this distinguishes the burner contract from the basket contract. Here, there is a strong case to support the conclusion that the agent had apparent authority; if he did, then the owner is liable to the burner manufacturer.

The agent also is liable as a party to the contract because he did not fully disclose his agency relationship. Although he told the burner manufacturer that he represented a well-known hot-air balloon operator, he did not disclose the owner's name. Generally even an authorized agent of a partially disclosed or unidentified principal is liable as a party to a contract with a third person. RESTATEMENT (SECOND) OF AGENCY § 321 (1958) ("unless otherwise agreed"); RESTATEMENT (THIRD) OF AGENCY § 6.02(2) (2006) ("unless the agent and the third party agree otherwise").

Point Three (30%)
Under the Second Restatement of Agency, the owner is not liable on the contract for solar cells because the agent did not have actual or apparent authority and the owner, as an undisclosed principal, cannot ratify the contract. Under the Third Restatement, the owner could be liable, as she ratified the contract. Under either Restatement, the agent is liable as a party to the contract.

The owner is not liable to the solar cell manufacturer for breach of the contract for the solar cells because the agent had no actual or apparent authority to purchase solar cells on the owner's behalf, and the owner, under the Second Restatement of Agency, did not ratify the contract with knowledge of the material facts. Thus, she is not liable as a ratifier of the contract.

The facts state that the agent had authority to purchase only propane fuel tanks. In addition, he had no apparent authority to purchase solar cells. The owner made no manifestations to the solar cell manufacturer that would lead a reasonable person in the manufacturer's position to believe that the agent had the authority to bind the owner to a contract to purchase solar cells. In fact, the agent made no manifestations at all to the solar cell manufacturer. Unlike with the basket manufacturer and the burner manufacturer, the owner did not notify the manufacturer of solar cells that an agent *might* contact it to purchase solar cells. In addition, the solar cells were delivered to the agent and not to the owner's address. In sum, the manufacturer was unaware of any relationship between the owner and the agent. As to the solar cell manufacturer, the owner is an undisclosed principal. There can be no apparent authority in the case of an undisclosed principal because there are no manifestations from the principal to the third person. *See* RESTATEMENT (SECOND) OF AGENCY § 8 cmt. a (1958) ("there can be no apparent authority created by an undisclosed principal"); RESTATEMENT (THIRD) OF AGENCY § 2.03 cmt. f (2006) ("apparent authority is not present when a third party believes that an interaction is with an actor who is a principal").

The owner also did not ratify the contract. Although the owner used the solar cells, generally a principal cannot ratify an unauthorized transaction with a third person "unless the one acting purported to be acting for the ratifier." RESTATEMENT (SECOND) OF AGENCY § 85(1) (1958).

The result differs under the Third Restatement, which expressly rejects the Second Restatement on this issue. The Restatement (Third) of Agency § 4.03 (2006) states, "A person may ratify an act if the actor acted or purported to act as an agent on the person's behalf." According to comment b, "an undisclosed principal may ratify an agent's unauthorized act." Under the Restatement (Third) of Agency rule, the owner probably ratified the transaction. The agent clearly acted on the owner's behalf, and in addition, the owner's conduct in using the solar cells "justifies a reasonable assumption that [she] is manifesting assent that the act shall affect [her] legal relations." See id. § 4.01(2).

The agent also is liable to the solar cell manufacturer for breach of the contract for the solar cells because he is a party to the contract. The facts indicate that the agent never told the solar cell manufacturer that he represented the owner or any other principal. Consequently, *even if* the agent were authorized (which, as discussed above, he is not), he would be liable as a party to the contract. See RESTATEMENT (SECOND) OF AGENCY § 322 (1958); RESTATEMENT (THIRD) OF AGENCY § 6.03(2) (2006). Here, he has no authority or apparent authority and is liable as a party to the contract.

The agent would also be liable under the Third Restatement. Under Restatement (Third) of Agency § 4.02(1) (2006), ratification generally relates back and the transaction is treated as if it were authorized at the time of the transaction. However, this does not relieve the agent of an undisclosed principal who ratifies an unauthorized transaction of liability under the ratified contract. See id. § 6.03(2) (authorized agent for undisclosed principal is a party to the contract) and § 4.03 cmt. b ("An undisclosed principal's ratification does not eliminate the agent's liability to the third party on the transaction . . . .").

[NOTE: An examinee may discuss the concept of inherent agency power. This concept is recognized by the Restatement (Second) of Agency § 8 A (1958), but the concept is not used in the Restatement (Third) of Agency (2006). Here, there are no facts to support that the agent had inherent authority.

As to contracts with agents for partially disclosed principals (e.g., the contract for the burners), the basic question is whether the acts done "usually accompany or are incidental to transactions which the agent is authorized to conduct." RESTATEMENT (SECOND) OF AGENCY § 161 (1958). If so, the principal is bound if the other party "reasonably believes that the agent is authorized to do them and has no notice that he is not so authorized." *Id.* The purchase of burners without whisper technology was not authorized, nor was it incidental to an authorized transaction. Therefore, there should not be inherent agency power.

As to contracts on behalf of undisclosed principals (e.g., the other two contracts), the basic question is whether the acts done are usual or necessary in the transactions the agent is authorized to transact. RESTATEMENT (SECOND) OF AGENCY § 194 (1958). The other two contracts seem fundamentally different from the authorized transactions. Therefore, there should not be inherent agency power.

Only minimal credit should be given for discussion of inherent agency power.]

Commercial Paper

(February 2000)

Legal Problems:

1. Did Bob's tender of payment discharge his own liability on the note to Frieda?

2. Did Bob's tender of payment discharge the liability of his co-maker, Cathy, on the note to Frieda?

3. Did Bob's tender of payment discharge the liability of Debra, an indorser, to Frieda on the note?

4. Did the crossing out of Aaron's name by Edward discharge Aaron's liability to Frieda on the note?

DISCUSSION

Point One: (25-35%)

As an obligor on a negotiable instrument, Bob's tender of full payment at maturity did not discharge his obligation on the instrument except with respect to future interest.

Frieda, as the current holder of the note, is the party who is entitled to enforce the note. Uniform Commercial Code § 3-301. As the co-maker of the note, Bob is jointly and severally liable on the instrument. UCC §§ 3-103(a)(5) & 3-116(a). A party who is jointly and severally liable as an obligor on a negotiable instrument is responsible to the holder for the entire amount of payment. Nevertheless, if such a party is forced to pay the entire amount of the instrument, he or she will have a right of contribution against the co-obligor. UCC § 3-116(b).

When Bob made the tender of full payment on the note's due date and Frieda refused it, the refusal by Frieda served to discharge only the obligation of indorsers and accommodation parties with a right of recourse against Bob. UCC § 3-603(b). As for Bob's own liability to Frieda, her refusal of his tender served merely to discharge Bob's obligation to pay interest following the refused tender. UCC § 3-603(c). Thus, under these facts, Bob would still be liable to Frieda for the $2,000 in principal but would not be liable for the $100 in interest on the note that had accrued since Bob's tender was refused by Frieda.

Point Two: (15-25%)

Bob's offer was not sufficient to cause Cathy's liability to be discharged when Frieda refused Bob's tender of payment.

Cathy, as co-maker on the note with Bob, was jointly and severally liable on the note. UCC § 3-

103(a)(5) & 3-116(a). Cathy's status as co-maker gave her the potential right of contribution against Bob in the event that she ended up paying the holder of the note more than her pro-rata share of liability. UCC § 3-116(b). However, Cathy's potential right of contribution would not be sufficient to discharge her obligation to pay Frieda, the holder, when Bob, her fellow co-maker, made a tender to Frieda that was refused. The only obligations discharged by Bob's tender would be those of an "indorser or accommodation party having a right of recourse" regarding the obligation to which the tender related. UCC § 3-603(b). Cathy's status as a co-maker fits neither of those categories. Thus, Cathy's liability as co-maker on the instrument would not be discharged as to principal.

Cathy's obligation to pay interest is less certain. Section 3-603(c) says that "[i]f tender of payment of an amount due on an instrument is made to a person entitled to enforce the instrument, the obligation of the obligor to pay interest after the due date on the amount tendered is discharged." Section 3-603(c) does not make clear in a case such as this whether "the obligor" being benefited must be the party making tender (which was the result under pre-1990 UCC § 3-604(1)) or whether instead the no-interest result applies to all obligors on the instrument. The latter interpretation of § 3-603(c) would at least discharge Cathy with respect to the $100 in accrued interest; the former interpretation would not.

Point Three: (20-30%)

As an indorser with a right of recourse against Bob, Debra's obligation on the note was discharged by Frieda's refusal of Bob's tender.

By signing on the back of the instrument as she did, Debra assumed the obligation of an indorser. UCC § 3-204(a) & (b). As an indorser, Debra had a potential right of recourse with respect to Bob, the co-maker whose tender was refused. UCC § 3-412. Accordingly, Debra benefited from the rule that completely discharges an indorser with a right of recourse where the obligor on a negotiable instrument makes a proper tender of full payment to the holder at or after maturity and payment is improperly refused. UCC § 3-603(b).

Point Four: (20-30%)

Even in the absence of Bob's tender, Edward's crossing out of Aaron's signature discharged Aaron's liability as indorser on the instrument.

Under UCC § 3-604(a), Edward, as the holder of an instrument, may discharge any party's obligation on an instrument by cancellation. Cancellation would include "striking out of the party's signature," as Edward did here with respect to Aaron's signature as indorser. UCC § 3-604(a). To be effective, cancellation does not require consideration, but it must be done by someone entitled to enforce the instrument (which Edward clearly was as a holder under UCC § 3-301) and it must be intentional (which the cancellation was here since Edward did it as an act of friendship).

Commercial Paper

(July 2000)

Legal Problems:

1. Will Lender be able to enforce the note against Brother free of Brother's personal defense against Roofer?

2. Will Lender be able to enforce the note against Sister given Lender's partial release of collateral against Brother?

3. Will Sister have a right of reimbursement against Brother?

DISCUSSION

Point One: (15-25%)

Lender can enforce the note against Brother because Lender was a holder in due course. Therefore, Lender took the note free of Brother's claim in recoupment.

As the maker and issuer of the note, Brother is obligated under Uniform Commercial Code § 3-412 to pay the instrument according to its terms to any person, such as Lender, who is entitled to enforce the instrument. UCC § 3-301 (person entitled to enforce the instrument includes the holder of the instrument). However, Brother's obligation to pay the instrument is not absolute. Sections 3-305(a)(2) and (a)(3) say that the right to enforce an obligation of a party on the instrument is subject to any defense that would be available on a simple contract as well as to claims in recoupment arising from the underlying transaction. In an action by Lender to enforce the note, Brother could raise a claim in recoupment based on Roofer's poor roofing job.

The rules of § 3-305(a), however, are specifically made subject to § 3-305(b), which says that a holder in due course is not subject to the contract defenses described in § 3-305(a)(2). Lender should qualify as a holder in due course under § 3-302(a)(2) since it took the instrument for value, in good faith, and without notice of any claims to the instrument. Therefore, Lender should take free of Brother's claim in recoupment and should be able to enforce the note in full against Brother.

Point Two: (55-65%)

Lender's ability to recover on the note from Sister is reduced by $2,000, the extent to which Lender impaired Sister's right of recourse by releasing its collateral interest in one of Brother's computers.

Because Sister received no direct benefit for signing the note, Sister is an accommodation party on the note. UCC § 3-419(a). Even though Sister is an accommodation party, she is still liable in

74

the capacity that she signed, here as an indorser. UCC § 3-419(b). Sister's obligation to pay the instrument as an indorser is not affected by her accommodation status except to the extent of the special provisions regarding accommodation party discharges contained in § 3-605. UCC § 3-419(c). As an indorser, Sister is obligated to pay the amount due to Lender, if Brother, as maker, were to dishonor the note and proper notice of dishonor were given to Sister. UCC § 3-415(a) & (c); § 3-503(a).

However, if a person entitled to enforce the instrument impairs the value of the collateral that secures the instrument's obligation, then an accommodation party having a right of recourse against the obligor is discharged to the extent of the impairment. UCC § 3-605(e). In this case, Lender impaired the value of the collateral securing the instrument through its binding release of rights to one of Brother's three computers that secured Brother's obligation under the instrument. UCC § 3-605(g)(ii). Because Lender impaired the value of the collateral by $2,000, Lender's own rights to recover against Sister (which would have been $8,000) are reduced to $6,000. UCC § 3-605(e).

Even though Lender is a holder in due course, Sister's partial discharge will still be effective against Lender. Since Sister's signature appeared on the back side of the note, her signature was an "anomalous indorsement" that gave notice to Lender and to any other later party that she was signing as an accommodation party. UCC § 3-419(c). Even putting aside Sister's anomalous indorsement, Lender knew that Sister was an indorser and therefore knew that Sister was a party with a right of recourse against Brother. UCC § 3-412 ("The obligation [of the issuer of a note] is owed to . . . an indorser who paid the instrument under Section 3-415.") Although personal discharges such as Sister's here are not effective against holders in due course without notice of the discharge, UCC § 3-601(b), here the holder in due course had notice of Sister's right of discharge and in fact caused the partial discharge. *Cf.* UCC § 3-302(b) ("discharge is effective against a person who became a holder in due course with notice of the discharge").

For the same reason that Brother's obligation to Lender is not reduced, Sister's obligation to Lender is not reduced because of the shoddy roof job.

Point Three: (15-25%)

Sister will have a right of reimbursement against Brother for the full amount that she pays Lender on the note.

Sister would have two different theories for recovering from Brother for any amount that Sister had to pay on the note to Lender. First, Sister signed in the capacity of an indorser. By that fact alone Sister has a right of recourse against Brother, the issuer of the note, if Sister has to pay a later holder of the note. UCC § 3-412. Second, if Sister had not signed as an indorser, she would nevertheless have a right of reimbursement against Brother because of her independent status as an accommodation party under UCC § 3-419(a). UCC § 3-419(e) ("An accommodation party who pays the instrument is entitled to reimbursement from the accommodated party and is entitled to enforce the instrument against the accommodated party.")

Commercial Paper
(February 2001)

Legal Problems:

1. Did Maker have an obligation to pay Neighbor when Neighbor demanded payment?

2. Did Maker have an obligation to pay Bank?

DISCUSSION

Point One: (45-55%)

Maker had no obligation to pay Neighbor when Neighbor demanded payment. Neighbor lost the right to enforce the note when Neighbor transferred possession of the note to Bank.

Under the Uniform Commercial Code, the document prepared by Maker is a negotiable instrument, i.e., it is "an unconditional promise or order to pay a fixed amount of money" that is "payable to bearer or to order," that is "payable on demand or at a definite time," and that "does not state any other undertaking." UCC § 3-104(a). The document prepared by Maker satisfies this definition because Maker promised to pay $1,000 to the order of Neighbor, and Maker did not promise to do anything else in the document. The document is a note because it is a written and signed undertaking to pay money. See § 3-104(e) (defining a "note" as a "promise"); § 3-103(a)(9) (defining a "promise" as a "written undertaking to pay money signed by the person undertaking to pay"). It is payable "on demand" because it does not state any time of payment. See UCC § 3-108(a)(ii).

In order for Maker to have been obligated to pay the money to Neighbor upon Neighbor's demand, Neighbor would have had to have been a person entitled to enforce the note when he demanded payment. In circumstances like those present in this case, the UCC defines a "person entitled to enforce" a negotiable instrument as "the holder of the instrument."

Neighbor was not a holder when he demanded payment because he had delivered the note to Bank and was not in possession of it. See UCC § 1-201(20) (requiring the "holder" of a negotiable instrument to have "possession").

In short, Maker should not have paid Neighbor without insisting that Neighbor exhibit the note before Maker paid the money. See UCC § 3-501(b)(2) ("Upon demand of the person to whom presentment is made, the person making presentment must. . . exhibit the instrument").

Point Two: (45-55%)

Maker is obligated to pay Bank. Bank is a person entitled to enforce the note against Maker, and Maker cannot assert any defense to payment.

Bank is the holder of the note. The "holder" of a negotiable instrument is "the person in posses-sion . . . in the case of an instrument payable to an identified person, if the identified person is in possession." UCC § 1- 201(20). Bank is in possession of the note and the note is payable to Bank because Neighbor wrote "Pay to the order of Bank" on it and indorsed it. *See* UCC § 3-204(a) (describing indorsement). As the holder, Bank is entitled to enforce the note against Maker, who issued the note. *See* UCC § 3-301 (defining "person entitled to enforce"); UCC § 3-412 (obligating issuer to pay the note to a person entitled to enforce the note).

Although Maker has paid Neighbor, Maker cannot assert this payment as a defense to enforce-ment by Bank. There are two independent reasons for this conclusion, either of which is suffi-cient. First, the payment to Neighbor did not discharge Maker's obligation because Neighbor was not entitled to enforce the note. *See* UCC § 3-602(a) (stating that payment discharges an instru-ment only "to the extent payment is made. . . to a person entitled to enforce"). As explained above, Neighbor was not a person entitled to enforce the note because Neighbor did not have possession of the note.

Second, Bank is a "holder in due course." A holder in due course is a holder who takes an instru-ment in good faith, for value, and without notice of any defenses or various other problems. *See* UCC § 3-302(a),(b). From all indications, Bank acted in good faith. *See* UCC § 3-103(a)(4) (defining "good faith" as "honesty in fact and observance of reasonable commercial standards of fair dealing"). Bank took the note for value because it canceled Neighbor's outstanding debt. *See* UCC § 3303(a) (stating that an instrument is transferred for "value" if it is transferred "as payment of . . . an antecedent claim"). The facts do not suggest that Bank had notice of any defenses or other problems with the note.

As a holder in due course, no discharge would be effective against Bank unless Bank had notice of it at the time Bank took the note. *See* UCC § 3-601(b) ("Discharge of the obligation of a party is not effective against a person acquiring rights of a holder in due course of the instrument without notice of discharge."). Bank could not have had notice of the payment to Neighbor because the payment occurred after Bank acquired the note. Maker must pay Bank even though Maker already has paid Neighbor. *See Lambert v. Barker,* 348 S.E.2d 214 (Va. 1986).

Commercial Paper

(July 2001)

Legal Problems:

1. Can Singer recover from Bank Two for conversion on the ground that Bank Two took the instrument with notice of a breach of Agent's fiduciary duty to Singer?

2. Was the instrument properly paid by Bank One?

3. Was Concert's obligation to Singer discharged by payment to Agent?

DISCUSSION

Point One: (45-50%)

Singer may recover from Bank Two for conversion on the ground that because Bank Two took the instrument with notice that Agent had breached her fiduciary duty. Bank Two was not a holder in due course.

The facts state that the check was issued to "Agent, as agent for Singer," and was issued for money owed to Singer by Concert. As between Singer and Agent, Singer is the owner of the check, and is the principal in a principal-agent relationship with Agent. In UCC terms, Singer is a "represented person" (UCC § 3-307(a)(2)) and Agent is a "fiduciary" (UCC § 3-307(a)(1)).

When Agent convinced Bank Two to deposit the check into Agent's personal account and use the proceeds for Agent's personal benefit, Agent violated her fiduciary duty to Singer and misappropriated Singer's property. This misappropriation of the Concert check gives rise to a claim by Singer to the instrument or its proceeds based on Agent's breach of fiduciary duty. UCC §§ 3-306, 3-307(b)(iii).

Singer's claim to the instrument and its proceeds may be asserted against Agent and against subsequent takers of the instrument. Therefore, because Bank Two also misused Singer's property (by receiving payment of the check and using the proceeds to cover Agent's overdrafts and increase her personal account balance), Bank Two may be liable for converting Singer's property-the check and its proceeds. See UCC § 3-420. But, if Bank Two is a holder in due course, it takes free of such claim UCC § 3-306. If Bank Two is not a holder in due course, it will be subject to Singer's claim. UCC § 3-306.

To be a holder in due course, Bank Two must be a holder, and it must have taken the check in good faith, for value and without notice of any claims or defenses. In this case, Bank Two, as the depository bank of a check bearing a proper restrictive endorsement (UCC § 3-206 (c)), is a holder and it has given value, the extinguishment of the overdraft (UCC § 3-303(a)(3)). Bank Two appears to have acted in good faith, though it could be argued that the Bank Two manager failed to follow "reasonable commercial standards of fair dealing," when he allowed Agent to deposit the check into Agent's personal account, at clear variance with past practice with regard to checks written to Agent as Singer's agent. The more powerful argument for Singer, however, is that Bank Two had notice of Singer's claim to the instrument and for that reason could not be a holder in due course.

Section 3-307(b)(1) of the UCC provides expressly that a taker's "notice of a breach of fiduciary duty" by a fiduciary is "notice of the claim of the represented person." Thus, to the extent that Bank Two had notice of a breach of fiduciary duty, it cannot be a holder in due course because it will be treated as having notice of Singer's claim to the check.

To be charged with *notice* under UCC § 3-307(b)(1), the taker, here Manager on behalf of Bank Two, must have had *knowledge* of two facts. First, the taker must have knowledge of the fiduciary status of the fiduciary. UCC § 9-307(b)(ii). Second, the taker must know that the check payable to the fiduciary is being taken in payment of a personal debt of the fiduciary (UCC § 9-307(b)(2)(i)), or deposited to an account other than the account of the fiduciary, as a fiduciary. UCC § 9-307(b)(2)(iii). Manager clearly knew that Agent was the fiduciary of Singer, given that the check was payable to Agent in her fiduciary capacity and Manager knew that Agent had deposited similar checks in Singer's account. Manager also knew that the check was being deposited to extinguish the personal overdraft of Agent and was deposited in Agent's personal account. Thus, Bank Two had notice of the breach of the fiduciary duty of Agent and therefore had notice of the claim of the represented person UCC § 3-307(b)(1). Accordingly, Bank Two is precluded from holder in due course status because of such notice (UCC § 3-302(a)(2)(v)) and is, therefore, subject to the claim of Singer. UCC §§ 3-306, 3-420.

The check from Concert has long since been negotiated and paid by Bank One, so Singer no longer has any claim to the instrument. He does, however, have a claim to recover the proceeds against Bank Two as a converter of the instrument and its proceeds. Under UCC § 3-420, "The law applicable to conversion of personal property applies to instruments." The measure of Singer's recovery is presumed to be the amount payable on the instrument, here $20,000.

Point Two: (25-35%)

Singer has no rights against Bank One because Bank One had no notice of Agent's breach of fiduciary duty or that the check was taken by Bank Two for Agent's debt.

Because the check was issued payable to the order of Agent and it was indorsed with Agent's signature, there was no forged indorsement. UCC § 3-110(c). Moreover, because Bank One did not take the instrument from Agent, it had no knowledge that the check had been taken for the debt of Agent.

Bank One is not liable to Singer in conversion because Agent was authorized to collect payment on behalf of Singer. Furthermore, the check was payable to the order of Agent, properly indorsed, and properly paid by Bank One upon presentment by Bank Two. Under UCC § 1-201(20), Bank Two was a "holder" and therefore a "person entitled to enforce the instrument." UCC § 3-301. This is true even though Bank Two was not a holder in due course.

Accordingly, Singer has no rights against Bank One.

Point Three: (15-25%)

Singer has no rights against Concert because Concert had paid an agent authorized to receive payment. and payment of the check discharged all underlying obligations.

Agent was authorized to collect funds owed to Singer *for* Singer's performance. Payment to an agent authorized to receive payment on behalf of the principal is considered payment to the principal. As stated in the RESTATEMENT (SECOND) *OF* AGENCY § 178(1) (1957), "If an agent, authorized to receive only money in payment of a debt, receives a check or other thing *from* the debtor and obtains the amount of the debt *from* the negotiation or sale of the thing received, the debt is paid. "

Under the UCC, issuance of the check to the authorized agent suspends Singer's right to collect on the underlying obligation, and payment of the check results in discharge of the underlying obligation to the extent of the amount of the check. UCC § 3-310(b)(1).

Here the debt Concert owed Singer was $20,000, and the amount of the check was $20,000. The check was indorsed by the payee, presented by the depository bank, a holder under these facts, and paid by Bank One. Therefore payment of the check by Bank One, which resulted in Agent's receiving the full amount, discharged the $20,000 debt owed by Concert to Singer. *See* UCC §§ 3-602,3-310(b)(1).

Singer has no rights against Concert.

Commercial Paper

(February 2002)

Legal Problems:

1. Is an instrument that is not negotiable because of omissions still enforceable if the payee fills in the blanks consistent with the payee's underlying agreement with the maker?

2. Can a person without physical possession of an instrument still enforce the instrument in a case where the instrument has been stolen?

3. Is the obligor on an instrument discharged by paying the instrument in good faith where there has been a forgery of the payee's signature?

4. Does the obligor on an instrument who pays the instrument that has a forged payee's signature have any rights of recovery against the party that presented the instrument for payment?

Point One: (15-25%)

Because Lender filled in the two blanks according to his actual agreement with Borrower, the note is enforceable as completed.

DISCUSSION

Before Lender filled in the blank lines on the note form, the note that Borrower gave Lender was not negotiable. That is because one of the requirements of negotiability under Article 3 of the Uniform Commercial Code is an unconditional promise to pay a fixed amount of money. UCC § 3-104(a) (1991). In this case, the amount due line was left blank by Borrower, the issuer of the note. Therefore, the note was an "incomplete instrument" under § 3-115(a). It is an instrument because Borrower signed the note and issued it to Lender; it is incomplete because the two lines for payee and amount due were left blank.

Section 3-115(b) indicates that an instrument that is not negotiable because of omissions is still enforceable "according to its terms as augmented by the completion." However, if the words or numbers were added to the incomplete instrument without the authority of the signer, the instrument is treated as an altered instrument and special rules apply.

In this case, although there was no mention of specific authority given by Borrower to Lender to fill in the blanks, the burden would be on Borrower to show lack of authority. UCC § 3-115(d). Because Lender did fill in the blanks consistent with the actual agreement of the parties, it seems likely that authority would be presumed. *See* Official Comment 2 to § 3-115 (1991). ("If the payee completes the note by filling in the due date *agreed to by the parties,* the note is payable on the due date stated.") (Emphasis added.)

(By leaving the payee space blank, Borrower made the note a bearer instrument, which the bearer could convert to an order instrument by filling in his name. 2 James J. White & Robert S. Summers, UNIFORM COMMERCIAL CODE § 17-3 (4th ed. 1995). Failure to include a payee does not diminish the negotiability or enforceability of the instrument.)

Point Two: (25-35%)

Because Lender was entitled to enforce the instrument at the time it was stolen, Lender would still be able to enforce it if Lender can prove the terms of the note and provide adequate assurance to Borrower against the risk of possible loss for future claims.

Even though Lender no longer has physical possession of the note, Lender would still be able to qualify as a "person entitled to enforce" the instrument under UCC § 3-301 (1991). Section 3-301(iii) specifically refers to a person who is not in possession of an instrument as nevertheless being entitled to enforce the instrument under § 3-309. Section 3-309(a) contains three requirements that enable a person not in possession of an instrument to enforce it. In this case, Lender satisfies all three requirements: (1) Lender was the person entitled to enforce the instrument when loss of possession occurred; (2) Lender's loss of possession was not the result of his own transfer or of a lawful seizure; and (3) the whereabouts of the note are unknown to both parties, at least before Borrower paid Innocent.

Section 3-309(b) requires that Lender prove both the terms of the instrument and his right to enforce it. Neither should be problematic in this case. Lender would have to give Borrower assurances against double payment because Borrower, by the terms of § 3-309(b), would be entitled to demand adequate protection against possible loss from future claims on the missing note.

Point Three: (25-35%)

Given the forgery of the payee's signature, Innocent did not qualify as a person entitled to enforce the instrument, and thus Borrower was not discharged by paying Innocent.

Under UCC § 3-602(a) (1991), the obligor on an instrument is ordinarily discharged by paying a person entitled to enforce the instrument. Borrower will not get the benefit of a discharge in making the payment to Innocent because Innocent does not qualify as a "person entitled to enforce" the instrument. In order for Innocent to be a person entitled to enforce the instrument under § 3-301, Innocent must be either a holder or a person who has the rights of a holder.

Innocent cannot be a holder because the chain of good title was broken by Robber's forged indorsement of the payee's (Lender's) signature. UCC § 3-201(b) (1991) provides that, "If an instrument is payable to an identified person, negotiation requires transfer of possession of the instrument *and its indorsement* by the holder" (emphasis added). *See also* UCC § 1-201(20) (1989) (A "holder" of a negotiable instrument means "the person in possession if the instrument is payable to bearer or, in the case of an instrument payable to an identified person, if the identified person is in possession.") Nor will Innocent qualify as a nonholder entitled to enforce the instrument because Innocent inherits only the rights of Robber, which are non-existent because of the theft and forgery. Accordingly, Innocent was not a person entitled to enforce the note, and Borrower's payment to Innocent does not discharge Borrower.

Point Four: (15-25%)

Because Innocent was not entitled to enforce the instrument, Borrower may recover from Innocent for breach of presentment warranty.

Even though Innocent knew nothing about either the theft or the forgery, Innocent nevertheless breached a presentment warranty to Borrower under Dee § 3-417(d)(1) (1991). At the time Innocent presented the note to Borrower for payment, Innocent was warranting to Borrower that Innocent was "a person entitled to enforce the instrument or authorized to obtain payment on behalf of a person entitled to enforce the instrument." *Id.* As noted above, Innocent cannot be a person entitled to enforce the instrument because of Robber's forgery of a necessary signature in the chain of title. Therefore, under § 3-417(d)(2), Innocent will be liable to Borrower for the amount that Borrower paid Innocent plus interest and expenses resulting from the breach of the presentment warranty.

Commercial Paper

(July 2002)

Legal Problems:

(1)   Is Motors' claim against First Bank subject to the defense of failure of consideration?

(2)(a) Did Motors' taking of the cashier's check discharge Driver's obligation to pay for the sports car under the sales contract?

(2)(b) May Motors recover from Driver for breach of transfer warranty?

DISCUSSION

Summary: First Bank is liable as issuer of the cashier's check to pay a person who is entitled to enforce the check. Motors is the holder of the cashier's check and is entitled to enforce it. However, Motors is not a holder in due course because the check was overdue on its face when Motors took it from Driver. Thus, First Bank can assert defenses to payment against Motors, including the defense of failure of consideration as a result of the dishonor of the check it received in payment for its cashier's check.

Driver's obligation to pay for the car was discharged when Motors accepted a cashier's check as payment. Moreover, Driver apparently was not a party to that check and did not indorse it, so Driver has no direct liability on the check, even if Bank dishonors it. However, Driver did transfer the check to Motors and therefore warranted that the check was not subject to any defenses. That warranty was breached, and Motors can recover from Driver for the breach of warranty.

Point One: (40-50%)

Motors' claim against First Bank is subject to the defense of failure of consideration. Motors had notice that the cashier's check was overdue and therefore Motors is not a holder in due course.

Motors is the holder of the cashier's check because the cashier's check is payable to Motors and Motors is in possession of it. *See* UCC § 1-201(20) (definition of holder). As a holder, Motors has a right to enforce the cashier's check against First Bank. *See* § 3-301(i) (holder's right to enforce); § 3-412 (obligation of issuer of a cashier's check).

First Bank, however, may assert a defense of failure of consideration because the Auto-Loans check that First Bank took in exchange for the cashier's check was dishonored. *See* § 3-303(b) (defense of failure of consideration); § 3-305(a)(2) (right of a holder to enforce is subject to ordinary defenses, such as failure of consideration). *See, e.g., Laurel Bank & Trust v. City National Bank,* 365 A.2d 1222 (Conn. Super. App. 1976) (bank refused to pay cashier's check because checks tendered to purchase the cashier's check were dishonored).

A holder in due course would not be subject to the defense of failure of consideration. *See* § 3-305(b) (defenses applicable to a holder in due course). Motors has met many of the requirements for becoming a holder in due course because Motors took the cashier's check in good faith, for value, and without notice of First Bank's defense. *See* UCC § 3-302(a) (requirements for holder in due course status). Motors, however, is not a holder in due course because Motors had notice that the cashier's check was overdue. *See* UCC § 3-302(a)(2)(iii) (holder in due course must not have notice that the instrument is overdue). Checks become overdue after 90 days. *See* UCC § 3-304(a)(2) (overdue instruments). A cashier's check is a "check" under UCC § 3-104(f). Motors should have known that the cashier's check was more than 90 days old on September 15 because the cashier's check was dated May 11 and thus was 126 days old.

<u>Point Two:(a) Motors' taking of the cashier's check from Driver discharged Driver's obligation & (b)(40-50%) to pay the purchase price of the car under the sales contract. However, Driver is liable to Motors for breach of a transfer warranty because the cashier's check is subject to a defense or a claim in recoupment.</u>

If a cashier's check is taken for an obligation, the obligation is completely discharged. *See* § 3-310(a) (effect of instrument on obligation). Accordingly, Driver's obligation to pay the purchase price of the car under the sales contract was discharged when Motors took the cashier's check in payment. (Note: At common law, this rule was referred to as the "doctrine of merger" because the underlying debt was said to be "merged" into the negotiable instrument.)

Driver is not liable on the cashier's check as a party because he did not sign or indorse it. Nothing in the problem's facts suggests that Driver indorsed the cashier's check. Accordingly, Motors could not enforce the check against Driver based on an indorsement. *See* § 3-415(a) (liability of indorser upon dishonor of an instrument) However, he did transfer the instrument. *See* § 3-203(a). When Driver transferred the cashier's check to Motors in exchange for the sports car, Driver warranted that the instrument was not subject to a defense or claim in recoupment. *See* § 3-416(a)(4) (transfer warranty). (See § 3-305(a), comment 3, for an explanation of claim in recoupment.) Driver breached this warranty because First Bank could have asserted a claim against Driver for the purchase price of the cashier's check after the Auto-Loans check was dishonored. *See* § 3310(b)(1) (rights when an ordinary check taken for an obligation is dishonored, i.e., Driver's obligation to pay for the cashier's check is suspended until Auto-Loans' check was dishonored). Motors could recover the amount of the check in damages from Driver. *See* § 3-416(b).

Commercial Paper

(February 2003)

Legal Problems: (1)   May Financier enforce the note against Mariner despite Mariner's defense that Chandler did not return the nets?

                  (2)   May Financier recover from Chandler for breach of transfer warranty because the note was subject to a defense when Chandler transferred it?

                  (3)   Did Trawler acquire good title to the fishing nets when Trawler purchased them from Chandler?

DISCUSSION

Summary: Financier, the holder of the note, cannot recover against Mariner, the maker of the note, because Mariner has a valid defense: Chandler, the original payee of the note, breached his contract to repair and return the nets. Financier is not a holder in due course because the note was overdue on its face when Financier took it from Chandler.

Financier can, however, recover from Chandler. Although Chandler endorsed the note "without recourse," that language only limits Chandler's liability as an indorser. In addition to indorsing the note, Chandler transferred it for value, thus making certain transfer warranties, including a warranty that the note was not subject to any defenses. Because Chandler breached that warranty (as the note was in fact subject to Mariner's breach of contract defense), Financier can recover its loss ($4,000) from Chandler.

Mariner may not recover his nets from Trawler because Mariner entrusted them to a merchant who deals in fishing nets (Chandler) and Trawler purchased them from Chandler in the ordinary course of business. In this case, the UCC protects the purchaser, even though Chandler had no right to sell the nets.

Point One: <u>Mariner is not liable to Financier on the note because Mariner has a</u>
(35-45%)   <u>defense to payment that it may assert against Financier.</u>

Chandler negotiated the note by indorsing it and delivering it to Financier. Uniform Commercial Code § 3-201(b). Financier became the holder of the note when he took the note from Chandler with Chandler's indorsement. UCC § 3-201(a) (specifying consequence of negotiation).

The holder of a note is a person entitled to enforce the note against its maker. UCC § 3-301. Accordingly, Financier is a person entitled to enforce the note against Mariner. Mariner, however, has a defense to payment because Chandler breached the contract to repair and return the nets. Mariner may assert this defense against Financier, unless Financier is a holder in due course. *See* UCC § 3-305(a)(2) (permitting the maker to assert contract defenses); § 3-305(b) (limiting the assertion of defenses against a holder in due course).

To be a holder in due course, among other requirements, a holder must take a note without notice that the note is overdue. UCC § 3-302(a)(2)(iii). In this case, the note was payable on March 1 and therefore became overdue after that date. UCC § 3-304(b)(2) (specifying when a note becomes overdue). Financier took the note after it was due. Financier had notice on the face of the note that it was overdue. Financier therefore is not a holder in due course and Mariner may assert against Financier the breach of contract defense Mariner has against Chandler.

Point Two: Chandler is liable to Financier for breach of transfer warranty
(35-45%)   because the note was subject to a defense to payment when Chandler transferred
             it.

A person who transfers a note for consideration warrants that the instrument is not subject to a defense to payment. UCC § 3-416(a)(4). Chandler is deemed to have made this warranty to Financier when Chandler transferred the note and Financier paid $3,500 to Chandler in consideration for it. UCC § 3-303(b) (defining consideration). The warranty was violated because, as explained in Point One, Mariner was entitled to assert Chandler's breach of contract as a defense to payment.

For breach of warranty, a person who took the instrument in good faith may recover damages from the warrantor in an amount equal to the loss suffered as a result of the breach. UCC § 3-416(b) (specifying the measure of damages). In this case, Financier appears to have taken the instrument in good faith because Chandler did not tell Financier anything about the origin of the note. *See* UCC § 3-103(a)(4). The amount of Financier's loss equals the difference between what the note is worth and what it would have been worth if it had been as warranted. *See* William D. Hawkland, 6 HAWKLAND UNIFORM COMMERCIAL CODE § 3-416:10 (2001). In this case, the note has no value to Financier because Mariner has a defense to payment. If the note had been as warranted, it would have been worth $4,000 to Financier because Mariner would have had to pay that amount. Accordingly, Financier may recover $4,000 from Chandler, not just the $3,500 he paid for the instrument.

Ordinarily upon dishonor, one who indorses a note is liable for payment based on the indorsement. UCC § 3-415(a). In this case, however, Chandler is not obliged to pay the note based on his indorsement because he indorsed the note "without recourse." UCC § 3-415(b). Financier therefore cannot enforce the note against Chandler based on Chandler's indorsement. Financier's claim against Chandler is limited to the breach of warranty claim. The indorsement "without recourse" is not effective to disclaim warranties. UCC § 3-416 cmt. 5.

Point Three: Trawler owns the fishing nets and may retain them because Mariner
(15-25%) entrusted the nets to Chandler, a merchant who deals in goods of the kind, and Chandler sold them in the ordinary course of business to Trawler.

A seller who does not have title to goods generally may not transfer title to the buyer. UCC § 2-403(1). This general rule, however, contains an important exception that sometimes permits a seller to transfer title to goods that the seller does not own. In particular, "[a]ny entrusting of possession of goods to a merchant who deals in goods of that kind gives him the power to transfer all rights of the entruster to a buyer in the ordinary course of business." UCC § 2-403(2).

In this case, Chandler is a merchant with respect to the fishing nets because he deals in all kinds of fishing equipment. UCC § 2-104(1). Mariner entrusted the fishing nets to Chandler when Mariner left them to be repaired. UCC § 2-403(3) (specifying that entrusting includes "any delivery and acquiescence in retention of possession"); Hawkland, *supra*, § 2-403:7 (citing the leaving of goods for repair as a typical example of entrusting). Trawler purchased the goods in the ordinary course of business because Chandler regularly sells used goods and because Trawler believed that Chandler owned the fishing nets. Accordingly, Chandler had the power to transfer to Trawler good title to the fishing nets. Trawler now has title to the fishing nets and may retain them.

Commercial Paper

(July 2003)

Legal Problems: (1)   When a negotiable instrument contains contradictory terms, is it enforceable and, if so, which terms prevail?

(2)   When does payment discharge a negotiable instrument?

(3)   What does one who loses a negotiable instrument have to show and do in order to enforce the note?

DISCUSSION

Summary: Finance Co. can enforce the note for $10,450. The rule is that words prevail over numbers. If Garden Shop paid the missing note, whether the payment discharged its obligation would depend on whether Finance Co. had already indorsed or negotiated the note. In either of those cases, it is possible that a "holder in due course" could later appear and enforce the note against Garden Shop. To avoid this contingency, a court would require Finance Co. to prove that it had lost the note and provide adequate security to Garden Shop against double liability before the court would order Garden Shop to pay.

Point One: The enforceability of the note is not affected by the inconsistency in
(15-25%)   its terms. The amount of the note is $10,450 because words prevail over numbers.

If Finance Co. can find the note, it can enforce it in the amount of $10,450. Despite the inconsistency as to the amount payable between the numbers and the words of the note, the note is still negotiable. The note contains an unconditional promise to pay a fixed amount of money to the order of a specific party at a definite time, with no other promises stated by the maker other than to pay. Uniform Commercial Code § 3-104(a). As payee, Finance Co. qualifies as a person entitled to enforce the instrument under § 3-301. Garden Shop's obligation as the issuer of the note under § 3-412 would be to pay the note according to its terms to a person entitled to enforce the instrument.

Section 3-114 covers the situation where there are contradictory terms within an instrument. Under § 3-104(b), this promissory note qualifies as an "instrument" because it is a negotiable instrument. The rule under § 3-114 is that in a case of contradiction such as this one, words prevail over numbers. Therefore, this note is enforceable for $10,450 rather than for $10,000.

Note: The note will be *overdue* if Finance Co. finds it and presents it at a later time (i.e. after the due date) but this fact will not affect Finance Co.'s right to enforce the note. Finance Co. might not be able, however, to collect any interest that accrues after the due date. With respect to possible third party holders, any holder that took the note after the due date (and therefore with notice that it was overdue) could not be a holder in due course. But a holder who took the note before the due date could be a holder in due course and could enforce the note even after it became overdue. Therefore, the fact that the note becomes overdue will not affect this part of the analysis or either of the other two basic points.

Point Two:	Because Finance Co. cannot produce the note, if Garden Shop pays
(35-45%)	Finance Co., it would discharge its obligation to pay against all persons as long as Finance Co. has not negotiated or indorsed the note.

If Garden Shop pays Finance Co. despite the loss of the note, Garden Shop's obligation on the note is discharged as against all persons unless Finance Co. had voluntarily transferred the note or had indorsed the note in blank prior to losing it. Section 3-602(a) says that a party obligated to pay the instrument is discharged on the instrument when it makes payment to a person entitled to enforce the instrument. Section 3-601(b), however, states that discharge of a party is not effective against a person acquiring the rights of a holder in due course of the instrument who has no notice of the discharge. However, if Finance Co. did indeed lose the note and had not indorsed the note in blank prior to losing it, then no other party could become a holder, much less a holder in due course. *See* UCC § 3-201(b) and § 3-301, discussed in Point One above, and Official Comment to § 3-309. On the other hand, if Finance Co. had voluntarily transferred the instrument rather than losing it, then payment to Finance Co. does not discharge Garden Shop because Finance Co. would not be a person entitled to enforce the instrument. *See* UCC § 3-309(a).

Alternatively, if Finance Co. indorsed the note in blank prior to losing it, the note would now be bearer paper. Thus, a third party in possession of the note would be a holder. *See* UCC § 3-201(a) (negotiation may occur even by means of an involuntary transfer) and Official Comment 1 to § 3-201 ("For example, if an instrument is payable to bearer and it is stolen by Thief or is found by Finder, Thief or Finder becomes the holder of the instrument when possession is obtained.") If that third party then negotiated the note for value to a good-faith purchaser who had no notice of any defense or discharge, that purchaser would be a holder in due course under § 3-302(a)(2) and would not be subject to Garden Shop's discharge defense under § 3-601(b).

Point Three:	Finance Co. must prove that it lost the note and must provide
(35-45%)	adequate protection against double liability before a court can enter judgment against Garden Shop.

If Finance Co. sues on the note without producing it, it can obtain a judgment against Garden Shop only if it meets the conditions set out in UCC § 3-309. First, Finance Co. must qualify under § 3-309(a) as a person entitled to enforce the instrument even though it is not in possession of the instrument. In order to do this, Finance Co. must show that (1) it was in possession of the instrument and entitled to enforce it at the time of its loss, (2) the loss was not the result of a transfer by Finance Co. or a lawful seizure, and (3) the instrument's whereabouts cannot be determined.

Second, Finance Co. must prove the terms of the instrument.

Third, Finance Co. must provide adequate protection to Garden Shop against loss that might occur to Garden Shop by reason of a claim by another person to enforce the instrument. The court must decide what protection to require. A surety bond is a common source of protection. If Finance Co. can convince the court that it lost the note and never indorsed it, then the need to provide protection is diminished because, without an indorsement by Finance Co., no later party could be a holder of the note. Thus, Garden Shop would not face a credible risk of being forced to pay the note again. *See* Point Two above and Official Comment to UCC § 3-309 ("On the other hand if the instrument was payable to the person who lost the instrument and that person did not indorse the instrument, no other person could be a holder of the instrument. In some cases there is risk of loss only if there is doubt about whether the facts alleged by the person who lost the instrument are true.")

Commercial Paper
(February 2004)

ANALYSIS

Legal Problems: (1)   Does the payee of a certified check have rights against the drawer when the check is stolen and payment is received by a person not entitled to enforce the instrument?

(2)   Does the payee of a stolen certified check have rights against the banks that collect or pay the stolen check when the payee's indorsement was forged and the check is paid to a person not entitled to enforce it?

(3)   Does a bank that pays a forged-indorsement check have the right to recover the amount of payment from a bank that presented the check for payment?

DISCUSSION

Summary: Sally cannot recover from Bill because he has no liability on a certified check, and his underlying obligation was discharged when Sally took the certified check from him in satisfaction of that obligation. Sally does have a conversion claim against both banks because they allowed Thief, a person not entitled to enforce the check, to receive payment on it. As between the banks, Local Bank can recover from Depositary Bank, which should bear the loss because it took the check from Thief and breached a warranty (no unauthorized indorsements) when it presented the check to Local Bank for payment.

Point One: Because Bill paid Sally with a certified check, his underlying obligation to pay for
(30-35%)   the car was discharged when Sally accepted the check. Moreover, Bill's obligation as drawer of the check was discharged when the check was certified by Local Bank.

When Sally accepted a certified check from Bill in payment for the car, Bill's underlying obligation to pay for the car was discharged "to the same extent discharge would result if an amount of money equal to the amount of the instrument were taken in payment." *See* UCC § 3-

310(a). The certified check is treated as the equivalent of cash. Sally's acceptance of the certified check fully discharges Bill's obligation on the underlying transaction.

Bill's obligation as drawer of the check was fully discharged by Local Bank's certification of the check. *See* UCC § 3-414(c). This is because the certified check is an obligation of Local Bank, *see* UCC § 3-413, and the Code assumes that the holder of a certified check takes or holds the check in reliance on the certifying bank's obligation rather than on the drawer's obligation. UCC § 3-414, cmt. 3.

Point Two: As the owner of the check, Sally has a conversion claim against both Depositary Bank and Local Bank.

(30-35%)

UCC § 3-420(a) provides that a bank that makes or obtains payment for a person not entitled to enforce the instrument is liable for conversion of the check. The liability runs in favor of the true owner or the person entitled to enforce the instrument, and is "presumed to be the amount payable on the instrument." UCC § 3-420(b).

Sally is the owner of the check. In addition, Sally is the only person entitled to enforce the instrument because the check was payable to Sally at the time of the theft. *See* UCC §§ 3-201(a) & (b), 3-301. Absent Sally's indorsement, Thief could not become a person entitled to enforce the check. Thus, when Local Bank made final payment on the check for Thief's benefit, it became liable in conversion to Sally, the true owner of the check. UCC § 3-420(a). Similarly, Depositary Bank, which ultimately gave Thief final credit for his deposit of the check, is liable in conversion to Sally because it obtained payment for a person not entitled to enforce the check (i.e., Thief).

Sally's damages for conversion against either of the two banks would be $15,000, the face amount of the check, under UCC § 3-420(b). She can recover no more than $15,000.

Point Three: Local Bank may recover from Depositary Bank because Depositary Bank breached a presentment warranty.

(30-35%)

As the first party to pay Thief, Depositary Bank will bear the loss if Thief is not found. The reason for this result is the operation of the warranty rules in Article 3 of the UCC. Under UCC § 3-417(d)(1), any party (including a bank) that presents a certified check for payment warrants to the person making payment that the person obtaining payment is entitled to enforce the instrument or is acting on behalf of someone entitled to enforce the instrument. That warranty was breached by Depositary Bank because Sally was the only person entitled to enforce the instrument (the check was payable to her and she had not indorsed it). Depositary Bank clearly was not acting on Sally's behalfCit presented the check on behalf of Thief and credited the amount of the check to Thief's account after receiving payment from Local Bank. Section 3-417 (d)(1) is "in effect . . . a warranty that there are no unauthorized or missing indorsements." *See* Comment 2 to § 3-417. Because the check included an unauthorized indorsement, the warranty was breached and Depositary Bank is liable to Local Bank.

The amount recoverable for this breach of warranty is the amount Local Bank paid on the check plus expenses and loss of interest resulting from the breach. UCC § 3-417(d)(2). Here the recovery from Depositary Bank would be at least the face amount of the check, $15,000.

Commercial Paper

(February 2005)

ANALYSIS

Legal Problems: (1)   Is a promissory note a negotiable instrument if, in a separate document, the obligor promises to do an act in addition to paying money?

(2)   Does a person entitled to enforce an instrument need to attempt recovery from the obligor before seeking recovery from an accommodation party that signed in the capacity of maker?

(3)   Does tender of partial payment by the accommodated party discharge an accommodation party?

(4)   Does an extension of time discharge an accommodation party?

DISCUSSION

Summary

The promissory note is a valid negotiable instrument. Kit's promise to paint Art's house is set forth in a separate document and is not referenced in the promissory note; therefore, the separate promise does not destroy the note's negotiability. Art is an accommodation party because he signed the instrument and did not receive any direct benefit from the loan proceeds. Art signed in the capacity of maker without any limiting language. Therefore, Dealer, a holder and a person entitled to enforce the instrument, may proceed directly against Art without first pursuing Kit.

However, Art is not obligated to pay Dealer anything. When Dealer refused Kit's tender of $2,000, Dealer released Art to the extent of $2,000. When Dealer extended Kit's time to pay without consulting Art, Art was released from his obligation to pay the remaining $3,000 because Art can demonstrate loss with respect to his right of recourse against Kit. Kit had the money on the day the loan was due, but currently cannot be found.

Point One: The promissory note is a valid negotiable instrument. Kit's promise in a separate
(20-30%)   agreement to paint Art's house does not affect the note's negotiability.

The promissory note satisfies the requisites of negotiability set forth in § 3-104 of the Uniform Commercial Code (UCC). It is an unconditional promise to pay ("I promise to pay") a fixed amount of money ($5,000) payable at a definite time (November 4, 2003) and payable to order ("to the order of Dealer"). The promissory note does not contain any other undertakings or instructions. Kit's undertaking to paint Art's house constitutes compensation to Art for being an accommodation party. But because their separate agreement is not included or referenced in the note, it is not an additional undertaking or a condition that destroys negotiability. *See* UCC § 3-106.

Point Two:	Dealer, a person entitled to enforce the instrument (UCC § 3-301), may collect from
(20-30%)	Art, an accommodation maker, without first proceeding against Kit.

Dealer is a holder of the instrument because the instrument was issued to him and he is the identified person in possession. UCC § 1-201(20). As a holder, he is a person entitled to enforce the instrument. UCC § 3-301. Art is an accommodation party because he signed the instrument and did not receive any direct benefit from the loan proceeds. UCC § 3-419(a). The loan proceeds were used to purchase Kit's car. Kit's promise to paint Art's house constitutes consideration for Art's agreement to guarantee the loan; it does not constitute a direct benefit from the loan proceeds.

An accommodation party "is obliged to pay the instrument in the capacity in which [he] signs." UCC § 3-419(b). When Art signed the promissory note directly under Kit's name, he signed in the capacity of maker. A maker is liable to pay the note "according to the terms at the time it was issued." UCC § 3-412. Art did not include any words unambiguously "guaranteeing collection rather than payment." Therefore Dealer, a person entitled to enforce the instrument, can proceed against Art, an accommodation maker, under UCC § 3-412 without first proceeding against Kit. *See* UCC § 3-419(d).

Point Three:	When Dealer rejected Kit's tender of payment of $2,000, Art was discharged to the
(20-30%)	extent of the amount of tender. *See* UCC § 3-603(b).

"If tender of payment of an obligation to pay an instrument is made to a person entitled to enforce the instrument and the tender is refused, there is discharge, to the extent of the amount of the tender, of the obligation of an indorser or accommodation party having a right of recourse with respect to the obligation to which the tender relates." UCC § 3-603(b).

Art, as an accommodation party, has a right of recourse against Kit in the event Art pays the note. UCC § 3-419(e). Thus, when Kit tendered $2,000 to Dealer, a person entitled to enforce the instrument (*See* above), and Dealer rejected the payment, Art was released to the extent of the tender ($2,000).

Point Four:	When Dealer extended Kit's time to pay without Art's consent, Art was discharged from
(20-30%)	his obligation to pay the remaining $3,000 because Art can prove the extension caused him
	loss with respect to his right of recourse against Kit.

"If a person entitled to enforce an instrument agrees, with or without consideration, to an extension of the due date of the obligation of a party to pay the instrument, the extension discharges an indorser or accommodation party having a right of recourse against the party whose obligation is extended to the extent the indorser or accommodation party proves that the extension caused loss to the indorser or accommodation party with respect to the right of recourse." UCC § 3-605(c).

Dealer, a person entitled to enforce the promissory note (*See* Point Two above), granted Kit an extension of time from November 4, 2003, until January 2, 2004. As a result, Art, an accommodation party who has a right of recourse against Kit if he is obligated to pay the loan (*See* UCC § 3-419(e)), is discharged to the extent he can prove that this extension caused loss with respect to his right of recourse. Here, Art can show that the extension caused him a loss of the remaining $3,000. On the due date, Kit had the money necessary to pay the debt. Kit has since disappeared with the money. Accordingly, Art should be discharged from having to pay Dealer the remaining $3,000.

NOTE: If an applicant missed the tender of payment argument, the applicant could correctly conclude that Art was discharged from the entire $5,000 based solely upon this extension of time.

Commercial Paper

(July 2005)

ANALYSIS

Legal Problems: (1)   What right, if any, does Cousin have to enforce the note?

          (2)   Who is liable on the note?

          (3)   How much are Ben and Frank liable for on the note?

          (4)   To what extent does Ben have a right of contribution from Frank?

DISCUSSION

Summary

Ben and Frank are jointly and severally liable as co-makers of the note, so a person entitled to enforce the note can recover the amount due from either of them. Cousin is a person entitled to enforce the note because Vendor transferred his rights to Cousin. However, Cousin is not a holder in due course both because Vendor did not indorse the note and because Cousin did not pay value for it. Accordingly, Cousin is subject to all defenses Ben and Frank might have and those defenses will reduce the amount due on the note.

Ben's payment of $4,000 to Vendor reduces the amount Cousin can recover. The outstanding balance for which Ben and Frank are liable is $3,000 because the contract provided that Ben and Frank would pay Vendor the lesser of $10,000 *or* the amount of the appraisal, which came in at $7,000.

Finally, Ben is entitled to contribution of $500 from Frank because Ben paid $500 more than his share of the debt.

NOTE: The National Conference of Commissioners on Uniform State Laws (NCCUSL) has approved amendments to articles 1 and 3 of the Uniform Commercial Code (UCC). These amendments will take effect only if and when state legislatures enact them. These amendments do not change the substance of any provisions applicable to this question. The amendments, however, alter the text and numbering of a few sections in articles 1 and 3. In the following discussion, citations in brackets refer to the amended versions of these articles. For more information on the amendments to the UCC, *see* NCCUSL's website at http:\\www.nccusl.org.]

Point One: Cousin is entitled to enforce the note but will be subject to any applicable defenses
(20-30%)   because Cousin is not a holder in due course.

Cousin's right to recover on the note and the amount Cousin may recover depend on whether Cousin is a holder in due course of the note. To be a holder in due course, Cousin must be a holder of the note and must have taken it for value, in good faith, and without notice of any defenses to the note. UCC § 3-302(a).

On these facts, Cousin is not a holder in due course for two reasons. First, when Vendor gave the note to Cousin as a gift, Vendor did not indorse it. The lack of an indorsement left the note payable to Vendor, and Cousin did not become its holder. UCC § 1-201(20). Second, Cousin did not take the note for value. *See* § 3-303 (defining value).

Nonetheless, Cousin is entitled to enforce the note. Under the "shelter rule," Vendor's transfer of the note to Cousin was also a transfer of all of Vendor's rights on the note, including Vendor's rights as a holder. UCC § 3-203(b). A non-holder in possession with the rights of a holder is entitled to enforce a note. *See* §§ 3-301(ii), 3-203 cmt. 2 ("If a transferee is not a holder because the transferor did not indorse, the transferee is nevertheless a person entitled to enforce the instrument under Section 3-301 if the transferor was a holder at the time of transfer."). However, the "shelter rule" only permits Cousin to assert the same rights that Vendor had to enforce the note, and Vendor held the note subject to Ben and Frank's defenses.

Because Cousin is not a holder in due course, Cousin took the note subject to those same defenses. *See* § 3-305(a) & (b) and Point Three below. As explained in Point Three, Ben and Frank have defenses based on their separate agreement with Vendor and on the partial payment by Ben.

Point Two: Ben and Frank, as co-makers, are jointly and severally liable for the outstanding
(10-20%)   balance of the note.

Ben and Frank are co-makers of the note because they both signed it. As a result, they are jointly and severally liable on the note. *See* § 3-116(a). Their joint and several liability means that a person entitled to enforce the note, such as Cousin, may recover the entire outstanding balance of the note from either Ben or Frank.

Point Three: Ben and Frank's outstanding liability on the note is $3,000.
(25-35%)

Although the original amount of the note was $10,000, Ben and Frank have two defenses to payment that limit their outstanding liability to $3,000. Cousin is subject to these defenses. (*See* Point One above.)

The first defense comes from the sales contract with Vendor. The contract limited Ben and Frank's total liability to the appraised value of the equipment if that value was less than $10,000. The appraised value turned out to be $7,000, which of course is less than $10,000. The UCC permits parties to assert defenses to payment based on separate agreements. *See* § 3-117 (specifying that "the obligation of a party to an instrument to pay the instrument may be modified . . . by a separate agreement of the obligor and a person entitled to enforce the instrument, if the instrument is issued . . . as part of the same transaction giving rise to the agreement"). Accordingly, Ben and Frank's liability before payment was limited to $7,000.

Ben and Frank also have a defense based on Ben's payment of $4,000 to Vendor. As explained above (Point One), Vendor was a holder of the note at the time of payment, and was entitled to enforce it. Payment to a person entitled to enforce a note discharges liability on the note to the extent of payment. *See* § 3-602(a)(ii) [rev. § 3-602(a)]. The $4,000 payment by Ben to Vendor thus reduced Ben and Frank's liability on the note from $7,000 to $3,000.

<u>Point Four:</u>   <u>Ben has a right to contribution from Frank for $500.</u>
(25-35%)

A co-maker may recover from other co-makers to the extent permitted by the law of contribution. *See* § 3-116(b). The law of contribution says that a co-maker who pays more than his or her proportionate share of a debt may recover the excess payment from other co-makers. *See* RESTATEMENT OF THE LAW OF RESTITUTION § 85 cmt. e (1937) ("If in partial satisfaction one [co-debtor] pays less than the entire amount but more than his share, he is entitled to recover from any [other co-debtor] who has not paid his share such excess up to the amount of the unpaid share of the other . . . ."); 12 AM. JUR. 2D *Bills and Notes* § 440 ("if one of two or more . . . makers of a note pays the note or an amount greater than his or her proportionate share, the maker is entitled to proceed against his or her comakers for contribution").

As explained above (in Point Three), Ben and Frank's total liability on the note before payment was $7,000. The proportionate share of this liability for each of them was $3,500. In paying $4,000 to Vendor, Ben paid $500 more than his proportionate share. Ben therefore has a right to recover $500 from Frank.

If Ben pays additional sums to Cousin in the future, Ben also will be able to recover these additional sums from Frank under a theory of contribution. Frank can have no right to contribution from Ben because Ben already paid more than Ben's proportionate share.

Commercial Paper

(July 2006)

ANALYSIS

Legal Problems: (1)   Was Consumer's attempt at an accord and satisfaction effective?

                    (2)   (a)   Was Thief's forgery of Consumer's signature on the check effective as Consumer's signature?

                            (b)   Did Consumer act negligently in leaving her handbag unattended on a table in a restaurant and thereby contribute to the forgery of her signature?

                            (c)   If Consumer was negligent, could Grocer bring a claim against Consumer for $150 following the bank's dishonor of the check?

DISCUSSION
Summary

Consumer's attempted accord and satisfaction was ineffective because Consumer acted in bad faith in attempting to avoid a debt about which there was no dispute. As to the forged check, Consumer probably has no liability because she never signed it. She would be liable on the check only if it were concluded that she was sufficiently negligent in leaving her handbag unattended on the restaurant table so that she should be estopped from denying the validity of the signature.

[NOTE: Although a bank is involved in the fact pattern, this question does not raise any questions under UCC Article 4. The check payable to Grocer was presented for payment over the counter and dishonored immediately, so there was no "collection" of the check. Article 4 is not included in the commercial paper specifications for the MEE, and references to UCC Article 4 in answers to this question are not on point.]

Point One (30-40%)

Consumer's attempt at an accord and satisfaction is not effective because there is no bona fide dispute about the amount owed.

A person tendering an instrument in payment of a claim may use the instrument to resolve a dispute surrounding the claim by an accord and satisfaction. UCC § 3-311. If there is a proper accord and satisfaction, then the claim is discharged. To achieve an accord and satisfaction, the following requirements must be met: (i) the person against whom the claim is asserted must in good faith tender an instrument to the claimant as full satisfaction of the claim; (ii) the claim must have been unliquidated or subject to a bona fide dispute; (iii) the instrument must contain a conspicuous written statement to the effect that it is tendered in full satisfaction of the claim; and (iv) the claimant must obtain payment of the instrument. UCC § 3-311(a) & (b).

In this case, requirements (iii) and (iv) are clearly satisfied. Department Store obtained payment on the instrument when it cleared Consumer's account. Also, Consumer clearly marked the check "Payment in Full for All Amounts Owed," which is a conspicuous statement to the effect that the instrument is tendered in full satisfaction of the claim. UCC § 3-311(b).

Nonetheless, there is no accord and satisfaction because neither requirement (i) nor (ii) is met. First, Consumer did not act in good faith in tendering the full payment check. She wanted to keep the sofa without actually paying for it. There are no facts to suggest that she thought she didn't actually owe the money to Department Store. Her attempted "accord and satisfaction" was a bad faith effort to avoid a proper debt, not a good faith effort to resolve a dispute. For the same reason, the second requirement is not met. There was no bona fide dispute about the amount owed. There is no evidence that the sofa was defective or that Consumer thought the amount stated on her monthly statement was incorrect for any reason. UCC § 3-311(a).

[NOTE: Article 3 contains a special rule allowing organizational creditors like Department Store to avoid inadvertent accord and satisfaction by requiring their debtors to send accord and satisfaction checks to an address other than the one used to collect routine payments. See UCC § 3-311(c). Some examinees may suggest that Department Store could raise this as an issue, but there are no facts in the question to indicate that the defense is available. Moreover, it is clear there was no sufficient accord and satisfaction in any event.]

Point Two(a) (30-40%)

Thief's signature is not effective as Consumer's signature because it was made without Consumer's authorization, so it is effective only as Thief's signature.

The general rule in Article 3 is that no one is liable on an instrument unless that person signed the instrument or authorized someone to sign on his or her behalf. UCC § 3-401(a). There is no evidence that Consumer authorized Thief to sign her check. The signature on the check will be effective as Thief's signature, not Consumer's. See UCC § 3-403. Accordingly, Consumer will not be liable on the check unless she is precluded from proving that the signature is a forgery. (See Point Two(b).)

Point Two(b) (15-25%)

Consumer's carelessness in leaving her unattended handbag with her checkbook in it on a table in a restaurant probably would not preclude her from raising a claim of forgery in defense of Grocer's attempt to enforce the check.

UCC § 3-406 provides that anyone whose "failure to exercise ordinary care substantially contributes" to the making of a forged signature on an instrument is precluded from asserting the forgery against a person who, in good faith, takes the instrument for value.

It is unlikely that Consumer's carelessness in leaving her handbag unattended on her table at the restaurant would preclude her from asserting that her signature had been forged. First, the comments to § 3-406 suggest that the preclusion rule in that section is primarily aimed at behavior that makes it relatively easy for a bad actor to commit the physical act of forgery, such as leaving the signature stamp readily available to an employee who is not authorized to endorse a check. To justify preclusion, negligence must "substantially contribute" to the "making of" the forgery. Section 3-406 has not been interpreted to impose any special duty on individuals to guard their checkbooks from theft by forgers. Even if Consumer were deemed to have been negligent in leaving her handbag unattended, a court is not likely to view that as the sort of negligence that satisfies the requirement of § 3-406 that the negligent act "substantially contribute" to the "making of a forged signature."

In addition, there is a good argument that Consumer's carelessness does not rise to the level of a "failure to exercise ordinary care." Thief's behavior in snatching Consumer's handbag was unlawful, and Consumer is not obliged by Article 3 to constantly be on the alert for any kind of unlawful behavior that might deprive her of possession of her checkbook. There is nothing in the fact pattern to indicate that this was a particularly dangerous neighborhood or that Consumer should have known there was a significant risk her handbag would be stolen.

[NOTE: It is more important that the examinees recognize and discuss the two elements of the § 3-406 preclusion rule ("substantially contributes . . . to the making of a forged signature" and "failure to exercise ordinary care") than that they reach the same conclusion as does this analysis. Credit should be given to an answer that favors precluding a forgery defense if the answer displays an understanding of the basic rule.]

Point Two(c) (5-15%)

If Consumer failed to exercise ordinary care and that failure contributed to the making of the forgery, then Grocer has a claim against Consumer for $150 because Bank dishonored the check when Grocer presented it.

If Consumer is found to have been negligent in having left her handbag where it could be stolen, and if that negligence substantially contributed to the making of the forgery, then she would be precluded from asserting the forgery of her signature as drawer as a defense to a claim by Grocer for $150. UCC § 3-406. If Consumer is precluded from asserting the forgery, then the signature is treated as her signature and she is the drawer of the check. As the drawer, she would be obliged to pay the amount of the check to a person entitled to enforce it if the check was dishonored. UCC § 3-414(b). Because Grocer is the payee of the check, Grocer is entitled to enforce the instrument. UCC § 3-301. The check was dishonored by Bank. UCC § 3-502. Thus, Consumer would be liable to Grocer for the amount of the check if the forged signature were treated as Consumer's signature.

Commercial Paper

(February 2007)

ANALYSIS

Legal Problems: (1)   To what extent is a "guarantor" of a note liable to the holder of the note?

                                      (2)   Is Acme's claim against Mom subject to the defense that Uncle negotiated the note contrary to his agreement and without authorization?

                                      (3)   May Mom raise a defense against Acme based on Acme's discharge of Nephew, the principal obligor on the instrument?

DISCUSSION

Summary

Acme can recover the $9,000 still due on the note from Mom. Although Mom has a defense against payment based on Uncle's violation of his promise not to negotiate the note without Nephew's and Mom's consent, this defense is not good against Acme because Acme is a holder in due course. A holder in due course can enforce the note free of any personal defense of this sort. *See* UCC § 3-305(b).

Even though Acme discharged Nephew, Mom's liability is intact. Mom signed as a guarantor or "accommodation party." An accommodation party remains liable on a note, even if the creditor discharges the primary obligor. *See* UCC § 3-605. Mom's liability is of course reduced by the amount paid on the debt by Nephew. *See* UCC § 3-419(e).

Point One (35-45%)

Mom signed the note in the capacity of a maker of the note and is liable to Acme in that capacity, even though she signed for accommodation only, unless she has a valid defense.

Mom signed the front of the note, immediately under Nephew's signature, and under the word "guaranteed." She also clearly indicated that she was signing as "a guarantor." Moreover, it is clear, in UCC terms, that Mom signed the note only for the purpose of incurring liability on it; she was not a direct beneficiary of the value given for the note, as Nephew, not Mom, received an interest in the sandwich shop. Thus, Mom signed the instrument "for accommodation," *see* UCC § 3-419(a), and the language she used ("as guarantor" and "guaranteed") gave notice that she had signed only for accommodation, *see* UCC § 3-419(c).

An accommodation party is "obliged to pay the instrument in the capacity in which the accommodation party signs." UCC § 3-419(b). Mom signed on the front of the note as a person undertaking to pay and thus signed in the capacity of a maker. UCC § 3-103(a)(7). As a maker, she would be obliged to pay the instrument to a holder. UCC § 3-412. Moreover, this obligation to pay arises even if the person seeking to enforce the instrument has notice of the party's accommodation status. UCC § 3-419(c). Thus, unless Mom has some other valid defense to payment (*see* Points Two and Three, below), the fact that she signed for accommodation will not relieve her of her obligation to pay the instrument according to its terms to a person entitled to enforce it.

Acme is a holder of the note because Uncle indorsed the note to Acme, which took possession of it. *See* UCC § 1-201(20) (definition of holder). As a holder, Acme has a right to enforce the note against any party who signed it. *See* UCC §§ 3-301 (right of party to enforce an instrument), 3-401(a) (effect of signature). Thus, Mom has an obligation to pay Acme unless Mom can assert a valid defense to payment that is good against Acme.

[NOTE TO GRADERS: The analysis and result are unchanged under the 2002 Revisions to Article 3-419. *See* Revised Article 3, § 3-419(e).]

Point Two (30-40%)

Acme is not subject to Mom's defense of unauthorized negotiation. Acme had no notice of the oral agreement among Uncle, Nephew, and Mom regarding a limitation on Uncle's power to negotiate the note. Acme gave value for the note in good faith. Thus, Acme is a holder in due course and can enforce the note against Mom free of any defense she could have asserted against Uncle.

Mom has a defense based on Uncle's breach of his agreement not to enforce or negotiate the note. *See* UCC § 3-117 (separate agreement modifying an obligation in a note can provide a defense to payment). The problem for Mom is that Acme appears to be a holder in due course of the note. Acme gave value for the note, taking it in good faith (from all that appears in the facts). The agreement restricting Uncle's right to negotiate the note does not appear on the face of the note, and Acme had no notice of that oral agreement. So Acme gave value in good faith and without notice of any defenses to the note. It is therefore a holder in due course. As a holder in due course, Acme took the note free of ordinary defenses, including Mom's defense of unauthorized negotiation. *See* UCC §§ 3-302(a) (requisites of holder in due course status), 3-305(b) (defenses applicable to a holder in due course).

[NOTE TO GRADERS: The analysis is unchanged under Revised Article 3.]

Point Three (20-30%)
Mom's liability on the note was not discharged by Acme's release of Nephew's liability.

As an accommodation party, Mom is liable to Acme if Nephew does not pay the full amount of the note, and this liability survives even if Acme discharges Nephew. Section 3-605(b) of the UCC expressly provides that an intentional voluntary discharge of the principal obligor by a person entitled to enforce a note "does not discharge the obligation of an . . . accommodation party . . . ." Mom has a right of recourse against Nephew, and she can seek reimbursement from

Nephew to the extent she pays on the note. *See* UCC § 3-419(e). Mom is, of course, only liable to Acme for $9,000, the amount of the note that remains unpaid.

[NOTE TO GRADERS: Revised Article 3 includes significant changes to § 3-605. Those changes would dramatically alter the analysis and result on this issue. This note details the revised analysis.

Because Mom is an accommodation party, she qualifies as a "secondary obligor" on the instrument signed by Nephew. UCC Revised § 3-103(a)(17). As a secondary obligor, Mom has the defenses set out in Revised § 3-605. In particular, when, as here, a person entitled to enforce the instrument releases the obligation of the principal obligor to pay the instrument, then "the secondary obligor is discharged to the same extent as the principal obligor from any unperformed portion of its obligation on the instrument." UCC Revised § 3-605(a)(2). The person entitled to enforce the instrument could retain rights against the secondary obligor by so specifying in the release, but absent such an explicit retention of rights, the secondary obligor is discharged.

Thus, when Acme accepted $1,000 and released Nephew from his obligation to pay the remaining amount due on the note, Mom was discharged. There is nothing in the facts to indicate that Acme expressly retained its rights against Mom.]

Commercial Paper

(July 2007)

ANALYSIS

Legal Problems: (1)   Under what circumstances would Lender take the check free from Corporation's claim of ownership?

        (2)   Was Sam's fraudulent indorsement effective to negotiate the check to Lender and make Lender a holder?

        (3)   Did Lender give value for the check merely by reducing Sam's loan balance?

        (4)   Did Lender have notice of Corporation's claim to the check when it took the check in payment of a personal debt owed by Sam?

DISCUSSION

Summary

Lender will not be subject to Corporation's claim to the check because Lender is a holder in due course. Sam's forged indorsement of the check is treated as valid (as against Corporation) because Corporation gave Sam responsibility for handling its checks. Lender took the indorsed check in good faith. It also gave "value" for the check because it took it in payment for an antecedent debt. Finally, Lender had no notice of Corporation's claim to the check or of any other claim or defense that might be raised. Lender is therefore not obligated to return the check to Corporation.

[NOTE: The Uniform Commercial Code (UCC) governs this problem. The American Law Institute and National Conference of Commissioners on Uniform State Laws approved a revision of UCC Article 1 in 2001 and approved amendments to UCC Article 3 in 2002 and 2003. This discussion cites the current revised and amended versions of these articles, but the problem has been designed so that the amendments do not affect the analysis.]

Point One (20-30%)

Lender will be free of Corporation's claim if Lender took the check under circumstances that satisfy the requirements for being a holder in due course.

A check is a negotiable instrument, UCC § 3-104(f), and a "person taking an instrument . . . is subject to a claim of a property or possessory right in the instrument . . . ." UCC § 3-306 (2003). In this case, Corporation was the original payee of the check, the check belonged to Corporation, and Corporation therefore has both a property and possessory right in the check. In most cases, Corporation would be able to assert this right and recover the check from a thief (e.g., Sam) or from a person who took the instrument from a thief (e.g., Lender).

However, a "claim of a property or possessory right in the instrument" may not be successfully asserted against a "person having rights of a holder in due course." *Id.* Therefore, if Lender is a holder in due course of the check, Lender will not be subject to Corporation's claim to the check. *See American Parkinson Disease Ass'n, Inc. v. First Nat. Bank of Northfield*, 584 N.W.2d 437, 441 (Minn. 1998) (holder in due course not subject to the claim of an organization from which the check was embezzled).

A "holder in due course" is a holder of a negotiable instrument who took the instrument in good faith, for value, and without notice of certain problems with respect to the instrument, including a claim to the instrument. UCC § 3-302(a)(2). The question stipulates that Lender took the check in good faith. Accordingly, whether Lender is a holder in due course depends on whether Lender is a holder of the check, whether Lender took the check for value, and whether Lender had notice of Corporation's claim to the check. The following points address these issues, ultimately concluding that Lender is a holder in due course.

Point Two (30-40%)

Lender is a holder of the check because a fraudulent indorsement of a check by an employee entrusted with responsibility with respect to the check is effective to negotiate the check.

Lender must be a "holder" of the check in order to be a holder in due course. A person can become a holder of a negotiable instrument by taking the instrument through the process of negotiation. *See* UCC § 1-201(b)(21)(A) (defining holder), § 3-201(a) (defining negotiation). Negotiation of an instrument payable to an identified person requires a transfer of possession of the instrument and the indorsement of the person to whom the instrument is payable. UCC § 3-201(b). In this case, the check was payable to Corporation, and possession was transferred to Lender. Therefore, if the check was indorsed by Corporation, Lender took the instrument through a negotiation and became a holder of the instrument.

Sam made an unauthorized indorsement of the check in the name of Corporation. Ordinarily, an unauthorized signature would not suffice to negotiate a check. UCC § 3-403(a). But an exception exists for unauthorized signatures made by an employee entrusted with responsibility for handling checks. The exception says: "if an employer entrusted an employee with responsibility with respect to the instrument and the employee . . . makes a fraudulent indorsement of the instrument, the indorsement is effective as the indorsement of the person to whom the instrument is payable if it is made in the name of that person." UCC § 3-405(b). An employer may entrust an employee with responsibility with respect to a check in several ways, including giving the employee authority to handle the check "for deposit to an account." UCC § 3-405(a)(3)(ii); *see Cable Cast Magazine v. Premier Bank, Nat'l Ass'n*, 729 So. 2d 1165, 1167 (La. Ct. App. 1999) (holding that a fraudulent indorsement by an employee who had authority to deposit checks was effective as the indorsement of the employer).

In this case, Corporation entrusted Sam with responsibility for the check because it authorized him to deposit it. Sam made a fraudulent indorsement of the check in the name of Corporation. This fraudulent indorsement therefore was effective as the indorsement of Corporation. Accordingly, the check was negotiated to Lender, and Lender became a holder of the check. The underlying policy is that the risk of unauthorized indorsement should fall upon Corporation because Corporation put Sam in a position that facilitated his commission of a forgery. Section 3-405(b) treats the fraudulent endorsement as effective only as to a person who took the instrument for value and in good faith. For a discussion of the value issue, see Point Three.

[NOTE: The facts stipulate that Lender took the instrument in good faith. Although the question asks only whether Lender must return the check to Corporation, some applicants might note that any loss caused by this fraud must be shared by Lender if Lender "fail[ed] to exercise ordinary care in . . . taking the instrument and that failure substantially contribute[d] to [the] loss . . . ." UCC § 3-405(b).]

Point Three (15-25%)

An instrument is taken for value if it is taken in payment of an antecedent debt.

In order to be a holder in due course, Lender must have taken the check for "value." UCC § 3-302(a)(2)(i). Section 3-303(a)(3) says that "[a]n instrument is issued or transferred for value if . . . the instrument is issued or transferred as payment of . . . an antecedent claim against any person, whether or not the claim is due." In this case, Lender took the $3,000 check in payment of Sam's antecedent mortgage debt. Therefore, even though Lender may not have given anything tangible to Sam, Lender still took the check for value. *See Fedeli v. UAP/Ga. Ag. Chem., Inc.*, 514 S.E.2d 684, 690 (Ga. Ct. App. 1999) (holding that a lender who took checks in payment of an existing indebtedness gave "value" for the checks).

Point Four (15-25%)

Lender did not have notice of Corporation's claim to the check.

To be a holder in due course, Lender must take the check without notice of any claim to the check. UCC § 3-302(a).

The system of negotiability of checks presumes that checks will be transferred in payment of obligations by persons other than the original payees of the checks. Thus, there is nothing inherently suspicious about a person transferring an indorsed check that was not originally payable to that person. Indeed, the holder-in-due-course rule is designed to encourage persons and businesses like Lender to accept and transfer checks in this manner.

Lender had no knowledge of Sam's fiduciary status; therefore, Lender cannot be charged with knowledge of Sam's breach of a fiduciary duty. *Cf.* UCC § 3-307(b)(2) (notice of certain acts constituting breach of fiduciary obligation gives notice of represented person's claim only where person taking an instrument from a fiduciary "has knowledge of the fiduciary status"). *See Jelmoli Holding, Inc. v. Raymond James Financial Serv., Inc.*, 470 F.3d 14, 19 (1st Cir. 2006) ("plaintiff must show knowledge by the taker, and not just warning clues, that the person tendering the check is a fiduciary"); *United Catholic Parish Schools of Beaver Dam Educ. Ass'n v. Card Serv. Ctr.*, 636 N.W.2d 206, 212-213 (Wis. Ct. App. 2001) (holding that the taker of an unauthorized check in payment of a personal debt did not have notice of a breach of a fiduciary duty because it did not have actual knowledge of any fiduciary relationship).

Thus, Lender is a holder in due course. It is a holder. It took the instrument in good faith and for value. And it did not have notice of Corporation's claim to the instrument even though Sam was using the check to pay a personal debt. As a holder in due course, Lender is not subject to Corporation's claim to the check.

[NOTE: Credit should be given for a reasonable discussion of the notice issue, regardless of the conclusion reached by the applicant.]

Commercial Paper

(July 2008)

ANALYSIS

Legal Problems: (1)(a) Did Law Firm's check and letter constitute an accord and satisfaction of Finisher's claims against Law Firm?

(1)(b) Can Finisher avoid the accord and satisfaction?

(2) Is CheckNow liable to Finisher for conversion of the Restaurant check?

DISCUSSION

Summary

Under UCC § 3-311, the Law Firm check together with the letter from Law Firm constituted an accord and satisfaction against Finisher if: (1) Law Firm tendered the check in good faith as payment in full; (2) the amount of Finisher's claim was subject to a bona fide dispute; (3) Finisher obtained payment of the check; and (4) Law Firm included on the check or an accompanying written communication a conspicuous statement to the effect that the check was tendered as payment in full. Although an accord and satisfaction can sometimes be avoided, Finisher will not be able to avoid it in this case because the check was received and deposited by Administrator, who was not merely a processing clerk for Finisher but instead had direct responsibility for resolving the dispute between Finisher and Law Firm.

CheckNow is not liable to Finisher because Administrator's indorsement on behalf of Finisher was not a forgery and even if it was, it was nonetheless effective under UCC § 3-405(b).

Point One(a) (40–50%)
The Law Firm check constituted an accord and satisfaction.

UCC § 3-311 governs accord and satisfaction by use of an instrument. An accord and satisfaction occurs when a debtor offers a sum of money, or some other stated performance, in settlement of a debt, and the creditor accepts the proposed performance in satisfaction of the debt. The purpose of accord and satisfaction is to allow parties to resolve disputes without judicial intervention. Section 3-311 provides statutory requisites for an accord and satisfaction accomplished by use of an instrument.

UCC § 3-311 follows the common law rule regarding accord and satisfaction with minor variations to reflect modern business conditions. UCC § 3-311, cmt. 3. To accomplish an accord and satisfaction by use of an instrument, certain conditions must be met. The person seeking satisfaction must do so in good faith, the amount of the claim must be subject to dispute, and the person to whom the instrument is tendered must obtain payment of the instrument. UCC § 3-311(a). In addition, "the instrument or an accompanying written communication" must clearly state that the instrument is tendered in full satisfaction of the debt. UCC § 3-311(b). If those conditions are satisfied, then an accord and satisfaction is accomplished, subject to limited exceptions discussed in Point One(b).

On our facts, the requirements of an accord and satisfaction are met. First, the Law Firm check is an instrument. UCC § 3-104(c). Second, it appears that Law Firm acted in good faith. "Good faith" means honesty in fact and the observance of reasonable commercial standards of fair dealing. UCC § 3-103(a)(4). There is nothing in the facts to suggest that Law Firm was trying to take advantage of Finisher or otherwise acting in bad faith. Thus, the good faith requirement is met.

Third, the amount that Law Firm owed was subject to a bona fide dispute. Not only did Law Firm have a claim in recoupment regarding damage to the carpet (that might reduce what was owed to Finisher), but that claim was unliquidated because there was no agreement on the amount of the damage to the carpet.

Lastly, Finisher obtained payment of the instrument, which was plainly marked "payment in full" and was attached to a letter making a clear assertion that the check was sent in settlement of the dispute about the damage to the carpet.

Point One(b) (10–20%)
Because Administrator had direct responsibility to resolve customer complaints, the accord and satisfaction was not inadvertent, and Finisher cannot avoid it.

Under some circumstances, a creditor can avoid an accord and satisfaction that is made inadvertently (e.g., when a creditor obtains payment of a check without realizing that the check was offered in full satisfaction of the creditor's claim). Thus, despite entering into an apparent accord and satisfaction, a creditor can sometimes preserve its rights by tendering repayment of the amount it received in satisfaction within 90 days after it obtains payment of the instrument. *See* UCC § 3-311(c).

However, an accord and satisfaction cannot be avoided where it was *not* inadvertent. Thus, when the claimant, "or an agent of the claimant having direct responsibility with respect to the disputed obligation," actually knows that an instrument is tendered in full satisfaction, then the claimant's claim is discharged if payment is obtained on the instrument. *See* UCC § 3-311(d).

Here, the full satisfaction tender was made in plain terms to Administrator, an agent to whom Finisher had given responsibility for the resolution of customer disputes. Moreover, given that the check was clearly marked as a "full satisfaction" check and was accompanied by a letter to that effect, it is likely that Law Firm could prove that Administrator knew that the check was tendered in discharge of Law Firm's debt.

Point Two (35–45%)
Finisher cannot recover in conversion against CheckNow because Administrator's indorsement on the check in Finisher's name is effective.

UCC § 3-420 governs whether CheckNow is liable for its conversion of the Restaurant check. Subpart (a) provides that an instrument [in this case the Restaurant check] is converted "if it is taken by transfer, other than a negotiation, from a person not entitled to enforce the instrument . . . ." Section 3-420 permits the true owner of a check to recover the amount of the check from a person who "takes an instrument bearing a forged indorsement" and obtains payment on that instrument for himself or herself. *See* § 3-420, cmt. 1.

Finisher made Administrator an agent for purposes of handling checks and gave Administrator express authority to indorse checks on Finisher's behalf as part of Administrator's job responsibilities. So even though Administrator was not authorized to cash the check and keep its proceeds, Administrator's signing of the check in Finisher's name was authorized and not a forgery. *See* UCC § 3-402, cmt. 1 (signature by a representative binds the represented person if the represented person would be bound under ordinary agency law principles).

The properly indorsed check was bearer paper, and Administrator was a holder of it. UCC § 3-205(b). (The facts do not indicate that the check was restrictively indorsed, i.e., "for deposit only.") As a holder, Administrator was a person entitled to enforce the instrument. Thus, when CheckNow cashed the check, it gave value for the check to a person "entitled to enforce the instrument." This is not a conversion under UCC § 3-420.

[NOTE TO GRADERS: Some applicants might conclude that Administrator's indorsement of the check was not authorized because Administrator had authority to indorse *only* for the purpose of deposit into Finisher's account. But even if Administrator's indorsement were unauthorized, it would be effective. When an employer gives an employee the authority to indorse or deposit instruments for the employer, then a fraudulent indorsement of the instrument by the employee "is effective" as the employer's indorsement, at least in favor of a person "who, in good faith, . . . takes [the instrument] for value." UCC § 3-405(b). The rationale for this rule is that the employer ought to bear the consequences of his bad judgment in giving responsibility for checks to a dishonest employee because the employer is in the best position to insure against or avoid the risk of employee defalcations.

The facts are clear that Finisher gave Administrator "responsibility with respect to the instrument" involved in this dispute, the Restaurant check. CheckNow gave value for the Restaurant check, and no facts suggest that CheckNow acted other than in good faith. As a result, it is likely that the forged indorsement will be treated as effective for purposes of determining CheckNow's liability to Finisher. Applicants who fail to recognize that the indorsement was authorized could receive some credit for this analysis.]

Commercial Paper

(February 2009)

ANALYSIS

(Negotiable Instruments (Commercial Paper) IV.A.; V.A., C., H.; VI.)

Legal Problems: (1)   Is a person in possession of a check that has been transferred by means of a forged indorsement entitled to enforce the check against the payee whose signature was forged?

    (2)   Is a person in possession of a check that has been transferred by means of a forged indorsement entitled to enforce the check against the drawer of the check?

    (3)   Is a person in possession of a check that has been transferred by means of a forged indorsement entitled to enforce the check against the drawee bank?

    (4)   Is a person in possession of a check that has been transferred by means of a forged indorsement entitled to enforce the check against the forger from whom he received the check?

DISCUSSION

[NOTE: Although a bank is involved in the fact pattern, this question does not raise any questions under UCC Article 4. When Seller tried to present the check payable to Payee for payment over the counter, Bank did not pay it or accept it for collection, so there are no Article 4 issues raised by these facts. Article 4 is not included in the negotiable instruments specifications for the MEE, and references to UCC Article 4 in answers to this question are unnecessary.]

Summary

Even though Seller acted in good faith and gave value in exchange for Payee's check, Seller has no rights against Payee because Payee never signed the check and is therefore not liable on it. Furthermore, the lack of a valid indorsement of the check by Payee means that Seller cannot be a holder of the check and is therefore not entitled to enforce it against Drawer or Bank. Moreover, Bank would not be liable to Seller in any event, as a drawee is not liable to the payee or holder of a check (draft) unless it has accepted it. Accordingly, Seller's only recourse will be against Thief on a theory of breach of transfer warranty or on Thief's indorser's contract.

Point One (20–30%)
Seller cannot recover from Payee because Payee is not liable on the instrument. Thief's forgery of Payee's signature is not effective as an indorser's signature because Payee was not negligent, and Thief is not Payee's agent.

UCC § 3-401(a) provides that a person is not liable on an instrument unless that person signed the instrument or that person's agent or representative signed the instrument. Payee did not sign the instrument and Thief is not Payee's agent or representative, so his forgery of her signature is not effective as her signature. An exception to this general rule is found in UCC § 3-406, which provides that if a person's failure to exercise ordinary care substantially contributes to the making of a forged signature, then that person will be precluded from asserting the fact of the forgery to avoid liability. Nothing in the facts suggests that Payee was negligent, so this exception does not apply.

Point Two (30–40%)

The check is payable to Payee, so without Payee's indorsement, Thief is not a holder of the instrument; when Thief transferred the check to Seller, Seller acquired only the rights that Thief had and so is not entitled to enforce the instrument.

When a negotiable instrument has been dishonored, a "person entitled to enforce the [instrument]" ordinarily may bring an action to enforce the instrument against the drawer of the instrument. UCC § 3-414(b). In this case, however, Seller has no legal right to enforce the instrument against Drawer because Seller is not a person entitled to enforce the instrument.

The check Drawer wrote was originally payable to Payee and was therefore "order paper." *See* UCC § 3-109. Until Payee indorses the check, Payee is the only person who can be a holder of the instrument. UCC § 1-201(b)(21)(A). When Thief acquired the check as a result of stealing Payee's handbag, he did not become a holder in his own right because Payee had not indorsed the check. Thief also did not acquire any of Payee's rights as a holder because Payee did not deliver the check to Thief for the purpose of giving Thief a right to enforce it. *See* UCC § 3-203(a) & (b). Thus, Thief was neither a holder of the check nor a person with the rights of a holder, and Thief was not entitled to enforce the check. *See* UCC § 3-301.

When Thief transferred the check to Seller, Seller did not become a holder because, as noted earlier, the forged indorsement of the check was ineffective and the check remained payable to Payee. Seller did receive all the rights Thief had in the check, but Thief had no right to enforce the check. In short, Seller is not a person entitled to enforce the check and therefore has no claim against Drawer.

[NOTE: Some examinees might also note that Seller's attempt to cash the check was not a presentment because he was not a person entitled to enforce. UCC §§ 3-301, 3-501. Since dishonor of a check is a condition precedent to the drawer's liability on a check, UCC § 3-414(b), and presentment is a condition precedent to dishonor, Seller also cannot recover from Drawer because the check has not yet been dishonored.]

Point Three (10–20%)

Bank is not liable to Seller on the check both because Seller is not entitled to enforce the check and because a drawee bank is not liable, even to a holder, on an uncertified personal check.

Bank is not under any obligation to the holder to pay a check that it has not already accepted (certified), so Seller could not recover from Bank even if it had wrongly dishonored the check because a drawee bank is not liable on an unaccepted draft. *See* UCC § 3-408. Moreover, Seller was not a holder and not entitled to enforce the check, so it was entirely proper for Bank to refuse to pay.

Point Four (30–40%)

Seller is entitled to recover the amount of the check from Thief because Thief breached the transfer warranties that Thief is entitled to enforce the instrument and that all signatures are genuine.

A person who transfers an instrument for consideration makes certain standard warranties to the transferee of the instrument. In particular, the transferor warrants that he is entitled to enforce the instrument and that all signatures on the instrument are authorized and authentic. UCC § 3-416(a).

When Thief transferred the check to Seller in exchange for the car, Thief breached these transfer warranties. Thief was not a person entitled to enforce the instrument, and the forged Payee signature was neither genuine nor authorized. Seller took the instrument in good faith and so is entitled to recover the amount of the check from Thief for breach of these warranties. UCC § 3-416(b).

[NOTE: Seller arguably has a contract claim against Thief. Thief's forgery of Payee's signature is effective as Thief's own signature, UCC § 3-403(a), with respect to a person, like Seller, who takes the instrument for value. So as to Seller, Thief is an indorser of the check (even though he indorsed in Payee's name) and owes Seller an indorser's obligation. *See* UCC § 3-415(a). When Bank refused to pay the instrument, that refusal arguably triggered Thief's liability as an indorser.

There are difficulties with that analysis, however. First, only a person entitled to enforce the instrument can bring a claim against an indorser, and Seller is not entitled to enforce. Second, dishonor is a condition precedent to the indorser's liability on a check, UCC § 3-415(a), and (as noted earlier) the check has not yet been dishonored. Consequently, examinees who mention Thief's indorser's liability might receive some credit, but only if they also discuss the more likely basis for Thief's liability to Seller, that is, breach of transfer warranties.]

Commercial Paper

(February 2010)

Legal Problems: (1)(a) Is Dealer entitled to enforce the $10,000 check against Lawyer?

(1)(b) Does Lawyer have a defense to payment of the check to Dealer?

(1)(c) Is Lawyer's defense of ordinary fraud available against Dealer, the holder of an instrument who received it in exchange for a promise that has not yet been performed?

(2) When a check with a forged indorsement is transferred to a check-cashing service, is the original payee of the check entitled to recover from the check-cashing service when the forgery was committed by an employee to whom the payee had given responsibility for handling the check?

DISCUSSION

Summary

Dealer is a holder of the $10,000 check that was dishonored and can enforce the check against Lawyer. However, Lawyer signed the check only because of Employee's fraud, and Lawyer therefore has a defense to payment that can be asserted against anyone who is not a holder in due course. Dealer is not a holder in due course because Dealer did not give value for the check— Dealer never delivered the car to Employee. Thus, although Dealer can enforce the check, Dealer will be subject to Lawyer's defense of fraud in the inducement.

Checkco is not liable to Lawyer for taking the $5,000 check with the forged indorsement because Employee was entrusted by Lawyer with responsibility for the check and, therefore, for these purposes, Employee's forgery is effective as the indorsement of Lawyer.

[NOTE: Because the facts of this question include the collection of checks by banks, UCC Article 4 (Bank Deposits and Collections), which is not included in the Negotiable Instruments specifications for the MEE, is implicated. However, the issues raised by this question are Article 3 (Negotiable Instruments) issues, and reference to UCC Article 4 is not necessary to resolve them.]

Point One(a) (20%)
Dealer is entitled to enforce the check against Lawyer because Dealer is a holder of the check.

The $10,000 check is payable to the order of Dealer and is in Dealer's possession. Dealer is accordingly a holder of the check, UCC § 1-201(b)(21), and is "a person entitled to enforce" it. UCC § 3-301. Lawyer signed the check as drawer and the check has been dishonored. Therefore

Lawyer is obliged to pay the check to a person entitled to enforce it. UCC § 3-414. Consequently, Dealer has a *prima facie* claim to payment from Lawyer.

Point One(b) (25%)
Lawyer has a personal defense of fraud in the inducement.

Lawyer has a defense to payment. Lawyer signed and issued the check because of Employee's fraudulent act of including the check among a group of checks intended to pay Lawyer's ordinary business expenses. Under UCC § 3-305, this fraud is a defense to Lawyer's obligation to pay the check. *See* UCC 3-305(a)(2) & cmt. 2 ("the obligation of a party to pay an instrument" is subject to any defense that would be available to the party in an action to enforce "payment under a simple contract," including defenses of fraud, misrepresentation, and mistake). Dealer, as a person entitled to enforce Lawyer's check, will be subject to this defense unless Dealer is a holder in due course. *See* UCC §§ 3-305(a), 3-305(b) (in general, the right to enforce an instrument is subject to both real and personal defenses, but a holder in due course is subject only to the so-called "real defenses," which do not include ordinary fraud).

[NOTE: Some applicants may erroneously argue that this defense is good even against a holder in due course because there was fraud in the factum—Lawyer did not know what he was signing. But UCC § 3-305(a)(1) allows a fraud defense to be asserted against a holder in due course only if the fraud induced the obligor to sign the instrument without a "reasonable opportunity" to learn its terms. Here Lawyer knew he was signing a check and had an opportunity to learn its terms—he could have read it.]

Point One(c) (25%)
Dealer is not a holder in due course because he did not give value for the check.

A holder in due course is a holder who took the instrument for value, in good faith, and without notice of, *inter alia*, any defenses to it. UCC § 3-302(a). Although Dealer does not appear to have acted in bad faith or to have had notice of Lawyer's defense, Dealer has not given "value" for the instrument within the meaning given to that term in Article 3 of the UCC.

Here Dealer took the negotiable instrument (the check) as payment for the car. However, Dealer has not delivered the car. When a negotiable instrument "is issued or transferred for a promise of performance," the promisor gives value only "to the extent the promise has been performed." UCC § 3-303(a)(1). Thus, because Dealer did not perform its promise—delivering the car—it did not take the check for value.
Because Dealer did not take the check for value, Dealer is not a holder in due course. Dealer, as a mere holder, is therefore subject to Lawyer's defense. Lawyer does not have to pay $10,000 to Dealer.

Point Two (30%)
Even though Checkco took the stolen check, it is not liable to Lawyer because Lawyer had entrusted responsibility for the check to Employee, and Employee's fraudulent indorsement of the check in Lawyer's name therefore is treated as an effective indorsement.

The check that was transferred to Checkco was originally made payable to the order of Lawyer. While the check appeared to carry Lawyer's indorsement, the indorsement had been forged by Employee. Normally, the forged indorsement would be ineffective, Employee would not be a holder of the check or a person entitled to enforce it, and Checkco's action of taking the check by transfer from Employee would be a conversion of that check for which Checkco would be liable to Lawyer. UCC § 3-420(a). *See also* UCC §§ 1-201(b)(21) (definition of holder),   3-301 (definition of person entitled to enforce).

In this case, however, the result is different. According to the facts, Employee had the authority to process checks and to deposit those checks in Lawyer's business account. This constitutes "responsibility" for those checks. *See* UCC § 3-405(a)(3). Because the fraudulent indorsement of Lawyer's signature on the instrument was perpetrated by Employee, a person to whom Lawyer entrusted "responsibility with respect to the instrument," the indorsement is effective as Lawyer's indorsement. UCC § 3-405. Inasmuch as the indorsement was effective, Employee was a holder of the check and, thus, a person entitled to enforce it. As a result, Checkco did not obtain transfer of the check from a person not entitled to enforce it and, accordingly, Checkco's action did not constitute conversion and Checkco is not liable to Lawyer for the amount of the check.

[NOTE: Lawyer would have a claim to recover some part of the loss from Checkco if Checkco "fail[ed] to exercise ordinary care" in taking the instrument from Employee and that failure contributed to the loss. *See* UCC § 3-405(b). There are no facts in the problem to suggest a lack of care by Checkco, but some applicants may note the possibility that Lawyer could recover some portion of the value of the check from Checkco if Lawyer proved that Checkco failed to exercise ordinary care.]

[NOTE: References to UCC § 1-201 are to the current official text. In states in which former Article 1 is still in effect, citations will be slightly different. There is no difference in substance.]

Commercial Paper

(July 2010)

Includes Sales/Contracts Issues

Legal Problems: (1)   Is a seller bound by statements about goods made by him in conjunction with their sale?

                 (2)   Under what circumstances may a buyer revoke acceptance of goods that do not conform to the contract?

                 (3)   What are the rights of a buyer who has revoked acceptance of goods?

                 (4)   What are the rights of a holder of a dishonored check?

DISCUSSION

Summary

The transaction between Buyer and Seller is a contract for the sale of goods governed by Article 2 of the Uniform Commercial Code, as well as by common law doctrines (e.g., involving fraud and misrepresentation) that supplement the Code. Under both UCC principles and common law principles, Seller's untrue statements about the brakes and clutch provide a basis for Buyer to avoid the contract, recover the purchase price, and recover any other allowable damages for losses that he may have suffered as a result of the breach.

The false statements about the brakes and the clutch were misrepresentations under common law principles. They also constituted express warranties under the UCC, which Seller breached because the statements were untrue. Under common law rules, Seller's misrepresentations provide a basis for Buyer to avoid the contract because the misrepresentations were fraudulent and material, they induced Buyer to complete the car purchase, and Buyer was justified in relying on them. Similarly, under the UCC, Buyer was entitled to revoke his acceptance of the car because acceptance was induced by Seller's false assurances. If Buyer avoids or rescinds the contract under common law principles, or revokes his acceptance under UCC rules, Buyer is entitled to return of any payments made plus any damages for breach of contract.

Checkco, as the holder of the check, can recover the amount of the check from Buyer (as drawer) or Seller (as indorser). Checkco is a holder in due course, and Buyer will have to pay the amount of the check even though the car did not conform to the contract.

Point One (20%)

Seller's statements about the brakes and clutch constituted express warranties that became part of the contract under the Uniform Commercial Code. They were also misrepresentations that could provide Buyer with a basis to avoid the contract under common law principles.

This is a contract for the sale of goods and as such is governed by Article 2 of the UCC. In addition, basic principles relating to fraud and misrepresentation can be applied to supplement the rules in the Code. *See* UCC § 1-103.

Buyer and Seller clearly entered into a contract for the sale of the car. There was offer and acceptance, and the basic terms of the bargain were reflected in a writing.

Under the UCC, affirmations of fact relating to the goods that are part of the basis of the bargain create express warranties that the goods will conform to those affirmations and descriptions. UCC § 2-313(1). Seller's statements that the brakes and clutch had been replaced were clearly such affirmations of fact and, thus, constituted express warranties. The more general statements that the car was in "tip-top shape" and was "good for another 100,000 miles," however, may be "an affirmation merely of the value of the goods or a statement purporting to be merely the seller's opinion or commendation of the goods" and, therefore, may not constitute express warranties. UCC § 2-313(2).

[NOTE: Although the warranties are not included in the writing the parties signed, UCC § 2-202 (Article 2's parol evidence rule) allows that writing to be supplemented by "consistent additional terms" unless the court finds that the writing was intended to be a "complete and exclusive" statement of the terms. There are no facts in the problem to suggest that the parties intended their writing to be the exclusive statement of their terms, and the express warranties made by Seller were not inconsistent with anything in the writing.]

Under common law principles, a misrepresentation is any "assertion that is not in accord with the facts," Restatement (Second) of Contracts § 159, and a misrepresentation is "material" if it is likely to induce assent to the contract, *id.* § 162. Here, Seller's misrepresentations about the brakes and the clutch were clearly not in accord with the facts, and were also the sort of claims that would contribute directly and substantially to a buyer's decision to purchase the car. Furthermore, there is strong reason to believe that Seller's statements were fraudulent, as Seller very likely knew that the brakes and clutch had not been repaired within the last six months (although the facts are not completely clear on this point). Seller will be bound by his fraudulent or material misrepresentations. *See* RESTATEMENT (SECOND) OF CONTRACTS § 164 (buyer may void a contract if assent is induced by a fraudulent or material misrepresentation on which the buyer is justified in relying).

Point Two (20%)
Buyer accepted the car, but was entitled to revoke his acceptance under UCC rules because the car's nonconformity substantially impaired its value to him and because the car was accepted without discovery of the nonconformity and acceptance was induced by Seller's false assurances. Under the common law doctrine of misrepresentation, Buyer may avoid the contract because his assent to it was induced by Seller's misrepresentations.

Buyer took the car and drove it for a week. Since this time span was well beyond a reasonable period in which to inspect the car, Buyer's failure to reject the car means that he accepted it. UCC § 2-606. Having accepted the goods, Buyer can no longer reject them. UCC § 2-607(2). However, under proper circumstances, a buyer can revoke acceptance of goods. *See* UCC § 2-608. In particular, a buyer may revoke acceptance if (i) the goods do not conform to the contract, (ii) the nonconformity "substantially impairs" the value of the goods to the buyer, and (iii) the buyer accepted the goods either on the reasonable assumption that a nonconformity would be cured or without discovery of a nonconformity if acceptance was induced by either difficulty of discovery before acceptance or the seller's assurances; revocation must occur within a reasonable time after the buyer discovers or should have discovered the nonconformity and before any change in condition of the goods not caused by the nonconformity. *Id.*

In this case, all conditions for revocation are met. First, there is no doubt that the goods do not conform to the contract. The car was warranted to have new brakes and a new clutch. (*See* Point One.) Second, it is obvious that those nonconformities substantially impair the value of the car to Buyer. Third, Buyer accepted the car without discovery of the nonconformities, and this acceptance was induced by Seller's false assurances. Moreover, Buyer communicated the revocation to Seller immediately upon learning of the grounds for it, and there was no change in the condition of the car that was unrelated to its nonconformity. Therefore, Buyer's revocation is effective. *See* UCC § 2-608(2).

Under the common law doctrine of misrepresentation, a buyer can avoid (rescind) a contract if his assent was induced by fraudulent or material misrepresentations and he was justified in relying on those misrepresentations. RESTATEMENT (SECOND) OF CONTRACTS § 164. Those conditions are met here. Although the facts do not explicitly say so, Buyer asked specifically about the car's condition and even contemplated taking it to a mechanic. Seller's specific statements about the recent work done on the brakes and clutch (relatively expensive items to repair) probably were a significant factor in Buyer's decision to assent to the contract without inspection. *See id.* § 167, cmt. a ("It is enough that the manifestation substantially contributed to his decision to make the contract.") Buyer was justified in relying on Seller's statements about the car's condition, as Seller was in possession of the car, was offering it for sale, and represented that he knew its condition. Under these circumstances, Buyer can avoid the contract as a result of Seller's misrepresentations.

Point Three (20%)
Because Buyer's revocation of acceptance is effective, Buyer may cancel the contract, recover the purchase price that has been paid, and recover any damages. If Buyer chooses to rescind or avoid the contract under common law principles, Buyer is entitled to restitution of the purchase price that has been paid, and may also recover any damages.

A buyer who has justifiably revoked acceptance of goods is entitled to recover so much of the price as has been paid. *See* UCC § 2-711. Similarly, a buyer who rescinds a contract due to a seller's misrepresentation is entitled to restitution of any portion of the purchase price that has been paid. RESTATEMENT (SECOND) OF CONTRACTS § 376. Thus, Buyer is no longer obligated to pay for the car and can recover the purchase price that has been paid (the $4,000 in cash and the $1,000 amount of the check).

Moreover, Buyer is also entitled to damages under UCC § 2-712 or § 2-713. Under UCC § 2-713, Buyer is entitled to the difference between the market price of a car conforming to the contract and the contract price, plus incidental and consequential damages. Because, according to the mechanic, the market price of a car conforming to the contract was equal to the contract price, Buyer is entitled only to any incidental and consequential damages under UCC § 2-713. Alternatively, under UCC § 2-712, Buyer may "cover" by buying a car in substitution for the car bought from Seller. Such a covering purchase must be a commercially reasonable substitute as opposed to an upgrade to a better car. If Buyer makes a covering purchase, Buyer may recover the excess, if any, of the cover price over the contract price of $5,000, plus incidental and consequential damages. UCC § 2-712(2). Pursuant to UCC § 2-721, these additional remedies are also available to a buyer who chooses to rescind the contract based on a claim of material misrepresentation or fraud.

Point Four(a) (20%)
Checkco, as a holder of the check, can assert a claim for the amount of the check against either Seller or Buyer.

The facts state that Buyer paid $1,000 of the purchase price of the car with a check drawn on First Bank. A check is a negotiable instrument governed by Article 3 of the Uniform Commercial Code. UCC § 3-104. Buyer was the "drawer" of the check. *See* UCC § 3-103(a)(3). Seller was an "indorser." *See* UCC § 3-204(b).

If a check is dishonored, the drawer (Buyer, in this case) has an obligation "to pay [it] . . . according to its terms at the time it was issued" to a "person entitled to enforce" it. UCC § 3-414(b). Similarly, if a check is dishonored, an indorser (Seller, in this case) has an obligation to pay the amount of the check to a person entitled to enforce it. *See* UCC § 3-415(a). The refusal of First Bank to pay the check when it was presented by Checkco constituted dishonor. UCC § 3-502(b)(2).

A "holder" of a check is a person entitled to enforce it. UCC § 3-301. When Seller indorsed the check in blank (i.e., by signing only his name), the check became payable to the bearer. UCC § 3-205(b). When Seller handed this "bearer instrument" to Checkco, Checkco became a holder of the check because it was in possession of an instrument that was payable to the bearer. UCC § 1-201(b)(21)(A). Thus, under UCC §§ 3-414 and 3-415, Buyer and Seller are liable to Checkco for the amount of the check.

[NOTE: Seller is liable on the check because Seller indorsed it. Some applicants might also note that Seller could be liable to Checkco for breach of a transfer warranty because, at the time Seller transferred the check to Checkco, Seller would have been aware that Buyer had a defense to payment of the instrument. UCC § 3-416(a). An examinee might be given credit for a correct analysis of this point, but the more direct route to Seller's liability is that Seller has an indorser's obligation to pay the holder of a dishonored instrument. UCC § 3-415(a).]

Point Four(b) (20%)
Checkco is a holder in due course and will not be subject to defenses that may be asserted by either Seller or Buyer.

Seller has no defenses to his obligation under UCC § 3-415, so Checkco may recover from Seller. Buyer, however, might claim that he has a defense to that obligation or a "claim in recoupment" arising from Seller's breach of contract in the transaction that gave rise to the check. If Checkco qualifies as a holder in due course, Buyer will not be able to raise any claims in recoupment and will be able to raise only the four "real" defenses listed in UCC § 3-305(a)(1). None of those defenses (infancy, illegality of the transaction, fraud that induced the obligor to sign the instrument without knowledge of or reasonable opportunity to learn its terms, and discharge in insolvency proceedings) is present. Thus, if Checkco is a holder in due course, it will be able to recover from Buyer despite the fact that Seller breached the contract giving rise to the check.

A holder in due course is a holder of an instrument who takes an instrument that is not questionable on its face for value, in good faith, and without notice of, *inter alia*, any defenses to it. UCC § 3-302(a).

Each of these elements has been fulfilled. First, it has already been established that Checkco is a holder. Second, there are no facts to suggest that the check was questionable on its face. Third, Checkco took the check for value because it performed its promise of paying $950 for it. *See* UCC § 3-303(a)(1). The fact that $950 is less than the face amount of the check is irrelevant. Fourth, Checkco appears to have taken the check in good faith. "Good faith" is defined to include "honesty in fact and the observance of reasonable commercial standards of fair dealing." UCC § 3-103(a)(4). Nothing in these facts suggests a lack of good faith on the part of Checkco. There is no evidence of dishonesty and no indication that its actions were outside the bounds of commercial standards of fair dealing. Finally, there are no facts to suggest that Checkco had notice of any defenses to the check.

Accordingly, Checkco is a holder in due course and may recover from Buyer notwithstanding the fact that Seller breached the contract giving rise to the check.

[NOTE: Of course, Checkco is entitled to only one recovery.]

Commercial Paper

(July 2011)

ANALYSIS

Legal Problems

(1)   Can Bank recover from Checkco, which presented a check with a forged indorsement, for the loss Bank incurred in recrediting Manufacturer's account?

(2)   Can Checkco recover its loss from Jeweler, who was neither a party to the check nor transferred it?

(3)   Can Checkco recover its loss from Supplier, who indorsed the check and transferred it to Jeweler?

DISCUSSION

Summary

When Checkco presented the check to Bank, it warranted that it was entitled to enforce the check. This warranty was breached because, as a result of the forgery of Jeweler's signature, Checkco was not a person entitled to enforce the check; thus, Bank can recover its loss from Checkco. Checkco cannot recover from Jeweler, who neither indorsed the check nor made any transfer warranties. Supplier was a transferor who transferred by indorsement, so Supplier made transfer warranties to Checkco. None of the transfer warranties was breached and, because the check was not dishonored, Supplier is not liable on his indorser's obligation. Thus, Checkco cannot recover from Supplier.

Point One (40%)
By presenting the check to Bank and obtaining payment, Checkco warranted that it was entitled to enforce the check. This was not the case because of the forged indorsement of Jeweler. Thus, Bank may recover from Checkco the damages flowing from this breach of warranty.

When a check is presented to the drawee for payment and the drawee pays the check, the person making presentment warrants that, *inter alia*, it is a person entitled to enforce the check (or is authorized to obtain payment on behalf of such a person). UCC § 3-417(a)(1). Checkco presented the check to Bank, the drawee (UCC § 3-103(a)(4)), and Bank paid the check; therefore Checkco made this warranty.

Checkco was not a person entitled to enforce the check. Under UCC § 3-301, to be a person entitled to enforce the check in these circumstances, Checkco would need to be either a holder of the check or a nonholder of the check in possession of it who has the rights of a holder. Checkco is not the holder of the check because, in order to be the holder, Checkco would need to be in possession of the check and it would have to be payable either to bearer or to Checkco. UCC § 1-201(b)(21)(A). While Checkco was in possession of the check, the check was not payable to either bearer or Checkco. Once the check was indorsed "Pay to Jeweler" by Supplier, the check became payable to Jeweler and could only become payable to bearer or another person if indorsed by Jeweler. UCC § 3-205(a). Jeweler never indorsed the check, however. (The forgery of Jeweler's signature is ineffective. UCC § 3-403.) Thus, Checkco was not the holder of the check. While Checkco was a nonholder in possession of the check, it did not have the rights of a holder. It could have obtained the rights of a holder if Jeweler—the former holder—had transferred those rights, but Jeweler did not do so because transfer requires delivery of the check to a person for the purpose of giving that person the right to enforce the check (*see* UCC § 3-203) and Jeweler never delivered the check to Checkco (or anyone else) with such intent. Thus, Checkco was neither a holder of the check nor a non-holder in possession with the rights of a holder; accordingly, it was not a person entitled to enforce the check and, as a result, breached its presentment warranty. The fact that Checkco acted in good faith and without notice of the forged indorsement does not alter Checkco's status.

Bank was damaged by this breach because, had Checkco been a person entitled to enforce, the facts giving rise to Bank's obligation to recredit Manufacturer's account would not be present and Bank would not have suffered the loss it incurred when it recredited Manufacturer's account after paying the check. Accordingly, Checkco is liable to Bank for this loss.

Point Two (25%)
Checkco cannot recover from Jeweler, who is not a party to the check and did not make any warranties with respect to it.

A person is not liable on an instrument unless the person has signed the instrument. UCC § 3-401(a). Jeweler did not sign the check and thus is not liable on it. (The forgery of Jeweler's signature as an indorsement does not count as Jeweler's signature. UCC § 3-403.) While a person who is not a party to an instrument can still make warranties with respect to it, Jeweler has made no warranties to Checkco in this case. Presentment warranties are not relevant because they run only to a drawee or acceptor of the check and Checkco is neither. UCC § 3-417(a). Jeweler made no transfer warranties because Jeweler did not transfer the check for consideration. UCC § 3-416(a).

Point Three (35%)
Supplier indorsed the check, but has no liability as an indorser because the check was not dishonored. Supplier made a transfer warranty to Checkco, but it was not breached. Thus Supplier has no liability for breach of transfer warranty.

When Supplier indorsed the check, he incurred the obligation of an indorser. The obligation is to pay the check if it has been dishonored. UCC § 3-415(a). This check was paid by Bank and was not dishonored, so Supplier has no liability as an indorser. [NOTE: Alternatively, an examinee could conclude that Supplier has no liability to Checkco as an indorser because Checkco is neither a person entitled to enforce the check nor a subsequent indorser who paid it.]

When Supplier transferred the check for consideration and by indorsement, he made transfer warranties not only to its transferee (Jeweler) but also to any subsequent transferees, including Checkco. UCC § 3-416(a). As of the time of the transfer, none of the transfer warranties set out in UCC § 3-416(a) was breached—Supplier was a person entitled to enforce the check (as the payee in possession of the check, Supplier was its holder and, thus, a person entitled to enforce it); all signatures on the check were authentic and authorized; the check had not been altered; it was not subject to any claims or defenses that could be raised against Supplier; and no insolvency proceedings had been instituted against Manufacturer. Therefore, Supplier was not liable for breach of transfer warranty.

[NOTE: An examinee might cite UCC § 4-208 rather than UCC § 3-417 in Point One, and UCC § 4-207 rather than UCC § 3-416 in Point Three. Those citations are equally valid.]

Commercial Paper

(February 2012)

ANALYSIS

Legal Problems

(1)   Does Dealer have a claim against Uncle?

(2)   Does the fact that Uncle received no consideration for his indorsement give him a defense?

(3)   Can Uncle assert Ned's defense that he was induced to enter into the transaction and issue the note because of Steve's misrepresentation?

(4)   Can Uncle's defense be raised successfully against Dealer?

DISCUSSION

Summary

Dealer is likely to be successful in his action against Uncle. Dealer, who is the holder of the note and thus a person entitled to enforce it, will sue Uncle based on his indorser's obligation. Because Uncle is an accommodation party, the lack of consideration for his indorsement is not a defense. Although Uncle has no defenses of his own, because he is an accommodation party he is permitted to raise Ned's defense that he was induced to enter into the transaction by Steve's misrepresentation. This defense will not be successful against a person who has the rights of a holder in due course. Thus, it is necessary to determine whether Dealer is such a person. Although Dealer is not a holder in due course because he did not take the note for value as defined in UCC Article 3 (the unperformed promise to deliver the car does not constitute "value"), Dealer has the rights of a holder in due course by transfer from Cal, who was a holder in due course. Accordingly, Dealer is not subject to Uncle's defense, and Uncle is liable to Dealer for the amount of the note.

Point One (15%)
Dealer has a claim against Uncle as an indorser of the note.

If an instrument has been dishonored and notice of dishonor has been given or is excused, an indorser of the instrument is liable to a person entitled to enforce it. UCC §§ 3-415, 3-503. Ned's failure to pay the note constituted dishonor (UCC § 3-502(a)), and Uncle is an indorser of the note. Thus, as long as he has been given notice of dishonor (or such notice is excused), Uncle is liable to a person entitled to enforce the note.

Dealer is a person entitled to enforce the note because he is the holder of the note. UCC § 3-301. Although the note was issued payable to the order of Steve, Dealer, who is in possession of the note, is now the holder because when Steve indorsed the note by signing his name on the back, the note became a bearer instrument (*see* UCC § 3-205), and anyone in possession of a bearer instrument is a holder. UCC § 1-201(b)(21).

Uncle has been given timely notice of dishonor. As a result, subject to possible defenses (*see* Points Two, Three, and Four), Uncle is liable on the note to Dealer.

Point Two (10%)
Uncle cannot successfully raise as a defense lack of consideration for his indorsement.

Uncle incurred the obligation of an indorser on the note without receiving consideration for incurring that obligation. This lack of consideration would, in most circumstances, be a defense against his liability on the note. UCC § 3-305(a)(2). But in this case, a different rule applies because Uncle is an "accommodation party." He is an accommodation party because he signed an instrument for the purpose of becoming liable on it, even though he was not a direct beneficiary of the value given for the instrument. UCC § 3-419(a). The obligation of an accommodation party may be enforced whether or not the accommodation party received consideration. UCC § 3-419(b). Accordingly, Uncle cannot raise as a defense the fact that he received no consideration for his indorsement.

[NOTE: An examinee might state that Uncle received consideration because Steve agreed to sell the chemical on credit in exchange for Uncle's willingness to be liable on the note. The facts do not explicitly indicate such a *quid pro quo*, but an examinee should receive credit for this analysis.]

Point Three (15%)
Uncle can raise as a defense Ned's claim that he was induced to enter into the transaction by Steve's misrepresentation.

Parties to an instrument generally are not permitted to assert another party's defense to liability on the instrument. UCC § 3-305(c). There is an exception to this principle: because Uncle is an accommodation party, he is entitled to raise the defenses of the "accommodated party"—Ned. UCC § 3-305(d). Thus, Uncle would be able to raise, as a defense to his obligation on the note, the defense that Ned would be able to raise—that he was induced to enter into the transaction by Steve's misrepresentation. As explained in Point Four, however, Uncle will be unsuccessful in this defense because Dealer has the rights of a holder in due course and will be free of that defense.

Point Four(a) (25%)
Ned's defense of misrepresentation is a "personal" defense that cannot be raised successfully against someone who has the rights of a holder in due course.

Except when a holder in due course is enforcing an instrument, a person liable on the instrument can raise any defense to liability that could be raised against liability on a simple contract. UCC § 3-305(a)(2). Under this principle, Uncle, raising Ned's defenses (*see* Point 3), could defend on the ground that Ned would not be liable on the promissory note because he was induced to enter into the obligation by Steve's misrepresentation.

However, this defense would be effective only if the person enforcing the note did not have the rights of a holder in due course. The right of a holder in due course to enforce the obligation of a party to an instrument is subject to the four "real" defenses listed in UCC § 3-305(a)(1) but is not subject to any other defenses (usually referred to as "personal" defenses). The four "real" defenses are (i) infancy; (ii) duress, lack of capacity, or illegality that nullifies the obligation under other law; (iii) fraud that induced the obligor to sign the instrument with neither knowledge nor reasonable opportunity to learn of its character or essential terms; and (iv) discharge of the obligor in insolvency proceedings. The defense that Ned was induced to enter into the transaction by Steve's misrepresentation is not a real defense listed in UCC § 3-305(a)(1). Accordingly, if Dealer has the rights of a holder in due course, Dealer will not be subject to the defense.

Point Four(b) (35%)
Although Dealer is not a holder in due course, Dealer has the rights of a holder in due course under the shelter principle of negotiable instruments law and thus is not subject to Uncle's defense.

Dealer is not a holder in due course of the note. This is because one of the criteria under UCC § 3-302(a) that must be satisfied for a person to be a holder in due course is that the person must have taken the instrument for "value." As that term is defined in Article 3 of the UCC, an unperformed promise does not constitute value. UCC § 3-303. Accordingly, because Dealer has not yet delivered the car to Cal, he did not take the note for value. Thus, Dealer is not a holder in due course. (This is the case even if Dealer took the note without notice of Steve's misrepresentation.)

However, when Cal owned the instrument, he was a holder in due course. This is because Cal was a holder of the instrument and satisfied the other requirements listed in UCC § 3-302(a). Cal was a holder because he was in possession of a bearer instrument (*see* Point One). In addition, Cal satisfied the other elements of UCC § 3-302: he gave value by paying $19,000 for the note, took the note in good faith (honesty in fact and the observance of reasonable commercial standards of fair dealing, UCC § 1-201(b)(20)), and took the note without notice of any claims or defenses to it or that it was overdue. Although Cal subsequently learned of Steve's misrepresentation, holder-in-due-course status is determined at the time the instrument is negotiated and value is given. In this case, that was October 14, and Cal did not receive notice of the misrepresentation until the next day. Therefore, Cal was a holder in due course.

When Cal transferred the note to Dealer, Dealer obtained Cal's rights as a holder in due course. This is because of the "shelter principle" of UCC Article 3: "transfer of an instrument . . . vests in the transferee any right of the transferor to enforce the instrument, including any right as a holder in due course." UCC § 3-203(b). As a result, Dealer has the same rights as Cal. As a holder in due course, Cal would not have been subject to Uncle's defense based on Steve's misrepresentation. Therefore, Dealer is not subject to Uncle's defense and is entitled to payment of $20,000 from him.

Commercial Paper
(February 2013)

ANALYSIS

Legal Problems

(1)(a) What rights does a person in possession of a note that has been indorsed in blank by the payee have against the maker of the note?

(1)(b) Which defenses may the maker of a note raise against a person entitled to enforce it who is not a holder in due course but is a transferee from a holder in due course?

(2) What rights does a person entitled to enforce a note have against an indorser who transferred it for consideration with no warranties?

(3) What rights does a person entitled to enforce a note have against a previous holder who transferred it as a gift without indorsing it?

DISCUSSION

Summary

The niece is a holder of the note and is thus a person entitled to enforce it. The chef, the issuer of the note, is obligated to pay it to the niece as the person entitled to enforce it. The niece is not subject to any defense or claim of the chef relating to the improper repair of the oven because the niece has the rights of a holder in due course. When the buyer bought the note from the repairman, the buyer became a holder in due course of the note and thus took it free of any personal defenses the chef had against the repairman. Even though the niece is not herself a holder in due course of the note, the niece succeeded to the buyer's rights as holder in due course and thus took free of the chef's personal defenses.

Because the chef refused to pay the note, the niece can recover from the repairman on the repairman's obligation as indorser. The niece cannot recover on the note against the buyer, however, because the buyer did not indorse the note (and thus incurred no indorser's obligation) and the buyer did not receive any consideration for transfer of the note to the niece (and, therefore, made no transfer warranty).

[NOTE: Although Article 9 of the Uniform Commercial Code governs the sale of promissory notes (a point that might be correctly noted by examinees), that Article does not determine the answer to any of the questions posed.]

Point One(a) (20%)
The niece is the holder of the note and thus may enforce it against the chef, who is the issuer of the note.

The chef is the maker of the note and, thus, its issuer. *See* UCC §§ 3-103, 3-105. The issuer of a note is obligated to pay it in accordance with its terms to a "person entitled to enforce" it. UCC § 3-412. The niece is a "person entitled to enforce" the note. This is because the niece is the holder of the note, and a holder of a note is a person entitled to enforce it. UCC § 3-301. The niece is the holder of the note because (i) the repairman's signature on the back of the note not accompanied by words indicating a person to whom the note was made payable was a "blank indorsement," which had the effect of making the note a bearer instrument, (ii) anyone in possession of a bearer instrument is a holder of it, and (iii) the niece is in possession of the note. *See* UCC §§ 1-201(b)(21)(A), 3-204, and 3-205. Accordingly, the chef has an obligation to the niece to pay the note in accordance with its terms, and the niece may enforce that obligation.

Point One(b) (40%)

The niece is not a holder in due course of the note, but, because she is a transferee from the buyer, who was a holder in due course, she has the same enforcement rights as the buyer. Because the buyer, as a holder in due course, would have been able to enforce the note against the chef without being subject to defenses or claims arising from the improper repair, the niece has the same rights and will not be subject to the chef's defenses or claims about the repair.

As noted in Point One(a), the chef has an obligation to the niece to pay the note in accordance with its terms. However, except against a person with the rights of a holder in due course, the chef can raise any defenses or claims in recoupment that he would have if the claim on the note were an ordinary contract claim. UCC § 3-305. Thus, except against a holder in due course, the chef would be able to raise the improper repair as a defense or a claim in recoupment (a claim in response to the niece's claim).

But claims in recoupment and most defenses cannot be raised against a person with the rights of a holder in due course. Against a holder in due course, the chef can raise only the four "real" defenses listed in UCC § 3-305(a)(1) (infancy; duress, lack of legal capacity, or illegality that nullifies the obligation of the obligor under other law; fraud in the *factum*; discharge in insolvency proceedings), none of which is present here.

The niece is not a holder in due course because she did not take the note for value. *See* UCC §§ 3-302(a)(2)(i) (criteria for holder in due course status) and 3-303(a) (definition of "value"). But this does not mean that the niece is subject to the chef's claim arising out of the improper repair. The buyer was a holder in due course of the note because he took the note for value ($9,500), in good faith, and without notice of any facts that would have alerted him to the chef's defense against the repairman. UCC § 3-302(a)(2). As a holder in due course, the buyer owned the note free of the chef's claim because that claim did not constitute a "real" defense. UCC § 3-305(b). When the buyer gave the note to the niece, this constituted a "transfer" of the note. *See* UCC § 3-203(a). When a note is transferred, the transferee receives "any right of the transferor to enforce the instrument, including any right as a holder in due course." UCC § 3-203(b). Under this rule (also known as the "shelter principle"), the buyer transferred his freedom from the chef's defenses to the niece and the niece can enforce the note free of the chef's defenses.

Point Two (20%)

Because the chef dishonored the note, the niece can recover from the repairman on the repairman's obligation as indorser.

The chef's refusal to pay the note constituted dishonor. *See* UCC § 3-502. The repairman, as an indorser of the note (*see* Point One(a)), incurred the obligations of an indorser under UCC § 3-415(a). When a note has been dishonored, one of the obligations of an indorser is to pay the amount of the note to a person entitled to enforce it. Therefore, the repairman is liable for the amount of the note to the niece, a person entitled to enforce the note (so long as the niece gives proper notice of dishonor to the repairman).

[NOTE: Because the repairman indorsed the note without warranties, there are no transfer warranties. UCC § 3-416 cmt. 5.]

Point Three (20%)
The niece cannot recover on the note against the buyer as either indorser or warrantor because the buyer did not indorse the note and did not receive consideration for transferring the note to the niece.

The buyer did not indorse the note and, therefore, did not incur the obligation of an indorser to pay the note upon dishonor.

The niece cannot recover from the buyer under a transfer warranty theory because transfer warranties are made only by a person "who transfers an instrument for consideration." Here, the buyer gave the instrument to the niece as a gift. So the buyer made no transfer warranty. UCC § 3-416(a). Therefore, the niece cannot recover from the buyer on that theory.

The Examiners have indicated that Conflict of Laws will only appear as a sub-issue in a question primarily testing another subject.

Conflict of Laws

(February 1995)

Legal Problems:

(1)   Does the seizure of Foodco's sausage in State D provide a constitutional basis for the assertion of jurisdiction over Spiceco's claim against Foodco?

(2)   Does the contractual relationship between Foodco and Spiceco create sufficient contacts with State D to justify the assertion of long--arm jurisdiction over Foodco?

(2)(a) What significance, if any, should the State D court ascribe to the seizure of Foodco's property in its analysis of minimum contacts?

(2)(b) Assuming that Foodco has the requisite contacts with State D, is the assertion of jurisdiction reasonable?

DISCUSSION

Point One: (10--20%)

Seizure of property within a state, standing alone, no longer supplies a constitutional basis for the assertion of jurisdiction over claims against nonresidents.

In *Shaffer v. Heitner*, 433 U.S. 186 (1977), the Supreme Court held that all assertions of judicial jurisdiction over nonresidents, including those that begin with the attachment of property, must comport with the minimum contacts standard of *International Shoe v. Washington*, 326 U.S. 310 (1945). The court thus abandoned the suggestion in *Pennoyer v. Neff*, 95 U.S. 714 (1878), that a state can adjudicate claims against the owner of property found within the state merely by attaching or otherwise asserting control over the property. (Presence of the property may still be relevant in assessing minimum contacts. See Point Three, infra.) As applied to Spiceco's seizure of Foodco's sausage, Shaffer teaches that the mere fact of the seizure of property does not suffice to empower the court of State D to adjudicate the claim. Rather, the State D court must find that Foodco has minimum contacts with the state such that the assertion of jurisdiction does not offend "traditional notions of fair play and substantial justice." International Shoe, 326 U.S. at 316.

Point Two: (40--50%)

Foodco's contractual relationship with Spiceco may not be a sufficient contact with State D to justify the assertion of jurisdiction over Foodco.

State D's long--arm statute, allowing creditors to proceed by attachment and to assert claims against nonresident corporations that "transact any business" in the state, provides the necessary authorization for its courts to exercise the specific type of jurisdiction invoked here. The statute will be construed to reach the full extent of jurisdiction permitted by the due process clause, so this analysis proceeds to a consideration of "minimum contacts."

The leading minimum contacts case in the field of contract, Burger King v. Rudzewicz, 471 U.S. 462 (1985), provides the framework for analyzing the assertion of jurisdiction here. Burger King held that Florida could constitutionally assert jurisdiction over the defendant Rudzewicz in an action seeking to recover unpaid installments due under a franchise contract. Consistent with such earlier cases as World--wide Volkswagen Corp. v. Woodson, 444 U.S. 286 (1980), and Hanson v. Denckla, 357 U.S. 235 (1958), the court required evidence that the defendant has engaged in some form of conduct sufficient to support a finding that the defendant had purposefully availed himself of the benefits and protections of the forum.

In Burger King, the court found that Rudzewicz, a Michigan resident with no other ties to Florida, had purposefully availed himself of the benefits of Florida law by entering into a franchise relationship with Burger King, a large restaurant company with its headquarters in that state. The court emphasized both the commercial significance of, and the tight controls imposed by, the franchise contract-pointing out that the contract regulated all aspects of the enterprise, resulted in the purchase by Rudzewicz of $165,000 worth of equipment, and called for payment of $1 million over the 20-year life of the relationship. It also emphasized a provision in the contract that made Florida law applicable to all disputes. The fact that Rudzewicz had not set foot in Florida was not fatal to the assertion of jurisdiction, inasmuch as parties often conduct business by mail or telephone. The court was nonetheless quick to point out that each jurisdictional inquiry would turn on its particular facts, that not every breach of contract would justify the assertion of jurisdiction over nonresident contract debtors-a dictum apparently aimed at protecting consumers and small debtors from default judgments obtained in inconvenient fora.

Burger King provides some support for the assertion of jurisdiction over the claim against Foodco. Foodco, after all, did reach out repeatedly to Spiceco in State D as a source of supply and can be said to have purposefully availed itself of the benefits and protections of State D law on that basis. Moreover, the relationship had been established for some years; it was not a one--shot order. On this basis, it seems unlikely that the fact that Foodco's employees had never met personally with Spiceco in State D will carry much weight. Foodco can reach out as purposefully to State D by placing telephone orders as Rudzewicz did to Florida.

On the other hand, the relationship between Spiceco and Foodco was not as closely regulated as that in Burger King. Nothing suggests that the parties had negotiated any written contract to govern their relationship (aside perhaps from the writings contained in order forms and bills), let alone a detailed contract with a State D choice--of-law provision. Moreover, Foodco retains complete control over the management of its affairs-a fact that undercuts the claim that Foodco has purposefully affiliated itself with an out--of-state enterprise. (But while the Burger King court made much of the extent of contract negotiations and the scope of the contract's controls, one might at least question whether such factors enjoy dispositive weight. After all, the Uniform Commercial Code or the otherwise applicable common law of the two states supplies much of the detail that Foodco and Spiceco omitted when they entered into a more informal relationship.) In any case, the contract here does not involve the same degree of commercial significance as that in Burger King. While it does not involve a consumer purchase of the kind that had troubled the lower court and led to the limiting dictum in the court's opinion in Burger King, a few thousand dollars worth of spice does not match the amount owing in Burger King.

The leading minimum contacts case in the field of contract, Burger King v. Rudzewicz, 471 U.S. 462 (1985), provides the framework for analyzing the assertion of jurisdiction here. Burger King held that Florida could constitutionally assert jurisdiction over the defendant Rudzewicz in an action seeking to recover unpaid installments due under a franchise contract. Consistent with such earlier cases as World--wide Volkswagen Corp. v. Woodson, 444 U.S. 286 (1980), and Hanson v. Denckla, 357 U.S. 235 (1958), the court required evidence that the defendant has engaged in some form of conduct sufficient to support a finding that the defendant had purposefully availed himself of the benefits and protections of the forum.

Point Two(a): (20--30%)

The contacts implicated by the presence of Foodco's sausage in State D lend some additional support to the assertion of jurisdiction.

Given that the spice orders and the failure to pay, standing alone, may not suffice to establish Foodco's minimum contacts with State D, the property seizure deserves attention. Shaffer suggests that the assertion of power over property unrelated to the claim adds little to the jurisdictional inquiry. But here, one can argue that the presence of property counts. To begin with, one might argue that the sausage contains Spiceco spices, and thus bears some relationship to the claim. But such an argument seems speculative-we do not know whether Spiceco spices were used in making the specific sausage that was seized in State D. In any case, a focus on the claimed relationship tends to make the inquiry more formalistic than the Shaffer court intended. Rather, the analysis should properly focus on the extent to which use of State D facilities to ship sausage to State C establishes additional ties that support the assertion of jurisdiction.

Consideration of this question involves the role of the independent distributor. The problem states that Foodco relies on the distributor to sell its product and, in particular, that the distributor arranges the shipments to State C. The presence of the property in a warehouse in State D thus appears to owe more to the convenience of the distributor than to any purposeful involvement by Foodco, and could be characterized as the kind of "unilateral conduct" that Hanson v. Denckla considered insufficient for minimum contact purposes. It is nonetheless undeniable that Foodco derives indirect benefits in the form of revenues derived from the distributor's use of State D facilities to make the shipment to State C. While these benefits have little to do with the relationship between Spiceco and Foodco, they do establish ties to State D. A court concerned about the absence of sufficient contractual ties between Spiceco and Foodco might well ascribe dispositive significance to such additional contacts.

Point Two(b): (5--15%)

Assuming that Foodco has established the requisite minimum contacts with State D, the assertion of jurisdiction satisfies the test of reasonableness.

Assuming State D concludes that Foodco has the requisite minimum contacts, it should have little difficulty in regarding the assertion of jurisdiction as reasonable-the second aspect of the International Shoe test. State D appears to have an interest in making a forum available to its domestic spice firm, and a good many of the witnesses (those employed by Spiceco) will find the State D forum more convenient. In recent years, the court has declared unreasonable only the California court's assertion of jurisdiction over a claim for indemnity involving companies whose relationship bore no connection to the United States. See, Asahi Metal Industry Co. v. Superior Court, 480 U.S. 102 (1987). State D's more obvious stake in providing a convenient forum for Spiceco probably establishes a reasonable basis for the assertion of jurisdiction that overcomes any claim of inconvenience by Foodco.

Conflict of Laws

(July 1995)

Legal Problems:

1. In the initial phase of the federal diversity action, as filed in the federal district court of State Y, which choice--of--law rules apply?

2. After the change of venue to the federal district court for State X, which law applies?

3. Do the appropriate choice--of--law rules of State Y call for application of the substantive law of State Y, which would allow Petrol to claim the proceeds from Insurer under its insurance contract, or the substantive law of State X, which would give effect to the denial--of--coverage clause?

DISCUSSION

Point One: (15--25%)

In the initial phase of the federal diversity action filed in State Y. the choice--of--law rules of State Y would apply under the Erie doctrine.

The Erie doctrine, set forth in Erie R.R. Co. v. Tompkins, 304 U.S. 64 (1938), applies to choice-of--law rules. Klaxon Co. v. Stentor Electric Mfg. Co. Inc., 313 U.S. 487 (1941). Under Klaxon, the choice--of--law rules of the state in which the federal court sits-that is, of State Y in the initial phase-would be used to determine which state's law governs the validity of the denial--of--coverage clause in the contract (see Point Three, infra). The principal reason for this application of Erie is to deter forum--shopping as between federal and state courts in the same state and thereby to protect the integrity and uniformity of state law within its territory.

Point Two: (15--25%)

Following the transfer or change of venue from the federal district court of State Y to that of State X, the State X court must follow State Y choice--of--law rules.

Van Dusen v. Barrack, 376 U.S. 612 (1964), established that a transfer of a civil action initiated by a defendant in a federal case, under 28 U.S. Code § 1404(a), does not affect the choice--of-law rule that was or would have been adopted by the transferor court. Ferens v. John Deere Co., 110 S.Ct. 1274 (1990), carries the Erie--based, anti--forum--shopping rule of Van Dusen one step further. Ferens held that even where the plaintiff institutes the transfer, the transferor court's rules generally would govern in the transferee court. Thus, State Y choice-of--law rules would govern after the transfer of the action to the federal court in State X.

Point Three: (55--65%)

<u>Under governmental interest analysis, this case presents a situation where neither state has a significant interest in applying its law. Under such circumstances, a court would probably apply local law. Thus, the law of State Y would apply to the losses in both State Y and State X. Therefore, Insurer's denial--of--coverage clause would not bar recovery by Petrol against Insurer.</u>

Because the federal district court in State X will use State Y choice--of--law rules, it will decide whose law to apply by following the governmental interest analysis approach favored by State Y courts. Governmental interest analysis requires a step--by--step series of considerations. Although many states have adopted variations of this approach, the basic scheme is as follows:

1. When a court is asked to apply the law of a foreign state different from the law of the forum, it should inquire into the policies expressed in the respective laws and into the circumstances in which it is reasonable for the respective states to assert an interest in the application of those policies. In making these determinations the court should employ the ordinary processes of construction and interpretation.

2. If the court finds that one state has an interest in the application of its policy in the circumstances of the case and the other has none, it should apply the law of the only interested state.

3. If the court finds an apparent conflict between the interests of the two states, it should reconsider. A more moderate and restrained interpretation of the policy or interest of one state or the other may avoid conflict.

4. If, upon reconsideration, the court finds that a conflict between the legitimate interests of the two states is unavoidable, it should apply the law of the forum.

Currie, Comments on <u>Babcock v. Jackson</u>, 63 Colum.L.Rev. 1233, 1242(1963).

It should be noted that under the facts State Y has substituted the First Restatement for the law of the forum as a "tie--breaker" in the event of a true conflict.

State X law requires prompt notice to the insurer and thereby validates the denial--of--coverage clause in the Insurer contract. Such a law is designed to protect State X insurers, purely and simply. See, <u>Sandefer Oil & Gas, Inc. v. AIG Oil Rig of Texas, Inc.</u>, 846 F.2d 319 (5th Cir. 1988). The contrary policy of State Y, on the other hand, is to protect local (State Y) insured parties. Neither state presumably has an altruistic interest in protecting the interests of the other state's natural or corporate citizens; the laws are designed to protect local persons. As a result, neither state has a real interest in application of its law to this case. State X has no interest in seeing its insurer--protective policy applied to protect a State Y insurer. State Y has no interest in applying its pro--coverage policy to protect an insured party from State X. Thus, this a classic "unprovided--for case," with neither a false conflict (only one state has an interest, as in step 2, above) nor a true conflict (both states have an interest, as in steps 3 and 4, above).

There is no uniform method by which state courts resolve this kind of case. It is possible that

State Y courts might apply the First Restatement because that is the technique by which they resolve a true conflict. Under the First Restatement, the question of the validity of a clause in the contract would be governed by the place of contracting. For insurance contracts delivered by mail, that is the place of posting, presumably State Y. See, First Restatement, Conflict of Laws, § 317 (1934). If the issue is viewed as a performance issue, the law of the place where notification of a loss would be completed (Petrol's performance, in this case) would apply. In this case, the law of the place of performance would be the law of State Y, which invalidated the notice clause in the insurance contract. Finally, the law of State Y might also be applied to invalidate the clause on another theory: that courts will apply their own law, especially in borderline cases such as this one, unless there are compelling reasons for choosing foreign law. In any event, it would appear that State Y law would apply to resolve this "unprovided--for case."

It might be argued that State Y does have an interest in applying its law to protect Petrol with respect to the State Y well. The argument would be that State Y has an interest in ensuring insurance coverage of all local losses, regardless of the domicile of the insured party (in this case, State X). The general rationale would be that protection of out--of--state insureds would promote external insurance coverage of local losses and relieve the state of the potential economic burden that might result if insurance was unavailable to cover a particular loss within the state.

Thus, State Y law would apply, either by determining that this is an unprovided--for case to be resolved in favor of the local law (for any of the reasons mentioned above) or by finding a false conflict (with respect to the State Y well) because only State Y would have an interest in applying its pro-coverage law in order to confirm insurability and thereby encourage external insurance coverage of losses in State Y.

MBE SUBJECTS – RELEASED ESSAY ANALYSIS

CONSTITUTIONAL LAW
MEE Question - July 2008

ANALYSIS

Legal Problems: (1) To what extent does the First Amendment shield a newspaper from liability in a defamation action for publishing a false statement about a public figure?

(2) Does the First Amendment shield a reporter from liability in a civil trespass action for trespassing on private property while investigating a news story on a matter of public concern?

(3) Does the First Amendment shield a newspaper from liability in an invasion-of-privacy action based on disclosure of private facts in a newspaper story about a matter of public concern if the reporter did not break the law in obtaining the story?

DISCUSSION

Summary

New York Times v. Sullivan requires plaintiffs who are public figures to prove "actual malice" in order to receive money damages for defamation. If *News* was merely negligent in identifying the unknown woman as Star, Star cannot recover damages. But because of the conflicting stories about Star, *News* may have acted with reckless disregard of the truth and, therefore, with actual malice. The First Amendment does not shield Scoop from liability for trespass under generally applicable tort law; here, because Scoop's acts constituted trespass under generally applicable tort law, he is liable for damages. Finally, Lex's action for invasion of privacy should fail. Truthful disclosure of private facts is protected by the First Amendment unless the press did not obtain the information lawfully or the disclosure is not on a matter of public concern. Here, the published facts were on a matter of public concern because Lex is a public figure and his hypocrisy about adultery is newsworthy. Because neither *News* nor Scoop broke the law in obtaining the photograph, *News* is not liable to Lex under the First Amendment.

Point One (40–50%)
Star cannot successfully sue *News* under a libel theory because the facts do not appear to support a finding that the reporting was done with actual malice.

In *New York Times v. Sullivan,* 376 U.S. 254, 280 (1964), the United States Supreme Court held that public officials seeking to recover damages in a defamation action (libel or slander) must prove that the defendant reporter acted with "actual malice," defined as "knowledge that [the published defamation] was false" or "reckless disregard of whether it was false or not." Proof of negligent falsehood is insufficient to permit liability for defamation.

The Supreme Court has extended this standard to public figures who assume "roles of especial prominence in the affairs of society. Some occupy positions of such persuasive power and influence that they are deemed public figures for all purposes. More commonly, those classed as public figures have thrust themselves to the forefront of particular public controversies in order to influence the resolution of the issues involved." *Gertz v. Robert Welch, Inc.*, 418 U.S. 323, 345 (1974).

Here, Star, a world-famous actress, is undeniably a public figure. She can recover only if she proves that *News* acted with actual malice, i.e., that *News* knew that the woman Scoop photographed was not Star, or that it acted with reckless disregard with regard to that fact. There is no indication that *News* acted with knowledge of falsity; indeed, we are told that Scoop "honestly believed" that Star was Lex's adulterous partner. But it is a much closer question whether *News* acted with "reckless disregard" for the truth. While logical or factual consistency is not demanded by *New York Times*, the fact that the same edition of *News* reported Star to be in another state shows that *News* very easily could have discovered Scoop's report to be untrue. The fact that "most people" could have seen that Star was not the woman in Scoop's photograph also provides some support for recklessness in reporting. These factors probably are inadequate to show that *News* acted with reckless disregard for the facts, but it is a close question.

[NOTE TO GRADERS: An applicant's analysis of this part is more important than his or her conclusion.]

Point Two (15–25%)
There is no First Amendment privilege giving the press immunity from liability arising under generally applicable law, even when in pursuit of a news story on a matter of public concern.

The First Amendment does not shield the press from liability arising under generally applicable law not aimed at suppression of free speech. In *Cohen v. Cowles Media Co.*, 501 U.S. 663 (1991), the United States Supreme Court stated that "generally applicable laws do not offend the First Amendment simply because their enforcement against the press has incidental effects on its ability to gather and report the news. . . . [E]nforcement of such general laws against the press is not subject to stricter scrutiny than would be applied to enforcement against other persons or organizations." *Id.* at 669–70.

Here, Scoop's actions in breaking into the hotel constituted trespass under generally applicable law that does not single out the press for special treatment. Scoop, like any other member of the public, is subject to tort law that applies to all members of society, even when he is engaged in the journalistic activities of gathering and reporting the news. Thus, the First Amendment is no shield to liability for him, and the hotel can collect damages for his trespass.

Point Three (30–40%)
News is probably immune from liability for invading Lex's privacy because the published information was lawfully obtained and involves a matter of public concern.

In a series of cases, the United States Supreme Court has held that where a media defendant has lawfully obtained a private fact, such as the identity of a rape victim, the First Amendment shields the media from liability as long as the news story involves a matter of public concern. *See, e.g., Cox Broadcasting v. Cohn*, 420 U.S. 469 (1975); *Florida Star v. BJF*, 491 U.S. 524 (1989); *Bartnicki v. Vopper Corp.*, 532 U.S. 514 (2001). In some jurisdictions, the First Amendment protection is incorporated directly into the tort rule, and the disclosure of private facts is not tortious if the facts are "of legitimate concern to the public." RESTATEMENT (SECOND) OF TORTS § 652D.

In this case, the First Amendment would shield *News* from liability. First, neither *News* nor its employee Scoop acted unlawfully in procuring the picture. Scoop took the photograph from a public vantage point and was not breaking the law in doing so. Indeed, publication of the picture was not really publication of a "private" fact at all. Lex was kissing the young woman on a public street. Although he was in a private car, passersby (e.g., Scoop) apparently could observe the kiss. A court might well conclude that Lex had no reasonable expectation of privacy under the circumstances.

Moreover, the news story about Lex's adultery addresses a matter of public concern. Lex is undeniably a public figure under the *Gertz* test, *see* Point One, as he is a nationally famous lawyer and television personality. In addition, given the strong position he has taken publicly opposing marital infidelity, evidence that his personal actions belie his public arguments is relevant to the public debate that Lex has voluntarily thrust himself into. Accordingly, because the photograph was newsworthy and lawfully obtained, *News* cannot be held liable for invasion of privacy.

MBE SUBJECTS – RELEASED ESSAY ANALYSIS

CONSTITUTIONAL LAW
MEE Question - July 2009

ANALYSIS

Legal Problems: (1) Does the First Amendment permit Anti-Tax's conviction under the state sedition statute based on advocacy of (a) illegal nonpayment of a future tax increase, or (b) "mak[ing] Tax pay up . . . [and] show[ing] him what a taking really means"?

(2) Does the First Amendment permit Anti-Tax's conviction under the state's broad abusive-words statute?

DISCUSSION

Summary

Under the *Brandenburg* test, a conviction for violation of the Sedition Statute based on inciting illegal conduct is consistent with the First Amendment if there is advocacy of illegal conduct that is imminent and likely to occur and if the statute is limited to criminalizing advocacy of such conduct. Anti-Tax's advocacy of nonpayment of the proposed tax increase does not meet the "imminent and likely" test because the proposed tax legislation has not been enacted. It is unclear whether Anti-Tax's advocacy of "mak[ing] Tax pay up . . . [and] show[ing] him what a taking really means" satisfies the *Brandenburg* test.

Anti-Tax may not be convicted under the Abusive Words Statute because the statute is overbroad and facially unconstitutional.

Point One (45–55%)
Anti-Tax cannot be convicted for advocating nonpayment of the tax increase because the proposed illegal conduct could not be performed imminently. It is possible, but not certain, that Anti-Tax could be convicted for urging viewers to "make Tax pay up" and "show him what a taking really means."

In *Brandenburg v. Ohio*, 395 U.S. 444 (1969), the Supreme Court of the United States held that the First Amendment precludes the conviction of individuals who incite or advocate breaking the law unless (1) there is *advocacy* of illegal conduct and not just an abstract expression of ideas, (2) the advocacy calls for *imminent* lawbreaking, and (3) the lawbreaking is *likely* to occur. Moreover, a person cannot be convicted on the basis of a statute that does not distinguish between abstract expression of ideas and such advocacy.

In this case, Anti-Tax made two statements. He advocated nonpayment of the proposed tax increase and he urged viewers to "make Tax pay up" and "show him what a taking really means."

Anti-Tax's statement urging nonpayment of a future tax increase does not satisfy the *Brandenburg* requirements. Although the statement satisfies the illegality requirement, the imminence requirement cannot be satisfied because the proposed tax legislation had not been enacted. It also seems doubtful that the state could show likelihood; it is unclear that the tax increase legislation will ever be passed, and there is no evidence that anyone will take seriously Anti-Tax's suggestion.

It is unclear whether Anti-Tax's statement urging viewers to "make Tax pay up" and "show him what a taking really means" meets the *Brandenburg* requirements for advocacy of imminent lawbreaking. The statement does not expressly advocate immediate, illegal conduct.

On the other hand, the statement does urge a "taking," which implies theft or property destruction. This implication, coupled with the fact that Anti-Tax provided Tax's home address, suggests that Anti-Tax was calling for immediate action. Although there is no evidence of the likelihood that a viewer would act on Anti-Tax's suggestion, the short time lapse between the broadcast and the arson provides circumstantial evidence that a viewer did act on it. It is thus possible, but not certain, that Anti-Tax's statement will be found to satisfy both *Brandenburg* requirements.

While the Sedition Statute is not limited on its face to punishing advocacy of imminent lawbreaking, it has been construed to apply only to such advocacy. Accordingly, overbreadth of the statute is not a bar to conviction under it.

Point Two (45–55%)
The First Amendment "fighting words" doctrine does not permit Anti-Tax's conviction under the Abusive Words Statute.

In *Chaplinsky v. New Hampshire*, 315 U.S. 568, 572 (1942), the Supreme Court excluded from the protection of the First Amendment so-called "fighting words," i.e., words "which by their very utterance inflict injury or tend to incite an immediate breach of the peace." Fighting words are unprotected speech because they play little or no part in the exposition of ideas. *Id.*

Speech does not come within the fighting-words doctrine unless it is likely to cause a violent reaction from others. *See Cohen v. California*, 403 U.S. 15 (1971) (wearing of a jacket reading "F*ck the Draft" in a courthouse did not constitute fighting words because it was not likely to cause a violent reaction from others under the circumstances). Here, it is possible, but not certain, that the state can establish that Anti-Tax's statement urging viewers to "make Tax pay up," etc., was likely to cause a violent reaction.

However, even if the state establishes a likelihood of a violent reaction, Anti-Tax may not be convicted under the Abusive Words Statute because of its overbreadth. In *Gooding v. Wilson*, 405 U.S. 518 (1972), the Court held that a man who told a police officer "I'll kill you" and "I'll choke you to death" could not be punished for uttering what were clearly fighting words because the statute under which conviction was sought was overbroad and unconstitutional on its face.

Here, the Abusive Words Statute, which punishes "directing any abusive word or term at another," is clearly overbroad. Commentary on matters of public concern is afforded the highest level of First Amendment protection, and this protection extends to "vehement, caustic, and sometimes unpleasantly sharp attacks on government and public officials." *New York Times Co. v. Sullivan*, 376 U.S. 254, 270 (1964). A statute which punishes language that is merely rude or abusive will of necessity reach protected speech. Indeed, Anti-Tax's statement "You're a dishonest imbecile" is a textbook example of rude and abusive speech protected by the First Amendment.

Thus, even if Anti-Tax's statement urging viewers to "make Tax pay up" represented fighting words that threatened personal violence against Tax, Anti-Tax's conviction under this overbroad statute would violate the First Amendment.

MBE SUBJECTS – RELEASED ESSAY ANALYSIS

CONSTITUTIONAL LAW
MEE Question - July 2010

ANALYSIS

Legal Problems: (1)   May a municipality prohibit leafleting in a public forum based on an anti-leafleting rationale?

                (2)   May a public school deny use of classroom space to a student religious group when, by making that space available to other student groups, it has created a limited public forum?

                (3)   May a speaker be convicted for trespassing on government property that is not a public forum when the government has an interest unrelated to speech in preventing the trespass?

DISCUSSION

Summary

For First Amendment purposes, there are three types of forums: the public forum, the limited public forum, and the nonpublic forum. A public street or sidewalk is a public forum. In a public forum, the state may not regulate speech based on its content, nor may it penalize speech based on an anti-leafleting rationale. Thus, Homestead may not fine Chapter under the anti-leafleting ordinance.

When a governmental entity deliberately opens government property to the public for meetings or other forms of speech, it creates a limited public forum subject to the same First Amendment requirements as a traditional public forum. Thus, because High School created a limited public forum, Principal may not deny Church Club the right to use that forum.

In a nonpublic forum, governmental actors may restrict speech as long as their actions are reasonable and content-neutral. Principal's office was a nonpublic forum because it was clearly off-limits to the public except by invitation, and Principal's actions were reasonable under the circumstances. Thus, Father has no First Amendment grounds to vacate his trespass conviction.

Point One (40%)
Homestead cannot enforce its anti-leafleting ordinance against Chapter because a municipality must allow speech in a traditional public forum even if doing so imposes costs on the municipality.

The First Amendment, as applied to the states and local governments through incorporation in the Fourteenth Amendment, applies to Homestead's enforcement of its anti-leafleting ordinance, which is a state action.

Although the United States Supreme Court once granted local governments broad powers to regulate speech in streets and parks, *see Davis v. Commonwealth of Massachusetts*, 167 U.S. 43 (1897), for the better part of a century, the Court has treated a public street or sidewalk as a First Amendment "public forum." In a public forum, government may regulate speech only if certain conditions are met. If the regulation is not content-neutral, it must meet the requirements of strict scrutiny. If the regulation is content-neutral, it must meet the requirements of intermediate scrutiny; to pass muster under this standard, the regulation must impose only reasonable restrictions on the time, place, or manner of speech that are narrowly tailored to serve a significant governmental interest, and it must leave open ample alternative opportunities to engage in speech. *See Ward v. Rock against Racism*, 491 U.S. 781 (1989); ERWIN CHEMERINSKY, CONSTITUTIONAL LAW: PRINCIPLES AND POLICIES 1127 (3d ed. 2006).

Here, Homestead's regulation of speech under its anti-leafleting ordinance is content-neutral; the ordinance forbids one means of communication, leafleting, without regard to the content of the speech. Thus, Homestead must show that its ordinance passes intermediate rather than strict scrutiny.

The Homestead ordinance is unlikely to pass muster under intermediate scrutiny because Homestead has not left open an alternative channel for the prohibited speech. Instead of regulating the time, place, and manner of leafleting, Homestead has banned it entirely. Particularly where a form of speech is inexpensive and available to all, a governmental entity may not prohibit it altogether. *See City of Ladue v. Gilleo*, 512 U.S. 43, 56 (1994).

The fact that the prohibited speech imposes costs upon the governmental entity does not alter this result. In the seminal case of *Schneider v. State of New Jersey, Town of Irvington*, 308 U.S. 147 (1939), the Supreme Court struck down an anti-leafleting ordinance much like the Homestead ordinance. In so doing, the Court held that

> "the purpose to keep the streets clean and of good appearance is insufficient to justify an ordinance which prohibits a person rightfully on a public street from handing literature to one willing to receive it. Any burden imposed upon the city authorities in cleaning and caring for the streets as an indirect consequence of such distribution results from the constitutional protection of the freedom of speech and press." *Id.* at 162.

Thus, Homestead may not fine Chapter for leafleting.

Point Two (35%)
A public school that makes classroom space available to student groups has created a limited public forum and may not discriminate as to use of that forum based on the content of speech. Thus High School cannot deny use of a classroom after school hours to Church Club.

A "limited public forum" (also known as a "designated public forum") is created when a governmental entity could close a location to speech but instead opens it to speech. All the rules applicable to a traditional public forum apply to a limited public forum. Thus, under the First Amendment, as applied to the states and local governments through incorporation in the Fourteenth Amendment, the government may not discriminate among speakers based upon the content of their speech. *See* CHEMERINSKY, *supra*, at 1137.

There is no exception to the requirement of content neutrality when religious speech is at issue. The Supreme Court has repeatedly held that, in a public forum, religious speech stands on an equal footing with nonreligious speech, and content-neutral access rules do not violate the Establishment Clause. Many of the cases have involved student or community groups that wanted to use, for religious speech, limited public forums created by public schools. *See, e.g., Widmar v. Vincent*, 454 U.S. 263 (1981); *Lamb's Chapel v. Center Moriches Union Free School Dist.*, 508 U.S. 384 (1993); *Good News Club v. Milford Central School*, 533 U.S. 98 (2001). In *Good News*, the case most like this one, the Supreme Court held that, when a school opens its classrooms for use by student groups, it creates a limited public forum and may not deny access to a student religious club that intends to use the classroom for prayer based on the religious content of that speech. The Court also held that a school that opens its facilities to religious speech under a content-neutral policy does not violate the Establishment Clause under the standard established in *Lemon v. Kurtzman*, 403 U.S. 642 (1971). *See Good News*, 533 U.S. at 103–04.

Thus, High School may not deny Church Club use of its classrooms for after-school meetings.

Point Three (25%)
The First Amendment does not shield Father from a trespass conviction. First, government can regulate conduct that is not imbued with communicative value. Second, even if the conduct has communicative value, the state can regulate such conduct in a nonpublic forum if the state's interest is important or substantial, and is unrelated to the suppression of expression, and if the regulation is no greater than necessary to serve the state's interest. Here, Principal's office was a nonpublic forum, Father's act of trespass was not communicative, and High School had an important and substantial interest in preventing trespassers from entering Principal's office.

Father was convicted for his physical entry into Principal's office, not for what he said while there. The act of marching into Principal's office—which is the act for which Father was convicted—is not conduct imbued with communicative value and does not implicate the First Amendment. Thus, Father's trespass conviction will likely survive a First Amendment challenge.

Even if Father's conduct is viewed as conduct imbued with communicative value because he entered Principal's office to express an opinion, the conviction would be upheld under *United States v. O'Brien*, 391 U.S. 367 (1968). The test in that case is whether a law that regulates speech-related conduct serves an interest within the government's regulatory powers that is important or substantial and that is both unrelated to the suppression of expression and no greater than necessary to serve the state's interest. Here, Principal's office was clearly not a public forum. The door was closed, a sign announced that there was "no admittance without an appointment," and Principal was meeting with another parent at the time that Father marched in.

High School clearly has a legitimate and important interest in prohibiting trespassers from entering Principal's office where private conversations about individual students or official school business may be taking place. High School's interest is not related to suppression of expression. Moreover, the means of protecting that interest (prohibiting admittance without appointment) are closely related to advancement of High School's interest.

MBE SUBJECTS – RELEASED ESSAY ANALYSIS

CONSTITUTIONAL LAW
MEE Question - July 2011

ANALYSIS

Legal Problems

(1)   Are the actions of a private nursing school subject to the Equal Protection Clause of the Fourteenth Amendment if the school receives no direct state funds, but the state regulates the school and certifies its graduates as eligible to become licensed nurses?

(2)(a)   Does it violate the Equal Protection Clause of the Fourteenth Amendment for a state-owned nursing school to deny admission to a male applicant because of his gender?

(2)(b)   Does it violate the Equal Protection Clause of the Fourteenth Amendment for a state to have an in-state nursing program reserved for female students, and an out-of-state program for male students, where the facilities of and employment from the all-female program are superior?

DISCUSSION

Summary

Private has not violated the man's rights under the Equal Protection Clause of the Fourteenth Amendment by denying him admission, because the actions of Private are not the actions of the state for purposes of the Equal Protection Clause. By contrast, as an arm of the state itself, Public's actions are state action. When Public denied the man admission based upon his gender, Public denied him equal protection of the laws. The creation of the Male Nursing Opportunity Program fails to cure this constitutional violation. As in *United States v. Virginia*, 518 U.S. 515 (1996), if a state creates two separate single-gender educational institutions, the institutions must (at a minimum) provide equivalent educational experiences. Because in this case the Male Nursing Opportunity Program is clearly inferior as an educational institution, it fails to pass scrutiny under the Equal Protection Clause.

Point One (30%)
Private's actions are not subject to the Equal Protection Clause because it is not a state actor.

The Fourteenth Amendment provides that "No State shall . . . deny to any person within its jurisdiction the equal protection of the laws." The U.S. Supreme Court has interpreted this language as applying not only to the states themselves but also to private parties whose actions constitute "state action." Simply put, in order for there to be a violation of the Fourteenth

Amendment, the allegedly unconstitutional action (here, denial of admission based upon gender) must be attributable to the state. Actions of private parties are not typically considered state action, but the actions of otherwise "private" parties can constitute state action in certain exceptional cases. For instance, private parties have been held to be state actors where (1) they have performed a traditional public function, *Jackson v. Metropolitan Edison Co.*, 419 U.S. 345, 352–53 (1974), (2) there is the enforcement of certain private contracts, (3) there is joint action or "entanglement" between a state and private actor, or (4) there is state encouragement of private discrimination, *Blum v. Yaretsky*, 457 U.S. 991, 1004 (1982) ("A State normally can be held responsible for a private decision only when it has exercised coercive power or has provided such significant encouragement, either overt or covert, that the choice must in law be deemed to be that of the State.").

Private is a private entity and none of the factors described above contribute to a conclusion that its actions constitute state action. Running a private school or college is not state action. *Rendell-Baker v. Kohn*, 457 U.S. 830 (1982). First, Private is not performing a traditional public function. Second, there has been no judicial enforcement of a private contract here. Third, it is highly unlikely that a court would hold that mere state regulation of the curriculum and state certification of graduates is sufficient to constitute entanglement. Fourth, there is no evidence that the state has directly encouraged Private to discriminate on the basis of gender.

Point Two(a) (40%)
Public has violated the Equal Protection Clause because a state college may not deny admission on the basis of gender absent an "exceedingly persuasive justification."

Laws that classify on the basis of gender are typically assessed under heightened scrutiny. *Reed v. Reed*, 404 U.S. 71, 75 (1971). Although some early cases suggested that strict scrutiny was the correct standard, modern cases have settled on intermediate scrutiny. *See Craig v. Boren*, 429 U.S. 190 (1976). In *United States v. Virginia*, 518 U.S. 515, 531 (1996), the U.S. Supreme Court held that state laws that make classifications on the basis of gender are unconstitutional unless the state can establish an "exceedingly persuasive justification" for the classification. An "exceedingly persuasive justification" is one that serves "important governmental objectives" and which does not rely upon outdated or overbroad generalizations and stereotypes about differences between men and women. The burden of justification is demanding and rests entirely on the state. The state must at least show that the "[challenged] classification serves important governmental objectives and that the discriminatory means employed are substantially related to the achievement of those objectives." *Mississippi Univ. for Women v. Hogan*, 458 U.S. 718, 724–25 (quoting *Wengler v. Druggists Mut. Ins. Co.*, 446 U.S. 142, 150 (1980) (internal quotations omitted)). These objectives must be real in the sense that they are real state purposes rather than hypothetical justifications for the gender classification. Moreover, gender classifications must be "substantially related" to the achievement of such important governmental objectives. "[A] State can evoke a compensatory purpose to justify an otherwise discriminatory classification only if members of the gender benefited by the classification actually suffer a disadvantage related to the classification." *Id.* at 728.

Because the man has been denied admission to Public solely on the basis of his gender, the action of Public—clearly the action of the state, as Public is the state nursing school—is presumptively unconstitutional. The state interest in this case is remedying past discrimination against women—as the letter states, "[m]indful of the historical discrimination that women have faced in State A, our state has established Public to remedy this discrimination and provide opportunities for women who want to work in the growing field of health care as nurses." Remedying past discrimination is certainly an important governmental objective; in the contexts of race and gender classifications, the Supreme Court has upheld this governmental objective in the face of heightened scrutiny. However, it is unclear whether this quote from Public's letter sets forth the actual state purpose. Although there has been gender discrimination in the field of health care in State A in the past, there is no evidence that there has been discrimination against women in the nursing field. Indeed, the evidence that 95 percent of nurses have historically been women suggests that State A is more likely reinforcing outdated stereotypes of women as nurses (rather than, say, doctors) by restricting Public admissions to women. Finally, if the goal of the admissions policy is to end discrimination against women in the health care field, it is not clear how the admissions policy advances this objective.

Point Two(b) (30%)
The Male Nursing Opportunity Program is inconsistent with the guarantees of equal protection.

In certain cases, a state may treat men and women differently consistent with the equal protection guarantee and provide separate facilities for each gender (for example, male and female sports teams, dormitories, and bathroom facilities at state universities). In such cases, moreover, the state must bear the burden of (1) demonstrating the "exceedingly persuasive justification" for the separate treatment, and (2) demonstrating that the separate facilities are substantially equivalent. Thus, for example, in *United States v. Virginia*, the Supreme Court suggested that the Commonwealth of Virginia could offer all-male and all-female public military-style education consistent with the Equal Protection Clause. However, because the new all-female "Leadership Program" in that case provided facilities and career opportunities inferior to those that the Commonwealth was providing in its established all-male program at the Virginia Military Institute, the Court concluded that the separate program violated the Fourteenth Amendment.

In this case, because the Male Nursing Opportunity Program is markedly inferior to the all-female Public program, it is insufficient to satisfy the Equal Protection Clause. Although graduates of the all-male program are still eligible to become nurses in State A, the two programs are not substantially equivalent. They differ in both overall quality and the employment opportunities they offer to their graduates. The facilities of the Male Nursing Opportunity Program are not as modern as those at Public, the faculty is not as experienced, and graduates of the Male Nursing Opportunity Program do not enjoy the same employment opportunities as graduates of either Public or Private. For these reasons, the Male Nursing Opportunity Program is inferior to the regular all-female Public program, and it cannot be offered as a substitute consistent with Equal Protection.

ANALYSIS

Legal Problems

(1)   Does Congress have authority under the Commerce Clause to regulate employer precautions against workplace violence?

(2)   Do federalism principles bar Congress from applying the Act to state agencies as employers?

(3)   Does the Eleventh Amendment bar the employee's suit against the state?

DISCUSSION

Summary

Under the Commerce Clause, Congress has power to regulate economic activities that substantially affect interstate commerce. Here, the Act regulates a non-economic aspect of an economic activity (i.e., the employment relationship) that has a substantial effect ($5 to $10 billion per year) on interstate commerce. This regulation probably falls within the scope of the Commerce Clause, although at least one case can be read to suggest the opposite possibility. The Act does not violate federalism principles embodied in the Tenth Amendment to the Constitution by improperly commandeering states or by regulating state employers differently than private employers. However, the employee's federal court lawsuit is barred by the state agency's Eleventh Amendment immunity, and the Act cannot abrogate that immunity.

Point One (50%)
Congress has power under the Commerce Clause to regulate workplace violence only if the court concludes that the Act regulates an economic activity with a substantial aggregate effect on interstate commerce.

In *United States v. Lopez*, 514 U.S. 549 (1995), the Supreme Court of the United States clarified that Congress may enact three types of regulations under the Commerce Clause. First, Congress may regulate the channels of interstate commerce, which are the pathways through which interstate travel and communications pass. Examples of the channels include interstate highways and phone lines. Second, Congress may regulate the people and instrumentalities that work and travel in the channels of interstate commerce. Examples include people such as airline pilots and flight attendants, as well as the airplanes on which they travel. Third, Congress may regulate activities that substantially affect interstate commerce.

The Act does not fit within either of the first two *Lopez* categories. First, the statute applies to any workplace, regardless of its location, and so it does not narrowly regulate the channels of interstate commerce. Second, the Act applies to all employees and not only those people or instrumentalities in the channels of interstate commerce. Consequently, the Act will be valid only if it regulates an activity that substantially affects interstate commerce.

The key to satisfying the substantial effects requirement is the threshold determination of whether the regulated activity is economic or commercial in nature. When Congress regulates an economic or commercial activity, the Court will uphold the regulation if Congress had a rational basis for concluding that the class of activities subject to regulation, in the aggregate, has a substantial effect on interstate commerce. Aggregation on a national scale typically makes this an easy standard to meet. On the other hand, if the regulated activity is not economic or commercial in nature, the Court will not aggregate to find a substantial effect, and the standard becomes extremely difficult to meet. *See Gonzales v. Raich*, 545 U.S. 1 (2005); *United States v. Morrison*, 529 U.S. 598 (2000); *Lopez, supra*.

Therefore, the key question is whether violence in the workplace is an economic or commercial activity. In *Morrison*, the Court held that Congress exceeded its commerce power by enacting a statute giving a cause of action to the victims of gender-motivated violence. It therefore can be argued here, as *Morrison* held, that acts of violence are not economic or commercial in nature, and thus in applying the substantial effects test, the court may only measure the effect of the particular act of violence at issue in the suit and not the aggregate effect of all acts of violence in the workplace.

One could argue that *Morrison* is distinguishable because the statute at issue here is limited to violence in the workplace. The workplace is an economic environment, and workplace violence directly impedes productivity of the workplace. The court therefore should conclude that the statute at issue here is an economic regulation and thus is within the commerce power of Congress because, based on the facts given in the problem, Congress had a rational basis for concluding that workplace violence, in the aggregate, has a substantial effect on interstate commerce.

Point Two (20%)

<u>The Act does not violate federalism principles because it regulates both public and private employers on the same terms.</u>

In *Garcia v. San Antonio Metropolitan Transportation Authority*, 469 U.S. 528 (1985), the Supreme Court held that Congress may regulate the states on the same terms as private actors. For example, *Garcia* upheld application of the federal minimum wage and maximum hour law to both public and private employers. In *New York v. United States*, 505 U.S. 144 (1992), however, the Court held that Congress may not "commandeer" the states to regulate private conduct. In *New York v. United States*, the Court struck down a federal statute that commandeered states to regulate private disposal of low-level hazardous waste.

The Act does not commandeer the state to regulate private conduct. Instead, the Act merely requires both public and private employers to obey the same federal requirement—to address workplace violence under the threat of civil liability. It is true that the state, as an employer, must adopt policies and regulations to implement the Act's mandates. But *Reno v. Condon*, 528 U.S.

141 (2000), clarifies that a federal mandate requiring state personnel to alter their own activities is not unconstitutional commandeering.

Point Three (30%)

The Eleventh Amendment bars the employee's federal court lawsuit against the state, and the Act does not validly abrogate that immunity.

The Eleventh Amendment provides: "The Judicial power of the United States shall not be construed to extend to any suit in law or equity, commenced or prosecuted against one of the United States by Citizens of another State, or by Citizens or Subjects of any Foreign State."

Despite the text of the Eleventh Amendment, the Supreme Court has interpreted it to bar lawsuits between a state and one of its own citizens, as well as lawsuits that arise under federal law. *See Seminole Tribe of Florida v. Florida*, 517 U.S. 44 (1996). Further, this immunity extends to state agencies. Consequently, the Eleventh Amendment would bar the employee's lawsuit against the state agency in federal court, unless the Act validly abrogates the state's immunity.

A federal statute abrogates Eleventh Amendment immunity if, first, the statute unambiguously asserts that it does so, and second, Congress enacted the statute under a power that may abrogate Eleventh Amendment state immunity. Here, the Act satisfies the first requirement because Section 204 unequivocally attempts to abrogate state Eleventh Amendment immunity. The Act fails the second requirement, however, because Congress did not pass the Act under a grant of power that may abrogate state immunity. In *Seminole Tribe*, the Court held that Article 1, section 8 of the Constitution does not grant Congress power to abrogate state sovereign immunity. (The Supreme Court has held that Congress can abrogate state immunity when it exercises its powers under amendments that postdate the Eleventh Amendment. By way of contrast, Section 5 of the Fourteenth Amendment does grant Congress that power. *See Fitzpatrick v. Bitzer*, 427 U.S. 445 (1976) (Fourteenth Amendment)). Because the Act does not validly abrogate the state's Eleventh Amendment immunity, the District Court should dismiss the employee's lawsuit.

MBE SUBJECTS – RELEASED ESSAY ANALYSIS

CONSTITUTIONAL LAW
MEE Question – February 2013

ANALYSIS

Legal Problems

(1) Does AutoCo's operation of a "company town" result in its actions counting as those of the state for purposes of constitutional analysis?

(2) Does the expulsion of a schoolchild for failure to recite the Pledge of Allegiance violate the First Amendment as applied through the Fourteenth Amendment?

(3) Does the arrest of a pamphleteer in connection with violation of an anti-littering rule, where the littering is done by the recipients of leaflets distributed by the pamphleteer, violate the First Amendment as applied through the Fourteenth Amendment?

DISCUSSION

Summary

The First Amendment, as applied through the Fourteenth Amendment, applies only to state action. It does not typically govern private actors. However, courts have found state action where the private actor has exercised a "public function," such as running a privately owned "company town," as AutoCo has done here. Thus, First Amendment protections apply. By requiring the son to participate in a mandatory Pledge of Allegiance ceremony, AutoCo has compelled the expression of political belief in violation of the First Amendment as applied through the Fourteenth Amendment. The father's arrest in connection with breaching the anti-litter rule also violated the First Amendment as applied through the Fourteenth Amendment. Although state actors can regulate the incidental effects of speech on the public streets on a content-neutral basis, this power is limited and cannot extend to punishing a distributor of literature because of littering by third parties.

Point One (30%)
AutoCo's operation of a company town (including a school) makes it a state actor under the public function strand of the state action doctrine.

The individual rights protections of the Constitution apply only where there is "state action"— either direct action by the government or some action by a private party that is fairly attributable to the government. As a general rule, the actions of a private company like AutoCo or of a private school like the school operated by AutoCo would not constitute state action, and the protections of the Constitution (in this case the First Amendment) would not apply.

However, there are situations in which the actions of a private actor are attributed to the state. One such situation is when the private actor undertakes a public function. There are not many bright-line rules in the Supreme Court's state action doctrine, but one of them is this: Where a private actor undertakes a "public function," the Constitution applies to those actions. Where a corporation operates a privately owned "company town" that provides essential services typically provided by a state actor, the public function doctrine applies and the Constitution binds agents of the town as if they were agents of the government. *See, e.g., Marsh v. Alabama*, 326 U.S. 501 (1946). Here, AutoCo does more than own the town; it provides security services, fire protection, sanitation services, and a school. Thus the actions of AutoCo constitute state action and are governed by the Fourteenth Amendment.

Point Two (35%)
The son's expulsion for failure to recite the Pledge of Allegiance violates the First Amendment as applied through the Fourteenth Amendment as a compelled expression of political belief.

As explained in Point One, the First Amendment applies to the school as a state actor.

Although children in public schools (and in schools subject to the First Amendment like the Oakwood school) have some First Amendment rights, *Tinker v. Des Moines Independent Community School District*, 393 U.S. 503, 506 (1969), schools have greater leeway to regulate the speech of students and teachers than the state would have outside the school context. *Hazelwood School Dist. v. Kuhlmeier*, 484 U.S. 260 (1988); *Morse v. Frederick*, 551 U.S. 393 (2007). However, the Supreme Court has long held that public schools may not force their students to participate in a flag salute ceremony when it offends the political or religious beliefs of the students or their families. *West Virginia Board of Educ. v. Barnette*, 319 U.S. 624 (1943) (invalidating a mandatory public school flag salute ceremony); *see also Wooley v. Maynard*, 430 U.S. 705 (1977) (invalidating compelled expression of political belief on state-issued license plates).

In this case, the school requires its students to participate in a flag salute and Pledge of Allegiance ceremony and punishes them when they refuse to participate. Pursuant to this policy, the school has expelled the son. This expulsion violates the First Amendment ban on compelled expression.

Point Three (35%)
Because the father was distributing leaflets in a traditional public forum, his trespass arrest violated the First Amendment as applied through the Fourteenth Amendment.

As explained in Point One, AutoCo is treated as a state actor. Thus, Oakwood's commercial district is treated as government-owned property for purposes of the First Amendment. Thus, the leafleting here is subject to the First Amendment because it is an expressive activity. *Schneider v. State of New Jersey, Town of Irvington*, 308 U.S. 147 (1939). When expression takes place on government-owned property, government regulation of the expression is assessed under the public forum doctrine. Public streets and sidewalks have long been held to be the classic example of a "traditional public forum" open to the public for expression. *Hague v. CIO*, 307 U.S. 496,

515–16 (1939). Because the father was distributing leaflets while standing on a street corner in the commercial district, his expressive activity occurred in a traditional public forum.

When a state tries to regulate expressive activity in a traditional public forum, it is prohibited from doing so based on the expressive activity's content unless its regulation is narrowly tailored to achieve a compelling governmental interest ("strict scrutiny"). In this case, however, AutoCo is regulating the father's expressive activity on the ostensibly neutral ground that his expressive activity has produced litter and made the street unsightly. When a state tries to regulate expressive activity without regard to its content, intermediate scrutiny applies. Under intermediate scrutiny, the true purpose of the regulation may not be the suppression of ideas (if so, then strict scrutiny applies), the regulation must be narrowly tailored to achieve a significant governmental interest, and it must leave open ample alternative channels for expressive activity. *Ward v. Rock Against Racism*, 491 U.S. 781, 791 (1989).

Here, the application of the ordinance to the father will fail for two reasons. First, the Supreme Court has held that the government's interest in keeping the streets clean is insufficient to ban leafleting in the public streets, as the government power to regulate with incidental effects on public sidewalk speech is very limited. *See, e.g., Schneider,* 308 U.S. at 162 (leafleting/littering). Second, the regulation (a blanket ban on distribution that results in littering) is not narrowly tailored to protect expression. A narrowly tailored alternative would be prosecution only of people who litter. Moreover, the effect of the littering rule is likely to be a ban on all leafleting, thus eliminating an entire class of means of expression. This raises the possibility that there are not "ample alternative channels of communication" open to the father as required under the Court's standard of review for content-neutral regulation of speech.

[NOTE: Some examinees might argue that this is a "time, place, and manner" restriction, and that AutoCo might have greater latitude to regulate the public sidewalks under this theory. This argument is incorrect for two reasons. First, the Supreme Court has held that the power to regulate speakers through littering laws is very limited, for the reasons given and in the cases cited above. But more generally, a "time, place, and manner" restriction involves the shifting of speech from one time and place to another or to another manner; here, there is no shifting, but a direct punishment for expressive activity (albeit one couched in content-neutral terms). In addition, some examinees might read the ordinance to be, in effect, a total ban on leafleting, since most leafleting will produce some litter. Those examinees might note that the Court has required total bans on an entire mode of expression to satisfy strict scrutiny and analyze the father's prosecution here accordingly. *See United States v. Grace*, 461 U.S. 171, 177 (1983) (invalidating ban on display of signs on public sidewalks surrounding U.S. Supreme Court; "[a]dditional restrictions such as an absolute prohibition on a particular type of expression will be upheld only if narrowly drawn to accomplish a compelling governmental interest").]

MBE SUBJECTS - PRACTICE ESSAY QUESTIONS

CONSTITUTIONAL LAW
Answer to Question 1

Dormant Commerce Clause

The commerce clause has negative implications that limit a state's ability to burden interstate commerce. When a state's law discriminates against interstate commerce, the law is per se invalid unless an exception applies. In this case, it's not clear if there's a law discriminating against interstate commerce. The law passed by the Alpha legislature merely authorizes the Department of Agriculture to promulgate rules for the preservation of seed stocks. This law does not discriminate against commerce on its face. If, however, the promulgated rule is treated as the law, then it arguably discriminates against other states. The rule gives preference to in-state farmers. If the law gives preference to in-state residents, it must be narrowly tailored to a compelling state interest. Hence, Wickard can argue that the rule is per se invalid or that it doesn't meet strict scrutiny.

If the law is treated as non-discriminatory, it can still violate the dormant commerce clause. A law that burdens interstate commerce must not place an unreasonable burden on interstate commerce. If a law does burden interstate commerce, the courts will apply a balancing test. First, a court will look at the state's interest. In this case, it might be preserving farms. Second, it will look at the burdens on interstate commerce. In this case, there will be a high burden whenever there aren't enough seeds. Third, the court will ask whether this is the least restrictive means available. In this case, there are other ways that the state could achieve the same end. It doesn't have to discriminate against out-of-state residents to protect farmers.

Market Participant Exception

Even if there is a dormant commerce clause problem, Wickard might not be successful because an exception might apply. The state is likely acting as a market participant. The state funded the development of the new seeds and a state university developed the seeds. Furthermore, the state is selling the seeds through the Department of Agriculture.

When a state acts as a market participant, it can engage in activities that otherwise would violate the dormant commerce clause. Hence, under the market participant doctrine, Wickard will be unsuccessful with his commerce clause challenge. The state can offer lower prices to state farmers and it can give them preference in the distribution of seeds.

Privileges and Immunities

Under the Privileges and Immunities Clause of Article V, the state cannot discriminate against out-of-state U.S. citizens in matters relating to commercial activities and civil liberties. In order to be protected under the privileges and immunities clause you must be a natural citizen. Therefore, Wickard, unlike the large corporate farms, would be able to make this argument. Furthermore, in this case, the state is limiting his ability to farm – a commercial activity – by denying him seeds. Hence, Wickard can argue that Alpha is violating the Privileges and Immunities Clause.

There is, however, an exception to this general rule. A state can discriminate against out-of-state citizens when there's an important state interest, the law is narrowly tailored to that interest, and there are no reasonable non-discriminatory alternatives to the law. In this case, the law does advance an important state interest – it's trying to protect the state's farmers. The corn blight devastated the state's corn harvest and caused tremendous economic harm. The state should be able to remedy this. Furthermore, the law is likely narrowly tailored to advancing that interest. It's not like the law completely excludes the out-of-state farmers. It gives the seeds as long as there are enough available. It's also not clear that there are non-discriminatory alternatives. Given that there's a limited supply of the seeds, the state will need to provide some preferences to in-state farmers in order to advance its interests.

Hence, Wickard's challenge under the Privileges and Immunities clause would also be unlikely to succeed. This, however, is probably his strongest argument. It's unclear whether the exception applies.

Contracts

The Alpha Department of Agriculture just told him that it would be unable to fulfill his order. If Wickard already had a contract for the seeds before the rule was passed, then he could argue that the law impaired an existing contract. Hence, it would be invalid at least for the current contract. That would at least allow Wickard to avoid facing ruin this season.

Due Process

Similarly, an existing contract might give Wickard a legitimate entitlement. Hence, Substantive Due Process would apply and he could argue that he's entitled to a hearing.

Equal Protection

Wickard might want to raise an equal protection challenge. This will not be successful. Wickard is not in a suspect or quasi-suspect class. Therefore, rational basis review will apply. Given in-state farmers preference is rationally related to the goal of improving the state's farm industry.

Similarly, a Due Process challenge would fail because there's no fundamental right at issue.

MBE SUBJECTS - PRACTICE ESSAY QUESTIONS

CONSTITUTIONAL LAW
Answer to Question 2

Federal courts may hear any case where state action has violated the federal constitution. Depending on the constitutional right affected, the court may apply one of three tests: (1) the strict scrutiny test which requires that the state law narrowly tailor the necessary law to achieve an important government interest, (2) the intermediate scrutiny test which requires the law to be substantially related to an important government interest, or (3) the rational basis test, which only requires that the law be rationally related to a legitimate government interest. Depending on the subject matter of law, a specific test will be applied.

Unmarried minors

Both people who are unmarried, and minors, are not protected groups of people. When a group is unprotected, the rational basis test is applied to the law that specifically addresses these classes of people. Under the 14th Amendment of the U.S. Constitution, a state cannot discriminate against certain classes of people and treat them differently than others based on their classification. Here, because unmarried people and minors are not a highly protected class, the court only needs to address if Section 1 of the State Sexual Responsibility Act (SSRA) is rationally related to a legitimate government interest.

Just based on the classification, Section 1 is rationally related to the legitimate government interest of discouraging sexual intercourse among unmarried minors. However, the use of contraceptives is a fundamental right, married or unmarried, and strict scrutiny applies.

Contraceptives

The 4th Amendment of the U.S. Constitution gives individuals the fundamental right to privacy. In accordance with this fundamental right, individuals have the right to get an abortion, get married, raise and educate their children as they please, and use contraceptives. Fundamental Rights are strongly protected and if a state law encroaches on these rights, strict scrutiny is applied and the law must be narrowly tailored to achieve a compelling government interest. Here, the law is not narrowly tailored. There are many other ways for State to discourage sexual intercourse among minors through perhaps sexual education, parenting responsibility classes, etc. Thus, although this may be a compelling government interest, the law is not narrowly tailored and must be struck down. Section 1 is unconstitutional.

Billboards and the 1st Amendment

Commercial speech may be barred if it is false or a misrepresentation or misleading. Aside from these restrictions, commercial speech is protected by the First Amendment to the U.S. Constitution and is protected by strict scrutiny. Speech may be restricted only by reasonable time, place and manner restrictions as long as the restrictions are content neutral. Here, barring advertisements for any contraceptive devise is not content neutral. The state is directly attacking the content of the Billboards and restricting their use because of their content. The time, place and manner restriction of Section 2 (2) would be legitimately upheld if all billboards were reduced without banning particular types of billboards due to their content. It seems as though advertisers have other avenues for advertising their products and that this restriction would not limit speech. However, as mentioned above, Section 2 (2) is unconstitutional because it is not constitutional. Furthermore, as there are other ways in which to advance the state's esthetic interests without suppressing speech, this section of the act is not narrowly tailored for achieving a compelling gov't interest (esthetics) and this law does not pass the strict scrutiny test.

Offensive Material & the 1st Amendment

Offensive or obscene speech cannot be regulated unless: (1) it applies to the sexual prurient interest of the average person, (2) the statute specifically describes what is obscene or offensive, or (3) the materially seriously lacks any literary, artistic, political, or scientific value. Here the statute in Section 2 (1) is attempting to ban the advertising for contraceptives on billboards because they may offend some state residents. However, the state has failed to explain what is offensive about contraceptives and why they should be banned from billboards.

Again, because commercial speech is protected under the 1st Amendment's freedom of speech, strict scrutiny applies. Here, the state lacks a compelling gov't interest. The fact that a billboard advertising contraceptives may offend "some" state residents is not sufficient for banning speech, and Section 2 (1) does not pass the strict scrutiny test.

For these reasons, both Sections 1 and 2 are unconstitutional and should be repealed.

MBE SUBJECTS - PRACTICE ESSAY QUESTIONS

CONSTITUTIONAL LAW
Answer to Question 3

Memo: To State Representative

This legislation will likely be challenged by parents adopting children, pursuant to their Equal Protection Rights afforded by the 14th Amendment of the United States Constitution.

Under the Equal Protection Clause, one class of people must not be treated differently than another absent a state interest that is to the degree necessary in each case. This case is treating people differently than others based on race. Under the law, race is a suspect classification. When there is a suspect classification, the courts will apply a strict scrutiny test. This test is that the law will be upheld only if it is necessary to achieve a compelling state interest. The state has the burden of proof under strict scrutiny.

The state would argue this law is necessary to obtain the best fit for adoptive children. The state would argue this law is not discriminating on its face, but rather has a discriminatory impact and when the state law is not discriminating on its face the discriminatory impact must be intended by the state and here the state did not intend to discriminate. The state would argue that race is not the sole factor in the adoption process, but merely one factor in adoption placement.

However, a citizen adopting a child that was not given a child based on their race could argue that this law is not necessary to further the intent of the state to make the best adoption fit because the law refers to race on the face and does not refer to other factors that should be considered. This law is not the least restrictive means to achieve the state's goal of obtaining the best fit.

This legislation should be redrafted accordingly to eliminate foreseeable litigation that will arise when the adopting parents sue pursuant to their equal protection rights.

CONSTITUTIONAL LAW
Answer to Question 4

Domestic Violence Act

Congress has broad powers under the commerce clause and its other enumerated powers. However, the Supreme Court's decision in <u>Lopez</u> indicated that there were limits on Congress' power under the commerce clause. The <u>Lopez</u> decision indicated that some laws have nothing to do with interstate commerce. For example, possession of a firearm within a certain distance of a schoolyard is not an economic activity and does not relate to interstate commerce. The <u>Lopez</u> decision stated that the areas of crime, education and family law have traditionally been the domain of the states. Purely local activities with no economic impact should be reserved to the state legislatures.

Section #1

Section #1 is probably not a constitutional exercise of the commerce power. Although the act states that domestic violence crimes often result in economic loss, it is still unconstitutional. <u>Lopez</u> stated that under its commerce power, Congress can pass laws that regulate:

    1. the instrumentalities of interstate commerce,

    2. the channels of interstate commerce, and

    3. activities that substantially affect interstate commerce.

Additionally, Congress may regulate purely local activities if they are economic activities and taken together cumulatively, they substantially affect interstate commerce.

Crimes of domestic violence are not economic activities. It is very unlikely that the court would apply the cumulative effects doctrine to domestic violence crimes. Congress would need to provide some evidence of the effect on interstate commerce, because it is not obvious that domestic violence crimes substantially affect interstate commerce. Furthermore, criminal law is a traditional domain of the states. Therefore, it is likely that Section #1 is unconstitutional. It is not within Congress' power under the commerce clause.

Section #2

This section, like Section #1, appears to be invalid. Congress does not have the power under the commerce clause to regulate possession of firearms. This is a purely local activity, and is not economic in nature. In fact, this law is similar to the law struck down in <u>Lopez</u> as unconstitutional (possession of a firearm near school grounds). As mentioned previously, it does not matter that the act states that "domestic violence crimes often result in economic losses." Congress has to show that domestic violence crimes substantially affect interstate commerce.

Section #3

This section is probably valid under the commerce clause, but invalid under the First Amendment. This section, unlike Sections #1 and #2, is valid under the commerce clause. This section regulates the instrumentalities of interstate commerce – the mail.

However, this section probably violates the First Amendment. It regulates the <u>content</u> of speech, by outlawing transmission of certain materials in the mail. The government can regulate and even ban obscene material. However, this law is overbroad because it regulates material that is not obscene. Obscene material is defined as:

        1. appealing to the prurient interest in sex, as defined by community standards,

        2. patently offensive, as defined by community standards,

        3. lacking serious value, as defined by a rational reasonable person standard.

This law is overbroad because it is not limited to obscene material. It also regulates "indecent or sexually explicit material." The word "indecent" is also vague, making it difficult to comply with the statute. The law is unconstitutional because it is overbroad and vague. Furthermore, it regulates <u>content</u> of speech, and is invalid under the strict scrutiny test. The law is not narrowly tailored to a compelling government interest.

MBE SUBJECTS - PRACTICE ESSAY QUESTIONS

CONSTITUTIONAL LAW
Answer to Question 5

There are many constitutional issues presented by the instant fact scenario. To begin, it is important to set forth some general principles of constitutional law applicable to the instant cases.

The Constitution grants to Congress several powers. However, these powers are limited to those enumerated in the Constitution. Therefore, unless the power is expressly granted to the Congress, it is reserved to the states. Some provisions, such as the Necessary and Proper Clause and the Commerce Clause, have given Congress great powers over the years. However, their exercise must ultimately be tied to the Constitutional mandates. Further, the Necessary and Proper Clause can be used only in conjunction with another enumerated power.

Among the powers greatest in scope for Congress are those found in the Commerce Clause, 13th Amendment, and the 14th Amendment. In the instant case there is no indication that Congress has tied the law in any way to commerce and thus the Commerce Clause is inapplicable.

The 13th Amendment grants power to Congress to eliminate all "badges of slavery" and this power is not limited to use against the states; that is, the 13th Amendment power can be used against private individuals and entities.

The 14th Amendment grants to Congress, *inter alia*, the power to proscribe denial of Equal Protection of the Laws. This power can be used only against states or individuals acting intimately with the states, that is, where the state and private individual are so wrapped up as to give it the appearance of state action. The 14th Amendment prohibits classifications based on race, gender, religion, etc. unless they meet particular tests (outlined below).

Before analyzing the three suits, it should be noted that it is presumed the constitutional concerns of standing, etc. are not in issue given that the facts state the Court "will decide all three cases."

Suit #1

The first suit is brought by a private school engaging in racial discrimination. Congress will argue that the law is proper as applied to this group under both the 13th and 14th Amendments. Their argument under the 13th Amendment is quite strong given the prior rules set forth. Congress is not barred from acting on private entities under the 13th Amendment because that Amendment allows proscription of all badges of slavery, by states and private individuals. Further, the discrimination in issue, admitting only whites, is certainly a badge of slavery. Thus, Congress should win this case under the 13th Amendment as they are merely prohibiting the badges of slavery.

Congress will also argue that the 14th Amendment grants them this power. However, unlike the 13th, the 14th Amendment does not allow them this power. However, if it had, Congress would argue that the school is classifying based on race and as such has to meet the strict scrutiny standard, which they cannot, and thus the power is valid. The strict scrutiny standard applies to the suspect classifications of race and alienage, along with classifications including fundamental rights. This standard holds that the classification is invalid unless the state can prove it is necessary to meet a compelling state interest. Congress would argue, and likely succeed if it could get there, that the instant classification fails the test. In the end, Congress should win under the 13th Amendment, but fail under the 14th.

Suit #2

Suit #2 involves a private school discriminating on the basis of gender. Because this is not a badge of slavery, the 13th Amendment is inapplicable. Also, because only the 14th Amendment is pertinent, and it applies to states – not private entities, Congress is without power as to this school. However, if it were allowed, Congress would argue that the school is classifying based on gender and cannot meet the test of intermediate scrutiny. Intermediate scrutiny is applied to gender and legitimacy classifications. The test requires the state prove that it is substantially related to an important government interest. However, because the Congress has no power over private entities under the 14th Amendment, the school should win this case.

Suit #3

The final suit involves a private school discriminating on the basis of religion. Again, the 13th Amendment is inapplicable here because this is not a badge of slavery. Also, like the previous cases, the 14th Amendment gives Congress no power here because the actors are private actors, not state actors. If Congress could argue that it was enforcing the Equal Protection Clause like it would argue in all the previous cases, there is some question as to the standard to apply. While religion is not currently thought of as an intermediate scrutiny category, the Court would be within reason to find it so. If so, it would be tested under the same standard set forth earlier for intermediate scrutiny. If not, the classification would be analyzed under rational basis under the 14th. This test requires the challenging party to prove that the law is not rationally related to a proper government purpose. This test is very hard to challenge. However, because the instant actors are beyond the state's power under the 14th Amendment, the school will win.

Another potential argument is that the Congress is someone using a 1st Amendment power, via the 14th, to prohibit the "state" from discriminating on the basis of religion. If that was so, the Congress would argue that strict scrutiny applies because the state cannot endorse religion unless they meet that high standard. First, the Congress would have to prove that the school is a state actor, which they will not be able to do. If they could, Congress would argue the state must meet strict scrutiny.

MBE SUBJECTS - PRACTICE ESSAY QUESTIONS

CONSTITUTIONAL LAW
Answer to Question 6

1. The first issue concerns the action of Alice Allen, asserting that the statute is unconstitutional.

The issue is whether Alice Allen has standing to pursue such a suit. Typically to bring a suit there must be a case or controversy and an actual injury, not newly ideological has to be suffered, furthermore there has to be re-dressibility, meaning the court can remedy the injury.

A taxpayer may only have standing as such if they are directly "injured" by the tax or if they feel congress has excluded its spending authority as promulgated by in the Establishment Clause.

In this case, Alice Allen is not bringing her action based on taxes, but to assert Congress exceeding its authority. Whether or not easily ascertainable. Provided Congress isn't in violation of other constitutional rights what they spend money on is up to them if reasonably based on providing the general welfare. Without providing that landowners will be justly compensated. Congress' act would be a violation of a fundamental property interest. But, as stated in the facts, Congress has provided for just compensation for the taking of people's land.

In light of the above, it does not appear that Congress acted beyond their powers, and therefore Alice Allen has no standing and the case should be dismissed.

2. The next issue concerns Billy Burton's refusal to sell his land to the Interior Department and their suit to effectuate the appropriation. As discussed above, the government can take land under the "Takings Clause" provided it's reasonably based on providing for the general welfare and landowners are justly compensated.

Whether congress was acting for the general welfare is debatable. But assuming they were, plus the fact they were willing to pay fair market value, is reason to decide in their favor. The fact that the land was unusual and was extremely profitable makes no difference, as long as the compensation is just.

3. The final action to consider is that of the State of Adam seeking declaratory judgment that the President's order was unconstitutional. Outside of the President's initial veto power of Congress' acts with or without his approval (overriding his veto), the President does not have constitutional authority to effect a change or act inconsistently with an act of Congress. In fact, it is his duty to uphold congressional acts.

In this case, the President's order to reduce the annual spending is contrary to Congress's act, and is therefore unconstitutional.

MBE SUBJECTS - PRACTICE ESSAY QUESTIONS

CONSTITUTIONAL LAW
Answer to Question 7

Alberts was convicted on the Federal 1996 law that required all cars (vehicles) affecting interstate commerce be equipped with a "Clean Pipe" for the exhaust system. The Federal government, Congress, had the authority to regulate interstate commerce via the United States (US) constitution. This is a very broad power and anything that tends to relate to interstate commerce is a valid law as long as it is rationally related to an important government (Gov't.) interest. The 1996 legislation was aimed at reducing the pollution. This is an important government interest. Is it rationally related to that interest?

The law does appear to be rational; they require a pipe that is aimed at reducing pollution. However, Alberts may argue that the punishment, arrest and conviction, was not rational, and that a stiff fine is a better punishment. Although this may be true, if pollution is a problem, the gov't. has an interest to reduce the pollution.

I forgot to mention above whether A's arrest by the federal law, was this within the commerce clause, i.e.: Within the federal governments power? As stated above, the Congress has broad discretion with regulating under the commerce clause. However, A was driving between 2 small towns within State A (s), A did not cross between state lines, affecting interstate commerce; i.e. that A's vehicle was not engaged in affecting interstate commerce.

The gov't. can argue that this was interstate commerce because all roads within every state, and all cars have some impact at some time, therefore A's car did impact interstate commerce in some way (even if small way).

However, I think this is a weak argument because A's vehicle was being driven within the state, and was not engaged in affecting interstate commerce. Additionally, a small dirt road has little impact on interstate commerce. The dirt roads are primarily for small communities, especially ones where there are few out of state visitors. Therefore, A's conviction should be overturned.

B's and C's convictions.
B's and C's convictions were in 1999 and were for violation of the state law requiring that all cars driven in S have the "Scrub Pipe." This law is expressly different than the federal law. Where a federal law and a state law are in direct conflict, the federal law applies because of the Supremacy Clause of the U.S. Constitution. This provides that the laws of the federal gov't. are superior to those of the states if there is a conflict. This is true in the case at hand. The federal law requires a Clean Pipe and State law requires a Scrub Pipe. Applying the Supremacy Clause, the State law is invalid. If there is no direct conflict, a state law is OK if it does not conflict with the intent of Congress with respect to the federal law. In this case at hand, there is a direct conflict, so the State law is invalid.

Because B and C were convicted under an <u>invalid</u> state law, their convictions should be overturned.

The answer (analysis, not results) would be different with respect to B's and C's convictions if the federal law had been repealed before their arrests in 1999. If the law had been repealed, then the state law would not have been invalid, and the Supremacy Clause would not have invalidated the state law. Although I think the end results would be the same (that B's and C's convictions should be overturned), the analysis would be different.

Analysis if the law had been repealed:

A state may not make a law that negatively impacts interstate commerce. Here, S wants all vehicles in its state to have a certain kind of exhaust pipe (Scrub Pipe) for all vehicles driven in the state. This puts an undue burden on interstate commerce. Vehicles, such as the one B was driving, would have to re-route through a different state, or change the vehicle's exhaust system every time it went through S. This is especially true if there are other viable pollution reducing pipes available and are OK to use within other states.

Because Barton was driving across many states, so it involved in interstate commerce, and so this statute directly affects B. This is the type of thing that the Constitution is trying to prevent by prohibiting states to unduly burden interstate commerce. B's conviction should be overturned.

C was not driving across state lines, but he was a federal employee. The state may not impose its laws against the federal government. It can't impose its laws against individual government workers, ex: a state may not assess tax on a federal agency, but it may tax the income its employees earn. In the case at hand, the mail truck is federal property. S may not impose its pipe restrictions on property of the federal government. In addition, the mail carrying business has a direct impact on interstate commerce. So C's conviction should be overturned for this reason (unduly burdening interstate commerce) as well as the limitations states have in applying their laws to the federal gov't.

MBE SUBJECTS – RELEASED ESSAY QUESTIONS

CONTRACTS
MEE Question – July 2007

ANALYSIS

Legal Problems: (1)(a) Did Baker's letter of May 1 constitute an offer?

(1)(b) Did Café Owner's oral response on the morning of May 7 constitute a counteroffer?

(2)   Did Café accept Baker's offer?

(3)   Did the contract between Baker and Café satisfy the Statute of Frauds?

DISCUSSION

Summary

A valid contract requires an offer, an acceptance and, when as here, the contract cannot be performed within one year, a writing that satisfies the Statute of Frauds. Here, Baker made an offer to work for Café that was accepted when Café's Owner sent an acceptance by express mail to Baker. It is irrelevant that Baker did not read the acceptance. The fact that an earlier rejection was mailed is also irrelevant because a rejection, unlike an acceptance, is effective only upon receipt, and Baker did not receive the rejection before receiving the acceptance. When both a rejection and an acceptance are sent, whichever is received first is effective. Lastly, the writings, being signed, satisfy the requirements of the Statute of Frauds. Therefore, Café has an enforceable contract.

Point One(a) (20-30%)
Baker's signed letter of May 1 to Café agreeing to work as a pastry chef for Café is a valid offer.

A person makes an offer when the person communicates to another a statement of "willingness to enter into a bargain, so made as to justify" the other person who hears the statement "in understanding that his assent to that bargain is invited and will conclude it." RESTATEMENT (SECOND) OF CONTRACTS § 24 (1981). Here, Baker's letter of May 1 to Café was an offer because an objective recipient of the letter, such as Café, would reasonably conclude that assent would create a contract.

An offer cannot ripen into a contract by acceptance unless its terms are reasonably certain. *Id.* § 33(1). Here, the terms were clear and certain and identified the parties, the subject matter, and the price.

Point One(b) (20-30%)

Café Owner's phone call to Baker on the morning of May 7 asking if he would possibly work for less was not a counteroffer but merely a request for changed terms.

A counteroffer is a statement from the offeree to the offeror, relating to the same subject matter as the original offer but suggesting a substituted bargain from the original terms. *Id.* § 39(1). Generally, if an offeree makes a counteroffer, the offeree can no longer accept the original offer. *Id.* § 39(2). Here, Café's Owner said to Baker "The $100,000 is pretty stiff. Could you possibly consider working for less?" This utterance is not a counteroffer because it did not offer substitute terms to Baker and did not indicate any unwillingness to conclude the bargain on Baker's terms if Baker would not accept an alternative salary. All Café's Owner did was ask Baker if he could possibly work for less. Café's Owner proposed no alternative salary. Because Café's Owner's call to Baker was not a counteroffer, but merely a request for unspecified changed terms, it did not preclude Café's later acceptance of Baker's offer.

Point Two (25-35%)

Although Café's Owner initially rejected Baker's offer in writing, he later accepted the offer. Because Baker received the acceptance before he received the rejection, Baker's offer is deemed accepted.

A rejection is a manifestation of intent not to accept an offer. *Id.* § 38(2). A rejection terminates the offeree's power to accept an offer. *Id.* § 38(1). However, a rejection does not extinguish the offeree's right to accept an offer until the rejection is received by the offeror. *Id.* § 40. Here, Café's Owner's letter stating "I am no longer interested in hiring you" clearly manifests an intent not to go forward with the bargain and constitutes a rejection of Baker's offer.

However, Café's Owner's second letter, in which Café agreed to Baker's terms, was an acceptance because it was a manifestation of assent to the terms of an offer made in a manner invited by the offer. *Id.* § 50(1). The question then becomes which of the two letters sent by Café's Owner is effective, the rejection or the acceptance.

An acceptance is effective upon dispatch under the so-called "mailbox rule." *Id.* § 63. A rejection is effective only upon receipt. But when an acceptance is sent after a rejection (that is, both the acceptance and the rejection are sent), whichever gets to the recipient first is effective. *Id.* § 40. Here, Café's letter of acceptance was received by Baker first, while the letter containing the rejection was still on the way to Baker. *See id.* § 68 (a communication is received when it comes into the possession of the person to whom it is addressed). The fact that Baker did not read the letter does not alter this result. Because the acceptance was the first communication received, it is effective. Therefore, Café accepted Baker's offer to work for Café, and a contract was created.

Point Three (25-35%)

If a contract cannot be performed within a year, it must meet the requirements of the Statute of Frauds. Here the contract satisfies that statute and, therefore, is enforceable.

A contract must satisfy the Statute of Frauds if it cannot be fully performed within one year. *Id.* § 130. Here, the two-year employment requirement cannot be completed in one year, and therefore the contract is within the purview of the Statute of Frauds and must satisfy the requirements of the Statute of Frauds to be enforceable.

A contract within the Statute of Frauds satisfies that statute and is enforceable if it is evidenced by a writing signed by "the party to be charged," which (a) reasonably identifies the subject matter of the contract; (b) is sufficient to indicate that a contract has been made; and (c) "states with reasonable certainty the essential terms" of the contract. *Id.* § 131.

Here, each party signed a writing that is sufficient under these criteria as it identifies the position, person, term, and salary. Therefore, the Statute of Frauds is satisfied and the employment contract is enforceable. Because this is a personal services contract, if Baker refuses to work for Café, Café can sue Baker for damages, but cannot get specific performance.

MBE SUBJECTS – RELEASED ESSAY QUESTIONS

CONTRACTS
MEE Question – July 2008

ANALYSIS

Legal Problems: (1)   Should Rancher's damages for harm to Ranch be measured by the cost of completion ($500,000) or by the difference in value ($20,000)?

             (2)   Were Rancher's losses from the roping clinics foreseeable?

             (3)   Were Rancher's losses from the roping clinics ascertainable with reasonable certainty?

             (4)   Should the award of damages for Rancher's losses from the roping clinics take into account expenses he avoided?

             (5)   Did the damage award properly account for losses Rancher could reasonably have avoided by mitigation?

DISCUSSION

Summary

Under basic principles of contract law an injured party is entitled to a damage award that will put him in the position he would have been in had the contract been performed. Here, with regard to the harm to Ranch, the question is whether the proper measure of damages is the cost of completion or the difference in value. Although the answer is not certain, the court probably did not err in awarding the cost of completion. With regard to the roping clinics, damages for Rancher's inability to conduct the clinics are recoverable only if foreseeable and reasonably certain. Here, while the damages are likely foreseeable, it is less clear that they are sufficiently certain. Even if the loss from the inability to conduct the clinics was foreseeable and certain, damages should have been reduced by any amount saved due to not conducting the clinics. Further, damages should be reduced by any amounts that could have been avoided through mitigation.

Point One (40–50%)
Rancher is entitled to cost-of-completion damages because the breach appears to be willful and only cost-of-completion damages will enable Rancher to use Ranch for its intended purpose.

For breach of contract, the injured party may be entitled to expectation damages. These damages are intended to put the injured party in the same position as if the contract had been performed. *See* E. ALLAN FARNSWORTH, FARNSWORTH ON CONTRACTS § 12.8, at 190 (2004). Since Ranch was not restored to its pre-exploration condition, Rancher is entitled to damages. One measure of damages is the cost of restoration—here, $500,000. *Id.* § 12.13. However, where an award might be wasteful, such as when the cost to restore (here $500,000) would greatly exceed the difference in value (here $20,000), damages may be measured by the difference in value. *See Jacob & Youngs v. Kent*, 129 N.E. 889 (N.Y. 1921). But when the breach appears to be willful, as is the case here, and only completion of the contract will enable the non-breaching party to use the land for its intended purposes, the cost of completion is considered the appropriate damage award. *See American Standard, Inc. v. Schectman*, 439 N.Y.S.2d 529 (App. Div. 1981). Therefore, the court probably did not err in awarding Rancher the cost of returning Ranch to its pre-exploration condition.

Point Two (5–10%)
Rancher's losses based on his failure to conduct roping clinics were foreseeable.

Contract damages must be foreseeable to be recoverable. FARNSWORTH ON CONTRACTS § 12.14. Damages are foreseeable if a reasonable person in the position of the breaching party would have known at the time the contract was made that the damages were likely to occur as a result of the breach. *Hadley v. Baxendale*, 156 Eng. Rep. 145 (Ex. 1854). Here, it is likely that Gasco would have known that if it did not restore Ranch, Rancher would not be able to hold his roping clinics. In fact, Rancher specifically told Gasco of his plans to hold the clinics on Ranch. Because of this direct communication, the damages caused by Rancher's inability to conduct the roping clinics were foreseeable.

Point Three (5–10%)
Rancher can recover foreseeable losses from his inability to conduct the roping clinics only if those losses also were sufficiently certain.

Contract damages must be proved with reasonable certainty to be recoverable. FARNSWORTH ON CONTRACTS § 12.15. Here, Rancher faces the problem of a "new business." Although Rancher had conducted clinics on the road in the past, Rancher had not conducted clinics on Ranch. While most states no longer apply a per se rule denying recovery to all new businesses, courts still are reluctant to award lost profits to new businesses, because such profits "are regarded as being too remote, contingent and speculative to meet the standard of reasonable certainty." *Western Publ'g Co. v. Mind Games, Inc.*, 944 F. Supp. 754, 756 (E.D. Wis. 1996).

Here, it is a close call whether there is sufficient certainty to award Rancher his lost profits from the roping clinics. On one hand, there is no reasonable certainty that the clinics would have been a success, or that 50 people would have attended each year. On the other hand, Rancher has run roping clinics in the past and so has some track record on which to base a damage award. *See Fun Motors of Longview v. Gratty, Inc.*, 51 S.W.3d 756 (Tex. Civ. App. 2001) (experience of the person involved relevant in determining certainty of damages).

[NOTE TO GRADERS: An applicant could reasonably reach either conclusion on this point. An applicant may receive extra credit for noting that this award would be reduced to its present value amount.]

Point Four (10–20%)

Rancher's award should have been reduced by the expenses Rancher would have incurred in conducting the roping clinics.

Contract damage awards must take into account costs avoided because of the breach. FARNSWORTH ON CONTRACTS § 12.9, at 209. Here, even if Rancher's claimed damages of $300,000 were foreseeable and certain, that amount represents the gross amount that Rancher would have received. In order to receive that amount, Rancher would have incurred expenses. Gasco's breach saved him those expenses. Therefore, even if the award of $300,000 was foreseeable and reasonably certain, it should be reduced to the net amount Rancher would have earned after expenses. *See, e.g., Lieberman v. Templar Motor Co.*, 140 N.E. 222, 225 (N.Y. 1923).

Point Five (10–20%)
It is uncertain whether Rancher's award should have been reduced by the amount of loss Rancher could have avoided by going on the road with his roping clinics.

The $300,000 award of damages may be reduced by the amount Rancher could have earned by mitigating his loss. Mitigation requires the injured party to take reasonable steps to reduce the damages. FARNSWORTH ON CONTRACTS § 12.12, at 232. Here, Rancher offered clinics on the road before he bought Ranch. After the breach Rancher could have resumed these activities as mitigation, as that alternative may not be viewed as substantially different from or inferior to the clinics he planned to offer on the ranch. *Id.* However, the need to travel might make this alternative inferior. *See Parker v. Twentieth Century-Fox Film Corp.*, 474 P.2d 689 (Cal. 1970). Therefore, it is uncertain whether Rancher's award should be reduced by the amount he could have earned by offering the roping clinics on the road.

MBE SUBJECTS – RELEASED ESSAY QUESTIONS

CONTRACTS
MEE Question – July 2009

ANALYSIS
(Contracts II.A. & C.; VII.D.)

Legal Problems: (1)   Was Resident's promise to pay Sam $1,000 supported by consideration?

                           (2)   In the absence of bargained-for consideration, can Sam enforce Resident's promise under the material benefit (moral consideration) rule?

                           (3)   In the absence of bargained-for consideration, can Sam enforce Resident's promise under the theory of promissory estoppel?

DISCUSSION

Summary

Sam cannot recover the $1,000 under the theory that Resident's promise was supported by consideration as there is no evidence of a bargained-for exchange. Sam may be able to recover if the material benefit (or moral consideration) rule applies because Resident made the promise to pay $1,000 in recognition of a benefit received. Sam may also be able to recover under the theory of promissory estoppel if he acted in reasonable reliance on Resident's promise. However, Sam may recover less than the full $1,000 under both the material benefit rule and the theory of promissory estoppel.

Point One (25–35%)
Sam cannot recover under the theory that Resident's promise was supported by consideration because that promise was not part of a bargained-for exchange.

To be legally enforceable, a promise generally must be supported by consideration, which is shown through bargained-for exchange. This means that the promisor must have sought and received something of legal value in exchange for the promise. *See* RESTATEMENT (SECOND) OF CONTRACTS § 71. Here, there was no bargained-for exchange.

Sam might argue that his action in rescuing the dog and/or Sam's promise to apply for paramedic training constitutes consideration for Resident's promise to pay $1,000. However, neither of those arguments will prevail. Resident's promise to pay the $1,000 was not made in exchange for Sam's rescue of the dog, but instead was made in recognition of that prior action. With regard to Sam's promise to apply for paramedic training, Resident did not seek that promise in exchange for the promise to pay the $1,000. Resident's promise was not part of an exchange and therefore the consideration necessary to make Resident's promise legally enforceable is absent.

Point Two (15–25%)
Sam may be able to recover if the material benefit (moral consideration) rule applies, but possibly may not receive the full $1,000 Resident promised him.

Some states recognize an exception to the past consideration limitation in cases in which the promise is made after receipt of a significant benefit. This exception is set out in the Restatement (Second) of Contracts § 86 (the material benefit rule) and encapsulates cases in which moral consideration was found to provide a basis for recovery. The material benefit rule states that a promise not supported by consideration may be enforceable if it is "made in recognition of a benefit previously received by the promisor from the promisee . . . ." RESTATEMENT (SECOND) OF CONTRACTS § 86(1); *see Webb v. McGowin*, 168 So. 196 (Ala. 1935). Here, Resident promised to give Sam $1,000 in recognition of Sam's act of saving Resident's dog. Thus, it could be argued that the material benefit rule applies because Resident received a benefit from Sam and made the promise to give Sam $1,000 in recognition of that benefit.

However, the material benefit rule does not apply (and the promise is not enforceable) if the promisee conferred the benefit as a gift, or to the extent that the value of the promise is disproportionate to the benefit conferred. RESTATEMENT (SECOND) OF CONTRACTS § 86(2). Here, it is unclear whether Sam intended to confer a gift upon Resident. He may have been acting out of pure selflessness when he rescued the dog, or he may have believed that his heroic action would result in a financial reward.

Even if it is determined that Sam did not intend to confer a gift (and that Resident's promise is therefore enforceable), a court might limit recovery to something less than the full $1,000 if it finds that $1,000 is disproportionate to the value of the rescue of the dog.

Point Three (35–45%)
Sam may be able to recover some or all of the $1,000 if the doctrine of promissory estoppel applies. Promissory estoppel requires that the promisee show that a promise existed, that a detrimental change in position was made in reasonable reliance on the promise, and that enforcement of the promise is the only way to avoid injustice.

The doctrine of promissory estoppel allows the enforcement of gratuitous promises to avoid harm to individuals who have relied on those promises. *See* RESTATEMENT (SECOND) OF CONTRACTS § 90. In order to establish a promissory estoppel claim, all of the following must be shown: (1) the promisor, when making the promise, should have reasonably expected that the promisee would change his position in reliance on the promise; (2) the promisee did in fact change position in reliance on the promise; (3) the change in position was to the promisee's detriment and injustice can be avoided only by enforcing the promise. *Id.*

Here, the facts state that Resident promised to pay $1,000. Sam did change his position in reliance on that promise by incurring a $1,000 debt. Resident might argue that Sam's applying to the cosmetology program was not reasonable reliance because the promise was specific to a different program—Resident said, "If you are going to start paramedic training, I want to help you." However, Resident also said, "I want to compensate you for your heroism," and Sam could reasonably interpret that remark as indicating that Resident's promise to give him $1,000 was a promise to compensate him for rescuing Resident's dog and was not conditioned on his career choice. Thus, it is possible that Sam could recover that portion of the $1,000 promised by Resident that is determined to be the amount required to avoid injustice.

MBE SUBJECTS – RELEASED ESSAY QUESTIONS

CONTRACTS
MEE Question – February 2011

ANALYSIS

Legal Problems: (1)(a)   Was a contract formed when Designer offered Retailer a discounted payoff in exchange for early cash payment; Retailer responded, "Thanks. That's a good deal. I don't have the cash to pay you now. I'll do it if I can get a loan"; and Designer replied, "That will be great"?

                (1)(b)   If a contract was formed, did Retailer breach that contract by making only minimal efforts to obtain the necessary cash?

                (2)   If Retailer breached the contract, is Retailer liable for Designer's loss caused by Designer's inability to make a planned investment that would have netted a $35,000 gain for Designer?

                (3)   If Retailer breached the contract, is Retailer liable for punitive damages?

DISCUSSION

Summary

Retailer and Designer entered into a new, modified contract which Retailer breached. Designer's opening statement was an offer. However, because Retailer's response added a condition, his need to take out a loan to obtain the cash to pay early, the response did not constitute acceptance of Designer's offer. Rather, Retailer's response was a counteroffer, which Designer accepted, thereby creating a contract. That contract contained Retailer's implied promise to make a good-faith effort to borrow the needed cash. Retailer did make some efforts to get the cash, but these efforts were not sufficient to constitute good faith. Therefore, Retailer breached the contract by not acting in good faith.

The ordinary measure of damages in a contract action is expectation damages, which aim to put the nonbreaching party in the position he expected to be in following full performance. Here, if Retailer had not breached, Designer would have had $15,000 to make an investment that would have netted a $35,000 gain. Because these losses were foreseeable and reasonably certain, Designer will be able to recover his actual damages.

Designer will not be able to collect punitive damages because Retailer's conduct was not tortious.

Point One(a) (40%)

Designer made an offer to Retailer to modify their existing contract. Retailer did not accept the offer. Instead, Retailer made a counteroffer, which Designer then accepted, forming a modified contract.

Designer's statement "I need cash quickly to make an investment. . . . [I]f you promise now to pay me $15,000 in cash by the 25th of this month, I will accept that payment as satisfying your obligation under our contract for this year" was an offer to enter into a new, modified contract. Retailer did not accept this offer. Instead, Retailer said, "Thanks. That's a good deal. I don't have the cash to pay you now. I'll do it if I can get a loan." This response, impliedly making Retailer's obligation to perform conditioned upon his getting a loan, contained an additional term and was, therefore, a counteroffer. *See* RESTATEMENT (SECOND) OF CONTRACTS § 59. Designer's response, "That will be great," indicated assent to the terms of Retailer's counteroffer even though it did not include specific words of acceptance. There was consideration for the modified contract under the bargained-for-exchange test because Designer agreed to accept a reduced payment and Retailer agreed to pay early if he could get a loan. *See id.* § 71.

It might be argued that Retailer's response did not constitute a counteroffer because Retailer did not explicitly state that his performance was conditioned upon getting a loan. However, Retailer's response made it clear that Retailer could not complete the contract unless Retailer obtained a loan, and Designer certainly understood this. Therefore, the parties entered into a contract on the terms offered by Retailer.

[NOTE: An examinee may discuss this issue in terms of an amendment to the existing contract. Such an analysis should receive full credit.]

Point One(b) (30%)
Retailer breached the contract by failing to make good-faith efforts to obtain the necessary loan.

Retailer might argue that because he did not get the loan, his obligation to pay never arose and he was not in breach. In fact, the language used only suggested that Retailer's obligation to perform would be subject to a condition precedent, that is, his getting the loan.

However, the contract contained an implied obligation to make good-faith efforts to obtain a loan. Without such an implied obligation, the contract would be illusory because Retailer would have no obligation. *See Wood v. Lucy, Lady Duff-Gordon*, 222 N.Y. 88, 118 N.E. 214 (1917); *Mezzanotte v. Freeland*, 200 S.E.2d 410 (N.C. Ct. App. 1973).

To satisfy the requirement of making good-faith efforts, Retailer must have taken reasonable steps to obtain the necessary cash. Here, Retailer did no more than pick up two loan applications which he did not even submit. His actions were not sufficient to constitute a good-faith effort to obtain the loan. Retailer therefore breached the contract.

Point Two (20%)
Designer is entitled to recover from Retailer his actual damages, which would include the gain that he would have realized on the investment he intended to make.

The normal measure of damages for breach of contract is expectation damages, which aim to give the nonbreaching party the benefit of his bargain. *See* FARNSWORTH, CONTRACTS § 12.1 (3d ed. 2004). Expectation damages must be foreseeable, *see Hadley v. Baxendale*, 156 Eng. Rep. 145 (1854), and proved with reasonable certainty, *see* FARNSWORTH, *supra*, § 12.1.

Here, when Designer made the initial offer, he stated that he needed cash quickly to make a potentially profitable investment. On these facts, it is foreseeable that Designer would not be able to make the investment when Retailer failed to make timely payment. It is not necessary that the profitability of the investment be foreseeable at the time of the breach. It is enough that the fact of the investment is foreseeable, and here it was, because Designer told Retailer that Designer needed the cash to make an investment, making the damages foreseeable. The facts state that Designer can prove that he would have made $35,000 on the investment, making the damages reasonably certain. Therefore, Retailer is liable for Designer's actual damages.

Point Three (10%)

Designer is not entitled to recover punitive damages because such damages are not ordinarily recoverable in a contract action.

Punitive damages are not generally recoverable as an element of damages in a breach of contract action "unless the conduct constituting the breach is also a tort for which punitive damages [can be recovered]." RESTATEMENT (SECOND) OF CONTRACTS § 355. The facts do not indicate any conduct on the part of Retailer that would constitute a tort compensable through punitive damages. Therefore, Designer is not entitled to recover punitive damages.

MBE SUBJECTS – RELEASED ESSAY QUESTIONS

CONTRACTS
MEE Question – February 2012

ANALYSIS

Legal Problems

(1)   Did RepairCo substantially perform its contractual obligations by the contract due date?

(2)   Can RepairCo recover some portion of the contract price on the theory that the contract was divisible?

(3)   Can RepairCo recover some portion of the contract price as restitution for part performance?

DISCUSSION

Summary

RepairCo neither fully nor substantially performed its contractual obligations. Therefore, RepairCo is not entitled to recover the full contract price. However, RepairCo may be entitled to recover some portion of the contract price if the contract is divisible. If the contract is not divisible, RepairCo may be entitled to restitution for part performance.

Point One (50%)
RepairCo did not substantially perform its contractual obligations when it repaired only 6 of the required 10 cars by the contract due date.

RepairCo did not fully perform its contractual obligations. However, RepairCo might argue that it substantially performed its obligations under the contract and therefore is entitled to recover on that contract. Substantial performance is present when a party completes its contractual obligations with "no uncured material failure." RESTATEMENT (SECOND) OF CONTRACTS § 237. Whether a failure to perform is material depends on several factors, including (1) the extent to which the injured party will be deprived of the benefit he reasonably expected, (2) the extent to which the injured party can be adequately compensated for the part of that benefit of which he will be deprived, (3) the extent to which the other party failing to perform or to offer to perform will suffer forfeiture, (4) the likelihood that the party failing to perform will cure his failure, and (5) the extent to which the behavior of the party failing to perform comports with standards of good faith and fair dealing. *Id.* § 241.

Here, because its failure to perform was a material breach, RepairCo did not substantially perform. First, it repaired only 6 of the 10 vehicles, thereby denying GreenCar a material portion of the benefit GreenCar reasonably expected. GreenCar could not make other arrangements to obtain that lost material benefit (the use of 4 "green" cars on April 22) because it was the only company with the specialized cars, and GreenCar was not aware until April 21 that only 6 of the 10 cars had been repaired. Second, while GreenCar might be compensated in damages for some of the harm caused by not having a full fleet of vehicles for the Earth Day parade, it could not be compensated for such non-economic harms as lost reputation. Third, RepairCo will not suffer forfeiture—it will not have to undo any work done and might recover some amount for the work it completed (*see* Points Two and Three). Fourth, RepairCo cannot cure its failure because the contract required it to deliver 10 cars on April 21, which it did not and cannot do. Finally, RepairCo's failure to perform likely did not comport with standards of good faith and fair dealing. This is because it allowed the work stoppage to continue so that it could teach its workers a lesson, rather than accepting their terms, as it intended to do eventually, and completing the contract.

Because RepairCo failed to substantially perform its contractual obligations, GreenCar is excused from its obligation to pay on the contract. "Where a contract is made to perform work and no agreement is made as to payment, the work must be substantially performed before payment can be demanded." *Stewart v. Newbury*, 115 N.E. 984, 985 (N.Y. 1917). Here, the facts do not indicate that progress payments or periodic payments were negotiated or agreed to. Thus, RepairCo is not entitled to recover on the entire contract on the theory of substantial performance.

Point Two (25%)
If RepairCo establishes that the contract with GreenCar is divisible, RepairCo may be entitled to recover an amount less than the full $10,000 contract price.

If RepairCo's performance is divisible, RepairCo may be entitled to some payment. *See Gill v. Johnstown Lumber Co.*, 25 A. 120 (Pa. 1892). A contract is said to be divisible if the performances to be exchanged can be divided into corresponding pairs of part performances in such a way that a court will treat the elements of each pair as if the parties had agreed they were equivalents. E. ALLAN FARNSWORTH, FARNSWORTH ON CONTRACTS § 8.13 (3d ed. 2004). Here, RepairCo could argue that although the contract stated one total contract price ($10,000), the contract also stated an amount per vehicle. Thus, the total payment could easily be divided among the 10 very similar vehicles, which required similar work, with each car repair corresponding to $1,000 of GreenCar's payment. RepairCo could argue, therefore, that it is entitled to 6/10 of the $10,000, or $6,000, less any additional incidental or consequential losses resulting from its failure to repair the remaining 4 cars on April 21.

GreenCar could argue, however, that the contract is not divisible. GreenCar needed all 10 cars to meet its contractual obligation to supply 10 cars for the local Earth Day parade. "[T]here is no set formula which furnishes a foolproof method for determining in a given case just which contracts are severable and which are entire." *John v. United Advertising*, 439 P.2d 53, 56 (Colo. 1968). Thus, it is possible, but far from certain, that RepairCo could recover some part of the contract price from GreenCar on the theory that the contract is divisible.

Point Three (25%)
Even if the contract is not divisible, RepairCo may be entitled to restitution from GreenCar for the benefit it conferred in part performance.

Even if the contract is not divisible and RepairCo cannot recover on the contract, RepairCo may be entitled to some recovery from GreenCar as restitution for part performance so that GreenCar is not unjustly enriched. A party "is entitled to restitution for any benefit that he has conferred by way of part performance…in excess of the loss that he has caused by his own breach." RESTATEMENT (SECOND) OF CONTRACTS § 374(1); *Lancellotti v. Thomas*, 491 A.2d 117 (Pa. Super. Ct. 1985). RepairCo partially performed by delivering 6 of GreenCar's vehicles with the work done on the contract due date. Thus RepairCo may be entitled to restitution for the work done on those cars, less any additional incidental or consequential losses resulting from its failure to repair the remaining 4 cars on April 21. [NOTE: An examinee might properly refer to this form of possible recovery as either unjust enrichment or *quantum meruit*.]

MBE SUBJECTS – RELEASED ESSAY QUESTIONS

CONTRACTS
MEE Question – February 2013

ANALYSIS

Legal Problems

(1) What was the legal effect of the sailor's October 31 letter to the builder?

(2)(a) What was the legal effect of the builder's November 25 response to the sailor's October 31 letter?

(2)(b) What was the legal effect of the sailor's refusal to take and pay for the boat on December 15?

DISCUSSION

Summary

This is a sale of goods governed by the Uniform Commercial Code. Because the sailor had reasonable grounds for insecurity about the builder's ability to deliver the boat in a timely manner when the sailor learned about the strike on October 31, the sailor was legally justified in sending the letter to the builder seeking adequate assurance of the builder's performance pursuant to the contract. The builder's failure to provide such assurance within a reasonable time operated as a repudiation of the contract. However, the builder was free to retract the repudiation before the sailor either cancelled the contract or materially changed position in reliance on the builder's repudiation. The builder retracted the repudiation when he informed the sailor that the workers were back and that the boat would be delivered by the date stipulated in the parties' contract. Because the sailor had taken no action in response to the original repudiation, he no longer had the right to cancel the contract with the builder. The sailor's subsequent statement that "our contract is over" may have constituted repudiation by the sailor. In any event, when the sailor failed to perform on December 15, that constituted breach.

Point One (35%)

Because the sailor had reasonable grounds for insecurity with respect to the builder's performance, the sailor's letter to the builder was a justified demand seeking assurance of the builder's performance under the contract; failure of the builder to provide such assurance within a reasonable time constituted repudiation of the contract.

The sailor was legally justified in sending the letter to the builder on October 31. Contract parties are entitled to expect due performance of contractual obligations and are permitted to take steps to protect that expectation. UCC § 2-609 states that "[w]hen reasonable grounds for insecurity arise with respect to the performance of either party, the other may in writing demand adequate assurance of due performance . . . ." Here, the sailor learned on October 31 that the builder's workers were on strike. This gave the sailor reasonable grounds for insecurity about the builder's ability to complete performance on time and thus gave the sailor the right to seek adequate assurance from the builder. Because the sailor's demand for assurance was justified, the builder was required to provide assurance that was adequate under the circumstances within a reasonable time (not to exceed 30 days) or be held to have repudiated the contract. UCC § 2-609(4).

Point Two(a) (30%)
The builder did not, within a reasonable time, provide the sailor adequate assurance of due performance; this failure to provide assurance constituted a repudiation of the contract.

Because the sailor, with legal justification (*see* Point One), demanded from the builder assurance of due performance, the builder's failure to provide such assurance within a reasonable time was a repudiation of their contract. *See* UCC § 2-609(4) ("After receipt of a justified demand[,] failure to provide within a reasonable time not exceeding thirty days . . . assurance of due performance . . . is a repudiation of the contract."). On October 31, the sailor requested that the builder provide adequate assurance regarding the completion of the boat by December 15. The builder did not respond to the sailor's letter until November 25—nearly a month later. Even if that response had been given in a reasonable time, it nonetheless did not provide assurance of due performance. It simply stated, "I'm sorry about the strike, but it is really out of my hands. I hope we settle it soon so that we can get back to work." Therefore, the builder's November 25 response did not provide adequate assurance in response to the sailor's justified request. Thus, the builder had repudiated the contract.

Point Two(b) (35%)
Although the builder repudiated the contract with the sailor, the builder probably retracted that repudiation on December 3 and the sailor was no longer entitled to cancel their contract. Thus, the sailor's failure to perform the sailor's obligations under the contract constituted a breach.

The builder's failure to provide adequate assurance of performance constituted a repudiation of their contract (*see* UCC § 2-609(4)), but the builder was free to retract that repudiation until the sailor cancelled the contract or materially changed his position or indicated by communication or action that the sailor considered the repudiation to be final. *See* UCC § 2-611(1) ("Until the repudiating party's next performance is due, he can retract his repudiation unless the aggrieved party has since the repudiation cancelled or materially changed his position or otherwise indicated that he considers the repudiation final.").

Here, the facts state that before the builder's December 3 telephone call to the sailor, the sailor did nothing in response to the builder's repudiation, such as contracting with a third party for a boat. The builder's December 3 call, informing the sailor that the boat would be timely delivered, probably constituted a retraction of the repudiation because it clearly indicated to the sailor that the builder would be able to perform. UCC § 2-611(2). Thus, after being so informed, the sailor did not have the right to treat their contract as cancelled. UCC § 2-611(3). Accordingly, the sailor's failure to perform the sailor's obligations under the contract by taking the boat and paying for it constituted a breach of the contract.

MBE SUBJECTS - PRACTICE ESSAY QUESTIONS

CONTRACTS
Answer to Question 1

A contract is an agreement that is legally enforceable. An agreement is legally enforceable if there is a meeting of the minds between the contracting parties and each party gives consideration. Consideration is some bargained—for exchange between the parties. The consideration may take many different forms, including performance of the contract, a promise to pay, or forbearance from doing legal acts. Generally courts do not consider the amount of consideration given, as that is a decision between the parties to the contract. A court will, however, consider the consideration given if it appears that the consideration is a sham (i.e. has not been paid).

A contract is formed by an offer of one party and the acceptance of another. An offer is a statement or conduct by one party manifesting an intent to create a contract with the other party. An acceptance is a statement or conduct by the other party manifesting an intent to enter into a contract. Generally an offer may only be accepted by the person that the offeror intends to accept it. Therefore, advertisements are generally not construed as an offer unless it is specific as to quantity and who may accept. The more broadly disseminated an offer is, the more likely it is to be construed as an advertisement, and not as an offer.

The offeree's acceptance must be made before the offeror revokes the offer and before the offeree rejects the offer. An offeror may revoke an offer in various ways, including (1) by an unambiguous statement to the offeree that the offeror does not intend to go through with the contract or (2) by unambiguous conduct of which the offeree is aware, manifesting an intent not to go through with the contract. An offeree may reject an offer in various ways, including (1) by an unambiguous statement to the offeror that the offeree does not accept the offer or (2) by attempting to accept something other than what was offered (i.e. a counteroffer). The counteroffer becomes a new offer that the original offeror may accept or reject.

Contracts concerning the sale of real estate must satisfy the statute of frauds. With regard to real estate, the statute of frauds may be satisfied either by performance or by a writing. For performance to satisfy the statute of frauds in the real estate context, the buyer must meet two of the following three tests: paid consideration to the seller, have possession of the premises, or made improvements upon the property. For a writing to satisfy the statute of frauds, the writing must include all material terms and must be signed by the party to be charged (i.e. the party who is claiming that the statute of frauds has not been satisfied). It is not necessary, however, that all of the terms of the agreement be in only one writing. Multiple writings will also satisfy the statute of frauds.

An option contract is an offer that the offeror promises to hold open to the offeree for a certain period of time and agrees not to revoke. If an option contract is made without consideration, the offeror has no obligation to hold it open as promised. If the offeree pays consideration to the offeror, the offeror is legally obligated to hold the contract open for the designated period of time.

The notice posted at the bank stating that Mary's recreational property was for sale did not constitute an offer, but was merely an invitation to bargain. John's call to Mary asking whether she would be willing to sell for $250,000 is just a negotiation or an invitation to negotiate since he only asked whether she would be willing to sell, and did not make an unambiguous offer to pay that amount. Mary's response that she would need at least $300,000 is probably an offer because John is led to believe that by simply saying "yes" or "okay" that there would be a contract. However, because they are dealing with a contract to sell land, the contract must meet the statute of frauds, and their oral agreement does not do so (because there is neither performance nor a writing as required by the statute of frauds). However, once they put their agreement in writing, the writing requirement of the statute of frauds is satisfied. Unfortunately, their attempted option contract does not appear to meet the requirements of an option contract for consideration. While a court normally will not inquire as to the value of the consideration, if no consideration is actually paid, there is no valid and enforceable contract. Here, $1.00 is only nominal consideration and John failed even to pay that amount. Therefore this option contract is without consideration. While John may still accept within the 30 days provided by the option contract, he will have no recourse against Mary if she revokes the option contract or if she offers the property to someone else.

John's letter to Mary two weeks later does not qualify as a counteroffer because John did not say in the letter that he would accept the offer only on the condition that Mary agree to a lower purchase price. John instead is trying to get a better bargain by asking for a lower price – this is merely an inquiry. Asking for a lower price is not the same as accepting on the condition that the offeror accept a lower price, and therefore does not qualify as a counteroffer and therefore does not qualify as a rejection of Mary's offer. Even if this letter does constitute a conditional acceptance (that would normally be construed as a counteroffer), the offer would remain open because it is an option contract and Mary has agreed to keep the contract open for 30 days. The fact that the option contract is without consideration will only bear upon acts made by Mary (i.e. only Mary has the right to revoke the option).

The information that Tim gave to John that Mary either sold the property or was offering to sell it to Bob has no effect on Mary's offer. Mary's offer can only be revoked by an unambiguous statement or conduct and the information from a third person that Mary may have taken some other action with the property is not unambiguous.

Because the option contract still appears to be valid, John's letter is a valid acceptance. Under the mailbox rule, mail is deemed to come into effect when it is received. There is an exception to this rule for acceptances of offers; an acceptance is valid when it is mailed. Therefore assuming the option was still open, John's acceptance of the offer was effective on the date that the acceptance was mailed. The fact that the contract consists of multiple writings still satisfies the statute of frauds.

Mary's death will not affect the enforcement of the contract because she died the day after a valid contract was formed. The period between the time the contract was made and the time of performance is called the executory period. The death of a party to a contract during this period does not affect the rights or obligations of the parties under that contract (unless the contract is for something requiring personal performance of the decedent). However, if a party dies before an offer has been accepted, then the acceptance is void (unless it was an option). Here the contract for the sale of land is not personal, and the acceptance was made while Mary was still alive, even though she may not have been aware of it, and is therefore enforceable even though Mary has died.

For these reasons, there is a valid contract for the sale of land between John and Mary.

MBE SUBJECTS - PRACTICE ESSAY QUESTIONS

CONTRACTS
Answer to Question 2

The contract between builder and owner will be governed by common law contract law because it does not involve the sale of goods over $500. Under common law, if Builder (B) has performed, B is entitled to be paid the contract price minus any damages. Here, the parties are in dispute about the contract price and the amount of damages.

What is the total contract price?

The original contract price of $300,000 is in dispute.

Is the $450,000 contract price enforceable?

The contract explicitly states that a modification will only be allowed if there is a signed writing. Is this contract provision controlling? Under the common law, modification provisions requiring that modifications only be in writing, were often not enforced. Although under the UCC, they are usually enforced, in this case the common law governs, and the contract provision will likely not control the outcome of the dispute. Therefore, the new contract price may be enforceable.

Pre-existing duty rule

Under the pre-existing duty rule, a contract governed by the common law cannot be changed without additional consideration. If the builder was already under the duty to complete a construction contract, he cannot hold up the process by demanding more money without additional consideration. Here, B has tried to increase the amount he is paid with no additional consideration on his part. The pre-existing duty rule says that unless there is additional consideration, the amount cannot be increased. The rule protects the contract makers from one party being a holdout to the deal. Here, B's threat to quit performance may fall under this rule, and the new contract price may be unenforceable.

Impossibility/Impracticability/Commercial Frustration

Under these doctrines, if something happened outside of the control of the parties to greatly change the deal they have made (extreme conditions creating a dramatic change in circumstances), the parties may be let off the hook or may be allowed to change the terms of the contract. Here, B experienced a dramatic change in the price of bricks, based on a national shortage. Such an event is likely to qualify under the Impracticability exception and the new contract price may be enforced as a result. Without more facts, it is unclear how extreme is the event that caused the shortage, but it is likely that based on the agreement of the parties and the national shortage, the new contract price is enforceable.

Is Owner required to pay the contract price?

The second part of the analysis concerns whether or not the Owner is required to pay the contract price. Here, it is important to look at whether or not the contract was performed, the doctrine of substantial performance, and issues of breach.

Substantial Performance

Under construction contracts and the common law, the doctrine of substantial performance says that if the contract was substantially performed (e.g. all express conditions were satisfied and the material obligations were substantially completed), the buyer must tender payment. Here, whether or not there was substantial performance is unclear. Builder was obligated to build a house for Owner, yet he did not install Kitchen cabinets, gutters and downspouts and sidewalks. Whether or not this was substantial performance will likely turn on what is standard in the industry. It is likely that the installation of kitchen cabinets, gutters, and downspouts are standard and must be installed before the house complies with housing code regulations (if in effect in the area). However, the installation of sidewalks is less certain, and that omission may not bear on whether or not there was substantial performance. The misplaced wall that reduces the housing value by $5,000 is not necessarily evidence that substantial performance did not occur. However, it will almost certainly be relevant in the discussion of damages and payment (see below).

If any of these conditions were expressly mentioned in the contract, then substantial performance was not completed. However, if not expressly conditioned, Builder may argue he has substantially completed his obligation and should be paid. It is likely that the uncompleted kitchen and the lack of gutters, etc, will count against substantial completion of the contract.

If the contract was substantially performed, Builder will still be liable for any breach. Here, his omission of gutters, kitchen cabinets, and wrong placement of the wall, will all entitle the owner to a remedy for breach.

If work does not constitute substantial performance.

If Builder is not considered to have substantially performed, Owner will be allowed to rescind the contract and is not obligated to pay the contract price. In such a situation, however, Builder is entitled to a quasi-contract remedy to prevent unjust enrichment by the Owner. In that situation, Builder will be paid for the amount of enrichment the Owner benefited from the building (likely the amount the building/work is worth).

What remedies are available to Owner?

Assuming the new contract price of $350,000 (see above discussion), the Owner is entitled to several possible remedies.

Expectation damages

If the Builder is considered to have substantially completed his performance obligations, Owner is entitled to have the amount owed decreased by the amount of damages. Expectation damages put the non-breaching party in the position he would be in had no breach occurred. Here, if the breach by builder is immaterial (kitchen, gutters, wall sidewalk), Owner will pay the contract price ($350,000) minus the breach of kitchen cabinets, gutters and sidewalks ($17,000). Owner would also be entitled to either a reduction of $60,000 (the cost of tearing down the wall) or ($5,000) the diminution in value from the breach. Based on what Owner would have had with no breach, Owner is entitled to either of the two amounts ($5,000 or $60,000). Thus, Owner would be obligated to pay either $273,000 or $328,000 for the completed building. Given these damages, Owner would be in the position he would have been in had no breach occurred.

Consequential Damages.

Consequential damages are allowed when the parties both knew of special circumstances that would be affected by a breach of the contract. Here, there is no evidence of such a situation, so there would be no consequential damages.

Punitive Damages.

Even if the breach was willful, punitive damages are not allowed under contract law, so Owner will not be entitled to any claim for punitive damages.

Specific Performance.

Specific performance is allowed in situations where the court can require that a party to a contract specifically perform the contract. The remedy of specific performance is never used to force a party to do work, however. Therefore, Owner is not entitled to specific performance from Builder, e.g. in requiring him to fix the misplaced wall. A court will not force a party to a contract to work, so Owner is only allowed to recover damages from Builder.

MBE SUBJECTS - PRACTICE ESSAY QUESTIONS

CONTRACTS
Answer to Question 3

First, Ben's (B) claims are going to be in contract. The claims at issue regard the sale of goods and as a result, the Uniform Commercial Code (UCC) applies. For a contract to be formed, there must be a mutuality between the parties, (i.e., an offer and agreement) consideration, and no defenses to preclude formation. An offer is a statement made to another that induces or requests assent or agreement by the other party. Consideration is a bargained for legal detriment. The main defenses in this case would be statute of frauds.

Here a contract was formed when B sent the offer, which was a letter requesting the air purifiers. Silent Air (SA) accepted the offer when it responded by saying it would deliver the two and that a $50 delivery fee would be added. The added term does not make this a counter offer because under the UCC an acceptance does not have to be a mirror image to the offer, as the common law requires. Also B accepted the delivery term by paying the price.

The consideration is $1,300 on B's side and the purifiers on SA's side.

SA would claim the statute of frauds (SOF) applies to this transaction. The SOF requires the sale of goods contracts that are for $500 or more to be in writing and signed by the person to be charged. The agreement here is in writing. Two writings can be read together to satisfy the SOF. The offer and acceptance are both in writing and lay out the contract terms. The facts are silent about whether SA signed the writing. If they did not, they have a valid defense. If they did, then no defense is available and a contract has been formed.

B's first claim will be for breach of warranty for a particular purpose (WPP). The WPP requires the seller to know or have reason to know that the buyer has a particular purpose for the goods and for the seller to reassure the buyer the goods will perform for the particular purpose.

In this case, SA knew (vicariously through Stella the Salesperson) that B needed an exceptionally high level of indoor air quality because many of the children at the day care center had asthma/severe allergies.

Stella assured B that SA's model that B later bought would clean and purify the air to the highest level recognized. Relying on Stella's statements, B bought the air purifiers. However, the purifiers did not clean the air as evidenced by the air quality consultant's tests. Therefore SA breached its WPP.

SA will argue that the manual disclaimed all warranties, including WPP. Generally a merchant can disclaim implied warranties; however, a merchant cannot disclaim express warranties. WPP is an express warranty and therefore cannot be disclaimed.

SA would also argue that parol evidence cannot be used because the entire agreement was in writing. (SA would only argue if the SOF defense does not work.) The parol evidence rule

(PER) prohibits the introduction of inconsistent new terms when a contract is completely integrated. Here the inconsistent terms would be the disclaimer and the WPP. B would have to claim an ambiguity exists or that the writing is not a complete integration. This is so that B could either explain the ambiguity or show consistent additional terms. However, this does not look likely because the terms B is attempting to add are not consistent but contradictory, and therefore excluded by the PER.

B could argue that he did not receive the manual until after the contract was formed and therefore this disclaimer was not part of the original contract and not enforceable.

Warranty of Merchantability

B could claim that SA breached its warranty of merchantability (WM). The WM warrants that all products are fit for the general purpose for which it is sold.

Here the general purpose is to purify the air. However, the products are not purifying the air, as set out by the air consultant's test results. Also, the purifiers would run only a few days at a time before malfunctioning. Also, one of the purifiers made a loud noise which is not what it should do and not what can be used for the general purpose of domestic use. Therefore SA breached the WM.

SA again will claim the manual disclaims the WM. The WM is an implied warranty that can be disclaimed by statements such as that in the manual. However, the disclaimer must be conspicuous, i.e., in a different font, bold, or larger size. B could argue that because it was not conspicuous, it does not apply. Unfortunately, we do not have enough information to determine this issue.

Remedies

In contract cases, the buyer is entitled to expectation damages. Expectation damages place the non-breaching party in the same position had the contract been performed. Also the non-breaching party is entitled to incidental and consequential damages.

With regard to expectation damages, B is entitled to the fair market value of the goods he should have received at the time of the breach subtracted from replacement cost. So B can replace and get the difference between the replacement and the contract.

B is also entitled to consequential damages that are foreseeable to both parties at the time the contract was performed. Here it should have been foreseeable that if the purifiers do not work, B might lose clients. Therefore, SA would be liable for what B lost because he lost the two families.

If B incurred any incidental damages for getting new purifiers, then SA is liable for those as well. These include the time and money spent finding comparable purifiers.

B is not going to get specific performance because specific performance is rarely granted unless for specifically manufactured goods, which we do not have here.

This appears to be a standard good that SA manufactures.

MBE SUBJECTS - PRACTICE ESSAY QUESTIONS

CONTRACTS
Answer to Question 4

Mary's Claims Against Grandpa

There are three key components to a valid contract – offer, acceptance and consideration. All three of those factors are present here. Grandpa made an offer to Mary on May 2 that she accepted by moving to Smallville and taking care of Grandpa. Grandpa's letter is a valid offer because it states what he wants (to be taken care of) and what consideration is giving up in exchange for that (Tara). Further contracts involving land must state the land to be transferred with specificity. Here, Grandpa refers to "my Tara." This would indicate to anyone who is familiar with the town or the family which property he is referring to. Thus, this is a valid offer.

Next we look for acceptance. Some contracts can be accepted only through performance while others are accepted with a promise. Courts generally construe contracts as bilateral unless they specifically state that they can only be accepted through performance, then it is a unilateral contract. This is no exception. Mary moved to Smallville and began taking care of Grandpa the day after receiving the offer. This sufficient evidence for a court to find a valid acceptance.

Finally, there must be consideration, a bargained-for exchange. In this contract, the consideration is the estate of "Tara." Courts will not take the value of the benefit bestowed or detriment incurred into consideration when determining whether something is consideration. It only must meet one of those two things. Here, Mary is incurring a detriment by moving to Smallville. She could live anywhere and do anything, but she is picking up her life and moving in order to take care of Grandpa. In return, she is receiving Tara in his will. Most courts will consider this valid consideration. Thus, a contract was formed on May 3 when Mary moved to Smallville.

The Historical Society and Grandpa's estate might argue that Grandpa revoked the contract on May 21. Unilateral contracts, those contracts requiring full performance as acceptance, cannot be revoked once performance has begun. There is a valid argument that this contract was a unilateral contract. The offer stated that Mary was to take care of Grandpa and the estate for the rest of his life. This requires ongoing care until Grandpa is dead. Then and only then will the contract be fulfilled and performance complete. That is when Mary will be entitled to Tara. Until performance is complete, revocation is not valid. Thus, the May 21 revocation was not valid. Mary was not discharged from her duties, the contract was still valid, and Mary is entitled to take Tara by way of the contract.

In the very least, Mary should be able to recover for the care that she gave Grandpa under a theory of quasi-contract. In that case, she should be able to recover for any expenses she may have incurred, for her time and possibly moving expenses.

Mary's Claims Against the Historical Society

Mary could raise two different claims against the Historical Society receiving Tara. First, she could argue undue influence on the part of Stella. Undue influence in the making of a will requires (1) the existence and application of influence over the will, (2) the intent of such influence to cause the testator to change his will, and (3) that the testator would not have changed his will but for the influence. Here, however, there is no clear evidence that Stella or the Historical Society put any undue influence on Grandpa, although it is suspicious that he changed his will the day after being with Stella. Mary would need more evidence to support this claim.

Second, Mary could argue that Grandpa lacked competency to change his will. To be competent a testator must be aware of (1) the extent of all of his property, (2) the natural objects of his bounty, (3) that he is changing/making his will, and (4) the dispositions that he is making. This is fairly broad and only requires a "lucid" moment, even for the insane. Again, there does not seem to be evidence of a lack of competency here. Mary would need more evidence to prove this.

Tom's Rights

As stated previously, a valid contract needs offer, acceptance and consideration. The agreement between Tom and Mary seems to have all three of these requirements. Contracts for the sale of land must be in writing and must include a reasonably accurate description of the land in question, a price term (this will not be inserted by the Court) and method of payment. Mary's letter of May 10 seems to include all of these things. The one question would arise concerning method of payment. The letter merely states that Tom will pay Mary $100,000 when she received title to Tara. Although this is not too specific, a Court would likely find that this is a valid offer. That Mary did not at the time have title to the property does not impair the contract, especially considering that Tom knows that. The contract is only concerning a future interest in land.

Tom accepted Mary's offer on May 23 by letter. An offer must be accepted within a reasonable period of time. Here the time is only 13 days and time is not of the essence with the contract. So a Court would find this within the reasonable period of time requirement. Tom accepted Mary's offer by mail. When an offer is accepted by mail, the acceptance is effective upon mailing, not upon receipt of the acceptance. Thus, Mary's offer was accepted by Tom when he mailed his acceptance. This is called the Mailbox Rule. The question will arise concerning the fact that Mary never received the acceptance. Although Mary might have a good argument, a Court will likely find in favor of Tom. When an acceptance is mailed properly with the correct address and proper postage, the acceptance is presumed to have gotten to its destination. Such will be the case here. The acceptance was effective when mailed and Mary is presumed to have received it. Thus, a valid contract came into being once Tom mailed the acceptance.

As previously discussed, a Court will not look too hard into amount of consideration given. It appears, and there is no evidence here to the contrary, that $100,000 is sufficient consideration to support this contract. Because of the foregoing, Tom will be able to enforce the contract.

Further, property is considered sufficiently unique such that specific enforcement is often ordered by a Court. If it is determined that Mary owns the property (the gift to the Historical

Society is voided), Tom will be able to specifically enforce the contract and make Mary sell him Tara for $100,000. If the Court determines that the Historical Society owns the property through a validly executed will, Tom will not likely have any recourse against Mary. The contract specifically stated that she would sell Tara to Tom when she received it. Because she never received the property (it went to the Historical Society) the contract is excused as to both parties.

MBE SUBJECTS - PRACTICE ESSAY QUESTIONS

CONTRACTS
Answer to Question 5

Is there a valid, enforceable contract?

A valid contract requires an offer, accept, consideration or a consideration substitute, and no defenses to enforcement like the Statute of Frauds.

The UCC applies to this contract because it is for the sale of goods. For the most part, the common law and UCC are the same, but there are relevant differences that apply to these facts.

Offer and Acceptance: No mirror image rules under the UCC.

An offer is a manifestation of an intention to contract. Here, the order that Becky sent is an offer. Under the common law, an acceptance that adds additional terms is treated as a counter offer rather than an acceptance. Here, Samz sent a form confirming the order with the additional term that all complaints concerning defects must be made in a reasonable time. The mirror image rule doesn't apply to the UCC; rather the acceptance is valid if it adds a new term if it is a seasonable expression of acceptance (not a conditional acceptance). Thus, supported by consideration (promise to pay and promise to deliver furniture), a valid contract was formed.

Is the new term a part of the contract? Where both parties are merchants, the new term is a part of the contract unless it materially changes the offer or the offeror objects. Here, Becky is in retail clothing and she needs the furniture for a business and Samz sells furniture, thus both parties are merchants. The term does not materially alter the contract and Becky didn't object so it is part of the contract. (If a party wasn't a merchant, the additional term would merely be a proposal to be separately accepted or rejected.)

Statute of Frauds satisfied.

This contract is for a sale of goods for $500 or more ($1,500). There is a writing(s) and thus it is satisfied and not a defense to enforcement, assuming Becky signed the order or it was on stationary with her business' letterhead.

Becky's Acceptance of the Goods.

The UCC requires perfect tender. (Common law substantial performance.) Here, Samz delivered the goods and they were conforming. Becky may try to argue she rejected the goods; however, a seller does not have a right to reject unless the goods are not perfect. Additionally, she had an opportunity to inspect them and did not; thus this would be implied acceptance of the credenza.

Sue Becky for Breach of the Contract.

Samz may sue Becky for breach because there is an enforceable contract and Becky's attempted rejection of the goods is invalid. Even though Samz picked up the goods, he did not waive the breach. When the buyer breaches and the seller has the goods, the seller may get damages in the amount of the market price at the time of delivery, minus the contract price or the resale price minus, the contract price, or may even get lost profits if the breach prevented him from getting two sales.

Here, Samz mitigated his damages, as is his duty, by selling to Bob at a discount. Therefore, he can collect $50 in damages for the credenza in addition to the $1,000 that Becky still owes Samz.

He may also get lost profits if Bob would've also purchased a credenza. This would be the contract price ($500) minus the costs to acquire the credenza and wax it ($375), totaling $125, in addition to the $1,000 owing.

He may not seek to reclaim the goods if Becky still hasn't paid, assuming the time period (10 days) has passed since Becky received the goods and there is no evidence that Becky was insolvent at that time.

Conclusion.

Samz will likely be successful in a suit against Becky.

MBE SUBJECTS - PRACTICE ESSAY QUESTIONS

CONTRACTS
Answer to Question 6

Contract

In common law services contracts there must be an offer, acceptance and supported by consideration.

An offer is the manifestation to enter into an enforceable agreement if the other party understands all the terms of the offer and accepts. The contract is not enforceable until it is supported by consideration. This is where the offeror has bargained for and the offeree has detrimentally agreed to a promise. In other words, the offeror promises to do something and the offeree promises to give up something in exchange.

Addams has offered to give Jones her legal work. Addams made an offer to have Jones do all of her legal work for a three-month period for $150 per hour.

S.O.F.

This is a services contract that can be performed within a year. The statute of frauds requires all agreements to perform something beyond one year to be in writing. This contract can be performed within a year. It is out of the statute of frauds.

Nevertheless, both parties have reduced the agreement to writing. Addams and Jones appear to have agreed on the terms. Both have supported with consideration.

When Addams gave Jones a difficult task that appeared to have modified their agreement. It appears Addams orally told Jones to complete a difficult mortgage.

The next question is whether the $300 per hour fee is a modification to the original agreement? If it is, it will require consideration. If no consideration, then Addams may refuse to pay the bigger fee because Addams will argue pre-existing duty. The rule is, if a party had a pre-existing duty to do something, then there is no consideration. Jones will argue that adhering to the higher fee she is consideration enough. Addams on the other hand, will argue Jones agreed to do all of Addams legal work for $150 per hour. Jones had a pre-existing duty to work. No consideration. If that is the case, then Addams would not have to pay for the extra $150 per hour.

On the other hand, if Jones argues that she had to give up her precious time to complete the mortgage within 24 hours, that is enough consideration and that Addams should pay the bill.

Perhaps Jones put Addams under duress. Was Addams pressured into agreeing with the new fee? If so, it should be set aside. A party under duress has no right to enter into a contract if they were forced into it. If Addams felt she was pressured, then the agreement to pay the higher fee should be excused.

Furthermore, there appears to be a condition attached to the later agreement. Jones demanded that before doing the mortgage, he would want a higher fee. When Addams agreed, then Jones completed the work.

It appears Addams is in breach. Jones can recover the extra $150 at the time of breach. That will put Jones back in the place he would have been in but for the breach.

Addams on the other hand, may not have to pay. Perhaps Jones had a pre-existing duty to perform for $150/hr. No consideration. No breach.

Furthermore, Jones may sue Addams for breach of original contract. The original agreement was for a 3-month period. Addams hired another lawyer. When a party rescinds a contract, the non-breaching party has a remedy against the breaching party. If that is the case, Jones can demand the $300 fee, plus the amount of fees remaining on the contract. This is provided they are $150/hr.

Under the rules of professional conduct, there is nothing preventing a lawyer from entering into a contract with their client, as long as the agreement does not limit the lawyer's liability or ability to practice.

Jones did not limit his liability. Nor did the contract limit his ability to practice.

A lawyer can charge a flat fee for services rendered, as long as it was not a contingent fee on a criminal case or domestic relations case.

If Jones felt that $300/hr. was reasonable for a mortgage to be drafted in 24 hours, then that was OK. Addams may argue, but it may not be unethical.

However, when Jones threatened not to work, if he did not get paid, may be unethical. Addams will argue a lawyer should not pressure clients into doing something they shouldn't.

I would advise Addams not to bring a complaint unless she felt she was pressured beyond her will.

On the other hand, she may have a claim for breach of contract when Jones refused to work. Addams had no choice, but to seek outside help.

Maybe when Addams agreed to pay the higher fee it created an accord.

When parties disagree on a disputed claim and subsequently create a new claim, satisfaction of payment will suffice.

Jones will argue Addams agreed to the new fee creating an accord. But Addams refused to pay. No satisfaction.

MBE SUBJECTS - PRACTICE ESSAY QUESTIONS

CONTRACTS
Answer to Question 7

Original Agreement

A contract is an enforceable agreement. A contract is formed when there has been a valid offer, a valid acceptance and consideration.

The first issue is whether the March 15th offer was a valid offer. An offer must be sufficiently definite, such that the offeree would reasonably believe that acceptance would create a contract. Here, the offer for the sale of real property described the property by name and gave the price. Property description is sufficient even without a legal description as long as it would identify a unique parcel. "Happyacres" is enough to meet this standard. This was a valid offer.

Next is the issue of whether the offer was an option contract. An option contract is created when one party pays value to the other for a promise to keep the offer open for a certain time period. Here, there is a recital of consideration for that promise to keep it open for 30 days, but it is not clear whether Buyer actually paid that consideration. It seems like this is not a valid option contract. As a regular offer, then, it could be revoked unless it induced detrimental reliance in Buyer, which doesn't seem to have occurred.

The next issue is whether the offer was revoked prior to any acceptance by Buyer. A revocation of an offer is valid when it is received if it is sent by mail, because revocation must be communicated to the offeree. Buyer received Owner's written revocation on March 26th, before he had accepted. Thus, the revocation is valid.

The next question is whether Buyer's March 2nd letter was a valid acceptance. An acceptance is only valid if the offer is still open. Because the revocation was valid, this could not have been an acceptance.

If the value of $10 was in fact paid to Owner by Buyer, then the offer would have been irrevocable. An option contract is irrevocable until the end of the option period. Any acceptance during that period that is received by the Offeror is valid, so if (contrary to my finding of no option contract earlier) there was a valid option, then this was a valid acceptance because it was received during the 30-day period. If valid acceptance, then there was a valid contract with promises as consideration.

Oral Agreement

Contracts for the sale of land are within the statute of frauds. Thus, in order for an agreement to be valid, it must be in writing, or Buyer must have two of these factors: possession, improvements, and part payment. If the original agreement was not valid (because March 15th letter not valid option contract), then this later agreement would have an issue relating to the Statute of Frauds. A writing must exist to satisfy the statute that contains the party's names, property description, price and signature of party to be bound. Possibly the entire record here, with all letters, would suffice as a writing, but since the price term had changed, this argument would fail and the agreement would be invalid under the statute of frauds.

Next, if the original contract was enforceable (if the option was valid), there may be a pre-existing duty problem. In a common law situation, there must be consideration to support any modification. If Owner was already bound to close by April 13th, then Owner gave no consideration for the modification -- he had a pre-existing duty to close by that date. If that is the case, then the promise to pay $250,000 cannot be enforced. However, time is not considered of the essence unless the parties so state, if Owner was agreeing to perform at a date earlier than he was required to, that would be enough consideration, and the modification would be fine.

Also, a modification under common law must be in writing if the contract as modified would have to be in writing. Here, there is a sale of land, which is within the statute of frauds so a new contract would have to be in writing. Because of this, the modification would be invalid and the promise to pay $250,000 unenforceable.

Promise to pay creditor

First, there is an issue of whether the promise to pay the old debt barred by the statute of limitations is a pre-existing duty. A contract requires offer, acceptance and consideration; a pre-existing duty is not valid consideration unless it is owed to a third person or voidable due to minority age, etc. A promise to pay a past due undisputed debt is not sufficient for consideration. But, if the claim is barred by the statute of limitations, a promise to repay the debt is a consideration substitute. Thus, Owner's promise would be enforceable.

The oral promise is also sufficient. The statute of frauds requires the promise to act as a guarantor for the debts of another to be in writing. But here, Owner is promising to pay his own debt.

Owner's promise to pay the past debt had a condition precedent. If a condition precedent fails, performance is excused. Here, there was a condition that Owner receive $100,000 from the sale of Happyacres. It is not clear whether Owner received $100,000 in profits (he may have had a mortgage). But if Owner did receive $100,000, he must pay it to Creditor.

If profits were less than $100,000, Creditor may try to argue that he was a third party beneficiary of the Owner-Buyer Contract, and then try to sue Buyer for the extra $50,000. But he was not an intended beneficiary because Buyer didn't know about him, so this would be a losing argument.

Oral Agreement Complied with Creditor Agreement

Owner's last argument regarding the agreement with Creditor and Buyer is that Owner relied on the modification, (200,000 – 250,000), which was manifested by his agreement with Creditor. For this, he could assert a claim of promissory estoppel against Buyer, since the oral modification was probably not enforceable as a contract. Promissory estoppel exists where there is 1) a promise, 2) reasonable, foreseeable, detrimental reliance, 3) injustice. Here, Buyer promised to pay $250,000. In reliance on that promise, Owner made the promise to pay Creditor. To now let Buyer get out of that promise would be unjust to Owner. Because Buyer was the one who offered the extra money, it seems foreseeable and reasonable that Owner would thereupon act on that promise, even if Buyer was not aware of the Creditor-Owner situation. Under this theory, Owner could recover the extra $50,000.

Corporations

(February 2000)

Legal Problems:

(1)(a) Can a corporation award an executive stock options in that corporation as part of the executive's compensation?

(1)(b) Can a corporation issue stock options when all of the authorized shares of such corporation are issued and outstanding?

(2) Can a corporation issue additional shares of an existing class of common stock that have greater rights and preferences than the outstanding shares of that class?

(3) Is the consent of all common shareholders required for the issuance of preferred shares by a corporation?

(4) Are a common shareholder's preemptive rights triggered by an award of common stock options to an executive, by the issuance of additional common stock, or by the issuance of preferred stock?

DISCUSSION

Point One(a): (15-25%)

Subject to Point One(b) PrattCo has the right to award options to its officers for purchase of shares as part of the officers' compensation.

A corporation may issue options for the purchase of its shares on terms and conditions determined by the board of directors. Revised Model Business Corporation Act (RMBCA) § 6.24. Shares may be issued, and options extended, for different types of consideration, including both "services performed" and "contracts for services to be performed." RMBCA § 6.21(b). Thus, the board could agree to give Leslie the requested options either on an "as earned" basis as Leslie completes periods of service with the company, or "up front" in consideration for a contract for future services. Therefore, the board would normally be entitled to issue the options to Leslie subject to all necessary actions to authorize sufficient shares as discussed below.

Point One(b): (15-25%)

PrattCo has issued all of its authorized shares; therefore, the stock options cannot be issued unless the board and the shareholders vote to increase the number of common shares authorized.

A corporation must have a sufficient number of authorized shares to cover all issued and outstanding shares, as well as all shares subject to options that have been issued. Articles of incorporation are required to state the number of authorized shares of the corporation. RMBCA § 2.02(a)(2). PrattCo's articles of incorporation authorize three million shares of Class A Common stock, of which all three million shares have been issued and are outstanding. This means that PrattCo cannot issue the stock options to Leslie unless its articles are amended to provide for additional authorized shares of Class A Common stock in a number at least sufficient to meet Leslie's options.

An increase in the number of Class A Common shares authorized requires approval of both the board of directors and the Class A Common shareholders. RMBCA §§ 10.03, 10.04. Although a supermajority vote for certain changes to a corporation's articles may be specified in the articles of incorporation, RMBCA § 7.27, no supermajority requirement is found in PrattCo's articles, so a majority of the shares voted will be sufficient to approve the change. RMBCA §§ 7.25, 10.03(e)(2). Since all Class A shareholders (other than William) will vote to authorize the additional shares, PrattCo will be able to carry out its plan to issue the options and hire Leslie.

Point Two: (30-40%)

Brenda's proposal to purchase Class A Common shares cannot be implemented because it provides for preferential dividend rights within an undifferentiated class of stock.

Brenda's proposal cannot be implemented because it gives Brenda's Class A Common shares preferential dividend rights beyond that given to the other Class A Common shares. All shares within a class of stock must have identical rights and preferences unless the shares within a class are divided into separate series. RMBCA § 6.02 (c); Hamilton, *Corporations,* V.CA, at 243 (1992). In addition, shares that have a preferred right to receive dividends or distributions on liquidation should not be called "common" shares. Henn and Alexander, *Laws of Corporations* § 160, at 403 (1983). *See McKinney's N. Y. Business Corporation Law* § 501(b). Since Brenda's shares would have preferred rights to receive dividends, they cannot be issued as Class A Common shares.

Point Three: (20-30%)

PrattCo could create a new class of shares (Preferred Stock) and sell Brenda shares of Preferred Stock with preferential rights if the board and the shareholders approved amendments to the articles to provide for such Preferred Stock. Amendment of the articles of incorporation to create Preferred Stock requires board approval and a majority vote of the Class A Common shareholders, which, under the facts, can be obtained.

PrattCo could accomplish Brenda's objective by issuing shares of Preferred Stock instead of Class A Common shares. To do so, PrattCo would have to amend the articles of incorporation to create the Preferred Stock and designate the shares to be sold to Brenda as Preferred Stock with the preferential rights that Brenda has requested. Amendment of the articles of incorporation to create Preferred Stock requires board approval and a majority vote of the Class A Common shareholders. RMBCA §§ 10.03, 10.04. Since William holds only 30% of the Class A Common shares and all shareholders other than William will vote in favor of creating the Preferred Stock, William will not be able to block the creation and issuance of the Preferred Stock.

Point Four: (10-20%)

William has preemptive rights under the articles and generally would be entitled to his proportional share of any Class A Common stock issued. However, no preemptive rights exist with respect to shares issued as compensation to officers, such as those to be issued to Leslie, and no preemptive rights exist for common shareholders with respect to referred shares that are not convertible into common, such as the Preferred Stock that could be issued to Brenda.

The PrattCo articles of incorporation include language that "the corporation elects to have preemptive rights." This triggers the preemptive rights provisions of the RMBCA. RMBCA § 6.30(b). Under the RMBCA and many state statutes, a corporation must "opt in" to create preemptive rights by expressly including the right in its articles of incorporation. In other states, preemptive rights are presumed to exist unless the corporation "opts out" and expressly excludes such rights in its articles. Regardless of the type of law in this jurisdiction, the statement in the PrattCo articles establishes preemptive rights for its shareholders.

However, there are several widely recognized exceptions to preemptive rights. Under the RMBCA and many state statutes, no preemptive rights exist as to "shares issued to satisfy. . . option rights created to provide compensation to . . . officers. . . of the corporation. . . ." RMBCA § 6.30(b)(3)(ii). Therefore, William has no preemptive right to buy any PrattCo shares as a result of the issuance of Leslie's options.

If Brenda were to purchase Class A Common shares, the sale would not come within any of the statutory exclusions of preemptive rights, and William would have the right to purchase 30% of the Class A Common shares sold to Brenda. RMBCA § 6.30(b)(3). However, since Brenda's shares must be issued as Preferred Stock (not Class A Common), as discussed in Point Three above, William's preemptive rights claim can be defeated. Holders of common shares have no preemptive rights to preferential shares unless those shares are convertible to common. RMBCA § 6.30 (b)(5). So long as the Preferred Stock, which is entitled to preferential rights to dividends, is not convertible into Class A Common and carries no rights to acquire Class A Common, William would have no preemptive rights in the Preferred Stock sold to Brenda.

Corporations

(July 2000)

Legal Problems:

1. Are restrictions on a shareholder's ability to transfer stock of a close corporation that require the consent of all other shareholders to the transfer and the transferee enforceable against a transferring shareholder?

2. Are restrictions on a shareholder's ability to transfer stock of a close corporation that require the consent of all other shareholders to the transfer and the transferee enforceable against a third party that lacks notice?

3. Will a court order the dissolution of Store to protect the minority shareholders?

DISCUSSION

Point One: (35-45%)

Restrictions on the transfer of stock that require approval of the transfer and transferee by all other shareholders are generally enforceable as long as the restrictions are created for reasonable purposes.

As a general rule, share transfer restrictions are invalid if they are unreasonable restraints on alienation of stock. Thus, an absolute restraint on alienation of stock is *per se* unreasonable and void. Usually, however, courts will permit share transfer restrictions if they are adopted for a lawful purpose. Lawful purposes include keeping a corporation closely held or keeping a corporation in the family. H. Henn & J. Alexander, *Laws o/Corporations* § 281, at 756-58 (3d ed. 1983).

The share transfer restriction described in the facts requires the consent of all other shareholders and the approval by such shareholders of the proposed transferee. Consent restraints, such as this one, are among the most restrictive stock transfer restraints because they make stock unassignable if one shareholder refuses to vote to approve the transfer. The courts are split on the enforceability of consent restrictions. Some jurisdictions have considered such a restriction to be tantamount to an absolute restraint on alienation, manifestly unreasonable and void. *See Hill v. Warner, Berman & Spitz P.A.,* 197 N.J. Super. 152, 484 A.2d 344 (1984); *Rae v. Hindin,* 29 A.D.2d 481, 288 N.Y.S.2d 662 (Sup. Ct. N.Y. 1968), *aff'd,* 23 N.Y.2d 759, 296 N.Y.S.2d 955 (1968). Other jurisdictions, however, have enforced transfer restrictions of this type. *See Gray* v. *Harris Land & Cattle Co.,* 227 Mont. 51, 737 P.2d 475 (1987); *Benson* v. *RMJ Securities Corp.* 683 F. Supp. 359 (S.D.N.Y. 1988); Henn & Alexander, *Laws of Corporations* at 759; Del. Gen. Corp Law § 202(c)(3).

Modern statutory law frequently permits many types of restrictions on the transfer of stock. The

Revised Model Business Corporation Act (RMBCA) permits restrictions established in a corporation's "articles of incorporation, bylaws, an agreement among shareholders, or an agreement between shareholders and the corporation." RMBCA § 6.27(a). "A restriction on the transfer or registration of transfer of shares is authorized for any . . . reasonable purpose." RMBCA § 6.27(c)(3). The RMBCA also provides that a stock transfer restriction may "require the corporation, the holders of any class of its shares, or another person to approve the transfer of the restricted shares, if the requirement is not manifestly unreasonable." RMBCA § 6.27(d)(3).

An initial determination must be made as to whether the restriction on transfer is reasonable and therefore enforceable against Dave, a shareholder. Arguably, it is not manifestly unreasonable to allow family members to approve new shareholders so they can keep control in the family or in people acceptable to the family. Therefore, the restriction would be enforceable against Dave. Alternatively, it could be argued that the restriction would not be enforceable because the restriction might unreasonably result in the current shareholders never having the right to transfer their shares in Store.

Point Two: (10-15%)

Restrictions on the transfer of stock would be enforceable against Bank if it had actual knowledge of the restrictions and would not be enforceable against Bank if it did not.

Assuming that the share transfer restriction is enforceable against Dave, it must be determined whether the restriction is binding on Bank. Both the RMBCA and the Uniform Commercial Code (UCC) address the issue of whether the share transfer restrictions are binding on third parties to whom restricted stock is conveyed. The RMBCA states:

A restriction on the transfer or registration of shares is valid and enforceable against the holder or a transferee of the holder if the restriction is authorized by this section and its existence is noted conspicuously on the front or back of the certificate. . . . Unless so noted, a restriction is not enforceable against a person without knowledge of the restriction. RMBCA § 6.27(b).

Section 8-204(1) of the UCC similarly provides that a stock transfer restriction is invalid unless the restriction is noted conspicuously on the stock certificate.

The facts state that Store's Articles of Incorporation provide for the share transfer restrictions. Therefore, the restriction is "authorized" as required by the RMBCA. RMBCA § 6.27(a)(b). However, the facts do not indicate whether the transfer restriction is conspicuously noted on the stock certificates. Therefore, it is not clear whether Bank knew of the share transfer restriction on the Store stock that Dave had pledged to the Bank. If the restriction is conspicuously noted on the certificates, the restriction is valid and enforceable against Bank. If it is not conspicuously noted, the restriction is enforceable only if Bank had actual notice of it through other means. Because the facts are silent as to whether Bank had knowledge of the restriction, it cannot be determined whether the restrictions are enforceable against Bank.

Point Three: (45-55%)

<u>A court is likely to order the dissolution of Store in order to protect the minority shareholders from oppressive conduct by the majority.</u>

In this case, the directors and controlling shareholders may have embarked upon a plan to freeze out Dave, the minority shareholder. The plan appears to have two elements: to deprive Dave of a voice in management and to eliminate shareholder dividends while increasing salaries to the majority shareholders and the directors.

The RMBCA permits courts to intervene in the affairs of closely held corporations under limited circumstances. A court may dissolve a corporation "in a proceeding by a shareholder if it is established that. . . the directors or those in control of the corporation have acted, are acting, or will act in a manner that is illegal, oppressive or fraudulent." RMBCA § 14.30(2)(ii).

The issue here is whether the conduct of Anne, Bob, and Clyde, the majority shareholders, is "illegal, oppressive or fraudulent." Shareholder dividends were eliminated while directors' and employees' compensation was dramatically increased, and the minority shareholder was given no voice in management. It appears that the directors and controlling shareholders are attempting to pay to themselves what had formerly been regarded as corporate profits.

The majority shareholders will argue that they have a right to accumulate profits, that dividends are usually discretionary and within the business judgment of the board of directors, and that their actions had a legitimate business purpose. Henn & Alexander, *supra,* § 327, at 913-14. Nonetheless, the combination of eliminating dividends while substantially increasing the compensation of majority shareholders in their capacities as directors and employees of the corporation raises the issue of whether the minority shareholders have been oppressed.

The standard for oppressive conduct is not clearly established. Some courts define oppression as violating the reasonable expectations of shareholders. "One of the most significant trends in the law of close corporations in recent years is the increasing willingness of courts to look to the reasonable expectations of shareholders to determine whether 'oppression' or similar grounds exist as a justification for involuntary dissolution or another remedy." F. Hodge O'Neal & Robert Thompson, *Close Corporations* § 9.30, at 9-141 (1988).

Many courts have taken an alternative approach, finding that in closely held corporations, controlling shareholders have a higher fiduciary duty to minority shareholders than in publicly held corporations. *See Nelson* v. *Martin and Gammon,* 1996 Tenn. App. Lexis 63; Henn & Alexander, *supra,* § 268, at 735. Under such a view, majority shareholders "are required to deal fairly, honestly and openly with minority shareholders and may not use their corporate control to prevent the minority from having an equal opportunity in the corporation." *Nelson* v. *Martin and Gammon,* 1996 Tenn. App. Lexis 63, citing *W&W Equipment Co., Inc.* v. *Mink,* 568 N.E. 2d 564, 570 (Ind. Ct. App. 1991). In addition, some courts have held directors in a closely held corporation to higher fiduciary duties than those of directors in public corporations. Henn & Alexander, *supra,* § 276, at 747.

Whether the standard is reasonable expectations of shareholders or the duty of good faith and loyalty from majority to minority shareholders, it is clear that attempts to freeze out minority shareholders are oppressive if the majority shareholders profit from the corporation to the detriment of minority shareholders. If what is properly a dividend is converted to salary for majority shareholders, the expectations of the minority shareholders have been frustrated and the obligations of the majority shareholders have been breached, thereby justifying judicial dissolution.

The RMBCA provides that if a proceeding is started to dissolve a corporation, the corporation may terminate the action if it, or a shareholder, purchases the complaining shareholders' shares for fair value. RMBCA § 14.34(a).

Thus, Dave, the minority shareholder, is likely to get a court-ordered dissolution of Store. The corporation or any of its shareholders may choose to purchase Dave's stock to stop the proceeding.

Corporations

(February 2001)

Legal Problems:

1. Under what circumstances would Henry, as beneficial owner but not record owner of 20 shares, be entitled to vote at the Acme annual meeting?

2. Was there a quorum present for shareholder action at the Acme annual meeting?

3. Did Candace, Fran, and David receive sufficient votes to be elected as directors of Acme meeting?

DISCUSSION

Point One: (25-35%)

Without having obtained a proxy, Henry was not entitled to vote at the annual meeting because only shareholders of record are entitled to vote.

Generally only shareholders of record are entitled to vote at a meeting of shareholders. *See* Model Bus. Corp. Act § 1.40(22) (1984) (definition of shareholder); Del. Gen. Corp. Law. § 219 (stating that the share ledger is the only evidence as to who are the shareholders entitled to vote, in person or by proxy, at any meeting of shareholders). A mere beneficial owner of shares is not entitled to vote at a meeting of shareholders. *Salgo v. Matthews,* 497 S.W.2d 620, 628 (Tex. Civ. App. 1973) (stating that beneficial ownership of shares does not carry with it the right to vote without having the shares transferred on the corporate books).

Where corporate shares are transferred between the record date for a meeting of shareholders and the date of the meeting, the transferee is not entitled to vote the shares at the meeting. *Wick v. Youngstown Sheet & Tube Co.,* 46 Ohio App. 253, 188 N.E. 514, 517-18 (1932) (holding that election inspectors did not err in permitting voting of shares by shareholders as of record date, regardless of subsequent transfers of the shares), *petition dismissed,* 127 Ohio St. 379, 189 N.E. 4 (1933). The corporation is not required to determine the "true" owners of corporate shares on the day of the meeting. Rather, the corporation is entitled to rely on its share ledger as of the record date for the meeting in determining who is entitled to vote.

The establishment of a record date is for the convenience of the corporation. *McDonough v. Foundation Co.,* 7 Misc. 2d 571, 155 N.Y.S.2d 67, 68 (1956). A transferee of shares after the record date who wants to vote at a scheduled shareholder meeting should obtain a proxy from his or her transferor to vote the shares. *Wick,* 188 N.E. at 518.

Point Two: (25-35%)

A quorum was present for shareholder action at the Acme annual meeting.

Neither the articles of incorporation nor the bylaws of Acme contain a provision relating to the quorum for a meeting of shareholders. Consequently, a quorum is a majority of the votes entitled to be cast by the voting group. *See* Model Bus. Corp. Act § 7.25(a) (1984); Del. Gen. Corp. Law § 216. The voting group in this case consisted of all the common shareholders of Acme.

A shareholder may vote his or her shares either in person or by proxy. Candace and Fran were present at the meeting in person. Brenda granted a proxy appointment to George to vote her shares, as is the right of a shareholder, and, thus, was present by proxy. A proxy should be accepted as valid if on its face it appears to be "free from all reasonable grounds of suspicion of its genuineness and authenticity." *In re Election of Directors of the St. Lawrence Steamboat Co.,* 44 N.LJ. 529, 534 (N.J. Sup. Ct. 1882). The facts do not suggest that the proxy from Brenda was suspicious on its face. Consequently, 60 shares entitled to vote were present at the annual meeting of Acme. Since, as discussed above, Henry (as a mere beneficial owner) was not entitled to vote, his shares are not counted as present for quorum purposes.

There were 100 shares entitled to vote at the Acme annual meeting. A majority of 100 is 51. Since, as discussed above, there were 60 shares entitled to vote present at the Acme annual meeting, a quorum was present for shareholder action even though only two of the five shareholders owning only 40 of the 100 shares were physically present at the meeting.

Point Three: (25-35%)

Candace, Fran, and David each received sufficient votes to be elected as directors at the Acme annual meeting.

In most states the election of directors requires only a plurality vote of the shares entitled to vote at a meeting at which a quorum is present. *See* Model Bus. Corp. Act § 7.28(a) (1984); Del. Gen. Corp. Act § 216(2). As discussed above, a quorum was present at the Acme annual meeting.

The plurality vote requirement for directors simply means "that the individuals with the largest number of votes are elected as directors up to the maximum number of directors to be chosen at the election." Model Bus. Corp. Act Ann. § 7.28 Official Comment (3rd ed. 1996). Three directors were to be elected at the Acme annual meeting of shareholders. Candace, Fran, and David each received 40 votes, which was more than any other candidates received. George, Brenda, and Henry only received 20 votes each. Consequently, Candace, Fran, and David were elected as directors.

In a minority of states, directors must be elected by a majority of the shares entitled to vote at a meeting of shareholders at which a quorum is present. Model Bus. Corp. Act Ann. § 7.28 annot. (3rd ed. 1996). A majority of the 60 shares present and entitled to vote was 31. (As discussed above, Henry was not entitled to vote at the meeting.) Since 40 shares voted for the election of Candace, Fran, and David, they received enough votes to be elected as directors even in those few states requiring a majority vote.

In voting his or her shares, each shareholder can cast no more than 20 votes for each directorship to be filled unless cumulative voting is authorized. If cumulative voting is authorized (which it is not here), then each shareholder has a number of votes equal to the number of shares owned times the number of directorships to be filled and the shareholder can allocate those votes among any of the persons running for director.

Corporations

(February 2002)

Legal Problems:

Analysis

(1)   What is the applicable legal standard when a shareholder brings a derivative action based on breach of a director's fiduciary duties?

(2)(a) Do directors violate their duty of care to the corporation when they vote to recommend action after only one hour of discussion?

(2)(b) Does a director violate her duty of loyalty to the corporation when she votes to issue herself shares of the corporation?

(3)   If the court finds sufficient evidence of a breach of a fiduciary duty to overcome the Business Judgment Rule (BJR), can the director prevail with a defense of (i) disinterested director approval, (ii) shareholder approval, or (iii) fairness?

DISCUSSION

Summary: The Class B Shareholder is unlikely to prevail in this derivative action. Ordinarily, the Business Judgment Rule (BJR) would preclude the court from second-guessing the board of directors on an issue of this sort (i.e., how best to finance a business expansion). In this case, however, even though the directors did not breach their duty of care to the corporation, Dart clearly did breach the duty of loyalty by voting to cause the corporation to enter into a transaction that provided her with a financial benefit. Because of the breach of the duty of loyalty, the BJR does not immunize the transaction from scrutiny. Nevertheless, the court would not enjoin the transaction because it was carried out in a manner that removes the taint of the breach of loyalty.

Point One: (5-10%)

In a shareholder derivative action, decisions of the board on business issues are presumptively correct under the Business Judgment Rule (BJR).

In order to prevail in this derivative action to enjoin the issuance of Class C Preferred, the Class B shareholder must overcome the BJR. The BJR is a legal presumption. Absent a showing that the directors have violated a fiduciary duty to the corporation or committed fraudulent or illegal acts, the court will not second-guess their judgments. *See Davis* v. *Louisville Gas & Electric Co.,* 142 A. 654, 659 (Del. Ch. 1928) (court refused to enjoin the directors from amending the certificate of incorporation, stating "it is not [the court's] function to resolve. . . questions of policy and business management. The directors are chosen to pass upon such questions and their judgment unless shown to be tainted with fraud is accepted as final").

If the Class B shareholder puts forth sufficient evidence to demonstrate that the directors breached a fiduciary duty to Ergo, the BJR will no longer apply.

Point Two (a): (25-35%)
Although the directors discussed the matter for only one hour, they did not violate their duty of care to Ergo when they voted to recommend to shareholders the amendment to the Articles.

Directors owe a duty of care to Ergo; they must act on an informed basis, in good faith in the honest belief that the action taken is in the best interest of the corporation. *See Aronson v. Lewis,* 473 A.2d 805,812 (Del. 1984). Under the Revised Model Business Corporation Act (RMBCA), directors are required to discharge their duty "in good faith and in a manner the director reasonably believes to be in the best interests of the corporation." RMBCA § 8.30(a). When becoming informed to make a decision, directors must discharge their duty "with the care that a person in a like position would reasonably believe appropriate under similar circumstances." RMBCA § 8.30(b). The duty of care is procedural (process oriented), not substantive.

The facts do not support an argument for lack of good faith or failure to act "with the care that a person in a like position would reasonably believe appropriate under similar circumstances." RMBCA § 8.30(b). Even if the other funding alternatives might have been better for Ergo, directors are not liable for bad decisions so long as they follow the appropriate procedures, which they did here. *See Kamin v. American Express Co.,* 383 N.Y.S.2d 807 (N.Y. Sup. Ct. 1976), *aff'd,* 387 N.Y.S.2d 993 (N.Y. App. Div. 1976).

The directors spent only one hour considering and deciding the issue. In *Smith v. Van Gorkom,* two hours was held insufficient for a major corporate decision. *See Smith v. Van Gorkom,* 488 A.2d 858 (Del. 1985) (Duty of care violated when directors approved a merger after a 20-minute oral presentation without reviewing the documents or assessing the valuation at a meeting that was called without much notice.) However, courts are generally concerned with major corporate decisions, like the sale of control in *Van Gorkom. See Cede & Co. v. Technicolor, Inc.,* 634 A.2d 345, 370 (Del. 1993). In Ergo's case, the issue was only the source of funding, as the directors had already properly approved the expansion plan.

Point Two (b): (10- 20%)

Dart violated her duty of loyalty to Ergo when she voted to issue the Class C Preferred to herself.

The duty of loyalty requires a director to put the interests of the corporation before the director's own interests. If a director enters into a transaction with the corporation that provides the director with financial benefit, it is a violation of the duty of loyalty. The purchase of the Class C Preferred by Dart is a transaction with Ergo that provides Dart with a financial benefit. Therefore, Dart violated her duty of loyalty to Ergo when she voted to issue the Class C Preferred to herself. This was also a conflicting interest transaction under the RMBCA because Dart knew she could benefit. RMBCA § 8.60.

Dart has a conflicting interest transaction because, at the time she voted to issue the Class C Preferred to herself, she knew she had a significant financial interest.

Point Three: (35-45%)

Although the directors did not violate their duty of care to Ergo, Dart violated her duty of loyalty. Regardless, the court would not enjoin the issuance of the Class C Preferred because Dart could show the transaction was (1) approved by a majority of disinterested directors after full disclosure, (2) approved by a majority of shareholders after full disclosure, or (3) fair to Ergo.

Even though the directors did not violate their duty of care, Dart violated her duty of loyalty to Ergo, and that fact prevents the application of the BJR. Nonetheless, the court would NOT enjoin the issuance of the Class C Preferred if Dart could demonstrate that the sale of Class C Preferred to her was (1) approved by a majority of disinterested directors after full disclosure, (2) approved by a majority of shareholders after full disclosure, or (3) fair to Ergo. See Robert C. Clark, CORPORATE LAW § 5.2 (1986); Revised Model Bus. Corp. Act (RMBCA) §§ 8.61-.63. In this case, Dart can demonstrate all three.

Disinterested Director Approval: All seven directors voted to offer the Class C Preferred to Dart after full disclosure of all material facts relating to the transaction. Disclosure of all material facts constitutes full disclosure. Approval must also be by a majority of disinterested directors. Dart is interested because she is a party to the transaction. The three remaining Class A directors are arguably interested because their positions as Ergo directors are dependent upon election by Dart, the sole Class A shareholder. If they failed to support Dart, Dart could remove them from their positions as directors. The three Class B directors, however, are disinterested directors. They all voted in favor of issuing the shares to Dart. Therefore, a majority (indeed all three) of the disinterested directors approved the offering of the Class C Preferred to Dart. Under the RMBCA (and most state statutes), the three disinterested directors who voted are sufficient to constitute a quorum when voting on a conflicting interest transaction.

Shareholder Approval: According to the facts, the proxy solicitation provided full disclosure of all relevant information regarding the plan to issue the Class C Preferred to Dart for $5 million. The fact that the directors did not disclose that they had considered and discarded other financing options is unimportant because information on other options was properly considered and discarded. All Class A shares voted in favor of the transaction, as did a majority of Class B shares (720,000 of 820,000 shares). Therefore, a majority of shareholders approved the transaction after full disclosure. Note that there is no requirement that the shareholders be disinterested.

Fair: Alternatively, Dart can show that the transaction was fair to Ergo at the time the Class C Preferred shares were issued. In assessing fairness, directors may rely on expert opinions. *See* RMBCA §8.30(e). To demonstrate that the price was fair to Ergo, Dart would offer the opinion of the independent investment bank stating that (1) $5 million would be fair value for the Class C Preferred, and (2) in the long run, payment of the Class C Preferred dividend would be less costly to Ergo than interest payments on a loan.

Corporations

(February 2003)

Legal Problems: (1)   Can a judgment creditor "pierce the corporate veil" of a wholly owned subsidiary corporation to recover the creditor's judgment from the parent corporation shareholder?

                  (2)   Assuming that a judgment creditor can pierce the corporate veil of a wholly owned subsidiary corporation, can it further pierce the parent corporation's corporate veil to recover its judgment from the parent corporation's shareholders?

DISCUSSION

Summary: Stuart's estate will probably be able to pierce the corporate veil to hold Corn Corp liable for the estate's judgment against GCI. Whether a court will pierce the corporate veil depends heavily on the facts of a particular case, and here the facts support holding Corn Corp liable. In the first place, the usual facts supporting veil-piercing are present here: the business records of Corn Corp and GCI were completely intermingled, GCI did not observe the formalities of a separate corporate existence, GCI was inadequately capitalized, and GCI's business (selling Super Corn Plus) was held out to the public as a mere extension of Corn Corp's business. In addition, the activities that led to the judgment against GCI were the result of decisions made and directed by an officer of Corn Corp at a time when Super Corn Plus was still a Corn Corp product.

It is less likely that a court would pierce the corporate veil of Corn Corp in order to hold its shareholders liable to pay Stuart's estate's claim. There is nothing to suggest that the shareholders used Corn Corp as a "mere instrumentality" or their "alter ego." They respected corporate formalities, and Corn Corp appears to have been adequately capitalized.

Point One: <u>Stuart's estate will likely be able to pierce GCI's corporate veil and</u>
(50-60%)   <u>recover its judgment from Corn Corp, the "parent" corporation, because GCI failed to maintain a formal separate existence as evidenced by its inadequate capitalization and failed to maintain corporate formalities, and because justice requires piercing to prevent Corn Corp from insulating itself from its wrongdoing.</u>

Shareholders generally are not liable for the corporation's debts. *See* Revised Model Business Corporation Act § 6.22. A court, however, will "pierce the corporate veil" when circumstances indicate that the privilege has been misused or when necessary to do justice. *See Pepper v. Litton*, 308 U.S. 295, 310 (1939). The decision to pierce the corporate veil will be based on a determination of the facts.

While a parent corporation is expected to exert some measure of control over a subsidiary corporation, the subsidiary corporation is expected to be separate, at least in form. When a parent corporation so dominates a subsidiary corporation that the subsidiary has no real separate existence, and justice so requires, a court will disregard the corporate form and hold the parent corporation personally liable for the subsidiary's debts.

One basis for piercing the corporate veil is fraud or illegitimate purpose. In the absence of fraud or illegitimate purpose, a court may still pierce the corporate veil when justice so requires if (a) the parent and subsidiary intermingle their respective business transactions, accounts, and records; (b) the subsidiary fails to observe the formalities of separate corporate procedures; (c) the subsidiary is not adequately financed in light of its foreseeable normal obligations; or (d) the parent and subsidiary do not hold themselves out to the public as separate enterprises. *See* Harry Henn & John R. Alexander, LAWS OF CORPORATIONS § 148 (1983).

Based on the facts, GCI is a wholly owned subsidiary of Corn Corp. Corn Corp had a legitimate purpose for organizing GCI. Creating a separate entity for marketing reasons (because some food processors might not have wanted genetically engineered corn) is an acceptable business reason. Despite this legitimate purpose, a court might still pierce the corporate veil because GCI did not formally maintain a separate existence from Corn Corp (internally or externally). GCI did not formally maintain corporate formalities and was not initially adequately capitalized.

Corn Corp and GCI intermingled their assets and business transactions. GCI operated out of the offices of Corn Corp and had exactly the same directors and officers. GCI did not keep separate records of its business transactions. Additionally, while the two corporations each had separate bank accounts, the fact that GCI received "informal" loans from Corn Corp is further evidence of the blurred boundaries between the parent and subsidiary.

GCI did not observe corporate formalities. It did not keep separate minute books. Additionally, Corn Corp did not adequately finance GCI in light of its foreseeable normal obligations. Corn Corp funded GCI with only the patent, which was new and of speculative value, and $6,000, which was only enough to produce the seed for the first crop. The inadequate initial capitalization was further evidenced by GCI's need for "emergency loans" from Corn Corp to meet day-to-day cash flow needs.

Finally, Corn Corp and GCI marketed products with very similar names (Super Corn and Super Corn Plus). These similar product names could be reasonably interpreted by the public to be from the same entity. The decline in sales experienced by Corn Corp after Stuart's death seems to indicate that the public viewed Corn Corp as the same entity as GCI. Further, as discussed above, both Corn Corp and GCI operated from the same location, which could lead the public to conclude that the businesses were not distinct.

Justice requires piercing because Super Corn Plus was developed by Corn Corp, and an officer and director of Corn Corp negligently rushed it to market without the proper testing. Corn Corp should not now be able to use a wholly owned subsidiary that did not maintain a separate existence to insulate itself from liability.

Point Two: The facts do *not* support piercing Corn Corp's corporate veil to hold
(40-50%) and Alan, Bruce, Kathy, as shareholders, liable for Stuart's estate's judgment.
Kathy, however, might be liable for her negligent acts.

While the facts support piercing the corporate veil to hold Corn Corp liable for the judgment against GCI, this will not help Stuart's estate because the facts indicate that Corn Corp cannot pay its bills (so it will be unable to pay the judgment). Therefore, Stuart's estate would like to recover the judgment against GCI from the shareholders of Corn Corp (Alan, Bruce, and Kathy). However, the facts do *not* support a claim to recover from Alan, Bruce, or Kathy in their capacity as shareholders of Corn Corp.

Shareholders generally are not liable for the corporation's debts. *See* RMBCA § 6.22. Courts generally respect the corporate form and shield shareholders from liability unless the shareholders use the corporation as a "mere instrumentality" or "alter ego" to carry out an improper or illegal purpose (e.g., to perpetrate fraud, to evade the law, to escape obligations). "[W]here corporate formalities are substantially observed, initial financing reasonably adequate, and the corporation not formed to evade an existing obligation or a statute or to cheat or to defraud, even a controlling shareholder enjoys limited liability." *See* Henn and Alexander, LAWS OF CORPORATIONS § 146 (3d ed. 1983).

There are no facts to support a conclusion of an illegal or improper purpose when Corn Corp was incorporated. There is also no suggestion that Corn Corp was inadequately capitalized when it was incorporated. Corn Corp had $500,000 of initial capitalization and had been profitable for 20 years. The fact that Corn Corp cannot currently pay its bills is irrelevant to this determination.

Further, there is no evidence that the shareholders did not respect the corporate formalities. For example, Kathy scrupulously kept Corn Corp's minute books. Nor is there any evidence that Alan, Bruce, or Kathy ignored the "separateness" of Corn Corp. In summary, there are no facts to indicate that any of the shareholders of Corn Corp treated Corn Corp as their "alter ego" or a "mere instrumentality," and the interests of justice do not require piercing the corporate veil in this case.

Although the facts do not support a holding that Kathy is liable in her capacity as a shareholder of Corn Corp, Stuart's estate could bring a separate action against Kathy for her negligent acts as the head of Corn Corp's product development.

Corporations

(July 2003)

Legal Problems: (1)(a)   In a parent-subsidiary merger, does the board of directors of the subsidiary corporation have to approve the merger?

(1)(b)   In a parent-subsidiary merger, do the shareholders of the parent corporation have to approve the merger?

(1)(c)   In a parent-subsidiary merger, do the shareholders of the subsidiary corporation have to approve the merger?

(2)   In a parent-subsidiary merger, if the subsidiary's minority shareholders believe that the parent corporation is paying less than fair value, can they force the parent corporation to pay more money?

DISCUSSION

Summary: None of the objections presented by Pat and Dale will suffice for unwinding this merger. Corp's ownership of 95 percent of Sub's shares gives it the power to merge Sub into itself without securing the approval of Sub's board of directors and without holding any vote of Corp's or Sub's shareholders. However, Pat and Dale are entitled to receive the fair value of their shares, provided they properly invoke their appraisal rights.

Point One (a): The approval of Sub's board of directors is not required for this
(20-30%)   parent-subsidiary merger.

A merger between two corporations is normally effectuated by adoption of a plan of merger by the board of directors of both corporations. Revised Model Business Corporation Act (RMBCA) § 11.04(a) (1999 Rev.). However, when a parent owns at least 90 percent of the outstanding shares of each class of stock of a subsidiary, the parent may merge the subsidiary into itself without the approval of the subsidiary's board of directors. *See* RMBCA § 11.05 (1999 Rev.). The rationale for this rule is that the parent owns sufficient shares of the subsidiary to remove any members of the board of directors voting against the merger and replace them with members who would vote in favor of the transaction.

The facts of this problem present such a parent-subsidiary situation. Because Corp owns 95 percent of Sub, approval of the merger by the Sub board of directors is not necessary. Thus, Corp could proceed with the merger despite the Sub board's negative vote on the plan of merger, and the negative vote provides no basis for unwinding the merger.

Note: Some state's parent-subsidiary merger statutes require that the parent corporation own at least 95 percent (e.g., Arkansas), while other states require only 80 percent (e.g., Alabama).

Point One (b): Approval by the shareholders of Corp is not required for this parent-
(20-30%)   subsidiary merger.

A plan of merger usually must be submitted to shareholders for their approval. *See* RMBCA § 11.04 (1999 Rev.). However, RMBCA § 11.04(g) provides that approval by shareholders of the surviving corporation is not required when the merger will not result in a fundamental change in the corporation or the ownership rights of its shareholders. In particular, no shareholder approval is required if

> (1) the corporation will survive the merger . . . ; (2) . . . its articles of incorporation will not be changed; (3) each shareholder of the corporation whose shares were outstanding immediately before the effective date of the merger . . . will hold the same number of shares, with identical preferences, limitations, and relative rights, immediately after the effective date of change; and (4) the issuance in the merger . . . of shares or other securities . . . does not require a vote under § 6.21(f).

RMBCA § 11.04(g)(1999 Rev.).

The facts presented satisfy the requirements for this exception insofar as Corp's shareholders are concerned. First, Corp will survive the merger because Sub is being merged into it. Second, Corp's articles of incorporation will not change as a result of the merger. Finally, no vote to issue shares is required because this is a cash-out merger (the Sub shareholders are receiving cash, not securities). The cash-out nature of the merger also means that no Corp shareholder will experience a change in the number of shares owned or the rights and preferences of those shares. Therefore, the fact that the Corp shareholders did not vote does not constitute a basis to unwind the merger.

Note: Prior to the RMBCA 1999 revision, approval by Corp's shareholders would not have been required simply because this was a short-form merger (parent's subsidiary). See old RMBCA § 11.04. Under the revised act, the analysis is more elaborate but the result is the same.

Point One (c): The shareholders of Sub are also not required to approve this parent
(20-30%)   subsidiary merger.

As noted above, shareholder approval of a plan of merger is generally required. *See* RMBCA § 11.04(b)(1999 Rev.). However, parent-subsidiary mergers are an exception to this rule when the parent owns at least 90 percent of the outstanding shares of each class of the subsidiary. *See* RMBCA § 11.05 (1999 Rev.). Shareholder approval is not required in these circumstances because the parent corporation owns a sufficient number of shares to ensure that the plan of the merger will be adopted. In our problem, because Corp owns 95 percent of Sub, it would easily prevail in any shareholder vote and, accordingly, the law does not require a vote by the shareholders of Sub for the merger to proceed. Therefore, the failure of the Sub shareholders to approve the transaction does not constitute a basis to unwind the merger.

Point Two: Pat and Dale are entitled to exercise appraisal rights and seek the
(30-40%)   "fair value" of their shares.

Appraisal rights (also referred to as dissenter's rights) allow shareholders to force the corporation to pay fair value for their shares in the event of certain fundamental changes, including a parent-subsidiary merger for which shareholder approval is unnecessary. *See* RMBCA § 13.02 (a)(1)(ii) (1999 Rev.). Thus, Pat and Dale, as minority shareholders of Sub, are entitled to exercise appraisal rights in connection with this merger. As Pat and Dale believe that each share is worth $5 more than Corp paid them in the merger, they will exercise their appraisal rights. Assuming that they follow the procedure established by the applicable statute (including notifying the corporation of their assertion of appraisal rights and demanding payment), they will be entitled to receive the fair value of their shares.

If Corp and Pat and Dale cannot agree on fair value, a court will decide the matter. In the court proceeding, Pat and Dale would offer the testimony of the independent financial advisor, stating the fair value of Sub shares to be between $21 and $26 per share, to support their contention. They might not get $25 per share, but based on this independent evaluation, they would probably get more than $20 per share.

Corporations

(February 2004)

ANALYSIS

Legal Problems: (1)   Must shareholders show cause to remove a director?

                (2)   May a shareholder revoke a proxy that states it is irrevocable by issuing a subsequent proxy?

                (3)   What vote is required to remove a director when cumulative voting is authorized by the corporation?

DISCUSSION

Summary: Zeta's shareholders may remove Diane without cause so long as they get the appropriate vote. Under cumulative voting, at least 60,001 votes would be sufficient to elect Diane as a director. Diane cannot be removed if the votes cast against removal would be sufficient to elect her as a director at an annual meeting to elect directors. Under either vote, there were sufficient votes cast against removing Diane and thus, she should not be removed.

Sam's proxy to Arnie was revoked when he issued a subsequent proxy to Betty. Even though the proxy stated it was irrevocable, words alone are not sufficient to create an irrevocable proxy. A proxy is only irrevocable if coupled with an interest, and there are no facts to indicate that this proxy was coupled with an interest.

Point One: <u>Shareholders need not show cause to remove a director.</u>
(35-45%)

Under the common law, shareholders had the inherent power to remove a director, but only for cause. *See Frank v. Anthony*, 107 So. 2d 136 (Fla. Ct. App. 1958); *Toledo Traction, Light & Power Co. v. Smith*, 205 F. 643 (N.D. Ohio 1913). Cause is defined as substantial grounds, such as directorial breach of duty or malfeasance in office. *See Eckhaus v. Ma*, 635 F. Supp. 873 (S.D.N.Y. 1986); *Doolittle v. Morley*, 292 P.2d 476 (Idaho 1956). "Rocking the boat" and being critical of management, as alleged here, do not constitute cause for removal.

However, most modern statutes, including the Revised Model Business Corporation Act (RMBCA), permit shareholders to remove a director without cause. *See* RMBCA § 8.08(a) ("The shareholders may remove one or more directors with or without cause unless the articles of incorporation provide that directors may be removed only for cause"); *Mitchell v. Concerned Citizens of CVEC, Inc.*, 486 So. 2d 1283 (Ala. 1986). As Zeta's articles of incorporation contain no special provisions concerning removal of directors, the shareholders may remove Diane without showing cause. Therefore, the first ruling was incorrect.

Point Two:	By issuing a subsequent proxy to Betty, Sam revoked the proxy he issued to Arnie, even though the proxy stated it was irrevocable.

(35-45%)

Under the common law and state corporation statutes, a proxy is revocable unless it expressly provides that it is irrevocable and the appointment of the proxy is "coupled with an interest." *See* RMBCA § 7.22(d); *Stein v. Capital Outdoor Advertising, Inc.*, 159 S.E.2d 351 (N.C. 1968); *In re Chilson*, 168 A. 82 (Del. Ch. 1933). Thus, unless it was coupled with an interest, Sam could revoke the proxy he gave Arnie even though the proxy states it is irrevocable.

The concept of "coupled with an interest" is not completely clear, but, in general, the proxy holder must have "either (1) a charge, lien, or some property right in the shares themselves; or (2) a security interest given to protect the proxy holder for money advanced or obligations incurred." James D. Cox et al., CORPORATIONS 332 (1997). The RMBCA specifies various categories of people who qualify: (1) a pledgee; (2) a person who purchased or agreed to purchase the shares; (3) a creditor of the corporation who extended it credit under terms requiring the appointment; (4) an employee of the corporation whose employment contract requires the appointment; or (5) a party to a voting agreement created under RMBCA § 7.31.

Sam's proxy to Arnie was not coupled with an interest. The facts indicate only that Arnie was Sam's friend. Because the proxy to Arnie was not coupled with an interest, it was revocable in spite of the language to the contrary.

Where two or more revocable proxies have been given, the last given revokes all previous proxies. FLETCHERS CYCLOPEDIA OF PRIVATE CORPORATIONS § 2026. When Sam gave Betty a proxy on August 15, he revoked the proxy he had given to Arnie on August 1. Therefore, the second ruling was incorrect. Betty was entitled to vote Sam's shares.

Point Three:	Under cumulative voting, a director is not removed if the number of votes cast against removal would be sufficient to elect the director at an annual meeting. Here, the number of votes cast against Diane's removal would have been sufficient to assure her election. Diane would not be removed under either vote.
(10-20%)	

In a corporation with straight voting, a shareholder vote removes a director if the number of votes for removal exceeds the number of votes against removal. RMBCA § 8.08(c). However, this corporation's articles require cumulative voting. "If cumulative voting is authorized, a director may *not* be removed if the number of votes sufficient to elect him under cumulative voting is voted against his removal." RMBCA § 8.08(c)(emphasis added). *See* Ark. Stat. Ann. § 4-27-808; Miss. Code Ann. § 79-4-8.08; Utah Code Ann. § 16-10a-808(3). Diane could have been elected a director with 60,001 votes, and more votes than that were voted against her removal (123,000 or 75,000, depending on how the proxies were counted). Therefore, the third ruling was correct. Diane could not have been removed.

NOTE: Directors are elected by a plurality of the votes cast, so the directors with the greatest number of votes are elected. According to Zeta's articles, the nine directors have staggered terms, and three directors are elected at each annual meeting. Therefore, under cumulative voting, each share is entitled to three votes (number of shares x number of directors up for election). *See* RMBCA § 7.28(c).

As stated in the facts, a director must receive at least 60,001 votes to assure election under the following formula:

$$\left(\frac{\text{number of votes eligible to be cast}}{\text{number of directors to be elected} + 1} \right) + 1$$

Corporations

(February 2005)

ANALYSIS

Legal Problems: (1)   Did Presley, as president of Corp, have authority to retain an attorney to file suit against FS for payment of $11,000 on behalf of Corp?

               (2)   Did Presley, as president of Corp, have authority to declare a dividend payable to Corp's shareholders?

               (3)   Did Presley, as president of Corp, have the authority to enter into a purchase agreement with Large to acquire its local manufacturing plant for Corp?

DISCUSSION

Summary

According to the bylaws of Corp, Presley, as president, is the CEO and has authority to manage the business of the corporation. Therefore, Presley had authority to retain an attorney to file suit against FS to collect the $11,000 FS owed Corp so long as collecting on this type of obligation (an account receivable) was in the ordinary course of business and the lawsuit was filed to preserve corporate assets. Presley did not have authority to declare a dividend to Corp's shareholders. Dividends can be authorized only by the board of directors. Finally, Presley did not have authority to enter into a purchase agreement with Large to acquire its local manufacturing plant for Corp. The purchase of an additional manufacturing plant would be outside the ordinary course of business.

Point One: As president of Corp, Presley had authority to retain an attorney to file suit against FS to
(30-40%)   collect the $11,000 FS owed Corp because retaining an attorney to collect an account receivable was in the ordinary course of Corp's business. Further, as FS was on the verge of bankruptcy, Presley was attempting to preserve one of Corp's assets.

Corporations are managed by or under the direction of their boards of directors. *See* Revised Model Business Corporation Act (RMBCA) § 8.01. The board of directors generally delegates day-to-day management of the corporation's business to officers. *See* RMBCA §§ 8.40, 8.41. Traditionally, officers had only those powers conferred on them by the bylaws or resolutions of the board of directors. *See Black v. Harrison Home Co.*, 99 P. 494 (Cal. 1909); *Daniel Webster Council, Inc. v. St. James Assoc., Inc.*, 533 A.2d 329 (N.H. 1987). Today, most states presume that the president has the inherent power to act for the corporation so long as the matter is within the scope of its ordinary business. *See, e.g., Lee v. Jenkins Bros.*, 268 F.2d 357, 365-66 (2d Cir.

1959); *Belcher v. Birmingham Trust National Bank*, 348 F. Supp. 61 (N.D. Ala. 1968); *Gunter v. Novopharm USA, Inc.*, 2001 U.S. Dist. LEXIS 2117 (N.D. Ill. 2001).

Presley was appointed president of Corp by its board of directors. The bylaws provide that "the president, as the chief executive officer of the corporation, shall manage the business of the corporation and perform such other duties as the board of directors may from time to time direct." Pursuant to the bylaws, Presley, as chief executive officer responsible for managing the business, had the authority to retain an attorney to file suit against FS for the following reasons: Corp manufactures computer desks and sells them to furniture stores like FS. FS purchased computer desks but has not paid for them. Presley was attempting to collect on an account receivable. Hiring an attorney to bring suit against a retailer for payment is part of Corp's ordinary course of business.

Absent a prohibition contained in bylaws or imposed by the board of directors, Presley had authority to bring suit on behalf of Corp, so long as it was in the ordinary course of business. *See Custer Channel Wing Corp v. Frazer*, 181 F. Supp. 197, 200 (S.D.N.Y. 1959); *West View Hills, Inc. v. Lizau Realty Corp*, 160 N.E.2d 622, 624 (N.Y. 1959) (absent direct prohibition, a president has presumptive authority to prosecute suits in the name of the corporation). *See generally* 2A FLETCHER'S CYCLOPEDIA OF PRIVATE CORPORATIONS § 618 (discussing presidents' authority to bring legal proceedings). There are no facts indicating that the board of directors has withheld authority from Presley to commence litigation on behalf of Corp.

Some case law indicates that the president may only commence litigation to preserve corporate assets or prevent dissipation. *See Lloydona Peters Enterprises v. Dorius*, 658 P.2d 1209, 1211 (Utah 1983). Even under this test, Presley had authority to sue FS. As FS was on the verge of bankruptcy, by retaining an attorney to file suit, Presley was attempting to preserve a corporate asset.

Point Two: Presley did not have authority to declare a dividend payable to Corp's shareholders.
(25-35%)   Corporate law reserves the authority to declare dividends to the board of directors.

Although the president of a corporation has the authority to bind the corporation by acts that are in the ordinary course of business (*see* Point One above), the president does not have the authority to declare or pay dividends to shareholders. Corporate law confers this authority only on the directors of the corporation. *See* RMBCA § 6.40(a); Del. Gen. Corp. Law. § 170(a). Consequently, only the board of directors has the power to declare a dividend. *See* 1 PRINCIPLES OF CORP. GOVERNANCE § 3.01 Reporter's Note ("some matters, such as the declaration of dividends, are required by statute to be decided by the board"). Therefore, Presley, as an officer, did not have the authority to declare a dividend payable to Corp's shareholders.

Point Three: Presley has no power, as president, to enter into a purchase agreement to acquire Large's
(30-40%)   local manufacturing plant on behalf of Corp because the transaction is extraordinary in
              nature.

The president of a corporation has the authority to bind the corporation by acts that are in the ordinary course of business, but does not have the authority to bind the corporation by extraordinary acts. *See* Point One above. While some acts are clearly ordinary or extraordinary, in many cases there is no bright line demarcation. "Any attempt at precision in drawing this line would almost certainly be futile, because the issue is highly dependent on the context in which it arises, and the types of business transactions that may arise are endlessly variable." *See* 1 PRINCIPLES OF CORP. GOVERNANCE § 3.01 Reporter's Note. Factors that a court might consider in determining whether a transaction is extraordinary include "the economic magnitude of the action in relation to corporate earnings and assets, the extent of the risk involved, the time span of the action's effect, and the cost of reversing the action." *Id. See also Joseph Greenspon's Sons Iron & Steel Co. v. Pecos Valley Gas Co.*, 156 A. 350, 352-53 (Del. Super. 1931) (factors include "the character of the goods ordered, the amount thereof in relation to the size and condition of the company, the nature of the company, its purposes and aims").

The facts surrounding Presley's planned purchase of Large's local manufacturing plant do not provide numbers to calculate the economic impact of the purchase on the corporation, but they do suggest that the impact would be significant. Additionally, while Presley believes the price is "very reasonable," the payment process could span 10 years. Finally, it seems likely that it would be costly to reverse the transaction if it turned out not to be beneficial to Corp.

Consequently, it is very likely that entering into a purchase agreement to acquire Large's local manufacturing plant would be viewed as an extraordinary act. As such, Presley, as president, would not have actual authority to sign the purchase agreement without the approval of the board of directors.

Further, there are no facts that gave Large a reasonable basis to believe that Presley was authorized to enter into this purchase agreement. Therefore, Presley also lacked apparent authority to enter into the purchase agreement.

Corporations

(July 2005)

ANALYSIS

Legal Problems: (1) Is Peg, as promoter of a corporation to be formed, personally liable on the contract with Chem Corp.?

(2) Is Acme, Inc., liable on the contract with Chem Corp.?

DISCUSSION

Summary

Peg, as a promoter, is personally liable on the contract unless the parties did not intend for her to be personally liable. This is a question of fact, which an applicant could argue either way. Acme, Inc., is liable on the contract with Chem Corp. if it adopted the contract. Although Acme did not expressly adopt the contract, by accepting delivery of and paying for the chromite, it impliedly adopted the contract with Chem Corp.

Point One: Under the contract, Peg, as a promoter, is personally liable unless the parties, as
(45-55%)   evidenced by their words and actions, did not intend for Peg to be liable.

Peg is a "promoter." A promoter is someone who "forms a corporation and procures for it the rights, instrumentalities and capital to enable it to conduct its business." *Stap v. Chicago Aces Tennis Team, Inc.*, 379 N.E.2d 1298 (Ill. App. 1 Dist. 1978). *See* 1A William Meade Fletcher et al., FLETCHER CYCLOPEDIA OF THE LAW OF PRIVATE CORP. § 189 (perm. ed., rev. vol. 2002).

Generally, a promoter who signs a contract in the name of a proposed corporation is personally liable on that contract unless the parties agree otherwise. *See* REVISED MODEL BUS. CORP. ACT § 2.04 (2003); *Spence v. Huffman*, 486 P.2d 211 (Ariz. App. 1971); RESTATEMENT (SECOND) OF AGENCY § 326, cmt. b (1958). This is true even if the contract does not mention the promoter's liability. Subsequent adoption by the corporation does not relieve the promoter of liability unless the third party and the corporation expressly or impliedly enter into a novation, by which they agree to relieve the promoter from personal liability on the contract. *See Malisewski v. Singer*, 598 P.2d 1014 (Ariz. App. 1979). Therefore, absent a novation, Peg ordinarily would be personally liable to Chem Corp. for the liquidated damages.

However, if a party who contracts with a promoter knows that the corporation has not yet been formed and agrees to look only to the corporation for performance, the promoter is not liable. The facts clearly state that Chem Corp. knew that Acme, Inc. had not yet been formed. The facts, however, do not indicate that Chem Corp. agreed to look only to the future corporation or that the contract expressly relieved Peg of liability. Peg signed the contract "as agent for Acme, Inc., a corporation to be formed." However, Peg cannot act on behalf of a nonexistent principal. *See* RESTATEMENT (SECOND) OF AGENCY § 326 (one who acts for a nonexistent principal is himself liable on the contract). Therefore, Peg would be personally liable for the liquidated damages unless she can show that Chem Corp. did not intend to hold Peg liable. This is a fact-based analysis, which an applicant could argue either way.

Chem Corp.'s statement, "No problem. We know with whom we are dealing and what the chromite's for. Do not waste our time. If you are serious, lock in the deal," could be interpreted to support either argument. It could be interpreted as an indication that Chem Corp. planned only to look to the corporation for payment, in which case Peg bears no personal liability for the contract. *See Quaker Hill, Inc. v. Parr*, 364 P.2d 1056 (Colo. 1961). Alternatively, the statement "if you are serious" could be interpreted to mean "if you, Peg, are willing to be personally liable."

The fact that Peg signed the contract as an agent for the corporation to be formed is ineffective to eliminate personal liability, as a matter of agency law. However, it does evidence her belief that she was not signing in her personal capacity and that Chem Corp. would look to the corporation, not to her, for performance on the contract.

The facts do not suggest an express novation of the contract. However, some jurisdictions imply novation upon formation and adoption by the corporation. In such a jurisdiction, Peg might argue that she is not liable because Acme adopted the contract (*see* Point Two below).

Point Two: Acme, Inc., is liable under the contract if it expressly or impliedly adopted it.
(45-55%)   While there was no express adoption, by receiving and paying for chromite for three months, Acme, Inc., implicitly adopted the contract.

A contract with a promoter is not a contract with the subsequently formed corporation. The newly formed corporation is not automatically bound by the contracts executed by its promoter prior to formation. The newly formed corporation is only liable on such a contract if: (1) a statute mandates liability, (2) charter documents mandate liability, or (3) the contract is adopted or ratified by the corporation. *See Bishop v. Parker*, 134 P.2d 180 (Utah 1943); 1A Fletcher et al., *supra* § 207.

NOTE: Although there are technical differences between the terms "adoption" and "ratification," many courts use them interchangeably.

Adoption of a contract can be either express or implied. Express adoption requires the unequivocal action by someone, with knowledge of all material facts, who would have had the authority to bind the corporation to this type of contract. The fact that "[n]either the board of directors nor the officers of Acme, Inc., formally reviewed or approved the contract with Chem Corp." indicates that Acme never expressly adopted the contract.

A corporation can impliedly adopt a contract so long as it is done with knowledge of all material facts by someone who would have had the authority to bind the corporation to this type of contract. Implied adoption requires that the corporation receive some benefit or accept some service. *See Stolmeier v. Beck*, 441 N.W.2d 888 (Neb. 1989); *Fortune Furniture Mfg. Co., v. Mid-South Plastic Fabric Co.,* 310 So. 2d 725 (Miss. 1975). This test is clearly satisfied. Acme received three shipments of chromite at the contract price and paid each invoice promptly. Because Vic acted pursuant to the direction of Acme's board of directors, he had the authority to bind the corporation to this type of contract (raw materials needed for production). Vic approved the invoice after checking that the invoice price agreed with the contract price. Because Acme received a benefit after Vic checked the material facts, Acme, Inc., adopted the contract and is liable to pay the liquidated damages.

Corporations

(February 2006)

ANALYSIS

Legal Problems: (1)   Was the special shareholder meeting to vote on the proposal to dissolve Green properly called?

                   (2)   Could the Class A Preferred shares vote at the special shareholder meeting called to vote on the proposal to dissolve Green?

                   (3)   Did Deb properly appoint Ed as her proxy?

                   (4)   If Ed was permitted to represent both his own and Deb's shares, was there a quorum present at the special shareholder meeting so that a vote could be taken, and, if so, what vote was necessary to approve the proposal to dissolve Green?

DISCUSSION

Summary

Green's board of directors has the authority to call a special shareholder meeting to vote on the proposal to dissolve the corporation. The corporation must provide proper notice of the meeting. The notice for this special meeting was defective for two reasons. First, the notice of the meeting failed to specify the purpose of the meeting. Second, Ed, a shareholder entitled to vote on the proposal, was not given notice. Although Ed waived his objection to failure to receive notice when he attended the meeting without objection, this objection was not waived by Deb because neither she nor her valid proxy attended the meeting. Thus, the meeting was not properly held. Even if the meeting were deemed to have been properly held, the proposal failed.

At the meeting, Ed properly voted his 200 shares of Class A Preferred because the articles of incorporation of Green provided that these shares were entitled to voting rights if the corporation failed to make dividend payments for four successive quarters and had outstanding arrearages. Ed, however, could not vote Deb's shares as Deb did not properly appoint Ed as her proxy. A valid proxy must be evidenced by a signed writing or verifiable electronic transmission.

If Ed had been permitted to represent both his own and Deb's shares at the meeting, a quorum was present and the vote could occur. However, the proposal could not be adopted. The vote would be a tie and therefore there would be no majority (the minimum requirement to approve the action).

Point One: (35-45%)

While the board of directors may call a special meeting to vote on the proposal to dissolve Green, this special meeting was not properly called for two reasons. First, the notice for the special meeting did not specify the purpose of the meeting. Second, all shareholders entitled to vote at a special shareholder meeting are entitled to notice of the meeting, and Ed was not given notice.

A proposal to dissolve the corporation adopted by the board of directors must be submitted to a shareholder vote. *See* REVISED MODEL BUSINESS CORPORATION ACT ("RMBCA") § 14.02(a). For this purpose, the board of directors has the authority to call a special meeting. *See* RMBCA §§ 7.02(a)(1), 3.04 (board of directors will always be empowered to call a special meeting). After the Green board unanimously agreed to recommend dissolution of the corporation, they sought to call a special meeting to submit the proposal to a shareholder vote. However, as discussed below, the meeting was not properly called.

The corporation must provide proper notice of the special meeting. Furthermore, notice of the special meeting must include a full description of its purpose. RMBCA § 7.05(c). The notice providing for this meeting did not include a statement of purpose. While Deb discovered the purpose of the meeting during Ed's phone call to her, she did not waive the notice impropriety because neither she nor her duly appointed proxy attended the meeting.

In order to properly call a meeting, the corporation also is obligated to notify all shareholders entitled to vote at the special meeting in a timely manner. RMBCA § 7.05(a) (more than 10 and less than 60 days before the meeting); *Gray v. Bloomington & N. Ry.*, 120 Ill. App. 159 (1905) (meeting held under written waiver of notice). Here, notice for this special meeting was deficient because, although Deb was given timely notice, Ed was not. Ed learned of the meeting accidentally two days prior to the meeting during his dinner conversation with Deb. However, Ed, unlike Deb, waived his objection to lack of notice by attending the meeting without objection. *See* RMBCA § 7.06(b)(1); *In re P.B. Mathiason Mfg. Co.*, 99 S.W. 502 (Mo. App. 1907); *Germer v. Triple-State Natural Gas & Oil Co.*, 54 S.E. 509 (W.Va. 1906); FLETCHER CYCLOPEDIA OF THE LAW OF PRIVATE CORPORATIONS § 1999.

[NOTE: An exceptional answer might add that under the RMBCA, even if the Class A Preferred shares were not entitled to voting rights at this time (*see* Point Two), they would still be entitled to notice of this special meeting because all shareholders are entitled to notice of a meeting to consider fundamental corporate change, including dissolution. RMBCA § 14.02(d).]

Point Two: (5-15%)
Ed was entitled to vote his 200 Class A Preferred shares because under Green's articles of incorporation these shares were entitled to voting rights as Green had missed more than four successive dividend payments and there were arrearages outstanding.

Unless the articles of incorporation provide otherwise, each outstanding share, regardless of class, is entitled to one vote on each matter voted on at a shareholders' meeting. *See* RMBCA § 7.21(a). Green's articles of incorporation provided that the Class A Preferred shares were non-voting shares unless certain conditions were fulfilled. Therefore, absent the occurrence of those certain conditions, the Class A Preferred shares were not entitled to vote on a proposed dissolution, though in an RMBCA jurisdiction they were entitled to notice of the vote. RMBCA § 14.02(d).

Under these facts, Ed was entitled to vote his 200 Class A Preferred shares because the conditions specified in the articles of incorporation had occurred. Green had missed four successive dividends and there were arrearages outstanding.

Point Three: (20-30%)
Ed could not vote Deb's shares because Deb did not properly appoint Ed as her proxy.

A shareholder may vote in person or by proxy. RMBCA § 7.22(a). Therefore, Deb was entitled to appoint Ed as her proxy to vote her shares at the special meeting when she was unable to attend. However, an oral proxy appointment is not sufficient. To appoint a valid proxy, Deb must sign an appointment form or make a verifiable electronic transmission. RMBCA § 7.22(b). In this case, Deb orally asked Ed to serve as her proxy. This appointment was insufficient.

Point Four: (30-40%)
The proposal to dissolve Green was not properly approved because the meeting was not properly held. Even if the meeting had been properly held, the votes cast in favor of dissolution were insufficient to adopt the dissolution proposal because Ed did not have a valid proxy and no majority was cast in favor of the proposal.

First, as noted above, the special meeting was not properly held as it was not called in the proper manner, and the impropriety was not effectively waived. Furthermore, even if the meeting had been properly called, there was no quorum. Unless the articles of incorporation provide otherwise, a quorum is usually a majority of votes entitled to be cast on a matter. RMBCA § 7.25(a). As no dividend had been paid in more than four consecutive quarters, the Class A Preferred shares were entitled to vote. *See* Point Two above. Therefore, there were 400 shares entitled to vote on the proposal to dissolve Green. Thus, at least 201 votes must be represented in order to establish a quorum. If Ed had been permitted to represent all of Deb's and his own shares at the special meeting, all 400 shares would have been present and the quorum satisfied. However, Ed was not entitled to vote Deb's shares. Because only 200 shares were represented at the meeting, no quorum was present, and the dissolution proposal failed.

Even if the special meeting had been properly held, the votes cast in favor of dissolution were insufficient to adopt the dissolution proposal because Ed did not have a valid proxy and no majority was cast in favor of the proposal. The vote required to approve the proposal to dissolve depends on the jurisdiction. Under the RMBCA, the proposal will be approved if, of the votes represented at a properly held meeting, more votes are cast in favor of the proposal than against. Under the older Model Business Corporation Act standard, the proposal to dissolve must be approved by a majority of shareholders entitled to vote. Any other applicable statute would require an even greater vote in favor of the proposal.

Thus, regardless of the standard applied, the proposal to dissolve Green, even assuming the meeting was properly held and Ed had properly cast Deb's votes, would fail because, if Ed had voted Deb's 200 shares (100 Common, 100 Class A Preferred) in favor of the proposal and his 200 Class A Preferred shares against, there would have been a tie vote, and neither a super-majority or even a majority in favor of the proposal.

Corporations

(July 2006)

ANALYSIS

Legal problems: (1)   Did Parensco breach any of its fiduciary duties by failing to disclose the Aster proposal to the minority shareholders of Subco?

                     (2)   Did the Subco board breach its duty of care to the Subco shareholders in approving the merger?

                     (3)   Did Parensco breach any duty owed to the minority shareholders of Subco by offering to pay them only $120 per share?

DISCUSSION
Summary

Parensco probably did breach its fiduciary duties by failing to disclose the Aster proposal to the minority shareholders of Subco. A majority shareholder has a duty to disclose information if it is material and if non-disclosure will cause a loss to minority shareholders. The Subco board probably did breach its duty of care by approving the merger after only brief discussion. Parensco probably did breach its fiduciary duty of fair dealing because it did not offer a fair price and did not engage in a fair process when it failed to make full disclosure of the Aster proposal.

Point One (45-55%)
Parensco probably breached its fiduciary duties to the minority shareholders of Subco by failing to disclose the Aster proposal.

As majority shareholder, Parensco has a duty to disclose any information that it knew or should have known if that information was material. Here, Parensco will be found to have breached this duty to disclose if the information regarding the Aster proposal was material, and the nondisclosure caused a loss to the minority shareholders.

As to the materiality of the nondisclosure, the minority shareholders would argue that the information regarding Aster went to the fairness of the price that Parensco was offering and, therefore, a reasonable shareholder would consider it important in deciding how to vote on the transaction. *See Rosenblatt v. Getty Oil Co.*, 493 A.2d 929, 944 (Del. 1985). Although the $200 per share price arose in the context of a preliminary conversation, and may not have been a firm offer, the shareholders would argue that they are capable of assessing the importance of the information, and they can take into account that any further discussions regarding the proposal might have broken down or the deal might not have been consummated. *See Basic Inc. v. Levinson*, 485 U.S. 224 (1988).

Parensco will counter that the price offered by Aster was immaterial for two reasons. First, the price offered by Aster was preliminary in nature and there is no obligation to disclose a preliminary conversation. Second, the price that Aster might have offered for control of Subco bears little relationship to a fair price for a minority interest, which is what Parensco was offering to acquire in the merger. Aster was negotiating to buy control of Subco, something that the minority shareholders could not sell. The question of materiality is a close one, but on balance it appears that the information was material.

Assuming that the information was material, the next question is whether its nondisclosure caused any loss to the minority shareholders. Parensco would argue that the nondisclosure caused no loss; it had sufficient votes to approve the transaction without any of the minority shareholders' votes. The minority will counter that, although the merger could have been approved without their vote, had they had the disclosure, the minority shareholders could have exercised their rights under the state appraisal statute. *See Alabama Farm Bureau Mut. Cas. Co. v. American Fid. Life Ins. Co.*, 606 F.2d 602, 614 (5th Cir. 1979) (minority shareholders need only demonstrate that nondisclosure deprived them of a state remedy that would otherwise have been available). As the merger has now been consummated, this remedy is foreclosed. Thus, they would argue that the nondisclosure caused them loss.

Point Two (25-30%)
The Subco board appears to have breached its duty of care to the Subco shareholders in approving the merger.

Ordinarily the Subco board's action would be protected by the business judgment rule. Here, however, even though the facts are not extensive on this point, they do suggest that the Subco board was only minimally involved in the approval of the merger, and failed to exercise due care. The Subco board relied solely on a report of an investment banker and a presentation from Carr, the president of Parensco, and voted to approve the deal after a "brief discussion." The nature of the transaction, resulting in a cash-out of the minority shareholders, called for high degree of care by the directors. They apparently failed to undertake much of an investigation. *See Smith v. Van Gorkom*, 488 A.2d 858 (Del. 1985). While their reliance on Banker's report appears to be justified, it might not be enough to discharge their duty of care.

The Subco board might argue that the approval by the minority shareholders "cured" any breach of the duty of care and that since this approval was by a majority of the minority shareholders, the burden of proof shifts to the complaining minority shareholders to prove that the merger was unfair. In fact, however, the approval by the minority shareholders is without legal effect because there was not full disclosure, as noted above.

Point Three (15-25%)
Parensco probably breached its fiduciary duty of fair dealing when it offered to pay the minority shareholders of Subco only $120 per share.

When a majority shareholder purchases the interest of the minority, it has a duty of fair dealing. *Weinberger v. UOP, Inc.*, 457 A.2d 701 (Del. 1983). The transaction is reviewable to determine whether the majority shareholder discharged this duty. Under the facts of this case, it is doubtful that Parensco did. Parensco bears the burden of demonstrating that the process it employed was fair and that the price that it selected was fair. *See id.* at 710-11. As to the former, the discussion above in Points One and Two demonstrates that Parensco failed to engage in a fair process. As to the latter, the negotiations with Aster and the subsequent sale of Subco assets for $3 billion, not $800 million, so soon after the acquisition of the minority shares for only $120 each, suggest that the minority shares of Subco were worth more than Parensco was offering in the merger. As a result, Parensco probably breached its fiduciary duty of fair dealing.

Corporations

(July 2007)

ANALYSIS

Legal Problems:

(1)(a) Can the members of an LLC maintain a direct action against the manager of the LLC for mismanagement of the LLC?

(1)(b) Can the members of an LLC maintain a derivative action against the manager of the LLC for mismanagement of the LLC?

(2) Were Art's actions a breach of his fiduciary duty of care as the manager of LLC?

(3) Can Peter pierce the veil of limited liability of LLC and hold any or all of its members liable for LLC's debt?

DISCUSSION

Summary

If Brett and Chad bring an action against Art for mismanagement of LLC, that action must be a derivative (not direct) action because the harm Brett and Chad suffered was derivative of the injury Art caused LLC. To bring a derivative action, Brett and Chad must comply with the procedural requirements set forth in the Uniform Limited Liability Company Act (ULLCA). These requirements typically mandate a demand upon the managing partner before initiating an action. However, here demand is likely to be excused because Art is unlikely to bring an action against himself.

If Brett and Chad bring a derivative action, they are likely to lose. Under the ULLCA, Art would be liable for a breach of the duty of care only if he acted in a grossly negligent or reckless manner. In jurisdictions that have not adopted the ULLCA, Art would be protected by the business judgment rule.

Most LLC statutes provide that neither members nor managers are personally liable for the debts of an LLC. Courts generally recognize the equitable concept of piercing the veil of limited liability of an LLC. However, the facts in this case do not seem to provide a basis for piercing, and Peter probably cannot recover from Art, Brett, or Chad.

Point One(a) (15-25%)

Members of an LLC cannot maintain a direct action against the manager of the LLC for mismanagement of the LLC.

Members of a manager-managed LLC do not have the right to maintain a direct action against the manager of the LLC when the alleged misconduct caused harm only to the LLC. *See Wright v. Herman*, 230 F.R.D. 1, 10 (2005) (overwhelming majority rule that a claim for an injury to a corporate entity against a manager or officer must be brought derivatively). The operating agreement provides that Art manages LLC. Therefore, this is a manager-managed LLC. It does not matter that Art is also a member of LLC.

Here, the harms that Art caused—failing to manage the business profitably and failing to insure the business properly—were harms to the business and reputation of LLC, not harms directly to Brett and Chad. Because the harms were derivative, not direct, Brett and Chad may not bring a direct action against Art.

[NOTE: If Art breached a contractual obligation to Brett and Chad, they could maintain a direct action against Art. ULLCA § 410(a)(1) permits a member to sue the LLC or another member to enforce the member's rights under the operating agreement. The facts do not suggest that any violation of the operating agreement occurred.]

Point One(b) (15-25%)

<u>Members of an LLC can maintain a derivative action against the manager of the LLC for mismanagement of the LLC. Normally, members must make a demand on the manager to bring the action. Here, however, demand will likely be excused.</u>

Members of an LLC can maintain a derivative action against the manager of the LLC for mismanagement of the LLC. In order to maintain such an action members must normally first make a demand that the manager bring the action and allege in their complaint the efforts that they made to "secure initiation of the action by [the] . . . manager or the reasons for not making the effort." ULLCA §1103. Here, however, it is likely that demand would be excused, as Art would have to agree to bring an action against himself. Obviously, this demand would be futile. Therefore, Brett and Chad probably could bring a derivative action without first making a demand on Art, although that action would likely fail. (*See* Point Two.)

Point Two (20-30%)

<u>Simple negligence does not constitute a violation of a manager's fiduciary duty of care to the LLC.</u>

Under the ULLCA, managers (or members in a member-managed LLC) owe a duty of care to the LLC, but they are not liable for simple negligence. ULLCA § 409(c) provides that the duty of care consists of "refraining from engaging in grossly negligent conduct or reckless conduct, intentional misconduct, or a knowing violation of law." Under this standard, the question would be whether Art's failure to manage LLC profitably and to insure the business rose to the level of gross negligence or reckless conduct.

Some state statutes reject the gross negligence standard of the ULLCA and impose an ordinary negligence standard for evaluating breaches of an LLC manager's duty of care. Where that is the case, however, the business judgment rule may be applied to protect LLC managers from liability for business decisions made in good faith. *See* Elizabeth Miller and Thomas E. Rutledge,

The Duty of Finest Loyalty and Reasonable Decisions: The Business Judgment Rule in Unincorporated Business Organizations, 30 DEL. J. CORP. L. 343, 366-68 (2005). *See also* Revised Uniform Limited Liability Company Act § 409(c) (2006) (adopting an ordinary negligence standard but making an LLC manager's liability for breach of the duty of care subject to the business judgment rule).

Although the precise operation and content of the business judgment rule will vary from state to state, its impact is to shield managers from liability for business decisions. *Brehm v. Eisner*, 746 A.2d 244, 264 n.66 (Del. 2000). Under this rule, a court will not second-guess a manager's decision, even if the decision was a bad one, if the manager acted "on an informed basis, in good faith, and in the honest belief that the action taken was in the best interests of the company." *Aronson v. Lewis*, 473 A.2d 805, 812 (Del. 1984).

Under any of these tests, Art is unlikely to be held liable for the fact that LLC's business failed. The mere fact that LLC was unprofitable does not indicate that Art violated his duty of care. Many businesses operate unprofitably, and no facts suggest that Art was either grossly negligent (as required by the ULLCA) or even negligent in his general operation of LLC's business. In addition, in those jurisdictions that apply a negligence standard, Art would also have the protection of the business judgment rule, and there are no facts to suggest that Art behaved in a way that would take his decisions outside the scope of that rule.

On the other hand, Art is arguably liable for his failure to insure LLC. His failure to sign the insurance premium payment check was clearly negligent and could be characterized as grossly negligent. What's more, in a jurisdiction that imposed an ordinary negligence standard, the business judgment rule might not protect Art from liability for this sort of breach of the duty of care. Generally, the business judgment rule protects business managers from liability for their good faith business decisions; it does not protect them from liability for negligent failures to perform ministerial acts such as signing corporate checks.

[NOTE: An applicant may note that Art is subject to a duty to act in good faith. The ULLCA includes an obligation of good faith and fair dealing among the statutory duties of a manager. *See* §409(d). The facts, however, suggest that Art did act in good faith; thus, Brett and Chad could not maintain a claim for a breach of this duty.]

Point Three (30-40%)

To pierce the veil of an LLC and hold the members personally liable, a claimant must demonstrate either that the LLC was a mere instrumentality of the individual defendants or that there was a unity of interest and ownership between the LLC and the individual defendants. Here, it is unlikely that Peter can pierce the veil of LLC.

Ordinarily, members of an LLC are not liable for the debts, obligations, or liabilities of an LLC "solely by reason of being or acting as a member." ULLCA §303. However, either by statute, *see, e.g.,* Minn. Stat. § 322B.303(2), or by judicial decision, *see, e.g., Kaycee Land & Livestock v. Flahive,* 46 P.3d 323 (Wy. 2002), most states to consider the issue have recognized the possibility of piercing the veil of limited liability of an LLC, under appropriate circumstances.

Courts that pierce the veil rely on various theories to do so. Two of the most prominent are the "mere instrumentality" and "unity of interest and ownership" theories. *See, e.g., Litchfield Asset Mgmt. Corp. v. Howell*, 799 A.2d 298 (Conn. App. Ct. 2002).

Under the "mere instrumentality" test, Peter would have to show that (1) the members dominated the entity in such a way that LLC had no will of its own, (2) the members used that domination to commit a fraud or wrong, and (3) the control and wrongful action proximately caused the injury complained of.

Under the "unity of interest and ownership" test, Peter must demonstrate that there was such a unity of interest and ownership between the entity and the members that, in fact, LLC did not have an existence independent of the members and that failure to pierce through to the members would be unjust or inequitable.

Whereas a failure to follow formalities in the operation of the corporation is a factor in corporate veil piercing cases, it is less frequently relevant in LLC cases. This is because many LLC statutes, including the Uniform Limited Liability Company Act, provide explicitly that "the failure of a limited liability company to observe the usual company formalities . . . is not a ground for imposing personal liability on the members of managers." ULLCA § 303(b). However, in the absence of a statutory bar, some courts will cite a failure to follow formalities in the LLC context as part of the rationale for piercing the LLC veil. *See, e.g., Bonner v. Brunson*, 585 S.E.2d 917 (Ga. Ct. App. 2003).

The decision to pierce the LLC veil is highly fact dependent. The factors that are most likely to lead to an affirmative decision to pierce the veil are facts suggesting that the LLC was simply the "alter ego" of the owners, evidence of serious undercapitalization of the company, or a lack of substantive separation between the business of the company and the personal business of the owners. *See* Rapp, *Preserving LLC Veil Piercing: A Response to Bainbridge*, 31 IOWA J. CORP. L. 1063 (2006).

Under any of these tests, it seems probable that neither Brett nor Chad could be held liable for the liabilities of LLC as they had no authority to act on behalf of LLC. As to the "mere instrumentality" test, neither Brett nor Chad dominated LLC in a way that it became a "mere instrumentality." As to the "unity of interest" test, there was not, in any sense, a unity of interest and ownership between Brett and Chad and LLC.

The case against Art may appear stronger, because Art may have dominated LLC, but it is still not likely that Peter could prevail. Under the mere instrumentality test, even if Peter could show that Art dominated LLC, it is not likely that Peter would be able to prove that Art used his domination to commit a fraud or wrong. Although Art sent in the insurance premium without signing the check, this negligence is not sufficiently wrongful to justify piercing the limited liability shield. Under the unity test, Peter could not show that Art had a "unity of interest in ownership with LLC" because Chad and Brett had substantial interests in LLC. Although it might be argued that LLC was undercapitalized because it could not meet its obligations, its initial capitalization was substantial ($100,000), and there are no facts to suggest that amount would not have been sufficient capitalization for a business of this sort had it been run more effectively (and had Art purchased insurance as intended).

Corporations

(February 2008)

ANALYSIS

Legal Problems: (1)   Did Cal violate his duty of loyalty to Prime by failing to make full disclosure of all relevant information to the Board about a partnership in which he has an interest and with which Prime is considering entering into a transaction?

         (2)   Assuming that Cal violated the duty of loyalty, does he have any defenses to avoid liability?

         (3)   Did the members of Prime's board of directors, other than Cal, violate their duty of care by approving a more expensive contract without full information?

DISCUSSION

Summary

Cal, the CEO and chairman of the board of Prime, owes a fiduciary duty of loyalty to Prime. Even though Cal did not participate in the Board's discussion of the consulting project and even though the contract with Smart was approved by a majority of disinterested directors, Cal breached his duty of loyalty by failing to disclose the substantially higher fee charged to Prime by Smart, a partnership in which Cal has a financial interest. Here, a court would be unlikely to find that the contract was objectively fair to Prime, given Smart's substantially higher fee. Therefore, Cal has no defense to a claim of breach of his duty of loyalty.

The Board may have violated its fiduciary duty of care when it approved the contract with Smart after only a 10-minute discussion and without seeking or receiving full information about the fees to be charged.

Point One (5–15%)

Cal violated the fiduciary duty of loyalty by allowing Prime to contract with a partnership in which Cal is a partner without fully disclosing all relevant information.

Cal is the CEO and chairman of the board of Prime and therefore has a fiduciary duty of loyalty to Prime. Here, he may have breached that duty because he stands to benefit personally if Smart is hired, since he is a partner in Smart. As a partner, he is presumably entitled to a share of any profits derived from Smart's work for Prime, even if he himself performs no services.

Point Two (40–50%)

The RMBCA provides three safe harbors for a director who breaches his duty of loyalty: approval by disinterested directors, approval by disinterested shareholders, or fairness. It is unlikely that any of these safe harbors will protect Cal.

The Revised Model Business Corporation Act §§ 8.60–8.63 (1984, with 2000 amendments) (RMBCA) includes three safe harbors that may protect a director who breaches his duty of loyalty. However, it is unlikely that any of these safe harbors will protect Cal under the facts of this case.

Under the first RMBCA safe harbor, approval by disinterested directors insulates a director's conflicting interest transaction from judicial scrutiny if the interested director disclosed his or her interest and "play[ed] no part, directly or indirectly, in [the disinterested directors'] deliberations or vote." RMBCA §§ 8.61(b)(1) & 8.62(b). The statute also requires disclosure of any information in Cal's possession that "an ordinarily prudent person would believe to be material to a judgment about whether or not to proceed with the transaction." *Id.* § 8.60(4).

Applying the first prong of this test, it appears that the Prime board, except for Cal, was disinterested when it approved the Smart consulting contract. As far as disinterested approval is concerned, the entire Prime board, with Cal abstaining, approved the Smart consulting contract. The facts do not suggest that any of the directors besides Cal had a personal interest in this matter. Nothing indicates that the other directors are subject to Cal's control or serve at his pleasure. Three board members are also senior officers of Prime and therefore arguably dependent on Cal's continued goodwill, but the remaining eight are outside directors with no other connections to the corporation. Accordingly, even if there is some possible doubt as to the independence of the three inside or management directors, there is no doubt as to the independence of the other eight, all of whom voted in favor of the contract. Thus, the disinterested directors approved the transaction and there is no evidence that Cal played any part in the deliberations or vote.

However, applying the second prong of this test, Cal did not make adequate disclosure. Cal informed the Board of his status as a partner in Smart before the Board's approval and therefore disclosed the fact of his conflict. However, he did not inform them that the fee to be charged by Smart was substantially higher than would ordinarily be expected for work like this. This is material information a prudent director would want to know. Therefore, because of the nondisclosure, it is unlikely that the contract with Smart can be defended on the basis of the disinterested directors' approval.

Under the second RMBCA safe harbor, approval by disinterested shareholders would insulate a director's conflicting interest transaction from judicial scrutiny. *See id.* § 8.61(b)(2). No facts support that defense.

Under the third RMBCA safe harbor, a duty of loyalty claim could be rebutted by proof that "the transaction, judged according to the circumstances at the time of commitment, is established to have been fair to the corporation." *Id.* § 8.61(b)(3). Although there is some room to argue this point, the fact that Smart's proposed fee is substantially higher than what it normally charges for comparable work suggests strongly that a finding of objective fairness could not be supported.

Point Three (35–45%)

Prime's disinterested directors likely breached their duty of care when they approved, with minimal discussion and without full information, a contract in which a director had an interest.

If the directors do not qualify for the protection of the business judgment rule, they likely will be found to have breached their duty of care in approving the contract with Smart. The business judgment rule creates a presumption that "in making a business decision, the directors . . . acted on an informed basis, in good faith and in the honest belief that the action taken was in the best interests of the company." *Aronson v. Lewis*, 473 A.2d 805, 812 (Del. 1984).

In this case, there is no evidence of bad faith. At least eight directors were entirely disinterested. Nor is there any evidence that the directors did not have an honest belief that they were acting in the best interests of Prime.

However, a court could find that the directors did not act on an informed basis in reviewing the two alternatives. Because the business judgment rule presumes that the Board was adequately informed, a party claiming that the directors breached their duty of care has the burden of showing that the Board did not have sufficient information to justify going with the higher-priced firm. The fact that Smart was going to charge Prime more than its customary rate suggests that the rate was not justified by added value. Arguably, the $150,000 price difference required the Board to at least ask more about Smart's rates. Moreover, if the Board had discussed the contract for more than 10 minutes, it might have realized that it lacked full information.

Therefore, it is likely that a court would find that the Board violated its fiduciary duty of care by approving the contract with Smart.

Corporations

(February 2009)

ANALYSIS

(Corporations VI.A.)

Legal Problems: (1) Does the business judgment rule protect from liability a director who authorizes a transaction in which another director has a financial interest without obtaining full disclosure?

(2) Does the business judgment rule protect from liability a director who is interested in a transaction and who does not make full disclosure about that transaction?

(3) Does the approval of the transaction by the disinterested members of the board of directors protect from liability a director who is interested in a transaction and who does not make full disclosure about that transaction?

(4) Does an exculpatory provision in the articles of incorporation protect from liability a director who authorizes a transaction in which another director has an interest without obtaining full disclosure?

(5) Does an exculpatory provision in the articles of incorporation protect from liability a director who is interested in a transaction and who does not make full disclosure about that transaction?

DISCUSSION

Summary

The directors (other than Major) will not be protected from liability by the business judgment rule because they did not exercise adequate care in authorizing the transactions with Major. Major will not be protected from liability by the business judgment rule because he is interested in the transactions and did not disclose all relevant facts about the transactions to the other directors. Nor will Major be protected from liability by the approval of the transactions by a disinterested board of directors because he failed to make full disclosure regarding the transactions to the directors who approved the transactions. The directors (other than Major) will be protected from liability by the exculpatory provision in the articles of incorporation because their breach was of the duty of care, not the duty of loyalty, and the exculpatory provision protects against breaches of the duty of care. Major, however, will not be protected from liability by the exculpatory provision because he breached his duty of loyalty when he received an improper financial benefit through the transactions with Corporation.

Point One (30–40%)
The directors (other than Major) will not be protected from liability by the business judgment rule because they did not exercise adequate care when they failed to seek and receive sufficient information about the transactions.

Directors owe a duty of loyalty and a duty of care. The directors other than Major received no personal benefit from the transactions that they approved and did not stand on both sides of the transactions being approved. Thus the directors, other than Major, did not violate the duty of loyalty.
Consequently, the claims against them are for failure to exercise the level of care required of directors. In this case, the claim is likely to be that the directors failed to exercise care in informing themselves regarding the transactions that they approved. *See generally Smith v. Van Gorkom*, 488 A.2d 858, 872–73 (Del. 1985) (directors have a duty to exercise an informed business judgment); MODEL BUS. CORP. ACT § 8.30(b) (directors shall exercise care in becoming informed).

The exercise of managerial powers by a director is generally subject to the business judgment rule. The business judgment rule "is a presumption that in making a business decision, the directors of a corporation acted on an informed basis, in good faith and in the honest belief that the action taken was in the best interests of the company." *Aronson v. Lewis*, 473 A.2d 805, 812 (Del. 1984) (overruled on other grounds). Consequently, "the party attacking a board decision as uninformed must rebut the presumption that its business judgment was an informed one." *Smith*, 488 A.2d at 872. *See also* MODEL BUS. CORP. ACT § 8.31(a)(2)(ii)(A) (to similar effect).

Under the facts, the directors (other than Major) did not exercise adequate care in becoming informed about the transactions in question: they relied entirely on Major's assurances that the prices paid by Corporation represented the fair market value of the properties purchased, they did not ask how he determined the fair market value, and they never employed any independent party to evaluate the properties being purchased, despite their awareness of Major's interest in the transactions. In sum, the directors exercised scant, if any, care in becoming informed.

In performing their duty to become informed, directors are generally entitled to rely upon information, opinions, reports, or statements of corporate officers. *See* DEL. GEN. CORP. LAW § 141(e); MODEL BUS. CORP. ACT § 8.30(d) & (e)(1). In this case, however, the directors had knowledge that made such reliance unwarranted. They knew that Major was interested in the transactions being presented to the board for approval. *See* MODEL BUS. CORP. ACT § 8.30(d) (director is not protected from liability in reliance where he or she has knowledge that makes reliance unwarranted). In addition, Major's statement that "I have investigated the value of my property to be purchased by Corporation and I assure you that the purchase price to be paid by Corporation represents its fair market value" probably lacked enough substance to be relied upon. *See Smith*, 488 A.2d at 874–75.

In sum, the directors (other than Major) are not entitled to the protection of the business judgment rule because their decisions were uninformed.

Point Two (10–20%)

Major will not be protected from liability by the business judgment rule because Major has an interest in the transactions in question.

Where a director stands on both sides of a transaction, the business judgment rule does not apply. *See* AM. LAW INST., PRINCIPLES OF CORPORATE GOVERNANCE: ANALYSIS AND RECOMMENDATIONS § 4.01(c)(1) (1994) (good faith business judgment of director fulfills duty of director where director is, among other things, not interested in the subject of the transaction); *cf.* MODEL BUS. CORP. ACT § 8.31(a)(2)(v) (director not liable to corporation unless party asserting liability establishes one of a number of elements including receipt of financial benefit by the director to which director is not entitled or other actionable breach of duty by the director to deal fairly with the corporation). Instead, the director has the burden of proving the fairness of the transaction. *See, e.g., HMG/Courtland Properties, Inc. v. Gray*, 749 A.2d 94, 115 (Del. Ch. 1999) (directors who were on both sides of transactions in question had burden of establishing entire fairness of the transactions).

Major will not be protected from liability by the business judgment rule because Major was interested in the transactions and, consequently, Major will be required to establish the fairness of the transactions in question in order to avoid a claim that he breached a fiduciary duty of loyalty.

Point Three (10–20%)

Major will not be protected from liability by the approval of the transactions by a disinterested board of directors because Major failed to make full disclosure regarding the transactions to the directors who approved the transactions.

Major may argue that since the transactions in question were approved by disinterested directors, the transactions should be subject to the business judgment rule and the party challenging the transactions should be required to prove that the transactions were unfair to the corporation or, perhaps, even to prove that the transactions constituted waste. *See* DEL. GEN. CORP. LAW § 144(a)(1); *Marciano v. Nakash*, 535 A.2d 400, 405 n.3 (Del. 1987) (dictum) ("approval by fully informed disinterested directors under § 144(a)(1) . . . permits invocation of the business judgment rule and limits judicial review to issues of gift or waste with the burden of proof upon the party attacking the transaction"). In a Model Act jurisdiction, Major may also argue that the transaction should be within the statutory "safe harbor" for transactions approved by disinterested directors and, therefore, immune from attack. *See* MODEL BUS. CORP. ACT §§ 8.61(b) & 8.62.

None of these arguments is available to Major because approval by disinterested directors does not trigger the business judgment rule where the director has not disclosed *all* material facts about the director's interest in the transaction. *Cf. id.* § 8.60(4) (defining "required disclosure" to include, among other things, "all facts known [by the director] respecting the subject matter of the transaction that an ordinarily prudent person would reasonably believe to be material to a judgment about whether or not to proceed with the transaction"). Clearly Major did not make adequate disclosure to the board of directors. In fact, Major misrepresented the facts by assuring the board that the price being paid for his properties was the fair market value. Certainly an ordinarily prudent board member would find the fact that the price is vastly more than market price is material to a judgment about whether to proceed with a transaction.

In sum, Major is not protected from liability by the approval of the transactions by a disinterested board of directors because Major failed to make full disclosure to the directors.

Point Four (5–15%)
The directors (other than Major) will be protected from liability by the exculpatory provision in the articles of incorporation.

A corporation's articles of incorporation may include a provision shielding its directors from liability for money damages for the failure to exercise adequate care in the performance of their duties as directors. Delaware, for example, permits provisions that protect directors from liability for breaches of the duty of care, but does not permit provisions that protect directors from liability for any breach of the duty of loyalty, for acts or omissions that are not in good faith, or for any transactions from which the director received an improper personal benefit. *See* DEL. GEN. CORP. LAW § 102(b)(7). Similarly, the Model Business Corporation Act permits provisions that protect directors from liability for breaches of the duty of care, but does not permit provisions that limit or eliminate liability "for the amount of a financial benefit received by a director to which he is not entitled." MODEL BUS. CORP. ACT § 2.02(b)(4).

Here, there is no suggestion that the directors (other than Major) received an improper personal benefit. The directors (other than Major) do not appear to have breached the duty of loyalty. They have not engaged in self-dealing and the facts do not suggest they usurped any corporate opportunity or received excessive compensation. Although their actions in taking Major's assertions at face value appear very foolish, negligence does not establish bad faith.

In sum, the directors (other than Major) are protected from liability for money damages for breach of the duty of care by the exculpatory provision in the articles of incorporation.

[NOTE: An applicant may argue that the directors (other than Major) acted in bad faith because they failed to take any meaningful action to determine the facts underlying the transactions. If that inaction is found to constitute gross negligence, it may constitute an action "not in good faith" and so subject the directors (other than Major) to liability. Applicants who raise this argument should receive extra credit.]

Point Five (5–15%)
Major will not be protected from liability by the exculpatory provision in the articles of incorporation because Major breached his duty of loyalty and received an improper personal benefit from Corporation.

Major will not be protected from liability by the exculpatory provision in the articles because that provision does not protect directors for actions undertaken in bad faith or for a breach of the duty of loyalty, such as the receipt of an improper personal benefit. Major acted in bad faith by intentionally misrepresenting to the board that the purchase prices represented fair market value when they in fact reflected vastly inflated prices. Major's conduct probably violated the duty of loyalty since he had a personal interest in the transactions, they were not properly approved, and they probably were not fair to the corporation. Major received an improper personal benefit by getting proceeds for his property at inflated prices. For these reasons, the exculpatory provision will not protect Major from liability.

Corporations

(February 2010)

ANALYSIS

Legal Problems: (1)   Does Smith have a right to inspect Omega's corporate books and records to determine whether $35 per share is a fair price for his shares?

               (2)   Is Smith required to make a demand on the corporation prior to bringing a suit to compel a dividend?

               (3)   Is a suit to compel the payment of a dividend likely to be successful?

DISCUSSION

Summary

Smith has a right to inspect corporate books and records to determine the value of his shares because this purpose is reasonably related to Smith's interest as a shareholder. Smith is not required to make a demand upon the corporation prior to bringing a suit to compel the payment of a dividend because such a suit attempts to vindicate an individual right of Smith as a shareholder. It is not a suit by Smith as a representative of Omega to vindicate a corporate right. However, a suit to compel the payment of a dividend is unlikely to be successful because, even if funds are legally available to pay dividends, Smith can compel the payment of a dividend only by showing that the decision to withhold dividends was made in bad faith.

Point One (25%)
As a shareholder, Smith has a right to inspect corporate books and records for a proper purpose. Determining the value of Smith's shares for purpose of sale is a proper purpose.

A shareholder has a right to inspect corporate books and records for a proper purpose. MODEL BUSINESS CORP. ACT (MBCA) § 16.02(b) & (c) (1984); DEL. GEN. CORP. § 220(b). A proper purpose is a purpose reasonably related to a person's interest as a shareholder. DEL. GEN. CORP. § 220(b). The determination of the value of one's own shares for purposes of sale is a proper purpose. *CM & M Group, Inc. v. Carroll*, 453 A.2d 788, 792 (Del. 1982); *Matter of Smilkstein v. J. Smilkstein & Sons, Inc.*, 223 N.Y.S.2d 561, 563 (N.Y. Sup. Ct. 1961). The fact that Smith has not definitely decided to sell does not prevent the valuation from being a proper purpose. *CM & M Group, Inc.*, 453 A.2d at 792–93 (involving shares in a closely held corporation); *Macklowe v. Planet Hollywood, Inc.*, 1994 WL 560804 (Del. Ch., Sept. 29, 1994) (involving shares in a closely held corporation; no present intention to sell or concrete steps to sell shares required in order for valuation of shares to be a proper purpose).

In contrast to a publicly traded corporation, a closely held corporation has no market that continuously values its shares. The fact that Omega is a closely held corporation reinforces the conclusion that valuing the shares is a proper purpose for inspection. Thus, "[w]hen a minority shareholder in a closely held corporation whose stock is not publicly traded needs to value his or her shares in order to decide whether to sell them, normally the only way to accomplish that is by examining the appropriate corporate books and records." *Macklowe*, 1994 WL 560804 at *4.

In sum, Smith has a right to inspect Omega's corporate books and records because this purpose is reasonably related to Smith's interest as a shareholder.

[NOTE: An applicant might receive extra credit for recognizing that in order to exercise his inspection rights, Smith must comply with procedural requirements, which generally include making a written demand for inspection and allowing the corporation a certain length of time (typically five days) to respond.]

Point Two (30%)
A suit to compel the payment of a dividend is a suit seeking to enforce an individual right of the shareholder and not a suit in a representative capacity seeking to enforce a right of the corporation. Therefore, no demand on the corporation is required prior to bringing suit.

A shareholder is generally required to make a demand on the corporation to take remedial action prior to bringing a derivative suit. *See* MBCA § 7.42 (requiring a demand in all cases); Del. Chancery Court Rule 23.1 (requiring complaint to allege demand or reason for failure to make demand). However, a shareholder is not required to make a demand on the corporation prior to bringing suit where the shareholder brings a suit in his or her individual capacity to enforce an individual right of the shareholder. The important question, then, is whether a suit to compel the payment of a dividend is a suit to enforce a right of the corporation or, conversely, a suit to enforce an individual right of the shareholder.

A suit to compel the payment of a dividend is not a suit to enforce a right of the corporation. It is a suit to enforce a right of the individual shareholder, that is, the shareholder's right to share in the net profits of the corporation. *Doherty v. Mutual Warehouse Co.*, 245 F.2d 609, 612 (5th Cir. 1957); *Knapp v. Bankers Securities Corp.*, 230 F.2d 717, 721–22 (3d Cir. 1956) (noting also that the right to dividends is an incident of the ownership of stock). Consequently, there is no requirement that Smith make a demand on the corporation prior to bringing suit to compel the payment of a dividend.

[NOTE: In some jurisdictions, a derivative suit may be appropriate and graders are encouraged to ascertain local law on this issue. If an applicant approaches this issue solely from the perspective of the shareholder bringing a derivative suit, then the grader should also expect some analysis of demand futility. Presumably, Baker and Jones, having made the decision not to pay a dividend, are unlikely to agree to have the corporation sue the directors for failure to declare a dividend.]

Point Three (45%)
The decision as to whether to distribute corporate earnings as dividends or to retain those earnings in order to expand the business is a matter that is generally within the business

judgment of the corporate directors. Smith's suit to compel the payment of a dividend is unlikely to be successful because, in order to succeed, Smith would be required to prove that dividends were withheld in bad faith.

While directors have fiduciary duties, the business judgment rule protects them from liability for breach of their fiduciary duties. The business judgment rule is a presumption that in making business decisions, the directors act on an informed basis, in good faith, and in the honest belief that the action being taken is in the best interests of the corporation. *Aronson v. Lewis*, 473 A.2d 805, 812 (Del. 1984), *overruled on other grounds by Brehm v. Eisner*, 746 A.2d 244 (Del. 2000). The decisions regarding whether to declare a dividend and the amount of any dividend declared are generally matters within the business judgment of the directors. *Dodge v. Ford Motor Co.*, 170 N.W. 668, 682 (Mich. 1919).

To prevail in a suit to compel the payment of a dividend, a shareholder must prove that there are funds legally available for the payment of a dividend and that the directors acted in bad faith in their refusal to pay. *Gay v. Gay's Super Markets, Inc.*, 343 A.2d 577, 580 (Me. 1975); *Zidell v. Zidell, Inc.*, 560 P.2d 1086, 1089 (Or. 1977) (plaintiff must show bad faith, fraud, breach of fiduciary duty, or abuse of discretion on the part of the directors); *Gottfried v. Gottfried*, 73 N.Y.S.2d 692, 695 (N.Y. Sup. Ct. 1947). "The essential test of bad faith is to determine whether the policy of the directors is dictated by their personal interests rather than the corporate welfare." *Gottfried*, 73 N.Y.S.2d at 695.

Usually the plaintiff-shareholder will attempt to prove bad faith by establishing various "earmarks of bad faith." These earmarks include "[i]ntense hostility of the controlling faction against the minority; exclusion of the minority from employment by the corporation; high salaries, or bonuses or corporate loans made to the officers in control; the fact that the majority group may be subject to high personal income taxes if substantial dividends are paid; [and] the existence of a desire by the controlling directors to acquire the minority stock interests as cheaply as possible." *Id.* Here, there may be several earmarks of bad faith. Baker and Jones seemed hostile toward Smith, telling him to "go away and let us run the show." They refused to disclose their salaries. Further, it could be argued that Baker and Jones were trying to acquire Smith's shares as cheaply as possible. The facts do not establish whether $35 per share is a fair price.

The earmarks "are not, however, invariably signs of improper behavior by the majority." *Zidell*, 560 P.2d at 1089. If these earmarks are not the "motivating causes" of the board's dividend decision, they do not constitute bad faith. *Gottfried*, 73 N.Y.S.2d at 695. In a number of cases, courts have recognized that a good-faith decision to retain corporate earnings for business expansion is an appropriate exercise of business judgment. *Gay*, 343 A.2d at 580; *Gottfried*, 73 N.Y.S.2d at 700–01. In judging the decision of the board of a closely held corporation, a court may also consider that "[d]irectors of a closely held, small corporation must bear in mind the relatively limited access of such an enterprise to capital markets." *Gay*, 343 A.2d at 582.

In sum, a suit to compel the payment of a dividend is unlikely to be successful because, even if funds are legally available to pay dividends, Smith could succeed only by showing that the decision to withhold dividends was made in bad faith or, in other words, was dictated by the personal interests of the directors rather than the corporate welfare. It is unlikely that he can do this when a proper motive for withholding the payment of dividends exists, as it does here.

Corporations

(July 2010)

Legal Problems: (1)   Were the shares owned by Amy on the record date but then sold to Zach properly voted by Amy or Zach?

    (2)   Were the shares subject to the proxy given to Dell by Brian properly voted by Dell, or by Brian, who attended the meeting?

    (3)   Were the shares held by Carter properly voted by Carter?

    (4)   Were the shares voted by X Corporation's president properly voted?

    (5)   When the articles of incorporation of a corporation conflict with the bylaws of a corporation regarding how many shares must vote in favor of a shareholder proposal, which takes precedence?

DISCUSSION

Summary

Amy's shares were properly voted by Amy in favor of the proposal even though she no longer owned the shares when the meeting was held. Zach did not acquire ownership of those shares until after the record date, and Amy did not grant Zach a proxy to vote those shares at any time. Brian's shares were properly voted in favor of the proposal because his earlier proxy to Dell was revoked when Brian attended the meeting and voted his shares. Carter's shares were properly voted against the proposal because he properly attended the meeting and voted them. X Corporation's president was not permitted to vote the shares reacquired from Amy.

When the articles of incorporation of a corporation conflict with its bylaws regarding how many shares must be voted in favor of a shareholder proposal in order for that proposal to be approved, the articles of incorporation preempt the bylaws. Therefore, the proposal must receive a two-thirds vote of the outstanding shares entitled to vote on the matter to be approved. Here, the shareholder proposal received sufficient votes in favor and was approved.

Point One (25%)
Only shareholders of record on the record date are entitled to vote at an annual shareholders' meeting. Here, Amy was the owner of the 50 shares on the record date, and Zach is not entitled to vote them. Therefore, Amy's vote of 50 shares in favor of the shareholder proposal is counted, and Zach's vote of 50 shares against the proposal is not.

A record date determines who is entitled to vote at a particular shareholder meeting, "namely, those persons who were registered as shareholders 'of record' on that date." ROBERT CHARLES

CLARK, CORPORATE LAW § 9.1.2 (1986); *Brizzolara v. Sherwood Mem. Park, Inc.*, 645 S.E.2d 508, 518 (Va. 2007). Here, on the record date of December 30th, Amy was the owner of the 50 shares. Therefore, absent her proxy to another, Amy is entitled to vote the 50 shares. The fact that Zach bought the shares does not give Zach the right to vote the 50 shares because he did so after the record date.

[NOTE: If Amy had given Zach a legally binding proxy together with the shares, Zach might have had the right to vote them even though Zach was not the record owner on the record date. The facts do not suggest that any proxy was given, however, and therefore Amy's vote of 50 shares in favor of the proposal should be counted, and Zach's vote of 50 shares against the proposal should not be counted.]

Point Two (25%)

Generally, a shareholder proxy is revocable. Any action taken inconsistent with a proxy revokes that proxy. Here, Brian attended the meeting and voted, which was inconsistent with Brian's prior grant of a proxy to Dell. Therefore, Brian effectively revoked the proxy, and his vote of 25 shares in favor of the shareholder proposal should be counted.

Brian gave Dell a proxy to vote Brian's shares. Shareholder proxies generally are revocable, and any action inconsistent with the grant of a proxy works as a revocation of that proxy. *See* Anish Monga, *Using Derivatives to Manipulate the Market for Corporate Control*, 12 STAN. J.L. BUS. & FIN. 186, 213 (2006); Richard A. Epstein, *Why Restrain Alienation?*, 85 COLUM. L. REV. 970, 985 n. 32 (1985) ("Proxies must be revocable unless coupled with an interest."); *see, e.g.,* N.Y. BUS. CORP. LAW § 609 (McKinney 1984). A proxy may be made irrevocable only if the proxy form explicitly so states and the proxy is "coupled with an interest." *See* MODEL BUSINESS CORP. ACT (MBCA) § 7.22(d) (1984 with 2000 amendments) ("An appointment of a proxy is revocable unless the appointment form or electronic transmission states that it is irrevocable and the appointment is coupled with an interest.").

Here, the proxy given by Brian to Dell did not state that it was irrevocable, nor was it coupled with an interest, and therefore it was revocable. Brian's attendance at the shareholders' meeting and his vote of the 25 shares were actions inconsistent with the grant of a proxy covering those shares to Dell. Therefore, Brian effectively revoked the proxy, and Brian's vote of 25 shares in favor of the proposal should be counted while Dell's vote of 25 shares against the proposal should not be counted.

Point Three (10%)

A shareholder of record may attend and vote at an annual shareholders' meeting. Thus Carter's vote of 25 shares will be counted against the proposal.

A shareholder of record is entitled to attend and vote at an annual shareholders' meeting unless he or she has executed a valid, irrevocable proxy covering his shares. *See* MBCA § 7.22(a). Here, Carter attended the meeting and properly voted his 25 shares against the proposal.

Point Four (20%)

Shares that are repurchased by a corporation are not outstanding shares and therefore may not be voted. Therefore, the vote of 50 shares by X Corporation's president against the proposal cannot be counted.

Shares that are reacquired by a corporation are considered authorized but not outstanding. MBCA § 6.31(a). Some jurisdictions refer to these as "treasury shares."

In counting shareholder votes, "each outstanding share . . . is entitled to one vote on each matter voted on at a shareholders' meeting." *Id.* § 7.21(a). The facts indicate that X Corporation's president voted 50 shares that the corporation reacquired from Amy. Because reacquired shares are not outstanding, they cannot be voted. Therefore the 50 shares voted by the president do not count.

Point Five (20%)
When the articles of incorporation conflict with a corporation's bylaws regarding how many shares must vote in favor of a shareholder proposal in order for that proposal to be approved, the articles of incorporation prevail over the bylaws. Here, the shareholder proposal received sufficient votes in favor and was approved.

When a corporation's articles of incorporation conflict with its bylaws regarding how many shares must vote in favor of a shareholder proposal in order for that proposal to be approved, the articles of incorporation preempt the bylaws. *See Boatmen's First Nat'l Bank of West Plains v. Southern Mo. Dist. Council of the Assemblies of God*, 806 S.W.2d 706, 713 (Mo. Ct. App. 1991) ("[A]ny bylaw provision that conflicts with the articles of incorporation is void."). Here, X Corporation's Articles of Incorporation requiring approval of two-thirds of the shares outstanding and entitled to vote on the matter to approve any shareholder action will preempt the bylaws' requirement of unanimity.

Here, Amy's 50 votes and Brian's 25 votes in favor of the proposal are counted, while only Carter's 25 votes against the proposal are counted. Therefore, the proposal received the necessary approval by two-thirds of the shares outstanding and entitled to vote on the matter and should pass.

Corporations

(February 2011)

ANALYSIS

Legal Problems: (1)   When did Delta's corporate existence begin?

(2)   Is Adam, Baker, or Clark personally liable on the Mega contract?

(3)   Is Adam, Baker, or Clark personally liable on the Sole contract?

DISCUSSION

Summary

Delta's corporate existence began only upon Adam's filing of Delta's articles of incorporation on November 15. The recitation in the articles of a stated earlier effective date (September 1) is of no legal consequence. Only Adam is personally liable on the Mega contract because Adam alone participated in entering into the contract with knowledge that the articles had not been filed. Adam and Baker, but not Clark, are liable on the Sole contract. That contract was executed by Delta before its articles were filed. Adam and Baker, but not Clark, participated in entering into the contract with knowledge that Delta's articles had not been filed. Thus, Adam and Baker are personally liable for the Sole contract, and Clark is not personally liable.

Point One (20%)

Delta achieved corporate status upon the filing of its articles of incorporation on November 15. The filing of Delta's articles of incorporation does not relate back to the earlier date of September 1 specified in the articles.

Under the Model Business Corporation Act (MBCA) § 2.03(a) (1984, with 2000 amendments), ". . . corporate existence begins when the articles of incorporation are filed." Because "[i]ncorporation under modern statutes is so simple and inexpensive . . . nothing short of filing articles of incorporation should create the privilege of limited liability." *Id.*, ch. 2 official cmt.

This date-of-filing rule applies even if the filed articles recite an effective date prior to the date of filing. The MBCA allows the parties to specify "a delayed effective date" but not an earlier effective date. *Id.* § 2.03(a). Thus, the recitation in Delta's articles of an earlier effective date is ineffective; Delta's corporate existence began on the date that Adam filed the articles.

Point Two (40%)

When a corporation's articles of incorporation have not been filed, persons purporting to act for the corporation are personally liable for corporate debts if they knew when the debt was incurred that there was no incorporation.

The fact that Delta's articles of incorporation were not filed when Delta entered into the contract with Mega does not automatically make Adam, Baker, and Clark liable to Mega for amounts due on that contract. Under the MBCA, "[a]ll persons purporting to act as or on behalf of a corporation, knowing there was no incorporation under this Act, are jointly and severally liable for all liabilities created while so acting." § 2.04. Thus, under § 2.04 both the participation and knowledge requirements must be met to hold any of Adam, Baker, and Clark liable.

With regard to the Mega contract, only Adam purported to act on Delta's behalf and only Adam knew that Delta's articles had not been filed. Therefore, Adam is personally liable on the Mega contract. On the other hand, neither Baker nor Clark satisfies either the participation or knowledge requirement. Thus, neither is liable on the Mega contract.

[NOTE: The facts clearly state when Baker learned that the articles had not been filed: October 15. Clark, however, at all times believed that Delta's articles of incorporation had been filed.]

[NOTE: Examinees may discuss the de facto incorporation doctrine under which a shareholder is not liable for the obligations of a defectively incorporated corporation when there was "a bona fide attempt to organize . . . and colorable or apparent compliance with the requirements of the law." *Gillette v. Aurora Ry. Co.*, 81 N.E. 1005, 1009 (Ill. 1907); *Milligan v. Milligan*, 956 So. 2d 1066, 1074 (Miss. Ct. App. 2007). Such analysis is inapplicable here. First, the MBCA (which the facts state governs this problem) abolished the doctrine. Even in a non-MBCA jurisdiction, the doctrine would not apply here because Adam did nothing to attempt compliance with the statutory requirements. "Without allegations that a certificate of formation was ever prepared or filed, there is no basis . . . to claim a good-faith attempt to comply with [statutory requirements]." *Leber Associates, LLC v. The Entertainment Group Fund, Inc.*, No. 00 Civ. 3759, 2003 U.S. Dist. LEXIS 13009 at *33 (S.D.N.Y. July 29, 2003) (applying Delaware law).]

Point Three (40%)
Persons purporting to act for a corporation are personally liable for a corporate contract if they entered into the contract with knowledge that there was no incorporation.

When a corporation's articles of incorporation have not been filed, a person is liable for pre-incorporation transactions only when the person purporting to act on behalf of a corporation not yet formed possesses actual knowledge that the corporation's charter has not yet been issued. *See* MBCA § 2.04; *Weir v. Kirby Construction Co., Inc.*, 446 S.E.2d 186 (1994). It is not enough to establish liability that a person should have inquired about the entity's status and should have known that the corporation was not formed, as those facts do not rise to the level of actual knowledge required. *See Sivers v. R & F Capital Corp.*, 858 P.2d 895, 898 (Or. Ct. App. 1993).

Here, with regard to the Sole contract, Adam and Baker knew that Delta's articles of incorporation had not been filed at the time Delta entered into that contract, while Clark did not know. Baker might argue that, as a mere prospective shareholder, he was not a "[person] purporting to act as or on behalf of a corporation," MBCA § 2.04, and thus has no liability. This argument is likely to fail. With regard to the Sole contract, Baker was more than a prospective shareholder—he participated in the negotiation of the contract and therefore purported to act on behalf of a corporation. Further, the official commentary to § 2.04 suggests that its protection does not extend to individuals in Baker's position. ("[Section 2.04] does not foreclose the possibility that persons who urge defendants to execute contracts in the corporate name knowing that no steps to incorporate have been taken may be estopped to impose personal liability on individual defendants.") Rather, the provision is intended to shield those who erroneously but in good faith believe that the necessary documents have been filed. *See Cranson v. IBM*, 200 A.2d 33 (Md. 1964). Here, at the time of the Sole contract, Baker knew that Delta's articles had not been filed and therefore did not have the necessary good-faith belief to the contrary. Thus, Baker, together with Adam, will be personally liable on the Sole contract. Clark, however, is not liable because he does not meet the participation requirement nor does he satisfy the knowledge requirement; he believed at all relevant times that the articles had in fact been filed. However, even if Clark had knowledge that the articles had not been filed, he would not be liable on the Sole contract because he does not meet the participation requirement.

<u>Corporations</u>

(February 2012)

ANALYSIS

Legal Problems

    (1)(a) Did the directors other than Claire receive proper notice of the special meeting of the board of directors?

    (1)(b) Did Claire receive proper notice of the special meeting of the board of directors and, if not, did she waive notice?

    (2)   Was a quorum present at the special meeting of the board of directors?

    (3)   Did the purchase of the asset receive the required number of votes in favor to be approved?

DISCUSSION

Summary

Proper notice of the special meeting of the board of directors was given to all directors other than Claire. Claire did not receive proper notice of the special meeting, but she waived the right to object to actions taken at the special meeting when she attended the special meeting and voted. A quorum (a majority of the directors) is required for action taken at a meeting to be proper. Here, a quorum was present at the special meeting. However, Alan and Barb were not able to hear each other and therefore cannot be counted as participating in the meeting. Therefore, in determining whether the purchase of the asset received the required number of votes to be proper, the votes of Alan and Barb may not be counted. Thus, the purchase of the asset was not properly approved by the board because it did not receive the required number of votes.

Point One(a) (25%)
<u>The directors other than Claire received proper notice of the special meeting of the board of directors.</u>

Unless the articles of incorporation or bylaws provide otherwise, notice of a special meeting of a corporation's board of directors must be given at least two days prior to the date of the meeting. MODEL BUS. CORP. ACT (MBCA) § 8.22(b). The notice must include information regarding the time, location, and date of the meeting but does not need to include information regarding the purpose of the meeting. *Id.*

Here, the facts state that the corporation's articles of incorporation and bylaws do not contain any special provisions regarding the board of directors. Notice of the special meeting was sent to six of the seven directors 29 days before the meeting was to be held, and it specified a time, location, and date. Therefore, with respect to those six directors, the notice of the special meeting was proper.

[NOTE: Although the references in the analysis are to the MBCA, the result throughout is the same under the Delaware General Corporation Law.]

Point One(b) (25%)
Claire did not receive proper notice of the special meeting of the board of directors; however, she waived such notice.

A director who does not receive notice of a special meeting of the board of directors at least two days prior to the meeting does not receive proper notice of that meeting. (*See* Point One(a).) However, a director who attends a special meeting of the board of directors despite not receiving proper notice waives such notice unless the director objects to the holding of the meeting and thereafter does not vote at the meeting. MBCA § 8.23(b). Here, there is no doubt that Claire did not receive proper notice of the special meeting. No notice was sent to Claire, who learned of the meeting through a phone call with another director. Even if that phone call constitutes notice, it was not received at least two days prior to the special meeting and therefore is not proper. (*See* Point One(a).)

However, Claire attended and voted at the special meeting. By these actions, Claire waived the notice requirement and therefore cannot claim that proper notice of the special meeting was not given.

Point Two (25%)
A quorum was present at the special meeting of the board of directors.

In order for action taken at a special meeting of directors to be proper, a quorum must be present at the meeting. MBCA § 8.24(c). Unless the articles of incorporation or bylaws provide otherwise, when a corporation has a fixed number of directors, a quorum consists of a majority of that fixed number. *Id.* § 8.24(a)(1).

Here, the facts state that the corporation's articles of incorporation mandate a seven-member board of directors and its articles of incorporation and bylaws contain no special provisions regarding the board of directors. Therefore, a quorum for the corporation's purposes consists of four directors. Here, while not all seven members of the board of directors were legally present at the special meeting, five of them (all but Alan and Barb) were (*see* Point Three). Therefore, a quorum was present, and the meeting was legally held.

Point Three (25%)
The purchase of the asset did not receive the required number of votes and was therefore not properly approved by the board of directors.

Unless the articles of incorporation or bylaws provide otherwise, if a quorum is present when a vote is taken, a majority vote of directors present is the act of the board of directors. MBCA § 8.24(c). Here, a quorum was present when the vote was taken (*see* Point Two). However, there were only five members of the board of directors present at the special meeting. Alan and Barb were not legally present.

While directors generally are entitled to participate in special meetings over the telephone, as Alan and Barb attempted to do, such participation is valid only if *all* directors participating "may simultaneously hear each other during the meeting." MBCA § 8.20. Only directors who satisfy this requirement are deemed to be present at the meeting. *Id.* Here, the facts state that Alan and Barb could hear and be heard by the five directors present in the conference room but that Alan and Barb could not hear each other. Because Alan and Barb could not hear each other, neither was legally present at the meeting.

Because Alan and Barb were not legally present at the meeting, their votes on the purchase of the asset may not be counted. Therefore, the vote on the purchase of the asset was two votes in favor and three votes against, and the purchase of the asset was not approved by the board of directors.

Corporations
(July 2012)

ANALYSIS

Legal Problems

    (1)   Does Acme have fiduciary duties as majority voting member that would require it to have A-B LLC bring the concrete claim against Acme?

    (2)   Can Brown bring the concrete claim against Acme?

    (3)   Does Brown have sufficient grounds to seek the dissolution of A-B LLC?

    (4)   Should A-B LLC's losses be borne by Acme and Brown and allocated between them in the same way as its profits?

DISCUSSION

Summary

Acme's lawyer is wrong in almost every respect. As the member of A-B LLC with management control, Acme has breached its fiduciary duties of loyalty and care by refusing to have the LLC bring the concrete claim. Brown can bring the concrete claim on behalf of the LLC against Acme as a derivative action, though not as a direct action against Acme. Brown may have sufficient grounds to seek judicial dissolution of A-B LLC, because Acme's failure to have the LLC bring the concrete claim likely constitutes oppression. Finally, under the rule of limited liability, the members and managers of an LLC generally are not liable for LLC losses. Thus, the A-B LLC losses arising from the judgment against the LLC are not borne by Acme or Brown, nor are they allocated between them.

[NOTE: The resolution of the issues in this problem would generally be the same in all jurisdictions. The following MEE jurisdictions have adopted the Uniform Limited Liability Company Act (ULLCA) (2006): the District of Columbia, Idaho, Iowa, Nebraska, and Utah.]

Point One (25%)

Acme owes A-B LLC and Brown fiduciary duties of loyalty and care. Refusing to have the LLC bring the concrete claim violates Acme's fiduciary duties because the refusal is self-interested and not in the LLC's best interests.

A-B LLC is a member-managed limited liability company (LLC). The operating agreement varies the statutory default to give Acme a 55% voting interest, which is permissible under ULLCA § 110. In exercising its management powers, Acme has fiduciary duties under ULLCA

§ 409 as a member in a member-managed LLC to both A-B LLC and Brown. These fiduciary duties include both a duty of loyalty and a duty of care.

The ULLCA does not specifically address whether the duty of loyalty precludes a majority member from refusing to have the LLC bring a surefire claim against the member. But the ULLCA provides that members have a duty of loyalty to "account to the company and to hold as trustee for [the company] any . . . benefit derived by the member . . . in the conduct . . . of the company's activities." ULLCA § 409(a)(1)(A). The benefit that Acme derives by virtue of A-B LLC not bringing a claim against Acme is an improper benefit, and thus keeping the benefit is a breach of Acme's duty of loyalty.

The ULLCA provides that, subject to the business-judgment rule, the duty of care requires the member to "act with the care that a person in a like position would reasonably exercise under similar circumstances and in a manner the member reasonably believes to be in the best interests of the company." ULLCA § 409(c). Because refusing to have the LLC bring the concrete claim against Acme is self-interested, the business-judgment rule is inapplicable. Under the facts given, Acme cannot reasonably believe that it is in A-B LLC's best interest to not bring the surefire concrete claim against Acme.

Point Two (25%)

The claim based on the defective concrete sold by Acme to A-B LLC is a claim of the LLC as an entity, not of the LLC's members. Thus, Brown can maintain a derivative action on behalf of A-B LLC, in which the LLC brings its concrete claim against Acme. But Brown cannot maintain a claim on Brown's own behalf directly against Acme.

Brown, as a member of the LLC, may maintain a derivative action under ULLCA § 902 to enforce A-B LLC's concrete claim against Acme. A derivative action in a member-managed LLC may be brought only if (1) a demand is made on the other member to bring an action and the member fails to do so, or (2) such demand would be futile. Here, Brown has made a demand on Acme and Acme has failed to have the LLC bring an action against Acme. Therefore, Brown may bring a derivative action against Acme.

Under ULLCA § 104, an LLC is an entity distinct from its members. The claim based on the faulty concrete is a claim of A-B LLC as an entity, not a claim of its constituent members. For this reason, Brown cannot advance the concrete claim on its own behalf. This is consistent with the direct action provision, ULLCA § 901, under which Brown would have to "plead and prove an actual or threatened injury that is not solely the result of an injury suffered or threatened to be suffered by the limited liability company."

Point Three (25%)

Based on Acme's unjustified refusal to advance the concrete claim, Brown may have grounds to seek judicial dissolution of A-B LLC.

Brown could apply to the court for an order of involuntary dissolution under ULLCA § 701(a)(5), alleging that Acme, as the member in control of the company, is acting in a manner that is oppressive and directly harmful to Brown.

The comment to ULLCA § 701 states that courts have begun to apply close corporation "oppression" doctrine to LLCs. Courts in the close corporation context have found oppression when actions by controlling shareholders violate the reasonable expectations of non-controlling shareholders. Thus, the question becomes whether Acme's refusal to have the LLC bring a surefire claim against Acme violates Brown's reasonable expectations. At a minimum, Brown had reasonable expectations that Acme would not violate its fiduciary duties (*see* Point One). In addition, Acme's refusal to have the LLC bring the concrete claim violates Brown's reasonable expectation that Acme would manage the LLC in the best interests of the LLC. Finally, Acme's refusal directly harms Brown, because unless Acme makes good on the LLC losses, Brown will suffer reputational harm for being involved in a construction project where the customers lost all their money.

Point Four (25%)

Under the rule of limited liability, LLC members and managers are not liable beyond their investment in the LLC for losses incurred by the LLC. There are no facts to support piercing the LLC veil, nor did the homeowners bring direct claims against Acme or Brown.

Although allocation of losses among partners in a partnership follows the allocation of profits, no allocation rule applies in an LLC because of limited liability. Under the rule of limited liability, if the LLC becomes indebted, obligated, or otherwise liable to an outside party, no member or manager becomes liable on that debt, obligation, or liability solely by reason of acting as a member or manager. *See* ULLCA § 304(a)(2). Thus, if A-B LLC lacks the assets to satisfy the judgment awarded to the homeowners, there can be no liability of either Acme or Brown on this judgment—unless a court pierces the LLC veil or finds that one of the members had acted to create direct liability.

Under the facts, there is no indication of fraud or other inequitable conduct in the formation or operation of A-B LLC that would support a piercing claim against Acme or Brown. Although state courts have recognized piercing in the LLC context, there must exist some circumstances that would justify piercing on equitable grounds, such as undercapitalization of the business, failure to follow formalities, commingling of assets, confusion of business affairs, or deception of creditors. None of these factors exists here.

At most, the homeowners may have had a direct claim against Acme for supplying defective concrete, but the homeowners did not bring this claim against Acme. Nor is there any indication that Brown was responsible for losses caused by the defective concrete. Therefore, because no claims were brought against either Acme or Brown, there are no losses for which either of them is liable directly, and there is no basis for allocating losses between them. If A-B LLC lacks the assets to satisfy the judgment awarded against it, any shortfall will be a loss borne by the homeowners.

MBE SUBJECTS - RELEASED ESSAY QUESTIONS

CRIMINAL LAW & PROCEDURE
MEE Question – July 2007

ANALYSIS

Legal Problems: (1)   Did Defendant act with the *mens rea* sufficient to be found guilty of second-degree murder?

                  (2)   Was Defendant's accidental shooting of Friend the legal cause of Friend's death?

DISCUSSION

Summary

Defendant need not have acted with deliberation or premeditation to be guilty of second-degree murder. However, Defendant must have acted with the *mens rea,* or mental state, of "malice aforethought." Malice aforethought is present where a defendant acts with "depraved indifference to the value of human life." On these facts, a jury could conclude that Defendant's act of shooting at a lamp to "scare Friend" evidenced a disregard of the risks to Friend and of the value of Friend's life sufficient to amount to depraved indifference.

Defendant's act of shooting Friend was the legal cause of Friend's death. First, it was the "but for" cause of Friend's death. Had Friend not been shot, Defendant would not have been driving him to the hospital, there would have been no accident, and Friend would not have bled to death. The fact that the accident contributed to Friend's death does not relieve Defendant of liability. The accident occurred as a result of Defendant's response to the shooting and would not be held to break the chain of causation. Thus, if Defendant were found to have acted with the requisite *mens rea,* Defendant would be responsible for Friend's death and guilty of second-degree murder.

Point One (45-55%)

A jury could find that Defendant's act of shooting at a lamp to scare Friend evidenced an extreme indifference to the value of human life and thus conclude that Friend acted with "malice aforethought."

To be guilty of second-degree murder, Defendant must have acted with the requisite *mens rea,* or mental state, of malice aforethought. Malice aforethought is a term of art, and it encompasses several different mental states. In most jurisdictions, the malice aforethought requirement is satisfied if Defendant acted with intent to kill, with knowledge that his acts would kill, with intent to inflict great bodily harm, or with reckless disregard of an extreme risk to human life (a depraved heart). J. DRESSLER, UNDERSTANDING CRIMINAL LAW 512-13 (2001); *see* MODEL PENAL CODE § 210.2(1)(b).

In this case, the evidence does not suggest that Defendant acted with intent or knowledge that Friend would be harmed. However, the evidence probably does support a conclusion that Defendant acted with "a depraved heart" and therefore with the malice aforethought necessary for Defendant to be guilty of murder.

Although the precise terminology used to describe "depraved-heart" murder differs from jurisdiction to jurisdiction, most states require (i) that the defendant act "recklessly" (i.e., with an awareness of the risk that his acts could cause death) and (ii) that the defendant's conduct show a high degree of indifference to the value of human life. Thus, convictions for depraved-heart murder have been upheld when a defendant intentionally shot a gun into a crowded room, *People v. Jernatowski*, 144 N.E. 497 (N.Y. 1924), or played Russian roulette with a partially loaded revolver, *Commonwealth v. Malone*, 47 A.2d 445 (Pa. 1946).

Here, Defendant probably acted recklessly. Defendant shot a gun in the general direction of Friend, while aiming at a lamp that was behind Friend. This behavior carries an obvious risk to Friend: if Defendant's aim was slightly off or if Friend moved (as happened here), Friend could be shot and fatally injured. From the facts of Defendant's behavior, and the obvious risks attending that behavior, a jury could infer that Defendant must have been aware of those risks and thus acted recklessly.

Did Defendant's recklessness evidence an "extreme indifference to the value of human life?" Courts have held that behavior that carries a substantial risk of causing death, when it has no legitimate purpose and is done solely for the amusement of a defendant, is a sufficient predicate for a conclusion that the defendant acted with the necessary indifference to human life to be liable for depraved-heart murder. *See Malone*, 47 A.2d 445. Here Defendant ran a high risk of causing serious harm to Friend for no purpose other than to amuse himself by scaring Friend. This is the kind of behavior that provides a sufficient predicate for a jury to find "extreme indifference to the value of human life" and to convict Defendant of second-degree murder.

Point Two (45-55%)

Defendant's act of shooting Friend was the legal cause of death because Friend would not have died "but for" having been shot by Defendant, and the injuries suffered by Friend in the car accident do not break the chain of proximate causation.

Defendant is criminally liable for Friend's death only if Defendant's acts were both the actual and proximate cause of Friend's death. *See generally* WAYNE R. LAFAVE, CRIMINAL LAW 331-358 (4th ed. 2003).

Defendant's act of shooting Friend was the actual cause of Friend's death. First, Defendant's act was the "but for" cause of Friend's death. Had Defendant not shot Friend, they would not have been driving to the hospital, the accident would not have occurred, and Friend would not have bled to death. Quite apart from that, however, it is well established that where a defendant's wrongful act (the gunshot wound) works in combination with some other cause (the injuries in the accident) to cause a victim's death, the defendant's act is an actual cause of the death because it "accelerated the death process." DRESSLER, *supra*, at 185; *see also Oxendine v. State*, 528 A.2d 870 (Del. 1987) (defendant who inflicts a second non-mortal wound can be considered the cause of child's death only if his actions caused child to die sooner than he otherwise would). Here, the facts state that Friend's death was the result of loss of blood caused by *both* the gunshot wound and the automobile accident. In that case, the gunshot wound is an actual cause of death.

Defendant's acts were also the proximate cause of Friend's death. The accident was a "dependent intervening cause"—a consequence of Defendant's prior wrongful conduct. It is widely held that such an intervening cause breaks the chain of causation from the original act to the death only if the intervening force was "so out-of-the-ordinary that it is no longer fair to hold [the defendant] criminally responsible for the outcome." DRESSLER, *supra*, at 190. Courts routinely say that the intervening event must have been "abnormal or bizarre" to prevent a defendant's original action from being regarded as the proximate cause of death. *See Kibbe v. Henderson*, 534 F.2d 493, 498-99, n.6 (2d Cir. 1976), *rev'd on other grounds, Henderson v. Kibbe*, 431 U.S. 145 (1977). Here, there is nothing abnormal about Defendant's response to his wrongful act (he tried to rush Friend to the hospital). Nor is there anything abnormal or bizarre about the fact that Defendant was involved in an accident while rushing to the hospital with a wounded friend. Even if Defendant was not at fault in causing the accident, the fact that it occurred is not sufficiently "out-of-the-ordinary" to warrant breaking the chain of causation from the shooting to the death. Therefore, Defendant's act of shooting Friend was the legal cause of Friend's death, and Defendant is guilty of second-degree murder if that act was committed with malice aforethought (*see* Point One).

MBE SUBJECTS - RELEASED ESSAY QUESTIONS

CRIMINAL LAW & PROCEDURE
MEE Question – February 2008

ANALYSIS

Legal Problems: (1)   Did the police interview of Student violate Student's Fourth Amendment right to be free from unreasonable seizure such that Student's statements (including the confession) should be suppressed as "fruit of the poisonous tree"?

    (2)   Should Student's statements be suppressed because the police failed to read him his *Miranda* rights when they questioned him in the manager's office?

    (3)   Should Student's confession be suppressed because it was involuntary?

DISCUSSION

Summary

Student was "seized" within the meaning of the Fourth Amendment when he was brought into the manager's office to be questioned by the police. However, that seizure did not violate Student's Fourth Amendment rights because the police had "reasonable articulable suspicion" that Student had been the perpetrator of an armed robbery. This allowed them to detain him for the purposes of investigation and will not taint any statements that Student made during the detention.

Whether the police were required to read Student his *Miranda* warnings depends on whether he was subject to in-custody interrogation. In this case, the only real question is whether Student was in custody. Applying the objective standard, Student was probably not in custody when he spoke with the officers in the manager's office, and *Miranda* warnings were not required.

The last question is whether Student's confession to the officers was voluntary or whether it was the product of police coercion that overcame Student's will. Here a court must look at the totality of the circumstances in ruling on the voluntariness of the confession. Most courts would probably conclude that Student's confession was voluntary.

Point One (25–35%)

Student was seized by the police within the meaning of the Fourth Amendment, but the seizure was a lawful investigative detention.

Student has a Fourth Amendment right to be free from unreasonable seizure. However, this Fourth Amendment right was violated in this case only if: (a) Student was in fact "seized" by the police when they spoke with him in the manager's office, and (b) that seizure was unreasonable for Fourth Amendment purposes. If the seizure did violate Student's Fourth Amendment rights, then Student's statements would be suppressible because they were the direct result of that seizure (i.e., "the fruit of the poisonous tree"). *Wong Sun v. United States*, 371 U.S. 471 (1963).

A person has been seized if, in light of all of the circumstances, "a reasonable person would have believed that he was not free to leave." *United States v. Mendenhall*, 446 U.S. 544, 554 (1980). In this case, a court could legitimately find that Student was seized by law enforcement. Student was taken into his manager's office where he remained for approximately 25 minutes with two police officers, one of whom had a visible weapon. One officer sat between Student and the door, and the door was closed. Student was not told that he was free to leave. Under these circumstances, a reasonable person in Student's position would probably have believed that he was required to stay in the room until the police officers gave him permission to leave.

Assuming that there was a seizure, the next question is whether it was a violation of Student's Fourth Amendment rights. Although the police did not have probable cause to arrest Student for the armed robbery, the Fourth Amendment permits detention of an individual for a relatively brief period of time if the police have a "reasonable articulable suspicion" that the individual in question has been recently involved in criminal activity. *Terry v. Ohio*, 392 U.S. 1 (1968).

In this case, three people said that the person on the tape of the convenience store robbery "could be," "might be," and "looked like" Student. These identifications, although far from certain, gave the law enforcement officers sufficient specific facts to form the basis of a reasonable suspicion that Student was the robber. The fact that one of the identifiers was an anonymous caller does not affect the reasonableness of law enforcement's actions since the police officers corroborated the possible identification with Student's principal and Student's homeroom teacher.

Thus, Student's Fourth Amendment rights were not violated, and his statements should not be suppressed.

Point Two (30–40%)

The police were probably not required to read Student the *Miranda* warnings because he was probably not in custody until they placed him under arrest.

Law enforcement officers are required to read *Miranda* warnings to a suspect when the suspect is subjected to an in-custody interrogation. *Miranda v. Arizona*, 384 U.S. 436, 444 (1966). If the officers were required to read the warnings and failed to do so, the statements should be suppressed.

Student was clearly subject to interrogation, which has been defined not only as questioning initiated by law enforcement but as "any words or actions on the part of the   police . . . that the police should know are reasonably likely to elicit an incriminating response" from the suspect. *Rhode Island v. Innis*, 446 U.S. 291, 301 (1980) (quoting *California v. Beheler*, 463 U.S. 1121,

1125 (1983) (*per curiam*)). The only question then is whether Student was "in custody" when he was being questioned.

Custody is a substantial seizure and is defined as either a formal arrest or "restraint on freedom of movement of the degree associated with a formal arrest." *New York v. Quarles*, 467 U.S. 649, 655 (1984). A suspect need not be in a police station to be in custody. Whether a suspect is in custody is determined by "how a reasonable person in the suspect's situation would perceive his circumstances." *Yarborough v. Alvarado*, 541 U.S. 652, 662 (2004). In assessing the question of custody, courts consider the facts surrounding the interrogation. The test to be applied is purely objective. Therefore, a suspect's age, experience, and other personal characteristics are not considered. *Id.* at 666–67.

In this case, two police officers had Student summoned to the manager's office, into which they escorted him and closed the door. Student was outnumbered two to one, and one officer, with a visible firearm, sat between Student and the door. The police did not tell Student that he was free to leave. Nonetheless, Student was probably not in custody. The police officers told Student that they would "like to talk" with him; he was not told that he was under arrest until the end of the interview. During the interview, Student was not in any restraints, the two officers were seated in chairs, and the interview took place in an office. While Student may not have felt that he was free to leave, a reasonable person would probably not have believed that he had been arrested or otherwise taken into formal custody. If Student was not in custody, then the police were not required to read him *Miranda* warnings before talking with him. Therefore, there should be no suppression for a *Miranda* violation.

[NOTE TO GRADERS: Credit should be given for reasonable arguments on either side of this issue.]

Point Three (25–35%)

Based on the totality of the circumstances, Student's confession was probably voluntary.

The voluntariness of a confession is based on (1) whether the police subjected the suspect to coercive conduct, *see Colorado v. Connelly*, 479 U.S. 157, 167 (1986), and (2) whether the conduct was sufficient to overcome the will of the suspect, *see Rogers v. Richmond*, 365 U.S. 534, 543–44 (1961).

There is certainly some evidence of coercion. Here, the police interviewed Student in a small, closed room, two against one, with a firearm displayed. The police did not tell Student that he was free to go if he chose, did not tell him that he was not obliged to answer their questions, and did not advise him of his *Miranda* rights. The police also lied to Student about the strength of their case. By itself, the lie would not be a ground for suppression. Trickery and deceit do not render a confession inadmissible. *United States v. Kontny*, 238 F.3d 815, 817 (7th Cir. 2001). "Far from making the police a fiduciary of the suspect, the law permits the police to pressure and cajole, conceal material facts and actively mislead." *United States v. Rutledge*, 900 F.2d 1127, 1131 (7th Cir. 1990). But in conjunction with the other factors, this deception pushes this case closer to the line of coercion.

The more difficult question is whether this coercive conduct was sufficient to overcome the will of the suspect. Here, courts consider the totality of the circumstances and take into account both the conduct of the police and the suspect's individual characteristics such as age, level of education, and familiarity with the criminal justice system. *Alvarado*, 541 U.S. at 667–68; *Schneckloth v. Bustamonte*, 412 U.S. 218, 226 (1973).

A court could conclude that the police behavior was insufficiently coercive to have overcome Student's will. The facts indicate that Student is an adult (18 years old) of at least average intelligence and that he has some experience with the juvenile justice system. The interview in his manager's office lasted less than 30 minutes. Although the police statements about the identification were not 100 percent true, the fact that a suspect has been deceived about the strength of evidence does not automatically render a statement involuntary. *Frazier v. Cupp*, 394 U.S. 731, 739 (1969). The statement by the police officers that the prosecutor might be more lenient when a defendant is young and cooperates could be construed as an accurate observation of how the justice system operates rather than as a promise of leniency. Similarly, the police officers' general description of prison as "not being a nice place" was not a threat but simply a statement of fact.

On the other hand, a court that focuses on Student's youth and inexperience might consider the confession to have been involuntary. Student is a high school senior with minimal experience with the criminal justice system. He was questioned in his manager's office by two police officers. His confession was in direct response to police conduct that could be considered "overreaching." First, the police deliberately lied about the strength of the evidence against him. When it appeared that Student was reacting to that tactic, the police upped the ante by telling him that a confession might result in leniency. Finally, the police officers made what could be taken as a veiled threat about what would happen to Student in prison if he did not confess.

[NOTE TO GRADERS: Credit should be given for reasonable arguments on either side of this issue.]

MBE SUBJECTS - RELEASED ESSAY QUESTIONS

CRIMINAL LAW & PROCEDURE
MEE Question – July 2009

ANALYSIS

Legal Problems: (1)   Does John have standing to challenge the search of Crystal's parents' home and the seizure and search of the leather bag?

    (2)   Did the prosecution produce sufficient evidence to prove all of the elements of attempted armed robbery?

    (3)   Is "withdrawal," "abandonment," or "change of mind" a defense to a charge of an attempted crime?

DISCUSSION

Summary

John does not have a reasonable expectation of privacy in Crystal's parents' home and therefore does not have standing to challenge the legality of the search of that home. Nor can he claim a reasonable expectation of privacy in the leather bag and its contents since he turned it over to Crystal.

The trial court correctly denied the motion for judgment of acquittal. The prosecution presented sufficient facts to prove all the elements of attempted armed robbery. Specifically, the state showed that John had the intent to commit an armed robbery and that he had performed sufficient acts toward the commission of the robbery to have gone beyond mere preparation.

The trial court was probably correct to deny the motion for the jury instruction on abandonment. In many jurisdictions, abandonment is not a defense in any case in which an individual has committed sufficient acts to constitute an attempt, as John has in this case. Even in jurisdictions where abandonment is a defense, it must be a voluntary and complete renunciation by the defendant of the criminal scheme. John's decision not to complete the robbery was not due to his voluntary abandonment of his criminal purpose. It was the result of his accomplice's flight from the scene.

Point One (30–40%)
John does not have standing to challenge the search of Crystal's parents' home because he lacks a reasonable expectation of privacy in that home. Similarly, he cannot challenge the seizure of his bag and the search of its contents because he had surrendered control of the bag to Crystal and therefore had no reasonable expectation of privacy in its contents.

Although the police did not have a warrant, Crystal's mother consented to the search of her home when she let them in after they stated that they could get a warrant. Even if her consent to the search of her home was considered coerced or involuntary and therefore invalid, John could not raise the issue. In *Rakas v. Illinois,* 439 U.S. 128 (1978), the Supreme Court of the United States held that only those who are actual victims of the alleged Fourth Amendment violation have "standing" to challenge it. As the Court put it, "[a] person who is aggrieved by an illegal search and seizure only through the introduction of damaging evidence secured by a search of a third person's premises or property has not had any of his Fourth Amendment rights infringed." *Id.* at 134. Here, John can claim no reasonable expectation of privacy in his girlfriend's family's home.

Similarly, a person challenging a seizure and search of an object such as a bag must have a reasonable expectation of privacy in the object seized and searched. John cannot claim that he had a reasonable expectation of privacy in his bag found in Crystal's closet. While he might have a property interest in the bag, he surrendered his reasonable expectation of privacy in the bag when he turned the bag over to Crystal and asked her to "get rid of it." *See Rawlings v. Kentucky,* 448 U.S. 98 (1980). Once John gave the bag to Crystal, he had no way to control who had access to his bag and how Crystal was to dispose of it.

Accordingly, the trial judge correctly denied John's motion to suppress the bag and its contents.

Point Two (30–40%)
The prosecution produced sufficient evidence to prove that John intended to commit an armed robbery and that he committed acts going "beyond mere preparation" and constituting an attempt to commit the robbery.

A motion for judgment of acquittal should be granted only if the prosecution has failed to present sufficient evidence for a reasonable jury to find that the defendant committed each element of the charged offense beyond a reasonable doubt. *Jackson v. Virginia,* 443 U.S. 307, 319 (1979); *State v. Thompson,* 88 S.W.3d 611, 614–15 (Tenn. Crim. App. 2000). In this case, there is more than enough evidence to support a conviction for attempted armed robbery.

In order to prove that John attempted an armed robbery, the prosecution must prove two elements. First, the prosecution must prove that John intended to commit an armed robbery. Second, the prosecution must prove that John's actions went sufficiently beyond "mere preparation" to constitute an actual "attempt" to commit the crime. *See* MODEL PENAL CODE § 5.01.

As to John's intent, the e-mails and the testimony of the clerk and Crystal provide ample evidence that John planned to either use a weapon or threaten the imminent use of a weapon against the store clerk to compel the store clerk to turn over money. This evidence shows clearly that John intended to commit the essential elements of armed robbery—he intended to use force or the threat of force to steal the property of another. Accordingly, the prosecution has more than met its burden of proving that John intended to commit armed robbery.

The evidence is also sufficient to show that John's actions to carry out his plan went beyond "mere preparation" and constituted an actual "attempt" to commit the crime. States use various tests for determining when a defendant's conduct has gone far enough to constitute an attempt to commit a crime. Some state courts say that the actor's conduct must be "proximate" to the crime; others say that it must be "dangerously proximate" to the crime. The Model Penal Code requires only that a defendant's conduct be a "substantial step" toward commission of the crime and corroborative of his criminal intent. JOSHUA DRESSLER, UNDERSTANDING CRIMINAL LAW § 27.09 (4th ed. 2006). Some states say that the defendant's behavior must "unequivocally" manifest the criminal intent. *See id.* § 27.06.

In this case, the prosecution's evidence demonstrates that John's conduct went beyond mere preparation and constituted an attempt. John's behavior—loading a gun, taking it into a store, and approaching the store clerk—ought to satisfy any test of proximity: John was dangerously close to completing his crime. Moreover, the conduct on its face bespeaks an intention to rob the store clerk by force or threat of force, and the clerk said that he thought John intended to rob him. Indeed, from all the facts, it appears that John would have robbed the clerk but for the fact that John's accomplice started to cry and left the store. Most courts would find that these actions were "near enough to the accomplishment of the substantive offense to be punishable." *Commonwealth v. Peaslee*, 59 N.E. 55, 56 (Mass. 1901); *see also People v. Terrell*, 443 N.E.2d 742 (Ill. Ct. App. 1982); *State v. Stewart*, 420 N.W.2d 44 (Wis. 1988).

Point Three (20–30%)

Although John left the Minit Mart without completing the robbery, the circumstances of his departure do not support a defense of withdrawal or abandonment.

In most jurisdictions, voluntary withdrawal or abandonment is not a defense to the crime of attempt once the actor's conduct has gone beyond mere preparation. *See Dixon v. State*, 559 So. 2d 354, 355–56 (Fla. Dist. Ct. App. 1990); DRESSLER, *supra*, § 27.08. In those jurisdictions, if John's conduct had gone far enough toward completion of a crime to constitute an attempt, he would be guilty of attempt even if he subsequently decided to renounce his criminal plans completely and voluntarily. *See, e.g., Stewart*, 420 N.W.2d at 49–51. In a jurisdiction taking this view of attempt, the court was correct to refuse a jury instruction on the defense of abandonment because no such defense exists.

A minority of jurisdictions take the view that the abandonment of an attempt before the crime is completed is an affirmative defense. However, the abandonment must be utterly voluntary. An abandonment that is the result of any extrinsic factor is not considered voluntary. *Wilkinson v. State*, 670 N.E.2d 47, 49 (Ind. Ct. App. 1996) (passing out from intoxication not voluntary abandonment of an attempted crime).

Here, John abandoned the robbery only after his 14-year-old accomplice got scared and ran out of the store. Whether his decision to leave the store without completing the robbery was motivated by a concern for Crystal, a belief that he needed her participation, or some other factor, it was taken in response to Crystal's behavior and was not an entirely voluntary decision by John. It does not satisfy the requirements for the abandonment defense, and the trial judge was correct to deny an instruction on that defense.

MBE SUBJECTS - RELEASED ESSAY QUESTIONS

CRIMINAL LAW & PROCEDURE
MEE Question – July 2010

ANALYSIS

Legal Problems: (1)   What are the elements of the crime of larceny by false pretenses?

                       (2)   Did Owner make a false representation of a material present or past fact that caused Customer to pass title to the property (the $250) to Owner?

                       (3)   Did Owner act with the *mens rea* required to be found guilty of false pretenses?

DISCUSSION

Summary

To be guilty of larceny by false pretenses in most jurisdictions, Owner must have made a false representation of a material fact that caused Customer to pass title to property to Owner. Owner must have acted with knowledge of the falsity of the fact and with an intent to defraud.

While Owner did not believe that Star had the best refurbished computers in town, his claim to the contrary was a false representation of opinion, not fact, and could not support a conviction for larceny by false pretenses. However, Owner's statement that the computer technician installed a new hard drive in each refurbished computer was a false statement of a material fact because the technician did not install new hard drives. Owner obtained title to Customer's property when Customer paid Owner $250 for the computer. The fact that Customer purchased the computer after being satisfied by Owner's claims suggests that Customer relied upon Owner's false representation of fact in passing title to property.

A court would likely find that Owner knowingly made the false representation about new hard drives because Owner believed that it was very likely that the computer technician used by Star did not install new hard drives, and Owner deliberately decided not to question the technician. Owner also had the requisite intent to defraud because Owner made the false claim about the new hard drives based upon the belief that it was one of the most important factors that would lead to a purchase by Customer.

Point One (25%)
To be guilty of larceny by false pretenses, a defendant must knowingly make a false representation of material fact to a person, with the intent to defraud, and the false representation must cause the victim to pass title to something of value to the defendant.

The crime of "larceny by false pretenses" or, as it is sometimes called, "obtaining property by false pretenses" or just "false pretenses," is a type of theft offense. In most jurisdictions, the *actus reus* elements of false pretenses are (i) a false representation of material fact (ii) that causes another person to transfer title to property (including money) to the defendant. The *mens rea* required is knowledge that the representation of fact is false and an intent to defraud. *See generally* JOSHUA DRESSLER, UNDERSTANDING CRIMINAL LAW § 32.10 (5th ed. 2009). *See, e.g.,* MODEL PENAL CODE § 223.3 (theft by deception).

Here, Owner is charged with the crime of false pretenses on the theory that Owner stole Customer's money (the $250 that Customer paid for the computer) by lying to Customer in order to induce Customer to give the money to Owner in exchange for the computer.

Point Two (35%)
The *actus reus* elements of the crime of false pretenses are met because Owner made a false representation of a material present or past fact that caused Customer to pass title to something of value (the $250) to Owner.

As noted above, to be guilty of false pretenses in most jurisdictions, Owner must have made a false representation of a material present or past fact that caused Customer to pass title to property to Owner. *See State v. Agosta*, 787 A.2d 1252, 1254 (Vt. 2001). The false representation must be one of fact, not opinion. *See McMurphy v. State*, 455 So. 2d 924, 927 (Ala. Crim. App. 1984). Commercial puffery is not generally considered "false pretenses." *See* DRESSLER, *supra*, § 32.10[C][2][a]. While Owner did not believe that Star had the best refurbished computers in town, his claim to the contrary was a false representation of opinion, not of fact, and could not support a conviction for larceny by false pretenses. *See id.*

On the other hand, Owner's statement that the technician had installed a new hard drive in each refurbished computer was a false statement of a material fact. *See People v. Taurianen*, 300 N.W.2d 720, 725 (Mich. Ct. App. 1980) (per curiam) (misrepresentation of fact where defendants accepted payment for repair work that was not performed). Owner claimed that the technician had installed a new hard drive in every refurbished computer when no such installation had occurred.

Through this false representation, Owner succeeded in obtaining title to Customer's property when the purchase of the computer was completed and Customer gave Owner $250. *See People v. Long*, 294 N.W.2d 197, 200 (Mich. 1980).

It does not matter that Customer may have had additional reasons for purchasing the computer—reasons that had nothing to do with Owner's false representation. It is enough that Owner's false representation contributed to Customer's parting with property. *See State v. Handke*, 340 P.2d 877, 883 (Kan. 1959). The fact that Customer purchased the computer after being satisfied by Owner's claims, including the claim that the computer technician installed a new hard drive in every refurbished computer, suggests that the false representation contributed to Customer's parting with $250, thus establishing the causal link between Owner's false representation and the transfer of title to the property. *See id.*

Point Three (40%)
The *mens rea* element of the crime of false pretenses is likely met because Owner made the false representation knowingly and with the intent to defraud Customer.

To be guilty of false pretenses, Owner must have made the false representation knowingly and with the intent to defraud Customer. *See Trevino v. State*, 142 P.3d 214, 216 (Wyo. 2006). Most courts find that a defendant acts knowingly and has knowledge of a particular fact when, *inter alia*, the defendant is aware of a high probability of the fact's existence and deliberately avoids learning the truth. *See United States v. Guay*, 108 F.3d 545, 551 (4th Cir. 1997); MODEL PENAL CODE § 2.02(7). A court would likely find that Owner knowingly made the false representation based upon both Owner's belief that it was very likely that the computer technician used by Star did not install new hard drives and Owner's deliberate decision not to question the technician. *See Guay*, 108 F.3d 545 at 551. The markedly low rates and fast service provided by the technician would provide additional evidence that Owner knew or should have known that the technician was not installing new hard drives. *See Commonwealth v. Franks*, 340 A.2d 456, 459–60 (Pa. Super. Ct. 1975) (Price, J., dissenting).

A few states, however, reject this "willful blindness" standard and require actual knowledge. *See Love v. Commonwealth*, 55 S.W.3d 816, 825 (Ky. 2001) (actual knowledge of each element of offense required, but such knowledge may be proved by circumstantial evidence). In these states, Owner would lack actual knowledge that the technician failed to install new hard drives and could not be found guilty of false pretenses. *See id.*

With respect to the second element, a defendant has the intent to defraud required to establish false pretenses when the defendant intends that the person to whom the false representation is made will rely upon it. *See Commonwealth v. Cheromcka*, 850 N.E.2d 1088, 1094 (Mass. App. Ct. 2006). Because Owner made the claim about the new hard drives based upon the belief that it would help persuade Customer to buy a computer, Owner also had the requisite intent to defraud.

MBE SUBJECTS - RELEASED ESSAY QUESTIONS

CRIMINAL LAW & PROCEDURE
MEE Question – July 2011

ANALYSIS

Legal Problems

(1)   Was it constitutional for Officer to stop and arrest Suspect for a petty traffic offense when Officer's real motive was to find evidence of other crimes?

(2)   Was it constitutional for Officer to seize evidence from Suspect's car?

(3)   Did Officer's questioning of Suspect violate Suspect's rights under *Miranda*?

(4)(a)   Did Officer's questioning of Suspect make Detective's subsequent interrogation of Suspect unconstitutional?

(4)(b)   Was Suspect's ambiguous statement regarding a lawyer sufficient to invoke Suspect's right to an attorney and to require Detective to cease interrogation?

DISCUSSION

Summary

Officer had probable cause to believe that Suspect was violating traffic laws based on his own observations of Suspect. Officer therefore acted constitutionally in stopping and arresting Suspect. The stop and the subsequent arrest are constitutional despite the fact that the traffic infraction was minor, Officer had never previously arrested anyone for a seat belt violation, and Officer had another motive for making the stop.

It was also lawful for Officer to engage in a "plain view" search of the front seat of Suspect's car by looking into the window after the arrest of Suspect.

Officer violated Suspect's constitutional rights by interrogating Suspect at the scene after arresting him without first providing *Miranda* warnings and obtaining a valid waiver. Thus, Suspect's responsive statement to Officer at the scene is inadmissible. However, Officer's *Miranda* violation does not make Suspect's subsequent interrogation by Detective unconstitutional. A violation of *Miranda* does not taint derivative evidence (e.g., Suspect's statement made during the second interrogation). Moreover, Detective's second interrogation was a separate interrogation that involved a change in time, place, and circumstance. Prior to Detective's second interrogation, *Miranda* warnings were given and a knowing and valid waiver was obtained. Suspect's equivocal and ambiguous statement about possibly needing a lawyer was not an invocation by Suspect of his *Miranda* right to silence, so Detective did not need to cease his interrogation and provide Suspect with an attorney.

Point One (25%)
A traffic stop and arrest with probable cause does not violate the Fourth Amendment even if the offense was minor and the stop served as a pretext for investigating other criminal wrongdoing.

Under the Fourth Amendment, the constitutional reasonableness of a traffic stop does not depend on the motivation of the officer involved or the petty nature of the offense charged, as long as state law permits an arrest. *See Whren v. United States*, 517 U.S. 806, 810 (1996) ("As a general matter, the decision to stop an automobile is reasonable where the police have probable cause to believe that a traffic violation has occurred."). If the officer has probable cause to believe that a suspect has committed an offense, then a stop and arrest of that suspect is reasonable if authorized under the applicable state statute. *See Atwater v. City of Lago Vista*, 532 U.S. 318, 354 (2001) ("If an officer has probable cause to believe that an individual has committed even a very minor criminal offense in his presence, he may, without violating the Fourth Amendment, arrest the offender.").

Here, the arrest was constitutional because Officer had probable cause, based on his personal observations, to believe that Suspect was committing a traffic violation and the state seat belt statute permitted arrest. The stop and subsequent arrest were constitutional despite the fact that the traffic infraction was minor and Officer had never previously arrested anyone for a seat belt violation. In addition, the stop and arrest were constitutional even if Officer used the seat belt violation as a pretext to investigate criminal wrongdoing based on Officer's knowledge that Suspect was a reputed drug dealer. *Whren*, 517 U.S. at 813–14.

Point Two (25%)
Officer's seizure of evidence from the front seat of Suspect's car did not violate the Fourth Amendment.

Under the Fourth Amendment, a police officer is lawfully permitted to seize evidence without a warrant if the evidence is found in plain view during lawful observation. *See Coolidge v. New Hampshire*, 403 U.S. 443, 465 (1971) ("It is well established that under certain circumstances the police may seize evidence in plain view without a warrant."). Under the plain view doctrine, "if police are lawfully in a position from which they view an object, if its incriminating character is immediately apparent, and if the officers have a lawful right of access to the object, they may seize it without a warrant." *Minnesota v. Dickerson*, 508 U.S. 366, 375 (1993).

In this case, Officer had probable cause to stop and arrest Suspect for a traffic law violation based on his own observation of Suspect's violation of the seat belt law. Following the arrest, Officer was lawfully permitted to look into the car window while the car was stopped on a public road. Officer had probable cause to believe that white powder contained in a clear plastic bag in the car of a reputed drug dealer is likely to be an illegal drug, and Officer had additional cause to support that belief after Suspect stated, "That cocaine isn't mine," in response to Officer's question about the bag. The fact that Suspect's statement is inadmissible, *see* Point Four(a), does not prevent Officer from relying on the statement to establish probable cause. The lawful access requirement "guard[s] against warrantless entry onto premises whenever contraband is viewed from off the premises . . . but does not bar the seizure of evidence in a parked car" that is observed by an officer who is viewing contraband from a lawful vantage point. *Boone v. Spurgess*, 385 F.3d 923 (6th Cir. 2004). *See also United States v. Gillon*, 348 F.3d 755, 759–60 (8th Cir. 2003) (once officers saw "what appeared to be bags containing crack cocaine" in a parked car "they had a right of access to the passenger compartment of the car" to seize the likely contraband). *Cf. United States v. Ross*, 456 U.S. 798 (1982) (police officers who have probable cause to believe a vehicle contains contraband had lawful right to enter and search vehicle and seize contraband found therein).

Point Three (15%)
Officer violated Suspect's *Miranda* rights when Officer arrested Suspect and interrogated him without providing *Miranda* warnings and obtaining a valid waiver.

A person under arrest is in custody and must first receive *Miranda* warnings before being subjected to interrogation. *Miranda v. Arizona*, 384 U.S. 436, 444 (1966) (Prior to any questioning, a person under arrest "must be warned that he has a right to remain silent, that any statement he does make may be used as evidence against him, and that he has a right to the presence of an attorney, either retained or appointed."). Here, Officer arrested Suspect and then interrogated Suspect, asking him "Are these drugs yours?" without first providing *Miranda* warnings. This custodial interrogation involved express questioning of Suspect by Officer that violated Suspect's *Miranda* rights. *See Rhode Island v. Innis*, 446 U.S. 291, 300–01 (1980) ("[T]he *Miranda* safeguards come into play whenever a person in custody is subjected to either express questioning or its functional equivalent.").

Point Four(a) (25%)
Officer's *Miranda* violation did not taint Detective's subsequent interrogation.

Statements taken during custodial interrogations conducted in violation of *Miranda* are excluded from the prosecution's case-in-chief. However, a violation of *Miranda* is a violation of a constitutional "rule," *see Dickerson v. United States*, 530 U.S. 428, 444 (2000), not a direct violation of the constitution. Unlike direct violations of the constitution, *Miranda* violations do not taint derivative evidence and the "fruit of the poisonous tree" doctrine does not apply. *See United States v. Patane*, 542 U.S. 630, 631–32 (2004) ("Unlike . . . actual violations of the Self-Incrimination Clause, there is, with respect to mere failures to warn, nothing to deter . . . [and] therefore no reason to apply [*Wong Sun's*] 'fruit of the poisonous tree' doctrine.").

In *Oregon v. Elstad*, 470 U.S. 298, 305–09 (1985), the U.S. Supreme Court held that, if a suspect was subjected to custodial interrogation without the benefit of *Miranda* warnings, a subsequent confession by the suspect may nonetheless be admitted if the totality of circumstances establishes that the second statement was knowing and voluntary. Unless the police engage in an interrogation process that must "realistically [be] seen as part of a single unwarned sequence of questioning," *see Missouri v. Seibert*, 542 U.S. 600, 612 n. 4 (2004), subsequent custodial interrogation following a break in the initial proceedings, *Miranda* warnings, and a waiver of rights is constitutional. *See id. See also Elstad*, 470 U.S. at 318 ("a suspect who has once responded to unwarned yet uncoercive questioning is not thereby disabled from waiving his rights and confessing after he has been given the requisite *Miranda* warnings.").

Here, Officer's initial unwarned custodial interrogation should not prevent the prosecution from using Suspect's later confession to Detective. After Officer's original *Miranda* violation, Suspect was taken to the police station where Detective provided proper *Miranda* warnings and obtained Suspect's knowing and voluntary waiver before interrogating Suspect. Detective's provision of *Miranda* warnings at a later time and in a different place rendered Suspect's later statements to Detective admissible.

Point Four(b) (10%)
Suspect's statement that he might want an attorney was too ambiguous to require Detective to cease interrogation.

Pursuant to *Davis v. United States*, 512 U.S. 452, 458 (1994), if an arrestee makes an unambiguous and unequivocal request or demand for an attorney, the police must cease the interrogation and honor the request.

Suspect did not make such a request or demand; the statement "I'm not sure about this. Maybe I need a lawyer" was ambiguous and equivocal. *Id.* at 459–62. *See also United States v. Johnson*, 400 F.3d 187, 195 (4th Cir. 2005), citing *Burket v. Angelone*, 208 F.3d 172, 197–98 (4th Cir. 2000) ("I think I need a lawyer" is not an unambiguous request for an attorney.). Therefore, Detective was not required to cease the interrogation and provide Suspect with an attorney. Indeed, Detective was not even obliged to seek clarification of Suspect's intentions. *Davis*, 512 U.S. at 461–62 (declining to "adopt a rule requiring officers to ask clarifying questions" and concluding that when a suspect's statement "is not an unambiguous or unequivocal request for counsel, the officers have no obligation to stop questioning him"). Detective therefore did not violate Suspect's rights by ignoring Suspect's equivocal statement about an attorney, and the court should not suppress Suspect's confession.

MBE SUBJECTS - RELEASED ESSAY QUESTIONS

CRIMINAL LAW & PROCEDURE
MEE Question – July 2012

ANALYSIS

Legal Problems

    (1)(a)   What are the elements of involuntary manslaughter?

    (1)(b)   Did Adam act with mens rea required to be guilty of involuntary manslaughter?

    (1)(c)   Were Adam's actions the legal cause of the child's death?

    (2)   Can Bob be liable as an accomplice for the child's death?

DISCUSSION

Summary

A jury could find Adam guilty of involuntary manslaughter both in a jurisdiction that requires recklessness and in one that requires only gross negligence (sometimes referred to as criminal or culpable negligence). In a jurisdiction that requires recklessness, Adam's statements indicate that he was aware that his conduct created an unreasonable (or high and unreasonable) risk of death or serious bodily injury and that he consciously disregarded that risk. In a jurisdiction that requires gross negligence, a jury could find Adam guilty because a reasonable person under similar circumstances would have been aware that his conduct created an unreasonable (or unreasonable and high) risk of death or serious bodily injury.

Adam's conduct was the cause of the child's death. Adam's conduct was the but-for cause of the child's death because if Adam had not placed the marbles on the road, the child would not have died. The fact that the child was not properly secured in the vehicle does not break the chain of causation because this outcome was foreseeable.

Bob did not commit an act that resulted in the death of the child, nor did he have a duty to stop Adam from committing that act. However, a jury could find Bob liable as an accomplice to Adam's involuntary manslaughter if he assisted in the act with the required mental state. Here, Bob intentionally assisted Adam in the act by driving him to the scene of the crime. In a jurisdiction that requires recklessness, Bob's statements indicate that he was not aware that his assistance created an unreasonable (or high and unreasonable) risk of death or serious bodily injury. Bob is more likely to be found guilty as an accomplice in a state that requires gross/criminal/culpable negligence, if a reasonable person under similar circumstances would have been aware of this risk.

Point One(a) (25%)

To be guilty of involuntary manslaughter, a person must cause the death of another human being by conduct that creates an unreasonable (or high and unreasonable) risk of death or serious bodily injury. The precise mens rea requirement will vary from jurisdiction to jurisdiction.

In most jurisdictions, a defendant is guilty of involuntary manslaughter when the defendant causes the death of another human being by engaging in conduct that creates an unreasonable (or high and unreasonable) risk of death or serious bodily injury. WAYNE R. LaFAVE, CRIMINAL LAW § 15.4(a) (5th ed. 2010).

The modern and majority view is that the defendant must have acted "recklessly" to be convicted of involuntary manslaughter (i.e., the defendant must have been aware of the unreasonable (or unreasonable and high) risk of death or serious bodily injury that his conduct created). Recklessness is typically defined as conscious disregard of a known risk, *see, e.g.,* MODEL PENAL CODE § 2.02(c).

In other jurisdictions it is enough if the defendant acted with greater than ordinary negligence, which some states call "gross," "criminal," or "culpable" negligence. *See* C.T. Foster, Annotation, *Test or Criterion of Term "Culpable Negligence," "Criminal Negligence," or "Gross Negligence," Appearing in Statute Defining or Governing Manslaughter*, 161 A.L.R. 10 (1946). In these states, even if the defendant was unaware of the risk, the defendant could be found guilty if an ordinary person in the defendant's situation would have been aware that her conduct created an unreasonable (or unreasonable and high) risk of death or serious bodily injury.

Adam will be guilty of involuntary manslaughter only if he acted with the requisite degree of culpability and his conduct was the legal cause of the child's death.

Point One(b) (25%)

A jury could conclude from Adam's statements and actions that he acted with a mens rea of recklessness or gross negligence.

In order to determine whether Adam has committed involuntary manslaughter, his mens rea with regard to the result must be assessed.

In most jurisdictions, Adam can only be convicted of involuntary manslaughter if the fact finder concludes that he acted "recklessly" by consciously disregarding the unreasonable (or high and unreasonable) risk of death or serious bodily injury that his conduct created. In these jurisdictions, the prosecution will argue that Adam's statements indicating that he knew that the marbles could cause an accident, including his statements that "When cars come by, they'll slip on the marbles and they won't be able to stop," and that "They'll have trouble; maybe there will even be a crash," demonstrate that Adam was aware of the risk. The prosecution will also argue that Adam (like everyone else) knows that serious bodily injury and death are frequent outcomes of car crashes.

Adam will likely respond in several ways. First, he will contend that he was not reckless because he did not consciously disregard an unreasonable (or unreasonable and high) risk of death or serious bodily injury resulting from the accident. His statements indicated, he will argue, that he believed that drivers would lose control of their vehicles and would get mad and that there might be a crash, but did not suggest any awareness of the risk that someone would die or suffer serious bodily injury. He could also argue that no crash occurred while he watched the intersection, that traffic at the intersection was usually light, and that he was not aware of the risk that two cars would crash into each other, particularly at 2 a.m.

On the whole, a jury could conclude that Adam's statements indicate that he was clearly aware that his actions could cause a car crash and every reasonable person knows that car crashes can cause death or serious bodily injury. Adam's statement "I'll bet someone will come" specifically suggests that he believed that cars would drive through the intersection that evening.

To prove that Adam had a mens rea of recklessness, the prosecution does not need to prove that Adam knew the precise time or circumstances of the resulting crash. If, however, the fact finder accepts that Adam did not consciously disregard an unreasonable (or unreasonable and high) risk of death or serious bodily injury from the resulting crash, he would not be guilty of involuntary manslaughter in a jurisdiction that requires recklessness for the crime.

In some jurisdictions, Adam can be convicted of involuntary manslaughter if the fact finder concludes that he acted with "gross," "criminal," or "culpable" negligence. In these jurisdictions, Adam can be convicted if a reasonable person in his situation would have been aware that his conduct created an unreasonable (or unreasonable and high) risk of death or serious bodily injury. It is highly likely that a fact finder would conclude that a reasonable person would be aware that conduct likely to cause vehicles to slip at an intersection creates an unreasonable (or unreasonable and high) risk of car crashes and death or serious bodily injury as a result of the crashes.

Point One(c) (25%)

Adam's conduct was the but-for cause of the child's death. His conduct was also the legal cause because no intervening event occurred that would be sufficient to break the chain of causation.

The state will need to prove that Adam caused the child's death in order for Adam to be found guilty of involuntary manslaughter. Causation requires a showing of both causation in fact—otherwise known as but-for causation—and proximate causation. "[A] defendant's conduct is a cause-in-fact of the prohibited result if the said result would *not* have occurred 'but for' the defendant's conduct." *Velazquez v. State*, 561 So. 2d 347, 350 (Fla. Dist. Ct. App. 1990) (emphasis in original). Adam was plainly the but-for cause of the child's death. If Adam had not dumped the marbles at the intersection, the child would not have died.

The next question is whether Adam's conduct was also the "proximate" cause of the child's death. Proximate cause under the criminal law is complex to define (Prof. Joshua Dressler, in his hornbook UNDERSTANDING CRIMINAL LAW § 14.03[A] (5th ed. 2009), calls it "obscure"), but its core is foreseeability. *Kibbe v. Henderson*, 534 F.2d 493, 499 (2d Cir. 1976). Adam may argue that the child would not have died but for the fact that the man did not have his child properly secured in the vehicle. He may argue that this failure was an unforeseeable intervening cause—another but-for cause of the child's death—and that in this case it should be treated as a superseding cause that should cut off his liability for the result. He may bolster this argument by noting that seat belts are required under state law. This argument should fail. It is true that the man's failure to properly secure the child was an intervening cause of the child's death. However, this intervening cause was not unforeseeable. Adam should have anticipated that some people, including children, who ride in cars are not properly secured by seat belts or child restraints.

Adam might also argue that the resulting car crash was such an extraordinary consequence of his action of dumping the marbles at the intersection that it would be unfair to hold him accountable. This argument should also fail because in these circumstances a car crash resulting in the death of a child who was not wearing a seat belt is not such an unusual or extraordinary consequence of Adam's act as to justify relieving him of liability. *See State v. Hallett*, 619 P.2d 335, 339 (Utah 1980) ("[W]here a party by his wrongful conduct creates a condition of peril, his action can properly be found to be the proximate cause of a resulting injury, even though later events which combined to cause the injury may also be classified as negligent, so long as the later act is something which can reasonably be expected to follow in the natural sequence of events.").

Point Two (25%)

Bob intentionally assisted Adam in his act of dumping the marbles on the road, but Bob may not have acted with the mens rea required to be held liable as an accomplice to involuntary manslaughter.

Two elements are necessary for Bob to be found guilty of involuntary manslaughter on a theory of accomplice liability. First, Bob must have assisted Adam in the commission of the crime. DRESSLER, *supra*, § 30.04[A][1]. Second, Bob must have acted with dual intentions: (1) "the intent to assist the primary party" and (2) "the intent that the primary party commit the offense charged." *Id.* § 30.05[A]. In cases where the primary party's crime is one involving recklessness or negligence, most jurisdictions hold that the second intent element is satisfied if the defendant intended to assist the primary party and otherwise acted with the mens rea required for the underlying offense (i.e., recklessness or negligence, as the jurisdiction requires). *Id.* § 30.05[B][3].

Here, Bob assisted Adam by driving him to the intersection. Even a small amount of assistance can suffice to create accomplice liability.

[NOTE: An examinee might also argue that Bob assisted Adam by staying with him and watching, on the theory that he provided some kind of encouragement to Adam. However, mere presence at a crime scene is not sufficient to constitute assistance, so accompanying Adam is probably not enough. *See State v. Noriega*, 928 P.2d 706, 708 (Ariz. Ct. App. 1996).]

Bob also appears to have acted with the intent of assisting Adam. When Bob drove Adam to the intersection, he knew that it was for the purpose of bringing Adam to that place so that Adam could dump the marbles in the intersection. Bob had no other purpose.

The next question is whether Bob's mens rea with regard to the child's death was sufficient for involuntary manslaughter. Bob will argue that he had no mens rea at all with regard to the child's death and therefore can be guilty of no offense. He will also argue that his statements to Adam suggest that he believed (1) that no one was likely to drive through the intersection and (2) that the marbles would not cause any danger to any drivers who would simply drive over them. Accordingly, Bob will argue that he did not act with the culpability required to be held liable as an accomplice to involuntary manslaughter.

In most jurisdictions, Bob must have acted "recklessly" to be convicted as an accomplice to involuntary manslaughter (i.e., he must have been aware of the unreasonable (or unreasonable and high) risk of death or serious bodily injury that his conduct created). Based on Bob's statements, he does not appear to have been reckless. The prosecution's best argument would be that Bob knew about the risk because Adam told him that cars might crash. In response, Bob can argue that his statements demonstrate that he thought Adam was wrong about the risks of dumping the marbles.

In some jurisdictions, Bob can be convicted if he demonstrated "gross," "criminal," or "culpable" negligence (i.e., if an ordinary person in his situation would have been aware that his conduct created an unreasonable (or unreasonable and high) risk of death or serious bodily injury). In these states, Bob could be found guilty of involuntary manslaughter on a theory of accomplice liability if the fact finder believes that an ordinary person would have realized that placing 2,000 marbles on a road would interfere with the ability of cars to stop when they drove over the marbles, thereby creating an unreasonable (or unreasonable and high) risk of death or serious bodily injury.

In a few jurisdictions, Bob cannot have accomplice liability for involuntary manslaughter as a matter of law. In these jurisdictions, the courts adhere strictly to the requirement that an "accomplice must want the crime to be committed by the other party," and they reason that it is "logically impossible" for a person to be an accomplice to a crime of recklessness or negligence because one cannot "intend" a negligent or reckless killing. DRESSLER, *supra,* § 30.05[B][3]. In most jurisdictions, however, courts hold an accomplice responsible for a crime like manslaughter if the accomplice intentionally provided assistance to the principal and acted with recklessness or negligence, as the case may be, with respect to the risk that the principal's behavior would cause death.

[NOTE: With respect to the "dual intent" issue, the key is whether examinees recognize that accomplice liability requires two levels of culpability. It is less important which approach examinees adopt than that they see the problem—Bob cannot be guilty as an accomplice unless he was culpable with respect to the underlying crime, and Bob, in fact, not only did not intend any car crash or resulting death, he actually did not believe that such an event would occur.]

MBE SUBJECTS - PRACTICE ESSAY QUESTIONS

CRIMINAL PROCEDURE
Answer to Question 1

I. Introduction

A motion to suppress evidence will depend on the exclusionary rule. The exclusionary rule is a judge-made rule which excludes evidence that was unlawfully obtained. If it is determined that evidence was unlawfully obtained, then the issue is if other evidence will be excluded as well through the use of "Fruit of a Poisonous Tree" Doctrine. Under that doctrine, all evidence obtained from an illegal search or seizure or from an improper interrogation will also be excluded, unless the evidence could have been found or seized through one of the three exceptions to this doctrine. The three exceptions are: (1) if the evidence could have been obtained through an independent source; (2) if the evidence would have been inevitably discovered; or (3) the evidence was seized/obtained through an intervening act of free will on part of the defendant.

II. Suppression of Confession

Miranda warnings must be given to a person who is in custody and being interrogated, because under the 5th Amendment everyone is given the right from self-incriminating themselves. The 5th Amendment gives each person in police custody the right to counsel, which is not offensive specific; therefore if after a police officer gives a person in custody a Miranda warning and he clearly and definitively says he needs a lawyer, that police officer cannot resume interrogation, unless the person in custody reinitiates it.

A police officer must give a person in custody Miranda warnings any time he feels he could get an incriminating statement.

In the situation at hand, the facts say that they had a reliable informant tell the police about the burglary and about Rogers (R); therefore the police had probable cause to bring R into custody to question her, because probable cause can be from an anonymous informant. Also, to do a stationhouse detention, as was done here, the police can bring a person in for questioning.

Because it is stipulated that R was in custody, it can be reasonable to think that one would give an incriminating statement if interrogated. Moreover, when Officer Stevens (S) began questioning in the "interrogation room" he had to give R her Miranda warnings, which he did.

R's statement, "I think I want a public defender" was an attempt to say that she wanted a lawyer, but was not clear enough; therefore normally if a person in custody doesn't give a clear and definitive answer, he isn't invoking his right to remain silent and right to counsel, and can be questioned.

However, S's comments to R that "it's only right that I tell you what's what" and that "once we get you a lawyer I won't be able to help you" was improper and from that in telling R that she'll have to give up her Miranda rights if she wants his help was totally out of line. S used improper means of bribery to get R to talk. S knew that R might give incriminating statements and her waiver was not voluntary – it was coerced; therefore R's confession given afterwards should not be admitted, as it falls within the exclusionary rule mentioned in the introduction.

Therefore, R's motion to suppress the confession should be granted.

III. Suppression of Jewelry

As stated in the introduction, the "Fruits of a Poisonous Tree" Doctrine will exclude any evidence obtained or derived from an illegal search and seizure or an improper Miranda warning. Generally, if a person is improperly mirandized, and is later searched for weapons or contraband on his person, that physical evidence will still be admitted, as Miranda warnings apply to statements made. However in this case the evidence was not found on R, but rather found after R gave incriminating statements. The police officers were able to get probable cause from R's statements to S during interrogation. Unless the officers believe that they could have gotten probable cause through one of the three exceptions to the Fruits Doctrine (stated in Intro), this evidence should be suppressed.

The prosecution can argue that they could have gotten probable cause to search her house from the credible, reliable informant and therefore have obtained the jewelry through an independent source, which if the court agreed, the next step would be to determine if it was seized properly. For one to challenge an illegal search and seizure they must challenge it under the 4th Amendment.

Under this if they had a reasonable expectation of privacy and the search was by a government official, then she has standing to challenge. Here, R did have a reasonable expectation of privacy (it was in her home) and the search was done by a government police officer; therefore that test is met.

Next, we need to look to see if there was a validly issued search warrant. There was a search warrant and assuming it properly stated the place to be searched and the things to be seized and it was issued by a neutral magistrate judge, it is valid, because the facts state they used R's testimony as its probable cause.

Therefore, if a court determines that the probable cause was proper (i.e. from R's coerced testimony), which I think is incorrect, then the jewelry should be admitted.

However, if there was no probable cause, because her statement was coerced and the evidence was obtained using illegal interrogation, then the jewelry should be excluded as fruits of a poisonous tree, assuming no exceptions apply.

Therefore, the motion to suppress the jewelry should be granted.

MBE SUBJECTS - PRACTICE ESSAY QUESTIONS

CRIMINAL LAW AND PROCEDURE
Answer to Question 2

Jimmy wants the $1000 and the cocaine suppressed.

The 4th Amendment prohibition against unreasonable search and seizure is extended to state action through the 14th Amendment. The 4th Amendment provides that a person will not be subject to an unreasonable search or seizure unless there is a warrant based on probable cause. In order for a person to attempt to have evidence excluded based on a violation of their 4th Amendment rights, the defendant must show first that there was state action and that he/she had a 4th privacy interest in the thing that was searched. Action of the publicly paid police is always presumed to be state action. The question remains whether Jimmy had a privacy interest in the car and its contents such that his rights were violated and the items found should be excluded.

The facts indicate that there was probable cause to arrest Jimmy and there are a variety of exceptions that allow the police to conduct a search without a warrant, they include a search incident to a lawful arrest, the automobile exception, plain view, stop and frisk, consent, hot pursuit and evanescent evidence. The search in this case of Jimmy would be considered a search incident to a lawful arrest. Therefore, the police can search him and whatever is in his "wingspan." The search of Jimmy's body would be reasonable under these circumstances because she was looking for possible weapons or other contraband which he might have on his body. There might have been a question of how much of a "full body search" was reasonable, but if she patted down his clothes and felt the packet in his pants pocket, it would be reasonable. The plain view exception doctrine has been extended to include the plain feel as well. In other words, if she could tell that there was something suspicious feeling from the outside of his clothing that gave rise to the articulable suspicion that there was some contraband in his pocket, Jones would be allowed to reach in and discover the drugs. As such the drugs would be admissible as falling under the search incident to a lawful arrest exception to the warrant requirement.

In addition, Jones could search anything in Jimmy's wingspan. This means wherever he could reach to hide evidence or gain access to a weapon. The Supreme Court has decided that the interior of the car is considered the wingspan for searches of this type. Therefore the entire interior of the car was fair game for the police to search. Jimmy was suspected of committing a robbery and there was a substantial amount of money missing from the store that had been held up. Because money is not very cumbersome and it could be hidden in a glove compartment it would have been reasonable for Officer Jones to check there. Therefore the $1,000 should be allowed to be used as evidence against Jimmy since it was obtained through a lawful search of his wingspan following a lawful arrest.

Once she finished through the car, Jones opened the trunk. The wingspan of the driver of the car does not extend to the trunk of the car. In addition, the automobile exception does not apply in this case because that exception to the warrant requirement only applies when the automobile is part of the activity that gave rise to the probable cause in the first place. In this case, Jimmy escaped on foot, there was no description of a car for police to be on the lookout for and there was nothing criminal about the way that Jimmy was driving that would have given rise to suspicion about the car itself. Therefore the search of the trunk was not under any exception to the warrant requirement. But, since Jimmy was arrested and the car would probably have been impounded, there will be a good argument to allow the evidence in because if there would be an inevitable discovery of the evidence apart from the unreasonable search then the evidence should be able to come in against Jimmy.

Jimmy will not be able to succeed on any of his motions to suppress because of the exceptions to the warrant requirements.

Leonard and Lana

Officer Jones ordered Leonard and Lana out of the car. This is allowed when a police officer stops a car, he can either request that the occupants stay in the car or get out depending on the circumstances and what he thinks is safest. Lana had her backpack on her back and it was clearly hers. In order for Lana and Leonard to assert a 4th Amendment right, they have to have a privacy interest as discussed above. The facts do not indicate that either of them claimed to own the car and the S.C. has said that passengers do not have a privacy interest in the car that they are a passenger in when it is subject to an otherwise lawful search. As for Lana, she might be able to claim that she had a privacy interest in her backpack. It was on her back when she was asked to get out of the car. She had done nothing to arise the suspicion and the only reason that it was in the car and subject to the search was because she was ordered to leave it there, otherwise she was going to take it out. The search of the backpack was done after the money (the subject of the arrest) had been found. This might therefore be more accurately characterized as an arrest incident to a search because Lana was arrested after the backpack was searched. It is possible that Lana will be able to successfully have the marijuana found in her backpack suppressed based on these facts.

As for Leonard, a police officer can detain the people that are in the car while an arrest and subsequent search is being conducted, but in order for there to be a search conducted of that person there has to be some articulable reason. It does not seem from the facts that there was any reason to suspect that Leonard had been doing anything wrong other than being with Jimmy in the same car. Jones arrested him and then searched his pants and found the marijuana in the pocket, but unless there was some other reason to search or arrest Leonard, his motion to suppress should be granted.

MBE SUBJECTS - PRACTICE ESSAY QUESTIONS

CRIMINAL LAW AND PROCEDURE
Answer to Question 3

The issues in this question all surround the legality of searches and seizures. Searches and seizures by police officers are governed by the 4th amendment. Evidence of an illegal search or seizure can be suppressed at trial by an individual who has standing to object. Normally, searches require a warrant supported by probable cause. There are a number of exceptions to this rule where the police simply need probable cause. And there are still other exceptions where the police don't even need that. I will address the issue of each search and seizure in the chronological order that it occurred.

Consensual search.

First, the police knocked on the door. Since the police had no warrant and no probable cause, they could not have just entered the house. Police are also entitled to perform a search if they have consent. The individual can refuse to consent. The police are, however, entitled to knock because it is not a search. In this case, the police knocked and Smith refused to let the police in and asked them to leave. Smith was entitled to do this and the police would normally have had to comply with the request. They had no consent to search.

Plain view.

The Plain view doctrine allows the police to seize contraband if it is in "plain view." This exception applies as long as the police are not otherwise violating the 4th amendment. In this situation, the police were lawfully knocking on the door of a resident. Jones then saw the cocaine, which gave him probable cause to seize it.

Even when the police have probable cause to search a house, they normally should not just search it. Instead, the police are required to go to a neutral and detached magistrate and seek a warrant based upon the probable cause. The police can skip the warrant requirement in exigent circumstances. Exigent circumstances exist if the police have reason to believe that the items in question will be moved in the time that it will take to get the warrant.

In this situation, the police did not get a warrant, but instead, entered upon their own determination of probable cause. The police could argue that exigent circumstances required immediate entry since Smith could have flushed the cocaine while they were getting the warrant. Smith could argue that officer Adams could have waited with Smith and prevented him from entering the house and destroying the cocaine while Jones went to get a warrant. At that point, the officers had no reason to think that someone else in the house would have been able to destroy the evidence. The likelihood of success on this issue is very questionable and it is probably about 50-50.

Full body search.

The police may perform a limited search incident to arrest in order to find weapons that might hurt the police. The police may perform a further search incident to arrest to inventory all of the belongings on the arrestee. In this case, the police did a full body search on Smith. Although this isn't limited enough to be a search just to find weapons (it is a full search), it is allowed in order to inventory Smith's possessions.

Searching the rest of the room.

As part of the search incident to arrest, the police are allowed to search not only the person, but also the grab area or jump area of the defendant. This area may extend to an entire room provided that the room is not too big. The police may only search an area where a weapon could be. In this case, the police searched Smith's grab area legally. The facts state, however, that the woman was found in the corner of the room farthest from the door. If this is not within Smith's grab or jump area, then the search would be illegal. (Also assuming that Spencer was not in the officer's plain view)

Standing.

In order to have illegally seized evidence excluded from trial, the defendant must have standing to object to the illegal search or seizure. One has standing if he or she has a reasonable expectation of privacy in the place searched. An owner or resident of a house has such a reasonable expectation in her home. There is not a reasonable expectation of privacy when simply visiting a friend unless you are an overnight guest. One does have a reasonable expectation of privacy in their own person.

Here, Smith owns the home and Spencer is just a guest. Unless Spencer also lives there or is an overnight guest, she has no reasonable expectation of privacy. Smith does have such an expectation. Therefore, Smith would have standing to object to the search of the house or his body, but Spencer would not. Since the police did not search her body (they could see the pipe in her hand) Spencer cannot object to that either. Therefore, if any of the evidence is illegally searched or seized, only Smith could even object to it at trial.

Derivative evidence.

If the police perform an act that violates the 4th amendment, all evidence obtained in a derivative of the search is also inadmissible at trial as "fruits of the poisonous tree." In this case, if the initial entry into the house was illegal, all further evidence will also be illegal because it wouldn't have been found, but for the initial entry. Smith would be able to object to all evidence being admitted at trial if the initial entry was illegal.

MBE SUBJECTS - PRACTICE ESSAY QUESTIONS

CRIMINAL LAW AND PROCEDURE
Answer to Question 4

This scenario presents questions under the 4th Amendment, of whether the searches and seizures at issue here were lawful. I address each piece of evidence in turn.

The Cocaine

Initially, Officer Sarah's investigation was lawful. She was simply checking out a loud argument in a quiet residential area. After she inquired into what was happening, the two men quickly quieted down and ran away.

When she followed Jerry, he began running. At this point, reasonable suspicion existed for Sarah to stop Jerry. With reasonable suspicion that criminal activity is occurring, an officer is permitted to stop to investigate their suspicions. If the officer has reasonable suspicion that a suspect is armed, they are also allowed to pat down the suspect and seize anything that is plainly a weapon or contraband (as long as the contraband's criminal character is immediately apparent).

So, Sarah was justified in stopping Jerry. However, the only way she would be justified in patting him down would be with reasonable suspicion he was armed (probably not the case here), or if probable cause to arrest existed. I believe probable cause existed at this point, because Jerry was involved in an argument, left immediately when he saw the police, ran when followed by the police and ditched his backpack in the garbage.

The only remaining problem is whether she was justified in tearing open the envelope. Generally, containers on a suspect can be seized and searched if there is probably cause to arrest, so this search was OK.

Pursuant to probable cause, an officer can search a suspect, and seize whatever is found, including the envelope. (This is the search incident to arrest exception).

Additionally, even if no probable cause for the search/arrest existed, the cocaine should be admissible via inevitable discovery, since probable cause arose when Sarah found the stolen DVD (as will be discussed) and therefore he would have been searched incident to arrest at this point, or possibly subject to an inventory search of his belongings at the police station.

Bottom Line: Admit the cocaine.

The DVD

In order for something to qualify as a search, a two prong test must be satisfied?

    1. Did defendant manifest a subjective intent to keep the thing searched private (Did he expect privacy?)

2. Does society accept this expectation as legitimate?

Here, Jerry probably manifested an intent to keep the backpack private (and society would recognize this as legitimate), up until he threw it into the dumpster.

The Supreme Court has repeatedly said that a suspect does not have a legitimate expectation of privacy in garbage, therefore it can be searched without a warrant. After all, anyone can search garbage, why should police be excluded?

Sarah's search of the bag was OK then, even without a warrant. Once she identified the DVD player as stolen, probable cause to arrest Jerry existed. Once an arrest can lawfully be made, a search incident to arrest can be conducted of the defendant's person. Therefore, the cocaine, even if found via an unlawful search earlier, would have inevitably been discovered.

It should also be noted here that Jerry has standing to challenge the search only if the backpack is his. One cannot object to the search of another's person or possession, even if evidence incriminating them is discovered. (No legitimate expectation of privacy in another's stuff).

Here, it is likely the backpack was stolen, as it was a student backpack, and Jerry ditched it into the garbage.

Therefore, Jerry probably has no standing to challenge the search of the backpack, and even if he did the search would likely be found valid, since it was not only abandoned, but was thrown into a garbage dumpster.

The Statement

The admissibility of the statement requires a discussion of <u>Miranda</u>. Under Miranda, statements made by a defendant during police custodial interrogations are deemed coercive unless the following Miranda warnings are given prior to the statement:

    1. Right to remain silent.

    2. Anything you say can be used against you in court.

    3. You have a right to an attorney.

    4. If you can't afford an attorney, one will be provided for you.

As long as the "gist" of the warnings are conveyed to the suspect, that is sufficient. In this case, it appears no Miranda warnings were given. Therefore, it must be determined whether Jerry's statement was made during a "custodial interrogation."

Custody is determined by a number of factors. Where did the alleged interrogation occur? What are the surrounding circumstances? Here, it is likely Jerry did not feel free to leave, given that Sarah had just found cocaine on him, had just patted him down after chasing him and now found a stolen DVD player. Given these facts, I believe Jerry probably felt as if he were in custody, given the totality of the circumstances (Not free to leave).

So was Sarah's statement "likely to elicit" incriminating information, whereby it would be deemed an interrogation for <u>Miranda</u> purposes?

This could go either way. On one hand, Sarah didn't specifically ask Jerry anything, or even specifically direct her comment at him. If she had, the comment would more likely be interpreted as "likely to elicit."

On the other hand, as she said it, she was confronting Jerry with incriminating evidence (the stolen DVD).

The Supreme Court has found interrogation to be more likely when a suspect is confronted with incriminating evidence, because it is much more likely to elicit an incriminating response. Given this precedent, I believe that since Sarah confronted Jerry with the evidence, this will be deemed an interrogation.

As there was custody and interrogation in the absence of <u>Miranda</u> warnings, the statements should be excluded from the evidence against Jerry. However, the DVD and the cocaine should be allowed in as evidence in the case against him.

MBE SUBJECTS - PRACTICE ESSAY QUESTIONS

CRIMINAL LAW AND PROCEDURE
Answer to Question 5

MEMORANDUM

TO: Bar Examiners

FROM: Bar Applicant

RE: Sufficiency of the Evidence in State v. Dennis

DATE: July 29, 2003

Evidence of Intoxication with Respect to Attempted First Degree Murder.

Generally, relevant evidence is admissible. A piece of evidence is relevant if it tends to make a fact in issue in the case more probable or less probable than it would be without the evidence. Dennis here was charged with Attempted First Degree Murder. In order to convict a person of Attempted First Degree Murder the prosecution must prove that the defendant premeditated and deliberated about the killing of the victim, had the intent to kill the victim, and took a substantial step in furtherance of carrying out the crime. Here, there is not a lot of evidence regarding Dennis' premeditation. Dennis was in an argument with Vickie and picked up a gun only after seeing Vickie with a knife. Therefore, the state may or may not be able to prove Dennis had the required premeditation and deliberation to kill Vickie. However, if the court does find sufficient evidence of premeditation and deliberation, Dennis' conviction on attempted first degree murder may be upheld. The evidence does show that Dennis said "I will kill you..." to Vickie, that he picked up a gun he believed to be loaded, aimed it at Vickie and pulled the trigger twice. This would probably be sufficient to prove that Dennis took a substantial step toward committing the crime of first degree murder. A mistake of fact is not a defense to attempt, and therefore, the fact that the gun was not loaded will not enable Dennis to avoid conviction. However, Voluntary intoxication is a defense to specific intent crimes such as attempted first degree murder if it negates the defendant's specific intent. Here, evidence of the defendant's voluntary intoxication could have negated the state's proof that Dennis intended to kill Vickie. Accordingly, the evidence of Defendant's intoxication was relevant because it made a material issue in Dennis' defense more likely than it would be without the evidence. Therefore, the evidence should have been admitted, and it should be argued on appeal that this was reversible error.

Jury instruction that "the law presumes that a person intends the natural and probable consequences of his actions."

At issue here is whether the court erred in instructing the jury that "the law presumes that a person intends the natural and probable consequences of his actions." In criminal cases, the prosecution must prove each of the elements of the crime beyond a reasonable doubt. As discussed above, in order to be convicted of attempted first degree murder, one of the elements that must be proven by the prosecution is that the defendant intended to kill the defendant. While it is sometimes said that a person intends the natural and probable consequences of his actions, in this case, the court likely erred in giving this instruction because it relieved the prosecution of the burden of proof on the element of intent. Here, the facts state that Dennis aimed the gun at Vickie and pulled the trigger. However, if it was the case that Dennis did not intend to kill Vickie, but only intended to injure her, then allowing the jury to assume that a person intends the natural and probable consequences of his actions would result in the prosecution not having to prove that Dennis actually intended to kill Vickie. The facts state that Dennis aimed the gun at Vickie and pulled the trigger, but as mentioned above, he may have only intended in injure Vickie. Accordingly, because the jury was instructed that the law presumes that a person intends the natural and probable consequences of his actions, the prosecution was effectively relieved of its burden of proof on the element of intent, and as such, Dennis' conviction must be overturned.

Jury Instruction on Self-Defense.

At issue here is whether the court erred by instructing the jury that Dennis bore the burden of proving self-defense by a preponderance of the evidence. As discussed above, in criminal cases, the prosecution must prove the elements of the case against a defendant beyond a reasonable doubt. However, it is permissible for the burden of proof on an affirmative defense to be placed on a criminal defendant, provided the burden is only of proving the defense by a preponderance of the evidence. Here, by placing the burden of proving self-defense by a preponderance of the evidence on the defendant, the court did not unconstitutionally shift the burden of proof onto the defendant, (as it did with its instruction re: how the law presuming that persons intend the natural and probable consequences of their actions). Thus, the court's instruction that Dennis had to prove that he acted in self-defense by a preponderance of the evidence is likely fine, and does not result in reversible error. Accordingly, the conviction of Dennis will not be overturned on these grounds on appeal.

It may have been error for the court to instruct the jury that Dennis was required to retreat prior to employing force in self-defense. Generally, one using force in self-defense is not under a duty to retreat prior to using force in self-defense. However, some jurisdictions do require the defendant to retreat prior to using deadly force, so it is unclear whether the court erred in so instructing the jury in this case. However, in those jurisdictions that do require a person to retreat prior to using deadly force in self-defense, there is the so-called "castle exception" which provides that a person does not need to retreat before using deadly force if the person is inside his/her home. Here, the facts indicate that Dennis was inside his home and therefore the court may have erred in not instructing the jury regarding this exception to the rule requiring retreat prior to using deadly force. It is also possible that Dennis would not have the "castle exception" available to him because his actions were not done in an attempt to protect his home from an outsider, but rather he was attacking the co-owner of the home.

MBE SUBJECTS - PRACTICE ESSAY QUESTIONS

CRIMINAL LAW AND PROCEDURE
Answer to Question 6

In the prosecution against Dave, he probably will only be able to exclude the last statement he made to Officer Petra. The others will be admissible.

Under the Exclusionary Rule, a defendant will be able to exclude evidence offered by the prosecution against him that was the product of an illegal search or coerced confession. In this case, we are dealing with improper confessions.

A defendant must be read his Miranda rights before a police officer can commence with a custodial interrogation. A defendant is in custody when he is not free to leave. An interrogation includes not just pointed questions, but also any police conduct that is likely to produce an incriminating or damaging response from the defendant.

Statement 1: "Just a peaceful robbery."

When Dave responded to Officer Petra's question as to what he was doing, Dave offered this joking reply. Because Officer Petra had not yet issued Dave his Miranda warnings, this statement would be inadmissible if it was given during a custodial interrogation.

The court is likely to hold the statement admissible. Officer Petra's question about Dave's activities was certainly within the scope of an interrogation, but the court is likely to find that Dave was not yet in custody. Determining this depends on one's perspective. Dave most assuredly did not believe he was in custody. He did not even know that Petra had observed him through a one-way mirror. Thus, Dave's statement was made while he was not under the impression that he was not free to leave.

In fact, Dave may have not been free to leave. Officer Petra probably would have used force to stop Dave had he tried to escape. Thus, from the officer's perspective, this may have been a custodial interrogation. But the Court will probably look at it from Dave's perspective and hold the statement admissible – almost like a spontaneous statement made prior to Miranda warnings.

Spontaneous statements are admissible and Dave's will be too.

Statement 2: Sold more swamp

After Dave's first response, Petra promptly gave Dave his Miranda warnings. He was told of his right to remain silent and to have an attorney present during his interrogation. Dave responded by saying maybe he needed a lawyer.

Courts generally hold that a criminal defendant must expressly and without a doubt invoke his Miranda rights. Dave's half-hearted invocation will be deemed insufficient. The exclusionary rule and Miranda warnings exist to deter police from conduct they know or should know violates the law and the rights of others. Dave's meager attempt to ask for a lawyer was insufficient to put Petra on notice. Thus, Petra was not aware that continued inquiry would violate Dave's rights.

As such, Dave's subsequent response that he sold another parcel of swamp is admissible. He had been given his Miranda warnings. He did not unequivocally invoke them. Therefore, Officer Petra's question was valid. Dave's admission is admissible.

Statements 3 & 4: Cutting corners

After admitting that he had sold another parcel of swamp, Dave definitely invoked his rights and stated he wanted a lawyer. Given that the conversation between Petra and Dave jumped back and forth between the crime he was caught committing and one for which he was indicted the day before, there might be an issue of whether Dave was invoking the 6th Amendment right to counsel, which is offense-specific, and his 5th Amendment right to counsel, which is not offense-specific and which protects individuals during police interrogation. It is not clear why Dave asked to speak with counsel after addressing the alleged crime of the previous day.

In any case, Petra ended all inquiry as he was required. They waited for more officers.

At some point, Dave reinitiated the conversation by saying he had a real estate broker.

A defendant who reinitiates conversation after the police have stopped an interrogation because of an individual's invocation of his right to an attorney can be questioned further. But the police should re-Mirandize.

There is also the issue of whether Dave had invoked his 5th and 6th Amendment right to counsel. Assuming it was his 5th Amendment right, Dave reinitiated the conversation and offered that his friend knew how to cut corners. Even if the first statement, which was offered prior to Petra's re-reading Dave his Miranda warnings is inadmissible, Dave repeated the statement after hearing them again. Thus, one way or another, the trier of fact will know Dave has a friend who knows how to cut corners.

The only way Dave could hope to exclude this is by saying his earlier invocation was his right to counsel under the 6th Amendment for the prior days activities. As such, he had an offense-specific right to counsel at all critical stages of the charge. But since Dave did not even know he had been indicted on that charge, the court is likely to hold that Dave invoked his 5th Amendment right. When he reinitiated the conversation, additional inquiry was proper. His admission that he knew a friend who cut corners is admissible.

Statement 5: A couple of forms

Dave can exclude his last statement from his prosecution. After stating for the second time he had a friend who helped him cut corners, Dave unequivocally again asserted that he wanted a lawyer.

Thus, Officer Petra had to stop all further interrogation. An individual who re-initiates a conversation, but then re-invokes his Miranda rights has the right to prevent the police from further custodial interrogation. If the police continue to question the defendant, the evidence obtained is inadmissible.

Dave effectively re-invoked his Miranda rights. Nonetheless, Petra told Dave he was indicted on a charge the previous day. While not a direct question, Officer Petra's statement was, nevertheless, a custodial interrogation because Petra should have known it was likely to produce an incriminating response from Dave.

It did. Dave made a statement about forms he had used. The prosecution will not be able to admit this last statement into evidence because it was obtained in violation of Dave's rights.

MBE SUBJECTS - PRACTICE ESSAY QUESTIONS

CRIMINAL LAW AND PROCEDURE
Answer to Question 7

The issue here is whether Andy and Beth can suppress the evidence of drugs due to an illegal search. First, one must determine whether a 4th Amendment violation occurred. This is a two-part question. The first part requires government action. The second is whether the individual had a reasonable expectancy of privacy in the first place. To determine whether the individual's expectation of privacy was reasonable, one must determine whether the individual has standing to object and whether the individual was holding themselves/possession out to the public. If there was government action, and the individual had a reasonable expectancy of privacy, than there was a 4th Amendment violation, unless police either had a warrant or were under an exception to the warrant requirement.

In this case, Andy will most likely fail in suppressing the marijuana found in his waistband. There was government action taken by Officer Miller. Andy does have standing to object because both himself and his car were being searched therefore there was a violation of his reasonable expectation of privacy. However, no warrant is required because one of the six exceptions to the warrant requirement apply. These exceptions are search incident to arrest, automobile exception, plain view, not pursuit, consent and stop and frisk. Here, we use the search incident to arrest.

Officer Miller was fully within the scope of his position to pull over Andy for the state traffic ordinance and arrest him if he was in violation. An officer can't randomly stop a driver, but can once the driver has violated an ordinance. Had the officer pulled him over simply for looking like "druggies" or not recognizing them he would not have met the standard of probable cause to make arrest or even just to stop which requires a reasonable suspicion. However, this is not the case here, Andy had violated an ordinance and therefore was properly stopped and arrested.

As noted earlier, search incident to arrest is proper without a warrant, therefore, Andy can't object to the marijuana found in his waistband. Also, subject to an arrest, an officer may search the entire passenger compartment of the car. In fact, he may search the entire car except for the trunk. This is where Beth's suppression motion comes in.

She was also subject to a government action in the officer pulling her over, but the issue is whether or not one has standing to object or whether she was holding her possessions out to the public. She does not have standing to object to the search of the car. However, generally, when a passenger is holding a personal item at the time of the stop and arrest of the driver, they may be asked to step out of the car, but are allowed to take their personal possessions in their immediate control with them. Beth was wearing her backpack and therefore should have been able to keep it with her free from search. If Beth had thrown it on the back seat however, it would no longer have been in her immediate possession and therefore would have been subject to the search. Therefore, she has standing to object to the search of her backpack, unless the officer saw something which gave him probable cause to search it which doesn't appear to be the case. Furthermore, there is no exception to the warrant requirement, since Beth herself was not arrested. The only argument state could make, is that finding drugs on Andy gave him probable cause to search Beth (and her backpack), but that most likely wouldn't be enough.

Andy alone can object to the search of the trunk. As noted earlier, as a search incident to arrest, an officer can search everything, but the trunk. The only way that the evidence won't be suppressed is if officer argues "independent source." Therefore, although the drugs in trunk were "fruits of a poisonous tree" the causal chain between the illegal search and the evidence is broken because the evidence would have been found anyway. Normally, after an arrest, the car that driver was arrested in, is impounded and inventoried. In this case, the car would have been searched anyway, if the car were impounded and the drugs would have been found. However, Beth may have driven the car home and if that's the case, the evidence of the drugs in the trunk would not come in as fruits of an illegal search.

The 5A objection concerns Andy's statement to the police. Because he simply blurted the statement out, it would not be found to violate his 5A privilege against the right against self-incrimination. For this right to take hold, there must be 1) custody, and 2) interrogation. Andy is not free to go once he is under arrest, so in that sense he is under police custody. However, the interrogation prong has not been met. The officer had not asked him any questions – Andy blurted out a statement. Therefore, the statement can be used against him and is not suppressible.

*Under 5A, an officer must inform an individual who is under custodial interrogation of his right to remain silent and his right to an attorney.

Decedent's Estates

(February 2000)

Legal Problems:

1. Can the 1998 will witnessed only by interested witnesses be challenged on the grounds that it was not executed with testamentary intent, it was witnessed by interested persons, or it was revoked?

2. Assuming that only the 1997 will is entitled to be probated, can the testator's nieces claim any share of the testator's estate on the theory that they have a claim against his estate?

3. Assuming that only the 1997 will is entitled to be probated, can the testator's residuary estate be distributed to the Opera Society in lieu of the Banks Foundation for Opera under the *cy pres* doctrine, or does the bequest to the foundation fail, so that the residue of the testator's estate is distributed only to his heirs?

DISCUSSION

Point One: (40-60%)

Testator's 1998 purported will can be denied probate because it was not executed with the requisite testamentary intent. If evidence of a lack of intent is inadmissible such that on its face the will is valid, the 1998 document might arguably have been revoked by cancellation or by codicil and therefore is not entitled to be probated. If not so revoked, it is entitled to be probated.

The facts indicate that Banks intended to have the 1998 document executed in such a way that it would be invalid. He did this because he wanted his property to pass to the Banks Foundation for Opera under the terms of his 1997 will without his nieces knowing this, so they would continue to take care of him. What Banks failed to appreciate was that the mere fact that a will is witnessed by beneficiaries under the will does not mean the will is invalid. In fact, in almost all jurisdictions, the validity of the will is unaffected by whether a witness is interested, although interestedness on the part of a witness may have an adverse impact on the witness's right to receive the bequest. *See generally* William M. McGovern, Jr., Sheldon F. Kurtz & Jan Ellen Rein, *Wills, Trusts and Estates* § 4.3 (1988). Jurisdictions which have adopted the Uniform Probate Code (UPC) are even less restrictive since in those jurisdictions an interested witness does not forfeit the testamentary gift. Unif. Prob. Code § 2-505.

Although Banks's will was properly executed, it is invalid as a will if it was not executed with any testamentary intent. In the absence of testamentary intent, a document, even though executed with the statutory formalities, is invalid. *See generally* 79 Am. Jur. 2d *Wills* § 12. Testamentary intent can be established by extrinsic evidence, Unif. Prob. Code § 2-502(c), and while cases such as this-where it is the absence of intent that is at issue-are rare, presumably lack of intent can also be shown by extrinsic evidence.

The evidence in this case, that Banks executed the 1998 will without testamentary intent and to accomplish his goals used his nieces as witnesses mistakenly believing this would invalidate his will, is also reaffirmed by Banks's handwritten note on the back of the last page of the will. This note would likely constitute sufficient evidence to prove that the will was not executed with testamentary intent. On the other hand, if the note were not admissible for that purpose (e.g., in jurisdictions with a very restrictive view regarding the admissibility of extrinsic evidence), the handwritten note might be a sufficient revocation of the will by cancellation, at least in some jurisdictions.

Under § *2-507* of the Uniform Probate Code, a will can be revoked by a number of acts, including a cancellation. Under the UPC, words of cancellation need not touch any of the words of the will, but they must be somewhere on the will. Under UPC § *2-507,* the note revokes the will because it was written on the will. A different result follows in jurisdictions that follow the common-law rule, requiring words of cancellation to "touch" the words of the will. *See, e.g., Thompson* v. *Royall,* 163 Va. 492, 175 S.B. 748 (1934) (words of cancellation ineffective because they did not come in contact with the will).

Could the 1998 will be viewed as having been revoked by a codicil? That would depend upon whether local law recognized holographic wills, whether holographic wills had to be signed, and whether Banks's initials on the envelope would meet any signing requirement, information that is not provided here.

Point Two: (10-20%)

Banks's nieces probably cannot establish a claim against his estate on the basis of breach of contract to make a will. but they may be entitled to recover the reasonable value of their services to him.

Ordinarily, contracts to make a will must be in writing. *See, e.g.,* N.Y. EPTL § 13-2.1; Unif. Prob. Code § 2-514. In the absence of a writing, such contracts are unenforceable. Jurisdictions that do not expressly address this matter in their probate codes may reach the same result by applying a statute of frauds. On the facts given, Banks's agreement with his nieces was made orally. No facts suggest that it was reduced to writing. Accordingly, any claim by the nieces for breach of a contract to make a will would face the hurdle that they never put their agreement with their uncle in writing, as required by most probate codes.

On the other hand, it could be argued that there is enough written evidence of the agreement to satisfy any writing requirement even though there is no formal written contract. The 1998 will itself combined with the note on the back of that will provide some written evidence of Banks's promise to his nieces. In addition, if a local statute of frauds (rather than the probate code) creates the requirement of a writing, arguably the doctrine of part performance or estoppel may avoid the operation of that statute. *See,* William M. McGovern, Jr., Sheldon F. Kurtz, & Jan Ellen Rein, *Wills, Trusts, and Estates* 46-59 (1988). On that basis the nieces may be able to assert against Banks's estate a claim of breach of contract to make a will.

If a jurisdiction does not require a writing to establish a contract to make a will, the nieces should be able to recover the amount of their damages, assuming the 1997 will is probated.

If the nieces' claim cannot be sustained as a contract to make a will, they may be able to recover damages in an amount equal to the reasonable value of their services or impose a constructive trust for such amount on the successor of Banks's estate. *Id.*

Point Three: (30-40%)

Assuming that the 1997 will is probated and the nieces are not entitled to the whole estate, the residue of Banks's estate should be distributed to the Opera Society in lieu of the Banks Foundation by application of the *cy pres* doctrine.

The residuary bequest in favor of the Banks Foundation for Opera cannot be given effect, even if this will is probated, because the Foundation was never organized prior to Banks's death. Where a charitable bequest becomes impossible or impracticable to fulfill, a court may use the doctrine of *cy pres* to reform that gift to accomplish the testator's general charitable intent. *See generally Restatement (Second) of Trusts* § 399 (1959). *Cy pres* is appropriate unless a court determined that Banks's intent was limited only to benefiting the foundation that was never formed. This seems unlikely under the facts of the case since the purpose of the foundation was itself to benefit the Opera Society, which can just as easily be accomplished by substituting it as the residuary legatee under the will.

Decedent's Estates

(July 2000)

Legal Problems:

(1)(a) Is the March 2 will entitled to be probated because it was revived when Testator's September 10 will was revoked?

(1)(b) Assuming the March 2 will is entitled to be probated, should $10,000 be distributed to Charity Y or was the bequest to Charity Y satisfied before Testator died by Testator's gift to the charity of $15,000 on February 1, 1990?

(1)(c) Assuming the March 2 will is entitled to be probated, did Cory timely disclaim his interest in the $50,000 bequest and, if so, does the bequest pass to Gary or to the residuary legatees under Testator's will?

(2) If the March 2 will was not revived, can the September 10 will be probated under the doctrine of dependent relative revocation and, if so, how will the estate be distributed?

DISCUSSION

Point One(a): (30-40%)

The March 2 will can be probated if State A permits a will that has been revoked by the execution of a later will to be revived if the later will is revoked. If the March 2 will is revived, Andy and Billy take the residue but how the general bequests will be distributed depends on the resolution of two separate issues.

The execution of the September 10 will revoked the March 2 will under the laws of all states. Under the common law, however, the later revocation of the second will revives the first will. This rule followed from the principle that wills only speak at the time of death and, since the second will was revoked and therefore is a nullity, only the prior will had legal effect. Because of the belief that the common-law rule frustrated the intent of testators who revoked the later will with the intent of dying intestate, many states adopted statutes rejecting the common-law revival rule. These statutes can take at least two forms. One is that the revocation of the second will does not revive the earlier will. *See, e.g.,* Iowa Code § 633.284. The other form, as exemplified by the Uniform Probate Code § 2-509(a), is that the revocation of the second will does not revive the earlier will unless "it is evident from the circumstances of the revocation of the subsequent will or from the testator's contemporary or subsequent declarations that the testator intended the previous will to take effect as executed."

A will may be revoked by a cancellation. *See generally* Unif. Prob. Code § 2-507. When revoking the September 10 will by cancellation, the result of writing "VOID" across the face of the will, Testator explicitly indicated that he preferred his March 2 will. This statement is evidence of his intent to revive the earlier will. Thus, under either the common-law revival rule or a statutory substitute incorporating an intent standard, the March 2 will is entitled to be probated. Only if State A has an absolute no-revival rule would the March 2 will not be entitled to be probated.

Point One(b): (10-20%)

If the March 2 will is probated, then $10,000 should be distributed to charity Y. Testator's lifetime gift to Charity Y is not a gift in satisfaction of this general bequest.

Under the common law, if, subsequent to the execution of a will, a testator gives property to a person who is named as a general legatee in a will executed by the testator prior to the making of the gift, a rebuttable presumption arises that the testator intended the gift to be in satisfaction of the general legacy. This is known as the doctrine of "satisfaction" or "ademption by satisfaction." *See generally* W. McGovern, S. Kurtz & J. Rein, *Wills, Trusts and Estates* 30 (1988). The common-law rule is often abrogated or modified by statute. For example, under the Uniform Probate Code § 2-609(a)(ii), a gift to a legatee is not in satisfaction of the legacy unless the testator declared in a contemporaneous writing that he/she intended the gift to be in satisfaction of the bequest. In other states, the gift is not in satisfaction absent some writing evidencing testator's intent that the gift be in satisfaction of the bequest.

However, the ultimate result in this case is arguably the same whichever version of the doctrine applies because it appears Testator did not intend the $15,000 gift to be taken into account in determining the amount distributable to Charity Y under the will. This is evident from the language in the document found with the check that the $15,000 was one of many gifts and that Testator hoped to be in a position to make future gifts to Charity Y because the charity's work was so important to him. While it might be argued that the mere fact that Testator kept the check and note with his will evidences an intent that the gift of $15,000 be in satisfaction of the bequest, that argument seems weak in light of the more specific language on the note evidencing Testator's intent to continue making gifts to the charity.

Point One(c): (10-20%)

If the March 2 will is entitled to be probated, Cory timely disclaimed his interest in the $50,000 bequest. The bequest should pass to his child, Gary.

The typical disclaimer statute provides that a disclaimer must be made within nine months of the testator's death. The nine-month period is typical because state disclaimer statutes are designed to comport with the federal disclaimer rules. *See generally* Int. Rev. Code § 2518(2). Since Cory disclaimed on October 30, 1998, Cory's disclaimer was made within nine months of Testator's death and therefore was timely.

The typical disclaimer statute further provides that if a timely disclaimer is made, the disclaimed property interest passes as if the disclaimant died before the testator. *See, e.g.,* Unif. Prob. Code § 2-801 (d)(1). In this case, the disclaimed property interest would pass in accordance with any applicable lapse statute to Cory's child, Gary. The lapse statute applies because (1) Cory is a descendant of Testator (a typical requirement of a lapse statute), (2) Cory has issue who survive

Testator (another typical requirement of a lapse statute), and (3) Testator's will did not specially condition Cory's bequest on Cory surviving Testator. *See generally* J. Ritchie, N. Alford, R. Effland & J. Dobris, *Decedent's Estates and Trusts* 1021 (8th ed. 1993); *cf.* Unif. Prob. Code § 2-603 (applying the lapse statute, in some cases, even if the bequest is expressly conditioned on survivorship).

Point Two: (35-45%)

If the March 2 will was not revived. then the September 10 will is entitled to be probated under the doctrine of dependent relative revocation (DRR) if it is established that Testator would have preferred the disposition in the September 10 will to intestacy. Otherwise, Testator died intestate.

The March 2 will was revoked by the execution of the September 10 will regardless of whether the latter will was revoked. *See generally* Unif. Prob. Code § 2-507(a)(I). If the March 2 will is not revived, either the revocation of the September 10 will is ignored under DRR or Testator died intestate. Most likely Testator died intestate.

If a valid will is revoked by a physical act (such as cancellation) under Testator's mistaken belief that in doing so Testator could revive an earlier will, the revocation of the will can be ignored under DRR. Because DRR is an intent-effectuating doctrine, it applies only when the court determines that the testator would prefer the disposition in the revoked will to that resulting from a determination that the testator died intestate. *See generally Estate of A/burn* 18 Wis. 2d 340, 118 N.W.2d 919 (1963). Courts are more likely to apply DRR if the distribution of the estate using DRR approximates more closely the distribution testator actually intended than the distribution that would occur if DRR did not apply. When that is not the case, courts are more likely to reject using DRR.

For example, if the intended revocation of the September 10 will is ignored using DRR and, thus, that will is entitled to probate, Testator's entire $100,000 estate would be distributed equally to Andy and Billy. Cory, on the other hand, would take nothing. Alternatively, if the September 10 will is revoked and DRR is not applied, Testator would be deemed to have died intestate and Testator's entire estate would be distributed in equal thirds to Andy, Billy, and to Cory, since Cory's disclaimer did not apply to any intestate share.

It would appear that a distribution of $33,000, $33,000, and $33,000 to Andy, Billy, and Cory (ignoring DRR and using intestacy) approximates more closely what Testator actually intended - $50,000 to Cory, $10,000 to Charity Y, $20,000 to Andy and $20,000 to Billy, which was the distribution under the March 2 will-than a distribution of $50,000 to Andy and $50,000 to Billy (applying DRR and distributing the estate under the September 10 will). Here, Cory gets less than intended but at least something, while Andy and Billy get somewhat more than Testator intended. Thus, not applying DRR arguably more closely approximates Testator's intent. Of course, this is a close question, and examinees could argue either way.

Decedent's Estates

(February 2001)

Legal Problems:

1. Was either the will or the bequest to Ben invalidated because Ben was one of the two witnesses to Testator's will?

2. Was the bequest to Wendy revoked as a result of her divorce from Testator?

3. Since the assets of Testator's estate of $132,000 are insufficient to satisfy all of the bequests under the will, how should the bequests abate?

DISCUSSION

Point One: (30-40%)

The validity of the will is unaffected by the fact that Ben was a witness to the will. However, in most states Ben forfeits the $40,000 bequest because two disinterested witnesses did not witness the will. On the other hand, in states that have adopted the Uniform Probate Code, Ben does not forfeit that bequest.

At common law, if a witness who received a benefit under a will witnessed the will, the will was invalid unless two disinterested witnesses also witnessed the will. The will was invalid because the interested witness was not competent to testify about the validity of the will in court; thus, its validity could not be judicially established. *See generally* RESTATEMENT (THIRD) OF PROPERTY (Donative Transfers) § 3.1, Comment 0 (Tent. Draft No. 2, 1998). In virtually every state, the common-law rule has been abolished and the witnessing of a will by an interested witness does not affect the validity of the will. *See, e.g.,* Unif. Prob. Code § 2-505. On the other hand, most states have statutes that provide that unless two disinterested witnesses witness the will, the interested witness forfeits the bequest to that witness. Some states temper that result if the interested witness would have been an heir of the testator by limiting the amount forfeited to the amount, if any, by which the bequest to the interested witness exceeds the beneficiary-witness's intestate share. *See generally* William McGovern, Sheldon Kurtz, and Jan Rein, WILLS, TRUSTS AND ESTATES (1988). If such statutes applied here, Ben would forfeit the entire $40,000 bequest, as he is not an heir of Testator.

Under the Uniform Probate Code, on the other hand, an interested witness does not forfeit any portion of the bequest to the witness. The Uniform Probate Code justifies that approach by noting that the interested witness statute rarely prevents undue influence (an argument usually made to justify such statutes) and typically adversely affects bequests to innocent persons who act as witnesses to wills at a testator's express request. Under the Uniform Probate Code, Ben would not forfeit any portion of the $40,000 bequest.

Point Two: (30-40%)

The bequest of $100,000 to Wendy is revoked as a result of her divorce from Testator after the execution of the will.

At common law, divorce did not revoke a bequest to a former spouse by operation of law. In most states today, a divorce revokes a provision in a will for the testator's former spouse unless the will, a contract between the former spouses, or a court order expressly provides otherwise. *See generally* Unif. Prob. Code § 2-804. In other states, divorce revokes a will provision for the spouse but only if the divorce is accompanied by a property settlement agreement. *See* Dukeminier & Johanson, WILLS, TRUSTS AND ESTATES 283 (5th ed. 1995). Here, Testator's divorce from Wendy was accompanied by a property settlement agreement. Thus, the provision for Wendy was revoked and she is not entitled to any share of Testator's estate.

Where a provision in favor of a former spouse is revoked by operation of law, as in this case, the bequest passes as if the former spouse predeceased the testator. While Testator's will did not expressly require Wendy to survive to take, by virtue of the statutory fiction that Wendy predeceased Testator, the bequest lapses. It lapses because lapse statutes do not apply to bequests to former spouses. Typically, lapsed general legacies are distributed as part of the residuary estate. *See, e.g.,* Unif. Prob. Code § 2-804(d).

Point Three: (40-60%)

Legacies abate in the following order: residuary, general, and specific. Testator's $132,000 estate is insufficient to satisfy all of the general and specific legacies under the will. Thus, the residuary estate fully abates, the specific bequest of the portrait can be fully funded, and the remaining bequests abate to a limited extent.

Both at common law and under the typical state abatement statute, legacies abate in the following order: (1) residuary bequests, (2) general bequests, and (3) specific bequests. For purposes of abatement, a demonstrative bequest is treated as specific to the extent of the designated fund from which it is payable, and treated as general to the excess, if any. *See* Unif. Prob. Code § 3-902(a).

Under Testator's will, Testator specifically bequeathed the family portrait to Susan. Testator created two effective general legacies of $100,000 each in Leslie and Doris. (The bequest to Wendy was revoked by operation of law. *See* Point Two.) The legacy to Ben is forfeited under the interested witness statute in most jurisdictions. *(See* Point One.) In those states where it is not forfeited, the bequest of $40,000 to Ben is treated as a demonstrative legacy that is specific to the extent of the value of the stamp collection ($20,000) and general as to the remaining $20,000 of value. *See* Unif. Prob. Code § 3-902(a).

If the bequest to Ben is forfeited because of an interested witness statute, there are $130,000 of assets (not counting the specifically devised portrait) available for distribution to Leslie and Doris, who would each take $65,000. Susan would take the portrait valued at $2,000. The residuary bequest to University is totally abated.

If the bequest of $40,000 to Ben is not forfeited, then $20,000 of that bequest (the portion that cannot be satisfied by the specific bequest of the stamp collection) as well as the $100,000 bequests to Leslie and Doris are treated as general legacies for a total of $220,000. Thus, the $110,000 of the estate remaining after $22,000 of assets is distributed to Ben and Susan, the two specific legatees, would have to be allocated among the three general legatees to whom $220,000 had been bequeathed. Of that, $10,000 (1/11th) would be payable to Ben, $50,000 (5/11th) would be payable to Leslie, and $50,000 (5/11th) would be payable to Doris. The residuary estate is totally abated.

Decedent's Estates

(July 2001)

Legal Problems:

1. Was the bequest of the watch to Ben properly revoked, such that the watch passes to Chris?

2. Is Sarah entitled to receive the dining room table, the automobile, or neither?

3. Is Nicole entitled to the balance of Testator's tangible personal property under the doctrine of incorporation by reference?

4. To whom should the undisposed of property (the $10,000 bank account) be distributed?

DISCUSSION

Point One: (25-30%)

The gift of the watch to Ben was not revoked by either physical act or cancellation. It was revoked, however, by a subsequent will since State A law permits testators to execute holographic wills. Thus, the watch passes to Chris.

State A law permits wills to be completely or partially revoked by the execution of a subsequent will or by physical act or cancellation. In this case, no physical act was done to the face of the will to evidence that either the entire will or any of its provisions were revoked. On the other hand, on the back of the will, Testator, in her own handwriting, stated: "I don't want Ben to have my watch. I want it to go to my first cousin, Chris." Because these words do not come into physical contact with the words of the will, they are not words of revocation. *Thompson* v. *Royall,* 175 S.E. 748 (Va. 1934). *But see* Unif. Prob. Code § 2-507 (permitting revocation by cancellation even though words of cancellation do not touch words of the will). However, under the laws of State A, these words can be construed as a holographic codicil.

In some states, the handwriting on the back of the will would not be a valid holographic will because of underlying state statutes requiring holographic wills to be signed. *See, e.g.,* Unif. Prob. Code § 2-502(b) (requiring holographic wills to be signed). State A, however, has no signature requirement.

A holographic will can revoke an earlier typewritten will. *See generally Mangum* v. *Fuller,* 797 S.W.2d 452 (Ark. 1990). If the subsequently executed holographic will only disposes of a part of the estate disposed of in the typewritten will, then the typewritten will is revoked only to the extent that it is inconsistent with the provisions o(the holographic will. *See Gilbert* v. *Gilbert,* 652 S.W.2d 663 (Ky. Ct. App. 1983). *See also* Unif. Prob. Code § 2-507(a)(1) (partial revocation by inconsistency). Here, the holographic will is inconsistent with the typewritten will only to the extent that it leaves the watch to Chris, rather than Ben. Thus, no other disposition in the typewritten will is revoked.

Point Two: (35-50%)

The bequest of the dining room table to Sarah was revoked by physical act. Testator revoked the original bequest with the apparent intent of substituting for it a bequest of the automobile. However, the substituted bequest cannot be sustained as a holographic will because it was typewritten. Furthermore, the doctrine of dependent relative revocation is not likely to apply to prevent the bequest of the table from being revoked.

Under State A law, a bequest may be revoked by cancellation if the cancellation is accompanied by an intent to revoke. When a will is found with marks of cancellation upon it (here, the scratches through the phrase "dining room table"), a presumption arises that such marks were made by the testator with the intent to revoke. *See generally* W. McGovern, S. Kurtz, and J. Rein, WILLS, TRUSTS AND ESTATES § 5.2 (1988). Here, no facts suggest that such marks of cancellation could have been done by anyone but Testator and in light of the presumption, such marks were done by the Testator with the intent to revoke. However, typing the word "automobile" above "dining room table" suggests that Testator revoked the bequest of the dining room table in order to substitute for it a bequest of the automobile. Unfortunately, that typed bequest was neither signed nor witnessed and cannot be sustained as a valid holographic codicil because it was not in Testator's handwriting. Thus, Sarah takes nothing unless the revocation of the bequest of the dining room table can be avoided under the doctrine of dependent relative revocation.

Under the doctrine of dependent relative revocation, a revocation can be deemed conditional on the validity of a subsequently executed will or codicil if that would accomplish the testator's intent. W. McGovern, S. Kurtz, and J. Rein, WILLS, TRUSTS AND ESTATES § 5.3 (1988). Under this doctrine, if the subsequently executed will is invalid, then the revocation which was dependent upon it is ignored. *Id.* Typically, however, courts apply that doctrine only when there is a sufficiently close identity between the bequest that was revoked and the bequest that was expressed in the invalid subsequent will. Here, there is no such close identity between a dining room table and an automobile, and accordingly a court is unlikely to apply the doctrine of dependent relative revocation to prevent the bequest of the dining room table from being revoked. If, on the other hand, Sarah could find evidence that Testator's revocation was conditional, then she would be entitled to the dining room table. See Point Three for disposition of the automobile and the dining room table.

Point three: (15-20%)

Under the Doctrine of incorporation by reference, Nicole should be entitled to the balance of the Testator's tangible personal property.

Under the doctrine of incorporation by reference, a will may refer to an unattested written document and incorporate its terms into the will so long as that written document was in existence at the time the will was signed and the evidence is clear that testator intended to incorporate its terms into her will. *See, e.g., Smith* v. *Weitzel,* 338 S.W.2d 628 (Tenn. Ct. App. 1960); W. McGovern, S. Kurtz, and J. Rein, WILLS, TRUSTS AND ESTATES § 6.3 (1988). *See also* Unif. Prob. Code § 2-510. Where such a document is incorporated the dispositive provisions in it are given the same effect as if they had been set forth in the duly attested will. Here, the letter referred to in Testator's will was dated May 17, 1997, the day before Testator signed her will. Thus, it was in existence on the date Testator signed the will. Testator's will specifically refers to the letter by date and reflects a clear intent that the disposition in the letter be given effect. Thus, Nicole should be entitled to all of Testator's remaining tangibles, and probably the specific tangibles ineffectively bequeathed to Sarah. *See* Point Two. (This presumes that item three of the will operates like a residuary clause but with respect to the tangibles only.) Some states have statutes that specifically authorize the bequest of tangibles in the manner used here and validate such bequests even if the memo was executed after the will. *See, e.g.,* Unif. Prob. Code § 2-513.

Point Four: (15-20%)

The bank account should be distributed to Sarah and Ben as the sole heirs of Testator.

Where a testator's will fails to dispose of all of the testator's property, the undisposed of property passes to the testator's heirs. *See, e.g., Levy* v. *Hebrew Technical Institute,* 196 So. 2d 225 (Fla. Ct. App. 1967). Typically, the intestacy laws of the states provide that, absent descendants or a spouse, an intestate's property is distributed to (1) parents, (2) the descendants of the parents, (3) more remote ancestors, and (4) their descendants, in that order. Here, Testator's closest living relatives are Sarah and Ben and as such they are equally entitled to all of Testator's property not disposed of by Testator's will.

Decedent's Estates

(February 2002)

Legal Problems:

(1)(a) Did Testator's will, which included a general residuary clause purporting to exercise all of the donee's powers of appointment (a so-called "blanket exercise" clause), effectively exercise the special testamentary power of appointment that was created in Mary's will ?

(1)(b) Did Testator's will, which included a blanket exercise clause, effectively exercise the general testamentary power of appointment created in Frank's will?

(2) Does Daughter, the devisee of specifically devised encumbered property, take that property subject to the mortgage where the will contains a clause directing that the decedent's debts be paid by the executor?

(3) Is Son, the specific legatee of the watch, entitled to the insurance proceeds on the watch that were payable as a result of the theft of the watch shortly before Testator's death?

DISCUSSION

Point One(a): (15-25%)

The "blanket exercise" clause in Testator's will did not effectively exercise the power of appointment given to Testator by Mary's will because Mary's will required Testator to refer specifically to the power when exercising it.

In most states, a general residuary clause in a will (e.g., "I give all of my estate. . .") does not exercise powers of appointment. The situation is different if the general residuary clause is coupled with what is called a "blanket exercise" clause (e.g., "including all property over which I have a power of appointment"), as is the case here. Under these circumstances, any power of appointment held by the donee is exercised, unless the donor of the power of appointment specifically required the donee to refer to the instrument creating the power when exercising the power. *See generally* Unif. Probate Code § 2-608. *See also* Restatement (Second) of Property §§ 17.1-.2 (1984); *accord Holzbach* v. *United Virginia Bank,* 216 Va. 482, 219 S.E.2d 868 (1975).

Here, Mary, the donor of Testator's special power, expressly required that Testator specifically refer to her will in which the power was created if Testator, as donee of the power, sought to exercise the power. Testator's will contained only a blanket exercise clause, which failed to satisfy a condition on the exercise of the power imposed by the donor. Thus, the power was not effectively exercised.

Point One(b): (10-15%)

Testator's general testamentary power created by Frank's will was effectively exercised by a blanket exercise clause.

No facts indicate that Frank imposed a specific reference requirement with respect to the general testamentary power that Frank, as donor, granted Testator, as donee. Therefore, under the rule that a blanket exercise clause is effective to exercise powers absent a specific reference requirement. Testator's will effectively exercised the general testamentary power of appointment.

Point Two: (20-30%)

At common law. Daughter takes the family home free of the mortgage. Under the law of most states today. Daughter takes the home subject to the mortgage on which Testator was liable at the time of his death. The mortgage is not payable from the assets of Testator's estate.

Under the common-law doctrine of exoneration, the specific devisee of encumbered real property was entitled to have the mortgage on the property paid from the estate as a debt of the decedent unless there was evidence of a contrary intent on the part of the testator. *See, e.g., Martin* v. *Johnson,* 512 A.2d 1017 (D.C. 1986).

On the other hand, many states have adopted statutes contrary to this common-law rule of exoneration. For example, the Uniform Probate Code provides that "a specific devise passes subject to any mortgage interest existing at the date of death, without right of exoneration, regardless of a general directive in the will to pay debts." Unif. Probate Code § 2-607. In states with statutes of this type, the specific devisee of encumbered property takes subject to the mortgage notwithstanding the fact that the will contained a clause directing the executor to pay the decedent's debts.

Courts have also held that a general directive to pay debts is insufficient to evidence an intent to exonerate the devisee of specifically devised property. *See, e.g., Griffin* v. *Gould,* 72 Ill. App. 3d 747, 391 N.E.2d 124 (1979). Depending on the underlying state law, Daughter takes either subject to the mortgage or free of the mortgage.

Point Three: (25-35%)

The insurance proceeds payable as a result of the theft of the watch shortly before Testator's death should pass to Son as the specific devisee of the watch. There is, however, contrary authority.

Under the doctrine of ademption, if the subject matter of a specific devise is not in the probate estate at the time of the testator's death, the bequest to the devisee adeems (or fails). *See generally* William H. McGovern, Jr. & Sheldon F. Kurtz, WILLS, TRUSTS AND ESTATES 295 (2d ed. 2001). However, if the property was destroyed by fire or lost by theft and proceeds of insurance are paid to the executor of the estate in settlement of claims against the insurance company, some courts hold that the insurance proceeds are payable to the specific devisee as a substitute for the specifically devised property. *See White* v. *White,* 105 N.J. Super. 184,251 A.2d 470 (1969); *accord In re Estate of Wolfe,* 208 N.W.2d 923 (Iowa 1973); Unif. Probate Code § 2-606.

However, some state courts have held to the contrary, finding that the insurance proceeds pass as part of the testator's residuary estate. *In re Estate of Wright,* 7 N.Y.2d 365, 197 N.Y.S.2d 711, 165 N.E.2d 561 (1960). They find that the insurance policy is a separate and distinct asset from the property subject to the specific devise and that the proceeds, as specifically undisposed property, pass to the residuary legatees under the will.

It seems that the majority rule stated in *Wolfe*, 208 N.W.2d 923, as well as in the Uniform Probate Code and some other state codes is the better rule because it is more likely to accord with the reasonable expectations of a testator.

Decedent's Estates

(July 2002)

Legal Problems:

(1)   Is Nephew liable in wrongful death for causing Testator's death?

(1)(a) Was Testator's durable health care power of attorney validly executed?

(1)(b) Was Nephew, a beneficiary under Testator's will and a witness to Testator's health care power of attorney, prohibited from acting as an agent?

(2)   Can the nieces successfully challenge the will because Testator lacked the mental capacity to execute her will?

(3)   Does Nephew forfeit the bequest under the interested witness statute?

DISCUSSION

Summary: Nephew would not be liable in wrongful death if, as it appears, he acted under a valid durable health care power of attorney and in good faith. His decision to direct the withdrawal of life support was entirely consistent with the doctor's medical advice.

Testator's will appears to have been validly executed. Arguments that Testator lacked mental capacity should fail because the facts show that she knew both the objects of her bounty and the nature and extent of her property.

Lastly, Nephew would not forfeit his share under typical state interested witness statutes because the will bequeathed him a share less than what would have been his intestate share. Likewise, under the UPC, he would take his share as that statute has no interested witness forfeiture statute.

Point One: (35-40%)

Under the typical durable health care power of attorney statute, if Nephew acted under a valid durable health care power and in good faith, he would be shielded from civil liability that might otherwise arise as a result of his directing the withdrawal of the life-support systems.

The typical durable health care power of attorney statute immunizes the agent of the principal from civil liability for health care decisions made in good faith. *See, e.g.,* Unif. Health Care Decisions Act § 9(b)(1993). Health care decisions include the decision to withhold or withdraw life-sustaining treatment, including food and hydration. *See* Unif. Health Care Decisions Act § 1(6).

Agents act within the scope of the statute when they act pursuant to a properly executed durable health care power of attorney. State laws vary, however, on whether the person designated as the agent can be a witness to the durable health care power of attorney. For example, under the Uniform Health Care Decisions Act, the designated agent is not prohibited from being a witness. In fact, under the Uniform Act, no witnessing of the power is required. On the other hand, in many states, the person designated as the agent cannot be a witness to the power.

Even if Nephew was not legally constituted as Testator's agent, he may nonetheless have acted appropriately under so-called "family consent" laws. These laws permit close family members (typically in the order listed in the statute) to act as a surrogate decision maker for a patient where there is no properly authorized agent acting under a durable power. For example, under § 5 of the Uniform Health Care Decisions Act, Nephew could act as a surrogate decision maker since there are no more closely related relatives and Nephew is an adult "who exhibited special care and concern for the patient."

Whether Nephew was acting as a properly constituted agent or as a surrogate under the family consent law, ultimately the issue of civil liability most likely depends on whether Nephew acted in "good faith." Here the facts suggest that he did. Testator had suffered a massive stroke and had lapsed into a coma, and Nephew's direction to withdraw Testator's life support appears to be consistent with sound medical advice to the effect that more care would be futile. While the fact that Nephew is named in Testator's will as a beneficiary may create the appearance of impropriety, this fact alone is not sufficient evidence of bad faith; empirically most agents and surrogates are persons who are both close to the principal and named as beneficiaries under the principal's will.

Point Two: (35-40%)

Testator's will is valid notwithstanding that Testator was sometimes forgetful, as the facts support the conclusion that Testator had the mental capacity to execute a will.

In order to validly execute a will, Testator must have "mental capacity." A testator has mental capacity if the testator knows (1) the nature and extent of the testator's property, (2) those persons who are the natural objects of the testator's bounty, (3) the nature of the instrument that the testator is signing, and (4) the disposition that is being made in the will. See generally William H. McGovern & Sheldon F. Kurtz, WILLS, TRUSTS AND ESTATES 272 (2d ed. 2001).

Here Testator was forgetful, which at first blush suggests the absence of mental capacity. But simply relying on that fact is insufficient to determine whether Testator had mental capacity since the criteria that determine mental capacity for purposes of validating a will look specifically to Testator's understanding of her property interests, her beneficiaries, and her disposition. On these issues, the facts suggest that Testator did have mental capacity.

Testator appears to have been actively involved in the management and administration of her property affairs, suggesting that she knew the nature and extent of her property. She knew those persons who might be the objects of her bounty as evidenced by the fact that she frequently visited with her 20 relatives, including those not mentioned in her will. Furthermore, the bulk of her estate is bequeathed to Charity, an organization with which she had had a long association. Thus, the will does not reflect a disposition that would likely be inconsistent with Testator's testamentary intent.

Given that the burden of proof to establish the lack of testamentary capacity rests on the contestants, it is most unlikely that they could sustain that burden on these facts.

Point Three: (20- 30%)

Nephew would not forfeit any of his bequest under the will.

Under the Uniform Probate Code, Nephew would not forfeit his bequest even though Nephew was a witness to the will because the Code does not have an interested witness statute barring interested witnesses from taking under a will.

At common law, if a will was not witnessed by two disinterested witnesses the will was invalid. *See* McGovern & Kurtz, *supra,* at 177. In the United States, this harsh rule has been replaced by statutes in most states barring the interested witness from taking the bequest but not invalidating the will. *Id.*

The typical interested witness statute, however, contains one or two important exceptions. The first is that if the will is witnessed by three or more persons such that the will would have been valid without the witnessing by the interested witness, the interested witness does not forfeit the bequest. *Id.* That exception would not apply here as Testator's will was witnessed only by two persons.

The second exception is that if the interested witness also would have been an heir of the testator, the witness forfeits only so much of the bequest as exceeds what would have been that witness's intestate share. Under that exception, Nephew forfeits nothing, as the bequest to Nephew of $100,000 is less than what his intestate share would have been. Nephew's intestate share would have been in excess of $250,000, as the estate is valued at more than $1 million and there are four heirs.

In light of the discussion under Point One, there is no reasonable basis on which to argue that Nephew's bequest is invalid under the slayer statutes.

Likewise, the facts state that Nephew was wholly unaware of the will provision in his favor. Thus, there is no basis to invalidate the will on undue influence grounds.

NOTE: If the will is valid, the nieces would probably have no standing to raise the interested witness issue. If the interested witness statute applied and the bequest, or some portion of it, were forfeited, the forfeited portion would pass to Charity as the residuary legatee under Testator's will.

Decedent's Estates

(February 2003)

Legal Problems: (1)   Was Testator's October 1, 1998, will properly executed?

(2)   Did Testator's codicil effectively incorporate her earlier will by reference?

(3)   Did Testator's gift of the diamond ring to Betty adeem the codicil's bequest of the ring to Nora?

DISCUSSION

Summary: Although Testator's will was not validly executed because it was signed in her name but outside of her presence, it was validly incorporated by reference into Testator's duly executed codicil, which expressly referred to it by date. Thus, the will, as incorporated by reference into the codicil, is valid to pass title to Blackacre to Charity, the beneficiary under the will.

Because the bequest of the ring in the codicil to Nora adeemed by virtue of Testator's gift of the ring to Betty, Nora is not entitled to the ring.

Point One: Testator's October 1, 1998, will was not effectively executed because
(35-45%)   Lawyer, while signing it at Testator's direction, did not sign it in her presence.

Will execution statutes commonly provide that another person may sign a testator's will if it is done at the testator's direction and in the testator's conscious presence. *See, e.g.*, Uniform Probate Code (UPC) § 2-502(2). A few statutes additionally require that persons who sign for the testator must also sign their own names and sometimes also give their addresses. *See* Restatement (Second) of Property: Donative Transfers, Statutory Note to § 33.1. Many wills statutes require one or both of the following additional requirements: (1) that the testator declare the instrument to be his or her will to the witnesses, or (2) that the testator ask the individuals selected as witnesses to witness his or her execution of the instrument.

In this case, Lawyer signed Testator's name at her direction, but the question is whether he did so in her presence. The likely answer is that he did not. Courts have used two tests to determine presence: the majority "line-of-sight" test and the minority "conscious presence" test. Under the "conscious presence" test, the will execution is sufficient "if it was done in the testator's conscious presence, i.e., within the range of the testator's senses such as hearing." *See* Unif. Prob. Code § 2-502 cmt.

Lawyer clearly did not satisfy the "line-of-sight" test because Testator did not see Lawyer signing the will on her behalf. Under the "line-of-sight" test, the testator should be capable of seeing the witnesses and the person who is signing the will on the testator's behalf actually sign the will. In those cases where the testator must specifically ask the witnesses to act as such, the witnesses should be capable of hearing that request. *Matter of Jefferson's Will*, 349 So. 2d 1032 (Miss. 1977). Even under the more liberal "conscious presence" test (which the UPC expressly adopts), it is very unlikely that the court will conclude that the presence requirement was satisfied. In the analogous situation where a testator acknowledges her signature to witnesses over the telephone, courts have held that this does not satisfy the "conscious presence" requirement. *See In re Estate of McGurrin*, 743 P.2d 994 (Idaho Ct. App. 1987). There is too much room for fraudulent or mistaken substitution of one document for another under these circumstances to permit the will to be admitted to probate.

The defect with the signature requirement is itself sufficient reason to conclude that the will was defectively executed. Additionally, since Testator did not sign the will, acknowledge her signature, acknowledge the will to the witnesses in their presence (under either test), or ask them to act as witnesses, there was defective execution with respect to the witnessing requirements of the will statutes in most states.

The Uniform Probate Code's harmless error provision, UPC § 2-503, would not likely allow the October 1, 1998, writing to be admitted as a will. There are two defects here, signature and attestation, and the Comment to § 2-503 provides that the greater the departure from the required formalities of execution, the less likely that the provision will cure the defects. This is especially true with respect to defects in the signature requirement. *See* UPC § 2-503 cmt.

Point Two: The validly executed codicil incorporated the October 1, 1998, will
(25-35%)   by reference, and therefore the October 1, 1998, will can be given legal effect even
             though it was defectively executed. Therefore, Charity is entitled to Blackacre.

The codicil is Testator's only duly executed will. A properly executed codicil can incorporate by reference an earlier will that was defectively executed, as here. *See Allen* v. *Mattock*, 14 Eng. Rep. 757 (P.C. 1858); Jesse Dukeminier & Stanley Johanson, WILLS, TRUSTS, AND ESTATES 303 (6th ed. 2000). Therefore, if the jurisdiction recognizes the doctrine of incorporation by reference, the court should give effect to the October 1, 1998, will as an incorporated extrinsic writing.

The doctrine of incorporation by reference is recognized in most states. Either by statute (e.g., UPC § 2-510) or by judicial decision, several requirements must be met in order for a properly executed will to incorporate an extrinsic writing by reference. The usual requirements are: (1) the extrinsic writing must in fact have been in existence at the time the incorporating will was executed; (2) the incorporating will must refer to the extrinsic writing as having been in existence at the time of execution; (3) the incorporating will must refer to the extrinsic writing in such a way as to reasonably identify it; and (4) the incorporating will must manifest the testator's intent to incorporate the extrinsic writing. *See Wagner v. Clauson*, 78 N.E.2d 203 (Ill. 1948). All four of the requirements were met here. The codicil's reference to the existing October 1, 1998, will is sufficiently clear, as is the intention to incorporate the earlier writing. Therefore, Charity is entitled to Blackacre.

Note: If the jurisdiction does not recognize the incorporation doctrine, the probate court should not give any effect to the October 1, 1998, writing. Specifically, the doctrine of republication by codicil cannot be used to republish an earlier will that was defectively executed. The republication requirement can be used to give effect to an earlier will that was invalid for reasons other than defective execution. The October 1, 1998, will was invalid solely because it was defectively executed, so republication is not available here. If the will was not incorporated by reference, Blackacre would pass to Nora and Betty equally as Testator's heirs.

Point Three: The bequest of the diamond ring to Nora was adeemed by Testator's
(25-35%)   gift of the ring to Betty. Therefore, Nora is not entitled to the ring and Betty keeps
             it.

The doctrine of ademption by extinction provides that if the subject matter of a specific bequest is not part of the estate at the testator's death, the bequest is adeemed. The doctrine applies only to specific bequests. The bequest here was specific because the will referred to a specific asset. Under the traditional approach to ademption—the so-called "identity theory"—the testator's intent as to ademption is irrelevant. All that matters is whether or not the specifically bequeathed asset is part of the estate at death. Accordingly, Testator's gift of the ring to Betty caused the bequest to Nora to adeem.

Even under the Uniform Probate Code's non-ademption provision, UPC § 2-606(a)(6), which adopts the so-called "intent theory" of ademption, the result would be the same. In the Comment to § 2-606, the drafters provide a hypothetical problem with facts similar to those of this case. The Comment states, "G's deliberate act of giving away the specifically devised property is a fact and circumstance indicating that ademption of the devise was intended." Therefore, § 2-606(a)(6) would yield the same result as the traditional ademption doctrine, particularly because the facts state that Testator gifted the ring to Betty in order to ensure that Nora did not take under the codicil.

Decedent's Estates

(July 2003)

<u>Legal Problems:</u>   (1)   Was the 1988 will that was destroyed by Testator's lawyer outside of Testator's presence legally revoked by physical destruction?

    (2)   Is Testator's 1996 handwritten will entitled to be probated, and if so, as a subsequent testamentary instrument, did it revoke Testator's 1988 will?

    (3)   Is Greg entitled to any share of the estate as a "pretermitted heir"?

DISCUSSION

<u>Summary:</u> Blackacre is distributable to Earl under the terms of the valid holographic will and the balance of the estate is distributed as follows: $100,000 to Carrie under the 1988 will, $2,500,000 to Fred under the 1996 will, and the residue to Doris under the 1988 will. Adam and Greg take nothing. This distribution results from the fact that the 1988 will was not wholly revoked by destruction but only partially revoked by the inconsistent provisions of the codicil. Furthermore, Greg is not entitled to a forced share because he was alive when the wills were signed.

<u>Point One:</u>   <u>The 1988 will was not revoked because it was physically destroyed</u>
(25-30%)   <u>by someone other than the testator and not in the testator's presence.</u>

Most states require that a revocatory act (such as physical destruction of a will) by someone other than the testator be done in the testator's presence, or at least in the testator's "conscious presence," and at the testator's request. *See, e.g.,* Uniform Probate Code (UPC) § 2-507. Therefore, in most states, the 1988 will would not have been legally revoked. Testator asked Lawyer to destroy the will, but the destruction did not occur in Testator's presence.

Although the 1988 will was physically destroyed, it was not revoked and the unexecuted copy is available to prove its content.

<u>Point Two:</u>   <u>Because holographic wills are valid in State A, the 1996 will can be</u>
(35-45%)   <u>probated. The 1988 will was revoked by the 1996 holographic will only to the extent that it was inconsistent with the later holographic will.</u>

The 1996 document is a holographic will because it is entirely in Testator's handwriting; under the laws of State A holographic wills are valid and therefore the 1996 will is entitled to be probated. The fact that the 1996 will is entitled to be probated, however, does not preclude the possibility that the 1988 will can also be probated so long as it was not revoked. Wills may be revoked either by physical destruction, accompanied by an intent to revoke, or by the execution of a subsequent will. Typically, if a will has been executed and then another will is executed, the latter will revokes the former will only to the extent that they are inconsistent, unless, of course, the latter will has an express revocation clause. *See generally* UPC § 2-507(a)(1). Here, the 1996 will did *not* have an express revocation clause. Because it did not have a residuary clause (it contained only a specific bequest and a general bequest), its terms are not wholly inconsistent with the terms of the 1988 will. In fact, the only inconsistency between them is the disposition of Blackacre. Under the 1988 will, Blackacre was bequeathed to Adam; under the 1996 will, it was bequeathed to Earl. Since the later will trumps the earlier will, Blackacre is distributable to Earl.

Assuming that both documents can be probated for the reasons stated, the probate estate should be distributed as follows: Blackacre to Earl, $100,000 to Carrie, and $2,500,000 to Fred; Doris, the residuary legatee under the 1988 will, takes the remaining $2,400,000. Adam takes nothing.

Point Three: Greg, Testator's child and only heir, is not entitled to any share of
(20-25%)   Testator's estate because he is not a pretermitted heir.

In most jurisdictions, pretermitted heir statutes have been enacted permitting children of a testator under certain circumstances to claim a share of the estate even though they were omitted from the deceased testator's will. Typically, these statutes apply only if the child was born or adopted after the execution of the will. *See generally* UPC § 2-302. Here, Greg was alive when both the 1988 will and the 1996 will were executed. Thus, Greg would not be entitled to a "forced share" under the typical pretermitted heir statute. However, if the statute protects children born before the will was executed who were not expressly disinherited, then Greg would take the entire estate.

Decedent's Estates

(February 2004)

ANALYSIS

Legal Problems: (1)   Do Mary and Grandchild each have standing to contest Testator's will?

                  (2)   Can Testator's will be successfully contested on the grounds of:
                          (a) lack of mental capacity?
                          (b) lack of due execution?

DISCUSSION

Summary: Mary has standing to contest the will because, if the will were denied probate, she would be Testator's sole heir. On the other hand, Grandchild lacks standing to contest the will because if the will were denied probate, Grandchild would not be entitled to any share of Testator's estate. Mary, who is entitled to contest the will, is not likely to be successful on the ground of lack of mental capacity but might prevail on the ground of lack of due execution in states applying the strict compliance doctrine.

Point One: <u>Mary has standing to contest the will. However, Grandchild does not have standing to</u>

(20-30%)   <u>contest the will.</u>

Wills can be contested only by persons who would be better off financially if the will were denied probate than they would be if the will were admitted to probate. *See generally* William M. McGovern & Sheldon F. Kurtz, WILLS, TRUSTS, AND ESTATES 464 (2d ed. 2001). If the rule were otherwise, wills would be subject to suits by persons seeking to extort money from legitimate beneficiaries who want to avoid litigation.

Under the laws of all states, an intestate's children take to the exclusion of their own descendants. Thus, if Testator's will were denied probate, Testator's entire estate would pass to Mary; nothing would pass to the grandchildren or great-grandchild. Mary, therefore, would have standing to contest the will because as Testator's only child she would be her only heir if the will were denied probate. On the other hand, Grandchild would not be financially better off if the will were denied probate and, thus, would lack standing to contest the will.

Point Two (a): (30-40%)	Testator probably had the mental capacity to execute a will at the time she executed it.

In order to execute a will, a testator must have mental capacity. A testator meets this requirement if the testator knows (1) the nature and extent of her property, (2) the persons who are the natural objects of the testator's bounty and have the highest moral claims to the testator's property, (3) the disposition the testator is attempting to make, and (4) the interrelationship of these items in connection with the testamentary plan formulated in the will. *See generally* Jesse Dukeminier & Stanley M. Johanson, WILLS, TRUSTS AND ESTATES 163 (6th ed. 2000).

All persons are afforded the presumption that they have mental capacity. As a result, the burden of proving that the testator lacks mental capacity rests on the contestant to the will. Here, there are two arguments to support a will contest on mental incapacity grounds, although Bank has good responses to both arguments.

First, Testator arguably did not know the nature and extent of her property. Testator could not identify the stocks that she owned or name the stockbroker who managed them. Also, she could not recall the addresses of her two residences. On the other hand, she did know what she was worth and she did know that she owned two residences. Thus, whether she lacked mental capacity on this ground may ultimately depend on how precise a testator must be regarding the nature and extent of her property. Courts often are very lenient and uphold the wills of elderly testators who at least grasp the big picture about their financial affairs. Furthermore, because of the burden of proof, in a very close case the contestant will lose.

Second, Testator could not identify one of the persons with a high moral claim to her property, namely her great-grandchild. On the other hand, Testator could identify her more closely related relatives, and in particular Mary, whom she was intending to disinherit. Her failure to recall whether she had a great-grandchild probably would not be dispositive of her mental capacity. Courts have not required elderly testators to know the number of their remote descendants, particularly in a mobile society where people may have infrequent contacts with grandchildren and great-grandchildren.

Point Two (b):	Testator's will was not duly executed under the strict compliance doctrine but could be

(30-40%)   upheld as valid if the court either adopts the substantial compliance doctrine or infers that Testator requested the witnesses to sign.

At common law, if the execution of a will did not strictly adhere to the required formalities, the will would be invalid and the testator would have died intestate. The facts state that under the governing law, a properly executed will must be signed by the testator in the presence of two witnesses after the testator has declared the instrument to be her will and has requested that the witnesses act in such capacity. Here, the signing, witnessing, and declaration requirements have been satisfied, but the facts state that Testator did not specifically request the witnesses to act as such. Thus, courts adhering to the strict common-law approach (known as the strict compliance doctrine) would invalidate the will. *See generally* McGovern & Kurtz, *supra,* at 170-72.

On the other hand, statutes in some states and a judicial decision in at least one state have tempered the harsh consequences of the common-law rule by adopting a "substantial compliance" approach to determining whether a will has been validly executed. *See generally* John H. Langbein, *Substantial Compliance with the Wills Act*, 88 HARV. L. REV. 489 (1975). Under this approach, if the execution of a will substantially complies with most of the formalities, or at least the most important of them, the will is valid. *See, e.g., In re Will of Ranney* 124 N.J. 1, 589 A.2d 1339 (1991) (will valid even though witnesses only witnessed the self-proving will affidavit and did not witness the actual will).

Similarly, § 2-503 of the Uniform Probate Code (UPC) grants a court a so-called "dispensing power" under which a court can probate a will when its execution failed to comply with all of the execution formalities so long as the evidence is clear and convincing that the decedent intended the document to be her will. In this case, the failure to request that the witnesses act as such when they signed in the physical presence of Testator can easily be ignored under this statute if, as the facts suggest, Testator clearly intended Charity to take under her will. The statement, "My family has enough" is evidence of Testator's intent.

It might also be argued from the context and surrounding circumstances that Testator implicitly asked the witnesses to sign even if she did not do so expressly. She saw them sign, and she declared the instrument to be her will. At least one court has adopted that approach and thus avoided an all-out adoption of the substantial compliance theory. *See Matter of Graham's Estate*, 295 N.W.2d 414 (Iowa 1980).

Decedent's Estates
(July 2004)

ANALYSIS

Legal Problems: (1)   Did Clara survive Decedent such that Decedent's estate passes under Clara's will to Son-in-Law?

(2)   Is Half-Sister an heir of Decedent?

(3)   Is Adopted-Sister an heir of Decedent?

(4)   Does the $90,000 gift to Brother reduce Brother's share of Decedent's estate?

(5)   Is Gramps entitled to any share of Decedent's estate?

DISCUSSION

Summary: Under the Uniform Simultaneous Death Act, Clara is deemed to have predeceased Decedent. Likewise, Clara predeceased Decedent under the 120-hour survivorship rule of the Uniform Probate Code(UPC). Therefore, Son-in-Law cannot claim any share of Decedent's estate. Decedent's heirs are his siblings: Brother, Half-Sister, and Adopted-Sister. However, their respective shares of Decedent's estate may differ depending upon underlying state law. The gift to Brother is not an advancement and thus does not reduce Brother's share of Decedent's estate. If Half-Sister takes an equal share, then Brother, Half-Sister, and Adopted-Sister are each entitled to $100,000. Gramps would take only in a state determining heirship under the civil law method of consanguinity, which very few states apply.

Point One: Under the Uniform Simultaneous Death Act, there is a presumption that Clara
(30-40%)   predeceased Decedent and there is no evidence here to rebut that presumption. Likewise, under the UPC's 120-hour survivorship rule, Clara predeceased Decedent because she did not survive him by 120 hours. Thus, Son-in-Law is not entitled to any share of Decedent's estate.

Son-in-Law, as the sole beneficiary under Clara's will, would be entitled to Decedent's estate only if Clara had been entitled to inherit Decedent's estate. Clara would be an heir of Decedent only if she survived Decedent, because an heir must be alive at the time of the intestate's death. However, in a situation such as this one, where the two decedents were killed in the same traffic accident, Clara is deemed to have predeceased Decedent if there is insufficient evidence that she and Decedent died other than simultaneously. Unif. Simul. Death Act § 2. Since the evidence here is insufficient to establish that they did not die simultaneously, under the Uniform Act, Clara is deemed to have predeceased Decedent.

While it might be argued that Clara survived because the truck hit her car from the rear and presumably hit Decedent first, it is also possible that the mere impact at the rear of Clara's car was sufficient to cause both their deaths. Furthermore, the only direct evidence of their deaths was that neither appeared to be alive at the scene of the accident. Thus, there is no direct evidence to establish that Clara survived Decedent. The fact that Decedent was declared dead first should not be controlling because the declarations of death were made simply in the order in which they were removed from the ambulance, and the factual evidence supports the conclusion that neither was alive when they were placed into the ambulance.

Under § 2-104 of the UPC, Clara is also not an heir of Decedent because she failed to survive him by 120 hours.

Point Two: Half-Sister is an heir of Decedent. Depending on state law, she is entitled either to the
(10-20%)   same share as a whole sibling or a lesser share.

Decedent's heirs will be the descendants of his deceased parents and perhaps Gramps. *See* Point Five. The issue therefore arises whether siblings of the half-blood and adopted siblings inherit along with siblings of the whole blood.

Half-Sister and Decedent are half-bloods because they share only one common parent. Under § 2-107 of the UPC, relatives of the half-blood inherit the same share as relatives of the whole blood. Thus, Half-Sister would take $100,000.

However, in some jurisdictions they inherit a smaller share. *See, e.g.*, Iowa Code § 633.219.

Point Three: Adopted-Sister is an heir of Decedent.
(20-30%)

At common law, an adopted child could not take from or through an adopting parent. Thus, at common law, Adopted-Sister would not be Decedent's heir. By the end of the twentieth century, motivated by a policy to treat the adopted child as part of the adopting parents' nuclear family, most state laws were changed to provide that an adopted child is treated as a biological child for purposes of inheritance. Thus, under the UPC, Decedent's estate is distributed equally to the descendants of his deceased parents. *See* UPC § 2-103(3). The descendants of Decedent's parents include both their biological and adopted children. *See* UPC § 2-114(b). Thus, Adopted-Sister would take $100,000.

Point Four: Decedent's lifetime gift to Brother is not an advancement and thus does not reduce Brother's share of Decedent's estate.
(20-30%)

At common law, a lifetime transfer to a child who would be the transferor's heir was treated as a down payment on the child's intestate share. Under the common-law rule, the gift to Brother would not be an advancement as Brother is not Decedent's child. *See generally* Joel C. Dobris, Stewart E. Sterk & Melanie B. Leslie, ESTATES AND TRUSTS 155 (2d ed. 2003); *see also* 755 Ill. Comb. Stat. 5/2-5.

Many states have broadened the common-law rule to include transfers to any person who is an heir. However, most states also provide that a lifetime transfer to a person who would be the transferor's heir is presumptively a gift and not an advancement. *See* UPC § 2-109.

States differ in what it takes to rebut the gift presumption. Some states permit any competent evidence to be used to rebut the presumption. Others have a heightened evidentiary requirement. For example, under the UPC, the presumption that a lifetime transfer was a gift can be rebutted by a contemporaneous writing of either the decedent or the donee stating either that the gift was an advancement or that it was to be taken into account in computing the distribution of the decedent's estate. UPC § 2-109. Here, however, there is neither a writing nor any other competent evidence that Decedent intended an advancement when he made the transfer to Brother. Consequently, the transfer to Brother would be treated as a gift, not an advancement, and Brother would take $100,000 of Decedent's estate.

Lastly, in some states an advancement only occurs when the donee would have been an heir of the decedent at the time the transfer was made. *See, e.g.,* Iowa Code § 633.224. If that rule applies here, the transfer could not be an advancement because at the time Decedent transferred the money to Brother, Clara was living and thus would have been Decedent's only heir.

Point Five: Gramps is not entitled to receive any share of Decedent's estate unless heirship
                in the state was determined under the civil law method of consanguinity.

(5-15%)

Under the civil law method of consanguinity, Gramps as well as Decedent's siblings would be related to Decedent within the second degree of consanguinity and Gramps would share equally with the siblings in the estate. Most states have rejected this method of determining heirship. In those states, including all those that have adopted the UPC and those that follow the parentelic method of descent, Gramps would not be entitled to share in Decedent's estate.

Decedent's Estates
(February 2005)

ANALYSIS

<u>Legal Problems:</u> (1) Does the physical destruction of one executed copy of the 1994 will, done with the intent to revoke, effectively revoke the 1994 will if the other executed copy has not been physically destroyed?

(2) Is the 1991 will revived by the revocation of the 1994 will?

(3) Assuming the 1991 will is revived, is Cousin entitled to $100,000, $10,000, or nothing?

(4) Assuming the 1991 will is revived, did the bequest to Sister adeem?

DISCUSSION

<u>Summary</u>

Testator's 1994 will was revoked by physical destruction even though only one of the two executed copies was physically destroyed because in doing so Testator intended to revoke the 1994 will. Under the State A statute, revocation of the 1994 will revived the 1991 will. Under the 1991 will, $10,000 passed to Cousin because the handwritten cancellation of that bequest was conditioned on the effectiveness of the $100,000 bequest. However, the $100,000 bequest cannot be given effect because it was not witnessed. Furthermore, while under the common law the bequest to Sister adeems, in some states Sister is entitled to Whiteacre, the replacement property for Blackacre. If an applicant concludes that the 1994 will was not revoked because there was one remaining executed copy, Cousin and Sister take nothing.

<u>Point One:</u> Testator's 1994 will was revoked by the physical destruction of one of two executed
(25-35%) copies of that will.

All states permit the revocation of a will by physical destruction if that act is accompanied by an intent to revoke. *See generally* Uniform Probate Code (UPC) § 2-507. If Testator had not executed the 1994 will in duplicate, there would be no question that it was revoked because the facts evidence both a physical destruction and an intent to revoke.

However, the 1994 will was executed in duplicate, and the physical destruction of one copy may have been motivated by a desire either to revoke the will or to revoke only the copy. While the matter has not been considered in all states, the prevailing view is that the revocation of one copy presumptively revokes the will. *See, e.g., In re Betts' Will*, 107 N.Y.S.2d 626 (N.Y. Sur. 1951); *In re Estate of Mettee*, 694 P.2d 1325 (Kan. Ct. App. 1985). The proponent of the copy of the will that was not destroyed must then prove that Testator did not intend to revoke the will. Here, Testator's statement accompanying the destruction of one copy as well as the other surrounding facts suggest that Testator intended to revoke the 1994 will for the purpose of reviving the 1991 will. Thus, Testator would not have intended the other copy of the 1994 will to remain in effect.

Point Two: Under the State A statute, the 1991 will was revived by the revocation of the 1994 will
(5-15%) because there is no evidence that Testator did not intend a revival of the earlier will.

The State A statute provides that "the revocation of a will that revoked an earlier will revives the earlier will in the absence of a contrary intention." Here, the facts support the conclusion that Testator, by revoking the 1994 will, intended to revive the 1991 will. In particular, when revoking the 1994 will, Testator made reference to the fact that by revoking the 1994 will Cousin would be taken care of. That result would only be true if the 1991 will were revived. Given that intent and the statutory directive, the 1991 will is revived.

Point Three: Under the doctrine of dependent relative revocation, Cousin is entitled to $10,000.
(35-45%) Cousin is not entitled to $100,000 because that intended bequest was made by an unattested act.

On the assumption that the 1991 will was revived, the question arises whether Cousin takes $100,000 as Testator likely intended, $10,000 under the doctrine of dependent relative revocation, or nothing because the typewritten bequest to Cousin was revoked by cancellation.

While Testator may well have intended Cousin to take $100,000 as evidenced by the handwriting on the will and the statement accompanying the revocation of the 1994 will, since State A does not permit holographic wills, that writing cannot be given effect as a valid will or codicil because it was not witnessed. While the facts do not state what the State A statute requires for execution formalities, all states minimally require two witnesses to create a valid will unless they permit holographic wills.

Given that Cousin cannot take the $100,000, the issue arises whether Testator's scratching out of the $10,000 bequest to Cousin results in the revocation of that bequest under the typical revocation statute.

Under the doctrine of dependent relative revocation, the physical revocation of a bequest can be ignored if evidence exists to suggest that the testator revoked that bequest on the mistaken assumption that some other bequest would be effective. *See generally* William M. McGovern & Sheldon F. Kurtz, WILLS, TRUSTS AND ESTATES § 5.3 (2d ed. 2001). Such evidence appears here not only from the fact that immediately above the scratching out of the bequest appeared the words of the greater, albeit ineffective, bequest, but also from the statements Testator made to his neighbor regarding Cousin when the 1994 will was revoked. If the doctrine does not apply, however, then Cousin takes nothing because the $100,000 is ineffective as a bequest and the $10,000 bequest was revoked by cancellation.

Point Four: Under the common law, the bequest to Sister adeemed, although some states have
(15-25%) statutes substituting the new home for the home that was sold.

An ademption of a bequest occurs when the subject of a specific devise has been sold by the testator between the time the will was executed and the time the testator dies. *See generally* McGovern & Kurtz, *supra,* § 8.1 (2d ed. 2001); *In re Estate of Brown*, 922 S.W.2d 605 (Tex. App. 1996) (devise of family home at specified address adeemed where home at time will was signed was not the home at time of testator's death). The theory behind ademption is that a testator, knowing of the disposition of the specifically devised property, could execute a new will to take account of that disposition if the testator wanted some substitute bequest to pass to the beneficiary. Absent the execution of a new will, Testator presumably does not intend the beneficiary to take any substituted property.

Some states, however, have adopted statutes that substitute so-called replacement property for the specific property disposed of by the testator. For example, § 2-606 of the Uniform Probate Code (UPC) provides that a specific devisee (here, Sister) is entitled to any property acquired by a testator as "replacement property" for the property that the testator sold. The facts support the conclusion that Whiteacre was acquired by Testator as a substitute for Blackacre. Thus, under the UPC, or a similar statute, Sister would be entitled to Whiteacre. Absent such a statute, Sister would be entitled to nothing under the common law.

In the absence of a statute, a court might also reach the same result by noting that the will reflects the intent to devise Sister the family home, arguably without regard to whether the family home was Blackacre or Whiteacre.

Decedent's Estates
(July 2005)

ANALYSIS

Legal Problems: (1)   Can an insured change a life insurance beneficiary designation by will?

    (2)   Does a joint tenant who deposited all funds into a joint tenancy bank account retain the right to bequeath this asset to an individual who is not the surviving joint tenant?

    (3)   With respect to the state lapse statute:

    (a) Does it apply to class gifts? If yes,
    (b) Does it apply to class members who died before the testator executed his will?
    (c) Does it apply to class members who predeceased the testator but were alive when his will was executed?

DISCUSSION

Summary

The life insurance proceeds should probably be distributed to Sam because a beneficiary designation cannot, in most states, be changed by will. The joint tenancy bank account should be distributed to Sam unless it is established that, in creating the joint tenancy, Testator intended to give Sam check-writing privileges instead of an ownership interest. In some states, evidence of such intention would be sufficient to void the joint tenancy. Sam's surviving child is clearly entitled to share in Testator's estate; whether Sam's deceased children also share depends on whether the state lapse statute applies to class gifts and, if so, whether it extends to class members who died before Testator's will was executed.

Point One: In most states, a life insurance beneficiary designation cannot be changed by
(10-20%)   will. Thus the insurance proceeds are probably payable to Sam.

In most jurisdictions, life insurance proceeds are payable to the beneficiary named in the beneficiary-designation form filed with the insurance company even if the insured names a different beneficiary in a later-executed will. This rule is typically justified as a matter of contract: as in this case, life insurance policies generally provide that policy proceeds will only be paid to a beneficiary named on an appropriate form filed with the insurance company; other possible methods of changing a beneficiary are thus viewed as being excluded by the insurance contract. *See generally Cook v. Equitable Life Assurance Society of the U.S.*, 428 N.E.2d 110 (Ind. 1981).

However, some courts have rejected the majority rule on the grounds that the requirement that a beneficiary change be evidenced by a form filed with the insurance company is for the exclusive benefit of the company. These courts permit an insured to change a beneficiary designation by will if his insurance company does not object. *See, e.g., Burkett v. Mott*, 733 P.2d 673 (Ariz. 1986). If State A has adopted this minority approach, the insurance proceeds would pass to Doris under the terms of Testator's will.

NOTE: An applicant need not describe both the majority and minority approaches to receive credit. The revocability of a life insurance beneficiary designation by will does not appear to be addressed by any state statute.

Point Two: The surviving tenant of a joint bank account is ordinarily entitled to the account
(30-40%)   balance on the death of the other tenant. Some states would distribute the account balance as part of the deceased tenant's probate estate if the evidence shows that the deceased tenant created the joint tenancy for his own convenience and had no intent to give the surviving tenant an ownership interest.

Ordinarily, a bank account in the name of "A and B" as joint tenants creates a right of survivorship. Upon the death of one tenant, the survivor takes the entire account balance. *See* UNIF. PROBATE CODE (UPC) § 6-212 (amended 2003).

Where a joint tenancy was created merely for a depositor's convenience, for example, to give the other co-tenant check-writing privileges, some courts will set aside the joint tenancy if the evidence shows that the depositor intended to convey only a power of attorney to write checks. The UPC has adopted this approach. *See* UPC § 6-212 cmt. Other courts invariably affirm a joint tenancy, relying on the parol evidence rule to exclude evidence of the depositor tenant's intentions. *See* William M. McGovern Jr. & Sheldon F. Kurtz, WILLS, TRUSTS, AND ESTATES § 6.3 (3d ed. 2004); *Bielecki v. Boissel*, 715 A.2d 571 (R.I. 1998). And even among courts that permit a joint tenancy to be set aside, some require clear and convincing evidence of the depositor tenant's intentions. *See Franklin v. Anna National Bank*, 488 N.E.2d 1117 (Ill. App. 1986).

In this case, there is no direct evidence that Testator intended to convey only check-writing privileges in Account #1. That Testator made all deposits and received all statements demonstrates nothing about his intentions, nor does the fact that Testator was concerned about his physical health. However, one might infer an intention to create a convenience account from Testator's belief that he could bequeath this asset by will. Thus, Sam would prevail in a state that disallows evidence of depositor intentions and in a state that requires clear and convincing evidence to overturn a joint tenancy designation; it is possible that Doris would prevail in a state that permits a joint tenancy designation to be overturned by a preponderance of the evidence.

A constructive trust theory has sometimes been utilized to award a joint tenancy bank account to the beneficiary named in the depositor tenant's will. Under a constructive trust approach, Sam would take the account but would hold the balance in the account in trust for Doris. However, the imposition of a constructive trust ordinarily requires evidence of misconduct, and there is no evidence of wrongdoing by Sam. *Id.*

<u>Point Three:</u> <u>The children of Ann and Bill can share in the residuary estate only if the shares</u>
(30-40%) <u>they would have taken had they survived Testator pass to their issue under the</u>
<u>governing lapse statute. This determination will depend on statutory interpretation.</u>

The State A lapse statute provides that, "if a beneficiary who is a descendant of the testator predeceases the testator, the beneficiary's surviving issue take the share the deceased beneficiary would have taken had the beneficiary survived." The statute is silent regarding its application to class gifts and, if it applies to class gifts, whether it also applies to persons who died before the execution of the will creating a class gift.

At common law, a gift to a class (such as a group of persons related to each other through a common ancestor) implied a survivorship condition, with the result that only those class members who survived the testator shared in the gift. Under the common law approach, only Sam's surviving child would take the balance of Testator's estate. Some states with lapse statutes that do not specify whether they apply to class gifts utilize the common law approach.

Most state lapse statutes, either expressly or by judicial construction, do apply to class gifts. In these states, Bill's child would take the share that Bill would have taken had Bill survived Testator because Bill was alive when Testator's will was executed. *See* McGovern & Kurtz, *supra* § 8.3 at 332. However, even when a lapse statute applies to class gifts, some states, by statute or case law, refuse to extend its reach to persons, like Ann, who predeceased both the testator and the execution of the testator's will. The theory behind such a limitation is that, because the testator would have known that such person was dead when the testator executed his or her will, the testator would not have intended to include either the deceased person or that person's issue in the class gift, unless the testator specifically made such a bequest in his will.

The 1990 UPC takes a different approach; anti-lapse protection is extended even to potential class members who died before the class gift was created. *See* UPC § 2-603(b)(2). The UPC approach is based on the view that testators would not typically want to exclude the family line of a deceased class member. Under this approach, the children of both Ann and Bill would share in Testator's residuary estate.

Decedent's Estates
(February 2006)
ANALYSIS

Legal Problems: (1) Is the lifetime gift of $60,000 to Grandchild 6 an advancement?

(2) Is Grandchild 1 barred from sharing in Dorothy's estate by a "slayer statute"?

(3) To whom should the probate estate be distributed and what is each person's share?

DISCUSSION

Summary

The transfer to Grandchild 6 is presumptively a gift, not an advancement. Grandchild 1 is not barred from sharing in the estate because Grandchild 1 did not feloniously take Dorothy's life. Thus, Dorothy's estate is distributable to her surviving grandchildren. The shares they take will depend on whether they take per stirpes or per capita under the applicable intestacy statute.

Point One: (30-40%)
There are potentially two reasons the gift to Grandchild 6 is not an advancement. First, the advancement doctrine is inapplicable when the decedent dies with a will. Second, under a typical advancement statute, lifetime gifts are not an advancement absent evidence that the transferor intended them as such.

The doctrine of advancements usually applies only to intestate succession. *See* William H. McGovern & Sheldon F. Kurtz, WILLS, TRUSTS AND ESTATES § 2.6 at 66 (2001). In states that follow this rule, the $60,000 gift to Grandchild 6 would be ignored when computing the "heirs" share of Dorothy's estate. However, there is some authority for the proposition that the doctrine of advancements would apply if, as here, a will leaves property to the testator's heirs. *Id.* Furthermore, here Dorothy has expressly directed an intestate-style distribution. Whether the $60,000 would be taken into account in determining Grandchild 6's share of Dorothy's estate would depend on the applicable advancement statute.

Under the common law, a lifetime transfer to an heir was presumptively treated as a down payment on the heir's intestate share. In most, if not all, states today, a lifetime transfer is presumed to be a gift and is ignored in computing the heir's intestate share unless there is evidence to show a contrary intent. *See generally* UNIF. PROBATE CODE § 2-109. Here, there is no evidence that Dorothy intended the $60,000 to be an advancement.

Point Two: (15-25%)
Grandchild 1 should not be barred from sharing in Dorothy's estate under the typical slayer statute because Grandchild 1 did not act with felonious intent.

Under the typical slayer statute, an heir or beneficiary is barred from taking from the decedent if the heir or beneficiary feloniously and intentionally killed the decedent. *See, e.g.,* UNIF. PROBATE CODE § 2-803(b). The typical slayer statute excludes accidental killings even if they amount to manslaughter. Here, Grandchild 1 acted both inadvertently and negligently and thus is not barred by the slayer statute.

[NOTE: If an applicant concluded that Grandchild 1 would be barred by the slayer statute, Grandchild 1's forfeited share of Dorothy's estate would be disposed of as if Grandchild 1 predeceased Dorothy. Here, that would mean that Grandchild 1's share would pass to Great-Grandchild, Grandchild 1's child.]

Point Three: (40-50%)
Assuming both Grandchild 1 and Grandchild 6 share in Dorothy's estate, all six grandchildren take equal shares if the estate is distributed to them per capita. If the estate is distributed per stirpes, the same six grandchildren receive the entire estate but in different amounts. Under either system, Great-Grandchild takes nothing.

Dorothy's will incorporates by reference the state intestacy scheme. Thus, the distribution of the estate is determined as if Dorothy died intestate. State laws differ regarding the distribution among issue where the decedent died intestate. Many states make the initial division of shares by computing the number of the decedent's children who had either survived the decedent or who left issue who survived. In such states, the initial division would be into thirds (per stirpes system). In many other states, including Uniform Probate Code states, the initial division is made by counting the number of heirs at the generational level at which there is at least one living member (per capita per generation system). Here, that would be six, since the first level at which there are surviving descendants of Dorothy is the grandchild level.

Taking the latter (Uniform Probate Code approach) first, since no advancement was made to Grandchild 6 (*see* Point One) that grandchild shares in the estate. In addition, Grandchild 1 is not barred by the typical "slayer statute" because he did not intentionally take Dorothy's life. (*See* Point Two.) Thus, under the latter approach, all six grandchildren take equal $20,000 shares of Dorothy's estate.

In those states that initially divide the estate into thirds, Dorothy's estate would be divided into three $40,000 shares. Abel's two children would be entitled to split 1/3 of the estate, taking $20,000 each. Each of Brandon's three children would be entitled to 1/3 of a $40,000 share and Carrie's $40,000 share would pass entirely to Grandchild 6. Great-grandchild (the child of Grandchild 1) takes nothing because Grandchild 1 is entitled to take a share of Dorothy's estate and in all states a remote descendant is excluded from inheriting when that descendant's ancestor survives.

[NOTE: The foregoing discussion assumes that no advancement was made to Grandchild 6 and that Grandchild 1 was not barred by a slayer statute. If an applicant made other assumptions, the applicant should be expected to have a different analysis to Point Three.

Decedent's Estates
(July 2006)

ANALYSIS

Legal Problems: (1)   Did Husband and Wife have a contractual will such that Child is entitled to receive the portion of Wife's estate bequeathed to Child under that joint will?

                (2)   Does either the doctrine of facts of independent significance, or the rule that wills "speak at the time of death," apply to save the bequest in the 1995 will to the pastor?

                (3)   Is Robin entitled to the $1,000 bequest notwithstanding that her status as a beneficiary was evidenced by an unattested writing?

DISCUSSION
Summary

Wife's estate should be distributed as follows: $1,000 to Ted, pastor of First Avenue Church, and the residue to Child. Child is a contract creditor of the Wife's estate because Wife and Husband signed a contractual will in 1995. Robin is entitled to nothing because the attempted bequest to her was evidenced by an unattested writing.

John, who would have been entitled to the bulk of Wife's estate under the 2002 will, takes nothing because Wife's entire estate is exhausted by the claims of Ted and Child. John would take from Wife's estate only if the 1995 will was not contractual and the 2002 will could not be successfully contested.

Point One (30-40%)
The joint will executed by Husband and Wife constituted their contract that the survivor would not change their joint plan for distribution of their assets. As a result, Ted and Child can enforce the provisions of the 1995 will without contesting the 2002 will.

Although the existence of a joint will does not by itself establish the existence of a contract between the two testators to dispose of their property in a certain way, a will contract is created when the joint will includes material provisions of the contract or has language in it that refers to a contract between the testators. UNIF. PROBATE CODE § 2-514. Here, the language of the joint will "each of us agrees" should be more than sufficient to establish the existence of a contract between Husband and Wife to dispose of the property in a certain way.

The contract became irrevocable upon the death of Husband. *See* 1 William J. Bowe & Douglas W. Parker, PAGE ON THE LAW OF WILLS § 10.2 (1960) [hereinafter "PAGE ON WILLS"] ("On the death of one party, leaving in effect a will which contains the provisions prescribed by the contract, the transaction is said to become an irrevocable contract as to the survivor."); *see also Estate of Wiggins*, 360 N.Y.S.2d 129 (App. Div. 1974). Because the terms of the contract mandated that Wife, the survivor, distribute all of "her property" in accordance with the joint plan of distribution, Wife was obligated to distribute not only the couple's joint property, but also the property she acquired after Husband's death, in accordance with the will contract as reflected in the 1995 joint will.

The will contract does not by itself invalidate Wife's 2002 will. Instead, the will contract makes the beneficiaries under the joint will contract creditors of Wife's estate. *See* 1 PAGE ON WILLS § 10.3. Here, the contract required distribution of the entire estate to the beneficiaries of the joint will. As a result, although the 2002 will would properly be admitted to probate, the beneficiaries under that will would take nothing; rather, the entire estate would be paid to the creditors, Child and Ted (*see* Point Two), under the prior will.

If applicants conclude that the phrase "each of us agrees" does not sufficiently state contractual intent, then the 1995 will would not be contractual and would be revoked by the 2002 will to the extent they were inconsistent. Therefore, Ted would take $1,000. (*See* Point Two.) Child would take only $100,000 under the 2002 will and John would take the residue.

Point Two (20-30%)
Under either the doctrine of facts of independent significance, or the general rule of construction that wills "speak at the time of death," Ted, the current pastor of First Avenue Church, takes $1,000.

In general, a testator must identify beneficiaries in the will itself; a testator may not change will beneficiaries without testamentary formalities. The doctrine of facts of independent significance, however, gives effect to a will provision that disposes of property "by reference to acts and events that have significance apart from their effect upon the dispositions made by the will." UNIF. PROBATE CODE § 2-512; *see also* 2 PAGE ON WILLS § 19.34. The principle behind the doctrine is that the possibility of undue influence or fraud is reduced when the change in beneficiary has significance apart from the change in the testator's will. Hence, since the church was unlikely to choose its pastor in order to assure that the pastor chosen would inherit $1,000 from the estate of Husband and Wife, that fact, the pastor's identity, has significance apart from the bequest. Hence, the doctrine would give effect to the $1,000 bequest to the then-current pastor, which was Ted, not George.

By contrast, the memorandum in the safe deposit box directing that $1,000 be distributed to Robin cannot be given effect under this doctrine because that memorandum had no purpose independent of an attempt to make a bequest. *See* 2 PAGE ON WILLS § 19.34 at 122; *see also* Point Three.

The bequest to the pastor also is effective under the general rule of construction that a will "speaks" as of the time of death and at that time Ted is the only person qualifying for the bequest to the pastor of the First Avenue Church.

[NOTE: Applicants could reach the same result using the so-called "plain meaning" rule. Under this rule, Ted takes because the words in the will are unambiguous that the bequest passes to the church pastor who survives Wife.]

Point Three (20-30%)
The $1,000 bequest to Robin is invalid because it is not evidenced by a testamentary instrument.

While a will may incorporate an attempted bequest in a document not executed with the formalities required of a will, here the attempted bequest to Robin in such a document is invalid because the incorporation by reference doctrine requires that the document to be incorporated be in existence at the time the will was signed. Here the document to be incorporated was executed after both the 1995 and the 2002 wills were executed.

Furthermore, even if the jurisdiction had adopted a statute like Unif. Probate Code § 2-513, the bequest would still be invalid. That statute permits tangible personal property to be disposed of in accordance with the terms of an unattested memorandum without regard to when it was executed. However, § 2-513 applies only to tangibles; here, Wife attempted to bequeath Robin money, which is not a tangible.

Lastly, this bequest cannot be sustained under the doctrine of independent significance because the memorandum's only significance was to make a testamentary gift.

[NOTE: Applicants who assume that the memorandum is in Wife's handwriting and that holographic works are valid under state law could conclude that the $1,000 gift to Robin was valid. However, no facts state that the memorandum was in Wife's handwriting.]

Decedent's Estates
(February 2007)

ANALYSIS

Legal Problems: (1)   How many shares of XYZ Company stock is Brother entitled to claim?

(2)   What is the effect of Sister's disclaimer?

(3)   Does the inter vivos gift of $5,000 satisfy the bequest to Uncle?

(4)   Given that there are insufficient assets to carry out all of Testator's directions, how should the bequests abate?

DISCUSSION

Summary

Sister's disclaimer effectively deletes her bequest from the will. The treatment of the remaining bequests turns on their classification. The specific bequest to Brother entitles him to 100 shares under the common law view and 106 shares under the Uniform Probate Code and like statutes. The general bequest to Uncle is not satisfied by the inter vivos gift. The general bequest to Uncle and the general bequest to Cousin will abate pro rata because the estate assets are insufficient to pay their $15,000 aggregate general legacies. There are insufficient assets to satisfy the residuary bequest to Polytech. If Brother is not entitled to the six additional shares, two of them go to Uncle and four of them to Cousin in payment of their general legacies.

Point One (20-30%)

Whether Brother is entitled to 100 or 106 shares of XYZ stock depends on whether state law allocates stock dividends to a specific legatee.

The bequest to Brother of "my 100 shares" is a specific bequest. States following the **common law** hold that a stock dividend, like a cash dividend, is a property interest distinct from stock given by specific bequest. In these states, Brother is entitled only to 100 shares of XYZ stock. *See* Note, *Rights to Stock Accretions Which Occur Prior to Testator's Death,* 36 ALB. L. REV. 182, 188-192 (1971); Annotation, *Change in Stock or Corporate Structure, or Split or Substitution of Stock of Corporation, as Affecting Bequest of Stock,* 46 A.L.R.3d 7 §§ 8, 9 (1972).

In states that have adopted Uniform Probate Code § 2-605 or a like statute, a stock dividend is treated like a stock split instead of a cash dividend. Under this approach, which aims to maintain the legatee's percentage of ownership in the corporation, Brother is entitled to all 106 shares.

Point Two (20-30%)

The effect of Sister's disclaimer is that the property passes as if Sister had failed to survive Testator.

At common law and under the Uniform Probate Code, Sister's disclaimer causes Testator's property to pass as if Sister had failed to survive Testator. *See* UNIF. PROBATE CODE § 2-1106 (current version, incorporating the 1999 Uniform Disclaimer of Property Interests Act); UNIF. PROBATE CODE § 2-801 (earlier versions). Because Sister has no descendants who survive Testator, the state's anti-lapse statute will not be applicable to the bequest to Sister. The $3,000 bequest to Sister lapses.

Point Three (20-30%)

The inter vivos gift of $5,000 does not satisfy the bequest to Uncle.

The bequest of $5,000 to Uncle is a general pecuniary bequest. Under the common law, an inter vivos gift made after a will's execution can satisfy a general bequest, but only if the testator so intends. Here, there is no evidence of such intention. Moreover, no presumption of such intention exists where, as here, the testator does not stand in loco parentis to the legatee. *See* THOMAS E. ATKINSON, HANDBOOK OF THE LAW OF WILLS § 133 (2d ed. 1953). Uniform Probate Code § 2-609 produces the same result because none of the statutory bases for satisfaction of a bequest by inter vivos gift have been met: the will does not provide for deduction of the gift, and neither the testator nor the legatee has declared in a contemporaneous writing that the gift is in satisfaction of the bequest.

Point Four (20-30%)
The bequests abate according to their classifications, hence in the following order: first the residuary gift to Polytech, then the general gifts to Uncle and Cousin, pro rata, and last, the specific gift to Brother.

Under both the common law and the Uniform Probate Code, the shares of distributees abate in the following order: (1) property not disposed of in the will, (2) residuary gifts, (3) general gifts, and (4) specific gifts. Abatement within each category is pro rata. *See* UNIF. PROBATE CODE § 3-902; WILLIAM M. MCGOVERN JR. & SHELDON F. KURTZ, WILLS, TRUSTS, AND ESTATES § 8.2 (3d ed. 2004). Thus, the residuary gift to Polytech abates first; Polytech receives nothing. The general gifts to Uncle and Cousin abate next and pro rata, meaning that the 1-to-2 ratio of Uncle-to-Cousin is maintained. Thus, Uncle and Cousin receive $3,000 and $6,000, respectively, plus (under the common law but not under the Uniform Probate Code) two and four shares, respectively, of XYZ Company stock. Finally, Brother receives the XYZ Company stock to which he is entitled: 100 shares under the common law view and 106 shares under the Uniform Probate Code and like statutes.

Decedent's Estates
(February 2008)

ANALYSIS

Legal Problems: (1)   Did Harriet unduly influence Testator to make her a beneficiary under his will?

          (2)   If Harriet unduly influenced Testator, is his will partially or entirely invalid?

          (3)   To whom should Testator's estate be distributed if:
(a) the will is entirely invalid?
(b) the will is partially invalid?

DISCUSSION

Summary

Testator's will is invalid, in whole or in part, if it was the product of undue influence. Here, the facts are not conclusive, but may support an undue influence finding. If the will is valid, the estate will pass in equal shares to Harriet and Doris.

If the bequest to Harriet was the product of undue influence, the court may invalidate the entire will or only Harriet's bequest. If the entire will is invalidated, the estate would pass under the laws of intestate succession: Doris, Sam, and Fred, who would take as the representative of his deceased parent, Bob, would take equal 1/3 shares.

If only the bequest to Harriet is invalidated, one-half of the estate would pass to Doris under the will and the remaining half would pass either to Doris as the remaining residuary legatee or, if the common law "no residue of a residue" rule is applied, to Doris, Sam, and Fred under the laws of intestate succession. In that case, Doris would take 2/3 of the estate, and Sam and Fred would each take 1/6.

Point One (35–45%)

The court may find that Testator's will, in whole or in part, was the product of Harriet's undue influence.

If a will or portion of a will is the product of undue influence, it may be set aside. Undue influence occurs when the "wrongdoer exerted such influence over the [testator] that it overcame the [testator's] free will and caused the [testator] to make a donative transfer that the [testator] would not otherwise have made." RESTATEMENT (THIRD) OF PROPERTY (WILLS AND OTHER DONATIVE TRANSFERS) § 8.3(b) (2003). The burden of establishing undue influence is on the will contestant, who must show that: (1) the testator was susceptible to undue influence, (2) the alleged wrongdoer had the opportunity to exert undue influence upon the testator, (3) the alleged wrongdoer had a disposition to exert undue influence, and (4) the will appears to be the product of undue influence. *Id.* at cmt. e. Undue influence may be established by circumstantial evidence. *See generally Estate of Kamesar*, 259 N.W.2d 733, 737–38 (Wis. 1977).

The facts of this case, if proven at trial, would certainly establish that Harriet had opportunity and a disposition to influence Testator. Harriet lived in Testator's home, criticized and limited his contacts with Doris, a natural object of Testator's bounty, and urged him repeatedly to make a will in her favor. The will contestant should also be able to show that the bequest to Harriet was linked to her attempts to influence the will, as Testator executed the will only after Harriet threatened to quit and at a time when he had become increasingly dependent upon her; Testator also bequeathed to Harriet, an employee who was not the natural object of his bounty, one-half of his probate estate.

The facts do not so clearly establish Testator's susceptibility to undue influence. On the one hand, Testator was increasingly ill and dependent on Harriet. He also agreed to see an attorney after Harriet threatened him. On the other hand, Testator maintained control over his financial affairs until his death, continued to play an active role as trustee of various nonprofits, refused to see the attorney Harriet suggested, and communicated his dispositional plan to his own attorney through handwritten instructions.

Because the evidence is inconclusive, the outcome might depend on who bears the burden of proof. Normally, this rests on the party challenging the will. However, in many jurisdictions, a presumption of undue influence arises when there is a confidential relationship between the testator and the alleged influencer and suspicious circumstances surround the drafting of the will. Most of the cases involving confidential relationships involve attorneys and close relatives; it is not clear that a confidential relationship between Testator and Harriet could be established in this case. But if it were, then the burden of proof on the issue of undue influence would shift to Harriet.

[NOTE TO GRADERS: Applicants' conclusions are less important than their knowledge of the relevant legal principles and ability to apply those principles to the facts.

NOTE TO GRADERS: Some applicants may also discuss testamentary capacity and duress. The facts strongly support a finding of testamentary capacity because Testator continued to manage his financial affairs and appeared to know his family and the disposition he made of his assets. Some applicants may confuse "duress" with "undue influence"; others discuss them separately, but duress (a greater intrusion into a testator's mind) is not supported on these facts.]

Point Two (10–20%)

If the court finds that the bequest to Harriet was the product of undue influence, it may invalidate the entire will or only the bequest to Harriet.

A finding of undue influence may lead a court to invalidate the entire will or only a portion of it. Most courts will invalidate only those portions that are "infected" by undue influence. *See*

Williams v. Crickman, 405 N.E.2d 799 (Ill. 1980). Clearly, if there was undue influence, it affected the bequest to Harriet and that bequest should be invalidated.

It is less clear whether the entire will was infected by Harriet's undue influence. Given his estrangement from Sam, it is possible that Testator would have left his entire estate to Doris had he not left a one-half share to Harriet. However, it is also possible that Testator might have left a share of the estate to his grandchild, Fred; the facts do not show that Testator was estranged from either Fred or Fred's deceased parent, Bob. Testator might also have left a share to Sam's child, Ella, or even to Sam himself. Indeed, Testator might not have executed a will at all. Given this uncertainty, the court might invalidate the entire will or only the bequest to Harriet.

Point Three(a) (10–20%)
If the entire will is invalidated, Testator's estate would pass to his heirs, Doris, Sam, and Fred.

Assuming that the court invalidates the entire will as the product of undue influence, Testator's estate will be distributed to his heirs. In every jurisdiction, Testator's heirs would be his two surviving children, Doris and Sam, and his grandchild, Fred, who takes as the representative of Testator's deceased child, Bob. Doris's child, Ella, would not take as an heir because Doris survived Testator and there is no basis for Ella to represent her mother. *See* UNIF. PROB. CODE §§ 2-101, 2-106.

Point Three(b) (15–25%)
If the bequest to Harriet alone is invalidated, Harriet's one-half share of the estate would either pass to Doris in its entirety or be distributed equally to Doris, Sam, and Fred, depending on whether the jurisdiction applies the common law "no residue of a residue" rule.

When a residuary bequest fails, the question arises as to whether the invalidated share passes to the testator's heirs or to the remaining residuary legatee(s). Under the common law "no residue of a residue" rule, the invalid share passes to the testator's heirs. *See* WILLIAM M. MCGOVERN & SHELDON F. KURTZ, WILLS, TRUSTS AND ESTATES 335 n. 73 (3d ed. 2004). The theory behind this approach is that, if the invalid share were to pass to the remaining residuary legatee, it would increase her share without an executed bequest and thus violate the policies that underlie typical statutory execution requirements. Under the common law approach, Doris would take one-half of the estate under the will, and the remaining half would be distributed in equal shares to Doris, Sam, and Fred under the law of intestate succession. (*See* Point Three(a) above.)

Many courts today reject the common law rule, theorizing that the testator's execution of a will evidences an intention to benefit the legatees named in the will to the exclusion of heirs, particularly would-be heirs not mentioned in the will. This "residue of a residue" approach has been adopted in Uniform Probate Code § 2-604. Under this approach, Harriet's invalid share would go to Doris, the only other residuary legatee. Neither Sam nor Fred would take a share of Testator's estate.

[NOTE TO GRADERS: Applicants who are answering according to local law may not discuss both options if their jurisdiction has a clear rule that addresses this issue.]

**Decedent's Estates
(February 2009)**

ANALYSIS

(Decedents' Estates II.I.1., 2., 3. & 7.)

Legal Problems: (1)   Does a bequest of a specific number of shares of stock owned by Testator when the will was executed include other shares of the same stock acquired after the will was executed as a result of a stock dividend?

        (2)   Does a bequest of a specifically described home include another home acquired with the proceeds from the sale of the specifically described home?

        (3)   Does a bequest of a generically described automobile adeem when the automobile owned when the will was executed is traded for another automobile?

        (4)   Does Donna's disclaimer of the $10,000 bequest result in that bequest passing to her daughter or to the residuary legatee?

DISCUSSION

Summary

In most jurisdictions today, Andy would be entitled to all 200 shares of XYZ stock. Ben might be entitled to the condo as replacement property. Carrie would be entitled to the blue automobile. The $10,000 bequest to Donna would fail as a result of her disclaimer and would pass to Ed, as the residuary legatee. However, in jurisdictions that do not follow the modern approach, Andy would only be entitled to 100 shares of the XYZ stock and Ben would not be entitled to the condo because that request adeemed. Any property not passing to Andy, Ben, or Carrie passes to Ed, the residuary legatee.

Point One (20–30%)
Andy is entitled to the 200 shares of XYZ stock Testator owned at the time of death unless the jurisdiction does not follow the modern approach.

Historically, a bequest of stock owned by a testator when the testator's will was signed excluded subsequently acquired shares of the same stock acquired by the testator as the result of a stock dividend. *See, e.g., Hicks v. Kerr*, 104 A. 426 (Md. 1918). The rule was justified on the ground that, if the testator had wanted the legatee to take the later-acquired shares, the testator could have changed the will to take those additionally acquired shares into account. A contrary rule applied to shares acquired as a result of a stock split. *See, e.g., Bostwick v. Hurstel*, 304 N.E.2d 186 (Mass. 1973).

Today, stock dividends are typically treated like stock splits because, in each case, nothing of value has been distributed by the corporation to the shareholder. Additional shares of the same company, when acquired by stock split or stock dividend, are, from the shareholder's economic perspective, merely a change in form, not substance. *See* UNIF. PROBATE CODE (UPC) § 2-605 (a devise of stock owned by the testator when the will is executed includes such additional stock owned by the testator at death, whether acquired by a stock split or a stock dividend). Under the UPC or a like statute, Andy would be entitled to all 200 shares of XYZ stock owned by Testator at her death.

Point Two (20–30%)
In most states, the bequest of the home to Ben adeems. However, in some states Ben would be entitled to the substitute home.

Under common law, an ademption occurs when the subject matter of specific devise is not found in the probate estate at the time of the testator's death. *See* WILLIAM M. MCGOVERN & SHELDON F. KURTZ, WILLS, TRUSTS AND ESTATES 315–16 (3d ed. 2004). Here, Testator specifically bequeathed to Ben Testator's home located at 4 Cypress Garden. Since Testator did not own that home when she died, the bequest adeems. *Id.* at 316. As a result, the condo passes to Ed, the residuary legatee.

Under UPC § 2-606(a)(5) or a like statute, however, Ben would be entitled to Testator's condominium. This section provides that the devisee of specifically devised real estate is entitled to any "real property . . . owned by the testator at death which the testator acquired as a replacement for specifically devised real property . . . ." The facts support the conclusion that Testator purchased the condominium as a replacement home for the home that was specifically devised to Ben.

The "replacement property" concept appears to have little support in case law. However, RESTATEMENT (THIRD) OF PROPERTY (WILLS AND OTHER DONATIVE TRANSFERS) § 5.2, cmt. d urges that the provision of the UPC should be applied by courts in those cases "in which the result appears to be consistent with the testator's intent."

Point Three (20–30%)
Carrie is entitled to the blue automobile.

Because of the time-honored rule of construction that a will "speaks" at the time of death, a bequest of generically described property (e.g., my automobile) applies to property that meets the generic description at the testator's death. *See generally* MCGOVERN & KURTZ, *supra*, at 316; RESTATEMENT (THIRD) OF PROPERTY (WILLS AND OTHER DONATIVE TRANSFERS) § 5.2, cmt. e. Thus, the bequest of the automobile is unlike the bequest of the home in that the latter, but not the former, is described in a non-generic manner and thus is subject to the rules of ademption.

[NOTE: At first blush an examinee might think that the bequest of the automobile raises an ademption problem because the automobile owned when the will was signed (the white automobile) was not the same as the automobile owned when Testator died (the blue automobile). However, this is not an ademption problem because Testator did not refer to a specific automobile when executing her will. Also, an examinee might analyze this under the doctrine of independent significance and get to the same result.]

Point Four (20–30%)
<u>The $10,000 bequest to Donna fails because of Donna's disclaimer and because Donna is not the type of legatee typically described in an anti-lapse statute. The bequest passes to Ed, the residuary legatee.</u>

If Donna had not disclaimed the $10,000 legacy, it would have passed to her under the provisions of Testator's will. However, she did disclaim the bequest. Under the typical disclaimer statute, if a legatee disclaims a general bequest, the bequest passes as if the disclaimant had predeceased the testator. *See generally* UPC §§ 2-1106, 2-901(d).

When a disclaimant is deemed to have predeceased the testator, the question arises whether the bequest to that disclaimant passes to her issue. The answer here depends upon the application of the anti-lapse statute. The typical anti-lapse statute would not apply here because Donna was a friend, not a relative, of Testator. *See generally* UPC § 2-603 (anti-lapse statute applicable to legatee who was a grandparent or issue of grandparent of the testator). If the anti-lapse statute is inapplicable, then the $10,000 passes to Ed as the residuary legatee.

[NOTE: If the anti-lapse statute did apply, as it might in a distinct minority of states, then the bequest to Donna would pass to Donna's daughter. However, given how few states have adopted this view, an examinee who merely said that Donna's disclaimed bequest passed to her issue should receive little or no credit unless that is the rule in the applicant's state.]

Decedent's Estates
(July 2009)

ANALYSIS

Legal Problems: (1)   Is Testator's will invalid because it was the product of undue influence?

    (2)   Is Testator's will invalid because it was induced by fraud?

    (3)   If Testator's will is valid, did Friend effectively exercise her general power of appointment over trust assets with the general residuary clause in her will?

    (4)   If Testator's will is invalid, who are Testator's heirs?

DISCUSSION

Summary

If a will was procured through undue influence or induced by fraud, it is invalid. In this case, the facts, if proven at trial, would not establish undue influence but would establish that Testator's will was induced by fraud in the execution. If the will is valid, under the majority view, Testator's estate will probably pass to Charity following Friend's death because Friend did not effectively exercise her power of appointment by the general residuary clause in her will. If Testator's will is invalid, his estate passes to Niece if the intestacy statute utilizes the parentelic method of determining heirship and to both Niece and Uncle if the statute utilizes the civil law consanguinity method. If only the general power of Friend is set aside as a product of either undue influence or fraud but the court rules that the remaining provisions of Testator's will are valid, then Charity takes.

Point One (20–30%)
The facts do not establish that Testator's will is invalid as the product of undue influence.

A will is invalid if it was executed as the result of undue influence. Undue influence occurs when the "wrongdoer exerted such influence over the [testator] that it overcame the [testator's] free will and caused the [testator] to make a donative transfer that the [testator] would not otherwise have made." RESTATEMENT (THIRD) OF PROPERTY (WILLS AND OTHER DONATIVE TRANSFERS) § 8.3(b).

The burden of establishing undue influence is on the will contestant, who must show that (1) the testator was susceptible to undue influence, (2) the alleged influencer had the opportunity to exert undue influence upon the testator, (3) the alleged influencer had a disposition to exert undue influence, and (4) the will appears to be the product of undue influence. *See id.* at cmt. e. *See also Estate of Kamesar*, 259 N.W.2d 733, 737–38 (Wis. 1977).

In this case, there are facts showing that Friend had both the opportunity and the disposition to exert undue influence. Friend and Testator were intimates over a two-year period. Friend showered Testator with affection. Friend told Brother that she would "be generous" to him if Testator left her everything, suggesting her desire to influence Testator's will.

It is less clear that Testator was susceptible to undue influence. Susceptibility is typically based on "age, personality, physical and mental health, and ability to handle business affairs." *Kamesar*, 259 N.W.2d at 738. Testator was 70 years old and a successful business executive. There is no evidence that he was in poor physical or mental health. On the other hand, Testator does seem to have been influenced by Friend's demonstrations of affection, interest, and commitment.

The more important weakness in a will contest based on undue influence is the fact that neither Friend nor Brother attempted to persuade Testator to give Friend a general power of appointment or bequeath other assets to her, nor did they attempt to dissuade Testator from making bequests to others or interfere with his relationships. Instead, Brother used deception to achieve Friend's goal of obtaining control of Testator's assets. While this deception is important to a claim of fraud (*see* Point Two), it does not fit the usual pattern of undue influence claims.

Point Two (20–30%)
Because the facts establish that Testator's will was induced by fraud in the execution, it is invalid in whole or in part.

A will or provision in a will procured by fraud is invalid. Fraud occurs when a testator is deceived by a misrepresentation and is thereby led to execute a will that the testator would not otherwise have made. Most courts additionally require a finding that the misrepresentation was made with the intent to deceive the testator and for the purpose of influencing the testamentary disposition. *See* JESSE DUKEMINIER & STANLEY M. JOHANSON, WILLS, TRUSTS, AND ESTATES 213 (6th ed. 2000). Fraud in the inducement occurs when a person misrepresents facts—for example, whether a proposed beneficiary is alive. Fraud in the execution occurs when a person misrepresents the character or contents of the instrument signed by the testator. *Id.* at 214–15.

The facts of this case support a finding of fraud in the execution. Testator told Brother that he wanted to leave the trust remainder to Charity. Brother told Testator that the will he had drafted was in accordance with Testator's instructions. It was not, because the will gave Friend a general power of appointment over trust assets; she could appoint those assets to herself and deprive Charity of the remainder. Because Friend told Brother that she wanted the will to leave her "everything," the evidence supports a finding that Brother intended to deceive Testator. If the will contestant succeeds in establishing these facts at trial, the court should invalidate the will.

If the court finds that the will was tainted by fraud or undue influence, it may invalidate the entire will or only those portions "infected" by the fraud or undue influence. *See Williams v. Crickman*, 405 N.E.2d 799 (Ill. 1980). As there are no facts to suggest that Friend or Brother played a role in the selection of Charity as taker in default, a court might invalidate the general power alone, leaving Charity as the residuary taker.

Point Three (20–30%)
If Testator's entire will is valid, whether Charity or Sister takes Testator's estate depends on whether Friend effectively exercised her general power of appointment. Under the majority view, a residuary clause in a will that makes no reference to the power is an ineffective exercise.

If fraud cannot be proven and Testator's entire will is valid, Friend's lifetime interest in the trust and general power of appointment would be valid also. Whether Charity or Sister takes the trust principal depends on whether Friend, who survived Testator, effectively exercised her general power.

Whether a power is effectively exercised depends on the donee's intent and any formalities mandated by the donor. *See* RESTATEMENT (SECOND) OF PROPERTY (DONATIVE TRANSFERS) § 17.1. In this case, the donor required no formalities. However, since the donee's (i.e., Friend's) will does not specifically refer to the power, it is unclear whether she intended to exercise her general power. Under the majority approach, also followed by the Restatement of Property, a residuary article in a donee's will that makes no reference to a power of appointment is not an effective exercise of a general power. *See id.* § 17.3. Under this approach, Charity, the taker in default of appointment, would take Testator's estate because Friend did not effectively exercise the power of appointment. Under the minority view, a general residuary clause does effectively exercise a power of appointment. If this approach is followed, Sister would take Testator's estate.

[NOTE: Friend survived Testator by a week; thus, under the Uniform Probate Code and the Simultaneous Death Act, she survived Testator because she survived him by 120 hours. If the state has the old version of the Uniform Simultaneous Death Act, Friend might be deemed to have predeceased Testator if they are viewed as having died in a common accident or disaster. In such a case, Charity takes as well.]

Point Four (15–25%)
If Testator's entire will is invalid, Testator's entire estate would pass to Niece under the parentelic method of determining heirship, but it would pass equally to Niece and Uncle under intestacy schemes governed by the civil law consanguinity method.

If the court finds that Testator's entire will is the product of fraud, his estate will be distributed based on state rules of intestate succession. Had the accident taken place after Testator and Friend were married, Friend would have taken Testator's entire estate. But given that the wedding had not yet taken place, no state grants Friend a share of Testator's assets.

Under the so-called parentelic method of determining heirship employed in the Uniform Probate Code and most state intestacy rules, the issue of an intestate's parents take to the exclusion of any issue of the intestate's grandparents. Niece is a grandchild of Testator's parents; Uncle is a child of Testator's grandparents. Thus, Niece takes to the exclusion of Uncle. *See* UNIF. PROBATE CODE § 2-103. Under the civil law consanguinity method employed in a minority of jurisdictions, Niece and Uncle would share equally because both of them are in the third degree of consanguinity to Testator.

[NOTE: An applicant might argue that only a portion of the will, the power of appointment, is invalid due to fraud. In such a case, the power would be excised from the will and upon Friend's death the trust assets would pass to Charity.]

Decedent's Estates
(July 2010)

Legal Problems: (1)   Did Testator execute a valid will when he did not sign the only page containing bequests, but all three pages of the will were physically present at the time he signed the last page and Testator intended them to be his will?

                         (2)   Was Testator's handwritten codicil valid?

                         (3)   Did Testator revoke the bequest to Sister by striking out the clause in his will giving her $20,000?

                         (4)   Does Testator's gift to "children" include adopted children and nonmarital children?

                         (5)   May a court reform Testator's will when Testator's likely intention conflicts with the will as drafted?

DISCUSSION

Summary

Under the doctrine of integration, all pages of a will that are together when the last page is signed and witnessed are deemed to have been validly executed. Thus, Testator's will is valid. Testator's handwritten codicil is invalid because it was neither signed by Testator nor witnessed. However, although crossing out a portion of a will (here, the bequest to Sister) would normally revoke that bequest under this state's law, because of the doctrine of dependent relative revocation, Testator's bequest to Sister was not revoked because it appears that Testator struck out this bequest on the mistaken assumption that the handwritten codicil was valid. In all states, a gift to children includes adopted and marital children. In most states, a gift to children would include a nonmarital child if clear and convincing evidence of paternity was available. Although Testator appears to have intended to benefit only some of his children, Abby and Bruce, the will gives the residuary estate to all of Testator's "children," and most courts do not allow the admission of extrinsic evidence to alter the plain meaning of a will. Thus, Sister would receive $20,000 from Testator's estate and the balance would likely be distributed, in equal shares, to Abby, Bruce, Carl, and Don, if Don can establish Testator's paternity.

If the will was not validly executed Testator would have died intestate and his estate would be distributed only to his heirs. His heirs would be Abby, Bruce, and Carl in all states and, depending upon the state rules relating to proof of paternity, possibly Don.

Point One (25%)

Because all pages of Testator's will were present at the same time that Testator signed the last page of his will and the pages were intended by Testator to be his will, the will is valid.

Under the relevant state statute, a will, to be valid, must be signed by the testator and witnessed by two witnesses. Like all wills statutes, the statute applicable here does not require that the pages of the will be stapled or that the testator and witnesses sign each page.

Under the doctrine of integration, a multi-page will is valid even if only the last page is executed as long as the proponent of the will can establish that all pages were physically present and together when the testator and witnesses signed the last page of the will and that each page was intended by the testator to be part of his will. *See* THOMPSON ON WILLS § 124 (3d ed. 1947); 2 PAGE ON THE LAW OF WILLS §§ 19.10, 19.11 (2003). Here, all three pages of the will were present and together when Testator signed the will, and Testator intended the document to be his will. The proponent of the will may also rely upon a presumption that all pages of the will were present and together when the last page was signed if the pages, when read together, set out an orderly dispositional plan. *See* THOMPSON, *supra*, § 105; Comment, *Wills: Integration and Incorporation by Reference*, 4 BAYLOR L. REV. 211 (1952); Comment, *Wills—Integration*, 50 MICH. L. REV. 915 (1952). Here, page 1 of the will contained a bequest consistent with Testator's instructions to the attorney, and this page was followed by other pages containing matters commonly included in wills.

In sum, the will was executed properly and is valid.

Point Two (15%)
Testator's handwritten codicil to the will is invalid because state law requires all testamentary provisions to be signed by the testator and witnessed by two attesting witnesses.

Under state law, all testamentary provisions, to be valid, must be signed by the testator and witnessed by two attesting witnesses. Here, Testator attempted to change the bequest to Sister with a handwritten, unsigned, and unwitnessed writing. This provision is ineffective under state law.

Point Three (30%)
Notwithstanding the fact that Testator crossed out the bequest to Sister, the bequest is not revoked. Under the doctrine of dependent relative revocation, a revocation based on a mistaken assumption of law or fact (here, the validity of the handwritten bequest) is not given effect if it appears that the testator would not have revoked his will or some portion thereof had he known the truth.

Testator crossed out the bequest to Sister with the intention of substituting for it a larger bequest. This alternative bequest was invalid because it was neither witnessed nor signed by Testator. (*See* Point Two.)

Under the doctrine of dependent relative revocation, if a testator revokes a will or bequest based on a mistaken assumption of law or fact, the revocation is ineffective if it appears that the testator would not have revoked the bequest had he had accurate information. Here, Testator's cancellation of the bequest to Sister was motivated by a desire to give Sister *more* money. Had Testator known that the alternative larger bequest would be invalid, he would not have wanted to cancel the lesser bequest to Sister, leaving her with nothing at all. Thus, under the doctrine of dependent relative revocation, the revocation of the bequest to Sister is ignored and she is entitled to the $20,000. *See* WILLIAM M. MCGOVERN & SHELDON F. KURTZ, 242–43 (3d ed. 2004).

Point Four (25%)
The bequest to "my children" would include Testator's two biological children born during marriage and his adopted stepchild. It is unclear whether it would include Testator's nonmarital child.

State laws generally provide that the word "children" in a will should be interpreted consistently with the definition of the word "children" used in determining rights to intestate succession. *See, e.g.*, UNIF. PROBATE CODE § 2-705.

Biological children born to a married couple and adopted children are included within the category of children entitled to take through intestate succession. Thus, Abby, Bruce, and Carl are all included in Testator's bequest to his "children." *See* MCGOVERN & KURTZ, *supra*, at 100–04.

In all states, a nonmarital child (here, Don) is included within a bequest to children only if paternity is established under the relevant statute. In most states, paternity for purposes of intestate succession may be established by evidence of subsequent marriage of the parents, by acknowledgment by the father, by an adjudication of paternity during the life of the father, or by other clear and convincing evidence. *See* JESSE DUKEMINIER & STANLEY M. JOHANSON, WILLS, TRUSTS, AND ESTATES 115 (6th ed. 2000). It is unclear whether Testator's paternity of Don was adjudicated or acknowledged during Testator's lifetime; it is also unclear whether there is clear and convincing evidence of Testator's paternity.

In sum, it is uncertain whether Testator's nonmarital child, Don, will be included within the bequest to Testator's "children."

[NOTE: If evidence of Testator's paternity is not currently available, Don might seek an order requiring decedent's marital children to submit to blood testing in order to establish Testator's paternity; some courts have granted such petitions. *See Sudwischer v. Estate of Hoffpauir*, 589 So. 2d 474 (La. 1991). In recent years, some courts have also permitted exhumation of a decedent's remains for purposes of establishing paternity. *See Brancato v. Moriscato*, 2003 WL 1090596, 34 Conn. L. Rptr. 208 (Super. Ct. 2003). Other courts have refused to grant such requests. *See In re Estate of Bonanno*, 745 N.Y.S.2d 813 (Sur. Ct. 2002) (request for exhumation denied when postmortem DNA analysis of decedent's blood samples established that petitioner was not decedent's son).]

Point Five (5%)

Most jurisdictions disallow reformation of a will to correct a mistake. In those states, the bequest to "my children" would stand despite Testator's apparent intention to benefit only his biological children, Abby and Bruce.

The fact that Testator identified only Abby and Bruce as his children when talking with his lawyer is unlikely to result in an interpretation of the will limiting the word "children" to Abby and Bruce. Although the "controlling consideration in determining the meaning of a donative document is the donor's intention" (RESTATEMENT (THIRD) OF PROPERTY: WILLS AND OTHER DONATIVE TRANSFERS § 10.1 (2003)), a majority of jurisdictions bar the admission of extrinsic evidence to vary the literal meaning of the words used in a will and refuse to allow reformation of a will to correct a mistake. "Hypothetical or imaginary mistakes of testators cannot be corrected. . . . The only means for ascertaining the intent of the testator are the words written and the acts done by him." *Sanderson v. Norcross*, 136 N.E. 170, 172 (Mass. 1922). Under this formalist approach, Testator's attorney could not testify that Testator intended to leave his estate to only Abby and Bruce, based on their conversations.

In recent years, a few states have begun to move away from the formalist approach and toward the more liberal approach adopted in the Restatement (Third) of Property. Under the Restatement, a court may reform even an unambiguous donative document based on clear and convincing evidence of (a) a mistake of fact or law or (b) the donor's intention. *See* RESTATEMENT (THIRD) OF PROPERTY: WILLS AND OTHER DONATIVE TRANSFERS § 12.1; *Estate of Herceg*, 747 N.Y.S.2d 901 (Sur. Ct. 2002) (reforming will based on drafting attorney's testimony that omission of particular beneficiary was due to computer error); UNIF. PROBATE CODE § 2-805 (2008 amendment). Using this approach, a court would admit the attorney's testimony to show that Testator's bequest to "children" was based on a mistake of law (the meaning of "children" for purposes of intestate succession) and that Testator intended to benefit only Abby and Bruce. However, it is unclear whether such testimony would meet a clear and convincing evidentiary standard given that Testator did not discuss his intentions toward Carl and Don with the attorney.

In sum, Abby and Bruce will certainly take a share of Testator's estate. It is highly probable, but not certain, that Carl will. It is uncertain whether Don will as well, depending on whether Testator's nonmarital children are included in the class gift to "children" under state law. *See* Point Four.

Decedent's Estates
(February 2011)

ANALYSIS

Legal Problems: (1)   Was Testator's will validly executed?

                        (2)   Should the life insurance proceeds be distributed to Niece or Cousin?

                        (3)   Does the handwritten memorandum found in Testator's safe-deposit box determine the disposition of Testator's jewelry?

                        (4)   Did the bequest to Husband lapse?

                        (5)   How should the general bequests in Testator's will abate?

DISCUSSION

Summary

Testator's will is valid and should be admitted to probate because Testator complied with the statutory requirements in executing the will. Testator's life insurance proceeds will probably go to Niece because life insurance contracts almost always disallow alteration of a beneficiary designation in a life insurance contract by will, and most states have upheld such contractual requirements. Testator's jewelry will probably go to Niece because the memorandum describing the gift to Niece preexisted Testator's will and thus was incorporated by reference into Testator's will. The gift of $40,000 to Husband lapsed because he predeceased Testator, and bequests to spouses are not typically saved from lapse by an antilapse statute. It is irrelevant that Husband had a child who survived Testator. The general bequests of $25,000 each to Church, Library, and School must be abated because there are insufficient funds ($60,000) to pay these bequests. Because there are no indications in the will specifying a different abatement scheme, Church, Library, and School will take equal shares (i.e., $20,000) of Testator's bank account. As a result of the abatement, nothing remains in the estate to pass to Son. Niece need not contribute to those general bequests because life insurance proceeds are nonprobate assets not governed by the will. Furthermore, the devise of items listed in a memorandum was specific, and specific devises are the last to abate.

Point One (20%)
Because Testator complied with the statutory execution requirements, her will is valid.

Here, state law disallows "all holographic wills and codicils." A holographic will is an unwitnessed will in a testator's handwriting. Testator's will was not holographic even though written in the testator's hand because it was signed and witnessed.

State law does provide that a will is not valid unless it is "acknowledged by the testator to the witnesses and signed by the testator in the presence of at least two attesting witnesses, who shall sign their names below that of the testator within 30 days." Testator signed her will in the presence of three witnesses who, on the same day, signed their names below hers. Testator acknowledged the instrument to be her will when she stated, "This is my will. I would like each of you to witness it." Therefore, Testator's will is valid because its execution complied with the law of the state.

Point Two (20%)
Niece will probably take Testator's life insurance because, in most states, Testator could not change her life insurance beneficiary except as specified in her life insurance contract.

If an insured dies while a life insurance policy is in effect, the policy proceeds are payable to the named beneficiary. Although the owner of a life insurance policy typically retains the right to change the named beneficiary without obtaining that beneficiary's consent, the owner must do so in accordance with procedures specified in the life insurance contract.

Life insurance contracts almost never permit a change of beneficiary by will, and courts have almost invariably upheld such restrictions. *See* ROBERT J. LYNN & GRAYSON M.P. MCCOUCH, INTRODUCTION TO ESTATE PLANNING IN A NUTSHELL 131–32 (5th ed. 2004); *Cook v. Equitable Life Assurance Society*, 428 N.E.2d 110 (Ind. Ct. App. 1981). Courts have sometimes found that a beneficiary change that does not comply with the terms of the insurance contract is valid if the policyholder has "substantially complied" with the contract by taking all reasonable steps within his or her power to make the change in accordance with the contract terms. *See* LYNN & MCCOUCH, *supra,* at 131–32. Courts in a few states have also upheld a change of beneficiary by will. *See, e.g., Burkett v. Mott*, 733 P.2d 673 (Ariz. Ct. App. 1986) (relying on insurance company's failure to object); *Connecticut Gen. Life Ins. Co. v. Peterson*, 442 F. Supp. 533 (W.D. Mo. 1978).

Here, Testator attempted to change the beneficiary of her policy by naming Cousin as the beneficiary in her will. Assuming that Testator had a standard life insurance contract, such a change would be disallowed. There is nothing in the facts to show that Testator made any attempt to comply with the formalities required by the insurance contract. Thus, unless this state follows the minority approach, Niece, the named beneficiary in the policy, will take the policy proceeds.

Point Three (20%)
Niece will probably take Testator's jewelry because, in most states, the memorandum describing the bequest was incorporated by reference into Testator's will.

In most jurisdictions, a writing that exists at the time a will is executed may be incorporated by reference into the will. The will must describe the writing with sufficient particularity that it can be identified, but the writing need not be witnessed or executed with testamentary formalities. *See* LYNN & MCCOUCH, *supra*, at 183–84; UNIF. PROBATE CODE § 2-510.

Here, the memorandum describing the bequest of jewelry to Niece is clearly identified in Testator's will, and it was found in the location described by Testator. The memorandum is dated on the day before Testator's will was executed, so it qualifies as a document that can be incorporated by reference. Thus, assuming that this state follows the approach of the overwhelming majority of states and allows incorporation by reference, Niece will take the jewelry.

In addition, some states recognize the right of a testator to dispose of tangible personal property by a signed memorandum, whether prepared before or after the execution of the will, even though it is not executed with the formalities required of wills. *See, e.g,* Iowa Code § 633.276; UNIF. PROBATE CODE § 2-513.

[NOTE: The difference between UPC § 2-513 and the incorporation-by-reference doctrine is that the former allows a testator to dispose of tangible personal property by a signed memorandum executed both before and after the will was signed. Under the incorporation-by-reference doctrine, the memorandum must be in existence at the time the will is executed.]

Point Four (20%)
The bequest to Husband lapsed because he predeceased Testator. Under the typical antilapse statute, the bequest to Husband would not be saved from lapse even though he left issue who survived Testator.

If a beneficiary does not survive the testator, the bequest lapses and falls into the residue of the estate. Under the common law, lapse occurred whenever a beneficiary predeceased the testator and the testator specified no alternate disposition of the assets in question. A lapsed bequest passes into the residue of the testator's estate. *See* WILLIAM M. MCGOVERN, JR. & SHELDON F. KURTZ, WILLS, TRUSTS AND ESTATES 328–29 (3d ed. 2001).

Today, all states have antilapse statutes. Under a typical antilapse statute, if a beneficiary dies before the testator and the beneficiary was both related by blood to the testator within a certain degree of relationship and had issue who survived the testator, the bequest to the deceased beneficiary is saved from lapse and the deceased beneficiary's issue takes in lieu of the deceased beneficiary. *See, e.g.,* UNIF. PROBATE CODE § 2-603.

The typical antilapse statute, therefore, would not save a bequest to a spouse even if the spouse predeceased the testator leaving issue who survived the testator. *Id.*

Thus, the $40,000 bequest to Husband lapses and passes into the residuary estate.

Point Five (20%)
Testator's general legacies must be abated because there are insufficient assets to pay all named beneficiaries. Under standard abatement principles, Son will receive nothing and Library, Church, and School will receive equal, pro rata general bequests. Niece will take the jewelry because specific devises abate last. She also will take the life insurance because it passes outside the will.

When the assets of a testator's estate are insufficient to pay all of the bequests payable under the testator's will, these bequests are reduced, or abated. Under the common law and in most states, unless the testator specifies a different abatement scheme, testamentary bequests abate in the following order: (1) residuary bequests, (2) general bequests (i.e., bequests of a fixed dollar amount), and (3) specific bequests (i.e., identifiable property such as "my jewelry"). Abatement within each category is pro rata. *See* UNIF. PROBATE CODE § 3-902; LYNN & McCOUCH, *supra*, at 47–48.

Here, there are insufficient assets in Testator's estate to pay the bequests made under her will, and Testator specified no abatement scheme. Thus, the residuary bequest to Son abates first; Son will receive nothing. The general bequests to Church, Library, and School, totaling $75,000, abate next and pro rata as each of them was bequeathed $25,000. Thus, Church, Library, and School will each receive $20,000 from the available $60,000. Niece need not contribute because the bequest of jewelry is a specific devise and, assuming this state follows the majority view, the life insurance is a nonprobate asset that will not be taken into account when abating the testamentary bequests. *See* UNIF. PROBATE CODE § 3-902.

[NOTE: If Husband's daughter is entitled to the $40,000 bequest to Husband, there will be $115,000 of general legacies to abate proportionally when distributing the $60,000.]

Decedent's Estates
(February 2012)

ANALYSIS

Legal Problems

(1)   Was the document captioned "Last Will and Testament" republished by codicil?

(2)   Was the document captioned "Last Will and Testament" incorporated by reference into Testator's valid partial will?

(3)   Assuming that the document captioned "Last Will and Testament" drafted by Testator's attorney is not a valid will, will Daughter be barred from inheriting from Testator by the state "slayer statute"?

(4)   Did Testator's bequest of her house located at 340 Green Avenue adeem?

(5)   Did the dividend of 200 shares of XYZ Corporation common stock pass to the devisee, Aunt?

DISCUSSION

Summary

Because the document captioned "Last Will and Testament" was never executed by Testator, it cannot be republished by codicil. Because the partial will (an intended codicil) did not specifically refer to the document captioned "Last Will and Testament," that document cannot be incorporated by reference. Thus, although the partial will is valid and determines the disposition of the assets named therein, the rest of Testator's estate passes to Daughter, Testator's sole heir, through partial intestacy. Nephew gets nothing.

Daughter is not barred from inheriting from Testator, because slayer statutes bar from inheriting only a beneficiary who killed the decedent whose estate is at issue. Here, Daughter was convicted of murdering Testator's husband, not Testator. Thus, Daughter takes the $200,000.

Under the common law ademption doctrine, the bequest of Testator's house at 340 Green Avenue was adeemed by extinction, and Cousin would take nothing. Under the Uniform Probate Code or a like statute, however, Cousin would take Testator's home at 12 Elm Street as replacement property.

Under the law of most states, Aunt would be entitled to both the 400 shares of XYZ Corporation common stock devised to her and the 200 shares Testator received as a stock dividend.

Point One (20%)

Testator's valid partial will did not republish the unexecuted, unwitnessed document captioned "Last Will and Testament."

The document captioned "Last Will and Testament" is not a valid will because it was never executed. However, the document the attorney next sent was properly executed by Testator, and it is a valid partial will. It thus determines the disposition of the assets named therein (Testator's home and 400 shares of XYZ stock).

A valid partial will, or codicil, that refers to an earlier will is said to republish that will. When republication takes place, the republished will is deemed to be executed on the same day as the codicil. *See generally* RESTATEMENT (THIRD) OF PROPERTY: WILLS AND OTHER DONATIVE TRANSFERS § 3.4 (1999). Republication can cure defects that might otherwise affect the validity of bequests made under a will. For example, in a jurisdiction that voids bequests to interested witnesses, a bequest to such a witness can be saved if the will is republished by a later-executed codicil witnessed by two disinterested witnesses.

However, by most accounts, a document that is not a valid will cannot be republished by codicil. *See generally* JESSE DUKEMINIER AND STANLEY M. JOHANSON, WILLS, TRUSTS, AND ESTATES 303 (6th ed. 2000). There is some contrary authority, but those cases involve codicils written on the unexecuted dispositive document itself. *See, e.g., Johnson v. Johnson*, 279 P.2d 928 (Okla. 1954). Here, the codicil was a separate document.

Thus, the "Last Will and Testament" unexecuted by Testator (and which left Testator's entire estate to Nephew) was not republished when Testator properly executed a partial will, and it will have no effect on the distribution of Testator's assets. Nephew gets nothing.

[NOTE: Colorado, Hawaii, Montana, and Utah have adopted the dispensing power in the Uniform Probate Code § 2-503. That power allows a court to validate a will not executed in accordance with the statute of wills if the evidence is clear and convincing that the testator intended the document to be a will. It is not clear, however, whether that statute can apply where the will was neither signed by the testator nor witnessed by anyone. It is also unclear that Testator intended the first, unsigned document to be her will. Examinees who believe that the document captioned "Last Will and Testament" can be saved under the dispensing power would have to conclude that the later document was a codicil only and that assets not disposed of by the later codicil pass to Nephew under the earlier will.]

Point Two (15%)
The document captioned "Last Will and Testament" was not incorporated by reference into Testator's valid partial will because the partial will did not specifically refer to the earlier document or reflect Testator's intent to incorporate that will.

"A writing that is not valid as a will but is in existence when a will is executed may be incorporated by reference into the will if the will manifests an intent to incorporate the writing and the writing to be incorporated is identified with reasonable certainty." RESTATEMENT (THIRD) OF PROPERTY: WILLS AND OTHER DONATIVE TRANSFERS § 3.6. *See also* UNIF. PROBATE

CODE § 2-510 (allowing for incorporation by reference when the will describes "the writing sufficiently to permit its identification").

Here, the document captioned "Last Will and Testament" drafted by Testator's attorney was in existence at the time Testator executed the second, partial will disposing of Testator's real estate and stock. However, it is unclear whether the partial will identifies the "Last Will and Testament" with "reasonable certainty."

More importantly, the partial will does not evidence an intention to incorporate the prior "Last Will and Testament" by reference. Indeed, quite to the contrary, the only possible "reference" to the first document is in the statement "I republish my will." "I republish" is not the type of reference to a prior document that an experienced attorney would use to incorporate a document by reference; "republish" is a term of art that has legal consequences. *See* Point One.

Thus, the "Last Will and Testament" first drafted by the attorney was not incorporated by reference into the second document, Testator's valid partial will. Therefore, assets not passing under the valid partial will should pass to Testator's heir(s) by intestacy.

Point Three (15%)
Daughter is Testator's sole heir, and she is not barred from inheriting from Testator by a slayer statute because these statutes apply only when the heir has murdered the decedent whose estate is at issue.

Because Testator's valid will did not dispose of Testator's entire estate, the remaining assets will pass to Testator's heirs. Under all intestate succession statutes, Daughter would be Testator's only heir.

Although murderers are often barred from inheriting under a "slayer statute," such a statute would not bar Daughter from inheriting from Testator because these statutes apply only when the heir killed the decedent whose estate is at issue. *See* UNIF. PROBATE CODE § 2-803 (barring legatee or heir from taking share of estate when he or she killed the decedent). No slayer statute bars an heir from inheriting from a decedent's estate because the heir killed another person, even if the heir's victim left property to the decedent that is included in the decedent's estate.

[NOTE: If an examinee erroneously concludes that Daughter is barred from taking a share of Testator's estate, the examinee should conclude that whatever Daughter would have taken will pass to her child, Grandson, absent a statute that bars both the slayer and the slayer's descendants from taking.]

Point Four (35%)
Under the common law ademption doctrine, the bequest of Testator's house to Cousin adeemed because Testator's house at 340 Green Avenue, Springfield, State A, was not in Testator's probate estate. Possibly under the intent theory of ademption, and certainly under Uniform Probate Code § 2-606 or a like statute, the house located at 12 Elm Street could pass to Cousin as a substitute gift.

Under the common law ademption doctrine, if specifically devised property (i.e., property that is specifically described in the will) is not in the testator's estate when the testator dies, the bequest adeems (i.e., fails). *See generally* WILLIAM MCGOVERN & SHELDON KURTZ, WILLS, TRUSTS, AND ESTATES 315 (3d ed. 2004). Under this common law doctrine, the testator's intentions are irrelevant; all that matters is whether the testator owned the specifically devised asset at his or her death.

Some modern courts have rejected the common law "identity test" for ademption in favor of an intent test. Under the intent test, a beneficiary of specifically devised property is entitled to substitute property that was owned by the testator at his or her death if the beneficiary proves that the testator intended the beneficiary to take the substitute property. *See generally* Note, 23 DRAKE L. REV. 478 (1974); *Estate of Austin*, 113 Cal.App.3d 167 (1980).

Testator's bequest of the property at 340 Green Avenue was a specific bequest and thus subject to the ademption doctrine. Under the common law identity test, the bequest would adeem because Testator did not own this property at her death. The home would then pass to Daughter as Testator's heir. *See* Point Three.

Under the intent test, Cousin would be entitled to Testator's home at 12 Elm Street if he or she could establish that Testator wanted Cousin to take this home as a substitute for the property at 340 Green Avenue. It is unclear whether Cousin could make such a showing. Indeed, the fact that Testator told her attorney that she wanted Cousin to have the five-bedroom house at 340 Green Avenue because "Cousin has such a large family" arguably suggests that Testator did not want Cousin to take the two-bedroom house at 12 Elm Street, which would likely be too small for Cousin's family.

[NOTE: An examinee who demonstrates an understanding of the intent theory of ademption should not be penalized if he or she reaches a different conclusion.]

Under the Uniform Probate Code, a specific devisee has the right to any "real . . . property owned by the testator at death which the testator acquired as a replacement for specifically devised real property." UNIF. PROBATE CODE § 2-606(5). Under this or a like statute, Cousin would be entitled to the property at 12 Elm Street because Testator acquired that property as a replacement for 340 Green Avenue.

Point Five (15%)
Aunt is entitled to both the 400 shares of XYZ Corporation common stock bequeathed to her by Testator and the 200 additional shares of XYZ Corporation common stock distributed to Testator as a stock dividend. Thus, Aunt takes all 600 shares of that stock.

Under the common law, a devisee of common stock was entitled to additional shares of that stock obtained by the testator through a stock split, but not to additional shares acquired as a stock dividend. Under this approach, Aunt would be entitled to only 400 shares of XYZ common stock. *See* JESSE DUKEMINIER AND STANLEY M. JOHANSON, WILLS, TRUSTS, AND ESTATES 464 (6th ed. 2000); *Hicks v. Kerr*, 104 A. 426 (1918).

Today, virtually all jurisdictions treat stock splits and dividends the same way; in each case, additional shares obtained by the testator go to the specific devisee. *See, e.g.*, UNIF. PROBATE CODE § 2-605. Under this approach, Aunt would be entitled to all 600 shares of XYZ common stock.

Decedent's Estates
(July 2012)

ANALYSIS

Legal Problems

(1)   Which state's laws govern the disposition of Zach's bank account, Zach's house, and Zach's farm?

(2)   Is Zach's will valid in (a) State A and (b) State B?

(3)   If Zach's will is invalid, which of Zach's children are entitled to a share of his assets in State A and State B?

DISCUSSION

Summary

The postmortem distribution of personal property is governed by the law of the state in which the decedent was domiciled at the time of his death. The postmortem distribution of real property is governed by the law of the situs. Thus, State A law controls the disposition of Zach's bank account and Zach's house, and State B law controls the disposition of Zach's farm. In State A, Zach's will is invalid because Zach did not sign it at the end. In State B, Zach's will is invalid because it was not signed by two witnesses. Thus, Zach died intestate in both states.

Under the laws of both State A and State B, Alex is entitled to a share of Zach's estate. In State A, Brian is entitled to a share if the word "children" in the State A statute is construed to include adopted children.

Although the State A intestate-distribution statute excludes nonmarital children, Carrie is nonetheless entitled to a share because intestate-distribution laws that exclude nonmarital children whose paternity has been established are unconstitutional.

Under State B law, Alex and Carrie are clearly entitled to shares of Zach's assets. Brian also is entitled to a share because the State B statute specifically includes adopted children.

Point One (30%)

Because the disposition of real property is governed by the law of the situs, State A law will govern the disposition of Zach's house and State B law will govern the disposition of Zach's farm. State A law also governs the distribution of the personal property, the bank account, because State A was the decedent's domicile at the time of his death.

The law of the state where the real property is located governs the disposition of real property. *See* RESTATEMENT (SECOND) OF CONFLICT OF LAWS § 223(1). This approach reflects the situs state's interest in the regularity of titles and the interests of third parties who rely on local land records. *See Baker v. General Motors Corp.*, 522 U.S. 222 (1998) (dictum); EUGENE F. SCOLES ET AL., CONFLICT OF LAWS (4th ed. 2004). Therefore the law of State A controls the disposition of the house and the law of State B controls the disposition of the farm. Each state's statutes must be consulted to determine the validity of Zach's will and, if the will is invalid, the rules governing intestate succession. *See* RESTATEMENT (SECOND) OF CONFLICT OF LAWS § 236.

The law of the state in which the decedent was domiciled at his death governs the disposition of personal property. Because Zach was a domiciliary of State A, State A law governs the disposition of his bank account even though the account was maintained at a bank in State B.

[NOTE: Comments to the Second Restatement suggest that when the situs state (State B) has a statute recognizing the validity of a will properly executed in the state where the testator was domiciled, it may determine the validity of a landowner's will under the law in his state of domicile (State A). Most states have such will-validation statutes, but the facts provide that State B has no such law and instead expressly requires nonresidents to comply with its will-execution requirements. The question is designed, in part, to test the examinee's ability to read and apply a specific statute. Zach's will is invalid under State A law in any event. *See* Point Two.]

Point Two (30%)

Zach's will is invalid under the law of State A because Zach did not sign it at the end. The will also is invalid under the law of State B because it was not signed by two witnesses. Therefore, Zach died intestate under the laws of both states.

Although State A permits holographic (i.e., handwritten and unwitnessed) wills, State A law expressly requires the testator to have "signed" the holograph at the end. Zach's will is shown in its entirety in the facts; Zach did not sign it at the end. Therefore, the will is invalid under the laws of State A and Zach's bank account and his house in State A pass in accordance with State A's laws of intestate succession. *See* Point One.

State B validates signed holographic wills only if they have been signed by two witnesses, and Zach's will was not. Therefore Zach's farm passes in accordance with State B's laws of intestate succession.

Therefore, in both State A and State B, University, the beneficiary under the invalid will, takes nothing.

Point Three(a) (5%)

Alex is entitled to share in the house, the farm, and the bank account under the applicable laws of each state, as Alex is a biological child of Zach and was born in wedlock.

The intestacy laws of both State A and State B provide that the property of an intestate decedent passes to his surviving children. There is no possible argument, under either state's law, that a marital child like Alex would be excluded from the class of surviving children who take.

Point Three(b) (15%)

Brian takes a share of the house and the bank account under State A law if "children" includes adopted children; Brian takes a share of the farm under State B law because adopted children are treated the same as biological children.

Under State A law, an intestate's property passes to his "surviving children," excluding nonmarital children. The statute is silent on the status of adopted children.

At common law, only blood relations could inherit from an intestate decedent. *See* WILLIAM M. MCGOVERN, JR. & SHELDON F. KURTZ, WILLS, TRUSTS AND ESTATES 100 (3d ed. 2001). Although all states today grant adopted children inheritance rights in at least some circumstances, there is typically an explicit statutory command that achieves this result. *See, e.g.,* UNIF. PROBATE CODE § 2-114. State A has no statutory provision expressly altering the common law. In the absence of such a statute, a court might conclude that had the legislature intended to give adopted children the same rights as biological children, it would have said so; alternatively, it might conclude, based on general nondiscrimination goals, that the legislature must have intended to give adopted children the same rights as biological children. *See* THOMAS E. ATKINSON, WILLS 87 (2d ed. 1953). There are cases going both ways on this issue. *Id.*

In State B, Brian clearly inherits because the statute says so.

[NOTE: The examinee's conclusion on this point is less important than his or her demonstrated ability to recognize the statutory ambiguity and formulate arguments in support of a position.]

Point Three(c) (20%)

Because State A's law disallowing inheritance by all nonmarital children does not meet constitutional standards, Carrie is entitled to take as a child of Zach.

Under the common law, a nonmarital child could not inherit from either parent. Today, all states grant nonmarital children the right to inherit from their mothers and to inherit from their fathers when at least one statutorily defined method of establishing paternity has been satisfied. *See* MCGOVERN & KURTZ, *supra*, at 93–94. The Supreme Court has held that a statute disallowing inheritance by a nonmarital child from her father when the father's paternity has been adjudicated during his lifetime is unconstitutional. *See Trimble v. Gordon*, 430 U.S. 762 (1977). *See also Reed v. Campbell*, 476 U.S. 852 (1986). Because Zach's paternity of Carrie was adjudicated during his lifetime, Carrie would be entitled to a share of Zach's estate despite the language of the State A statute. Carrie also takes under the laws of State B because she is Zach's biological child.

MBE SUBJECTS – RELEASED ESSAY QUESTIONS

EVIDENCE
MEE Question – February 2008

ANALYSIS

Legal Problems: (1)(a) When a hospital record is offered into evidence to prove the truth of an out-of-court statement contained therein, must the record itself, the out-of-court statement, or both be covered by a hearsay exception?

(1)(b) Is Nurse's notation of Victor's statement a business record that can be admitted to prove the content of Victor's statement?

(1)(c) Is Victor's statement, which relates both to the general cause of his injuries and to the identity of the person causing the injuries, admissible to prove the truth of the matter stated?

(2) May a spouse assert the marital privilege in order not to testify with respect to communications with a deceased spouse?

(3) When a hearsay statement has been admitted, is an inconsistent hearsay statement admissible to attack the credibility of the hearsay declarant?

DISCUSSION

Summary

Both the hospital record and Victor's statement in it are hearsay, and each must fall within an exception to the hearsay rule in order for Victor's statement to be admissible for its truth. The hospital record falls within the business-records exception to the hearsay rule. Victor's statement that he was stabbed may fall within the hearsay exception for statements relating to medical diagnosis and treatment, but Victor's identification of Dan as his assailant is not pertinent to his medical treatment and would not fall within the medical diagnosis or any other hearsay exception. Consequently, that portion of Victor's statement is inadmissible to prove that Dan stabbed Victor and should have been excluded from evidence.

In most jurisdictions, Wife will be able to invoke the privilege for confidential marital communications and refuse to testify to what Victor told her. In some jurisdictions, however, only the "communicating spouse" can invoke the privilege, so in those jurisdictions, Wife would be required to testify.

If Wife cannot invoke the marital privilege, her testimony as to Victor's identification of his assailant is admissible only for the purposes of impeaching Victor's hearsay declaration that Dan stabbed him. If that hearsay declaration is not admitted, Victor's statement to Wife should also be excluded.

Point One(a) (20–30%)

Because the hospital record is being offered to prove both that Victor made certain statements to Nurse and that those statements are true, it is double hearsay and is admissible only if both the hospital record and the statements made by Victor fall within hearsay exceptions.

Hearsay is an out-of-court statement "offered in evidence to prove the truth of the matter asserted." FED. R. EVID. 801(c). Hearsay is generally inadmissible. FED. R. EVID. 802.

Here, the hospital record is "double hearsay," and both levels of hearsay must fall within a hearsay exception or the record is inadmissible. The record itself is the first level of hearsay. The record is an "out-of-court statement," and the prosecutor is offering it to prove the truth of what it says—that Victor told Nurse that Dan stabbed him. Without Nurse present to prove what she heard Victor say, her "out-of-court statement" about Victor's words, in the form of her notation in his hospital record, is admissible only if the record falls within a hearsay exception. (*See* Point One(b).)

The prosecutor is also seeking to prove that what Victor said ("Dan stabbed me") is true. This is also hearsay because Victor's statement was made out of court and is offered for its truth. Therefore, the prosecutor must show that Victor's statement falls within a hearsay exception. (*See* Point One(c).)

Point One(b) (20–30%)

The hospital record satisfies the business-records exception to the hearsay rule.

A record of "acts, events, conditions, opinions, or diagnoses" is admissible under the business-records exception to the hearsay rule if it is "made at or near the time" of the recorded event by "a person with knowledge" of the event. FED. R. EVID. 803(6). Additionally, the making of the record must occur in the course of a regularly conducted business activity, and it must be the regular practice of the business to make the record. *Id.* This foundation can be introduced through the testimony of a record custodian or other person with knowledge of the method of record keeping. It is not necessary that the person with knowledge of the matter entered testify at trial. *United States v. Duncan*, 919 F.2d 981, 986 (5th Cir. 1990).

Nurse's notation in the hospital record concerning Victor's statements to her falls within the business-records exception. Nurse had personal knowledge of what Victor said, and she wrote down his statements "at or near the time" that he made them. The facts state that it is the regular practice of the hospital to record this sort of information in a patient's record.

Point One(c) (20–30%)

Victor's statement to Nurse that he was stabbed may be admissible for the truth of the matter stated because it falls within the hearsay exception for statements made for the purpose of receiving medical diagnosis and treatment; however, Victor's identification of his assailant as "Dan" is not admissible because it was not pertinent to diagnosis or treatment.

As noted earlier, Victor's statement is itself hearsay because the prosecutor is offering it to prove the truth of the matter asserted—that Dan stabbed Victor. Therefore, even if the hospital record is admissible to prove what Victor said, the statement should still be excluded unless Victor's statement itself falls within a hearsay exception.

Statements made by a person who is seeking medical treatment are exempted from the ban on hearsay if the statements concern medical history, symptoms, "or the inception or general character of the cause" of the symptoms. FED. R. EVID. 803(4). Hence, Victor's statement to Nurse about the cause of his injuries may qualify for this hearsay exception.

However, the rationale for this hearsay exception is that statements made by people seeking medical treatment will generally be reliable because of the declarants' knowledge that medical diagnosis or treatment will be facilitated by such statements (or hindered if the statements are false). Thus, this hearsay exception is limited to statements that are "reasonably pertinent to diagnosis or treatment." *Id.*

Statements which relate to the cause of the medical condition being diagnosed or treated are generally viewed as "pertinent to diagnosis or treatment." Thus, Victor's statement that he was stabbed with a knife would fall within the exception and would be admissible. But statements of fault ordinarily are not admitted under this exception, because the identity of the person who was at fault in causing the injury is not relevant to the treatment that is to be given. Thus, the portion of Victor's statement identifying Dan as the assailant is inadmissible. CHRISTOPHER B. MUELLER & LAIRD C. KIRKPATRICK, EVIDENCE § 8.75 (3d ed. 2007).

In short, although the hospital record of what Victor said is admissible even though it is hearsay, Victor's identification of his assailant is also hearsay and is inadmissible because it does not fall within an exception. Therefore, the trial court should not admit the record containing that statement.

[NOTE TO GRADERS: Other hearsay exceptions are also inapplicable to Victor's identification of his assailant. Although Victor died a week after making the statement, the statement would not be admitted as a dying declaration or statement made under belief of impending death. The exception requires that the declarant believe that death is imminent at the time of the making of the statement. Victor died unexpectedly; thus, there is no indication that he had the necessary expectation of impending death at the time the statement was made. FED. R. EVID. 804(b)(2). The exception for an "excited utterance" probably would not apply because the facts do not show that Victor was still under the "stress of excitement" of the stabbing when he made the statement to Nurse. *See* FED. R. EVID. 803(2).]

Point Two (20–30%)

The testimonial spousal privilege may only be asserted by a spouse who is testifying against an accused spouse. The marital-confidential-communications privilege can be asserted by either spouse. Wife may assert the privilege and refuse to testify concerning her confidential communications with Victor.

Two evidentiary privileges apply to the marital relationship. The federal courts recognize a testimonial or witness privilege under which a witness-spouse has the right not to testify against an accused spouse in a criminal case. *Trammel v. United States*, 445 U.S. 40 (1980). This privilege is inapplicable in this case because Wife has not been asked to testify against her husband, Victor.

The federal courts and most states also recognize a second privilege for confidential communications between spouses when those communications occur during the marriage. *United States v. Acker*, 52 F.3d 509, 514 (4th Cir. 1995). The privilege protects communications during marriage even if the marriage no longer exists and even if one of the parties to the marriage is dead.

Under the majority view, both spouses hold the privilege for all communications between them. Here, Wife could invoke the privilege and be excused from testifying as to Victor's statements to her because all the requirements of the privilege are met: Victor's statements were statements of one spouse to another in private (it appears that no one overheard them), and neither Wife nor Victor revealed their exact content to anyone else. These confidential communications between spouses are protected by the privilege.

Some courts, however, have taken the position that only the communicating spouse can assert the privilege. Under that minority view, Wife could not assert the privilege and would have to reveal what Victor said. *See* 1 KENNETH S. BROUN ET AL., MCCORMICK ON EVIDENCE § 83 (6th ed. 2006).

Here, however, it is possible that Wife will not be allowed to invoke the privilege because she broke the confidentiality of her communications with her husband when she told Friend, a third party, some of what her husband told her. The marital communications privilege is intended to protect the confidentiality of spousal discussions. Where one spouse has revealed the content of those communications to a third person, then confidentiality no longer exists and the privilege probably should not apply. At the very least, Wife might be required to testify to the fact that she has already revealed to Friend: that Victor told her that he was attacked by someone other than Dan.

Point Three (10–20%)

The prosecutor's hearsay objection to testimony about Victor's statement to Wife should not have been sustained because the court had previously admitted Victor's hearsay statement that Dan was his assailant. Once an out-of-court statement is offered for its truth, the credibility of the hearsay declarant may be attacked with an inconsistent statement by that declarant, including statements that would otherwise be hearsay. Thus, once Victor's identification of Dan as his assailant was admitted into evidence, his inconsistent statement to Wife could be admitted to attack his credibility.

Victor's statement to Wife that Dan was not his assailant is hearsay (because it was made outside the courtroom) and could not have been admitted to prove the truth of the matter stated. Victor's statement is nonetheless admissible to impeach his credibility.

On the facts, the court has admitted Victor's hearsay statement to Nurse that Dan attacked him. Once a hearsay statement is admitted into evidence, the hearsay declarant's credibility may be attacked just as though the hearsay declarant were a witness at trial. In addition, *any* inconsistent statement made by the hearsay declarant may be admitted to impeach the declarant's credibility. FED. R. EVID. 806. Thus, if the hospital record is admitted to prove that Victor identified Dan as his assailant, then Victor's statement to Wife (identifying someone else as his assailant) is admissible to attack Victor's credibility, despite the existence of the hearsay rule. 4 CHRISTOPHER LOUISELL & LAIRD C. KIRKPATRICK, FEDERAL EVIDENCE § 511 (2d ed. 1994). (Of course, Wife's privilege claim may still prevent admission of the statement.)

MBE SUBJECTS – RELEASED ESSAY QUESTIONS

EVIDENCE
MEE Question – February 2009

ANALYSIS

(Evidence I.A.2. & 3., C.1., D.1. & 5.; II.C.1. & 2.)

Legal Problems: (1) Under Rule 608(b), was it proper to cross-examine Witness about his alleged lie on his job application?

(2) Under Rule 608(b), was Witness's job application admissible to contradict Witness's denial that he had lied, or was it inadmissible extrinsic evidence?

(3) If Witness's job application was not admissible for impeachment purposes under Rule 608(b), could the exhibit be admitted into evidence to refresh recollection under Rule 612?

(4) Under Rule 608(b), was Contractor's testimony admissible to impeach Witness, or was it inadmissible extrinsic evidence?

DISCUSSION

Summary

Under Rule 608(b), a trial court has discretion to permit cross-examination of a witness concerning a specific instance of untruthful conduct. Lying on a job application represents untruthful conduct and an important issue in this case—whether Plaintiff removed the safety guard—will probably turn on the credibility of the witnesses. Thus, the Court was within its discretion in permitting the cross-examination. With respect to the job application, Rule 608(b) expressly forbids the admission of extrinsic evidence of a prior bad act. Some federal courts hold that any document is extrinsic evidence; others hold that a document is not extrinsic evidence if it can be authenticated by the witness. Thus, the Court was within its discretion in excluding Exhibit 37, the job application. Exhibit 37 was inadmissible even if it had been used to refresh Witness's recollection because the use of Exhibit 37 to refresh Witness's recollection does not make it automatically admissible. Rule 612 authorizes admission of a recollection-refreshing exhibit only if offered by the lawyer who has not used the exhibit to refresh the recollection of the witness. Finally, Contractor's testimony was not admissible under Rule 608(b) because, although probative of untruthfulness, it was clearly extrinsic evidence.

Point One (25–35%)

<u>The trial court acted within its discretion in permitting cross-examination concerning the alleged lie on Witness's job application because lying about one's job experience is probative of untruthfulness.</u>

The standard of review regarding an alleged error in an evidentiary ruling is abuse of discretion. *United States v. Alexander*, 849 F.2d 1293, 1301 (10th Cir. 1988). A trial court's ruling should be affirmed, even if the court of appeals would make a different ruling, if the challenged ruling lies within the zone of reasonable disagreement.

Character evidence is generally inadmissible to prove action in conformity with the character trait. FED. R. EVID. 404(a). However, when a person testifies as a witness, that person's credibility becomes a material issue; a witness's credibility thus may be attacked by showing that the witness has an untruthful character. FED. R. EVID. 404(a)(3). Accordingly, a court may, in its discretion, admit evidence relating to a prior bad act if it is offered during cross-examination of the witness being impeached and is "probative of . . . untruthfulness." FED. R. EVID. 608(b). Conduct that involves falsehood or deception is generally considered probative of untruthfulness. *See United States v. Cole*, 617 F.2d 151 (5th Cir. 1980) (submitting a false excuse for being absent from work); *United States v. Mansaw*, 714 F.2d 785, 789 (8th Cir. 1983) (giving a false name); *United States v. Reid*, 634 F.2d 469, 473–74 (9th Cir. 1980) (giving false name, occupation, name of business, and purpose in information request to government).

In this case, the trial court acted properly in allowing counsel to ask Witness if he had lied about his job experience on his application. The facts suggest Witness's testimony was critical to establish that Plaintiff had removed a safety guard from the table saw. This testimony could be devastating to Plaintiff's claim. Consequently, this line of inquiry was relevant and probative of Witness's truthfulness and the court was reasonable in its decision to permit counsel to cross-examine Witness about his job application. FED. R. EVID. 608(b).

[NOTE: Admission into evidence of a *document* containing the falsehood might violate the extrinsic evidence rule (*see* Point Two), but questioning the witness about such a document does not. *See United States v. Jackson*, 882 F.2d 1444, 1448–49 (9th Cir. 1989); *Cole*, 617 F.2d at 154.]

Point Two (20–30%)

<u>The trial court was within its discretion in excluding Exhibit 37 because Rule 608(b) forbids the use of extrinsic evidence to attack a witness's character for truthfulness.</u>

Rule 608(b) expressly prohibits the use of extrinsic evidence to impeach a witness's character for truthfulness: "Specific instances of the conduct of a witness, for the purpose of attacking or supporting the witness's character for truthfulness . . . may not be proved by extrinsic evidence." FED. R. EVID. 608(b). Thus, although a witness may be cross-examined about a prior alleged lie, if he refuses to admit to lying, he may not be contradicted with extrinsic evidence. Rule 608(b) does not define "extrinsic evidence," and there is disagreement among federal courts and evidence scholars about the term's meaning. With respect to documents, one approach holds that a document is extrinsic evidence in all circumstances. The other, more lenient approach holds that a document is not extrinsic evidence if the witness being impeached can provide the foundation for admission of the document. *See* Kevin C. McMunigal & Calvin W. Sharpe, *Reforming Extrinsic Impeachment*, 33 CONN. L. REV. 363, 372–73 (2001) (concluding that a job application containing a lie would be extrinsic under the former approach, but not under the latter); *United States v. Elliott*, 89 F.3d 1360, 1368 (8th Cir. 1996) (holding that the trial court did not abuse its discretion in excluding the résumé of a witness offered to impeach the witness under Rule 608(b) by showing a misrepresentation of educational and employment experience).

Thus, whether the Court should have admitted Exhibit 37 depends on which approach prevails in this jurisdiction.

[NOTE: An applicant should receive full credit if the applicant recognizes the extrinsic evidence issue.]

Point Three (15–25%)
Exhibit 37 was not admissible to refresh Witness's recollection because Rule 612 permits only counsel for the opposing party to offer such a document into evidence.

Since the Court permitted cross-examination concerning Exhibit 37, it was proper to allow the cross-examiner to try to get Witness to change his denial of lying on the job application. The cross-examiner need not take the first answer a witness offers. *See Carter v. Hewitt*, 617 F.2d 961, 969–73 (3d Cir. 1980); *United States v. Ling*, 581 F.2d 1118, 1121 (4th Cir. 1978). The cross-examiner thus appropriately showed Exhibit 37 to Witness to refresh his recollection before asking him again whether he had lied.

However, when an otherwise inadmissible document is shown to a witness to refresh his recollection, the witness must read it to himself. It is improper to allow such a document to be read aloud to the jury, and it may be admitted as an exhibit only if offered by the lawyer who has not used the exhibit to refresh the recollection of the witness. *See* FED. R. EVID. 612; CHRISTOPHER B. MUELLER & LAIRD C. KIRKPATRICK, FEDERAL EVIDENCE § 6:96 (3d ed. 2007).

[NOTE: It may have been improper for the Court to permit Plaintiff's Counsel to attempt to "refresh" Witness's recollection, given that Witness did not testify to any lack of memory about what was said on the job application. However, Defense Counsel did not object to the attempt to refresh recollection, but only to the admission of the job application as an exhibit. Accordingly, only the admission of the exhibit is at issue.]

Point Four (10–20%)
The trial court properly excluded the testimony of Contractor because testimony by another witness represents extrinsic proof of the prior bad act and therefore is not admissible under Rule 608(b).

The trial court correctly refused to permit testimony from Contractor that Witness had claimed 12 years of experience on his job application. This testimony was relevant only to the witness's credibility and clearly constituted extrinsic evidence. FED. R. EVID. 608(b); *see also United States v. Abel*, 469 U.S. 45, 55 (1984) (witness's testimony about defendant's gang membership was inadmissible extrinsic evidence of defendant's veracity; however, evidence of gang membership was admissible to show defendant's bias).

MBE SUBJECTS – RELEASED ESSAY QUESTIONS

EVIDENCE
MEE Question – February 2010

ANALYSIS

Legal Problems: (1)   Should the court exclude Witness's opinion that Driver was speeding?

               (2)   Should the court exclude Spouse's testimony as to Pedestrian's character for being cautious and risk-averse?

               (3)   Should the court exclude evidence of Pedestrian's habit of lowering her cell phone or ending a call when crossing a street?

               (4)(a) Should the court admit evidence of Pedestrian's memory loss?

               (4)(b) If the court does admit evidence of Pedestrian's memory loss, should it then also admit the evidence of Pedestrian's other injuries?

DISCUSSION

Summary

Witness's proffered testimony that Driver was speeding is relevant to the issues of Driver's negligence and causation. Although it is an opinion, it is admissible because non-experts may offer opinions on relevant, non-technical issues, rationally based on their personal perceptions.

The court should exclude Spouse's testimony that Pedestrian is cautious and risk-averse. Evidence of character traits is not admissible to prove action in conformity with those character traits in civil cases.

Pedestrian's testimony that she always lowers her cell phone and checks for traffic before entering intersections is admissible evidence of a habit and may be offered to prove that she acted in conformity with that habit on the day in question.

Proof of Pedestrian's concussion and memory loss is relevant and admissible to show that Pedestrian is not a reliable witness and that the facts to which Pedestrian is testifying are therefore "less probable" than they would otherwise be.

However, even if the court admits evidence of Pedestrian's concussion, it should not admit evidence of her other injuries. Because the parties have stipulated the extent of injury and the resulting damages, evidence of those injuries is irrelevant and likely to unfairly prejudice the jury.

Point One (20%)
The court should allow Witness to offer an opinion on the speed of Driver's car.

To be admissible, evidence must be relevant. FED. R. EVID. 402. Relevant evidence is any evidence that tends "to make the existence" of a "fact that is of consequence to the determination of the action more probable or less probable than it would be without the evidence." FED. R. EVID. 401. Witness's testimony is relevant to the determination of the action because the fact that Driver was speeding, if true, would make it more likely that Driver was acting negligently and was the cause of the accident. Under Rule 403, relevant evidence can be excluded under certain circumstances, but there are no facts in this question to suggest an appropriate ground for exclusion under this rule. *See* FED. R. EVID. 403 (relevant evidence may be excluded if it is unduly prejudicial, confusing, cumulative, a waste of time, or a source of undue delay in the proceedings).

However, Witness's testimony is in the form of an opinion. Rule 701 places restrictions on non-expert opinion evidence. A witness who is not testifying as an expert may offer an opinion only if

(a) the opinion is "rationally based on the [witness's] perception" of what happened;
(b) the opinion helps determine "a fact in issue"; and
(c) the opinion is "not based on scientific, technical, or other specialized knowledge" that is governed by Rule 702.

FED. R. EVID. 701.

In this case, Witness's testimony meets all three requirements. First, Witness saw Driver's car as it approached the intersection and was able to perceive its speed. In addition, Witness was able to observe Driver's speed relative to that of other cars around it, and Witness observed that Driver's car was moving noticeably faster than surrounding cars. These perceptions provide a rational and logical basis for Witness's opinion that the car was speeding.

Second, there is no question that whether Driver was speeding is a fact relevant to Pedestrian's claim. If Driver was speeding, that fact would make it more likely that Driver was driving negligently and that Driver's negligence caused the collision.

Finally, Witness is not an "expert in disguise" who is attempting to sneak in an opinion based on scientific or engineering principles. Witness's opinion that Driver was speeding is a commonsense conclusion based on direct observations. No specialized training, experience, or education is necessary to form a valid opinion on such a basis.

[NOTE: How much weight the jury should give this opinion is an issue for the jury and does not affect admissibility.]

Point Two (25%)
The court should not admit Spouse's testimony regarding Pedestrian's character trait of being cautious and risk-averse.

Spouse's proposed testimony that Pedestrian is very cautious and risk-averse is testimony about Pedestrian's character. The purpose of offering the testimony is to suggest that Pedestrian would have acted consistently with that character on the day in question and would have checked before entering the intersection. If true, that would tend to establish that Pedestrian was not negligent. The evidence is therefore relevant.

However, Federal Rule of Evidence 404(a) restricts the use of character evidence, even when such evidence is relevant. Rule 404(a) provides that "evidence of a person's character or a trait of character is not admissible for the purpose of proving action in conformity therewith on a particular occasion," except in three situations that apply exclusively to criminal trials. Here, Spouse's testimony that Pedestrian generally is cautious and risk-averse is relevant precisely because it suggests that on the day of the collision Pedestrian was acting in a cautious and risk-averse manner. This is exactly what Rule 404(a) forbids, and the testimony is inadmissible.

Point Three (25%)
The court should admit Pedestrian's testimony about Pedestrian's cell phone usage habits.

Habit evidence is admissible to prove that a person acted in conformity with that habit. FED. R. EVID. 406. This is true even if the only evidence of a habit is Pedestrian's own testimony. Rule 406 specifically authorizes the use of habit evidence "whether corroborated or not and regardless of the presence of eyewitnesses." Pedestrian's testimony will provide sufficient background information to establish that she actually has a habit of lowering her cell phone and looking both ways when crossing a street. Pedestrian claims to have acted in conformity with this habit when entering the intersection, which is relevant to Pedestrian's defense against Driver's claim that Pedestrian was contributorily negligent. Therefore, this evidence is admissible.

Point Four(a) (15%)
The court should admit the evidence of Pedestrian's memory loss.

Pedestrian's concussion is relevant, albeit indirectly, to determining who is liable for the collision. Pedestrian intends to testify at trial about what happened, but the concussion has erased some of her memory. Evidence of memory loss is relevant because it has a tendency to suggest to the jury that Pedestrian's testimony concerning the events related to the collision is less reliable. The evidence of memory loss may make the facts to which Pedestrian testifies "less probable." FED. R. EVID. 401. Rule 403 is not a basis to deny Driver's motion because it would not be "unfairly prejudicial" to Pedestrian to allow Driver to benefit from Pedestrian's inability to recall what happened. *Cf. Davis v. Alaska*, 415 U.S. 308, 316 (1974) ("[T]he cross-examiner is . . . permitted to delve into the witness'[s] story to test the witness'[s] perceptions and memory . . . .").

Point Four(b) (15%)
The court should exclude the evidence of Pedestrian's other injuries.

Rules 401–403 also establish that evidence of Pedestrian's fractures is not relevant and not admissible. The parties have stipulated to these injuries and have agreed on the value of the compensation due to Pedestrian if Driver is responsible for these injuries. Therefore, the fact that Pedestrian suffered these additional injuries does not, by itself, tend to prove any fact of consequence in dispute that will aid in the determination of who caused the collision. Therefore, such evidence is a "waste of time" under Rule 403. It is also "unfairly prejudicial in the sense that the evidence is unnecessary and might cause the jury improperly to sympathize" with Pedestrian without advancing the factual inquiry at all. *See, e.g., Miller v. New Jersey Transit Authority Rail Operations*, 160 F.R.D. 37, 42 (D.N.J. 1995) (bifurcating damages phase of trial from liability necessary because "the severity of Plaintiff's injuries would prejudice the defendants so severely if issues of liability and damages were not bifurcated that the defendants would not receive a fair trial").

[NOTE: To the extent that Driver's introduction of evidence of Pedestrian's memory loss includes evidence of the severity of Pedestrian's injuries, Pedestrian can argue, and the judge could find, that the parties' stipulation has been violated. If the stipulation is no longer in effect, this could open the door to admission of evidence of Plaintiff's other injuries, subject to Federal Rules of Evidence 401 and 403.]

MBE SUBJECTS – RELEASED ESSAY QUESTIONS

EVIDENCE
MEE Question – February 2011

ANALYSIS

Legal Problems: (1) May a witness who testifies to a lack of memory at trial be impeached with a prior inconsistent statement, and may extrinsic evidence of the prior inconsistent statement be admitted?

(2) May a prior statement of identification be admitted?

(3) May a prior inconsistent statement made to the police be admitted to prove the elements of the charged offenses?

(4) May a defense witness's testimony about what his friends think of a criminal defendant whom they met recently just a few times be admitted to prove that the defendant is honest and gentle?

DISCUSSION

Summary

Witness's statement to Police Officer contradicted her testimony at trial. This is a "prior inconsistent statement" that can be used at trial to impeach her credibility. Because Witness's testimony that she did not remember the incident and did not recognize Defendant was inconsistent with her written statement, because her lack of memory was likely feigned, and because she was given an opportunity to explain the statement, the court should have permitted Prosecutor to question Witness about her prior inconsistent statement and admitted the authenticated copy of Witness's statement to impeach Witness.

Part of Witness's statement—"I was walking in City Park on May 5, at 2 p.m., when I saw Defendant. I know Defendant from the neighborhood and recognized Defendant as suspect number 1 on the 12-person photograph display shown to me today by Police Officer"—should have been admitted as a statement of identification, which is not hearsay as defined in the Federal Rules of Evidence. FED. R. EVID. 801(d)(1)(C). The remainder of Witness's statement—"I saw Defendant attack Victim and then run away with Victim's bag"—was properly excluded because, although inconsistent, the statement was not made "under oath subject to the penalty of perjury at a trial, hearing, or other proceeding, or in a deposition." FED. R. EVID. 801(d)(1)(A).

Buddy's testimony was properly excluded because even relevant character evidence must be introduced in the form of proper opinion or reputation evidence. Buddy did not testify to his own opinion, and Buddy's knowledge of his friends' opinions did not provide evidence of Defendant's reputation.

Point One (25%)

A prior inconsistent statement is ordinarily admissible for the purpose of impeaching the credibility of a witness. Extrinsic evidence of the prior statement, such as the written statement itself, may be admitted when the witness has been given an opportunity to explain or deny the statement.

It is generally permissible for a litigant to impeach the credibility of any witness, including a witness called by that litigant. FED. R. EVID. 607. Moreover, it is common and proper to impeach a witness's credibility "by showing that the witness has made prior statements inconsistent with his [or her] testimony at trial." GRAHAM C. LILLY, AN INTRODUCTION TO THE LAW OF EVIDENCE § 8.5, at 414 (3d ed. 1996).

In order to introduce a prior out-of-court statement to impeach a witness's credibility, there must be an inconsistency between the prior out-of-court statement and the witness's trial testimony. The inconsistency must involve a relevant issue. If a witness testifies to a lack of memory regarding a relevant issue contained in a prior out-of-court statement, the judge may find that this testimony is inconsistent with the out-of-court statement on the same issue. Moreover, if the judge finds that the lack of memory is feigned, the court is more likely to find that the testimony and statement are inconsistent. *See* MICHAEL H. GRAHAM, HANDBOOK ON FEDERAL EVIDENCE § 613.2 (5th ed. 2001). Here, there is more than a claimed lack of present memory concerning the facts. Witness testified that she had never seen Defendant in her life and denied that she had told Police Officer that she saw Defendant rob Victim. Thus, her trial testimony is inconsistent with her previous written statement. Her testimony is also strongly suggestive of feigned memory loss.

Thus, the court should have allowed Prosecutor to question Witness about the entire statement. The written statement may also be admitted as extrinsic evidence. Witness should also have been given an opportunity to explain or deny all or part of the written statement, and the statement should have been admitted to impeach Witness's credibility by proving that she made prior inconsistent statements. Admission of Witness's statement for the limited purpose of impeaching her trial testimony does not raise hearsay concerns because it is not admitted to prove the truth of the matter asserted in the statement.

[NOTE: At Defense Counsel's request, the judge should instruct the jury that the prosecution cannot rely on Witness's prior written statement, which was admitted solely to impeach Witness's credibility, to prove any of the elements of the charged offenses.]

Point Two (25%)

Part of Witness's statement—"I was walking in City Park on May 5, at 2 p.m., when I saw Defendant. I know Defendant from the neighborhood and recognized Defendant as suspect number 1 on the 12-person photograph display shown to me today by Police Officer"—should have been admitted as a statement of identification, which is not hearsay.

A prior statement of identification of a person made after perceiving the person is not hearsay if the witness who made the statement testifies at trial and is subject to cross-examination concerning the statement. FED. R. EVID. 801(d)(1)(C). The rationale for this rule is that the opportunity to cross-examine the witness concerning the statement takes it outside the scope of the hearsay rule. FED. R. EVID. 801(d)(1). For the statement to be admissible to prove the truth of the matter asserted under this provision, it is not necessary that the speaker be able to confirm the identification at trial or remember the identity of the person. If the declarant testifies and is subject to cross-examination concerning the identification, the declarant's lack of memory at trial does not defeat admissibility and the requirements of Rule 801(d)(1)(C) are fulfilled. *United States v. Owens,* 484 U.S. 554 (1988).

In this case, Witness's prior written statement included an identification of Defendant. That identification was made by Witness based on Witness's knowledge of Defendant from the neighborhood, Witness's direct observation of Defendant in City Park on May 5 at 2 p.m., and Witness's recognition of Defendant's photograph. That prior statement of identification of Defendant is excluded from the general definition of hearsay when, as here, Witness testifies and is subject to cross-examination concerning the statement.

Point Three (20%)
The remainder of Witness's prior inconsistent statement made to the police—"I saw Defendant attack Victim and then run away with Victim's bag"—may not be admitted to prove the elements of the charged offenses because it is hearsay.

Under the Federal Rules of Evidence, certain prior inconsistent statements are not hearsay. FED. R. EVID. 801(d)(1)(A). However, to be admissible to prove the truth of the matter asserted, the prior inconsistent statement must be made "under oath, subject to the penalty of perjury at a trial, hearing, or other proceeding, or in a deposition." *Id.* Witness's statement to the police does not fit within this rule, nor does it fit within any hearsay exception.

Point Four (30%)
A criminal defendant may introduce evidence of his good character relating to a relevant character trait. Character may be proved only through testimony of reputation or opinion.

Character evidence is generally inadmissible to prove that a person acted in conformity with a particular character trait. However, a defendant in a criminal case is permitted to offer evidence of a relevant character trait to prove that the defendant did not commit the charged offense. FED. R. EVID. 404(a)(1). Because Defendant is charged with robbery and assault (both crimes of violence), evidence that Defendant is a "gentle person who would never hurt anyone" would be relevant. FED. R. EVID. 401. Evidence that Defendant is "honest" is a closer call. Committing a robbery or an assault is not inconsistent with having a reputation for truth-telling, if being "honest" means being a truth-teller. *See United States v. Darland,* 626 F.2d 1235 (5th Cir. 1980). On the other hand, robbery is a form of theft, and theft is dishonest. So a court might admit evidence of Defendant's honesty, as well as evidence of his gentleness.

However, the Federal Rules of Evidence limit the ways in which a defendant's character traits may be proven. *See* FED. R. EVID. 405(a). In particular, "proof may [only] be made by testimony as to reputation or by testimony in the form of an opinion." *Id. See also Michelson v. United States,* 335 U.S. 469 (1948).

Here, Buddy did not testify as to his own opinion or Defendant's community reputation. Rather, he said that a few of his friends think that Defendant is honest and gentle. Buddy's testimony about his friends' opinions of Defendant does not qualify as evidence of Defendant's "reputation in the community." "Community" includes circles of associates where one lives, works, or regularly socializes. *United States v. Oliver*, 492 F.2d 943 (8th Cir. 1974); *United States v. Parker*, 447 F.2d 826, 830–31 (7th Cir. 1971). Buddy's friends' opinions do not qualify as reputation testimony because the friends met Defendant recently and only a few times.

MBE SUBJECTS – RELEASED ESSAY QUESTIONS

EVIDENCE
MEE Question – February 2012

ANALYSIS

Legal Problems

(1)   Should the court admit evidence of the hospital's subsequent remedial measures when those measures would have prevented or mitigated the woman's injuries if they had been in place at the time of the alleged tortious conduct?

(2)   Should the court admit evidence of the hospital's offer to pay the woman when that offer was made after her lawsuit had been filed?

(3)(a) Should the court admit evidence of the man's offer to pay the woman when the offer was made before the woman's claim was in dispute?

(3)(b) Should the court admit evidence of the man's offer to pay the woman's medical expenses?

(4)   Should the court admit evidence of the woman's past sexual relations in a civil suit alleging that she was sexually assaulted?

DISCUSSION

Summary

While evidence of the hospital's subsequent remedial measures may be relevant to a determination of its liability for the woman's physical and psychological injuries, this evidence is inadmissible because subsequent remedial measures that would have made an injury less likely to occur are not admissible to prove negligence or other culpable conduct.

Although evidence of the hospital's offer to settle with the woman may be relevant to a determination of the hospital's negligence, settlement offers are inadmissible to prove negligence.

Evidence of the man's offer to pay the woman $10,000 may be relevant to a determination of his liability. This evidence is admissible because his offer was made before the woman's claim was disputed and before she filed her civil suit.

Evidence of the man's offer to pay the woman's medical expenses may be relevant to a determination of his liability. However, this evidence is inadmissible because evidence of an offer to pay medical and other similar expenses caused by an injury is inadmissible to prove liability for the injury.

Evidence that the woman has engaged in sexual relations in the past with another student should be admitted. This evidence has significant probative value because the woman has specifically alleged psychological injuries attributable to her belief in abstinence before marriage and her lack of prior sexual experience. On these facts, the court should find that the probative value of this evidence "substantially outweighs" the potential harm that could inure to the woman when the jurors hear evidence that she engaged in sexual relations with another student.

Point One (20%)
The court should exclude evidence of the hospital's subsequent remedial measures.

Evidence is relevant if it has "any tendency to make a fact" either "more or less probable than it would be without the evidence." FED. R. EVID. 401 (as amended December 1, 2011). "Relevant evidence is admissible," unless it is inadmissible pursuant to some other rule. FED. R. EVID. 402. The woman has alleged that the hospital caused the exacerbation of her injuries by negligently delaying her medical treatment for three hours pursuant to its then-existing standard policy. The hospital's decision to change its policy and provide immediate treatment to all sexual assault victims suggests that it has concluded that its old policy was inappropriate. This may be relevant to the woman's claim that the hospital's decision to deny her immediate treatment was negligent.

However, evidence of the policy change is nonetheless inadmissible. Rule 407 of the Federal Rules of Evidence provides that "[w]hen measures are taken that would have made an earlier injury or harm less likely to occur, evidence of the subsequent measures is not admissible to prove negligence." FED. R. EVID. 407. Here, the hospital's policy change is a subsequent measure that could have made the woman's alleged injury less likely had the policy been in place at the time she visited the hospital. The woman wishes to introduce evidence of the policy change to establish that the hospital's behavior pursuant to its prior policy was negligent. There are no facts indicating that this evidence is relevant to prove anything other than the hospital's negligence in this case. But such evidence, even when relevant, is excluded based on "a social policy of encouraging people to take, or at least not discouraging them from taking, steps in furtherance of added safety." FED. R. EVID. 407 advisory committee's note. *See Werner v. Upjohn Co., Inc.*, 628 F.2d 848, 857 (4th Cir. 1980) (explaining that Rule 407 is intended to guard against the fact that people "would be less likely to take subsequent remedial measures if their repairs or improvements would be used against them in a lawsuit").

Point Two (20%)
The court should exclude evidence of the hospital's offer to settle with the woman.

Evidence of the hospital's offer to settle with the woman may be relevant to a determination of its negligence because this evidence has some tendency to make it more probable that the hospital engaged in negligent conduct. FED. R. EVID. 401. However, the Federal Rules of Evidence bar evidence that a party "furnish[ed] or promis[ed] or offer[ed] . . . a valuable consideration in compromising or attempting to compromise the [disputed] claim." FED. R. EVID. 408. Rule 408 excludes settlement offers and statements made during settlement negotiations. Evidence of offers to settle "disputed claim[s]" is excluded based on "the promotion of the public policy favoring the compromise and settlement of disputes." FED. R. EVID. 408 advisory committee's note.

Here, the hospital's offer to settle with the woman falls squarely within this rule and should be excluded from evidence. Its offer was an effort to settle with the woman. Because the offer was made after the woman filed her claim, it was made at a time when her "claim was disputed as to validity or amount." She seeks to admit the offer to help prove the hospital's liability for her claim. Rule 408 bars admission of the evidence under these circumstances.

[NOTE: In their discussion of this issue and of Point Three, some examinees might discuss whether any out-of-court statements by the man or the hospital would be excluded from evidence by the hearsay rule. In this case, the hearsay rule would not exclude these statements because they were made by an opposing party. FED. R. EVID. 801(d)(2). A statement by the man is "an opposing party's statement." *Id.* A statement by the hospital is either a statement "made by a person whom the party authorized to make a statement on the subject," FED. R. EVID. 801(d)(2)(C), or a statement "made by the party's agent or employee on a matter within the scope of that relationship and while it existed." FED. R. EVID. 801(d)(2)(D).]

Point Three(a) (20%)
The court should admit evidence of the man's offer to pay the woman $10,000.

Evidence of the man's statement "If you are upset about what happened, I can send you a check for $10,000 to help you forget the whole thing" may be relevant to a determination of his liability. This evidence has some tendency to make it more probable that the man believed that the woman might have some valid basis for filing a complaint against him. FED. R. EVID. 401. The question is whether this offer to the woman, like the hospital's offer, is barred from admission by Rule 408.

As noted above, an offer to compromise is barred from admission only if it is made in response to a "disputed claim." FED. R. EVID. 408. In this instance, the man made his offer to the woman almost four months before she filed this suit. Rule 408 excludes settlement offers and statements made during settlement negotiations. Although Rule 408 does not require that a lawsuit be filed, here the man made his offer before the woman had made any claim at all against him, much less a "disputed claim," and therefore his offer is not excluded under Rule 408.

Point Three(b) (20%)
The court should exclude evidence of the man's offer to pay the woman's medical expenses.

Evidence of the man's offer to pay the woman's medical expenses is probably relevant, but the court should nonetheless exclude the evidence. Federal Rule 409 precludes admission of "[e]vi-dence of furnishing, promising to pay, or offering to pay medical . . . expenses resulting from an injury . . . to prove liability for the injury." FED. R. EVID. 409. Such evidence is excluded because "such payment or offer is usually made from humane impulses and . . . to hold otherwise would tend to discourage assistance to the injured person." FED. R. EVID. 409 advisory committee's note (*quoting* 20 A.L.R. 2d 291, 293). Unlike Rule 408, Rule 409 does not require that the statement be made in response to a disputed claim.

Point Four (20%)
The court should admit evidence of the woman's past sexual behavior because the probative value of the evidence substantially outweighs the danger of harm to her.

In any "civil or criminal proceeding involving alleged sexual misconduct," the "Rape Shield" rule of the Federal Rules of Evidence generally bars the admission of "evidence offered to prove that a victim engaged in other sexual behavior." FED. R. EVID. 412(a). The purpose of the rule is "to safeguard the alleged victim against the invasion of privacy, potential embarrassment and sexual stereotyping that is associated with public disclosure of intimate sexual details and the infusion of sexual innuendo into the fact finding process." FED. R. EVID. 412 advisory committee's note.

However, in civil cases, Federal Rule of Evidence 412 permits the admission of otherwise inadmissible evidence of an alleged victim's sexual behavior "if its probative value substantially outweighs the danger of harm to any victim." FED. R. EVID. 412(b)(2). In this case, evidence of the woman's past sexual behavior with another student has significant probative value because the woman has specifically alleged psychological injuries attributable to her belief in abstinence before marriage and her lack of prior sexual experience. Here, the court is likely to find that the probative value of this evidence "substantially outweighs" the potential harm that could inure to the woman when the jurors learn that she previously had sexual relations with another student.

MBE SUBJECTS – RELEASED ESSAY QUESTIONS

EVIDENCE
MEE Question – February 2013

ANALYSIS

Legal Problems

(1) Is the authenticated copy of the mechanic's text message relevant and admissible?

(2) Is the woman's question, "Is my scooter safe to drive for a while?" relevant and admissible?

(3) Is the woman's testimony describing the mechanic's thumbs-up relevant and admissible?

DISCUSSION

Summary

The mechanic's text message to the woman is relevant to whether (1) the woman lost control of the scooter due to its defective brakes, (2) the woman knew that the brakes needed repair, and (3) it was negligent for the woman to drive the scooter knowing that its brakes needed repair.

The mechanic's text message is hearsay if it is offered by the pedestrian to prove that the scooter's brakes needed repair. However, it fits the hearsay exception for present sense impressions and probably also fits the exception for business records. The mechanic's text message is not hearsay if it is instead offered by the pedestrian to prove the woman's state of mind (i.e., that she had notice that her brakes needed repair).

The woman's question to the mechanic and his response are also relevant to whether the brakes caused the accident and whether the woman was negligent. The question is not hearsay because the woman did not make an assertion.

The mechanic's thumbs-up response is nonverbal conduct intended by the mechanic as an assertion and is therefore an out-of-court statement. If the woman offers the mechanic's statement to prove that the scooter was actually safe to ride, the woman's testimony about the statement is hearsay.

However, the mechanic's statement is not hearsay if it is offered by the woman to prove her state of mind. Therefore, the woman's question and the mechanic's response are admissible to prove the woman's state of mind.

Point One(a) (20%)
The mechanic's text message to the woman should be admitted because it is relevant.

Evidence is relevant if it has "any tendency to make a fact more or less probable than it would be without the evidence." FED. R. EVID. 401. "Relevant evidence is admissible," unless it is inadmissible pursuant to some other rule. FED. R. EVID. 402.

The mechanic's text message to the woman, "When you pick up your scooter, you need to schedule a follow-up brake repair. We'll order the parts," is relevant for two reasons. First, this evidence has some tendency to make it more probable that the brakes malfunctioned and caused the accident. Second, it has some tendency to make it more probable that the woman was negligent in riding her scooter after being told by the mechanic that it required further repair.

Point One(b) (30%)
The mechanic's text message fits either the hearsay exception for present sense impressions or the exception for business records, or it is admissible non-hearsay.

The mechanic's text message is a statement under Rule 801(a) because it is "a written assertion." FED. R. EVID. 801(a). The text message is hearsay if the pedestrian offers it to prove the "truth of the matter asserted in the statement" (i.e., that the scooter's brakes required repair), which resulted in the woman losing control of the scooter and causing the accident. FED. R. EVID. 801(c).

However, the mechanic's text message fits the hearsay exception for "present sense impressions" under Rule 803(1) because it is "[a] statement describing or explaining an event or condition made while or immediately after the declarant perceived it." FED. R. EVID. 803(1). Here, the mechanic's text message described the condition of the scooter immediately after he perceived it during the maintenance service.

The mechanic is a person with knowledge of the condition of the scooter, so if text messages regarding repairs were made and kept by the mechanic in the ordinary course of business, this text message also fits the business records exception. Under Rule 803(6), a business record is a record of an act "made at or near the time by . . . someone with knowledge" and "the record was kept in the course of a regularly conducted activity of a business" and "making the record was a regular practice of that activity." FED. R. EVID. 803(6).

However, the text message is not hearsay if it is instead offered to prove that the woman was negligent because she rode her scooter after the mechanic told her it required repair. If offered for this purpose, it would not be offered for the truth of the matter asserted in the statement, but to show the woman's belief about the condition of the scooter (her state of mind).

Point Two (10%)
The woman's question to the mechanic should be admitted because it is not hearsay.

The woman's question to the mechanic is relevant because, along with the mechanic's thumbs-up response (*see* Point Three), it has some tendency to make it more probable that the woman was not negligent and/or that the scooter brakes did not malfunction and cause the accident. FED.

R. EVID. 401. The woman's question does not raise hearsay concerns because it is not an assertion.

Hearsay is defined under Rule 801(a) as "an oral assertion, written assertion, or nonverbal conduct." Although "assertion" is not further defined, "a favorite [definition] of writers in the [evidence] field for at least a century and a half [is that] the word simply means *to say that something is so,* e.g., that an event happened or a condition existed." 2 MCCORMICK ON EVIDENCE § 246 (6th ed. 2006). Under this definition, the woman's question is not hearsay because it is not an assertion.

Point Three(a) (20%)
The mechanic's thumbs-up to the woman is a nonverbal assertion that is relevant, and the woman's testimony about that response is admissible.

Hearsay is defined under Rule 801(c) as a "statement," that is, "a person's oral assertion, written assertion, or nonverbal conduct, if the person intended it as an assertion." FED. R. EVID. 801(a). Here, when the mechanic responded to the woman's question ("Is my scooter safe to ride for a while?") with a thumbs-up gesture, the facts suggest that he intended his nonverbal conduct as an assertion that, in his opinion, the scooter was safe to ride.

The mechanic's assertion is relevant and admissible to prove that the woman was not negligent because the evidence makes it more probable that, at the time of the accident, she believed that the scooter was safe to ride, despite the fact that the brakes required repair. FED. R. EVID. 401. Admission of the woman's description of the mechanic's thumbs-up for this purpose does not raise hearsay concerns because the evidence would not be offered for the truth of the matter asserted, but to show the woman's belief about the condition of the scooter (her state of mind).

Point Three(b) (20%)
The mechanic's thumbs-up is relevant to determine whether the scooter's brakes malfunctioned, causing the accident, but if offered for this purpose it is also hearsay.

The mechanic's nonverbal assertion is relevant to the determination of whether the scooter's brakes malfunctioned, causing the accident. However, if offered to prove the "truth of the matter asserted in the statement" (i.e., that the scooter was safe to ride for a while), it is hearsay that does not fit any hearsay exception.

MBE SUBJECTS - PRACTICE ESSAY QUESTIONS

EVIDENCE
Answer to Question 1

When assessing an evidentiary issue, the first rule is all evidence is admissible if relevant. Evidence is relevant if it would assist the trier of fact in determining an issue of the claim more or less probable. Here, the witnesses presented raise the issue of relevance and should be assessed as to each witness.

When dealing with witnesses, the issue of hearsay invariably arises. Hearsay is any out-of-court statement offered to prove the truth of the matter asserted. All hearsay is inadmissible unless it falls under one of the exceptions. There are out-of-court statements that do not qualify as hearsay such as a party admission. The reason is the veracity of the statement is upheld by the context or circumstances under which the statement is made. Therefore, the court can trust some out-of-court statements, but others are hearsay and are presumed inadmissible.

Witness – psychologist –

The psychologist may appear as an expert witness for the prosecution. An expert witness may appear after people foundation is laid. The expert must be qualified by training, education, experience and industry standards. If such foundation is established, the expert may testify by giving opinion on issues that may be used as substantive evidence by the jury. The expert may also review tapes or material, observe in court or conduct examination to make an opinion. This differs from a lay witness who may only give opinion based on personal knowledge. Here, W#1 will testify on her review of the police interview and interviews conducted by her with the parents. W#1 may give opinions on the CSAAS diagnosis, which is relevant as it would assist the trier of fact in understanding the condition V suffers from the abuse. As a relevant expert witness, W#1 may testify to her work and give her expert opinion on the issues relevant to the case.

Witness #2

Witness #2 is not likely able to testify. A witness cannot impeach a party using specific bold acts. Additionally, the relevancy of W#2 is questionable since child molestation and rape are two very different crimes. Here, the defendant is charged with child molestation. The prosecution wishes to bring in witness to show defendant raped her. This bad act would only go to the propensity to commit a crime.

Under the federal rules, evidence is inadmissible when the prejudicial harm substantially outweighs any probative value. Showing conformity to commit sexual assault is highly prejudicial. The relevance or probative value of merely showing his sexual problems is slight at best. Therefore, because of its prejudicial harm and showing conformity, the testimony of W#2 is likely inadmissible.

Prosecution could argue these past sexual problems show identity or state of mind. Bad conduct is allowed if going to lack of mistake, identity, or state of mind. Here, the prosecution could argue the testimony of W#2 goes to show state of mind or identity of the sexual abuser. However, with the analysis above, it is not likely such witness will survive judicial review.

As a child abuse case, the court may allow past sexual convictions in. A past sexual conviction is relevant in a child abuse claim. If W#2 charged and convicted defendant, she might be relevant in showing identity or state of mind, enough to overcome the prejudicial harm or risk in showing conformity. Under this standard, therefore, W#2 may be able to testify.

Witness #3

Witness #3 wants to testify to a hearsay statement. As defined above, Ms. X's prior out-of-court statement would be offered to prove the truth asserted in the statement that she initiated a false claim against D about molesting V. W#3 would be able to testify on the grounds Ms. X's statement is a party admission if she were a party to the claim. A party admission is non-hearsay and admissible. Here, Ms. X initiated the claim on the behalf of her child. She may qualify as a party to the claim and therefore her statement is admissible as non-hearsay. However, Ms. X is not a party to the claim since it is between the state and the defendant. Therefore, her out-of-court statement is hearsay and inadmissible.

When a declarant is unavailable, his or her past statements are limited in admissibility. An unavailable declarant's statement may be admissible only if a dying declaration, excited utterance or against self interest at the time stated. Here, Ms. X's statement that she framed D is against her self-interest. She does not need to be available to make the statement admissible. Therefore, the statement is admissible.

Witness #4

A defendant may raise his character first unless it is a material element in a claim. A character witness may testify by opinion and reputation to the relevant character of the defendant. Here, W#4 wishes to testify to D's trustworthiness with children. W#4 wishes to testify to her opinion in this area. She may not use specific instances where D was trustworthy, but may give her general opinion to D's reputation. Therefore, W#4 may testify to D's reputation to being trustworthy with kids.

W#4 may also testify to D's reputation for sexual and social propriety. Again, using the reasoning from above, W#4 may testify in her opinion and in general terms regarding the character relevant to D's defense. W#4 will undergo cross examination where the prosecution may test her knowledge and soundness of D. However, as a person with personal knowledge of D's reputation, W#4 may testify using general terms to the character and reputation of D.

Witness #5

Witness #5 may not testify as character impeachment to Witness #1. A character of a witness may be attacked, but not by extrinsic evidence. Here, Witness #5 would serve as extrinsic evidence to impeach W#1's character and truthfulness. This is not allowed. Therefore, Witness #5 is inadmissible as a witness.

Alternately, Witness #5 may testify to show bias. A witness may be impeached using extrinsic evidence if showing bias. Here, Witness #5 would go to showing Witness #1 bias in diagnosing V. If Witness #1 adopts a policy of lenient diagnosing then that could be a bias. Therefore, if offered to show bias, Witness #5 may be admissible as a witness for D.

MBE SUBJECTS - PRACTICE ESSAY QUESTIONS

EVIDENCE
Answer to Question 2

I. Introduction

A motion to suppress evidence will depend on the exclusionary rule. The exclusionary rule is a judge-made rule which excludes evidence that was unlawfully obtained. If it is determined that evidence was unlawfully obtained, then the issue is if other evidence will be excluded as well through the use of "Fruit of a Poisonous Tree" Doctrine. Under that doctrine, all evidence obtained from an illegal search or seizure or from an improper interrogation will also be excluded, unless the evidence could have been found or seized through one of the three exceptions to this doctrine. The three exceptions are: (1) if the evidence could have been obtained through an independent source; (2) if the evidence would have been inevitably discovered; or (3) the evidence was seized/obtained through an intervening act of free will on part of the defendant.

II. Suppression of Confession

Miranda warnings must be given to a person who is in custody and being interrogated, because under the 5th Amendment everyone is given the right from self-incriminating themselves. The 5th Amendment gives each person in police custody the right to counsel, which is not offensive specific; therefore if after a police officer gives a person in custody a Miranda warning and he clearly and definitively says he needs a lawyer, that police officer cannot resume interrogation, unless the person in custody reinitiates it.

A police officer must give a person in custody Miranda warnings any time he feels he could get an incriminating statement.

In the situation at hand, the facts say that they had a reliable informant tell the police about the burglary and about Rogers (R); therefore the police had probable cause to bring R into custody to question her, because probable cause can be from an anonymous informant. Also, to do a stationhouse detention, as was done here, the police can bring a person in for questioning.

Because it is stipulated that R was in custody, it can be reasonable to think that one would give an incriminating statement if interrogated. Moreover, when Officer Stevens (S) began questioning in the "interrogation room" he had to give R her Miranda warnings, which he did.

R's statement, "I think I want a public defender" was an attempt to say that she wanted a lawyer, but was not clear enough; therefore normally if a person in custody doesn't give a clear and definitive answer, he isn't invoking his right to remain silent and right to counsel, and can be questioned.

However, S's comments to R that "it's only right that I tell you what's what" and that "once we get you a lawyer I won't be able to help you" was improper and from that in telling R that she'll have to give up her Miranda rights if she wants his help was totally out of line. S used improper means of bribery to get R to talk. S knew that R might give incriminating statements and her waiver was not voluntary – it was coerced; therefore R's confession given afterwards should not be admitted, as it falls within the exclusionary rule mentioned in the introduction.

Therefore, R's motion to suppress the confession should be granted.

III. Suppression of Jewelry

As stated in the introduction, the "Fruits of a Poisonous Tree" Doctrine will exclude any evidence obtained or derived from an illegal search and seizure or an improper Miranda warning. Generally, if a person is improperly mirandized, and is later searched for weapons or contraband on his person, that physical evidence will still be admitted, as Miranda warnings apply to statements made. However in this case the evidence was not found on R, but rather found after R gave incriminating statements. The police officers were able to get probable cause from R's statements to S during interrogation. Unless the officers believe that they could have gotten probable cause through one of the three exceptions to the Fruits Doctrine (stated in Intro), this evidence should be suppressed.

The prosecution can argue that they could have gotten probable cause to search her house from the credible, reliable informant and therefore have obtained the jewelry through an independent source, which if the court agreed, the next step would be to determine if it was seized properly. For one to challenge an illegal search and seizure they must challenge it under the 4th Amendment.

Under this if they had a reasonable expectation of privacy and the search was by a government official, then she has standing to challenge. Here, R did have a reasonable expectation of privacy (it was in her home) and the search was done by a government police officer; therefore that test is met.

Next, we need to look to see if there was a validly issued search warrant. There was a search warrant and assuming it properly stated the place to be searched and the things to be seized and it was issued by a neutral magistrate judge, it is valid, because the facts state they used R's testimony as its probable cause.

Therefore, if a court determines that the probable cause was proper (i.e. from R's coerced testimony), which I think is incorrect, then the jewelry should be admitted.

However, if there was no probable cause, because her statement was coerced and the evidence was obtained using illegal interrogation, then the jewelry should be excluded as fruits of a poisonous tree, assuming no exceptions apply.

Therefore, the motion to suppress the jewelry should be granted.

MBE SUBJECTS - PRACTICE ESSAY QUESTIONS

EVIDENCE
Answer to Question 3

Relevant evidence is evidence that makes any material fact or issue in a case any more or less probable. Generally, all relevant evidence should be admitted. The court has the discretion to exclude evidence that is more prejudicial than probative even if relevant. There is also evidence, such as hearsay, that is generally inadmissible because it lacks reliability. However there are a number of exceptions to the hearsay rule.

1. Acme Salesperson's Testimony

The defense counsel would have objected to the salesperson's testimony as hearsay. Hearsay is an out of court statement sought to be admitted in court for the truth of the matter asserted. In this case, the statement was made by Fred at Acme (out of court) and Betty is likely seeking to have it admitted to prove Fred was buying the car for her (truth). The hearsay objection is valid. However it may, have been an error to sustain it if it falls into one of the exceptions to the rule. A weak argument could be made that Fred's statement was not hearsay, but legally operative words of contract, and excluded from hearsay. However, a better argument could be made that his statement was a present sense impression. A statement of present sense is one made by the declarant, in the moment, and is admissible if the declarant is unavailable to testify. The sustaining of the objection is likely error because the salesperson's testimony is admissible as the present sense exception to the hearsay rule.

2. E-mail

The defense counsel would have made two objections here; first, that the e-mail is hearsay; and second, that is was improperly authenticated. The best evidence rule does not apply because the e-mail is not a legally operative document.

The hearsay rule is set forth above. The e-mail from Fred is hearsay since it is an out of court statement (e-mail) used to prove Fred intended Betty to have the Jag (truth). Sustaining the objection would only have been error if the e-mail was admissible under an exception to the rule or was excluded from hearsay.

Betty would have a good argument that the e-mail falls into the hearsay exception of admission of a party opponent. This is available when the declarant is unavailable to testify and allows statements by the opposing party (here Fred/Fred's estate) into evidence.

This evidence may not be available to Betty if the jurisdiction has a Dead Man Statute. These types of statutes bar testimony by interested parties regarding conversations had with the decedent prior to death regarding distribution of their estate. An argument could be made that Fred's e-mail to Betty is a prior conversation.

The Authentication objection would be that the e-mail was not properly authenticated. However, sustaining it would have been in error because Betty's testimony that she replied to Fred at the e-mail address would have been enough.

3. Cross Examination of Betty

The objection here would have been that defense counsel improperly asked about prior crimes of Betty. Generally evidence of prior crimes is not admissible to show criminal propensity. However, crimes involving dishonesty may be inquired about to impeach a witness and show a propensity for un-truth.

In this case, Betty is testifying as a witness and defense counsel is allowed to impeach her with evidence of un-truth. Although where fraud is primarily a crime of theft, an argument can be made that the fraudulent nature shows a dishonest propensity. It should be admitted against Betty and the court's overruling of the objection was not error.

MBE SUBJECTS - PRACTICE ESSAY QUESTIONS

EVIDENCE
Answer to Question 4

Federal Rules of Evidence require first, that the evidence be logically relevant, and second, that it be subjected to and survive a discretionary filter so as to support underlying public policy of ensuring credible testimony for the fact finder when a declarant is not present and under oath, and/or to prohibit evidence where the probative value is substantially outweighed by its prejudicial effect.

<u>Logical relevance</u> – it must assist the trier of fact in understanding, determining or ascertaining the facts presented.

<u>Hearsay</u> – is when an out-of-court declarant's statement is being offered to prove the matter asserted. Generally this is not allowed. However, statements such as notice or warning, admissions, intent, are not viewed as hearsay. Second, statutorily the rules provide that statements with regard to state of mind – and identifications, present sense impression, excited utterances – are excluded or non-hearsay and may be allowed.

The judge has final discretion in whether to allow evidence as testimony to enter the trial. Further, under writings, there is a best evidence rule which requires that a writing, being offered to prove facts asserted, must be the original.

Statements made to interpreter

Here the statements being offered came from persons who are unavailable for court; they were not made under oath or during another judicial proceeding.

1. However, the statement that 9 paid Mary is an admission, thus it would be permissible under an exception to hearsay. Further, it appears logically relevant to the defendant's case.

2. The statement about the van's location may be brought under testimony by either the Agent or the interpreter because it is actual knowledge and does not require special training or knowledge.

3. "Mary left them in the van," may be offered under a hearsay exception. However, the second part is hearsay within hearsay, thus not permissible because the statement "saying she was going to go get help" would be offered to prove the matter asserted and Mary is an out-of-court declarant, thus barred.

4. Mary never returned. That statement may not be brought in by the Agent, other than to state she was not there when the nine were found.

The 10th man Victor –Statements to Agent

Great pain, but made an identification of Douglas as smuggler; the identification may be brought in as an exception to hearsay. The witness is unavailable and this statement is includable under dying declaration.

If Victor were dying, or believed he were dying, it may have been a dying declaration, but there are insufficient facts. Victor would need to have been under the impression he was dying soon and that he was relaying the facts of his situation because of his perceived imminent death. In addition, he would have to be unavailable for Court which he appears to be. It is unclear whether he died or not, because only 9 men were deported. So assuming he died, it could be a dying declaration.

Agent – may testify to those aspects of the arrest to which he has personal knowledge. However, his testimony is limited to his observations and opinions. If being offered as an expert, he must be introduced as such and comport with the educational and experience requirements of an expert. If so, he can make other testimonial statements. However, facts would not lead to this. Therefore, his own personal experience/knowledge is the limit, so long as it is logical and relevant. His testimony of Victor's Identification of Douglas discussed prior.

Further, the foundation must be laid to ensure that the interpretive services used, adequately meet requirements for presenting statements in court as those of the declarant and not the interpreter.

Douglas

- May identify Mary as smuggler. He is providing logically relevant information that he has personal knowledge of.
- May testify to the van breakdown, and Mary leaving, and did not return, and that he left, set camp until rescued.
- May testify as to Mary stating she was leaving and would return, because although it is hearsay it is under the exception which allows statements relative to the declarant's state of mind to be admitted.

Notes of Agent

The notes are hearsay. However, Douglas could offer the notes as recollection refreshed and have the information read into the record.

However, the court would need to ensure there were no violations under hearsay etc. within the content of the notes.

MBE SUBJECTS - PRACTICE ESSAY QUESTIONS

EVIDENCE
Answer to Question 5

I. Prosecution's Evidence – case-in-chief

A) Prosecution calling all 5 victims to testify concerning the robbery (of each individual).

Under the Federal Rules of Evidence all relevant evidence is admissible unless it is inadmissible for some other reason under the Federal Rules (FRE). Evidence is relevant if it makes a fact of consequence to the determination if the action more or less probable than without that fact. However, even if evidence is relevant and not inadmissible under any FRE, a judge may exclude the evidence if its probative value is outweighed by its prejudicial effect, it is unnecessarily cumulative, etc. Here, the testimony of all five victims is likely relevant and admissible (and not unnecessarily cumulative). The prosecution is charging the defendants with robbing in all five cases. Thus, each victim should be able to testify to the circumstances of their robbery. The evidence is relevant and not unnecessarily cumulative (because there were 5 robberies) and even though prejudicial, their probative value is for proving the crime at issue so they are extremely relevant. The prosecution will have to lay a proper foundation for each witness (personal knowledge, etc.).

B) Prosecution Witness #1:

The police officer's testimony will likely be admitted as non-hearsay under the exclusions to the hearsay definition. The police officer's testimony as to the victim's description of the young male is probably hearsay. Hearsay is an out-of-court statement offered to prove the truth of the matter asserted. Here, the officer is testifying as to the victim's statements (out-of-court statement) concerning the identity of the perpetrator by the victims. It is offered to prove the truth of the matter asserted. Here, the statement is offered to prove that the person who stopped in front of the victim was indeed a young male. The statement meets the definition of hearsay. However, the Federal Rules exclude from the definition of hearsay both party admissions and prior statement of witnesses. Prior statements of identification by the witness are generally deemed to be non-hearsay under the prior identification (prior statements) by witness. Thus, the officer would likely be able to testify as to the prior identification by the witness of the perpetrator as a young male. If the judge determines that it is admissible hearsay by the officer, the prosecution will get it in under the victim's testimony of the prior identification. However, the witness' testimony is likely admissible as non-hearsay.

C) Prosecution Witness #2:

As a general rule, the prosecution is permitted to call expert witnesses to testify in their case-in-chief. Expert witnesses generally must be qualified as experts by laying a foundation. This expert testimony foundation can be laid by showing the expert's knowledge is based on a reliable science, he/she followed reliable methodology, accepted practice, etc. However, experts may also be qualified from experience in the field. This includes police officers. If the prosecution establishes that the police officer is qualified as an expert in police work, particularly that he/she has experience with such scams, he will be allowed to testify as to this experience. (i.e. lay a foundation to qualify as an expert witness. In addition, experts are also qualified to give opinions based upon hypothetical facts. They need not have personal knowledge of the particular facts of the case. Here, if the expert is qualified by proper foundation, he/she can testify as to the common "bump and go" two-person scam.

D) Prosecution evidence of 6 months earlier robberies:

In a criminal case, the prosecution, in this case-in-chief, cannot use character evidence of specific acts to show conduct in consistency with these acts. The prosecution may be able to use character evidence in rebuttal to the defendant's putting his good character in evidence, but cannot do so in its case-in-chief. Here, the prosecution would not use character evidence of specific bad acts or crimes to show that defendant's action in conformity with that conduct on this occasion. Thus, the evidence is likely inadmissible as character evidence (because defendant's haven't put in issue). However, the prosecution may be able to use "specific acts" in a criminal case to show motive, intent, absence of mistakes, or common plan or scheme. Here, the prosecution may be able to get the bad acts in to show common plan or scheme.

II. Defendant's Evidence

A) Defense Witness #1

1. Church Membership

As a rule, irrelevant evidence is inadmissible. (Please see definition of relevance in I.A.). Here, membership of the witness in a church does not seem to make any fact in issue more or less probable. Thus, this is likely an inadmissible question as it is irrelevant.

However, if the prosecution is attempting to impeach the witness, perhaps by evidence of bias because they go to the same church, and thus she has some motive for lying, this may be admissible as impeachment evidence. It is unlikely, however, to be considered sufficient for bias and will be inadmissible.

2. Defendant #3, statement to police

Prior inconsistent statements of a witness now on the stand can be used to impeach. They cannot, however, come in as substantive evidence unless they are made under oath at a prior proceeding. However, to impeach by prior inconsistent statement, the prosecution must give the witness an opportunity to explain or deny the statement. This opportunity can come at anytime. Here, the witness has stated on the stand that she and D1 and D2 were in Mountain View at the time of the crimes. However, she had previously stated to the police that D1 and D2 and herself were in River City on the days the crimes were committed. Thus, this is a prior inconsistent statement and the prosecutor is entitled to use it for impeachment, but not substantive (beware it is hearsay) purposes.

B) Witness #4 – Impeachment by crime:

In some circumstances, the prosecutor is entitled to impeach the credibility of a witness by previous criminal convictions. Previous criminal convictions of a witness are allowed (by reputation, opinion, or record of conviction) without laying a foundation and by extrinsic evidence of the record. To impeach a witness by criminal conviction, the crime must be either 1) a felony or misdemeanor involving dishonestly (this is not), or a felony not involving dishonesty. For felonies not involving dishonesty, the judge has discretion whether or not to admit the crime. The judge may exclude the evidence if its probative value is outweighed by its prejudicial effect. No crimes over 10 years (convictions) are admissible. Here, the conviction is a 2-yr. old felony <u>not</u> involving dishonesty. (Unless judge determines hit and run is dishonest – then must be admitted, no discretion to exclude). Here, the probative value of the conviction is probably outweighed by its prejudicial effect. The conviction does not appear to be relevant to the witness' credibility, and will likely confuse/prejudice the jury. The evidence is probably inadmissible for this reason.

MBE SUBJECTS - PRACTICE ESSAY QUESTIONS

EVIDENCE
Answer to Question 6

There are numerous evidentiary issues with regard to each item of evidence to be offered as follows:

I. <u>Dobbs'   1999   Federal   Income   Tax   Return</u>.
The defense will raise an objection of authentication, hearsay and possibly best evidence rule. They should be resolved as follows:

a) The document must be authenticated. This must be accomplished by (1) Dobbs admitting it is his, or (2) proof that the signature is his. The jury may compare this tax return signature with another specimen of his signature; the prosecutor may introduce a handwriting expert; or the prosecutor may put a lay person on the stand who was familiar with Dobbs' signature <u>before</u> he was indicted/charged to verify it is his. This should not be difficult to accomplish.

b) The defense will argue that the tax return is hearsay. However, it is not being offered for the truth of the matter asserted (i.e. that Dobbs made $200K income in 1999), but rather to show that this is what he claimed. Therefore, it is not hearsay. Moreover, it is a party admission (out of court party statement offered against party in court) therefore excluded from the definition of hearsay.

c) Defense will raise a 'best evidence' rule – objection which applies to legally operative documents or documents which contain evidence that constitutes a witness' sole knowledge of the matter re: which one witness is testifying. The tax return is a legally operative document, so the original or a photocopy must be produced. This is unlikely to be difficult to do.

II. <u>Tom Tubman</u>.

Tubman ("T") seeks to testify re: his illegal arrangement with Dobbs. Defense will object that character evidence may not be introduced to prove that Defendant acted in conformity with such character in the present occasion under Rule 406. That is, defense will argue that T may not testify that Dobbs previously committed tax evasion to prove that he did so again in this occasion, and this is correct. However, prior acts of misconduct <u>may</u> be admitted to show (1) motive, (2) intent, (3) plan, (4) common scheme, (5) control, or similar non-propensity matters. Here, the evidence that Taxpayer Dobbs received illegally obtained income (i.e. the $10K he charged T) shows motive to conceal such income; therefore it should be admitted, provided its probative relevance is not substantially outweighed by its prejudicial effect. Here its probative value is very high; therefore it should be admitted.

Moreover, Dobbs' statements to T should be admitted in any case, as they are party admissions (statements made by a party out of court, offered <u>against</u> the party in court).

Finally, the check for $10K must be (1) authenticated (see discussion above – T will likely authenticate it since he signed the check) and (2) must qualify as non-hearsay or an exception to hearsay. A check is a legally operative document, therefore by definition non-hearsay and should be admitted.

III.   <u>Kerri Kurner</u>.

First, defense will again raise a character evidence objection to admission of Kerri's evidence. However, the same exception applies (see Tubman analysis); this is evidence of specific prior misconduct offered to show motive – so it's not character evidence/should be admitted.

The amount Kerri paid Dobbs is clearly relevant ($8,500 indicates suspicion of illegality). Since she cannot recall the exact amount, the defense will object to the use of her diary, saying the diary is hearsay.

Two hearsay exceptions may apply, as follows:

a) <u>Refreshing recollection</u> – if Kerri is testifying on the stand and states she can't remember what she paid Dobbs, prosecutor may show her the diary for her to <u>silently</u> read to refresh her recollections. The diary, as used for this limited purpose, need not be authenticated, as it will not come into evidence (except at defense's request). Defense must be given an opportunity to review the diary.

b) If Kerri still cannot remember, she will be able to read the diary statements to the jury as a "<u>recorded recollection</u>" (exception to hearsay). If she can show (1) that she wrote it, (2) at a time when she had a clear memory, (3) she had personal knowledge of the matter and (4) she wrote the material in a reliable way. (Moreover the diary must also be authenticated which should not be a problem since Kerri will testify it is hers).

Re: the requirements above, they may be met if Kerri admits she wrote it; it appears she wrote it when it was still fresh in her mind (facts state she wrote in her diary "every evening describing the events of the day," – this probably satisfies that requirement). It appears that her memory/writing is reliable (may possibly be shown by other evidence of accurate recordings).

If these requirements are met, the diary may be read into evidence (but the jury may not actually <u>read</u> the diary).

<u>Mr. Dobbs' wife</u>.

Three issues arise with respect to her testimony: (1) whether the testimony is privileged under spousal immunity; 2) whether it's privileged as a confidential mental communication; or (3) whether it's a party admission.

The 'spousal immunity' privilege states that a spouse may not be compelled to testify against his or her spouse in a criminal proceeding, but may choose to do so if s/he wishes. Since Dobbs and his wife are separated, but not divorced, Ms. Dobbs may invoke the privilege if she wishes. The facts state that she is willing to testify – so she may. Mr. Dobbs is not the holder of the privilege.

Confidential Marital Communications.

A spouse may not disclose communications by the other spouse that were made in reliance on the confidential marital relationship. If Dobbs and his wife were married in the late fall of 1999, and Dobbs told her re: his 'side business' income in confidence, she may not testify re: this fact (note this would be true even if they were now divorced, as long as they were married at the time of the confidential communication).

This statement is probably protected by this privilege, which will not be trumped by the fact that it is also a party admission and thus an exception to the hearsay rule. Absent evidence that (1) they were not married at the time or (2) the statement was made in the presence of others/in public, some other indicia of non-confidentiality, Ms. Dobbs' testimony is not admissible.

MBE SUBJECTS - PRACTICE ESSAY QUESTIONS

EVIDENCE
Answer to Question 7

In this case the defendant is charged with felony murder, and the issues revolve around the evidence and testimonies that each of the parties want to introduce during the hearing.

Imogene

Imogene's testimony could be considered to be hearsay. Hearsay is an out-of-court statement used to prove the declarant's statement for its truth and veracity. Hearsay testimony can be excluded if it can be proven, as in this case, to outweigh the benefit of using the statement, by its extreme prejudicial effect on the defendant.

The statement made by Imogene, first of all, is prejudicial to the defendant's case because it shows bias to the Witness's testimony. She was granted immunity in exchange for her testimony. The prejudicial effect of the statement outweighs the relevancy and use of the statement.

Police Officer

The police officer's statement is also Hearsay, which is an out-of-court statement used to prove the truth of the matter asserted by the declarant. In this case, the statement will fall under one of the exceptions to the Hearsay rule, which is the out-of-court identification of the defendant by a witness to the criminal event. In showing the photos, the state will have to prove that the defendant's picture was not discriminatorily placed and that the photo identification was performed as to not violate the defendant's fifth amendment rights. With the proper foundation, the photo identification of the defendant will be allowed to prove that the security guard saw the defendant at the robbery.

Teller

The teller's testimony goes to the truth of the matter. It is relevant information, which shows that the defendant was present during the bank robbery. It will not be hearsay testimony, but will be testimonial evidence that goes directly to the criminal matter asserted.

Bank Customer

The bank customer's testimony will go also to the truth of the matter asserted and will be relevant as eyewitness testimony. She states that she looked directly at all of the robbers and the defendant was not one of them.

The prosecution will rebut this in cross-examination. He will try to prove that the witness is lying because she stated in her testimony that she was making a withdrawal and she was actually making a deposit. In cross-examination, the adverse party may direct examination towards any evidence and testimony that is introduced during the direct examination. Because the defendant introduced Bank Customer as a witness and introduced her statement, the prosecution may cross-examine her and try to prove inconsistencies in her statement. In this case, Defendant is going to argue that the withdrawal or deposit is a collateral matter and is not dispositive of the evidence used against him. He will argue that to attack such collateral matter is prejudicial to his case and could confuse the jury.

The prosecution will argue that the inconsistencies in her statement go to the veracity of her testimony and that he is allowed to rebut her truthfulness and inconsistencies. He will want to introduce the bank records under the business record exception to the hearsay rule in order to prove that she is lying about whether she was making a deposit or withdrawal, inferring that her testimony lacks truthfulness. The court will allow the testimony if the prosecutor is able to lay the proper foundation for the business record.

In cross-examination, the fact that the prosecution is going to ask the bank customer that she, in grand jury testimony stated that the defendant looked a little like the bank robber, can be introduced under the hearsay exception for inconsistent statements dealing with prior identification. The grand jury testimony was taken during the proceeding where the witness was sworn in and could have been subjected to cross-examination, so the inconsistent statement will be allowed in, in order to prove bank customer's truthfulness and inconsistent statement at trial.

The defendant will rebut the prosecution's attack on his witness' truthfulness by bringing in Friend who will testify that the Bank Customer is a good friend and that in her opinion she is an honest person. Normally one must be wary when introducing character evidence. If the evidence was directed at the defendant then . . .

In this case, character evidence can be brought in by the defendant, in rebuttal to an attack of his witness' truthfulness and veracity. The prosecution has tried to show that the Bank Customer is inconsistent in her testimonies and has lied, so the defendant must now prove that she is not. Her honesty is on the line, and the defendant is allowed to let opinion testimony come in to protect her statement. If the opinion testimony was going to be used in relation to the defendant to show that he could not have done the crime, it would not be allowed, because of its hearsay attributes. But in this case the defendant's character is not on the line, the witness' is, so the opinion testimony is admissible.

Family Law

(February 2000)

Legal Problems:

1. Did the court in State X have jurisdiction to dissolve the marriage such that State Y is precluded from granting a divorce?

2. Did the court in State X violate due process by denying Wife spousal support?

3. Does the obligation of the court in State Y to give full faith and credit to the State X divorce decree preclude it from awarding spousal support to Wife?

DISCUSSION

The power of State Y to grant a divorce decree and award spousal support depends on the validity and effect of the divorce and support decree issued by State X. Under the doctrine of divisible divorce, the State X decree may be valid and effective as to the divorce, but not as to spousal support. Points One and Two concern the validity of the State X decree in these respects. Point Three addresses State Y's power to award spousal support, in the event that State X's decree is valid as to the divorce but not as to the spousal support.

Point One: (30-40%)

A divorce decree dissolving a marriage is entitled to full faith and credit if the court in the rendering state had jurisdiction to enter it. A court has jurisdiction if at least one of the spouses is domiciled in the rendering state.

The in-state domicile of at least one of the parties is sufficient for a state court's jurisdiction in a divorce action. *Williams* v. *North Carolina,* 317 U.S. 287 (1942). A change of domicile is effected by moving to the new location with intent to remain there, regarding it as one's home. Friedenthal, Kane & Miller, *Civil Procedure* 31 (1996). Whether Husband intended to regard State X as his home is, of course, problematic, as he left State X immediately upon receiving his divorce. Arguably, at least, Husband lacked the intent required for domicile and hence for State X to exercise jurisdiction.

As the burden of proof is on the litigant who is contesting the jurisdiction, jurisdictional challenges based on lack of domicile when the durational residency requirement has been complied with rarely succeed. Nonetheless, State Y can independently examine whether State X had jurisdiction. *Williams* v. *North Carolina,* 325 U.S. 226 (1945) *(Williams II).* Since Husband does appear to have satisfied the durational residency requirement, most courts would hold that the court in State X did have jurisdiction to dissolve Husband and Wife's marriage and, therefore, State Y cannot issue a divorce decree. *E.g., Newport* v. *Newport,* 219 Va. 48 (1978).

Point Two: (30-40%)

A court that does not have in personam jurisdiction over a person may not constitutionally assert jurisdiction to deny that person spousal support.

In personam jurisdiction over a nonresident defendant is not needed for a court to take jurisdiction to grant a divorce terminating the marital status of a party properly before it. But personal jurisdiction is required before a court may assert jurisdiction to determine the defendant's support rights and duties. This is the doctrine of "divisible divorce." *See generally Estin* v. *Estin,* 334 U.S. 541 (1948); *Vanderbilt* v. *Vanderbilt,* 354 U.S. 416 (1957); H. Clark, *The Law of Domestic Relations in the United States* § 12.4, at 443-56 (2d ed. 1988). Thus, a court's decree can be entitled to full faith and credit with respect to its marriage dissolution order, but not with respect to its order granting or foreclosing alimony. Whether a court can constitutionally assert in personam jurisdiction over a nonresident defendant depends on whether the nonresident defendant has or has had minimum contacts with the rendering state such that the maintenance of the support action against him or her does not offend traditional notions of fair play and substantial justice. *See Kulko* v. *Superior Court of California,* 436 U.S. 84 (1978).

The fact that the parties were married in State X might seem to give State X a very strong interest in all aspects of the marriage's dissolution, including the financial aspects. Since both Husband and Wife voluntarily chose to be married in State X and under the laws of State X, it might seem fair to conclude that they purposefully availed themselves of the benefits and protection of the laws of State X. But the U.S. Supreme Court in *Kulko* showed a marked reluctance to apply its minimum contacts theory to personal relations matters as broadly as it has in ordinary commercial litigation. The parties in *Kulko* were married in the rendering state, but the Court held that this contact alone was not sufficient in the context of a claim for child support. It is also unlikely that it would be sufficient in the context of a claim for spousal support or separate maintenance. That is especially the case where, as here, the marriage took place many years ago and the wife has had no significant contact with the rendering state during the intervening period. Following *Kulko,* a court would probably conclude that Wife does not have sufficient contact with State X for courts in that state to have asserted in personam jurisdiction over her. Therefore, the State X order cutting off her right to spousal support is not entitled to full faith and credit in State Y.

Point Three: (30-40%)

State Y can probably award spousal support because State X granted an *ex parte* divorce in which it did not have jurisdiction to deny Wife support.

While a valid divorce decree issued by the state in which the plaintiff's domiciled can terminate the marital status of the parties, the state must have personal jurisdiction over the defendant spouse to determine spousal support. Thus, even if State X's divorce decree is accorded full faith and credit, the effect of the decree is limited to a determination of marital status unless the court had personal jurisdiction over the defendant.

Although courts typically do not have subject matter jurisdiction to award spousal support if it is not awarded at the time of the divorce, most states have statutes or case law that allows the spouse who was not subject to the in personam jurisdiction of the court granting the divorce to seek support notwithstanding the valid divorce. H. Clark, *The Law of Domestic Relations in the United States* § 12.4, at 452-53, citing cases and statutes. Some states do not provide an exception, finding that once a divorce decree entitled to full faith and credit with respect to marital status is issued, then spousal support cannot be awarded. *See, e.g., Loeb* v. *Loeb,* 118 Vt. 472, 114 A.2d 518 (1955). Nonetheless, regardless of the validity of the State X divorce decree, under the laws of most states, State Y could determine spousal support.

Family Law

(July 2000)

Legal Problems:

1. Can the child consent to surgery or is parental consent required?

2. Can a court order an operation over the objection of the parents, even when the parents' objections are based on their religious beliefs?

3. Must the child obey the parents' commands about the child's religious education?

DISCUSSION

Point One: (25-35%)

Parental consent is required for Fred's surgery because his situation does not fit any of the usual exceptions to the general rule that the parent, not the child, decides what medical care the child should receive.

A doctor who performs surgery on a minor child without the parents' consent is liable in tort. Homer Clark, *The Law of Domestic Relations in the United States* § 9.3 (2d ed. 1988). There are exceptions to this general rule, but none applies here. For example, consent is not necessary in emergency cases when there is no time to obtain parental consent. And, by statute, most states do not require parental consent for particular types of medical care, usually related to public health concerns, such as treatment for venereal disease (although sometimes even these statutes exempt children whose parents object to treatment on religious grounds). Some states, by statute or case law, make an exception to the parental consent requirement for older children, either specifying an age or indicating that the minor must be mature. Typically, however, the "mature minor" must be near the age of majority, and the medical procedure must not be major. Leslie Harris, Lee Teitelbaum, & Carol Weisbrod,. *Family Law* 985 (1996). Since none of these exceptions fits these facts, Fred's consent is not sufficient and parental consent is necessary.

Point Two: (35-45%)

Although a court can order medical treatment for a child over the objections of the parents when the medical treatment is urgently needed to prevent serious harm to the child's health, even when the parents' objections are based on their religious beliefs, the court would probably not do so here.

Under the *parens patriae* authority of the state, the state can intervene to protect children when parents deny them needed medical care. The child labor case, *Prince* v. *Massachusetts*, 321 U.S. 158 (1944), is often cited to support the state's right to protect children. "Parents may be free to become martyrs themselves. But it does not follow they are free. . . to make martyrs of their children." *Id.* at 170. Generally, if a parent fails to provide needed medical care, a child can be adjudicated neglected and the state can order the medical treatment. In addition, many states have exemptions to the abuse and neglect statutes that allow the state to order the medical care without a finding of parental fault if the parents object to the child's treatment on religious grounds. Homer Clark, *The Law of Domestic Relations in the United States* § 9.3 (2d ed. 1988).

When parents object to the medical care, however, the concept of "need" is interpreted narrowly. Here, no strong facts are presented that the care is "needed," because Fred does not face imminent death or serious injury. The medical condition is not life threatening and can be postponed until Fred is an adult. In these medical treatment cases, the courts weigh the risks and benefits of treatment. The strongest facts for ordering the operation are that Fred will suffer some physical damage and is suffering psychological harm that is having a negative impact on his school performance. In addition, Fred wants the surgery. On the other hand, the state has a strong respect for parents' autonomy, the parents are concerned about the risks inherent in the surgery, and the parents' religious beliefs are a major basis for their objection. On balance, a court would probably not order that Fred's surgery proceed. Nonetheless, even where the child is not in imminent danger, some courts will order medical treatment, notwithstanding the parents' religious objections. Leslie Harris, Lee Teitelbaum, & Carol Weisbrod, Family *Law* 982 (1996).

Point Three: *(20-30%)*

The right of parents to direct the upbringing of their child includes control over the child's religious education. and children have a duty to obey their parents.

Parents generally have a right to raise their children as they see fit. *Wisconsin* v. *Yoder,* 406 U.S. 205 (1972)(compulsory education case). A child who fails to follow parental commands is disobedient, and the state seeks to reinforce the parents' control over their child, not undermine it. Leslie Harris, Lee Teitelbaum, & Carol Weisbrod, *Family Law* 1484-85 (1996). The state would have authority to intervene only if the parents' commands were so extreme as to constitute abuse or neglect. Here, the requirement that Fred attend religious services once per week and follow his parents' religion is not likely to rise to that level. Thus, Fred must obey his parents' instructions with respect to religious services.

Family Law

(February 2001)

Legal Problems:

1. Under what circumstances will a parent be deemed to have abandoned her child so the child could be adopted by a third-party custodian without the parent's consent?

2. In a custody dispute between a parent and a third party with whom the child has lived for a number of years, to whom is the court likely to award custody?

3. Would a third party who has developed a substantial relationship with a child be awarded visitation rights over the objections of the child's parent?

DISCUSSION

Point One: (35-45%)

In some states, a parent cannot be found to have abandoned her child so long as she subjectively intends to maintain a relationship with the child: in other states, if a parent has failed to express substantial interest in her child, she may be found to have abandoned the child, regardless of her subjective intent.

Under the traditional law of adoption, to establish "abandonment" courts required proof that the parent subjectively intended to abandon the relationship; proof of behavior that objectively suggests a fixed loss of interest in the child was not sufficient. *E.g., In re Adoption of Walton,* 123 Utah 380,259 P.2d 881 (1953). In a state that uses the subjective test, Mother has not abandoned Daughter because (1) Mother insists that she never intended to terminate her relationship with Daughter, and (2) she asked Caretaker to keep Daughter only until Mother "got her life back together." Accordingly, Caretaker could not adopt Daughter because Mother has not abandoned Daughter and will not consent.

On the other hand, some states use an objective test for abandonment under which a court might find that Mother had abandoned Daughter. The inquiry under this test is whether the parent has acted in ways that indicate a commitment to maintaining the parent-child relationship, and includes factors such as whether the parent paid support or visited the child. *See, e.g., In the Matter of the Appeal in Pima County Juvenile Severance Action No.* S- *II* 4487, 179 Ariz. 86, 876 P.2d 1121 (1994) (en banc). Here, a court might well find that Mother's failure to pay even a minimal amount of support and her very infrequent visits constituted abandonment, though her recent efforts to reestablish her relationship with Daughter cut against this finding. If Mother is found to have abandoned Daughter, then Daughter would be available for adoption, and Caretaker would probably be able to adopt her.

Point Two: (35-45%)

In a custody contest between a parent and a third party. custody in the parent is presumed to be in the best interest of the child. To rebut this presumption. the third party must generally prove either that the parent is unfit or that granting custody to the parent would be highly detrimental to the child. In some states, however, the court may award custody to the third party upon finding that doing so would be in the child's best interest.

In custody cases between two parents, the standard is the best interest of the child. However, in most states this standard is not used in parent vs. third party disputes. Instead, there is a strong presumption that a child should be in the custody of the parents; therefore, Caretaker has the burden of proving that she should have custody of Daughter. H. Clark, THE LAW OF DOMESTIC RELATIONS § 19.6 at 821 (1988). In many jurisdictions, as long as the parent is considered fit, the court will not even consider whether third-party custody would be better for the child. Clark, *supra* § 19.6 at 823. Therefore, in such a jurisdiction, Mother would almost certainly receive custody of Daughter. She is currently fit, has employment, is attending Alcoholics Anonymous (and has been for six months), and has not lost contact with her child (i.e., no abandonment). In those jurisdictions, the court would not consider Daughter's strong attachment to Caretaker to mitigate Mother's claim.

In other jurisdictions, however, the presumption in favor of parental custody can be overcome by showing that awarding custody to the parent would be very detrimental to the child. *See, e.g., Painter v. Bannister,* 258 Iowa 1390, 140 N.W.2d 152 (1966), *Guardianship of Phillip B.,* 139 Cal. App. 3d 407, 188 Cal. Rptr. 781 (1983). Under this standard it is not unusual for courts to find that breaking a long-term, stable, parent-child bond between the child and the third-party caretaker will be harmful to the child, at least when expert testimony to this effect is presented. In our case, the expert would testify that the strength of Daughter's attachment to Caretaker means that a disruption would be harmful to her psychologically. This might be sufficient to overcome the preference for Mother. Daughter has lived four of her five years with Caretaker (almost her entire life), and has seen her mother only occasionally. For courts less focused on parental rights, these would be critical facts. *See, e.g., Ortner v. Pitt,* 187 W. Va. 494, 419 S.E.2d 907 (1992).

A minority of states use the best interest test in all custody contests including those between parents and nonparents. *See, e.g., In re Custody of C.C.R.S.,* 892 P.2d 246 (Colo. 1995) (en banc). Under the best interest test, a court would probably award custody to Caretaker because she has become Daughter's psychological mother.

An examinee might receive extra credit for noting that awarding custody to Caretaker might raise a question of unconstitutional interference with Mother's parental rights. *See Troxel v. Granville,* 530 U.S. 57 (2000). Although *Troxel* concerned visitation and not custody (see Point Three), the plurality in *Troxel* held that there is a presumption that fit parents act in their children's best interest, and that courts must award "special weight" to a parent's decisions. Prior to *Troxel,* the *C.C.R.S.* court rejected the argument that the best interest standard violates parents' constitutional rights. The court reasoned that the Supreme Court cases on parental rights, *e.g., Santosky v. Kramer,* 455 U.S. 745 (1982); *Lassiter v. Dept. of Soc. Serv.,* 452 U.S. 18 (1981), all concerned permanent termination of parental status. A custody ruling, the court said, is less drastic and therefore constitutionally permissible when supported by good reasons (the child's best interest). Other courts, however, might find that the best interest standard unconstitutionally infringes on parental rights if it denies parental custody in favor of a nonparent in cases where the parent is legally "fit." *See Troxel* v. *Granville,* 530 U.S. 57 (2000).

Point Three: (15-25%)

In most states, a court cannot award visitation rights to a third party without statutory authority, but in a minority of states, courts may make such an award if it is in the child's best interest, at least to parties who have stood in loco parentis to the child.

In some states, statutes authorize courts to order visitation for a nonparent who has a substantial relationship with a child if visitation is in the child's best interest. *E.g.,* Or. Rev. Stat. § 109.119; Cal. Fam. Code § 3100(a); Alaska Stat. § 25.24.150(a). In the absence of such a statute, courts generally lack jurisdiction to enter such orders because they are inconsistent with the parents' custodial rights, which include determining with whom a child will associate. *See Troxel v. Granville,* 530 U.S. 57 (2000). Some courts, however, have held that they have inherent authority to make visitation orders in a child's best interest. *See, e.g., Spells v. Spells,* 250 Pa. Super. 168, 378 A.2d 879 (1977) (awarding visitation to a former stepparent); *Simpson v. Simpson,* 586 S.W.2d 33 (Ky. 1979) (adopting the in loco parentis approach in holding that visitation with a surrogate parent may be in the child's best interest); *Gribble v. Gribble,* 583 P.2d 64 (Utah 1978); *Rhinehart v. Nowlin,* 111 N.M. 319, 323, 805 P.2d 88,92 (1990) (holding that the trial courts are given "exclusive jurisdiction of all matters relating to the guardianship, care, custody, maintenance and education of the children," which includes "the granting of visitation rights to a person or persons who the trial court determines are significant and important to the welfare of the children" (emphasis in original)); *Looper v. McManus,* 581 P.2d 487 (Okla. App. 1978); *Wills v. Wills,* 399 So. 2d 1130 (Fla. App. 1981); *Evans v. Evans,* 302 Md. 334, 488 A.2d 157 (1985).

If a court had the authority to grant nonparental visitation, the facts of this case might support such an order. Arguably, it would be in Daughter's best interest to continue visiting Caretaker, rather than having their relationship abruptly terminated. A court must, however, give "special weight" to Mother's opposition. *See Troxel v. Granville,* 530 U.S. 57 (2000). Moreover, the court might conclude that it would be better not to allow visitation if it found that Daughter would be adversely affected by the animosity between Caretaker and Mother.

NOTE: *Troxel* does not affect the outcome of this question, as it is distinguishable from the facts here. In *Troxel,* grandparents who never had custody of the grandchildren, sought visitation contrary to the wishes of the children's custodial parent. Here, Caretaker had custody of Daughter for most of Daughter's life prior to bringing her petition. In these circumstances, the court would most likely find that granting Caretaker visitation rights would not violate the mother's constitutional rights.

Family Law

(July 2001)

Legal Problems:

1. Is State B required to recognize the child support order of State A?

2. Does State B have jurisdiction to modify the child support order?

3. When will a court reduce a child support award due to changed circumstances, and can the reduction be made retroactive?

4. When will a court increase or extend a spousal support award due to changed circumstances?

DISCUSSION

Point One: (20-30%)

State B is required to recognize the child support order of State A.

Under federal law, states are required to give full faith and credit to child support awards from other states. Under 28 U.S.C. § 1738B(a) each state: "(1) shall enforce according to its terms a child support order made consistently with this section by a court of another State." Section 1738B is known as the Full Faith and Credit for Child Support Orders Act.

Section IV-D of the Social Security Act also requires a state, as a condition of participation in the federally funded child support programs, to have procedures that require that "any payment or installment of support under any child support order. . . [be] . . . entitled as a judgment to full faith and credit in such State and in any other State." 42 U.S.C. § 666(a)(9). This amendment to the Social Security Act may also be called The Child Support Enforcement Act or the IV-D Program.

Hence, Father cannot evade the State A child support order by moving to State B. State B must recognize and enforce the State A order. It is no longer the case that child support orders are not entitled to full faith and credit.

The same result is mandated by the Uniform Interstate Family Support Act (UIFSA), legislation which states are required to adopt under federal law. Section IV-D of the Social Security Act requires that a state, as a condition of participation in the federally funded child support pro-grams, have UIFSA in effect. 42 U.S.C. § 666(f). UIFSA provides a simple procedure for the registration of the child support order of another state. The order is then enforced in the same manner as an order issued by the registering state. UIFSA § 603. Mother can use UIFSA to enforce the State A order in State B.

Point Two: (10-20%)

State B does not have jurisdiction to modify the child support order.

State B does not have jurisdiction to modify the State A child support order. Under federal law, each state "shall not seek or make a modification of . . . [a child support] order except in accordance with subsection [ ](e)." 28 U.S.C. § 1738B(a). (Full Faith and Credit for Child Support Orders Act). Subsection (e) of the Full Faith and Credit for Child Support Orders Act prohibits the modification of child support orders issued by a court with continuing exclusive jurisdiction, unless no contestant or child resides there, or unless each contestant has agreed in writing to allow another state to assert jurisdiction. Those requirements are not met here because Mother and children still reside in State A, and Mother has not consented to State B's assuming jurisdiction to modify.

This same result is mandated by UIFSA. Section 205 of UIFSA confers continuing, exclusive jurisdiction on the state issuing the child support order unless no litigant or child resides there, or unless each party has consented to another state's modification jurisdiction. State A continues to have jurisdiction, and State B cannot modify. Section 603(c) of UIFSA requires that states enforce without modification the child support orders of other states.

Point Three: (35-45%)

A court will reduce a child support award when there has been a material and substantial change in circumstances: however, such a change in circumstances has not been demonstrated here. Further, a court cannot order a retroactive modification of a child support order.

In most jurisdictions, modifications of child support orders may be made only upon a showing of a substantial and continuing change in circumstances making the prior order unreasonable. Under the Uniform Marriage and Divorce Act (UMDA), modification of a child support order is allowed "only upon a showing of changed circumstances so substantial and continuing as to make the terms unconscionable." Unif. Marriage and Div. Act § 316(a), 9A U.LA. 102 (1987). However, modifications based on changed circumstances are allowed in most jurisdictions upon the less stringent showing of a material or substantial change of circumstances, although the burden on the party requesting the modification is still a heavy one. Donald T. Kramer, LEGAL RIGHTS OF CHILDREN § 4.07 (2d ed. 1994 and Supp. 1997). Under any standard, however, the changes must be more or less permanent, rather than temporary. *Id.* Although Father has been unemployed for three months, he did receive 50 percent of his annual salary in severance pay and other benefits at the time of his termination. Since his job prospects are good, it is likely that his unemployment will only be temporary. In addition, the stated reasons for Father's move to State B provide some evidence of bad faith by Father. Therefore, it is unlikely that his child support payment will be reduced at this time. If, however, the court were to reduce Father's child support obligation, the reduction would be calculated under the state's child support guidelines and would not likely be the $1,000 that Father requests. If Father turns out to be unable to find a job after a lengthy period, the court would be more likely to reduce the amount of the payments.

The court could also impute income to Father, based upon his prior employment history, education, and efforts (or lack thereof) to find employment.

Moreover, under UMDA, a modification of support can be made retroactive only from the date of service of the motion to modify on the other party. Unif. Marriage and Div. Act § 316(a), 9A U.L.A. 102 (1987). Here, if the court were able to modify the child support obligation, the modification could only be made retroactive to the date of service on Mother and cannot be made six months retroactive. Therefore, Father will owe the full amount of the child support arrearage, which is $12,000.

Federal law requires the same result with respect to retroactive modification of child support orders. Section IV-D of the Social Security Act requires a state, as a condition of participation in the federally funded child support programs, to have procedures that require that "any payment or installment of support under any child support order. . . [be] . . . not subject to retroactive modification by such State or by any other State." 42 U.S.C. § 666(a)(9).

Point Four: (25-35%)

An award of spousal support is modifiable only when there has been a substantial change in circumstances.

Modification of spousal support is allowed only upon a showing of a substantial and continuing change in circumstances making the prior order unreasonable. Under UMDA, a modification of spousal support is allowed "only upon a showing of changed circumstances so substantial and continuing as to make the terms unconscionable." Unif. Marriage and Div. Act § 316(a), 9A D.L.A. 102 (1987). Most jurisdictions are not as stringent as UMDA, but most place a heavy burden on the party requesting the modification (*e.g.*, requiring a "substantial change in circumstances that rendered the original award unreasonable and unfair." *Hecker v. Hecker*, 568 N.W.2d 705 (Minn. 1997)). Courts consider whether the change in circumstances was anticipated at the time the original award was made and the good faith of the party asking for the modification. *See, e.g., Pope v. Pope*, 559 N.W.2d 192 (Neb. 1997).

A change in the payor's ability to payor in the recipient's needs would be the type of change a court would consider. Mother now has increased need because her income has been reduced by one-fourth. Since her workload includes being the custodial parent of the parties' two children, it seems very reasonable that she would follow her doctor's orders not to resume full-time work. Her loss of income was unanticipated and may be permanent. There is no indication of bad faith on her part. Mother presents a sympathetic case for an extension and an upward modification of her maintenance award. However, Father's circumstances have also changed. His circumstances are discussed under Point Three above.

Overall, it is debatable whether Mother would succeed in having her award increased, particularly in a jurisdiction that took as strong a stand against modification as reflected in UMDA. Although her income has been reduced by one-fourth, there is no indication of other, unexpected expenses. Since her original award was for five years, she will be receiving maintenance for four more years under the original award. Her age, work experience, and duration of the marriage were factors that would have been considered in making the original award and would have tended not to support an award of long-term maintenance since she has been employed, she is not near retirement age, and the marriage was not of extremely long duration. Therefore, it seems unlikely that the court would order an increase in the duration of the maintenance award at this time.

On the other hand, it is possible that the spousal support amount should be increased at this time because of the permanent decrease in her earnings. She seems unable to provide adequate self-support based on the change in her physical condition. It is probably premature, however, to ask for a change in duration.

Family Law

(February 2002)

Legal Problems:

1. If a wife sues her husband for injuries resulting from her husband's negligence, is such action barred by spousal immunity?

2. If a child sues her parents for negligence in an area of parental discretion, is the action barred?

3. Maya bystander who is an unmarried cohabitant and who witnesses her fiancé's death recover for negligent infliction of emotional distress or for loss of consortium, or is such recovery limited only to close family members?

DISCUSSION

Point One: (25-35%)

In the great majority of jurisdictions, negligence suits between husbands and wives are no longer barred by spousal immunity.

For many years, husbands and wives could not sue each other for negligence. The usual reasons for such immunity were that such suits would be destructive of marital harmony and would encourage fraud and collusion against insurance companies. Homer Harrison Clark, THE LAW OF DOMESTIC RELATIONS IN THE UNITED STATES § 11.1 (2d ed. 1987).

In the vast majority of jurisdictions, however, interspousal immunity has been abolished as courts have dismissed fears of disrupting familial harmony and of collusion. John DeWitt Gregory et al., UNDERSTANDING FAMILY LAW § 6.02 (2d ed. 1993). In these jurisdictions, if Wife can prove that Husband's negligence caused her injuries (as it appears from the facts that it did), then she may receive compensation for her injuries.

Point Two: (30-40%)

The majority of courts have abolished absolute immunity for most parent-child lawsuits. However. in areas dealing with the exercise of ordinary parental discretion. no suit would be allowed.

Historically, just as husbands and wives could not sue each other, and for comparable concerns about family harmony, minor children could not sue their parents for personal injury torts. Many jurisdictions, probably a majority, have abolished this absolute immunity. Clark, *supra,* § 11.2.

Even though parents are not absolutely immune from suits by their children, they have substantial discretion in making decisions concerning their children's upbringing. Because of this discretion, children cannot recover for acts that might otherwise result in liability. Courts are reluctant to substitute their judgment for that of parents (to act *in loco parentis)* and to interfere in the arena of family privacy. Matters falling within the exercise of parental discretion include providing food. (This is clearly not a case of true child neglect, where Daughter's parents have failed to provide sufficient food at all.) Clark, *supra.* Therefore, it is unlikely that Daughter could successfully maintain a lawsuit against her parents for not giving her more calcium in her diet.

Point Three: (30-40%)

Both a claim for negligent infliction of emotional distress and a claim for loss of consortium are likely to fail because Emily was not married to Frank at the time of the accident.

In many jurisdictions, when a bystander witnesses an accident which kills or seriously injures a close family member, and the bystander suffers from severe emotional distress, there may be a cause of action against the tortfeasor for negligent infliction of emotional distress. *See* W. Page Keeton & William L. Prosser, PROSSER & KEETON ON TORTS § 54 (5th ed. 1984); *Dillon v. Legg,* 441 P.2d 912 (Cal. 1968). In this situation, Emily witnessed the accident, which was due to Husband's negligence. After Frank's death (which occurred while she was holding him), she suffered the severe distress required to pursue a tort action.

The problem for Emily's recovery, however, is that she was not Frank's wife. At the time of his death, they were engaged and were cohabiting.

A majority of jurisdictions would be unlikely to expand liability, even to a cohabiting fiancée. This reluctance is based on the difficulties of determining which cohabitants should be allowed to recover and problems of proving the importance of the relationship. *See Elden v. Sheldon,* 758 P.2d 582 (Cal. 1988). Some courts might also take the position that recognition of cohabitants' rights in this cause of action would undermine the strong public policy in support of marriage. Harry D. Krause, FAMILY LAW IN A NUTSHELL § 6.5 (3d ed. 1995).

On the other hand, some jurisdictions have allowed engaged cohabitants to recover in a tort suit of this type. *See, e.g., Dunphy v. Gregor,* 642 A.2d 372 (N.J. 1994); Krause, *supra,* § 6.3. Emily would argue that her claim should be recognized. Her relationship with Frank was like that of a husband and wife. They lived together and were to be married in a week. Witnessing his death was emotionally devastating to her. She had strong emotional ties to Frank, and she should receive compensation for her severe loss.

Emily might also try to bring a loss of consortium claim. This tort, which is recognized in almost all U.S. jurisdictions, is intended to compensate a spouse for loss of such things as the other spouse's companionship, sexual relations, and affection. *See Millington v. Southeastern Elevator Co.,* 239 N.E.2d 897, 899 (N.Y. 1968); Laura M. Raisty, Note, *Bystander Distress and Loss of Consortium: An Examination of the Relationship Requirements in Light of Romer v. Evans,* 65 Fordham L. Rev. 2647, 2650-51 (1997). While originally only the husband could recover for loss of consortium, the right was extended to wives during the mid-twentieth century. *See, e.g., Hitaffer v. Argonne Co.,* 183 F.2d 811 (D.C. Cir. 1950). Compensation for loss of consortium typically is available only to the legally recognized spouse of the injured party, not to a fiancée or cohabitant. Raisty, *supra,* at 2652. Thus, Emily would not have a claim for loss of consortium because she and Frank were not yet married.

Note: Emily might also try to bring a suit for wrongful death, a statutory tort unrecognized at common law. It is intended to compensate family members for the death of a relative, typically a spouse, child, parent, etc. Again, however, since Emily and Frank were not married, Emily would not have a claim worth pursuing.

Family Law

(July 2002)

Legal Problems:

(1)   Is the husband of a married woman who conceives a child by artificial insemination regarded as the legal father of the child if the artificial insemination was performed by a medical doctor with the husband's written consent?

(2)   If a married woman conceives a child by a man other than her husband, who is the child's legal father?

(3)   Under what circumstances can the presumption favoring custody in the legal parent be overcome?

DISCUSSION

Summary: A child's legal parent is *presumptively* entitled to custody both because parental rights are protected by common-law and constitutional principles and because parental custody is typically consistent with a child's best interest. Under the presumption, Bert is Daughter's legal father because he consented to his wife's artificial insemination and the procedure was performed by a doctor. Bert, as Ann's husband, is also presumptively Sonny's father *but* this presumption is rebutted by the fact that Walt is Sonny's biological parent. Presumptively the legal parent is entitled to custody. On the facts, however, Bert may be able to rebut the presumption that Walt should have custody of Sonny. The third point considers whether, on the facts given, the presumption favoring custody in a legal parent could be rebutted.

Point One: (10-20%)

Bert is the legal father of Daughter because he consented in writing to Ann's artificial insemination, and the procedure was performed by a doctor.

Even though Bert is not the biological father of Daughter, he is regarded as her legal father in virtually all American jurisdictions because he consented to his wife's artificial insemination. The leading case is *People* v. *Sorensen,* 68 Cal. 2d 280, 66 Cal. Rptr. 7, 437 P.2d 495 (1968). The 1973 Uniform Parentage *Act* provides that a child conceived by artificial insemination by donor is the legal child of the mother's husband if he consented in writing and if the insemination was performed by a medical doctor. Uniform Parentage Act of 1973 § 5. Statutes in many states contain similar provisions. Both these conditions are satisfied here, and Bert is, therefore, the legal father of Daughter.

Point Two: (30-40%)

Bert, as Ann's husband, is presumed to be Sonny's father. In most jurisdictions, the presumption is rebuttable. Here, Walt the biological father of Sonny, can rebut the presumption.

At common law and under the statutes or case law of most states, a child born to a married woman is presumed to be her husband's child. Homer H. Clark, Jr., THE LAW OF DOMESTIC RELATIONS IN THE UNITED STATES § 4.4 at 191 (2d ed. 1988); Uniform Parentage Act of 1973 § 4; Uniform Parentage Act of 2000 § 204(a)(1). The presumption could generally be rebutted by proof of the husband's infertility or his lack of access to his wife. *See* Clark, *supra.*

In those states that would allow the presumption of paternity in the mother's husband to be rebutted, Walt could rebut the presumption because Bert is infertile, and because he and Ann were living apart at the time of Sonny's conception.

Because Walt can show that he is Sonny's biological father, Walt will have all the legal rights of a married father in many states. *E.g.,* Uniform Parentage Act of 1973 § 2; *In the Interest of ROC,* 496 N.W.2d 239 (Iowa 1992); *In re Petition of Kirchner,* 649 N.E.2d 324 (Ill. 1995). However, in some states, Walt may still be denied the status of legal father if Walt has not attempted to assume his parental responsibilities. *Cf. In re Raquel Marie* X, 570 N.Y.S.2d 604 (App. Div. 1991) (finding father's consent to the adoption of his child was unnecessary because father's conduct did not demonstrate intent to pursue a meaningful relationship with child). Walt has offered to pay the expenses of Sonny's birth and to support Sonny, even though his offers were rejected. He also informally acknowledged paternity upon Sonny's birth, although he did not file suit or assert his paternity in a registry before Ann's death. On balance, Walt has attempted to exercise his parental responsibilities, and it would arguably violate Walt's due process rights to accord him fewer legal rights than other biological fathers. *Cf. John* S. v. *Kelsey S.,* 4 Cal. Rptr. 2d 615 (Cal. 1992) (invalidating California statute that allowed mother to unilaterally thwart father's efforts to become "presumed father," thereby allowing father's rights to be terminated on best interest grounds).

In some jurisdictions, however, courts have authority to exclude evidence that would rebut the presumption favoring paternity in the wife's husband if rebutting the presumption would be con-trary to the child's best interest. *E.g., Ban v. Quigley,* 812 P.2d 1014 (Ariz. Ct. App. 1990); *Turner v. Whisted,* 607 A.2d 935 (Md. 1992); *R.H. v. K.D.,* 506 N.W.2d 368 (N.D. 1993). Bert might argue that rebutting the presumption that he is Sonny's father is inconsistent with Sonny's best interest for essentially the same reasons discussed in Point Three below.

Point Three: (45-55%)

Bert will argue that as the legal father of Daughter, he is presumptively entitled to custody of her. The man who is determined to be the legal father of Sonny will argue that he is presumptively entitled to Sonny's custody. The presumption of custody in the legal father can be rebutted, although what is required to rebut the presumption varies from state to state. Bert would be likely to rebut the presumption, but Walt would not be likely to rebut the presumption.

A child's fit legal parent is presumptively entitled to custody as against a nonparent. *See* Homer

H. Clark, Jr., THE LAW OF DOMESTIC RELATIONS IN THE UNITED STATES 811 (2d ed. 1988). In most jurisdictions, to rebut the presumption favoring custody in the legal parent, a third party must show that awarding custody to the legal parent will be detrimental to the child. *E.g., Painter v. Bannister,* 140 N.W.2d 152, 156 (Iowa 1966); *Guardianship of Phillip B.,* 188 Cal. Rptr. 781,788 (Cal. App. 1983). This standard is clearly intended to be more favorable to the legal parent than is the best interest of the child test, which is used in custody disputes between parents and does not imply a preference in favor of either claimant. Some states, however, apply a best interest test to custody disputes between third parties and parents, although this test typically applies when the nonparent is living with the child and functioning as a parent. An application of the best interest standard in other situations arguably raises constitutional concerns. *Cf. Troxel v. Granville,* 530 U.S. 57, 69-70 (2000) (invalidating application of visitation statute where lower court gave no weight to the presumption that fit parents act in their children's best interest).

The presumption of parental fitness applies to the man deemed to be the legal father. Bert, Daughter's legal father, benefits from this presumption, and he will undoubtedly be awarded custody of Daughter. There is no evidence that he is not the fit and proper person to have custody of her. The fact that Walt has spent "some time" with Daughter and is fond of her is not enough to rebut the presumption. Walt's best argument is that if he is awarded custody of Sonny, he should also be awarded custody of Daughter because separating Daughter from Sonny would be detrimental to Daughter. Yet, on balance, this argument would not succeed as Bert can make the same argument (and more persuasively) in the context of Sonny's custody.

It is less clear who will be awarded custody of Sonny. The presumption of parental fitness applies to the man deemed to be the legal father. See Points One and Two above. Bert has a realistic chance of rebutting the presumption if Walt is Sonny's legal father. Walt has virtually no chance of rebutting the presumption if Bert is Sonny's legal father.

Assuming Walt is Sonny's legal father, Bert will argue that it would be detrimental to award Sonny to Walt. Bert is a fit and proper parent, Ann named him as guardian in her will, Sonny is currently living with him and Daughter, and separating siblings is generally disfavored. Moreover, Bert will argue that Walt's history of physical and mental abuse present a question of his fitness for custody.

Assuming Bert is Sonny's legal father, Walt will have difficulty arguing that an award of custody to Bert would be detrimental to Sonny. There are no facts given that would support this argument.

Therefore, Walt's best hope of obtaining custody of Sonny is if he is Sonny's legal father and the court rejects Bert's arguments that an award of custody to Walt would be detrimental to Sonny.

Family Law

(February 2003)

Legal Problems: (1)   Under the Uniform Child Custody Jurisdiction Act (UCCJA), the Uniform Child Custody Jurisdiction and Enforcement Act (UCCJEA), or the Parental Kidnapping Prevention Act (PKPA), must the State X court enforce the State Z decree awarding custody to Husband?

    (2)   Should the State X court give preclusive effect to Husband's State Z judgment and therefore bar Wife's claims for divorce and property division?

DISCUSSION

Summary: The State X court is not required to enforce the State Z decree awarding custody to Husband. Although the custody provision entered by the State Z court was the first custody order entered, the State Z court lacked jurisdiction under both the Uniform Child Custody Jurisdiction Act (UCCJA) and Uniform Child Custody Jurisdiction and Enforcement Act (UCCJEA). Consequently, a court in State X applying the UCCJA or UCCJEA need not recognize or enforce the custody provision in the State Z decree. Also, the Parental Kidnapping Prevention Act (PKPA) would not require that the State X court give the State Z decree full faith and credit. The assertion of jurisdiction by State Z was not consistent with the requirements of the PKPA.

The State X court should give preclusive effect to Husband's State Z judgment of divorce. The State Z court had jurisdiction to adjudicate the divorce, given Husband's domicile. However, the State X court should adjudicate Wife's claim for property, since the State Z court lacked *in personam* jurisdiction over Wife to adjudicate that claim, and since the State X court has such jurisdiction over Husband.

Point One: The State X court is not required under the UCCJA, the UCCJEA, or
(45-55%)   the PKPA to enforce the State Z decree awarding custody to Husband.

Every state has adopted either the UCCJA or the UCCJEA. These acts require that states recognize and not modify sister state custody judgments that were based upon jurisdictional requirements similar to those found in the UCCJA or UCCJEA.

The UCCJA and UCCJEA both set forth four bases upon which a state court may assert jurisdiction to make an initial child custody determination. A court has jurisdiction to make an order if (1) the state is the home state of the child at the time of the commencement of the proceeding (*i.e., home state jurisdiction*); (2) the child and at least one contestant have a "significant connection" with the state (*i.e., significant connection jurisdiction*); (3) the child is physically present in the state and has been abandoned or subject to abuse (*i.e., emergency jurisdiction*); or (4) no other state appears to have jurisdiction under the Act, or the state with jurisdiction has declined to exercise it, and it is in the best interest of the child for the court to assert jurisdiction (*i.e., default jurisdiction*).

State Z did not have jurisdiction on any of these bases. The children had resided in State X since they were born, so State Z was not the children's home state. The children had never been to State Z, so there was no basis for "significant connection" jurisdiction. State Z also lacked "default" jurisdiction because State X could have exercised "home state" or "significant connection" jurisdiction, and State X had not declined to exercise jurisdiction. Finally, the children were not present in State Z when the court issued its custody decree, nor was there any evidence that they were in danger, so the State Z court lacked emergency jurisdiction. *See* UCCJA § 3.

Note: Although § 204 of the UCCJEA deals more directly than does the UCCJA with issues of emergency jurisdiction in situations of spousal abuse, the UCCJEA still requires that the child be present in the state issuing the emergency order.

Therefore, under both the UCCJA and UCCJEA, the State Z court lacked jurisdiction to adjudicate custody and the State X court need not enforce this aspect of the State Z decree.

Nor does federal law require that the State X court enforce the State Z decree. The federal Parental Kidnapping Prevention Act (28 U.S.C. § 1738A) dictates the circumstances in which the courts of one state must give full faith and credit to an earlier custody decree from a sister state. The PKPA contains provisions that are substantially similar to those of the UCCJA and UCCJEA. First, under 28 U.S.C. § 1738A(c)(1), the issuing court must have had jurisdiction under its own state laws. Here, State Z surely did not. Second, under 28 U.S.C. § 1738A(c)(2), even if State Z had jurisdiction under its own law, the PKPA requires enforcement only if the initial assertion of jurisdiction was consistent with the jurisdictional standards set out in the PKPA, which are very similar to the standards required by the uniform acts.

Note: The principal difference between the jurisdictional requirements of the PKPA and the UCCJA is that the PKPA permits jurisdiction to be based upon a "significant connection" only if the child does not have a "home state." For the reasons noted above, State Z's assertion of jurisdiction was not consistent with those standards. Since neither prong (c)(1) nor (c)(2) is satisfied here, the decree need not be enforced.

Accordingly, under all three statutes, State Z lacked jurisdiction to award Husband custody, and therefore, State X need not enforce the custody decree.

Point Two: The State X court must give preclusive effect to Husband's State Z
(45-55%) judgment of divorce, but not to the State Z determination respecting property division.

The principle of "divisible divorce" provides that the jurisdictional basis for termination of marriage is different from the jurisdictional basis for deciding the incidents of marriage such as alimony, property division, and child support. *Estin v. Estin*, 334 U.S. 541 (1948); *Vanderbilt v. Vanderbilt*, 354 U.S. 416 (1957). Divorce jurisdiction is based on "domicile" or some equivalent long-term connection between at least one of the parties to the marriage and the forum state. *Id.*

In this case, it appears that Husband had changed his domicile from State X to State Z. He had moved to State Z and his new job there demonstrated his intent to remain there for the foreseeable future. Thus, State Z was his new domicile at the time he filed for and obtained his default divorce decree. *Williams v. North Carolina (I)*, 317 U.S. 287 (1942).

Because Wife neither answered nor otherwise appeared in Husband's State Z divorce action, she now may collaterally attack that judgment in State X. However, Wife may challenge only the jurisdictional basis for the State Z divorce decree, not the merits. *Williams v. North Carolina (II)*, 325 U.S. 226 (1945). Unlike the situation in *Williams (II)*, where the deserting spouses stayed only temporarily in Nevada to get divorced and then immediately returned to their previous home state, Husband has remained in State Z and has accepted a new job there. Because there is substantial evidence that State Z became the bona fide domicile of Husband when he moved there, Wife's collateral attack on the validity of the State Z divorce decree obtained by Husband will fail. Thus, the State Z dissolution of the marriage must be recognized and will preclude Wife's action for divorce.

On the other hand, Husband's claim that the State Z judgment precludes Wife's claim in State X for property division should be rejected. The jurisdictional basis for such claims is *in personam*. *Estin*, 334 U.S. 541; *Vanderbilt*, 354 U.S. 416. No factual basis for *in personam* jurisdiction over Wife by the State Z court has been shown. As Wife had never been in State Z, and did not answer the divorce petition, there were no "minimum contacts" sufficient to support the assertion of *in personam* jurisdiction in State Z over Wife with respect to property division. *See Kulko v. Superior Court of California*, 436 U.S. 84 (1978). Thus, the State Z judgment would have no preclusive effect on Wife's property division claim in State X. *Estin*, 334 U.S. 541; *Vanderbilt*, 354 U.S. 416.

Family Law

(July 2003)

<u>Legal Problems:</u> (1)(a) Should the State X court enforce the premarital agreement even though the party challenging the agreement lacked legal counsel?

(1)(b) Should the State X court uphold the provisions that waive the right to marital property and child support upon divorce?

(2) Is Ann's trust fund subject to distribution as marital property?

<u>DISCUSSION</u>

<u>Summary:</u> The court will probably enforce the premarital agreement's provisions regarding property division. Ann appears to have voluntarily entered the agreement despite the fact that she lacked legal counsel. Although the absence of legal counsel would be a factor a court would consider in assessing voluntariness, the other facts suggest that the agreement was voluntarily entered into. However, the court will not enforce the premarital agreement's provision waiving child support because parents cannot waive a child's right to support. If the premarital agreement is upheld, then consistent with the terms, Burt cannot reach Ann's trust fund. If the premarital agreement is invalid, in most states Burt will not be able to obtain Ann's trust fund because it is separate property. The entire amount is separate property because the base amount was acquired before marriage and the appreciation in the fund is not the result of spousal labor.

<u>Point One (a):</u> The court in State X will probably enforce the premarital agreement,
(40-50%) except for the provision on child support (see Point One(b)), because the agreement was voluntarily entered into.

Today in all states premarital agreements are enforceable and not void as "contemplating divorce." However, the premarital agreement will not be enforceable against Ann if she can prove that she involuntarily entered the agreement. American Law Institute, PRINCIPLES OF THE LAW OF FAMILY DISSOLUTION: ANALYSIS AND RECOMMENDATIONS § 7.04 cmt. b (2001) [hereinafter ALI PRINCIPLES] (both case law and statutes generally require that consent to a premarital agreement be voluntary); *see also* Uniform Premarital Agreement Act § 6(a)(1), 9B U.L.A. 373 (1987) [hereinafter UPAA]. Here no facts support duress, oppression or unfair surprise. *See generally* ALI PRINCIPLES, *supra,* § 7.04 cmt. b; *see* Ira Mark Ellman, Paul M. Kurtz & Elizabeth S. Scott, FAMILY LAW: CASES, TEXT, PROBLEMS 800-01 (1998).

The fact that Ann did not have a lawyer will probably not affect the court's determination of whether Ann entered into the agreement voluntarily. Neither any state nor the UPAA mandates the assistance of independent counsel. Courts generally have not required independent counsel as a precondition to enforcing an agreement against an objecting party. *See* ALI PRINCIPLES, *supra,* § 7.04 cmt. e, reporter's note. Moreover, the lack of independent counsel is probably not enough to invalidate the agreement here. Ann was advised to obtain a lawyer, she had plenty of time before the marriage to do so, and her trust fund and job gave her the resources to do so.

Factors suggesting that the agreement was entered into voluntarily include the length of time between the date the premarital agreement was presented and the wedding (three months), and the fact that Ann's background permitted her to read and understand the agreement (she had a high school education); the factual history also indicates that Ann read the agreement, that she did not express any reservations about signing it, that Burt's lawyer told her of the agreement's exact effect, and that she had more assets than Burt when entering the marriage. The facts, on the whole, suggest that Ann voluntarily entered into the agreement.

Point One (b): A premarital agreement can address property division upon divorce
(15-25%)   but cannot bind a court on matters of child support.

In virtually all states, premarital agreements can include provisions about the disposition of property upon marital dissolution. *See, e.g.,* UPAA § 3(a)(3). *See also* ALI PRINCIPLES, *supra,* § 7.04 cmt. a. Therefore, the provisions on property division are not objectionable because of their subject matter.

However, almost all states agree that a child's right to support cannot be adversely affected by a premarital agreement. *See* UPAA § 3(b); Ellman, Kurtz & Scott, *supra,* at 839 ("The traditional rule is that a contract between prospective spouses cannot bind a court in deciding child support.").

The fact that the child support provision is probably invalid does not preclude enforcement of the rest of the agreement. Even if the court declares one or more provisions of the premarital agreement to be unenforceable, the remaining provisions may be valid and enforceable. Typically, if an agreement contains some unenforceable terms (such as an impermissible waiver of child support), the remaining terms may be enforced if the parties intended them to be enforceable even without the unenforceable terms. 17A C.J.S. CONTRACTS § 332, p. 309-310; Arnold H. Rutkin, 5 FAMILY LAW & PRACTICE § 59.04(4) (1999) ("The standard rules of contract law apply to antenuptial agreements."). *See, e.g., Rogers v. Yourshaw,* 448 S.E.2d 884, 887 (Va. Ct. App. 1994). Here there is no provision specifying whether the contract is entire or severable, and in all likelihood, the court would find it is severable and uphold the rest of the agreement.

Point Two: (15-25%)	If the premarital agreement is valid, then it would independently shield the trust fund from Burt's claim. If the premarital agreement is valid, Burt will probably not be entitled to any of Ann's trust fund because it was separate property.

If the premarital agreement is valid (see Point One(b)), Burt waived his rights in Ann's separate property and would not be entitled to any part of the trust fund.

Even if the agreement were not enforced, property acquired before marriage is generally considered separate property. *See* ALI PRINCIPLES, *supra,* § 4.03 cmt. b. Therefore, Ann's trust fund of $200,000 is her separate property. Typically, separate property is not subject to division in an equitable distribution or a community property regime.

Regarding the additional $600,000 that represents the appreciation in the value of the trust fund, the general rule is that appreciation of separate property remains separate property if the appreciation is not attributable to spousal labor. ALI PRINCIPLES, *supra,* § 4.04 cmt. a. Since the facts state that Ann's father solely managed the trust, the property would be considered separate. About fourteen states, however, make all property subject to division upon divorce. *See* Uniform Marriage and Divorce Act (UMDA) § 307, Alternative A, 9 U.L.A. (Part I) 288 (1988). But even in these states, there is little to support Burt's contribution to the appreciation of the asset or his claim of need, the two factors primarily considered by courts in distributing property.

Family Law
(February 2004)

ANALYSIS

Legal Problems: (1)   What property is subject to division on divorce?

(2)   Will a court consider Harold's adultery or his gifts to Carol in dividing property upon divorce?

(3)   Will a long-term homemaker's role be relevant to a determination of that spouse's share of the property upon divorce?

DISCUSSION

Summary: The real estate business, the joint bank account, the jointly titled family home, and the pension are all subject to division as "marital property" because they were acquired with funds earned by a spouse during the marriage. In most states, Wendy's stock would not be subject to division because it was acquired by inheritance and is Wendy's separate property. However, a minority of states allow courts to divide even this separate property.

Most states would not consider Harold's affair with Carol relevant to the division of property but would consider Harold's large gifts to Carol as relevant.

All equitable distribution statutes require consideration of both need and contribution. Wendy's homemaking services would be relevant because they provide a basis for arguments about both her need and contribution. Wendy and Harold will make very different arguments about how Wendy's role as a homemaker and mother should affect property distribution. Ultimately, it is impossible to predict the weight the court would place on Wendy's contribution or her need in making the overall property award.

Point One: All of Harold and Wendy's assets that were acquired with funds earned by Harold
(25-35%)   during the marriage are marital property subject to division on divorce. Wendy's stock, which was acquired by inheritance, would be subject to division only in those states that authorize the division of all property.

A majority of states require the court to first classify the property held at the time of the divorce as marital or separate and authorize the court then to divide the marital property. In the eight community property states, community property is treated much the same as marital property. Definitions of marital and community property are nearly identical. Homer H. Clark, Jr. & Ann L. Estin, DOMESTIC RELATIONS: CASES AND PROBLEMS 732 (6th ed. 2000). As a result, all states will allow the court to distribute marital or community property, which includes all property derived from earnings during the marriage. *See* American Law Institute, PRINCIPLES OF THE LAW OF FAMILY DISSOLUTION § 4.03, Proposed Final Draft, Part I (1997).

All of the property, except Wendy's stock, will be considered marital property in a common-law state or community property in a community property state. The *real estate business,* the *pension,* the *jointly titled family home,* and the *joint bank account* were acquired with spousal earnings. How the assets are titled is irrelevant.

Wendy's *stock* will not be subject to division in the majority of states. It is Wendy's separate property because Wendy inherited it. *See* ALI PRINCIPLES, *supra,* § 4.03. An inheritance is the separate property of the spouse who inherits it, even if the spouse acquires it during the marriage. *Id.*

A minority of states (about fourteen) authorize the courts to divide all the property held by the spouses at the time of divorce without regard to when, how, or by whom the property was acquired or how the title was heldCthe so-called "hotchpot" approach. *See* Uniform Marriage and Divorce Act (UMDA) § 307, Alternative A, 9 U.L.A. (Part I) 288 (1988). In those states, the stock will be subject to division.

Point Two:	<u>In the majority of jurisdictions, adultery is not relevant to division of property</u> <u>at divorce, but dissipation of assets is relevant. Harold's large gifts to</u>
(20-25%)	<u>Carol would qualify as dissipation.</u>

The majority of states do not allow for consideration of adultery in the division of property. Harry Krause, FAMILY LAW 163 (2d ed. 1996). A minority of states could consider Harold's adultery when making a division of property. *See* Ira Mark Ellman, Paul M. Kurtz & Elizabeth S. Scott, FAMILY LAW: CASES, TEXT, PROBLEMS 284 (3d ed. 1998) (citing those few states in which the courts will consider adultery as a factor in property division). Therefore, in most jurisdictions the fact that Harold had an affair would not be relevant to the property distribution.

In virtually all states, however, "economic" fault, including dissipation of marital assets, is relevant to property distribution. *See* Ellman, Kurtz & Scott, *supra,* at 414 (mentioning general agreement that dissipation of assets is a relevant factor in the equitable distribution of property). *See also* Uniform Marriage and Divorce Act (UMDA) § 307, Alt. A. (directing a court to divide property "without regard to marital misconduct," yet to consider, *inter alia*, "the contribution or dissipation of each party in the acquisition, preservation, depreciation, or appreciation in the value of the respective estates").

Dissipation is generally thought to be "the use of marital property for the sole benefit of one of the spouses for a purpose unrelated to the marriage at a time that the marriage is undergoing an irreconcilable breakdown." *In re Marriage of O'Neill*, 563 N.E.2d 494, 497 (Ill. 1990). Harold's expenditures on Carol were large, were for a nonmarital purpose, inured solely to the benefit of Harold, and were made during the breakdown of the marriage. Therefore, these expenditures would be relevant in dividing the property. The remedy would be either to include the value of the gifts to Carol in the marital estate or to consider the dissipation when making the ultimate distribution of the remaining property. Ellman, Kurtz & Scott, *supra*, at 416.

Point Three:	In most jurisdictions, Wendy's role as a homemaker and parent would be relevant to equitable property distribution, both as a contribution
(20-25%)	to the marriage and as an indicator of need.

In all equitable distribution states, spousal contribution and need are the primary factors in property division. Homemaking and parenting are recognized forms of spousal contribution. These same services, when they substitute for paid employment over a lengthy period, will also evidence a spouse's need. *See* ALI PRINCIPLES. Therefore, Wendy's services would provide the basis for two different types of property distribution arguments.

Most states do not assign any particular value to homemaking services and would permit Harold to argue that Wendy's contribution was minimal, given her modest homemaking skills and heavy reliance on paid help. *See Ferguson v. Ferguson,* 639 So. 2d 921 (Miss. 1994); *In re Betz,* 880 S.W.2d 618 (Mo. Ct. App. 1994); *Williams v. Massa,* 728 N.E.2d 932, 942 (Mass. 2000). But some equitable distribution states have a presumption that a homemaker's contribution is equal to a breadwinner's and that an equal division is most just. *See, e.g., Brown v. Brown,* 914 P.2d 206, 209 (Alaska 1996); Or. Rev. Stat. § 107.105(1)(f). Whether such a presumption can be rebutted by evidence that the contribution of the homemaker was not equal to that of the breadwinner varies by state. *Compare* Wis. Stat. Ann. § 767.255(3)(d) with *Hammond v. Brown,* 1995 WL 546903, *2 (Ohio App. 8 Dist., Cuyahoga County, Sep. 14, 1995).

Wendy will likely argue that her homemaking contributions played a significant role in the acquisition of the marital property. She would emphasize the fact that her role as a full-time homemaker and parent freed Harold to devote time to building his business. She would also emphasize her services in entertaining Harold's clients.

Wendy will also argue that her role as a long-term homemaker has greatly increased her need for marital property by reducing her capacity for self-support and asset accumulation. This claim would be difficult for Harold to rebut.

Given that equitable property distribution is highly discretionary, it is impossible to estimate how much weight the court would place on Wendy's need as compared to her contribution. It is also impossible to determine how the court would evaluate Wendy's and Harold's contribution-based arguments.

In the small minority of states that require equal division of marital property, arguments about Wendy's contribution and need would, of course, be unavailable to both parties.

Family Law

(July 2004)

ANALYSIS

Legal Problems: (1)   Did Secretary's move into Husband's home and Boy's testimony about missing his mother constitute a substantial change of circumstances justifying reevaluation of the custody decree?

(2)   Was joint custody in Boy's best interests given that his parents did not agree to joint custody and had a hostile relationship?

DISCUSSION

Summary: The trial court erred in modifying the custody order. A substantial change of circumstances that would justify custody reevaluation probably did not exist given the short time that had elapsed since entry of the original custody order. Although a custodial parent's nonmarital cohabitation might, in some states, constitute an unforeseen and substantial change of circumstances justifying custody reevaluation, Wife did not show that the cohabitation negatively affected Boy or his relationship with his father. Nor did Wife show that Boy's feelings of sadness were attributable to the cohabitation or even that they were new.

Assuming that a substantial change of circumstances existed, joint custody would not be in Boy's best interests: the parents did not agree to joint custody, they would not cooperate, and the mother already had liberal visitation.

Point One: Because the motion to modify was made within three months of the original custody
(65-75%)   order and the evidence did not show that either Secretary's move into Husband's home or Boy's feelings of sadness threatened his well-being, an appellate court would likely find that Wife had failed to establish a substantial change of circumstances.

Custody orders are invariably modifiable, but modification is impermissible unless there has been a change in circumstances since the order was entered. Most states require that the change in circumstances be substantial and unforeseen. For example, the Uniform Marriage and Divorce Act (UMDA), 9A U.L.A. 211 § 409(b) (1979) requires that there be "facts that have arisen since the prior decree or that were unknown to the court at the time of entry of the prior decree."

Most states also disfavor modification when sought shortly after a custody decree has been entered; the principle of res judicata and the belief that children's interests are served by stable custody arrangements both contribute to this view. Thus, if a modification petition is filed within two years of the original decree, UMDA § 409(a) authorizes a modification hearing only if the evidence suggests "there is reason to believe that the child's present environment may endanger seriously his physical, mental, moral or emotional heath." In states that do not have statutory standards restricting early modification, case law typically disfavors it unless the evidence shows that the child is at risk. Because the modification petition was brought within three months of the original order and the evidence did not show any risk of harm to Boy, appellate courts in most states would likely find that there was an insufficient basis to modify custody.

In some states, appellate courts have held that a custodial parent's post-decree nonmarital cohabitation represents a change of circumstances sufficient to warrant a modification hearing. *See Todd v. Casciano*, 569 S.E.2d 566, 570 (Ga. Ct. App. 2002); *Word v. Remick*, 58 S.W.3d 422, 427 (Ark. App. 2001). In these states, an appellate court would likely find that the trial court did not err in hearing evidence on modification. But, even in states that authorize a hearing in these circumstances, modification is typically disallowed unless the petitioner shows that the nonmarital cohabitation has an adverse impact on the children. *See* UMDA § 402 ("The court shall not consider conduct of a proposed custodian that does not affect his relationship to the child."); *Todd v. Casciano*, 569 S.E.2d 571. Wife presented no evidence at the hearing to show such an impact nor did she even show that Boy's feelings of sadness were attributable to Secretary's presence in the home. In other states, however, the mere fact of cohabitation may disqualify a parent to have custody.

A child's custody preference is relevant to a custody determination, and alteration of a child's custody preference thus can constitute a substantial change of circumstance. *See Butland v. Butland*, 1996 WL 362038 (Ohio Ct. App. June 27, 1996). Here, Boy's testimony does not clearly indicate any alteration of his custody preference; Boy testified that he missed his mother, not that he wanted to live with her. Nor did the evidence show that Boy's feelings of sadness are attributable to living with his father instead of facing his parents' divorce. But even if Boy's testimony were interpreted to mean that he wants to live with his mother, the feelings of young children are typically given less weight than feelings of those who are mature. Consequently, it is highly unlikely that Boy's statement would be sufficient to qualify as a substantial change of circumstance. *See, e.g., Mulkey-Yelverton v. Blevins*, 884 P.2d 41, 43-44 (Wyo. 1994); *Butland*, (whether child's views qualify as a substantial change of circumstance depends upon the "depth, sincerity, and the extent they reflect changed circumstances within the parent-child relationship or relationship between the parties").

Point Two: Because the parents did not agree to joint custody and had a high-conflict relationship,
(25-35%)   an appellate court would likely find that joint custody was not in Boy's best
                 interests.

Even if there is a substantial change in circumstances, a court may not modify a custody order unless the change will serve the child's best interests. *See* UMDA § 409(b). It is generally understood that requiring hostile parents to share custody can be harmful to children. Thus, "[w]ith few exceptions, courts and commentators agree that joint custody is a viable option only for parents who are able and willing to cooperate with one another in making decisions for their child." *Taylor v. Taylor*, 508 A.2d 964, 971 (Md. 1986). *See also Braiman v. Braiman*, 378 N.E.2d 1019, 1020-21 (N.Y. 1978); *Word v. Remick*, 58 S.W.3d at 426.

Most courts will not impose joint custody on unwilling parents. Even in states that do permit the imposition of joint custody over a parent's objection, a court may not order joint custody unless it finds that this arrangement is in the child's best interests. In making such an assessment, it would be reversible error if the court did not consider the extent of parental conflict and the likelihood of achieving both cooperation between the parents and a stable living situation for the child. *See* Annotation, *Propriety of Awarding Joint Custody of Children,* 17 A.L.R. 4TH 1013 (1982 & Supp.).

The joint custody order in this case also fails to address the basis for Wife's modification petition. Boy will still be living in the same home with Husband's nonmarital cohabitant for substantial periods of time.

An appellate court is thus likely to find that the trial court erred both in modifying the custody decree and in ordering joint custody.

Family Law

(February 2005)

Legal Problems: (1) May a custodial parent relocate to another state when the move infringes on the noncustodial parent's right of visitation, and was it proper to allow relocation of the children in this case?

(2) May a court in a state other than that of the original child support order enforce the collection of child support in a case where the obligor still resides in the original state but has been personally served in the state where modification is sought?

(3) May a court in a state other than that of the original child support order modify the order based on its own law in a case where the obligor still resides in the original state but has been personally served in the state where modification is sought?

(4) May a court in a state other than that in which the original child custody order was entered modify a child custody decree when the parent-contestant still resides in the original state but has been personally served in the state where modification is sought?

DISCUSSION

Summary

Although the various states utilize a variety of decision-making standards in judging parental relocation requests that inhibit visitation with the noncustodial parent, a move sought in good faith that will serve the children's best interests ordinarily will be granted. Although State B obtained personal jurisdiction over Harold when he was personally served in State B, jurisdiction over the interstate enforcement and modification of child support orders is governed by the Uniform Interstate Family Support Act (UIFSA). Under that Act, State B would have jurisdiction to enforce the State A order as long as Wendy registers it, but because Harold is still a resident of State A, State B would *not* have jurisdiction to modify the order.

Jurisdiction over the interstate modification of a child custody order is governed by the federal Parental Kidnapping Prevention Act (PKPA). Under the PKPA, as well as the Uniform Child Custody Jurisdiction and Enforcement Act (UCCJEA), the State B court would not have jurisdiction to modify the State A custody order because Harold is still a resident of State A.

Point One: If a custodial parent's relocation petition is made in good faith and not for the purpose
(30-35%)   of defeating the other parent's visitation rights and if the move is in the best interests of the children, permission to move with the children will be granted.

In enunciating standards to govern relocation disputes, courts have balanced the impact on visitation by the noncustodial parent against the benefits of the move to both the children and the custodial parent. *See* Homer Clark, THE LAW OF DOMESTIC RELATIONS IN THE UNITED STATES § 19.4 at 814 (2d ed. 1988). Although the law in this area "has been unusually unstable, with some states having undergone rather significant shifts in their standards over recent years . . . , [t]he clear trend has been that of increasing leniency toward the parent with whom the child has been primarily living." American Law Institute, PRINCIPLES OF THE LAW OF FAMILY DISSOLUTION § 2.17 cmt. d (2002). Some states now permit the custodial parent and child to move unless the parent's motives for moving are vindictive. *See, e.g., Aaby v. Strange*, 924 S.W.2d 623 (Tenn. 1996). Other states require the parent who wishes to relocate to show that the proposed move serves the child's best interests. *See, e.g., Pollock v. Pollock*, 889 P.2d 633 (Ariz. 1995). Yet others will permit the custodial parent to relocate unless the evidence shows that the move will be detrimental to the child. *See, e.g., Marriage of Pape*, 989 P.2d 1120 (Wash. 1999). Some courts have also emphasized the availability of an alternative reasonable visitation schedule; if such an alternative exists, the court will almost always grant the relocation request. *See Schwartz v. Schwartz*, 812 P.2d 1268 (Nev. 1991).

Under any of these approaches, Wendy should be permitted to relocate to State B. There is no evidence that Wendy's proposed move was aimed at defeating Harold's visitation rights, and the court found that her request was made in good faith. Wendy was offered a job in State B at a salary twice that of her job in State A, an improvement in her economic circumstances that would clearly benefit the children. There is no evidence that the move would adversely affect the children socially or educationally. Both are very young (ages 5 and 7) and thus highly unlikely to suffer from the loss of long-term relationships or the disruption of an academic program. Because Wendy's new home in State B is only 100 miles from Harold's, it is likely that a reasonable alternative visitation schedule that will fully protect the children's relationship with Harold can be worked out: the original visitation order called for visitation on alternate weekends and during the month of July; certainly the July visitation schedule could be preserved and some of Harold's alternate weekends could be replaced with longer visitation periods during school holidays; if Harold and Wendy were to share the job of transporting the children to Harold's home, weekend visits also seem quite plausible. Accordingly, the court was correct in allowing Wendy to relocate with the children.

NOTE: Applicants who analyze this issue on the basis of the constitutional right to travel should not receive credit. However, applicants who note that some courts use that right as a rationale for a consensual relocation standard might receive a modicum of extra credit.

Point Two: A registered child support order is enforceable in a nonissuing state. (20-30%)

The interstate enforcement of child support is governed by UIFSA, which has been adopted by all states. Although the courts of State B have personal jurisdiction over Harold based on in-state personal service (*See Burnham v. Superior Court of California*, 495 U.S. 604 (1990)), personal jurisdiction is not enough to give a State B court jurisdiction to enforce or modify the State A support and custody decrees.

Under UIFSA § 603(b), a registered child support order issued in another state is "enforceable in the same manner and is subject to the same procedures as an order issued by a tribunal of this State." Thus, the State B court may exercise personal jurisdiction over Harold and enforce the State A child support order because Wendy registered that order.

NOTE: Applicants could receive extra credit for noting that Wendy could still enforce the State A order through a State B court even if State B did not have personal jurisdiction over Harold. To do so, she would utilize UIFSA's two-state procedures.

Point Three: The state that issued a child support order retains exclusive jurisdiction to modify that
(20-30%)   order as long as the support obligor continues to reside in that state.

The interstate modification of a child support order is also governed by UIFSA. Under UIFSA, the state that originally issued a child support order has continuing, exclusive jurisdiction to modify the order if that state remains the residence of the obligee, the child, or the obligor, and at least one of the parties does not consent to the jurisdiction of another forum. *See* UIFSA § 205. *See also* UIFSA § 603 ("A tribunal of this State shall recognize and enforce, but may not modify, a registered order if the issuing tribunal had jurisdiction."). Harold continues to reside in State A and has not consented to the jurisdiction of another forum. Thus, a State B court does not have jurisdiction to modify the State A order. An extension of the child support obligation from 18 to 21 years would represent an impermissible modification because, under UIFSA, the law of the issuing state, State A, governs the support obligation, not the law of the enforcing state, State B. *See* UIFSA § 604. The fact that Harold was personally served in State B does not change this result. *See* Point Two above.

Point Four: Only the courts of the state that originally issued a child custody order may modify that
(20-30%)   order while the child or any contestant continues to reside in the issuing state.

The interstate modification of a child custody order is governed by the federal Parental Kidnapping Prevention Act (PKPA). The joint decision-making provision that Wendy sought to modify is part of the State A custody order, and the PKPA provides that a state may not modify a custody order issued by another state if either the child or any contestant continues to reside in the issuing state and the issuing state's courts do not decline to exercise jurisdiction. *See* 28 U.S.C. § 1738A(c)). State B's personal jurisdiction over Harold does not alter this result. Under the Supremacy Clause, the PKPA takes precedence over any conflicting state law. *See, e.g.*, *Murphy v. Woerner*, 748 P.2d 749 (Alaska 1988).

It is also unlikely that State B law would conflict with the PKPA, as the Uniform Child Custody Jurisdiction and Enforcement Act (UCCJEA), which in 2003 had been adopted in 31 states, contains custody-modification standards virtually identical to those of the PKPA. Under the UCCJEA, a state that properly issued a custody decree retains continuing, exclusive jurisdiction until all parties and the child have left the state, or an issuing state court has determined that there is no longer any significant connection between the child and the person remaining in the state and that substantial evidence is no longer available in that state. *See* UCCJEA § 202.

Since there are no facts to suggest that State A would decline to exercise jurisdiction, a State B court may not modify the State A custody decree. Thus, if Wendy wishes to modify the custodial arrangement, she will be required to institute proceedings in State A.

Family Law

(July 2005)

ANALYSIS

Legal Problems: (1)   Are a biological father's parental rights under the U.S. Constitution violated if he has only two years after the child's birth to establish that he is the father of a married woman's child?

            (2)   Is a husband who was married to a child's mother at its birth obligated to support a child who is not biologically related to him if he has failed to challenge his paternity in a timely manner and has induced reliance on his continued parental support?

            (3)   Are a mother's parental rights violated by granting visitation to a biological father when the mother's ex-husband is the child's legal father and the court grants no deference to the mother's views on visitation?

DISCUSSION

Summary

Fred's parental rights were not violated when the State X court dismissed his untimely petition. Although unwed fathers who have established a significant relationship with their biological children have a substantive due process right entitled to protection, it is unlikely that Fred could show such a relationship given his limited contact with Child and his failure to file a paternity action when he was entitled to do so. Moreover, even if Fred were found to possess the requisite relationship because his attempts to establish contact with Child were thwarted by Wife, Fred's rights would be limited because Husband is presumed to be Child's father. The statute of limitations that restricts Fred's ability to challenge the paternity of Wife's husband is a more lenient provision than the conclusive presumption of legitimacy that was upheld against a substantive due process challenge in *Michael H. v. Gerald D.*, 491 U.S. 110 (1989).

Husband is obligated to pay child support for Child. He will be estopped from denying his paternity because he induced reliance on his continued support and failed to challenge his paternity within the two-year statute of limitations.

Wife's constitutionally protected parental rights were violated by granting visitation to Fred when the court gave no deference to Wife's assessment of Child's best interest.

Point One: The statute of limitations in State X's paternity statute does not violate the substantive
(40-50%)   due process rights of Fred, the biological father, under the U.S. Constitution.

Under the U.S. Constitution, an unwed biological father who has a significant relationship with his biological child has a substantive due process right in that relationship. *See Stanley v. Illinois,* 405 U.S. 645 (1972); *Quilloin v. Walcott,* 434 U.S. 246 (1978); *Caban v. Mohammed,* 441 U.S. 380 (1979); *Lehr v. Robertson,* 463 U.S. 248 (1983). But the Supreme Court has also held that it is only "[w]here an unwed father demonstrates a full commitment to the responsibilities of parenthood by '[coming] forward to participate in the rearing of his child,' [that] his interest in personal contact with his child acquires substantial protection under the Due Process Clause." *Lehr,* 463 U.S. at 249. Fred lived with Child for only three months and communicated with him only twice a year thereafter. He paid no support and did not offer to do so. He could have established his paternity when Wife moved out, but chose to wait until Child was four years old. Consequently, a court would almost certainly hold that Fred lacked the type of relationship warranting substantive due process protection.

Even if Fred could establish a significant parental relationship with Child, the fact that Husband is Child's presumed father would limit Fred's constitutional rights. Under the common law, if a mother was married at the time she gave birth, her husband was presumed to be her child's father. Like State X, most U.S. jurisdictions generally retain, in statutory form, some version of the common law presumption of legitimacy. *See, e.g.,* UNIFORM PARENTAGE ACT § 204(a)(1) (2002). In *Michael H. v. Gerald D.,* 491 U.S. 110 (1989), the U.S. Supreme Court upheld a California statute that precluded a biological father from bringing a paternity action when the mother of his child was married and she did not join in his paternity petition. In a plurality decision, the Court held that, because of the state's interest in protecting the marital family and the lack of any established tradition recognizing an extramarital father-child relationship, there was no substantive due process violation even though the father wishing to establish his paternity had had a significant residential relationship with his child. If an unmarried father whose child has a presumed father can be completely foreclosed from unilaterally establishing his paternity, a two-year statute of limitations is certainly constitutional.

In the wake of the *Michael H.* opinion, many states have enacted statutes which give an unmarried father no more than two years to establish his paternity when his alleged child has a presumed father. *See* CAL. FAM. CODE § 7541(b) (1994); UNIF. PARENTAGE ACT § 607(a) cmt. (2002) ("a two-year period allows an adequate period to resolve the status of a child within the context of an intact family unit; a longer period may have severe consequences for the child in that circumstance").

NOTE: An applicant may erroneously discuss procedural due process or equal protection. If the above points are made within the context of a procedural due process or equal protection analysis, an applicant should get credit. However, an answer concluding that a two-year statute of limitations is per se unconstitutional is incorrect. While the U.S. Supreme Court has struck down one- and two-year paternity statutes of limitation *(see, e.g., Mills v. Habluetzel,* 456 U.S. 91 (1982); *Pickett v. Brown,* 462 U.S. 1 (1983)), these cases involved the right of a child to establish a parental relationship and obtain a support order. Here, by contrast, Husband is liable for Child's support. *See* Point Two, below.

Point Two: Husband is conclusively presumed to be Child's father and is estopped from denying his child support obligation.

(10-20%)

Husband could have challenged the presumption of legitimacy within two years of Child's birth, but chose not to do so even though he knew he was not Child's biological father. Instead, he held Child out as his own and supported him. He encouraged or, at the very least, acquiesced in Wife's decision not to establish Fred's paternity within the statutory period and in her termination of Fred's visits with Child.

Even if the State X paternity statute permitted Husband to challenge his paternity, here he would be obliged to pay child support. When a nonparent consents to act as a parent and the child's interests would be harmed by termination of the parental relationship, the nonparent is estopped from disclaiming parental responsibilities. *See, e.g., W. v. W.*, 779 A.2d 716 (Conn. 2001) (stepparent); *L.S.K. v. H.A.N.*, 813 A.2d 872 (Pa. Super. 2002) (same-sex partner who encouraged mother to utilize artificial insemination to bear a child). Courts have often applied the estoppel principle when, as here, a mother's husband who knew her child was not his induced detrimental reliance on his continued willingness to act as a parent. *See, e.g., Watts v. Watts*, 337 A.2d 350 (N.H. 1975). Wife is now statutorily barred from seeking support from Fred, and Child has had no meaningful paternal relationship except with Husband. By assuming the rights of a parent, Husband also assumed the responsibilities of parenthood: he is now Child's father for all purposes.

Point Three: Wife's due process rights were probably violated when the court granted Fred
(30-40%)   visitation without any deference to her determination of what is in Child's best interest.

The State X statute is similar to the Washington statute that was held unconstitutional, as applied, in *Troxel v. Granville*, 530 U.S. 57 (2000). In its plurality decision, the *Troxel* Court noted that the statute "effectively permits any third party seeking visitation to subject any decision by a parent concerning visitation of the parent's children to state-court review," *id.* at 67, and that the state court had given no deference to the parent's decision that visitation was not in her child's best interest. The Court held that, before "a fit parent's [visitation] decision . . . becomes subject to judicial review, the court must accord at least some special weight to the parent's own determination." *Id.* at 71.

Here, the State X court accorded Wife's decision no weight at all. Instead, it ruled, as a matter of law, that "it is always in a child's best interests to know his or her biological parents, regardless of the custodial parent's views about the child's needs."

Although some state courts have held that *Troxel* is inapplicable to visitation petitions from a nonparent who lived with the child and acted as a "de facto" parent, it is highly unlikely that Fred could establish such a relationship with Child. *See, e.g., Rubano v. DiCenzo*, 759 A.2d 959 (R.I. 2000). Fred lived with Child for only three months after Child's birth and thereafter saw Child on only a handful of occasions. Child may not even remember Fred.

Nor can *Troxel* be distinguished because Fred is a biological parent. A child has only one legal father. *See Michael H. v. Gerald D.*, 491 U.S. 110 (1989). Fred's opportunity to establish parental rights was foreclosed with the dismissal of his paternity suit. Therefore Fred is a "third party" and has no more rights to visitation than any other "third party."

NOTE: An exceptional answer might try to distinguish *Troxel* from the case at hand based on the fact that, given Husband's attempt to disclaim paternity of Child, Child may not have a meaningful opportunity to enjoy a paternal relationship unless Fred's visitation petition is granted. It could be argued that this fact makes Fred different from the typical third-party visitation petitioner and more like the de facto parents to which some state high courts have refused to apply the *Troxel* standard.

It is difficult to determine how a court would rule on this argument. Fred is Child's biological parent and appears to be more interested at this point in maintaining a relationship with Child than does Husband, Child's legal father. But to award Fred visitation would perhaps undercut the policies that underlie the paternity statute of limitations. In addition, Fred's earlier relationship with Child was insubstantial.

Family Law

(February 2006)

ANALYSIS

Legal Problems: (1)   Will a husband's alimony obligation that terminated upon his former wife's remarriage be reinstated if the former wife's new marriage is annulled?

(2)   Can an annulment be obtained based on a spouse's misrepresentation of that spouse's assets?

(3)   Is a marriage void if contracted after the filing of a divorce petition but before the final decree is entered?

DISCUSSION

Summary

The court is unlikely to reinstate a spousal maintenance award based on the annulment of the recipient spouse's remarriage. Although an annulment legally "erases" a marriage, the weight of modern authority does not permit reinstatement of alimony based on annulment of the marriage that terminated the alimony obligation. The court is also unlikely to grant an annulment based on misrepresentation of the value of a stock portfolio. Fraud is a basis for annulment only if it goes to the "essentials" of the marriage, and courts typically have not found asset misrepresentation to meet this test. Finally, the court is likely to declare Herb's bigamous marriage valid based on one or another curative doctrine and thus deny Herb's motion to dismiss.

Point One: (30-40%)
The court is not likely to reinstate a spousal maintenance award that terminated upon remarriage even if the remarriage is annulled.

When a marriage has been annulled, it is typically declared invalid from the date of its inception. By contrast, divorce terminates a marriage upon the date of the divorce. Because an annulment legally "erases" a marriage, most courts have held that alimony may not be granted in annulment cases without statutory authority; it seems illogical to say that a marriage never existed and then impose a duty that arises only from a valid marriage. The same logic would support reinstatement of a prior spousal maintenance award. If the award terminates on remarriage and no remarriage occurred, then it would seem that the alimony entitlement still exists.

Some of the older cases apply the "logic of annulment" doctrine and order reinstatement of prior alimony awards. But, recognizing the payor's interest in certainty as to the termination of his obligations, the vast majority of the modern cases deny petitions to revive alimony entitlements that were terminated by an annulled marriage. *See* Homer H. Clark, THE LAW OF DOMESTIC RELATIONS IN THE UNITED STATES 144 n. 25 (2d ed. 1988) (collecting cases).

Modern statutory standards typically follow this "no-revival" approach. *See, e.g.,* UNIF. MARRIAGE & DIVORCE ACT § 208 (providing that the court granting an annulment may, in the interests of justice, make the decree prospective only and thus equivalent to a divorce decree).

Some modern courts have reinstated alimony awards when the equities strongly favor the former alimony recipient. For example, in *In re Marriage of Weintraub*, 167 Cal. App. 3d 420, 213 Cal. Rptr. 159 (1985), the wife alleged that her second marriage took place only because she was abducted and physically coerced into marriage; the court held that proof of an involuntary marriage was enough to support reinstatement. Here, there are no facts that justify reinstatement: Ann chose to marry Charles; although Charles misrepresented his assets, he could have suffered financial reverses even had he told the truth. Ann is neither disabled nor infirm. Moreover, Ann could have divorced Charles and thus preserved her entitlement to obtain alimony from him. In many jurisdictions, statutory law today permits the spouse who obtains an annulment to also seek alimony.

Point Two: (20-30%)
Fraud is a basis for annulment only if it goes to the "essentials" of the marriage, and asset value is not generally considered an essential.

In most states, a marriage is voidable and may be annulled based on fraud. Even in states without explicit statutory authority, courts have often found that their inherent equity power permits the grant of a fraud-based annulment. Although some case law permits annulment based on a "material" misrepresentation, most courts have "required fraud going to the 'essentials of the marriage.'" Krause et al., FAMILY LAW: CASES, COMMENTS, AND QUESTIONS 561 (4th ed. 1998).

The line between fraud going to the "essentials" and lesser misrepresentation is not always easy to discern. The cases are fact-based, and some jurisdictions have interpreted the materiality requirements more liberally than others. But even in "liberal" annulment states, "false representations regarding one's character, social standing, or fortune do not constitute fraud sufficient to annul a marriage. While such factors constitute a species of fraud, they do not afford a basis for destruction of the marriage." 4 AM. JUR. 2D, *Annulment of Marriage* § 24.

Annulment is particularly unlikely here as Charles seems to have misrepresented only the value of his stock. The case is simply one in which a spouse thought her intended was wealthier than he actually was. Such a situation could arise as a result of market forces as well as misrepresentation. Therefore, Ann is highly unlikely to obtain an annulment of her marriage to Charles based on his misrepresentation of his stock portfolio's value.

Point Three: (30-40%)
For purposes of ascertaining the validity of a subsequent marriage, curative doctrines are likely to prevail over the argument that Herb's marriage to Betty is void for bigamy because it was entered prior to a final decree of divorce.

If Herb's divorce from Ann was not final at the time he married Betty, his marriage to Betty was bigamous. A bigamous marriage is void *ab initio*; it has no legal effect.

However, public policy favors finding a marriage to be valid: "the law presumes morality and not immorality." *Hynes v. McDermott*, 91 N.Y. 451 (1883). Betty might rely on either of two "marriage-saving" doctrines to avoid the conclusion that her marriage to Herb is void:

1. There is a presumption that the latest of a series of marriages is valid. The presumption is "one of the strongest presumptions known to the law" and can be rebutted only by "strong . . . evidence that the prior marriage still subsists or by cogent and conclusive evidence." Clark, *supra*, § 2.7. The presumption is designed to protect the parties' expectations; some cases thus hold that its strength increases with the lapse of time and the birth of children.

In some jurisdictions the presumption of validity could be rebutted by evidence that Herb was still married to Ann when he married Betty, even though his divorce from Ann was later granted. The fact that Herb's marriage to Betty was short might also lead a court to find the presumption rebutted. But because the presumption is essentially an equitable doctrine, many courts would estop Herb from rebutting the presumption of validity based on his "unclean hands," Betty's innocence, and the fact that Ann will not be harmed by a finding that the marriage to Betty is valid because she has been divorced from Herb for a period of time.

[NOTE: This issue can be argued either way. Applicants should receive credit for correctly stating the legal principles and making a cogent argument.]

2. Removal of the impediment (the divorce) renders the subsequent marriage valid. Under the Uniform Marriage & Divorce Act § 207(b), parties to "a marriage prohibited under this section who cohabit after removal of the impediment are lawfully married as of the date of the removal of the impediment."

Using one or the other or some combination of these marriage-saving doctrines, it is probable that the court would find that Herb was married to Betty, and therefore deny Herb's motion to dismiss the divorce petition.

Family Law

(July 2006)

ANALYSIS

Legal Problems: (1)   (a)   Must a state that does not permit common law marriage recognize a common law marriage that was valid in the state where contracted?

                    (b)   Did Wendy and Matt enter into a valid common law marriage?

            (2)   Did Wendy and Matt enter into an enforceable agreement to share property?

            (3)   Should the court grant Steve's adoption petition over Matt's objection?

DISCUSSION
Summary

If Matt and Wendy entered into a valid common law marriage in State A, it would be recognized in State B even though State B law does not permit common law marriage. However, Matt and Wendy did not enter into a valid common law marriage in State A. Although the "ceremony of commitment" might arguably represent an agreement to be married, Matt and Wendy did not publicly hold themselves out as a married couple. Thus, Matt may not claim a spousal entitlement to a share of Wendy's property acquired during their relationship.

However, if State B recognizes oral cohabitation agreements, the court could find that Matt's and Wendy's agreement to "treat each other as an equal owner of all worldly goods acquired during our life together" was enforceable and award Matt a share of Wendy's property acquired during the period they cohabited. Many states recognize such oral agreements.

The court may not grant Steve's adoption petition over Matt's opposition. Although the U.S. Supreme Court has upheld restrictions on the right of an unmarried father to veto his child's adoption, it has also required the states to give fathers who have been committed parents the opportunity to veto a stepparent adoption.

Point One(a) (5-15%)
A common law marriage that is valid where contracted is also valid in a state that does not permit common law marriage.

Under universally accepted conflict-of-laws principles, a marriage valid under the law of the place in which it was contracted will be valid elsewhere unless it violates a strong public policy of the state that has the most significant relationship to the spouses and the marriage. *See* RESTATEMENT (SECOND) OF CONFLICT OF LAWS § 283. Perhaps because the vast majority of states once permitted common law marriage, courts in states that do not recognize common law marriage have consistently held that, if a man and woman are domiciled in a state that permits common law marriage and their conduct meets the requirements of that state's law for establishing such a marriage, recognition of the marriage does not violate a strong public policy. Thus, if Matt and Wendy entered into a valid common law marriage in State A, it would be recognized by a State B court.

Point One(b) (25-35%)
The court may not find that Wendy and Matt entered into a common law marriage because they did not hold themselves out as a married couple.

A common law marriage creates marital obligations and rights identical to those flowing from a ceremonial marriage, including the equitable distribution of marital property. To establish a common law marriage, the proponent must show: (1) capacity to enter a marital contract, (2) a present agreement to be married, (3) cohabitation, and (4) "holding out" a marital relationship to the community. The evidence here clearly establishes capacity and cohabitation. Arguably, the commitment ceremony shows an agreement to be married as it involved an exchange of vows much like those made in a traditional marriage ceremony. (A court might also find that there was no agreement to marry because the ceremony did not include any references to marriage or use the terms husband and wife.) But Matt and Wendy did not hold themselves out to the public as a married couple; they consistently referred to each other as "companion" rather than husband and wife, and Wendy retained her own name.

Point Two (15-25%)
The court may find that Matt's and Wendy's mutual vows to share "our worldly goods" constituted
an enforceable agreement to share property acquired during their relationship if state law permits a cohabitant to recover based on a verbal cohabitation agreement.

Agreements between cohabitants creating property or support rights were once unenforceable because they were made in the context of a "meretricious relationship." But since the California Supreme Court's landmark decision in *Marvin v. Marvin*, 557 P.2d 106 (Cal. 1976), many states have abandoned this approach and declared cohabitation agreements enforceable as long as they do not involve the explicit exchange of money for sex. *See* Joel E. Smith, *Annotation, Property Rights Arising from Relationship of Couple Cohabiting Without Marriage*, 3 A.L.R. 4th 13 (1979 & Supp.) (surveying state laws). Again following *Marvin*, and in contrast to the approach applied to premarital agreements, most courts in states that permit enforcement of cohabitation agreements do not require such agreements to be in writing or even to be clear and specific; oral agreements that vaguely require the cohabitants to share or "do right by" each other have been held to create enforceable claims to post-relationship property division and/or support. *See, e.g., Morone v. Morone*, 413 N.E.2d 1154 (N.Y. 1980). Many states, yet again following *Marvin*, will even imply an agreement from the parties' behavior.

Because Matt and Wendy vowed at their "ceremony of commitment" to "treat each other as an equal owner" of goods acquired during the relationship, Matt would not face the evidentiary problems that many cohabitants confront; the "agreement" was made before fifty guests, all of whom are now potential witnesses. The fact that Matt and Wendy thereafter had a child together, jointly participated in the child's care, pooled their earnings in a joint bank account, and remained together in a stable relationship for nearly a decade provides further behavioral evidence of an agreement to share property.

If applicants find that a valid common law marriage existed, then their discussion should address equitable principles of property division and/or community property principles if applicable in their jurisdictions.

[NOTE: Applicants who recognize the alternate theories of constructive trust, *quantum meruit*, partnership, or partition may receive additional credit. *See, e.g., Tapley v. Tapley*, 449 A.2d 1218 (N.H. 1982) (limiting cohabitant's *quantum meruit* recovery to compensation for business services); *Tarry v. Stewart*, 649 N.E.2d 1 (Ohio Ct. App. 1994) (disallowing cohabitant's *quantum meruit* claim for improvements to house because of benefit received from living in house during the relationship).

Point Three (35-45%)

The court may not grant Steve's adoption petition over Matt's opposition because Matt has been an involved father who lived with his child for a substantial portion of the child's life and who wishes to maintain an active, custodial relationship with the child.

Although the U.S. Supreme Court has upheld state statutes that grant the unmarried father only a limited opportunity to object to his child's adoption (*see, e.g., Lehr v. Robertson*, 463 U.S. 248 (1983); *Quilloin v. Walcott*, 434 U.S. 246 (1978)), it has also stated that, "[w]hen an unwed father demonstrates a full commitment to the responsibilities of parenthood by [coming] forward to participate in the rearing of his child, his interest in personal contact with his child acquires substantial protection under the Due Process Clause." *Lehr*, 463 U.S. at 261 (internal citation omitted). Applying this standard, the Supreme Court upheld a statute authorizing a court to dispense with the requirement of the unmarried father's consent to the adoption of his child, at least when the father had "never shouldered any significant responsibility with respect to the daily supervision, education, protection, or care of the child." *Quilloin*, 434 U.S. at 256. By contrast, the Court struck down a statute dispensing with the requirement of the unmarried father's consent as applied to a man who had maintained joint custody of his children from the time of their birth until they were two and four years old. *Caban v. Mohammed*, 441 U.S. 380 (1979). Both *Quilloin* and *Caban* involved stepparent adoptions like that sought by Steve and Wendy.

The evidence unequivocally shows that Matt has demonstrated "a full commitment to the responsibilities of parenthood." Not only did he live with Child for most of Child's life, but the evidence suggests that he was an equal participant in Child's care. Moreover, since Wendy's marriage, Matt has consistently visited Child despite Wendy's rigid visitation restrictions. Matt has volunteered to pay child support, and he took the initiative to establish his paternity and obtain joint custody.

Because Matt is a committed father entitled to protection under the due process clause, his parental rights cannot be severed without his consent or a showing of parental unfitness. As there is no evidence of abuse, neglect, or other grounds for termination, the adoption petition must be denied.

[NOTE: Examinees could receive extra credit for noting that the Supreme Court's decision in *Michael H. v. Gerald D.*, 491 U.S. 110 (1989), upholding a statute that denied an unmarried father the opportunity to establish his paternity over the combined opposition of the mother and her husband, does not alter this result. The statute at issue in *Michael H.* applied only when the mother was married to the husband at the time she gave birth; the Court relied heavily on the state's interest in preventing disruption of intact marital families in its analysis. Those applicants who find that a common law marriage existed could discuss the presumption of paternity because Child was born in wedlock. However, because the common law marriage was not registered, they should still go on to analyze Matt's rights under the unmarried father principles as discussed above in concluding that Steve's adoption petition must be denied.

Family Law

(February 2007)

ANALYSIS

Legal Problems: (1) (a) Does a court have jurisdiction to grant a divorce when one spouse has no contacts with the forum state?

(b) Does a court have jurisdiction to divide marital property when one spouse has no contacts with the forum state?

(2)   May a spouse who did not consent to a separation and believes that reconciliation is possible successfully oppose a divorce petition brought on grounds of separation and irreconcilable differences?

(3)   When are assets owned by one spouse subject to division at divorce?

DISCUSSION

NOTE: Applicants answering this question in a community property state should use community property principles. For this purpose, the phrase "marital property" means community property.

Summary

A court that lacks personal jurisdiction over one spouse may grant a divorce, but may not issue a binding property division or support order. On the facts of this case, Husband could secure a divorce without Wife's consent and despite Wife's claim that the marriage could be saved if Husband entered counseling.

In all states, a court may divide marital property regardless of which spouse holds title. Property acquired during the marriage with employment income is marital property subject to division; inherited property and property acquired before marriage are separate property that is typically not subject to division. If the value of a separate asset is increased through marital funds or significant spousal labor, it may be apportioned into separate and marital components.

Point One(a) (15-25%)

A court that lacks jurisdiction over one spouse may grant a divorce.

Jurisdiction over both spouses is not necessary to dissolve a marriage. If the plaintiff spouse is a domiciliary of the forum state, courts of that state have jurisdiction to dissolve the plaintiff's marriage. In *Williams v. North Carolina*, 317 U.S. 287 (1942) (*"Williams I"*), the United States

Supreme Court likened a divorce action to an *in rem* proceeding in which the *res* is marital status. The court found that each spouse "carried" the marital status to the forum state when he or she established a new domicile in that state; thus a state court may grant its domiciliary's divorce petition as long as he or she has satisfied the state's jurisdictional requirements.

Domicile—residence with the intent to remain indefinitely—is a question of fact. *See Williams v. North Carolina*, 325 U.S. 226, 229-30 (1945) (*"Williams II"*). On these facts, Husband is almost certainly a domiciliary of State B. Husband moved to State B one year ago; he rented an apartment and obtained employment there; he has indicated that he never intends to return to State A. State B could thus grant Husband a divorce.

Point One(b) (15-25%)

A court that does not have jurisdiction over both spouses may not issue a binding property division order.

In an *ex parte* divorce, the court's jurisdiction extends only to the marriage itself. Unless the court also has personal jurisdiction over the defendant spouse, it may not issue a binding order affecting personal rights such as property division. The divorce decree is thus "divisible." *See Estin v. Estin*, 334 U.S. 541 (1948).

Unless the defendant is personally served within the forum state, a court does not have personal jurisdiction over a defendant who lacks "minimum contacts" with the state. *See Kulko v. Superior Court*, 436 U.S. 84 (1978). Wife was served with Husband's divorce petition in State A. She has never been to State B; indeed, she knows no residents of State B except Husband. A State B court thus may not issue a binding support or property division order.

[NOTE TO GRADERS: An applicant could receive extra credit for noting that a State B court could issue a binding property division order if Wife participates in the State B divorce action. When both spouses participate in the divorce proceeding, principles of preclusion apply; because the participating spouse could have raised the jurisdictional issue in the forum state, he or she is bound by the forum state's determination on this issue. *See Sherrer v. Sherrer*, 334 U.S. 343 (1948).]

Point Two (20-30%)

A court may order a divorce based on separation and irreconcilable differences even if the separation was nonconsensual and one spouse believes that reconciliation is possible.

In virtually all states, a spouse may obtain a divorce without a showing of fault or consent of the other spouse. The typical basis for a no-fault divorce is irreconcilable differences, a minimum period of separation, or both. *See* HARRY D. KRAUSE ET AL., FAMILY LAW: CASES, COMMENTS, AND QUESTIONS 557, 566 (5th ed. 2003).

Today, a no-fault divorce may be granted without any attempt at reconciliation. Even if one spouse establishes that marital discord arose from a curable condition (for example, addiction or profligate spending), the fact that one spouse believes that the marriage can be saved is not an adequate basis to deny the other spouse a divorce. *See, e.g., Hagerty v. Hagerty*, 281 N.W.2d 386 (Minn. 1979); *Eversman v. Eversman*, 496 A.2d 210 (Conn. App. Ct. 1985).

In states that require a minimum period of separation as the basis for a no-fault divorce, separation need not be consensual. *See, e.g.,* HOMER H. CLARK, THE LAW OF DOMESTIC RELATIONS IN THE UNITED STATES 517-18 (2d ed. 1988). The mandated period of separation is usually one year or less.

Thus, any effort by Wife to prevent the divorce would be unsuccessful. The parties have been separated for a year, Husband appears determined to secure the divorce, and Wife's belief that the marriage can be saved is legally irrelevant.

Point Three (30-40%)

Assets acquired before marriage or by inheritance are separate, not marital, property. In most states, neither separate property nor appreciation in its value is subject to division at divorce. However, the use of marital funds to add value or obtain increased equity in separate property creates marital property. Property acquired during the marriage with marital funds is marital property.

In all states, marital property is divided at divorce without regard to how that property is legally titled. Thus, the fact that the marital home, the stock, and the bonds are titled in Husband's name alone is not determinative of how the assets should be divided.

In a majority of states, "marital property" may be divided between the spouses, but "separate property" remains the property of the owning spouse. In a minority of "hotchpot" jurisdictions, the court may divide all assets, whenever or however acquired; a few states permit the division of separate property in special circumstances, such as hardship.

An asset is marital property if it was acquired during the marriage by any means other than gift, descent, or devise. An asset that is initially separate property may be transformed into marital property if marital funds or significant effort by the owner-spouse during the marriage enhances its value or build equity. The fact that a separate asset appreciates in value during the marriage does not in itself transform that asset into marital property. *See* KRAUSE ET AL., *supra*, at 752, 763-64.

If State A is a majority jurisdiction, Husband's stock would be classified as separate property, the bonds as marital property, and the marital home as partly separate and partly marital. The stock was inherited, and there is no evidence that its value has been enhanced by Husband's efforts or with marital funds. The bonds, on the other hand, were purchased with marital property (money Husband earned during the marriage) and are therefore marital property. The marital home was purchased before the marriage, but with a mortgage; employment income was used to reduce the mortgage indebtedness and obtain additional equity in the house. In most states, such equity-building payments create marital property. *See* J. THOMAS OLDHAM, DIVORCE, SEPARATION AND THE DISTRIBUTION OF PROPERTY § 7.05 (2006) (describing apportionment principles and noting that, in a few states, installment payments create only a marital lien against the value of the separate asset).

Thus, Wife is entitled to have a court make an equitable division of the bonds and the post-marriage increase in Husband's home equity. In most states, however, Husband's stock would be separate property, not subject to division upon divorce.

Family Law

(July 2007)

ANALYSIS

<u>Legal Problems:</u>   (1)(a) Does Husband's conduct provide a basis for setting aside the divorce settlement agreement?

(1)(b) Does Mediator's conduct provide a basis for setting aside the divorce settlement agreement?

(2)   Is Wife entitled to spousal maintenance?

DISCUSSION

<u>Summary</u>

A spouse's fraud, duress, or coercive behavior provides a basis for setting aside a settlement agreement that is unfair. In this case, there is evidence to support findings of unfairness and impermissible misconduct by Husband. Additionally, a mediator's substantial misconduct is a basis for setting aside a settlement agreement. Such substantial misconduct is clearly evident in this case. Wife has a strong spousal maintenance claim given her disproportionate contributions to the marriage and to Husband's education, the substantial disparity in Husband's and Wife's economic circumstances, and the duration of the marriage.

Point One(a) (15-25%)

<u>A divorce settlement agreement may be set aside when a spouse's fraud, duress, or coercive behavior results in an unfair agreement. Husband's collusion with Mediator, his implicit threats against Wife, and his failure to disclose his relationship with Mediator provide a basis for setting aside the settlement agreement.</u>

When a divorce settlement agreement is attacked before a final judgment of divorce is entered, the court generally "has great freedom . . . to reject the agreement, to accept it, or to accept it with modifications." HOMER H. CLARK, THE LAW OF DOMESTIC RELATIONS IN THE UNITED STATES 760 (2d ed. 1988). Although the case law is far from uniform and often relies heavily on the facts of the case at hand, courts in most states have held that an agreement may be set aside based on fraud, duress, or coercive behavior that results in an agreement substantively unfair to one of the parties. *See id.* at 761; UNIF. MARRIAGE AND DIVORCE ACT (UMDA) § 306(b) (1982) (written separation agreement is binding on the court unless unconscionable).

Courts have been particularly solicitous of divorce litigants who are unrepresented by legal counsel. Even when there is no general duty of disclosure, a number of courts have held that when negotiating a separation agreement, a represented spouse has a fiduciary obligation toward an unrepresented spouse. *See, e.g., Terwilliger v. Terwilliger*, 64 S.W.3d 816 (Ky. 2002). Although lack of independent legal counsel will not by itself invalidate an agreement, courts will generally examine the circumstances that led to the waiver of counsel. Moreover, an attorney may not ethically represent both spouses in drafting an agreement.

Here, Wife had no attorney before the mediation session, while Husband met with Mediator, an attorney who had represented his family for many years. Husband also failed to tell Wife about that meeting and his family's relationship with Mediator. Taken together, these facts may establish that the agreement was procured through fraud. Husband's collusion with Mediator to pressure Wife into signing an agreement favoring his interests also appears to be coercive; so does Husband's fist-clenching and "menacing" look.

Husband's behavior thus offered the trial court a basis for invalidating the settlement agreement if that agreement was substantively unfair to Wife. Because, in most states, there are strong arguments in favor of a spousal maintenance award to Wife (*see* Point 2), the trial court would be justified in finding that the agreement was substantively unfair.

[NOTE: Cases refusing to invalidate fraudulently obtained settlement agreements that already have been incorporated into a divorce judgment are inapplicable to this fact pattern. *See, e.g., Daffin v. Daffin*, 567 S.W.2d 672 (Mo. Ct. App. 1978); *Hewett v. Zegarzewski*, 368 S.E.2d 877 (N.C. Ct. App. 1988).]

Point One(b) (15-25%)

A divorce settlement agreement may be set aside based on serious mediator misconduct. Because Mediator was guilty of such misconduct, the trial court would not err in setting the agreement aside.

Substantial mediator misconduct is a basis for setting aside a divorce settlement agreement. *See Vitakis-Valchine v. Valchine*, 793 So. 2d 1094 (Fl. Ct. App. 2001). In this case, Mediator was guilty of serious misconduct. First, a mediator must be impartial and disclose potential conflicts of interest. *See ABA Model Standards of Practice for Family and Divorce Mediation*, Standard IV, 35 FAM. L.Q. 27 (2001) (mediator must "conduct the mediation process in an impartial manner" and "disclose all actual and potential grounds of bias and conflicts of interest reasonably known to the mediator . . . ."). In this case, a number of facts suggest bias: Mediator was the attorney for Husband's family and met with Husband prior to the mediation session; Mediator failed to reveal these sources of bias and showed partiality toward Husband by requesting only his proposal. Second, a mediator is required to explain the mediation process and make sure that the parties have enough information to ensure informed decision making. *See id.* at Standard III ("mediator shall facilitate the participants' understanding of what mediation is"). In this case, Mediator did not explain the mediation process, the law, or the parties' entitlement to independent counsel. Third, a mediator should recognize and control a situation, such as domestic violence, that would result in unfairness or prejudice to one of the parties. *See id.* at Standard X ("mediator shall recognize a family situation involving domestic abuse and take appropriate steps to shape the mediation process accordingly"). Here, Mediator did not screen for domestic violence and did nothing to adjust the power imbalance between Husband and Wife. Fourth, a mediator may not coerce or improperly influence any party to make a decision. *See id.* at Standard I ("mediator shall recognize that mediation is based on the principle of self-determination by the participants"); *Vitakis-Valchine*, 793 So. 2d at 1099. Here, Mediator characterized Husband's proposal as "fair" and failed to ask Wife what she would propose as a settlement.

Mediator's misconduct offered the trial court another, independent basis for setting aside the settlement agreement.

Point Two (40-50%)

Wife has a strong claim to spousal maintenance given her disproportionate contributions to the marriage and to Husband's education, the substantial disparity in Husband's and Wife's economic circumstances, and the duration of the marriage.

Rules governing the award of spousal maintenance vary from one state to the next, but they almost invariably require the trial court to consider the parties' financial resources and needs, the marital contributions, and the marital duration. Some state statutes require consideration of spousal misconduct. Some require the court to consider one spouse's support for the other's education or training or mandate reimbursement for such contributions. *See* Robert Kirkman Collins, *The Theory of Marital Residuals: Applying an Income Adjustment Calculus to the Enigma of Alimony*, 24 HARV. WOMEN'S L.J. 23 (2001) (describing and categorizing factors in determination of spousal maintenance). Spousal maintenance statutes also accord substantial discretion to the trial court.

In this case, Husband's salary will soon be five times that of Wife's, and his economic prospects are extremely good. Wife is minimally educated and relatively unskilled; her economic prospects are extremely poor. The marriage lasted eleven years. During that time, Wife made greatly disproportionate economic and non-economic contributions to the marriage, Wife greatly facilitated Husband's medical training, and Husband was consistently abusive to Wife.

In the vast majority of states, this combination of facts would amply support a spousal maintenance award to Wife during the three-year period needed to complete her college education. Given Husband's anticipated $150,000 annual salary, Wife's earning capacity (apparently no greater than $30,000 per year), and her likely inability to work full time while attending college, a $25,000 spousal maintenance award also seems to be fully justified.

In some states, however, a spouse must establish that she lacks the capacity for self-support as a precondition to obtaining a spousal maintenance award. *See, e.g.,* UMDA § 308(a) (court may not award spousal maintenance unless spouse (1) "lacks sufficient property to provide for his reasonable needs; and (2) is unable to support himself through appropriate employment . . . ."). Wife has no property, but she is capable of self-support. Under a standard like that of the UMDA, she would be ineligible for spousal maintenance unless her employment was not "appropriate." Some courts have thus refused to award spousal maintenance to a wife capable of self-support even when she supported her husband's professional education. *See, e.g., McDermott v. McDermott*, 628 P.2d 959 (Ariz. Ct. App. 1981) (schoolteacher wife who supported husband through graduate school not eligible for spousal maintenance because she could support herself); *Morgan v. Morgan*, 383 N.Y.S.2d 343 (App. Div. 1976) (overturning spousal maintenance award to wife who had supported husband's legal education and planned to finish college and go to medical school because she was capable of self-support).

Decisions denying spousal maintenance on facts like those in the problem are typically quite old, however. Today, courts and commentators tend to view spousal maintenance as compensation for loss rather than relief of need. *See Principles of the Law of Family Dissolution: Analysis and Recommendations* § 5.04 *et seq.*, A.L.I. (2002) (treating spousal maintenance as a remedy for "unfair loss allocation"). Some jurisdictions also employ a quasi-contract or unjust enrichment approach. The problem contains facts that would support this type of argument given that Husband and Wife both expected to benefit from Husband's enhanced earning capacity.

Even in a jurisdiction with case law strongly emphasizing self-support, Wife could rely on the fact that she and Husband had an understanding that she would return to school after his education was completed. *See Morgan*, 383 N.Y.S.2d at 344 (basing denial of spousal maintenance in part on fact that wife's current educational plan was "never in the contemplation of the parties during marriage"). That agreement would also provide Wife with an argument that her current employment is inappropriate.

[NOTE: The applicant's conclusion should be given less weight than his or her command of the relevant legal principles and use of the facts.]

Family Law

(February 2008)

ANALYSIS

<u>Legal Problems:</u> (1) May an adoptive parent dissolve the adoption of a stepchild based on a quarrelsome relationship with the child?

(2) May a support obligor obtain retroactive modification of a support obligation?

(3) May a support obligor obtain downward modification of his future support obligation based on a voluntary reduction of his income?

(4) May a divorced parent of a 19-year-old college student refuse to support that student when the student has refused to obey reasonable parental commands?

DISCUSSION

Summary

A quarrelsome relationship with an adoptee is not a valid basis for dissolving an adoption. Husband is thus obligated to support Ann and Bert. Moreover, because retroactive modification of a child support obligation is forbidden by federal law, Husband may not obtain termination or reduction of his support obligation for the period before he sought modification. Modification of a future support obligation may be obtained based on a substantial change in circumstances, but a voluntary reduction in income does not warrant downward modification unless it was made in good faith. Many courts also take the needs and interests of the supported child into account. Thus the court probably did not err in denying Husband's petition to modify his obligation to support Ann. But the court probably did err in denying Husband's petition to modify his obligation to Bert, as Bert, an employable college student, had refused to obey reasonable parental commands.

Point One (20–30%)

<u>The court did not err in refusing to dissolve Husband's adoption of Ann and Bert.</u>

An adoption order works as a complete—and final—transfer of parental rights and responsibilities. Traditionally, an adoption order could not be dissolved for any reason. In recent years, some states have enacted statutes authorizing dissolution of adoption in special circumstances, such as the discovery of an undisclosed mental or physical illness. *See, e.g.,* CAL. FAM. CODE § 9100 (2007). Stepparent adoptions are no easier to undo than stranger adoptions.

In evaluating dissolution claims, courts typically look to the length of the relationship, the child's needs, and the parent's motives. *See* Annot., *Annulment or Vacation of Adoption Decree by*

Adopting Parent or Natural Parent Consenting to Adoption, 2 A.L.R.2d 887, § 8 (1948). Here, Husband has been Ann's and Bert's parent for more than a decade and the only father they have known. Ann needs Husband's continuing support. The fact that Husband has reduced his income strongly suggests that he seeks dissolution, at least in part, for financial reasons. Moreover, the only reason that Husband can offer for dissolution, the fact that he had disagreements with teenagers Ann and Bert, is clearly inadequate. The trial court thus did not err in denying Husband's petition to dissolve the adoption.

Point Two (10–15%)

The court did not err in refusing to retroactively modify Husband's support obligation.

Federal law absolutely forbids retroactive modification of child support obligations. *See* 42 U.S.C. § 666(a)(9). The trial court thus did not err in refusing to retroactively modify Husband's child support obligation.

Additionally, state courts have long held that the obligation to pay accrued and unpaid installments of child support may not ordinarily be modified. "If the hardship is particularly severe, the courts [have] sometimes devise[d] a way to protect the obligor, but in most instances the courts hold that retroactive modification of this kind is beyond their power and indeed the governing statute may so provide." HOMER H. CLARK, THE LAW OF DOMESTIC RELATIONSHIPS IN THE UNITED STATES 725 (2d ed. 1988). Here, because Wife commenced an enforcement action within a few months of when Husband ceased making payments and thereby limited the accrual of arrears, Husband has no basis for establishing a particularly severe hardship.

[NOTE TO GRADERS: An applicant who discusses only federal law should get full credit.]

Point Three (25–35%)

The trial court probably did not err in refusing to reduce Husband's future support obligation to Ann. A support obligor's voluntary income reduction cannot be used to obtain downward modification of his future support obligation unless the reduction was made in good faith. Even a good-faith income reduction may be inadequate to obtain downward modification if the court finds that the child(ren) would suffer hardship without an offsetting benefit.

In order to obtain modification of a future support obligation, the petitioner must show a substantial change in circumstances. Courts will generally find that a significant *involuntary* income reduction represents a substantial change warranting relief. But when the income loss is *voluntary*, they invariably require a showing that the reduction was made in good faith and not for the purpose of depriving the child or punishing the custodial parent.

Some courts will grant downward modification based solely on a showing of good faith on the theory that, if a married parent can reduce his income even if it negatively affects his children's living standard, a divorced parent should have the same right. Others will not grant downward modification if the support reduction would impose a significant hardship on the children. Many take a multifactor approach that balances the short- and long-term interests of both parent and child. *See* HARRY D. KRAUSE ET AL., FAMILY LAW: CASES, COMMENTS, QUESTIONS 1015 (5th ed. 2003).

If the court were to consider hardship or engage in an interest-balancing analysis, the facts support denial of Husband's petition. A temporary income reduction for training that will produce a future income gain is sometimes a valid basis for modification. However, Husband's income reduction does not have any obvious end point nor is it calculated to give the children future benefits. Even if Husband succeeds in becoming a successful novelist, the children's ages (16 and 19) would likely preclude a higher future support award to offset the current income loss. *See, e.g., Harvey v. Robinson*, 665 A.2d 215, 218 (Me. 1995); *In re Marriage of Ilas*, 16 Cal. Rptr. 2d 345 (1993). Wife, who already works full time, cannot easily make up the lost income nor can she continue to borrow indefinitely. But Husband could easily defer his plan to write a novel or reduce his income much less drastically.

Even if the court looked only at whether the income reduction was made in good faith, there is evidence to support denying Husband's petition. Although Husband's prior work on the novel provides evidence of good faith, the timing of the decision to reduce his income—the very same time that he wanted to stop supporting Ann and Bert—is suspect and suggests bad faith. Thus, the court probably did not err in denying Husband's petition to modify his support obligation to Ann.

[NOTE TO GRADERS: An applicant's conclusion is less important than his or her understanding of the legal issues. An applicant should receive full credit if he or she discusses the relevant factors.]

Point Four (15–20%)

Because the support rights of an employable child are contingent on compliance with reasonable parental demands, the trial court probably erred in denying Husband's request for future modification of his support obligation to Bert.

In a number of states, a divorced parent may be required to provide college or other educational support for a child over the age of majority. *See* KRAUSE ET AL., *supra,* at 881. But both married and divorced parents may terminate support to employable children who disobey reasonable parental commands. *See* 67A C.J.S. *Parent and Child* § 16 (2002).

Husband's commands to Bert seem reasonable and calculated to serve Bert's best interests. A regular, late-night job at a bar would either prevent Bert from getting enough sleep or prevent him from attending morning classes; the fact that Bert's grades have fallen supports Husband's view that Bert cannot keep up with his studying while performing with the band. Bert's arrest for driving while intoxicated also suggests that he should not be working in a bar. The evidence thus suggests that the trial court erred in denying Husband's request for modification of his college-tuition obligation to Bert.

Family Law

(July 2008)

ANALYSIS

Legal Problems: (1)   Which state's law governs enforceability of the premarital agreement?

(2)   Is the waiver-of-property-rights provision in the premarital agreement enforceable?

(3)   Is the child-custody provision in the premarital agreement enforceable?

(4)   Are profits from the songs Wendy wrote after separation but before the divorce filing marital property subject to division at divorce?

DISCUSSION

Summary

In determining the enforceability of a premarital agreement, some states apply the law of the state in which the contract was signed and others apply the law of the state with which the parties have the most significant relationship. Under either test, the law of State A will probably govern here. State A has adopted the Uniform Premarital Agreement Act (UPAA), under which an agreement will be enforced unless (1) the party against whom enforcement is sought did not execute the agreement voluntarily, or (2) that party did not receive or waive fair and reasonable disclosure of the assets and obligations of the other party and can show that the agreement was unconscionable when executed. Thus the property-distribution provision of the agreement would be enforceable under State A law. In all states, a premarital agreement respecting child support or custody is voidable based on the child's best interest. In most states, marital property continues to accrue at least until a divorce petition has been filed. Profits from property, such as a song, created by a spouse during the marriage are subject to distribution at divorce.

Point One (15–25%)
In determining the enforceability of a premarital agreement, states apply either the law of the state in which the contract was executed (here State A) or the state with the most significant relationship to the parties and the transaction. Under either test the court will likely apply the law of State A.

Some states apply the law of the state in which a premarital contract was executed in determining its enforceability. *See, e.g., Hill v. Hill*, 262 A.2d 661 (Del. Ch. 1970). Under this approach, the court should apply the law of State A.

Others, probably more numerous, apply the law of the state with the most significant relationship to the matter at hand. *See* RESTATEMENT (SECOND) OF CONFLICT OF LAWS § 188. Hal and Wendy entered into a premarital agreement in State A, married there, had a child there, and lived there for all but a few months of their six-year marriage. Wendy and Child are in State A and Wendy plans to remain there. Wendy has a strong argument that State A's law should govern because of its interest in assuring that contracts executed and marriages consummated within its borders comply with its policies. On the other hand, Hal is in State B, State B was the marital home when Hal and Wendy separated, and some marital assets may be located there. Thus, State B may also have an interest in applying its law.

On these facts, it is likely, but not certain, that State A's interests are stronger, and State A's law will likely apply under either test.

Point Two (35–45%)
In determining whether a premarital agreement governing property distribution at divorce is enforceable, courts consider whether the agreement was voluntarily made, whether it is substantively fair, and whether full disclosure of assets and obligations was made. The weight assigned to these factors varies from state to state, but under the UPAA, an agreement entered voluntarily and with reasonable disclosure of assets and obligations is enforceable.

Although courts were once hostile to premarital agreements, today all states permit spouses to contract premaritally with respect to rights and obligations in property. In all states, the enforceability of a premarital agreement turns on three factors: voluntariness, fairness, and disclosure. How courts apply these factors varies significantly from one state to the next.

In many states, an agreement is unenforceable if the party against whom enforcement is sought succeeds in showing *any one of* involuntariness, unfairness, or lack of adequate disclosure. However, under the UPAA, which has been adopted in 25 states and State A, the party against whom enforcement is sought must prove (1) involuntariness or (2) that "the agreement was unconscionable when it was executed" *and* that he or she did not receive or waive "fair and reasonable" disclosure and "did not have, or reasonably could not have had, an adequate knowledge" of the other's assets and obligations. UPAA § 6(a). Thus, under the UPAA, a court may not refuse to enforce a premarital agreement based on substantive unfairness unless it also finds inadequate disclosure or lack of knowledge.

Wendy is highly unlikely to succeed in establishing inadequate disclosure or lack of knowledge. Lawyer gave Wendy copies of Hal's tax returns for the past three years and an accurate list of his assets. Under the UPAA, Wendy would thus be required to show that her execution of the agreement was involuntary in order to avoid its enforcement.

In considering whether a premarital agreement was voluntarily executed, courts look to whether there was fraud, duress, or coercion. They agree that one party's insistence on signing the agreement as a condition of the marriage does not, by itself, render the agreement involuntary, but there is no consensus on what additional facts are sufficient to establish involuntariness. *See* AMER. LAW INST., PRINCIPLES OF THE LAW OF FAMILY DISSOLUTION § 7.04, Reporter's Notes, cmt. b. & d.

Many of the reported cases, like this one, involve a claim of involuntariness based on presentation of an agreement very close to the wedding date. In analyzing whether an agreement signed under these circumstances is voluntary, courts have looked at a wide range of factors, including the difficulty of conferring with independent counsel, other reasons for proceeding with the marriage (for example, a preexisting pregnancy), and financial losses and embarrassment arising from cancellation of the wedding. HARRY D. KRAUSE & DAVID D. MEYER, FAMILY LAW IN A NUTSHELL 73 (4th ed. 2003). In this case, Hal presented the proposed agreement a full two weeks before the wedding. Wendy was mature, had been previously married, and made her decision to sign after conferring with her family. There are no facts indicating lack of opportunity to confer with counsel or any particular hardship that would result from canceling the wedding. On these facts, it is unlikely, although not impossible, that Wendy can establish involuntariness. Under the UPAA, the agreement is likely enforceable.

[NOTE TO GRADERS: If a court were to apply the law of State B, it would probably also consider whether the agreement is unfair. State standards vary for determining whether an agreement is so unfair as to be unenforceable. Some states demand a showing of unconscionability. Other states utilize a lesser standard. In some states, courts consider whether the agreement was unconscionable when signed; in others, they may also consider unconscionability at the time of divorce. "Courts do not consider every hard bargain to be unconscionable, but will withhold enforcement from agreements that would leave one spouse truly impoverished." *Id.* at 74–75. Here, while there is no information on how much divisible property Hal acquired during the last year of the marriage, Wendy will certainly receive child support, and the agreement does not restrict the court's capacity to award alimony. Whether Wendy could successfully show that the agreement is unconscionable on these facts is unclear.]

Point Three (5–10%)
In all states, a premarital agreement regarding child support or custody is unenforceable if it is not in the best interest of the child.

The traditional rule is that a premarital agreement cannot bind a court deciding child support or custody. Although the UPAA does not explicitly bar an agreement respecting child custody, "[l]ong tradition . . . would seem to ensure . . . that courts would not consider themselves bound by custody provisions they believe injurious to the child's interest. The law of separation agreements in every state is explicit on that point, and there is no reason why premarital agreements would be treated differently." IRA M. ELLMAN ET AL., FAMILY LAW: CASES, TEXT, PROBLEMS 839 (3d ed. 1998).

Point Four (20–30%)
Profits from a song written after separation but before a final divorce decree is entered are likely to be classified as marital property subject to division at divorce.

In the majority of states, marital property continues to accrue until a final divorce decree is entered. *See* HARRY D. KRAUSE ET AL., FAMILY LAW: CASES, COMMENTS, AND QUESTIONS 756–57 (5th ed. 2003). In some states, however, marital property ceases to accrue after the date of permanent separation (*see, e.g.,* N.C. GEN. STAT. § 50-20) or the date of filing for a divorce (*see, e.g.,* N.Y. DOM. REL. L. § 236B). Wendy's songs were written after the five-year property-distribution waiver period provided for in the premarital agreement. Thus, because no divorce petition has been filed, Wendy's songs are probably marital property.

The fact that Wendy has not yet received profits from the songs does not change this result. Today, even contingent expectancies such as nonvested pension rights are subject to division at divorce if they were acquired through spousal effort during the marriage. Thus profits from Wendy's songs, even if payment has not yet been made, would be divisible at divorce if the songs were created during the marriage. *See* KRAUSE ET AL., *supra* at 774–75. Of course, a court might find that the songs were worthless or that their value was too speculative for distribution.

Family Law

(February 2009)

ANALYSIS

(Family Law IV.A., B., E.1.; V.B., B.3.; VI.B.)

Legal Problems: (1)   Did State A's assertion of personal jurisdiction over Dad to determine paternity and child support based on his sexual activity in State A more than 14 years earlier meet due process requirements?

                  (2)   Will a court enforce an agreement between parents that relieves a parent of support duties in exchange for that parent relinquishing parental rights?

                  (3)   Will a court base the support obligation of an unmarried father who has had no relationship with his child on public-assistance benefit levels?

                  (4)   Will a court award custody or visitation of a 14-year-old child to a parent whom the child has never met and who lives in a different state from the child?

DISCUSSION

Summary

Because Dad's State A contacts that provide a statutory basis for long-arm jurisdiction are closely related to the nature of the claim against Dad and Dad has a continuing support obligation, State A's assertion of personal jurisdiction over Dad probably met the requirements of the Due Process Clause. The contract between Mom and Dad waiving Dad's child-support obligation is unenforceable. Dad's child-support obligation will be based on his earnings and income, not state public-assistance benefit levels. Dad is highly unlikely to succeed in obtaining custody of Child, but may obtain visitation.

Point One (25–35%)

State A's assertion of personal jurisdiction over Dad probably met due process requirements because the nature of the claim—paternity and child support—is closely related to Dad's State A contacts, and Dad has a continuing obligation to support Child, a State A domiciliary.

The long-arm statute quoted in the fact pattern is § 201(6) of the Uniform Interstate Family Support Act (UIFSA), which has been adopted by all states. The Supreme Court of the United States has not ruled on the constitutionality of this provision.

The leading case on the due process requirements governing jurisdiction over a nonresident parent in a child-support action is *Kulko v. Superior Court,* 436 U.S. 84 (1978). In *Kulko,* the Supreme Court employed the "minimum contacts" test laid out in *International Shoe Co. v. Washington,* 326 U.S. 310, 316 (1945), and reversed a state-court ruling extending long-arm jurisdiction over a nonresident parent based on his "consent[] to the permanent residence of the . . . child" in the forum state. The *Kulko* court noted that due process demands "some act by which the defendant purposefully avails [him]self of the privilege of conducting activities within the forum state," *Hanson v. Denckla,* 357 U.S. 235, 253 (1958), before the forum state may legitimately exercise long-arm jurisdiction. *Kulko,* 436 U.S. at 94. The Court also held that a father "who agrees, in the interests of family harmony and his children's preferences, to allow them to spend more time in [the forum state] . . . than was required under a separation agreement can hardly be said to have 'purposefully availed himself' of the 'benefits and protection' of [the forum state's] laws." *Id.*

The long-arm statute at issue in this case does rely on purposeful activity, i.e., sexual intercourse. Although the Supreme Court has not ruled on the constitutionality of such a provision, state courts have found that statutes like this one meet due process requirements. *See, e.g., Poindexter v. Poindexter,* 594 N.W.2d 76 (Mich. Ct. App. 1999); *County of Humboldt v. Harris,* 254 Cal. Rptr. 49 (Cal. Ct. App. 1988); *Lake v. Butcher,* 679 P.2d 409 (Wash. Ct. App. 1984); *Larsen v. Scholl,* 296 N.W.2d 785 (Iowa 1980). These courts have relied on the voluntary nature of the conduct, the fact that the child's birth could easily be anticipated, and the state's strong interest in ensuring that the child is supported.

Dad might argue that the state's assertion of jurisdiction in this case would violate due process standards given that more than 14 years have passed since the State A acts that serve as a jurisdictional basis. In making this argument, Dad might rely on *Kulko,* in which the Supreme Court stated that the forum state could not have relied on the defendant's marriage during a three-day visit to the forum state 13 years before the support action was brought as a basis for jurisdiction. *See Kulko,* 436 U.S. at 93. But, in contrast to the marriage in *Kulko,* the sexual activity that serves as the jurisdictional basis in this case is directly related to the basis for asserting jurisdiction and Dad continues to have a support obligation to Child. It is thus likely that a court would find that the assertion of jurisdiction is constitutional. *See* UIFSA § 201 cmt. ("No time frame is stated for filing a proceeding; this is based on the fact that the absent parent has a support obligation that extends for at least the minority of the child (and often longer in many states).") There are also state-court decisions exercising long-arm jurisdiction on similar facts. *See Dambakly v. Patire,* 754 N.Y.S.2d 308 (App. Div. 2003).

Point Two (15–25%)
The agreement between Mom and Dad eliminating Dad's child-support duty is inconsistent with the best interests of the child and is unenforceable.

Although the agreement between Mom and Dad appears to satisfy other basic contract law requirements, it is unenforceable. Courts have long held that parents may not enter into enforceable agreements that adversely affect the rights of their children; courts always retain authority to enter support and custody orders that are in the children's best interests. *See* AM. LAW INST., PRINCIPLES OF THE LAW OF FAMILY DISSOLUTION: ANALYSIS & RECOMMENDATIONS §§ 2.06, 3.13, 7.06 &

comments (2002); HOMER H. CLARK, JR., THE LAW OF DOMESTIC RELATIONS IN THE UNITED STATES § 18.5 (2d ed. 1988). The agreement at issue in this case would eliminate the relationship between Dad and Child for the convenience of the parents; all courts would find that this conflicts with the child's interests in having two parents who can provide support and care.

Point Three (20–30%)
The State A court will determine the value of Dad's child-support obligation to Child on the same basis that it would use to determine support for a child born to married parents. Because the court must consider, at a minimum, all of Dad's income and earnings, it will not base the value of a child-support award on state public-assistance benefit levels.

Federal legislation enacted during the 1980s requires all states, as a condition of federal funding, to employ numerical child-support guidelines and establish a rebuttable presumption that the award which would result from application of the guidelines is correct, *see* 42 U.S.C. § 667; the guidelines must be applied in all cases, regardless of the parents' marital status.

Although state guidelines vary considerably in the way support is calculated, none sets presumptive awards at a public-assistance level. Federal regulations require state support guidelines to "take into consideration all earnings and income of the noncustodial parent, . . . be based on specific descriptive and numeric criteria and result in a computation of the support obligation." 45 C.F.R. § 302.56.

Thus the State A court should determine the value of Dad's support obligation based on his income, not the value of state public-assistance benefits.

[NOTE: Support laws that disregard marital status may be constitutionally mandated. In *Gomez v. Perez*, 409 U.S. 535 (1973), the Supreme Court held that a state law which based the existence of a support obligation on the parents' marital status violated the Equal Protection Clause. *Gomez* has often been interpreted as forbidding marital-status variation in the *value* of support, although there are some state court opinions that have taken a contrary view. *See* AM. LAW INST., *supra*, § 3.01 Reporter's Notes.]

Point Four (20–30%)
The State A court will determine custody and visitation based on Child's best interests. It will almost certainly award primary custody to Mom because Dad has had no prior relationship with Child, but it will likely award Dad visitation.

Custody and visitation disputes are governed by the court's determination of the child's best interests. *See* CLARK, *supra*, §19.1; AM. LAW INST., *supra*, § 2.02 & cmt. Residential and relational continuity are both widely recognized as important sources of child well-being. It is thus highly unlikely that a court would award custody to Dad, who lives at some distance from Child's current home and with whom Child has had no relationship whatsoever.

However, meaningful contact with both parents also is recognized as an important source of child well-being. It is thus extremely rare for a court to deny an adjudicated parent visitation, even when the parent and child have had no significant relationship. *See id.* The presumption in favor of visitation and the lack of any evidence in the fact pattern that visitation would be harmful to Child suggest that Dad's petition for visitation would be granted.

The court might nonetheless deny Dad's visitation petition if it finds that visitation is not in Child's best interests. This outcome is more likely if the court finds that the petition was brought in bad faith as a means of deterring Mom from proceeding with the paternity/support action and if Child strongly objects to visitation; because Child is 14, most states would require the court to consider Child's wishes in fashioning a visitation order. *See Family Law in the Fifty States 2003–2004*, 38 FAM. L. Q. 810, Chart 2 (custody criteria) (2005).

Family Law

(July 2009)

ANALYSIS

Legal Problems:　　(1)　May a court in a non-issuing state enforce a child support order against an obligor over whom it does not have personal jurisdiction?

　　　　　　　　　(2)　May a court in a non-issuing state modify a custody decree when one party continues to reside in the issuing state?

　　　　　　　　　(3)　When should a court modify a custody decree based on the relocation of a parent in a situation where the parents share joint physical custody?

　　　　　　　　　(4)　When should a court grant a support obligor downward modification of a child support order?

DISCUSSION

Summary

Interstate enforcement and modification of child support is governed by the Uniform Interstate Family Support Act (UIFSA), which has been adopted by all states. Here, UIFSA would permit State B, the non-issuing state, to enforce a registered support order against Husband through a "two-state" procedure.

The interstate modification of the child custody decree is governed by the federal Parental Kidnapping Prevention Act (PKPA) and the Uniform Child Custody Jurisdiction and Enforcement Act (UCCJEA). Neither the PKPA nor the UCCJEA give the State B court authority to modify the State A custody decree.

Custody modification is based on a substantial change in circumstances. Wife's relocation to State B has significantly impaired Husband's ability to exercise his custodial rights and represents a substantial change in circumstances. On these facts, it is unclear whether Husband will obtain modification of the custody decree in State A.

Under UIFSA, State A has exclusive jurisdiction to modify the State A child support order prospectively if it finds a substantial change in circumstances. If Husband obtains modification of the custody decree, he can probably succeed in eliminating his child support obligation. If he does not obtain modification, he will not be able to eliminate his child support obligation, although it is possible that he will be able to obtain prospective downward modification.

Point One (10–20%)

State B should enforce the State A child support order because a registered child support order is enforceable in a non-issuing state even if the non-issuing state does not have personal jurisdiction over the respondent.

The interstate enforcement and modification of child support is governed by the Uniform Interstate Family Support Act (UIFSA), which has been adopted by all states. Under UIFSA § 603(b), a registered child support order issued in another state is "enforceable in the same manner and is subject to the same procedures as an order issued by a tribunal of [the adopting state]."

State B does not have personal jurisdiction over Husband because he has no State B contacts. *See Kulko v. Superior Court*, 436 U.S. 84 (1978). However, UIFSA provides a two-state procedure that avoids the need to obtain personal jurisdiction over Husband. Using this approach, Wife can obtain an enforcement order in State A (the issuing state) by filing an enforcement petition in a court of State B (the initiating state) that will be forwarded to the relevant State A court. *See* UIFSA § 203. Thus, a State B court may enforce the State A child support order.

Because Husband has not paid child support required under the State A order, support enforcement is appropriate, and State B should enforce the State A child support order.

Point Two (20–30%)

A State B court may not modify the State A custody order because, under the PKPA, only courts of the issuing state may modify a custody order so long as the child or any contestant continues to reside in the issuing state and the issuing state does not decline to exercise jurisdiction.

The federal Parental Kidnapping Prevention Act (PKPA) provides that a state may not modify a custody decree issued by another state if either the child or any party continues to reside in the issuing state and the issuing state's courts do not decline to exercise jurisdiction. *See* 28 U.S.C. § 1738A(d). Under the Supremacy Clause, the PKPA takes precedence over any conflicting state law. *See, e.g., Murphy v. Woerner*, 748 P.2d 749 (Alaska 1988).

Virtually all states have now enacted the Uniform Child Custody Jurisdiction and Enforcement Act (UCCJEA), which contains custody-modification standards virtually identical to those of the PKPA. Under the UCCJEA, a state that properly issued a custody decree (here, State A) retains continuing, exclusive jurisdiction until all parties and the child have left the state, or until an issuing-state court has determined that there is no longer any significant connection between the child and the person remaining in the state and that substantial evidence is no longer available in that state. *See* UCCJEA § 202.

It is highly unlikely that a State A court would decline to exercise jurisdiction under UCCJEA § 202 because Husband remains in State A, Wife moved only two months ago, and Son and Husband had ongoing weekly contact until that time. Son thus maintains a significant connection with Husband and substantial evidence is still available in State A. Thus, if Wife wishes to modify the custody arrangement, she must do so in State A; a State B court may not modify the custody decree.

Point Three (25–35%)
Custody modification is based on a substantial change in circumstances. One parent's relocation that significantly impairs the other parent's ability to exercise his or her custodial rights represents a substantial change in circumstances. It is unclear whether the court will grant Husband's modification petition.

Because of the need to protect the best interests of a child, custody orders are subject to modification throughout the child's minority. But because stability and finality are also important values in child custody litigation, most states permit modification only when there has been a substantial change in circumstances since the original custody decree. *See* HARRY D. KRAUSE ET AL., FAMILY LAW: CASES, COMMENTS AND QUESTIONS 740–41 (6th ed. 2007). One parent's physical relocation that significantly impairs the other parent's opportunity to exercise custody and visitation rights provided in the divorce decree is almost invariably considered a substantial change in circumstances. *See id.*

Parental relocation is a common triggering factor in custody-modification cases, and "[t]his area of law has been unusually unstable. . . . [However, t]he clear trend has been that of increasing leniency toward the relocating parent with whom the child has been primarily living." AM. LAW INST., PRINCIPLES OF THE LAW OF FAMILY DISSOLUTION: ANALYSIS AND RECOMMENDATIONS § 2.17, Reporter's Notes, cmt. d (2002). One group of states places the burden of proof on the relocating custodial parent and requires that parent to show that the move serves the child's best interests. *See Pollock v. Pollock*, 889 P.2d 633, 635 (Ariz. Ct. App. 1995). In some of these states, the relocating parent must additionally show that the move is for a legitimate purpose and reasonable in light of that purpose. *See, e.g.,* CONN. GEN. STAT. 46b–46d. Other states place the burden of proof on the objecting parent to show that the move does not serve the child's best interests; some additionally require the objecting parent to show that the move would be harmful to the child. *See, e.g., Pennington v. Marcum*, 266 S.W.3d 759, 768–69 (Ky. 2008) (best interests test applicable when modification petition brought more than two years after initial decree or when objecting parent seeks merely to preserve initial visitation schedule; harm standard applicable when custody modification petition brought within two years of initial decree); TENN. CODE ANN. § 36-6-108 (2005) (objecting parent must show that move is not for a reasonable purpose, that "relocation would pose a threat of specific and serious harm to the child that outweighs the threat of harm to the child of a change of custody," or that parent's motive for moving is vindictive).

Some states, in joint-custody cases, apply standards that are more protective of the parent who is not relocating. *See, e.g., O'Connor v. O'Connor*, 793 A.2d 810 (N.J. Super. Ct. App. Div. 2002); OKLA. STAT. ANN. tit. 43 § 109(f) (best interests test applicable to modification of joint-custody order); TENN. CODE ANN. § 36-6-108 (2005) (best interests test applicable when parents share equal visitation). Even if State A does not have a special rule for joint-custody cases, relocation, of necessity, has a much larger impact when, as here, the parent who is not relocating has had more than 40 percent of total residential time with the child.

In this case, a number of facts support Husband's petition. Under the custody decree, Husband not only had joint custody, but Son resided with Husband more than 40 percent of each week. Wife's move 600 miles away precludes weekly visits by Husband, let alone substantial residential time with Son. Wife's move was not necessary; she could have stayed at her former employment. Ten-year-old Son undoubtedly had established school and social relationships that were disrupted by the move. Perhaps most important, Wife moved without notifying Husband or seeking court approval; Wife should have sought modification of the custody decree so as to accommodate her proposed move *before* physically removing Son from State A. Her failure to do so will certainly place her at a disadvantage in contesting Husband's modification petition.

On the other hand, some facts support Wife's relocation. Wife's relocation will provide Son with a higher family income and better access to his maternal relatives. There are no facts to suggest that Wife's move was motivated by vindictiveness.

It is thus possible, but not certain, that Husband will obtain modification of the custody decree.

[NOTE: An applicant's conclusion about case outcome is less important than his or her analysis of the relevant issues.]

Point Four (15–25%)
Under UIFSA, State A has exclusive jurisdiction to modify the State A child support order. Although federal law forbids *retroactive* modification of the support order, a State A court may modify the order prospectively if it finds a substantial change in circumstances. It is possible that Husband could obtain elimination of his child support obligation if his petition for custody modification is granted.

Under UIFSA, an issuing state has continuing, exclusive jurisdiction to modify a support order if the child or any party continues to reside in that state and all parties do not consent to the jurisdiction of another forum. *See* UIFSA § 205. *See also* UIFSA § 603 ("[A] tribunal of this State shall recognize and enforce, but may not modify, a registered order if the issuing tribunal had jurisdiction."). Because Husband continues to reside in State A, State A courts have exclusive jurisdiction to modify the State A child support order.

A State A court may not *retroactively* modify the child support order because federal law forbids retroactive modification in all circumstances. *See* 42 U.S.C. § 666(a)(9)(C).

If Husband succeeds in obtaining modification of the custody decree, a State A court might grant Husband *prospective* elimination of his child support obligation. In all states, modification of a support order is based on a finding that there has been a substantial change in circumstances that significantly reduces the child's need for support or the obligor's capacity to pay. *See* KRAUSE ET AL., *supra*, at 991. If Husband succeeds in obtaining modification of the custody decree, Wife would have residential time with Son for only eight weeks per year. This would certainly represent a substantial change in circumstances, as Wife would no longer be a custodial parent. Moreover, Wife's net monthly income has increased by $1,000 per month. On these facts, a court could *prospectively* eliminate Husband's child-support obligation.

If Husband does not obtain modification of the custody decree, the court should not eliminate Husband's child support obligation. There is a strong public policy favoring the establishment and maintenance of legal support obligations, and even poor obligors whose income falls below a value that the state deems essential for self-support are typically required to make token child support payments. *See id.* at 905–06. A court might *reduce* Husband's support obligation based on Wife's increased income if that income is available to support Son. However, Wife's move to State B may have increased her expenses and, assuming that Husband does not obtain sole custody of Son, Son's increased residential time with Wife would almost certainly increase her child-related expenses. It is thus unclear whether a State A court would find that Wife's increased income warrants a prospective reduction in Husband's support obligation.

Family Law

(February 2010)

ANALYSIS

Legal Problems: (1)   Did Harry's behavior constitute fraud or overreaching sufficient to invalidate the settlement agreement?

(2)   Would a divorce obtained on grounds of adultery significantly enhance Wendy's prospects of obtaining a monetary award?

(3)(a)   Is Harry's law degree marital property subject to division at divorce?

(3)(b)   Can Wendy obtain alimony (spousal support)?

DISCUSSION

Summary

Courts generally will invalidate a settlement agreement resulting from fraud, overreaching, or duress if it results in a settlement that is substantively unfair. Harry's preparation of the agreement, his failure to advise Wendy to seek independent counsel, and his biased account of Wendy's legal rights will likely lead the court to conclude that the agreement should be invalidated if the court also concludes that Wendy should have obtained an award. A divorce obtained on grounds of adultery will not likely give Wendy a significant advantage in obtaining an award. In only about half of the states is fault a factor in alimony determination or property division, and even in those jurisdictions in which fault is relevant, it rarely plays a major role in judicial decision making. Wendy is not entitled to a cash award based on the value of Harry's law license, and the facts do not reveal any other assets that might provide the basis for such an award. Given that state law does not authorize claims for reimbursement alimony, it is unclear whether Wendy can obtain an alimony award.

Point One (30%)

The settlement agreement will be invalidated if the court finds that (1) it was procured by fraud, duress, or overreaching, and (2) it is substantively unfair. A court will likely find that Harry's conduct in drafting and negotiating the agreement satisfies the first part of this test. It is unclear whether the court will conclude that the agreement is substantively unfair to Wendy.

In most states, a settlement agreement resulting from fraud, overreaching, or duress may be set aside if it is substantively unfair. *See* JOHN DEWITT GREGORY, PETER N. SWISHER & SHIRLEY L. WOLF, UNDERSTANDING FAMILY LAW 112 (3d ed. 2005). *See also* UNIF. MARRIAGE AND DIVORCE ACT (UMDA) § 306(b) (written settlement agreement is binding on the court unless unconscionable). A few courts have also held that spouses have fiduciary obligations toward each other that continue, when one spouse is unrepresented by counsel, during the negotiation of a settlement agreement. *See, e.g., Crawford v. Crawford*, 524 N.W.2d 833 (N.D. 1994).

Here, Wendy was unrepresented and Harry, an attorney, failed to advise her to seek independent legal counsel. Although a lack of independent legal counsel will not by itself invalidate a settlement agreement, courts will generally examine the circumstances that led a spouse to forgo counsel or waive marital rights. Harry also advised Wendy that a court would "definitely not" impose any post-marital obligations on him, which is probably untrue. Taken together, these facts suggest fraud and overreaching.

However, if Harry's conduct did not result in an agreement substantively unfair to Wendy, the agreement should not be invalidated. The agreement is not unfair as to Harry's law degree. (*See* Point Three(a).) It might be unfair as to alimony. (*See* Point Three(b).)

[NOTE: Some applicants may state that the court can ignore the settlement agreement because the divorce is not yet final. This is incorrect, and an applicant who resolves the issue in this way should not receive credit.]

Point Two (20%)
Obtaining a divorce on grounds of adultery is unlikely to significantly improve Wendy's prospects of obtaining alimony or a cash award representing her share of marital property.

Even if Wendy is able to obtain a divorce on grounds of adultery, it is unlikely to give her a financial advantage. About a third of the states have eliminated fault-based divorce grounds. In these states, Wendy could not obtain a divorce on grounds of adultery; she could obtain only a no-fault divorce.

Although most states permit consideration of *financial* misconduct, only about half permit consideration of *marital* misconduct, such as adultery, in either property division or alimony determination. Of the group of states that permit consideration of marital misconduct, about half restrict its use to alimony determination. And while a claimant's marital fault was once, in many states, a bar to an alimony award, in virtually all states that today permit consideration of fault in alimony decision making, it is simply one factor among many. *See* AM. LAW INST., PRINCIPLES OF THE LAW OF FAMILY DISSOLUTION: ANALYSIS AND RECOMMENDATIONS 46–53 (2002) (describing state-by-state survey). Some appellate courts in states that permit consideration of marital misconduct have required trial courts to consider fault only when egregious. *See O'Brien v. O'Brien*, 489 N.E.2d 712, 719 (N.Y. 1985) (fault excluded except in "egregious cases that shock the conscience"); *O'Loughlin v. O'Loughlin*, 458 S.E.2d 323, 326 (Va. Ct. App. 1995) (party's fault relevant to award determination when fault had an economic impact on marriage). Some states have explicitly ruled that adultery is not sufficiently egregious to have an impact on alimony. *See In re Marriage of Sommers*, 792 P.2d 1005, 1009 (Kan. 1990) ("It is difficult to conceive of any circumstances where evidence of marital infidelity would be a proper consideration in the resolution of the financial aspects of a marriage."); *Stevens v. Stevens*, 484 N.Y.S.2d 708 (App. Div. 1985). In other states, there is older case law permitting consideration of adultery or similar misconduct, but virtually no modern cases do so. *See* AM. LAW INST., *supra*. Commentators reviewing the case law have thus concluded that "the current judicial trend in many states today . . . [is] to ignore or severely limit the ultimate effect of fault-based statutory divorce factors except in serious or egregious circumstances." Peter Nash Swisher, *The ALI Principles: A Farewell to Fault—But What Remedy for the Egregious Marital Misconduct of an Abusive Spouse?*, 8 DUKE J. GENDER L. & POL'Y 213, 227 (2001).

Thus, in most states, proving Harry's adultery is unlikely to significantly enhance Wendy's prospects of obtaining either a property-distribution or an alimony award. In some states, however, this factor might play a role in the court's decision.

Point Three(a) (10%)
Harry's law degree is not marital property subject to division at divorce, and the facts do not show that there are any other significant assets.

The states, by an overwhelming margin, have rejected the claim that a professional degree or license is property subject to division at divorce; the notable exception is New York. *See* HARRY D. KRAUSE, LINDA D. ELROD, MARSHA GARRISON & J. THOMAS OLDHAM, FAMILY LAW CASES, COMMENTS, AND QUESTIONS 788 (6th ed. 2007). *See also O'Brien v. O'Brien*, 489 N.E.2d 712 (N.Y. 1985). Wendy thus has no property interest in Harry's degree, and a court could not grant her a cash award in compensation for such an interest. The facts also fail to reveal any other assets that could be classified as marital property. Thus, a cash award to Wendy representing a share of marital property would be inappropriate.

Point Three(b) (40%)
It is not clear whether Wendy will receive alimony.

If the court invalidates the settlement agreement, Wendy could seek an alimony award. But permanent or long-term alimony is seldom awarded except in the case of a long marriage and a significant, long-term gap between the husband's and wife's economic prospects. *See* GREGORY ET AL., *supra*, at 307–08, 411. It is virtually certain that Wendy could not obtain such an award, given the short duration of the marriage and the possibility that Wendy could pursue a career that would generate an income equal to or higher than Harry's since Wendy is still young and without children.

In a state, like this one, that does not permit reimbursement alimony, Wendy could seek a short-term, "rehabilitative" alimony award to complete her college education. In some states a spouse must establish that she lacks the capacity for self-support as a precondition to obtaining a rehabilitative award. *See, e.g.*, UMDA § 308(a) (court may not award alimony unless spouse (1) "lacks sufficient property to provide for his reasonable needs; and (2) is unable to support himself through appropriate employment . . . ."). Wendy has no property, but she is capable of self-support. Under a standard like that of the UMDA, she would be ineligible for alimony unless her employment was not "appropriate." Some courts have thus refused to award alimony to a wife capable of self-support even when she supported her husband's professional education. *See, e.g., McDermott v. McDermott*, 628 P.2d 959 (Ariz. App. 1981) (schoolteacher wife who supported husband through graduate school not eligible for alimony because she could support herself); *Morgan v. Morgan*, 383 N.Y.S.2d 343 (App. Div. 1976) (overturning alimony award to wife who had supported husband's legal education and planned to finish college and go to medical school because she was capable of self-support).

Most of these decisions are old; courts today typically view capacity for self-support as only one factor among many in awarding rehabilitative alimony. Here, Wendy's contributions to the couple's support and to Harry's education and Harry's ability to contribute to Wendy's future support would weigh in her favor. But the process of alimony determination is highly discretionary, and several factors—Wendy's youth, the short duration of the marriage, the fact that the marriage produced no children, Harry's probably modest salary as a public defender— would all weigh against Wendy's claim for rehabilitative alimony. *See* GREGORY ET AL., *supra*, at 312–14.

In sum, Wendy's prospects of obtaining an alimony award are quite uncertain.

[NOTE: Spousal support and spousal maintenance are alternative terms for alimony. An applicant should not be penalized for using one of these terms instead of alimony. The applicant's conclusion should be given less weight than his or her command of the relevant legal principles and use of the facts. A number of jurisdictions now authorize "reimbursement" or "restitutional" alimony to compensate one spouse for significant contributions to the other's education or career. *Id.* at 411–13. Given Wendy's support of Harry during law school, Wendy would have a strong claim to this form of alimony, but it is not authorized in the state where her claim was brought.]

Family Law

(July 2010)

ANALYSIS

Legal Problems: (1)   Under what circumstances is a premarital agreement enforceable?

(2)   What property is subject to division at divorce?

(3)   When is an alimony award appropriate?

DISCUSSION

Summary

Although state rules governing the enforceability of a premarital agreement vary considerably, a premarital agreement will generally be enforced unless the party against whom enforcement is sought can show involuntariness, inadequate disclosure by the other spouse, or unconscionability. Although Husband cannot show involuntariness or inadequate disclosure, it is possible that he can show unconscionability if this jurisdiction evaluates unconscionability at the time enforcement of the agreement is sought. If the agreement is unenforceable, in most states Husband's inherited real estate would not be divisible at divorce; the marital home titled in Wife's name would be, and Wife's pension would be partly marital and partly separate. In considering whether to award alimony, courts consider a variety of factors, including the parties' ages, length of the marriage, contributions by both parties, and the parties' physical and mental health. Here, it is unclear whether a court would award Husband alimony.

Point One (50%)

In determining whether a premarital agreement governing property distribution at divorce is enforceable, courts consider whether the agreement was voluntarily made, whether it is unconscionable, and whether disclosure of assets and obligations was made. The weight assigned to these factors varies from state to state. Here, Husband may have a basis for challenging the validity of the premarital agreement in a state that allows a court to strike down an agreement based on unconscionability at the time enforcement is sought.

Although courts were once hostile to premarital agreements, today all states permit spouses to contract premaritally with respect to rights and obligations in property. In all states, the enforceability of such agreements turns on three factors: voluntariness, unconscionability, and disclosure. How courts apply these factors varies significantly from one state to the next. In many states, an agreement is unenforceable if the party against whom enforcement is sought succeeds in showing *any one of* the three factors: involuntariness, unconscionability, or inadequate disclosure.

Under the Uniform Premarital Agreement Act (UPAA), which has been adopted in 27 jurisdictions, the party against whom enforcement is sought must prove (1) involuntariness *or* (2) that "the agreement was unconscionable when it was executed" *and* that he or she did not receive or waive "fair and reasonable" disclosure and "did not have, or reasonably could not have had, an adequate knowledge" of the other's assets and obligations. UNIF. PREMARITAL AGREEMENT ACT § 6(a). Thus, under the UPAA, a court may not refuse to enforce a premarital agreement based on unconscionability unless the court also finds lack of adequate disclosure or knowledge.

Under the UPAA, Husband and Wife's premarital agreement would be enforceable. The facts show that Husband and Wife both disclosed their assets, and there is no evidence that Husband signed the agreement involuntarily. Although lack of independent legal advice is a factor in determining whether a party entered into an agreement voluntarily, Husband had ample opportunity to obtain legal counsel and decided against it. Husband also had ample time to review the agreement before signing it, and, perhaps most importantly, he proposed the agreement. *See* ROBERT E. OLIPHANT & NANCY VER STEEGH, FAMILY LAW §§ 14.11, 14.13 (2d ed. 2007); *Hengel v. Hengel*, 365 N.W.2d 16 (Wis. Ct. App. 1985) (agreement upheld when wife received proposed agreement two weeks before wedding and had it reviewed by legal counsel).

In states that have not adopted the UPAA, courts employ a range of standards. In most of these states, a court may invalidate a premarital agreement on grounds of unconscionability even if both parties have fully disclosed their assets. In evaluating unconscionability, some states require courts to determine whether the agreement was unconscionable when signed; others require a determination of unconscionability at the time of divorce; yet other states permit courts to invalidate an agreement based on unconscionability at either point in time or to invalidate an agreement simply because it is unfair. And some states specifically disallow spousal support waivers or apply special standards to such waivers. *See* HARRY D. KRAUSE, ET AL., FAMILY LAW: CASES, COMMENTS AND QUESTIONS 208 (6th ed. 2007).

Here, the agreement initially benefited Husband by ensuring payment of his debts and protecting him against his own imprudent speculation; if unconscionability is analyzed at the time the agreement was signed, the court will likely find it enforceable. At the time of divorce, however, the agreement is arguably unconscionable in that it would grant Wife not only all marital assets, but also Husband's inherited real estate, an asset that, in most states, would be Husband's separate property. (*See* Point Two.) Moreover, Husband has suffered a serious injury and might succeed in establishing that he is incapable of self-support. Thus, in a state that permits invalidation of an agreement based on unconscionability at the time of divorce, a court could find that the premarital agreement between Husband and Wife is unconscionable and unenforceable. In a state that disallows spousal support waivers, this provision might also be struck down even if the property division provision were upheld.

[NOTE: A number of states that have adopted the UPAA have varied its enforcement provisions. For example, although the UPAA provides that "parties to a premarital agreement may contract with respect to . . . the modification or elimination of spousal support," UPAA § 3(a)(4), some UPAA states have disallowed spousal support waivers (*see* S.D. CODIFIED LAWS § 25-2-18 (2009); *Sanford v. Sanford*, 694 N.W.2d 283 (S.D. 2005)) or allowed such waivers only in limited circumstances. *See* 750 ILL. COMP. STAT. ANN. § 10/7 (West 2010) (a spousal-support waiver is unenforceable if it causes the waiving spouse undue hardship in light of circumstances not reasonably foreseeable at the time of signing). Some states permit a court to invalidate a premarital agreement on grounds of unconscionability even when there has been full asset disclosure. *See, e.g.,* WIS. STAT. ANN. § 766.58(6) (2009).]

Point Two (30%)

Unless a valid premarital agreement specifies otherwise, in most states, property acquired during the marriage through spousal effort is divisible at divorce, but property acquired through gift, descent, or devise is not. Thus Husband could be awarded part of Wife's pension and a share in the marital home.

In all states, a divorce court may divide marital property without regard to title. In the majority of states, a divorce court may not divide separate property. In a minority of "hotchpot" jurisdictions, the court may divide all assets, whenever or however acquired; a few states permit the division of separate property in special circumstances, such as hardship. *See* KRAUSE, *supra*, at 752, 763–65 (6th ed. 2007).

An asset is marital if it was acquired during the marriage by any means other than gift, descent, or devise. An asset that is initially separate property may be transformed into marital property if marital funds or significant efforts by the owner-spouse enhance its value or build equity during the marriage. *See id.*

Here, if State A is a majority jurisdiction, Husband's real estate would be classified as separate property, the marital home as marital, and Wife's pension as partly marital and partly separate. The real estate was inherited, and there is no evidence that its value has been enhanced by Husband's efforts or marital funds. The marital home was purchased after marriage with Wife's employment income. The value of Wife's pension reflects both marital employment income and premarital employment income; a court would thus apportion its value. *See* J. THOMAS OLDHAM, DIVORCE, SEPARATION AND THE DISTRIBUTION OF PROPERTY § 7.10[5] (2006) (describing apportionment principles).

Thus, absent an enforceable premarital agreement, a divorce court could award Husband a share of Wife's pension and the marital home. In most states, it could not award Wife a share of Husband's real estate.

Point Three (20%)

Even if the premarital agreement is unenforceable, it is unclear whether Husband can obtain alimony. Husband's failure to contribute to the marriage weighs against his alimony claim, but, if Husband can establish that his injury precludes employment, that factor coupled with his age and the duration of the marriage may support an alimony award.

State A terms spousal support "alimony."

Rules governing the award of alimony vary from one state to the next, but they almost invariably require the trial court to consider the parties' financial resources and needs, their marital contributions, and the marital duration. Some state statutes also require consideration of spousal misconduct. *See* Robert Kirkman Collins, *The Theory of Marital Residuals: Applying an Income Adjustment Calculus to the Enigma of Alimony*, 24 HARV. WOMEN'S L.J. 23, 46 (2001) (describing and categorizing factors in alimony determination); LYNN D. WARDLE & LAURENCE C. NOLAN, FUNDAMENTAL PRINCIPLES OF FAMILY LAW 718 (2d ed. 2006); AMERICAN LAW INSTITUTE, PRINCIPLES OF THE LAW OF FAMILY DISSOLUTION: ANALYSIS AND RECOMMENDATIONS §§ 5.02, 5.03 (2002). Although alimony statutes typically accord substantial discretion to the trial court, they are invariably gender neutral. *See Orr v. Orr*, 440 U.S. 268 (1979).

In evaluating need, a court typically considers the standard of living enjoyed by the parties during the marriage and whether the recipient spouse will be able to achieve that level of economic self-sufficiency within a reasonable period of time following the divorce; health, the existence of separate assets, and the share of marital assets that the recipient spouse will receive may also be taken into account. *See* OLIPHANT & VER STEEGH, *supra*, §§ 11.14–11.18.

In evaluating a spouse's contributions to the marriage, a court may consider negative as well as positive actions, including a spouse's failure to make economic or noneconomic contributions and misuse or dissipation of marital funds. *Id.* § 11.13.

In this case, both Husband and Wife are minimally educated. The 15-year marriage was relatively lengthy. The marital standard of living has not been high, and throughout the marriage, Wife has made greatly disproportionate contributions. For most of the marriage, Husband's failure to contribute more was unexcused. Although Husband suffered a major injury five years ago, a court may be skeptical of his claim that he cannot work given Husband's employment history, his apparent lack of noneconomic contributions, and his failure to make use of the pilot's license he acquired with Wife's help. Wife does not earn a high salary that would permit her to pay alimony easily. Finally, because the question assumes that the agreement is invalid, Husband would, in most states, retain his inherited real estate, which would provide him with an asset that he could use to defray his expenses.

On the other hand, if Husband succeeds in establishing his disability, a court might find that his current need outweighs his lack of economic contributions, particularly given the length of the marriage, Husband's age, Wife's earning ability, and the fact that Wife will receive a share of marital assets.

Thus, on these facts, it is possible, but by no means certain, that Husband will obtain an alimony award if the premarital agreement is found to be invalid.

Family Law

(February 2011)

ANALYSIS

Legal Problems: (1) On what basis may the property-division and support provisions of a separation agreement be invalidated, and is there evidence to support invalidation in this case?

(2) When, if ever, may the property-division provisions of a divorce decree be modified?

(3) When, if ever, may the spousal- and child-support provisions of a divorce decree be modified?

(4) May the nonpaternity of a mother's husband be established after entry of a divorce judgment when the child is 10 years of age and the husband is the only father the child has ever known?

DISCUSSION

Summary

Both the support and property-division provisions of a separation agreement may be invalidated based on a finding of unconscionability or fraud. Here, there are insufficient facts to support a finding of unconscionability with respect to the property-division or spousal-support portions of the agreement. Given the variety of approaches currently applied by the states to paternity misrepresentation and disestablishment, it is unclear whether the court erred in denying Husband's petition to invalidate the child-support provisions of the separation agreement.

A spousal- or child-support order may be modified based on a change of circumstances after the order was entered. However, there has been no change of circumstances in this case because Husband knew or should have known of the economic needs of his intended wife and stepchildren before signing the agreement, and there is no evidence that those needs have changed. It is unclear whether Husband can obtain modification of his child-support obligation based on his nonpaternity of Child.

Point One (40%)

A separation agreement may be invalidated, in whole or in part, based on unconscionability or fraud. Here, there are insufficient facts to support a finding of unconscionability with respect to the property-division or spousal-support portions of the agreement. Given the variety of approaches currently applied by the states to paternity misrepresentation and disestablishment, it is unclear whether the trial court erred in denying Husband's petition to invalidate the child-support provisions of the separation agreement based on fraud.

All states authorize invalidation of a separation agreement, or a specific portion of such an agreement, based on a finding of fraud or unconscionability. Here, there is no evidence of asset or income misrepresentation. And, although judicial interpretations of the unconscionability test vary (*compare Jameson v. Jameson*, 239 N.W.2d 5 (S.D. 1976) *with Williams v. Williams*, 508 A.2d 985 (Md. 1986)), the facts do not appear to support an unconscionability finding with respect to the property-division or spousal-support portions of the agreement. The parties were represented by separate counsel, and there is no evidence of asset nondisclosure. Nor will the unconscionability doctrine serve to relieve a spouse whose complaint is simply that he believes he made a bad bargain. *See Jameson*, 239 N.W.2d at 7. It is not even clear that Husband made a bad bargain. Although he did receive fewer assets than Wife, most states require *equitable*, not equal, division of assets, and equity is determined through a complex assessment of contribution and need-based factors. *See* HARRY D. KRAUSE ET AL., FAMILY LAW: CASES, COMMENTS, AND QUESTIONS (6th ed. 2007) at 752. Moreover, the agreement requires Husband to pay only $10,800 per year (13.5 percent of his total income) in *combined* child and spousal support. Many state child-support guidelines would require Husband to pay this much or more in child support alone. *See id.* at 891–93 (reviewing support guidelines). Thus, it is highly unlikely that an appellate court would find reversible error in the trial court's refusal to invalidate these portions of the agreement based on unconscionability.

It is unclear whether an appellate court would find reversible error in the trial court's refusal to invalidate the child-support portion of the agreement, however. It is now apparent that Husband is not Child's biological parent. Arguably, Wife's failure to alert Husband to this possibility was a form of misrepresentation which might support a finding of fraud. A few courts have permitted tort actions against a wife who misrepresented her husband's paternity. *See Miller v. Miller*, 956 P.2d 887 (Okla. 1998); *G.A.W., III v. D.M.W.*, 596 N.W.2d 284 (Minn. App. 1999). In a state with such case law, it is possible that an appellate court might conclude that Wife's conduct provided a basis for invalidating the child-support provisions of the agreement. *See* Point Three, *infra.*

Point Two (10%)
A divorce property-division award is not subject to modification.

Although a support award may be modified after a divorce decree has been entered, a property-division award, whether it results from a judicial decision or a divorce settlement agreement, may not be modified after a divorce decree has been entered. *See* KRAUSE ET AL., *supra*, at 991. This distinction rests on a fundamental difference between support and property division. A support order requires payment, over what may be a long period of time, of post-divorce income, while a property-division award divides assets accrued during the marriage based on the equities at the time of divorce. Property division thus reflects an evaluation of the past, and support determination reflects an evaluation of the future. Because the future is unpredictable, courts are empowered to modify a support award to take account of changed circumstances. Because the past can be ascertained, courts are not empowered to reconsider that evaluation and modify a property-division award once it has been embodied in a final judgment of divorce. Thus, the trial court did not err in refusing to modify the property-division provisions of the divorce decree.

Point Three (25%)

A spousal-support award may be modified when the court finds that there has been a substantial change in a party's circumstances. Because Husband knew of his future obligations to his new spouse and stepchildren at the time he signed the agreement, there is no change of circumstances in this case.

In all states, a spousal-support award may be modified based on a change in a party's circumstances. Most courts require that such a change be substantial. *See* HARRY D. KRAUSE & DAVID D. MEYER, FAMILY LAW IN A NUTSHELL, 303–05 (5th ed. 2007).

A court may take into account legal obligations to a new spouse and/or children in determining whether there has been a change in circumstances that warrants modification of a support award. *See id.* However, in this case, Husband does not have new adopted or biological children to whom he owes support; he has stepchildren. In most states, a stepparent relationship creates no legal support obligations. *See id.* at 175–76.

More importantly, a change in circumstances that is *anticipated* may not serve as a basis for modification of a support order. *See* M.L. Cross, Annotation, *Change in Financial Condition or Needs of Husband or Wife as Ground for Modification of Decree for Alimony or Maintenance,* 18 A.L.R.2d 10 § 3 (1951 & Supp.). Here, Husband knew about the support needs of Fiancee and her children at the time he signed the separation agreement; Husband was living with Fiancee and the children at the time the agreement was signed, and his planned marriage to Fiancee was the reason Husband was willing to sign the agreement as presented. Thus, because Husband's decision to sign the agreement and accept these support obligations was made with full knowledge of his impending marriage, he cannot now claim that marriage as a change of circumstances that warrants modification of his obligations under the divorce decree. Therefore, the trial court should not modify the spousal-support award based on the needs of Husband's new wife and her children.

Point Four (25%)
It is unclear whether the trial court erred in refusing to modify the child-support award based on Husband's nonpaternity of Child.

Traditionally, courts have been extremely reluctant to terminate an established parent-child relationship and have relied on a wide range of equitable and procedural principles to avoid doing so. Some courts have found that a prior legal judgment, such as the divorce decree terminating Husband's and Wife's marriage, bars the introduction of nonpaternity evidence based on application of res judicata or collateral estoppel principles. *See* Alan Stephens, Annotation, *Parental Rights of Man Who Is Not Biological or Adoptive Father of Child but Was Husband or Cohabitant of Mother When Child Was Conceived or Born,* 84 A.L.R.4th 655 (1991 & Supp.) (collecting cases). Other courts have relied on the equitable doctrines of estoppel and laches to achieve the same result. *See* AM. LAW INST., PRINCIPLES OF THE LAW OF FAMILY DISSOLUTION: ANALYSIS & RECOMMENDATIONS § 3.03 cmt. d (2002); John C. Williams, Annotation, *Laches or Acquiescence as Defense, so as to Bar Recovery of Arrearages of Permanent Alimony or Child Support,* 5 A.L.R.4th 1015 (1981 & Supp.). Moreover, some courts have simply cited the child's best interest, without relying on any specific legal principle, as justification either for denying permission to introduce evidence of nonpaternity or for denying a petition to disestablish paternity. *See, e.g., Godin v. Godin*, 725 A.2d 904, 911 (Vt. 1998). *See also* Stephens, *supra*. Under this latter approach, the trial court correctly denied Husband's petition to modify his support obligation based on his nonpaternity because Child is 10 years old, Husband is the only father Child has known, and there is no evidence that another father-child relationship could be established.

However, in recent years, a number of courts have placed greater emphasis on the interests of erroneously identified fathers. For example, in *M.A.S. v. Mississippi Department of Human Services*, 842 So. 2d 527 (Miss. 2003), the Mississippi Supreme Court held that a paternity judgment could be vacated more than nine years after its entry based on DNA tests performed in an unrelated matter which revealed that the petitioner was not the child's biological father. Although *M.A.S.* involved a nonmarital child, the Mississippi courts have since applied its reasoning in a case brought by a divorced petitioner. Although the petitioner had lived with the child only during its first month of life and had limited contact thereafter, the court did not rely on the tenuous parent-child relationship in granting the disestablishment petition. Instead, the court stated its belief that "the best interest of the child . . . is to know the identity of the natural father" and "refuse[d] to sanction the manifest injustice of forcing a man to support a child which science has proven not to be his." *Williams v. Williams*, 843 So. 2d 720, 723 (Miss. 2003). *See also Doran v. Doran*, 820 A.2d 1279 (Pa. Super. Ct. 2003) (utilizing similar approach).

Some states have also adopted new paternity disestablishment legislation that places greater emphasis on the interests of erroneously identified fathers. *See, e.g.,* GA. CODE ANN. § 19-7-54 (2009) (mandating paternity disestablishment in certain circumstances when genetic testing demonstrates a zero percent probability of paternity). *See also* Paula Roberts, *Truth and Consequences: Part II. Questioning the Paternity of Marital Children*, 37 FAM. L.Q. 55, 94 (Appendix F) (2003) (listing 12 state statutes allowing paternity disestablishment by a married father and noting a strong trend toward enactment of such legislation). Under a legislative or judicial standard which permits paternity disestablishment without regard to the child's relational and financial interests, a court could appropriately accept the blood tests offered by Husband, enter a finding of nonpaternity, and terminate Husband's support obligation.

In a state where the courts or the legislature has adopted rules favoring the ability of erroneously identified fathers to prove nonpaternity, Husband's motion to disestablish his paternity and eliminate his child-support obligation would be more likely to succeed. Even in such states, if Husband was aware of his nonpaternity and had an opportunity to litigate the issue at the time of entry of the divorce decree, courts are likely to treat the divorce decree as res judicata on the paternity issue and conclude that there are no changed circumstances warranting a modification of the child-support order. *Nancy Darlene M. v. James Lee M., Jr.*, 400 S.E.2d 882 (W. Va. 1990). However, some courts have allowed motions to modify a child-support order in a divorce decree on the basis of nonpaternity, even when that issue was litigated in the original action, reasoning that a motion to modify is a direct attack on the judgment, not a collateral attack, and therefore is not barred by res judicata principles. *Dixon v. Pouncy*, 979 P.2d 520, 524 (Alaska 1999).

Family Law

(July 2011)

ANALYSIS

Legal Problems

(1)   Is a common law marriage that is valid where contracted also valid in a state that does not recognize common law marriage?

(2)   What are the requirements for a valid common law marriage?

(3)   Does a state statute that permits the adoption of an unmarried father's child when he has not "maintained a residential relationship" with the child for "at least 9 of the 12 months immediately preceding the filing of an adoption petition" violate the U.S. Constitution when applied to a committed residential parent?

(4)   Under the UCCJEA, when may a state issue an order (a) terminating parental rights and (b) making an initial custody determination?

DISCUSSION

Summary

A common law marriage valid where contracted is valid in all states. To enter into a valid common law marriage, a couple must cohabit, hold themselves out as a married couple, and enter into a present agreement that they are married. Although Meg and Dave may have agreed to be married in the future and Meg has held Dave out as a future husband (her fiancé), this conduct is inadequate to establish a common law marriage. Thus, Dave would be treated as an unmarried father under State B's adoption-consent statute.

Dave cannot satisfy the statutory requirements to veto his child's adoption because he has not lived with Child for at least 9 of the 12 months prior to filing of the adoption petition. However, the State B statute is almost certainly unconstitutional as applied to Dave because Dave is a committed father who consistently held himself out as Child's father and both lived with and supported Child until Meg's unannounced departure to State B.

The UCCJEA permits a state to make an "initial child-custody determination" only if it is the child's "home state" when the child-custody proceeding was commenced or was the home state of the child within six months before the commencement of the proceeding and a parent continues to live in the state. A child-custody proceeding includes a proceeding to terminate parental rights. Thus, because Meg took Child from State A only five months ago, State B does not have jurisdiction to terminate Dave's parental rights or to issue a child custody order.

Point One (20%)

A common law marriage that is valid where contracted is also valid in a state that does not permit common law marriage.

Under accepted conflict-of-laws principles, a marriage valid under the law of the place in which it was contracted is valid elsewhere unless it violates a strong public policy of the state which has the most significant relationship with the spouses and the marriage. *See* RESTATEMENT (SECOND) OF CONFLICT OF LAWS § 283. Perhaps because the vast majority of states once permitted common law marriage, courts in states that do not recognize common law marriage have consistently held that, if a man and woman were domiciled in a state that permits common law marriage and their conduct met the requirements of that state's law for establishing such a marriage, recognition of the marriage does not violate a strong public policy. Thus, if Dave and Meg entered into a valid common law marriage in State A, it would be recognized by a State B court. *See* Point Two(b).

A common law marriage, once established, is the equivalent of a ceremonial marriage. Thus, if Dave can show that he and Meg entered into a common law marriage, he would be treated as a married father under State B's adoption law.

Point Two (20%)
Dave and Meg did not enter into a common law marriage.

To establish a common law marriage, the proponent must show: (1) capacity to enter a marital contract, (2) a present agreement that the two parties are married, (3) cohabitation, and (4) "holding out" a marital relationship to the community. *See* HARRY D. KRAUSE ET AL., FAMILY LAW: CASES, COMMENTS, AND QUESTIONS 129 (6th ed. 2007). The evidence here clearly establishes capacity and cohabitation. It also suggests an agreement to *become* married. However, a common law marriage requires a *present* marriage agreement. If Dave and Meg made any marriage agreement, it was an agreement to be married *in the future*: Meg told Dave that she was "committed to marrying him," but that she "wanted a real wedding, and we can't afford that now;" Meg also proposed that Dave move in with her so that "we can save money to get married." There is also no evidence that Dave and Meg held themselves out as a married couple. Although Meg said to friends and family that Dave was her fiancé, a fiancé is an intended spouse, not a current marriage partner.

Thus, Dave and Meg did not enter into a valid common law marriage, and Dave would be categorized as an unmarried father under State B's adoption-consent statute.

Point Three (40%)
Dave is a committed father who consistently held himself out as a parent, resided with his child, and provided support for his child and the child's mother. Thus, Dave has a strong argument that State B is constitutionally precluded from permitting his child's adoption without his consent.

"When an unwed father demonstrates a full commitment to the responsibilities of parenthood by '[coming] forward to participate in the rearing of his child,' his interest in personal contact with his child acquires substantial protection under the [Fourteenth Amendment's] Due Process Clause." *Lehr v. Robertson*, 463 U.S. 248, 261 (1983). *See also Stanley v. Illinois*, 405 U.S. 645 (1972); *Quilloin v. Walcott*, 434 U.S. 246 (1978); *Caban v. Mohammed*, 441 U.S. 380 (1979).

Interpreting this standard, the U.S. Supreme Court has held that a father who lived with his children and their mother and held the children out as his own is entitled to a hearing to demonstrate his parental fitness before his parental rights may be terminated. *Stanley*. The Court has also held that the equal protection clause requires the state to give a father the opportunity to veto his child's adoption when state law grants a similarly situated unmarried mother a veto. *See Caban.*

On the other hand, the Court has held that a state adoption law that failed to grant an unmarried father a right to veto his child's adoption was constitutional when applied to a nonresidential father who provided minimal support and did nothing to establish his legal paternity until after the adoption petition was filed. *See Quilloin*, 434 U.S. 246. The Court has also held that an adoption order entered without notice to the unmarried father was constitutional when the state provided him with an opportunity to obtain notice and a hearing through registration with a "putative father registry." *See Lehr*, 463 U.S. at 264.

Dave has demonstrated the kind of commitment that triggers protection under the Fourteenth Amendment. Like the fathers whose constitutional rights were recognized in *Stanley* and *Caban*, Dave held himself out as Child's father; he consented to be identified as Child's father on Child's birth certificate and sent birth announcements identifying himself as Child's father. Like the fathers in *Stanley* and *Caban*, Dave lived with Child and Child's mother and provided support to them. After Child's birth, Dave was the only family breadwinner and held down two jobs in order to provide for Meg and Child. He also had volunteered to marry Meg and thus would have been a marital father had Meg agreed. Dave is also blameless for his failure to satisfy the statutory veto requirements; Dave would have lived with Child and Meg for the relevant nine-month period but for Meg's abrupt and unannounced departure from their home. State courts have typically held adoption-consent statutes that would deny a veto right to a father who has done everything in his power to establish a full relationship with his child are unconstitutional as applied in such a case. *See e.g., Adoption of Kelsey S.*, 823 P.2d 1216 (Cal. 1992); *In re Raquel Marie X*, 559 N.E.2d 418 (N.Y. 1990).

Although Dave does in some respects resemble the unsuccessful unmarried father in *Lehr*, it is likely that Dave would still prevail. The *Lehr* father, like Dave, was forced to hire an investigator to find his child and her mother. By the time he succeeded in doing so, an adoption petition had been filed. However, the *Lehr* father did not receive notice of this petition because he had not established his paternity and had failed to enter his name in the state's putative father registry. Given that he could have obtained notice and a hearing, the Supreme Court held that the state did not violate his constitutional rights when a judge refused to delay signing the adoption petition in order to give the father time to file the appropriate papers and participate in a hearing at which his objection could be heard. *See Lehr*, 463 U.S. 248.

Here, by contrast, Dave established his paternity by voluntarily acknowledging Child and causing his name to be placed on Child's birth certificate. Under federal law, a voluntary acknowledgment of paternity is binding if unchallenged by the named father within 60 days. *See* 42 U.S.C. § 666(a)(5). Additionally, State B does not provide unmarried fathers with a putative father registry, and Dave thus had no way of obtaining notice of an adoption proceeding.

Thus, State B's adoption consent statute appears to be unconstitutional as applied to Dave, a committed parent who has fully participated in the rearing of his child.

Point Four (20%)
Because State A has been Child's home state within the past six months and Dave, a parent, continues to live in State A, State B does not have jurisdiction to terminate Dave's parental rights or to make an initial child-custody determination respecting Child.

Under the Uniform Child Custody Jurisdiction and Enforcement Act, which has been adopted in 48 states, a child's "home state" has exclusive jurisdiction to issue an initial custody decree. UCCJEA § 201(a)(1). A "home state" is a state where the child has lived with "a parent, or a person acting as a parent, for at least six consecutive months immediately before the commencement of a child-custody proceeding." *Id.* § 102(7). A "child-custody proceeding" includes a "proceeding for . . . termination of parental rights." *Id.* § 102(4). A home state continues to have exclusive jurisdiction to issue an initial custody order even if the child is absent from the state when a custody petition is brought, so long as no more than six months has elapsed since the child's departure from the jurisdiction and "a parent or person acting as a parent continues to live in" the home state. *Id.* § 201(a)(1). The "[p]hysical presence of, or personal jurisdiction over, a party or a child is not necessary . . . to make a child-custody determination." *Id.* § 201(c).

Here, Meg took Child from the family home in State A only five months ago, and Dave still lives in State A. Thus, State A has exclusive jurisdiction to issue an initial custody decree and also to terminate parental rights. State B lacks jurisdiction to do either.

[NOTE: The UCCJEA does not apply to adoption proceedings, but termination of a parent's rights is typically a precondition for an adoption. Thus, as a practicality, the UCCJEA should preclude a State B court from granting petition for Husband's adoption of Child.]

<u>Family Law</u>

(July 2012)

ANALYSIS

Legal Problems

(1)   When a child has no "home state," what state has jurisdiction to issue a valid child-custody decree?

(2)   Must a court defer to the preference of an older child when awarding custody?

(3)   Under the U.S. Constitution, may a state statute authorize a court to grant a grandparent custody of a child without giving any special weight to the best-interests determination of a fit and available parent?

DISCUSSION

Summary

Under the Uniform Child Custody Jurisdiction and Enforcement Act (UCCJEA), when a child has no "home state," i.e., a state in which the child has resided for the prior six months, a state may exercise jurisdiction based on (1) "significant connections" with the child and at least one parent and (2) the existence of "substantial evidence" relating to child custody in the forum jurisdiction. Here, State A has significant connections with Daughter and Mom; substantial evidence related to child custody exists in State A, where Daughter and Grandparents are currently located and where Daughter was domiciled until very recently. Thus, State A has jurisdiction to make a custody award.

On the merits, a court may deny Grandparents' custody petition even though Daughter strongly prefers to live with them. In all states, the preferences of a child are relevant to a determination of the child's best interests in a custody proceeding, but they are not determinative.

However, the State A statute under which Grandparents have brought a custody petition is probably unconstitutional. In *Troxel v. Granville*, 530 U.S. 57 (2000), a plurality of the Supreme Court ruled that a state statute which authorized a court to grant visitation to "[a]ny person" based on a finding that such visitation was in "the best interest of the child" unconstitutionally interfered with the fundamental right of parents to rear their children. Although State A's statute authorizing the award of custody to a nonparent based on the best interest of the child is limited to grandparents, it similarly grants "no special weight" to a parent's determination of her child's best interest and thus does not comport with the standards set forth in *Troxel*.

Point One (40%)

<u>State A has jurisdiction because no state is Daughter's "home state." Daughter and Mom both have significant connections with State A, and substantial evidence is available in State A regarding Daughter's care.</u>

Under the Uniform Child Custody Jurisdiction and Enforcement Act, which has been widely adopted, a state has jurisdiction to make an initial child-custody determination if "this State is the home state of the child on the date of the commencement of the proceeding, or was the home State of the child within six months before the commencement of the proceeding and the child is absent from this State but a parent or person acting as a parent continues to live in this State" and no other state's courts would have jurisdiction under the above standard or other courts having jurisdiction have declined to exercise it. UCCJEA § 201(a)(1) & (2).

Neither State A nor State B can claim jurisdiction under § 201(a)(1). A "home state" is the state in which the child "lived with a parent or a person acting as a parent for at least six consecutive months immediately before the commencement of a child-custody proceeding." *Id.* § 102(7). Here, Daughter and Mom moved to State B only four months before the State A custody petition was filed in State A, so State B is not Daughter's home state. State A was the home state of Daughter within six months of the proceeding commenced in State A. However, State A does not have home-state jurisdiction because neither statutory condition has been met: a parent (Mom) does not continue to live in State A, and the child is not absent from State A.

Under the UCCJEA, when—and only when—"a court of another state does not have jurisdiction under paragraph 1" (i.e., the home-state rule), a court may exercise jurisdiction over a child-custody determination if

> (2)(A) the child . . . and at least one parent . . . have a significant connection with this State other than mere physical presence; and
> (B) substantial evidence is available in this State concerning the child's care, protection, training, and personal relationships. *Id.* § 201(a)(2).

Here, a State A court would have jurisdiction under § 201(a)(2) because Daughter and Mom both have a significant connection with State A and substantial evidence relating to Daughter's care is available in State A: Mom was married in State A, gave birth to Daughter there, and lived there with Daughter from the time of her birth until four months ago. Daughter is currently in State A, and so are Grandparents. Other evidence related to Daughter's schooling, friendships, and other personal relationships is also available in State A.

[NOTE: State B would also have jurisdiction under § 201(a)(2): Daughter and Mom both have a significant connection with State B as it is where they both lived until Daughter's recent return to State A and substantial evidence from Mom, Stepdad, Daughter's school, etc., is available in State B. However, under UCCJEA § 206(a), a court "may not exercise its jurisdiction . . . if . . . a proceeding concerning the custody of the child has been commenced in a court of another State having jurisdiction substantially in conformity with this [Act] . . . ." Thus, State B could not exercise jurisdiction under § 201(a)(2) because a petition has been filed in State A.]

The federal Parental Kidnapping Prevention Act (PKPA) sets out child-custody jurisdictional standards much like those contained in the UCCJEA. Under the PKPA, a State A court would have jurisdiction because no state is Daughter's home state, "the child and at least one contestant[] have a significant connection with . . . State [A] other than mere physical presence . .

. and there is available in such State substantial evidence concerning the child's present or future care. . . ." 28 U.S.C. § 1738A(c)(2)(B). Like the UCCJEA, the PKPA provides that where a court of another state is exercising jurisdiction that complies with the federal standard, another court shall not exercise jurisdiction. *Id.* § 1738A(g).

Thus, State A has jurisdiction over the custody action initiated by Grandparents.

[NOTE: In 2012, the UCCJEA had been adopted in all states except Massachusetts.]

Point Two (25%)

Although the wishes of an older child are relevant to a custody determination and are typically given great weight, they are not determinative; a court may thus deny Grandparents' custody petition over the express opposition of Daughter.

In all states, the views of a child who is mature enough to form and express a preference are relevant to a custody determination. The wishes of older children like Daughter are typically given substantial weight. *See* D.W. O'Neill, Annotation, *Child's Wishes as Factor in Awarding Custody*, 4 A.L.R. 3d 1396 (1965). However, the child's wishes "are not treated equally in every case":

> Sometimes the child's wishes are given controlling effect, while at other times the wishes are disregarded altogether. The circumstances determining what effect, between these two extremes, should be given to a child's wishes in a particular case are, in addition to the comparative effect of objective factors affecting its welfare generally, . . . and in addition to the natural right of the child's parent to have its custody (frequently invoked successfully, at least in the absence of the parent's long-term abandonment of the child to another's custody): the child's age and judgment capacity; the basis for and strength of its preference, generally; the treatment extended to the child by the contestants for its custody; and the wrongful inducement of the child's wishes.

Id. § 2(a). *See also* Wanda Ellen Wakefield, Annotation, *Desire of Child as to Geographic Location of Residence or Domicile as Factor in Awarding Custody or Terminating Parental Rights*, 10 A.L.R. 4th 827 (1981).

Although there are a handful of states in which, by statute, the court must defer to the wishes of an older child when choosing between fit parents (*see* 10 A.L.R. 4th § 4*)*, even if State A has such a statute it would not be applicable here, as the custody contest is between a fit parent and a nonparent.

Thus, although the wishes of Daughter are relevant in an action regarding her custody, a court may disregard those wishes and deny Grandparents' custody petition.

Point Three (35%)

Because the State A statute gives "no special weight" to a parent's determination of her child's best interests, under the Supreme Court's plurality opinion in *Troxel v. Granville,* the statute is unconstitutional.

In *Troxel v. Granville,* 530 U.S. 57 (2000), the Supreme Court addressed the constitutionality of a state statute under which "[a]ny person" could petition for visitation rights "at any time" and authorized a court to grant such visitation whenever it concluded that "visitation may serve the best interest of the child." A plurality of the Court found that the statute provided inadequate protection for a parent's constitutionally protected liberty interest in the care, custody, and control of her child. The statute at issue was, in the Court's view, "breathtakingly broad," and it required the court to give "no special weight at all to [a parent's] . . . determination of her daughter's best interests." 530 U.S. at 67, 69. Moreover, the court that awarded visitation pursuant to the statute used a decision-making framework that "gave no weight" to the parent's having "assented to visitation" on a schedule different from that preferred by the grandparent petitioners and that "contravened the traditional presumption that a fit parent will act in the best interest of his or her child." *Id.* at 69.

Under *Troxel*, the State A grandparent-custody statute is almost certainly unconstitutional. Like the statute struck down in *Troxel*, the State A statute does not require the court to give any special weight to a parent's determination of her child's best interest; in fact, it does not appear to require the court to give *any* weight to a parent's determination of a child's best interest. Moreover, the State A statute permits a much larger intrusion upon parental prerogatives than did the statute considered in *Troxel*; that statute permitted a court to grant a nonparent *visitation*, while the State A statute authorizes a court to award a nonparent *custody.*

Although the State A statute does restrict nonparent custody petitions to grandparents and additionally requires that the child have been abandoned or have a parent who has died, this should not alter the constitutional analysis. These facts are not relevant to the Supreme Court's reasoning in *Troxel*. Moreover, *Troxel* itself involved a visitation petition brought by grandparents whose son had died.

Federal Civil Procedure

(February 2000)

Legal Problems:

1. Does the federal district court in State B have subject matter jurisdiction?

2. Does the federal district court in State B have personal jurisdiction?

3. Should venue be transferred to the federal district court of State A?

DISCUSSION

Point One: (10-20%)

The federal district court has subject matter jurisdiction based upon diversity of citizenship and the required amount in controversy.

The challenge to jurisdiction raises issues as to personal jurisdiction as well as subject matter jurisdiction. Subject matter jurisdiction exists under 28 U.S.C. § 1332 if there is diversity of citizenship and the amount in controversy exceeds $75,000. Diversity of citizenship exists between Barbara, a citizen of State B, and Adam, a State A citizen.

Barbara's claim for $80,000 on its face satisfies the statutory amount in controversy. Adam's supporting affidavit suggests the possibility that Barbara may ultimately recover less than the statutory minimum, but that does not defeat the federal court's jurisdiction. "[T]he sum claimed by the plaintiff controls if the claim is apparently made in good faith. It must appear to a legal certainty that the claim is really for less than the jurisdictional amount to justify dismissal." *St. Paul Mercury Indemnity Co.* v. *Red Cab Co.*, 303 U.S. 283, 288-89 (1938). Barbara's actual recovery will depend upon factual issues and cannot be said to a legal certainty to be less than the statutory minimum.

Point Two: (45-55%)

The federal district court has personal jurisdiction based upon requisite minimum contacts and the state's long-arm statute.

Determining the existence of personal jurisdiction requires analysis both of whether personal jurisdiction can be constitutionally exercised by the State B federal district court and of whether the appropriate state statute allows the federal court to assert personal jurisdiction.

The constitutional question is dependent on the classic line of cases beginning with *International Shoe Co.* v. *Washington,* 326 U.S. 310 (1945). *International Shoe* requires the defendant to have sufficient "minimum contacts" with State B such that requiring defense in State B would not "offend 'traditional notions of fair play and substantial justice. ", *Id.* at 316, quoting *Milliken* v.

Meyer, 311 U.S. 457, 463 (1940).

The sufficiency of contacts required under *International Shoe* and subsequent decisions depends on whether the court is seeking to assert general or specific jurisdiction. General jurisdiction is involved where the subject matter of the lawsuit is not related to the contacts the defendant has with the forum state. Specific jurisdiction is involved when the lawsuit arises out of the contacts which form the basis for determining whether there are minimum contacts. Fewer contacts are required to assert specific personal jurisdiction than to assert general personal jurisdiction:

> [W]here a forum seeks to assert specific jurisdiction over an out-of-state defendant who has not consented to suit there, this "fair warning" requirement is satisfied if the defendant has "purposely directed" his activities at residents of the forum, and the litigation results from alleged injuries that "arise out of or relate to" those activities.

Burger King Corp. v. Rudzewicz, 471 U.S. 462, 472 (1985) (quoting *Keeton v. Hustler Magazine, Inc.,* 465 U.S. 770, 774 (1984), *Helicopteros Nacionales de Colombia S.A. v. Hall,* 466 U.S. 408, 414 (1984)).

Were this a general jurisdiction case-for example, if Barbara were suing Adam on an unrelated personal injury claim-the contacts would clearly be insufficient. *See Helicopteros Nacionales de Colombia, S.A. v. Hall,* 466 U.S. 408 (1984).

Here, however, Barbara seeks to assert specific jurisdiction, since the cause of action arises out of Adam's contacts (the fee-splitting contract) with State B. The contacts appear sufficient to assert personal jurisdiction. Purposeful activity was directed toward State B. Although there are factual points to the contrary, including where the contract was written, the contacts with State B are sufficient for an action arising out of such contacts. Adam initiated the contact, solicited the contract, and had further related contacts with Barbara.

Recognizing that personal jurisdiction is constitutionally permissible, the question remains whether there is statutory authority to assert that jurisdiction. Under Federal Rule of Civil Procedure 4(k)(I), Barbara must look to the law of State B to determine whether personal jurisdiction maybe asserted in a diversity action. This requires interpreting State B's long-arm statute. The statute clearly contemplates the exercise of jurisdiction in an action such as this because contracting with Barbara constitutes transacting business within the state.

Point Three: (25-35%)

Venue should not be transferred to the federal district court of State A because the convenience of the parties and the convenient administration of justice would not be better served there than in the federal district court of State B.

Venue transfers are controlled by 28 U.S.C. § 1404, which provides "in the interest of justice, a district court may transfer any civil action to any other district or division where it might have been brought." The action could have been brought in State A. The subject matter jurisdiction is the same. Adam is doing business within the state sufficient to confer personal and subject matter jurisdiction, and venue is proper since all the defendants are in State A. The question is whether the interests of justice require the transfer. It would appear not. The relative difficulty to Barbara and Adam seems the same. The evidence necessary at trial is not predominately in one jurisdiction rather than the other. There appears to be no hardship on any third party who might be a witness. The logical conclusion would be that the preference for allowing Barbara to choose the forum has not been overcome.

Federal Civil Procedure

(July 2000)

Legal Problems:

1. Does the district court have the power to issue a pretrial order that dictates the order in which issues will be tried to a jury?

2. Was the court justified procedurally in granting the motion for judgment as a matter of law before the close of evidence?

3. Was the court justified substantively in granting the motion for judgment as a matter of law?

DISCUSSION

Point One: (25-35%)

Under Rule 16. the district court has the power to enter a pretrial order that specifies the order in which issues will be tried.

Rule 16 of the Federal Rules of Civil Procedure gives district court judges the power to structure trials in a manner that facilitates their expedited disposition. In particular, Rule 16(c) empowers courts to take action to simplify potentially difficult or complex litigation. Rule 16(c)(14) specifically authorizes courts to direct the parties "to present evidence early in the trial with respect to a manageable issue that could, on the evidence, be the basis for a judgment as a matter of law under Rule 50(a)." This language offers ample support for the court's decision to require Claimant to present evidence of Fiberco exposure early to facilitate a motion for judgment as a matter of law.

Point Two: (25-35%)

A motion for judgment as a matter of law may be granted before the close of evidence if the opposing party has been fully heard on the dispositive issue.

Rule 50 simplifies and clarifies federal practice on what were once called motions for directed verdicts, bringing the practice into line with that on motions for summary judgment. In brief, Rule 50 permits a party like Fiberco to move for judgment as a matter of law at any time during the course of a jury trial if the opposing party "has been fully heard" on an issue. Fed. R. Civ. P. 50(a)(1). Thus, Claimant's indication that the testimony of BrakeCo's manager concluded his proof on the issue of exposure to Fiberco asbestos suggests that the motion for judgment as a matter of law was procedurally proper at the time it was made. Fiberco was not required to await submission of Claimant's entire case to make a procedurally proper motion for judgment as a matter of law, and the trial court is not obliged to wait before ruling on it.

Point Three: (25-35%)

A motion for Judgment as a matter of law is properly granted when it is clear that there is no legally sufficient basis for a verdict in favor of the nonmoving party.

It also appears that the court correctly resolved the motion in Fiberco's favor. Rule 50 specifies the standard for the grant of a motion for judgment as a matter of law, indicating that such motions may be granted whenever "there is no legally sufficient evidentiary basis for a reasonable jury to find for" the nonmoving party. Fed. R. Civ. P. 50(a)(1). In this case, the problem specifies that the relevant jurisdiction has rejected the so-called market share theory of liability and places the burden on the plaintiff to produce specific evidence establishing exposure to the defendant's asbestos product. While the manager's testimony places Fiberco products in the firm's storeroom, it does not establish that the products were there at the time Wife worked at the firm. One can argue that the presence of Fiberco products at one point in time provides evidentiary support for an inference that they were there on other occasions as well. However, the manager appears to negate that inference with the admission that he had never seen the Fiberco products in the storeroom until after Wife's employment had ended. Claimant might have attempted to bolster his case with other evidence of Fiberco exposure, either through company records or other testimony. In failing to do so, Claimant appears to have failed to provide evidence sufficient to support a rational jury verdict in his favor on the issue of Fiberco exposure.

Federal Civil Procedure

(February 2001)

Legal Problems:

(1)   Did the federal district court abuse its discretion when it ordered Bus to participate in settlement discussions and cited it for contempt for violating that order?

(2)(a) What standard governs a motion to amend pleadings and to amend a pretrial order to allow a litigant to introduce a new issue during trial?

(2)(b) Should a party be permitted to amend a pretrial order to introduce evidence that the party did not mention or disclose during discovery or the pretrial conference?

DISCUSSION

Point One: (35-45%)

A federal district judge has explicit authority under Fed. R. Civ. P. 16 to order litigants to participate in settlement discussions, although sanctions to compel participation should be used with caution.

Until the 1993 amendments of Rule 16 of the Federal Rules of Civil Procedure, the question of whether federal courts could order litigants to participate in settlement talks was in dispute. *See, e.g.*, G. *Heileman Brewing Co. v. Joseph Oat Corp.*, 871 F.2d 648 (7th Cir. 1989) (en banc 6-5 split decision) (holding that district judges have inherent authority to order represented parties to appear at pretrial settlement conferences); CA. Wright, A.R. Miller, M.K. Kane, FEDERAL PRACTICE AND PROCEDURE § 1525.1 (1990 & 2000 Supp.). In the 1993 amendments to Rule 16, the drafters added the following language to Rule 16(c):

> If appropriate, the court may require that a party or its representative be present or reasonably available by telephone in order to consider possible settlement of the dispute.

As explained in the Advisory Committee Notes, the change was intended, in part, to make it clear that courts may issue orders designed to facilitate settlement. There is, therefore, no question that the court had authority to require a corporate representative of Bus to be present or available for settlement discussions.

The judge also had authority to hold Bus in contempt for failing to attend the conference. Rule 16(f) explicitly provides that "if no appearance is made on behalf of a party at a scheduling or pretrial conference. . ., or if a party or a party's attorney fails to participate in good faith, the judge, upon motion or the judge's own initiative, may make such orders with regard thereto as are just, and among others, any of the orders provided for in Rule 37(b)(2)(B),(C),(D)." Rule 37(b)(2)(D) permits the court to treat "as a contempt of court the failure to obey any orders." Because Bus failed to attend the conference and failed to participate in settlement negotiations in good faith, the court did not abuse its discretion under Rules 16 and 37 by holding Bus in contempt.

The Advisory Committee Notes to Rule 16 caution that settlement talks will be unproductive if a party is uncooperative. Bus, then, has a reasonable argument on appeal that the district judge should not have imposed the contempt sanction once Bus's counsel made it clear that Bus was recalcitrant about settlement and that discussions would be pointless. It is not likely, however, that the district court's decision was an abuse of discretion sufficient to warrant reversal. There is no evidence that the order for party participation imposed great hardship on Bus, and the court may have believed that Bus's recalcitrance was merely posturing that could be overcome by serious discussion. Thus, although a case for reversal can be made, it does not seem likely to succeed on these facts.

Point Two(a): (45-55%)

Under Rule 16. a final pretrial order may be modified only to prevent manifest injustice. That standard supersedes the more liberal policy governing amendment of pleadings under Rule 15.

In the fact pattern, the defendant has sought to introduce the issue of a "waiver of liability" at trial, without having raised that issue in the pleadings or having included it in the pretrial order. Ordinarily, when evidence is objected to at trial on the ground that it is not within those issues raised by the pleadings, Rule 15(b) authorizes the court to allow an amendment of the pleadings at trial and directs the court to "do so freely when the presentation of the merits of the action will be subserved thereby and the objecting party fails to satisfy the court that the admission of such evidence would prejudice the party in maintaining the party's action or defense upon the merits." An amendment allowing Bus to raise the waiver as a defense would sub serve the presentation of the merits. Any prejudice that Victim might suffer presumably could be minimized by granting an extension to permit Victim to meet the new evidence. Thus, an examination of Rule 15(b) alone suggests that the court abused its discretion in declining to permit Bus to amend its answer and to offer the ticket stub at trial.

But Rule 15(b) cannot be read in a vacuum. Under Rule 16(e) of the Federal Rules of Civil Procedure, "[t]he order following a final pretrial conference shall be modified only to prevent manifest injustice." According to the Advisory Committee Notes, pretrial orders should not be changed lightly, but total inflexibility is undesirable. In determining whether to admit evidence and to allow issues that were not identified in the pretrial order, the courts have discretion to consider such factors as the prejudice to the opposing party, the extent to which introduction of the new evidence would disrupt the orderly presentation of the trial, and the possible bad faith of the party seeking to disregard the pretrial order. *See, e.g., Morfeld v. Kehm,* 803 F.2d 1452 (8th Cir. 1986); C.A. Wright, A. R. Miller, M.K. Kane, FEDERAL PRACTICE AND PROCEDURE § 1527 (1990 & 2000 Supp.). Thus, Rule 16 imposes a heavy burden on a party seeking to amend a pretrial order, but the trial court has such discretion when the danger of prejudice is slight and the failure to amend might result in an injustice. On the other hand, if the evidence or issue was within the knowledge of the party seeking modification at the time of the pretrial conference, the argument for amending the order is considerably weakened. *Id.*

On the given facts, Bus does not have a strong argument that the trial court abused its discretion in barring introduction of the evidence of a waiver of liability. It is difficult to imagine that "manifest injustice" would result from denying Bus the opportunity to present evidence on a defense that the court could reasonably conclude has been available to it from the beginning. Bus likely knew that the terms of its ticket included a waiver. It apparently had the ticket stub in its possession throughout the proceedings. Moreover, introduction of the new issue of waiver would probably prejudice Victim unless a continuance were granted, and that would result in trial delay. In short, any harm caused to Bus by restricting it to the evidence and claims allowed by the pretrial order does not appear to be a "manifest injustice."

How should one resolve the tension between Rule 15(b), on the one hand, and Rule 16(e), on the other? It appears that the Rule 16(e) amendment standard should apply because, according to the Rule itself, the pretrial order "shall control the subsequent course of the action." Fed. R. Civ. P. 16(e). One should note, however, that "several courts have permitted pretrial orders to be amended by concluding that Rule 16 must be read in conjunction with Rule 15(b)." 6A C. A. Wright, A. R. Miller & M. K. Kane, FEDERAL PRACTICE AND PROCEDURE § 1527 at 290 (1990); *see, e.g., Phaneuf v. Tenneco, Inc.,* 938 F. Supp. 112 (N.D.N.Y. 1996). Thus, while it appears that the district court did not abuse its discretion in declining to amend the final pretrial order, one could make a reasonable argument that the more liberal Rule 15(b) standard should have been applied.

However, even if that argument is successful, it appears that the court properly barred Bus from offering the ticket stub into evidence as a sanction for failing to produce it pursuant to Rule 26(a)(1). *See* Point Two(b), *infra.*

Point Two(b): (5-15%)

If a party fails to produce a document that should have been disclosed under the mandatory disclosure provisions of the federal discovery rules, the party ordinarily will not be permitted to use the document as evidence at trial.

Bus's failure to disclose the ticket stub pursuant to its mandatory disclosure obligation provides an additional reason for the court to bar introduction of the evidence. Under Rule 26(a), a party must provide a copy or description of "all documents. . . that are relevant to disputed facts alleged with particularity in the pleadings." Rule 26(a)(1)(B), Fed. R. Civ. P. Here, the waiver of liability contained on the tour ticket is relevant because it would tend to defeat Victim's claim for recovery. The trial court's decision to prevent Bus from using the evidence is an appropriate sanction for non-disclosure of the ticket. "A party that without substantial justification fails to disclose information required by Rule 26(a) . . . shall not, unless such failure is harmless, be permitted to use [such information] as evidence at a trial." Rule 37(c)(1), Fed. R. Civ. P.

Federal Civil Procedure

(July 2001)

Legal Problems:

(1)   Maya litigant who was not a party to a prior judgment invoke that judgment against another litigant who was a party in order to preclude relitigation of the identical issue previously decided?

(2)(a) Is a federal district court's order refusing to grant summary judgment on collateral estoppel grounds a final judgment?

(2)(b) Are there any exceptions to the final judgment rule that would permit review of an order refusing to grant summary judgment?

DISCUSSION

Point One: (45-55%)

Plaintiff, a non-party to the *SEC* v. *Silver* action, may rely on the decision in that action to prevent Silver from relitigating the question of whether Silver's registration statement was false and misleading.

This question involves the scope of the doctrine of collateral estoppel and the right of a non-party to an action to use collateral estoppel offensively against a losing party in the action. If Silver is precluded by the *SEC* v. *Silver* judgment from relitigating the question of whether its registration statement was false or misleading, and if Plaintiff is entitled to assert that preclusive effect against Silver, then Plaintiff's motion for summary judgment on that issue should have been granted.

The doctrine of collateral estoppel (or issue preclusion) generally prevents a litigant from relitigating issues that have been previously litigated and determined in a prior action. The traditional requirements for asserting collateral estoppel are: (1) a valid and final judgment was rendered in a prior action; (2) an issue of fact was actually litigated, determined, and essential to the judgment in the prior action; (3) the same issue arises in a subsequent action; and (4) the same parties are litigants in both actions. RESTATEMENT (SECOND) OF JUDGMENTS § 27 (1982).

The first three elements of this test are clearly satisfied. First, the judgment in the prior case *(SEC* v. *Silver)* was final according to the facts. Second, the issue of fact relating to the misrepresentation was actually litigated, determined, and essential to the judgment in the prior action. Here, Silver vigorously contested the misrepresentation claims in the SEC lawsuit. Moreover, the finding of misrepresentation in that lawsuit was the basis for a grant of both declaratory and injunctive relief. Thus, the factual misrepresentation issues were actually litigated, determined (e.g., declaratory judgment), and essential to the judgment enjoining Silver. Third, the misrepresentation issues in the prior action, SEC v. *Silver,* were identical to the misrepresentation claims in the subsequent action, *Plaintiff* v. *Silver*. Both actions revolved around whether the registration statement contained false and misleading representations of fact. However, the parties to the current action are not the same, and that fact alone would prevent collateral estoppel under traditional doctrine.

The modern approach to collateral estoppel, however, allows a non-party to the prior litigation (like Plaintiff) to invoke collateral estoppel against a party to the prior litigation, at least under certain circumstances. Section 29 of the RESTATEMENT (SECOND) OF JUDGMENTS reflects the modern view in stating that "[a] party precluded from relitigating an issue with an opposing party, in accordance with Sections 27 and 28, is also precluded from doing so with another person unless the fact that he lacked full and fair opportunity to litigate the issue in the first action or other circumstances justify affording him an opportunity to relitigate the issue." When § 29 applies, there is a new fourth element in place of the "same parties" requirement. The new fourth element is that the party to be precluded had a full and fair opportunity to litigate the same issue in the prior action.

In *Parklane Hosiery Co. v. Shore*, 439 U.S. 322 (1979), the U.S. Supreme Court adopted this approach, upholding the use of offensive collateral estoppel against Parklane, which had litigated the relevant misrepresentation issues in a prior action brought by the SEC Shore, a non-party to the prior lawsuit, was allowed to use collateral estoppel against Parklane in a subsequent lawsuit to preclude Parklane from relitigating the same issue a second time. The Court held that Parklane was not unfairly prejudiced because it had had a full and fair opportunity to litigate the issues in the earlier lawsuit. Thus, the *Parklane* case is consistent with the requirements of § 29, and it adopts offensive collateral estoppel as controlling federal law in federal courts.

Thus, while Plaintiff was not a party to the *SEC* lawsuit, and therefore could not have been bound if the *SEC* lawsuit judgment had been for Silver, Plaintiff is permitted to use collateral estoppel offensively in the subsequent lawsuit provided that Silver had a full and fair opportunity to litigate the same issue in the prior lawsuit. Here, Silver had that opportunity, and it vigorously litigated those issues. Accordingly, the trial judge erred in denying Plaintiff's motion for summary judgment.

Point Two(a): (30-40%)

The appellate court should dismiss Plaintiff's interlocutory appeal because there is no final judgment. and the appeal is premature.

The basic policy governing appeals from district court decisions is embodied in the final judgment rule, which prohibits appeals, with some exceptions, prior to entry of a final judgment by the trial court at the completion of the case in the trial court. This policy is designed to prevent the negative impact on trial and appellate courts that would occur if there were several appeals from rulings of the trial court during the course of the trial of a case. Frequent appeals would disrupt the trial court's ability to move forward with the case and would strain the judicial resources of the appellate courts. The final judgment policy is embodied in Title 28 U.S.C. § 1291, which provides in relevant part that "the courts of appeals. . . shall have jurisdiction of appeals from all final decisions of the district courts of the United States."

Plaintiff's appeal of the denial of the motion for summary judgment is clearly interlocutory and not final. Although the statute does not define "final decision," the courts hold that a "final decision is one that ends the litigation on the merits so that the only thing left for the district court to do is to execute the judgment." MOORE'S FEDERAL PRACTICE § 201.10 (3d ed. 1998). Here, the denial of Plaintiff's motion does not end the litigation; to the contrary, the trial on the merits will be more complex because of the decision. There was, accordingly, no final decision, and Plaintiff's appeal was premature under § 1291 unless an exception applies. *See generally Cunningham v. Hamilton County, Ohio,* 527 U.S. 198 (1999).

Point Two(b): (10-20%)

There are no exceptions to the final judgment rule that are likely to apply to these facts.

The applicants are asked to discuss the following exceptions to the final judgment rule: (1) the collateral order doctrine, *Cohen v. Beneficial Life Insurance Co.,* 337 U.S. 541 (1949), and (2) mandamus review under 28 U.S.C. § 1651(a); *Kerr v. U.S. District Court,* 426 U.S. 394 (1976).

The collateral order doctrine allows review of final orders of district court judges when those orders are collateral to (or separate from) the merits of the lawsuit, and the orders are effectively unreviewable on appeal. *Cunningham v. Hamilton County, Ohio,* 527 U.S. 198 (1999); *Cohen v. Beneficial Life Insurance Co.,* 337 U.S. 541, 546. Here, however, the order at issue (allowing relitigation of the issue of misrepresentation) is intimately connected with the merits of the lawsuit and is certainly subject to review on appeal of any final judgment. The collateral order doctrine is therefore inapplicable.

Plaintiff will not be able to rely on mandamus review because this requires a showing that the trial court decision is beyond its jurisdiction or violated a mandatory duty owed by the trial court. *Will v. United States,* 389 U.S. 90, 95 (1967); *Kerr v. U.S. District Court,* 426 U.S. 394 (1976). Although the trial court should have granted the motion for partial summary judgment, the fact that the trial court made an error of law does not warrant mandamus where there is otherwise no abuse of judicial authority. A wider use of mandamus to review legal errors would effectively eviscerate the final judgment rule, and appellate courts have accordingly been wary of a broad application of mandamus review. "A party may not use a writ of mandamus to correct ordinary error by the district court. . . . The burden is on the applicant to show intolerable error or misbehavior." MOORE'S FEDERAL PRACTICE § 201.44 (3d ed. 1998). The error in this case would not cross that high threshold, at least absent some evidence of extraordinary hardship to Plaintiff as a result of the error.

Federal Civil Procedure

(February 2002)

Legal Problems:

1. Were the requirements of the diversity jurisdiction statute met here, even though at the time of the accident Passenger, the plaintiff, and Teacher, the defendant, were citizens of the same state?

2. Were the requirements of the venue statute met here, given that Passenger filed in her home state, which was where the accident occurred?

3. Is supplemental jurisdiction available over Passenger's claim against Rentco, the third-party defendant, given that they are citizens of the same state?

DISCUSSION

Point One: (35-45%)

Because Passenger and Teacher were citizens of different states when the complaint was filed and the amount in controversy exceeds $75,000, Passenger properly invoked federal diversity jurisdiction. It is irrelevant that the plaintiff and the defendant were citizens of the same state at the time of the accident.

The court should deny Teacher's motion to dismiss for lack of subject matter jurisdiction. The requirements for federal diversity jurisdiction have been established in this case.

Passenger's complaint states only a state-law negligence claim, so federal question jurisdiction under 28 U.S.C. § 1331 is unavailable. Diversity jurisdiction is available under 28 U.S.C. § 1332(a)(1) only if Passenger and Teacher are citizens of different states and the amount in controversy exceeds $75,000, exclusive of costs and interest. An individual is a citizen of the state in which he or she is domiciled. In order to change one's domicile, one must be physically present in the new place with the intent to make that place one's permanent home. *See, e.g., Mississippi Band of Choctaw Indians* v. *Holyfield*, 490 U.S. 30, 48 (1989).

The problem states that Passenger is a citizen of State A. At the time of the accident, Teacher had sold his home in State A, quit his job in State A, and accepted a new job in State B. Teacher was, however, still a domiciliary of, and hence a citizen of, State A because he had not yet reached State B after having formed the requisite intent to change his domicile. Had the suit been filed the day of the accident, diversity jurisdiction would have been unavailable because both the physical and mental elements must be present for a change of domicile. Jack H. Friedenthal et al., CIVIL PROCEDURE 30 (3d ed. 1999).

It is well settled, however, that the availability of diversity jurisdiction is determined *as of the date the suit is commenced.* 13B Charles Alan Wright, Arthur R. Miller & Edward H. Cooper, FEDERAL PRACTICE AND PROCEDURE § 3608 (2d ed. 1984 & Supp. 2001). Having purchased a home in State B and begun his new job shortly after his arrival there, Teacher had established a new domicile in State B. Hence, at the time suit was filed in this case, nine months after the accident, Teacher had become a domiciliary and citizen of State B. Thus, diversity of citizenship existed between Passenger and Teacher.

In addition to diversity of citizenship, the amount in controversy must exceed $75,000, exclusive of costs and interest. 28 U.S.C. § 1332(a). Because Passenger's complaint seeks damages in excess of $100,000, the amount in controversy requirement is met.

The motion to dismiss for lack of jurisdiction should be denied: there is diversity of citizenship, and the amount in controversy requirement is satisfied.

Point Two: (15-25%)

Because venue is proper in a diversity case in the judicial district in which a "substantial part of the events or omissions giving rise to the claim occurred," and because the accident occurred in State A, venue is proper in the federal district court of State A.

The court should deny Teacher's motion to dismiss for improper venue. The requirements of the venue statute, 28 U.S.C. § 1391, are met.

Venue is a geographical concept that localizes lawsuits in places that are connected either to the parties or to the events giving rise to the action. Stephen C. Yeazell, CIVIL PROCEDURE 1991-92 (4th ed. 1996). Under 28 U.S.C. § 1391(a), which applies to civil actions in which jurisdiction is founded solely on diversity of citizenship (as is the case here), venue is proper in "(1) a judicial district where any defendant resides. . ., [or] (2) a judicial district in which a substantial part of the events or omissions giving rise to the claim occurred. . ." 28 U.S.C. § 1391(a). Here, Teacher resides in State B. However, the accident itself occurred in State A. Thus, a substantial part of the events giving rise to the claim occurred in State A, and venue in State A is proper under § 1391(a)(2).

NOTE: Some examinees might suggest that venue is proper in the federal district court of State A because the plaintiff, Passenger, resides there. Although under the pre-1990 version of the venue statute, venue in diversity cases was proper in the district "where all plaintiffs. . . reside," that language was eliminated by enactment of the Judicial Improvements Act of 1990. Thus, under current law, the plaintiff's residence in State A is irrelevant to venue.

Point Three: (35-45%)

Although Passenger's claim against Teacher and her claim against third-party defendant Rentco derive from a common nucleus of operative fact and hence are part of the same case for purposes of Article III of the Constitution, Supplemental jurisdiction is *statutorily* unavailable over claims by plaintiffs against persons made parties under Rule 14.

The district court cannot exercise subject matter jurisdiction over Passenger's direct claim against Rentco. There is no independent basis for jurisdiction (neither diversity nor federal question), and supplemental jurisdiction is not available for this type of claim.

Rule 14(a) of the Federal Rules of Civil Procedure permits a defendant to bring a third party into an action if the defendant believes the third party "may be liable" to defendant for all or part of any judgment against defendant in the action. Pursuant to this rule, defendant Teacher brought Rentco into the action as a third-party defendant. Passenger sought thereafter to amend the original complaint to state a claim directly against Rentco. The issue is whether the court has jurisdiction over Passenger's direct claim against Rentco. For reasons explained below, the court cannot take jurisdiction over Passenger's claim.

In the first place, there is no independent basis for federal jurisdiction over this claim. Plaintiff Passenger and third-party defendant Rentco are both citizens of State A, so diversity jurisdiction is not available for Passenger's claim against Rentco. Under § 1332(c)(1), a corporation is deemed a citizen of both its state of incorporation and the state in which it maintains its principal place of business. 28 U.S.C. § 1332(c)(I). Hence, Rentco is a citizen of both State A and State C. Because Passenger is a citizen of State A as well, there is no independent basis for diversity jurisdiction over Passenger's direct claim against third-party defendant Rentco. Further, because Passenger's claim against Rentco is a state-law negligence claim, there is no federal question jurisdiction.

Supplemental jurisdiction is also not available. Section 1367(a) provides that in a civil action of which the district court has original jurisdiction, the court has supplemental jurisdiction over "all other claims that are so related to claims in the action within such original jurisdiction that they form part of the same case or controversy under Article III of the United States Constitution." 28 U.S.C. § 1367(a). In *United Mine Workers of America* v. *Gibbs,* 383 U.S. 715, 725 (1966), the U.S. Supreme Court held that two claims will have that requisite connection if they "derive from a common nucleus of operative fact." Here, Passenger's claim against Teacher and Passenger's claim against third-party defendant Rentco derive from a common nucleus of operative fact: the failure of the brakes, the accident, and Passenger's resultant injuries. Without regard to their federal or state character, we would expect plaintiff to bring these claims together in a single action. *Id.*

However, Congress created statutory exceptions to supplemental jurisdiction. One of those exceptions, 28 U.S.C. §1367(b), applies here to prevent the court from taking jurisdiction. Section 1367(b) provides that supplemental jurisdiction in diversity cases shall not extend to "claims by plaintiffs against persons made parties under Rule 14. . . ." 28 U.S.C. § 1367(b). Because Passenger's claim against Rentco is a claim by a plaintiff against a person made a party under Rule 14 (Rentco was brought into the suit when Teacher filed a third-party complaint against it under Rule 14), supplemental jurisdiction is unavailable. Passenger could proceed directly against Rentco only if there were an independent basis for jurisdiction (e.g., diversity), and there is none. Because there is no independent basis for jurisdiction over this claim and because supplemental jurisdiction is unavailable, the district court should dismiss Passenger's claim against Rentco.

Federal Civil Procedure

(July 2002)

Legal Problems:

(1)(a)   What effect should the federal district court give to the forum selection clause?

(1)(b)   Is the court likely to transfer the case to State N in these circumstances?

(2)   Can a foreign-based party to U.S. litigation refuse to make its officers available for depositions on the ground that they are "beyond the subpoena power" of the court?

DISCUSSION

Summary: A motion for transfer of a case from one federal venue to another should be granted if a transfer would serve the convenience of the parties and the witnesses, if it would be in the interests of justice, and if the transferee court would have been a proper venue in the first instance. All of these requirements are satisfied here. The existence of a freely and fairly negotiated forum selection clause favoring State N is strong evidence that State N is a convenient forum, and the facts support the conclusion that State N is generally convenient for both parties, although State A is more convenient for plaintiff. Justice also favors upholding the expectations of the parties when they have freely selected State N as an appropriate forum. The action could also have been brought in State N initially.

When a corporate party is properly before a court (and no objection to personal jurisdiction was made here), the opposing party may depose an appropriate officer or director to speak for the corporation. The deposing party does not need to rely upon the court's subpoena power for the exercise of authority over the officer or director. A protective order is proper only if there is some other basis to oppose the deposition (e.g., the party that noticed the deposition did not proceed in accordance with the federal rules governing the timing of discovery).

Point One(a): (25-35%)

Because Buyer is seeking to transfer the case from one federal court to another federal court the motion to transfer is governed by 28 U.S.C. § 1404(a). State's policy against forum-selection clauses is irrelevant and the forum-selection clause is an important factor the court should consider in deciding whether to grant the motion to transfer.

Motions to transfer cases from one federal court to another are governed by 28 U.S.C. § 1404(a), which provides:

> For the convenience of parties and witnesses, in the interest of justice, a district court may transfer any civil action to any other district or division where it might have been brought.

Under this statute, motions to transfer are determined by weighing a number of factors, including the "convenience of witnesses and parties," and "public-interest factors of systemic integrity and fairness." *Stewart Org., Inc.* v. *Ricoh Corp.*, 487 U.S. 22, 29-31 (1988).

When a venue-transfer motion is predicated on the existence of a forum-selection clause in a contract, the forum-selection clause "will be a significant factor that figures centrally in the district court's calculus." *Id.* at 29. This is because "the presence of a forum-selection clause," bears upon the "convenience of [the proposed] forum," given the parties' expressed preference for that venue. Thus, the court must evaluate the fairness of the proposed transfer in light of the forum-selection clause. *Id.* Further, the existence of a state law rule invalidating the forum-selection clause does not excuse the court from considering the clause as one factor bearing on the propriety of a venue transfer.

Although the forum-selection clause must be treated as a "significant factor" when the district court evaluates Buyer's transfer motion, the U.S. Supreme Court has said that the existence of a forum-selection clause is not "dispositive." *Id.* For instance, an inequality of bargaining power between the parties may warrant giving less effect to the forum-selection clause. Similarly, litigating in the proposed forum may impose significant and unusual hardships on one of the parties. Absent such special factors, however, many courts hold that transfer motions under § 1404(a) should always be granted when doing so will give effect to a freely negotiated and fair forum-selection clause. *See, e.g., REO Sales, Inc.* v. *Prudential Ins. Co.*, 925 F. Supp. 1491 (D. Colo. 1996); *Riviera Finance* v. *Trucking Serv., Inc.*, 904 F. Supp. 837 (N.D. Ill. 1995).

Point One(b): (45-55%)

The federal district court in State A should grant the motion to transfer because the transfer would uphold the parties' expectations and provide them with the neutral and experienced forum for which they bargained.

Applying the factors set out in Point One(a) should lead to transfer of this action. The forum-selection clause in this case was a bargained clause in a contract between parties of apparently equal bargaining power. State N appears to be a neutral forum, and State N courts are well known for their expertise in commercial matters. Although State N does not appear to be an especially convenient forum, the parties' decision to select that forum in their contract indicates that each party believed State N to be a reasonably convenient alternative to less desirable options, including the option of litigating in either party's home jurisdiction. Absent some evidence to suggest that a transfer to State N would result in special hardship or a denial of justice to either party, the court is likely to take the view that the parties' decision to select the State N forum was ample evidence of the general superiority of that forum to State A.

This conclusion is bolstered by the fact that this is an international case. In *MIS Bremen v. Zapata Off-Shore Co.*, 407 U.S. 1 (1972), the Supreme Court adopted the view that a forum-selection clause in an international contract "should control absent a strong showing that it should be set aside." According to the Court, the need for a neutral forum, the desirability of avoiding uncertainty about where litigation might occur, and the need for a forum with expertise in the subject matter all justify giving deference to the parties' choice of forum when that choice is made in "a freely negotiated private international agreement, unaffected by fraud, undue influence, or overweening bargaining power." *Bremen,* 407 U.S. at 12.

NOTE: Although *MIS Bremen* was an admiralty case, the Supreme Court has described the decision as "instructive" for other cases, including motions under § 1404(a) to transfer diversity actions. *See generally* C. Wright, A. Miller & R. Marcus, FEDERAL PRACTICE AND PROCEDURE § 3803.1 (1995).

A transfer under § 1404(a) must be to a "district or division" where the case "might have been brought" initially. Here, it might be argued that the case could not have been brought in State N because there are no connections with State N sufficient to give State N courts jurisdiction over the defendant. However, personal jurisdiction can be based on consent, and both parties clearly consented to State N jurisdiction in their contract. Pre-lawsuit contractual consent serves as a basis for State N service of process on the defendant corporation, and would therefore have been an adequate basis for personal jurisdiction and venue had the action been brought in State N originally. *See American Airlines, Inc. v. Rogerson ATS,* 952 F. Supp. 377 (N.D. Texas 1996). In addition, because the defendant corporation is an alien corporation, venue in a suit brought against it would be proper in any district in the U.S., including in a federal district court in State N. *See* 28 U.S.C. § 1391(d); *Naegler v. Nissan Motor Co., Ltd.,* 835 F. Supp. 1152 (W.D. Mo. 1993).

Point Two: (20-30%)

Under Federal Rule of Civil Procedure 30, Seller has the right to compel the deposition of an officer of Buyer without resorting to the court's subpoena power.

A party to an action may secure the deposition of another party simply by providing notice to the other party. No subpoena of a party deponent is necessary, and a party is subject to sanctions for failing to provide a deponent, even if the party would be beyond the reach of the court's subpoena power if the party were a non-party witness. *See* Fed. R. Civ. P. 30(b)(1), 37(b)(2), 37(d)(1). *See generally* Wright, Miller & Marcus, *supra,* §§ 2103, 2112 (1995).

As a corporate party, Buyer cannot speak for itself but requires a natural person to speak for it. Seller could have noticed Buyer's deposition and required Buyer to nominate a representative to be deposed. *See* Fed. R. Civ. P. 30(b)(6). Alternatively, Seller can do what it did here - it can identify an officer or director of Buyer to be deposed as Buyer's representative. *See, e.g., Triple Crown America, Inc. v. Biosynth AG,* 1998 WL 227886 (B.D. Pa. 1998). If the person fails to appear, sanctions are authorized by Rule 37(d)(1). *See generally* Wright, Miller & Marcus, *supra.* Hence, Buyer's argument that its officers are "beyond the court's subpoena power" does not present a valid reason to prevent the deposition of an officer. Buyer, as a party to the litigation, is obliged to produce its officers for deposition. Accordingly, Buyer's request for a protective order should be denied, unless Buyer can offer sound reasons for resisting the deposition other than the simple claim that its CEO is beyond the reach of the court's subpoena power.

NOTE: If the court had no personal jurisdiction over defendant corporation, the claim that the officers and directors are beyond the court's subpoena power might be a colorable basis to resist the notice of deposition. The facts, however, suggest that personal jurisdiction is not a real issue. First, any problem with the State A federal court's personal jurisdiction over defendant Buyer was waived when Buyer responded to Seller's complaint without raising the personal jurisdiction issue. (*See* Fed. R. Civ. P. 12(h)(l).) Second, if the case is transferred, the federal court in State N would have personal jurisdiction over defendant Buyer because of its contractual consent to the jurisdiction of that court.

Federal Civil Procedure

(February 2003)

Legal Problems: (1)   Under Fed. R. Civ. P. 56, should summary judgment be granted to a defendant who supports his motion with evidence negating the plaintiff's claim when the plaintiff's response fails to directly controvert that evidence?

(2)(a) Does claim preclusion arising from a prior federal suit against a product's manufacturer bar a subsequent suit against the product's distributor?

(2)(b) In this case, may the distributor successfully invoke issue preclusion against the plaintiff?

DISCUSSION

Summary: In the federal court action, defendant Acme's motion for summary judgment was premised on the claim that a proper warning label was attached to its widget at the time the widget was delivered to the distributor. Under the applicable state law, Acme's duty to warn was fully discharged if that fact were true. To support its claim, Acme provided affidavits of witnesses who said the label was present at the relevant time. In the face of this evidence, Plaintiff had a duty to present evidence of "specific facts" showing that there was a genuine issue for trial. Plaintiff's affidavit, which asserted only the absence of a label *when she purchased the widget*, did not contradict Acme's evidence that a label was present when it delivered the widget to the distributor. Hence, summary judgment was appropriate on that issue.

Nothing that happened in the federal court action should preclude Plaintiff from proceeding with the state court action. Claim preclusion is inappropriate because there is no mutuality of estoppel: the defendant in the state court action was not the same as, or in privity with, the federal defendant and would not have been precluded or otherwise affected by the result in the federal action. Issue preclusion is inappropriate because the only issue *actually decided* in the federal action (whether a warning label was present when the manufacturer delivered the widget *to the distributor*) is not an issue in the state action, where the question is whether a warning label was present when the widget was delivered *to the retailer*.

Point One: Because Plaintiff's response to Acme's motion for summary

(30-40%) <u>judgment failed to demonstrate a genuine issue of material fact as to Acme's supported assertion that a warning label was affixed to the product at the time of delivery to the distributor, the court properly granted summary judgment to Acme on the failure to warn claim.</u>

A motion for summary judgment should be granted in favor of a party if "there is no genuine issue as to any material fact" and the party is "entitled to a judgment as a matter of law." Fed. R. Civ. P. 56(c). A defendant on a claim may move for summary judgment by attacking any *necessary* element of the plaintiff's case. *See Celotex Corp. v. Catrett*, 477 U.S. 317 (1986). In determining whether there are any genuine issues of material fact, the court should construe all factual matters in the light most favorable to the non-moving party. However, where the moving party presents evidence of facts that would defeat the non-moving party's claim, the non-moving party "may not rest upon the mere allegations" of her pleading. The non-moving party has a responsibility to offer, "by affidavits or as otherwise provided" in Rule 56, evidence of "specific facts showing that there is a genuine issue for trial." Fed. R. Civ. P. 56(e).

On the facts of this problem, the court properly granted Acme's motion for summary judgment on the failure to warn claim. The law of State Y (which the federal court is obliged to apply under the *Erie* doctrine in this diversity case) states that a manufacturer fully discharges its duty to warn if adequate warning labels are affixed to the product *at the time of delivery to its distributor.* Thus, to win on her failure to warn claim, Plaintiff must prove that no proper warning label was affixed to the widget at the time of delivery to the distributor.

Defendant Acme's summary judgment motion alleged that adequate warning labels were, in fact, affixed to the product at the relevant time, and that allegation was supported by affidavits attesting to the presence of the warning label at the time of delivery to the distributor. This properly supported motion therefore negates a key element of Plaintiff's claim, thereby discharging Acme's duty to support its summary judgment motion under Fed. R. Civ. P. 56(e).

At this point, the burden shifted to Plaintiff to come forward with controverting evidence. Plaintiff responded to the summary judgment motion with her own affidavit, in which she attested that no warning label had been present on her widget when she purchased it. This does not directly controvert Acme's motion, since it does not contend that the warning label was missing at the point of delivery to the distributor, the critical moment for manufacturer liability under applicable state law. Consequently, Plaintiff failed to meet her burden to produce evidence controverting Acme's version of the facts. *See* Jack H. Friedenthal, Mary Kay Kane & Arthur R. Miller, CIVIL PROCEDURE 461 (3d ed. 1999).

Thus, Acme has demonstrated that no genuine issue of material fact exists on a key element of Plaintiff's claim, and that it is, therefore, entitled to judgment as a matter of law. Fed. R. Civ. P. 56(c).

<u>Point Two (a): Because Widgets was not a party to the prior action, it probably</u>
(20-30%) <u>cannot bar Plaintiff's action against it on claim preclusion grounds.</u>

Note: Even though the current suit is in state court, the effect of the Acme judgment is governed by federal law because the judgment came from a federal court. A state court is required to give to a federal judgment the same preclusive effect that the judgment would have *in federal court*. *See generally* Eugene F. Scoles & Peter Hay, CONFLICT OF LAWS § 24.2 (2d ed. 1992). The preclusive effect of a judgment by a federal court sitting in diversity ordinarily would be determined by the preclusion rules of the state in which the federal court sits. *Semtek Int'l, Inc. v. Lockheed Martin Corp.*, 531 U.S. 497 (2001).

In order to bar a plaintiff's subsequent lawsuit on claim preclusion grounds, a defendant must show (1) that the prior judgment is final, valid, and on the merits (which is true here), (2) that the present claims are within the scope of the prior judgment, as measured by the same transaction test (also true here), and (3) that there is mutuality of estoppel (i.e., that the defendant urging preclusion is the same as, or in privity with, the defendant in the prior suit). Although the first two elements of claim preclusion are easily satisfied on the facts of the problem, Widgets' claim preclusion argument will probably fail on the final prong: mutuality of estoppel.

Here, there are no facts to suggest that Widgets had such a close relationship with Acme that Widgets would have been bound by the prior judgment had that decision gone against Acme. Widgets apparently did not control or participate in the Acme litigation. Nor are Widgets and Acme in any agency or representative relationship that would warrant treating Acme's actions as binding on Widgets. In short, there is nothing to suggest that Widgets bore such a close relationship to the first suit or to Acme that it would be proper to treat the first action as binding on Widgets. Under the circumstances, the usual rule that a judgment operates only against parties to the first suit seems fully applicable. *See* Charles A. Wright, Arthur R. Miller & Edward H. Cooper, FEDERAL PRACTICE AND PROCEDURE § 4406.

Where, as here, a plaintiff brings separate suits against alleged joint tortfeasors whose liability is joint and several (and not derivative), the courts traditionally hold that the plaintiff is entitled to maintain separate actions and that a judgment in a case involving one tortfeasor does not preclude the bringing of a claim for the same harm against another tortfeasor. *See* Restatement (Second) of Judgments § 49, cmt a. *See, e.g., Drescher v. Hoffman Motors Corp.* 585 F. Supp. 555, 558 (D.C. Conn. 1984); *U.S. v. Manning Coal Corp.*, 977 F.2d 117, 122 (4th Cir. 1992); *Levy v. Verser, Inc.*, 882 F. Supp. 736, 740 (N.D. Ill. 1995). *But see Meshulam v. General Motors Corp.*, 995 F.2d 192, 194 (11th Cir. 1993) (under Florida law, the manufacturer, the wholesale distributor, and the retailer of an allegedly defective product are treated as identical parties for *res judicata* purposes and an action against a retailer is a bar to a subsequent action against the manufacturer on product liability grounds).

Note: Although the doctrine of mutuality of estoppel has been widely abandoned in relation to *issue preclusion*, it is still largely operative in the context of *claim preclusion. See, e.g., Sidag A.G. v. Smoked Food Products Co.*, 776 F.2d 1270, 1275 (5th Cir. 1985). The traditional rule requiring mutuality of estoppel for claim preclusion purposes appears to be undergoing some modification in federal courts. Wright, Miller and Cooper report that increasing numbers of federal courts now allow claim preclusion against a party to a prior action by litigants who would not themselves have been bound by the results of the prior case if there are "good reasons why [the new defendant] should have been joined in the first action and the old party cannot show any good reasons to justify a second chance." Wright, *supra,* § 4464 (2000 Supp.) In the present case, however, there is no evidence of a good reason why Plaintiff ought to be required to sue both Acme and Widgets at the same time.

Point Two (b): Widgets will not be able to assert issue preclusion against Plaintiff
(20-30%)   because the issues in Plaintiff's suit against Widgets are not the same as the issues that were actually litigated in Plaintiff's prior suit against Acme.

Widgets' attempt to invoke issue preclusion will also fail. The problem for Widgets is that none of the issues involved in Plaintiff's suit against it were actually decided in Plaintiff's suit against Acme. As to the failure to warn issue, although evidence was presented in Acme's suit on whether the required warning was present at the time Widgets delivered the product to the retailer (in the form of the employee affidavits), the court did not need to use that evidence to decide the summary judgment motion, since the key point there was whether the label was affixed at the point of delivery *to the distributor*, not the retailer. As to the dangerous defect issue, the settlement in Acme's case obviated any actual litigation on the point. The settlement also precluded any actual litigation as to the amount of Plaintiff's damages. It is well settled that a judgment entered pursuant to a settlement cannot serve as the basis for issue preclusion in a later case. *See generally* Jack H. Friedenthal, Mary Kay Kane & Arthur R. Miller, CIVIL PROCEDURE § 14.11 (3d ed. 1999).

Because issue preclusion essentially exports the factual findings of one case into another, any issue to be precluded must be precisely the same one that was actually litigated, decided, and necessary to the judgment in the prior suit. Here, that is not the case.

Federal Civil Procedure

(July 2003)

<u>Legal Problems:</u>   (1)   Does the pendency of a parallel state court proceeding in State Z require the federal district court to abstain from adjudicating the class action?

(2)   Is class certification appropriate in this case under the guidelines set forth in Fed. R. Civ. P. 23?

DISCUSSION

<u>Summary:</u>   The court's refusal to abstain was correct. The court is not required to abstain merely because the federal litigation is duplicative of state litigation. The facts do not present any other basis for abstention.

The district court properly denied class certification because Farmer's breach-of-warranty claim is not typical of the claims of those class members who have suffered personal injuries. In addition, Farmer is not an adequate representative of the class because his interests differ significantly from the interests of the personal injury claimants and Farmer's attorney is inexperienced with this kind of litigation.

<u>Point One:</u>   <u>Although duplicative federal and state court litigation is wasteful, no</u>
(30-40%)   <u>federal rule requires abstention simply on the basis of duplication. The court's</u>
<u>denial of abstention was correct because no existing federal abstention rule would</u>
<u>support abstention in this case.</u>

In general, parties may proceed to judgment in a federal district court action without regard to the pendency of state proceedings that seek similar relief. *See Kline v. Burke Construction Co.,* 260 U.S. 226 (1922). Indeed, a federal district court has a "duty . . . to adjudicate a controversy properly before it," and it may abstain "only in the exceptional circumstances where the order to the parties to repair to the State court would clearly serve an important countervailing interest." *Colorado River Water Conservation District v. United States,* 424 U.S. 800, 813 (1976).

The facts of this problem do not support abstention under any established abstention rule. *Pullman* abstention, *see Railroad Comm'n of Texas v. Pullman Co.,* 312 U.S. 496 (1941), operates only when the state court's resolution of unsettled state law issues may obviate the necessity of resolving a difficult federal law issue. *Burford* abstention is appropriate only if federal adjudication would interfere with the state's administration of a complex regulatory scheme, *Burford v. Sun Oil Co.,* 319 U.S. 315 (1943), and *Younger* abstention is limited to cases where the federal court is asked to enjoin the actions of state officials, *Younger v. Harris,* 401 U.S. 37 (1971). Nothing in this problem implicates any of these standard abstention doctrines.

There is an argument that the district court should dismiss the action under the U.S. Supreme Court's decision in *Colorado River*, 424 U.S. 800. Viewed expansively, the *Colorado River* doctrine, which is based on "principles of federalism, comity, and conservation of judicial resources," could be said to warrant federal court restraint when parallel state proceedings mean that pursuit of federal proceedings will waste judicial resources and potentially involve federal resolution of issues also pending before state courts. *See Black Sea Investment, Ltd. v. United Heritage Corp.*, 204 F.3d 647, 650 (5th Cir. 2000). Such an argument could be bolstered by observing that dismissal under *Colorado River* is not governed by a "hard and fast rule," but by the application of an elaborate balancing test. *See Moses H. Cone Mem. Hosp. v. Mercury Const. Corp.*, 460 U.S. 1, 16 (1983).

However, *Colorado River* does not justify abstention in this case. In *Colorado River*, the Supreme Court emphasized that the dismissal of the federal action in that case (in favor of parallel state proceedings) was an "extraordinary and narrow exception," 424 U.S. at 813, to the "virtually unflagging obligation of the federal courts to exercise the jurisdiction given them." 424 U.S. at 817.

The mere fact of duplicative litigation, which is all that appears to justify abstention on our facts, is not enough to justify abstention under *Colorado River*. *See Black Sea Investment, Ltd.*, 204 F.3d at 650. ("Duplicative litigation, wasteful though it may be, is a necessary cost of our nation's maintenance of two separate and distinct judicial systems.") There must be evidence of other factors that militate against federal litigation, such as the risk of inconsistent rulings with respect to a particular piece of property or clear evidence of a federal policy favoring unitary adjudication of the claims at issue. In conducting the necessary balancing inquiry, moreover, "the balance [is] heavily weighted in favor of the exercise of jurisdiction." *Cone Mem. Hosp.*, 460 U.S. at 16. In our case, there appears to be no special state interest to protect, no federal policy supporting unified state court adjudication of these product liability claims, and no apparent risk of inconsistent adjudications. It thus appears that the court's ruling was correct, as the class action here falls under the general rule of no abstention, rather than the narrow exception in *Colorado River*.

Point Two: (60-70%)	The district court was justified in ruling that class certification was unwarranted because the facts suggest the absence of claim typicality and adequate representation.

Federal Rule of Civil Procedure Rule 23(a) identifies the prerequisites that must be satisfied before any class may be certified. Rule 23(a) requires evidence that:

> (1) the class is so numerous that joinder of all members is impracticable, (2) there are questions of law or fact common to the class, (3) the claims or defenses of the representative parties are typical of the claims or defenses of the class, and (4) the representative parties will fairly and adequately protect the interests of the class.

If the Rule 23(a) prerequisites are satisfied, a class action may be certified if it falls within one of the categories specified in Rule 23(b). Of particular relevance to this case is Rule 23(b)(3), which also requires that "questions of law or fact common to the members of the class predominate over any questions affecting only individual members, and . . . a class action is superior to other available methods for the fair and efficient adjudication of the controversy."

For a number of reasons, the district court's refusal to certify Farmer's class action was appropriate. While Farmer has satisfied a few of the prerequisites specified in Rule 23(a), he has not satisfied all of them. With respect to the few, the 100,000 members of the class easily satisfy the numerosity requirement, and there are issues of law and fact common to the members of the class. In particular, there are the questions whether the shock absorbers are defective and, if so, whether relief is appropriate under federal warranty law.

Farmer has not likely, however, satisfied the typicality and adequacy of representation requirements. As for typicality, the claims of representatives and class members are typical when they stem from a single event or are based on common legal theories. *Rall v. Medtronic*, 1986 WL 22271 (D. Nev. 1986). Here, Farmer's individual claim seeks to recover for out-of-pocket losses resulting from replacement of the shocks. While Farmer's claim is "typical" of other class members' claims to the extent that all the claims involve the question of the defectiveness of the shock absorbers, Farmer's warranty claim otherwise differs significantly from claims for personal injuries, which some members of the class have here. Personal injury claims are highly individualized, involving issues of causation, extent of damages, contributory negligence, etc., that are not present with respect to Farmer's breach-of-warranty claim. Because of differences of this sort, federal courts have been reluctant to grant class certification where the claims of injured persons will be represented by class representatives who have no personal injury or where personal injury claims are lumped with claims that do not involve personal injury. Moreover, personal injury claimants have a strong interest in individually controlling the prosecution of their claims and in making individual decisions on whether to settle. A class action is designed for situations where individual claims are too small to warrant individual prosecution. *See, e.g., Walsh v. Ford Motor Co.*, 106 F.R.D. 378, 404-408 (D.D.C. 1985). *See generally Amchem Products, Inc. v. Windsor*, 521 U.S. 591, 615-619 (1997). Consequently, a typicality problem arises here. *Cf. Hanlon v. Chrysler Corp*, 150 F.3d 1011 (9th Cir. 1998) (class certification proper because class limited to economic loss claimants; personal injury claimants excluded).

The adequacy of representation requirement involves a two-part inquiry. First, the court must ask whether the representative's interests are aligned closely enough with other class members to ensure fair representation of the absentee class members. Second, the court must ensure that class counsel is experienced and qualified to carry out the litigation in order to fairly and adequately protect the interests of the class. Both requirements pose problems in this case. *See, e.g., Gen. Tel. Co. of the Southwest v. Falcon*, 457 U.S. 147, 157 n. 13 (1982); *Emig v. American Tobacco Co., Inc.*, 184 F.R.D. 379, 387 (D. Kan. 1998). The difference between the nature of the contract and warranty claims of Farmer and those of the personal injury victims presents a potential conflict of interest that raises doubts about Farmer's adequacy as a representative of the interests of the personal injury claimants. Farmer might be more willing to accept a modest settlement than would the personal injury claimants in the class. This adequacy of representation problem is magnified in view of the lawyer's inexperence with class litigation. There is a real question as to whether a new bar admittee is appropriate counsel for such complex litigation.

Even if the district court were satisfied that the Rule 23(a) prerequisites were satisfied, these same concerns would warrant denial of class certification pursuant to Rule 23(b). As noted above, the court may certify the class action only if common questions predominate over questions affecting individual members of the class. Given the existence of personal injury claimants in the class, some of whom have already filed independent claims, and given the existence of questions about the adequacy of the representation being provided by Farmer for the class, it was certainly within the scope of the court's discretion to conclude that the efficiency to be had by litigating "common questions of law and fact" in a class action would be overwhelmed by the problems posed by the presence of litigants with diverse personal injury claims, raising non-common issues of fact and law. *See, e.g., Amchem,* 521 U.S. at 622-25. In this regard, the personal injury claimants probably have a strong interest "in individually controlling the prosecution . . . of [their] separate actions." *Georgine v. Amchem Products, Inc.,* 83 F.3d 610, 633 (3d Cir. 1996). Moreover, given the potential variability in the nature of the claims asserted by the class members, and the inexperience of class counsel, the "difficulties likely to be encountered in the management" of an action involving such diverse claims would probably significantly reduce the efficiencies stemming from class litigation. *Id.*

Accordingly, although the class is large and there are some common issues of law and fact, given the wide discretion residing with the court, it appropriately refused to certify the class.

Federal Civil Procedure

(February 2004)

ANALYSIS

<u>Legal Problems:</u>

(1)   Can Husband and Wife join their respective personal injury and loss-of-consortium claims in a single action in the U.S. district court?

(2)   Can Husband and Wife join their respective claims against the United States and Motorist in a single action in the U.S. district court?

(3)   Does the U.S. district court have subject matter jurisdiction over the state law claims?

DISCUSSION

<u>Summary:</u>   Rule 20(a) of the Federal Rules of Civil Procedure permits Husband and Wife to assert their federal and state law claims against the United States and Motorist because their claims arose out of the same transaction. Although the court would not have diversity jurisdiction in an action by Husband and Wife against Motorist if such an action were brought on its own, the court has supplemental jurisdiction over that claim because it shares a "common nucleus of operative fact" with Husband and Wife's federal question claim against the United States.

<u>Point One:</u>   <u>Federal Rule 20(a) permits Husband and Wife to join their respective personal injury</u>

(15-25%)   <u>and loss-of-consortium claims in a single action.</u>

Federal Rule of Civil Procedure 20(a) permits plaintiffs to join their claims in a single action when those claims arise out of a single event and share at least one common issue of law or fact. The rule provides, in relevant part:

> All persons may join in one action as plaintiffs if they assert any right to relief jointly, severally, or in the alternative in respect of or arising out of the same transaction, occurrence, or series of transactions or occurrences and if any question of law or fact common to all these persons will arise in the action.

The requirements of Rule 20(a) are satisfied by the facts stated in this problem. The claims of Husband and Wife arise out of the same occurrence (the traffic accident) and involve at least one common issue of fact or law (for example, whether either the soldier who was feeling drowsy or Motorist or both were negligent). Accordingly, Husband and Wife may join their claims in a single action.

NOTE: Rule 20(a) does not confer subject matter jurisdiction on the U.S. district court to hear the respective claims of the plaintiffs. It simply provides the mechanism for joining claims over which the Constitution and the Congress have given it subject matter jurisdiction. Accordingly, the joinder of Husband and Wife as party plaintiffs is proper, provided the U.S. district court has subject matter jurisdiction over the claims by each plaintiff. *See* Point Three below.

Point Two:	Federal Rule 20(a) permits Husband and Wife to join their respective claims against the United States and Motorist in a single action.
(15-25%)	

Just as Rule 20(a) permits plaintiffs to join in an action, it permits a plaintiff or plaintiffs to join defendants where the plaintiff(s)' claims against each defendant arise from a single transaction and share a common issue of fact or law. The rule provides, in relevant part:

> All persons . . . may be joined in one action as defendants if there is asserted against them jointly, severally, or in the alternative, any right to relief . . . arising out of the same . . . occurrence . . . and if any question of law or fact common to all defendants will arise in the action.

Again, the requirements of Rule 20(a) are clearly met on these facts. The claims of each plaintiff against the United States and Motorist arise out of the same occurrence and involve at least one common issue of fact or law (for example, the extent of Husband's injuries). When this is so, the Federal Rules permit (but do not require) a party to join two or more defendants in a single action.

NOTE: As is the case with joinder of plaintiffs, this rule does not confer subject matter jurisdiction on the federal court to hear a claim against a joined defendant. Thus, joinder may be defeated where the court lacks subject matter jurisdiction over the joined claim. *See* Point Three, below.

Point Three:	Even though the federal court lacks diversity jurisdiction over Husband's and Wife's claims against Motorist, it has "supplemental jurisdiction" over those claims.
(50-60%)	

Federal courts are tribunals with limited subject matter jurisdiction in civil cases. Basically, they may decide only "federal question" and "diversity" cases. The claims of Husband and Wife against Motorist do not involve a federal question; they are state tort law claims. Nor do their claims against Motorist qualify for diversity jurisdiction. First, diversity is determined on the date the suit is filed. Although Husband and Wife were citizens of a different state than Motorist on the day of the accident, they were all citizens of State X on the date that suit was filed. Second, their claims do not satisfy the amount in controversy requirement. Neither claim is for an amount in excess of $75,000, so an effort to pursue their claims in a federal court under its diversity jurisdiction would fail.

However, a state cause of action may be heard in a federal court under supplemental jurisdiction (formerly termed "ancillary" or "pendent" jurisdiction). Where a party has both a federal question claim and a state law claim and both claims arise out of a common nucleus of operative fact, it has long been recognized that the federal court may, in the interest of the economical and efficient administration of justice, decide both the federal and the state claims in a single action. *See United Mine Workers v. Gibbs*, 383 U.S. 715 (1966).

Subsection (a) of Section 1367 of the Judicial Code authorizes a federal court to exercise "supplemental jurisdiction" over any state law claim that has a nucleus of operative fact in common with a claim that is itself within the subject matter jurisdiction of the federal court. The statute not only codifies the "pendent claim" jurisdiction as formulated in the *Gibbs* case, but the final sentence of subsection (a) expands supplemental jurisdiction expressly to include "pendent party" jurisdiction. "Such supplemental jurisdiction," the statute reads, "shall include claims that involve the joinder or intervention of additional parties."

Accordingly, since the State X tort claims of Husband and Wife against Motorist arise out of the same occurrence as their federal question claims against the United States, the federal court in State X has supplemental jurisdiction over these State X claims. The claims against Motorist share a "common nucleus of operative fact" with the claims against the United States, and it is reasonable to expect them to be resolved in one action. Under such circumstances, the courts have routinely held that 21 U.S.C. § 1367(a) confers supplemental jurisdiction over such claims. *See, e.g., Roche v. John Hancock Mut. Life Ins. Co.*, 81 F.3d 249 (1st Cir. 1996); *Spiegel v. City of Chicago*, 920 F. Supp. 891 (N.D.Ill. 1996) (supplemental jurisdiction appropriate when disparate tort claims arise from same basic occurrence). Thus, even though the state law claims, standing alone, would be outside the court's subject matter jurisdiction, they may be joined to the case against the United States, over which the court has exclusive jurisdiction pursuant to the Federal Tort Claims Act, 28 U.S.C. § 1346(b).

NOTE: The statute gives the court discretion to reject claims on prudential grounds, including when the pendent claims raise novel issues of state law, when they substantially predominate over the claims over which the federal court has original jurisdiction, when the claims over which the court had original jurisdiction have all been dismissed, or in other "exceptional circumstances." However, none of these prudential reasons for denying supplemental jurisdiction is present on our facts.

Federal Civil Procedure

(July 2004)

ANALYSIS

Legal Problems:

(1)(a) Were the requirements for federal diversity jurisdiction satisfied, even though Plaintiff and decedent Tortfeasor were citizens of the same state?

(1)(b) Was Executor precluded from raising the issue of subject matter jurisdiction because it failed to raise the issue earlier in the case and, in fact, conceded jurisdiction?

(2) When suit is filed to enforce a federal judgment in a state court, may the defendant collaterally attack the federal judgment for lack of subject matter jurisdiction?

DISCUSSION

Summary:

The federal district court of State Y should have dismissed the action for lack of subject matter jurisdiction. The federal court lacked jurisdiction because there was no diversity. Defendant Executor's citizenship is deemed to be the same as decedent Tortfeasor's. Tortfeasor and Plaintiff were both citizens of State X. The lack of diversity defeats diversity subject matter jurisdiction and is not waivable. Defendant may raise subject matter jurisdiction at any time, and the federal court erred in denying the motion. But the issue of subject matter jurisdiction was fully litigated in federal court, so Defendant is precluded from raising it in a collateral attack on the judgment. The state court in State X must therefore enforce the federal judgment.

Point One(a):
(20-30%)

Even though Plaintiff and Executor were from different states, diversity jurisdiction was unavailable because, under 28 U.S.C. § 1332(c)(2), "the legal representative of the estate of a decedent shall be deemed to be a citizen only of the same State as the decedent." Plaintiff and Executor's decedent, Tortfeasor, were both citizens of State X and consequently the requirements for diversity jurisdiction were not met.

Plaintiff's complaint included only a state-law negligence claim. The court, therefore, had subject matter jurisdiction only if diversity jurisdiction existed under 28 U.S.C. § 1332. To satisfy the diversity statute, the amount in controversy in the action must exceed $75,000 and the parties must be diverse.

Plaintiff's complaint alleged damages in excess of $500,000. The facts state that Plaintiff was severely injured and there is nothing to suggest that Plaintiff's damages claim was made in bad faith. Consequently, Plaintiff will be deemed to have satisfied the amount-in-controversy requirement of $75,000. 28 U.S.C. § 1332(a).

The diversity of citizenship requirement, however, is not satisfied in this case. For purposes of determining citizenship, an individual is a citizen of the state in which he or she is domiciled. *See, e.g., Mas v. Perry,* 489 F.2d 1396, 1399 (5th Cir. 1974). Plaintiff and decedent, Tortfeasor, were both citizens of State X. Defendant, Executor, was a citizen of State Y. On the face of it, the plaintiff and defendant were citizens of different states, satisfying the diversity requirement. However, diversity jurisdiction should have been unavailable because Executor stands in the shoes of Tortfeasor and takes Tortfeasor's citizenship for purposes of diversity. Under 28 U.S.C. § 1332(c)(2), "the legal representative of the estate of a decedent shall be deemed to be a citizen only of the same State as the decedent." Thus, because Executor was sued as a representative of Tortfeasor's estate, Executor was deemed to be a citizen of the same state as Tortfeasor, State X. Plaintiff, of course, is also a citizen of State X, so diversity jurisdiction should have been unavailable.

Accordingly, the district court erred in denying the motion to dismiss for lack of jurisdiction. The motion was proper when made, and it should have been granted because the parties were not diverse. (*See* Point One(b) below.)

Point One(b): (15-25%)	Executor's motion to dismiss for lack of subject matter jurisdiction must be considered on the merits, even if it was raised a year after Executor answered and admitted jurisdiction.

Although the motion to dismiss for lack of subject matter jurisdiction was filed a year after Executor's answer to the complaint admitted the existence of jurisdiction, the court was nevertheless obliged to consider the motion on its merits. The defense of lack of subject matter jurisdiction is not waivable and may be raised "*whenever* it appears by suggestion of the parties . . . that the court lacks jurisdiction of the subject matter." Fed. R. Civ. P. 12(h)(3) (emphasis added). Accordingly, the court was obliged to consider the merits of Executor's jurisdictional challenge.

Point Two: (50-60%)	The state court is required to give the federal court judgment the same credit it would receive in federal court. Because Executor litigated the issue of subject matter jurisdiction before the federal court, lost, and did not appeal, Executor is precluded from relitigating the issue of jurisdiction in state court.

State courts are required to give full faith and credit to the judgments of other states. U.S. Const. art. IV, §1. Likewise, state, federal, and territorial courts are required to give state court judgments the same credit that they would receive in the courts of the rendering state. 28 U.S.C. § 1738. Although neither Article IV nor the full faith and credit statute explicitly requires state courts to honor federal judgments, "it is well recognized that the same compulsion controls and thus state courts must treat federal judgments as those judgments would be treated by the federal courts themselves." Jack Friedenthal et al., CIVIL PROCEDURE § 14.15 at 711 (3d ed. 1999) (footnote omitted); *see also Stoll v. Gottlieb*, 305 U.S. 165, 172 (1938).

In *Durfee v. Duke*, 375 U.S. 106, 111 (1963), the United States Supreme Court announced the "general rule that a judgment is entitled to full faith and credit even as to questions of jurisdiction when the second court's inquiry discloses that those questions have been fully and fairly litigated and finally decided in the court which rendered the original judgment." *See also Treinies v. Sunshine Mining Co.*, 308 U.S. 66, 78 (1939). Here, Executor raised the lack of subject matter jurisdiction in the federal court action. The issue was briefed, argued, and decided. Although the court's decision on the issue was mistaken, no appeal was taken and the court's judgment became final. If the second suit had been filed in federal court, the doctrine of issue preclusion or collateral estoppel would bar the defendant from relitigating the issue of subject matter jurisdiction since the identical issue was fully and fairly litigated in the first suit. Full faith and credit requires that the federal judgment have the same effect in the state court. Thus, the state court should enforce the federal judgment notwithstanding the challenge to the federal court's subject matter jurisdiction. If Executor had wished to continue the jurisdictional challenge, Executor should have filed an appeal from the decision of the federal district court.

NOTE: The U.S. Supreme Court has ruled that the preclusive effect of the judgment of a federal court sitting in diversity should be determined by the law of the state in which the federal court sits. *See Semtek Int'l, Inc. v. Lockheed Martin Corp.*, 531 U.S. 497 (2001). Thus, the preclusion rules of State Y would determine whether the State X court should enforce the federal judgment. It is likely, however, that State Y would follow a rule of jurisdictional finality similar to the rule in *Durfee v. Duke*: if the question of subject matter jurisdiction was fully and fairly litigated, the judgment is not subject to collateral attack. *See* RESTATEMENT (SECOND) OF JUDGMENTS § 12.

Federal Civil Procedure

(February 2005)

ANALYSIS

<u>Legal Problems:</u> (1)(a) Were the requirements for federal diversity jurisdiction satisfied as to the tort claim, given that Buyer and Seller were citizens of different states when the suit was filed but subsequently became citizens of the same state?

(1)(b) Does the federal district court have jurisdiction over Buyer's contract claim, even though it does not independently satisfy the jurisdictional amount-in-controversy requirement?

(2) May the court transfer a case to another district when venue did not lie in the other district at the time the suit was filed?

DISCUSSION

Summary

Because Buyer and Seller were citizens of different states at the time the suit was filed, the requirements for diversity jurisdiction were met with respect to the tort claim. Moreover, the contract claim was properly aggregated with the tort claim to satisfy the amount-in-controversy requirement, and in any event there was supplemental jurisdiction over the contract claim because both claims derive from a common nucleus of operative fact. Transfer to the federal court in State Y would be inappropriate because the claim could not have been brought there in the first instance.

Point One(a):   Buyer properly invoked federal diversity jurisdiction as to the tort claim because Buyer
(30-40%)   was a citizen of State Y and Seller was a citizen of State X when the complaint was filed, and the
               amount in controversy exceeds $75,000.

The court should deny Seller's motion to dismiss for lack of subject matter jurisdiction over the tort claim. The requirements for federal diversity jurisdiction have been established in this case.

Buyer's claims are based on state law. Therefore, to proceed in federal court, he must satisfy 28 U.S.C. § 1332(a), which establishes the requirements for federal subject matter jurisdiction based on diversity of citizenship. According to the plain terms of the statute, "the matter in controversy [must] exceed the sum or value of $75,000," and be between "citizens of different states." The courts have interpreted § 1332 as requiring the parties to be diverse *at the time the suit is filed*, and not at the time the cause of action arises. *See, e.g., Gordon v. Steele*, 376 F. Supp. 575 (W.D. Pa. 1974) (citing cases); Charles A.Wright, Arthur R. Miller & Edward H. Cooper, FEDERAL PRACTICE AND PROCEDURE § 3608 (1998). Here the amount-in-controversy requirement has been met with regard to the claim for personal injury and lost wages ($500,000), and the only question is whether the diversity requirement is met.

In determining the citizenship of the parties, the courts look to the domicile of each party, examining "[t]he fact of residency . . . coupled with a finding of intent to remain indefinitely." *Gordon, supra*, quoting cases; *see also Mas v. Perry*, 489 F.2d 1396 (5th Cir. 1974). A change of domicile is effected "by a combination of two elements: (a) taking up residence in a different domicile with (b) the intention to remain there." *Id.* The important question is whether Buyer was a citizen of State Y *at the time the suit was filed*. Having completed his move to State Y at that time, and having the intent to remain in State Y, Buyer was then a State Y citizen. Buyer was therefore diverse from Seller, who was still a citizen of State X when the suit was filed.

Some applicants may conclude, based on Buyer's rental of an apartment and his intent to remain in Big City, that he was already a citizen of State Y at the time of the accident (and hence before the time the suit was filed).

Because citizenship is determined at the time suit is filed, Seller's post-filing move to State Y does not affect the court's diversity jurisdiction. The parties were diverse at the time the suit was filed and changes in citizenship after filing are irrelevant, absent bad faith on the part of a party. Wright, Miller & Cooper, FEDERAL PRACTICE AND PROCEDURE § 3608 (1998).

Point One(b):   <u>Although the $2,500 contract claim alone would not satisfy the amount-in-controversy</u>
(30-40%)   <u>requirement for a diversity action, Buyer may aggregate the contract claim with his tort claim in</u>
              <u>order to satisfy the amount-in-controversy requirement.</u>

Buyer's effort to join the small contract claim to his large tort claim can be analyzed in two ways. First, under traditional aggregation rules, a single plaintiff with "two entirely unrelated claims against a single diverse defendant" may bring them in federal court as long as the aggregate of the claims exceeds the $75,000 amount-in-controversy requirement. Charles Alan Wright, LAW OF FEDERAL COURTS 210 (5th ed. 1994). The rationale is that "the diversity statute confers federal jurisdiction over 'civil actions' satisfying the required minimum amount in controversy . . . not over counts, thus permitting the plaintiff to aggregate the stakes in his separate claims or counts to come up to the minimum." *Herremans v. Carrera Designs, Inc.,* 157 F.3d 1118, 1121 (7th Cir. 1998). Thus, because the aggregate of Buyer's tort and contract claims exceeds $75,000, the court has jurisdiction to hear them all, including the contract claim for $2,500.

Second, under the federal supplemental jurisdiction statute, 28 U.S.C. § 1367(a), district courts "shall have supplemental jurisdiction over all claims that are so related to claims in the action within such original jurisdiction that they form part of the same case or controversy." *See also United Mine Workers v. Gibbs*, 383 U.S. 715 (1966). The standard test is whether the claims "derive from a common nucleus of operative fact." *Id.* In this problem, the tort and contract claims, which both derive from the sale of a car with defective brakes, are "so related" as to arise from the "same case or controversy," and the district court may, accordingly, take supplemental jurisdiction over the contract claim. None of the exceptions in § 1367(b) apply.

Point Two: <u>The State X federal district court cannot transfer the action to the federal court in State Y because</u>
(30-40%) <u>venue would not have been proper in State Y at the time the action was first filed.</u>

Seller's motion for a change of venue should be denied. In a diversity case, venue properly lies, and a civil action may only be brought, in a judicial district "where any defendant resides . . ." or "in which a substantial part of the events or omissions giving rise to the claim occurred . . ." 28 U.S.C. § 1391(a). At the time the case was commenced, Seller, the defendant, resided in State X. Moreover, all relevant events occurred in State X. Hence, at the time the suit was filed, venue was proper only in the State X federal district court.

Seller's subsequent move to State Y does not warrant a change of venue. The change of venue statute, 28 U.S.C. § 1404, permits a district court to transfer actions "for the convenience of parties and witnesses, in the interest of justice." However, a change of venue is only permitted "to any other district or division where [the case] *might have been* brought." *Id.*

The relevant time frame under both the basic venue statute and the venue transfer statute is the time that the suit is filed. As a consequence, the court should deny Seller's motion for a change of venue. At the time Buyer's suit was brought, the only possible venue was State X. As noted above, State X was both Seller's residence and the place where a substantial part of the events giving rise to Buyer's claim—the sale of the car and the accident—occurred. There was little or no connection between State Y and the events giving rise to the action. Accordingly, because the case could not have been brought in State Y, the requirements of § 1404 are not met, and the motion for a change of venue must be denied. It is irrelevant that Seller now resides in State Y.

In addition, it is possible to argue that discretionary factors also would justify denial of a transfer. Because the events occurred in State X, and most, if not all, of the witnesses are from State X (the mechanic, those responding to the accident, the hospital employees treating Buyer, and Friend), it can be argued that "the convenience of the parties and witnesses, and . . . the interests of justice" are all best served by permitting the case to go forward in State X.

NOTE: While an answer that mentioned only the discretionary factors might lead to a correct result, it would *not* be an adequate answer. The key point, which controls the result, is that the action could not have been brought originally in State Y and therefore could not be transferred there.

Federal Civil Procedure

(July 2005)

ANALYSIS

Legal Problems: (1) Does the federal district court have authority immediately and during the pendency of the lawsuit to enjoin Claire from violating the non-compete provision in the contract and/or from retaining the chem sheets and pricing information?

(2) Is the federal district court likely to enjoin Claire from violating the non-compete clause throughout the pendency of the lawsuit?

(3) Is the federal district court likely to compel Claire to return to Drugco the chem sheets and pricing information throughout the pendency of the lawsuit?

DISCUSSION

Summary

The district court has the power to issue a temporary restraining order, followed by a preliminary injunction, prohibiting Claire from soliciting customers in violation of her contract with Drugco. In determining whether to grant an injunction, the court will consider Drugco's likelihood of winning the lawsuit, the possibility of irreparable injury if the injunction is not granted, the balance of hardships between the parties, and any relevant public interest factors. The court will also consider the same factors in determining whether to issue a preliminary injunction ordering Claire to return Drugco's chem sheets and pricing information. On the facts of this problem, the court is likely to grant both preliminary injunctions.

Point One: The district court in State A has authority under Rule 65 of the Federal Rules of Civil
(10-20%) Procedure to issue a temporary restraining order prohibiting Claire from violating the non-compete provision in her contract, but such an order must expire within a few days and Drugco must seek a preliminary injunction.

A preliminary injunction is an equitable remedy that enjoins a person from engaging in specified behavior, or requires a party to engage in specified behavior, during the pendency of the action. A temporary restraining order (TRO) is an equitable remedy that may be issued *ex parte* (without notice) to prevent irreparable harm until the court has an opportunity to rule on a motion for a preliminary injunction. Rule 65 of the Federal Rules of Civil Procedure governs the issuance of both TROs and preliminary injunctions by federal district courts. Although the Federal Rules permit the issuance of a TRO without notice and on an *ex parte* basis, all TROs must expire within ten days, and courts generally set an earlier expiration date for TROs issued *ex parte*. Moreover, local rules may require that notice be given prior to the issuance of a TRO. *See generally* FED. R. CIV. P. 65(b). Rule 65(c) requires an applicant seeking either a TRO or a preliminary injunction to post bond or provide some other security in the event that a party is later "found to have been wrongfully enjoined or restrained." FED. R. CIV. P. 65(c).

Point Two: The district court may grant a preliminary injunction to enjoin Claire from violating
(45-55%) the non-compete provision in the contract during the pendency of the lawsuit if it finds that Drugco is likely to succeed on the merits of the lawsuit, that Drugco is likely to suffer irreparable injury if an injunction is not granted, and that the potential injury to Drugco is greater than any harm that Claire would suffer as a result of an injunction.

The substantive prerequisites for a preliminary injunction derive from traditional principles of equity jurisdiction. *See* 11A Charles Alan Wright et al., FEDERAL PRACTICE AND PROCEDURE § 2941 (2d ed. 1995). Courts generally consider four factors in deciding whether or not to grant a preliminary injunction: (1) the risk of irreparable harm to the plaintiff if the preliminary injunction is not granted; (2) the likelihood that the plaintiff will succeed on the merits; (3) the likelihood that the harm the plaintiff will suffer in the absence of preliminary injunctive relief outweighs the harm the defendant will suffer if the injunction is granted; and (4) the public interest. *Id.* The first two factors are the most important.

In assessing irreparable harm in the preliminary injunction context, courts ask whether the threatened harm would impair the court's ability to grant an effective remedy at the conclusion of the case. 11A Wright et al., *supra* § 2948.1. Numerous courts have granted preliminary injunctions to enforce non-compete clauses in employment agreements, concluding that an employer would suffer irreparable harm if a former employee solicited its customers. *See, e.g., Safety-Kleen Sys., Inc. v. Hennkens*, 301 F.3d 931, 935-36 (8th Cir. 2002); *JAK Prods., Inc. v. Wiza*, 986 F.2d 1080, 1084 (7th Cir. 1993). "[W]hen the failure to grant preliminary relief creates the possibility of permanent loss of customers to a competitor or the loss of goodwill, the irreparable injury prong is satisfied." *Multi-Channel TV Cable Co. v. Charlottesville Quality Cable Operating Co.*, 22 F.3d 546, 552 (4th Cir. 1994) (citation omitted).

In assessing whether the plaintiff is likely to prevail on the merits, courts most commonly ask whether the plaintiff has demonstrated "a reasonable probability of success. . . . All courts agree that plaintiff must present a prima facie case but need not show that he is certain to win." 11A Wright et al., *supra* § 2948.3 (footnotes omitted). In this case, both States A and B enforce non-compete clauses as long as they are reasonable in geographical scope and duration. Since Claire's contract with Drugco barred her from competing only within a three-county area of State A and only for one year, and since there is strong evidence that she is breaching the contract, a court is likely to conclude that Drugco will prevail on the merits.

In balancing the relative hardships, courts not only consider the injuries that the parties are likely to suffer, but also consider the likelihood of success on the merits. Thus, the stronger the showing on the merits, the less weight is given to the harm the defendant will suffer if the injunction is issued erroneously. Here, the harm to the plaintiff—the loss of customers—has already been discussed. The potential harm to the defendant—loss of her job or at least the inability to continue to work for Medico in the same geographical area for the remainder of the year—is likewise significant. But if the plaintiff demonstrates a substantial likelihood of success on the merits (as here), the preliminary injunction will be issued even if the harm factor favors the defendant. *See* 11A Wright et al., *supra* § 2948.3.

Finally, courts consider the public interest or policy considerations that militate in favor of or against issuance of the preliminary injunction. The decision here is not likely to have a significant impact on strangers to the litigation, so this factor is not likely to influence the outcome of the motion for preliminary injunctive relief.

On balance, it is likely that a court would issue a preliminary injunction to enjoin Claire from violating the non-compete provision in the contract during the pendency of the lawsuit. It is far less important that applicants reach this conclusion, however, than that they discuss intelligently Rule 65 and the factors that would guide the court's analysis.

Point Three: The district court in State A is likely to issue a preliminary injunction to compel Claire
(35-45%)   to return the chem sheets and pricing information to Drugco during the pendency of the
           lawsuit.

Just as Rule 65 allows a federal district court to issue an injunction restraining Claire's action, it also permits the court to issue an injunction compelling Claire to engage in particular acts (a "mandatory injunction") if the four-part test for a preliminary injunction is satisfied. On our facts, the four factors favor an order compelling Claire to return the chem sheets and pricing information.

First, the chem sheets, which reveal the chemical composition of the drugs sold by Drugco, are trade secrets, and their disclosure would give rise to irreparable harm. *See, e.g., Myers v. Williams*, 819 F. Supp. 919 (D. Or. 1993). Second, pricing information is highly confidential and Drugco's competitive position would be compromised if its pricing structure were available to a competitor. *See, e.g., Patio Enclosures, Inc. v. Herbst*, 39 Fed. Appx. 964, 968-69 (6th Cir. 2002). Such harm could not be remedied at the conclusion of the case, so preliminary relief is warranted.

Given that the chem sheets and pricing information are trade secrets under state law and given that the employment agreement required Claire to return them to Drugco upon termination of her employment, it is quite likely that Drugco will succeed on the merits of its claim to obtain the return of this data. Because neither Medico nor Claire is entitled to retain this information, the balance of hardships tips decidedly in favor of Drugco, and the public interest (as embodied in the law of States A and B) favors the preservation of trade secrets. Thus, it is likely that a court would issue a preliminary injunction to require Claire to return the chem sheets and pricing information during the pendency of the lawsuit.

NOTE: In addition to its authority to grant a preliminary injunction, the court also has authority to grant any preliminary remedy for the seizure of property that would be available under state law. *See* FED. R. CIV. P. 64. In some states, for example, a pre-judgment writ of replevin to secure the return of property is available to a movant who demonstrates a superior right of possession to the property and a likelihood of success on the merits of the underlying claim to possession. *See, e.g., Center Capital Corp. v. Burmac Metal Finishing Co.*, 2002 U.S. Dist. LEXIS 14872 (N.D. Ill. Aug. 13, 2002) (describing Illinois statute). Graders should consider awarding extra credit to applicants who note the possibility of pursuing state law replevin remedies as an alternative approach to recovering the chem sheets and pricing information.

Federal Civil Procedure

(February 2006)
ANALYSIS

Legal Problems: (1) (a)   Does a federal district court have federal question jurisdiction over a claim based on the state law of defamation when the plaintiff's complaint alleges that an anticipated First Amendment defense is invalid?

(1) (b)   Does a federal district court have diversity jurisdiction when the defendant previously resided in the same state as the plaintiff, still considers that state "home," and plans to return someday?

(2)   Can a federal district court in State A assert personal jurisdiction over a defendant whose activities occurred outside State A when those activities included posting allegedly defamatory material concerning a State A plaintiff on a website viewable by State A residents and when the defendant knows that the website is viewed by State A residents and derives revenue as a result of that fact?

DISCUSSION

Summary

Federal question jurisdiction is not available in this case because the complaint asserts a tort claim under state law. The well-pleaded complaint rule governs here; thus the negation of the federal defense in the complaint would not create federal question jurisdiction under 28 U.S.C. § 1331.

Whether the court has diversity jurisdiction over the case depends on whether Defendant is considered to have established a domicile in State B. If he is domiciled in State B, the parties are diverse and the amount in controversy is sufficient for jurisdiction. If he is still a State A domiciliary, then diversity is defeated. The matter can be argued either way, but the facts appear to support a conclusion that Defendant's current domicile is in State B because his intent is to remain and live there for the time being.

The question of personal jurisdiction over Defendant based on his publication of an alleged defamation over the Internet asks whether Defendant had sufficient contact with State A to justify the assertion of personal jurisdiction. Under the approach of most courts, this will turn on the degree to which Defendant targeted State A readers and the State A-based Plaintiff and published the story with knowledge that it might cause harm to Plaintiff in State A. A consideration of the "fairness/reasonableness" factors would also be necessary.

Point One(a): (10-20%)
<u>The federal district court does not have federal question jurisdiction because the complaint alleges a state law tort claim and federal issues exist only as a possible defense.</u>

Plaintiff's complaint does not raise a federal question but, instead, asserts a tort claim under state law. According to the well-pleaded complaint rule, a plaintiff's anticipation of a federal defense in the complaint does not create federal question jurisdiction. *Louisville & Nashville R.R. Co. v. Mottley,* 211 U.S. 149 (1908). Thus, Plaintiff's allegation that Defendant has no defense under the First Amendment does not, in itself, create subject-matter jurisdiction. 28 U.S.C. § 1332(a).

Point One(b): (30-40%)
<u>The federal district court will have subject-matter jurisdiction based on diversity of citizenship under 28 U.S.C. § 1332 only if Defendant is considered a domiciliary of State B.</u>

The complaint states a claim well in excess of the $75,000 jurisdictional threshold required for diversity jurisdiction. 28 U.S.C. § 1332(a). Thus, the question is whether there is complete diversity between Plaintiff and Defendant. *See Strawbridge v. Curtiss,* 7 U.S. 267 (1806) (establishing the rule of "complete diversity"). Plaintiff is a citizen of State A by virtue of her residence and domicile in State A. If Defendant is a citizen of State B, there is diversity. If Defendant is still a citizen of State A (where he lived until three years ago), then there is no diversity between Defendant and Plaintiff, and the court lacks jurisdiction.

For purposes of the diversity statute, a person is considered a citizen of the state in which he is domiciled. A person's domicile is his or her permanent home, the place where a person intends to remain indefinitely, and the place to which the person intends to return when temporarily absent. *See Mas v. Perry,* 489 F.2d 1396 (5th Cir. 1974).

Under the facts, there is a strong argument that State B has become Defendant's new domicile. He has lived there for three years; he votes, pays taxes, and owns property there. The center of his life appears to be State B, and he appears to intend to establish his permanent home there for the time being at least.

One might argue, on the other hand, that Defendant's expressed intent to return to State A someday and his statement that he views State A as his home mean that his domicile is still in State A; State B is but a temporary sojourn. While such an argument is plausible, the facts that Defendant's residence in State B has some permanence, that he treats it as his current permanent home for all purposes, and that he has no intention of returning to State A at any definite future time, make it most likely that a court would conclude that his domicile is in State B and that he has become a State B citizen for diversity purposes.

Point Two: (40-50%)
<u>Defendant may be subject to personal jurisdiction in State A because he appears intentionally to have targeted State A readers from his State B-based website.</u>

Under Rule 4(k)(1) of the Federal Rules of Civil Procedure, the federal district court can assert jurisdiction over a defendant who could be subjected to jurisdiction in the state courts of State A. Because of State A's long-arm statute (which is a general long-arm statute that extends to the constitutional limits), the only inquiry here is the constitutionality of the assertion of personal jurisdiction.

The Due Process Clause of the Fourteenth Amendment permits a court to exercise general personal jurisdiction over a foreign defendant when that defendant maintains substantial, continuous, and systematic contacts with the forum state. *See Helicopteros Nacionales v. Hall*, 466 U.S. 408 (1984). Where such contacts exist, the state may assert jurisdiction whether or not the claim is related to the defendant's contacts. Alternatively, a state may exercise specific personal jurisdiction where a nonresident defendant has purposefully availed itself of the benefits and protections of the forum state through minimum contacts, the claim arises out of or relates to those contacts, and the exercise of jurisdiction does not offend traditional notions of fair play and substantial justice. *International Shoe Co. v. Washington*, 326 U.S. 310 (1945).

Although the United States Supreme Court has not yet addressed the question of personal jurisdiction for Internet-based contacts, many lower courts have grappled with the question. Since websites on the Internet can be viewed everywhere, most courts have been reluctant to hold that the maintenance of a website alone is sufficient to subject the owner of the site to jurisdiction everywhere. One of the leading opinions is *Zippo Mfg. Co. v. Zippo Dot Com, Inc.*, 952 F. Supp. 1119 (W.D. Pa. 1997). *Zippo* suggested that the more interactive a website, the more likely courts should be to uphold personal jurisdiction, and that a purely passive website would not be sufficient to establish jurisdiction. Here, because Defendant's website, www.NBT.com, is passive, that is, it does not enable viewers to interact by posting their own messages, general jurisdiction based solely on the newsletter's accessibility across the United States would be unlikely.

However, Defendant did more than simply maintain a website that was accessed by State A residents. Defendant's website was largely devoted to commentary and reporting on events in State A, and Defendant knew (and profited from) the fact that many of his readers came from that area. In *Calder v. Jones*, 465 U.S. 783 (1984), the U.S. Supreme Court held that a California court could exercise jurisdiction over a Florida writer and a Florida editor of a defamatory article about a California resident's conduct in California. The Court reasoned that the defendants knew that their magazine (the *National Enquirer*) had its largest circulation in California and that the injury would be felt by the plaintiff in her home state. Under those circumstances, the defendants must have reasonably anticipated being haled into court in California when sued for the defamatory nature of their article. Lower courts have applied the logic of *Calder* to uphold jurisdiction where defamatory communications over the Internet intentionally targeted readers in the plaintiff's home state. *See Young v. New Haven Advocate*, 315 F.3d 256, 258 (4th Cir. 2002) (rejecting jurisdiction where Internet posting did not manifest intent to target audience in forum state); *Wagner v. Miskin*, 660 N.W.2d 593 (N.D. 2003) (upholding jurisdiction where Internet communication did target forum resident).

In this case, the facts likewise suggest a targeting of State A readers and a State A plaintiff in such a way that Defendant could "reasonably anticipate" being haled into State A courts to answer a complaint by Plaintiff against him. Not only did Defendant know that State A readers were likely to view his website, but Defendant could reasonably predict that the impact of the article would be felt by Plaintiff in State A. In addition, Defendant's commentary concerned actions taken in part in State A.

Although Defendant has not engaged in any physical conduct in State A, his targeting of a State A resident, the commercial benefits he derives from serving State A readers, and the large State A readership he has all add up to a strong case for specific personal jurisdiction over Defendant for purposes of this action. State A has a strong interest in the case, Plaintiff has a strong interest in having it tried in State A, and the needs of interstate commerce would be served if defendants who cause harm through instruments of commerce (e.g., the Internet) were subject to being held to account where foreseeable harm occurs, at least if the defendant's primary business activity is directed at the forum state. *Cf. Asahi Metal Industry Co. v. Superior Court*, 480 U.S. 102 (1987) (unreasonable to exercise jurisdiction in absence of forum interest, when defendant had no commercial or other ties to forum apart from product ending up there through stream of commerce). On the other hand, the proper reach of state court jurisdiction in Internet cases has not been definitively decided, and courts may be reluctant to extend jurisdiction to reach a defendant who, like Defendant, does not actively reach out to State A readers but simply maintains a passive website to which State A readers can direct their web browsers should they so choose.

Federal Civil Procedure

(July 2006)

ANALYSIS

Legal Problems:

(1)   Can Smith Brothers Transport assert a statute-of-limitations bar to an action when it was added to the action by an amended complaint filed after the applicable statute of limitations had run?

(2)   May a defendant immediately appeal a judge's denial of a motion to dismiss when the defendant claims that an action against it is barred by the statute of limitations?

(3)   Does the trial court have the power to dismiss a party's defense and enter default judgment against the party because the party's attorney failed to appear at a pretrial conference?

DISCUSSION
Summary

Pat's amendment of her complaint to name the proper defendant, Smith Brothers Transport, meets the requirements necessary for the amendment to relate back to the date of the original pleading. Thus, Pat's action against Smith Brothers Transport should be treated as timely filed, notwithstanding that Smith Brothers Transport was not added to the action until after the limitations period had run. The trial judge therefore correctly denied the motion to dismiss.

Smith Brothers Transport may not immediately appeal the denial of its motion to dismiss. The denial of a motion to dismiss is not a final judgment, and the judge's order in this case does not fall within any of the exceptions to the final judgment rule. Thus, the decision may be appealed only after the trial is concluded and the judgment is final.

Driver's attorney failed to appear as ordered at the pretrial conference because Driver didn't wish to discuss settlement. Although a trial judge has the power to sanction such behavior, including by entering a default judgment, the sanction in this case was probably so harsh as to be an abuse of discretion, at least absent other misbehavior by Driver or evidence that a lesser sanction would have been ineffective in securing future adherence to the judge's orders.

Point One (30-40%)
Because Pat's amended complaint was served on Smith Brothers Transport within the time for original service of process under Fed. R. Civ. P. 4(m), and because Smith Brothers Transport knew or should have known of the mistaken identity and would not be prejudiced by the delay, the court properly allowed the amended complaint to relate back to the date of the original filing.

Federal Rule of Civil Procedure 15(a) allows a complaint to be amended "once as a matter of course at any time before a responsive pleading is served." Thus, Pat's complaint was properly amended. *See* 6 Charles Alan Wright, et al., FEDERAL PRACTICE & PROCEDURE 2d ed. §§ 1484 & 1487 (1990) [hereinafter "FEDERAL PRACTICE & PROCEDURE"].

Not only can Pat amend her complaint to name the proper defendant, Smith Brothers Transport, but her amendment will "relate back to the date of the original pleading" if certain requirements are met. An amendment that "changes the party or the naming of the party against whom a claim is asserted" relates back to the date of the original pleading when:

- the claim asserted in the amended pleading "arose out of the conduct, transaction, or occurrence set forth or attempted to be set forth in the original pleading," and
- within 120 days of the original filing of the action (the normal time limit for service of the summons and complaint under Fed. R. Civ. P. 4(m)), the new party "has received such notice of the institution of the action" that it will "not be prejudiced in maintaining a defense on the merits," and the new party
- "knew or should have known that, but for a mistake concerning the identity of the proper party, the action would have been brought against" it.

Fed. R. Civ. P. 15(c).

Each of these requirements for relation back is met here. The amended complaint asserted the same claim, arising out of the same occurrence, as had been originally asserted against Smith Brothers Trucking, thus satisfying the first requirement. As to the second requirement, the facts suggest that both the original summons and complaint and the amended summons and complaint were served within the 120-day summons period. Given that Smith Brothers Trucking and Smith Brothers Transport have common owners, common premises, and the same agent for service of process (Robert Smith), either service of the summons and complaint would have given Smith Brothers Transport sufficient "notice of the institution of the action" that it would "not be prejudiced in maintaining" its defense.

Robert Smith received notice of the commencement of the original action and at that point he "should have known" that a lawsuit was being filed for Pat's accident and that a mistake had been made as to the proper defendant. Even if he did not know at that point, he surely knew when the amended complaint was served. Thus, the amendment naming Smith Brothers Transport relates back to the date of the original filing, and the motion to dismiss on statute of limitations grounds should be denied. *See Roberts v. Michaels*, 219 F.3d 775 (8th Cir. 2000); *Bowles v. Reade*, 198 F.3d 752 (9th Cir. 1999); *VKK Corp. v. Nat'l Football League*, 244 F.3d 114 (2d Cir. 2001). *See also* 6A FEDERAL PRACTICE & PROCEDURE § 1498 at 22-23 (2004 Supp.).

Point Two (30-40%)
<u>Because defendant Smith Brothers Transport's appeal does not fall within any of the exceptions to the final judgment rule, the denial of the motion to dismiss may be appealed only after the trial is concluded and the judgment is final.</u>

In most cases, a party may appeal only from a final judgment. *See* Larry L. Tepley & Ralph U. Whitten, CIVIL PROCEDURE 930-32 (3d ed. 2004). A final judgment is a controlling and dispositive order that "ends the litigation on the merits and leaves nothing for the court to do but execute on the judgment." *Catlin v. United States*, 324 U.S. 229, 233 (1945). In addition, Fed. R. Civ. P. 54(b) allows a trial judge to sever portions of a multi-claim case for appeal with a finding that "there is no just reason for delay" and with a direction for the entry of judgment on the decided claim(s) or defense(s). But unless this is done, early decided claims must ordinarily await final judgment as to all claims before they are eligible for appeal. Under either the standard final judgment rule or Fed. R. Civ. P. 54(b), Smith Brothers Transport cannot appeal the denial of its motion to dismiss. Rather than ending the litigation on the merits or terminating a particular claim, the trial judge's decision allowed the litigation to continue. Smith Brothers Transport was joined to the action and now faces trial.

This issue also does not qualify for any of the statutory exceptions to the final judgment rule. It is not an interlocutory appeal from an order granting or dissolving an injunction, *see* 28 U.S.C. § 1292(a), and it does not qualify as a certified appeal because the trial judge refused to certify the question, *see* 28 U.S.C. § 1292(b).

The judge-made collateral order exception to the final judgment rule is also inapplicable. The collateral order rule allows an immediate appeal from an order that (1) "finally determine[s]" a "claim of right," (2) that is separable from, and collateral to, the rights asserted in the main action, and (3) that is "too important to be denied review." *Cohen v. Beneficial Industrial Loan Corp.*, 337 U.S. 541, 546 (1949). The Court restated the doctrine in *Coopers & Lybrand v. Livesay*: "To come within the small class of decisions excepted from the final judgment rule by *Cohen*, the order must conclusively determine the disputed question, resolve an important issue completely separate from the merits of the action, and be effectively unreviewable on appeal from a final judgment." 437 U.S. 463, 468 (1978). The denial of Smith Brothers Transport's motion to dismiss fails on all counts. It does not conclusively determine the disputed question (whether the statute of limitations has run), the issue is not completely separate from the merits, but is instead intertwined with the merits, and the question is reviewable on appeal.

[NOTE: A writ of mandamus may sometimes be used to secure review of a trial court's action. Mandamus is a drastic remedy, to be used only when justice demands and less extraordinary remedies are unavailable. *Kerr v. United States*, 426 U.S. 394, 402 (1976). Mandamus is generally used by an appellate court "to prevent a district court from acting beyond its [subject matter] jurisdiction, or to compel it to take action that it lacks the power to withhold." 16 FEDERAL PRACTICE & PROCEDURE § 3932 at 472, citing *Will v. United States*, 389 U.S. 90 (1967). On the facts of this problem, mandamus is inappropriate because the trial court's decision in no way involved action beyond the court's power. To the contrary, the trial court clearly has the power under the Federal Rules to permit an amendment of a complaint to relate back to the date of the original complaint for statute-of-limitations purposes. Thus, there was no abuse of power here.]

Point Three (30-40%)

The trial judge may have abused her discretion in entering a default judgment against Driver for his attorney's failure to appear at the pretrial conference, at least absent any other instances of misbehavior by Driver or his attorney or any evidence that lesser sanctions would not work.

Federal Rule of Civil Procedure 16 authorizes a district judge to convene pretrial conferences for the purpose of ensuring that cases are processed effectively and efficiently. Although courts are not required to hold a pretrial conference, *see* FED. R. CIV. P. 16(a), once a conference is ordered, appearance is compulsory. *See Identiseal Corp. v. Positive Identification Sys., Inc.*, 560 F.2d 298, 301-02 (7th Cir. 1977). The scheduling and running of pretrial conferences is largely within the trial court's discretion. Moreover, the court has the power to sanction a party or the party's attorney if "no appearance is made on behalf of [the] party at a . . . pretrial conference." FED. R. CIV. P. 16(f). Possible sanctions include any order authorized under Fed. R. Civ. P. 37(b)(2)(B), (C), & (D), including "[a]n order striking out pleadings . . . or dismissing the action . . . or rendering a judgment by default against the disobedient party."

Thus, the trial judge had the power to sanction Driver for the nonappearance of Driver's attorney. Moreover, the sanction imposed (striking Driver's pleading and rendering judgment against him) is authorized by the rules. Nonetheless, Driver may prevail on appeal if he can show that the trial judge abused her discretion in light of the facts and the severity of the sanction. *See Link v. Wabash R.R. Co.*, 370 U.S. 626 (1962).

Driver's attorney stated that he did not attend the pretrial conference because Driver was unwilling to settle the case and, accordingly, did not want the attorney to waste money by attending an unnecessary hearing. This explanation of non-attendance is plainly inadequate. Pretrial conferences have multiple purposes. In addition to facilitating settlement, they are used to establish early court control over an action to ensure good case management and to discourage "wasteful pretrial activities." Driver's assessment that his attorney's attendance at the conference would be a "waste" does not justify the disregard of the court's order.

Nonetheless, the court's sanction against Driver was probably so harsh as to be an abuse of discretion. Dismissal of an action or the entry of a default judgment are the most severe sanctions available to a district court and are usually appropriate "only when [a party's] misconduct is serious, repeated, contumacious, extreme, or otherwise inexcusable." *Bachier-Ortiz v. Colon-Mendoza*, 331 F.3d 193, 195 (1st Cir. 2003). Lesser sanctions should be utilized before the more extreme sanctions, absent reason to believe that lesser sanctions would be ineffective to secure compliance with court orders. *See Berry v. CIGNA/RSI-CIGNA*, 975 F.2d 1188 (5th Cir. 1992). Absent additional facts showing repeated defiance of the court or the likely ineffectiveness of lesser sanctions, the trial judge's decision to enter a default judgment in this case was probably an abuse of her discretion to "make such orders [with regard to the attorney's failure to attend the conference] as are just." FED. R. CIV. P. 16(f).

Federal Civil Procedure

(February 2007)

ANALYSIS

Legal Problems: (1)   Are accident and investigative reports discoverable when they are prepared in the ordinary course of business and not in anticipation of any immediately pending litigation?

   (2)   Is information in a bus operator's personnel file about the operator's driving record, safety record, and disciplinary record discoverable in an action against the bus operator's employer that alleges the bus operator was driving negligently?

DISCUSSION

Summary

The motion to compel should be granted in part and denied in part. Federal Rule of Civil Procedure 37(a) provides that a party may be compelled to provide discovery. Here, the accident and investigative reports are not trial preparation materials that are protected under Fed. R. Civ. P. 26(b)(3). They are routine reports that were not prepared in anticipation of litigation. Records in the operator's personnel file regarding his driving and safety record are relevant and discoverable under Fed. R. Civ. P. 26(b)(1). That information is related to his driving skills and his employer's potential liability. On the other hand, the operator's disciplinary records may not be discoverable. While some disciplinary information may relate to the issues in the case, other disciplinary information may have nothing whatever to do with the bus operator's driving skills, and its disclosure would serve simply to harass and embarrass the bus operator. A court may order an *in camera* review to excise irrelevant material before allowing release of the personnel file.

Point One (35-45%)

The motion to compel production of the accident and investigative reports should be granted because they were not prepared in anticipation of litigation.

Under Fed. R. Civ. P. 26(b)(1), a party "may obtain discovery regarding any matter, not privileged, that is relevant to [a] claim or defense" in the action. Relevant information is discoverable even if it would be inadmissible at trial, so long as "the discovery appears reasonably calculated to lead to the discovery of admissible evidence." FED. R. CIV. P. 26(b)(1). There is no question that the bus operator's accident report and his supervisor's investigative report satisfy this relevancy requirement.

On the other hand, Fed. R. Civ. P. 26(b)(3) protects trial preparation materials from discovery. Materials "prepared in anticipation of litigation or for trial by [a] party" are discover-able only if the party seeking discovery can show a "substantial need" for the materials and an inability "without undue hardship to obtain the substantial equivalent of the materials by other means." FED. R. CIV. P. 26(b)(3).

Thus, the crucial question is whether the accident reports that the bus operator and the supervisor completed were "prepared in anticipation of litigation" within the meaning of this rule. *Broadnax v. ABF Freight Sys., Inc.*, 180 F.R.D. 343, 346 (N.D. Ill. 1998). On the facts of this problem, they were not. Both the bus operator's report and the supervisor's report appear to be standard Transit Authority business records that are routinely prepared in the event of an accident. The facts say that the bus operator was following standard procedure when he called his supervisor and when he completed the "Operator's Report of Accident" form. Similarly, the supervisor was following standard procedure when she went to the accident scene and completed the "Supervisor's Investigative Report" form. While Transit Authority may honestly claim that it has such procedures precisely because it "anticipates" that there may be litigation whenever there is an accident, routinely prepared records that are completed in the regular course of business do not become trial preparation materials merely because the business anticipates that they might be useful in litigation.

The timing for completion of the reports supports the conclusion that they were not prepared in anticipation of litigation. The bus operator began to complete his report immediately after the accident occurred. The supervisor completed the investigative report on the same day of the accident and within one hour of the time that the accident occurred. Accident and investigative reports like the ones described here are protected from discovery only when they are prepared in response to a threat of imminent litigation. *Id.*; *Wikel v. Wal-Mart Stores, Inc.*, 197 F.R.D. 493 (N.D. Okla. 2000). There was no threat of litigation when these reports were completed. Therefore, these materials are discoverable. *Id.*; *see also* FED. R. CIV. P. 26(b)(3) (Advisory Committee's note).

Point Two (55-65%)

Under Fed. R. Civ. P. 26(b)(1), the bus operator's driving and safety records are relevant because they address his driving skills and care in a case that involves his alleged negligent driving, but his disciplinary record may not be relevant. Thus, the court is likely to order disclosure of the personnel file, but it may restrict disclosure or use of the information in some fashion.

As noted above, parties to an action "may obtain discovery regarding any matter, not privileged, which is relevant to the claim or defense of any party." FED. R. CIV. P. 26(b)(1). Even if not directly relevant to a claim or defense, a matter that is relevant to the general "subject matter involved in the action" may be discovered if the court determines that there is good cause for such discovery. *Hill v. Motel 6*, 205 F.R.D. 490, 492 (S.D. Ohio 2001). The facts and the circumstances of each particular case determine the relevancy of information that a party seeks during discovery. *Id.* Accordingly, in its discretion, and in light of the facts of each case, the court decides whether requested information is relevant. *Coleman v. American Red Cross*, 23 F.3d 1091, 1096 (6th Cir. 1994).

Personnel records are discoverable, *Goldman v. Checker Taxi Co.*, 325 F.2d 853 (7th Cir. 1963), despite frequent claims that they should be protected for privacy reasons, *Gohring v. Case Corp.*, 43 F.3d 340, 342-43 (7th Cir. 1994). Where discovery is resisted, the court must balance the interest of the party seeking discovery against any alleged privacy interest that would be infringed by disclosure. *Eckstein Marine Serv., Inc. v. M/V Basin Pride*, 168 F.R.D. 38 (W.D. La. 1996).

Here, Tourist has alleged that the bus operator was negligent. To the extent that the driving and safety records in the personnel file include material about this accident, they are clearly relevant to Tourist's claim. The bus operator's more general driving and safety records are a closer question. If they reveal a pattern of poor driving, they might be relevant to the claim against Transit Authority.

Even if it cannot be shown that the driving and safety information is directly relevant to the specific claim in this case, this seems a good case for showing good cause to compel production of the information because it is relevant to the subject matter of the lawsuit. An investigation of the bus operator's driving and safety record might lead to information of direct benefit to Tourist's case. Therefore, information in the bus operator's personnel file about his driving skills, including his driving record and any other accident reports, is discoverable. The motion to compel production of the personnel file should be granted, with respect to the driving records.

Regarding the bus operator's disciplinary records, the discovery request is much more troubling. The personnel record may well contain disciplinary information about the bus operator that could be entirely irrelevant to the action and that would be embarrassing and damaging to the bus operator if disclosed (*e.g.*, that he has been disciplined for sexual harassment). On the other hand, it is conceivable that the records might include evidence that could bolster Tourist's case, such as evidence of disciplinary action taken against the bus operator for driving-related behavior.

Under these circumstances, a court may limit Tourist's access to the bus operator's personnel files by restricting access to those portions deemed clearly relevant to the action. *See Rintchen v. Walker*, 1996 WL 238701 at *4 (E.D. Pa. 1996) (requiring defendants in an action alleging driving negligence to make available information in a personnel file including driving records and disciplinary records related to his driving skills, but forbidding disclosure of other information). Alternatively, a court might order an *in camera* review of the records to determine whether they contain anything of "a particularly sensitive or private nature" that warrants protection. *See Eckstein Marine Serv.*, 168 F.R.D. at 40-41. Or, a court may order release of the entire file but enter a confidentiality order restricting access to the file to attorneys and parties reviewing it for purposes of the litigation. *Id.*

Federal Civil Procedure

(July 2007)

ANALYSIS

<u>Legal Problems:</u>

(1)(a) What are the requirements for an action to be removed from a state court to a federal court?

(1)(b) Are those requirements met in a suit against a decedent's estate executor who is a citizen of the same state as the plaintiff but the decedent was not?

(2)(a) Can the default judgment against Bert have preclusive effect in subsequent cases even though Bert never appeared to defend himself?

(2)(b) Is Bert's claim against Al so closely related to Al's original claim that Bert is barred from raising it in a subsequent action?

DISCUSSION

Summary

Bert's tort action against Al's estate raises a state law claim and may be removed to federal court only if the federal court would have had diversity jurisdiction over the action had it originally been filed in that court. Moreover, the case cannot be removed if any defendant is a citizen of the state in which the case is pending. In this case, removal was proper. The amount in controversy clearly exceeds the $75,000 threshold. Although Executor is a citizen of State B and not diverse from Bert, she is a party to the action only in her capacity as a representative of Al's estate, and for diversity and removal purposes she is "deemed to be a citizen only of the same state as the decedent." Thus, Executor is treated as a State A citizen, the diversity requirements are met, and removal is appropriate.

Bert's action is barred by the default judgment in the prior suit between Bert and Al and should therefore be dismissed by the federal court. A default judgment is conclusive and binding on the parties if, as here, the rendering court had jurisdiction over the subject matter and the parties. Bert's claim against Al arose out of the same transaction or occurrence as Al's original claim, and the same evidence would have been relevant to the disposition of both claims. Under Federal Rule of Civil Procedure 13(a), Bert's claim was a compulsory counterclaim which Bert was required to raise in the initial action and, under standard rules of preclusion, Bert is barred from bringing a subsequent action asserting that claim.

Point One(a) (25-35%)

Removal of a case from a state court is appropriate if the federal court in that state would have original jurisdiction over the action and the defendant is not a citizen of that state.

An action filed in state court may be removed to the federal district court of the district where the state action is pending if the district court has "original jurisdiction" over the action. 28 U.S.C. § 1441(a). The federal court would have jurisdiction over Bert's state law tort action against Al only if the requirements of diversity are met. The amount in controversy must exceed $75,000 and the parties must be diverse (citizens of different states). 28 U.S.C. § 1332. In addition, removal by a defendant is prohibited if the defendant is a citizen of the state where the action is pending. 28 U.S.C. § 1441(b).

Point One(b) (25-35%)

Because Executor is "deemed to be a citizen only of the same state as the decedent," the parties to the state court action were diverse and the case was properly removable to the federal court pursuant to the court's diversity jurisdiction.

The requirements for removal are met here. Bert's complaint seeks damages of $3 million for personal injuries leading to permanent disability. This clearly exceeds the required amount in controversy, and there is nothing to suggest that the damage claim is not made in good faith. The parties are diverse because diversity depends on the citizenship of Bert and the decedent, Al, not the citizenship of Bert and Executor. Although Executor is the named defendant, for diversity purposes Executor is "deemed to be a citizen only of the same state as the decedent," the person whose interest she represents. 28 U.S.C. § 1332(c)(2). The decedent, Al, was a citizen of State A and therefore was diverse from Bert, a State B citizen. The requirements of diversity jurisdiction were therefore satisfied and the case is removable.

Moreover, although the removal statute forbids a defendant from removing a case to federal court on the basis of diversity jurisdiction if the defendant is a citizen of the state where the action is pending, see 28 U.S.C. § 1441(b), the rule that an executor or administrator of an estate is deemed to be a citizen *only* of the state in which the decedent was a citizen is applicable here as well. 28 U.S.C. §1332(c)(2). Because Executor is treated as a State A citizen, removal was appropriate.

Point Two(a) (15-25%)

A default judgment is entitled to preclusive effect, subject only to the requirements that the rendering court had subject matter jurisdiction and personal jurisdiction over the defendant and that the defendant had notice of the action and an opportunity to appear and defend himself. Those requirements are met here.

A default judgment rendered by a court is entitled to preclusive effect so long as the court had subject matter and personal jurisdiction over the action and the parties. *See Sewell v. Merrill Lynch*, 94 F.3d 1514 (11th Cir. 1996); *Orca Yachts LLC v. Mollicam Inc.*, 287 F.3d 316, 318 (4th Cir. 2002). Although Bert did not appear and defend himself in the original action, the federal court clearly had jurisdiction over the action and over Bert. The parties were diverse (Bert was from State B and Al from State A) and the amount in controversy (the value of Al's automobile) exceeded $75,000. Moreover, as Bert was a citizen of the state in which the action was pending, and was domiciled in the state at the time, the court had personal jurisdiction over him. The facts also state that Bert was properly served and had notice of the action.

Point Two(b) (25-35%)

The judgment in the prior suit between Al and Bert precludes Bert from asserting his personal injury claim because that claim was a compulsory counterclaim that should have been raised in the original action.

Because the judgment in Al's suit against Bert was rendered by a federal court sitting in diversity, its judgment will be given the same preclusive effect as would be given under State B law to a State B state court judgment (because State B is the state in which the judgment-rendering court was located). *See Semtek Int'l Inc. v. Lockheed Martin Corp.*, 531 U.S. 497 (2001). The precise preclusive effect that should be given to a default judgment is subject to some variance among the states, *see, e.g.*, RESTATEMENT (SECOND) OF JUDGMENTS § 22 and comments (1982), but on this issue there is substantial uniformity. It is widely accepted that a default judgment bars the losing party from asserting defenses that could have been raised in the action or claims that were subject to a compulsory counterclaim statute or rule in the original action. *See generally* 3 MOORE'S FEDERAL PRACTICE § 13.14 (3d ed.).

The federal compulsory counterclaim rule, Federal Rule of Civil Procedure 13(a), would have required Bert to bring his claim against Al in the first action, had Bert actually defended that action. Rule 13(a) requires a defendant to "state as a counterclaim any claim" that he or she has against the plaintiff if the claim "arises out of the transaction or occurrence that is the subject matter" of the plaintiff's claim. Here, Bert's claim against Al for damages arises out of the same occurrence (the traffic accident) as Al's previous claim against Bert. Moreover, key issues of law and fact raised by both claims would be the same as both claims involve the basic question of who was at fault in the accident. Much of the evidence that would support or refute Al's claim against Bert is likely to be relevant to Bert's claim against Al. In short, the two claims are logically, factually, and transactionally related. These are precisely the circumstances under which the federal rules require Bert to assert his claim as a counterclaim. *See generally Tank Insulation Int'l, Inc. v. Insultherm, Inc.*, 104 F.3d 83, 85-86 (5th Cir. 1997). Because Bert's claim for damages was a compulsory counterclaim that should have been raised in the original action, the judgment in that original action bars the claim. It does not matter that Bert did not actually litigate in the prior case but merely allowed a default judgment to be entered against him.

[NOTE: Because the question of the preclusive effect of this judgment involves the effect of the federal counterclaim rule, some applicants might argue that the preclusion issue is governed by federal law and not by state preclusion rules. *Cf. Semtek*, 531 U.S. 497, 508 (state law governs the preclusive effect of a diversity judgment *absent substantial federal concern*). But it does not really matter whether an applicant concludes that state or federal preclusion rules apply. The basic rule—that a default judgment bars the defendant from raising in future litigation a claim that was subject to a compulsory counterclaim statute or rule in the original litigation—is well established in state and federal practice.]

Federal Civil Procedure
(February 2008)

ANALYSIS

Legal Problems: (1) Under Rule 50 of the Federal Rules of Civil Procedure, can a post-judgment motion for judgment as a matter of law be granted if the defendant moved for judgment as a matter of law at the close of the plaintiff's evidence but did not move for judgment as a matter of law at the close of all the evidence?

 (2) Should a court reject a jury verdict and grant judgment as a matter of law on the basis that the losing party's evidence was more persuasive than the evidence of the party in whose favor the jury ruled?

 (3) Should a court grant a motion for a new trial if the movant shows that the movant's evidence was more persuasive and more credible than the opponent's evidence?

 (4) Should a court grant a motion for a new trial on the ground that a juror during voir dire withheld information suggesting that she would be biased against one of the parties in the suit?

DISCUSSION

Summary

In Plaintiff's employment discrimination suit against Corporation, the post-trial motion by Corporation for judgment as a matter of law (JMOL) should be denied. First, Corporation did not move for JMOL at the close of all the evidence as required by Rule 50(b) of the Federal Rules of Civil Procedure. Corporation's motion at the close of Plaintiff's evidence does not satisfy the Rule's requirement. Second, Corporation's arguments in support of the motion do not state grounds sufficient for entering judgment for Corporation as a matter of law.

On the other hand, Corporation's motion for a new trial under Rule 59 of the Federal Rules of Civil Procedure may have merit. Corporation does not face a procedural bar such as that precluding its post-judgment motion for JMOL. Corporation's alternative motion for a new trial should be granted if Corporation can show that the jury's verdict was clearly against the weight of the evidence and a miscarriage of justice, or if a juror failed to reveal information indicating a strong bias against Corporation. It is unlikely that Corporation can show that the verdict is clearly against the weight of the evidence, but Corporation should be able to show juror bias.

Point One (20–30%)

Because Corporation failed to move for judgment as a matter of law at the close of all the evidence, Rule 50(b) bars it from moving for judgment as a matter of law after trial.

Under Rule 50(b) of the Federal Rules of Civil Procedure, a party may make a motion for judgment as a matter of law ("JMOL"; also called a judgment notwithstanding the verdict or JNOV) if the party makes the motion no later than 10 days after entry of judgment and if the party previously made a motion for JMOL at the close of all the evidence. Here, the defendant made its post-verdict motion in a timely manner, but it did not make an earlier JMOL motion "at the close of all the evidence." Even though Corporation moved for JMOL at the close of plaintiff's evidence, it must make the motion again at the close of the record or it loses its right to renew the motion after entry of judgment. Moreover, a post-trial motion for judgment can be granted only on grounds advanced in such a pre-verdict motion. *See, e.g.,* STEVEN BAICKER-MCKEE, WILLIAM M. JANSSEN & JOHN B. CORR, A STUDENT'S GUIDE TO THE FEDERAL RULES OF CIVIL PROCEDURE 800 (10th ed. 2007).

The federal courts are divided on how strictly to enforce Rule 50(b) when a party has moved for judgment at the close of the plaintiff's case but not at the close of all the evidence. Some circuits have required strict compliance and have held that a motion at the close of plaintiff's case never is sufficient to support a renewed motion for JMOL. *See, e.g., Mid-America Tablewares, Inc. v. Mogi Trading Co.*, 100 F.3d 1353, 1364 (7th Cir. 1996). Courts in these circuits would deny Corporation's renewed motion because no JMOL motion was made at the close of all evidence.

Other circuit courts have held that, if a JMOL motion was made at the close of plaintiff's case, the failure to again move at the close of all the evidence need not be fatal to a post-verdict motion if the evidence introduced by the defendant was brief and could not have possibly changed the court's decision on the earlier motion. *See, e.g., BE & K Constr. Co. v. United Bhd. of Carpenters & Joiners*, 90 F.3d 1318, 1325 (8th Cir. 1996). *See generally* 11 CHARLES ALAN WRIGHT & ARTHUR R. MILLER, FEDERAL PRACTICE AND PROCEDURE § 2537 n. 10 (3d ed. 2007). This exception would not help Corporation here, however, because the witness testimony it presented in defense was substantial and could well have changed the trial court's view on the merits of the motion if Corporation had made that motion at the close of all evidence after presenting its own case.

Thus, Corporation is now precluded from renewing its JMOL motion.

Point Two (20–30%)
Even if Corporation had preserved its right to file (or "renew") the motion for JMOL after the verdict, the motion should still be denied because Corporation has not advanced arguments that justify granting such a motion.

A motion for JMOL at the close of all the evidence, or a renewed motion after the return of the verdict, can be granted only if "there is no legally sufficient evidentiary basis for a reasonable jury" to find for the party opposing the movant. FED. R. CIV. P. 50(a). In ruling on such a motion, the trial judge is not authorized to weigh the evidence, pass on credibility of witnesses, or otherwise substitute the judge's view of the evidence for the jury's view. The standard expressed in Rule 50(a) makes clear that the grant of a motion for JMOL is "a performance of the court's duty to assure enforcement of the controlling law and is not an intrusion on any responsibility for factual determinations conferred on the jury by the Seventh Amendment." FED. R. CIV. P. 50 advisory committee's notes to 1991 Amendment. This standard is also used as a reference point for entry of summary judgment under Rule 56. *See Anderson v. Liberty Lobby,* 477 U.S. 242, 250–51 (1986).

Thus, Corporation's argument that its evidence was more persuasive and more credible than Plaintiff's evidence does not provide the court with a basis for overturning the jury's verdict. Even if true, the superior strength of Corporation's evidence does not mean that the jury acted unreasonably by returning a verdict for Plaintiff. Similarly, even if the trial judge agrees with Corporation that its witnesses were more credible than the witnesses for Plaintiff, that fact still would be insufficient to support a motion for JMOL. Assessments of witness credibility are core jury functions, and Rule 50 does not give the judge license to usurp that core function.

The verdict may be overturned only if, on the basis of the evidence, no reasonable jury could have found that Plaintiff had met her burden of proof. *See* WRIGHT & MILLER, *supra,* § 2524. Here the jury had an objective, reasonable basis for accepting Plaintiff's version of the facts: the suspicious timing of Plaintiff's firing and the testimony by a witness to the discriminatory statements by Plaintiff's supervisor. Even if the trial court thinks the jury erred, the trial court should defer to the jury's choice between competing versions of events when the jury choice is reasonably based on the evidence presented in the case. *Tennant v. Peoria & Pekin Union Rwy. Co.,* 321 U.S. 29, 35 (1944).

[NOTE TO GRADERS: The fact that a juror withheld evidence of possible bias against Corporation, while a potentially serious problem, would not warrant a JMOL in Corporation's favor. However, as explained below, the fact of such undisclosed bias might support an order for a new trial.]

Point Three (20–30%)

Corporation's alternative motion for a new trial should be granted if the court is convinced that the jury's verdict was clearly against the weight of the evidence and a miscarriage of justice, but such a result is unlikely here.

Corporation's motion for new trial was filed within 10 days of the entry of judgment, as required by Rule 59(b). Unlike motions for JMOL under Rule 50, no pre-verdict motions are required in order to make the post-verdict motion for new trial. Thus, Corporation's alternative motion for new trial is procedurally proper and can be considered on the merits.

Rule 59 does not specify any standard for the granting of a new trial, but instead provides that such motions can be granted "for any of the reasons for which new trials have heretofore been granted in actions at law in courts of the United States." In effect, Rule 59 gives the trial judge power and discretion to prevent a miscarriage of justice. Because an order for a new trial is not a final judgment, such motions are more freely granted than are motions for JMOL. In general, the grounds for a new trial are that the verdict is against the weight of the evidence, that the damages are excessive, or that for other reasons—such as errors of law—the trial was not fair. *See* WRIGHT & MILLER, *supra,* §§ 2805, 2806. Where the court is convinced that a mistake has been made, such as where the prevailing party's witnesses were wholly lacking in credibility, a new trial may be ordered. On a motion for new trial, unlike a motion for JMOL, the court is not required to view the evidence in the light most favorable to the verdict winner. *Id.* § 2806.

In this case, the first ground offered in support of the motion is Corporation's argument that its evidence was more persuasive and more credible than Plaintiff's evidence. Because the court is free to weigh the evidence itself on a motion for new trial, this argument may prevail. Courts have held that an order for a new trial is appropriate when the trial judge is convinced that the jury has reached a seriously erroneous result.

However, the trial judge must respect the collective wisdom of the jury. *See id.* It is not proper for a court to grant a new trial on the ground that the verdict is against the weight of the evidence unless the record shows that the jury's verdict resulted in a miscarriage of justice. *See, e.g., Tennant,* 321 U.S. at 35; *United States v. Landau,* 155 F.3d 93, 104–05 (2nd Cir. 1998). "[S]ince the credibility of witnesses is peculiarly for the jury, it is an invasion of the jury's province to grant a new trial merely because the evidence was sharply in conflict." *Latino v. Kaizer,* 58 F.3d 310, 315 (7th Cir. 1995). The issue here is simple and the facts were highly disputed at trial. Notwithstanding the fact that the court may believe that Corporation's evidence was "more persuasive," it would be improper for the court to grant Corporation's motion for a new trial on this basis.

Point Four (20–30%)

Corporation's motion for a new trial should be granted if a juror improperly failed to reveal information that would bias that juror against Corporation.

Corporation's second argument in support of a grant of new trial is stronger. By showing that a juror improperly failed to disclose information that would bias the juror against Corporation, Corporation has identified an error that could have influenced the verdict. Through questions during voir dire, jurors are screened for potential bias. Although motions for a new trial based on juror nondisclosures during voir dire are often unsuccessful, if the withheld information would have justified a disqualification for cause, a new trial should be granted. *See* WRIGHT & MILLER, *supra,* § 2810; *McCoy v. Goldston,* 652 F.2d 654, 659 (6th Cir. 1981). Here, had Corporation known of the juror's prior experience with employment discrimination suits and her hostility toward companies that are accused of discrimination, Corporation surely would have moved that the potential juror be struck for cause.

Of course, the fact that a juror has potential biases is not enough to warrant striking the juror from the jury for cause. The question is whether those potential biases are also actual biases. *See Smith v. Phillips,* 455 U.S. 209, 216 (1982). Here, there is evidence that the jury foreperson had actual bias and manifested that bias even before the trial began.

Under these circumstances, the trial court could find that the jury foreperson's apparent bias against Corporation fundamentally undermined the fairness of the trial. If the court so concludes, it should grant Corporation's motion for a new trial.

[NOTE TO GRADERS: Before doing so, the court might hold a hearing to determine whether the jury foreperson was actually biased. *See Olson v. Bradrick*, 645 F. Supp. 645, 653–54 (D. Conn. 1986).]

Federal Civil Procedure
(July 2008)

ANALYSIS

Legal Problems: (1)   Do the Federal Rules of Civil Procedure permit a defendant to compel a plaintiff to join other parties as additional defendants when the original defendant alleges that those other parties are responsible for the plaintiff's injury?

    (2)   Do the Federal Rules of Civil Procedure permit a defendant to join a counterclaim against the plaintiff when the counterclaim is for an unpaid bill relating to the transaction that gave rise to the plaintiff's claim?

    (3)   Does a federal court have jurisdiction over a defendant's state-law counterclaim when that counterclaim is for less than $75,000 but is related to the plaintiff's original claim?

DISCUSSION

Summary

Ron probably cannot force Guest to join CreamCorp as a defendant because CreamCorp is not a necessary party within the meaning of Rule 19 of the Federal Rules of Civil Procedure. Ron's claim that CreamCorp caused Guest's injury does not provide a sufficient justification for forcing the joinder of CreamCorp over Guest's objection.

The Federal Rules permit Ron to join any counterclaim he may have against Guest, regardless of whether the counterclaim arises out of or relates to Guest's claim against Ron.

A federal court ordinarily would not have jurisdiction over Ron's $50 state-law claim because it does not satisfy the amount-in-controversy requirement of diversity jurisdiction. Here, however, Ron's counterclaim arose out of the same transaction as Guest's tort claim. Therefore, it is likely that the federal district court will have subject matter jurisdiction to hear the counterclaim under the supplemental jurisdiction statute, 28 U.S.C. § 1367.

Point One (40–50%)
Rule 19 of the Federal Rules of Civil Procedure does not afford Ron a means to compel Guest to join CreamCorp as an additional defendant because CreamCorp does not qualify as a necessary party.

Ordinarily the plaintiff is the master of her suit and gets to decide whom to sue, with whom to sue, where to sue, and what claims to bring. Thus, if a plaintiff like Guest sues only one defendant when she has claims against two defendants, ordinarily there is nothing that a defendant, like Ron, can do to compel the plaintiff to join another party. *See* FLEMING JAMES, JR., ET AL., CIVIL PROCEDURE § 10.11 (5th ed. 2001).

But there are some checks on plaintiff autonomy. Rule 19, which governs the joinder of persons needed for just adjudication, authorizes joinder of defendants over the plaintiff's objection only when:

- "the court cannot accord complete relief among existing parties" if the absent person is not joined, or
- the absent person claims an interest in the action that would "as a practical matter" be impaired or impeded if that person is not joined, or
- the person's absence may leave any of the parties subject to a risk of multiple liability or inconsistent obligations.

FED. R. CIV. P. 19(a). Where any of these criteria is met, courts and commentators commonly refer to the absent party as a necessary party, and a court is empowered to join that party, even over the plaintiff's objection. *See generally* JACK H. FRIEDENTHAL ET AL., CIVIL PROCEDURE § 6.5 at 357–59 (4th ed. 2005).

In this case, none of these requirements is satisfied. First, CreamCorp's presence is not necessary for the court to afford complete relief as between Guest and Ron. If Guest got sick because the oysters were contaminated, the court can afford complete relief by holding Ron liable and awarding damages to Guest. If, on the other hand, Guest became sick because the ice cream was made from unpasteurized milk, then the court can afford complete relief between Ron and Guest by refusing to hold Ron liable. Either way, complete and proper relief can be accorded as between Ron and Guest, without CreamCorp's presence. If the jury or court finds that the oysters did not cause the food poisoning, Guest will have to initiate a separate suit to determine if she can recover from CreamCorp. While inefficient, this result does not render CreamCorp a necessary party under Rule 19. *See* FRIEDENTHAL, *supra*, at 359 n. 30. *Cf. Temple v. Synthes Corp.*, 498 U.S. 5, 7–8 (1990) (per curiam) (concluding that joint tortfeasors are permissive, not necessary, parties under Rule 19(a)). In short, Guest's ability to recover whatever (if anything) she is entitled to recover from Ron is unaffected by CreamCorp's absence.

Second, although CreamCorp may have an interest in the subject matter of the action if Ron attempts to prove that CreamCorp's product caused Guest's food poisoning, that interest is not likely to be impaired or impeded if CreamCorp is not joined. If the jury finds that Guest's illness was caused by the oysters, CreamCorp's interest would not be impaired. If the jury finds that Guest's illness was caused by CreamCorp's ice cream, CreamCorp will not be bound by the judgment since it was not a party, and it will be free to relitigate the issue of the ice cream's toxicity if Guest sues it in a separate lawsuit. *See Janney Montgomery Scott, Inc. v. Shepard Niles, Inc.*, 11 F.3d 399, 407 (3d Cir. 1993) (declining to hold that "any potential effect the doctrine [of stare decisis] may have on an absent party's rights makes the absent party's joinder compulsory under Rule 19(a)"); *Pujol v. Shearson/American Express, Inc.*, 877 F.2d 132, 136 (1st Cir. 1989) (stating that "[t]he mere fact . . . that Party A, in a suit against Party B, intends to introduce evidence that will indicate that a non-party, C, behaved improperly does not, by itself, make C a necessary party").

Third, Ron does not face a substantial risk of incurring inconsistent obligations or double liability if CreamCorp is not joined here. If Ron is held liable to Guest, Ron will pay Guest but face no other liability or obligation on the same claim. If Ron is not held liable, then the possibility of double liability or inconsistent obligations does not exist.

Therefore, under Rule 19 Ron cannot compel Guest to join CreamCorp as an additional defendant.

[NOTE TO GRADERS: If an examinee concludes that CreamCorp is a necessary party, the examinee must also consider whether CreamCorp can be joined without depriving the court of subject matter jurisdiction. In fact, joinder is possible because CreamCorp is subject to the personal jurisdiction of the State B courts and is diverse from plaintiff Guest, a citizen of State A.]

Point Two (20–30%)

Rule 13 of the Federal Rules of Civil Procedure not only permits, but requires, Ron to bring his claim for the unpaid restaurant bill as a counterclaim against Guest in the context of Guest's lawsuit against Ron because the counterclaim arises out of or relates to the same transaction or occurrence.

A claim for relief brought by a defendant against a plaintiff is called a counterclaim. Counterclaims are governed by Rule 13 of the Federal Rules of Civil Procedure. Rule 13 requires a defendant to bring a counterclaim against the plaintiff if the counterclaim arises out of the same transaction or occurrence as the plaintiff's claim against the defendant. FED. R. CIV. P. 13(a). Here, Ron's claim to be paid for the restaurant meal arises out of the same transaction and occurrence as Guest's claim that she became sick as a result of the meal. Both claims arose out of the meal Ron served to Guest.

Rule 13(b) further provides that an answer "*may* state as a counterclaim" any claim against the plaintiff "that is not compulsory" FED. R. CIV. P. 13(b) (emphasis added). Read together, these portions of the rule authorize Ron to bring a counterclaim against Guest for the unpaid $50 regardless of whether it arises out of the same transaction or occurrence as Guest's claim against Ron. Therefore, it is not necessary to determine whether Guest's claim and Ron's claim arose out of the same transaction or occurrence. In either case, Ron may bring the claim.

Point Three (25–35%)

The federal district court likely would have jurisdiction to hear the counterclaim under the supplemental jurisdiction statute, 28 U.S.C. § 1367, as long as the counterclaim for failure to pay the check and the plaintiff's claim for negligence form part of the same case for purposes of the case-or-controversy requirement of Article III.

Whether the federal court can assert jurisdiction over Ron's counterclaim is another matter. The counterclaim against Guest for failure to pay the $50 is a state-law claim that could not be brought on its own in federal court. While there is complete diversity of citizenship between Guest and Ron, the amount in controversy on the unpaid restaurant check claim is only $50 and doesn't come close to satisfying the $75,000 amount-in-controversy requirement for diversity jurisdiction. *See* 28 U.S.C. § 1332(a).

However, where a federal court already has jurisdiction over some claims, the supplemental jurisdiction statute, 28 U.S.C. § 1367, authorizes district courts to hear claims that could not otherwise be heard in federal court if those claims "are so related to [the primary] claims in the action . . . that they form part of the same case or controversy under Article III of the United States Constitution." 28 U.S.C. § 1367(a). In determining whether or not the primary claim and the supplemental claim "are so related," most courts apply the "common nucleus of operative fact" test announced by the United States Supreme Court in *United Mine Workers v. Gibbs*, 383 U.S. 715, 725 (1966) (stating that "[t]he state and federal claims must derive from a common nucleus of operative fact" to be part of the same "case" for constitutional purposes). *See* JAMES, *supra*, § 2.28 at 146–47.

Here, it is likely that Guest's claim against Ron for food poisoning and Ron's claim against Guest for the unpaid $50 arise out of a common nucleus of operative fact, namely the alleged food-poisoning incident. The reason that Guest stopped payment on the check and declined to pay for the food was because the food allegedly made her ill. *See, e.g., Geisinger Medical Ctr. v. Gough*, 160 F.R.D. 467, 470 (M.D. Pa. 1994) (concluding that the defendant's claim that the plaintiff committed medical malpractice was a compulsory counterclaim to the plaintiff's claim to recover for unpaid medical bills; "[t]he counterclaim is thus an offshoot of the same basic controversy as the plaintiff's claim and necessarily involves common issues of law and fact that would require duplicative effort if tried in a separate action").

Section 1367(c) affords the district court discretion to decline to exercise supplemental jurisdiction in four circumstances: "(1) the claim raises a novel or complex issue of State law; (2) the claim substantially predominates over the claim or claims over which the district court has original jurisdiction; (3) the district court has dismissed all claims over which it has original jurisdiction; or (4) in exceptional circumstances, there are other compelling reasons for declining jurisdiction." 28 U.S.C. § 1367(c). Here, the counterclaim for failure to pay the restaurant bill does not raise any novel or complex issues of state law. The restaurant bill claim does not predominate over the more factually complex claim of food poisoning. The district court has not dismissed the plaintiff's claim. Nor are there any compelling reasons to decline to exercise jurisdiction. Therefore, it is likely that the district court would have supplemental jurisdiction to hear Ron's counterclaim against Guest.

[NOTE TO GRADERS: Some applicants may approach the unpaid $50 restaurant bill under Article 3 of the Uniform Commercial Code because Guest paid by check and then stopped payment on the check. The facts state that Ron's claim against Guest was based on the unpaid restaurant bill, not on the check. Thus, a discussion of Article 3 is not necessary but would also be a correct approach. Regardless of whether applicants frame the counterclaim as arising under Article 3 or the unpaid bill, the jurisdictional analysis would be the same as both claims arise under state law.]

Federal Civil Procedure
(February 2009)

(Federal Civil Procedure I.D.; II.A.; Conflict of Laws III.B., C.1.)

Legal Problems: (1)(a) Do the Federal Rules of Civil Procedure permit a federal district court to authorize service of process on a foreign defendant by e-mail?

    (1)(b) Is e-mail service of process constitutional under the circumstances of this case?

    (2)(a) Which jurisdiction's choice-of-law rules should be used to select the applicable unfair-competition law?

    (2)(b) Under the "most significant relationship" test, what factors govern the choice among State A, Country X, and State B unfair-competition law?

DISCUSSION

Summary

Absent a governing international agreement, the district court has authority to order service of process by e-mail so long as the service is reasonably calculated to give notice to Copyco of the suit. Once it obtains jurisdiction over Copyco, the court should use State A's "most significant relationship" approach to determine the proper law to apply to the unfair-competition claim. The proper choice of law depends on several factors, including the policies underlying the competing laws. Here, given the many connections of the case to State A, it is likely that a court sitting in State A would apply State A law.

Point One(a) (20–30%)
Rule 4 of the Federal Rules of Civil Procedure permits service of process on a foreign corporation outside of the United States by any means directed by the court as long as it is not prohibited by international agreement.

In a proper case, a federal court has the power to permit a plaintiff to serve a foreign corporate defendant by e-mail. Rule 4 authorizes service of process upon a corporation outside the United States "in any manner prescribed by Rule 4(f) for serving an individual, except personal delivery . . . ." FED. R. CIV. P. 4(h)(2). Subdivision (f) of Rule 4, in turn, permits service in places outside the United States by a variety of methods, including means of service allowed by international agreement, by foreign law, and by general international practice. Importantly, subdivision (f) gives the district court broad authority to direct service by any "means not prohibited by international agreement." FED. R. CIV. P. 4(f)(3). In other words, the court can authorize any method of making service of process abroad, including e-mail, in its discretion, if no international agreement prohibits it. Moreover, the court's authority to direct non-traditional means of service "is neither a 'last resort' nor 'extraordinary relief,'" *Rio Props., Inc. v. Rio Int'l Interlink*, 284 F.3d 1007, 1015 (9th Cir. 2002); it is simply one of the tools the court has to ensure that procedural matters are handled sensibly and fairly.

On the facts of this case, it is likely that e-mail service of process would be approved by the court. First, the facts state that there are no applicable international treaties, so the court's power to direct any "means" of service, including e-mail, is not limited by international agreement. Second, this seems like a perfect case for e-mail: the defendant's street address cannot be ascertained, and the defendant's business conduct evinces a preference for communication through the Internet. It would seem that service by e-mail would be convenient for the defendant and reasonably calculated to give the defendant notice of the action. It would, moreover, prevent the significant hardship to the plaintiff that might result if the plaintiff were required to find other means to track down and serve this elusive corporate defendant. For these reasons, the court is likely to authorize e-mail service in this situation. For other recent cases authorizing e-mail service under such circumstances, see *Philip Morris USA Inc. v. Veles Ltd.*, 2007 WL 725412 (SDNY 2007); *Export-Import Bank of the U.S. v. Asia Pulp and Paper Co.*, 2005 WL 1123755 (SDNY 2005); *Williams v. Adver. Sex LLC*, 231 F.R.D. 483 (N.D. W.Va. 2005); *In re Int'l Telemedia Assoc., Inc.*, 245 B.R. 713, 719 (Bank. N.D. Ga. 2000).

Point One(b) (20–30%)
Service by e-mail is constitutional where it is reasonably calculated to give notice.

Even if permitted by the Federal Rules of Civil Procedure, a method of service of process cannot be employed if it would violate the United States Constitution. The due process clause guarantees litigants "notice reasonably calculated, under all the circumstances, to apprise interested parties of the pendency of the action and afford them an opportunity to present their objections. . . . The means employed must be such as one desirous of actually informing the absentee might reasonably adopt to accomplish it." *Mullane v. Central Hanover Bank & Trust Co.*, 339 U.S. 306, 314–15 (1950). Service by e-mail is reasonably calculated to reach Copyco, which lists its e-mail address on its website but does not list a street address or post office box. In fact, in these circumstances, service by e-mail may be the method of service most likely to reach Copyco. Since service via e-mail is reasonably calculated to reach Copyco, it comports with due process.

Point Two(a) (20–30%)
A federal court exercising diversity jurisdiction over non-federal claims must apply the choice-of-law rule of the state in which it sits.

In *Klaxon Co. v. Stentor Electric Manufacturing Co.*, 313 U.S. 487 (1941), the Supreme Court of the United States held that a federal district court sitting in diversity must apply the choice-of-law approach prevailing in the state in which it sits. The *Klaxon* rule is designed to ensure that a federal court sitting in diversity and the state court sitting next door would reach the same result if presented with the same case. If federal courts were free to craft their own choice-of-law rules, then the federal court might choose a different jurisdiction's substantive law to govern the dispute than the state court would, and the goals of uniformity and equal administration of justice would be frustrated. *Id.* at 496–97. Thus, the federal district court sitting in State A should apply the choice-of-law approach followed by the courts of State A. The facts indicate that State A applies the Second Restatement of Conflict of Laws.

Point Two(b) (20–30%)
Because the federal court will apply State A's choice-of-law rule, the Restatement (Second) of Conflict of Laws (the methodology employed by State A) applies here. Under the Second Restatement's approach, issues in tort are governed by the law of the state that has the most significant relationship to the occurrence and the parties.

Unfair competition is a tort claim governed by § 145 of the Restatement (Second) of Conflict of Laws (cmts. e & f (1971)). Section 145 states that "the rights and liabilities of the parties with respect to an issue in tort are determined by the local law of the state which, with respect to that issue, has the most significant relationship to the occurrence and the parties under the principles stated in § 6." *Id.* § 145(1). Section 145 lists four contacts to be considered in performing this analysis: "(a) the place where the injury occurred, (b) the place where the conduct causing the injury occurred, (c) the . . . place of incorporation, and place of business of the parties, and (d) the place where the relationship, if any, between the parties is centered. These contacts are to be evaluated according to their relative importance with respect to the particular issue." *Id.* § 145(2).

Here, an evaluation of the § 145 contacts reveals that a number of jurisdictions have important connections to the parties and the transaction. First, Bearco's injury—the loss of customers who bought Copyco's knockoff "Griz" bears—occurred in all 50 states and would have been felt most acutely in State A (where Bearco maintains its corporate and administrative offices) and State B (where Bearco's factories are located). Copyco's conduct occurred both in Country X, where it manufactured the knockoff bears, and also in all 50 states, where it sold bears in competition with Bearco. The two companies are incorporated in different locations, State A (Bearco) and Country X (Copyco), and their places of business are likewise in different locales.

Where the contacts are so thoroughly split among so many jurisdictions, courts applying the Second Restatement will pay special attention to the principles for making choice-of-law decisions as stated in § 6 of the Restatement. In a tort case like this one, a court will ordinarily focus its attention on the policies of the laws that are in conflict and, in particular, on any interest of its own state in having its policies apply to the case. *Id.* at § 6(2)(b) & (c).

Here it is likely that the purpose of State A's unfair-competition law is to protect businesses from the economic harm caused by the kind of unfair competition involved in this case. Given that Bearco is a local business, incorporated and headquartered in State A, and that the injury from Copyco's unfair competition will be felt in State A, State A would certainly have an interest in seeing its policy applied to force Copyco to compensate Bearco. On the other hand, Country X would be interested in seeing its law apply to protect Copyco if the policy behind Country X's failure to regulate unfair competition is intended to facilitate competition by its companies and to encourage their manufacturing operations in Country X.

Here, a federal court sitting in State A is likely to conclude that State A has the "most significant relationship" to the case. In a situation of conflict between local and foreign law, where both the local and foreign jurisdictions' policies would be furthered by applying their law, most courts will apply local law and further local policies unless there is a strong reason not to do so. There is nothing unfair in subjecting Copyco to State A law where its activities were directed in part at customers in State A, it injured a State A corporation, and it was foreseeable that it could be subject to State A law on account of its activities. The federal court will likely apply State A's unfair-competition law.

[NOTE: An applicant's conclusion is less important than his or her ability to state and use the relevant principles of the Restatement (Second) of Conflict of Laws. Applicants are expected to know that the federal court will apply State A's choice-of-law methodology to choose the law governing the supplemental state claim and that the Second Restatement requires application of the law of the state with the most significant relationship to the parties and the occurrence. They should also know that the Second Restatement requires consideration of a variety of personal and territorial factors and an analysis of the policies underlying the laws competing for application. Applicants are not expected to recall specific Restatement sections or comments, nor are applicants expected to reach the same results as the model analysis.]

Federal Civil Procedure
(July 2009)

(Federal Civil Procedure I.A.1., E.; IV.C.)

Legal Problems: (1)   What steps must be taken to effect removal from state to federal court?

                     (2)   Is the joinder of Ann and Bill as plaintiffs proper under the Federal Rules of Civil Procedure?

                     (3)   If Ann's and Bill's claims remain joined, will the federal court have jurisdiction over the case?

DISCUSSION

Summary

To remove a case from state to federal court, the defendant must file a notice of removal with the federal district court, give written notice of that filing to all adverse parties, and file a copy of the notice of removal with the state court.

The joinder of Ann and Bill as plaintiffs would be proper under Federal Rule of Civil Procedure 20 because their claims for relief arose out of "the same transaction [or] occurrence" and involve a "common question" of law or fact.

The case is within the subject matter jurisdiction of a federal court in State X. Both Ann and Bill, citizens of State X, are diverse from GlassCo, which is a citizen of State Y (the state of its incorporation and principal place of business). Ann's claim for $1,000,000 easily satisfies the required jurisdictional amount of $75,000. Although Bill's claim does not satisfy the required jurisdictional amount, the federal court will have "supplemental jurisdiction" over Bill's claim because it is sufficiently related to Ann's claim to be part of the same "case or controversy."

Point One (10–20%)
The defendant begins the process of removal by filing a notice of removal in the federal court "for the district and division within which [the state court action] is pending." Removal is then accomplished by giving notice of the filing to all adverse parties and filing a copy of the notice of removal with the state court.

Procedurally, the first step for removing an action from state to federal court is for the defendant to file a notice of removal in the federal district court for the district and division within which the state action is pending. 28 U.S.C. § 1446(a). The notice must be filed within 30 days of the defendant's "receipt . . . , through service or otherwise, of a copy of the initial pleading . . . , or within 30 days after the service of summons . . . if such initial pleading has then been filed and is not required to be served . . . , whichever period is shorter." *Id.* § 1446(b). The notice of removal must be signed and must include a statement of the basis for federal jurisdiction. *Id.* § 1446(a). A copy of the materials from the state court proceeding must also be filed. *Id.*

After filing the notice of removal, the defendant must serve notice of the filing on all adverse parties and file a copy of the notice of removal with the state court. *Id.* § 1446(d). Removal is "automatic." Once the state court has a copy of the notice of removal, the case is removed and the state court can take no further action in the case. *Id.*

[NOTE: If the defendant removes the action to federal court, and the plaintiff wishes to contest the removal, the plaintiff must file a motion to remand.]

Point Two (30–40%)
Federal Rule of Civil Procedure 20(a) permits the claims of Ann and Bill to be joined in a single action because those claims arose out of the "same transaction [or] occurrence" and involve "common questions" of law and fact.

Federal Rule of Civil Procedure 20(a)(1) provides that two or more plaintiffs may join their claims in a single lawsuit if the plaintiffs "assert any right to relief jointly, severally, or in the alternative with respect to or arising out of the *same transaction, occurrence* or series of transactions or occurrences; *and . . . any question of law or fact common to all plaintiffs [being joined] will arise in the action.*" (emphasis added)

Both requirements for joinder are met in this case. First, Ann and Bill are each asserting claims that arose out of a single occurrence—the accident involving the falling glass. Second, those claims will certainly raise some common questions of fact (e.g., whether the glass accident was caused by the negligence of GlassCo employees) and may also raise common questions of law (e.g., the legal standard for measuring damages). This is precisely the kind of case in which Rule 20 allows joinder of plaintiffs in the interest of promoting efficiency and consistency of results.

The fact that Ann and Bill are asserting separate claims and separate rights to relief does not matter. Rule 20 allows plaintiffs to join when they assert their rights to relief "severally."

Point Three (45–55%)
The federal court will have subject matter jurisdiction over the removed case because Ann's claim is within the diversity jurisdiction of the court and Bill's claim, although it does not satisfy the amount-in-controversy requirement for diversity jurisdiction, is within the federal court's supplemental jurisdiction.

Removal of a case from state to federal court is proper only when the "civil action" that is removed is within the "original jurisdiction" of the federal court. 28 U.S.C. §1441(a).
    In this case, Ann's tort claim against GlassCo would be within the original diversity jurisdiction of the federal district court of State X. Ann and GlassCo are citizens of different states, and Ann's claim for $1,000,000 exceeds the $75,000 amount-in-controversy requirement of the diversity statute, 28 U.S.C. § 1332.

Bill's tort claim, on the other hand, is not within the diversity jurisdiction of the court. Although Bill and GlassCo are diverse, Bill is seeking damages of only $5,000, which is substantially less than the $75,000 minimum amount-in-controversy for federal diversity actions.

Nonetheless, the federal court will have jurisdiction over Bill's claim pursuant to 28 U.S.C. § 1367, the "supplemental jurisdiction" statute. When a federal court has original jurisdiction over a claim in an action, § 1367(a) provides that the court "shall have supplemental jurisdiction over all other claims that are so related [to the main claim] that they form part of the same case or controversy under Article III of the United States Constitution."

On the facts of this problem, Bill's claim is sufficiently related to Ann's claim to be "part of the same case or controversy." Both claims arose out of a "common nucleus of operative fact" (the accident involving the glass) and are so similar in facts and law that it is sensible to expect them to be tried in a single judicial proceeding. *See, e.g., United Mine Workers of America v. Gibbs,* 383 U.S. 715, 725 (1966). Thus, the court has supplemental jurisdiction over Bill's claim. *See Exxon Mobil Corp. v. Allapattah Services, Inc.,* 545 U.S. 546 (2005).

Federal Civil Procedure
(February 2010)

Legal Problems: (1) Does a federal district court have diversity jurisdiction over an action between a plaintiff domiciled in one state and three defendants who are domiciled in another state when one of the defendants is a permanent resident alien and not a U.S. citizen?

(2) Does a federal district court have diversity jurisdiction over a case that arises out of a surrogacy agreement but does not seek a divorce, alimony, or child custody decree?

(3) Do the Federal Rules of Civil Procedure permit a plaintiff to join three defendants in a single action when her claims against the defendants, although based on different contracts, all seek recovery for expenses generated by a single occurrence?

DISCUSSION

Summary

The federal district court has jurisdiction to adjudicate Surrogate's claims against the defendants because there is complete diversity among all of the parties and the amount-in-controversy requirement is met. The domestic relations exception to diversity jurisdiction is not implicated by these facts because Surrogate does not seek a divorce, alimony, or child custody decree, and a state court already has determined legal parentage. Surrogate properly joined all three defendants in a single action because her claims against them arise out of the same transaction or occurrence (the birth and hospitalization of the baby) and involve a common question of law or fact.

Point One (35%)
<u>The federal district court has diversity jurisdiction to hear these breach-of-contract claims because complete diversity of citizenship exists between the plaintiff and all of the defendants, and the amount-in-controversy requirement is met.</u>

Surrogate is suing Insureco for breaching the terms of the insurance policy, in which it agreed to insure Surrogate and her dependent children. She is suing Husband and Wife for breaching the surrogacy agreement, in which they agreed to assume full financial and legal responsibility for any child resulting from the implantation of their embryo. These claims arise under state contract law and do not raise any federal questions. Therefore, federal court jurisdiction is proper only if the case satisfies the requirements of 28 U.S.C. § 1332, the diversity statute.

Section 1332 grants federal district courts original jurisdiction of all civil actions with an amount in controversy in excess of $75,000 if the plaintiff and defendant are "citizens of different States." 28 U.S.C. § 1332(a). In addition, the "diversity" between the parties on either side of the case must be "complete." *Strawbridge v. Curtiss*, 7 U.S. (3 Cranch) 267, 267 (1806). In other words, no plaintiff may be a citizen of the same state as any of the defendants. *See* 13E CHARLES ALAN WRIGHT ET AL., FEDERAL PRACTICE AND PROCEDURE § 3605 (2009).

On these facts, there is complete diversity. Plaintiff Surrogate is deemed to be a citizen of State B because she is domiciled there. *Id.* § 3611 at 464–65. Defendant Husband, similarly, is a citizen of State A, where he is domiciled. Surrogate and Husband are diverse.

Surrogate is also diverse from Insureco. Under the diversity statute, "a corporation shall be deemed to be a citizen of any State by which it has been incorporated and of the State where it has its principal place of business . . . ." 28 U.S.C. § 1332(c)(1). *See also* 13F WRIGHT ET AL., *supra*, §§ 3623–3624. Thus, Insureco is a citizen of both State A and State C and is therefore diverse from Surrogate, a State B citizen.

Even though Wife is not a U.S. citizen, § 1332 provides that "an alien admitted to the United States for permanent residence shall be deemed a citizen of the State in which such alien is domiciled." 28 U.S.C. § 1332(a). Since Wife has been admitted for permanent residence, she is deemed to be a citizen of State A, where she is domiciled. 13E WRIGHT ET AL., *supra*, § 3604 & n. 14. Thus, she is also diverse from Surrogate.

Because the plaintiff, Surrogate, is a citizen of only State B and none of the defendants is a citizen of State B, complete diversity exists.

Surrogate alleges that each defendant is obliged by contract to pay the $500,000 hospital bill. She seeks a court order compelling payment of that bill. She thus raises a claim against each defendant that exceeds the $75,000 amount-in-controversy threshold. *See* JACK H. FRIEDENTHAL, MARY KAY KANE & ARTHUR R. MILLER, CIVIL PROCEDURE 49–50 (4th ed. 2005) (in cases where plaintiff seeks equitable relief, the amount in controversy is the value to the plaintiff of what is sought to be obtained); *Burns v. Massachusetts Mut. Life Ins. Co.*, 820 F.2d 246, 248 (8th Cir. 1987).

Point Two (30%)

Under the domestic relations exception, federal courts do not have authority to issue divorce, alimony, and child custody decrees. Here, the district court would retain jurisdiction to adjudicate the plaintiff's claims, because they raise contractual questions.

The federal courts have long declined to exercise jurisdiction over domestic relations issues. More than a century ago, the Supreme Court of the United States announced that "[t]he whole subject of the domestic relations of husband and wife, parent and child, belongs to the laws of the States and not to the laws of the United States." *In re Burrus*, 136 U.S. 586, 593–94 (1890). Although the domestic relations exception is not grounded in the Constitution, the Supreme Court has concluded that such a long-established exception to diversity jurisdiction should be retained, absent a Congressional decision to repudiate it. *See Ankenbrandt v. Richards*, 504 U.S. 689, 695, 700–01 (1992) (stating that "[w]ith respect to such a longstanding and well-known construction of the diversity statute, and where Congress made substantive changes to the statute in other respects, we presume, absent any indication that Congress intended to alter this exception, that Congress 'adopt[ed] that interpretation' when it reenacted the diversity statute," quoting *Lorillard v. Pons*, 434 U.S. 575, 580 (1978) (internal citations and footnote omitted)).

Nonetheless, the mere fact that a case involves domestic relations (as the current problem arguably does) does not mean that there is no diversity jurisdiction over that case. According to one leading treatise, the domestic relations exception applies only to cases that are primarily marital disputes. *See* 13E WRIGHT ET AL., *supra*, § 3609. This conclusion was reinforced in *Ankenbrandt*, in which the Supreme Court limited the scope of the domestic relations exception, stating that it "encompasses only cases involving the issuance of a divorce, alimony, or child custody decree." 504 U.S. at 704. There, the Court held that a federal district court had diversity jurisdiction to adjudicate a tort claim brought by the mother of two children on their behalf against their father and his companion, alleging sexual and physical abuse, because the suit did not seek a divorce, alimony, or child custody decree. *Id. See generally* CHEMERINSKY, FEDERAL JURISDICTION § 5.3, at 302–03 (4th ed. 2003); 13E WRIGHT ET AL., *supra*, §§ 3609 & 3609.1.

On the facts of this question, the domestic relations exception does not apply. No one is seeking a divorce or alimony decree. And there is no dispute over custody of the baby. To the contrary, Husband and Wife already have obtained a state court declaration that they are the baby's parents and are entitled to sole custody; Surrogate's suit does not seek to alter that judicial custody determination. All Surrogate seeks is specific performance of Husband and Wife's contractual obligation to assume financial responsibility for the baby.

Finally, while Surrogate's claim against Insureco raises the issue of whether the baby is Surrogate's "natural child" within the meaning of the insurance policy, any determination of that issue would affect only Insureco's financial responsibility to cover the baby's hospital bills. Resolution of the issue would not affect the custody of the child.

Therefore, this case does not appear to fall within the domestic relations exception, and the district court should exercise its diversity jurisdiction and adjudicate Surrogate's claims. *See Mid-South Ins. Co. v. Doe*, 274 F. Supp. 2d 757 (D.S.C. 2003). As the Supreme Court held long ago, a federal court has "no more right to decline the exercise of jurisdiction which is given, than to usurp that which is not given." *Cohens v. Virginia*, 19 U.S. (6 Wheat.) 264, 404 (1821), *cited with approval in Marshall v. Marshall*, 547 U.S. 293, 298–99 (2006) (rejecting a broad interpretation of the probate exception to federal jurisdiction and requiring lower courts to exercise jurisdiction).

Point Three (35%)
Surrogate properly joined Husband, Wife, and Insureco as defendants because her claims against each of them arose out of the same transaction, occurrence, or series of transactions or occurrences and involve questions of law or fact common to all defendants.

The Federal Rules of Civil Procedure embody a liberal and flexible joinder policy. Rule 20(a), which governs permissive joinder of parties, permits the plaintiff to join multiple defendants whenever two conditions are met: (1) "any right to relief is asserted against [the defendants] jointly, severally, or in the alternative, with respect to or arising out of the same transaction, occurrence, or series of transactions or occurrences" and (2) "any question of law or fact common to all defendants [will] arise in the action." FED. R. CIV. P. 20(a). *See generally* 7

WRIGHT ET AL., *supra*, § 1651 *et seq*. Both of these conditions must be satisfied. *Id.* § 1653, at 403–04. Rule 20 is designed to "promote trial convenience and expedite the final determination of disputes, thereby preventing multiple lawsuits." *Id.* § 1652, at 395 (footnotes omitted). The Rule 20 requirements should be read as broadly as possible whenever doing so is likely to promote judicial economy. *Id.* § 1653, at 415.

In determining whether claims against the three defendants arise out of the same transaction or occurrence, courts often employ the logical-relationship test, under which "all logically related events entitling a person to institute a legal action against another generally are regarded as comprising a transaction or occurrence." *Id.* § 1653, at 409 (footnote omitted). Emphasizing the liberality and flexibility of this standard, one leading treatise notes that "courts are inclined to find that claims arise out of the same transaction or occurrence when the likelihood of overlapping proof and duplication in testimony indicates that separate trials would result in delay, inconvenience, and added expense to the parties and to the court." *Id.* § 1653, at 411–12. The inclusion of the language "in the alternative" was specifically intended to permit a plaintiff to join multiple defendants when she or he "is entitled to relief from someone, but the plaintiff does not know which of two or more defendants is liable under the circumstances set forth in the complaint." *Id.* § 1654, at 418–19.

Here, Surrogate's claims against all three defendants arise out of the same event—the baby's birth and hospitalization. In addition, certain factual questions will be common to both claims, including the circumstances of the birth and the terms of the surrogacy agreement between Surrogate and Husband and Wife, which are facts important both to Surrogate's claim against Husband and Wife and to Insureco's defense that the baby is not Surrogate's "natural child." Thus, joinder is appropriate in this case.

[NOTE: An applicant who demonstrates knowledge of the joinder rule and the ability to apply the rule to the facts of the problem in a sensible way should receive some credit, even if the applicant concludes that joinder is improper in this case. However, an applicant who concludes that joinder is improper should also note that dismissal of the action is not an appropriate remedy for improper joinder. The appropriate remedy is to sever the claims and allow Surrogate to proceed separately against the defendants. FED. R. CIV. P. 21.]

Federal Civil Procedure
(July 2010)

Legal Problems: (1)   May a federal district court exercise personal jurisdiction over a nonresident defendant that contracted outside the forum state to provide a loan to a plaintiff who lived in the forum state and that mailed loan paperwork to the plaintiff in the forum state, including the incorrectly mailed paperwork that gave rise to the plaintiff's lawsuit?

(2)   Does a federal district court have diversity jurisdiction when the plaintiff previously was domiciled in the defendant's state of citizenship and still returns there about once a month, but has moved to another state to work and may intend to stay there permanently?

(3)   Does a federal district court have federal-question jurisdiction over a lawsuit when the plaintiff's complaint refers to a potentially relevant federal statute but denies the applicability of the statute?

DISCUSSION

Summary

The State B district court may exercise specific personal jurisdiction over nonresident defendant Credit Union because Credit Union engaged in contacts with the forum state that demonstrated purposeful availment and that gave rise to Paul's claims. The exercise of personal jurisdiction would not be unfair.

Diversity of citizenship exists if Paul intends to remain in State B, which could be argued either way. Defendant Credit Union is a citizen of State A, where it is incorporated and has its principal place of business. Paul's complaint seeks sufficient monetary damages to satisfy the amount-in-controversy requirement.

The district court does not have federal-question jurisdiction in this case because Paul's complaint does not state a federal claim. It instead seeks to anticipate and rebut a potential federal defense. Under the well-pleaded complaint rule, federal-question jurisdiction is appropriate only when a federal claim is raised on the face of the complaint.

Point One (35%)
The United States District Court for the District of State B may exercise personal jurisdiction over Credit Union because Credit Union's contacts with the forum state gave rise to the suit and demonstrate purposeful availment and because the exercise of jurisdiction would not be unfair.

The United States District Court for the District of State B has personal jurisdiction over Credit Union. Federal district courts may exercise personal jurisdiction to the same extent as the courts of general jurisdiction of the state in which the district court sits. *See* FED. R. CIV. P. 4(k)(1)(A). State courts of general jurisdiction may exercise personal jurisdiction over nonresident defendants to the extent authorized by both the state's long-arm statute and the due process clause of the 14th Amendment of the U.S. Constitution. In this case, State B's long-arm statute authorizes jurisdiction as far as the Constitution allows, so the long-arm analysis is the same as the constitutional analysis.

The due process clause of the 14th Amendment permits states to assert personal jurisdiction over nonresident defendants who have established minimum contacts with the state such that the exercise of personal jurisdiction would not offend traditional notions of fair play and substantial justice. *International Shoe v. Washington*, 326 U.S. 310 (1945).

In this case, Paul's suit arises out of or relates to Credit Union's contacts with State B. Paul's claim is based on a loan agreement which informed Credit Union that Paul was a resident of State B at the time of the agreement and that loan information should be mailed to Paul in State B. Credit Union in fact sends information about the loan to Paul in State B, and receives payments from Paul from State B. Moreover, the lawsuit arises out of one of Credit Union's mailings to State B, albeit a mailing to an incorrect address.

Although these contacts probably fall short of the continuous and substantial contacts required for general jurisdiction, *see Helicopteros Nacionales v. Hall*, 466 U.S. 408 (1984), they are probably sufficient for the court to exercise specific jurisdiction over claims against Credit Union that arise out of its contacts with State B.

A nonresident defendant is subject to specific jurisdiction when its contacts with the forum state demonstrate purposeful availment of the benefits of the forum state and/or render it foreseeable that the defendant may be haled into the forum state's courts. *See Hanson v. Denckla*, 357 U.S. 235 (1958). While Credit Union might argue that its contacts with State B result from Paul's unilateral act of moving to State B and therefore do not demonstrate purposeful availment, this argument will fail. Credit Union entered a long-term contract with Paul knowing that he lived in State B and would be performing his part of the contract (making loan payments) in State B. Credit Union mailed several payment statements addressed to Paul in State B. As a result, Credit Union purposefully availed itself of the benefits of State B and could foresee being haled into court in State B on matters related to the contract with Paul. *See Burger King Corp. v. Rudzewicz*, 471 U.S. 462, 475–76 (1985).

Even when a nonresident defendant has established the necessary minimum contacts with the forum state, the exercise of personal jurisdiction over the defendant may offend due process if inconsistent with traditional notions of fair play and substantial justice. The defendant must make a compelling case for fairness considerations to outweigh the existence of minimum contacts. *Id.* at 477. Credit Union will not succeed in making such a case, as the fairness considerations tend to support the exercise of personal jurisdiction by the courts of State B. Paul, who now lives in State B, has an interest in convenient and effective relief close to home. State B has an interest in providing its residents with a forum for redress of injuries caused by out-of-state defendants.

And although litigation in State B will impose a burden on Credit Union, which maintains no branches in State B, that burden is minimized by modern transportation and communication. *See id.* at 483–84. As a result, the exercise of personal jurisdiction by the courts of State B will not offend notions of fairness.

Point Two (35%)

Credit Union is a citizen of State A. As a result, complete diversity will exist if Paul is a domiciliary of State B. However, it is uncertain whether Paul is a domiciliary of State B or is still a domiciliary of State A. If Paul is a State B domiciliary, then there is diversity jurisdiction; Paul's claim satisfies the amount-in-controversy requirement.

28 U.S.C. § 1332 vests the district courts with jurisdiction over cases in which (a) there is complete diversity of citizenship, meaning no plaintiff shares the state of citizenship of any defendant, and (b) the amount in controversy exceeds $75,000.

In determining citizenship, § 1332(c) directs that a corporation is a citizen where it is incorporated and where it has its principal place of business. *Hertz Corp. v. Friend*, ___ U.S. ___, 130 S.Ct. 1181, 1192 (2010) ("'[P]rincipal place of business' is best read as referring to the place where a corporation's officers direct, control, and coordinate the corporation's activities . . . the place where the corporation maintains its headquarters . . . i.e., the 'nerve center'"). Credit Union is incorporated in State A. Moreover, its principal place of business (indeed, its only place of business) is in State A. Credit Union is a State A citizen for diversity purposes.

An individual U.S. citizen's citizenship is determined by domicile, which is defined as the individual's "true, fixed, and permanent home . . . to which he has the intention of returning whenever he is absent therefrom." *Mas v. Perry*, 489 F.2d 1396, 1399 (5th Cir. 1974) (quotation omitted). Until recently, Paul's domicile was clearly State A, where he had lived his entire life. Six months ago, however, Paul moved to State B, where he now resides most of the time, although he sometimes returns for short visits to his vacation home in State A.

The question is whether Paul has changed his domicile to State B. To change domicile, an individual must both take up residence in a new state and intend to remain there. *Id.* at 1400. While Paul has taken up residence in State B, it is unclear whether he intends to remain there. He originally planned to stay in State B for a year and then decide whether he would remain or return to State A. Consistent with that plan, he took a job as a temporary employee. Recently, however, Paul decided to obtain more permanent employment, as he has really enjoyed living in State B. This change to more permanent employment suggests that Paul now intends to remain in State B on a permanent basis, in which case his domicile has changed to State B. On the other hand, his purchase of a vacation home in State A may suggest that he does not, in fact, intend to change his State A domicile.

[NOTE: The issue can be fairly argued either way.]

If Paul is a citizen of State B, complete diversity exists. If Paul remains a citizen of State A, complete diversity does not exist, as Paul and Credit Union would both be citizens of State A.

To determine whether the amount in controversy exceeds $75,000, courts rely on a plaintiff's good-faith allegations unless it appears "to a legal certainty" that the plaintiff cannot recover the amount alleged. *St. Paul Mercury Indemnity Co. v. Red Cab Co.*, 303 U.S. 283, 289 (1938). Paul's claim for $240,000 clearly satisfies the amount-in-controversy requirement, and there are no facts to suggest that it was not made in good faith. Even if the state statute providing for treble damages is preempted by the federal identity-theft statute, Paul's $80,000 claim for actual loss still satisfies the amount-in-controversy requirement.

Point Three (30%)

Paul's assertion of a defense to the possible applicability of a federal statute does not create federal-question jurisdiction.

28 U.S.C. § 1331 provides district courts with jurisdiction to hear suits arising under the laws of the United States. To determine whether such federal-question jurisdiction exists, a court looks at the allegations necessary for a well-pleaded complaint and asks whether the claims stated by those allegations are created by federal or state law. Claims created by federal, but not state, law generally fall within the scope of a district court's federal-question jurisdiction.

Paul's breach-of-contract claim is created by state law and therefore lies outside the district court's original federal-question jurisdiction. Although Paul's complaint mentions a federal statute, it does not state any claim that is based on the federal law. Instead, in order to rebut an anticipated defense, Paul's complaint asserts that certain provisions of federal law are unconstitutional.

Pursuant to the well-pleaded complaint rule, there is no federal-question jurisdiction when federal law is mentioned in the complaint only to deny the applicability of that law. Federal-question jurisdiction exists "only when the plaintiff's statement of his own cause of action shows that it is based upon [federal] laws or [the] Constitution." *Louisville & Nashville Railroad v. Mottley*, 211 U.S. 149, 152 (1908). Here, Paul is asserting a cause of action based only on state law; the only federal issue in the case is whether Paul's cause of action is preempted. Federal-question jurisdiction does not exist under these circumstances.

Federal Civil Procedure
(February 2011)

ANALYSIS

Legal Problems: (1)   May a defendant make a motion to dismiss for insufficiency of service of process when the defendant has already moved to dismiss for failure to state a claim upon which relief can be granted?

                 (2)   Do the Federal Rules of Civil Procedure permit a defendant to join a cross-claim against a co-defendant if it arises out of the same events as the plaintiff's claim against the defendants?

                 (3)(a)   Does a federal district court have independent subject-matter jurisdiction over a state law cross-claim for $20,000 between two defendants who are citizens of the same state?

                 (3)(b)   Does a federal district court have supplemental subject-matter jurisdiction over a state law cross-claim for $20,000 between two defendants who are citizens of the same state?

DISCUSSION

Summary

Because Bartender made a motion to dismiss the action against him for failure to state a cause of action without raising his defense of insufficiency of service of process, he was barred from raising that defense at a later time. The court therefore was correct in denying his motion, even if Bartender had a valid claim that the manner of service was improper.

Bartender's claim against Dave arises out of the same transaction or occurrence as Plaintiff's claim. The claim therefore qualifies as a cross-claim under Rule 13(g) of the Federal Rules of Civil Procedure, and Bartender may state that claim in his answer to the complaint.

A federal court would not have subject-matter jurisdiction over Bartender's claim against Dave if that claim were filed as an independent action. However, Plaintiff's original claim and Bartender's cross-claim are sufficiently closely related to form part of the same case or controversy under Article III of the United States Constitution. Accordingly, the supplemental jurisdiction statute authorizes the federal court to take jurisdiction over Bartender's cross-claim.

Point One (30%)
The court correctly denied Bartender's motion to dismiss for insufficiency of service of process because that defense was not raised when Bartender made his motion to dismiss for failure to state a claim.

Although it is likely that service of process was improper in this case, the district court nonetheless was correct to deny Bartender's motion to dismiss on that basis. Bartender initially responded to Plaintiff's complaint by making a motion to dismiss for failure to state a cause of action. FED. R. CIV. P. 12(b)(6). When that motion was denied, Bartender moved to dismiss for insufficiency of service of process. FED. R. CIV. P. 12(b)(5).

When a motion pursuant to Rule 12(b) is initially made, a party may join with that motion all other motions permitted by Rule 12 that are then available to the party. If a party makes a Rule 12(b) motion and fails to join certain other available defenses or objections, the party may not later raise those objections and defenses. In particular, a party that makes a Rule 12(b) motion but omits from that motion a defense of insufficiency of service of process is deemed to have waived that defense. FED. R. CIV. P. 12(h)(1).

Because Bartender made a Rule 12(b) motion to dismiss for failure to state a claim but did not join his available defense of insufficiency of service of process, Bartender waived that defense. Hence, the district court was correct to deny Bartender's motion to dismiss on that ground. It does not matter that Bartender appears to have had a valid claim that service was improper.

Point Two (30%)
Rule 13(g) of the Federal Rules of Civil Procedure permits a defendant, in the answer, to state a cross-claim against a co-defendant if it arises out of the same transaction or occurrence as the original claim.

Rule 13(g) of the Federal Rules of Civil Procedure provides that a defendant's answer may state as a cross-claim against a co-defendant any claim that "aris[es] out of the transaction or occurrence that is the subject matter of the original action" between the plaintiff and the defendants. The policy underlying Rule 13(g) is efficiency; multiple lawsuits are avoided if defendants bring related cross-claims in the context of the plaintiff's suit. 6 CHARLES ALAN WRIGHT ET AL., FEDERAL PRACTICE AND PROCEDURE CIVIL § 1431, at 267 (2010).

Here, Plaintiff's claims concern Dave's injury of Plaintiff and Bartender's service of alcohol to Dave. Bartender's cross-claim concerns Dave's injury of Bartender. The question is whether these various claims arise out of the same transaction or occurrence.

To determine whether two different claims arise out of the same "transaction or occurrence" for purposes of Rule 13, federal courts look at a number of factors: (1) whether the issues of fact and law in the plaintiff's claim and the defendant's cross-claim are essentially the same, (2) whether the same evidence would support or refute the plaintiff's claim and the defendant's cross-claim, (3) whether there is a logical relationship between the plaintiff's claim and the defendant's cross-claim, and (4) whether res judicata would bar a subsequent suit on the cross-claim. *See, e.g., Q Int'l Courier, Inc. v. Smoak*, 441 F.3d 214, 219 (4th Cir. 2006) (interpreting the same words in Rule 13(a), the compulsory counterclaim rule); 6 WRIGHT ET AL., *supra*, §§ 1410, 1431 at 277 (stating that "the standard for asserting a cross-claim is basically the same as that for a compulsory counterclaim"). The presence of any of these factors supports a conclusion that the "transaction or occurrence" requirement is met. *See Glass v. IDS Financial Serv., Inc.*, 778 F. Supp. 1029, 1061–62 (D. Minn. 1991); 6 WRIGHT ET AL., *supra*, § 1410 at 58.

The most frequently considered factor is whether there is a logical relationship between the defendant's cross-claim and the plaintiff's original claim. 6 WRIGHT ET AL., *supra*, § 1410 at 61, 65. Here, the alleged batteries of Plaintiff and Bartender occurred in the same place, within seconds of one another. Bartender's efforts to intercede in the initial battery presumably prompted Dave to injure Bartender. There appears to be a causal link, and thus a logical relationship, between the two claims.

In addition, the two claims involve almost identical factual and legal issues. Both Plaintiff's claim against Dave and Bartender's cross-claim against Dave are claims for battery arising under State A's law. Both claims involve factual questions about the cause and course of the fight in which Dave, Bartender, and Plaintiff were involved. Even though the factual issues may differ—whether Dave battered Plaintiff is a distinct question from whether Dave battered Bartender—the substantial overlap between the legal and factual issues supports the conclusion that the claims arise from the same transaction or occurrence. The identity-of-issues inquiry does not require a complete overlap between the claim and the cross-claim. *Id.* § 1410, at 59.

The "same evidence" test is also likely to be satisfied. To prove the battery claim against Dave, Plaintiff will need the testimony of witnesses to the brawl. It is likely that the patrons of the bar who witnessed Dave's alleged battery of Plaintiff also witnessed Dave's alleged battery of Bartender. Thus, a substantial amount of the evidence (i.e., the testimony of the witnesses to the event) will be the same.

The only factor that militates against allowing Bartender to bring a cross-claim is that a judgment on Plaintiff's claim against Dave would not preclude Bartender, who is not in privity with either Dave or Plaintiff, from suing on his own claim. Denying Bartender the ability to bring the claim would not prevent him from having his case heard at some future point. *Id.* § 1431, at 275–76. However, given that Bartender's claim against Dave is logically related to Plaintiff's claims, that it raises overlapping factual and legal issues, and that the same evidence is relevant to both claims, a court should allow Bartender's claim to be included as a cross-claim in Bartender's answer.

Point Three(a) (20%)
A federal district court would not have independent subject-matter jurisdiction over a state law cross-claim for $20,000 between two defendants who are citizens of the same state because the claim does not arise under federal law, the claimants are not diverse, and the amount-in-controversy requirement for diversity cases is not satisfied.

The federal question statute grants the federal district courts original jurisdiction "of all civil actions arising under the Constitution, laws, or treaties of the United States." 28 U.S.C. § 1331. A claim arises under federal law if federal law creates the cause of action. *Merrell Dow Pharms. Inc. v. Thompson*, 478 U.S. 804, 808 (1986); *Am. Well Works Co. v. Layne & Bowler Co.*, 241 U.S. 257, 260 (1916) (Holmes, J.) ("A suit arises under the law [that] creates the cause of action."). Here, state law creates Bartender's battery claim against Dave. Under this test, Bartender's cross-claim does not arise under federal law, and therefore the court would not have jurisdiction under the federal question statute, 28 U.S.C. § 1331.

Nor would a federal court have diversity jurisdiction over Bartender's claim. First, there is no diversity. Bartender and Dave are both citizens of State A. Second, Bartender is seeking damages of only $20,000, well below the $75,000 jurisdictional minimum in diversity actions. *See* 28 U.S.C. § 1332(a)(1).

Point Three(b) (20%)

A federal district court would have supplemental subject-matter jurisdiction over a state law cross-claim for $20,000 between citizens of the same state as long as it is so related to the plaintiff's claim against the defendants, of which the court has original jurisdiction, that the claims form part of the "same case or controversy" under Article III of the Constitution.

In the instant case, the federal district court has original diversity jurisdiction over Plaintiff's claims against Bartender and Dave. 28 U.S.C. § 1332. Each claim is for an amount in excess of $75,000, and Plaintiff, a citizen of State B, is diverse from both defendants, who are citizens of State A.

The supplemental jurisdiction statute permits federal district courts that have original jurisdiction of a civil action to assert "supplemental jurisdiction over all other claims that are so related to claims in the action within such original jurisdiction that they form part of the same case or controversy under Article III of the United States Constitution." 28 U.S.C. § 1367(a). Claims form part of the "same case or controversy" under Article III if they "derive from a common nucleus of operative fact." *United Mine Workers of America v. Gibbs*, 383 U.S. 715, 725 (1966). Cross-claims that satisfy Rule 13(g)'s "transaction or occurrence" test presumptively satisfy the *Gibbs* "common nucleus of operative fact" test and are within the court's supplemental jurisdiction. 13 WRIGHT ET AL., *supra,* § 3523, at 165–73. As noted in Point One, Bartender's claim and Plaintiff's claims arise out of the same occurrence, raise many of the same factual and legal issues, and will be proved, in part, by the same evidence. These claims clearly arise out of a "common nucleus of operative fact"—the bar fight that gave rise to all the claims in the case.

Because Bartender's claim is part of the "same case or controversy" as Plaintiff's original claims, it falls within the federal court's supplemental jurisdiction.

Federal Civil Procedure
(July 2011)

ANALYSIS

Legal Problems

(1)   Is a district court's grant of judgment on the pleadings with respect to a counterclaim a "final decision" subject to immediate appeal when the district court also orders judgment to be entered on the counterclaim?

(2)   Is a district court's refusal to enforce a contractual forum-selection clause a "final decision" subject to immediate appeal?

(3)   Does a district court's refusal to enforce a contractual forum-selection clause fall within any of the exceptions to the final-judgment rule?

(4)   If a district court makes several orders in a case and one of those orders is appealable, may an appellate court review the non-appealable orders on grounds of efficiency?

DISCUSSION

Summary

BritCo can appeal immediately from the district court's decision on BritCo's counterclaim. Where there are multiple claims or counterclaims in a case, a final disposition of one of those claims will be appealable when, as here, the trial court orders entry of judgment on that claim and certifies that there is no just reason for delay. FED. R. CIV. P. 54(b).

BritCo cannot appeal immediately from the court's refusal to enforce the forum-selection clause. The court's decision on this issue did not end litigation on the merits of the case and was therefore not an appealable final judgment.

In addition, the court's forum-selection order is not appealable under the collateral-order doctrine. Assuming the lower court's decision on the forum-selection clause was incorrect, immediate appeal is not necessary to vindicate BritCo's rights under the contractual forum-selection clause. Those rights can be protected after final judgment, by striking down any judgment issued in violation of the forum-selection clause. Nor do the facts of this problem present the kind of extraordinary abuse of power that would prompt an appellate court to review a lower court's action by writ of mandamus.

Even though the appellate court would have jurisdiction over another decision in the same case, considerations of efficiency do not give the court the power to hear an appeal from the lower court's decision on the forum-selection issue.

Point One (45%)

The district court's grant of judgment on the pleadings with respect to BritCo's counterclaim is immediately appealable because the district court judge stated that there was no just reason for delay and ordered entry of judgment on the counterclaim.

In the federal courts, litigants ordinarily may appeal only from final judgments of the district courts. *See* 28 U.S.C. § 1291. A final judgment is one that "ends the litigation on the merits and leaves nothing for the court to do but execute the judgment." *Catlin v. United States,* 324 U.S. 229, 233 (1945).

When, as in this problem, more than one claim for relief is presented in an action, Federal Rule of Civil Procedure 54(b) provides that a decision that "adjudicates fewer than all the claims" in the action "does not end the action as to any of the claims or parties. . . ." Under this default rule, a grant of judgment on one of several claims in an action is not a final judgment and is not subject to immediate appeal.

However, Rule 54(b) permits district courts to reverse the default rule and to designate their resolutions of particular claims as immediately appealable "final judgments" even when there are other claims in the action that have not yet been decided. A district court may "direct entry of a final judgment" as to a claim if the district court "expressly determines that there is no just reason for delay." This procedure "does not relax the finality required of each decision, as an individual claim, to render it appealable, but it does provide a practical means of permitting an appeal to be taken from one or more final decisions on individual claims, in multiple claims actions, without waiting for final decisions to be rendered on *all* the claims in the case." *Sears, Roebuck & Co. v. Mackey,* 351 U.S. 427, 435 (1956) (emphasis in original).

In this problem, multiple claims for relief were presented by the parties—OfficeEquip sued for breach of contract and BritCo counterclaimed for breach of the non-competition clause in the contract. When the district court granted judgment on the pleadings for OfficeEquip on BritCo's counterclaim, the court also expressly directed entry of judgment and expressly determined that there was no reason for delay. Thus, under Rule 54(b), the district court's decision constituted a "final judgment" on the counterclaim and is immediately appealable.

Point Two (40%)

The district court's refusal to enforce the forum-selection clause is not an appealable final judgment.

The district court's refusal to enforce the forum-selection clause did not resolve any of the claims in the action. Far from "end[ing] the litigation on the merits," *Catlin,* 324 U.S. at 233, the court's decision allowed the litigation to go forward on the merits. Under the final-judgment rule, this is a non-appealable interlocutory order.

Although there are certain exceptions to the final-judgment rule that BritCo could invoke in an attempt to secure immediate review of the court's decision, none of the exceptions would be applicable on the facts of this problem. *See* Point Three.

Point Three (10%)
A district court's order refusing to dismiss a case pursuant to a contractual forum-selection clause is not immediately appealable under the judge-made collateral-order doctrine or pursuant to any other exception to the final-judgment rule.

    a. Collateral-order doctrine.

In *Cohen v. Beneficial Industrial Loan Corp.*, 337 U.S. 541 (1949), the U.S. Supreme Court created the so-called "collateral order" doctrine as an exception to the final-judgment rule. Under the collateral-order doctrine, an immediate appeal may be taken from an interlocutory order that conclusively determines an important issue in a case if that issue is independent of (collateral to) the merits of the action and *if a delay in appellate review would effectively preclude the losing party from an opportunity to vindicate its rights on appeal.*

The collateral-order doctrine does not apply in this case because an immediate appeal is not necessary to preserve BritCo's contractual right to have contract disputes adjudicated in London. If the lower court's ruling on the forum-selection clause is wrong, BritCo's contractual rights can be vindicated on an appeal from a final judgment in the case. An appellate court could order dismissal of the case at that time, thus forcing OfficeEquip to pursue its claim in the appropriate court. *See Lauro Lines S.R.L. v. Chasser*, 490 U.S. 495 (1989) (collateral-order doctrine does not permit immediate appeal from an order denying enforcement of a contractual forum-selection clause because the right to have "binding adjudication" only in a particular forum can be vindicated on appeal from final judgment by reversing a judgment entered in violation of that right).

    b. Mandamus or prohibition.

Another means of obtaining immediate review of interlocutory orders is to seek an extraordinary writ (mandamus or prohibition) from the appellate court reversing the trial court's ruling. 28 U.S.C. § 1651(a). However, an appellate court is highly unlikely to grant an extraordinary writ in a case of this sort.

Mandamus and prohibition are available to allow appellate courts "to confine trial judges to the lawful exercise of their jurisdiction or to compel them to act if they have abdicated their jurisdictional obligations." J.H. FRIEDENTHAL, M.K. KANE, & ARTHUR R. MILLER, CIVIL PROCEDURE 624 (4th ed. 2005); *Roche v. Evaporated Milk Ass'n*, 319 U.S. 21, 26 (1943). Although courts often favor the enforcement of forum-selection clauses, *see The Bremen v. Zapata Off-Shore Co.*, 407 U.S. 1 (1972) (stating strong federal policy of enforcing forum-selection clauses in admiralty actions), their enforceability is not guaranteed and ultimately depends on the terms of the clause, the reasons for its adoption, and its impact on the parties to the litigation. *Cf. Carnival Cruise Lines, Inc. v. Shute*, 499 U.S. 585 (1991) (enforcing a forum-selection clause in a cruise line ticket on basis that clause is efficient tool for determining location of litigation in event of accident, use of clause avoids litigation in multiple forums, and plaintiffs did not satisfy their burden of establishing serious inconvenience if case were heard in chosen forum). Given that the writs of mandamus and prohibition are extraordinary writs to be used only in exceptional circumstances, s*ee Cheney v. U.S. District Court for the District of Columbia*, 542 U.S. 367, 380 (2004), it is highly unlikely that an appellate court would grant a writ to exercise immediate review over a district court's judgment about such matters.

[NOTES: (1) Technically, the writ that would be appropriately sought in this case is a writ of prohibition. But examinees who mention either writ should receive credit. (2) There are other statutory exceptions to the final-judgment rule, but none of them apply to this problem and you should not expect examinees to discuss them. *See, e.g.,* 28 U.S.C. § 1292(a) (immediate appealability of certain orders relating to injunctions, receiverships, and admiralty); 28 U.S.C. § 1292(b) (appealability of interlocutory orders when district judge certifies certain grounds for immediate appeal). *See generally* FRIEDENTHAL, *supra*, at 629–33.]

Point Four (5%)

The doctrine of pendent appellate jurisdiction would not authorize the appellate court to hear an appeal from the forum-selection decision, even though the court would have jurisdiction over another decision in the same case.

Otherwise non-appealable rulings are sometimes reviewed by appellate courts under the doctrine of "pendent appellate jurisdiction." The argument for pendent appellate jurisdiction is that the final-judgment rule "is designed to prevent parties from interrupting litigation by pursuing piecemeal appeals. Once litigation has already been interrupted by an authorized pretrial appeal, . . . there is no cause to resist the economy that pendent appellate jurisdiction promotes[,]" and a party should be able immediately to appeal any decisions in the case that can conveniently be reviewed along with the appealable order. *Swint v. Chambers County Comm.*, 514 U.S. 35, 45 (1995). BritCo might argue persuasively that judicial economy would be served if the appellate court would hear its appeal from the order denying enforcement of the forum-selection clause at the same time the court hears its appeal from the judgment on the pleadings order.

However, pendent appellate jurisdiction would not be available in this case. Although the U.S. Supreme Court has implied that the exercise of pendent appellate jurisdiction might sometimes be appropriate, it has also suggested that the scope of such jurisdiction should be narrowly confined. The appellate courts are bound by 28 U.S.C. § 1291, which limits their basic appellate jurisdiction to "final decisions," and reasons of judicial economy alone would not justify a court in expanding its jurisdiction to cover non-final orders. Rather, a party seeking review of a non-final order on the ground that it is pendent to an appealable order would need to show that the two rulings were "inextricably intertwined" or that "meaningful review" of the ruling over which the court has jurisdiction would not be possible unless the court also reviewed the otherwise non-appealable ruling. *Swint*, 514 U.S. at 51.

The forum-selection ruling and the ruling denying BritCo's counterclaim are not inextricably intertwined. Moreover, meaningful review of the counterclaim issue is possible without any consideration of the forum-selection question. Consequently, pendent appellate jurisdiction is not available in this case.

[NOTE: Even well-prepared examinees may be unfamiliar with the concept of pendent appellate jurisdiction. While the Supreme Court has mentioned the concept and it may be a useful label for some decisions, the Court has not expressly developed a doctrine of "pendent appellate jurisdiction." Nonetheless, examinees should be expected to spot the issue—raised by these facts—of how an appellate court ought to respond when a litigant seeks review of multiple orders of a lower court, some of which are appealable orders and some of which are not. What is important is that examinees recognize that there is a judicial economy argument in favor of reviewing all the orders simultaneously, but that *the judicial economy argument fails* because of the final-judgment rule, unless some special reason can be shown why simultaneous review will contribute to the court's ability to review the appealable order. Examinees who spot the problem and understand that judicial economy alone is not grounds for review of the forum-selection clause decision should receive full credit for this portion of the analysis, even if they make no mention of pendent appellate jurisdiction.]

Federal Civil Procedure
(February 2012)

ANALYSIS

Legal Problems

(1)   Does a federal court have removal jurisdiction when the parties to the state action are diverse, the amount in controversy exceeds $75,000, and the defendant is not from the state where the action was originally filed?

(2)   Should a federal court grant a change of venue pursuant to a forum-selection clause when the chosen venue is reasonable but the forum-selection clause is invalid under the law of the state where the case was originally filed?

(3) When federal jurisdiction is based on diversity, what effect does a change of venue have on the substantive law that applies?

DISCUSSION

Summary

Pursuant to 28 U.S.C. § 1441, a case filed in state court is removable by a defendant to federal court if the case falls within the original jurisdiction of the federal court. Here, the case was properly removed because it falls within the original diversity jurisdiction of the federal court: the two parties are of diverse citizenship, and the amount in controversy is in excess of $75,000. *See* 28 U.S.C. § 1332(a)(1).

Venue changes are proper under 28 U.S.C. § 1404(a) when they serve "the convenience of parties and witnesses" and are "in the interest of justice." Here, State B is arguably a more convenient forum for the litigation. Moreover, the Supreme Court has ruled that the "interest of justice" language in the statute provides a basis for a federal policy of enforcement of forum-selection clauses through venue transfers. Finally, venue in State B is proper under 28 U.S.C. § 1391(a)(1), because State B is a place where all defendants reside, and also under § 1391(a)(2), because a "substantial part" of the events relating to the dispute occurred in State B.

When a case is transferred under § 1404, the transferee court must apply the law of the original transferor forum, including that state's choice-of-law rules. Here, because the facts say that State A courts would apply State A law to the case, the federal court in State A is required to do so, and that law also must be applied in the transferee State B federal court. Therefore, the change of venue would not affect what law applies, and therefore contract rescission will be allowed.

Point One (30%)

It was proper to remove the action from a state court in State A to the federal court in State A because that federal court would have had diversity jurisdiction over the case had it been filed there originally.

A defendant may remove a civil action from state court to federal court if the action is a type over "which the district courts of the United States have original jurisdiction." 28 U.S.C. § 1441(a). In this case, if the action had been filed originally in a federal court, it would have been within the diversity jurisdiction of the federal court.

Federal diversity jurisdiction extends to "all civil actions where the matter in controversy exceeds . . . $75,000, and [which are] between . . . citizens of different States." 28 U.S.C. § 1332(a)(1). The restorer and owner are citizens of different states, so the diversity requirement is satisfied. Furthermore, the remedy sought by the owner—a return of the $100,000 contract price—exceeds the jurisdictional amount of $75,000. It does not matter that the owner may recover less than this: a plaintiff's claim of damages in excess of the jurisdictional amount will be accepted unless it "appear[s] to a legal certainty that the claim is really for less than the jurisdictional amount." *St. Paul Mercury Indemnity Co. v. Red Cab Co.*, 303 U.S. 283, 289 (1938). Here the facts relating to performance of the restoration contract, the amount paid on that contract, and the amount sought in rescission are adequate to avoid any suggestion that the recoverable damages are less than the jurisdictional amount "to a legal certainty."

Accordingly, because the case falls within the federal court's diversity jurisdiction, the federal court had removal jurisdiction over the action.

[NOTES: (1) Removal itself does not raise any personal jurisdiction issues, and discussions of personal jurisdiction are not relevant to the question asked, which is whether the federal court has removal jurisdiction. (2) In actions where federal jurisdiction is based on diversity, a defendant cannot remove the case to federal court if the case was filed in a state court in the defendant's home state. *See* 28 U.S.C. § 1441(b). That bar to removal is inapplicable on our facts because State A is not the defendant's (the restorer's) home state.]

Point Two (40%)

The change-of-venue motion is very likely to be granted because State B is a reasonably convenient forum in which to hear the action, the parties' contractual agreement to litigate in State B provides a strong reason for granting a transfer, and the State B federal court would have been an appropriate place in which to bring the action in the first place.

The motion for a change of venue is governed by 28 U.S.C. § 1404(a), which provides in its entirety, "For the convenience of parties and witnesses, in the interest of justice, a district court may transfer any civil action to any other district or division where it might have been brought." Transfer pursuant to the "convenience . . . and interest of justice" standard of § 1404 is discretionary ("may"), but transfer under § 1404 may be made only to a district in which the action might originally "have been brought."

In this case, the action originally could have been brought in a federal district court in State B. First, a State B federal court would have had diversity jurisdiction over the action. (*See* Point

One.) Second, a State B federal court would have been an appropriate venue for the action. Under 28 U.S.C. § 1391(a)(1), venue is proper in a district where "any defendant resides, if all defendants reside in the same State." On that basis, State B is a proper original venue simply because the restorer resides there. In addition, venue is proper in State B under § 1391(a)(2), which permits venue in any judicial district "in which a substantial part of the events or omissions giving rise to the claim occurred." The contract was signed in State B, and the restorer's work on the tapestry was performed there. Finally, because the restorer is a resident citizen of State B, the State B federal court would have had jurisdiction over him. In short, the action could originally have been brought in State B.

The question, therefore, is whether convenience and the "interest of justice" favor a transfer from State A to State B. Absent the forum-selection clause, the issue could be argued either way. Arguably, most of the evidence and witnesses in the case would be found in State B, which is where the work on the tapestry was performed and where the contract was drafted and signed. On the other hand, State A is the owner's home (and a convenient place for the owner to litigate), and it is also connected to the transaction—it was the situs of the negotiations. Judges have a good deal of discretion under § 1404(a), but normally a judge would allow a plaintiff's original venue choice to prevail where the facts are closely divided on the issues of convenience and interest of justice.

However, the presence of the forum-selection clause alters this analysis. In *Stewart Organization, Inc. v. Ricoh Corp.*, 487 U.S. 22 (1988), the Supreme Court ruled that a reasonable forum-selection clause is a relevant factor favoring a § 1404 change-of-venue motion, even if the forum-selection clause is unenforceable under the applicable state law. According to the Supreme Court, the presence of a reasonable forum-selection clause is an important consideration relevant to the "interest of justice" determination under § 1404. *See* 487 U.S. at 29. In this case, there are several connections between the transaction, the parties, and State B, and the parties' selection of a State B forum was certainly reasonable.

In sum, State B is an appropriate venue under the federal venue statute, there are several important connections between the case and State B, and the forum-selection clause provides a strong reason to grant the transfer. Therefore, the State A federal district court should grant the motion for change of venue.

Point Three (30%)

The United States District Court in State B must apply the law of State A to the transferred action, including State A's choice-of-law rules. Because State A would have applied its own rescission law, the federal court in State B must also apply State A rescission law.

In this diversity case based on a state law breach-of-contract claim, the *Erie* rule would have required the State A federal court to apply state substantive law. Moreover, for *Erie* purposes, the state substantive law includes any choice-of-law rules that a state court would apply as part of state law. *See Klaxon Co. v. Stentor Electric Mfg. Co.*, 313 U.S. 487 (1941). In this case, the facts state that State A choice-of-law rules would lead a State A court to apply its own rescission law.

Following a § 1404 transfer, the transferee court must apply the same law to the case as would have been applied by the transferor court. *See Van Dusen v. Barrack*, 376 U.S. 612 (1964). Thus, the State B federal court must apply whatever law would have been applied by the State A federal court. In short, the change of venue does not affect the law that will be applied to the substantive issues in the case.

Therefore, whether the case is heard in federal court in State A or federal court in State B, State A rescission law will be applied.

Federal Civil Procedure
(July 2012)

ANALYSIS

Legal Problems

(1)   Do the Federal Rules of Civil Procedure permit a defendant to amend its answer after discovery has closed in order to add an affirmative defense that has been suggested by facts revealed in discovery when that defense could have been raised at the outset of the action?

(2)   Should summary judgment be granted when facts revealed in discovery support a defendant's affirmative defense but when there are other facts at issue that would permit a jury to reject the defense?

DISCUSSION

Summary

Under Federal Rule of Civil Procedure 15(a)(2), leave to amend should be freely given when justice requires. Here, the merits of the case are advanced by allowing the amendment adding the affirmative defense, and there are no facts to suggest that Plaintiff would be prejudiced in the preparation and presentation of her case by allowing the amendment. Although Plaintiff will be harmed if Defendant is allowed to prove a valid defense, the harm of being subject to a valid defense is not the kind of "prejudice" that would warrant denying an amendment. On the applicable "abuse of discretion" standard, it is unlikely that the appellate court would reverse the trial court's decision on this issue.

The trial court erred in granting Defendant's motion for summary judgment. Under Rule 56(c), the standard for granting such a motion is that there is no genuine issue of material fact raised. Here, Plaintiff's deposition testimony suggests that there are genuine issues of material fact concerning whether Defendant exercised reasonable care to prevent and correct harassment and whether Plaintiff's failure to complain about the harassment was reasonable.

Point One (50%)

The trial court properly granted Defendant leave to amend its answer to the complaint, given that justice favors allowing Defendant to raise a potentially valid affirmative defense and no facts suggest that Plaintiff was unfairly prejudiced by the amendment.

A defendant has the burden of pleading all affirmative defenses. Federal Rule of Civil Procedure 8(c) is very clear when it states that a party defending a claim "must affirmatively state any avoidance or affirmative defense . . . ." Defendant had failed to raise a potentially valid affirmative defense in its answer and later sought to amend.

Under Rule 15(a)(2), a district court "should freely give leave [to amend] when justice so requires." The Supreme Court has defined this standard "negatively" by indicating that amendments should be allowed unless they result in a form of injustice. *See Foman v. Davis*, 371 U.S. 178 (1962). The categories of injustice the Court describes are undue delay, bad faith or dilatory motive, repeated failure to cure defects by amendment, undue prejudice to the party opposing the amendment, or futility of the amendment. Here, the only possible ground that Plaintiff might use to resist the amendment is "undue prejudice."

Defendant has a strong argument that it would be unjust to deny the amendment because doing so would deny Defendant an opportunity to have the case decided on its legal merits. Indeed, having cases decided on their merits is one of the key goals of the Federal Rules of Civil Procedure, *see, e.g.*, FED. R. CIV. P. 1 (seeking to achieve a "just, speedy, and inexpensive" determination) and one reason that the Rules direct courts to "freely give leave" to amend. Moreover, allowing a potentially valid defense does not cause "undue prejudice" to Plaintiff. Plaintiff's legal claim is only as good as its ability to overcome defenses, and it is not unjust to require that she respond to those defenses.

Plaintiff might argue that she is prejudiced by injecting the defense after the close of discovery. But no facts suggest prejudice, and it is difficult to know what the prejudice might be. The defense is supported by testimony of Plaintiff and is based upon matters known to her all along. Moreover, Plaintiff's counsel knew or should have known about this well-established affirmative defense. Finally, if Plaintiff requires more time for discovery, that is a matter that the court could address by granting more time (if the issue were raised) and is not itself a basis for denying leave to amend. In short, justice seems better served by allowing the amendment to ensure that the case is decided on its merits and not on the basis of Defendant's failure to plead an affirmative defense in its original answer.

Point Two (50%)

The trial court erred in granting summary judgment. Plaintiff's deposition answers, which were the basis of Defendant's summary judgment motion, raise genuine issues of material fact sufficient to preclude entry of judgment as a matter of law.

Federal Rule of Civil Procedure 56(a) allows a summary judgment motion to be granted only if "there is no genuine issue as to any material fact and the movant is entitled to judgment as a matter of law [JML]." *See Celotex Corp. v. Catrett*, 477 U.S. 317, 322 (1986); *Anderson v. Liberty Lobby, Inc.*, 477 U.S. 242, 247–48 (1986). An issue of fact is "genuine" if, based on the evidence presented by the nonmoving party, a reasonable jury could return a verdict for that party. A fact is "material" if it is relevant to an element of a claim or defense and its existence would affect the outcome of the case under the governing law. *Anderson*, 477 U.S. at 248. In determining whether there is a genuine dispute as to material fact, the court should consider the "depositions, documents, electronically stored information, affidavits or declarations, stipulations (including those made for purposes of the motion only), admissions, interrogatory answers, or other materials." FED. R. CIV. P. 56(c)(1)(A).

Here, Defendant has an affirmative defense to a claim of sex discrimination if Defendant can prove that no adverse job action was taken against Plaintiff, that Defendant exercised reasonable care to prevent and correct harassing behavior, and that the employee unreasonably failed to take advantage of protective or corrective opportunities. When, as here, a party moves for summary judgment on an issue on which it has the burden of persuasion at trial, it "must support its motion with credible evidence . . . that would entitle it to a directed verdict if not controverted at trial." *Celotex Corp.*, 477 U.S. at 331 (Brennan, J., dissenting). Defendant sought to establish facts supporting the elements of its affirmative defense by relying on Plaintiff's deposition testimony. The issue is whether that testimony establishes that there is no "genuine issue as to any material fact" relating to Defendant's affirmative defense and that, accordingly, Defendant should be granted judgment as a matter of law.

Plaintiff admitted that she suffered no adverse job action, that Defendant had policies against sexual harassment, and that procedures were available to her to complain about harassment. However, by itself this is not enough to warrant summary judgment, because Plaintiff's testimony also raised genuine issues with respect to two facts that are essential to Defendant's affirmative defense (as described in the facts of this question): whether Defendant exercised reasonable care to prevent and correct any sexually harassing behavior and whether Plaintiff unreasonably failed to take advantage of corrective opportunities provided by Defendant.

Although part of Plaintiff's deposition testimony suggests that Defendant did make reasonable efforts to address harassment by providing procedures that Plaintiff did not use, Plaintiff also testified that Defendant made no independent effort to enforce its policies (relying on Plaintiff to report or on supervisors to monitor the situation). In considering this evidence, the court must draw those inferences "most favorable to the party opposing the motion" for summary judgment. *United States v. Diebold, Inc.*, 369 U.S. 654, 655 (1962) (per curiam). A jury could reasonably find that this was not reasonable enforcement action for a workplace that had previously not had any women. Furthermore, Plaintiff testified that she was afraid to report the incidents for fear of retaliation. A jury might find her fear of retaliation to be a reasonable basis for her failure to use available procedures, given that the supervisor was himself one of the alleged harassers.

In short, it appears that there are genuine issues about the reasonableness of the employer's actions to prevent harassment and the reasonableness of Plaintiff's failure to report the behavior. Without a resolution of those factual issues, it is not clear whether Defendant's affirmative defense is valid, and summary judgment should not have been granted.

Federal Civil Procedure
(February 2013)

ANALYSIS

Legal Problems

(1) Does a judgment in a prior action preclude a nonparty from suing the same defendant on a closely related claim when the nonparty and the original plaintiff are in a family relationship?

(2) Does a judgment rendered in an earlier action preclude a nonparty from litigating an issue that was actually decided in the first suit?

(3) May a nonparty to an earlier action invoke the judgment in that action to preclude a party to the prior action from relitigating an issue that the party had a full and fair opportunity to litigate in the earlier action?

DISCUSSION

Summary

Pursuant to the doctrines of claim preclusion (res judicata) and issue preclusion (collateral estoppel), a judgment is binding on the parties thereto. In the absence of privity, nonparties to a prior suit cannot be bound by a judgment rendered in their absence. Thus, in the absence of privity, a nonparty to the first suit is not precluded from presenting her claim in a second suit even if it is factually related to the claims and defenses presented in the first suit; nor is she bound by determinations of issues made in the first suit. A family relationship, without more, does not support a finding of privity. For this reason, Mother, as a nonparty, is not bound by the judgment in the Son-Driver action. She may bring her separate claim for damage to her car, and she is not precluded from litigating the question of whether she was negligent in the maintenance of her car.

Driver, on the other hand, could be precluded from relitigating the issue of her negligence pursuant to the doctrine of non-mutual issue preclusion (also called non-mutual offensive collateral estoppel), which allows a nonparty to a prior action to invoke issue preclusion to prevent a party to that prior action from relitigating determinations of issues made therein. However, Mother may be prevented from invoking non-mutual collateral estoppel in this case because she could easily have joined her claim in the prior action but did not do so.

[NOTE: Federal common law governs the preclusive effect of a judgment rendered by a federal court sitting in diversity. *See Semtek Int'l, Inc. v. Lockheed Martin Corp.*, 531 U.S. 497, 508 (2001). But the *Semtek* Court concluded that federal common law, in this context, incorporates the preclusion law of the state in which the rendering federal court sits (unless the state law is incompatible with federal interests), *id.* at 508–09. Thus, State A's preclusion law determines the preclusive effect of the judgment rendered in Son's suit against Driver. The problem says that

State A preclusion law is identical to federal preclusion law, so the following analysis utilizes general principles of preclusion drawn from Supreme Court case law (announcing federal preclusion rules) and the Restatement (Second) of Judgments.]

Point One (35%)
Under the doctrine of claim preclusion, the judgment rendered in the first action does not preclude Mother, a nonparty, from suing Driver for the damage to her car because the judgment binds only parties or those in privity with them, and Mother and Son are not in privity.

Driver may contend that the doctrine of claim preclusion (res judicata) precludes Mother from presenting a claim arising from the same nucleus of facts that was presented in the first action brought by Son. According to the doctrine of claim preclusion, "when a court of competent jurisdiction has entered a final judgment on the merits of a cause of action, the parties to the suit and their privies are thereafter bound 'not only as to every matter which was offered and received to sustain or defeat the claim or demand, but as to any other admissible matter which might have been offered for that purpose.'" *Commissioner of Internal Revenue v. Sunnen*, 333 U.S. 591, 597 (1948) (citation omitted).

However, the doctrine of claim preclusion does not apply to Mother on the facts of this problem. First, Mother was not a party to the earlier case. "It is a principle of general application in Anglo-American jurisprudence that one is not bound by a judgment *in personam* in a litigation in which he is not designated as a party or to which he has not been made a party by service of process." *Taylor v. Sturgell*, 553 U.S. 880, 884 (2008) (citing *Hansberry v. Lee*, 311 U.S. 32, 40 (1940)); *see also* RESTATEMENT (SECOND) OF JUDGMENTS § 34(3) (1982). This rule reflects our "deep-rooted historic tradition that everyone should have his own day in court." *Martin v. Wilks*, 490 U.S. 755, 762 (1989) (citation omitted) (superseded by statute on other grounds). Since Mother was not a party to the first suit, she is not bound by the judgment unless an exception to the general rule applies.

Mother might be bound by the prior judgment if she were considered to have been sufficiently in privity with Son that Son represented her interests in that action. "A person who is not a party to an action but who is represented by a party is bound by and entitled to the benefits of a judgment as though he were a party." RESTATEMENT (SECOND) OF JUDGMENTS § 41(1). But there is no suggestion in the facts of the problem that Son, who is an adult, purported to represent Mother's interests in the first suit. "[C]lose family relationships are not sufficient by themselves to establish privity with the original suit's party, or to bind a nonparty to that suit by the judgment entered therein . . . ." *Cuauhtli v. Chase Home Finance LLC*, 308 Fed. Appx. 772, 773 (5th Cir. 2009) (citation omitted); *accord* 18A CHARLES ALAN WRIGHT ET AL., FEDERAL PRACTICE AND PROCEDURE § 4459 (2d ed. 2002).

In *Taylor v. Sturgell, supra,* the Supreme Court identified other special circumstances in which nonparties may be bound by a prior judgment—when a nonparty consents to be bound; when a nonparty is in a pre-existing substantive legal relationship with a party (such as preceding and succeeding property owners); when a nonparty assumed control of the prior litigation; when a party seeks to relitigate through a proxy; or where a special statutory scheme seeks to foreclose successive litigation by nonparties. *See Taylor*, 553 U.S. at 893–95. None of these circumstances exists here.

Because Mother was not a party to the first suit and is not in privity with Son, who is an adult, the judgment in the first action does not preclude her from bringing her own claim against Driver.

Point Two (35%)

Under the doctrine of issue preclusion, the judgment rendered in the first action does not preclude Mother, a nonparty, from litigating the issue of her negligence in maintaining her car's brake lights because the judgment binds only parties or those in privity with them, and Mother and Son are not in privity.

By its affirmative response to a special interrogatory, the jury in the first action expressly concluded that "Mother negligently failed to ensure that the brake lights on her car were in proper working order." Driver may attempt to invoke the doctrine of issue preclusion to preclude Mother from relitigating this issue in the second action.

> [I]ssue preclusion arises in a second action on the basis of a prior decision when the same 'issue' is involved in both actions; the issue was 'actually litigated' in the first action, after a full and fair opportunity for litigation; the issue was 'actually decided' in the first action, by a disposition that is sufficiently 'final,' 'on the merits,' and 'valid'; it was necessary to decide the issue in disposing of the first action, and . . . the later litigation is between the same parties or involves nonparties that are subject to the binding effect or benefit of the first action . . . . Once these requirements are met, issue preclusion is available not only to defend against a demand for relief, but also as offensive support for a demand for relief. Issue preclusion, moreover, is available whether or not the second action involves a new claim or cause of action.

18 CHARLES ALAN WRIGHT ET AL., FEDERAL PRACTICE AND PROCEDURE § 4416 at 392–93 (2d ed.); *see also* RESTATEMENT (SECOND) OF JUDGMENTS § 27 (1982).

Here, several of the elements necessary for issue preclusion are present. The same issue is involved in both actions—the issue of Mother's negligence in failing to maintain the brake lights on her car. That issue was actually litigated in the first action and decided by the jury. There is nothing to suggest anything less than a full and fair opportunity to litigate. The judgment disposing of the issue was final.

Nevertheless, the judgment will not preclude Mother from relitigating the issue for two reasons. First, Mother was not a party to the first action and, as explained above, Mother and Son are not in privity. Therefore, she cannot be denied an opportunity to litigate the issue of her negligence. Second, it does not appear that the jury's decision as to Mother's negligence was necessary to the prior judgment against Driver. Nothing suggests that the finding on Mother's negligence had any bearing on the outcome of the first action.

Point Three (30%)

Under the doctrine of non-mutual issue preclusion, the judgment rendered in the first action might preclude Driver from relitigating the issue of her negligence. However, Driver has a strong argument that such a result would be inconsistent with the policy against offensive use of non-mutual estoppel when the non-party plaintiff easily could have joined as a plaintiff in the first action.

Because Son already convinced the jury in the first action that "Driver was negligent in the operation of her vehicle," Mother may wish to invoke the doctrine of non-mutual issue preclusion to prevent Driver from relitigating the question of her negligence. As noted above, "issue preclusion arises in a second action on the basis of a prior decision when the same 'issue' is involved in both actions; the issue was 'actually litigated' in the first action, after a full and fair opportunity for litigation; the issue was 'actually decided' in the first action, by a disposition that is sufficiently 'final,' 'on the merits,' and 'valid'; it was necessary to decide the issue in disposing of the first action . . . ." 18 CHARLES ALAN WRIGHT ET AL., FEDERAL PRACTICE AND PROCEDURE § 4416 at 392 (2d ed.); *see also* RESTATEMENT (SECOND) OF JUDGMENTS § 27.

Here, these basic requirements for issue preclusion are met. First, the same issue is involved in both suits: whether Driver was negligent in the operation of her car. Second, this issue was actually litigated and decided in the first action; the jury answered a special interrogatory raising this very question. There is nothing to suggest that Driver lacked a full and fair opportunity to litigate the issue. Since a judgment was rendered against Driver for the injuries Son sustained as a result of Driver's negligence, resolution of the issue was necessary to dispose of the first action. Driver was a party to the first action, so she may be bound by the judgment.

[NOTE: Traditionally, issue preclusion required mutuality—both the party asserting issue preclusion and the party against whom issue preclusion was asserted were bound by the prior judgment. Under the traditional mutuality rule, Mother could not assert issue preclusion against Driver because Mother would not be bound by the judgment if Driver sought to rely on it. *See* Point One. There is no mutuality between Mother and Driver with respect to the prior judgment.

This traditional mutuality requirement has been abandoned in most jurisdictions. The Supreme Court rejected a strict mutuality requirement in *Blonder-Tongue Laboratories, Inc. v. University of Illinois Foundation*, 402 U.S. 313 (1971) (non-mutual defensive collateral estoppel used by a defendant to preclude a plaintiff from relitigating a claim the plaintiff previously litigated), and *Parklane Hosiery Co. v. Shore*, 439 U.S. 322 (1979) (non-mutual offensive collateral estoppel used by a plaintiff to preclude a defendant from relitigating a claim the defendant previously litigated). In *Parklane Hosiery*, the Court concluded (as a matter of federal preclusion law) that trial courts should have "broad discretion" to determine whether or not to permit a plaintiff to invoke non-mutual issue preclusion. "The general rule should be that in cases where a plaintiff could easily have joined in the earlier action or where . . . the application of offensive estoppel would be unfair to a defendant, a trial judge should not allow the use of offensive collateral estoppel." *Id.* at 331.

The *Parklane Hosiery* decision identified a number of circumstances that might make it unfair to allow a plaintiff to invoke non-mutual issue preclusion (non-mutual offensive collateral estoppel in the traditional terminology) against a defendant. In particular, the *Parklane Hosiery* court suggested that issue preclusion may not be appropriate if the plaintiff in the second action "could easily have joined in the earlier action." *Id.* Prohibiting plaintiffs from using non-mutual estoppel under such circumstances would promote judicial efficiency by encouraging plaintiffs to join the prior action. It would also discourage plaintiffs from staying out of prior litigation in order to secure, in effect, two bites at the apple: using the prior litigation offensively if the defendant loses and forcing the defendant to litigate a second time if the defendant wins the prior action.

An exceptional exam answer might therefore argue that non-mutual issue preclusion should be denied on these facts. Son and Mother both reside in State A; since they are related, they know each other well, and Son was driving Mother's car when the accident occurred. They could have sued together, and Rule 20 of the Federal Rules of Civil Procedure would have authorized joinder of their claims because those claims arose from the same transaction or occurrence and raised a common question of law or fact. FED. R. CIV. P. 20(a). The facts do not suggest that Mother had any reason not to join Son's suit other than a desire to see how Son's action concluded before bringing her own claim. *Cf. Nations v. Sun Oil Co. (Del.)*, 695 F.2d 933, 938 (5th Cir. 1983) (concluding that plaintiff "was entitled to await the development of his injuries and their predictable consequences"). Because it appears that Mother may be a "wait-and-see" plaintiff who could easily have joined the original action, a trial court might disallow, as a matter of discretion, her use of non-mutual issue preclusion.]

MBE SUBJECTS – RELEASED ESSAY QUESTIONS

REAL PROPERTY
MEE Question – July 2008

ANALYSIS

Legal Problems: (1)   What type of tenancy did the oral lease between Landlord and Tenant create?

               (2)   Did Tenant properly terminate the tenancy?

               (3)   Is Landlord entitled to collect $800 from Tenant?

DISCUSSION

Summary

Under the Statute of Frauds, a lease for a term of more than one year (in some states, three years) must be in writing or its electronic equivalent. When a tenant enters into an oral lease that violates the Statute of Frauds and the landlord accepts rent from the tenant, a periodic tenancy ensues if, as here, the tenant has been in possession and paying rent for a substantial period. Either party can terminate a periodic tenancy by giving proper notice. A proper termination notice provides notice for a period at least equal to the payment period specified in the lease agreement. Here, the payment period was one month, and Tenant's two-week notice was thus improper. As a result, Tenant still owes rent to Landlord. However, because the lease did not prohibit an assignment, Tenant's interest was freely assignable; Landlord's consent was not required. Because Tenant properly assigned her lease to Friend, who timely paid the $800 rent due to Landlord, Landlord cannot recover $800 from Tenant.

Point One (35–45%)
The oral five-year lease between Landlord and Tenant violated the Statute of Frauds. Because Tenant took possession two years ago and Landlord accepted monthly rent payments from Tenant throughout that time, a periodic month-to-month tenancy was created.

Most states have enacted a Statute of Frauds that requires leases of more than one year (in some states, three years) to be in writing. A lease subject to the Statute of Frauds is voidable until the tenant takes possession and the landlord accepts rent from the tenant. If the tenant takes possession and the landlord accepts rent, an at-will or periodic tenancy is created because there has been partial performance. *See* 3 GEORGE W. THOMPSON, COMMENTARIES ON THE MODERN LAW OF REAL PROPERTY, § 1021 (1980).

Here, Tenant took possession of the office and Landlord accepted rent. Thus, a periodic or at-will tenancy was created.

An at-will tenancy may be terminated without notice; a periodic tenancy requires notice for a period at least equal to the rent-payment term. Where, as here, rent has been paid for a substantial period of time, the tenancy is generally classified as periodic because payment over time evidences a commitment to the arrangement and creates expectations that justify notice of termination. Assuming that a periodic tenancy was created, most likely it was a month-to-month tenancy because the lease provided for monthly payments of rent.

Point Two (15–25%)
A periodic month-to-month tenancy is terminable by notice given at least one month prior to the termination date. Here, the tenancy was not properly terminated because Tenant gave Landlord only two weeks' notice.

A periodic month-to-month tenancy can be terminated by either party with a one-month notice of termination. *See* RESTATEMENT (SECOND) OF PROPERTY § 1.5, cmt. f. At common law, an oral notice was sufficient. Today, many states require written notice of termination. *See, e.g.*, CAL. CIVIL CODE § 1946 (West 1985) (requiring written notice minimum of 30 days before date specified in notice).

Here, Tenant gave Landlord a two-week notice of termination instead of the required one-month notice. Thus the notice to terminate was ineffective to terminate the month-to-month tenancy as of the beginning of the next month even if Tenant's oral notice of termination was acceptable under state law.

[NOTE TO GRADERS: The Restatement of Property takes the view, without any support in the case law, that a periodic *year-to-year* tenancy arises if monthly rent is paid and accepted for at least one year. RESTATEMENT (SECOND) OF PROPERTY § 2.3, cmt. d. This would affect the notice period required to properly terminate the tenancy, but it would not affect the case outcome. If a tenancy at will was created, then no notice of termination was required, and Tenant properly terminated the lease. In that case, Tenant would not owe any further rent.]

Point Three (35–45%)
Because the lease did not prohibit an assignment, Tenant was free to assign the lease to Friend. Because Friend properly took an assignment of the office lease from Tenant and timely paid the $800 rent to Landlord, Landlord has no claim against Tenant for unpaid rent.

Where a periodic tenancy arises, the terms of the unwritten lease, except the provision relating to the lease term, are enforceable. *See generally* STOEBUCK & WHITMAN, THE LAW OF PROPERTY § 6.15, at 261–62, § 6.17, at 265–66 (3d ed. 2000); RESTATEMENT (SECOND) OF PROPERTY § 2.3(2). In the absence of a contrary provision in a lease, a tenant's interest, like other property interests, is assignable. The assignee of a month-to-month tenant takes a month-to-month tenancy.

When a tenant assigns his interest in a lease, privity of estate arises between the assignee and the landlord. Privity of contract continues to exist between the landlord and the tenant. *See* HERBERT HOVENKAMP & SHELDON KURTZ, PRINCIPLES OF PROPERTY LAW § 9.10 (2005). The tenant is still contractually bound to pay rent, and thus serves as a surety for unpaid rent; if the assignee fails to pay the rent, the tenant is liable to the landlord. *See id.* at 302–03. Here, because the assignee,

Friend, paid the rent to Landlord when Friend sent Landlord the $800 check, no additional rent was due and Tenant is not liable to Landlord for $800.

MBE SUBJECTS – RELEASED ESSAY QUESTIONS

REAL PROPERTY
MEE Question – February 2009

ANALYSIS

(Real Property I.B.; III.D.1.; IV.B.2; V.D.2.)

Legal Problems: (1)   Does a deed conveying property "jointly in fee" to two daughters "equally, to share and share alike" create a tenancy in common or a joint tenancy with right of survivorship in the daughters?

    (2)   Assuming a joint tenancy with right of survivorship was created in the two daughters, was it severed when one of the two joint tenants granted a mortgage on, and entered into a contract for the sale of, the farm?

    (3)   Is a buyer subject to a prior recorded mortgage when the buyer has no actual notice of the mortgage and the previous deed in the chain of title to the seller was unrecorded?

    (4)   Does a deceased seller's interest in the proceeds of sale due under an executory real estate contract pass to the beneficiary of the real or personal property under the deceased seller's will?

DISCUSSION

Summary

The language in Parent's deed to Jessie and Karen probably is sufficient to overcome the statutory presumption that a conveyance to two or more persons creates a tenancy in common. Thus, Jessie and Karen probably became joint tenants in the farm. At Jessie's death her interest would terminate and Karen would own the farm in fee unless prior to her death Jessie severed the joint tenancy.

Whether the mortgage to Credit Union, executed only by Jessie, severs the joint tenancy depends upon whether the farm is located in a lien- or title-theory jurisdiction. However, even if the farm is located in a lien-theory jurisdiction where a mortgage would not sever the joint tenancy, when Jessie entered into a contract to sell Buyer her interest in the farm, she likely severed the joint tenancy and converted it into a tenancy in common. Thus, once the executor deeded Jessie's interest to Buyer, Karen and Buyer owned the farm as tenants in common.

Credit Union also has a mortgage on one-half of the farm. Because Credit Union recorded the mortgage before Buyer entered into the contract to purchase Jessie's interest, Buyer had constructive notice from the record of Credit Union's interest created by Jessie and takes subject to that mortgage even though the deed to Jessie was not recorded.

Because of the doctrine of equitable conversion, Jessie's interest in the farm at her death is characterized as personalty and passes to Legatee under Jessie's will.

Point One (20–30%)

Parent's deed of gift to Jessie and Karen created a tenancy in common unless the language in the deed overcame the statutory presumption that a conveyance to two or more persons creates a tenancy in common. Whether or not it does here is a close question. While the word "jointly" itself may not overcome the presumption, when used in conjunction with the phrase "share and share alike," it might.

A deed to two or more grantees may create a joint tenancy or a tenancy in common. To create a joint tenancy, the common law traditionally required the existence of four unities (time, title, interest, and possession). *See* WILLIAM B. STOEBUCK & DALE A. WHITMAN, THE LAW OF PROPERTY 182–83 (3d ed. 2000). Under the four-unities test, a joint tenancy presumptively is created by a conveyance to two or more persons if they acquire their interest at the same time, acquire their interest under the same instrument, acquire an equal interest in the property, and acquire the right to possession of the property.

The four unities are satisfied by Parent's deed to the daughters, so at common law they clearly took title as joint tenants with right of survivorship. With a joint tenancy, each joint tenant has the right of survivorship.

Today, in most states, there is a statutory presumption that a conveyance to two or more persons creates a tenancy in common rather than a joint tenancy. *See generally* SHELDON F. KURTZ, MOYNIHAN'S INTRODUCTION TO THE LAW OF REAL PROPERTY 282 (4th ed. 2005). Thus, if the presumption is not rebutted, Jessie and Karen took as tenants in common. Tenants in common have no right of survivorship.

The standard way to overcome the presumption favoring a tenancy in common is for the deed to use the term "joint tenancy" or "joint tenants," usually also adding an express reference to "survivorship" or "survivors," *id.* at 275–77, and it can be argued that where such language is absent the statutory presumption is not rebutted.

Although survivorship language is missing in Parent's deed to Jessie and Karen, the language of the deed could still be construed to overcome the statutory presumption favoring a tenancy in common. For example, some cases hold that the word "jointly" standing alone rebuts the presumption favoring a tenancy in common, although there are contrary cases holding that a grantor who uses the word "jointly" in the deed may intend that the grantees "own together" rather than that they own as joint tenants with the right of survivorship. STOEBUCK & WHITMAN, *supra,* at 185–86. Here, however, Parent's deed not only used the word "jointly" but added the phrase "equally, to share and share alike." This phrase, in common with the word "jointly," may point toward a joint tenancy as it evidences an intent by Parent to give each daughter an equal interest in the farm, another hallmark of a joint tenancy but not essential for a tenancy in common. This additional phrase also reflects the historic conception that joint tenants hold as a unit rather than as separate individuals. *See id.* at 184.

[NOTE: This is a close question, and applicants should receive equal credit for reasoned analyses that consider the possibilities, whether they conclude that the deed creates a tenancy in common or a joint tenancy. However, an applicant's conclusion should not affect the rest of the analysis because the remaining calls assume Jessie and Karen took from Parent as joint tenants with right of survivorship.]

Lastly, a deed is effective between the parties even if it is not recorded. *Id.* at 872. Thus, the daughters acquired a tenancy in common or a joint tenancy, notwithstanding their failure to record their deed of gift.

Point Two (25–35%)

If the deed of gift created a joint tenancy, Jessie's mortgage severed that joint tenancy as to her one-half interest if the state follows the "title theory" instead of the "lien theory" of mortgages. In any event, Jessie's contract of sale severed the joint tenancy. Therefore, Karen had no right of survivorship and the deed from the executor to Buyer caused Karen and Buyer to acquire a title to the farm as tenants in common.

When property is held by two persons in joint tenancy, a conveyance by one joint tenant of her entire ownership interest severs the joint tenancy as to the conveyed share. This is because the conveyance severs at least the unities of time and title between the remaining co-tenant and the new co-tenant. *See Jackson v. O'Connell*, 177 N.E.2d 194, 194–95 (Ill. 1961); KURTZ, *supra*, at 278–79.

When, as here, a joint tenant transfers a lesser interest, such as a mortgage, a severance of the joint tenancy may also occur. Courts usually resolve the issue by trying to decide whether the transfer destroyed any of the four unities.

In the case of mortgages, some states follow the "title theory," which says that the mortgagee takes title to the property for the duration of the mortgage. In "title theory" states, a mortgage granted by one joint tenant severs the joint tenancy as to the conveyed share. This would convert the joint tenancy into a tenancy in common. Other states follow the "lien theory" of mortgages, which says that the mortgagor retains title and the mortgagee takes only a lien on the property. This would leave the four unities intact, and thus Jessie would remain a joint tenant with her sister. *See People v. Nogarr*, 330 P.2d 858 (Cal. Ct. App. 1958); KURTZ, *supra*, at 279; STOEBUCK & WHITMAN, *supra*, at 184–85, 191.

If Jessie's grant of the mortgage did not sever the joint tenancy, her contract to sell her interest in the farm to Buyer almost certainly had that effect. *See* STOEBUCK & WHITMAN, *supra*, at 190–91; 2 A. JAMES CASNER, AMERICAN LAW OF PROPERTY § 6.2, at 11 (1952); Annotation, *What Acts by One or More of Joint Tenants Will Sever or Terminate the Tenancy*, 64 A.L.R.2d 918, 935–36 (1959). Although Jessie retained legal title until the contract closed, under the four unities analysis she no longer had the same interest as her sister. This follows from the doctrine of equitable conversion (discussed in Point Four below) because her interest (but not Karen's interest) is now subject to Buyer's equitable interest or title. Because the joint tenancy was severed, Karen had no right of survivorship and, therefore, did not become the sole owner of the farm at Jessie's death.

[NOTE: Many applicants may not address the distinction between the title- and lien-theory jurisdictions and should not be penalized for failing to do so. What is important is that applicants recognize the legal issue and come to a resolution. Furthermore, without regard to the mortgage, applicants should address the effect of the contract with Buyer. Also, if a jurisdiction does not recognize the doctrine of equitable conversion, the execution of the contract would not sever the joint tenancy.]

Since the joint tenancy was severed, the deed from the executor to Buyer caused Karen and Buyer to hold the farm as tenants in common.

Point Three (20–30%)
Buyer cannot qualify as a bona fide purchaser because Buyer had constructive notice of Credit Union's recorded mortgage. The failure to record the deed of gift from Parent to Jessie and Karen should not impair the mortgage because the non-recording of that deed would not interfere with Buyer's ability to find the mortgage during a title search. Thus, Buyer takes the farm subject to Credit Union's interest.

Assuming Buyer acquired an interest from Jessie, Buyer may claim to be a bona fide purchaser, who should take free of Credit Union's mortgage. To qualify as a bona fide purchaser, a person must (i) pay value for an interest and (ii) not have actual, inquiry, or constructive notice of the competing prior-in-time interest. *See* STOEBUCK & WHITMAN, *supra*, at 879–83.

Although Buyer paid value, *see id.* at 879–80, and lacked actual notice of the mortgage, Buyer had constructive notice of the mortgage because the mortgage was properly recorded before Buyer entered into the contract to buy Jessie's interest. Had Buyer made a proper title search by looking in the grantor-grantee index for all of Jessie's transactions as a grantor, the mortgage would have been discovered. Therefore, Buyer takes subject to Credit Union's interest.

[NOTE: The mortgage is not a "wild deed" that could be deemed unrecorded because it is outside of the buyer's chain of title or recorded out of sequence (too early or too late). Since the facts state that the grantor-grantee index operates in this jurisdiction, if Buyer had searched under Jessie's name as grantor, Buyer would have found her mortgage to Credit Union. In the typical wild deed case, the prior interest outside of the chain of title is created by someone other than the buyer's grantor.]

[NOTE: As an aside, Buyer's search would also reveal the fact that Jessie and her sister lacked record title because they never recorded the deed of gift from Parent. However, here that would not be a title objection because Buyer agreed to accept a title that was not marketable.]

Point Four (15–25%)

When Jessie entered into the contract of sale, the doctrine of equitable conversion transformed her interest into personalty. As a result, Devisee acquired no interest in the farm under Jessie's will. Rather, the sales proceeds pass to Legatee.

The doctrine of equitable conversion splits title to the property when a real estate contract is signed. Buyer obtained equitable title, and Jessie as seller retained legal title as trustee to secure payment of the remainder of the purchase price. *See* STOEBUCK & WHITMAN, *supra*, at 786–87. Equitable conversion only applies to a contract that is specifically enforceable; here there are no facts suggesting that Jessie or Buyer would be unable to obtain specific performance. Buyer cannot reject title because of the outstanding mortgage as Buyer agreed to accept a title without any warranties and regardless of its marketability. When equitable conversion applies, the seller's legal title is considered personal property, and the buyer's equitable title is considered real property. *Id.* When Jessie died, her share passed to Legatee, who took personal property under Jessie's will.

[NOTE: The preceding analysis depends upon Jessie's share prior to her death being classified as a tenancy in common because (1) the mortgage severed Jessie's joint tenancy share, or (2) the contract of sale to Buyer severed Jessie's joint tenancy share. If, on the other hand, Jessie died still owning a one-half interest as joint tenant, no part of the farm or its proceeds passed to Legatee or Devisee under Jessie's will. Rather, by right of survivorship, Karen owned the entire farm free and clear of the rights of Credit Union and Buyer because their interests, being wholly derivative from Jessie, would also expire at Jessie's death. *See* KURTZ, *supra*, at 279; STOEBUCK & WHITMAN, *supra*, at 191.]

MBE SUBJECTS – RELEASED ESSAY QUESTIONS

REAL PROPERTY
MEE Question – February 2010

ANALYSIS

Legal Problems: (1)   Did Bob take the land subject to a power-line easement when the easement was not recorded but the power lines were visible?

(2)   Did Bob take the land subject to a gas-line easement when the easement was not recorded and the gas line was not visible but Bob had actual knowledge of the gas-line easement?

(3)   If Bob took the land subject to the power-line easement, may he obtain damages from Owen based on the Owen-to-Abe warranty deed's covenant against encumbrances?

DISCUSSION

Summary

Under the state recording statute, a subsequent purchaser for value takes the purchased property free of prior unrecorded interests unless the purchaser has actual or inquiry notice of those interests. Both Abe and Bob had inquiry notice of the power-line easement, as the power lines were clearly visible. Had they looked, they would have discovered the power lines and been aware that they should make further inquiry regarding the possibility of an existing easement. Thus, Abe and Bob were on notice of any interest the electric company actually had that they could have ascertained by asking the electric company, and they take subject to that interest.

Abe had no notice of the underground gas-line easement, since it was not visible and it was not on the record. Thus Abe took the property free and clear of the gas-line easement. While Bob had actual knowledge of the gas-line easement, because of the shelter doctrine, Bob takes the land free of that easement. Because Bob is a remote grantee, he cannot recover damages from Owen for the power-line easement based on the covenant against encumbrances in the Owen-to-Abe deed.

Point One (40%)
Both Abe and Bob acquired the land subject to the unrecorded power-line easement. Because the power lines were visible, Abe and Bob were on inquiry notice of the easement.

In this state, a "conveyance of real property is not valid against any subsequent purchaser who, without notice, purchases said real property in good faith and for valuable consideration." Notice may be actual, constructive, or inquiry. JOHN G. SPRANKLING, UNDERSTANDING PROPERTY LAW § 24.04[D] (2d ed. 2007). Constructive notice comes from information that is on the public land records; inquiry notice arises from facts discernible through visual inspection of the premises or the applicable recorded instruments. *Id.* § 24.06. Some jurisdictions and authors equate constructive and inquiry notice.

Here, because Abe paid Owen for the land, he is a subsequent purchaser for value. Abe did not have actual notice of the power-line easement and, because that easement was never recorded, he did not have constructive notice of it based on the recorded instruments. However, because the power lines were discernible from visual inspection, Abe had inquiry notice of the power-line easement. Therefore, under the relevant statute, Abe took subject to the power-line easement. *See* WILLIAM B. STOEBUCK & DALE A. WHITMAN, THE LAW OF PROPERTY § 11.10, at 882 (3d ed. 2000).

The same analysis applies to Bob, who also takes subject to the power-line easement.

Point Two (30%)
Abe did not take the land subject to the unrecorded and invisible gas-line easement because he had no actual, constructive, or inquiry notice of it. While Bob had actual knowledge of the gas-line easement, because of the shelter doctrine, he takes free and clear of that easement.

The gas-line easement was never recorded. Thus neither Abe nor Bob acquired constructive notice of this easement from the land records. Abe had no actual notice of it, either. In contrast to the power-line easement, the gas-line easement was not discernible through visual inspection; the gas lines were underground, and the surface of the land had been restored to its pre-installation condition. Therefore, Abe had no inquiry notice of the gas-line easement. Thus, under the state recording statute, Abe took free of the gas-line easement.

At first blush, it would appear that Bob took the land subject to the gas-line easement because, in contrast to Abe, he had actual notice of it. However, under the "shelter doctrine," when a bona fide purchaser (here, Abe) acquires title free of a prior encumbrance, he can convey that title to a subsequent purchaser (here, Bob) free of that encumbrance. In order to ensure that the bona fide purchaser has an unlimited right to alienate his land in the future, the shelter doctrine applies even when the subsequent purchaser has actual notice of the prior, unrecorded encumbrance. *See* STOEBUCK & WHITMAN, *supra*, § 11.10 at 889.

Point Three (30%)
Bob cannot obtain damages from Owen for breach of the covenant against encumbrances because Bob is a remote grantee. However, some jurisdictions do not follow the common law rule. In those jurisdictions, a remote grantee may sue on the covenant against encumbrances.

Owen conveyed the land to Abe with a full covenant and warranty deed that made no mention of encumbrances. A full-covenant deed includes a covenant against encumbrances, i.e., a warranty that, at the time of conveyance, there are no outstanding third-party rights that negate the title the grantor purports to convey. That covenant is inconsistent with the fact that Abe and later Bob took subject to the power-line easement. (*See* Point One.) Abe clearly had a cause of action against Owen for breach of the covenant against encumbrances. The issue is whether Bob may also sue Owen.

Under the common law, the covenant against encumbrances is a "present covenant," breached, if at all, if there is an encumbrance at the time of the conveyance to Abe. Furthermore, the covenant does not run with the land. Therefore, it cannot benefit a remote grantee like Bob. *See* STOEBUCK & WHITMAN, *supra*, § 11.13 at 911; HERBERT HOVENKAMP & SHELDON F. KURTZ, THE LAW OF PROPERTY 617 (5th ed. 2001).

Some jurisdictions do not follow the common law rule. *See, e.g., In re Estate of Hanlin*, 133 N.W. 140 (Wis. 1907). In those jurisdictions, a remote grantee may sue on the covenant against encumbrances. *See* UNIFORM LAND TRANSACTIONS ACT § 2-312. Even in those jurisdictions, a remote grantee with notice of the easement may not sue on the theory that with such notice the grantee (1) never relied on the covenant or (2) bargained for a reduction in the purchase price to take account of the easement. *See Ford v. White*, 172 P.2d 822 (Or. 1946). Courts are divided on whether the covenant against encumbrances is breached when an unrecorded easement is ascertainable through visual inspection. Some courts say yes; others disagree, arguing that the grantee can sue even though the easement is visible because, if the warranty is in the deed, the grantee can reasonably assume that an easement is no longer valid when the grantor makes no exception for it when conveying title.

MBE SUBJECTS – RELEASED ESSAY QUESTIONS

REAL PROPERTY
MEE Question – July 2010

ANALYSIS

Legal Problems: (1)   What interest did School acquire in Blackacre and what interest did Owner retain?

(2)   Did School breach the condition or limitation in the deed from Owner when it stopped using the building erected on Blackacre to teach students and began using it for administrative purposes?

(3)   If Owner retained a future interest in Blackacre, did the statute of limitations run on that interest?

(4)   What interests, if any, do Ann and Mary have in Blackacre?

DISCUSSION

Summary

Owner conveyed either a fee simple determinable or a fee simple on condition subsequent to School. Because the Owner-to-School deed used language that did not conform to the classic formulations for creating either of these interests, it is unclear which interest School acquired. However, in the case of an ambiguous conveyance, there is a presumption in favor of the fee simple on condition subsequent.

If School has a fee simple on condition subsequent, either (1) Owner retained nothing to pass to Daughter because the Owner-to-School deed did not expressly specify that Owner retained a power of termination, or (2) Owner retained an implied power of termination which passed to Daughter and then through Daughter's estate to Ann and possibly, upon Bill's death, to Mary as well.

If School has a fee simple determinable, then Owner's retained possibility of reverter passed through Daughter's estate at least to Ann and possibly to Mary.

Any cause of action for breach of the condition or limitation (depending on the interest created in the School) accrued only three years ago and, thus, the statute of limitations on that action has not run.

Of course, whether School's interest has been lost depends upon whether using Blackacre for administrative purposes violates the requirement of using the property to teach children aged 5 to 13, which it probably does.

Point One (45%)

The terms of the conveyance to School were ambiguous. In construing an ambiguous instrument, courts typically adopt a preference for the fee simple on condition subsequent. If so construed, it is unclear what interest, if any, Owner retained. It is either no interest or a right of entry for condition broken (also called a "power of termination"). If, on the other hand, School acquired a fee simple determinable in Blackacre, then Owner retained a possibility of reverter.

If the Owner-to-School deed conveyed a fee simple determinable to School, then Owner retained a possibility of reverter, which became possessory immediately upon the happening of the event designated in the instrument. JOSEPH W. SINGER, INTRODUCTION TO PROPERTY 309 (2d ed. 2005). If, instead, the Owner-to-School deed conveyed a fee simple on condition subsequent, Owner may or may not have a power of termination or right of entry for condition broken, depending on whether the court would be willing to imply a forfeiture provision when none was expressly set forth in the deed. See RICHARD POWELL, REAL PROPERTY § 1:13.06[3] (Patrick J. Rohan ed., 1990); THOMPSON ON REAL PROPERTY § 17.01(d) (David A. Thomas ed., 1994)

Here, Owner conveyed Blackacre to School "if School uses Blackacre only to teach children aged 5 to 13." The language of the deed does not conform to the paradigms for creating either a fee simple determinable or a fee simple on condition subsequent. To create a fee simple determinable, the typical formulation would be "to School, so long as it uses Blackacre only to teach children aged 5 to 13." To create a fee simple on condition subsequent, the typical formulation would be "to School, but if School does not use Blackacre only to teach children 5 to 13, then the grantor may reenter and reclaim Blackacre." See SHELDON F. KURTZ, MOYNIHAN'S INTRODUCTION TO THE LAW OF REAL PROPERTY 44–48 (4th ed. 2005).

In this case, the deed language is ambiguous. The word "if" in the deed expresses the language of condition and suggests an intent to create a fee simple on condition subsequent, but the deed's lack of an express, retained power of termination suggests the intention to instead create a fee simple determinable. On the other hand, the deed's failure to use the typical formulation for creating a fee simple determinable, coupled with the absence of any language suggesting that Owner intended to retain a possibility of reverter (e.g., "Blackacre shall revert"), suggests that Owner did not intend to convey a fee simple determinable, but instead a fee simple on condition subsequent.

Where the terms of a conveyance are ambiguous, courts construe the instrument to effectuate the grantor's intentions. In construing an ambiguous instrument, courts typically adopt a preference for the fee simple on condition subsequent. See id. at 48; WILLIAM B. STOEBUCK & DALE A. WHITMAN, THE LAW OF PROPERTY 44 (3d ed. 2000).

Here, it doesn't matter whether the court finds that the Owner-to-School deed created a fee simple determinable or fee simple on condition subsequent if, in the latter case, it also implies a forfeiture provision. Either construction would allow Owner to regain possession of Blackacre if

School ceased using Blackacre only to teach children aged 5 to 13. The only practical difference that flows from these two constructions is that the fee simple on condition subsequent would require Owner (or his successors) to first make a demand, and the fee simple determinable would not because it becomes possessory immediately upon the happening of the limitation. In either case, the holder might have to sue the School to enforce her rights if Blackacre is not vacated voluntarily by School.

If, however, the court construes the deed as creating a fee simple on condition subsequent and does not imply a power of termination, then School has what amounts to a fee simple absolute because no one has the power of termination or right of entry for condition broken. In this case, School's decision to discontinue use of Blackacre for teaching children aged 5 to 13 has no effect on School's interest in Blackacre.

[NOTE: Applicants who conclude that School has a fee simple on condition subsequent may fail to realize that a right of entry must be expressly reserved in the deed and, thus, fail to discuss a court's reluctance to find a forfeiture.]

[NOTE: An applicant's conclusion on how the deed should be construed is much less important than demonstrating an understanding of the consequences that flow from the various constructions.]

Point Two (10%)
School has likely ceased using Blackacre "only to teach children aged 5 to 13." If Owner is treated as having either a possibility of reverter or a right of entry for condition broken (power of termination), then School's interest can come to an end and, subject to Point Four, Blackacre passes to the successors of Owner's estate. Otherwise, School continues to own Blackacre.

There is a factual question as to whether ceasing to only teach children aged 5 to 13 in the building on Blackacre and then using that building for administrative purposes is inconsistent with language in the deed from Owner to School. *See Mahrenholz v. County Bd. of School Trustees of Lawrence County*, 417 N.E.2d 138 (Ill. Ct. App. 1981). Here again applicants can make an argument either way, but the stronger argument appears to be that the terminating event occurred. No teaching appears to be going on in the building; rather, it is being used for administrative purposes, and that use seems to be beyond the intended purpose set forth in the Owner-School deed.

Point Three (10%)
If Owner's successors have an interest in Blackacre, the statute of limitations has not run on that interest.

Whether Owner conveyed to School a fee simple determinable or a fee simple on condition subsequent, the state statute of limitations applicable to actions for possession permits actions within "10 years after the cause of action accrues."

Because School ceased using Blackacre for the permitted purposes only three years ago, the period in which an action for possession may be brought has not yet expired.

Point Four (35%)

Ann has an interest in Blackacre if Owner retained either a possibility of reverter or a power of termination. In some jurisdictions, Mary (Bill's widow) would also have such an interest. If Owner retained only a power of termination, Ann will have to assert that right by exercising the power because possession will not automatically inure to her as it would have if Owner had retained a possibility of reverter.

If Owner retained a future interest in Blackacre, that interest passed to Daughter upon Owner's death because state law provides that such an interest is devisable. Upon Daughter's death, Daughter's devisable interest passed to Husband for life, with the remainder to "my surviving children."

Although Daughter was survived by two children, one of them, Bill, predeceased Husband. According to the Restatement of Property, which expresses what appears to be the current majority view, a survivorship contingency like that contained in Daughter's will applies at the termination of the interests that precede distribution of the remainder. *See* RESTATEMENT OF PROPERTY § 251 (1940). In this case, that point is Husband's death. Thus, under the Restatement approach, Mary has no interest in Blackacre because Bill, having predeceased Husband, had no interest in Blackacre to devise to Mary. This approach is typically justified on the ground that a testator would want an interest in property to pass only to children who could take possession.

There is another view that interprets a survivorship contingency to require surviving only the testator (here, Daughter) and not the life tenant (here, Husband). This view is typically justified by a preference for early vesting of estates. If it applies, then Bill's interest passed to Mary. *See* 3 POWELL ON REAL PROPERTY ¶ 27.03[2] (Michael Allen Wolf ed., LexisNexis Matthew Bender 2008).

If Owner bequeathed a possibility of reverter in Blackacre, instead of a power of termination, then Ann (and Mary, in a state that follows the non-Restatement view) is entitled to immediate possession of Blackacre. If Owner retained and bequeathed only a power of termination, then Ann's (and, in a non-Restatement jurisdiction, Mary's) interest would not become possessory until and unless the power of termination was exercised.

MBE SUBJECTS – RELEASED ESSAY QUESTIONS

REAL PROPERTY
MEE Question – July 2011

ANALYSIS

Legal Problems

(1)   Has Railroad abandoned its interest?

(2)   In the absence of a state recording act, as between Daughter and Purchaser, who owns the land?

(3)   Was Purchaser on constructive notice of the interests of Railroad and Daughter and thus not a bona fide purchaser for value?

(4)   Was Purchaser on inquiry notice of the interests of Railroad and Daughter and thus not a bona fide purchaser for value?

DISCUSSION

Summary

Railroad's interest would be lost only if it abandoned that interest, and abandonment is not supported by the facts. Under the common law, in the absence of a recording statute, Daughter would own the land in fee simple subject to the Railroad's easement because both of them acquired their interests before Purchaser bought the land from Oscar's estate. This result changes under the state's notice-type recording statute *only* if Purchaser is a protected bona fide purchaser without notice of either prior interest. Here, the most likely conclusion is that Purchaser, although having no actual or constructive notice of the interest of Railroad or Daughter, had inquiry notice of their interests and, thus, is not protected by the state recording statute. An argument can be made, however, that Purchaser had inquiry notice only of Railroad's interest, in which case Daughter would have no interest in the land, and Purchaser would own it subject to Railroad's interest.

Point One (30%)
Railroad's easement was not abandoned unless Railroad had an intent to abandon it.

Easements may be terminated in a variety of ways, such as by their express terms, written release, merger of the dominant and servient tenements, prescription, estoppel, condemnation, and abandonment. The only method of termination potentially applicable under these facts is abandonment. *See* HERBERT HOVENKAMP & SHELDON F. KURTZ, PRINCIPLES OF PROPERTY LAW 333–36 (6th ed. 2005). If a court were to find that either Daughter or Purchaser acquired a fee simple title (*see* Point Three) subject to Railroad's interest, either may argue that Railroad's easement was extinguished by abandonment because Railroad has not used the easement since 2000.

An abandonment theory is unlikely to succeed, however, because mere non-use of an easement is insufficient to establish abandonment. Instead, there must be a cessation of use coupled with evidence of the user's intent to abandon the easement. WILLIAM B. STOEBUCK & DALE A. WHITMAN, The Law of Property, 467–68 (3d ed. 2000). Here, there is insufficient evidence of Railroad's intent to abandon its easement. Notably, Railroad has not removed its tracks and there are no other facts to suggest that Railroad has voluntarily relinquished its interest. In the absence of such evidence, a court is likely to find that Railroad has not abandoned its easement.

Point Two (10%)
Under the common law first-in-time, first-in-right principle, Daughter, and not Purchaser, owns the land, unless the state's recording act mandates a contrary result.

Under the common law, a grantor can convey only those rights in land that the grantor had *at the time of the conveyance*. Thus, under the common law, priority among successive transfers is dictated by priority of time—the so-called "first-in-time, first-in-right" principle. *See* 14 POWELL ON REAL PROPERTY § 82.01[1][a] at 82-4 (2009).

Here, Oscar's conveyance to Sam in 1980 takes priority over the subsequent transfer by the executor of Oscar's estate to Purchaser. Once Oscar conveyed the land to Sam, neither Oscar nor his estate at his later death had a title left to convey to anyone, including Purchaser. Rather, title was then in Sam. Sam's conveyance of legal title to Daughter would prevail over the later conveyance by Oscar's executor to Purchaser. However, if the state recording act protects Purchaser, then Purchaser rather than Daughter would own the land. *See* Point Three.

Point Three (25%)
While the state has rejected the common law first-in-time, first-in-right principle by enacting a notice-type statute with a grantor-grantee index, Purchaser was not on constructive notice of the interest of either Daughter or Railroad. Although the deeds to Daughter and Railroad were recorded, they were not properly indexed and, thus, not discoverable, because the deed to their predecessor in title—Sam—was never recorded.

All states have recording statutes that, when applicable, overturn the results of the common law "first-in-time, first-in-right" principle. The recording statute here is a notice-type statute providing that unrecorded conveyances are not valid against a "subsequent purchaser for value and without notice" of the conveyance. Under a notice-type recording statute, Purchaser can prevail against either of or both Daughter and Railroad *only* if (1) the prior conveyances were unrecorded, (2) Purchaser paid value for the land, and (3) Purchaser took without either actual, constructive, or inquiry notice of the prior conveyances.

[NOTE: Some examinees may incorrectly conclude that the recording act is a race-notice statute because the last part of the statute states: "unless the same be recorded according to law." Placed in its proper grammatical context, however, "the same" relates to the instrument of prior *conveyance*. There is no requirement that the *subsequent purchaser* must record to take priority over an earlier transaction. By comparison, a typical race-notice statute protects only a subsequent purchaser who records. If he does not record, he is not protected, even though he is a bona fide purchaser.]

The facts clearly state that Purchaser paid value, so payment of value is not an issue here. Furthermore, no facts suggest that Purchaser had actual notice of the conveyances of the easement and fee to Railroad and Daughter, respectively. But there are two other possible ways for a subsequent purchaser to have notice. One is constructive; the other is inquiry.

Constructive notice arises through the recording system. A purchaser is placed on constructive notice of all information that is *properly* recorded on the public land records whether he sees it or not. *See* POWELL, *supra*, § 82.02[1][d][ii] at 82-33. While both Railroad and Daughter recorded their interests, Sam (from whom they both claimed) did not. Because Sam's deed from Oscar was not recorded, both the deed from Sam to Railroad conveying an easement and the later deed from Sam to Daughter conveying to her a fee are so-called "wild deeds," meaning they were recorded outside the chain of title. As such, they are undiscoverable by a reasonable search of the grantor-grantee indexes. A search of the public land records by Purchaser would have shown that as a matter of public record his seller, Oscar, had not conveyed the property to anyone because the Oscar to Sam deed was not recorded. As a result, a title searcher could not have discovered Sam's later conveyances to Railroad and Daughter even though they were recorded. Courts have uniformly held that a wild deed is not "properly recorded" and, therefore, imports no constructive notice to a subsequent purchaser. *See* WILLIAM B. STOEBUCK & DALE A. WHITMAN, *supra*, 894. Accordingly, Purchaser is not on constructive notice of the interests of Daughter and Railroad and his interest would appear to have priority to theirs. *But see* Point Four.

Point Four (35%)
Purchaser is not a bona fide purchaser for value under the state's notice-type recording statute because he had inquiry notice of Railroad's interest and, likely, of Daughter's interest as well.

Although Purchaser did not have constructive notice (*see* Point Three), the law also imputes knowledge to a subsequent purchaser in another way, namely through an obligation of inquiry. Here there is a strong argument that Purchaser had inquiry notice of Railroad's interest and, therefore, also that he had inquiry notice of Daughter's interest.

Inquiry notice exists when knowledge is imputed to a buyer from facts and circumstances suggesting the existence of a prior conveyance. *See* POWELL, *supra*, § 82.02[1][d][iii], at 82-39. Some courts have held that a purchaser who takes by quitclaim deed, as Purchaser did, is presumed to take with notice of any interests that could have been discovered by reasonable diligence. *See id.* § 82.02[1][d][iii][B], at 82-44 to 82-45. This perspective is based upon the theory that the title is suspicious if a grantor refuses to give covenants of title. The majority of courts, however, reject this rule because there are many legitimate reasons for a grantor to convey by quitclaim deed, particularly in an environment where title insurance is common. *See id.* § 82.02[1][d][iii][B], at 82-46. Accordingly, in most states, Purchaser would not have inquiry notice from the quitclaim deed alone.

[NOTE: In the minority of states that would require further inquiry based upon the quitclaim deed alone, it is unclear what further investigation is required. One could argue that Purchaser could have contacted Oscar's heirs or neighboring landowners, but there is no indication from the facts that such an inquiry would have revealed the prior conveyances. Another possibility would be to search the property tax rolls. The facts do not indicate who has been paying taxes on the property (or whether such taxes even exist in this state), but it is possible that such taxes were assessed against Sam (and later Daughter) after they acquired title to the property.]

The better argument is that inquiry notice arose from the possibility of a visual inspection of the property. Inquiry notice exists when someone other than the record owner is in possession or use of the property. *See id.* § 82.02[1][d][iii][A], at 82-41. Here, a visual inspection would have revealed the existence of railroad tracks on otherwise undeveloped land. Exercising reasonable diligence, Purchaser would have discovered the tracks, and then should have engaged in further inquiry to ascertain the interest of whoever put the tracks there. Accordingly, a court is most likely to find that even though Railroad's easement was recorded outside the chain of title, Purchaser had inquiry notice of Railroad's interest based upon the visible improvements on the land.

Would this inquiry notice also extend to the interest of Sam and then Daughter? Assuming that Purchaser was successful in making inquiries to find Railroad, Purchaser could have discovered that Railroad had acquired its interest from Sam. That discovery would have prompted further inquiry into the nature of Sam's interest. In addition, a search of the grantor index for Sam's name would reveal the deed to Daughter, which was recorded, albeit outside of the chain of title. Accordingly, if Railroad is still in existence and easily located, a court is likely to find that Purchaser had inquiry notice not only of Railroad's easement but also Daughter's fee simple interest.

In short, it seems fairly clear that Purchaser would be deemed to have inquiry notice of Railroad's easement, and it is likely that Purchaser also would have inquiry notice of Daughter's interest. [NOTE: Should an examinee, however, reason that Purchaser's inquiry obligation did not extend beyond asking Railroad what its interest was, then Purchaser would prevail as against Daughter, but not Railroad.]

[NOTE: Examinees may observe that Daughter does not qualify as a purchaser for value because Daughter received the land as a gift. However, Daughter's status as a donee is irrelevant to the analysis because she acquired legal title *before* Purchaser and, therefore, would prevail under the common law priority rule. Thus, Daughter is protected without having to prove her status as a purchaser under the recording act.]

MBE SUBJECTS – RELEASED ESSAY QUESTIONS

REAL PROPERTY
MEE Question – February 2012

ANALYSIS

Legal Problems

(1)   Was Sue's easement over Blackacre that she had acquired from Tom extinguished when she purchased Blackacre from Tom?

(2)   Did Dan acquire an easement implied from prior use over Blackacre when he purchased Whiteacre from Sue?

(3)   How should the proceeds from the sale of Whiteacre be distributed?

DISCUSSION

Summary

Immediately prior to Sue's sale of Whiteacre to Dan, Sue had no easement over Blackacre because the easement she had acquired from Tom was extinguished by merger. Immediately after the sale of Whiteacre to Dan, Dan had an easement over Blackacre. This easement arose by implication from Sue's prior use of the private gravel road over Blackacre for the benefit of Whiteacre.

Because Bank was obligated to advance the $700,000 to Dan under the terms of its loan commitment with Dan, Bank is entitled to all $1,500,000 from the $1,500,000 sales proceeds, and Finance Company is entitled to nothing.

Point One (25%)
The easement Sue acquired from Tom was extinguished by merger when Sue bought Blackacre from Tom. Thus, immediately prior to her sale of Whiteacre to Dan, Sue had no easement over Blackacre.

Sue purchased from Tom an easement for a right-of-way over Blackacre to be used in connection with her ownership of Whiteacre. This easement, an appurtenant easement of which Whiteacre was the dominant estate and Blackacre was the servient estate, was promptly and properly recorded. When the owner of the dominant estate (Sue) acquired the servient estate (Blackacre), however, the easement was extinguished by merger. *See generally* HERBERT HOVENKAMP & SHELDON KURTZ, PRINCIPLES OF PROPERTY LAW 334 (6th ed. 2005); *see also* II AMER. LAW OF PROPERTY § 8.90 (1957). This result follows from the fact that because of the post-sale unity of ownership of the two estates, Sue could enforce the easement only against herself, and lawsuits against one's self are impermissible.

Point Two (40%)
Upon the conveyance of Whiteacre, Dan acquired an easement implied from prior use with respect to use of the private gravel road traversing Blackacre.

An easement implied from prior use arises in favor of a grantee when (1) two parcels of land are in common ownership; (2) one of the parcels is conveyed to a grantee; (3) the parcel conveyed had been receiving a benefit from the parcel retained prior to the conveyance to the grantee, i.e., there was a use over the retained parcel in favor of the conveyed parcel which could have been the subject of an express easement appurtenant; (4) the usage is reasonably necessary or convenient; and (5) the usage is apparent. *See generally* WILLIAM B. STOEBUCK & DALE A. WHITMAN, THE LAW OF PROPERTY § 8.4 at 445 (3d ed. 2000); JOSEPH W. SINGER, INTRODUCTION TO PROPERTY § 5.3.3 at 194 (2d ed. 2005); HOVENKAMP & KURTZ, *supra*, at 331; *see also Romanchuk v. Plotkin*, 9 N.W.2d 421 (Minn. 1943).

Here, the first three criteria are clearly met: Sue owned both Blackacre and Whiteacre; she conveyed one parcel (Whiteacre) to Dan; and Whiteacre, the parcel conveyed, had been receiving a benefit from the parcel retained, i.e., use of the private gravel road traversing Blackacre, which could have been—indeed, was, before its extinction by merger—the subject of an express easement appurtenant.

Sue's use of Blackacre also appears to satisfy the "reasonably necessary" and "apparent" requirements. "The principle underlying the creation of an easement by implication is that it is so evidently necessary to the reasonable enjoyment of the granted premises, so continuous in its nature, so plain, visible and open, so manifest from the situation and relation of the two tracts that the law will give effect to the grant according to the presumed intent of the parties." *Rischall v. Bauchmann*, 46 A.2d 898, 902 (Conn. 1946); *see also Gemmell v. Lee*, 757 A.2d 1171 (Conn. Ct. App. 2000).

Most courts interpret the "reasonably necessary" requirement "to mean that the easement must be important to the enjoyment of the" conveyed land or "highly convenient." SINGER, *supra*, at 196. Courts are likely to find that an easement is implied from prior use where access to the transferred land is "extremely difficult by other routes" and to find that an easement is not implied when the transferred land has "easy access to public roads in another direction." *Id.* at 197. Sue's use of Blackacre for the benefit of Whiteacre meets this test; the facts specify that the private gravel road provided significantly better access to the four-lane highway than did the county road abutting Whiteacre.

Most courts have found that the "apparent" requirement is met when the usage is visible. *See* HERBERT HOVENKAMP & SHELDON F. KURTZ, THE LAW OF PROPERTY 367 (5th ed. 2001). Here, the private gravel road was open and obvious; indeed, the facts state that Dan was aware that Sue had used that road to more easily access the four-lane highway.

Thus, upon Sue's conveyance of Whiteacre to Dan, she conveyed to Dan an easement implied from prior use.

[NOTE: Dan did not acquire an easement by necessity over Blackacre, because Whiteacre is not landlocked, and he has access to it from the county road. An easement by necessity arises only when there has been a conveyance of a portion of the grantor's land, the grantor retains the remaining portion, and, after severance of the grantor's land, it is necessary for the grantee to pass over the grantor's retained portion to reach a public street or highway. *See generally* STOEBUCK & WHITMAN, *supra*, § 8.5 at 447. Landlocked land clearly satisfies the necessity test, and a few courts have found an easement where there is merely "reasonable" necessity. Additionally, this is not a case for easement by estoppel. An easement by estoppel arises when A gives B permission to use A's land and the licensee, here B, invests substantial funds in that land reasonably relying on the permission. The facts here do not support the conclusion that there is an easement by estoppel.]

Point Three (35%)
The proceeds from the foreclosure sale should be paid entirely to Bank because Bank gave Dan a future-advances mortgage.

The typical construction loan provides that the lender will advance funds to the borrower over a fixed time period. The lender secures a mortgage on the property for the entire amount of the money it has agreed to lend, including future advances. Such "future advances" mortgages may provide for obligatory advances, or they may provide for advances that are optional.

Whether the future-advances mortgage payments are obligatory or optional is critical to the rights of a junior lender. If payments under a future-advances mortgage are obligatory, then the junior lender's lien is junior both to amounts loaned to the debtor before the junior lien was recorded and to amounts loaned after the junior lien is recorded. If the payments under a future-advances mortgage are optional, the junior lender has a priority over amounts transferred to the debtor by the senior lender after the junior lender transfers funds to the debtor and records its mortgage. *See generally* GRANT S. NELSON & DALE A. WHITMAN, REAL ESTATE FINANCE LAW § 12.7 at 1088–90 (5th ed. 2007). The rationale for this rule is that in the case of an obligatory loan, the junior lender can ascertain from public land records the maximum amount of the senior lender's claim before loaning money to the creditor, while with an optional loan, the junior lender cannot know whether subsequent advances will be made and the senior lender can protect itself against junior lenders by searching the land records before making additional advances.

Here, Bank's loan commitment to Dan was secured by an obligatory future-advances mortgage, and Bank both recorded its mortgage and loaned Dan money before Finance Company did so. Thus, Bank is the senior lender in the amount of $1,500,000, the full value of its loan commitment to Dan, and it is entitled to all of the foreclosure sales proceeds. Finance Company is entitled to nothing.

MBE SUBJECTS – RELEASED ESSAY QUESTIONS

REAL PROPERTY
MEE Question – February 2013

ANALYSIS

Legal Problems

(1) Does the tenant have a defense to the landlord's action for unpaid rent based on constructive eviction?

(2) Does the tenant have a defense to the landlord's action for unpaid rent based on the tenant's surrender of the premises?

(3) What, if anything, may the landlord recover from the tenant for the period after the tenant vacated the building?

DISCUSSION

Summary

Under the common law, the tenant does not have a defense to the landlord's action for unpaid rent based on constructive eviction. Constructive eviction is based on the tenant proving that (1) the landlord breached a duty to the tenant, (2) the breach caused a loss by the tenant of the substantial use and enjoyment of the premises, (3) the tenant gave the landlord adequate notice and opportunity to repair, and (4) the tenant vacated the leased premises. Here, there was no constructive eviction because, although the tenant vacated and gave the landlord adequate notice, the landlord breached no express or implied duty to the tenant to repair the premises.

The tenant does not have a defense based on the landlord's acceptance of his surrender of the premises; a landlord's retention of keys does not constitute an acceptance of the tenant's surrender unless the landlord so intended, and here, the landlord's statements to the tenant at the time of the surrender of the keys do not evidence the intent to accept the tenant's surrender.

Under the common law, a landlord has no duty to mitigate damages but also cannot sue for rents due in the future. Under this approach, the landlord can sue only for past-due rents. Using this approach, on November 1, the landlord could recover all the rent past due (i.e., rent for September and October) but could not recover for rents due in the future. However, some courts have authorized recovery for future rent minus the fair market rental value of the premises. It is thus possible that the landlord could recover damages equal to the amount of rent due from September 1 to the end of the six-year lease term ($180,000) minus the property's fair-market rental value over that same period.

Point One (45%)

The tenant was not constructively evicted, because the landlord had no duty to repair the commercial premises that were the subject of the lease.

The landlord and the tenant entered into a term-of-years lease because the lease specified both a beginning and an ending date. HERBERT HOVENKAMP & SHELDON F. KURTZ, THE LAW OF PROPERTY 256 (5th ed. 2001). Although a term-of-years lease normally cannot be terminated by the tenant prior to the end of the term, a tenant may terminate a term-of-years lease if the tenant is constructively evicted. *See id.* at 286–88. Typically, as here, a claim of constructive eviction is made as a defense to a landlord's action for damages or unpaid rent.

In order to establish a constructive eviction, the tenant must prove that the landlord breached a duty to the tenant, such as a duty to repair, and that the landlord's breach caused a loss of the substantial use and enjoyment of the premises. The tenant must also show that he gave the landlord notice adequate to permit the landlord to meet his duty to the tenant and that the tenant vacated the leased premises. *Id.; see also* JOHN G. SPRANKLING, UNDERSTANDING PROPERTY LAW § 17.04 (2d ed. 2007).

Under the common law, there was no implied duty on the part of a landlord to repair leased premises; such a duty arose only if expressly set forth in the lease. SPRANKLING, *supra,* § 17.02[B]. Here, the written lease contained no term requiring the landlord to repair the air-conditioning. Even if the conversation created a lease term that the building had air-conditioning, that itself should not create a duty for the landlord to repair it.

Over the past several decades, courts have generally implied a duty to repair in *residential* leases either as part of a revised constructive eviction doctrine or based on an implied warranty of habitability. JOSEPH W. SINGER, PROPERTY 469–70 (3d ed. 2010). This shift has been justified based on the economic disparity between the typical landlord and tenant as well as the fact that residential tenants generally lack both the authority to authorize repairs to common areas of a building and the incentive to make repairs that will ultimately benefit the landlord.

However, courts have been more reluctant to imply a duty to repair in *commercial* leases, a context in which the tenant is often a valuable business and in a better position to assess and make repairs than is the landlord. *But see, e.g., Davidow v. Inwood North Professional Group,* 747 S.W.2d 373 (Tex. 1988). When courts have implied a duty to repair in a commercial lease, it is typically when the repair has been mandated by public authorities and involves work so substantial that it would not ordinarily fall within the tenant's common law repair duty and/or the value of the repair would primarily inure to the landlord's reversionary interest. *See Brown v. Green,* 884 P.2d 55 (Cal. 1994); Eugene L. Grant et al., *The Tenant as Terminator: Constructive Eviction in Modern Commercial Leases,* 2 THE COMMERCIAL PROPERTY LEASE ch. 15 (ABA 1997). Some courts have also permitted constructive eviction claims by commercial tenants of office buildings based on repairs required in common areas of the building. *See id.; Echo Consulting Services, Inc. v. North Conway Bank,* 669 A.2d 227 (N.H. 1995).

Here, the tenant is the owner of a valuable manufacturing operation and is the exclusive occupant of the building, the repair has not been mandated by public authorities, and the repair is not structural. To the contrary, the repair involves a feature of the building of unusual importance in the tenant's manufacturing operation, and the tenant is likely far more knowledgeable than the landlord about the air-conditioning specifications necessary for the manufacture of the tenant's product.

Based on these facts, it is unlikely that a court will find that the tenant in this case was constructively evicted. Although the tenant can show that he gave adequate notice to the landlord of the air-conditioning malfunction and vacated the premises, the lease was commercial, and it did not contain any promises or covenants by the landlord except a covenant of quiet enjoyment; a covenant of quiet enjoyment does not entail any repair obligations.

[NOTE: An examinee's conclusion is less important than his or her demonstrated awareness of the elements of constructive eviction and the need to imply a repair duty for such a defense to be viable here. Although the implied warranty of habitability is not available to this tenant, Texas, Minnesota, and Massachusetts imply a warranty of suitability in commercial leases in limited circumstances, and an examinee might argue that this warranty should apply here. If an examinee concludes that this warranty applies, he or she should discuss the other requirements for constructive eviction.

If the examinee wrongly concludes that the first element for a constructive eviction has been met, the examinee will then have to discuss the remaining three elements in order to conclude that the tenant can claim constructive eviction. The tenant would have a strong argument that the second element—substantial interference with the use and enjoyment of the premises—also is met. As indicated above, the landlord was aware that a functioning air-conditioning system was vital to the tenant's manufacturing operations. The facts further indicate that the system had failed three times in the past few months. The landlord may try to argue that the malfunctions did not substantially interfere with the tenant's use of the premises because the malfunctions caused the temperature to climb above 81 degrees for only a short period of time—3 hours, 6 hours, and 10 hours, respectively—on each occasion. The tenant will argue, however, that the landlord was aware that the tenant's manufacturing operations could tolerate temperatures above 81 degrees for no more than 6 hours. The final malfunction exceeded that limit, destroying $150,000 worth of the tenant's products.

The tenant would also have a strong argument that the third element is met: notice and opportunity to cure. The tenant notified the landlord of the problem immediately upon the system's first malfunction and did so again when it malfunctioned a second time and then a third time. The landlord might argue that there was insufficient time to cure the problem because the system corrected itself within a few hours on the first and second times. Although the malfunction lasted more than 10 hours the third time, the landlord might argue that the time period was insufficient to get a repair person on the premises. A court would be likely to find this argument unpersuasive, however, because the landlord could have attempted to correct the problem after the first and second malfunctions.

Assuming that the landlord was given sufficient notice and opportunity to cure, a court would be likely to conclude that the tenant also satisfied the final element of vacating the premises within a reasonable time. The landlord might argue that the tenant remained in the premises for almost four months after the air conditioning first failed, which would suggest that the problem was not so severe as to have constructively evicted the tenant. The tenant will argue, however, that he gave the landlord three months to cure the problem after the first two malfunctions threatened (but did not actually harm) his operations. The tenant then moved out shortly after the final malfunction caused temperatures to exceed the tolerance levels of his manufacturing operations.]

Point Two (10%)
The landlord did not accept the tenant's surrender of the lease.

When a tenant wrongfully moves from leased premises with the intent to terminate the lease, the landlord may either accept the tenant's surrender of the premises and terminate the lease or hold the tenant to the terms of the lease. *See* HOVENKAMP & KURTZ, *supra*, at 295–96. Here, the tenant's only basis for the claim that the landlord accepted his surrender is the landlord's retention of the keys. Many courts have considered whether a landlord's retention of keys delivered by a tenant constitutes acceptance of surrender. The weight of the case law holds that retention of the keys alone does not constitute acceptance of surrender without other evidence showing that the landlord intended to accept the surrender. *See generally*, 49 AM. JUR. 2d, *Landlord and Tenant* § 213.

Here, the landlord's note, saying "I repeat, the air-conditioning is not my problem. You have leased the building, and you should fix it," strongly suggests that the landlord did not intend to accept the tenant's surrender. The tenant might argue that the landlord's failure to make a similar statement when the keys were sent to her a second time and she retained them evidences a change of heart. However, it is likely that a court would find that the landlord's retention of the keys represented a decision to safeguard the keys, not to accept the tenant's surrender.

[NOTE: An examinee should receive credit for arguing the other way with a well-reasoned argument.]

Point Three (45%)
Under the common law, the landlord had no duty to mitigate damages. Additionally, a landlord was not entitled to recover unpaid rents due in the future but was only entitled to recover rents in arrears at the time of the commencement of the suit. Applying the common law here, the landlord could recover $5,000, the amount of rents due at the commencement of the suit ($2,500 for September and the same for October). Today, some courts allow the landlord, under certain circumstances, to sue the tenant for damages (not rent) equal to the difference, if any, between the unpaid promised rent for the balance of the term (here $175,000) and the property's fair rental value for the balance of the term.

Under the common law, because a lease was viewed as a conveyance instead of a contract, a landlord had no duty to mitigate damages resulting from a tenant's wrongful termination of a lease. A landlord could thus recover *the full value* of rents that were due and unpaid at the time of the suit. However, under the common law, a landlord could not sue a tenant for rents due in the future because there was always a possibility that the tenant might pay the rent when it was due. *See* SINGER, *supra* at 462. Thus, using the common law approach, on November 1, the landlord could only recover the full value of the two months' rent actually due and unpaid, i.e., $5,000 for September and October.

Some courts have rejected the no-mitigation-of-damages rule based on efficiency concerns and society's interest in assuring that resources remain in the stream of commerce rather than lying vacant, *see id.* at 464–65, and allow landlords to sue tenants who have wrongfully terminated a lease for damages equal to the difference between the unpaid rent due under the lease and the property's fair market rental value. Other courts have abandoned the no-recovery-for-future-rent rule. These courts, responding to the fact that a tenant may well disappear or be judgment-proof by the time a lease term is concluded, have allowed a landlord to collect damages equal to the value of rent over the entire lease term minus the property's fair rental value when a tenant has wrongfully terminated a lease and unequivocally shown an intention not to return to the premises or pay future rent. Under this approach, a landlord receives approximately the same amount he would have received were there a duty to mitigate damages. *See Sagamore Corp. v. Willcutt*, 180 A. 464 (Conn. 1935).

Here, because the tenant returned the keys to the landlord and said, "I will not be returning to the building or making further rent payments," the landlord could establish abandonment and an intention not to return. It is thus possible that the landlord might recover damages in the amount of $5,000 (for the months of September and October) plus the present value of $175,000 minus the fair market rental value of the property over the remaining months of the lease.

MBE SUBJECTS - PRACTICE ESSAY QUESTIONS

REAL PROPERTY
Answer to Question 1

A deed is a written instrument used to keep track of land ownership. It is not legal title. Legal title to land does not always pass when a deed passes. The first issue is whether or not Daughter ever got title to the land. Here, the Owner and Daughter agreed that a signed deed would be placed into a joint safe deposit box to which only Owner and Daughter have access. Owner is trying to avoid probate. It seems that this agreement is probably valid, and breached. The breach probably does not have an effect, for reasons discussed below.

One problem with the contract is that it was for land, and such contracts must be within the Statute of Frauds. Owner may use a statute of frauds defense to claim that the land is hers, so that she may escape suit by Friend against her. But this defense will probably fail, because the deed included a valid description of the land, mentioned the parties to the transaction, and was signed by the party to be charged (Owner). The deed conveyance will be assumed to be a total integration of the party's agreement, and any parol evidence (evidence outside the four corners of the deed) will not be considered. Because of this, it seems that the conveyance to Daughter will hold up.

Assume that there was no contract dispute. Another requirement of a conveyance is a valid delivery. A valid delivery happens when one party signs over the deed and gives the other party control of the deed. One claim here would be that Owner did not deliver the deed, and as such the conveyance never occurred. But the fact that the deed is signed and in Daughter's possession is pretty strong evidence otherwise. A court would not upset the conveyance just because of a story offered by Owner as to why the property should not have been conveyed. Many deeds around the country would be in dispute if this were the case.

Case 1: Daughter has legal title.

Assuming that the conveyance has a legally binding effect, the next question is what are the rights of Friend and Speculator. The parties are in a race-notice jurisdiction. This is because the statute says the party who takes is she who records "in good faith and for a valuable consideration" and who records first. In other words, the first bona-fide purchaser to record has the valid deed. There are several kinds of notice which the person recording must not be on. These are actual, record, and inquiry. If the party had reason to know someone is on the land, they are on inquiry notice. If the deed was recorded, they are on notice. Further, if someone was actually on the land and they knew this, they will be on notice.

In this case, Friend is not a BFP. He is on record notice that the land is not Owner's to sell. For this reason, he should have not entered the bargain. This also destroys any claim he may have to a superior title over Daughter. Further, Friend received a quitclaim deed for parcels 1-3. This means that Owner does not provide a guarantee against any title defects. If there are title defects, Owner is not liable for those title defects. Because of this, Owner probably is immune from suit over the property. Friend has no legal recourse, except against Owner for fraud or other harms which are beyond the scope of this question.

Additionally, if the transaction to Daughter was binding, then Speculator probably received a valid deed for parcel three. The quitclaim status of this transaction, while risky, probably has no legal effect, as title legally passed. Friend cleared parcel 1, built a house on it, and farmed it. This would have put Speculator on constructive notice of Friend's claim. Constructive notice is notice which a buyer is reasonably expected to take. It is not unreasonable to assume that Speculator would first inspect property before purchasing it. But this is all irrelevant, because Speculator has a legal title after he recorded.

Speculator takes.

Case 2: Owner has legal title.

But for the sake of argument, assume that the conveyance to Daughter was not valid. The first person to take as between Friend and Speculator will be the first bona-fide purchaser who records. Here, the issue will be whether Speculator was a bona-fide purchaser. If he is not a bona-fide purchaser, he will have taken with notice, and as such, will be prevented from claiming superior title. The facts which support a contention by Friend that Speculator took with record notice and constructive notice. As state above, Friend's presence on the land was probably sufficient to put Speculator on constructive notice. Further, when Friend recorded, this put Speculator on record notice. Speculator has a duty to inspect the land and the records. Because he did not do this, he has no claim. His claims against Daughter are limited because of the quitclaim deed. Again, any remedy to him will be against Daughter for harms which are outside the scope of this question.

MBE SUBJECTS - PRACTICE ESSAY QUESTIONS

REAL PROPERTY
Answer to Question 2

Neighbor's Easement

An easement is a non-possessory property interest that allows a dominant estate access to a certain part of a servient estate. In this case the dominant estate is Neighbor's and the servient estate is Lot 1 owned by Andy and Betty. There are 4 ways easements can be created: express easements, implied easements, easements by necessity, and prescriptive easements. In this case, there is an express easement given to Neighbor by Olivia. Easements generally run with the land, but in this case a court might find there is no easement at all because the dominant and servient lands are not adjoining --- there is a street between them.

Covenant

A court might determine that what the Neighbor had was a covenant to use Lot 1 to get to the lake. Covenants are promises to allow or not allow certain uses for land. To determine whether a covenant "runs with the land," courts look at whether the easement "touches and concerns" the land, and whether it was intended to run with land. In this case the covenant certainly touches and concerns the land since it involves a walkway to the lake, and it appears Olivia intended the covenant to run with the land because she granted the covenant to Neighbor and his heirs. Therefore, Neighbor most likely has a right to continue to use the walkway to the lake.

Sublease

Absent a contract clause prohibiting subleases or assignments, tenants are generally free to sublease or assign their interest in property at their will. Therefore, because no prohibition clause was on Tenant's rental contract with Olivia, the sublease to Tom is valid. It is a sublease and not an assignment because Tom will not occupy the lot for the entire term of Tenant's lease. Olivia will not be able to eject Tom.

Olivia also may not sue Tom for the rent due, but she may sue Tenant for the rent. Olivia is not in privity with Tom. Tenant may sue Tom for rent under the sublease contract, however.

Tenancy

There are two types of joint tenancies: tenants in common and joint tenancy with right of survivorship. If tenants are joint with right of survivorship, when one tenant dies that tenant's interest on the property will transfer to the surviving tenant. If tenants are in common, the death of a tenant does not extinguish that tenant's property interest, and it does not go to the surviving tenant.

Joint tenancies with right of survivorship require a unity of time, title, interest, and possession. If any of the requirements are not met, courts will assume a tenancy in common. Even if there was a unity of time, title, interest, and possession in this case, the tenancy created is still a tenancy in common because of the statute requiring joint tenancies to be expressly declared. The devise to Andy and Betty did not expressly create a joint tenancy. Even in the absence of such a statute, courts generally assume tenancies in common unless there is language to the contrary.

Therefore, Carol has a right to Lot 1 as a tenant in common with Andy. Because Andy refuses to let her in, this is an ouster, and Carol is entitled to half the fair market rental value of the lot.

MBE SUBJECTS - PRACTICE ESSAY QUESTIONS

REAL PROPERTY
Answer to Question 3

In determining who owns the property in question, it is important to first examine the legal significance of the language in the deed from Mother. Mother deeded the property "to Bob and Sue as joint owners in common." There is no right of survivorship unless it is clearly stated. Courts presume that co-tenants are tenants in common and not joint tenants with a right of survivorship absent clear language to the contrary. Bob and Sue held the property as tenants in common so she has no claim of a right of survivorship.

Connie will be protected against claims by Bob's son Junior because she is a bona fide purchaser for value. Bob validly conveyed his undivided one-half interest in the property (from Mother) to Connie before he died. Connie's status as a bona fide purchaser for value will be protected against claims by Bob's sole heir Junior.

Suits for partition are equitable remedies that courts in equity will consider when co-tenants cannot share the property. Under these facts, Sue has been using the property as her family home and does not want to leave the property or share it with Connie. Connie and Sue each own an undivided one-half interest in the entire property so partition may be proper.

Tenants in common each have the right to possess the entire property. Even if Connie and Sue have a one-half ownership interest, they both have a right to possess the entire property. If Sue had enough money to buy out Connie's interest and Connie agreed, that would likely be the best alternative. That way Connie would be compensated for her ownership interest and Sue could stay in her family home as she is very ill.

If Sue cannot afford to buy out Connie's interest due to her job loss and medical bills, partition may be necessary. If the property is big enough, it could possibly be divided between Connie and Sue.

If there is only one home on a small lot, it is more likely that a court will sell the entire property in a partition sale and divide the proceeds equally between Connie and Sue. Sue would be further compensated for any improvements she made on the property to increase its resale value and for all taxes she paid on the property while Connie was a joint tenant with her. Sue does not need to pay rent to Connie unless she has committed ouster against Connie by not allowing her any use of the property.

In conclusion, Connie and Sue own the property as tenants in common and, a partition sale may be the only way to equitably address the rights of both owners if they cannot live on the property together and if Sue cannot buy out Connie's one-half interest.

MBE SUBJECTS - PRACTICE ESSAY QUESTIONS

REAL PROPERTY
Answer to Question 4

1. Tenant's Transfer of interest to Sally was an Assignment.

The transfer from Tenant to Sally was an assignment and not a sublease because it was a transfer of all of Tenant's interest in Greenacres. A transfer of an entire leasehold estate is an assignment, while a transfer of less than the entire interest is a sublease. Here, Tenant transferred his entire estate in an assignment to Sally.

2. Tenant did not violate the lease by transferring his interest to Sally without getting owner's consent.

Unless a lease instrument provides otherwise, a lessee's interest in leased property is fully transferable – by assignment or by sublease. The facts say the lease was silent on the question of transferability, so under the common law rule, Tenant did not violate his lease by assigning his interest to Sally.

3. Tenant's Transfer of interest to Sally was an Assignment.

The transfer from Tenant to Sally was an assignment and not a sublease because it was a transfer of all of Tenant's interest in Greenacres. A transfer of an entire leasehold estate is an assignment while a transfer of less than the entire interest is a sublease. Here, Tenant transferred his entire estate in an assignment to Sally.

4. Tenant did not violate the lease by transferring his interest to Sally without getting owner's consent.

Unless a lease instrument provides otherwise, a lessee's interest in leased property is fully transferable – by assignment or by sublease. The facts say the lease was silent on the question of transferability, so under the common law rule, Tenant did not violate his lease by assigning his interest to Sally.

5. Did Owner properly terminate the lease?

Owner did not properly terminate the lease. This lease was a tenancy for years which terminates automatically at the end of the term. Here the term was set to be five years. Owner did not have the right to terminate the lease before the end of the lease term (Dec. 31, 2004). Since the lease did not have any restrictions on transferability, the assignment to Sally was valid and not a material breach of the lease that would entitle Owner to terminate the lease. Since there was no such material breach, the lease was not terminated, regardless of the fact Owner thought it was null and void.

6. Purchaser is entitled to protection under the jurisdiction's recording act.

The facts state that this jurisdiction has a race-notice recording statute. Under such a law the first bona fide purchaser for value who records his/her interest has the property right that will be recognized as valid by the courts. Since neither Tenant nor Sally recorded their interests in Greenacres, it appears that Purchaser takes the interest free of the lease. The facts that Purchaser paid valuable consideration and does not appear to have notice – actual or constructive of Sally or Tenant's claim to the property. He searched the chain of title and did not find any recorded encumbrances on the estate. In addition, it does not appear as though he had actual knowledge of Sally's possession of Greenacres – he did not visit the property until after he purchased it because he was an "out-of-town purchaser." Under these facts it appears Purchaser was a bona fide purchaser for value who bought Greenacres without notice of Sally's claim, and since Purchaser was the first to record his interest under the race-notice statute – Sally's interest is not enforceable against Purchaser. Purchaser takes Greenacres free of the lease.

7. <u>Sally's continued Possession of Greenacres Does Not Breach any Covenants in the Deed from Owner to Purchaser</u>.

Purchaser bought Greenacres from Owner and received a quitclaim deed, and not a warranty deed. Unlike a warranty deed that includes covenants that the deeded estate is encumbered and that the grantor owns the property and has the right to convey it, a quitclaim deed does not include any covenants of seisin or against encumbrances. A quitclaim deed merely purports to transfer the grantor's interest in the deeded property, but does not covenant that the property is not already in the possession of another; thus Sally's continued possession of Greenacres does not constitute a breach of any of the deed covenants.

MBE SUBJECTS - PRACTICE ESSAY QUESTIONS

REAL PROPERTY
Answer to Question 5

I. Easements and their Creation

An easement is the right of one landowner to use another landowner's land. The land that is benefited by use of an easement is called the dominant land while the land that is used by or serves the other landowner is called the servient land. An easement of the kind described in this fact pattern is specifically referred to as an appurtenant easement because the dominant and servient lands are immediately adjacent to each other and the use is personal. Easements can be created by 4 different methods: expressly, impliedly, prescriptively, or by necessity. The fact pattern states that Dan does not have an express easement (not in deed or conveyed by original landowner or expressly allowed) but Dan could argue that he has an easement by the other methods of easement formation. Requirements for those easement formations and counter arguments are discussed below.

a) Prescriptive Easement

Dan could obtain a prescriptive easement if he uses the easement in a manner that is 1) Continuous, 2) Openly, 3) Against claim of right or non-permissively, and 4) For a statutory period. (usually 10 years). All factors must exist concurrently. The facts state that Dan has used a road running from Highway 99 to his land (through Orla's land) since he bought the property. This would seem to indicate continuous use. Since Dan has not been hiding his use of this land, Dan would also meet the openly element. What seems unclear from the facts, however, is whether Orla had given Dan permission to use that road in the past and now wants to take it away or if he has been using the servient land non-permissively since he moved in. If Orla wants to prevent Dan from gaining this land (easement) prescriptively, she may try to argue that Dan was using the easement with her permission. The last element Dan would need to meet is use of the easement for a statutory period. The facts do not state any dates or length of duration. However, if Dan has been using this land for the statutory period, he would most likely be successful in gaining this easement by prescription.

b) Implied Easement

An implied easement is one where both parcels were owned by a common person in the past and where use of an area, the now servient land, was serving as an easement for the now dominant land (called quasi-easement) and the dominant land reasonably needs use of the easement. These factors seem to be met in this case. Orla used to own and use both parcels of land in question as a single lot. She must have used the same road that Dan uses to get to the Western half of the property because the facts state that there is no other possible route to the Western land by any Western, Northern, or Southern direction. Therefore, Dan reasonably must also use this same route for access to the highway. Dan could easily establish claim to the easement by implication. The only argument that I could foresee Orla making to counter Dan's claim is that Dan could build a bridge over the Western edge of his land, over the river, to Water Road. However, Dan is not legally required to do this to meet his elements in an implied easement. Sara's counter argument would fail.

c) Necessity

An easement by necessity is established when land is locked on all sides and the only access is through another's land. This is definitely the case in Dan's situation. Dan's land is bordered by Wetlands, a river and mountains on all sides. His only available route is the road through Orla's land. Again, Orla could make the same argument that Dan should build a bridge. This argument is faulty for the same reason as discussed above and would fail.

II. Who would prevail and Orla's other possible counter arguments.

For all of the reasons explained above, Dan would prevail in an action using any theory, prescription, implication, or necessity.

Orla's only hope is to argue that Dan's sale of the land would burden the use of his easements beyond the reasonable scope because now 4 families will use the easement rather than 1 individual. Case law has generally allowed a dominant landowner to continue use of an easement even when the dominant land is subdivided and increases traffic as long as the new use is within the reasonable scope. Since the land will be used only for recreational purposes, Dan has a strong argument that the land will not be burdened further because the land will most likely only be used occasionally.

III. Dan would likely be granted his easement and prevail over any arguments Orla would make.

MBE SUBJECTS - PRACTICE ESSAY QUESTIONS

REAL PROPERTY
Answer to Question 6

The conveyance of Greenacre by O in 1995 appears to be a valid conveyance. It clearly sets out the property that is conveyed by specifying Greenacre. It states the grantees of the conveyance. (B, C and Grandchildren) It makes the conveyance in the present tense. And it appears that there was delivery of the deed.

The conveyance does not violate the rule against perpetuities. A conveyance violates the rule against perpetuities if it will not vest or fail within 21 years of a life in being. The rule against perpetuities applies to contingent remainders, executory interests, interests subject to open, rights of first refusal and options. In this case, the grant to O's grandchildren is a vested remainder subject to open so the rule against perpetuities applies. However, the conveyance will vest or fail within a life in being. O grants B & C life estates and "upon the death of the last of them" remainder to her grandchildren. Because both B and C are alive, the gift to O's grandchildren must vest or fail when their life estates end. B and C are alive so it will vest or fail within a life in being. The language "upon the death of the last of them" is slightly ambiguous. It could be construed to mean upon the death of all of O's children. However, because the conveyance specifically states to B and C, the language "upon the death of the last of them" clearly refers to B and C. Therefore, the grant will vest or fail within the lifetime of B and C. Therefore, this conveyance does not violate the rule against perpetuities.

The grant to B and C conveyed life estates as joint tenants with right of survivorship. It is a life estate because both B and C have the right to possess Greenacre for their lifetime. B's life estate is measured by B's life and C's life estate is measured by C's life. B and C hold Greenacre as joint tenants with right of survivorship. In a conveyance, it is presumed that there is a tenancy in common unless the grant specifically states otherwise and the four unities are met. In this conveyance, it states that B and C are to have Greenacre for life "and upon the death of the last of them" it is to be given to someone else. This language demonstrates an intent for B and C to hold with rights of survivorship. When B died, C became the sole person with a present interest in Greenacre. The grant also meets the four unities of time, title, interest and possession. Greenacre was given to B and C at the same time and in the same conveyance. In addition, B and C have equal interest in the land and an equal right to possess it. Therefore, B and C each have life estates as joint tenants with right of survivorship.

The conveyance created a vested remainder subject to open in O's grandchildren. The conveyance is a remainder because it follows a life estate, it does not cut off a previous interest and there is no gap, or reversion in between the life estate and the vesting of the grandchildren's interest. The grant is also subject to open because it is granted to a class of people with the possibility that more may join. O has one grandchild D, however if C has more children, those grandchildren will also take Greenacre. Therefore, the class is not closed. This is called subject to open. The interest is vested because there is an ascertainable take, D. When C dies, D will have a possessory interest in Greenacre. Because D is ascertained, it is a vested remainder. D has a vested remainder subject to open.

Tenant Farmer does not have an interest in the land. Tenant Farmer entered into a lease with B. However, B held the land as a joint tenant with right of survivorship. This means that C had equal rights to possess the land. Tenant Farmer did not have a lease with C. Now C is the sole possessor of Greenacre and C did not take an interest subject to Tenant Farmer's lease. Therefore, Tenant Farmer does not have an interest in the land. Tenant Farmer could argue that the lease severed the joint tenancy and turned it into a tenancy in common. This argument is likely to fail however. Therefore, all B could lease was the extent of B's life estate. Since B is no longer alive, Tenant Farmer has no lease.

Syl has begun to adversely possess the back 60 acres, but does not have an interest in the land. Syl has begun adverse possession. Adverse possession requires continuous possession that is open and notorious, is exclusive, actual use of the land without permission for the statutory period. Syl's farming has met all of the elements of adverse possession except the statutory period. Usually, an adverse possessor must hold the land for 10 years in order to acquire an interest. In this case, Syl has only held the land for 6 years which is insufficient. In addition, Syl can only acquire the interest of the present holder, which is a life estate. If Syl did acquire an interest by adverse possession, it would only be for the life estate of C. Syl would have to start the statutory period again once O's grandchildren, the future interest holders, gained possession because presently they have no standing to bring an action for ejectment. Therefore, Syl has no interest in the land.

Greenacre is presently held by C who has a life estate. Neither Tenant Farmer nor Syl have an interest in the land. D has a vested remainder subject to open.

MBE SUBJECTS - PRACTICE ESSAY QUESTIONS

REAL PROPERTY
Answer to Question 7

Ashley (A) will argue that the restriction on use of the subdivided plots is a valid covenant that Barbara (B) must comply with. In order for the burden of a restrictive covenant to run with the land so that B is bound by it, there must be intent by the original owner(s) that the burden run with the land. Subsequent purchasers must have actual or inquiry notice of the burden. There must be horizontal privity between the original covenantors, there must be vertical privity between the selling covenantor and the buyer of the burdened land, and the covenant must touch and concern. A also has the option of pursuing the equitable servitude theory, under which she can get an injunction.

A may do better to pursue the equitable servitude theory here because this is not a situation where a subsequent purchaser is trying to avoid the running of the burden. B and Farmer are the original covenantors, rather. A can argue that Farmer's subdivision plan, with the covenant clearly marked, gave B notice of the common plan to which the subdivision was devoted – "single family residences." B's best defense is a lack of notice – it's not clear from the facts whether the subdivision map was recorded. However, we can assume recordation as it's given as an assumption in the facts. So B had at least record notice, which should be enough to support an injunction for A. B's other defense is that the 6 unrelated residents in her group home are living together as a family, that their use would be in the same spirit as the requirement, that the land be for "single family residences." This is a doubtful interpretation, since in real estate a "single family residence" is usually thought to mean one housing a group of people in fairly close relation by blood or law.

B will counterclaim for an injunction requiring A to desist from blocking the gravel drive. To do this, she must show the existence of a valid easement that has not been extinguished. B might claim a valid easement was created through implication by necessity. In that case, she must show that when Farmer divided their lots, he left her lot without any other access to a public road, except across another lot. In fact, when B bought the lot, this was the case, and until 1994 B used the drive across A's lot every day as the only way to reach her parcel. However, easements by necessity are generally extinguished when the necessity for them disappears. A's defense to this theory will be that the necessity supporting B's easement ended when B received permission to use Chuck's (C's) asphalt drive. This will probably succeed because at that point it was no longer true that there was no other way to reach B's parcel, and the permission from C apparently still stands.

B could also argue she received an easement by express reservation as written on her deed from Farmer. However, easements by reservation on behalf of another party are void. This is just such a situation: Farmer attempted to reserve an easement for B across Lot #9 after he'd already sold #9 to A. If he hadn't already sold Lot #9 to A, this might have been a successful easement by express grant, but having sold it, he couldn't grant an easement burdening land he no longer owns. So A's defense will be that Farmer couldn't grant an easement over land he didn't own, and he couldn't reserve an easement in favor of the buyer of another of his parcels, and it will probably defeat B's second theory.

B could lastly argue that she has gained an easement by prescription over A's land. Easements by prescription are gained through open and notorious, non-permissive, continuous use of the property over which the easement is claimed for the statutory period. B will have difficulty meeting these elements. B's use from 1988-1994 can be presumed to meet the first three, but falls short of the statutory period of 15 years. B might be able to tack Farmer's use of the driveway 2-3 times a year after A bought Lot #9 in 1985, adding 3 years to the period she can claim. But the period from 1994-1999, the apparent time of the present facts, she did not use the drive, preferring instead to use C's asphalt drive. Thus there is a problem with the requirement of continuous use. It may, but not likely, be sufficient that the gravel drive remained in existence, but probably not, because that is not continuous use.

Thus A is likely to succeed in her claim of an equitable servitude and get an injunction against B; B probably can't successfully claim there is an easement over A's property and enjoin A from blocking it.

Secured Transactions
(February 2000)

Legal Problems:

1. Should the computer be classified as a consumer good or as equipment?

2. Does Dealer have a perfected security interest?

3. Does Bank have a perfected security interest?

4. Does Dealer's security interest take priority over Bank's security interest?

DISCUSSION

Point One: (20-25%)

When Jane bought the computer, she expressed to Dealer an initial intent to use it for "personal, family, or household" use. Therefore, the computer would most likely be classified as a consumer good.

The relevant rules for resolving the priority dispute between Dealer and Bank will be determined by how one classifies the collateral. To do that, one must look at the expressed intent at the time of purchase and the use of the collateral in the hands of the debtor. The collateral's intended use at the time of the sale was as consumer goods under § 9-109 (1) of the Uniform Commercial Code. Jane originally intended to use the computer for "personal, family, or household" purposes. However, Jane's actual use turned out to be "primarily in business." If the latter use governs, the collateral will be "equipment" as defined in UCC § 9-109 (2) (excluding consumer goods from definition of "equipment").

Which use governs? One approach is that the debtor's intended use at the time of the sale should govern the classification. This approach is justified on the policy ground that the secured party should be able to rely on what the debtor represents as the intended use and should not be encouraged to police the collateral and keep the debtor under surveillance. J. White & R. Summers, *Uniform Commercial Code* 78-3-84 (4th ed. 1995). Moreover, UCC § 9-109 (1) states that goods are consumer goods if they are "used or bought" for personal use. Accordingly, the computer should be classified as a consumer good.

There is, however, authority for the proposition that the ultimate use controls. T. Crandall, R. Hagedorn, & F. Smith, *The Law of Debtors and Creditors* § 7.06[3][e] (1991). If the latter view is adopted, the computer will be deemed to be "equipment."

Point Two: (30-35%)

Dealer acquired a purchase money security interest, which attached and was automatically perfected at the moment of sale without the need for the filing of a financing statement.

Assuming that the collateral is correctly classified as a consumer good, Dealer enjoyed a purchase money security interest in it. Under UCC § 9-107(a), a purchase money secured creditor includes a seller who allows the debtor to purchase the goods on credit and takes a security interest in the goods sold. J. White, *supra,* at 765. Under UCC § 9-302(1)(d), filing is not required to perfect a purchase money security interest in consumer goods. The security interest is perfected automatically upon its <u>attachment </u>because the burden of filing in numerous small transactions would outweigh the benefits achieved from notice to the public. T. Crandall, *supra,* § 7.06[5][b]; J. White, *supra,* at 765. Accordingly, Dealer's failure to file a financing statement was of no consequence.

There is no doubt here that a security interest attached in Dealer's favor at the point of sale. Under UCC § 9-203(I) there are three requirements for attachment of a security interest: (1) The secured party must give value, which, under UICC § 1-201 (44)(a), includes "the extension of immediately available credit"; (2) The debtor must have sufficient property rights in the collateral, which Jane had when she took delivery of the computer, UCC § 2-501(1)(a); (3) Finally, for non-possessory collateral (i.e., collateral not in possession of the creditor), the debtor must have signed a security agreement, which Jane did.

If, on the other hand, the actual use of the computer governs the classification of the collateral, then the computer will be viewed as equipment. In such a case, Dealer's security interest would have attached by virtue of Jane's having signed the security assignment, but would have remained unperfected initially as a result of Dealer's failure to file. However, under UCC § 9-305 a security interest in goods may be perfected by the secured party's taking possession of the collateral. In this case, Dealer's perfection would have been delayed until December 1, when Dealer peacefully repossessed the computer following Jane's default.

Point Three: (20-25%)

<u>Bank's security interest attached and was perfected by filing on May 1.</u>

Bank's security interest attached because the three elements of UCC § 9-203(1) were met: (1) Bank gave value by extending credit to Jane, UCC § 1-201(44)(a); (2) Jane already owned the computer collateral and had the necessary property rights; and (3) Jane signed a security agreement. Because Bank properly filed a financing statement, Bank had a perfected security interest in Jane's equipment on May 1. J. White, *supra,* at 781-83.

Point Four: (20-25%)

<u>Assuming that the collateral is properly classified as a consumer good, Dealer's security interest takes priority over Bank's because Dealer was the first to perfect its security interest. Bank's security interest would take priority over Dealer's if the collateral were classified as equipment.</u>

Priority between two perfected security interests is governed by the first-to-file-or-perfect rule of UCC § 9-312(5)(a). T. Crandall, *supra,* § 7.07[4][a]. Assuming that Dealer's security interest was automatically perfected, it would take priority over Bank's later filing. Dealer's security interest was automatically perfected on January 15 when the security interest attached. Bank's security interest was perfected on May 1 when it made a conforming central filing.

On the other hand, if a court were to hold that actual use governed the classification of the computer for Dealer, it would be classified as equipment, and Dealer would not enjoy automatic perfection. Dealer's perfection would be delayed until December 1 when it perfected by taking possession of the computer. The priority result would then be reversed, because Bank would be the first secured party to file or perfect. Bank filed its financing statement on May 1, long before Dealer repossessed.

Secured Transactions
(July 2000)

Legal Problems:

1. Who has the superior claim to personal property, a previous owner from whom the property was stolen or a good faith purchaser for value?

2. May a secured party with a security interest in accounts and/or chattel paper require the obligors on the accounts to pay it directly upon the default of the debtor on the secured obligation?

3. May an account debtor raise defenses arising out of the underlying sales contract against the obligee of the account or assignees?

DISCUSSION

Point One: (30-40%)

An owner of stolen property may recover that property from a subsequent purchaser without reimbursing the purchaser and regardless of the purchaser's good faith in the transaction in which the purchaser acquired the property.

Section 2-403 of the Uniform Commercial Code adopts the common-law principle of *nemo dat:* no one can give or sell what he does not have. Thus, under Article 2, a purchaser of goods acquires only that title "which his transferor had or had power to transfer."

On the facts of this problem, the cedar chest was stolen from Owner. The thief who stole it had no title and no power to transfer title. Any purchaser from the thief would therefore acquire no title. Subsequent purchasers would likewise acquire only such title as their transferors had, i.e., no title.

There are exceptions to the *nemo dat* rule. In particular, good faith purchasers for value are sometimes able to acquire good title even if their transferors had no title or defective title. *See, e.g.,* UCC § 2-403(1), (2). However, the facts of this problem do not raise even a possibility of applying any of the recognized protections for good faith purchasers. In particular, the protection granted to buyers in the ordinary course from merchants who deal in goods of the kind purchased (e.g., the antique dealer in this problem) applies only if the goods were entrusted to the merchant by the true owner. Nothing of the sort happened in this problem.

Consequently, Owner will prevail in the replevin action, and Purchaser will be forced to give up the cedar chest with no reimbursement from Owner for payments already made to Dealer. Purchaser's remedy is against Dealer.

Point Two: (30-40%)

After default by the principal debtor, a secured party with a security interest in accounts or chattel Dealer is entitled to collect payments directly from the account debtors.

The obligation owed by Purchaser to Dealer under the installment sales contract is either an account or chattel paper (if the installment sales contract includes a provision creating a security interest in favor of Dealer). In either case, Uniform Commercial Code § 9-502 permits a secured party to "notify an account debtor. . . to make payment" when the account creditor (Dealer) is in default on the secured obligation. The purpose is to permit a party whose financing is secured by accounts or chattel paper to "liquidate by collecting whatever may become due on the collateral." UCC § 9-502, cmt. 1. The account debtor must, after notification from the secured party, make payments directly to the secured party rather than to the defaulting debtor, at least insofar as there is no question about the legitimacy of the secured party's claim. *See* UCC § 9-318(3) (after notice of assignment of an account and that payment is to be made to assignee, account debtor must pay assignee, subject to account debtor's right to demand proof of the assignment). *See generally* James J. White & Robert S. Summers, *Handbook on the Uniform Commercial Code-Practitioners' Edition* § 34-5(a) (4th ed. 1995).

Dealer's statements to Purchaser did not deny that Bank had a security interest or that Dealer was in default. Dealer simply denied that Bank had collection rights. Article 9, however, clearly grants Bank such rights in the event of Dealer's default, even if the security agreement does not give Bank collection rights. UCC § 9-502(1). Consequently, Purchaser should make payments to Bank and not to Dealer.

Point Three: (30-40%)

Purchaser has a breach of warranty claim against Dealer. This claim may be asserted against either Dealer or Bank as a defense to payment on the installment sales contract. Thus, Purchaser is not liable for payments to either Dealer or Bank.

As the facts make clear, Dealer had no title to the cedar chest that was sold to Purchaser. Under § 2-312 of the Uniform Commercial Code, every seller of goods makes a warranty of good title to the buyer, unless that warranty is "excluded or modified only by specific language or by circumstances" that put the buyer on notice that the seller claims no title. Nothing in these facts indicates any exclusion or modification of the warranty of good title.

Purchaser's remedies in the case of breach of warranty of good title for accepted goods include revocation of acceptance and include recovery for "the loss resulting in the ordinary course of events from the seller's breach." UCC § 2-714(1). In this case, of course, Purchaser has lost the cedar chest and its full value. This loss is an ample defense to any attempt on the part of Dealer to recover further payments on the installment sales contract. This argument can also be effectively couched in terms of failure of consideration, with the same result.

Bank's efforts to collect on the installment sales contract are also subject to Purchaser's claim against Dealer for losses due to Dealer's breach of the warranty of title. Section 9-318 of the Code provides that any assignee of accounts or chattel paper is subject to "any defense or claim arising" out of the contract between the account debtor and the assignor unless the account debtor has agreed not to assert defenses. On our facts, no such agreement is indicated. An assignee-secured creditor exercising collection rights under UCC § 9-502 is subject to the account debtor's defenses under § 9-318, just as any other assignee would be subject to those defenses. *See* James J. White & Robert S. Summers, *supra,* at § 34-5(b). Accordingly, Purchaser has no obligation to pay Bank.

Secured Transactions
(July 2001)

Legal Problems:

1. What is the relative priority of the security interests of Arcade's three creditors?

2. Does Oscar, as a buyer in the ordinary course of business, take free of security interests created by Arcade?

DISCUSSION

Point One: (60-70%)

Under the first-to-file-or-perfect rule, Bank would have priority over Finance and Supplier. However, Supplier's security interest qualifies for priority because it is a purchase money security interest (PMSI and Supplier complied with the requirements of UCC § 9-312(3) Revised 9-324(b)1. Accordingly, Supplier has priority, followed by Bank, then Finance.

As between secured creditors, the general priority rule is UCC § 9-312(5)(a) [Rev. 9-322(a)(1)]- the first to file or perfect has priority. Bank filed on February 12 although it did not perfect until July 1 when Arcade signed a security agreement on Bank's behalf. *See* UCC § 9-203, Dee § 9303 [Rev. 9-308] (noting that perfection requires attachment and that attachment typically requires a signed security agreement). Pursuant to the general rule, however, February 12 is Bank's priority date.

Finance filed and perfected on June 5 since its security interest had previously attached (i.e., on June 1, Arcade had rights in its existing inventory, Finance gave value through its loan, and Arcade signed a security agreement). *See* UCC § 9-203, UCC § 9-303 [Rev. 9-308]. Thus, June 5 is Finance's priority date. Bank, therefore, beats Finance in the remaining inventory. (Both have an after-acquired property clause in their security agreements that gives rise to a security interest in any new inventory that Arcade purchases.)

Supplier filed and perfected on August 21, assuming that Arcade had some rights in the collateral as of the purchase date of August 20. For example, the actual pinball machines that were the subject of the sale were identified on that date. *See* UCC § 2-501. In any event, perfection would occur no later than possession by Arcade on August 31. *See* UCC § 9-201, 9-203. Pursuant to the general rule, Supplier's priority is behind both Bank and Finance. Supplier, however, may take advantage of an exception to the general rule for purchase money security interests (PMSIs) in inventory. Section 9-312(3) of the Dee [Rev. 9-324(b)] states that a perfected PMSI in inventory has priority over a conflicting security interest in the same inventory if the PMSI is perfected at the time the debtor receives possession of the inventory, and if the conflicting security interest holders receive proper notice within five years before the debtor receives possession of the inventory. *See* UCC § 9-312(3)(a)-(d) [Rev. 9-324(b)(3)]

Supplier did take a PMSI because Supplier took a security interest to secure all or part of the price of the pinball machines that it sold to Arcade. *See* UCC § 9-107(a) [Rev. 9-103]. In addition, it is a PMSI in inventory because Arcade is a seller of pinball arcade games; thus, the machines purchased by Arcade are presumably "held by [Arcade] who holds them for sale. . . ." *See* UCC §9-109(4) [Rev. 9-102(a)(48)] (defining "inventory"). Indeed, the facts of the problem state that the machines were placed in Arcade's showroom "for sale to customers." Thus, the pinball machines are properly characterized as "inventory" of Arcade. *See* UCC § 9-109(4) [Rev. 9102(a)(48)].

As mentioned, Supplier filed and probably perfected on August 21, which indicates that the PMSI was perfected "at the time [Arcade] receive[d] possession of the inventory" on August 31. UCC § 9-312(3)(a) [Rev. 9- 324(b)(1)]. Finally, the facts of the problem indicate that "proper notice of [Supplier's] security interest [was sent] to all relevant creditors, including Bank and Finance," and that such notice was received before Arcade got possession of the machines on August 31. Thus, the notice requirements of UCC § 9-312(3)(b)-(d) [Rev. 9-324(b)(2)-(4)] are met. (The facts of the problem state that "proper" notice was sent so there is no need to discuss whether the content of the notice was correct.) Because the requirements of UCC § 9-312(3) [Rev. 9-324(b)] are met, Supplier has priority in the pinball machines over both Bank and Finance, as they hold "conflicting security interest[s] in the same inventory." UCC § 9-312(3) [Rev. 9-324(b)]. (Note that Bank and Finance hold conflicting security interests because their after-acquired property clauses attached to the pinball machines as soon as Arcade had rights in the collateral, which would be no later than possession on August 31. *See* UCC §§ 9-203, 9-204.)

In summary, therefore, the order of priority in the two remaining pinball machines is (1) Supplier, (2) Bank, and (3) Finance.

Point Two: (30-40%)

Because Oscar is a buyer in the ordinary course, he takes free of all security interests created by his seller (Arcade). Thus, Bank, Finance, and Supplier have no security interest to enforce in the pinball machine purchased by Oscar.

The general rule is that security interests are enforceable against purchasers of the collateral. *See* UCC § 9-201. Indeed, in general, security interests continue in collateral notwithstanding its sale, exchange, or other disposition. *See* UCC § 9-306(2) [Rev. 9-315(a)(1)]. Under UCC § 9-307(1) [Rev. 9-320(a)], however, a buyer in the ordinary course of business takes free of a security interest created by his seller even if the security interest is perfected and even if the buyer knows of the security interest. A buyer in the ordinary course means a person who, in good faith and without knowledge that the sale to him is in violation of the security interest of a third party, buys in the ordinary course from a person in the business of selling goods of that kind. *See* UCC § 1201(9). Arcade is in the business of selling pinball arcade games. There are no facts suggesting that Oscar acted in bad faith. In addition, the problem states that Oscar "had no actual knowledge" of any security interests in the pinball machine he purchased.

Because Oscar's purchase satisfies the requirements of UCC § 9-307(1) [Rev. 9-320(a)], Oscar takes the pinball machine free of all three security interests. Bank, Finance, and Supplier have no security interest to enforce in the pinball machine purchased by Oscar.

Secured Transactions
(February 2002)

Legal Problems:

1. Does a purchase money security interest perfected later than a general security interest prevail over the earlier perfected general security interest?

2. Does an initially unperfected purchase money secured creditor prevail over a later lien creditor?

3. Does a lien creditor prevail over a secured creditor with respect to a post-lien future advance?

DISCUSSION

Point One: (30-40%)

Because Seller perfected a purchase money security interest (PMSI) within 20 days after Debtor received possession of the computer, Seller prevails over Bank by virtue of the PMSI exception in UCC 9-324(b).

As between two secured creditors, the general priority rule is found in UCC § 9-322 (2000)-first to file or perfect has priority. Bank filed on January 3 and it perfected on that date as well, since its security interest had previously attached (i.e., on January 2, Debtor had rights in its existing equipment, Bank gave value through its loan, and Debtor signed a security agreement). See UCC § 9-203 (2000); § 9-308 (2000). Seller, however, did not file and perfect until February 20. Thus, under the general "first to file or perfect" rule, Bank would have priority over Seller.

There is, however, an exception to the general rule. Under UCC § 9-324(b) (2000), a PMSI in collateral other than inventory has priority over a conflicting security interest in the same collateral if the PMSI is perfected at the time the debtor receives possession of the collateral or within 20 days thereafter. Seller did take a PMSI because Seller took a security interest to secure all or part of the price of the computer that it sold. See UCC § 9-103(b) (2000). In addition, it is a PMSI in "collateral other than inventory" because the problem states that the computer is "for use in Debtor's business." Thus, the computer is properly characterized as "equipment" of Debtor. See UCC § 9-102(33) (2000). Finally, as mentioned, the PMSI was perfected on February 20, within 20 days after Debtor received possession of the computer, because Debtor received possession on February 12. Thus, pursuant to the PMSI exception, UCC § 9-324(b) (2000), Seller has priority over Bank. (Note that Bank does hold a conflicting security interest because its after-acquired property clause attached to the computer as soon as Debtor had rights in it, which was no later than February 12, when Debtor took possession. See UCC § 9-203 (2000); § 9-204 (2000).)

Point Two: (30-40%)

Because Seller filed within 20 days after Debtor received possession of the computer. Seller prevails over Larry by virtue of the PMSI exception in UCC § 9317(e) (2000).

Larry qualifies as a lien creditor because he acquired his lien on Debtor's computer by way of the sheriff's levy on February 14. UCC § 9-102 (2000). As between a secured creditor and a lien creditor, the general priority rule is found in UCC §§ 9-317(a)(2), 9-323 (2000)-a perfected security interest prevails over a lien creditor whose lien arises after the time of perfection. Under the majority rule, Larry became a lien creditor on February 14-the date of the sheriff's levy. *See* Lynn M. Lopucki & Elizabeth Warren, SECURED CREDIT: A SYSTEMS APPROACH 572 (2d ed. 1998). Another way of viewing it is to say that "The unperfected security interest is subordinate to the rights of a lien creditor." UCC § 9-317(a)(2) (2000). Seller did not perfect until February 20 (see above discussion). Thus, under the general rule, Larry would prevail over Seller.

There is, however, an exception to this general rule as well. UCC § 9-317 (2000) notes that a secured party who files with respect to a PMSI within 20 days after the debtor receives possession of the collateral takes priority over the rights of a lien creditor that arise between the time the security interest attaches and the time of filing. As previously explained, Seller's interest is a PMSI, and Seller filed within the 20-day period after Debtor received possession (filing on February 20; Debtor's possession on February 12). Moreover, Larry's lien arose on February 14, which is between the time of Seller's attachment (February 12) and the time of filing (February 20). Thus, under the UCC § 9-317(e) (2000) exception, Seller prevails over Larry.

Point Three: (20-30%)

Because Bank's future advance was made within 45 days of Larry's becoming a lien creditor. Bank has priority in the future advance.

The general rule for contests over future advances between lien creditors and secured creditors is found in UCC § 9-323(b)(2000). That section provides that lien creditors are subordinate to perfected security interests only to the extent that the interest secures advances made (1) before the lien arose; (2) within 45 days of the lien; (3) without knowledge of the lien; or (4) pursuant to a commitment entered into without knowledge of the lien.

The problem is somewhat complicated because the facts indicate that Bank had knowledge of the lien on February 16---one day *before* the future advance was made. Some applicants may believe, therefore, that Bank's knowledge of the lien precludes it from gaining priority in the future advance. Pursuant to UCC § 9-323(b)(2000), however, future advances made within 45 days of the lien, *even if the secured creditor is aware of the lien's existence,* take precedence over the lien. As previously explained, the lien arose on February 14. The advance was made on February 17 - well within the 45-day window of UCC § 9-323(b)(2000). Thus, Bank's security interest prevails over Larry's lien as to the future advance.

<u>**Secured Transactions**</u>
(July 2002)

Legal Problems:

1. Does a secured party have the right to a self-help repossession without prior notice of default to the debtor and without judicial process?

2. Under the circumstances of this case can it be reasonably argued that the repossession was carried out in breach of the peace?

DISCUSSION

Summary   After a debtor's default, a secured party may take possession of the collateral without notice and without judicial process. However, this right to self-help repossession exists only if the repossession can be accomplished without a "breach of the peace," a standard that the UCC leaves to the courts to define. Because the "breach of the peace" standard is open-ended and subject to judicial interpretation, the outcome of this case cannot be definitively stated. But the facts provide a basis for Debtor to make a reasonable argument that Uptown should have abandoned its attempt at self-help repossession and relied on judicial process to enforce its claim. First, Debtor had made it clear to Uptown that she would resist non-judicial repossession, and Uptown relied on trickery to avoid that resistance. A number of courts disfavor such "fraudulent" conduct by creditors. Second, the repossession was arguably done by an unauthorized entry into Debtor's "home," required "hotwiring" of the motor home (ordinarily the act of a thief), and involved the incidental (but intentional) seizure of possessions of Debtor to which Uptown had no lawful claim. Such "trespassory" conduct may also be disfavored. In addition, the creditor's use of a police officer (without securing judicial approval) is also treated by courts as improper, though the police officer did not actually effect this repossession.

<u>Point One</u>: (20-30%)

<u>Following default, a secured party has the right to take possession of the collateral without prior notice of default and without judicial process.</u>

The secured party's right to repossess the collateral arises on the debtor's default. UCC § 9-609. There is nothing in the Code that requires the secured party to give either notice of default or notice of intent to repossess. Repossession can be through self-help and without the need to commence judicial proceedings. *Id.* The only limitation is that the repossession must be accomplished without a breach of the peace. *Id.*

Under the facts, Debtor, having missed "several monthly payments," was clearly in default. Accordingly, Uptown was free to proceed with the self-help remedy of repossession.

Point Two: (70-80%)

<u>Debtor could argue that Uptown's repossession was in breach of the peace because it involved an unconsented entry into Debtor's place of residence, it was accomplished by "hot-wiring" the vehicle, it enlisted the aid of a law enforcement officer, and it was carried out over the verbal protests of Debtor.</u>

UCC § 9-609 authorizes the secured party to engage in self-help "without judicial process if this can be done without breach of the peace. . . ." See Point One. The term "breach of the peace" is not defined in the Code. Rather, the drafters relied on pre-Code case law to prescribe the parameters of permissible conduct. Particularly important facts include (1) whether the creditor has entered upon the premises of the debtor and (2) whether the debtor has consented to the entry and repossession. White & Summers, UNIFORM COMMERCIAL CODE § 34-7 (4th ed. 1995). Moreover, it is the potential for violence and not necessarily the occurrence or imminence of violence that defines a breach of the peace. Ordinarily, repossession of a vehicle from a driveway or public street or parking lot would not be found, without more, to be in breach of the peace. The matter is complicated in this case, however, because the motor home could be viewed as Debtor's residence.

Most courts would find that an unauthorized entry into the residence of a debtor would, in and of itself, constitute a breach of the peace. *Id.* In this situation, if the motor home is viewed as Debtor's home, it is likely that unauthorized entry would be held to be trespassory and a breach of the peace. The fact that Debtor lived in the motor home and it contained Debtor's "clothes and other stuff" supports Debtor's claim that the motor home was her residence, so that the unauthorized entry would be a breach of the peace. Any effort to take the motor home in that manner probably would be considered a breach of the peace.

Debtor might also argue that her initial objection was enough to preclude any further attempts at self-help repossession without her consent. Under this view, the fact that the repossession occurred a couple of weeks later and under circumstances where there was little potential for violence probably would not change the outcome. It was clear that Debtor opposed the repossession and would have resisted had she known that the motor home was about to be taken. On the other hand, it can be argued that the passage of time served to cool down the threat of violence. *See Wade* v. *Ford Motor Credit Corp.,* 668 P.2d 183, 189 (Kan. Ct. App. 1983). If so, Debtor's initial objection to repossession is irrelevant to an evaluation of the later action.

Even though Uptown's entry into the motor home was accomplished without force, the fact that Ernest, the employee, "hot-wired" the engine might arguably be found to be a breach of the peace. *See, e.g., General Electric Credit Corp.* v. *Timbrook,* 291 S.E.2d 383 (W.Va. 1982)(breaking lock to debtor's mobile home in order to gain entry constituted breach of peace); *Martin* v. *Darn Equipment Co.,* 821 P.2d 1025 (Mont. 1991)(cutting locked chain on ranch gate constituted breach of peace).

The fact that the repossession was accompanied by trickery (i.e., the fictitious coupon) may matter. The courts go both ways. *See, e.g., FA. North & Co.* v. *Williams,* 13 A. 723 (Pa. 1888) (trickery is not a breach of the peace); *Ford Motor Credit Co.* v. *Byrd,* 351 So. 2d 557 (Ala. 1977) (trickery is a breach of the peace). The fact that the deputy sheriff was standing by does not contribute to a finding of breach of the peace because the deputy did not participate or serve to intimidate Debtor. White & Summers, *supra*. There is no evidence that Debtor saw the deputy or was at all affected by the deputy's presence.

The argument could go either way. On balance, however, a court would probably find a breach of the peace under the circumstances and that the repossession was unlawfully carried out.

Secured Transactions
(July 2003)

<u>Legal Problems:</u>

(1)   When will a repossession be invalidated as having been conducted in breach of the peace?

(2)   What are the requirements for a valid waiver of the right of redemption, and what must the debtor tender if the security agreement contains an acceleration clause?

(3)   What are a debtor's remedies if a secured party fails to comply with the debtor's rights of redemption and seeks to recover a deficiency judgment?

DISCUSSION

<u>Summary:</u>

It is debatable whether the repossession, which Bank had the right to carry out, was or was not conducted without a breach of the peace. In any case, Bank's refusal of Debtor's tender of the entire balance violated Debtor's rights because the right of redemption cannot be waived in the security agreement. Given that the repossession was unlawfully carried out because of Bank's refusal to accept Debtor's tender of redemption, Debtor is entitled to recover any damages caused by Bank's failure to comply with the rules relating to the repossession. This might include damages for loss of business. Debtor can also challenge Bank's claim for a deficiency, but, since the sale was commercially reasonable, it is unlikely that Debtor will prevail on his challenge.

<u>Point One:</u>
(30-35%)

<u>Debtor can argue that Bank's repossession of the collateral was conducted in breach of the peace. Bank equally can assert that its repossession was peaceable.</u>

Section 9-609 of the Uniform Commercial Code provides that "after default, a secured party may take possession of the collateral," and may proceed without judicial process if this can be done "without breach of the peace." This "self-help repossession" is a significant right accruing to the secured party under Article 9's default provisions, and it may be exercised without giving prior notice to Debtor. Because Debtor was in default in its monthly payments in the amount of $1,600, Bank was within its rights in repossessing the kitchen equipment, so long as Bank did so without a breach of the peace. UCC § 9-609.

"Breach of the peace" is not defined in Article 9. White and Summers suggest that claims of breach of the peace be analyzed with a "crude two-factor formula of creditor entry and debtor response . . . refined by a consideration of third-party response, the type of premises entered and possible creditor deceit in procuring consent." James J. White & Robert S. Summers, UNIFORM COMMERCIAL CODE, 5th ed. § 25-7, at 219 (2000).

Applicants should discuss a number of facts in considering whether the repossession was carried out without a breach of the peace. First, the repossession took place on business property, rather than in a private home. The courts are most sensitive to unauthorized entries into a debtor's residence. *See* White & Summers, *supra*, § 25-7, at 220. Here, because the repossession took place at a business rather than at a home, the public policy against intrusion upon a debtor's solitude and safety is less compelling.

Second, although Debtor was not present, Debtor's employee was and Debtor's employee objected to the repossession. White and Summers state: "An opposition to the entry or seizure, however slight and even though merely verbal, normally results in a breach of the peace. The law should not make a debtor physically confront a repossessor in order to sustain a claim of breach of the peace." White & Summers, *supra*, § 25-7, at 221. On the other hand, some courts have held that oral protest alone does not unequivocally preclude self-help repossession. *See Clarin v. Minnesota Repossessors, Inc.*, 40 UCC Rep. Serv. 2d 316 (8th Cir. 1999) (no breach of peace where repossession took place in parking lot of debtor's place of work, notwithstanding debtor's initial oral protest). The Eighth Circuit in *Clarin* acknowledged that the "[c]ourts are divided on the issue of whether an unequivocal oral protest amounts to a breach of the peace." *Id.* at 318. Moreover, the employee's protest was less significant than the debtor's own protest would have been.

Apart from the oral protest, the facts do not suggest that entry was otherwise obtained by a breach of the peace. The repossessors did not attempt repossession during regular business hours; they did not pick the lock or break a door down or otherwise damage Debtor's business; the repossessors walked past the employee through an open door; the employee at first objected loudly, but later was quiet as the repossession proceeded; the employee did not physically attempt to halt the repossession or call law enforcement authorities; there was no threat of violence; Bank's representative did not use a ruse or stealth to gain entry, but honestly stated the purpose of the visit.

Point Two:
(30-35%)
The right of redemption cannot be waived in the security agreement, and Debtor was entitled to redeem the collateral by tendering fulfillment of all obligations before Bank had disposed of the collateral. Debtor had to tender the entire loan balance due because the security agreement contains an acceleration clause. Bank's refusal to accept a tender of the full balance due violated Debtor's rights.

Section 9-623 of the UCC provides that a debtor may redeem collateral "at any time before a secured party has disposed of collateral or entered into a contract for its disposition under Section 9-610." To redeem the collateral, debtor must tender "fulfillment of all obligations secured by the collateral" as well as the expenses reasonably incurred by the secured party in retaking, holding and preparing the collateral for disposition.

The right to redeem collateral is a mandatory right that may not be waived in the security agreement. *See* UCC § 9-602(11). As a result, the clause in the security agreement purporting to waive Debtor's right of redemption is ineffective. A waiver of Debtor's right to redeem is effective only if it is done "by an agreement to that effect entered into and authenticated after default." UCC § 9-624(c). There was no such agreement here. Thus, Debtor was entitled to redeem the collateral at the time he attempted to do so, because it was "before [the] secured party had disposed of the collateral . . . under Section 9-610." UCC § 9-623.

To redeem the collateral, a debtor must "tender fulfillment of *all* obligations secured by the collateral." UCC § 9-623. (emphasis added). Where, as here, the security agreement contains an acceleration clause, this would include the entire balance due on the loan. In addition, the redemption amount must include "the expenses reasonably incurred by the secured party in retaking, holding and preparing the collateral for disposition, in arranging for the sale, and to the extent provided in the agreement and not prohibited by law, [the secured party's] reasonable attorneys' fees and legal expenses." UCC § 9-623.

In this case, Debtor's initial tender of the amount of his arrearage in monthly payments was inadequate to redeem the collateral. When Debtor later offered to tender the full amount due, Bank made it clear that it would not accept any redemption. Bank based its refusal on the redemption waiver clause in the security agreement. But Part 6 of Article 9 deems such clauses unenforceable. In short, Bank's refusal to allow Debtor to redeem was a violation of Debtor's rights.

Point Three: Debtor is entitled to the remedies provided in UCC Sections 9-625
(30-35%)   and 9-627. Debtor may be able to recover damages if the repossession is found to be unlawful. It may also be able to challenge the imposition of a deficiency judgment.

Sections 9-625(a) and (b) of the UCC provide: "If it is established that a secured party is not proceeding in accordance with this article, a court may order or restrain . . . disposition of collateral. . . . A person is liable for damages in the amount of any loss caused by a failure to comply with this article."

A commercially reasonable sale under § 9-610 has already taken place. Thus, Debtor now must seek to recover from Bank for "any loss caused by a failure to comply" with Article 9. Presumably, this would include any loss attributable to the failure of Bank to allow Debtor to redeem and may include any loss attributable to improper repossession (assuming that Debtor can prove a breach of the peace was committed).

The collateral in this case—stove, refrigerator, freezers, and microwave oven for use in Debtor's restaurant business—would be classified as "equipment" ("used or bought for use primarily in business") under § 9-102(33). In the case of business equipment, Article 9 provides no clear guidance on the question of measuring damages for "any loss caused by a failure to comply with this article."

White and Summers state that a debtor's "loss" for these purposes "is probably the difference between the net amount actually realized on resale and the amount that would have been realized had the creditor complied with the Code's requirements." James J. White & Robert S. Summers, UNIFORM COMMERCIAL CODE § 25-11, at 931 (4th ed. 1995) (interpreting old § 9-507). The new Code states expressly, however, that damages should also include, in appropriate cases, such consequential losses as those caused by the "debtor's inability to obtain . . . alternative financing." UCC § 9-625(b). Some commentators endorse the possibility of punitive damages. *See* B. Clark, THE LAW OF SECURED TRANSACTIONS UNDER THE UNIFORM COMMERCIAL CODE ¶ 4.12[2], at 4-175 (1988).

In addition, UCC § 9-626 authorizes denial of a deficiency judgment when the creditor has failed to comply with Article 9's rules concerning the "collection, enforcement, disposition or acceptance" of collateral. Article 9 adopts the so-called "rebuttable presumption" rule: Where the creditor has violated a relevant rule, the creditor will not be allowed to obtain a deficiency judgment unless the creditor proves that the amount that "would have been realized" if the creditor had acted properly "is less than" the amount to which the creditor was entitled. UCC § 9-626(a)(4). However, reduction of a deficiency appears to preclude a debtor from also recovering actual damages. *See* UCC § 9-625(d).

In this case, Debtor might argue that consequential damages should include damages for loss of business opportunity, because Bank's wrongful repossession and/or refusal to permit redemption resulted in the closure of Debtor's business. Consequential damages must be reasonably foreseeable under the traditional rule of *Hadley v. Baxendale*, 156 Eng. Rep. 145 (1854). It is arguably foreseeable to the creditor that an improper refusal to allow redemption of essential kitchen equipment may result in substantial business losses to a restaurant operation. In addition, Debtor might argue that Bank's refusal to allow redemption interfered with Debtor's ability to secure alternative financing because it deprived Debtor of the collateral necessary for an alternative loan.

On the other hand, apart from these consequential damages, it will be difficult for Debtor to establish any loss. The sale of the kitchen equipment was commercially reasonable, and there is no evidence that Bank's wrongful conduct affected the price it received for the equipment. Consequently, Bank may well be able to establish that it is entitled to a deficiency judgment, despite its violations of Article 9.

Debtor had the absolute obligation to mitigate his damages. If he had enough money to pay off the balance and Bank's expenses, then he naturally had enough money to appear at Bank's foreclosure sale and buy the equipment back at the sale. Debtor would still have damages for interim loss of business, his own expenses, attorneys' fees, etc., but Debtor may be unable to recover for permanent loss of business.

Secured Transactions
(February 2004)

ANALYSIS

<u>Legal Problems:</u>

(1)   Did First Bank properly perfect its security interest in PC's equipment so that it has priority over a subsequent lien creditor?

(2)   Does First Bank's financing statement claiming a security interest in PC's accounts receivable give it a claim to those accounts when the security agreement does not mention those accounts and the financing statement was filed without PC's authorization?

(3)   Is First Bank liable for any damages PC sustained as a result of First Bank's filing of an overbroad financing statement and its subsequent refusal to terminate or amend the statement?

DISCUSSION

<u>Summary:</u>   First Bank will prevail over Luke, the subsequent lien creditor, if First Bank had a prior, perfected security interest in the disputed equipment. First Bank had a prior, perfected interest in PC's equipment, but not in PC's accounts receivable. Thus, First Bank prevails as to the equipment, but not as to the accounts receivable. Luke prevails as to the accounts receivable. Moreover, because First Bank improperly filed a financing statement covering PC's accounts, First Bank is liable to PC for any damages caused by that improper filing.

<u>Point One:</u>
(25-35%)   <u>Because PC had authenticated a security agreement granting First Bank a security interest in PC's equipment, First Bank perfected its security interest by filing, even though PC did not specifically authorize First Bank to file a financing statement. To that extent, First Bank had priority over Luke as to PC's equipment.</u>

As between a lien creditor and a secured party, the secured party has the superior claim to a debtor's assets if the secured party has a perfected security interest that predates the judicial lien. In this case, First Bank obtained a security interest in PC's equipment, filed a financing statement covering the equipment, and advanced funds to PC on the strength of that arrangement. As a result, First Bank had a perfected security interest in PC's equipment. Moreover, these steps were taken before Luke acquired a lien against PC's assets. Consequently, First Bank has the superior claim to PC's equipment. Uniform Commercial Code (UCC) § 9-201 (except as otherwise provided in the UCC, a security agreement is effective against other creditors of the debtor); § 9-317(a)(2) (a lien creditor prevails over a secured party only if the lien creditor obtains an interest before security interest is perfected).

It makes no difference that PC did not sign or expressly authorize the filing of the financing statement. Under the old version of Article 9, financing statements were required to be signed by the debtor. Under new Article 9, the debtor's signature is not necessary. *See* UCC § 9-502(a) and comment 3. Although filings must still be authorized by the debtor, *see* UCC § 9-509(a), the debtor's authentication of a security agreement covering particular collateral is *ipso facto* an authorization for the secured party to file a financing statement covering that collateral. UCC § 9-509(b)(1) and comment 4. Because PC authenticated a security agreement granting First Bank a security interest in equipment, First Bank was entitled to file a financing statement covering equipment, which was effective to perfect First Bank's interest.

Point Two: (25-35%)	Luke has a superior claim to PC's accounts because First Bank had no security interest in the accounts and the inclusion of the accounts in its financing statement was unauthorized and ineffective.

First Bank has no security interest in PC's accounts. To obtain a security interest in a debtor's assets, a creditor must receive the debtor's agreement to grant such an interest. In general, no security interest will attach to collateral unless "the debtor has authenticated a security agreement that provides a description of the collateral." UCC 9-203(b)(3)(A). Here, First Bank has absolutely no claim to a security interest in PC's accounts because the PC-First Bank security agreement did not include accounts receivable in the description of collateral, but mentioned only equipment. There is nothing in the facts to suggest that there was any intention to include accounts. To the contrary, the facts suggest that the security interest was intentionally limited to equipment.

If no security interest has attached, it cannot be perfected no matter what the creditor does. *See* UCC § 9-308(a). Here, no security interest ever attached to the accounts. Because First Bank has no security interest in the accounts and no other basis for claiming a property interest in the accounts, Luke's interest prevails.

The financing statement does not help First Bank in this regard because it is not a security agreement and, also, because it was overbroad. First Bank did not have the right to file a financing statement covering additional collateral unless PC authorized such a filing, which PC did not. A financing statement is effective "only to the extent that it was filed by a person that may file it." UCC § 9-510. Because First Bank was not entitled to file a financing statement covering PC's accounts receivable, the financing statement is not effective to cover those accounts. *See* UCC § 9-317(a)(2). Thus, Luke has a superior claim to the accounts receivable.

Point Three: (25-35%)	First Bank violated Article 9 by filing an overbroad financing statement and by refusing to correct that filing. As a result, it is liable to PC for any loss caused by those violations, including losses caused by PC's inability to secure financing from Second Bank.

Revised Article 9 provides generally that "a person is liable for damages in the amount of *any loss* caused by *a failure to comply with this article*." UCC § 9-625(b) (emphasis added). Damages may be recovered by a person who is a debtor at the time of the failure of compliance with Article 9. UCC § 9-625(c).

On our facts, First Bank filed an overbroad financing statement. The problem, as noted earlier, is that First Bank had no express authorization from the debtor to file the financing statement, and the authorization provided *ipso facto* by debtor's authentication of a security agreement extended *only* to the collateral mentioned in the security agreement, equipment. *See* UCC § 9-509(a), (b). Hence, by filing an overbroad financing statement, First Bank violated its "duty to refrain from filing [an] unauthorized financing statement." UCC § 9-625, cmt. 2. *See* UCC § 9-509(a) (a secured party may file a financing statement *only* if authorized). Moreover, a secured party has a duty to terminate an unauthorized filing when termination is requested by the debtor. UCC § 9-513(c)(4). First Bank also failed to comply with this duty.

First Bank is liable for any loss caused to PC by its breach of these duties. Recoverable losses include losses "resulting from the debtor's inability to obtain . . . alternative financing." UCC § 9-625(b). In this case, those losses may be substantial. First Bank's overbroad financing statement made it impossible for PC to secure a loan from Second Bank. PC's inability to secure financing for its business expansion prevented it from adequately servicing its contracts. As a result, the City of Eden canceled its contract, which had been expected to yield significant revenue for PC. PC must, of course, establish both the amount of the loss and that the loss was caused by First Bank's failure to comply with the Code. Moreover, damages should be limited to an amount "reasonably calculated to put [PC] in the position that it would have occupied had no violation occurred." UCC § 9-625, cmt. 3.

Secured Transactions
(July 2004)

ANALYSIS

<u>Legal Problems:</u>

(1) Did Finance Co.'s letter to Buyer informing it of the assignment of the purchase agreement to Finance Co. obligate Buyer to make future payments under the contract directly to Finance Co.?

(2) Can Buyer reduce the amount it owes Finance Co. by subtracting the expenses it incurred to add the attachments to the excavator?

DISCUSSION

<u>Summary:</u>

Once Finance Co. notified Buyer of the assignment of the right to receive payment and demanded payment of the balance, Buyer was obligated to pay Finance Co., notwithstanding Seller's instruction to the contrary. However, Buyer had the right to offset against Finance Co. its damages for Seller's breach of contract, even though Buyer had accepted delivery of the excavator.

<u>Point One:</u>
(45-55%)

<u>Once Finance Co. properly notified Buyer of the assignment of the purchase agreement and instructed Buyer to make payments directly to Finance Co., Buyer was obligated to make all payments under the contract to Finance Co.; Buyer's payments to Seller did not discharge that obligation.</u>

As a result of the security agreement signed by Seller, Finance Co. had a security interest in all of Seller's accounts and chattel paper. Moreover, the security agreement expressly provided that payments arising from Seller's "accounts and chattel paper" had been assigned to Finance Co. Under Article 9 of the Uniform Commercial Code, a security interest in "accounts" covers any "right to payment of a monetary obligation, whether or not earned by performance, . . . for property that has been or is to be sold." UCC § 9-102(a)(2). Consequently, Finance Co.'s security interest covered the amount owed by Buyer to Seller pursuant to Buyer's agreement to purchase the excavator.

Article 9 gives a secured party or assignee of an account (i.e., Finance Co.) the right to collect directly from the account debtor (i.e., Buyer) in the event of a default by the debtor (i.e., Seller).

UCC § 9-607(a)(1). To exercise that right effectively, Finance Co. must send an authenticated notification to the account debtor informing the account debtor that the amount due has been assigned and that payment is to be made to the assignee. The facts state that Finance Co. properly notified Buyer of the assignment of Seller's right to receive payment and directed Buyer to make future payments to Finance Co. *See* UCC § 9-406(a), cmt. 2. *See generally* James J. White & Robert S. Summers, UNIFORM COMMERCIAL CODE § 25-5 (5th ed. 2000).

Once an account debtor receives proper notification to make future payments directly to an assignee, the account debtor may discharge its payment obligation *only* by payment to the assignee. Payments made to the assignor do not result in discharge. UCC § 9-406(a).

The fact that Seller told Buyer to disregard the notice from Finance Co. is no defense. Proper notice from Finance Co. (assignee) is all that is required to obligate Buyer to make payment directly to Finance Co., and nothing in the UCC allows an assignor like Seller to interfere with the rights of the assignee in this way. Rather than ignoring the assignment and relying on Seller for instructions, Buyer should have demanded proof of the assignment from Finance Co. Had it done so, Buyer could have safely paid Seller until reasonable proof was offered. *See* UCC § 9-406(b)(c). What Buyer cannot do is what it did here—ignore the notification of the assignment and continue to pay Seller.

Consequently, Buyer was obligated to make the March and April payments to Finance Co., and it remains liable for those payments. Buyer was not discharged by reason of its payment to Seller. Buyer is also obliged to make the May payment to Finance Co., subject to an offset, as discussed below.

Point Two: Buyer can assert Seller's breach of contract as a defense to payment and offset its
(45-55%)   damages against the amount it owes Finance Co.

The rights of an assignee of an account (Finance Co.) are subject to "any defense or claim in recoupment arising from the transaction that gave rise to the contract." UCC § 9-404(a)(1). The account debtor may, of course, waive the right to assert defenses against an assignee, but there is nothing in the facts to suggest that Buyer waived this right.

Here, the facts establish that Buyer has a defense against full payment of the contract price. Seller agreed to supply Buyer with an excavator that was specially equipped. Moreover, Seller agreed to supply the excavator by a particular date, when Seller knew that Buyer needed it to begin work. When that date arrived, the excavator had not been equipped as required by the contract. Buyer nevertheless took delivery of the excavator, despite its failure to conform to the contract.

When a buyer takes goods in spite of a known nonconformity with the contract, the buyer has accepted the goods for the purposes of sales law. UCC § 2-606. Acceptance ordinarily obligates a buyer to pay the contract price. UCC § 2-607. However, acceptance of nonconforming goods does not bar a remedy for breach, so long as the buyer notifies the seller of the breach within a reasonable time of its discovery. Here, Buyer notified Seller of the nonconforming nature of the excavator at the time it took possession of the equipment and told Seller it intended to offset its costs for the attachments. As a result, Buyer is entitled to assert its remedies for breach, despite its acceptance of the goods.

In general, Buyer's remedy is the recovery of damages for the nonconformity, defined as "the loss resulting in the ordinary course of events from the seller's breach as determined in any manner which is reasonable." UCC § 2-714(1). Moreover, Buyer "may deduct all or any part of the damages . . . from any part of the price still due," so long as Buyer notifies Seller of the intention to do so. UCC § 2-717. Here, Buyer notified Seller of its intention in this regard.

Buyer's contract claims against Seller may be asserted against Finance Co., as assignee of the contract, to reduce the amount owed by Buyer. UCC § 9-404(b).

Under the contract, Buyer owes $75,000 to Finance Co. (the amount of the March and

April payments, which Buyer improperly sent to Seller, and the amount of the upcoming May payment). Buyer claims $30,000 in damages from Seller's breach, and it may deduct that amount from the amount owed under the contract. *See generally* James J. White & Robert S. Summers, UNIFORM COMMERCIAL CODE § 10-2 (5th ed. 2000)(techniques for measuring damages under UCC § 2-714). Consequently, Buyer owes Finance Co. $45,000.

Secured Transactions
(February 2005)

ANALYSIS

<u>Legal Problems:</u> (1)   Did Sal's purchase-money security interest in the oven, which involved a delayed filing, defeat Local Bank where Local Bank is an intervening judicial lien creditor?

(2)   Did Sal's purchase-money security interest in the oven, filed only with the Secretary of State's Office, defeat Finance Company, a subsequent mortgage lender that has filed a lien on the building in which the oven is located in the appropriate local real estate records office?

DISCUSSION

<u>Summary</u>

Sal's extension of credit to Bill provided the purchase money for Bill to buy the oven. When Bill signed the security agreement on March 1 granting Sal's a security interest in the oven, which was "goods" at the time of the purchase, a purchase-money security interest attached in favor of Sal's. It was not perfected as against other creditors at that time because Sal's had not filed a financing statement. However, a purchase-money secured creditor has 20 days *after delivery of the collateral* to perfect by filing. If the creditor does so, the security interest is perfected retroactively to the date of attachment. Under these facts, Sal's perfected by filing on March 28, which was less than 20 days after the March 14 delivery to Bill.

Ordinarily, a lien creditor, such as Local Bank, would have priority over an earlier unperfected secured creditor. However, because of the retroactive effect of Sal's filing its purchase-money interest, which related back to March 1 (the day Sal's security interest attached), Sal's prevails over Local Bank as to the oven.

However, Sal's failure to effect a valid "fixture filing" produces the opposite result vis-à-vis Finance Company. The oven is clearly a fixture. In order to perfect its security interest in the oven as a fixture against persons with interest in the real estate, Sal's was required to file a record of its interest in the local real estate records office designated by state law. Because Sal's did not do this, Sal's interest was not perfected as against Finance Company. Finance Company, as an "encumbrancer" by virtue of the mortgage granted to it by Bill, perfected its security interest in the building (and therefore in the fixtures as well) by filing in the appropriate real estate records office. Thus, Finance Company's interest in the oven prevails over Sal's.

<u>Point One:</u> Because Sal's interest in the oven was a purchase-money security interest, Sal's had
(55-65%)   priority over Local Bank, an intervening judicial lien creditor, even though Sal's failed to file its financing statement until after the judicial lien arose.

Because Sal's extension of credit enabled Bill to purchase the oven, Sal's had a purchase-money security interest in "goods." Uniform Commercial Code (UCC) § 9-103(1)(b). The oven qualified as "goods" under UCC § 9-102(44) because it was "moveable" when the security interest attached on March 1. Although a judicial lien creditor would normally have priority over an unperfected secured creditor, UCC § 9-317(a)(2), in this case Sal's lien had priority over the interest of Local Bank because Sal's perfected a purchase-money security interest within the grace period provided for in UCC § 9-317(e).

UCC § 9-317(e) provides that, if a purchase-money secured creditor files its financing statement within 20 days after the debtor receives delivery of the collateral, then the secured creditor will take priority over the rights of a judicial lien creditor whose lien arose between the attachment of the purchase-money security interest and the filing of the financing statement. In this case, Sal's perfected its interest on March 28 when it filed its financing statement in the Secretary of State's Office. UCC §§ 9-308(a), 9-310(a) (attachment plus filing a financing statement will qualify as perfection). That date was more than 20 days after Sal's security interest in the oven attached on March 1. UCC § 9-203(b) (attachment occurs where the creditor has given value, the debtor has rights in the collateral, and the debtor has signed a security agreement). However, Sal's perfected within 20 days after Bill received delivery of the collateral on March 14. Therefore, Sal's perfected security interest in the oven relates back to the date of attachment, March 1, and takes priority over Local Bank's judicial lien, which became perfected on March 26.

Point Two: (35-45%) Because Sal's failed to file in the local real estate records, Finance Company has priority over Sal's; Finance Company is a subsequent mortgagee that perfected its interest in the restaurant building where the oven is located by filing in the local real estate records.

The oven in which Sal's has a purchase-money security interest is a "fixture" under Article 9 and applicable state law because it is "so related to particular real property that an interest in [it] arises under real property law." UCC § 9-102(41).

The general rule under Article 9 for priority in fixtures is that a security interest in the fixture will be subordinate to "a conflicting interest of an encumbrancer or owner of the related real property other than the debtor." UCC § 9-334(c). Here the related real property is the restaurant building, and Finance Company's mortgage in that building qualifies as an encumbrance on it. Thus, Finance Company is as an "encumbrancer . . . of the related real property."

UCC § 9-334 includes a number of exceptions to the general rule that security interests in fixtures are subordinate to a conflicting interest of an owner or encumbrancer of the related real property. The only exceptions that might have been available to Sal's in UCC § 9-334(d) (purchase-money priority exception) and (e)(1) (where the debtor had a record interest in the realty) would require, among other things, that Sal's had effected a proper "fixture filing." UCC § 9-102(30). A fixture filing must be recorded in the local real estate records office. UCC § 9-502(b). In this case, Sal's failed to file in the local real estate records office.

Because Finance Company is an encumbrancer of the related real property and because Sal's fails to qualify for any of the exceptions listed in UCC § 9-334, Finance Company has priority as to the oven even though Finance Company's security interest was created after Sal's perfected its interest in the oven by filing in the Secretary of State's office.

Secured Transactions
(July 2005)

ANALYSIS

Legal Problems:

    (1) (a) What are the necessary requirements for attachment of an enforceable security interest and were they met in this case?

    (1) (b) May a secured party exercise self-help repossession and foreclosure remedies even if its security interest is unperfected?

    (2) (a) Were the repossession, foreclosure, and sale of the crane handled properly when Lender failed to give notice of any of these actions to a guarantor of the loan?

    (2) (b) What effect does a violation of UCC Article 9's notice rules have on the debtor's liability for a deficiency?

DISCUSSION

Summary

Lender has a security interest in the crane and is entitled to enforce that interest against Builder, even though the interest is unperfected. It can enforce through self-help repossession, as it did here, so long as there is no breach of the peace. However, Lender should have given notice to both Builder and Shareholder before it sold the crane. Because of Lender's failure to give proper notice of the sale, Article 9 of the Uniform Commercial Code (UCC) creates a rebuttable presumption that a proper sale would have generated enough money to entirely pay off Builder's debt. Thus, Lender is not entitled to recover any deficiency unless it can prove that even in a proper sale the crane would have sold for less than the amount outstanding on the loan. Moreover, Lender is liable for any damages that can be shown to have resulted from its failure to give notice (though the facts of this problem do not support a damages claim).

Point One (a) (b):   Lender's security interest is unperfected, but Lender nonetheless has the right to
(35-45%)   exercise self-help remedies after the debtor's default.

Lender can assert rights in the crane as collateral if lender has a security interest that has attached to the crane. On the facts of this problem, the requirements for attachment are satisfied. First, Builder signed an agreement granting Lender a security interest in the crane. Second, Lender gave value to Builder. Finally, Builder apparently had rights in the crane, as the facts indicate that the money was borrowed to purchase the crane and the crane was in Builder's possession. The security interest accordingly attached to the crane, and Lender has the right to enforce that interest against Builder.

Because Lender failed to file a financing statement, Lender's security interest is unperfected. *See* UCC § 9-310(a). However, a secured party may use Article 9's self-help remedies after default, regardless of the secured party's perfected or unperfected status. *See* UCC § 9-601(a). These self-help remedies include repossession and sale of the collateral and are inherent in a security interest. *See* UCC §§ 9-609, 9-610. Here, Builder was clearly in default, having missed three payments in a row. Thus, Lender was entitled to repossess and sell the collateral.

Point Two(a): <u>A secured party need not give notice or follow any established process in repossessing</u>
(35-45%)   <u>the collateral, so long as the repossession occurs without a breach of the peace. However, it must give advance notice of a foreclosure sale to the debtor, including any guarantor, and its failure to do so renders the foreclosure sale improper.</u>

Article 9's self-help remedies include repossessing the collateral. *See* UCC § 9-601(a)(1). No notice is required before repossession. *Id.* The only substantial restriction on self-help repossession is that no "breach of the peace" can result. *See* UCC § 9-609(b)(2). In this case, the facts indicate that there was no breach of the peace. The crane was repossessed from an unsecured job site and under circumstances where there was no opposition to the repossession and no dispute of any sort. Consequently, the repossession was conducted in a manner that complied with Article 9.

However, Lender's sale of the collateral did not fully comply with Article 9. Before conducting a foreclosure sale, a secured party must send reasonable notification to certain persons. *See* UCC § 9-611(b). These persons include not only the debtor, whom Lender did notify here, but also "any secondary obligor." *See* UCC § 9-611(c)(1), (2). Shareholder, as a guarantor of the secured debt, was a secondary obligor to whom notice should have been given. *See* UCC § 9-102(a)(71) and comment 2.a. Accordingly, Lender's failure to notify Shareholder of the foreclosure auction was a violation of the notice provisions of Article 9.

Shareholder's actual knowledge of the auction probably does not alleviate the sending-of-notice violation. Even though Shareholder's actual knowledge provided Shareholder with the opportunity to make a bid, thus serving the purpose of generating a more competitive auction, the statute plainly requires the sending of a notice, and the statute does not provide for actual knowledge to be a substitute for the sending of notice. In part, this is to avoid disputes over what information the debtor or secondary obligor did or did not have. Indeed, the statute requires that the notification be "authenticated," precisely to overturn earlier cases holding that oral notifications were sufficient. *See* UCC § 9-611 and comment 5.

In all other ways, Lender properly complied with the notice requirement. First, regarding the timing of the notice to Builder, the notice was sent more than 10 days before the auction, and it therefore falls within the timing safe-harbor provided by UCC § 9-612(b). Second, regarding the contents of the notice sent to Builder, the notice specifies that the sale will be by auction on a certain date, and it therefore satisfies the requirements of UCC § 9-613(1)(C) and (E) that the notice state the method and date of disposition.

Point Two(b): <u>When the secured party fails to comply with Article 9's foreclosure rules and the case</u>

(10-20%)   does not involve a consumer transaction, the debtor's liability for a deficiency is wholly eliminated, except to the extent that the secured party can prove that a deficiency would have existed even in a complying foreclosure.

Article 9 clarifies the rules on the availability of deficiency judgments in cases other than consumer transactions (that is, cases other than those in which the debt and collateral have personal rather than business purposes, *see* UCC § 9-102(a)(26)). Resolving a split of authority, Article 9 adopts the "rebuttable presumption rule" as its primary approach to evaluating deficiency claims in these situations. Under the rebuttable presumption rule, the court must rebuttably presume that, had the secured party complied with the foreclosure rules, the foreclosure sale would have generated enough money to fully discharge the secured debt. *See* UCC § 9-626(a)(3), (4).

In this case, the court will presume that a complying foreclosure sale would have generated $1.5 million (the amount of the debt), thus eliminating Builder's liability for the remaining $500,000 owed on the loan. The presumption that a compliant disposition would have generated $1.5 million is rebuttable. If Lender can prove that even a fully complying disposition (that is, one in which proper advance notice had been sent to Shareholder) still would have resulted in a deficiency of some amount, then Builder will be liable for that amount. The burden of proof is on Lender. *See* UCC § 9-626(a)(4).

NOTE: Some applicants will continue the analysis by examining whether Lender is likely to be able to rebut the presumption noted above. The two sides of this debate are fairly subtle and difficult, so applicants should get credit regardless of their conclusions on this point, so long as their conclusions are well-supported.

On the one hand, Shareholder's actual advance knowledge of the auction, though irrelevant in Point Two, might be important here. Since Shareholder declined to bid despite actual knowledge, Lender can make a strong argument that Shareholder would also have declined to bid even if Lender had sent Shareholder the statutorily required notice. In other words, there is apparently no reason to think that Lender's full compliance with the notice rules would have led to a smaller deficiency, and so the full $500,000 would be recoverable.

On the other hand, if Lender had sent notice to Shareholder and that notice had arrived earlier than the point at which Shareholder in fact gained actual knowledge, then Shareholder may have been able to react earlier and have arranged to make a substantial bid. If Builder can make a good enough case on this point to defeat Lender's burden of proof, then the deficiency to which Lender is entitled should be reduced by the amount by which Shareholder's participation would have increased the sale price of the cranes. Because Shareholder's bid would have been for up to $1.2 million ($200,000 more than the sale price), Lender's deficiency entitlement would be reduced by up to $200,000, leaving Builder liable for only the remaining $300,000.

Secured Transactions
(February 2006)

ANALYSIS

Legal Problems: (1)   Does a secured party's collateral include property that has been consigned to the debtor?

                (2)   What is the priority between the unperfected security interest of a consignor and the perfected security interest of an inventory lender, and how does that priority affect the consignor after foreclosure?

                (3)   How can a consignor achieve priority over an inventory lender?

DISCUSSION

Summary

The effect of Specialty's consignment of the speakers to Giant and Giant's grant of a security interest in "inventory" is that Bank acquired a security interest in the speakers. It does not matter that Specialty retained title to the speakers.

Specialty's interest in the speakers is a purchase money security interest under Article 9. Because Specialty did not file a financing statement to perfect its interest, the interest is junior to Bank's.

Specialty's interest could have been made senior to Bank's security interest if Specialty had filed a financing statement when it delivered the speakers to Giant.

Point One: (35-45%)
Bank's collateral includes the Specialty speakers, even though they are not owned by Giant, because Giant is deemed to have all the rights and title in the speakers that Specialty has, and Giant gave Bank a security interest that covered the speakers.

Bank had a security interest in Giant's inventory. Ordinarily, Bank's security interest would only attach to property in which the debtor (Giant) had rights, and it would only be effective to the extent of Giant's rights. *See* UCC § 9-203(b)(2). Under the terms of the consignment arrangement, the Specialty speakers are not owned by Giant (Specialty retains title), and accordingly, Giant would not ordinarily have ownership rights in them for purposes of attachment. However, UCC § 9-319(a) provides that, for purposes of determining the rights of a creditor of a consignee (e.g., the rights of Bank in this case), the consignee of goods under a consignment governed by Article 9 is "deemed to have rights and title to the goods identical to those [of] the consignor." Thus, if this consignment is governed by Article 9, Giant will be treated as having had the full ownership interest that Specialty had in the speakers, and Bank's security interest will attach to the speakers.

On these facts, the Giant-Specialty transaction created an Article 9 consignment. Under UCC § 9-102(a)(20), an Article 9 consignment exists where goods are delivered to a merchant (other than an auctioneer) for the purpose of sale, the merchant deals in those goods under a name other than the name of the consignor, the goods are not consumer goods immediately before their delivery to the merchant, the value of the goods exceeds $1,000, and the transaction does not otherwise create a security interest. Here, goods valued over $1,000 were delivered to Giant (a merchant dealing in goods of that kind under its own name). Although destined to be sold to consumers, the goods were not consumer goods before delivery; they were part of Specialty's inventory. *Compare* § 9-102(a)(23) (consumer goods are goods used or bought for "personal, family, or household purposes") *with* § 9-102(a)(48) (inventory means goods held for sale). There is no indication that the Specialty-Giant transaction otherwise created a security interest. In short, the transaction is a consignment governed by Article 9, and Giant will be treated as having right and title to the speakers for Article 9 purposes.

As a result, Bank's security interest attaches to the Specialty speakers. Now that Giant has defaulted on its debt, Bank has the right to repossess the speakers, sell them within the guidelines of Article 9, and be repaid on its debt from the proceeds. *See* UCC § 9-610(a). Specialty would have no cause of action against Bank for doing so unless Bank conducted its sale in a commercially unreasonable manner or otherwise violated the dictates of Article 9's foreclosure provisions.

[NOTE: The facts don't indicate any Article 9 violations by Bank, and the question does not invite applicants to hypothesize such violations. Points can be given for short mentions of violations that would actually result in monetary harm to Specialty, but the main thrust of answers should be that there is nothing inherently wrongful in Bank's proceeding against Specialty's property, due to the consignment and attachment rules discussed above.]

Point Two: (25-35%)
Specialty is treated as having a security interest in the speakers, and this interest is unperfected. Accordingly, Specialty's interest is junior to Bank's perfected security interest, and it is therefore extinguished upon Bank's foreclosure.

Although Specialty is the outright owner of the speakers, Article 9 treats Specialty as if its interest in the speakers were a purchase-money security interest in inventory. *See* UCC §§ 9-102(a)(72)(c), 9-103(d). So the question is whether Specialty's purchase-money security interest in inventory has priority over Bank's ordinary security interest in the speakers as inventory of Giant such that Specialty can recover the proceeds of the sale of the speakers.
On these facts, Bank's interest clearly prevails. Bank perfected its interest by filing a financing statement, whereas Specialty's interest is unperfected. Perfection of a purchase-money security interest in inventory would normally require Specialty to file a financing statement. *See* UCC § 9-310(a). There is no indication in the facts that Specialty took this step. Indeed, there is no hint that Specialty did anything to alert third parties to its interest, and the facts say explicitly that "as far as any third party can discern, the speakers are part of Giant's own inventory."

A perfected security interest in inventory has priority over an unperfected security interest in the same inventory, even if the unperfected interest is a purchase-money interest. UCC § 9-322(a)(2). This priority over the inventory extends to the proceeds of that inventory. *See* UCC 9-322(b)(1). Thus, Bank has priority over Specialty as to the proceeds of the sale of the speakers.

Point Three: (25-35%)
Specialty could have achieved priority over Bank by promptly filing a financing statement against Giant.

As noted above, Article 9 treats Specialty's ownership of the speakers as if it were a purchase-money security interest. *See* UCC § 9-103(d). Specialty could have protected its interest in the speakers had it filed a financing statement to perfect that interest. Had Specialty perfected its interest before Bank, Specialty would have achieved priority. *See* § 9-322(a)(1). Moreover, because Specialty's interest is treated as a "purchase-money security interest in inventory," it could have prevailed over Bank even if it perfected after Bank perfected, so long as it (1) filed a financing statement against Giant by the time Giant received the speakers, and (2) sent a notification to all holders of conflicting security interests in Giant's inventory explaining that Specialty was keeping a purchase money security interest in the consigned speakers.

[NOTE: Had Specialty achieved priority over Bank, Bank would technically still have had the right to foreclose on Specialty's speakers (because any junior party is free to foreclose, *see* UCC § 9-610(a)), but Specialty's senior security interest would not be discharged by such a foreclosure. *See* UCC §§ 9-617(a)(3), 9-201(a). In other words, Specialty's interest would attach to the proceeds of the sale. Moreover, Specialty's interest would follow the speakers into the hands of anyone who bought them at Bank's foreclosure sale, and Specialty would be able to take the speakers back from the buyer since they are, after all, Specialty's property. *See* UCC § 9-601(g).]

<u>**Secured Transactions**</u>
(July 2006)

ANALYSIS

Legal Problems: (1)   Did Dealer properly dispose of the collateral?

    (2)   What remedies are available to Joe as a result of Dealer's failure to properly enforce Dealer's security interest?

    (3)   Is Joe responsible for the $2,500 deficiency?

DISCUSSION
<u>Summary</u>

Dealer was required to dispose of the collateral in a "commercially reasonable" manner, which involves giving Joe reasonable advance notice of a public sale after adequate publicity preceding the sale. Here, Dealer's purchase of the boat for Dealer's own use without such advance notice and in a private sale did not satisfy the requirements for a commercially reasonable sale.

Where there has been a noncomplying disposition of consumer goods (the boat was purchased for Joe's family use, which makes it a consumer good), the consumer is entitled to recover actual damages and, in any event, a minimum statutory damage recovery. Because Dealer is still in possession of the boat, a court might also order Dealer to dispose of it through a proper public sale or even to permit Joe to redeem it.

Joe may or may not have the obligation to pay the deficiency. In consumer transactions, there is no "Code" rule. Some courts follow the absolute bar rule, under which a noncomplying sale completely bars recovery of a deficiency. Other courts adopt a rebuttable presumption that a complying sale would have produced proceeds sufficient to pay the existing debt, but the creditor is entitled to a deficiency judgment if it can rebut the presumption and prove that a complying sale would have produced less than the amount due.

Point One (30-40%)
<u>Dealer's disposition of the collateral failed to comply with UCC requirements in two respects. First, Dealer purchased the boat in a private sale, which was inappropriate under the circumstances. Second, Dealer failed to give Joe advance notice of the sale</u>.

Under the UCC, every aspect of a disposition must be commercially reasonable. UCC § 9-610(b). In addition, the UCC sets out some specific standards governing the disposition of collateral. One of these standards is the rule that a secured party may purchase the collateral *only* if the secured party buys it
    (1)   at a public disposition; or

    (2)   at a private disposition only if the collateral is of a kind that is customarily sold on a recognized market or the subject of widely distributed standard price quotations. UCC § 9-610(c). Neither requirement was met here.

First, Dealer purchased the collateral in a private, not a public, disposition. Public dispositions are those with some form of advertisement or public notice preceding the sale and where the public has access to the sale. *Id.* at cmt. 7. There is no suggestion that Dealer sought any third-party bids for the boat or made any public offer to sell it. Second, used boats are not sold under circumstances that would make a private sale appropriate. The facts make clear that used boats are not sold on a recognized market or pursuant to standard price quotations. To the contrary, boat prices fluctuate based on many factors and are subject to individual bids and negotiations. Thus, Dealer's private purchase of the boat was improper.

Dealer's disposition was also improper because Dealer did not inform Joe of the disposition until after it had occurred. The UCC requires a secured party to provide notice to the debtor before disposing of collateral. UCC § 9-611. A proper notice must describe the intended disposition and must be sent within a reasonable time before the disposition. UCC § 9-613. Under the facts, Joe was never informed of the impending disposition. The only notice he received was after the fact. This failure to notify was also a violation of the UCC.

[NOTE: The facts state that Dealer "disposed of the boat by purchasing it," which is one manner of disposition of collateral under UCC § 9-610. The problem is designed to force applicants to discuss the standards for disposition of collateral and whether Dealer met them. However, some applicants may incorrectly treat Dealer's actions as an "acceptance of collateral in full or partial satisfaction of the obligation," rather than as a disposition. *See* UCC § 9-620. Those applicants could receive some credit if their critique of Dealer's actions addresses the central problems of lack of notice and the commercial unreasonableness of Dealer's purchasing this type of collateral from itself in a private sale.]

Point Two

Joe has a number of potential remedies, including actual damages, statutory damages, and the possibility of a court-ordered alternative disposition of the collateral.

Point Two(a) (5-15%)

Joe may recover any actual damages.

Dealer is liable for actual damages in the amount of any loss caused by failing to comply with the UCC rules for notice of disposition and a commercially reasonable disposition. UCC § 9-625(b). Damages are "those reasonably calculated to put an eligible claimant in the position that it would have occupied had no violation occurred." *Id.* at cmt. 3. The most likely measure of Joe's actual loss is the difference between the amount credited to Joe by Dealer and the amount that would have been obtained in a sale that complied with UCC requirements. Under these facts, however, Joe would probably have trouble proving that a proper sale would have yielded a significantly better price for the boat.

Point Two(b) (5-15%)

Because this is a consumer transaction, Joe may recover "statutory damages" even if he suffered no actual damages.

Where the collateral is consumer goods, as here, the debtor is guaranteed a minimum recovery of "statutory damages" in an amount not less than the credit service charge (the interest payable on the loan) plus 10 percent ($1,000) of the principal amount of the loan. UCC § 9-625(c)(2). The purpose of this remedy is to "ensure that every noncompliance [with UCC requirements relating to the disposition of collateral] in a consumer goods transaction results in liability, regardless of any injury that may have resulted." *Id.* at cmt. 4.

Point Two(c) (5-15%)
Given that Dealer is still in possession of the collateral, a court could order Dealer to dispose of the collateral by a proper sale or even allow Joe to exercise his right of redemption.

Where a secured party is disposing of collateral improperly, a court "may order or restrain . . . disposition on appropriate terms and conditions." UCC § 9-625(a). Given the absence of any third-party purchaser of the collateral, a court might void Dealer's improper sale to itself and order Dealer to sell the collateral by a proper public disposition.

In addition, Joe has a right to redeem repossessed collateral by paying all amounts owed along with Dealer's repossession expenses. This redemption right is usually extinguished by a proper disposition of collateral. *See* UCC § 9-623. But a court might allow Joe to redeem under these circumstances (if he wishes to do so and can pay the required amounts), given the impropriety of the private sale by Dealer to itself and the fact that the boat is still in Dealer's possession.

Point Three (25-35%)
Joe's liability for a deficiency depends on whether the jurisdiction adopts the absolute bar rule or the rebuttable presumption rule.

Although ordinarily the secured party may recover a deficiency remaining after disposition, UCC § 9-615(d), Joe has several arguments to reduce or eliminate the claimed deficiency of $2,500.

Under UCC § 9-626(b), the impact of noncompliance with Article 9 on recovery of a deficiency in a consumer goods transaction is left to the court to determine. Courts tend to follow two approaches in consumer transactions. Under the so-called "absolute bar" rule, the creditor's noncompliance bars recovery of any deficiency. Under the "rebuttable presumption" rule (adopted in UCC § 9-626 for commercial transactions), the creditor's noncompliance results in a presumption that a complying disposition would have realized an amount of proceeds sufficient to cover the entire debt and expenses (and hence that there is no deficiency), but the creditor is given the opportunity to rebut this presumption by proving that even a complying sale would have realized less than the full amount due.

If the absolute bar rule is followed, Joe owes nothing to Dealer. If the rebuttable presumption rule is followed, Joe may be liable for a deficiency if Dealer can prove that a proper disposition of the collateral would have yielded less than what Joe owed (plus expenses). The facts state that the price the Dealer credited to Joe was within a range of likely prices, so it is possible that

Dealer could show that even a proper sale would have yielded less than the amount owed on the boat.

[NOTE: It is possible that Joe would be permitted both to recover his statutory damages and to have any deficiency eliminated through the application of one of these rules. Although double recovery or over-compensation of this sort is forbidden in a non-consumer context, the Code "is silent as to whether a double recovery or other over-compensation is possible in a consumer transaction." UCC § 9-625, cmt. 3. Some courts have therefore concluded that denial of deficiency does not preclude a consumer from also recovering statutory damages. *See Coxall v. Clover Commercial Corp.*, 781 N.Y.S.2d 567 (N.Y. City Civ. Ct. 2004).]

Secured Transactions
(February 2007)

ANALYSIS

Legal Problems: (1)   Was the financing statement filed by National Bank sufficient to perfect its security interest in the monies owed to Feagle by Hotel Corporation?

(2)   Was National Bank's security interest in the monies owed to Feagle by Hotel Corporation perfected automatically because National Bank did not receive a "significant part" of Feagle's accounts?

(3)   As between National Bank's unperfected interest and State Bank's perfected interest, whose interest prevails?

DISCUSSION

Summary

National Bank's financing statement was insufficient to perfect its interest in the Hotel Corporation account because the financing statement was filed under Feagle's trade name rather than under its true corporate name. Moreover, the facts suggest that the Hotel Corporation account constituted a significant part of Feagle's accounts, thus precluding National Bank's interest from being perfected automatically. By contrast, State Bank filed a proper financing statement and had a perfected security interest in Feagle's accounts, including the Hotel Corporation account. State Bank's perfected security interest has priority over National Bank's unperfected interest, even though State Bank acquired its interest three months after National Bank.

Point One (35-45%)

Security interests in accounts may be perfected by a financing statement that complies with Code requirements; a filing in the name of a debtor's trade name instead of its official corporate name is not effective unless the trade name is so similar that it is not seriously misleading.

National Bank obtained a security interest in the monies owed by Hotel Corporation to Feagle by having Feagle sign an agreement granting National Bank an interest in the specified collateral. That collateral—the monies owed to Feagle by Hotel Corporation—is an "account" for purposes of Article 9 of the UCC. See UCC § 9-102(2)(a "right to payment . . . for services rendered or to be rendered" is an "account"). A security interest in accounts must ordinarily be perfected by filing a proper financing statement in the appropriate government office. UCC § 9-310(a).

In this problem, National Bank filed a financing statement, but the financing statement was ineffective. In order to be effective, a financing statement must sufficiently provide the name of the debtor. UCC § 9-502(a)(1). Where the debtor is a registered organization such as a corporation, the financing statement must use the official registered corporate name of the debtor. UCC § 9-503(a)(1). A financing statement that provides only the debtor's trade name does not sufficiently provide the name of the debtor. UCC § 9-503(c).

Although the UCC forgives minor errors that do not render the financing statement seriously misleading, UCC § 9-506(a), an error in the debtor's name is seriously misleading unless a search of the records under the debtor's correct name (Feagle Construction Company, Inc.) using the filing office's standard search logic would disclose the financing statement. UCC § 9-506(b), (c). Because of the complete dissimilarity between the trade name (On Top Roofing) in which the financing statement was filed and the debtor's correct name (Feagle), this financing statement would be found ineffective and National Bank's security interest will not be perfected by filing.

Point Two (10-20%)

A security agreement in accounts may be perfected automatically if the assignment of accounts did not transfer a significant part of the assignor's outstanding accounts to the creditor. Given that the Hotel Corporation account appears to constitute a significant portion of all Feagle's outstanding accounts, and considering that National Bank is a professional lender, not a casual or isolated lender, National Bank's security interest will probably not be considered to have been automatically perfected.

In addition to providing for perfection of a security interest in accounts by filing, the UCC provides for perfection upon attachment (known as automatic perfection) for assignments of accounts that do not "transfer a significant part of the assignor's outstanding accounts" to the secured party. UCC § 9-309(2). Under the facts given, National Bank received an assignment of only one of Feagle's several outstanding accounts. However, the single Hotel Corporation account was, at the time of default, worth more than all Feagle's other accounts combined. The question, then, is whether this assignment of a single account was a transfer of "a significant part" of Feagle's outstanding accounts.

The UCC gives no guidance on the meaning of "significant part," but National Bank will have a difficult time arguing that an account amounting to more than 50 percent of the total value of Feagle's accounts is not significant. Moreover, the comments to UCC § 9-309(2) suggest that its purpose is to protect "casual or isolated assignments . . . which no one would think of filing," and that persons who "regularly" take assignments should file. National Bank took the assignment from Feagle as a part of a normal secured financing arrangement; it was a standard business transaction of the sort that almost always includes the filing of a financing statement. Indeed, National Bank did file (albeit ineffectively).

On these facts it is highly likely that a court would conclude that National Bank's interest was not automatically perfected.

[NOTE TO GRADERS: Few, if any, examinees will spot this issue. Those that do spot it are unlikely to analyze it correctly. As a result, Point Two should not be heavily weighted in your grading. It might be appropriate to treat it as a basis for extra credit rather than as an expected part of the analysis.]

Point Three (35-45%)

State Bank has first priority because its interest is perfected while National Bank's is not.

A perfected security interest has priority over a conflicting unperfected interest. UCC § 9-322(a). Because National Bank's interest was unperfected (*see* Points One and Two) and State Bank's interest was perfected, State Bank has priority under the UCC.

[NOTE TO GRADERS: If an applicant mistakenly concludes that National Bank's interest was perfected either by filing or automatically, then the applicant should conclude that National Bank would have priority over State Bank under the "first to file or perfect" rule. UCC § 9-322(a). Consider giving full credit for point three in this circumstance, at least if the applicant's answer shows full understanding of the priority rules and is wrong only because the applicant erroneously believes that National Bank's interest is perfected.]

Secured Transactions
(February 2008)

ANALYSIS

<u>Legal Problems:</u> (1)   As between the bank in which a deposit account is maintained and a bank that has filed a financing statement covering the account, whose security interest in the account has priority?

(2)(a) Is a financing statement effective to perfect a security interest when the financing statement does not give the debtor's correct name, but a search under the correct name would reveal the financing statement?

(2)(b) Does a perfected security interest have priority over a judicial lien that has attached to collateral?

DISCUSSION

Summary

A security interest in a deposit account is perfected only if the secured party has control of the account. First Bank did not have control of the deposit account; State Bank did. Thus, State Bank's interest is the only perfected interest, and State Bank's claim is superior to First Bank's claim.

First Bank's interest in Dart Corporation's office equipment was perfected even though its financing statement gave an incorrect name for Dart Corporation (DC). Because a search of the filing office records using DC's correct name would disclose the financing statement, it is effective to perfect First Bank's interest. Because First Bank is a perfected secured party, its interest prevails over the interest of State Bank, a judgment creditor whose lien attached after First Bank had perfected its interest.

Point One (45–55%)

<u>First Bank did not have control of DC's deposit account at State Bank. As a result, First Bank's interest is unperfected and is subordinate to State Bank's perfected interest, even though First Bank filed a financing statement and State Bank did not.</u>

DC's checking account at State Bank is a "deposit account" for Article 9 purposes. The facts state that the account is a demand account, and demand accounts are Article 9 "deposit accounts." *See* UCC § 9-102(a)(29) (definition of "deposit account"). Both State Bank and First Bank have enforceable security interests in the account because the following criteria are fulfilled: (1) DC's president signed a security agreement granting each bank an interest in the account, (2) DC has rights in the account, and (3) each bank extended value to DC by giving DC a loan. UCC § 9-203.

Although First Bank filed a financing statement covering the deposit account, First Bank's interest is not perfected. Under UCC § 9-312, "a security interest in a deposit account may be perfected only by control." Under UCC § 9-104, a creditor only has control of a deposit account if: (1) "the secured party is the bank with which the deposit account is maintained" (the bank account is at State Bank, not First Bank), (2) the bank where the account is held has agreed in writing to follow the instructions of the secured party (no such agreement exists), or (3) the secured party becomes the bank's customer with respect to the account (which was not done). Because none of the UCC § 9-104 requirements for control has been met by First Bank, First Bank's security interest in the bank account is unperfected.

State Bank, on the other hand, does have a perfected security interest in the deposit account, even though it did not file a financing statement, because State Bank is "the bank with which the deposit account is maintained," and therefore has control of the account. As between an unperfected secured creditor (First Bank) and a perfected secured creditor (State Bank), the perfected secured creditor has the superior claim to the collateral. *See* UCC § 9-322(a)(2).

Point Two(a) (20–30%)

<u>First Bank's security interest in DC's office equipment is perfected despite the error in DC's name on the financing statement.</u>

First Bank filed a financing statement covering DC's office equipment. For a financing statement to be effective under UCC § 9-502, it must contain three pieces of information: (1) the name of the debtor, (2) the name of the secured party, and (3) an indication of the collateral. In the case of First Bank's financing statement, the name of the secured party is correct and the collateral is sufficiently indicated as "office equipment." (DC's office equipment would be categorized as "equipment" under Article 9. *See* 9-102(a)(33).) The name of the debtor, however, contains an error. The issue is whether this error renders the financing statement ineffective.

Under UCC § 9-506(a), minor errors do not render a financing statement ineffective, unless those errors make the financing statement "seriously misleading." However, a corporation is a registered organization, and under § 9-503(a)(1), a financing statement sufficiently states the name of a "registered organization" only if the financing statement provides the name of the organization that is "indicated on the public record" that "shows the debtor to have been organized." Here, the financing statement should have stated the debtor's name as "Dart Corporation." Moreover, under § 9-506(b), "a financing statement that fails sufficiently to provide the name of the debtor in accordance with Section 9-503(a) is seriously misleading." Thus, First Bank's failure to include DC's correct name on the financing statement raises the possibility that the financing statement will be deemed "seriously misleading" and therefore ineffective.

Luckily for First Bank, however, § 9-506(c) provides a safe harbor that deals with this situation. Even where the debtor's name is incorrect on the financing statement,

"If a search of the records of the filing office under the debtor's correct name, using the filing office's standard search logic, if any, would disclose a financing statement that [otherwise] fails . . . to provide the name of the debtor . . . the name provided does not make the financing statement seriously misleading."

The facts state that a search in the State A filing office using DC's correct name, "Dart Corporation," will turn up the filed financing statement, even though it incorrectly states the name of the debtor as "Dart Incorporated." As a result, First Bank's financing statement is not "seriously misleading" under the relevant Article 9 provisions, and First Bank's interest is perfected.

[NOTE TO GRADERS: The safe harbor applies only to searches using the filing office's "standard search logic." Some states permit informal searches, not utilizing standard search logic. Some examinees may note that the fact pattern does not indicate whether the standard search logic was used. Examinees who note and discuss this problem could receive extra credit.]

Point Two(b) (20–30%)
First Bank's perfected security interest in the office equipment is superior to State Bank's judgment lien.

First Bank's claim to the office equipment is superior to State Bank's claim. First Bank is a perfected secured creditor, and State Bank is a judgment lien creditor. Under UCC § 9-317, a judgment lien creditor takes priority over a security interest only if the creditor becomes a "lien creditor" before the conflicting security interest is perfected. State Bank became a "lien creditor" when the sheriff levied on January 3. First Bank, however, perfected its security interest in the office equipment by filing on December 1, a month earlier.

Secured Transactions
(July 2008)

ANALYSIS

Legal Problems: (1) Does a prior security interest in equipment that is perfected by filing prevail over a later security interest that is perfected by notation on a certificate of title when the equipment in question is vehicles subject to a certificate-of-title statute?

(2)(a) Does a security interest in goods continue after the goods are attached to other goods in which someone else has a security interest?

(2)(b) Does a properly perfected purchase-money security interest in goods that are accessions to motor vehicles prevail over a prior security interest in the whole vehicle that is perfected by notation on the certificate of title?

(3) Does a properly perfected purchase-money security interest in goods that are equipment prevail over a prior perfected security interest in the same equipment?

DISCUSSION

Summary

Bank's filing of a financing statement was ineffective to perfect its interest in Debtor's delivery trucks because the trucks were covered by a certificate-of-title statute. Finance Company's interest is therefore superior to Bank's because Finance Company properly perfected its interest by notation on the trucks' certificates of title.

Global's security interest in the GPS units continued after the units were attached to the trucks, but that interest will be subordinate to Finance Company's interest if Finance Company's security interest in "delivery trucks" is interpreted to include the GPS units installed in the trucks.

Bank's security interest in the GPS units installed in the remaining 15 trucks is a perfected security interest in "equipment." However, its interest is subordinate to Global's perfected purchase-money security interest in the same equipment.

Point One (30–40%)
Finance Company has a superior claim to the 25 vehicles in which it has a security interest because its interest is perfected and Bank's is not. Where a motor vehicle certificate-of-title statute calls for perfection by notation on the certificate of title, the filing of a financing statement will not perfect an interest in the vehicles.

Debtor's fleet of delivery trucks is "equipment" for purposes of Article 9. *See* UCC § 9-102(a)(33). Bank has a security interest in that equipment. However, the facts tell us that the delivery trucks are subject to a certificate-of-title statute that provides for perfection by notation of a security interest on the certificate of title. Filing a financing statement is "not . . . effective to perfect a security interest in property subject to" such a statute. UCC § 9-311(a)(2). Thus, Bank did not perfect its interest in Debtor's delivery trucks by filing a financing statement.

Finance Company, on the other hand, did perfect its interest in the 25 trucks by complying with the applicable certificate-of-title statute and noting its interest on the certificates of title. *See* UCC § 9-311(b). Thus, Finance Company's perfected security interest in the 25 trucks is superior to Bank's unperfected interest. *See* UCC § 9-322(a)(2).

Point Two(a) (10–20%)
Once the GPS units were attached to Debtor's delivery trucks, they became accessions to those motor vehicles. Nonetheless, Global's interest in the GPS units continues after their attachment to the delivery trucks.

Where, as here, "goods . . . are physically united with other goods in such a manner that the identity of the original goods is not lost," the goods become accessions. UCC § 9-102(a)(1). A security interest in goods that is created and perfected before the goods become accessions continues after the goods become accessions. UCC § 9-335(a) & (b). Thus, Global's perfected security interest in the GPS units continued despite the fact that the units were attached to Debtor's trucks.

When the collateral of one creditor becomes united with the collateral of another, each creditor's collateral is an "accession" to the other creditor's collateral, and the two items of collateral together are regarded as "the whole." *See* UCC § 9-335, cmt. 3. Whether either creditor's security interest applies to "the whole," or applies only to its original collateral, "turns on the description of the collateral in [that creditor's] security agreement." UCC § 9-335, cmt. 5.

In this case, Global's security interest in the GPS units certainly does <u>not</u> cover "the whole" (i.e., delivery trucks with GPS units installed).

On the other hand, Finance Company's described security interest in the specifically identified delivery trucks expressly includes all installed accessories and therefore covers the GPS units.

Point Two(b) (10–20%)
Finance Company's interest in the delivery trucks and installed GPS units is superior to Global's interest in the GPS units.

The priority rules governing accessions are normally the same as the rules for other collateral. *See* UCC § 9-335(c). However, as it does in other places, Article 9 makes an exception when, as here, there is an applicable certificate-of-title statute. UCC § 9-335(d) provides that "[a] security interest in an accession is subordinate to a security interest in the whole which is perfected by compliance with the requirements of a certificate-of-title statute . . . ."

Thus, Global's security interest in the GPS units installed in the trucks claimed by Finance Company is subordinate to Finance Company's claim, which was perfected by notation on the trucks' certificates of title. The policy rationale for preferring Finance Company in these circumstances is to "enable[] a secured party to rely upon a certificate of title without having to check the UCC files to determine whether any components of the collateral may be encumbered." UCC § 9-335, cmt. 7.

[NOTE TO GRADERS: The policy expressed here also supports the conclusion that all components of the trucks, including the GPS units, should be treated as part of the trucks for purposes of applying Finance Company's security interest to them. *See* Point Two(a), *supra*.]

Point Three (30–40%)
Global's purchase-money security interest prevails over Bank's conflicting security interest in the remaining GPS units.

Bank's perfected security interest covers inventory and equipment, including after-acquired equipment and inventory. The GPS units are "goods" that are properly classified as equipment because they are not inventory, farm products, or consumer goods. UCC § 9-102(a)(33) (equipment); *see* UCC § 9-102(a)(34) (farm products), (44) (goods) & (48) (inventory). The after-acquired collateral clause in Bank's security agreement is valid, *see* UCC § 9-204(a), and Bank's priority dates to the time it filed its financing statement covering equipment, *see* UCC § 9-322(a)(1), even though its interest in the GPS units did not attach or perfect until Debtor acquired rights in the units. Thus, Bank has a perfected security interest in the GPS units.

Global, however, has a purchase-money security interest in the GPS units. A security interest in goods is a purchase-money security interest if the collateral "secures a purchase-money obligation incurred with respect to that collateral." UCC § 9-103(a)(1) & (b)(1). Global's interest in the GPS units secures a purchase-money obligation—the $40,000 debt to Global that Debtor incurred "as all or part of the price of the collateral." *See* UCC § 9-103(a)(2). Hence, the security interest is a purchase-money security interest. Global promptly filed a financing statement and its interest was perfected as soon as Debtor obtained possession of the GPS units.

A purchase-money security interest in equipment that is perfected when the debtor takes possession of the collateral prevails over a conflicting perfected interest in the same equipment, even if the conflicting interest is earlier in time. UCC § 9-324(a). Thus, although Bank's priority dates to June 1, its interest is nonetheless subordinate to Global's later-in-time purchase-money security interest.

Secured Transactions
(July 2009)

ANALYSIS

Legal Problems: (1)   What is the nature of Leaseco's interest in the printing press?

               (2)   Did Bank have a right to repossess and sell the printing press?

               (3)   As between Bank and Leaseco, which has a superior interest in the proceeds of the sale of the printing press?

               (4)   Does Leaseco have the right to recover the printing press from Purchaser?

DISCUSSION

Summary

The "lease" transaction between Leaseco and Printco created a security interest, not a lease. Therefore, Leaseco's interest in the press is governed by Article 9. Leaseco's security interest in the press is unperfected because it did not file a financing statement or take any other steps to perfect its interest.

Bank also has a security interest in the press by virtue of its security agreement with Printco. Bank's security interest is perfected.

Bank's perfected security interest has priority over Leaseco's unperfected interest. As the $50,000 recovered by the sale of the press did not fully cover Printco's debt to Bank, Bank is entitled to retain the $50,000 proceeds of the sale and Leaseco is not entitled to any recovery from Bank.

Leaseco cannot recover the press from Purchaser. Bank's proper foreclosure sale of the press to Purchaser transferred all of Printco's rights in the press to Purchaser and also discharged both Bank's and Leaseco's security interests.

Point One (25–35%)
Although Leaseco's arrangement with Printco was denominated a "lease," Leaseco actually transferred ownership of the press to Printco and retained an unperfected security interest.

Whether a transaction in the form of a lease actually creates a "true lease" or a security interest depends on the "economic realities" of the transaction, not on the form of the transaction or the supposed intent of the parties. *See* UCC § 1-203, Official Comments.

In this case, the lease transaction was structured so that Printco was obligated to pay an amount that would fully cover the cost of the printing press and also ensure Leaseco a 10% return. Moreover, Printco was not entitled to terminate the lease at any point prior to full performance. If Printco failed to perform, Leaseco could recover the printing press. If Printco performed, Printco could keep the printing press for the trivial sum of $10. In economic reality, this was not a lease of the printing press at all. It was the economic equivalent of an installment sale of the press, with Leaseco's retained title constituting only a security interest (the right to recover the press if payments were not made, thereby securing Printco's obligation to pay the purchase price).

UCC § 1-203(b) identifies certain situations in which a transaction creates a security interest, not a lease. In particular, § 1-203(b)(4) explicitly states that "a transaction in the form of a lease creates a security interest if" lease payments must be made for the full term of the lease and are not subject to termination, *and* the lessee has an option to "become the owner of the goods . . . for nominal additional consideration" at the conclusion of the lease agreement. That is precisely the structure of the Printco-Leaseco contract, and therefore this transaction should be treated as a sale of the press with Leaseco retaining a security interest.

The fact that the lease agreement provided for title to remain in Leaseco's name is immaterial. *See* UCC § 9-202. Leaseco's interest in the press is a security interest and is governed by Article 9. Because Leaseco did not file a financing statement, its security interest is unperfected.

[NOTE: Examinees need not know the details of the UCC rules. However, they should realize that the form of the transaction is not controlling, and that a so-called "lease" will be treated as a security interest if the "economic realities" so dictate. They should also be able to identify some of the facts that are relevant to a resolution of this issue.]

Point Two (20–30%)
Bank had a perfected security interest in the press and was entitled to repossess and sell the printing press.

In a signed agreement, Printco gave Bank a security interest in "all Printco's equipment, whether now owned or hereafter acquired." Bank advanced value to Printco by making a loan to Printco. Finally, Printco obtained rights in the printing press so that Bank's security interest attached to the press. A security interest attaches to collateral and is enforceable only if the debtor has rights in the collateral, but "limited rights in collateral, short of full ownership, are sufficient for a security interest to attach." UCC § 9-203(b), Official Comment 6. Here Printco had at least the right to possession of the press for the lease term.

In addition, because Bank filed its financing statement covering Printco's equipment, Bank's security interest was perfected. UCC § 9-310(a).

Following a debtor's default, a secured party may repossess and sell any collateral that secures its debt. *See* UCC §§ 9-609 (right to repossess), 9-610 (right to dispose of collateral by sale). As a secured party, Bank had the right to repossess and sell the printing press.

[NOTE: Moreover, the facts suggest that Bank fully complied with applicable laws: the repossession was peaceful, and the sale was made at a public auction, in a commercially reasonable manner, and after notice to the debtor.]

Point Three (20–30%)

Because Bank's security interest was superior to Leaseco's, Bank has a superior claim to the proceeds of the sale of the printing press, and it need not share those proceeds with Leaseco unless the proceeds exceed the amount due to Bank.

Bank had a perfected security interest. Leaseco's interest was unperfected. A perfected security interest has priority over an unperfected security interest. UCC § 9-322(a)(2).

[NOTE: If Leaseco had filed a financing statement within 20 days of delivery of the printing press to Printco, it would have had a perfected purchase-money security interest with priority over Bank's general security interest. UCC § 9-324(a). The facts state that Leaseco did not make such a filing.]

When a secured party with priority disposes of collateral, the proceeds of that disposition are applied in the following order: (1) the expenses of the disposition, (2) satisfaction of the obligation owed to the disposing secured party, and (3) satisfaction of any obligation secured by a subordinate interest. *See* UCC § 9-615(a).

Because Bank had priority over Leaseco, Bank was entitled to use the proceeds from the sale of the collateral to cover its expenses and any amounts owed to it by Printco before making any payment to Leaseco. The amount recovered from the sale of all of Printco's collateral, including the printing press, was only $75,000. The amount owed to Bank by Printco, on the other hand, was $150,000 (plus the expenses of the disposition). Thus, the proceeds of the collateral did not fully satisfy Printco's obligations to Bank, and there was no surplus that Leaseco could claim. Leaseco therefore has no valid claim to any of the proceeds of the sale of the printing press.

Point Four (15–25%)

Leaseco cannot recover the printing press from Purchaser because Bank's sale of the press to Purchaser discharged Leaseco's security interest and therefore eliminated its claim to the press,

A secured party's disposition of collateral after a debtor's default transfers the debtor's rights in the collateral to any transferee for value, and also discharges the secured party's interest in the collateral and "any subordinate security interest." UCC § 9-617(a).

Bank sold the printing press to Purchaser for $50,000. As a good-faith buyer of collateral at a foreclosure sale, Purchaser is a "transferee for value," and has the rights set out in UCC § 9-617. Thus, Purchaser takes free of Leaseco's interest, because Leaseco's interest is nothing more than a "security interest" that is subordinate to Bank's interest. *See* UCC § 9-617(b).

Secured Transactions
(February 2010)

ANALYSIS

Legal Problems:

(1)(a) When a contract provides that title to sold goods will not pass until payment has been made, what rights in the goods do seller and buyer have?

(1)(b) Does a secured party who has a security interest in the debtor's inventory have a security interest in raw materials that the debtor will use to manufacture its products?

(1)(c) What interest does a secured party with a security interest in goods have when the debtor receives goods pursuant to a contract providing that title to the goods does not pass to the debtor until they are paid for?

(1)(d) As between a lender with a security interest in inventory and an unpaid seller of the goods constituting inventory who has delivered the goods to the buyer but retained title to them until they are paid for, who has priority?

(2) Does a secured party with a security interest in a debtor's inventory have a security interest in goods that the debtor has contracted to buy but in which the debtor has no rights?

DISCUSSION

Summary

Copperco's interest in the copper sheet that has been delivered to Kitchenware is "limited in effect to a reservation of a security interest." UCC § 1-201(b)(35). Thus, Kitchenware is the owner of that copper sheet and Copperco has a security interest in it. The delivered copper sheet became part of Kitchenware's inventory and thus, Bank's security interest attached to it and was perfected. Copperco's security interest in the copper sheet is unperfected. As a result, Bank's security interest in the delivered copper sheet has priority over Copperco's security interest.

With respect to the second installment of copper sheet, the security agreement with Bank will create an enforceable security interest in that sheet only if Kitchenware "has rights in" the sheet. Because, under the Copperco-Kitchenware contract, Kitchenware has no rights in the second installment of copper sheet, Bank's security interest did not attach to that installment and only Copperco has an interest in it.

Point One(a) (30%)

Copperco's reservation of title to the delivered goods is ineffective except as retention of a security interest; Copperco's security interest is unperfected.

The sales contract between Copperco and Kitchenware provided that Copperco would retain title to the copper sheet until it received full payment for it. Under the Uniform Commercial Code, such "retention or reservation of title by a seller of goods notwithstanding shipment or delivery to the buyer under Section 2-401 is limited in effect to a reservation of a 'security interest.'" UCC § 1-201(b)(35). *See also* UCC § 2-401(1). Thus, Kitchenware owns the copper sheet, and Copperco has a security interest in it. Copperco has neither retained possession of the copper sheet nor filed a financing statement with respect to it, so Copperco's security interest is unperfected. *See* UCC § 9-308 *et seq.*

[NOTE: An applicant might note that Copperco's security interest is a purchase-money security interest. This statement is correct, but it does not change the analysis because only a purchase-money security interest *in consumer goods* is perfected without filing or possession by the secured party.]

Point One(b) (10%)
The copper sheet constitutes inventory, so it is covered by Bank's security interest.

Bank has a security interest in Kitchenware's "inventory." The copper sheet is inventory of Kitchenware because it constitutes "raw materials, work in process, or materials used or consumed" in Kitchenware's business. UCC § 9-102(a)(48)(D).

Point One(c) (20%)
Bank has a perfected security interest in the delivered copper sheet.

As noted in Point One(a) above, once the copper sheet was delivered to Kitchenware, Kitchenware became the owner of the sheet even though the contract provided that Copperco retained title. At that point, Kitchenware had rights in the delivered copper sheet, and Bank's security interest in inventory attached to it. *See* UCC § 9-203(b) (security interest attaches when value is given, security agreement has been signed, and debtor has rights in the collateral), § 9-204(a) (security interest may attach to after-acquired collateral). Bank filed a financing statement with respect to its security interest, so its security interest in the copper sheet is perfected. *See* UCC § 9-308 *et seq.*

Point One(d) (20%)
Bank's perfected security interest in the delivered copper sheet is superior to Copperco's unperfected security interest.

As noted above, Bank and Copperco both have security interests in the delivered copper sheet. Bank's security interest in the copper sheet was perfected by filing. Copperco's interest, on the other hand, was not perfected at all. As between the perfected and an unperfected security interests, Bank's perfected interest has priority. UCC § 9-322(a)(2).

Point Two (20%)

Because Kitchenware did not have rights in the undelivered copper sheet, Bank's security interest in it did not attach.

One of the elements of an enforceable and attached security interest is that the debtor have "rights in the collateral." *See* UCC § 9-203(b)(2). Thus, Bank has a security interest in the undelivered copper only if Kitchenware has rights in it. Under the terms of the contract between Copperco and Kitchenware, Kitchenware obtained no rights (even rights that are short of title) in the undelivered copper (and UCC § 2-401 does not limit Copperco's rights to a security interest because the goods were neither shipped nor delivered to Kitchenware). Thus, Kitchenware had no interest in the copper sheet. Accordingly, Bank's security interest did not attach to the undelivered copper sheet. Thus, as between Copperco and Bank, only Copperco has an interest in the undelivered copper sheet.

[NOTE: An applicant might argue that Kitchenware had some rights in the undelivered copper sheet because, when the copper sheet was identified to the contract by Copperco (when Copperco designated it for delivery to Kitchenware), this gave Kitchenware a "special property" in the copper sheet, *see* UCC § 2-501, and Bank's security interest could attach to that set of rights in the sheet. *See* UCC § 9-203(b)(2), cmt. 6 (limited rights in collateral are sufficient for attachment even if the rights are less than full ownership). However, that "special property" would not give Kitchenware (or Bank) any right to claim the goods from Copperco in the absence of payment of the contract price. *See* UCC §§ 2-502, 2-511. Moreover, Article 9 states expressly that a seller with a security interest created by retention of title under § 2-401 "has priority over a conflicting security interest created by the debtor" in any case where the debtor has not yet obtained possession of the goods. UCC § 9-110(4). Here, Copperco has at least a security interest in the goods under § 2-401 (*see* Point One(a), above). Because the goods were never in Kitchenware's possession, Copperco's security interest will be superior to Bank's interest, which was created by the debtor, Kitchenware. *See* UCC § 9-110. An applicant who makes these points should receive some credit.]

Secured Transactions
(February 2011)

ANALYSIS

Legal Problems: (1)(a) Did Bank have a security interest in the telescope before it was sold by Astronomy? Was the security interest perfected?

(1)(b) Did Bank's security interest in the telescope continue after the successive sales of the telescope to Johnson and Smith?

(2)(a) Did Astronomy have a security interest in the telescope before Johnson sold it to Smith? Was the security interest perfected?

(2)(b) Did Astronomy's security interest in the telescope continue to be enforceable after Johnson sold the telescope to Smith?

DISCUSSION

Summary

Bank had a perfected security interest in Astronomy's inventory. When one item of that inventory—the telescope—was sold to Johnson, Johnson took the telescope free of Bank's security interest in it because Johnson was a "buyer in ordinary course of business." Because Johnson owned the telescope free of Bank's security interest, Johnson transferred it to Smith free of that security interest. Astronomy retained a security interest in the telescope when Johnson bought it from Astronomy. The security interest was perfected even though Astronomy did not file a financing statement because the security interest was a purchase-money security interest in consumer goods. When Smith later bought the telescope from Johnson, he took free of Astronomy's security interest because of the protection afforded to buyers in consumer-to-consumer transactions by Article 9 of the Uniform Commercial Code.

Point One(a) (20%)
Bank had a perfected security interest in the telescope before it was sold.

Because Astronomy held the telescope for sale, the telescope was part of Astronomy's inventory. *See* UCC § 9-102(a)(48). Thus, it was covered by the security interest granted by Astronomy to Bank. The security interest was enforceable and attached because the three criteria in UCC § 9-203(b) were fulfilled: value had been given (Bank loaned money to Astronomy), Astronomy had rights in the telescope, and Astronomy had authenticated (signed or its electronic equivalent) a security agreement containing a description of the collateral. Bank's security interest in the telescope was also perfected. Filing the statement satisfied the requirement in UCC § 9-310 that a financing statement must be filed to perfect a nonpossessory security interest in goods.

Point One(b) (30%)

Bank's security interest in the telescope did not continue after the successive sales of the telescope to Johnson and Smith.

As a general rule, a security interest continues after sale of the collateral. UCC § 9-315(a)(1). However, that general rule is subject to many exceptions, one of which applies here: a buyer in ordinary course of business (BIOCOB) takes free of a security interest created by that buyer's seller. *See* UCC § 9-320(a). A BIOCOB is a buyer who buys goods in good faith, without knowledge that the sale violates the rights of another, from a person in the business of selling goods of the kind, in the ordinary course of the seller's business. *See* UCC § 1-201(b)(9) (UCC § 1-201(9) in states that have not enacted Revised Article 1). Johnson qualifies as a BIOCOB. Johnson bought the telescope from a person (Astronomy) in the business of selling goods of the kind in the ordinary course of Astronomy's business, and there is no indication in these facts that Johnson failed to act in good faith or had knowledge that the sale violated the rights of another. Because Johnson was a BIOCOB, he took the telescope free of Bank's security interest, which was created by his seller, Astronomy.

Since Johnson owned the telescope free of that security interest, under general property principles all of Johnson's property rights in the telescope were transferred to Smith when Johnson sold the telescope to Smith. *See also* UCC § 2-403(1). Thus, Smith acquired the telescope free of Bank's security interest. This is known in secured transactions law as the "shelter principle."

Point Two(a) (25%)

Before Johnson sold the telescope, Astronomy had a perfected security interest in it.

The security agreement between Johnson and Astronomy provided that Astronomy retained a security interest in the telescope to secure Johnson's obligation to pay the remainder of the purchase price. The security interest was enforceable and attached because the three criteria in UCC § 9-203(b) were fulfilled: value had been given (the telescope), Johnson had rights in the telescope, and Johnson had authenticated (signed or its electronic equivalent) a security agreement containing a description of the collateral.

Astronomy's security interest in the telescope was also perfected, even though Astronomy did not file a financing statement. This is because Astronomy's security interest was a purchase-money security interest (PMSI) in consumer goods. It was a PMSI because it was retained by the seller of the telescope to secure the buyer's obligation to pay the remainder of the purchase price. *See* UCC § 9-103. The telescope constituted consumer goods because it was bought by Johnson for personal, family, or household purposes. UCC § 9-309(1) provides that a PMSI in consumer goods perfects automatically upon attachment; thus, it was not necessary for Astronomy to file a financing statement to perfect its security interest.

Point Two(b) (25%)

Astronomy's security interest in the telescope is not enforceable against Smith.

Prior to the sale from Johnson to Smith, Astronomy had a perfected security interest in the telescope. (*See* Point Two(a).) Smith does not qualify as a BIOCOB because, *inter alia*, Smith did not buy the telescope from someone in the business of selling goods of that kind. (Johnson was not in the business of selling telescopes.) Thus, Smith did not take free of Astronomy's security interest pursuant to UCC § 9-320(a). However, a buyer of consumer goods takes free of a security interest in those goods if the buyer buys without knowledge of the security interest; gives value; buys for personal, family, or household use; and receives the goods before the filing of any financing statement covering them. *See* UCC § 9-320(b). Smith fulfilled these criteria. (Recall that Astronomy was not required to file a financing statement to perfect its security interest because it was a purchase-money security interest.) Thus, Smith took the telescope free of Astronomy's security interest in it.

[NOTE: Some examinees may note that Astronomy's rights against Johnson constitute chattel paper in which Bank has a security interest as proceeds of its original collateral. This is correct but does not affect the answer to the question posed because Smith is free of both security interests.]

Secured Transactions
(July 2011)

ANALYSIS

Legal Problems

    (1)   What interest does Clockwork have in the clocks?

    (2)   Does Lender have an interest in the clocks?

    (3)   Whose interest in the clocks—Clockwork's or Lender's—has priority?

    (4)   What interest does Vac have in the vacuum cleaner?

    (5)   Does Lender have an interest in the vacuum cleaner?

    (6)   Whose interest in the vacuum cleaner—Vac's or Lender's—has priority?

DISCUSSION

Summary

Clockwork's interest in the clocks is a security interest governed by Article 9 of the UCC. Because Clockwork did not file a financing statement with respect to its security interest in the clocks, its security interest is unperfected. The clocks are inventory of Decorator, so Lender also has a security interest in them. That interest was perfected when Lender filed a financing statement covering it. Lender's perfected security interest has priority over Clockwork's unperfected interest.

Vac's interest in the vacuum cleaner, although presented as a lease, is a security interest governed by Article 9 of the UCC. Because Vac did not file a financing statement with respect to its interest in the vacuum cleaner, its security interest is unperfected. The vacuum cleaner is equipment of Decorator, so Lender has a security interest in it. Because Lender filed a financing statement, Lender's security interest in the vacuum cleaner is perfected. Unperfected security interests are subordinate to perfected security interests, so Lender's security interest has priority over Vac's.

Point One (25%)
Clockwork has an unperfected security interest in the clocks.

The agreement between Clockwork and Decorator provides that Clockwork retains title to the clocks until their purchase price is paid. Under the Uniform Commercial Code, the substance of a transaction controls, rather than its form or the label given to it by the parties. Because Clockwork's interest exists to secure performance of Decorator's payment obligation, it is a security interest even though the parties did not label it as such. *See* UCC § 1-201(b)(35) [§ 1-201(37) in states that have not enacted revised Article 1 of the UCC].

Because the Clockwork-Decorator transaction created a security interest by contract, it is governed by Article 9 of the Uniform Commercial Code. UCC § 9-109(a)(1). The signed agreement between Clockwork and Decorator is sufficient to create an enforceable and attached security interest because value has been given to Decorator (the extension of credit), Decorator has rights in the clocks, and the agreement between them, providing for Clockwork's retained interest in the clocks, was signed by Decorator. *See* UCC § 9-203. However, in order for Clockwork's security interest to be perfected, Clockwork would need to either have possession of the clocks or file a financing statement with respect to the security interest. *See* UCC § 9-308 *et seq.* Clockwork's security interest in the clocks is not perfected because Clockwork neither filed a financing statement with respect to its security interest nor retained or took possession of the clocks.

[NOTE: An examinee might state that Clockwork's security interest is a purchase-money security interest and, therefore, perfected upon attachment without the necessity of filing a financing statement. This is incorrect. Only purchase-money security interests in *consumer goods* are perfected upon attachment without the filing of a financing statement. *See* UCC § 9-309(1). While Clockwork's security interest is a purchase-money security interest (*see* UCC § 9-103), the clocks do not constitute "consumer goods" in the hands of Decorator because the clocks are being held for sale to Decorator's customers and were not used or bought for Decorator's personal, family, or household purposes. *See* UCC § 9-102(a)(23).]

Point Two (10%)
Lender has a perfected security interest in the clocks.

Pursuant to its agreement with Decorator, Lender was granted a security interest in all Decorator's present and future inventory. Because the clocks are being held by Decorator for resale to its customers, they are inventory. *See* UCC § 9-102(a)(48). The security interest with respect to each clock that Decorator has or subsequently acquires is enforceable and attached because value has been given, Decorator has rights in the clocks, and Decorator has signed the security agreement. *See* UCC § 9-203. The after-acquired property clause is made enforceable by UCC § 9-204. The security interest is perfected because Lender filed a properly completed financing statement with respect to the security interest. *See* UCC §§ 9-308, 9-310.

Point Three (15%)
Lender's security interest in the clocks is superior to that of Clockwork.

While both Clockwork and Lender have security interests in the clocks, only Lender's security interest is perfected. (*See* Points One and Two.) Lender's security interest has priority over that of Clockwork because a perfected security interest is superior to an unperfected security interest in the same property. *See* UCC §§ 9-317(a)(1) and 9-322(a)(2).

[NOTE: An examinee might state that Clockwork's security interest has priority under UCC § 9-324 because it is a purchase-money security interest. This is incorrect. While Clockwork's security interest is a purchase-money security interest (*see* UCC § 9-103), § 9-324 gives priority only to certain *perfected* purchase-money security interests and Clockwork's security interest is unperfected.]

Point Four (25%)
Vac has an unperfected security interest in the vacuum cleaner.

The agreement between Vac and Decorator is presented as a lease. However, the UCC recognizes that the transaction is economically equivalent to a secured sale because Decorator will automatically become the owner of the vacuum cleaner after making all of the lease payments. Accordingly, the interest of Vac is a "security interest." *See* UCC § 1-203 [§ 1-201(37) in states that have not enacted revised Article 1 of the UCC]. Thus, the Vac-Decorator transaction is governed by Article 9 of the Uniform Commercial Code. UCC § 9-109(a)(1). The signed agreement between Vac and Decorator is sufficient to create an enforceable and attached security interest because value has been given to Decorator, Decorator has rights in the vacuum cleaner, and the agreement was signed by Decorator. *See* UCC § 9-203. However, in order for Vac's security interest to be perfected, Vac would need to retain or take possession of the vacuum cleaner or file a financing statement with respect to the security interest. *See* UCC §§ 9-308 *et seq.* Because Vac neither filed a financing statement with respect to its security interest nor retained or took possession of the vacuum cleaner, Vac's security interest in the vacuum cleaner is not perfected.

Point Five (10%)
Lender has a perfected security interest in the vacuum cleaner.

Pursuant to its agreement with Decorator, Lender was granted a security interest in all of Decorator's present and future equipment. Because the vacuum cleaner is used by Decorator in its business and is not inventory, farm products, or consumer goods, it constitutes equipment. *See* UCC § 9-102(a)(33). The security interest with respect to the vacuum cleaner is enforceable and attached because value has been given, Decorator has rights in the vacuum cleaner, and Decorator has signed the security agreement. *See* UCC §§ 9-203 & 9-204. Therefore, Lender's security interest attaches to the vacuum cleaner. The security interest is perfected because Lender filed a properly completed financing statement with respect to the security interest in inventory and equipment. *See* UCC §§ 9-308, 9-310.

Point Six (15%)
Lender's security interest in the vacuum cleaner is superior to that of Vac.

While both Vac and Lender have security interests in the vacuum cleaner, only Lender's security interest is perfected. (*See* Points Four and Five.) Lender's security interest has priority over that of Vac because a perfected security interest is superior to an unperfected security interest in the same property. *See* UCC §§ 9-317(a)(1) & 9-322(a)(2).

Secured Transactions
(July 2012)

ANALYSIS

Legal Problems

(1) What are the relative rights of a creditor with a perfected security interest in a debtor's inventory and a buyer who bought an item of the inventory in ordinary course of business?

(2) What are the relative rights of a creditor with a perfected security interest in a debtor's inventory and a lien creditor of the debtor with respect to an item of equipment that the debtor received in exchange for an item of inventory?

(3) What are the relative rights of a creditor with a perfected security interest in a debtor's inventory, a lien creditor of the debtor, and a supplier who has sold items of inventory to the debtor on credit, retaining title to the items, but has not filed a financing statement?

DISCUSSION

Summary

Bank has a perfected security interest in the present and future inventory of Recycled. That security interest covers both the bicycles in the inventory of Recycled and the bicycle helmets bought from Manufacturer. Although, as a general rule, a security interest continues in collateral notwithstanding its sale by the debtor, Bank does not have a claim to Consumer's bicycle. As a buyer in ordinary course of business from Recycled, Consumer took the bicycle free of the security interest in it that Recycled gave to Bank.

Bank also has a perfected security interest in the used computer. Although the computer is not inventory, it was received in exchange for an item of inventory and constitutes proceeds of that inventory to which Bank's security interest extends. Bank's security interest in the computer is superior to Utility's judgment lien, which was created after Bank had obtained its perfected security interest in the computer.

Manufacturer has a security interest in the helmets it sold to Recycled, but its unperfected security interest is subordinate to the perfected security interest of Bank and to Utility's judgment lien.

Point One (34%)

Because Consumer was a buyer in ordinary course of business with respect to the bicycle, Consumer took the bicycle free of Bank's security interest.

While a security interest in collateral generally continues in that collateral even after the collateral has been sold (*see* UCC § 9-315), that principle is subject to important exceptions. In particular, a buyer in ordinary course of business "takes free of a security interest" created by its seller "even if the security interest is perfected and the buyer knows of its existence." UCC § 9-320(a).

Here, Recycled sold the bicycle to Consumer. Consumer took free of Bank's security interest—which was created by Recycled, its seller—if Consumer was a "buyer in ordinary course of business." A buyer in ordinary course of business is "a person that buys goods in good faith, without knowledge that the sale violates the rights of another person in the goods, and in the ordinary course from a person . . . in the business of selling goods of that kind." UCC § 1-201(b)(9).

On these facts, Consumer is a buyer in ordinary course of business. First, Consumer bought the bicycle from Recycled, which is in the business of selling goods of the kind that Consumer bought—bicycles. Second, the sale occurred "in the ordinary course," i.e., in the seller's usual way. Third, Consumer acted honestly and in a manner consistent with reasonable commercial standards of fair dealing. Thus, Consumer acted in "good faith." UCC § 1-201(b)(20). Finally, there are no facts to suggest that Consumer knew that the sale was in violation of Bank's rights.

As a buyer in ordinary course of business, Consumer took the bicycle free of Bank's security interest, and Bank's security interest is extinguished.

Point Two (33%)

Although Bank's security agreement does not cover the equipment of Recycled, the used computer, which is equipment, constitutes proceeds of the inventory of Recycled, and Bank's security interest in the inventory extends to proceeds of the inventory. Because Bank's interest was perfected before Utility became a lien creditor, Bank has a prior claim to the used computer.

The security agreement pursuant to which Bank obtained its perfected security interest covers only inventory. The used computer was not held by Recycled for sale or lease, so it is not inventory. UCC § 9-102(a)(48). Rather, it is equipment. UCC § 9-102(a)(33). Thus, it is not included in the description of collateral in the security agreement.

However, Recycled obtained the computer in exchange for a bicycle that was inventory (and, thus, collateral). Because the computer was "acquired upon the . . . exchange . . . of collateral," the computer is "proceeds" of that collateral. UCC § 9-102(a)(64). A security interest in collateral extends to identifiable proceeds of that collateral. UCC § 9-315(a)(2). Thus, Bank has a security interest in the computer. In addition, the security interest in the computer as proceeds is perfected because the security interest in the original collateral (the bicycle) was perfected by the filing of a financing statement in the same office in which a financing statement would be filed in order to perfect a security interest in the computer. UCC §§ 9-315(c)–(d).

Because Bank has a perfected security interest in the used computer as proceeds, it has priority over Utility's later judgment lien. UCC § 9-317(a)(2).

Point Three (33%)

Bank's perfected security interest in the bicycle helmets is superior to Manufacturer's unperfected security interest and to Utility's later judgment lien. Manufacturer's security interest is subordinate to Utility's judgment lien.

While the contract with Manufacturer provides that Manufacturer retains title to the helmets until Recycled pays for them, the purported retention of "title" is limited in effect to retention of a "security interest." *See* UCC § 1-201(b)(35) (§ 1-201(37) in states that have not enacted the Revised Article 1). Manufacturer's security interest is not perfected because Manufacturer has not filed a financing statement, and there is no other basis for it to claim perfection of its security interest. *See* UCC §§ 9-308, 9-310.

Bank has a security interest in the inventory of Recycled. Bank perfected that interest by filing a financing statement. *See* UCC § 9-310(a). Because the bicycle helmets are held for sale by Recycled, they are inventory and are subject to Bank's security interest. *See* UCC § 9-102(a)(48) (definition of inventory).

Bank's security interest has priority over Manufacturer's security interest because a perfected security interest has priority over an unperfected security interest. *See* UCC § 9-322(a)(2).

Because Bank has a perfected security interest in the bicycle helmets, it has priority over Utility's later judgment lien. UCC § 9-317(a)(2). However, Utility's judgment lien has priority over Manufacturer's security interest in the bicycle helmets because Manufacturer's interest is unperfected. *Id.*

[NOTE: An examinee might correctly note that Manufacturer's security interest is a "purchase-money security interest." That point is irrelevant to the answer, however. A *perfected* purchase-money security interest can, under proper circumstances, have priority over other security interests, but Manufacturer's security interest was not perfected because no financing statement was filed and no other criterion for perfection has been satisfied. Thus, the general rule of UCC § 9-322(a)(2)—a perfected security interest has priority over an unperfected security interest—determines the priority of the competing security interests in this case. An examinee might erroneously state that Manufacturer's purchase-money security interest is automatically perfected without the need for filing pursuant to UCC § 9-309(1). This is incorrect, because only a purchase-money security interest *in consumer goods* qualifies for this special rule, and the helmets are "inventory" rather than "consumer goods." *See* definitions in UCC §§ 9-102(a)(23) and 9-102(a)(48).]

Secured Transactions
(February 2013)

ANALYSIS

Legal Problems

(1) Is a purchase-money security interest in consumer goods perfected even though there has been no filing of a financing statement?

(2) Does a person who buys consumer goods for personal use take those goods free of a prior perfected purchase-money security interest in the goods?

(3) Does a person who receives consumer goods as a gift take those goods subject to a prior perfected security interest in them?

DISCUSSION

Summary

The retailer's security interest in the bicycles was perfected, even though no financing statement was filed, because it was a purchase-money security interest in consumer goods. A purchase-money security interest in consumer goods is automatically perfected upon attachment.

The buyer is not subject to the retailer's security interest in the bicycle that the buyer bought from the man. Because the bicycle was consumer goods in the hands of the man, and the retailer never filed a financing statement covering the bicycle, the retailer's security interest is not effective against someone, like the buyer, who bought the bicycle for value, without knowledge of the retailer's security interest, and for personal use.

On the other hand, the retailer's security interest continues in the bicycle given to the friend, because the friend did not give value for the bicycle or buy it in the ordinary course of business.

Point One (35%)
The retailer's security interest in the bicycles attached on June 1. Because this interest was a purchase-money security interest in consumer goods, it was automatically perfected when it attached.

The retailer's security interest in the bicycles attached on June 1 when the man bought the bicycles (acquiring rights in the collateral), signed a security agreement containing a description of the collateral, and received value from the retailer (by being given credit with which to purchase the bicycles). UCC § 9-203(a) & (b).

Despite the retailer's failure to file a financing statement, its security interest was perfected. Pursuant to UCC § 9-309(1), a security interest is automatically perfected upon attachment if the goods are "consumer goods" and the security interest is a "purchase-money security interest."

In this case, the bicycles sold by the retailer to the man were consumer goods at the time of sale. The bicycles were "goods" because they were "movable when a security interest attaches." UCC § 9-102(a)(44). They were also consumer goods because they were "bought for use primarily for personal, family, or household purposes." UCC § 9-102(a)(23).

The retailer's security interest in these consumer goods was also a "purchase-money security interest." A purchase-money security interest is an interest that secures a debt that was incurred in order to "enable the debtor to acquire rights in or the use of the collateral." UCC § 9-103(a), (b)(1). Here, the man incurred an obligation to the retailer to purchase the bicycles, so the security interest he gave the retailer to secure that obligation was a purchase-money security interest.

Because the retailer's security interest was a purchase-money security interest in consumer goods, it was automatically perfected on June 1, when the interest attached to the bicycles.

Point Two (35%)
The buyer took the bicycle free of the retailer's security interest because (i) the retailer did not file a financing statement covering the bicycle, (ii) the bicycle was "consumer goods," and (iii) the buyer bought the bicycle for value, without knowledge of the retailer's security interest, and for personal use.

A security interest continues in collateral, even after a sale or other disposition of that collateral, unless the creditor authorized the disposition "free of the security interest" or another Article 9 exception applies. UCC §§ 9-201(a) and 9-315(a)(1).

However, a buyer of goods, like the buyer here, can take free of a prior security interest in those goods under certain circumstances. *See* UCC §§ 9-317(b) (buyers who give value and receive delivery of goods without knowledge of an unperfected security interest in the goods) and 9-320(a) & (b) (buyer in ordinary course of business; buyer of consumer goods in a consumer-to-consumer transaction who gives value). In this case, the retailer's security interest was perfected when the buyer purchased the bicycle, so UCC § 9-317(b) does not protect the buyer. The buyer also is not a protected "buyer in ordinary course of business" because he did not purchase from a person who is in the business of selling bicycles. *See* UCC § 1-201(b)(9).

The buyer can, however, qualify for the protection of UCC § 9-320(b). That section provides that a buyer of goods from a person who used them for personal, family, or household purposes takes free of a perfected security interest in the goods if (1) the buyer had no knowledge of the security interest, (2) the buyer gave value for the goods, (3) the buyer purchased the goods primarily for personal, family, or household purposes, and (4) the purchase occurred before the filing of a financing statement covering the goods.

The buyer met all of these criteria. The man used the bicycle for personal purposes. The buyer purchased the bicycle from the man, and the buyer had no knowledge of the retailer's security interest. The buyer gave value ($400) for the bicycle, and he bought it "primarily for personal, family, or household purposes," as he planned to use it for recreation, which is a personal rather than a business use. Finally, no financing statement had been filed. Therefore, under UCC § 9-320(b), the buyer took free of the retailer's security interest.

Point Three (30%)
The retailer's security interest continues in the bicycle that the man gave to the friend. Thus, the retailer can recover the bicycle from the friend because the friend did not give value for the bicycle or buy it in the ordinary course of business.

As noted in Point Two, the retailer did not authorize the man to dispose of the bicycle. Consequently, the retailer's security interest continued in the bicycle even after the man transferred ownership of the bicycle to the friend. *See* UCC §§ 9-201(a) and 9-315(a)(1). The retailer's security interest in the bicycle will be effective against the friend unless some other provision of Article 9 allows the friend to take the bicycle free of that security interest.

Unfortunately for the friend, there is no Article 9 provision that allows him to take free of the retailer's interest. The friend's basic problem is that he is not a buyer of the bicycle—he received the bicycle as a gift and did not give value for it. Thus, the friend is not protected by any of the applicable exceptions. *See* UCC §§ 9-317(b) (protecting *buyers* who give value for goods subject to an unperfected security interest), 9-320(a) (protecting *buyers* in ordinary course of business), and 9-320(b) (protecting *buyers* of consumer goods who give value).

In short, the retailer's security interest continues in the bicycle that the man gave to the friend. The friend took the bicycle subject to that security interest.

MBE SUBJECTS – RELEASED ESSAY ANALYSIS

TORTS
MEE Question – February 2008

ANALYSIS

Legal Problems: (1)   Is Library, an occasional, noncommercial product seller, strictly liable to Paul?

            (2)(a)   Is Supermarket, a commercial product seller, strictly liable for injuries to Paul when it did not produce or alter the defective product and did not sell the product to Paul?

            (2)(b)   Is a product defective when the risk cannot be eliminated and the product comes with adequate warnings?

            (3)   May Paul recover damages from any of Ann, Bill, or Chuck when he cannot show who was negligent and caused his injury?

' DISCUSSION

Summary

If Paul proves only the facts given in the problem, he will not be able to recover damages from any of the parties. Paul cannot recover damages from Library because, as an occasional, noncommercial seller of food, Library is not strictly liable for injuries caused by its food. Paul cannot recover damages from Supermarket either. Although Supermarket, as a commercial seller, is strictly liable for defective products, here the product was not defective as it was prominently labeled as possibly having salmonella bacteria, and the risk of salmonella contamination cannot be eliminated. There is evidence that at least one of Ann, Bill, or Chuck was negligent in the preparation of the chicken salad that caused Paul's injury. If Paul could establish which party was negligent, he could recover damages from that individual. However, Paul cannot establish which party was negligent, and the doctrines of res ipsa loquitur, alternative liability, and joint enterprise liability are all unavailable to assist Paul in his claim.

Point One (15–25%)
Strict products liability is only available against commercial product sellers. Thus Library cannot be liable because it is not a commercial product seller.

"One who sells any product in a defective condition unreasonably dangerous to the user or consumer . . . is subject to liability for physical harm thereby caused. . . ." RESTATEMENT (SECOND) OF TORTS § 402A (1966). The chicken salad sandwich that Paul consumed was unreasonably dangerous to the consumer because it contained salmonella bacteria. Thus, if Library had been a restaurant or other commercial entity, Paul would have a viable products liability action. In that action, he would not need to establish negligence on the part of Library.

However, a strict products liability action is only available against a "person engaged in the business of selling products for use or consumption." *Id.* § 402A cmt. f; RESTATEMENT (THIRD) OF THE LAW OF PRODUCTS LIABILITY § 1 (1998). Because the facts do not establish that Library is a commercial seller, Paul's action against Library will fail on that ground.

[NOTE TO GRADERS: An applicant could receive extra credit for noting that charitable immunity, which would probably have protected Library from liability in an earlier era, has been abrogated in virtually all jurisdictions.]

Point Two(a) (10–20%)
A commercial seller may be found strictly liable for a defective product it sells even if the seller did not produce the product and the injured party did not purchase the product from the seller.

Strict products liability applies to all commercial sellers. Even a retailer who has no control over the design and manufacture of a product may be found strictly liable if that retailer sells a defective product. Because Supermarket is a commercial seller, it may be found liable if the chicken it sold was defective. *See* RESTATEMENT (SECOND) OF TORTS § 402A.

The fact that Paul did not purchase the chicken himself does not alter the result. Modern products liability law applies to bystanders as well as purchasers. The "privity of contract" approach has everywhere been abandoned. *See id.* (establishing strict liability for injuries to "ultimate user or consumer"); *see also* 2 DAN DOBBS, THE LAW OF TORTS § 353 (2001).

Point Two(b) (15–25%)

A product seller is liable only for a defective product. Because the risk of salmonella contamination cannot be eliminated from raw chicken and the product was accompanied by detailed warnings, the chicken sold by Supermarket was not defective.

A product is defective when it is unreasonably dangerous. A product may be defective because it has a manufacturing defect, because it is defective in design, or because it provides inadequate instructions or warnings. The chicken sold by Supermarket carried adequate warnings of the risk of salmonella contamination and instructions on how to cook the chicken to ensure that it was safe for eating. The chicken sold by Supermarket did not contain a manufacturing or design defect as the risk of salmonella contamination is inherent in raw chicken and cannot be eliminated. Thus, the chicken conformed to the producer's specifications, and those specifications could not be altered. Because the chicken was not defective, Paul cannot recover damages from Supermarket. *See generally* DOBBS, *supra*, § 354.

Point Three (25–35%)

Paul could recover on a negligence theory against Ann, Bill, or Chuck *if, and only if,* he could show which of them was negligent in preparing the chicken salad. Furthermore, merely the fact that these batches of chicken salad were mixed together doesn't make Ann, Bill, and Chuck joint tortfeasors because there is no evidence they were engaged in a joint venture or joint enterprise.

In fact they acted independently of one another. Paul cannot recover on a strict liability theory because Ann, Bill, and Chuck are not product sellers.

The Health Department said that someone who made the chicken salad that Paul ate used improper precautions. The evidence thus shows that one of Ann, Bill, or Chuck was negligent, that is, failed to exercise reasonable care under the circumstances.

Even though Paul cannot show how the negligence occurred, he could still recover if only one individual had made the salad. In such a situation, Paul could use the doctrine of res ipsa loquitur, which permits the jury to infer negligence when "the event is of a kind which ordinarily does not occur in the absence of negligence; . . . other responsible causes . . . are sufficiently eliminated by the evidence; . . . and the indicated negligence is within the scope of the defendant's duty to the plaintiff." RESTATEMENT (SECOND) OF TORTS § 328D(1)(a)–(c). Paul can meet the first and third of these requirements: the Health Department has said that salmonella contamination does not occur when chicken is cooked and prepared properly. The salad preparers owed a duty to Paul as he was a lunch patron who would foreseeably have been expected to consume the chicken salad. However, Paul cannot establish that any *one* defendant had control of the chicken salad, as there were two other individuals who made salad independently. *See Samson v. Riesing,* 215 N.W.2d 662, 667–68 (Wis. 1974). Nor can Paul show that Ann, Bill, and Chuck have better information about who was negligent or are engaged in a conspiracy of silence. *See Ybarra v. Spangard,* 154 P.2d 687 (Cal. 1944).

There are other doctrines that permit the jury to find a defendant liable even when there is more than one defendant and the plaintiff cannot show which defendant's conduct caused his injury. However, none of these doctrines would help Paul to establish the liability of Ann, Bill, or Chuck. The "alternative liability" doctrine, which permits the jury to find two defendants liable when each was negligent and either individual could have caused the plaintiff's injuries, is unavailable because Paul cannot show that all defendants were negligent. *See Summers v. Tice,* 199 P.2d 1 (Cal. 1948); RESTATEMENT (SECOND) OF TORTS § 433B(3). The "joint venture" or "joint enterprise" doctrine allows the jury to impute one defendant's negligence to other defendants who are engaged in a common project or enterprise and who have an explicit or implied understanding about how the project is to be carried out. *See* DOBBS, THE LAW OF TORTS § 340. However, Paul cannot show that Ann, Bill, and Chuck had any common understanding. The facts state that Ann, Bill, and Chuck acted independently in making their respective batches of chicken salad.

Thus, because Paul cannot show which defendant was negligent, he cannot recover damages from Ann, Bill, or Chuck.

A strict products liability action would not be available against Ann, Bill, or Chuck because none is a product seller. Moreover, even if a products liability action were available, it would still be necessary to identify the source of the defective product, here the contaminated chicken salad.

MBE SUBJECTS – RELEASED ESSAY ANALYSIS

TORTS
MEE Question – February 2009

ANALYSIS

Legal Problems: (1)   Does Nephew have a cause of action against Tenant for negligence?

(2)   What is the standard of care applicable to Nephew?

(3)   Will Nephew's negligence prevent Nephew from recovering damages from Tenant or Landlord?

(4)   Did Landlord's violation of a state statute requiring that every part of a building be kept "in good repair" represent negligence *per se*?

(5)   Was Landlord's failure to repair the furnace a proximate cause of Nephew's injuries?

DISCUSSION

Summary

The jury could award Nephew damages in his action against Tenant. In a negligence action, an adult defendant's conduct is measured against that of a reasonable, prudent person engaged in a similar activity; a minor's conduct is measured against that of a minor of like age, intelligence, and experience. The determination of whether a party's conduct conforms to the applicable standard of care is a question of fact that is normally left to the jury. Here the jury could conclude that Tenant was negligent and that his negligence was the cause in fact and proximate cause of Nephew's injuries. Even if the jury also concluded that Nephew was negligent, under modern comparative negligence rules Nephew could still recover from Tenant.

It is less clear that the jury could award Nephew damages in his action against Landlord. Although violation of a state statute is normally considered negligence *per se*, it is unclear that the injuries Nephew suffered were within the category of harms the legislature aimed to prevent when enacting the statute. It is equally unclear whether Landlord's failure to repair the furnace was a proximate cause of the injuries.

Point One (15–25%)
A reasonable jury could conclude that Tenant was negligent and that his negligence caused Nephew's injuries.
In any negligence action, a plaintiff must show that the defendant owed the plaintiff a duty to conform his conduct to a standard necessary to avoid an unreasonable risk of harm to others, that

the defendant's conduct fell below the applicable standard of care, and that the defendant's conduct was both the cause in fact and the proximate cause of his injuries.

Nephew would have no difficulty in establishing that Tenant owed him a duty of care. Nephew was Tenant's household guest whose presence was known to Tenant. Thus, Tenant owed Nephew an obligation to exercise reasonable care to avoid foreseeable risks. *See* RICHARD A. EPSTEIN, CASES AND MATERIALS ON TORTS 154–55 (7th ed. 2000).

In determining whether Tenant's conduct fell below the standard of care, the jury would measure that conduct against the conduct of a reasonable, prudent person engaged in a like activity. A reasonable, prudent person takes precautions to avoid foreseeable risks. *See id.* at 162–63. A large pot of boiling water, if it spills, clearly poses a foreseeable risk of serious burns. A jury might also conclude that it was foreseeable that someone would come out of the bedroom quickly and collide with the boiling water. The burden of taking precautions to avert this possibility was small; Tenant could have yelled, "I'm coming with a pot of boiling water," or closed the bedroom door. Given the foreseeability of serious harm and the small burden of taking precautions, a jury might conclude that Tenant was negligent.

Tenant's conduct also was the cause in fact and proximate cause of the injuries. Tenant's failure to take precautions appears to have been a substantial factor in producing the accident. Burns were a foreseeable result of collision with a pot containing boiling water. Thus, based on the facts, a jury could properly award damages to Nephew.

Point Two (15–25%)
Although Nephew's age makes it unlikely, a jury could find that Nephew was negligent and that Nephew's negligence was a contributing factor in causing his injuries.

Nephew, like Tenant, had a duty to prevent foreseeable risks to himself and others. In judging whether Nephew exercised reasonable care under the circumstances, the jury would measure Nephew's conduct against that of a minor of like age, intelligence, and experience. *See* RESTATEMENT (SECOND) OF TORTS §§ 283, 283A (1965); *Roberts v. Ring*, 173 N.W. 437 (Minn. 1919). A few jurisdictions apply the so-called "tender years doctrine," under which a minor of less than seven years of age cannot be found negligent, but Nephew was age eight when the accident occurred.

Nephew chased a ball into the hall without looking or calling out. To an adult, this conduct would create a foreseeable risk of collision with someone walking in the hall. Age is the key factor here. A normal toddler does not foresee risks, particularly when engaged in an activity like chasing a ball; a normal adolescent does foresee such risks. Nephew, age eight, falls between a toddler and an adolescent. Therefore, it is possible, but not likely, that a jury would find that Nephew's conduct was negligent.

Point Three (10–20%)

Even if the jury found that Nephew was negligent in running into the hall, under modern comparative negligence rules, Nephew's negligence would reduce his recovery from Tenant but would not eliminate Tenant's liability.

At common law, if the jury found the plaintiff's negligence to be a cause in fact and proximate cause of his injuries, the plaintiff could not recover from the defendant. This all-or-nothing approach was frequently criticized; it has now been abandoned by virtually all states. *See* EPSTEIN, *supra*, at 369.

Under the modern "comparative negligence" approach, if the jury finds that two or more parties are negligent, it apportions fault between them. The plaintiff's fault share is subtracted from the total damages awarded by the jury. Thus, even if the jury found Nephew to be negligent, that finding would reduce his recovery from Tenant but would not eliminate Tenant's liability, except in a state that has preserved the all-or-nothing approach to contributory negligence or in a comparative negligence state where recovery is barred if the victim was more than 50 percent negligent.

Point Four (15–25%)
The unexcused violation of a statutory standard is negligence *per se* if the statute was designed to protect against the type of accident the actor's conduct caused and the injured party is within the class of persons the statute was designed to protect. Under this standard, it is unclear whether Landlord's conduct constituted negligence *per se*.

The governing state statute requires that "every apartment building . . . and every part thereof shall be kept in good repair." Arguably, Landlord violated the statute, as the furnace was "part" of the "apartment building" owned by Landlord, and it malfunctioned on three different occasions before Landlord took steps to correct the problem permanently. "An actor is negligent if, without excuse, the actor violates a statute that is designed to protect against the type of accident the actor's conduct causes, and if the accident victim is within the class of persons the statute is designed to protect." RESTATEMENT (THIRD) OF TORTS § 14 (P.F.D. NO. 1 2005). In such a case, the jury is *required* to find that the actor is negligent.

Landlord's failure to permanently fix the furnace was unexcused. On three earlier occasions, he was given notice of problems with the furnace but made only temporary repairs. Nephew, as the guest of a tenant, is within the class of persons the statute is designed to protect. Loss of heat and hot water is certainly among the types of harms the statute was designed to protect against. However, it is not clear that the accident which occurred—burns due to a collision—was within the category of harms the statute was designed to protect against. *See* EPSTEIN, *supra*, at 259–60 (describing conflicting authority on whether statutes criminalizing the act of leaving a key in a car ignition are designed to protect against injuries caused by a car thief).

Point Five (20–30%)
In a negligence action, a defendant is liable only if his conduct was the proximate cause of the plaintiff's injury. A reasonable jury could find that the type of harm Nephew suffered was too remote from Landlord's negligence in failing to provide adequate heat and hot water.

It is unclear whether Landlord's failure to repair the furnace was a proximate cause of Nephew's injuries. (Indeed, the "right type of harm" requirement for use of a statutory standard to establish negligence is probably just another way of stating the proximate cause requirement.) Even when the defendant is negligent, his conduct must have "such an effect in producing the harm as to lead reasonable men to regard it as a cause, using that word in the popular sense, in which there always lurks the idea of responsibility, rather than in the so-called 'philosophic sense,' which includes every one of the great number of events without which any happening would not have occurred." RESTATEMENT (SECOND) OF TORTS § 431, cmt. a.

Intervening actors or events that produce harm different in kind from that which one would normally anticipate from the defendant's negligence may break the chain of causation and lead a fact-finder to conclude that the defendant's acts are not the proximate cause of the plaintiff's injury. Thus, a defendant who negligently exceeds a speed limit and therefore happens to be on the spot where a tree falls during a violent windstorm is not liable for injuries caused by the tree (*see Berry v. Sugar Notch Borough*, 43 A. 240 (Pa. 1899)), and a defendant who negligently fails to stop a train at a station is not liable for the passenger's injuries when she elects to walk the mile back to the station along a dangerous route and is assaulted. *See Hines v. Garrett*, 108 S.E. 690 (Va. 1921). These harms are simply too remote from the defendant's negligent conduct.

On similar facts, courts have not agreed on whether a landlord's conduct was the proximate cause of a plaintiff's injury. Some courts have found that the landlord's negligence in failing to timely repair a furnace is too remote from burn injuries like Nephew's based on the intervening and arguably unforeseeable conduct of actors like Nephew and Tenant as well as the nature of the injuries, which are different in kind from those that would typically be produced by an inoperable heating system. Other courts have held that a jury might reasonably find heating hot water to be a foreseeable result of not having hot water and collisions from carrying hot water a foreseeable result of heating it. *Compare Martinez v. Lazaroff*, 399 N.E.2d 1148 (N.Y. 1979), with *Enis v. Ba-Call Bldg. Corp.*, 639 F.2d 359 (7th Cir. 1980). *See generally* Annotation, *Landlord and Tenant: Violation of Statute or Ordinance Requiring Landlord to Furnish Specified Facilities or Services as Ground of Liability for Injury Resulting from Tenant's Attempt to Deal with Deficiency*, 63 A.L.R.4th 883 (1988).

[NOTE: The applicant's conclusion on the proximate cause issue is less important than his or her analysis. The applicant should receive full credit if he or she recognizes and discusses the applicable legal principles.]

MBE SUBJECTS – RELEASED ESSAY ANALYSIS

TORTS
MEE Question – February 2010

ANALYSIS

Legal Problems: (1)   What must Penny establish in a battery action against Dennis?

(2)   What must Penny establish in a negligence action against Dennis?

(3)   What must Penny establish in an action against the Flies based on the team's employment relationship with Dennis?

(4)   What must Penny establish in a negligence action against the Flies?

(5)   If Penny succeeds in her action against either Dennis or the Flies, can she recover for damages for the neurological harm that resulted from a preexisting condition?

DISCUSSION

Summary

Penny does not have a viable battery action against Dennis because Dennis neither intended, nor knew with substantial certainty, that the ball he hit out of the Park would strike anyone. Penny does not have a viable negligence action against Dennis because there is no reasonable means by which Dennis could have avoided hitting Penny. Because Penny does not have a viable claim against Dennis, she has no viable claim against the Flies based on the team's employment of Dennis even though Dennis was acting within the scope of his employment. However, Penny might have a viable negligence action against the Flies based on the team's failure to attach netting to the fence adjoining Oak Street. The fact that the Flies have conformed to customary standards for minor league baseball fence construction is relevant but not determinative. If the jury finds that the Flies' failure to install netting along the Oak Street fence was negligent, Penny could recover for harm suffered as a result of her adverse reaction to medication even though this harm resulted from a preexisting condition.

Point One (25%)
Dennis did not commit a battery when the ball he hit struck Penny. Therefore Penny does not have a viable battery action against Dennis.

In a battery action, the plaintiff must show that the defendant *intentionally* caused a harmful or offensive bodily contact. A defendant intentionally causes such a contact if he "acts with the desire to bring about that harm" or engages "in action knowing that harm is substantially certain to occur." RESTATEMENT (THIRD) OF TORTS § 1, cmt. d. In this case, Dennis neither desired to bring about a harmful contact between the baseball and Penny nor, in light of his location inside the Park, could he have known that such a contact would or was substantially certain to occur. As a result, Penny does not have a viable battery claim against Dennis.

Point Two (25%)

Dennis was not negligent in hitting the ball that struck Penny over the Oak Street fence. Therefore Penny does not have a viable negligence claim against Dennis.

In a negligence action, the plaintiff must show that the defendant owed the plaintiff a duty to conform his conduct to a standard necessary to avoid an unreasonable risk of harm to others, that the defendant's conduct fell below the applicable standard of care, and that the defendant's conduct was both the cause in fact and the proximate cause of the plaintiff's injuries.

In determining whether Dennis's conduct fell below the standard of care, the jury would measure that conduct against the actions of a reasonable, prudent person engaged in a like activity. A reasonable, prudent person takes appropriate precautions to avoid foreseeable risks; in measuring whether a particular precaution was warranted, the jury weighs the burden of taking such precautions against the gravity of the risk and the likelihood that it will eventuate. *See* RICHARD A. EPSTEIN, CASES AND MATERIALS ON TORTS 150–51 (7th ed. 2004); *United States v. Carroll Towing Co.*, 159 F.2d 169 (2d Cir. 1947).

Here the burden of taking the precaution against the risk is high. The only meaningful precautions that Dennis might have taken were not hitting the ball at all or trying to hit it with less than maximum force. Either precaution would generally be inconsistent with Dennis's job as a professional baseball player, which includes the obligation to hit the ball and to hit a home run if possible. For Dennis, the cost of taking precautions could mean the loss of his career.

The gravity of the risk created by his hitting the ball cannot be determined easily. Being hit with an errant baseball could cause harm ranging from minimal bruising to far more serious injury. The likelihood of the harm occurring is low—in 40 years only 30 balls had previously been hit into Oak Street.

Thus Dennis was not negligent in hitting the ball that caused Penny's injury.

Point Three (10%)

Penny does not have a viable claim against the Flies based on the team's employment of Dennis.

An employer is vicariously liable for the tortious actions of his employee that are within the scope of the tortfeasor's employment. *See* RESTATEMENT (SECOND) OF AGENCY §§ 219, 229; RESTATEMENT (THIRD) OF AGENCY § 2.04. In this case, there is no question that Dennis was acting within the scope of his employment; he was a baseball player engaged in hitting a baseball. But Penny does not have a viable tort action against Dennis because Dennis's conduct was not tortious. Therefore, the Flies are not vicariously liable for his conduct.

Point Four (25%)

Penny may have a viable negligence action against the Flies based on the team's failure to attach netting to the Oak Street fence despite the fact that the fence conforms to customary standards within professional baseball.

Just as a jury would measure Dennis's conduct against the actions of a reasonable, prudent person engaged in a like activity, it would measure the Flies' conduct in constructing and maintaining the Oak Street fence against that of a reasonably prudent ballpark owner. And while Dennis had no means of avoiding the injury to Penny other than not hitting the ball, the Flies could have added netting to the Oak Street fence, and that netting would have prevented Penny's injury.

Custom is relevant in a negligence action, but it is not determinative. *See The T.J. Hooper,* 53 F.2d 107 (S.D.N.Y. 1931). Thus, even though the Flies' conduct conformed to the industry standard, Penny may succeed in her negligence action if she can establish that the cost of adding netting to the fence was relatively modest in relation to the risk of injuries from balls exiting the Park onto Oak Street. Given the changed character of the street, the increasing number of balls hit onto the street in recent years, and the widespread adoption of netting in another country, it is possible that Penny may succeed in making such a showing.

Point Five (15%)
Because a tort defendant "takes his victim as he finds him," Penny could recover for harm suffered due to her adverse reaction to medication.

A tort defendant takes his victim as he finds him. The plaintiff with an "eggshell skull" who suffers damage greatly in excess of those that a normal victim would suffer thus is entitled to recover fully for his injuries. *See* Epstein, *supra,* at 476–77. Because Penny's sensitivity to the prescribed medication was a preexisting condition, if Penny succeeds in her lawsuit against the Flies, she could recover for all injuries suffered as a result of that sensitivity.

MBE SUBJECTS – RELEASED ESSAY ANALYSIS

TORTS
MEE Question – February 2011

ANALYSIS

Legal Problems:	(1)(a)	Did use of a stun device to shock Claimant establish a prima facie case of battery?
	(1)(b)	Did frisking Claimant establish a prima facie case of battery?
	(2)	Did Claimant consent to either the frisk or the stun-device shock?
	(3)	Is the manufacturing defect in the Alertco device actionable in strict products liability?
	(4)	Can Claimant recover damages for her depressive reaction to the malfunctioning stun device even though that depressive reaction was unforeseeable?

DISCUSSION

Summary

A prima facie case of battery is established when the plaintiff shows that she suffered a harmful or offensive contact and that the defendant intended to cause such a contact. Guard's use of a stun device against Claimant meets this test because Guard intentionally administered a painful and physically incapacitating shock to Claimant's body. However, it is unclear whether Inspector's frisk of Claimant's body satisfies this test, as such a frisk may not be sufficiently offensive to constitute battery and Inspector may have been unaware that Claimant would be offended by the frisk. Moreover, because conduct can manifest consent, Claimant may have consented to the frisk when she walked through the metal detector. On the other hand, Claimant did not manifest consent to being shocked with the stun device.

A manufacturer is strictly liable for manufacturing defects. Alertco is thus liable for the defective stun device because the defect arose during the manufacturing process.

Because a tort defendant "takes his victim as he finds him," Claimant may recover for her unforeseeable depressive reaction to the stun device.

Point One(a) (20%)
A prima facie case of battery is established when the plaintiff shows that she suffered a harmful or offensive contact and that the defendant intended to cause such a contact. Guard's use of a stun device against Claimant satisfies this test. Thus, because Guard was acting within the scope of his employment, Claimant can establish a prima facie case against Metro.

An actor is subject to liability to another for battery if (a) he acts intending to cause a harmful or offensive contact with the person and (b) a harmful or offensive contact results. RESTATEMENT (SECOND) OF TORTS §§ 13 (Battery: Harmful Contact) & 18 (Battery: Offensive Contact) (1965). Intent, for purposes of establishing a battery, means either that "the actor desires to cause [the] consequences of his act" or that he "knows that the consequences are certain, or substantially certain, to result from his act . . . ." *Id.* § 8A & cmt. b.

Guard's use of a stun device to subdue Claimant meets these standards for an actionable battery. First, the use of a stun device both incapacitates the target and causes the target to suffer pain. Either effect constitutes "bodily harm" for purposes of establishing a prima facie case of battery. *See id.* § 15 ("bodily harm" includes "any physical impairment of the condition of another's body, or physical pain or illness"). Second, Guard certainly used the stun device for the purpose of physically impairing Claimant. His goal was to make it easier to subdue Claimant by causing physical impairment. Furthermore, although the facts do not say so explicitly, it is a reasonable assumption that Guard was aware that stun devices cause pain when they are used against someone. Thus, Guard's actions amount to battery: Guard intended to, and did, cause a harmful contact with Claimant. Because Guard was acting within the scope of his employment, Claimant can establish a prima facie case against Metro.

Point One(b) (20%)

It is unclear whether Inspector's frisk of Claimant establishes a prima facie case of battery. It is possible that Claimant will not be able to show intent to cause a harmful or offensive contact.

Inspector's frisk of Claimant was not harmful, but a contact can also constitute battery if it is *offensive.* "A bodily contact is offensive if it offends a reasonable sense of personal dignity." RESTATEMENT (SECOND) OF TORTS § 19 (1965). The facts make clear that Claimant found the contact offensive, but this is not determinative. Claimant must additionally show that being frisked offends a "reasonable" sense of dignity.

The frisk in this case was part of a routine screening process, and screening like this is now frequently encountered in airports and other public places. The routine nature of such screening may mean that it is no longer "reasonable" to be offended by it. On the other hand, the fact that Metro generally required employees to ask permission before frisking opera patrons suggests that frisking is often experienced by people as offensive, especially if it occurs without permission. It is thus possible, but not certain, that a routine frisk would be viewed by a court as a contact that "offends a reasonable sense of personal dignity."

Even if the frisk were considered offensive, a prima facie case of battery based on the frisk cannot be established unless Inspector is shown to have acted with intent to cause an offensive contact. To establish intent, Claimant must show that Inspector had the purpose of causing offense or knew he would cause offense by frisking Claimant. It is not enough to show that Inspector may have been aware of a risk that some patrons would be offended by a frisk. Battery's protection against "offensive contact" is intended to protect a person's "dignitary" interest. That interest "is protected *only* against intentional invasion. The actor is not liable for an act which involves a risk, no matter how great and unreasonable, that it will cause . . . an offensive contact." *Id.* § 18, cmt. g (emphasis added).

Because opera patrons were warned of the possibility of being frisked, Inspector may have assumed that they would not be offended by such a contact. On the other hand, Inspector did not warn Claimant before initiating the frisk in question, and it is unclear in what manner Inspector conducted that frisk. Claimant can establish a prima facie case if she can present some facts suggesting that Inspector knew with substantial certainty that Claimant's "reasonable sense of personal dignity" would be offended by Inspector's decision to touch her without warning, or that Inspector knew that the manner in which he touched Claimant would be offensive to her. But, absent some facts suggesting Inspector's knowledge that the frisk would be offensive, the mere fact that Inspector intentionally contacted Claimant's person does not satisfy the requirements for an actionable battery.

[NOTE: The examinee's analysis is more important than his or her conclusion.]

Point Two (30%)
Because conduct can manifest consent, Claimant may have consented to being frisked. Claimant did not manifest consent to being shocked with the stun device.

Consent—"willingness in fact for conduct to occur"—is a defense to battery. RESTATEMENT (SECOND) OF TORTS § 892. Consent "may be manifested by action or inaction and need not be communicated to the actor." Thus, "[i]f words or conduct are reasonably understood by another to be intended as consent, they constitute apparent consent and are as effective as consent in fact." *Id.*

Claimant did not intend to consent to Inspector's search of her person. Claimant told Friend, "I'm certainly not going to allow anyone to touch me," and told Inspector, "Leave me alone!"

However, a defendant is entitled to rely on objective manifestations of consent. Thus, because Claimant read the warning sign, saw opera patrons being frisked, and still proceeded through the metal detector, Metro can argue that its employee, Inspector, was entitled to infer that Claimant had consented to being frisked herself. *See O'Brien v. Cunard Steamship Co.*, 28 N.E. 266, 274 (Mass. 1891) (finding that the plaintiff consented to vaccination when she stood in line with other passengers and "there was nothing in [her] . . . conduct . . . to indicate . . . that she did not wish to obtain a [vaccination] card").

On the other hand, the fact that Metro usually required its employees to request permission before frisking patrons suggests that it did not infer consent to frisking from a patron's decision to proceed through the metal detector. A court thus might conclude that it was unreasonable to infer Claimant's consent to being frisked.

Metro has no possible argument that Claimant consented to being shocked with a stun device. Claimant did not see the stun device in use, and there were no signs warning of its use.

There are no other defenses available to Metro. The privilege to exercise force in self-defense or defense of others is unavailable because Claimant's statement ("Leave me alone!") could not reasonably be interpreted as a threat. *See* RESTATEMENT (SECOND) OF TORTS § 63 ("An actor is privileged to use reasonable force . . . to defend himself against unprivileged harmful or offensive contact or other bodily harm which he reasonably believes that another is about to inflict . . . .").

Point Three (15%)
A manufacturer is strictly liable for a defective product. Alertco is thus liable for the defective stun device even though Claimant cannot show that Alertco was negligent.

Alertco's product contained a manufacturing defect; it failed to meet Alertco's own specifications, and the defect occurred during the product's manufacture. *See* RESTATEMENT (THIRD) OF TORTS: PRODUCTS LIABILITY § 2 (1998). In order to recover for injuries sustained because of a manufacturing defect, a plaintiff need not show that the manufacturer was negligent. The manufacturer is strictly liable whenever "the product departs from its intended design even though all possible care was exercised in the preparation and marketing of the product . . . ." *Id.* In this case, the evidence establishes that the defect occurred during the manufacturing process. Thus, despite Alertco's excellent quality control, it is strictly liable to Claimant.

Point Four (15%)
Because a tort defendant "takes his victim as he finds him," Claimant may recover for her unforeseeable depressive reaction to the stun device.

"When an actor's tortious conduct causes harm to a person that, because of a preexisting physical or mental condition or other characteristics of the person, is of a greater magnitude or different type than might reasonably be expected, the actor is nevertheless subject to liability for all such harm to the person." RESTATEMENT OF TORTS: LIABILITY FOR PHYSICAL HARM § 31 (2010). Thus, the plaintiff with an "eggshell skull" who suffers injuries different from or greater than those that a normal victim would suffer is entitled to recover fully for his injuries.

Claimant's history of depression is a preexisting condition, like an eggshell skull. Thus, despite the fact that a depressive reaction to the stun device was unforeseeable, Alertco is liable for both Claimant's physical and psychological injuries. *See Bartolone v. Jeckovich*, 481 N.Y.S.2d 545 (N.Y. App. Div. 1984); *Steinhauser v. Hertz Corp.*, 421 F.2d 1169 (2d Cir. 1970).

MBE SUBJECTS – RELEASED ESSAY ANALYSIS

TORTS
MEE Question – February 2012

ANALYSIS

Legal Problems

    (1)   Could a jury properly find that Employee falsely imprisoned Paul by stopping the Ferris wheel for 30 minutes?

    (2)   Could a jury properly find that Funworld was negligent because Employee failed to take action to stop the two boys from rocking their car?

    (3)   Could a jury properly find that Mom is entitled to recover for her emotional distress and resulting miscarriage?

DISCUSSION

Summary

A jury could properly find that Employee falsely imprisoned Paul, because Employee knew with substantial certainty that Paul would be confined in the Ferris wheel car when he refused to restart the Ferris wheel, and the facts do not establish any defense to a false imprisonment claim. Because Employee was acting within the scope of his employment, a jury could impose liability on Funworld for Employee's actions. A jury could properly find that Employee's failure to take action to stop the two boys from rocking the car was negligent and that it caused Paul's injuries even though there has been only one similar accident over the past 40 years. It is unlikely that Mom can recover for her emotional distress and resulting miscarriage because she was not in the zone of danger and did not contemporaneously observe any injury to Paul.

Point One (40%)
Paul can establish the elements of a prima facie case of false imprisonment, and there is no defense here to a false imprisonment claim.

An actor is subject to liability to another for false imprisonment if "(a) he acts intending to confine the other or a third person within boundaries fixed by the actor, and (b) his act directly or indirectly results in such a confinement of the other, and (c) the other is conscious of the confinement or is harmed by it." RESTATEMENT (SECOND) OF TORTS § 35.

Confinement need not be physical, and it "need not be stationary." *Id.* § 36 cmt. b. The individual confined is not required to endanger his person through escape efforts. *Id.* § 36 cmt. a. *See also id.* § 38 ("confinement may be by actual or apparent physical barriers").

The requisite intent to confine can be shown through either motivation or knowledge. An actor may be found liable for false imprisonment both when "his act was done for the purpose of imposing confinement upon the other" and when he acted "with knowledge that such confinement would, to a substantial certainty, result from [his actions]." *Id.* § 35 cmt. d.

Here, Employee confined Paul by stopping the Ferris wheel. Given Paul's position in midair, he could not leave the car in which he was riding without endangering his person. Employee knew that Paul would be unable to leave the car when he acted. Thus, Paul can establish a prima facie case of false imprisonment. And because Employee was acting within the scope of his employment, Funworld is vicariously liable for his conduct.

Employee's actions would have been privileged if stopping the Ferris wheel had been necessary in order to protect "some interest of the actor or of the public which is of such importance as to justify the harm caused or threatened by its exercise." *Id.* § 10. *See also id.* § 890; *Sindle v. New York City Transit Authority*, 307 N.E.2d 245 (N.Y. 1973) (holding that a school bus driver who drove straight to police station instead of making regular stops was privileged to confine all students riding the bus when some students had committed acts of vandalism and continued to be abusive after being warned). Thus, for example, if Employee had stopped the Ferris wheel briefly to permit rescue workers to remove the two boys from the scene, Employee's conduct would likely have been privileged. However, Employee, for no apparent reason, failed to start the Ferris wheel for 30 minutes after the two boys were taken to the hospital.

Therefore, a jury could properly find that Employee falsely imprisoned Paul. Because Employee was acting within the scope of his employment, the jury could also find that Funworld was liable to Paul for injuries caused by Employee's actions.

While an argument could be made that Paul consented to being confined on the Ferris wheel, Paul's consent to be on the wheel was withdrawn once he begged to be taken off the wheel.

Point Two (25%)
A reasonable jury could properly conclude that Funworld was negligent for failing to take any action to stop the two boys from rocking the Ferris wheel car.

In any negligence action, a plaintiff must show that the defendant owed the plaintiff a duty to conform his conduct to a standard necessary to avoid an unreasonable risk of harm to others, that the defendant's conduct fell below the applicable standard of care, and that the defendant's conduct was both the cause in fact and the proximate cause of the plaintiff's injuries. Paul would have no difficulty in establishing that Funworld owed him a duty of care. Paul was a business visitor, and Funworld thus owed Paul reasonable care to avoid foreseeable risks. *See* RESTATEMENT (SECOND) OF TORTS §§ 332 & 343. Because Employee was acting within the scope of his employment, the jury could also find that Funworld was liable to Paul for injuries caused by Employee's negligence (*see* Point One).

In determining whether Employee's conduct was negligent, the jury should measure that conduct against the conduct of a reasonable, prudent person engaged in a like activity. A reasonable, prudent person takes precautions to avoid foreseeable risks, even if those risks have rarely materialized. *See* RICHARD A. EPSTEIN, CASES AND MATERIALS ON TORTS 177–78 (9th ed. 2008). If a Ferris wheel car is rocking vigorously, there is a small but nonetheless foreseeable risk that persons riding within the car or objects they are carrying may fall and cause injuries. Given the foreseeability of serious harm, and the small burden of taking steps to prevent the harm, a jury could properly conclude that Employee was negligent in failing to take any action to stop the two boys from rocking the car.

Point Three (35%)
Mom is unlikely to recover for her emotional distress and resulting miscarriage because she was not in the zone of danger nor did she contemporaneously observe an injury to Paul.

Although early cases typically denied recovery for negligent infliction of emotional distress to a plaintiff who experienced no physical contact or injury (*see Mitchell v. Rochester Railway Co.*, 45 N.E. 354 (N.Y. 1896)), today virtually all American jurisdictions have abandoned this approach; a plaintiff who is within the zone of danger created by the defendant and who suffers a physical manifestation of emotional distress occasioned by a threatened injury may recover in virtually all states. Here, however, Mom did not apprehend any personal danger. Her emotional harm and resulting miscarriage were due to her fears for *Paul's* safety.

In evaluating claims for emotional distress resulting from accidents involving other individuals, American jurisdictions have taken two different approaches. Some disallow recovery unless the plaintiff was herself within the zone of danger. *See, e.g., Tobin v. Grossman*, 249 N.E.2d 419 (N.Y. 1969); Michael Steenson, *Engler v. Illinois Farmers Insurance Co. and Negligent Infliction of Emotional Distress*, 32 WM. MITCHELL L. REV. 1335, n. 176 (2006) (reporting 13 jurisdictions that follow the zone-of-danger approach). A larger group permits recovery if the plaintiff was closely related to the victim, was located near the scene of the accident, and suffered shock resulting from "the sensory and contemporaneous observance of the *accident*." *Dillon v. Legg*, 441 P.2d 912 (Cal. 1968) (emphasis added); Steenson, *supra* (reporting 30 jurisdictions that follow some variant of the *Dillon* approach). In virtually all jurisdictions, emotional distress must result from sensory and contemporaneous observance of the accident itself, not the receipt of news relating to the accident. "All of us can expect at least once in our lives to be informed of the serious injury or death of a close family member . . . . Although the shock and grief growing out of such news is great, it is not compensable emotional distress." *Bowen v. Lumbermens Mutual Casualty Co.*, 517 N.W.2d 432, 445 (Wis. 1994). Some jurisdictions that follow the *Dillon* approach limit recovery to relatives who were at the scene when the accident happened. *See* Steenson, *supra*, n. 176. Some permit recovery by a relative who comes upon the scene shortly after the accident happens. *See id.* Only a handful of jurisdictions permit recovery based simply on the foreseeability of mental distress. *See id.* (reporting nine jurisdictions that use a foreseeability approach and noting that they typically require arrival at the scene shortly after the injury); *Ferriter v. Daniel O'Connell's & Sons, Inc.*, 413 N.E.2d 690 (Mass. 1980) (permitting recovery by wife who saw husband's injuries at hospital) (superseded by statute, M.G.L.A. 152 § 24).

Here, Mom was not within the zone of danger; she was some 100 yards away. Moreover, Mom's fright was occasioned solely by an erroneous report that "a little boy has been killed." Although

Mom was located near the scene of the accident, she did not see or hear the accident; she arrived on the scene after hearing emergency alarms. Indeed, even after she arrived, Mom could neither see nor hear Paul (nor could she see any other injured person) until several minutes after Paul exited the Ferris wheel, which was 40 minutes after the accident took place.

Thus, in virtually all jurisdictions, Mom will not be able to recover for her distress and resulting miscarriage even if Funworld is found negligent in failing to prevent Paul's injury. Mom was not within the zone of danger, and her emotional harm stemmed from an erroneous report that a boy had been killed, not from sensory and contemporaneous observance of injuries to Paul.

MBE SUBJECTS – RELEASED ESSAY ANALYSIS

TORTS
MEE Question – July 2012

Legal Problems

(1)(a)   Could a jury find that University had a duty of care to Susan and that its breach of that duty was the cause in fact and proximate cause of Susan's injuries?

(1)(b)   Could a jury find that Jim owed a duty of care to Susan and that his breach of that duty was the cause in fact and proximate cause of Susan's injuries?

(1)(c)   Could a jury find that Ann's Psychiatrist owed a duty of care to Susan and that Psychiatrist's breach of that duty was the cause in fact and proximate cause of Susan's injuries?

(2)   If any party is liable for Susan's injuries, may Susan also obtain damages for PTSD symptoms?

DISCUSSION

Summary

A jury could find that University is liable to Susan for failing to take reasonable precautions to protect Susan from foreseeable criminal activity resulting from unauthorized entrance into the dorm. University owed a duty of care to Susan, a resident of a dormitory controlled and maintained by University. University's failure to fix the broken lock or take other steps to prevent entry by an intruder violated that duty; it was also the cause in fact and proximate cause of Susan's physical injuries.

A jury could not find that Jim is liable to Susan unless Susan relied to her detriment on Jim's promise to obtain assistance or unless Jim increased the risk that Susan would suffer harm. Here, there is no evidence of reliance or increased risk as a result of Jim's failure to obtain assistance.

A jury could not find that Ann's Psychiatrist is liable to Susan. Although a therapist may be liable for failing to warn a patient's intended victim of credible threats of violence when that victim is reasonably identifiable, in virtually all jurisdictions, a therapist may not be found liable for failing to warn a victim who is a member of an indeterminate group.

If University is found liable to Susan, it will be responsible for damages related to Susan's PTSD injuries because a tort defendant takes his victim as he finds him.

Point One(a) (30%)

University owed a duty of care to Susan, a resident of a dormitory controlled and maintained by University, to take reasonable precautions to protect Susan from foreseeable criminal activity.

University's failure to fix the broken lock or take other precautions against unauthorized entry into Susan's dorm violated that duty. It was also the cause in fact and proximate cause of Susan's physical injuries.

A college does not stand in a *parens patriae* relationship with its students. *See Hegel v. Langsam*, Ohio Misc. 2d (Comp. Pl. 1971). However, although the common law imposed almost no duties on landlords to provide safe premises to tenants, modern courts have found that landlords, including landlords like University, have a duty to take reasonable precautions to protect tenants against foreseeable attacks. *See Kline v. 1500 Massachusetts Avenue Apartment Corp.*, 439 F.2d 477 (D.C. Cir. 1970). *See also* RESTATEMENT (SECOND) OF TORTS §§ 360, 361.

[NOTE: An examinee might also conclude that University owed a duty of care to Susan because she was an invitee. *See* DAN B. DOBBS, THE LAW OF TORTS § 235, at 605 (2000) (describing tenant in common areas of building as an example of an invitee encountering obvious dangers).]

Criminal activity of the sort that occurred here was foreseeable. Apartment buildings and college dormitories almost invariably have locked entrances to protect against intrusion by criminals. Indeed, recognizing this risk, University had taken steps to ensure that nonresidents could not enter the dormitory.

A jury could find that University's failure to repair the broken lock or to take other steps to secure the door through which Ann entered the dormitory represented a breach of its duty of care. The lock had broken four days before Ann's entry. Therefore, University employees had ample time to discover the break. Even if repairs were impossible within the relevant time period, University could have taken other steps to prevent the door from being opened from the outside. Such precautions were warranted given the foreseeability that unauthorized persons could enter the dormitory to engage in criminal acts. It is this risk that prompted University to issue key cards to the dormitory residents. *See Brauer v. New York Central & H.R.R. Co.*, 103 A. 166 (N.J. 1918) (finding railroad liable for theft resulting from failure to guard plaintiff's goods when theft foreseeable).

Because Ann's entrance into Susan's dorm was made possible by University's failure to secure the damaged door, a jury could find that University's failure to repair the lock was the cause in fact and proximate cause of Susan's physical injuries.

Point One(b) (25%)

There is no general duty to come to the aid of another. Jim assumed a duty to Susan only if Susan relied to her detriment on Jim's promise to obtain assistance or if Jim left Susan in a worse position. Here, the evidence does not show that Susan relied to her detriment or that Susan was in a worse position after Jim took charge.

Susan and Jim did not have a special relationship that created a duty to come to the aid of another. *See* DAN B. DOBBS, THE LAW OF TORTS §§ 314–319. However, when an actor "takes charge of another who is helpless adequately to aid or protect himself," he is subject to liability to the other for bodily harm caused by

a) "the failure of the actor to exercise reasonable care to secure the safety of the other while within the actor's charge, or

b) the actor's discontinuing aid or protection, if by doing so he leaves the other in a worse position than when the actor took charge of him."

RESTATEMENT (SECOND) OF TORTS § 324. *See also* RESTATEMENT OF TORTS § 323 ("One who undertakes, gratuitously or for consideration, to render services to another . . . [is liable] for physical harm resulting from his failure to exercise reasonable care . . . if (a) his failure to exercise such care increases the risk of such harm; or (b) the harm is suffered because of the other's reliance upon the undertaking.").

Here, Jim's failure to follow up his unsuccessful attempt to report Susan's injuries to the University security office with any other action was arguably negligent. Moreover, Jim's closing the library door made it less likely that anyone else would come to Susan's aid. However, there is no evidence that Susan actually suffered any harm as a result of Jim's conduct. Susan obtained medical assistance herself only half an hour after Jim left her, and there is no evidence that her minor physical injuries or PTSD symptoms were aggravated by delayed treatment.

Thus, because there is no evidence that Jim caused or exacerbated Susan's injuries, Susan cannot recover damages from Jim.

Point One(c) (30%)

A psychotherapist has a duty to warn a reasonably identifiable individual against whom her patient has made credible threats but has no duty to warn any individual who is a member of an indeterminate class against whom the patient has made threats.

In *Tarasoff v. Regents of University of California*, 551 P.2d 334 (Cal. 1976), the California Supreme Court held that the special relationship between a psychotherapist and patient justified the imposition of a duty to warn "persons threatened by the patient." Both the holding and reasoning of the *Tarasoff* court have been widely adopted. Today, in most states, a psychotherapist who fails to warn an intended victim against whom her patient has made credible threats of physical violence may be found liable for that victim's injuries. Many courts have also followed *Tarasoff* in permitting recovery either (1) when the therapist believed that the patient posed a real risk to the specified victim or (2) when the therapist negligently failed to take the threat seriously.

However, California courts have restricted the duty imposed on psychotherapists in *Tarasoff* to "potential victims . . . specifically known and designated" by the dangerous patient. *Thompson v. County of Alameda*, 614 P.2d 728, 736 (Cal. 1980). For example, in *Thompson*, the court refused to extend *Tarasoff* to a defendant that had released a youth who had a long history of violence and who had "indicated that he would, if released, take the life of a young child residing in the neighborhood." *Id.* at 730. The court held that, in contrast to *Tarasoff*, "the warnings sought by plaintiffs would of necessity have to be made to a broad segment of the population and would be only general in nature . . . . [S]uch generalized warnings . . . would do little as a practical matter to stimulate increased safety measures . . . [and] would be difficult to give." *Id.* at 736.

Courts and legislatures in other states have also generally confined the *Tarasoff* duty to intended victims who are readily ascertainable and subject to a serious threat of physical violence. *See, e.g.*, KY. REV. STATS. ANN. § 202A.400(1) (requiring "actual threat of physical violence against a clearly identifiable victim"); NEB. REV. STAT. § 38-2137(1) (requiring "serious threat of physical violence" against a "reasonably identifiable victim"); N.H. REV. STAT. § 329:31 (requiring "serious threat of physical violence against a clearly identified or reasonably identifiable victim" or "serious threat of substantial damage to real property"); N.J. STAT. ANN. § 2A:62A-16 (requiring "threat of imminent, serious physical violence against a readily identifiable individual"). Cases in which courts have imposed a broader duty have typically involved defendants who directly facilitated the patient's attack. *See, e.g., Lundgren v. Fultz*, 354 N.W.2d 25 (Minn. 1984) (imposing duty to victims where psychiatrist helped patient to obtain guns confiscated by police).

Under *Tarasoff* and the case law of most states, the fact that Ann's Psychiatrist did not find Ann's threats credible would not be a defense if the evidence showed that a reasonable therapist would have taken Ann's threats seriously. Here, Ann's Psychiatrist had a therapeutic relationship with Ann because Ann saw Psychiatrist weekly for several months. That relationship imposed on Psychiatrist a duty to warn Ann's ascertainable intended victims if Ann made serious threats of physical violence against them. Psychiatrist's decision not to warn anyone was likely reasonable based on Ann's lack of any history of violent behavior and the ambiguity of her vague threat to ensure that cheaters "get what is coming to them," which is not a clear threat of serious injury. More importantly, Ann's threats were general; she did not specify any ascertainable victims. Thus, in the vast majority of states, a jury could not find that Psychiatrist is liable to Susan.

Point Two (15%)

University is responsible for damages related to Susan's injuries because a tort defendant takes his victim as he finds him.

A tort defendant takes his victim as he finds him. The victim with an "eggshell skull" who suffers injuries greatly in excess of those that a normal victim would suffer is entitled to recover for the full extent of his injuries. *See* RICHARD A. EPSTEIN AND CATHERINE M. SHAKEY, CASES AND MATERIALS ON TORTS 471–74 (10th ed. 2012).

Here, although Susan sustained only minor physical injuries from Ann's attack, Susan suffered a preexisting condition, PTSD. Susan's PTSD symptoms that emerged after Ann's attack were attributable to her preexisting PTSD. Most of the "eggshell skull" cases involve unusual physical consequences of an underlying precondition. However, there is no reason why, with proper proof, the plaintiff should not also recover damages for mental symptoms such as anxiety or insomnia. *See Steinhauser v. Hertz Corp.*, 421 F.2d 1169 (2d Cir. 1970) (permitting recovery for plaintiff's post-accident schizophrenia when evidence showed that prior concussion created predisposition that was exacerbated by accident for which defendant was liable). Courts have sometimes been reluctant to award tort plaintiffs damages for mental distress unaccompanied by any physical injuries (*see Williamson v. Bennett*, 112 S.E.2d 48 (N.C. 1960) (disallowing mental-disorder damages when plaintiff suffered no physical harm in accident caused by defendant)). However, here Susan did suffer physical injuries during the attack, and the attack also triggered physical symptoms such as nausea, muscle tension, and sweating.

Thus, if Susan recovers damages from University for her physical injuries, she should also be able to recover damages for her PTSD symptoms.

MBE SUBJECTS - PRACTICE ESSAY QUESTIONS

TORTS
Answer to Question 1

I. Introduction

In any action for negligence, a plaintiff must prove that 1) defendant owed plaintiff a duty of care; 2) that defendant breached his duty; 3) that the breach was the factual and legal cause of plaintiff's injury; and 4) that plaintiff did indeed suffer harm (damages). A variety of defenses are available for defendants in negligence and will be discussed in turn below.

II. Passenger (P) v. Driver (D)

As stated above, P must prove that D owed P a duty of care. The general rule is that a defendant owes a duty to any foreseeable Plaintiff. Here, it should have been foreseeable to D that a passenger riding in this car might have been injured by any accident in which D's car was involved, so it should not be difficult for P to prove the duty element. The standard of care that governs D, as a child under 18, is that of a reasonably prudent person under the circumstances. This is so because although D is a child under 18 and would normally be judged by a special standard (that of a child of like age, experience, intelligence, and education), he was here engaged in an adult activity: driving. As such, he owes the duty of an adult.

P must next prove that D breached his duty of care. This will be difficult unless P can avail herself of negligence per se. The facts we have suggest that D was driving carefully, obeying the traffic laws, at the point he was unexpectedly hit by Thief. This being the case, there simply does not appear to be a breach. From the facts we have, D was acting as a reasonably prudent person would act under the circumstances.

However, D was in violation of a local criminal statute when the accident occurred. This being the case, P can still prove breach (and duty for that matter) conclusively, if she can use negligence per se. A conclusive breach will be established if a defendant is violating a criminal or regulatory law and 1) the person injured (here, P) was in the class of persons the law was designed to protect AND 2) the type of harm that defendant caused was the type of harm the law was enacted to prevent.

D was violating the law because, although he had a licensed driver with him in the front seat, he was driving between 11 P.M. and 6 A.M. The persons this law was enacted to protect were "others" who might be endangered by the permitted driver. P seems to fall in this case of persons, even though she was a passenger. And the type of harm – injury from auto accidents also appears to be (at least arguably) the type of harm the legislature sought to prevent. It appears that P can use negligence per se, for the reasons discussed above, to establish duty and breach by D.

The third element will be somewhat challenging for P to prove. She must prove that D's breach was both the factual and legal (proximate) cause of her injury. Factual cause is established using a "but for" test. Here, it is quite straightforward: <u>but</u> <u>for</u> D's negligence (driving at the time he should not have been), Thief would not have hit the particular car D was driving and P would not have been injured. Legal (proximate) cause is harder: Proximate cause will operate to <u>limit</u> a defendant's liability when intervening acts for factors, or other attendant circumstances, made a plaintiff's injuries completely unforeseeable. Unless the intervening act falls within a well-settled category, each case must be judged on a facts and circumstances basis.

Here, it arguably should have been foreseeable that another driver (a third person, like Thief) would have been negligent or even reckless in his own use of a vehicle. The world is filled with careless and even reckless drivers. With this in mind, it is not unfair to hold D liable for P's injuries – the intervening act of Thief was foreseeable.

Assuming P can prove her personal injuries (e.g. medical bills, lost wages, etc.), P has proved all elements against D and should therefore prevail (in her direct case).

<u>Defenses</u>: D has two colorable defenses to assert against P: assumption (implied) of risk and depending on the state law that governs, contributory or comparative negligence. Assumption of the risk merely requires D to show that the risk P took in riding in D's car was (1) apparent to the average person; and (2) P proceeded voluntarily, in light of the risk. As previously stated, the streets are filled with reckless and negligent drivers. Moreover, a reasonable person in P's shoes would have known that risks inhere in riding with an inexperienced 16-year-old. D therefore has a pretty strong assumption of the risk defense against P, assuming P was a voluntary passenger.

Failing to wear a seatbelt is something that a reasonably prudent person would not do under the circumstances. Because persons owe themselves a duty of reasonable care and P therefore breached this duty, to the extent that her failure to wear a seatbelt caused her injuries, she was also negligent. If the state law governing this claim follows common law rules for contributory negligence, P's own failure to wear a seatbelt will be a complete bar to her recovery. If the state follows pure comparative negligence, on the other hand, P will recover whatever portion of her damages were not attributable to her own negligence. If this is a modified comparative negligence state, P will only recover the portion of her damages not attributable to her negligence if her fault is no greater than the combined fault of D and any other defendants over whom she prevails.

III. P v. Thief

P must prove the same four elements that were discussed in detail above: duty, breach, factual/legal cause, and damages.

Duty: again, it should have been foreseeable to Thief that he could injure someone by driving as he did. Thief therefore owed a duty of care to P. Under the facts we have, Thief clearly breached his duty (the reasonable person standard) by running a red light. A reasonably prudent person would not run a red light. Moreover, P could probably avail herself of <u>negligence</u> <u>per</u> <u>se</u> (again), to conclusively establish duty and breach. It is against the law to run a red light. It takes little analysis to conclude that passengers in other cars are in the class of persons that the "red light" law is designed to protect, and that mid-intersection collisions are the type of harm to be prevailed.

As for cause, P can prove "but for" cause: but for Thief's negligence, P would not have been injured. And, because her injury was absolutely foreseeable to Thief from his breach, the issue of proximate cause is also incontrovertible here. Thief's negligence was both the factual and legal cause of her injury. The analysis for damages is the same as under P v. D above.

Defenses: There is no assumption of the risk likely available here. Persons don't assume that other drivers will run red lights. Contributory or comparative negligence would still be available to Thief to defend against P, however. Same analysis as above.

IV. P v. Dealer

Did Dealer owe a duty of care to P? Again, the answer turns on foreseeability. It is arguable that leaving keys in the ignition of a car creates the danger that cars will be stolen and potentially, crashed. Moreover, Dealer had had problems with similar thefts before, which should have put Dealer on notice as to the risk of theft and a resulting crash. One could foresee, in fact, that a thief may be especially likely to drive in a negligent or even reckless manner, having more urgent matters on his mind (i.e., to get away). If there is a case to be made that P was not a foreseeable plaintiff, I don't see it on these facts.

A reasonably prudent person would not leave keys in the ignitions of new cars on a car lot, especially in light of the past thefts. P can therefore prove breach.

Cause: Here, P's case gets harder. Even if Dealer had not left the keys in the ignition, it is possible that Thief could have broken into a car and driven it away, or stole a car from someone else. In short, it is questionable as to whether Dealer's breach was even a "but for" cause of P's injury, not to mention a proximate cause. But, to the extent that it was foreseeable that Thief would steal cars and drive them recklessly or negligently, as previously discussed, it is not unfair to hold Dealer liable, and Dealer's breach is therefore likely a proximate cause.

The damages analysis for the P v. Dealer claim is the same as the two above. In terms of damages, largely for the reasons stated in P v. Thief, assumption of the risk is not colorable as a defense put forward by Dealer. However, once again, contributory or comparative negligence (whichever the state allows) would be defenses for Dealer. Analysis as to contributory/comparative negligence would be the same as in P v. Driver above.

MBE SUBJECTS - PRACTICE ESSAY QUESTIONS

TORTS
Answer to Question 2

Neighbor May Recover $10,000 for Personal Injury

Normally a plaintiff is entitled to recover for the full amount of personal injuries caused by the defendant's negligence. Therefore Neighbor would normally be entitled to recover the full $20,000 of damages for personal injuries he sustained. However, this can be modified by contributory negligence or comparative fault statutes. The comparative fault statute in this jurisdiction is not a pure comparative fault regime. Instead, this comparative fault statute allows a plaintiff to recover damages only if his or her contributory fault was not greater than the fault of the defendant, and those damages would be reduced in proportion to the amount of fault attributable to the plaintiff. In this case, Neighbor was found to be 50% at fault and Driver was found to be 50% at fault. Since Neighbor's fault was not greater than Driver's fault (it was equal), Neighbor's recovery is not completely barred. However, it must be reduced in proportion to the amount of fault attributed to Neighbor, which is 50%. Therefore, under this jurisdiction's comparative fault statute, Neighbor is only entitled to recover $10,000 in damages from Driver.

Owner May Recover $5,000 for Property Damage to his Truck

Generally, a plaintiff may recover damages for property damage from a negligent defendant. Again, this can be modified by a contributory negligence or comparative fault statute. The comparative fault statute in this jurisdiction is not a pure comparative fault regime. Instead, this comparative fault statute allows a plaintiff to recover damages only if his or her contributory fault was not greater than the fault of the defendant, and those damages would be reduced in proportion to the amount of fault attributable to the plaintiff.

An employer may be held vicariously liable for the negligence of its employees. Therefore, the negligence of an employee can be attributed to an employer if the employee is acting in the scope of employment. However, this only applies to employees and not independent contractors. In determining whether a worker is an employee or an independent contractor, a court would look at many factors. For example, a court would consider how much control over the worker the employer had, whose tools and resources were used by the worker, the duration of the employment and how the worker was paid. A court would also consider how much control over his actions the worker had. Generally, if the employer has substantial control, provides the tools and resources for the job, and regulates most activities of the worker, and if the worker is salaried, the worker would be considered an employee and not an independent contractor. However, where the worker controls his actions, provides his own tools and resources, works short term or off-and-on, is paid by contract or hourly, and controls when he works, then the worker would be considered an independent contractor. In this case, Neighbor had little control over how and when he worked. He was closely supervised by Owner and was required to work 10 hours per week and on Saturdays. In addition, Neighbor was paid a weekly fixed salary rather than hourly or by set contract price for specific jobs. Neighbor also used tools, equipment and other resources that were provided by Owner. Moreover, the work is constant and there is always enough to keep Neighbor busy. Even though Neighbor only works part-time and has other full-time work, the facts here indicate that Neighbor is an employee of Owner rather than just an independent contractor.

Generally, an employee is not acting in the scope of employment if the employee is engaging in a frolic and detour. Therefore, an employer is generally not vicariously liable for the actions of an employee if the employee is on a frolic and detour. However, to be a frolic and detour, the conduct must be a substantial deviation from what the employee is supposed to be doing. In this case, Neighbor is supposed to be driving to the hardware store to purchase supplies. Neighbor deviated from what he was supposed to be doing when he stopped at the post office. However, this side trip was relatively minor. The post office was on the way to the hardware store, so Neighbor wasn't driving substantially out of the way, and he was only buying stamps so it didn't take very long. Therefore, a court would likely find that this minor deviation didn't constitute a frolic and detour and therefore Neighbor was acting in the scope of employment. Since Neighbor was an employee of Owner and was acting in the scope of his employment, his negligence may be vicariously attributed to Owner. Therefore, Owner is also considered to be 50% at fault. According to the comparative fault statute, Owner would only be able to recover $5,000 for property damage to his truck rather than the whole $10,000 because he is considered to be 50% at fault.

Even if Owner isn't vicariously liable for Neighbor's negligence, he may be found to be, because he was allowing Neighbor to use his truck. Generally, the owner of an automobile is not liable for torts committed by someone they allow to drive their automobile. However, the owner is sometimes vicariously liable if the driver is running an errand for the owner. Therefore, it is possible that Owner may be attributed Neighbor's negligence under this theory because he was running to the hardware store to purchase supplies for Owner. Again, he would then only be able to recover 50% of his damages so would only get $5,000.

If Neighbor's negligence were not attributed to Owner, he would recover the full $10,000 for property damage.

MBE SUBJECTS - PRACTICE ESSAY QUESTIONS

TORTS
Answer to Question 3

TO: File

FROM: Applicant

RE: Med Mal Case: Analysis of Plaintiff's Claims

Introduction

Assuming there are not ethical dilemmas in this case, the plaintiff has a number of claims that may be asserted: (1) negligence of the hospital – negligent supervision; (2) negligence of the surgeon based on simple negligence and res ipsa loquitor; (3) negligence of the nurse; (4) there could potentially be issues of intentional tort which will be briefly addressed.

Negligence in General

The issue is whether the hospital, surgeon or nurse were negligent.

Negligence has four elements: (1) duty owed by defendant to the plaintiff; (2) breach of duty by virtue of failure of the defendant to satisfy the relevant standard of case; (3) causation based on factual causation (but for causation) and legal causation (proximate causation); (4) damages. In order for the plaintiff to win a claim for negligence each of these elements must be satisfied. A plaintiff can also assert a claim for negligence based on res ipsa loquitur (res ipsa). Res ipsa allows the plaintiff to establish a prima facie case of negligence, but does not mean that the plaintiff will win the case – it just gets the case to the jury. Res ipsa means that the thing speaks for itself, or in other words, the thing would not happen without the negligence of the defendant, particularly if the defendant possessed exclusive control of the instrumentality or object involved in causing the harm to the plaintiff. There are defenses to negligence including assumption of risk which means that the plaintiff knew about the specific risk and either expressly or impliedly waived his or her right to make claim for injury arising out of that risk. In addition, in some jurisdictions, contributory negligence, or negligence on the part of the plaintiff entirely forbids the plaintiff to recover. Most jurisdictions have replaced contributory negligence with either pure or modified comparative negligence, meaning that even if the plaintiff is negligent, that is not a totally bar to recover, but instead will just reduce the amount of recovery that the plaintiff can have. In a modified jurisdiction, if the plaintiff is more than 50% at fault, he or she will not be able to recover.

Surgeon

The liability of the surgeon needs to be analyzed under the negligence framework and under the res ipsa framework.

Negligence

First, there is the issue of duty. The doctor owes a duty to the plaintiff if the plaintiff is a foreseeable plaintiff. Here, the plaintiff is foreseeable because he went to the doctor for surgery for hip replacement.

Second, there is the issue of breach of duty (here the duty owed will be examined along with the breach rather than examining the duty specifically as part of element 1 for purposes of analysis). The duty owed is that of a reasonable prudent person under similar circumstances. Or, at least that is the general duty owed by all members of society to one another. In some situations, there is a heightened level of duty – particularly when the defendant possesses some sort of specialized knowledge or if the defendant is a professional. Here, the surgeon is a professional doctor. He will be found to owe his patients, a duty to act as the reasonable prudent doctor based on local standards and based on the average member of his profession. Some jurisdictions have eliminated the locality portion of this rule, while others have retained it. Either way, a doctor must act as an average member of his professional would. So, the question is if the doctor breached his duty to the plaintiff by failing to act as the reasonably prudent average doctor would. Here, there is little indication of breach of duty. The hospital records indicate that the surgery went well, without apparent complications. Further, the surgeon states that nothing went wrong in the way of performance. There was explanation of risk to the plaintiff that 1/100 cases result in paralysis. In addition, there is indication that the surgeon advised the plaintiff of these risks. In this manner, there is apparently no breach of duty. This is likely why the plaintiff raised res ipsa which will be analyzed after the analysis of negligence is complete.

Third, there must be "but for" causation and proximate causation. It has already been suggested that it is difficult to show that there was a breach of duty since the doctor need only act like an average member of his profession and since he advised of the risk and the surgery went smoothly, there is no indication, or evidence at this juncture other than the paralysis (that happens 1/100 cases) to show breach. For purposes of analysis, however, two types of causation must be shown. First, but for or factual causation requires that the plaintiff show that but for the negligence of the defendant, his injuries would not have resulted. Here, but for the surgery the plaintiff would not have been injured would be his argument. At the same time, the surgeon can argue that even if the surgery were negligent, the plaintiff would have been injured because this (1) happens every 1/100 cases and (2) the plaintiff disobeyed the instructions of the nurse when it came to his recovery. This is really a fact question that will need to be argued. Second, proximate cause requires that the injury be foreseeable. Here, where there is a surgery where paralysis occurs in some of the cases, the injury is certainly foreseeable. The question then comes back to but for causation and if it can really be said that but for the surgery the paralysis would not have occurred.

Note that the causation in this case could turn to the substantial factor test since the negligence of both the surgeon or the nurse could be involved.

Finally, there must be damages. Here, the plaintiff is paralyzed. Therefore, there is injury.

Overall, there are two problems with the negligence case against surgeon. First, there is the issue of breach of duty. Based on the evidence as shown, there is not indication that there was a breach of duty, but greater fact investigation should be done. Second, there is a question as to whether but for causation is satisfied.

Res Ipsa

The plaintiff has raised res ipsa in all likelihood because his attorney recognized the problems with the negligence case against the surgeon. In this particular case, it is difficult to say that the thing speaks for itself or that the thing would not have occurred without the negligence of the doctor. Unlike the case where a doctor sews back up a surgical patient with a clamp still inside, this is a case of paralysis where paralysis is a risk that the plaintiff assumed. There is also no indication that the surgeon was entirely in control since here the paralysis can result from things that occurred during the recovery phase. Here, the recovery phase is marked by the plaintiff's failure to follow the nurse's instructions with regard to staying in bed for two weeks. It seems like it is difficult to apply res ipsa since the surgeon was not in exclusive control, there is no obvious problem that presented after the surgery, and the plaintiff knew the risks.

Defenses

Here, if the plaintiff has evidence that helps establish the negligence case discussed above, then the surgeon can raise defenses. First, the plaintiff expressly assumed the risk. Of course, the plaintiff will argue that if he can establish the elements of negligence, he did not assume the risk of a negligent surgery. Second, contributory negligence to either totally bar the plaintiff's recover or to lead to a reduction in recovery in a comparative jurisdiction. The plaintiff was arguably negligent by getting out of bed against orders. He may argue, however, that he was not in fact adequately warned.

The Nurse

The claims against the nurse is negligence in allowing the plaintiff to get out of bed. The elements of negligence are the same as above.

Duty: there was duty owed because the plaintiff was a patient of the nurse.

Breach of duty: here the duty owed would be either the reasonable prudent person under similar circumstances or the reasonable prudent professional nurse or the reasonable prudent nurse based on local standards and based on an average nurse. It is unclear if either of the heightened standards apply to nurses. While they are applied to the professions or to doctors, accountants, nursing is less clear. Even assuming that a nurse is held to a heightened standard of care, there is no indication of breach. Here, the nurse is said to have warned the plaintiff of the risks and that it was the plaintiff who disregarded her while she was with another patient. The facts further show that once she discovered the problem, she immediately put the plaintiff back in bed. Here, the nurse likely had other patients. There is no indication that the plaintiff had his own personal nurse. Since the nurse had others to look after, she could not monitor the plaintiff 24/7, but could only warn him and fix any mistakes that he made in choosing the course of his own recovery–getting back in bed. Unless there was some indication that the nurse needed to tie him down, there is no indication that there was any breach of duty by the nurse.

Causation: it is difficult to say that but for the nurse's breach (assuming there was a breach) there would not have been injury. The nurse did her best to warn. There may need to be a fact investigation as to if the plaintiff were still doped up and did not understand the warning or if the nurse should have stayed by his side because he was disoriented, but absent these indications, but for is hard because the real but for is but for the plaintiff's decision to walk. Assuming that it can be said that but for the nurse's negligence, there would be legal or proximate causation because it is foreseeable that the plaintiff would paralyzed if he walked prior to the end of his recovery period as evidenced by the warning. I would want more evidence as to the duties of the nurse and the state of the plaintiff.

Damage: there is damage due to paralysis of the plaintiff.

As with the surgeon, it appears that negligence is difficult to establish against because of the breach and but for elements. More evidence is necessary as discussed. Also, we may want evidence as to what the average nurse would do in this situation – is there any need to restrain such plaintiff – should he have been in traction or something similar?

Defenses

The defenses are the same as discussed with regard to the doctor. There is no indication that res ipsa is being applied against the nurse, but that analysis would be similar as well.

The Hospital

The hospital would be negligent either for negligent supervision of the surgeon or doctor or merely vicariously liable under the theory of respondeat superior. Under respondeat superior, an employer (the hospital) can be held liable for the torts or negligence of its employees or agents (nurse/surgeon) who are acting within the scope of their employment.

Vicarious liability is holding a third party liable for the torts or negligence of another.

Here, it is possible to hold the hospital responsible because the employees – nurse and surgeon – were acting in the scope of their employment – surgery and caring for the patient after surgery. The hospital can only be held vicariously liable under this theory of respondeat superior if it is shown that the surgeon and nurse are negligent. As discussed above, the plaintiff has an uphill battle on these elements.

There is the alternative of negligent supervision. If the hospital knew that the surgeon or nurse were new, inexperienced, or had been negligent in the past, then the hospital could be negligent in its own right, but there is no indication that this is the case.

The hospital could seek indemnification from the surgeon and nurse if it did in fact need to payout, but the hospital has already indicated that it is willing to indemnify the surgeon and the nurse. Therefore, there also do not appear to be any contribution issues between the surgeon and the nurse if negligence if found and they are found jointly and severally liable.

Intentional Torts

Since this case involved a surgery, it is possible that the plaintiff could bring a claim for the intentional tort of battery which requires: (1) intent to do the specific act or knowledge to a substantial certainty that the act will result; (2) causation; and (3) harmful or offensive contract to the plaintiff's person. Here, the intentional tort of battery is unlikely since there was informed consent to the operation and consent is a defense to the intentional torts.

Conclusion

Based on the foregoing, in the absence of additional evidence, there is no indication that the plaintiff will be able to succeed on any claim for simple negligence, res ipsa loquitur, or respondeat superior against the hospital. The particular pieces of evidence that could change the analysis have been indicated throughout the analysis.

MBE SUBJECTS - PRACTICE ESSAY QUESTIONS

TORTS
Answer to Question 4

Claims against Dunbar

Polly can assert two claims against Dunbar: strict liability for the injuries caused by a wild animal and negligence for allowing his daughter to tend to the sheep.

A defendant is strictly liable for injuries caused by a wild animal that are characteristic of that animal. Strict liability can also be imposed where the defendant knew the animal had a propensity to cause injury. Here, Dunbar owns a ram. And, it is somewhat debatable if it is a wild animal ("wild" is determined at birth). Arguably a ram is a wild animal even though now domesticated. Rams are known for their aggression and have to be penned. Even if the court concludes that the ram is not "wild," Dunbar can be held strictly liable because he knew (or should have known) that the ram might hurt someone. He grazes these animals and penned the ram. He also noticed the ram was causing injuries by butting the other sheep with its horns. Dunbar will be held to have known of the danger.

Furthermore, the injuries that Polly suffered are characteristic of a ram and of the type that Dunbar suspected – butting with the horns.

Dunbar may also be liable to Polly on a negligence theory. To show negligence, Dunbar must have owed a duty to Polly, breached that duty, his breach must have been the actual and proximate cause of Polly's injuries, and damages must be shown.

Duty of care is owed to all foreseeable plaintiffs. The standard of care is that of a reasonable person acting under similar circumstances. Actual cause is determined under a "but for" test – "but for" the defendant's negligence would the plaintiff have suffered harm. The defendant's negligence must also be the proximate (legal) cause of plaintiff's harm – was the harm within a foreseeable scope of risk created by the defendant. Finally, damages must be proven, they won't be presumed.

Polly was a foreseeable plaintiff. Dunbar was using her land to graze animals. He also probably breached his duty by allowing his 9-year old daughter to take care of the sheep alone without adult supervision. A reasonably prudent person would probably not allow a child to do such a task much less without adult supervision. Dunbar's negligence is the actual and proximate cause of Polly's harm. But for his negligence, the sheep and ram would not have escaped and hurt Polly. The risk that Claudia might make a mistake was within the risk of foreseeable harm. She is only 9, and likely to make such a mistake. Damages are asked and shown by Polly's injuries.

Claims against Claudia

Polly can assert a claim against Claudia for negligence. Please see elements of negligence as stated earlier. There is an issue as to what standard of care would be used in a case against Claudia.

Children over 4 can be held liable for negligence. But, they will not be held to the reasonable person standard. Children are held to a like-child standard. It is a subjective standard based on a child of similar age, intelligence, ability and experience. It is very difficult to prove. But, the child may be held to an adult standard of care if he/she is involved in "adult activities."

Claudia will probably be held to a like-child standard of care. Tending animals and helping out on the family farm is not likely an "adult activity." "Adult activities" are more like driving a car or operating machinery. If held to the like-child standard, Claudia will probably prevail. It is conceivable that a 9-year old will not completely secure the gate properly. That's why her father will be held negligent instead of her.

Claims Against Arthur

Generally there is not an affirmative duty to act unless one assumes the duty to help. Since Arthur told Claudia he would handle the emergency with Polly, he assumed the duty to help and an affirmative duty to act with reasonable care in assisting Polly. He turned away the only person that was aware of Polly's emergency, and thus will be found to have assumed the duty to help and use reasonable care. He breached that duty when he stayed on the phone and failed to help Polly.

Various defenses that may be used.

First, all of the defendants will assert that even if they are liable, Polly had a duty to mitigate damages which she failed to do when she refused medical help.

The defense of contributory negligence may also be asserted. Contributory negligence means that the plaintiff also acted negligently in causing her harm. It can be a total bar to recovery. The defendant will probably argue that Polly was contributorily negligent because she didn't look up when the sheep entered her land.

They may also defend on grounds of assumption of risk. That requires knowingly and voluntarily accepting a risk posed to the plaintiff. But, that will not work here against Polly because although she had knowledge that sheep would be on her land, she was not aware of the dangerous ram.

Finally, the defendants may argue that her harm was not foreseeable.

MBE SUBJECTS - PRACTICE ESSAY QUESTIONS

TORTS
Answer to Question 5

A partnership is not generally liable for intentional torts committed by partners or employees. However, when the business of the partnership involves force or confrontation, the partnership may be liable for the intentional torts committed by partners and employees during the ordinary course of business.

A general partner is personally liable for obligations of the partnership. A general partner is not personally liable for tortious conduct that took place before he became a partner, or more than 90 days after he disassociates from the partnership.

Paul may name the partnership as a defendant. The assets of the partnership may be used to pay for Paul's claims. Even though Cal became a partner after the tortious conduct and thus is not personally liable, his $100,000 capital contribution is a partnership asset that is available to pay for claims.

Paul may also name Art and Beatta as co-defendants. Art and Beatta were general partners when the tortious conduct took place, and as such are personally liable for obligations of the partnership. Art was also directly involved with the tort.

Art, Beatta and the partnership are all jointly and severally liable for the claim. This means that Paul can get the money from whomever has it.

In addition, Paul should name Dan as a co-defendant. Although Dan is not a general partner (only an employee) and is not liable for obligations of the partnership, he was an actor in committing the tort. Thus, he is personally liable for the tort. In addition, the Partnership may be vicariously liable for his tortious conduct. He committed the tort during business hours at the place of business, and the business involved force and/or confrontation.

Paul may bring claims against the above named defendants for conversion of chattels and battery.

Paul alleges that AB Repo mistakenly took his truck. Conversion of chattels is the taking and carrying away of the personal property of another with intent to keep it, and denying the owner substantial use of the property.

If AB Repo had no legal right to repossess Paul's truck, then he will win this claim. AB Repo took his truck without right and substantially impaired Paul's use of the truck.

As a remedy for conversion, Paul is entitled to the fair market value of the property at the time it was taken. Alternately, he could accept the truck back with damages to pay for damages to the truck and his loss of use for the truck.

Paul may also bring a claim against the defendants for battery. Battery is the intentional unwanted or offensive touching of another. Art and Dan committed battery when they grabbed Paul by the arms and threw him down the flight of stairs. As such, Paul is entitled to a remedy of damages for his medical expenses, pain and suffering, and other damages such as loss of income from being out of work.

Paul will definitely win this claim.

If Paul has suffered emotional distress from the incident, he may also file a claim for intentional infliction of emotional distress. Intentional infliction of emotional distress occurs when the defendant does extreme or outrageous actions that result in a physical injury to Plaintiff.

If Paul can show emotional distress (e.g., loss of sleep, loss of appetite, etc.) resulting from the battery, then he should win this claim. Being grabbed by the arms and thrown down a flight of stairs is outrageous conduct to one of ordinary sensibilities. Paul obviously can show physical damage with his broken leg and broken arm.

In summary, if the facts are as Paul has described, then all his claims have a strong probability of success.

MBE SUBJECTS - PRACTICE ESSAY QUESTIONS

TORTS
Answer to Question 6

<u>Lu v. Brad</u>

<u>Assault</u>

Assault is an intentional tort. Therefore, in order for the defendant to be liable, he must have the required intent. Assault is defined as causing apprehension or fear in another person of immediate harm.

When Brad's golf ball sailed past Lu's head, the ball caused apprehension of immediate harm – that is, being hit in the head with a golf ball. The issue is whether Brad had the requisite intent to cause that apprehension when he hit the golf ball.

Brad did not have intent to hit (or almost hit) Lu with a golf ball when he swung his club. However, the intent element may be satisfied by either transferred intent or substantial likelihood.

Transferred intent is a doctrine stating that intent may shift from tort to tort or from victim to victim. In order for it to apply to this case, Brad would've had to intend to hit someone else. This is clearly not the case.

Because Brad doesn't possess the required intent, Lu will not be successful on the assault claim.

<u>Trespass to Land</u>

Trespass to land requires the defendant, or the defendant's instrument, to enter the land of another. Trespass to land is also an intentional tort. In order for Brad to be liable, he must have intended to trespass. Brad's entry onto Lu's land must be without Lu's consent.

Brad, when he hits golf balls in his backyard, intends to hit golf balls. Although he may not specifically intend for the balls to go over the fence and into Lu's yard, there is a substantial likelihood that they will--especially given the fact that Brad is an unskilled golfer. This likelihood is also supported by the fact that balls have gone into Lu's yard almost daily. This satisfies the intent element of trespass to land.

The fact that Lu has asked Brad "on many occasions" to stop hitting balls into her yard is a clear indication that the balls are not in her yard with her consent.

Because Brad is responsible for hitting the balls into her yard, he will be liable for trespass to land.

<u>Brad v. Lu</u>

Conversion

Conversion is the same as trespass to chattels, but with a more serious outcome. Conversion is taking another's personal property for one's own use. The use must end in destruction, severe damage, loss or permanent deprivation for the rightful owner.

Brad's golf balls may have been on Lu's property wrongfully, but that does not give Lu the rightful ownership of the balls. When Lu sold the balls, she committed the tort of conversion. She used the balls as if they were her own and sold them.

Conversion is an intentional tort, so Lu must have the requisite intent in order to be liable for conversion. Although Lu probably did not originally intend to get Brad's golf balls and sell them, she did intend to sell them after she collected them from her yard.

Because Lu intentionally treated the balls as her own and as a result sold them, she will be liable for conversion.

Lu's other possible claims

Lu may try suing Brad for negligence if Lu can prove that Brad had a duty to her and by hitting golf balls into her yard breached that duty and caused damages, Lu would win a negligence action.

Lu may also try suing under a nuisance claim. The golf balls may be viewed as a private nuisance which is keeping her from enjoying her land.

MBE SUBJECTS - PRACTICE ESSAY QUESTIONS

TORTS
Answer to Question 7

A partnership is the union of two or more people carrying on business together. In a general partnership all parties are liable for the debts of the partnership. Additionally, partners are personally liable for the acts of other partners done in the course of business. Because partners are liable for each other's acts during the course of business, Pat has a cause of action against both Able and Baker, as well as the partnership, for battery and negligence. Pat does not have a cause of action against Carr, who joined the partnership after the torts occurred. Incoming partners are not liable for pre-incurred debt, or for torts committed in the scope of the partnership before the incoming partner joins.

1. Battery.

Baker committed common law battery when he struck Pat with a baseball bat. In order to show battery, Pat must prove that Baker intended to commit an offensive touching of Pat and that this touching was not consented to. There must also be damages caused by the offensive touching. This case is simple. Pat did not consent to being hit with a baseball bat, a touching that is clearly offensive. The damages are obvious. Baker will claim that the hitting was justified. However, this exceeds the amount of force justified by a "bouncer" to quiet a customer.

As a final note on battery, there was no assault because Pat was hit from behind. In order for there to be an assault, the defendant must, through words and an act, place the plaintiff in fear of imminent bodily harm. Pat did not fear imminent bodily harm because he was hit from behind.

As mentioned above, Able and the Partnership are liable for the intentional torts of partners. As such, Able is also liable for the battery of Pat.

2. Negligence.

In order to prove negligence, Pat must establish that there was a duty to act, that the D breached this duty, and that this breach was the cause of the injury. There must also be damages.

Baker is negligent. Normally there is no duty to come to the aid of others. However, when the defendant's actions place the plaintiff in danger, the defendant has a duty to use due care for the plaintiff. Here, Baker had a duty to help Pat after he hit him on the head, as he created Pat's peril. Baker breached this duty by allowing him to lay unconscious, on the floor for 30 minutes, then moved him to the street. The next issue is causation. The doctor's opinion that the delay in treatment aggravated the injury is probably sufficient to prove causation. The damages are the increased medical bills.

Able was also probably negligent. As an owner of the tavern, Able had a duty to his customers. Standing by while Baker hit Pat with a baseball bat breached this duty. As above, the delay in treatment caused further injury to Pat.

Even if Able is not negligent in his own right, he is liable for the negligent acts of his partner committed within the scope of the business. (See above for explanation)

As mentioned above, Carr is not liable for these acts because they occurred before he became a partner. It is important to note, however, that the $300,000 he invested in the partnership may be used to satisfy a judgment.

Finally, Pat is likely to succeed on his claims of battery and negligence. He can easily prove the elements of both. Although bouncers may use some force to maintain their taverns, this force was excessive and at least from these facts, completely unwarranted. Furthermore, both Able and Baker and "A-B Bar and Grill" are liable. Baker's acts was clearly within the scope of business. Pat is likely to succeed.

Trusts & Future Interests

(July 2000)

Legal Problems:

(1)   Does the trust violate the common-law Rule Against Perpetuities?

(2)(a) Are Cousin's children Adam (who was alive when Grantor created the trust), Ellen (born after Grantor's death), and Doris (a minor adopted child) included in the class gift of a remainder interest in the trust?

(2)(b) When, if at all, will Cousin's children be entitled to receive their   shares?

DISCUSSION

Point One: (10-15%)

The trust does not violate the common-law Rule Against Perpetuities.

The trust does not violate the Rule Against Perpetuities. Since the trust was revocable, the period of the rule begins to run from Grantor's death, not the date the inter vivos trust was created. At Grantor's death, Cousin was a life in being, and the non-vested interest created in Cousin's children vests or fails to vest no later than 21 years after Cousin dies. Thus, the non-vested interest vests within the permissible perpetuity period of lives in being plus 21 years. Brother's interest does not violate the Rule because the interest vests immediately at Grantor's death.

In some states, the common-law Rule Against Perpetuities has been repealed by statute. In such states, all interests in the trust would be valid.

Point Two(a): (40-50%)

Cousin's children Adam (who was alive at the time the trust was created) and Ellen (who was born after Grantor's death) are members of the class of "Cousin's children" and have remainder interests in the trust. Cousin's adopted child, Doris, also likely qualifies as a member of the class.

Grantor created a class gift in a contingent remainder when she created an interest in "Cousin's children who attain age 21." A class gift is a gift to a group of people collectively described, typically by reference to their relationship to a common ancestor, rather than a gift to named individuals. A class gift by its nature is capable of passing to multiple takers. The nature of a class gift is that the class membership, i.e., persons who may share in the gift, may fluctuate over time. Thomas F. Bergin & Paul G. Haskell, *Preface to Estates in Land and Future Interests* 136-37 (2d ed. 1984). At issue is the identity of the members of the class. This class consists of all of Cousin's children who join the class before it closes. However, only those class members who reach age 21 are entitled to a share of the property. See Point Two(b).

Cousin's child, Adam, who was alive at the time Grantor created the trust, is included in the gift of the remainder interest in the trust as of the time the gift was created. However, because the gift is a future interest, not an immediate gift, the class gift remains open until Brother's death, when the class closes. As long as the class remains open, new members may join the class. Therefore, since Cousin's other biological child, Ellen, was born prior to Brother's death and while the class was open, she is also a class member. Bergin & Haskell, *supra,* at 145.

The more difficult question is whether Doris, who is Cousin's adopted child, also is included in the class. While adopted children generally inherit from their adoptive parents, under the "stranger to the adoption" rule they were, until very recently, excluded from class gifts created by someone who did not know of the adoption and was not the adopting parent. *Id.* at 233-34.

Today, however, in many states, adopted children are more likely than they were in the past to be included in class gifts created by persons other than their parents. However, states differ in the criteria used for their inclusion in a class gift. For example, in states that follow the Uniform Probate Code, adopted children qualify as part of a class of "children" only if they "lived while a minor as a regular member of the household" of the named parent, unless the governing instrument indicates a contrary intent. UPC § 2-705 (and official comment). Under the UPC, Doris is likely to be included because she is under 21 and lives in Cousin's household.

In non-UPC states that have rejected the "stranger to the adoption" rule, an adopted child is included in a class gift created by someone other than the adopting parent on the theory that such child has been brought into the family of the adopting parent for all purposes and that society no longer distinguishes between adopted and biological children. In such states, adopted children are included in a class gift unless the governing instrument provides otherwise. *See generally* William M. McGovern, Jr., Sheldon F. Kurtz, & Jan Ellen Rein, *Wills, Trusts, and Estates* 46-59 (1988). In light of these modern reforms, it is most likely that Doris, Cousin's adopted child, will be included in the class gift since she was adopted before the class closed.

Depending on which of Cousin's children, as a group, qualify for an interest in the trust, those children, as earlier noted, acquired a contingent remainder in the trust. Two contingencies existed: (1) being born or adopted (becoming a child of Cousin) before the class closes and (2) attaining the age of 21. Once a child of Cousin reaches 21, that child's interest becomes vested, subject to open, i.e., subject to partial divestment by other children of Cousin. Once vested, the child is assured of obtaining a share of the trust principal because no other contingencies are stated, such as survival to any particular time, including the time for distribution. As more children attain the age of 21, the share of each becomes smaller because all the children in the class when it finally closes will ultimately share equally. Until the class closes, more potential class members may enter the class as they are born, but they may drop out of the class by not attaining the age of 21. Thus, the size of the class membership may fluctuate. *Id.*

<u>Point Two(b)</u>: (35-45%)

<u>Under the "rule of convenience," Adam may receive distribution of a *pro rata* portion of the principal of the trust at Brother's death since Adam has then fulfilled the condition precedent of</u>

attaining age 21 and there is then no outstanding present possessory estate. Ellen and Doris will receive their shares only if they reach age 21.

Although Brother has died, Cousin is still living and may have more children. Thus, the class of "Cousin's children" will not close physiologically until Cousin's death. However, absent any contrary intent of Grantor, the rule of convenience, which is a rule of construction, will close the class when any class member has a right to demand possession. Once a class closes, no new members can join the class.

A class member can demand possession of his share if there is no outstanding present possessory estate and the class member's interest is not subject to the happening of any unfulfilled condition precedent. Once the class closes, no new class members will be permitted to enter and take a share of the gift, although some may drop out of the class by failing to attain 21. "The rule strikes a balance between a donor's desire to include all possible members of the class and the desire to allow distribution to those who have qualified to take. It also avoids the administrative problems that would develop if living beneficiaries took property, subject to giving some back as new class members appeared." Roger W. Andersen, *Understanding Trusts and Estates* 233.

Under the rule of convenience, Adam can demand a share at Brother's death because both life tenants, Grantor and Brother, are dead, and Adam is a child of Cousin who has attained the age of 21. Adam will be entitled to a share of the trust principal in proportion to the total number of Cousin's qualifying children who are currently living. At the time the class closes, there are two (or three) members of the class since they were born (or adopted) before the class closed. If either Ellen or Doris attains age 21, she will receive her proportionate share. If either of them fails to attain age 21 , she falls out of the class and Adam (and the other member who has attained 21) will also receive *a pro rata* portion of that deceased class member's share. If Cousin has additional children after the class closes, those children will not be permitted to share in the trust because the class will have closed prematurely under the rule of convenience. *See* Bergin & Haskell, *supra,* at 146-47; Andersen, *supra,* at 234.

Trusts & Future Interests

(February 2001)

Legal Problems:

1. Can judgment claims against the income beneficiary for his failure to pay debts be paid by a trustee to the judgment creditor from either trust income or principal under these facts?

2. Can claims against the income beneficiary of a trust for unpaid alimony be paid by a trustee to the former spouse of the income beneficiary from either trust income or principal under these facts?

3. Can the income beneficiary of a trust be compelled to use trust income actually distributed to the beneficiary to pay judgment claims where the trust contains a spendthrift clause?

4. Are dividends paid to a trustee in stock, rather than cash, allocable to the income or principal accounts for trust accounting purposes?

DISCUSSION

Point One: (30-40%)

Most likely, Creditor will not be able to compel Bank to distribute trust income to it in satisfaction of its claim against Son because the trust instrument includes a spendthrift clause. Creditor also will not be able to compel distributions to it from the principal of the trust because Son is not entitled to any share of trust principal.

The creditors of the beneficiary of a trust have no greater rights in the trust property than the beneficiary has; however, they can have fewer rights. The trust instrument makes no provision for the distribution of trust principal to Son. Accordingly, because he has no right to receive trust principal, his creditors have no right to reach trust principal. If Son's creditors could reach trust principal, they would infringe on the property rights of the remainder beneficiaries of the trust.

Son, on the other hand, is entitled to trust income and, thus, absent a spendthrift clause in the instrument, his creditors would be able to attach that interest. However, if the governing instrument, as here, contains a spendthrift clause prohibiting a beneficiary's creditors from attaching the beneficiary's interest, the beneficiary's creditors usually cannot reach the beneficiary's trust interest in satisfaction of their claims. Most courts uphold spendthrift clauses, at least when applied against the claims of most creditors of a beneficiary, although a minority of states hold that spendthrift clauses are unenforceable. *See generally* George Bogert, TRUSTS § 40 (6th ed. 1987).

In the minority of states that bar the enforcement of spendthrift clauses, Creditor could compel

Bank to pay its claim against Son from trust income. However, in the large majority of states that uphold spendthrift clauses, Creditor could not compel payment of the claim from trust income while in the hands of Bank. Creditor stands on a different footing than Wife *(See* Point Two), and to date no state that generally upholds spendthrift clauses has found a countervailing public policy exception for the kind of claim Creditor has against Son.

Point Two: (30-40%)

Wife will not be able to compel distributions to her from the trust principal. Most likely, however, Wife will be able to compel Bank to distribute trust income to her in satisfaction of her unpaid alimony claims against Son notwithstanding the spendthrift clause in the trust.

Wife cannot reach the trust principal because Son has no interest in trust principal. *See* Point One. However, she may be entitled to distributions from trust income. Even in the large majority of states that uphold spendthrift clauses, if the particular creditor's claim is for unpaid alimony, the policy of effectuating the settlor's intent by generally upholding spendthrift clauses runs afoul of a stronger public policy favoring the payment of alimony and child support. *See, e.g., Bacardi v. White,* 463 So. 2d 218 (Fla. 1985). Today, most state courts hold that the policy favoring the payment of alimony and child support trumps the policy of generally supporting spendthrift clauses. In those states a trust beneficiary is not permitted to enjoy trust income while failing to support his children and former spouse. *See generally* RESTATEMENT (SECOND) OF TRUSTS § 157. Hence, Wife should be able to compel Bank to satisfy her claim for alimony from the trust's Income.

In a small minority of states, spendthrift clauses continue to be valid even as against unpaid alimony. *See, e.g., Erickson v. Erickson,* 266 N.W. 161 (Minn. 1936). In such states, Wife could not compel a distribution of trust income in payment of her claim.

Point Three: (10- 20%)

Son can be compelled to use trust income distributed to him from the trust to pay judgment claims against him even though the trust contains a spendthrift clause.

Spendthrift clauses in a trust do not operate to bar a trust beneficiary's creditors from reaching the distributed income or principal once it has actually been paid to the beneficiary. *See* Bogert, *supra* § 40 at 150. If Grantor had tried to restrain Son's ability to alienate the trust income once distributed to Son, that would have been an invalid restraint on alienation. Thus, once trust income is actually paid to Son, Wife and Creditor are entitled to reach that income in satisfaction of their claims by resorting to the customary legal processes for the enforcement of judgments.

Point Four: (10-20%)

Bank should hold the dividend paid in stock as part of the trust principal for ultimate distribution to Son's children when Son dies.

The Uniform Principal and Income Act treats distributions of stock, whether characterized as a stock dividend or as a stock split, as principal. *See* Unif. Prin. Inc. Act § 6(a). The Revised Act adopts the same position. Rev. Unif. Prin. Inc. Act § 401(c)(1).

The Revised Act gives Bank a limited power to allocate the stock dividend between income and principal in cases where the distributing corporation had made no distributions to shareholders except in the form of dividends paid in stock. In such cases, Bank might be justified in allocating some of the stock dividend to income to effectuate Grantor's intent to provide Son with trust income. However, the facts do not support such an allocation in this case.

In the absence of a statute, the law varies. In some states, dividends paid in the stock of the distributing corporation are income; in others, principal. Some states allocate the dividend between income and principal under the so-called "intact value" rule.

Trusts & Future Interests

(July 2001)

Legal Problems:

1. Is a promise to create a trust in the future legally enforceable if the promise is supported by consideration?

2. Is an oral trust of intangible personal property valid?

3. Did the trust terminate at Harry's death because there was then no trustee?

4. What is the effect of Wanda's disclaimer of the income interest and should the principal be immediately distributed (a) to Wanda and Charles, as Harry's heirs, (b) to Charles, as the implied remainder beneficiary of the trust, or (c) to Mary and Pat, as remainder beneficiaries of the trust?

DISCUSSION

Point One: (30-40%)

Harry's promise to create a trust of property he might inherit from his mother was legally enforceable.

A promise to create a trust in the future is unenforceable unless the promise is supported by consideration sufficient for the formation of a contract. *See generally* SCOTT ON TRUSTS § 30 (4th ed.); Bogert, TRUSTS § 24 (6th ed. 1987). Thus, if Harry had merely promised to create a trust of property he might later inherit from his mother, that promise would be unenforceable. Here, however, Harry's promise was incorporated into a prenuptial agreement in which the promise to create the trust was made in consideration of Wanda's waiver of alimony rights. This waiver is sufficient consideration to support Harry's promise to create the trust in the future, just as it is sufficient to support the validity of the prenuptial agreement.

Point Two: (30-40%)

A trust of intangible personal property may be declared orally. No writing is required. Thus, the trust for Wanda was validly created.

In order to create a trust, the grantor must have intended to create the trust and there must be a trust res (property), one or more trust beneficiaries, and a trustee. The intent to create a trust can be found in both the grantor's words and deeds. *See generally* SCOTT ON TRUSTS § 24.2 (4th ed.). Here, the evidence is clear that Harry intended to create a trust.

At the time of the declaration of trust there was also trust property ($1 million), one or more beneficiaries, and a trustee (Harry). Thus, the only possible remaining issue relating to whether the trust was validly created is whether an oral declaration of trust is valid. Most states require a writing to create an inter vivos trust of land. At common law, an inter vivos oral trust of personalty was valid. *See* Bogert, *supra* § 21. Generally, state statutes of frauds do not change this common-law rule. Thus, the trust was validly created even though created orally.

Point Three: (5-10%)

A trust will not fail for want of a trustee. Thus, even though no trustee is acting at Harry's death, the trust is valid and a court of equity can appoint a successor trustee.

A trust will not fail for want of a trustee. *See generally* Bogert, TRUSTS § 30 (6th ed. 1987). Thus, even if the sole individual acting as trustee dies, the trust does not terminate if the grantor intended the trust to continue beyond the death of the trustee. *Id.* Rather, the court of equity having jurisdiction over the trust can appoint another to act as a successor trustee. *Id.* Here, Harry's intent is clear-that the trust continue for Wanda's lifetime, not that the trust terminate at his death. This intent is evidenced not only by the provision that Wanda's income interest terminates at her death but also by the language of the orally declared trust specifically contemplating the appointment of a successor trustee. Thus, it is entirely appropriate for the court to appoint a successor trustee.

If the trust terminates as a result of Wanda's disclaimer *(See* Point Four), it would still be necessary to appoint a successor trustee to prepare the necessary accounting and distribute the trust principal to the correct beneficiaries. However, a court may simply direct the personal representative of Harry's estate to assume *these duties.*

Point Four: (30-40%)

Because Wanda has validly disclaimed her income interest in the trust, it is appropriate to accelerate the distribution of the trust principal under these facts and make an immediate distribution to the persons entitled to the trust principal without awaiting Wanda's death. However, it is unclear whether there is an implied gift to Harry's issue (Charles in this case). If so, Charles is entitled to the trust principal. If not, the trust principal is distributable to Harry's heirs (i.e.. one-third to Wanda and two-thirds to Charles}.

Under the doctrine of acceleration, if the income beneficiary of a trust disclaims his or her interest, the trust principal becomes immediately distributable to the presumptive remainder beneficiaries of the trust *provided no one would be harmed by making a distribution to them earlier than it would have been made had the income beneficiary not disclaimed. See generally Ohio National Bank of Columbus v. Adair,* 54 Ohio St. 2d 26,374 N.E.2d 415 (1978). *See also* Simes, THE LAW OF FUTURE INTERESTS § 110. For example, a remainder might not accelerate if to do so would result in the class gift to the remainder beneficiaries closing earlier than it otherwise would.

In this case, however, no one would be harmed by an acceleration because the identity of the persons entitled to the trust principal is not dependent on whether the distribution of the remainder accelerates or must await the death of Wanda. Rather, the ultimate identity of the takers of the trust principal depends on whether there is an implied gift to Harry's issue who survived Harry.

At the time the trust was created, Harry clearly specified what was to happen if he died without issue. He stated that in such case the principal should be distributed to his nieces and nephews - Mary and Pat. Thus, their interest could vest only if Harry died without issue. Because Harry died with issue, the gift to the nieces and nephews clearly fails.

Harry, however, failed to state who would take the trust property under the circumstances that actually occurred-if he died *with* issue. In such a case, the courts have split between inferring a gift to the issue (i.e., construing the trust to mean "upon [Wanda's] death, to Harry's issue but if Harry dies without issue, to Harry's surviving nieces and nephews") or finding that the gift of the remainder interest failed, resulting in the trust property reverting to the grantor's estate as undisposed of property. Theoretically, the controlling principle in construing the ambiguous instrument is to give effect to Harry's intent. Often, however, the grantor's intent is not readily determinable.

Some courts in these cases infer a gift to issue because "it is difficult to see why the [grantor] has made no provision for [his] issue although he has expressly provided for [his] death without issue." Simes, *supra* § 100. Thus, the court assumes that the intended gift to issue was inadvertently omitted and, therefore, constructs the gift to accomplish the grantor's presumed intent.

Other courts hold that the trust property is distributed to the successors of the grantor's estate on the theory that the grantor retained a reversion and that to construct a gift to issue is tantamount to writing a trust for the grantor and making a gift that is wholly speculative. If the trust property is distributable through Harry's estate by way of a reversion, it passes to his heirs via intestate succession, and it is distributable one-third to Wanda and two-thirds to Charles. Because Wanda's disclaimer was limited to her interest in the trust property, the disclaimer did not apply to any property distributable to her as part of Harry's estate.

Trusts & Future Interests

(July 2002)

Legal Problems:

(1)(a)   Can Testator's probate estate be disposed of according to the terms of a revocable inter vivos trust that was not executed in accordance with the Statute of Wills?

(1)(b)   Assuming the probate estate assets can be disposed of as a part of the revocable trust, do the terms of the trust in existence at the time the will was executed, or rather those as reflected in the subsequent amendment, apply?

(2)   Are the terms of the trust in favor of Wanda, Testator's former wife, revoked by operation of law because of their divorce?

(3)   Assuming the terms of the trust amendment apply, what is Hope's interest under the revocable trust?

DISCUSSION

Summary: The disposition of Testator's estate is governed by the will and the terms of the revocable trust as amended. Absent a governing statute or case law to the contrary, divorce does not revoke the provisions of a revocable trust in favor of a former spouse. Furthermore, if that interest is alienable and devisable (as is here the term interest in income), upon Wanda's death it would pass to Hope, the legatee under Wanda's will. As for Adam's interest in the remainder, which is limited to "surviving children," if governing law requires him to be alive when Wanda's two-year term ends, his interest fails since he died before the term ended. The remainder, thus, passes wholly to Testator's surviving children, Ben and Carrie.

Point One(a): (15-20%)

__Under the Uniform Testamentary Additions to Trust Act a will may pour over the probate estate assets to the trustee of an unfunded inter vivos trust even if the trust instrument was not executed in accordance with the Statute of Wills.__

At common law, the terms of the revocable trust could control the disposition of the testator's probate estate under the doctrine of incorporation by reference. Under this doctrine, if the will referred to an unattested document that was in existence at the time the will was signed, the terms of that document could be given effect in the same manner as if it had been properly executed. *See generally State Street Bank & Trust Co.* v. *Reiser,* 389 N.E.2d 768 (Mass. 1979).

This doctrine is no longer necessary to validate the so-called "pour over" will because of the almost universal enactment of the Uniform Testamentary Additions to Trust Act (1983)

(ÚTATA). Unif. Prob. Code § 2-511. Under UTATA, a trust, even an unfunded trust, as here, can be the beneficiary of the testator's probate estate so long as the trust is identified in the testator's will and its terms are set forth in a written instrument. The validity of the pour over arrangement is unaffected by the fact that the trust was amended after the execution of the will.

Point One(b): (15-20%)

Under the Uniform Testamentary Additions to Trust Act the disposition of the probate estate assets are governed by the terms of the revocable trust including all amendments to the trust.

Under the incorporation by reference doctrine, the terms of the amended revocable trust would not apply to the disposition of the probate estate assets as that amendment was not in existence when the will was executed. Under the Uniform Testamentary Additions to Trust Act, however, the amendment applies. Unif. Prob. Code § 2-511(b). Thus, as of Testator's death, the probate estate assets are to be held by Bank in trust to pay the income to Wanda for two years, and then to distribute the trust principal to Testator's surviving children.

Thus, the will and amended trust govern the disposition of Testator's estate.

Point Two: (20-30%)

Under the laws of most states today, Wanda's two-year term interest is not revoked by the divorce. Therefore, the trustee should hold the trust property and pay her the income for the next two years in accordance with the amended trust terms.

Many probate codes provide that if, subsequent to the execution of a will, the testator and the spouse are divorced, provisions in a will in favor of the former spouse are automatically revoked by operation of law. In such case, the property that would have passed to the spouse is disposed of as if the spouse had predeceased the decedent. If Testator had created a testamentary trust, then under such a statute, Wanda's two-year income interest would have been revoked by operation of law.

Here, however, Wanda's interest is created under the terms of the revocable trust. Typically, state statutes affecting a divorced spouse's interest under a will are inapplicable to interests created under a revocable trust and, therefore, Wanda's interest is not revoked.

However, the law in this regard is slowly changing. For example, § 2-804 of the Uniform Probate Code would cause Wanda's two-year interest in the revocable trust to be revoked upon her divorce from Testator. Some states have judicially reached that result by viewing the will and revocable trust as integrated estate planning documents and treating the probate statute's revocation of the spouse interest upon divorce as reaching the trust as well. See Clymer v. Mayo, 473 N.E.2d 1084, 1093 (Mass. 1985). See also Unif. Trust Code § 112. Of course, if her interest is revoked, then nothing passes to Wanda under the trust after Testator's death.

Point Three: (35-40%)

Assuming Wanda had an interest in the trust, it would pass under her will to Hope since an interest for a two-year term does not terminate at death. Whether University has an interest in the trust depends on whether the phrase "surviving children" means surviving Testator or surviving the two-year period set aside to pay the income to Wanda.

Trust interests are alienable, devisable, and descendible unless the terms of a trust expressly or impliedly provide otherwise.

Here, Wanda has a two-year term, which is devisable in the event she were to die within that period. Since Wanda has died prior to the expiration of the two-year term, her interest passes to Hope, the sole beneficiary of her estate. See Point Two.

University has an interest only if Adam had an interest. Whether Adam had an interest depends on whether the word "surviving" in the gift to Testator's "surviving children" means "surviving Testator" or "surviving the two-year period."

The preferred rule is to construe the word to mean surviving to the time of distribution. Under this rule, only those children of Testator alive two years after his death are entitled to the trust principal. *See generally* Simes & Smith, THE LAW OF FUTURE INTERESTS § 577 (3d ed. 1956). This would, of course, exclude Adam; if Adam has no interest to devise, then University, the beneficiary under Adam's will, would have no interest in the trust either.

On the other hand, in some states, surviving refers to surviving Testator. Under this interpretation, each of Testator's three children-Adam, Ben, and Carrie-had vested interests in the trust principal as of Testator's death. Vested interests are not forfeited even if the beneficiary dies within two years of Testator. Given that trust interests are devisable, the vested interest of Adam would pass under his will solely to University, at least under the common law. Construing "surviving" to mean surviving Testator results in the trust remainder vesting at the earliest time.

Under the Uniform Probate Code, the analysis would be somewhat different. Section 2-707(b)(3) provides that the word "surviving" does not evidence any intent that § 2-707 not apply, as that word often does under anti-lapse statutes on which § 2-707 is modeled. Under § 2-707(b), if a class gift is limited in favor of a class of children, only those children alive at the time of distribution are entitled to possession of the property (Ben and Carrie). However, if a deceased child left surviving issue, such issue would take the deceased child's share. Here, because Adam had no such descendants, the general rule applies and only those children of Testator alive at the time of distribution (Ben and Carrie) are entitled to possession. Under the Code, therefore, University would have no interest.

Trusts & Future Interests

(February 2003)

Legal Problems: (1) Should Trustee distribute $5,000 from the trust income to Susan in payment of her unpaid alimony claim?

(2) Should Trustee distribute $10,000 from the trust principal to John in payment of his tort judgment against Beth?

(3) Should the court terminate the trust and distribute the trust assets to Adam, Beth, and Charity?

DISCUSSION

Summary: Generally, an income interest subject to a spendthrift clause is not available for payment of claims against the income beneficiary. However, many states, for public policy reasons, do not apply this rule to unpaid alimony claims. In such states, Trustee should pay Susan's $5,000 claim. On the other hand, Trustee cannot pay John's claim from the trust because Beth is not entitled to any principal until the trust terminates and a payment to John would harm both Adam and Charity. Lastly, the court should refuse to terminate the trust because termination would be inconsistent with Decedent's intent as evidenced by the presence of a spendthrift clause in the trust instrument.

Point One: **Trustee should distribute $5,000 from trust income to Susan in**
(30-40%) **payment of her unpaid alimony claim notwithstanding that Adam's interest is subject to a spendthrift clause.**

The testamentary trust created by Decedent contains language that clearly indicates Decedent's intention to subject Adam's 10-year term interest to a spendthrift restriction. Spendthrift clauses are widely recognized. *See generally* Restatement (Second) of Trusts § 152(1) and Restatement (Third) of Trusts § 58 (Tent. Draft No. 2). The effect of a spendthrift clause is to bar a creditor from reaching the beneficiary's interest in satisfaction of the creditor's claim.

However, there are exceptions to the general rule for public policy purposes. A well-established exception enables a former spouse with an unpaid alimony judgment to reach a spendthrift trust interest of his or her former spouse. *See* Restatement (Second) of Trusts § 157(a); Restatement (Third) of Trusts § 59(a)(Tent. Draft No. 2); Uniform Trust Code § 503(b). This exception recognizes a strong public policy against allowing a trust beneficiary to enjoy a trust interest while neglecting to pay the court-ordered support of the beneficiary's former spouse. Accordingly, Trustee should pay Susan $5,000 to satisfy her unpaid alimony judgment against Adam.

Note: Even though Susan is entitled to receive $5,000 from the trust income, Trustee, as a practical matter, should not make that distribution to her without an authorizing court order. This protects Trustee from any possible liability for having made an inappropriate distribution to Susan. Also, if the jurisdiction does not adhere to the alimony exception, Trustee should distribute nothing from the trust to Susan.

Point Two: Trustee cannot properly pay $10,000 to John from the trust principal
(30-40%) of in payment his tort judgment against Beth because Beth's interest is a remainder interest.

The testamentary trust created by Decedent contains no language evidencing Decedent's intent to subject Beth's remainder interest to a spendthrift restriction. Absent such a restriction, Beth's interest would generally be alienable and reachable by her creditors. *See generally* Restatement (Second) of Trusts §§ 132 & 157 and Restatement (Third) of Trusts §§ 51 & 57 (Tent. Draft No. 2).

However, because Beth is a remainder beneficiary and not an income beneficiary, she has no immediate right to the possession and enjoyment of any trust property. Rather, she must await the termination of the trust to receive any trust property. John, as her creditor, can have no greater rights in the trust property than she had. As her creditor he simply steps into her shoes. Thus, he cannot obtain possession of her share any earlier than she could have obtained possession of it. Payment of trust principal to him at this time, therefore, would be premature.

Furthermore, if Trustee gave John any trust principal at this time, the rights of both Adam and Charity would be adversely affected since the income to which they are and will be entitled is generated from the principal. Any payment to John, therefore, would reduce the future income flow from the trust.

Accordingly, Trustee should not pay John's $10,000 claim from the trust principal.

Point Three: The court should refuse to terminate the trust and should not
(30-40%) distribute the trust assets to the beneficiaries.

It is a well-established rule that a testamentary trust can be terminated by a court upon the request and consent of all trust beneficiaries unless a material purpose remains to be accomplished. *See* Restatement (Second) of Trusts § 337. The bar against termination when a material purpose remains is referred to as the *Claflin* doctrine and is based on the seminal nineteenth-century case, *Claflin v. Claflin*, 20 N.E. 454 (Mass. 1889). The *Claflin* doctrine assures that a trust will not be terminated when termination would be inconsistent with the grantor's intent.

Accordingly, the question is whether there is a material purpose of the trust that would be defeated if the trust were to terminate. The traditional view is that a material purpose remains if any trust interest is subject to a spendthrift restriction that bars alienation of the spendthrift interest. Termination is inappropriate because, if trust assets are distributed to a beneficiary of a spendthrift interest, the beneficiary could later alienate the property. Under this view, the court should refuse to terminate the trust and should not order Trustee to distribute the trust assets to the beneficiaries.

Even under the third Restatement, the court should refuse to terminate the trust. This Restatement rejects the *per se* prohibition on trust termination where there is a spendthrift clause. It requires a finding that the trust grantor really intended the spendthrift provision to bar premature trust termination. Under this test, a spendthrift clause inserted in a trust as mere boilerplate might not bar a requested termination when all trust beneficiaries consent to the termination. Restatement (Third) of Trusts § 65, comment e (Tent. Draft No. 3). *See also* Uniform Trust Code § 411(c) (spendthrift clause is not presumed to constitute a material purpose of the trust). Here, however, the facts clearly indicate that Decedent would not have wanted Adam to prematurely reach his interest due to Decedent's unhappiness with Adam's lavish spending, and therefore the court should not terminate the trust.

Trusts & Future Interests

(February 2004)

ANALYSIS

<u>Legal Problems:</u>

(1) Does the bequest under Testator's will violate the Rule Against Perpetuities?

(2) Did Friend improperly delegate her duties to Bank?

(3) Did Bank, acting as agent of Friend, improperly invest the trust assets by failing to diversify the trust investments such that Friend, as trustee, is liable for any losses resulting from such failure?

DISCUSSION

<u>Summary:</u>

The bequest to great-grandchildren under Testator's will is invalid under the common-law Rule Against Perpetuities but valid under the wait-and-see doctrine because it actually vested before the perpetuity period had expired. Friend, as trustee of the revocable trust, breached the duty not to delegate and the duty to diversify trust investments and is liable for the resulting losses.

<u>Point One:</u>

(20-30%)

<u>The bequest under Testator's will would be void under the common-law Rule Against Perpetuities. However, the bequest is valid under the governing wait-and-see doctrine because it vested two months after Testator's death. Thus, the estate passes to Testator's great-grandchildren who are alive when the will is probated.</u>

Under the common-law Rule Against Perpetuities, "no interest is good unless it must vest, if at all, no later than twenty-one years after some life in being at the creation of the interest." John C. Gray, RULE AGAINST PERPETUITIES § 201 (4th ed. 1942). Furthermore, under the common-law rule, if there was any possibility, however improbable, that an interest might vest too remotely, that interest would be invalid even though in fact it actually vested in a timely manner.

For testamentary bequests, as here, the nonvested interest is deemed created at Testator's death. Thus, the testamentary gift to great-grandchildren is void if there is any possibility it could become possessory more than 21 years after the death of any of Testator's issue who survived him, a possibility that could occur here. For example, within one year after Testator died all of his issue who survived him except the 27-year-old grandchild could die. While that is improbable, it is certainly possible. Then the 27-year-old grandchild who survived Testator could have a child who would be a great-grandchild of Testator. And, then the 27-year-old grandchild could die. At this point, all of Testator's issue who survived him are dead, leaving only the later born great-grandchild. Then, 22 years later (more than 21 years after the death of all relevant lives) Testator's will could be probated. This would result (but for the Rule) in the gift vesting in Testator's great-grandchildren living when his will was probated. However, since this vesting occurs, as hypothesized, beyond the permissible period, the gift is invalid. It bears repeating that a nonvested interest is invalid if it might have vested too remotely even if, in fact, as here, that did not occur because Testator's will was probated two months after Testator died.

An invalid residuary gift is stricken from the will, and absent an alternative valid gift, the residue passes to the Testator's heirs, here Angela and Brian, his only two children.

This jurisdiction, however, has enacted the wait-and-see rule. Under the wait-and-see rule, the gift to the great-grandchildren is valid if it *in fact* vests within the perpetuity period. Here the will was probated two months after Testator died. Thus, the gift to the great-grandchildren vests in a timely manner. *See generally Merchants National Bank v. Curtis*, 97 A.2d 207 (N.H. 1953).

Point Two:	A trustee is responsible for administering the trust. Accordingly, at common law it is a breach of trust to delegate to a third party significant and
(35-45%)	discretionary duties, such as the duties to make distributions and investments. Under one or more Uniform Acts, however, at least the trustee's investment duty is delegable to a third party, although a breach of trust for that delegation could nonetheless occur for failing to properly supervise the third party.

The selection by the settlor of a trust of another person to act as a trustee evidences the settlor's trust and confidence in the designated trustee to properly administer the trust, including deciding what, if any, discretionary distributions of trust property should be made to beneficiaries, and how trust assets should be invested. Flowing from this confidence is the duty to exercise due care and the duty not to delegate those duties that the trustee can reasonably be expected to perform. *See* RESTATEMENT (SECOND) OF TRUSTS § 171.

According to the Restatement, a trustee cannot "delegate to another power to select investments." RESTATEMENT (SECOND) OF TRUSTS, § 171, cmt. h. According to Scott, "if . . . [the trustee] entrusts funds to the agent for this purpose and through the . . . negligence of the agent the funds are lost, the trustee is personally liable." SCOTT'S ABRIDGEMENT OF THE LAW OF TRUSTS § 171.2 (1960).

Similarly, Friend, as trustee, cannot delegate such an important function as determining how the trust property shall be distributed among the named beneficiaries, because this is an act that, in light of all the circumstances, it would appear Testator expected Friend to perform. Thus, Friend's discretionary power, as trustee, to distribute trust principal to the income beneficiaries cannot be delegated to Bank. *See generally* RESTATEMENT (SECOND) OF TRUSTS § 171, cmt. d.

Under the Uniform Trust Code, however, a trustee can delegate such duties that "a prudent trustee of comparable skills could properly delegate under the circumstances." Unif. Trust Code § 807. *Accord* RESTATEMENT (THIRD) OF TRUSTS § 171 (1992). Likewise, under § 9 of the Uniform Prudent Investor Act and § 3(2) of the Uniform Trustee's Powers Act, a trustee is given broad authority to delegate trust duties, effectively abrogating the common-law and Second

Restatement non-delegation rule, at least where a delegation would be deemed prudent under the circumstances. Nonetheless, it is highly unlikely that a prudent trustee who was a longtime friend of Testator's family and who presumably best knew how to make discretionary distributions among Testator's issue would delegate that function to a corporate agent that had no familiarity with Testator's family.

On the other hand, the Uniform Trust Code and Uniform Prudent Investor Act clearly contemplate the complete delegation of the trustee's investment responsibilities so long as the trustee exercises reasonable care, skill, and caution in selecting the agent and "periodically . . . [reviews] the agent's actions in order to monitor the agent's performance and compliance with the terms of the delegation." Unif. Trust Code ' 807(a)(3). *Accord* RESTATEMENT (THIRD) OF TRUSTS §171 (1992). Here, there may have been a proper delegation but there is also lack of supervision, which brings Friend outside of the protection of the Third Restatement's black letter rule. *See also* Point Three.

Point Three:	Friend probably acted imprudently with respect to the trust investments by failing in her oversight responsibilities to require that the trust investments be
(35-45%)	diversified.

"A trustee shall diversify the investments of the trust unless the trustee reasonably determines that, because of special circumstances, the purposes of the trust are better served without diversifying." Unif. Prudent Investor Act §3. *Accord* RESTATEMENT (SECOND) OF TRUSTS § 228. This rule reflects the time-honored principle that it is inappropriate to put all of your eggs into one basket. While in a limited number of instances diversification may not be necessary, none of them appear relevant here.

The rationale for diversification is clear. "Diversification reduces risk . . . [because] stock price movements are not uniform. They are imperfectly correlated. This means that if one holds a well-diversified portfolio, the gains in one investment will cancel out the losses in another." Jonathan R. Macey, AN INTRODUCTION TO MODERN FINANCIAL THEORY 20 (American College of Trust and Estate Counsel Foundation, 1991).

Even though it was Bank that failed to diversify, Friend, as trustee, is liable for this failure because (1) Bank was Friend's agent and (2) Friend, as trustee, had a duty to oversee the acts of the agent, including the duty to assure that investments were made in a prudent manner. *See* Unif. Prudent Investor Act § 9(a)(3) (trustee must exercise care, skill and caution in "periodically reviewing the agent's actions in order to monitor the agent's performance and compliance with the terms of the delegation"). Friend can be liable for the failure to diversify even though Friend committed no breach of trust by initially delegating her investment duties to Bank.

Trusts & Future Interests

(July 2004)

ANALYSIS

Legal Problems:

(1) Did the language in Settlor Trust specifying that Zack "use . . . income to send Zack's children to college" create a trust in favor of Zack's children?

(2) Is Debbie, a child born to Zack after the creation of Settlor Trust, included in the class gift in favor of Zack's children?

(3) Does the share of Settlor Trust that Abel would have taken had Abel survived Zack pass to Abel's children or to the surviving members of the class?

(4) Does the share of Settlor Trust that Carrie would have taken had Carrie survived Zack pass to Carrie's heirs or to the surviving members of the class?

DISCUSSION

Summary:

If Settlor imposed a trust upon Zack to use trust income to send Zack's children to college, Brian can impress a trust upon the funds distributed to Zack from Settlor Trust. There is a strong, but not conclusive, argument that Settlor did intend to impose a trust upon Zack. Upon Zack's death, the trust corpus passed to Brian, Spouse, Debbie, and Grandchild. The trust created a vested remainder in a class of persons (Zack's children) and that class remained opened until Zack's death. Thus Debbie is included in the class. Class members' interests were divested only if they failed to survive Zack and had issue who did survive him. Thus, Abel's share was divested in favor of his issue (Grandchild). Carrie's share was not divested and passes to her heir, Spouse, except in a state that has adopted § 2-707 of the 1990 Uniform Probate Code (UPC), or a like provision.

Point One:
(30-40%)

The language of Settlor Trust probably creates a trust for the benefit of Zack's children in the income of the trust. Thus, Brian can impress a trust upon the income distributed to Zack from Settlor Trust. It can be argued, however, that the college expenses condition was precatory.

Settlor Trust provided that trust income be distributed to Settlor's son Zack, with Zack "to use such income to send Zack's children to college." The question is whether this language merely expressed Settlor's desire or imposed on Zack a binding obligation in trust. The answer depends on Settlor's intent: a trust is created "only if the settlor properly manifests an intention to create a trust relationship." RESTATEMENT (THIRD) OF TRUSTS § 13.

In order to determine a settlor's intent, the courts consider:

> (1) the specific terms and overall tenor of the words used; (2) the definiteness or indefiniteness of the property involved; (3) the ease or difficulty of ascertaining possible trust purposes and terms, and the specificity or vagueness of the possible beneficiaries and their interests; (4) the interests or motives and the nature and degree of concerns that may reasonably be supposed to have influenced the transferor; (5) the financial situation, dependencies, and expectations of the parties; (6) the transferor's prior conduct, statements, and relationships with respect to possible trust beneficiaries; (7) the personal and any fiduciary relationships between the transferor and the transferee; (8) other dispositions the transferor is making or has made of his or her wealth; and (9) whether the result of construing the disposition as involving a trust or not would be such as a person in the situation of the transferor would be likely to desire. *Id.*

In cases where courts find "precatory language" not evidencing a trust, the settlor has typically used words such as "like," "request," "hope," or "wish" when stating what should be done with the funds. Settlor Trust did not contain such precatory language; instead, it specified that Zack was to use trust income for college expenses. The beneficiaries, purpose, and funds to be used can all be easily identified from the trust instrument. Thus, there is a strong argument that a trust was imposed upon Zack to use trust income for his children's college expenses. If a trust was imposed on Zack, then Brian can impose a trust on the income distributed to Zack before Zack died. It can also be argued that in light of the language in Settlor Trust, Brian could impose a constructive trust on the income distributed to Zack; otherwise Zack would be unjustly enriched.

The question could be argued the other way. Settlor was vague as to the amount to be spent on college, the period for which college expenses were to be paid, etc. Furthermore, Zack was to receive all of the income for life, including the period after which he had no children in college. This might be evidence that the direction to use the income for the children's college education was precatory.

Point Two: Debbie was born before the class gift to Zack's children closed and thus is a
              member of the class entitled to share in the trust corpus.
(20-30%)

Settlor created a class gift in the corpus of Settlor Trust with such gift to become possessory upon Zack's death. A class remains open and may admit new members until at least one class member is entitled to obtain possession of the gift. Because Settlor's class gift did not become possessory until Zack's death, Debbie is a member of the class and entitled to take a share of the corpus. *See generally* Cornelius J. Moynihan & Sheldon F. Kurtz, INTRODUCTION TO THE LAW OF REAL PROPERTY 156 (3d ed. 2002). Debbie's share of the corpus is one-quarter for the reasons described in Points Three and Four.

Point Three: Abel's share of the trust corpus passes to Grandchild as provided by the terms of
(20-30%)   Settlor Trust.

Settlor Trust expressly provided that the "issue of any deceased child . . . take his or her parent's share." This language in a trust instrument is typically interpreted to mean that, when the life tenant is predeceased by a child who otherwise would have shared in the remainder and that child has issue who survive the life tenant, the deceased child's issue are to take the share that the deceased child would have taken had he survived the life tenant. *See, e.g., In re Estate of Houston,* 201 A.2d 592 (Pa. 1964). This interpretation seems consistent with Settlor's intent and would result in Grandchild taking Abel's share.

UPC § 2-707 (1990) and similar statutes achieve the same result by different means. Under the 1990 UPC, all future interests in trust, whether or not the gift explicitly requires survival to take, are treated as if they require survival; Abel's interest is thus contingent on Abel's surviving Zack. However, if, as here, the governing instrument creates an alternative gift, then the takers of the alternative gift (the issue of Abel) succeed to that interest despite the implied survival condition. UPC § 2-707(b)(4) (1990).

Point Four   Under the common law, Carrie's interest was vested. Her interest was not divested
(20-30%)   when she died before Zack because she had no issue who survived Zack. Since
                    Carrie died intestate, her share passed to her mother, Spouse, who is her sole
                    heir. Under the 1990 Uniform Probate Code, Carrie's interest would fail and
                    go to Brian, Debbie, and Grandchild, the surviving members of the class.

Under the common law, a remainder interest to children that was not expressly conditioned on survival was not impliedly conditioned on survival. Here, the remainder to children was subject to a survival contingency, but that contingency applied only when the deceased child had issue who survived the life tenant. (*See* Point Three.) Thus in contrast to Abel's interest, Carrie's interest was not divested because the divesting condition was not applicable as to her. *See In re Estate of Houston,* 201 A.2d at 599. As Carrie died intestate, her one-quarter interest would pass to Spouse.

UPC § 2-707 (1990) and like statutes produce a different result. Under the 1990 UPC, Carrie's interest is impliedly conditioned on her being alive when Zack's estate terminated. Because she was not alive, her interest failed. And since she had no surviving issue, there is no alternative gift. Accordingly, the share to which Carrie would have been entitled had she survived Zack goes to Brian, Debbie, and Grandchild, in equal shares.

Trusts & Future Interests

(July 2005)

ANALYSIS

Legal Problems: (1) Is Friends' Trust invalid for failure to have "definite beneficiaries"?

(2) Can the donee of a special power of appointment exercisable in favor of the donee's issue exercise the power by appointing:
(a) only a life estate to a permissible object of the power?
(b) an interest in the property to a charitable organization?

(3) If a donee of a special power of appointment limited in favor of issue appoints assets subject to the power to an impermissible object of the power, who succeeds to the interest that was invalidly appointed?

DISCUSSION

Summary

A trust for "friends" is invalid because it does not have "definite beneficiaries." Thus, First Bank should make no distribution to George. Carrie's appointment of income to her son John is valid. Although Testator did not expressly state that appointments in further trust are permissible, the majority view is that, if the donee can appoint trust assets outright, the donee can also create lesser interests in permissible objects of the power. However, Charity is an impermissible object of Carrie's special power; thus Carrie made an ineffective appointment of the remainder. That interest will pass at John's death to University, the taker in default of appointment designated by Testator.

Point One: A trust for "friends" is probably invalid for want of definite beneficiaries.
(25-35%)

In order to create a valid trust, there must be intent, delivery, and acceptance. Additionally, there must be trust property, a trustee, and one or more beneficiaries. The Friends' Trust has a trustee, First Bank, and property, $100,000. The question is whether there is a beneficiary.

A trust for indefinite beneficiaries is invalid. This rule derives from the principle that trust beneficiaries must be able to enforce the terms of the trust. See RESTATEMENT OF TRUSTS (THIRD) § 46 (2003); George Gleason Bogert, TRUSTS § 34 (6th ed. 1984). A trust for the benefit of "friends" is a trust with indefinite beneficiaries. See RESTATEMENT OF TRUSTS (THIRD) § 46, General Comment.

The RESTATEMENT OF TRUSTS (THIRD) takes the position that a trust for friends may be valid if "some ascertainable group of friends . . . was intended . . . or . . . an implied term of the trust authorizes . . . [the trustee] to determine who the friends . . . are. . . ." *Id.* at Illustration 1. However, there are no facts to support such a finding in this case. The disposition cannot be saved by characterizing Friends' Trust as a power of appointment because a power that must be exercised (a so-called "imperative power"), as here, also requires definite beneficiaries. *See Clark v. Campbell,* 133 A. 166 (N.H. 1926). A discretionary power, vesting in the trustee the power both to select beneficiaries and to determine distributions, is valid and would permit a trustee to distribute to friends. But here the instrument creating Friends' Trust did not give First Bank discretion to select beneficiaries or determine distributions.

Point Two(a):	The donee of a special power of appointment exercisable in favor of the donee's issue
(10-20 %)	can exercise the power by appointing only a life estate to a permissible object of the power. Thus, the appointment to John is valid.

The language of Residuary Trust does not specify whether appointments in further trust (rather than outright) are permissible. In light of the language in Testator's will, applicants could argue that Carrie can appoint only principal to John. This argument, however, is rejected by the RESTATEMENT OF PROPERTY and the weight of the modern case law, which take the position that, if a donee can appoint trust assets (principal) outright, then the donee can also create more limited interests unless the evidence shows that the donor intended otherwise. *See* RESTATEMENT OF PROPERTY § 358(e) (1936); RESTATEMENT OF PROPERTY (SECOND) § 19.3 and accompanying comments (1986). Likewise, the Restatement permits donees to appoint property in trust for objects of the power. Therefore, the appointment of only a life estate to John is valid.
NOTE: Local law may contain contrary authority.

Point Two(b):	Carrie's purported exercise of her power in favor of Charity is invalid because Charity
(10-20%)	is an impermissible object of the power.

The donee of a special power of appointment (a power that excludes the donee, the donee's creditors, and the donee's estate as permissible objects) can only exercise the special power in favor of objects designated by the donor of the power. Here, the objects of the power were limited by Testator, the donor of the power, to Carrie's issue. Thus, Carrie's attempted appointment to Charity is invalid. *See* RESTATEMENT OF PROPERTY (SECOND) §§ 19.3, 20.1.

Point Three:	Because of Carrie's partially ineffective exercise of the special power, the remainder of
(15-25%)	the new trust at John's death will pass to University, the taker in default under Testator's will.

Carrie exercised her special power of appointment by attempting to appoint to both permissible (John) and impermissible (Charity) objects. As a general rule, "the ineffectiveness of the appointments to the non-objects does not affect the appointments to the objects. . . ." RESTATEMENT OF PROPERTY (SECOND) § 20.1 cmt. g. Thus, the purported appointment to Charity does not invalidate the otherwise effective appointment to John in trust. (*See* Point Two(a).)

Where a power has been ineffectively exercised, the property subject to the power not effectively exercised passes to the so-called "taker in default of appointment" designated by the donor of the power (here Testator). Testator's will specifies that University is the taker in default of appointment and that University takes to the extent that its interest has not been divested by an exercise of Carrie's special power. Here, University has been divested of the life estate effectively appointed to John but not the remainder interest ineffectively appointed to Charity. Thus, upon creation of the new trust John has a life estate and University has the remainder. Charity has no interest in this trust.

Trusts & Future Interests

(February 2006)

ANALYSIS

Legal Problems: (1)   Did Settlor create a valid trust?

(2)   Was In-Law's pour-over bequest to the Settlor's Family Trust valid?

(3)   Did Settlor effectively shield trust assets from creditors when he created a support trust with a spendthrift clause and named himself as the sole income beneficiary?

DISCUSSION

Summary

Settlor did not create a valid trust when he made a declaration of trust because the trust lacked assets. The trust became valid when Settlor deposited funds in the First Bank account and re-manifested his intention to create a trust by opening the account in the name of Settlor, as Trustee of the Settlor's Family Trust. In-Law's pour-over bequest was valid because the trust was clearly identified in In-Law's will and its terms were incorporated in a writing that predated that will. Victim can reach trust assets in the First Bank account because the spendthrift provision is ineffective, both because the trust was self-settled and, in some states, because it would be deemed revocable.

Point One: (30-40%)
Settlor's Family Trust became a valid trust when the First Bank account was opened in the name of Settlor, as trustee. The trust had both a trustee and beneficiaries and, once the account was opened, trust assets.

A trust of personal property is valid if it has a trustee, a beneficiary, and trust property. *See, e.g.,* UNIF. TRUST CODE § 407; RESTATEMENT (THIRD) OF TRUSTS § 20 (writing not necessary to create an enforceable inter vivos trust). After Settlor made his announcement and signed the napkin memorializing his intentions, the Settlor Family Trust had a trustee, Settlor, and two named beneficiaries, Settlor and Dawn. But it lacked assets because the stock sale proceeds that Settlor declared as trust assets did not yet exist. The announcement and napkin thus evidenced nothing more than the intent to create a trust in the future, and a promise to create a trust in the future is typically unenforceable without consideration.

However, the $100,000 deposit into the First Bank account three years later was sufficient to create a valid trust at that time. If a trust that is invalid for lack of assets is later funded, a trust arises at that time if the settlor re-manifests the intention to create the trust. By depositing $100,000 into an account at First Bank in the name of Settlor, as Trustee of the Settlor's Family Trust, Settlor re-manifested an intention to create a trust with the terms described in Settlor's original declaration. *See* RESTATEMENT (SECOND) OF TRUSTS §§ 26 & cmt. e, 86 cmt. c. Thus, while the trust was not valid when Settlor made his announcement, it was valid after the deposit into the First Bank account.

Point Two: (25-35%)

<u>The pour-over bequest is valid because the trust was clearly identified in In-Law's will and the trust's terms were incorporated in a writing antedating that will.</u>

Under the UNIFORM TESTAMENTARY ADDITIONS TO TRUST ACT and UNIFORM PROBATE CODE, a person may bequeath assets to a trust created during the testator's lifetime, by the testator or another, so long as the trust is identified in the testator's will and its terms are incorporated in a writing executed before or concurrently with the execution of the testator's will. Under these acts, such a bequest is valid even if the trust is unfunded, revocable, and amendable. *See* UNIF. TESTAMENTARY ADDITIONS TO TRUST ACT § 1(a); UNIF. PROBATE CODE § 2-511(a). In-Law clearly identified the "Settlor's Family Trust" in her will, and its terms were incorporated in a writing, the cocktail napkin, predating the execution of that will. As the acts do not require a formal document, the napkin satisfies the writing requirement. One of the uniform acts or a like statute has been enacted in *all* states. Therefore, In-law could pour her estate over to the Settlor's Family Trust.

The common law incorporation-by-reference doctrine, under which a testator may direct the distribution of his probate assets in accordance with the terms of another instrument that exists when the testator's will was executed and which is specifically referred to in the will, would also permit a court to distribute In-Law's estate in accordance with the provisions of the Settlor's Family Trust. *See* William H. McGovern & Sheldon F. Kurtz, WILLS, TRUSTS AND ESTATES § 6.2. Thus, under either the common law or modern uniform acts, Settlor, as trustee, would take In-Law's estate.

Point Three: (25-35%)
<u>The judgment creditor can reach trust assets to the extent the assets of this self-settled trust could be reached by Settlor.</u>

Because the Settlor's Family Trust is a self-settled trust, its spendthrift provisions are not enforceable on behalf of the trust settlor. *See* UNIF. TRUST CODE § 505 (a)(2); RESTATEMENT (THIRD) OF TRUSTS § 58(2) & cmt. e (Tent. Draft No. 2); RESTATEMENT (SECOND) OF TRUSTS § 156. The fact that Settlor's right of withdrawal is limited to funds "for my support" makes no difference; when the settlor of a trust is also a trust beneficiary, his creditors are entitled to the maximum amount that could be distributed from the trust to the settlor, even when withdrawals are discretionary or limited by a support standard.

Settlor's creditors might also argue that trust assets can be reached because the Settlor's Family Trust is revocable. Many states provide that creditors of the settlor of a revocable trust can reach trust assets in satisfaction of their claims. *See* UNIF. TRUST CODE § 505(a); RESTATEMENT (THIRD) OF TRUSTS § 25 cmt. e. Contrary to the common law, some states now presume that a self-settled inter vivos trust is revocable. *See* UNIF. TRUST CODE § 602; RESTATEMENT (THIRD) OF TRUSTS § 63 cmt. c. In other states, the creditors might argue that

Settlor's retained power to distribute income and principal to himself is effectively a power of revocation. *See* RESTATEMENT (SECOND) OF TRUSTS § 330.

[NOTE: Applicants should not receive credit for the conclusion that the spendthrift provision is invalid because the creditor is a tort victim. A few state courts have refused, on public policy grounds, to enforce spendthrift provisions against the claims of tort victims who can show gross negligence or intentional misconduct. *See, e.g., Sligh v. First Nat'l Bank*, 704 So. 2d 1020 (Miss. 1997). But the facts here do not show gross negligence or an intentional tort and only a handful of courts have adopted this position. *See* RESTATEMENT (THIRD) OF TRUSTS § 59 Reporters' Notes; UNIF. TRUST CODE § 504 cmt.]

Trusts & Future Interests

(February 2007)

ANALYSIS

Legal Problems: (1)   Does Testator's gift of trust income to friends fail for lack of definite beneficiaries?

    (2)   Does Claimant, as a judgment creditor of Sam, have a right to immediate payment of $25,000 from the trust?

    (3)   Should the gift to State University fail because State University ceased to exist shortly after Testator's death, or should it be paid to another charity?

DISCUSSION

Summary

The trust's income should be paid to Donna, the residuary legatee under Testator's will, because the gift of the income fails for want of definite beneficiaries. As to the principal, nothing should be paid to Claimant before the trust terminates because Claimant's rights cannot exceed those of Sam, the trust beneficiary, and Sam only has a right to receive trust principal after 10 years. When the trust terminates, one half of the corpus should pass to Sam and the other half, in all likelihood, to State Polytech, as a result of the probate court's exercise of its *cy pres* power.

Point One (35-45%)

<u>Trustee should pay the trust income to Donna, the residuary taker, because the gift of income to Testator's friends fails for want of definite beneficiaries.</u>

It is a well-established trust law principle that a private express trust must have definite beneficiaries. *See* UNIF. TRUST CODE (UTC) § 402(a)(3). The term "friends" is indefinite because it is impossible to determine the precise number of persons who fit this description. *Clark v. Campbell*, 133 A. 166 (N.H. 1926) (a leading case invalidating a trust where the trustee had the discretion to select among friends). Although the modern trend would allow a trustee to select a beneficiary from an indefinite class (*see* UTC § 402(c)), this liberalized position does not apply if the trustee must distribute equally to all members of an indefinite class. *See* WILLIAM M. McGOVERN JR. & SHELDON F. KURTZ, WILLS, TRUSTS, AND ESTATES at 377-79 (3d ed. 2004). Here the trust instrument requires Trustee to distribute income equally among all of Testator's friends. Thus, the income portion of the trust fails for want of definite beneficiaries. The fact that Walter and Janice may have been friends of Testator's does not entitle them to any distribution because the income must be distributed equally among all of Testator's friends.

Where an attempt to create a trust fails, the trustee holds a resulting trust for the settlor or the settlor's successors in interest. *See* RESTATEMENT (THIRD) OF TRUSTS § 8. Where a testamentary trust, as here, fails, the residuary legatee succeeds to the property interest. *See id.* Donna, the residuary legatee under Testator's will, would be Testator's successor-in-interest of the resulting trust. Accordingly, Trustee should pay over trust income to Donna during the trust term.

It could be argued that the income for the first ten years either be accumulated for ultimate distribution to the remainder beneficiaries or, alternatively, be distributed to the presumptive remainder beneficiaries currently. An applicant could reasonably argue in favor of accumulating trust income for ultimate distribution to the remainder beneficiaries when the trust terminates. However, because the trust prohibited a distribution to Sam and State University earlier than 10 years after Testator's death, the trust should not terminate under the acceleration of remainder doctrine. This fact makes the second alternative income distributions less likely.

Point Two (30-40%)

Trustee should not immediately pay over $25,000 to Claimant because, as a creditor of a trust beneficiary, Claimant's rights cannot exceed those of Sam, the beneficiary, and Sam has only a right to half of the principal in 10 years.

A creditor may reach a beneficiary's interest in a trust if the trust does not contain a spendthrift provision. *See* UTC § 501. But a beneficiary's creditor can have no greater rights in trust assets than the beneficiary, and a beneficiary of trust principal is not entitled to trust principal until the termination of all preceding estates. *See* RESTATEMENT OF PROPERTY § 156 (remainder as future right to property); RESTATEMENT (THIRD) OF TRUSTS § 2, cmt. d (trust beneficiaries have equitable estates). Thus, Claimant would not be entitled to any trust principal until the trust terminates. Indeed, if the trust principal were reachable during the 10-year period, then the rights of any income beneficiaries would be adversely affected because their rights are based on income derived from the entire principal.

Therefore, Claimant is not entitled to receive $25,000 of trust principal. Claimant can only reach what Sam had—a right to receive trust principal after 10 years. Of course, Claimant would be entitled to a $25,000 distribution from Trustee when the trust terminates, assuming that the judgment against Sam is still outstanding and that his interest in the trust at that time is at least $25,000.

Point Three (25-35%)

At the end of the 10-year period, one-half of the trust principal should be distributed to Sam. The other half should be distributed, in all likelihood, to State Polytech in lieu of State University by application of the court's *cy pres* power.

The trust provides that, at the end of ten years, the trust principal shall be distributed equally to Sam and State University. Sam is entitled to half the principal at that time, subject to a possible $25,000 reduction to pay Claimant. (*See* Point Two.)

The other half of the principal is payable to State University, but this gift cannot be paid because State University no longer exists. However, State University is a charity. It is a well-established principle of trust law that, when a charitable purpose cannot be carried out, the court should determine whether to exercise its *cy pres* power and redirect the charitable gift to another like charity. *See* UTC § 413; Restatement (Third) of Trusts § 67.

The *cy pres* doctrine requires an initial inquiry into the settlor's intent: if the court determines that the settlor had a specific charitable intention limited to the stated charitable purpose, the gift goes to the residuary legatee, in this case Donna. However, if the court determines that the settlor had a general charitable intention, it should substitute for the named charity another charity that is consistent with the settlor's intentions. *Id.* Both the UTC and Restatement (Third) of Trusts presume that a settlor has a general charitable intent. *Id.*

Given the presumption of general charitable intent, there is a strong argument that the court should exercise its *cy pres* power and substitute the fine arts program at State Polytech for that at State University. The will evidences a desire to benefit a fine arts program. It evidences no intention of limiting that benefit to the program at State University. Testator could not have known that State University would cease to exist after his death. The state legislature has already determined that State University's fine arts program largely duplicates that at State Polytech. Substituting State Polytech for State University would maintain Testator's commitment to the fine arts and public education in his state of residence. *Cf.* Restatement (Third) of Trusts § 67 cmt. e (providing that, if the testator leaves money to a particular university to teach courses in dianetics, and the university refuses to accept the funds on that basis, the court may permit the legacy to be applied to the establishment of such a course in another university, assuming the settlor has not provided otherwise).

If the court does not apply the cy pres doctrine, the gift to charity fails and the share it would have received either passes wholly to Sam as the only remainder beneficiary, or wholly to Donna, the residuary legatee under Testator's will.

Trusts & Future Interests

(July 2007)

ANALYSIS

<u>Legal Problems:</u>

(1)   How can Settlor retain full control of trust assets and income?

(2)   How can Settlor retain the right to make future additions to the trust?

(3)   How can Settlor ensure that trust assets are used so that Wife is comfortably provided for after his death?

(4)   How can Settlor ensure that assets remaining in the trust after Wife's death go to their children and give Wife the power to reward the children in her will?

(5)   How can Settlor ensure that issue of a child who predeceases Wife will take the deceased child's share of trust principal?

DISCUSSION

Summary

A redlined draft of the trust instrument showing alterations that would better meet Settlor's stated goals follows:

SETTLOR TRUST AGREEMENT

1.   I appoint ~~Bank~~ Settlor as trustee of the Settlor Trust <u>and, upon Settlor's death, I appoint Bank as trustee.</u>

2.   <u>I reserve the right to revoke this trust at any time, by deed or will.</u>

3.   <u>I reserve the right to withdraw and add assets to this trust at any time, by deed or will.</u>

~~2~~4.   I direct ~~Bank~~ the trustee to hold all assets listed on Schedule A in trust and to dispose of these assets as follows:

   a.   ~~Bank~~ Settlor, as trustee, shall pay all trust income to Settlor during Settlor's lifetime.

   b.   After Settlor's death, Bank<u>, as trustee,</u> shall pay such trust income and principal to Wife ~~in such amounts as Bank, in its sole discretion, deems appropriate~~ <u>as is necessary to comfortably provide for her support and maintenance.</u>

   c.   <u>Wife shall have the right to withdraw trust principal as is necessary to comfortably provide for her support and maintenance.</u>

   d.   After Wife's death, Bank shall distribute all remaining trust assets <u>to such one or more of Settlor's issue as Wife shall appoint by will. If Wife does</u>

not exercise her power of appointment, Bank shall distribute all remaining trust assets equally among Settlor's surviving children, share and share alike, provided, however, that if any child of Settlor predeceases Wife leaving issue surviving, the share of the deceased child shall be paid to that child's issue.

3~~5~~. ~~Bank~~ Settlor accepts and agrees to faithfully carry out the terms of this trust. [Signatures, dates, and acknowledgments are omitted]

SCHEDULE A
12,000 Shares of XYZ Corporation common stock
$150,000 (cash)

[NOTE: This new draft does not necessarily represent the best method of meeting Settlor's stated goals, but it does respond to the most obvious deficiencies in Attorney's draft.]

Point One (20-30%)

Because Settlor wants to retain full control of trust assets, he should retain a power of revocation. To give Settlor more control, he might be also given a right of withdrawal and be named sole trustee.

In some states an inter vivos trust is revocable unless the instrument expressly provides otherwise (*see* UNIF. TRUST CODE § 602(a)), but in most jurisdictions it is irrevocable unless the instrument expressly provides otherwise. Thus a well-drafted trust instrument should always expressly state whether it is revocable or irrevocable.

Here Settlor told Attorney: "I want to fully control trust assets . . . until I die." An irrevocable trust is incompatible with this aim. To ensure that Settlor has the power to revoke as part of a testamentary plan as well as during his lifetime, the revocation clause should expressly provide that it can be exercised by deed or will.

Additional control could be conferred upon Settlor through a retained right of withdrawal. This power would enable Settlor to withdraw assets from the trust without revoking it.

Finally, Settlor could be named sole trustee with Bank the successor trustee. This step would give Settlor complete control of the management and administration of the trust.

Point Two (10-15%)

Because Settlor contemplated the possibility of adding assets to the trust, the trust should have an additions clause.

As a general proposition, a trustee's duties cannot be unilaterally enlarged by the settlor after the trustee has accepted the office. *See* Unif. Trust Code § 801 (providing that "[u]pon acceptance of a trusteeship, the trustee shall administer the trust in good faith, in accordance with its terms and purposes . . . ."). Thus a well-drafted trust instrument should contain an additions clause if the settlor contemplates enlarging the trustee's responsibilities by augmenting the trust with additional assets. (Even then, however, a trustee may be able to reject additions. *See, e.g.,* UNIF. TRUST CODE § 816.)

Point Three (20-30%)

Because Settlor wanted to ensure that Wife would be comfortably provided for, the trust instrument should require distribution in accordance with an ascertainable standard relating to Wife's maintenance and support, and Wife should be granted a withdrawal power.

Settlor specified that he wanted Wife "to be comfortably provided for." Granting the trustee discretionary power to distribute income and principal to Wife cannot ensure this result because a beneficiary cannot compel a trustee to distribute trust property not otherwise subject to a standard unless he or she can show an abuse of discretion. *See* UNIF. TRUST CODE § 504(d). An ascertainable standard, such as "comfortable maintenance and support," sets bounds on the trustee's discretion and would empower Wife to compel distributions from the trust if necessary.

To further ensure that Wife is comfortably provided for, she could be given a right to withdraw trust principal. Such a power could be unconditional or, as in the revised instrument, might be limited to withdrawals necessary to ensure her comfortable support.

[NOTE: Unconditional withdrawal powers are often limited to $5,000 or 5 percent of trust principal in order to obtain tax advantages.]

Point Four (15-25%)

Because Settlor wanted to leave trust principal to his children and to enable Wife "to use trust assets as a way of rewarding, in her will, whichever children have been most helpful," and also expressed a desire that the descendants of a deceased child should take by substitution, Wife should have been given a special testamentary power of appointment. This power should extend to issue, not just children, to enable Wife to appoint to more remote descendants.

Settlor expressed the desire that his children take remaining trust principal and that Wife have the right to reward their children in her will. He also expressed a desire to have a deceased child's descendants take the deceased child's share. To accomplish these goals, Wife should have been given a special testamentary power of appointment. Such a power would enable Wife to favor some children over others, as Settlor wants. But because the exercise of a special power is limited to the group selected by the donor of the power (here, Settlor), Wife could not appoint trust assets to individuals other than Settlor's issue. The special power would both ensure that trust assets ultimately go to Settlor's children or more remote descendants and give Wife control. Exercise of a power can also be restricted, as Settlor has specified, to testamentary bequests. No other drafting tool can fully meet all of Settlor's goals. As drafted, Wife could appoint to a grandchild even if the grandchild's parent was alive. This could be avoided, if Settlor desired, by providing: "After Wife's death, Bank shall distribute all remaining trust assets to such one or more of the Settlor's children and issue of deceased children as Wife . . . ."

[NOTE: The word "issue" gives Wife the power to appoint to children as well as more remote descendants. This allows Wife the power, consistent with Settlor's intent, to give the property to the descendants of the deceased child. (*See* Point Five.)]

Point Five (10-20%)

Because Settlor wanted the issue of any deceased child to take his parent's share of trust assets, the trust instrument should have so specified.

Settlor stated that, "if Son dies before Wife, I'd want his share to go to Grandchild." Although Settlor did not specify that he would want surviving issue to take the shares of his other children, it's likely that he focused on Son because Son was the only child to have a child.

In many jurisdictions, the instrument drafted by Attorney will not accomplish the aim of ensuring that surviving issue take their deceased parents' shares. Many state anti-lapse statutes apply only to testamentary bequests, and the Settlor Trust was established during Settlor's lifetime. Thus the trust instrument should expressly state that issue take a deceased parent's share.

Trusts & Future Interests

(February 2008)

ANALYSIS

<u>Legal Problems:</u>

(1) Did Friend breach the duty of loyalty by investing trust assets in a closely held corporation in which he had a substantial financial interest?

(2) Did Friend breach the duty to invest prudently by investing 90% of trust assets in the illiquid stock of two closely held corporations?

(3) Did Friend breach the duty to diversify by investing 90% of trust assets in two corporations with virtually identical businesses?

(4) Did Friend breach the duty of care by making investments that produced no current income and made it impossible for James to exercise his 5% withdrawal power?

DISCUSSION

Summary

Friend breached the duty of loyalty, the duty to invest prudently, the duty to diversify the trust investments, and the duty of care when he invested 90% of the trust's assets in the preferred stock of two closely held corporations. Friend breached the duty of loyalty because he had a substantial financial interest in one of the closely held corporations. He breached the duty to invest prudently and the duty to diversify because the investments significantly diminished the liquidity of the trust principal and because A Corp. and B Corp. were involved in similar high-risk businesses. He breached the duty of care by investing in a manner that precluded carrying out the trust's obligations to James with respect to the payment of income and James's annual 5% withdrawal power.

Point One (15–25%)
<u>Friend breached the duty of loyalty by investing the trust assets in a corporation in which Friend, in his individual capacity, had a substantial investment.</u>

A trustee owes trust beneficiaries a duty of loyalty and must administer the trust exclusively in the beneficiaries' interests. Because the trustee must act on behalf of the beneficiaries, and not on behalf of himself, the duty of loyalty is breached when a trustee enters into transactions, on behalf of the trust, that involve a conflict of interest or self-dealing. Friend entered into a transaction involving a conflict of interest.

Uniform Trust Code § 802(c) provides that an investment in "a corporation . . . in which the trustee . . . has an interest that might affect the trustee's best judgment" is presumptively a breach of the duty of loyalty. Here, Friend invested in A Corp., in which he held 70% of the common stock. Although the comments to § 802 note that the presumption of a breach can be rebutted by showing that the terms of the transaction were fair or that the transaction would have been made by an independent party, there is no evidence to support such a showing in this case. It is also hard to imagine that an independent trustee would have made such a risky and illiquid investment.

Point Two (25–35%)
Friend breached the duty to invest prudently by investing the trust assets in the illiquid stocks of cash-poor, closely held corporations without proven, marketable products.

Almost all states have adopted, in one form or another, the Uniform Prudent Investor Act. Under this act, a trustee owes trust beneficiaries a duty to invest trust assets prudently. UNIF. PRUDENT INV. ACT § 1. In assessing whether a trustee has breached this duty, the Act requires consideration of a number of factors, including (1) the distribution requirements of the trust (*id.* § 2(a)), (2) general economic conditions (*id.* § 2(c)(1)), (3) the role the investment plays in relationship to the trust's overall investment portfolio (*id.* § 2(c)(4)), and (4) the trust's need for liquidity, regularity of income, and preservation or appreciation of capital (*id.* § 2(c)(7)). All of these factors support a finding that Friend's investment was imprudent.

The investments in A Corp. and B Corp. represented a very large share (90%) of the trust assets and dominated the portfolio. The investments drastically reduced the liquidity of the trust, making it impossible to meet the trust's distribution requirements. The investments also reduced the trust's annual income, resulting in a reduction in mandatory income distributions. The effects of the investments on the trust income and liquidity were not unexpected, but were known at the outset. Moreover, the technologies that both companies planned to develop were unproven; working prototypes had not been developed, and there was no evidence that such inventions would succeed in the highly competitive cell-phone market. (*See* Point Four.) Lastly, since the companies were developing competing technologies, there is a good chance that ultimately one of them would fail (e.g., Blu-ray vs. HD DVD).

Point Three (15–25%)

Friend breached the duty to diversify by investing 90% of the trust's assets in two corporations that were involved in the same type of business and subject to the same market risks.

A trustee owes a duty to diversify trust investments unless he "reasonably determines that, because of special circumstances, the purposes of the trust are better served without diversifying." UNIF. PRUDENT INV. ACT § 3.

The diversification duty rests on the assumption that it is risky to place all or substantially all of one's assets in the same investment basket. Although there is "no automatic rule for identifying how much diversification is enough," (*id.* § 3 cmt.), it seems highly unlikely that any fact finder would find the investment of 90% of trust assets in one narrow and unproven market sector sufficiently diverse.

Additionally, there are no facts in this case to support a finding that a lack of diversification was warranted because of special circumstances. Settlor funded the trust with publicly traded securities. The terms of the trust contemplated investments that would produce income and distributable principal.

Point Four (15–25%)

Friend breached the duty of care by investing the trust assets in a manner that precluded administration of the trust in accordance with its terms and purposes.

Under the common law, a trustee owes beneficiaries the duty to act with care, skill, and prudence. *See generally* GEORGE T. BOGERT, TRUSTS § 93 (6th ed. 1987). Although the Uniform Trust Code does not impose on trustees a duty of care, it does impose a duty to "administer the trust in good faith, in accordance with its terms and purposes and the interests of the beneficiaries . . . ." UNIF. TRUST CODE § 801.

Whichever formulation is used, Friend breached his duty by making investments that made it impossible to carry out the terms of the trust. The facts clearly evidence Settlor's intention to provide James with an annual income and imply that this income may have been intended to supplant the support Settlor provided James before creating the trust. The facts also clearly show that Settlor gave James the power to annually withdraw up to 5% of trust principal over the first 10 years of the trust. The investments in A Corp. and B Corp. effectively prevented James from exercising his withdrawal power and dramatically curtailed his income from the trust.

Trusts & Future Interests

(July 2008)

ANALYSIS

Legal Problems: (1)   Can Husband pour over the assets of his probate estate into a revocable trust he did not create and, if yes, does an amendment to that trust made after Husband executed his will apply to the disposition of Husband's probate estate?

    (2)   Is Son entitled to a share of the assets contributed to Wife's Trust given that he had not reached age 21 when Wife and Niece died?

    (3)   Is Grandchild entitled to a share of the assets contributed to Wife's Trust under either the amendment to or the original terms of Wife's Trust?

DISCUSSION

Summary

Wife retained the power to amend Wife's Trust and therefore her amendment to that trust was valid. Under the Uniform Testamentary Additions to Trusts Act and like statutes, if a testator (Husband) bequeaths assets to the trustees of a revocable trust created by another (Wife), the terms of such trust, including amendments made after the testator signed his will, govern the disposition of the bequeathed assets. The terms of Wife's Trust, as amended, thus govern the disposition of Husband's probate estate. Son will take a share unless the trust instrument is construed to mean that the age contingency had to have been met when Niece died. Grandchild will take if he is treated as a substitute taker of Daughter's remainder interest. Under traditional anti-lapse statutes, Grandchild would not be a substitute taker; under some modern survivorship statutes (*see* Point Three), Grandchild would be.

Point One (20–30%)
Husband can bequeath his probate assets to the trustees of a revocable trust created by Wife. The disposition of those assets will be governed by the terms of the trust, including amendments made after Husband executed his will.

Under the Uniform Testamentary Additions to Trusts Act and Uniform Probate Code (UPC), a person may bequeath assets to a trust created during the testator's lifetime, by the testator or another, so long as the trust is identified in the testator's will and its terms are incorporated in a writing executed before or concurrently with the execution of the testator's will. *See* UNIF. TESTAMENTARY ADDITIONS TO TRUSTS ACT § 1(a); UPC § 2-511(a). Under these acts, a devise is valid even if the trust is revocable or amendable. And, even if the trust is amended after the testator's will was executed, the terms of the amendment will govern the distribution of assets bequeathed to the trust. It makes no difference that the amendment was made by someone other than the testator. One of these uniform acts or a like statute has been enacted in *every* state. Thus

Husband could pour his estate over to Wife's Trust, and the amendments to that trust would govern the disposition of his estate.

[NOTE TO GRADERS: An applicant unfamiliar with the Uniform Testamentary Additions to Trusts Act or a similar statute might analyze this problem under the common law incorporation-by-reference doctrine. Under that doctrine, a testator may direct the distribution of his probate assets in accordance with the terms of another instrument that exists when the testator's will was executed and which is specifically referred to in the will. *See generally* WILLIAM MCGOVERN & SHELDON KURTZ, WILLS, TRUSTS AND ESTATES § 6.2 (3d ed. 2004). But the incorporation-by-reference doctrine would require the court to ignore the terms of trust amendments made after the execution of Husband's will. Because the original trust instrument directed the distribution of principal to Niece's "then living issue," Son and Grandchild (the representative of his deceased parent Daughter) would share equally in Husband's estate. (*See* Point Four.) On the other hand, under the cited uniform acts or a similar statute, Husband's probate estate assets will be distributed to "Niece's children ages 21 years or older who are living when Wife's Trust terminates."

It is also arguable that the amendment could apply to assets received from Husband's probate estate under the facts-of-independent-significance doctrine.]

Point Two (25–35%)
Whether Son takes depends upon the construction of the amendment to Wife's Trust. If the provision is construed to mean that Niece's children must be 21 or older at the time they survive Niece, Son will not take. If the provision is construed to require only that Niece's children who survive her eventually reach the age of 21, Son will take if and when he reaches age 21.

The amendment to Wife's Trust is capable of two interpretations. The narrower interpretation is that Niece's children must satisfy both the age and survivorship contingencies *at* Niece's death in order to take. The more liberal interpretation is that the age contingency can be satisfied *after* Niece's death. In construing the instrument, the court will attempt to effectuate Wife's intent. A strong argument can be made that only Niece's children satisfying both the age and survivorship contingencies at her death should take since the amendment specifies distribution to "children age 21 or older who are living" when the trust terminates. However, it is hard to imagine why Wife would have wanted to exclude a child of Niece simply because the child had not yet attained the age of 21 *at* Niece's death. It can also be argued that given Son was only 15 when the amendment was signed, the sole purpose of the age 21 requirement was to assure that a beneficiary was of sufficient maturity when he/she took possession of the property and that Wife never anticipated that Niece would die only five years later. Bank could easily keep the trust open until it was clear whether the underage child could meet the age contingency. The fact that the trust amendment specifies that principal must be paid when the trust terminates, not when income beneficiaries die, might also support this interpretation of the instrument.

[NOTE TO GRADERS: To receive credit, the applicant should not simply draw a conclusion but should demonstrate recognition that this is an issue of construction dependent on the grantor's intent and could go either way.]

Point Three (20–30%)

Grandchild can take a share of the trust only if Grandchild is a substituted taker for Daughter under state law. In most states, Grandchild would not be and thus would not take.

Grandchild is not a taker under the trust instrument because the gift was limited to Niece's *children* who survived the trust termination and the word "children" includes the ancestor's immediate offspring, not more remote descendants. Most state anti-lapse statutes apply only to wills and thus would not apply to the trust amendment. In these states, Grandchild would not take any share of the trust funded by gifts from Wife or from Husband's estate.

However, some states have enacted Uniform Probate Code § 2-707 or a like statute. Under this statute, when a remainder class gift is bequeathed to a class composed of children and a child dies before the event upon which the remainder becomes possessory (here Niece's death), a substitute gift is created in the descendants of the deceased child; words of survivorship (such as "who are living") do not affect the creation of a substitute gift. Thus, under Uniform Probate Code § 2-707 and like statutes, Grandchild would take as the representative of the deceased child beneficiary, Daughter. However, in some states with statutes similar, but not identical, to § 2-707, the survivorship contingency contained in the trust amendment could eliminate any subsequent gift to Grandchild.

[NOTE TO GRADERS: In answering Point One, if the applicant wrongly concluded that the trust amendment did not apply to the assets coming from Husband's estate, Son and Grandchild would take those assets under the original trust instrument which provided for distribution to Niece's then living *issue*. As a grandchild of Niece, Grandchild would be included in the distribution to issue and would take the share of his parent Daughter by right of representation. *See* UPC § 2-708.]

Trusts & Future Interests

(July 2009)

ANALYSIS

Legal Problems: (1) May a trustee with absolute and uncontrolled discretion be held liable for abuse of discretion?

                   (2) Does a trustee breach her duty of loyalty by purchasing trust property at its fair market value, and if so, must the trustee return the profits to the trust?

                   (3) When a charitable gift of trust assets cannot be carried out because the charitable beneficiary no longer exists, should these assets be returned to the settlor's estate?

DISCUSSION

Summary

Even when a trustee has absolute and uncontrolled discretion, she may be held liable for actions representing an abuse of discretion. Failure to distribute trust income to Edna based on a personal motive constitutes an abuse of discretion, and it is likely that Trustee would be liable for withholding income from Edna based on her disagreement with Edna's political opinions.

A trustee has a duty of loyalty to trust beneficiaries. A trustee breaches the duty of loyalty by purchasing trust assets from the trust in her personal capacity, even if she pays the trust the fair market value of those assets. Because Trustee breached her duty of loyalty by purchasing property from the trust, Trustee must return the profit to the trust.

When a charitable disposition of trust assets cannot be carried out and the trust has terminated, the court should determine whether, in making the gift, the settlor had a general or specific charitable purpose. If the court finds that the settlor had a general charitable purpose, as is likely in this case, it should exercise its cy pres power and authorize distribution of the trust property to a charity that falls within the settlor's general charitable purpose.

Point One (30–40%)
Even when a trustee has absolute and uncontrolled discretion, she may be held liable for actions representing an abuse of discretion. A failure to distribute trust income based entirely on a personal motive constitutes an abuse of discretion.

A trustee has a fiduciary duty to carry out the terms of the trust established by the settlor; failure to do so constitutes a breach of trust. In this case, the trust instrument conferred upon Trustee absolute and uncontrolled discretion to make income distributions, including distribution of all trust income to only one beneficiary. Trustee's distribution thus appears to be consistent with the terms of the trust, and a court will not ordinarily question a trustee's exercise of a discretionary power, particularly when the trustee is granted absolute and uncontrolled discretion. *See* RESTATEMENT (SECOND) OF TRUSTS § 187, cmts. g & j.

However, even when a trustee is granted absolute and uncontrolled discretion, her actions may be reviewed for abuse of discretion. *See id.* § 187; UNIF. TRUST CODE § 814(a). Application of this standard will insulate the trustee with respect to decisions about which reasonable individuals might disagree. But when the trustee's decision is based exclusively on personal reasons unrelated to the settlor's goals, the trustee's decision may be overturned. *See* RESTATEMENT (SECOND) OF TRUSTS § 187, cmts. g & j.

Here, Trustee withheld all income from Edna solely because of her personal disagreement with Edna's political opinions. Such vindictiveness probably represents an abuse of discretion. It is likely that a court would hold that Trustee's decision not to pay Edna any trust income during the last year of the trust was an abuse of discretion and therefore a breach of the duty to carry out the terms of the trust.

[NOTE: The call is structured in such a way that the applicant need not discuss what damages Edna might be entitled to for this breach. The amount of her damages may not be easily calculable.]

Point Two (30–40%)
Because Trustee breached her duty of loyalty by purchasing trust property in her personal capacity, Trustee must return the profits to the trust.

It is a fundamental trust concept that trustees have a duty of loyalty to trust beneficiaries. *See* RESTATEMENT (SECOND) OF TRUSTS § 170(1); UNIF. TRUST CODE § 802(a). The duty of loyalty includes the duty not to engage in self-dealing, such as purchasing property from the trust without court approval. The prohibition on self-dealing applies even if the purchase price is fair and reasonable. *See* RESTATEMENT (SECOND) OF TRUSTS § 170(1), cmt. b; UNIF. TRUST CODE § 802(b).

[NOTE: The trust standard differs from the corporate standard. Under the corporate standard, fairness, under certain circumstances, may shield directors from liability for a self-dealing transaction.]

Trustee clearly breached her duty of loyalty to the trust beneficiaries by buying trust assets in her personal capacity. Under the no-further-inquiry rule, the reasonableness of Trustee's action and her goal to save the trust the sales commission are irrelevant. Therefore, Trustee is liable to the trust beneficiaries for all profits resulting from the breach. *See* RESTATEMENT (SECOND) OF TRUSTS §§ 205, 206; UNIF. TRUST CODE § 1002(a)(2).

Point Three (30–40%)
The court should find that Settlor had a general charitable intent. Therefore, the trust property should not be returned to Settlor's estate. Instead, the court should exercise its cy pres power and

order that the property be distributed to a charity that falls within the general charitable purposes expressed in the trust.

Although a settlor or the settlor's estate is generally entitled to the return of any trust property that cannot be distributed in accordance with the terms of the trust, an exception applies to charitable trust dispositions that reflect a general charitable intention. *See* RESTATEMENT (SECOND) OF TRUSTS §§ 411, 413; RESTATEMENT (THIRD) OF TRUSTS § 8, cmt. g. In such a case, a court should exercise its cy pres power and direct distribution of the failed disposition to another charity. *See* RESTATEMENT (SECOND) OF TRUSTS § 399; RESTATEMENT (THIRD) OF TRUSTS § 67.

Until recently, it was necessary to demonstrate that the settlor had a general charitable intention before the cy pres doctrine could be applied. *See* RESTATEMENT (SECOND) OF TRUSTS § 399. However, the latest Restatement of Trusts adopts the position that there should be a presumption that the settlor had a general charitable intention. *See* RESTATEMENT (THIRD) OF TRUSTS § 67, cmt. b; *accord* UNIF. TRUST CODE § 413.

Under either approach, a court should find that Settlor had a general charitable intention given that the trust instrument itself specified that the gift to Business College derived from Settlor's "long-standing interest in the area of education." Because Settlor had a general charitable intention to benefit education, Settlor's estate is not entitled to a return of any portion of the trust property. Instead, a court should exercise its cy pres power and direct distribution to another educational institution. *See* RESTATEMENT (SECOND) OF TRUSTS § 399; RESTATEMENT (THIRD) OF TRUSTS § 67; UNIF. TRUST CODE § 413.

Trusts & Future Interests

(February 2010)

ANALYSIS

Legal Problems: (1) Did the class of "Settlor's surviving children" remain open following the creation of the trust so that Doris shares in the gift?

(2) Does the share of Alan, who predeceased Settlor, pass to Alan's child or Settlor's surviving children?

(3) Did Claire effectively disclaim her remainder interest in the trust, and, if so, to whom does her disclaimed interest pass?

(4) Did Bank breach its obligation to invest trust assets prudently by investing, at Settlor's direction and acquiescence, 90% of the portfolio in the stock of a closely held corporation and by maintaining this investment despite the stock's depreciation?

DISCUSSION

Summary

Doris is eligible to take a share of trust assets because the class of "Settlor's surviving children" did not close until Settlor's death. In all states, Ben and Doris would receive a share of the assets as surviving children of Settlor. Alan, who predeceased Settlor, would lose his share as would Claire, because her disclaimer is effective and precludes her from sharing in the estate. In most states Ben and Doris would each take one-half of the trust assets because Claire is deemed to have predeceased Settlor because of the disclaimer. However, in states that have adopted Uniform Probate Code § 2-707 or a like statute, trust assets would be divided into four equal shares, and the children of Alan and Claire would take, by representation, the shares their respective parents would have received. Because Settlor directed the investment in XYZ and acquiesced in its retention by Bank, Bank is probably not liable for losses on that investment.

Point One (20%)
Doris is entitled to share in the trust remainder because the class of "Settlor's surviving children" did not close until Settlor's death.

If a gift is made to a class of persons, such as a named person's children, the class closes (i.e., additional persons may no longer join the class) when the named person dies or the gift becomes possessory. *See* WILLIAM M. MCGOVERN, JR., AND SHELDON F. KURTZ, WILLS, TRUSTS AND ESTATES § 10.3 at 429 (3d ed. 2004); RESTATEMENT (THIRD) OF PROPERTY (WILLS AND OTHER DONATIVE TRANSFERS) § 15.1, cmt. e.

Here, Settlor's death closed the class of Settlor's "surviving children" under either test. Thus, all of Settlor's children, including Doris, who was born before the class closed, are eligible to share in the gift.

Point Two (20%)

The share that would have passed to Alan had he survived Settlor passes to Ben and Doris, the surviving members of the class, unless the state has adopted a survivorship rule like Uniform Probate Code § 2-707. If the Uniform Probate Code applies, Alan's share passes to his child.

When a remainderman (such as Alan) predeceases the life tenant, the trust assets are distributed based on the directives contained in the trust instrument. Here the assets pass to Settlor's other "surviving children" (i.e., Ben, Claire, and Doris) as the trust instrument specifically provided that, upon Settlor's death, the trust property should be distributed to Settlor's surviving children. (But see Point Three with respect to Claire's disclaimer of her interest.)

In states that have adopted Uniform Probate Code § 2-707 or a like statute, the outcome is different. Under § 2-707, if a gift is made in trust to a class of persons described as "children," a deceased child's descendants take the deceased child's share by representation. The use of the word "surviving," as here, does not change that result. *See* UNIF. PROBATE CODE § 2-707(b)(3). Thus, if the Uniform Probate Code or a like statute applies, Alan's share would pass to Alan's child.

[NOTE: The following states have enacted a form of Uniform Probate Code § 2-707: Alaska, Arizona, Colorado, Hawaii, Massachusetts, Michigan, North Dakota, New Mexico, and Utah.]

Point Three (30%)

Claire effectively disclaimed her interest in the trust. Under most state laws, her interest goes to those persons to whom it would have passed had she predeceased Settlor. In this case, the interest would pass to Ben and Doris, the remaining members of the class of "Settlor's surviving children." However, in states that have adopted a survivorship rule like Uniform Probate Code § 2-707, Claire's interest would pass to her child.

Almost all states have enacted disclaimer statutes that permit beneficiaries of wills and trusts to disclaim their interests in the estate or trust property. In most states, a disclaimer is not effective unless it is in writing and is made, for a testamentary transfer, within nine months of the decedent's death or, for a future interest in a nontestamentary transfer, within nine months after the future interest would become "indefeasibly vested." *See generally* UNIF. PROBATE CODE § 2-801(b) (1969). Both requirements were met in this case, with the result that Claire's disclaimer is effective. Claire's disclaimer would also be effective under the newest version of the Uniform Probate Code, which permits a disclaimer at any time prior to acceptance of the interest. *See id.* § 2-113.

When the holder of a future interest effectively disclaims that interest, the disclaimant is deemed to have predeceased the life tenant. Thus, Claire is deemed to have predeceased Settlor. *See, e.g., id.* § 2-1106 cmt. example 4(b). Under the common law, Claire's disclaimed share would pass to Ben and Doris, the surviving class members. However, under § 2-707 or a like statute, Claire's child would take Claire's share notwithstanding the express survivorship contingency in the trust instrument. *See id.* § 2-1106 cmt. example 4(b). (*See* Point Two.)

[NOTE: The following states have enacted a form of Uniform Probate Code § 2-707: Alaska, Arizona, Colorado, Hawaii, Massachusetts, Michigan, North Dakota, New Mexico, and Utah.]

Point Four (30%)
Bank may have breached its duties to invest prudently and diversify trust investments. However, whether Bank is liable for these breaches depends upon whether acting pursuant to the directions of the settlor of a revocable trust excuses Bank from its duties to diversify and act prudently.

A trustee is under a duty to "invest and manage trust assets as a prudent investor would." UNIF. PRUDENT INVESTOR ACT § 2. The obligation to invest and manage prudently normally requires the trustee to diversify trust investments. *Id.* § 3. A trustee is also expected to consider the trust's "needs for liquidity . . . and preservation or appreciation of capital." *Id.* § 2(c)(7).

If the trust here had been irrevocable, there is almost no doubt that Bank would be found to have breached its duties. First, by investing 90% of the trust assets in one stock, Bank failed to diversify. Second, Bank failed to preserve trust capital. Bank was aware that XYZ was declining in value and was suspicious of mismanagement by its directors, but Bank nonetheless retained the investment. XYZ was also a closely held stock. Although such an investment is not explicitly proscribed by the Uniform Act, it was disfavored in some earlier versions of the prudent investor rule. The commitment of 90% of trust assets to such an investment thus may have conflicted with the trustee's obligation to preserve liquidity and capital.

While a strong case can be made that Bank acted imprudently, Bank may not be liable because it acted in accordance with Settlor's express direction and continued acquiescence. Acting in accordance with a settlor's directives is inadequate to absolve a trustee from liability when a trust is irrevocable because the trustee's obligations are owed to trust beneficiaries. But when, as here, there were no income beneficiaries other than Settlor and Settlor held the power to revoke the trust, Settlor could be treated as the effective owner, thus absolving Bank of liability to Settlor and all other trust beneficiaries.

Uniform Trust Code § 603 specifically provides that, with respect to a revocable trust, a trustee's duties are "owed exclusively to" the settlor. Moreover, Uniform Prudent Investor Act § 3 provides that a trustee shall diversify trust investments unless the trustee "reasonably determines that, because of special circumstances, the purposes of the trust are better served without diversifying," and Uniform Prudent Investor Act § 2 directs the trustee to "consider[] the purposes, terms, . . . and other circumstances of the trust" in managing its assets. Under the Restatement of Trusts, the terms of a trust include the "intentions of the settlor manifested in any way that admits of proof." RESTATEMENT (THIRD) OF TRUSTS § 90 (1992 § 227), cmt. b. This approach reflects the view that the settlor of a revocable trust has an interest in trust assets that is the practical equivalent of ownership. In addition, trustees are not generally liable for "consented to" acts and can defend against charges of imprudence by proving a waiver.

Given these principles and the fact that Settlor directed Bank to invest in XYZ and was aware of the situation at XYZ, but told Bank that he expected things would turn around, an argument can be made that Bank is not liable for the imprudent investment in XYZ.

Trusts & Future Interests

(February 2011)

ANALYSIS

Legal Problems: (1)   Does a creditor of a beneficiary of a discretionary trust have the right to compel the trustee to make payments to the creditor?

                  (2)   When an income beneficiary of a testamentary trust adopts a child after the testator's death, does the adopted child qualify as a "grandchild" for purposes of sharing in a trust remainder?

                  (3)   In a class gift to grandchildren following the death of a life tenant, does the class close upon the life tenant's death when there is a grandchild eligible to take, even though more grandchildren could be born after that date?

                  (4)   When a trust instrument creates a remainder in "grandchildren, with the children of any deceased grandchild taking the deceased parent's share," does any interest vest in the estate of a grandchild who dies without issue before the remainder becomes possessory?

DISCUSSION

Summary

A creditor of the beneficiary of a discretionary trust may not compel the trustee to make payments to the creditor when the beneficiary cannot compel the trustee to make payments. Thus, Ron's friend had no claim against Trustee.

Adoption statutes generally treat adopted children equally with biological children for purposes of inheritance and taking as class gift members under a will. Thus Carol, Ron's adopted daughter, will be entitled to share in the remainder interest in the trust even though she was not adopted until after Testator's death, because the class of grandchildren was still open at that time.

When a trust instrument creates a future interest in grandchildren, the class of grandchildren closes when a grandchild becomes entitled to take, even if that means excluding other potential (but yet unborn) grandchildren. Here, grandchildren became entitled to take at the death of Testator's son Ron, and the class closed at that time, thus excluding any future-born grandchildren.

When a trust creates a future interest in grandchildren, with the children of any deceased grandchild taking the deceased parent's share, the estate of a grandchild who dies without issue before the time for distribution succeeds to the grandchild's interest unless the jurisdiction has adopted a statute akin to Uniform Probate Code § 2-707, which creates a presumption that future interests under the terms of a trust are contingent on survivorship until the distribution date.

[NOTE: There is no perpetuity issue in this question because Testator had a living grandchild when she died (Peter) and thus the remainder interest is guaranteed to vest no later than the death of Ron, who is a life in being.]

Point One (30%)

<u>Because the trust instrument conferred discretion on Trustee, Trustee was not obligated to make payments to Ron or to Ron's creditor.</u>

The language of the trust instrument conferred uncontrolled discretion on Trustee to make payments to, or withhold payments from, Ron. When, as here, a trustee's discretion is uncontrolled, there is no abuse of discretion if the trustee acts "honestly and in a state of mind contemplated by" the trust creator. RESTATEMENT (THIRD) OF TRUSTS § 50, cmt. c (2003). As a result, Ron would be able to compel payments only if Ron could demonstrate that Trustee had acted dishonestly or in a state of mind not contemplated by the trust's creator. There are no facts here to support such a finding. *See id.*; SCOTT ON TRUSTS § 128.3 (4th ed. 2001).

Because Ron's creditor could have no greater rights in the trust than Ron had, the creditor, Ron's friend, could not compel Trustee to make payments to him. *See* RESTATEMENT (THIRD) OF TRUSTS § 56 (2003); SCOTT ON TRUSTS § 155 (4th ed. 2001) (If the beneficiary himself cannot compel the trustee to pay over any part of the trust fund, his creditors are in no better position.). Moreover, even in the unlikely event that the friend could establish that Trustee's failure to make payments constituted an abuse of discretion, some modern authorities hold that a creditor cannot assert the beneficiary's right to complain of abuse of discretion. *See, e.g.,* UNIF. TRUST CODE § 504(b)(2) (providing that a creditor may not compel the trustee of a discretionary trust to make a distribution, even when failure to make the distribution would constitute an abuse of discretion).

[NOTE: This problem does not involve the law relating to the ability of creditors to come after a beneficiary's interest when the instrument includes a spendthrift clause, as no such clause appears in the instrument here.]

Point Two (25%)

<u>Carol, the adopted daughter of Ron, is entitled to a share of the remainder allocated to "grandchildren."</u>

Section 2-705(a) of the Uniform Probate Code provides that "[a]dopted individuals . . . are included in class gifts . . . in accordance with the rules for intestate succession." Section 2-114(b) of the Uniform Probate Code, which deals with intestate succession, provides that "an adopted individual is the child of his [or her] adopting parent or parents . . . ." Thus, for purposes of the trust, Carol is treated equally with a child born to Ron after Testator's death. *See also* RESTATEMENT (THIRD) OF PROPERTY (WILLS AND OTHER DONATIVE TRANSFERS) (Tentative Draft No. 4 (2004) § 14.5(2)(i) ("In construing a class gift created by someone other than the adoptive parent, the adopted child is treated as a child of the adoptive parent, but only if (i) the adoption took place before the child reached the age of majority.").

Because it is clear that Carol should be treated as though she were Ron's biological child, the question is whether she qualifies to take the remainder even though she was not yet adopted at

Testator's death. The answer is yes. The class of grandchildren closes when one person becomes entitled to possession of the remainder interest. *Id.* § 15.1. Because no person became entitled to a share of the trust principal/remainder interest until Ron's death, Carol is entitled to share because she was adopted before that time.

Point Three (20%)

Because at least one grandchild was entitled to take at the time of Ron's death, the class of grandchildren closed at that time, requiring distribution of the remainder at that time and excluding future grandchildren from sharing in the remainder.

A class gift closes to future entrants when at least one class member is entitled to distribution. RESTATEMENT (THIRD) OF PROPERTY (WILLS AND OTHER DONATIVE TRANSFERS) Tentative Draft No. 4 § 15.1 (2004). In this case, because grandchildren were entitled to take at Ron's death, the class closed, and any children subsequently born to Sam were excluded from sharing in the remainder.

Point Four (25%)

Ginny, the beneficiary of Peter's will, is entitled to share in the remainder to grandchildren unless the jurisdiction has adopted a statute akin to Uniform Probate Code § 2-707.

When a trust creates a vested remainder in a person or member of a class and then provides that the remainder should pass to that person's child if the remainder person predeceases the life tenant, the remainder is divested only if the deceased remainder person has a child. If, on the other hand, the remainder person dies childless, the remainder is not divested and passes to the remainder person's estate. *See, e.g., Swanson v. Swanson*, 514 S.E.2d 822 (Ga. 1999); *Matter of Krooss*, 99 N.E.2d 222 (N.Y. 1951). Here, Peter's remainder would have been divested in favor of his child if he had been survived by a child, but because he was not survived by a child, the remainder vested in his estate. And, because Peter left his entire estate to his wife, Ginny, she succeeds to Peter's interest in the remainder.

The result would be different if the jurisdiction has adopted § 2-707 of the Uniform Probate Code or a similar statute. Section 2-707(b), a controversial provision, makes future interests under the terms of a trust contingent on the beneficiary's surviving to the distribution date. Under UPC § 2-707(b), then, Peter's remainder was contingent on surviving Ron. Because Peter did not survive Ron, his interest did not vest. As a result, he had no interest to pass to Ginny.

Hence, at common law, Carol and Ginny would share the remainder equally; if UPC § 2-707 or a similar statute is in force, only Carol would succeed to the entire remainder.

Trusts & Future Interests

(July 2011)

ANALYSIS

Legal Problems

    (1)   May a court reform the terms of Testator's testamentary trust to permit the sale of the home?

    (2)   May a court reform the terms of Testator's testamentary trust to authorize the use of both the home's sale proceeds and the earnings on those proceeds to pay Daughter $2,000 monthly for her expected rent?

    (3)   Will the trust property pass to Testator's estate upon Daughter's death?

DISCUSSION

Summary

Under the "equitable deviation" doctrine, a court may modify an administrative provision of a trust based on unanticipated changed circumstances. Here, the trust's "no-sale" provision is administrative, and there is a strong argument that the change in the neighborhood around the home represents a circumstance not anticipated by Testator.

Under the common law, courts may not change the dispositive provisions of a trust. The trust provisions regarding disposition of the home's sale proceeds are dispositive. Thus, if the home is sold, a court may not alter the relative interests of Daughter and Charity in the sale proceeds. However, under Uniform Trust Code § 412(a) and like statutes, a court may modify the "dispositive terms of a trust . . . if, because of circumstances not anticipated by the settlor, modification . . . will further the purposes of the trust." It is unclear whether a court would reform the trust in the manner Daughter seeks under this provision.

If a charitable beneficiary no longer exists when a trust terminates, trust property reverts to the trust settlor or his or her estate unless the court, using its cy pres power, substitutes another charity for the nonexistent charity. Here, Testator's intentions are unclear. However, because there is a presumption of general charitable intent, the court would likely exercise its cy pres power. Under the Uniform Trust Code, which establishes a conclusive presumption of general charitable intent, the court would certainly exercise its cy pres power and substitute a different charity. Thus, the trust property would not revert to Testator's estate.

Point One (30%)
Under both the common law equitable-deviation doctrine and the Uniform Trust Code, a court could reform the provisions of the trust to authorize the trustee to sell the home instead of retaining it.

Under the common law, a court may order "equitable deviation" from the terms of a trust when an unanticipated change in circumstances would otherwise "defeat or substantial[ly] impair[] the accomplishment of the purposes of the trust." *See* AUSTIN W. SCOTT, ABRIDGEMENT OF THE LAW OF TRUSTS § 167 (1960). *See also* RESTATEMENT (SECOND) TRUSTS § 167; MARY F. RADFORD, GEORGE G. BOGERT & GEORGE T. BOGERT, THE LAW OF TRUSTS AND TRUSTEES § 994 (3d ed. 2006).

The Uniform Trust Code recognizes and expands the equitable-deviation doctrine. Under the Code, an administrative provision of a trust may be modified "if, because of circumstances not anticipated by the settlor, modification or termination will further the purposes of the trust." UNIF. TRUST CODE § 412(a). An administrative provision of a trust is one relating to the management of trust property instead of the allocation of benefits among trust beneficiaries. An unanticipated change in the character of the community where realty held by a trust is located represents the sort of change to which the equitable-deviation doctrine is applicable. *See* SCOTT, *supra*, at 315.

Here, the facts support application of the equitable-deviation doctrine. The trust provision in question is administrative: it directs the trustee to retain the home and not to sell it. The facts also show that the neighborhood in which the home is located has changed substantially and in a way that Testator did not anticipate. The trust instrument's directive that the trustee retain the home until Daughter dies seems to have been based on the view that the home would be in a desirable residential neighborhood. Instead, the neighborhood is now dominated by apartment houses and noisy commercial establishments. Thus, the equitable-deviation doctrine should permit reformation of the trust.

The Uniform Trust Code also provides that, even if circumstances have not changed in an unanticipated manner, an administrative provision may be modified if "continuation of the trust on its existing terms would be impracticable or wasteful or impair the trust's administration." *Id.* § 412(b). This expansion rests on the view that "a policy of rigid adherence to the letter of the donative instrument is likely to frustrate both the donor's purposes and the efficient use of resources." RICHARD POSNER, ECONOMIC ANALYSIS OF LAW 556 (5th ed. 1998).

Here, there is a strong argument that retention of the home would impair the trust goal of providing Daughter with adequate and desirable housing. Thus, reformation of the trust should also be permitted under Uniform Trust Code § 412(b).

[NOTE: Because the request to sell the home affects an administrative provision of the trust, the permission of the trust beneficiaries and/or trustee is *not* required to reform the trust. "Lack of consent by a beneficiary is no bar if a modification will have no effect on the non-consenting beneficiary." WILLIAM M. MCGOVERN, JR., AND SHELDON F. KURTZ, WILLS, TRUSTS AND ESTATES 385 (3d ed. 2004).]

Point Two (40%)
Under modern statutes, but not the common law, a court may alter a dispositive provision of a trust to further trust purposes. It is unclear whether a court would find that using the proceeds of the home's sale to fund Daughter's rent would further trust purposes.

Under the common law, the equitable-deviation doctrine applies only to administrative provisions of a trust. *See* RESTATEMENT (SECOND) OF TRUSTS § 167. Courts are not empowered to alter dispositive provisions that determine the allocation of trust assets and income among trust beneficiaries.

Here, although the trust provision directing that the home be retained until Daughter's death is administrative, the provisions directing that Daughter has the right to live in the home until her death and that the home sale proceeds go to Charity when Daughter dies are dispositive; effectively, these provisions grant Daughter an entitlement to trust income (but not trust principal) and grant Charity the proceeds from the home's sale. *See generally* UNIF. PRIN. & INC. ACT § 404(2) (1997). Thus, under the common law, a court may not alter the beneficial rights of Daughter and Charity in the proceeds obtained from selling the home.

However, under Uniform Trust Code § 412(a) and like statutes, a court may modify the "dispositive terms of a trust . . . if, because of circumstances not anticipated by the settlor, modification . . . will further the purposes of the trust. To the extent practicable, the modification must be made in accordance with the settlor's probable intention."

Here, it is unclear whether a court would find that trust modification would further the purposes of the trust. There is an argument that Testator intended to provide Daughter with a desirable residence during her lifetime and, although the home was such a residence during Testator's lifetime, an unanticipated change of circumstances has altered its desirability. (*See* Point One). Thus, a court could find that modification would further Testator's purposes, even if use of the proceeds would ultimately reduce the value of Charity's remainder interest.

There is an opposing argument, perhaps even stronger. Daughter has only a life interest in the home. However, her proposed modification would likely result in the complete loss of the remainder interest. Daughter proposes that the trust expend $24,000 annually from an estimated $300,000 trust. A payout of this size would likely cause a depletion of the entire trust corpus in due course and deprive the remainderman of its interest. In fact, if Daughter lives long enough, that payout would exhaust the trust principal, leaving no money to pay her either. On the other hand, the trustee could be authorized to purchase a new residence with the proceeds from the home's sale. This approach would both provide Daughter with a desirable place to live for the rest of her life, as Testator intended, and still preserve the remainder interest.

[NOTE: Extra points could be awarded to the examinee who notes that to the extent the remainder interest fails (*see* Point Three) and the property reverts to Testator's estate, the argument in favor of Daughter is strengthened if she is the sole beneficiary of Testator's estate.]

Point Three (30%)
Upon Daughter's death, the trust property likely will not pass to Testator's estate because of the cy pres doctrine.

Under the common law, when trust property to be used for a charitable purpose could not be distributed as directed in the trust instrument, the trust did not necessarily fail. *See* SCOTT, *supra*, § 399 (1960). Instead, the court determined whether to exercise its cy pres power and redirect the charitable gift to another like charity. *See* UNIF. TRUST CODE § 413; RESTATEMENT (THIRD) OF TRUSTS § 67.

The common law cy pres doctrine requires an initial inquiry into the settlor's intent: If the court determines that the settlor had a *specific* charitable intention limited to the charitable purpose stated in the trust instrument, the property reverts to the settlor or the settlor's estate. If the court determines that the settlor had a *general* charitable intention, it substitutes for the named charity another one with activities consistent with the settlor's intentions. *See* UNIF. TRUST CODE § 413; RESTATEMENT (THIRD) OF TRUSTS § 67. The common law and the Restatement (Third) of Trusts both presume that a settlor has a general charitable intent. *Id.*

Here, there is little evidence regarding Testator's intentions. Testator may have wanted to help the homeless generally; Testator may also have wanted to address homelessness in Capital City's business district specifically. There is no evidence that Testator viewed Charity as the sole means to either of these goals; nor is there evidence to the contrary. Therefore, the presumption of general charitable intent would likely prevail.

The Uniform Trust Code appears to establish a conclusive presumption of general charitable intention. Section 413(a) of the Code provides that "if a particular charitable purpose becomes unlawful, impracticable, impossible to achieve, or wasteful: (1) the trust does not fail, in whole or in part; (2) the trust property does not revert to the settlor or the settlor's successors in interest; and (3) the court may apply cy pres to modify . . . the trust by directing that the trust property be applied or distributed, in whole or in part, in a manner consistent with the settlor's charitable purposes." Thus, under § 413(a), the court should apply the cy pres doctrine and substitute a different charity for Charity. The trust assets would not revert to Testator's estate.

[NOTE: The following MEE jurisdictions have enacted the Uniform Trust Code: Alabama, Arkansas, District of Columbia, Missouri, Nebraska, New Hampshire, New Mexico, North Dakota, and Utah. The Uniform Trust Code has substantially influenced the Trust Code of Iowa as well.]

Trusts & Future Interests

(July 2012)

ANALYSIS

Legal Problems

 (1) Is there a material purpose of the trust yet to be performed?

 (2) Do Settlor's children have the only remainder interest in the trust?

 (3) Was the class gift in favor of Settlor's children open to admit Settlor's fourth child?

 (4) Would Trustee breach any fiduciary duties by terminating the trust as requested?

DISCUSSION

Summary

Husband and Settlor's four children may terminate the irrevocable trust if a court finds that they are the only trust beneficiaries and there is no material purpose of the trust yet to be performed. It is unclear whether Settlor's desire to terminate Husband's interest if Husband remarries would be viewed as a material purpose of the trust yet to be performed.

Under the common law, only Husband and Settlor's children have an interest in the trust, as the children's interest is not subject to any conditions. The children's interest is both vested and transmissible. However, if the jurisdiction has adopted a survivorship statute like Uniform Probate Code (UPC) § 2-707, then the children and Husband would not be the only trust beneficiaries. Under that statute, if a child dies before Husband leaving surviving issue, the issue would also have an interest in the trust.

Because Settlor's class gift to "Settlor's children" remained open until Settlor's death, all four children are entitled to share in the trust remainder.

The proposed distribution of principal, which would give Husband more than the actuarial value of Husband's interest, would not breach any fiduciary duty because it would be made at the request of all trust beneficiaries.

Thus, unless UPC § 2-707 or a like statute applies or there is a material purpose of the trust yet to be performed, Trustee's assertions are incorrect.

Point One (35%)

Husband and Settlor's four children may terminate the irrevocable trust if a court finds that there is no material purpose of the trust yet to be performed. However, if a court were to find that the limitation on remarriage was a material purpose, the trust could not be terminated merely with the consent of Husband and the four children.

Generally, even an irrevocable trust can be terminated prior to the death of all income beneficiaries if both the income beneficiaries and the remaindermen unanimously consent. *See generally* RESTATEMENT (THIRD) OF TRUSTS § 65(1) (2003). *See also* Point Two. However, if there is a material purpose of the trust yet to be performed, the beneficiaries alone may not terminate the trust. *Id.* § 65(2).

Here, it is unclear whether there is a material purpose yet to be performed. According to the Restatement, a material purpose should not be inferred from "[t]he mere fact that the settlor . . . created a trust for successive beneficiaries. . . . In the absence of additional circumstances indicating a further purpose, the inference is that the trust was intended merely to allow one or more persons to enjoy the benefits of the property during the period of the trust and to allow the . . . other beneficiaries to receive the property thereafter." *Id.* at cmt. However, the trust provision specifying that Husband's interest terminates upon his remarriage arguably demonstrates that a material purpose of Settlor was ensuring that trust assets did not benefit Husband's second wife. If Settlor did have such a material purpose, the proposed distribution of $250,000 to Husband could defeat that purpose should Husband remarry.

If the court were to find that Settlor had a material purpose that would be defeated by trust termination, it is unclear whether a court would permit termination of the trust. Under the First and Second Restatements of Trusts, "if the continuance of the trust is necessary to carry out a material purpose of the trust, the beneficiaries cannot compel its termination." RESTATEMENT (FIRST) OF TRUSTS § 337(2); RESTATEMENT (SECOND) OF TRUSTS § 337(2). Similarly, the Uniform Trust Code § 411(b) provides that "[a] noncharitable irrevocable trust may be terminated upon consent of all of the beneficiaries [only] if the court concludes that continuance of the trust is not necessary to achieve any material purpose of the trust."

However, under the Third Restatement of Trusts, which no court to date has followed, even if the court finds that the settlor had a material purpose that trust termination might defeat, it may nonetheless approve trust termination if "the reason for termination or modification outweighs the material purpose." RESTATEMENT (THIRD) OF TRUSTS § 65(2).

If the court were to employ the balancing approach approved by the Third Restatement, it is unclear what decision it would reach on the available facts. The reason for trust termination is to provide Husband with cash for his impending retirement. Without knowing more about Husband's finances and the income available from the trust, it is impossible to assess how Husband's goal compares to Settlor's goal of ensuring that no future spouse of Husband receives benefits traceable to trust assets.

[NOTE: While conditioning the continuation of a child's income interest on the child's marriage or divorce is void on public policy grounds, a similar marriage restriction tied to the surviving spouse's interest is not.]

[NOTE: The Uniform Trust Code has been adopted in Alabama, Arizona, Arkansas, the District of Columbia, Florida, Kansas, Maine, Massachusetts, Michigan, Missouri, Nebraska, New Hampshire, New Mexico, North Carolina, North Dakota, Ohio, Oregon, Pennsylvania, South Carolina, Tennessee, Utah, Vermont, Virginia, West Virginia, and Wyoming.]

Point Two (30%)

Under the common law, Settlor's children are the only trust remaindermen. Because each child's interest is vested and transmissible, it would pass to the child's estate, not the child's issue, should the child predecease Husband. Thus, the four children and Husband are the only beneficiaries of the trust and could consent to terminate the trust. However, under UPC § 2-707 alternative remainder interests are created in the issue of any of Settlor's children who predecease Husband.

A class gift is a gift to a group of persons described collectively, typically by their relationship to a common ancestor. See RESTATEMENT OF PROPERTY (WILLS AND DONATIVE TRANSFERS) § 13.1 (2004). Here, the gift to "Settlor's children" is a class gift.

Under the common law, when a class gift is made to a group who are equally related to a common ancestor *and* the gift is not expressly subject to a condition of survivorship, the gift is *not* impliedly subject to such a condition. See id. § 15.4 (incorporating the common law rule). If a member of such a class fails to survive until the time of distribution (here, Husband's death), that member's share passes to his or her estate, not to his or her issue. *Id.*

Here, the remainder interest in the trust is limited to a class of "Settlor's children." All class members are equally related to a common ancestor, Settlor, and the trust imposes no express condition of survivorship. Therefore, each child has a vested and transmissible interest that would pass to his or her estate should the child die before the distribution date. If the common law applies, then only Husband and the four children are the beneficiaries of the trust and, if there is no material purpose to be performed (*see* Point One), they could consent to a termination of the trust.

Critics of the common law approach have argued that it fails to carry out the intentions of the typical trust settlor, permits a deceased beneficiary to transmit her share of trust assets to persons who are "strangers" to the settlor, and increases administrative costs by requiring the reopening of deceased beneficiaries' estates and possibly successive estates. In response to these criticisms, some modern statutes do not follow the common law approach. For example, UPC § 2-707 provides that when a beneficiary does not survive to the distribution date, the beneficiary's interest passes to his or her issue unless the trust instrument specifies an alternate disposition. Here, under the Uniform Probate Code approach, issue of a deceased child would have beneficial interest in the trust and would have to be part of any termination effort unless their interest could be represented by another.

Section 304 of the Uniform Trust Code provides: "Unless otherwise represented, a minor, incapacitated, or unborn individual, . . . may be represented by and bound by another having a substantially identical interest with respect to the particular question or dispute, but only to the extent there is no conflict of interest between the representative and the person represented."

This statute permits one group of remaindermen to represent another group of remaindermen in the absence of a conflict of interest. Here, the four children and their issue would have a conflict in light of the proposed distribution that would exclude the issue from potentially sharing in any trust assets. Thus, under UPC § 2-707 or a like statute, the trust could not be terminated merely with the consent of Husband and the four children.

[NOTE: Section 2-707 of the Uniform Probate Code has been adopted in Alaska, Arizona, Colorado, Hawaii, Michigan, Montana, New Mexico, North Dakota, and Utah.]

Point Three (25%)

Settlor's youngest child is entitled to a share of the trust because that child was born and became a class member before the class closed.

As noted under Point Two, the gift to "Settlor's children" was a class gift. When a class gift is made to a group of individuals, such as the children of a named person, the class does not "close" (that is, additional individuals may join the class by satisfying the class eligibility requirements) until the named person dies or the gift becomes possessory. *See* WILLIAM M. MCGOVERN AND SHELDON F. KURTZ, WILLS, TRUSTS AND ESTATES 429 (3d ed. 2004); RESTATEMENT (THIRD) OF PROPERTY (WILLS AND OTHER DONATIVE TRANSFERS) § 15.1 cmt. e.

Here, Settlor's fourth child was born prior to Settlor's death and therefore joined the class before it closed. Thus, this child is entitled to a share of the trust property.

Point Four (10%)

While Trustee has a duty to carry out the terms of the trust, when the trust beneficiaries properly terminate the trust, they can direct that the trust property be distributed in a manner of their own choosing, and a distribution consistent with the beneficiaries' direction is not a breach of trust.

If trust beneficiaries properly terminate a trust, trust assets vest in them. After termination, the beneficiaries may themselves distribute trust assets in any manner they choose. They may also direct a trustee to distribute trust assets as their agent. A trustee who complies with such directions does not violate any fiduciary duty. *See* UNIF. TRUST CODE § 411.

Here, assuming that the trust beneficiaries may terminate the trust, Trustee may comply with their distribution instructions. The fact that Husband would receive more than the actuarial value of his life estate does not, under these circumstances, constitute a breach of trust. Moreover, even if Trustee were breaching a fiduciary obligation in complying with the children's directions, they would be deemed to waive any claims against Trustee because they ordered the distribution. *See, e.g., id.* § 1009.

Trusts & Future Interests

(February 2013)

ANALYSIS

Legal Problems

(1)(a) Was the revocable trust amendable?

(1)(b) If the trust was amendable, must the amendment have been executed in accordance with the state Statute of Wills in order to be valid?

(2) If the trust amendment was valid, does the amendment apply to the probate estate assets passing to the trust pursuant to Settlor's will?

(3) If the trust amendment was valid, should the trust property be distributed to University?

(4) If the trust amendment was not valid, should the trust property be distributed to Settlor's grandchild (her only heir) or held in further trust in accordance with the terms of the original trust instrument?

DISCUSSION

Summary

A revocable trust is amendable even if the trust instrument does not expressly grant to the trust settlor a power to amend. Both inter vivos trusts and amendments thereto are valid even though not executed in accordance with the requirements applicable to wills.

Under the Uniform Testamentary Additions to Trusts Act, a revocable trust may be amended at any time prior to the settlor's death, and the amendment applies to the disposition of assets conveyed to the trust pursuant to a will even if the will was executed prior to the date of the amendment.

At Settlor's death, trust assets, including probate assets passing to the trust under Settlor's will, would go to University if, as is the case here, the trust amendment was valid. If the amendment was invalid, the trust assets would continue to be held in further trust because there is no violation of the common law Rule Against Perpetuities.

Point One(a) (30%)
Settlor retained the right to amend the inter vivos trust despite her failure to expressly reserve this power.

At issue here is whether a retained power of revocation includes the power to amend, sometimes referred to as the power to modify. The Restatement (Second) of Trusts § 331 cmt. g provides that if a settlor has a power to revoke, that retained power ordinarily includes a power to modify (amend) as well. Comment g also notes that the power to amend includes both a power to withdraw trust assets and a power to "modify the terms of the trust." The Uniform Trust Code, which provides that a power to revoke includes the power to amend, is consistent with this view. UNIF. TRUST CODE § 602; *accord* RESTATEMENT (THIRD) OF TRUSTS § 63 cmt. The theory is that even though a power to amend was not expressly retained by a settlor, the goal of amendment, assuming the power was not included in the power to revoke, could easily be achieved by first revoking the trust and then creating a new trust with the same terms contemplated by the amendment. To require this would put form over substance.

Thus, by expressly retaining the power to revoke the trust, Settlor retained a power to amend the inter vivos trust despite her failure to expressly reserve this power.

[NOTE: Under the common law, a trust is irrevocable unless the settlor expressly retains a power to revoke the trust. Conversely, under the Uniform Trust Code, a trust is revocable unless the terms of the trust expressly provide otherwise. *See* UNIF. TRUST CODE § 602. The Trust Code's position on revocation follows the minority view in the United States and is inconsistent with prior Restatements of Trusts (*see* Restatement (Second) of Trusts § 330). Here, the trust is revocable because Settlor expressly retained a power of revocation.

The Uniform Trust Code has been adopted in 24 jurisdictions: Alabama, Arizona, Arkansas, District of Columbia, Florida, Kansas, Maine, Michigan, Missouri, Nebraska, New Hampshire, New Mexico, North Carolina, North Dakota, Ohio, Oregon, Pennsylvania, South Carolina, Tennessee, Utah, Vermont, Virginia, West Virginia, and Wyoming.]

Point One(b) (10%)
Settlor's amendment of the trust was valid despite her failure to have her signature to the trust amendment witnessed.

Neither the common law nor state statutes require a trust instrument or an amendment to a trust instrument to be executed in accordance with the formalities prescribed for execution of a will. Indeed, an inter vivos trust that does not involve real estate can be created orally. Under the Uniform Trust Code, the only requirements for creating a valid inter vivos trust are intent, the specification of beneficiaries, and the designation of a trustee. *See* UNIF. TRUST CODE § 402; *accord* RESTATEMENT (THIRD) OF TRUSTS § 13.

Here, the amendment meets the requirements of both the Uniform Trust Code and the common law. Thus, the fact that Settlor's signature was not witnessed when she signed the amendment to the trust does not make the amendment invalid.

Point Two (20%)
Under the Uniform Testamentary Additions to Trusts Act, a revocable trust may be amended at any time prior to the settlor's death, and the amendment applies to probate assets poured into the trust at the settlor's death pursuant to the settlor's will even when the will was executed prior to the date of the amendment.

Historically, property owned by an individual at her death passed to the individual's heirs or to beneficiaries designated in a will executed with the formalities (writing, signing, witnessing) prescribed by state law. However, when a will devises property to the trustee of an inter vivos trust, then the provisions of the trust—which may not have been executed in accordance with the formalities required for wills—effectively determine who will receive the property. Because of this possibility, some early cases held that if an inter vivos trust was not executed with the same formalities required for a valid will, then the trust was ineffective to dispose of probate assets poured into the trust at the settlor's death pursuant to the settlor's will.

This line of cases has been overturned by the Uniform Testamentary Additions to Trusts Act (the Act), now Uniform Probate Code § 2-511. Under the Act, adopted in almost all jurisdictions, a testamentary bequest to the trustee of an inter vivos trust established by the testator during his or her lifetime is valid if the trust is in writing, it is identified in the testator's will, and the trust instrument was executed before, concurrently with, or after the execution of the will. *Id.* The Act further specifies that such a bequest is valid even if the trust is amendable or revocable and that a later amendment applies to assets passing to the trust by a previously executed will.

Thus, because the trust amendment is valid, its terms apply to assets received by Bank from Settlor's estate.

Point Three (10%)
If the trust amendment was valid, then the trust assets, including assets passing to the trust under Settlor's will, should go to University.

Under the trust amendment, all trust assets (including the assets of Settlor's probate estate poured into the trust) pass to University. The facts provide no basis for failing to comply with Settlor's stated intentions.

Point Four (30%)
If the trust amendment was invalid, trust assets, including assets received pursuant to Settlor's will, should be held in accordance with the terms of the original trust instrument because those terms do not violate the Rule Against Perpetuities.

Under the dispositive terms of the original trust instrument, Settlor created successive income interests in her surviving children and grandchildren with a remainder interest in her great-grandchildren. Because the trust was revocable, the period during which the common law Rule Against Perpetuities requires that interests vest (i.e., 21 years plus lives in being) began to run from the date Settlor no longer had a power of revocation (here, her death), not the date on which the trust was created. *See* JESSE DUKEMINIER, STANLEY J. JOHANSON, JAMES LINDGREN & ROBERT SITKOFF, WILLS, TRUSTS, AND ESTATES 678 (7th ed. 2005).

Under the common law Rule Against Perpetuities, Settlor's trust is thus valid. At the time of Settlor's death, she was survived by no children, one granddaughter, and no great-grandchildren. Because Settlor cannot have more children after her death, the only income beneficiary of the trust is Settlor's surviving granddaughter. This granddaughter is the only person who can produce great-grandchildren of Settlor; thus, all great-grandchildren must, of necessity, be born during the lifetime of Settlor's only surviving granddaughter, who is a life in being. The granddaughter's interest vested at Settlor's death, and the great-grandchildren's interest will vest at the death of the granddaughter. There is no need to wait the additional 21 years permitted under the Rule. Thus, under the common law and the statute given in the facts, the nonvested interest in the great-grandchildren is valid.

[NOTE: Both modern wait-and-see statutes and the Uniform Statutory Rule Against Perpetuities upon which the statute in the facts is modeled provide that before using either reform to validate an otherwise invalid nonvested interest, one should first determine if the nonvested interest violates the common law Rule. If it does not, then there is no need to reform. This proposition, which is applicable in all MEE user jurisdictions that have not simply abrogated the rule, is tested by this problem.]

29432279R10459

Made in the USA
Charleston, SC
13 May 2014